Handbook of Innovative Career Counselling

Jacobus G. Maree
Editor

Handbook of Innovative Career Counselling

Springer

Editor
Jacobus G. Maree
Department of Educational Psychology
University of Pretoria
Pretoria, Gauteng, South Africa

ISBN 978-3-030-22798-2 ISBN 978-3-030-22799-9 (eBook)
https://doi.org/10.1007/978-3-030-22799-9

This Springer imprint is published by the registered company Springer Nature Switzerland AG
The registered company address is: Gewerbestrasse 11, 6330 Cham, Switzerland

Foreword

That there is a need for knowledge production and publications on career counselling is evident in the vast gaps worldwide. This is especially so in the application of this field of practice in less advantaged communities, marginalised groups and poorer countries generally. However, the necessity for a compilation of works that take an innovative approach to career counselling goes much further and extends the boundaries and vision for the field. This need emanates from the challenges facing most nations in the contexts of employment, schooling, vocational guidance, career guidance and education, career pathing and development, career counselling, life designing and the multitude of other career-related assessment and intervention needs.

Disciplines that are both theory-driven and applied sciences, especially in the human services sector, are duty bound to go beyond the ordinary in the quest for new knowledge and approaches that can meet the developing and emerging needs in society. It is no longer adequate to continue pushing techniques of old simply because of romanticised notions of their origins or developers, particularly when the methods start to be less suitable to current, Work 4.0-related demands or service users, and fail to produce the desired results. There are many examples of this in psychology-related work, and career counselling is one of those areas where the pursuit of newer, innovative ways of working is essential.

In addressing this crucial need, Prof. Maree has been particularly perceptive to the challenges in the field and those encountered by career counselling professionals. It is, therefore, not surprising to note the assemblage of leading researchers and academics in the field that he has put together to address this subject. A glance at the list of contributors and their academic affiliations reveals that a who's who in the field of career counselling has been gathered. The *Handbook of Innovative Career Counselling* is an impressive outcome of this painstaking endeavour.

In conceptualising this work and the component chapters that were needed, Prof. Maree has used his extensive experience in the field of career counselling to identify the needs at grassroots level against the current state of the science. It is, therefore, gratifying to see the chapters that were commissioned as well as the academics recruited to pen the desired works.

The book covers the broad areas that readers interested in innovative career counselling will want to access, opening with a series of chapters that provide a grounding and contextual look at the field. In particular, life design issues, contextual and interactional influences, developing and facilitating goals, career adaptability, mental health and well-being, as well as innovating with the arts in the workplace feature in the early part of the book. Considering the unemployment rates and job markets in many countries, especially the middle- and low-income countries, career adaptability is a skill that many are going to need, and the training of workers in this respect can be crucial in enabling people to put food on the table. Part II covers important life transitions that need to be managed and discusses innovative approaches to helping people cope with the various career–life stage shifts and transitions that are part of the developmental process. Innovative approaches to career counselling across the lifespan are included in Part III of the book and extend some of the transition work, while examining some specific advances in the field. Career counselling with children and youth are covered, as well as intervention approaches to helping specific adult groups like women and middle-aged and older people with career-related issues. Specific challenges in the education system relating to career development and advancement are explored in the next part addressing social justice issues. With the focus of Part V on career counselling in special populations, some current humanitarian concerns and needs are brought to the fore. Career-related difficulties in refugees, people with injuries and disabilities, those from socioeconomically challenged backgrounds, and individuals without the benefit of specific work-related skills are addressed. The next two parts discuss assessment and interventions in career counselling while advancing more innovative approaches to attain these goals and targeting previously underserved groups. The use of poetry, group-based interventions and working in rural contexts are some of the many aspects covered. A look at the use of a technological approach to career counselling rounds off the book.

Career counselling is vital for many reasons, the most obvious of which are the dilemmas and uncertainties facing young people in contemplating the future. Additionally, the extent to which young people are able to effectively match their abilities and strengths to their career ideals may be limited, given their developmental level and insufficient life experience. Moreover, being realistic and applying sound and reasoned judgment are not necessarily characteristic of the adolescent years when career choices come to the fore. We are also in an era of career fluidity where the job one originally trained to do is not necessarily the trajectory one follows for life, as was the scenario for previous generations. Early-, mid- and even late-career changes are no longer uncommon and individuals will need avant-garde skills and support to help them negotiate multiple transitions. The degree to which individuals will be able to adapt to new career opportunities is going to be critical for individual success and prosperity, as well as for national and global economic and social development. Career counselling using innovative approaches that are strategically directed at current and future job markets will be needed; more so in Global South countries with poorer economies where formal employment is scarce, and much creativity, adaptability, agility, resilience, and even self-employment, may be required.

The *Handbook of Innovative Career Counselling* is a well-researched and conceptualised collection of chapters that addresses a variety of issues from fresh perspectives which have posed challenges and demanded concerted focus. The editor and contributors are congratulated on an excellent compilation that will inform, educate and benefit many.

Durban, South Africa

Anthony L. Pillay
Department of Behavioural Medicine
University of KwaZulu-Natal

Acknowledgements

Thank you to the entire Springer publishing team for assisting us, the authors, in converting our ideas about innovation in career counselling into scholarly narratives. Special thanks to Chris Wilby, our accommodating, ever-kind and approachable assistant editor; Shinjini Chatterjee, our incomparable senior editor (psychology and health), for her exceptional guidance, commitment, patience and passion, and whose eternal smile always lifted me and my colleagues' spirits in challenging times; as well as Prashanth Ravichandran, our accomplished, committed and patient project coordinator. In addition, I also thank Tim Steward, who has been editing my work as only he can over so many years.

A very special thanks to Mark Savickas, the world's pre-eminent scholar in the field of career counselling, without whose inspiration and guidance this book would not have been possible. Mark, you are our collective and my personal role model. I admire you particularly for the way in which you steadfastly and unfailingly not only teach but also actually live the value and essence of true scholarliness.

To my outstanding co-authors (regrettably, it is not possible to list all your names here), thank you for your commitment, the esprit de corps we developed over time, and your cutting-edge, innovative insights. It is a privilege to have worked with you.

To Profs. Anthony Pillay and Wendy Patton, who graciously accepted my invitation to write the Foreword and Epilogue, thank you for your illuminating and outstanding contributions. It is much appreciated by the publisher, the editor and all the authors.

I thank everyone else with whom I had the pleasure of working, learning from and being inspired by. This includes the many thousands of research participants—often from extreme poverty backgrounds—who always embraced me and lifted my spirits when our research task threatened to become too daunting and overwhelming.

Lastly, I thank my late parents for their unwavering love, support and confidence in me. This volume is an attempt on my part to express my appreciation to them. I conclude by thanking my son, who never complains when I burn the midnight oil or seek his valuable input.

Jacobus G. Maree

Contents

Innovative Career Counselling Interventions

Editor and Contributors

About the Editor

Prof. Jacobus G. Maree [D.Ed. (Career Counselling); Ph.D. (Learning Facilitation in Mathematics); D.Phil. (Psychology)] is Full Professor in the Department of Educational Psychology at the University of Pretoria. His main research interests are career construction (counselling), life design (counselling), emotional–social intelligence, social responsibility, and learning facilitation in mathematics. Past editor of a number of scholarly journals, for instance, the *South African Journal of Psychology*, he is the current editor of the *African Journal of Career Development* and the regional editor for Southern Africa: *Early Child Development and Care*. He has received multiple awards for his research. In June 2014, he was, for instance, awarded the Stals Prize for exceptional research and contributions to education, and he received the Psychological Society of South Africa's Award for Excellence in Science in September 2014. He also received Honorary Membership of the Golden Key International Honour Society for exceptional academic achievements, leadership skills, and community involvement in 2014. He was awarded the Chancellor's Medal for Teaching and Learning from the University of Pretoria in 2010 and has been nominated successfully as an Exceptional Academic Achiever on four consecutive occasions. He has a B1 rating from the National Research Foundation.

He has authored or co-authored 115$^+$ peer-reviewed articles and 65 books/chapters on career counselling, research, and related topics since 2009. In the same period, he supervised 36 doctoral theses and master's dissertations and read keynote papers at 25$^+$ international conferences (e.g., Australia, Belgium, Canada, Croatia, Czechia, Egypt, England, France, Hungary, India, Italy, Mauritius, Namibia, Poland, Slovakia, South Africa, Turkey, and the USA) and at 25$^+$ national conferences. He has also presented invited workshops at conferences in 30$^+$ countries across the world on (a) integrating qualitative and quantitative approaches in career counselling, and (b) the art and science of writing scholarly articles. Over the past seven years, he has spent a lot of time abroad a visiting professor at various universities where he presented workshops on, for instance, contemporary developments in career counselling, scholarly article writing, and research methodology. He was awarded a fellowship of the International Association of Applied Psychology (IAAP) in 2014 and received the Psychological Society of South Africa's Fellow Award (lifetime award in recognition of a person who has made exceptional contributions to psychology in her/his life) in 2017.

Contributors

Peyman Abkhezr Faculty of Education, School of Early Childhood and Inclusive Education, Queensland University of Technology, Kelvin Grove, Queensland, Australia

A. J. Albien Department of Psychology, Stellenbosch University, Stellenbosch, South Africa

James A. Athanasou Discipline of Rehabilitation Counselling, Faculty of Health Sciences, The University of Sydney, Lidcombe, NSW, Australia

Jenny Bimrose The University of Warwick, Coventry, UK

David L. Blustein Boston College, Chestnut Hill, MA, USA

Michèle Boonzaier Department of Industrial Psychology, Stellenbosch University, Stellenbosch, South Africa

William C. Briddick Counselling and Human Development, College of Education and Human Sciences, South Dakota State University, Brookings, SD, USA

René Brohm De Nieuwe Kleren van de Wolf—Research Organization, Doorn, The Netherlands

Felix Bühlmann Institute of Social Sciences, Swiss National Centre of Competence in Research LIVES, University of Lausanne, Lausanne, Switzerland

Paulo Cardoso Department of Psychology, CEFAGE, University of Évora, Évora, Portugal

Laurie A. Carlson Colorado State University, Fort Collins, Colorado, USA

Melinde Coetzee Department of Industrial and Organisational Psychology, University of South Africa, Pretoria, Gauteng, South Africa

Valérie Cohen-Scali Conservatoire National des Arts et Métiers, Center of Research on Work and Development, Hesam Université, Paris, France

José Tomás da Silva Faculty of Psychology and Educational Sciences, University of Coimbra, Coimbra, Portugal

Nuraan Davids Stellenbosch University, Cape Town, South Africa

Maria Celeste Couceiro Gama de Almeida University of São Paulo, São Paulo, Brazil

Gideon de Bruin Department of Industrial Psychology, Stellenbosch University, Stellenbosch, South Africa

Marietha de Wet Department of Industrial Psychology, Stellenbosch University, Stellenbosch, South Africa

Annamaria Di Fabio Department of Education Languages, Intercultures, Literatures and Psychology, University of Florence, Florence, Italy

José F. Domene University of Calgary, Calgary, Canada

Aniek Draaisma Welten Institute, Open University, Heerlen, The Netherlands

Maria Eduarda Duarte Faculty of Psychology, University of Lisbon, Lisbon, Portugal

Gill Frigerio The University of Warwick, Coventry, UK

Xiaohe Gao Boston College, Chestnut Hill, MA, USA

Itamar Gati Hebrew University of Jerusalem, Jerusalem, Israel

Erna W. Gerryts Department of Educational Psychology, University of Pretoria, Pretoria, South Africa

Miguel M. Gonçalves School of Psychology, University of Minho, Braga, Portugal

Daniel Guttierez School of Education, College of William & Mary, Williamsburg, VA, USA

Paul J. Hartung Department of Family and Community Medicine, Northeast Ohio Medical University, Rootstown, OH, USA

Seth C. W. Hayden Department of Counselling, Wake Forest University, Winston-Salem, NC, USA

Carolina Henn Department of Industrial Psychology and People Management, University of Johannesburg, Johannesburg, South Africa

Erica M. Hines Community College of Aurora, Aurora, CO, USA

Amy E. Huff University of Colorado-Denver, Denver, Colorado, USA

Deirdre Hughes Exeter, England, UK

Elnaz Kashefpakdel London, UK

Maureen E. Kenny Boston College, Chestnut Hill, MA, USA

Lily Konowitz Boston College, Chestnut Hill, MA, USA

Saliha Kozan Boston College, Chestnut Hill, MA, USA

Marinka Kuijpers Welten Institute, Open University, Heerlen, The Netherlands

Reinekke Lengelle Athabasca University, Athabasca, Canada;
The Hague University of Applied Sciences, Hague, Netherlands

Belle Liang Boston College, Chestnut Hill, MA, USA

Yuliya Lipshits-Braziler Hebrew University of Jerusalem, Jerusalem, Israel

Stanske Lomans Berings & Lomans, Training and Storytelling Agency, Utrecht, The Netherlands;
University of Applied Sciences Utrecht, Utrecht, The Netherlands

Jacobus G. Maree Department of Educational Psychology, University of Pretoria, Pretoria, South Africa

Jonas Masdonati Institute of Psychology, University of Lausanne, Lausanne, Switzerland

Mary McMahon School of Education, The University of Queensland, Brisbane, Australia

Mary Beth Medvide Suffolk University, Boston, MA, USA;
Boston College, Chestnut Hill, MA, USA

Tera Meerkins Boston College, Chestnut Hill, MA, USA

Frans Meijers Research Group Pedagogy of Career Development, The Hague University of Applied Sciences, The Hague, The Netherlands

Brandon Morgan Department of Industrial Psychology and People Management, University of Johannesburg, Johannesburg, South Africa

Heidi S. C. A. Muijen Thymia—Philosophical Counselling, Weesp, The Netherlands

Anthony V. Naidoo Department of Psychology, Stellenbosch University, Stellenbosch, South Africa

Roberta A. Neault Vancouver, Canada

Spencer G. Niles School of Education, College of William & Mary, Williamsburg, VA, USA

Debra Sue Osborn Florida State University, Tallahassee, USA

Maria Paula Paixão Faculty of Psychology and Educational Sciences, University of Coimbra, Coimbra, Portugal

Jacqueline J. Peila-Shuster Colorado State University, Fort Collins, CO, USA

Harsha N. Perera College of Education, University of Nevada Las Vegas, Las Vegas, NV, USA

Steven I. Pfeiffer Florida State University, Tallahassee, USA

Deirdre A. Pickerell Vancouver, Canada

Jacques Pouyaud Laboratory of Psychology (EA 4139), University of Bordeaux, Bordeaux, France

Renata Muniz Prado Universidade de Brasília, Brasília, Brazil

Stephan Rabie Department of Global Health, Stellenbosch University, Stellenbosch, South Africa

Rachel S. Rauvola Department of Psychology, Saint Louis University, St. Louis, MO, USA

Marcelo Afonso Ribeiro University of São Paulo, São Paulo, Brazil

Shékina Rochat Vaud State Office of Career Counselling, Lausanne, Switzerland

Jérôme Rossier Institute of Psychology, Swiss National Centre of Competence in Research LIVES, University of Lausanne, Lausanne, Switzerland

Cort W. Rudolph Department of Psychology, Saint Louis University, St. Louis, MO, USA

Mark L. Savickas Northeast Ohio Medical University, Rootstown, USA

Suzanne Savickas Avenues of Counselling and Mediation, Medina and Fairlawn, OH, USA

Hande Sensoy-Briddick Counselling and Human Development, College of Education and Human Sciences, South Dakota State University, Brookings, SD, USA

Liezel Shirley Department of Psychology, Stellenbosch University, Stellenbosch, South Africa

Anna Shuqom Boston College, Chestnut Hill, MA, USA

Brian J. Taber Oakland University, Rochester, MI, USA

Ieva Urbanaviciute Institute of Psychology, Swiss National Centre of Competence in Research LIVES, University of Lausanne, Lausanne, Switzerland

Izanette van Schalkwyk Department of Psychology, Stellenbosch University, Stellenbosch, South Africa

Caitlin Venter Department of Psychology, Stellenbosch University, Stellenbosch, South Africa

Michelle Visser Department of Industrial Psychology, Stellenbosch University, Stellenbosch, South Africa

Esther M. Wafula Nairobi, Kenya

Yusef Waghid Stellenbosch University, Cape Town, South Africa

Mark Watson School of Behavioural and Lifestyle Sciences, Nelson Mandela University, Port Elizabeth, South Africa

Allison White Boston College, Chestnut Hill, MA, USA

Cassidy Wilson University of New Brunswick, Fredericton, Canada

Richard A. Young University of British Columbia, Vancouver, Canada

Hannes Zacher Institute of Psychology, Leipzig University, Leipzig, Germany

Conceptualising Innovative Career Counselling

Life Design: A Paradigm for Innovating Career Counselling in Global Context

Paul J. Hartung

Globalization … has one overarching feature – integration.
T. L. Friedman (2000, p. 8).

Abstract More than a decade has elapsed since the original statement of life design as an innovative and internationally-constructed paradigm for careers science and practice. Responding to the challenges of work and career in contemporary times, life design shifts the paradigm for career counselling from match-making to meaning making. This chapter situates life design in global context; reviews its core tenets, constructs, and practice methods; and considers its conceptual, empirical, and practice advance. Life designing offers positive direction for the careers field to foster human health and well-being through promoting work and employment in all people's lives. Continuing to adopt and advance life-design principles and practices helps transform career counselling from a straightforward logical pursuit to a complex therapeutic endeavor to assist people to use work as a way to imbue their lives with purpose and direction. Continuing advances in the emerging life design tradition led by approaches such as Career Construction Theory and Practice help dissolve long-held false distinctions between career and mental-health counselling. Such efforts give way to innovating a perspective on work as central to counselling for mental health and well-being. Goals of the life design paradigm continue to propel it as an innovative intervention model for meaningfully construing and constructing work and career in human life.

Keywords Life designing · Career construction theory and counselling · Career theory · Career intervention · Career development paradigms · Globalization

P. J. Hartung (✉)
Department of Family and Community Medicine, Northeast Ohio Medical University, Rootstown, OH 44240, USA
e-mail: phartung@neomed.edu

J. G. Maree (ed.), *Handbook of Innovative Career Counselling*,
https://doi.org/10.1007/978-3-030-22799-9_1

Introduction

The year was 1776. Swiss-born American patriot and artist Pierre-Eugène Ducimetière proposed a motto for a newly-formed nation: *E pluribus unum*—"Out of many, one." This now very well-known if unofficial motto of the United States (U.S.) resonates with the best spirit of globalization—the technological, economic, cultural, political, and social processes inherent in forming a single integrated world society (Albrow & King, 1990). In such a society, people around the globe ideally would have opportunity to grow stronger through shared interactions, knowledge, and access to resources—in short, through unity. Much like the phrase *e pluribus unum* intends to symbolize unity and strength through diversity, however, the realities of globalization and an integrated world society also, of course, pose real challenges. Prime among these challenges is for nations and peoples to preserve their diversity, dignity, individuality, identity, and rights to social justice; this, while many around the world running the human race pursue more unified and peaceful existences and ways of life.

Chapter Structure

With globalization as setting, careers scholars and practitioners continue to innovate and update the science and practice of career counselling on an international scale (Athanasou & Van Esbroeck, 2008; Nota & Rossier, 2015; Savickas et al., 2009). The collected works contained in the present volume provide convincing and perhaps the most immediate evidence of this point. To consider further how the careers field continues to innovate itself on a worldwide stage, in the present chapter I first consider career counselling theory, research, and practice within the context of globalization. Since the beginning of the 21st century, globalization, along with ever-burgeoning information technologies, has driven and shaped "a new social arrangement of work" wherein occupational instability and precarious work require workers to maintain their employability by learning and using new technologies, embracing flexibility, and creating their own opportunities (Savickas et al., 2009, p. 240). I then turn to examining three truths about the growing international reach of careers science and practice. These truths echo how the careers field has responded to globalization by innovating its paradigms and practices while internationalizing itself through integrative cross-national collaborative efforts. Life designing as an internationally-constructed paradigm for careers science and practice and a life-long, holistic, contextual, and preventive process of shaping self through work and relationships (Nota & Rossier, 2015; Savickas et al., 2009) stands out as a most compelling example of such efforts. The chapter culminates by considering the rise and growth of life design as an innovative 21st-century paradigm for career counselling theory, practice, and research that augments 20th-century models of person-environment fit and life-span development.

Globalization and Career Counselling

Responding to the many challenges of globalization has been and remains a core strength of career counselling and development (Hartung, 2012; Savickas & Baker, 2005; Watson & McMahon, 2012). In many places around the world career counselling grows more unified by internationalizing itself. The field remains and should remain divergent in its many indigenous counselling programs, principles, practices, and policies in countries around the world (Savickas, 2007). The field of career counselling also should, as in the view of many (e.g., Athanasou & Van Esbroeck, 2008; Gerstein, Heppner, Ægisdottir, Leung, & Norsworthy, 2009; Heppner, Leong, & Gerstein, 2008; Hohenshil, Amundson, & Niles, 2013; Leong & Blustein, 2000; Leong & Savickas, 2007; Watson & McMahon, 2012), increasingly become one; necessarily unified around the globe by a common mission to promote human psychosocial (including emotional) health and well-being through excellence in theory, practice, and research.

In unifying the field, we can recall the writing of Leong and Blustein (2000) who 20 years ago noted that the worldwide infusion of knowledge offers counsellors and psychologists across the globe great opportunity for continually learning from one another. And in so doing, we must listen to each other, as advised in the following well-known story:

> A university professor once traveled to visit a famous Zen master. While the master quietly served tea, the professor talked about Zen. The master poured the visitor's cup to the brim and then kept pouring. The professor watched the overflowing cup until he could no longer restrain himself. "It's overfull! No more will go in!" the professor blurted. "You are like this cup," the master replied, "How can I show you Zen unless you first empty your cup?"

Like the professor in this story, we must continually remind ourselves to "empty our cups" and listen carefully to one another.

Globalization, of course, may be new today in form but it is not new in fact. Nations and cultures have interacted for centuries through three discernible eras of globalization (Friedman, 2000, 2006). The first era, globalization 1.0 from 1492 to 1800, marked the rise of international trade and colonization. The second era, globalization 2.0 from 1800 to 2000, witnessed the growth of multinational companies and a world economy. The third era, globalization 3.0 that began in 2000 and continues today, involves the influence of non-Western countries and the emergence of individuals empowered to collaborate and compete globally. In short, globalization's three eras are characterized by internationalization at the level of countries, companies, and individuals, respectively. Thus, while not new in fact, globalization today proves very different in form and force from its historical predecessors. As Friedman (2000) put it in his landmark book *The world is flat*, "If globalization [today] were a sport, it would be the 100-m dash, over and over and over. And no matter how many times you win, you have to race again the next day" (p. 12). Remaining employable in today's globalized and digital world requires constant mastering and use of growing technologies, acquiring of individual flexibility and career adaptability, and enhancing proactive career self-management (Hirschi, 2018; Lent, 2018).

Huge advances in communication, robotics, automation, artificial intelligence, quantum computing, and other technologies leave virtually no one untouched by globalization 3.0's effects. While the digital age in the current era of globalization makes interconnection exponentially more possible than ever before, it ironically also leaves many people increasingly isolated and anxious. Again, to quote Friedman (2000):

> If the defining anxiety of the Cold War was fear of annihilation from an enemy you knew all too well in a world struggle that was fixed and stable, the defining anxiety in globalization is fear of rapid change from an enemy you can't see, touch or feel – a sense that your job, community or workplace can be changed at any moment by anonymous economic and technological forces that are anything but stable. (p. 12)

These facts and the opportunities and challenges of globalization confront career counselling on an international scale. While not quite as longstanding as globalization, the internationalization of career counselling is also not new and, in fact, closely parallels the timing of the end of globalization 2.0 and the beginning of globalization 3.0.

Innovating Career Counselling: Three Truths

With globalization and the internationalization of career counselling as backdrop, three truths emerge about innovating career counselling theory, research, and practice to promote inclusion and sustainable employment for all people. The first truth is that career counselling has responded and continues to respond to globalization by internationalizing itself (Arthur & McMahon, 2019; Gerstein et al., 2009; Hohenshil et al., 2013; McMahon, 2017; Watson & McMahon, 2012). The second truth is that collaborative efforts around the globe to propagate life design as a new paradigm for careers science and practice have yielded a prime and exemplary way to innovate and update career counselling theory, research, and practice (Nota & Rossier, 2015; Savickas et al., 2009). The third truth is that a substantial life-design conceptual and empirical literature (e.g., see Hartung, 2016; Nota & Rossier, 2015; Rudolph, Zacher, & Hirschi, 2019; Savickas & Guichard, 2016), along with rich career intervention practices in the life-design tradition (e.g., see Maree, 2013; McMahon, 2017; McMahon & Watson, 2015; Savickas, 2015b), have emerged in just the first decade since its original statement. These collective works now place life design alongside P-E fit and life-span development as the third principal paradigm for career theory building, research, and intervention (Savickas, 2013b). The life-design research and practice literature contain identifiable advances, gaps, and possible future directions for careers science and practice and for the continuing international advancement of career counselling to promote inclusion and sustainable employment. The next sections consider each one of these three truths in turn.

Career Counselling Innovates by Globalizing

The first truth is that career counselling has responded to globalization 3.0 by innovating its paradigms and practices through concerted global efforts. Rooted in the person-environment fit and life-span development paradigms and their respective practice methods of vocational guidance and career development (Savickas, 2015a), the field of career counselling has taken action to innovate itself, meet opportunities, and address challenges for globalizing the field. Particularly during the past 20 or so years, an international community of scholars and practitioners has worked to clarify career counselling and developments' mission, crystallize its identity, construct its knowledge base, and craft its practice methods around the world (e.g., see Arthur & McMahon, 2019; Athanasou & Van Esbroeck, 2008; Gerstein et al., 2009; Heppner et al., 2008; Hohenshil et al., 2013; Leong & Blustein, 2000; Leong & Savickas, 2007; Leung, 2003; Moodley, Gielen, & Wu, 2013; Pedersen & Leong, 1997). In so doing, the career counselling field joins globalizing efforts centered on building interconnections, increasing understanding among different cultures and peoples, and sharing common and unique knowledge and practices.

Forming international partnerships. Key among efforts to globalize career counselling has been the formation of vigorous international partnerships among counselling professionals on nearly every continent including Africa, Asia, Australia, Europe, North America, and South America (Gerstein et al. 2009). Groups like the Laboratory for Research and Intervention in Vocational Guidance (LaRIOS, http://www.larios.fisppa.unipd.it/it/) and the European Society for Vocational Designing and Career Counselling (ESVDC, https://uia.org/s/or/en/1122278214) have provided exemplary leadership in this regard. And, of course, counselling and psychology professional associations around the world—including the International Association of Applied Psychology (IAAP), the International Association for Educational and Vocational Guidance, and the International Association for Counselling—foster integrated and integral international partnerships. Meanwhile, cross-national collaborations between and among researchers and practitioners through visiting scholarships and other means have grown and strengthened career counselling's international reach.

Continuing to expand and strengthen international partnerships now more than ever proves necessary for a strong world community to effectively take shape to meet the challenges inherent in today's global and digital age and to develop career counselling principles and practices that promote inclusion and sustainable employment for all. A recent study of international collaborations in counselling psychology (Kivlighan, Adams, Deng, Ye, & Menninga, 2018) underscored this point. The study authors found that the number of publications involving international collaborations increased significantly during the period from 2005 to 2015. Yet, these publications involved authors representing just 28 countries, or less than 15% of the total number of the world's countries. While the study was limited to articles published in two U.S. journals, *The Counselling Psychologist* and *Journal of Counselling Psychology*, it makes the case that much additional collaborative work is needed to truly internationalize psychology and counselling generally and career counselling specifically. Toward this end, various professional associations have advanced career counselling on a global scale. Among the more recent of these associations, the counselling division within IAAP formed with a clear aim to advance career theory, research, and practice in the 21st century.

Organizing international collaborations. To further grow and advance global counselling psychology generally and career counselling in particular, an international group led by prominent career counselling scholar-practitioners (see Leong & Savickas, 2007) generated a proposal and petition to form a counselling division within IAAP. Founded in 1920 as the International Association of Psychotechnology (Association Internationalé de Psychotechnique) to promote collaboration and communication among psychologists worldwide, IAAP stands as the world's oldest international psychological association. In 2002, during the 25th International Congress of Applied Psychology (ICAP) in Singapore, the IAAP Board of Directors approved the formation of the Counselling Division (16) that has for nearly 20 years offered a home to scientist-practitioners concerned with the advancement of counselling psychology and especially career counselling on an international scale.

Consolidating international perspectives. On the heels of Division 16's founding, Leong and Savickas (2007) guest edited a special issue of the IAAP journal *Applied Psychology: An International Review*. The topic of the special issue was International Perspectives on Counselling Psychology. Scholars and practitioners from eleven nations—including Australia, Canada, China, Hong Kong, India, Israel, Japan, South Korea, Portugal, France, South Africa, and the United States—analyzed counselling psychology in their countries vis-à-vis its strengths, weaknesses, and opportunities for growth, as well as threats to its viability. In the concluding article of the special issue, Savickas (2007) culled four themes common among the diverse group of authors' SWOT analyses that suggested "a realistic and meaningful way forward" (Savickas, 2007, p. 182) for strategically consolidating counselling psychology and its subspecialty of career psychology. These themes included (a) defining counselling psychology in global context, (b) crystallizing its identity, (c) constructing indigenous principles and practices, and (d) collaborating cross-nationally. These themes clearly echoed and underscored Leung's (2003) earlier advice for global counselling psychology to form international partnerships, promote cross-national contacts and communication, and use international perspectives and knowledge to meet local needs.

Career Counselling Innovates Through a Paradigm Shift

Deepening the truth that career counselling grows increasingly global, a core group of leaders emerged early on in the formation of IAAP Division 16. This group of leaders impelled a second truth; that is, that international collaboration to propagate life design as a new paradigm serves as a tremendous force for innovating career counselling science and practice and unifying the field. This group assembled to take integrated, intentional, and concerted action in response to the challenges and opportunities of globalization and move career counselling forward in the ways suggested by Savickas (2007), Leung (2003), and the 11-nation counselling SWOT analysis (Leong & Savickas, 2007). Formed in 2006, the 7-nation Life Design International Research Group (see Savickas et al., 2009) provided instrumental leadership, vision, knowledge, and skills to develop career counselling models and methods in a multinational context.

Taking an international approach. The life-design group departed with past approaches whereby "counselling psychology has often looked to other disciplines and specialties in search of a paradigm to guide its practice" (Savickas, 2007, p. 185). Instead, as its first project the group took deliberate action to construct a new paradigm for psychological science and practice borne not of models and methods adopted from other disciplines, nor of one country context but multinational in scope and indigenous to counselling psychology and career counselling. The resulting new paradigm of life design first appeared in a seminal paper published in the *Journal of Vocational Behavior* (Savickas et al., 2009). This landmark work outlined the history, fundamental epistemology, principles, and practices of life design as a new paradigm for career theory and intervention. The paradigm intended to build on rather than replace its predecessors of person-environment fit and lifespan development. Life design was chosen because a decidedly central focus of Division 16 and a critical mass of scholar-practitioners within Division 16 concentrate on career development and vocational guidance. Indeed, counselling psychology on an international scale traces its roots to vocational guidance and career development (Arthur & McMahon, 2019; Athanasou & Van Esbroeck, 2008; Hartung, 2012; Watson & McMahon, 2012).

Today, the internet (of things) and the worldwide web have removed walls and opened doors and windows of opportunity for increased collaboration and knowledge sharing the world over. Likewise, life design as a 21st-century paradigm for career theory and intervention (Savickas et al., 2009) reflects the promulgation of a network of scholars who have substantially helped to coalesce and advance career counselling in international context. Borne over 10 years ago of the work of the seven-nation Life-Design Research team, life design has offered the field a paradigm for internationalizing career counselling. Rather than drawing from other disciplines and specialties, scholar-practitioners have evolved new perspectives on career theory and intervention to better account for the dynamic, non-linear, contextualized, diverse, and uniquely patterned nature of human work life within a rapidly changing and tumultuous global work environment (e.g., see Arthur & McMahon, 2019; Guichard, 2009; Maree, 2007, 2017; McIlveen & Patton, 2007; Savickas, 2013a). Based in constructivist and social constructionist theory (Collin & Guichard, 2011; McMahon, 2017; Young & Collin, 2004), these newer approaches shift the focus from a matching paradigm to a meaning paradigm culminating in life design as a new model and narrative (Hartung, 2013) as a prime practice method for 21st-century career and self-construction (Savickas et al., 2009).

Shifting the paradigm. Work on personal constructs, biographical hermeneutics, and the narrative paradigm over the past 30 years (for a review see Hartung, 2013), along with globalization and internationalization, led to the statement of life designing (Savickas et al., 2009). Life designing offers a paradigm shift by viewing self not as an object or subject, but rather as a project for making meaning (Savickas, 2015a). It most values narratability, or the capacity to tell one's own life story, along with adaptability and intentionality as the main outcomes of career counselling that assist people to answer the question "What purpose does work serve in my life?" The core elements of life design are reflexive consciousness and self-making.

Life designing enriches career counselling's venerable individual differences and developmental traditions with a focus on using work to construct and design a meaningful life. Life design adds to P-E fit and developmental traditions a lexicon of life themes, relationships, story, hope, and purpose to foster a sense of identity and security in self that organizations and workplaces once provided and rarely do any longer (Savickas, 2015a). Much as differential and developmental models predominated 20th-century career development, life designing offers a groundbreaking and powerful framework for comprehending the complexities of work and life in the 21st century. Exemplary career counselling models and methods within the life-design paradigm include self-constructing in France (Guichard, 2009), life construction in Portugal (Duarté, 2009), narrative career counselling in Iceland (Vilhjálmsdóttir & Tulinius, 2009), systems theory and practice in Australia (McMahon & Patton, 2017), career construction in the United States (Savickas, 2013a), and contextual action theory and counselling in Canada and the United Kingdom (Young, 2017; Young, Valach, & Collin, 2002).

Career counselling for life design advances a contextualist epistemology emphasizing human diversity, uniqueness, and purposiveness in work and career to make a life of personal meaning and social consequence. Life design has taken hold as the next major evolution of the field marking a progression in career counselling paradigms from (a) matching and vocational guidance (Holland, 1996) to (b) managing and life-span career development (Super, 1990) to (c) meaning making and life-design (Savickas et al., 2009; Savickas, 2012). This progression places life design alongside vocational guidance and career development as a contemporary model for innovating career counselling and assisting people to manage the exigencies of work and careers in a post-industrial world (Savickas, 2015a).

Innovating through three paradigms. Despite sustained efforts to apply career theories to counselling, the fact remains as Osipow (1994) stated some years ago that "Career theories are not counselling theories" (p. 222). Most career theories, unlike counselling and psychotherapy theories, do not explicitly guide counselling practice. Much of the disconnect between career theory and practice rests in imprecise definitions and inadequate models of career counselling. Over the years, work has helped to redress this problem; most notably in the form of a volume on career counselling theory and practice (Savickas & Walsh, 1996) and in the advancement of constructivist, social constructionist, ecological, systemic, and narrative counselling models and methods (see Arthur & McMahon, 2019; Maree, 2007; McMahon, 2017; McMahon & Watson, 2015). Consolidating these works, Savickas (2015a) provided a framework that distinguished vocational guidance, career development, and life design as three paradigms for career counselling.

Vocational guidance helps people match themselves to educational and occupational settings. Guidance methods assist clients to answer the question "What occupation shall I choose?" Vocational guidance activities count and categorize individual traits and match them to fitting occupational settings. Vocational guidance attends to the objective content of (a) people's self-characteristics such as interests, abilities, and personality and (b) work environment factors that require and reward those characteristics. It thereby helps clients identify the types of people they resemble most and the work environments those people populate. The central goal of vocational guidance is to promote *congruence* between self and occupational setting (Holland, 1997). Clients who match self to setting become *actors* who fit into corresponding work environments that allow them to enact their scripts (Savickas, 2019). Vocational guidance best serves clients who need to affirm an expressed occupational choice, identify alternative educational or occupational pathways to consider, and determine what occupations fit them best.

Career development helps clients develop adaptability for managing tasks and transitions associated with constructing a career and designing their lives. Career adaptability involves acquiring the attitudes, beliefs, and competencies needed for career planning, decision making, exploration, and problem solving (Maree, 2017; Savickas, 2002). Career development methods help clients answer the question "How do I adapt to life tasks and manage career transitions?" Career development activities place work within the context of a client's whole life and attend to subjective processes of (a) patterning life across domains of school, work, play, family, and community and (b) readying clients to make career decisions by teaching them planning attitudes and decision-making skills. It thereby helps clients develop concern about their futures, control of the decision-making process, curiosity to explore educational and vocational options, and confidence to make decisions and deal with barriers to their career development (Savickas, 2002). The central goal of career development is *adaptability* to navigate tasks and transitions (Maree, 2017; Savickas, 1997; Super & Knasel, 1981). Career development interventions best serve clients who need to learn how to balance life roles, gain occupational information, deal with making decisions, manage transitions, and adapt to change.

Life design denotes an interpersonal process of helping people comprehend their life stories and design their life-careers (Savickas, 2019). Counselling methods help clients answer the question "What meaning do I give to work in my life?" Life-design career counselling concerns the purpose work holds for clients with regard to their unique life stories. Its activities construe the themes that pattern clients' lives and give meaning to their life-careers and attend to the dynamics that shape clients' identities and self-concepts. Life design thereby helps clients reflexively comprehend and coherently narrate how they may use a career to advance their life projects. The central goal of life design is *narratability* to reflect on and retell one's own story to foster meaning (Savickas, 2019; Savickas et al., 2009). Clients who know their own stories succeed as *authors* of a life-career that holds meaning for them and that matters to others (Savickas, 2019). Career counselling for life design best serves clients who need to construe their lives holistically and comprehend how they can use work to be themselves more completely.

Enriching career counselling paradigms. In short, guidance involves what occupation to pick, development concerns how to prepare for career decision making, and life design construes what purpose work serves in people's lives. Life design adds richness and complexity to the career planning process by offering opportunity for critical self-reflection. Reflexive engagement with one's life-career story particularly assists individuals who do not benefit from traditional guidance and career development methods. Contemporary advancement of narrative counselling methods aims to assist people to clarify their (career-life) identities and shape the personal meaning of a life-career.

The life design paradigm, without question a signature outgrowth of concerted and collaborative international work and partnerships, now offers a conceptual model and life-long, holistic, contextual, and preventive counselling intervention framework for fostering human life-careers. The Life Design Group itself provides a blueprint for successful international collaborations that others having particular research and practice interests can emulate. These sorts of organized, concerted, and purposeful partnerships represent the important work needed and that is well underway to internationalize career counselling and simultaneously innovate its theories and practice methods.

Career Counselling Innovates Through Research and Practice Advances

With life design as a paradigm shift, a third truth about innovating career counselling emerges; namely, a considerable body of scholarly literature has propelled life design during its first decade as a paradigm for career theory and intervention. The launching point of all life design literature was, of course, the seminal 2009 *Journal of Vocational Behavior* (*JVB*) paper yielded by the Life Design Group's first project (Savickas et al., 2009). To prove the point of life design's growing influence on scholarship, I used PsychInfo to conduct a preliminary and cursory scan of the literature published between 2009 and 2018 that deals with life design. Using life design as well as various combinations of life design and its key principles as keywords, my search identified 363 articles, books, and chapters. This literature could be sorted, with some overlap, according to life design as a paradigm and its core principles and processes of career adaptability, reflexivity, narratability/identity, intentionality, and action.

Life design as a paradigm. A total of 102 articles and chapters from my search dealt with life design as a paradigm. Beginning with the seminal 2009 *JVB* paper (Savickas et al., 2009), these works have articulated and considered life design as a conceptual and intervention model. Among them, and offering the definitive resource on life design generally, Nota and Rossier (2015) edited the *Handbook of Life Design* with chapters contributed by a host of international scholar-practitioners. These chapters consider life design across a full spectrum of theory, developmental age periods, and intervention approaches. Five chapters in particular examine life design as a paradigm, elaborate on its core constructs, and deepen understanding of the model relative to P-E fit and developmental paradigms.

Career adaptability. As would be expected, my search indicated that the vast majority of the published literature dealing with life design focuses on career adaptability—the second project of the Life Design Group. This fact is evidenced in a total of 233 publications about career adaptability and its measurement since the original statement of life design in 2009. Of course, studies abound on the development and validation of the *Career Adapt-Abilities* Scale international form (Savickas & Porfeli, 2012), its use in a variety of country contexts, and its versions published in 13 countries including Belgium, Brazil, China, France, Iceland, Italy, The Netherlands, Portugal, South Africa, South Korea, Switzerland, Taiwan, and the United States (see Leong & Walsh, 2012). Principal among these works, four publications consolidate knowledge about career adaptability and provide go-to resources for researchers, practitioners, educators, and students alike: (a) a *JVB* special issue edited by Leong and Walsh (2012), (b) a 2015 chapter by Rossier (2015), (c) a 2017 volume edited by Maree (2017) with a host of international contributors, and (d) a 2018 literature review published in *Journal of Career Assessment* (Johnston, 2018). An abundant and expanding literature has amassed over the past nine years to map the nomological network and measurement of career adaptability, which has firmly taken its place as a cross-nationally valid construct and practical focus of career intervention and outcome research.

Reflexivity. A total of 12 entries in my literature search dealt with reflexivity. The Life Design Group took as its third collaborative project to examine the life design counselling process. A 2016 special issue of *JVB*, edited by Savickas and Guichard and featuring papers by authors from multiple nations, examined processes of life-design counselling that foster client reflexivity, defined as self-awareness coupled with intentional action directed toward the future (Savickas, 2019). On balance, the studies in the special issue indicated among other things that client reflection and reflexivity result from time-tested and proven core counselling conditions of "a safe environment, [an effective] working alliance, strategic questioning, attunement to client feelings, empathic responding, and encouragement" (Savickas, 2016, p. 88). To measure reflexivity, DiFabio, Maree, and Kenny (2018) constructed and initially validated the Life Project Reflexivity Scale that should stimulate and facilitate much-needed further research on the reflexivity construct.

Narratability/identity, intentionality, and action. Using the keywords of life design coupled with each one of the remaining core life-design principles yielded a total of just 16 entries. Most of these entries were chapters and could be categorized as dealing with narratives and action (e.g., Watson & McMahon, 2015). No articles could be found dealing principally with intentionality.

Conclusion. A preliminary and cursory review indicated that the conceptual and empirical literature dealing with LD can be linked primarily to one of three projects by the Life Design International Research Group (see Savickas & Guichard, 2016): (a) statement of life design as a paradigm, (b) life-design counselling outcome research, principally via constructing a measure of career adaptability, and (c) counselling process research focused on interventions to facilitate reflexivity. Most studies, then, understandably concentrate on these three areas. Little research deals with life design's other principal constructs and counselling processes and goals of narratability, intentionality, and action. Any one of these constructs appears ripe for the focus of future internationally-based research projects.

Meanwhile, work remains critical to mental (including emotional-social and psychological) health and well-being (Paul & Moser, 2009). And all people should have access and ability to engage in decent work (Duffy, Blustein, Diemer, & Autin, 2016). Life design clearly offers positive direction for the careers field to advance human health and well-being and to move the field from the margins to the mainstream of counselling and psychology. Continuing to adopt and advance life-design principles and practices should help transform career counselling from a straightforward, logical pursuit to a complex, therapeutic endeavor to inscribe people's lives with purpose and direction; further blurring the artificial yet long-held line between career and mental health counselling. With continuing efforts led by scholars and practitioners using life design-based career theories and counselling approaches, long-held distinctions between career and mental-health counselling should give way to evolving a perspective on work as central to counselling and essential for mental health and well-being. Doing so should yield the most desirable effect of promoting decent work, employability, and inclusion among all people and may attract more students and professionals to the careers field. Original goals set for life-design as a career intervention framework should continue to propel it for years to come as a theory and practice model for meaningfully construing and constructing work and career in human life.

Conclusion

Entering the third decade of the 21st century, career counselling has taken great strides to internationalize itself and promote theory, research, and practice that promotes inclusion and sustainable employment for all people. The contemporary context of sweeping advances in worldwide information and communication technologies, widespread social reform across many nations, ever-growing population diversity, increased life expectancies in many countries, a global economy, and a transformed world of work have necessitated this change. As the world evolves its new shape as an interconnected globalized system fueled by burgeoning information technology and confronted with ongoing economic fluctuations and widespread social and political upheaval, career counselling around the globe must and will respond and continue to transform, innovate, and unify its paradigms and practices.

A rising tide of revolutionary change in the nature of work itself began in the late 20th century and has accelerated during the first two decades of the 2000s. This change has been fueled by circumstances of the global and information age that affect virtually all human life on every corner of the globe. This change now takes firm hold at the dawn of the third decade of the 21st century in a transformed world of work that requires workers to adapt to living in "knowledge societies" (Savickas et al., 2009, p. 239). In response, career counselling practitioners and scholars around the world have evolved and advanced contemporary perspectives on career to better account for the dynamic, non-linear, contextualized, diverse, and uniquely patterned nature of human work life within a rapidly changing and tumultuous global work environment (Savickas et al., 2009). Based in constructivist and social constructionist theory (Maree, 2007; Savickas, 2002) these approaches shift the focus from a matching paradigm to a meaning paradigm for 21st-century career construction (Savickas, 2019; Savickas et al., 2009). Life designing augments career counselling's individual differences and measurement tradition with a focus on individual life scripts, narratives, and using work to construct and pattern a meaningful life. In so doing, it honors past accomplishments by seeking to manage the "great inheritance" (Savickas et al. 2009; p. 2) of 20th-century P-E fit and developmental career counselling practices, and enrich it with a life-long, holistic, contextual, and preventive counselling intervention framework that increases individuals' life-career adaptability, narratability, and intentionality.

The contemporary global age demands continued work to meet the needs of individuals across nations, societies, and cultures who strive to adapt themselves to changing social, familial, occupational, and other environments. Today's revolutionary times, unseen since the industrial revolution and in striking parallel to the first quarter of the 20th century, demand that career counselling as a field continues to respond to the present-day concerns of people across the globe facing tremendous uncertainty and instability in both themselves and in the world around them. Continually innovating career counselling to better assist people to manage the stresses, uncertainties, and vagaries of life in a post-industrial world requires continuous development as a global community of career counselling scholars and practitioners concerned with promoting inclusion and sustainable employment for all the world's people.

References

Albrow, M., & King, E. (Eds.). (1990). *Globalization, knowledge and society*. London, England: Sage.

Athanasou, J. A., & Van Esbroeck, R. (Eds.). (2008). *International handbook of career guidance*. Dordrecht, The Netherlands: Springer.

Arthur, N., & McMahon, M. (Eds.). (2019). *Contemporary theories of career development: International perspectives*. London, England: Routledge.

Collin, A., & Guichard, J. (2011). Constructing self in career theory and counseling interventions. In P. J. Hartung & L. M. Subich (Eds.), *Developing self in work and career: Concepts, cases, and contexts* (pp. 89–106). Washington, DC: APA Books.

DiFabio, A., Maree, J. G., & Kenny, M. E. (2018). Development of the Life Project Reflexivity Scale A new career intervention inventory. *Journal of Career Assessment*, published online https://doi.org/10.1177/1069072718758065.

Duarte, M. E. (2009). The psychology of life construction. *Journal of Vocational Behavior, 75*(3), 259–266.

Duffy, R. D., Blustein, D. L., Diemer, M. A., & Autin, K. L. (2016). The psychology of working theory. *Journal of Counseling Psychology, 63*(2), 127–148.
Friedman, T. L. (2000). *The Lexus and the olive tree: Understanding globalization*. New York: Farrar, Straus, & Giroux.
Friedman, T. L. (2006). *The world is flat: A brief history of the twenty-first century updated and expanded*. New York: Farrar, Straus, & Giroux.
Gerstein, L. H., Heppner, P. P., Ægisdottir, S., Leung, S. A., & Norsworthy, K. L. (Eds.). (2009). *International handbook of cross-cultural counseling: Cultural assumptions and practices world-wide*. Thousand Oaks, CA: Sage.
Guichard, J. (2009). Self-constructing. *Journal of Vocational Behavior, 75,* 251–258.
Hartung, P. J. (2012). Career development in global context: History, status, and prospects. In M. Watson & M. McMahon (Eds.), *Career development: Global issues and challenges* (pp. 11–26). Hauppauge, NY: Nova Science Publishers.
Hartung, P. J. (2013). Career as story: Making the narrative turn. In W. B. Walsh, M. L. Savickas, & P. J. Hartung (Eds.), *Handbook of vocational psychology* (4th ed., pp. 33–52). New York: Routledge.
Hartung, P. J. (2016). Introduction to the special issue: Advancing career intervention for life design. *The Career Development Quarterly, 64,* 2–3.
Heppner, P. P., Leong, F. T. L., & Gerstein, L. H. (2008). Counseling within a changing world: Meeting the psychological needs of societies and the world. In W. B. Walsh (Ed.), *Biennial review of counseling psychology* (Vol. 1, pp. 231–258). New York: Routledge.
Hirschi, A. (2018). The fourth industrial revolution: Issues and implications for career research and practice. *The Career Development Quarterly, 66,* 192–204.
Hohenshil, T. H., Amundson, N. E., & Niles, S. G. (2013). *Counseling around the world: An international handbook*. Alexandria, VA: American Counseling Association.
Holland, J. L. (1997). *Making vocational choices* (3rd ed.). Odessa, FL: Psychological Assessment Resources.
Johnston, C. S. (2018). A systematic review of the career adaptability literature and future outlook. *Journal of Career Assessment, 26,* 3–30.
Kivlighan, D. M., Adams, M. C., Deng, K., Ye, X., & Menninga, E. J. (2018). A social network analysis of international collaboration in counseling psychology. *The Counseling Psychologist, 46,* 274–295.
Lent, R. W. (2018). Future of work in the digital world: Preparing for instability and opportunity. *The Career Development Quarterly, 66,* 205–219.
Leong, F. T. L., & Blustein, D. L. (2000). Toward a global vision of counseling psychology. *The Counseling Psychologist, 28,* 5–9.
Leong, F. T. L., & Savickas, M. L. (2007). Introduction to special issue on international perspectives on counseling psychology. *Applied Psychology: An International Review, 56,* 1–6.
Leong, F. T. L., & Walsh, W. B. (2012). Guest editors' introduction to the special issue. *Journal of Vocational Behavior, 80,* 659–660.
Leung, S. A. (2003). A journey worth traveling: Globalization of counseling psychology. *The Counseling Psychologist, 31,* 412–419.
Maree, J. G. (Ed.). (2007). *Shaping the story: A guide to facilitating narrative career counselling*. Pretoria, South Africa: Van Schaik Publishers.
Maree, J. G. (2013). *Counselling for career construction: Connecting life themes to construct life portraits. Turning pain into hope*. Rotterdam, The Netherlands: Sense.
Maree, J. G. (Ed.). (2017). *Psychology of career adaptability, employability, and resilience*. NY: Springer.
McIlveen, P., & Patton, W. (2007). Narrative career counseling: Theory and exemplars of practice. *Australian Psychologist, 42,* 226–235.
McMahon, M. (Ed.). (2017). *Career counselling: Constructivist approaches* (2nd ed.). London, England: Routledge.

McMahon, M., & Patton, W. (2017). The systems theory framework: A conceptual and practical map for story telling in career counselling. In M. McMahon (Ed.), *Career counselling: Constructivist approaches* (2nd ed., pp. 113–126). London, England: Routledge.
McMahon, M., & Watson, M. (Eds.). (2015). *Career assessment: Qualitative approaches*. Rotterdam: Sense Publishers.
Moodley, R., Gielen, U. P., & Wu, R. (2013). *Handbook of counseling and psychotherapy in an international context*. New York: Routledge.
Nota, L., & Rossier, J. (Eds.). (2015). *Handbook of life design: From practice to theory and from theory to practice*. Boston, MA: Hogrefe Publishing.
Osipow, S. H. (1994). Moving career theory into the twenty-first century. In M. L. Savickas & R. W. Lent (Eds.), *Convergence in career development theories: Implications for science and practice* (pp. 217–224). Palo Alto, CA: CPP Books.
Paul, K. I., & Moser, K. (2009). Unemployment impairs mental health: Meta-analyses. *Journal of Vocational Behavior, 74*(3), 264–282.
Pedersen, P. B., & Leong, F. T. L. (1997). Counseling in an international context. *The Counseling Psychologist, 25,* 117–122.
Rudolph, C. W., Zacher, H., & Hirschi, A. (2019). Empirical developments in career construction theory. *Journal of Vocational Behavior, 111,* 1–6.
Savickas, M. L. (1997). Adaptability: An integrative construct for life-span, life-space theory. *Career Development Quarterly, 45*, 247–259.
Savickas, M. L. (2002). Career construction: A developmental theory of vocational behavior. In D. Brown and Associates, *Career choice and development*(4th ed., pp. 149–205). San Francisco: Jossey Bass.
Savickas, M. L. (2007). Internationalisation of counseling psychology: Constructing cross-national consensus and collaboration. *Applied Psychology: An International Review, 56,* 182–188.
Savickas, M. L. (2012). Life design: A paradigm for career intervention in the 21st century. *Journal of Counseling and Development, 90,* 13–19.
Savickas, M. L. (2013a). Career construction theory and practice. In S. D. Brown & R. W. Lent (Eds.), *Career development and counseling: Putting theory and research to work* (2nd ed., pp. 147–183). Hoboken, NJ: Wiley.
Savickas, M. L. (2013b). The 2012 Leona Tyler address: Constructing careers—Actors, agents, and authors. *The Counseling Psychologist, 41,* 648–662.
Savickas, M. L. (2015a). Career counseling paradigms: Guiding, developing, and designing. In P. J. Hartung, M. L. Savickas, & W. B. Walsh (Eds.), *APA handbook of career intervention* (Vol. 1, pp. 129–143)., Foundations Washington, DC: APA Books.
Savickas, M. L. (2015b). Life-design counseling manual. Rootstown, OH. www.vocopher.com.
Savickas, M. L. (2016). Reflection and reflexivity during life-design interventions: Comments on career construction counseling. *Journal of Vocational Behavior, 97,* 84–89.
Savickas, M. L. (2019). *Career counseling* (2nd ed.). Washington, D. C.: American Psychological Association Books Inc.
Savickas, M. L., & Baker, D. B. (2005). The history of vocational psychology: Antecedents, origins, and early development. In W. B. Walsh & M. L. Savickas (Eds.), *Handbook of vocational psychology* (3rd ed., pp. 15–50). Mahwah, NJ: Lawrence Erlbaum.
Savickas, M. L., & Guichard, J. (2016). Symposium introduction: Reflexivity in life designing interventions. *Journal of Vocational Behavior, 97,* 1–2.
Savickas, M. L., Nota, L., Rossier, J., Dauwalder, J., Duarte, M. E., Guichard, J., …. van Vianen, A. E. M. (2009). Life designing: A paradigm for career construction in the 21st century. *Journal of Vocational Behavior, 75*, 239–250.
Savickas, M. L., & Porfeli, E. J. (2012). Career adapt-abilities scale: Construction, reliability, and measurement equivalence across 13 countries. *Journal of Vocational Behavior, 80,* 661–673.
Savickas, M. L., & Walsh, W. B. (Eds.). (1996). *Handbook of career counseling theory and practice* Palo Alto, CA: Davies-Black Publishing.

Super, D. E., & Knasel, E. G. (1981). Career development in adulthood: Some theoretical problems *British Journal of Guidance and Counseling, 9*,194–201.

Super, D. E. (1990). A life-span, life-space approach to career development. In D. Brown & L. Brooks (Eds.), *Career choice and development: Applying contemporary theories to practice* (2nd ed., pp. 197–261). San Francisco, CA: Jossey-Bass.

Vilhjálmsdóttir, G., & Tulinius, T. H. (2009). Tales of two subjects: Narratives of career counseling. *Journal of Vocational Behavior, 75*, 267–274.

Watson, M., & McMahon, M. (Eds.). (2012). *Career development: Global issues and challenges.* Hauppauge, NY: Nova Science Publishers.

Watson, M., & McMahon, M. (2015). From narratives to action and a life design approach. In L. Nota & J. Rossier (Eds.), *Handbook of life design: From practice to theory and from theory to practice* (pp.75–86). Boston, MA: Hogrefe Publishing.

Young, R. A. (2017). Career counselling as and about goal-directed human action. In M. McMahon (Ed.), *Career counselling: Constructivist approaches* (2nd ed., pp. 185–195). London, England: Routledge.

Young, R. A., & Collin, A. (Eds.). (2004). Special issue on constructivism, social constructionism, and career. *Journal of Vocational Behavior, 64*(3), 373–532.

Young, R. A., Valach, L., & Collin, A. (2002). A contextualist explanation of career. In D. Brown (Ed.), *Career choice and development* (4th ed., pp. 206–252). San Francisco, CA: Jossey-Bass.

A Contextual Action Theory of Career

Richard A. Young

Abstract Action has always been central to many aspects of psychology but in recent years it has received renewed attention, particularly in light of developments in cognitive neuroscience and other fields. Specifically, cognitive or behavioral explanations in themselves have been seen as incomplete, focusing too exclusively on either internal states or the external world. Action is the proposed alternative, whose meaning and definition has several iterations from intentionality through embodiment. The view presented in this chapter is that action is not just another term to use instead of behavior, cognition, construction, or process (although all are involved). Rather, human action is presented as a unit of social meaning. It involves both the participants' subjective experience and includes manifest behavior. This view has implications for our understanding of career, the practice of career counselling, and how we conduct career-related research. In this chapter, contextual action theory, as a broad conceptual explanation, is presented as the basis for understanding and defining career differently. In this view, career is fully involved with and reflective of human action. By unpacking this approach, the basis for an innovative view of career, and by implication, for career counselling and research, is proposed. It moves away from the longstanding reliance on personality, aptitude, or context as primary explanatory factors for occupational and life choices. The temporal dimension of human action, that is, actions in the present as well as how they contribute to longer-term projects and career provide an important way in which clients can and do construct the present and future. In addition, this recent conceptualization of human action shifts the focus away from the individual to the joint action between people. Others have significant places in individual career lives; human action provides such a framework for how this is done. This approach is illustrated with examples from current career research and practice.

Arthur, Hall, and Lawrence (1989) identified theory as the life blood of scholars in the career field. However, these same scholars are people who act in their daily lives, who rely on the actions of others, and whose theories reflect and attempt to influence

---

R. A. Young (✉)
University of British Columbia, Vancouver, Canada
e-mail: richard.young@ubc.ca

J. G. Maree (ed.), *Handbook of Innovative Career Counselling*,
https://doi.org/10.1007/978-3-030-22799-9_2

the actions of lay persons and professional practitioners. Action can be proposed as the life blood of both career practitioners and lay persons. The challenge of this chapter is to draw these life bloods together in a meaningful way that speaks to both what we do and how we understand it in an organized and systemic way. Specifically, the questions that need to be addressed are whether career theory can represent and address the challenges of living life and the practices that such a life invites.

Over the approximately 11 decades that career has been a formal topic in the human sciences, any number of theories have been developed. These theories have had a variety of purposes and have contributed differently to understanding career and practices related to career. At the same time, practitioners are interested in action/practice and those of us engaged with clients are practice oriented, are action oriented. Ultimately, because it is a human science, the starting point of career theory should be about action or practice.

In this chapter, we describe the contextual action theory of career (e.g., Young & Valach, 2004; Young, Valach, & Collin, 2002). In the first part of this chapter, we articulate some of the fundamental issues career practitioners, theorists, and researchers face in coming to terms with any theory. In the second part of the chapter, we provide an overview of the theory. Interested readers can also consult earlier publications that address this theory and its use in research and practice. However, it is important is to. By doing so, we hope to show that contextual action theory addresses many of the pertinent theoretical issues in the career field and is particularly relevant to linking theory and practice.

Issues Pertinent to Career Theory

Career

One of the challenges of proposing a career theory is the definition of the word career itself. Recently, the term career has come to be associated closely with work, occupation, occupational choice, and occupational satisfaction. But its more traditional meaning allows us to go beyond a narrow occupational sense of the word. The Oxford English Dictionary defines career as a person's "course or progress through life, or a distinct part of life." This definition sanctions a focus on the occupational aspects of life as well as accounting for other aspects that contribute to the lives we live. This dictionary definition is a helpful starting point, but we are still in the domain of a loose collection of phenomena that people refer to and understand as career. Indeed, the range of meanings is so extensive that McMahon (2014) questioned whether career psychology, vocational psychology, and career guidance are the same disciplines. The fact that the term career represents a loose collection of phenomena is not necessarily a bad thing because it speaks to the complexity and to the different social meanings and uses attributed to the concept. This dictionary definition addresses the trend McMahon noted regarding the increasing move of theories about career away from a Western middle-class focus to ones that account for gender, social class, culture, and family background more explicitly.

It is because of the importance of career and its complexity that behavioural scientists have undertaken to explain it in a variety of ways, ranging from matching approaches in the early part of the 20th century (e.g., Parsons, 1909) to life design approaches in first decades of the 21st century (e.g., Nota & Rossier, 2015). These and other theories have provided important information about various aspects of the phenomenon that we know of as career. The study of vocational behavior has served and continues to serve many purposes: it assists people in making good decisions about their futures, it allows workplaces to operate in ways that are productive, efficient, and life enhancing, and it provides career professionals with the bases or frameworks for their interventions and assistance.

The theories of career that have developed since Parsons (1909) articulated his explanation have been responsive to the context in which they were developed. The phenomenon of career is highly representative of contexts and cultures. Guichard (2015) is one among several scholars who described the evolution of career theories from matching through trait-factor, developmental, and finally constructionist approaches. In each of these cases, the phenomenon of career, that is, what the theory was about, had changed. An important observation of the most recent iterations of career theories is the change from more structured, ideological, and organized social forms to one in which the individuals are left to determine what life means to them.

Career serves an important function in society because it is an invitation to action. It is what Gibson (1979) identified as an affordance. The view of a life dedicated to the welfare of others as a medic for Médecins Sans Frontières invites people to consider that possibility. Given many factors present in the environment, this interpretation offers the possibility of action and, in the long term, career. It invites action in the immediate term by the person perhaps Googling what the requirements are to study medicine, but it also provokes looking, in the longer term, at many of the actions that would be needed to become a medic for Médecins Sans Frontières. What is important in this example is the shared cultural and social meaning and the affective value the affordance of a career as a medic in Médecins Sans Frontières stimulates in the person. There is a meaning appraisal of the event, can I accomplish this, is it realistic for me, and there is a great deal of looking forward.

Theory

As we move forward in proposing an innovative theory for career, we must ask the more fundamental question of why are we seeking a theory of career. There are several pertinent reasons. First, we are driven by the scientific paradigm of the 20th and 21st centuries. It was no longer satisfactory to explain phenomena because society believed them to be so. In addition, the complexity and diversification of the world of work, precipitated by the Industrial Revolution, was another important factor in the development of career theory. Many career theories have taken one or other specific perspective, albeit usually an important perspective, to meet the cultural and historical context and career issues present at the time the theory was developed and used. Finally, the formalization of psychology and sociology as empirically oriented disciplines distinct from their philosophical and theological parents allowed the focus on specific domains of behaviour such as career.

The challenge of any theory that undertakes to explain career is the fuzziness of the concept itself, or the elasticity of its definition. But if we take a close look at the definition of career provided earlier in this chapter, we can attest to its meaning as a course or progress through life. A comprehensive theory that accounts for progress over a lifetime must be dynamic. A model that predicts simply from one point in time to another, while valuable in the moment, does not account for the innumerable processes involved. A dynamic theory is one that can account for change across time. In the case of career progress, a dynamic theory about progress over a life will be able to speak to the on-going interaction between the person and the context.

Implicit in the definition as pointed out above is the notion of goals, that is, progress toward what. The course or progress through life is not manifest simply in a job title. If we examine what would comprise a successful course or progress through life in 21st century Western cultures and other cultures as well, we know that it would include well-being, self-esteem, the sense of living a meaningful life, and the care and well-being of children and other significant persons in our lives. These human goals give rise to a complex of inter-related actions over various lengths of time.

Recently, Blustein, Olle, Connors-Kellgren, and Diamonti (2016) have been among those who have articulated criticism of much of what has transpired in vocational psychology as being without an inclusive, social justice perspective. They have suggested that it has excluded the unemployed, those experiencing poverty, and those in unpaid work. If career theory is a construct that excludes certain groups of people, then one can question the appropriateness of the explanation. The social justice challenge is not simply a matter of including marginalized groups in our career discussions, it is a matter of how practices related to these groups are understood and enacted. Career theory is challenged to address this understanding.

When we are addressing career theory, we must acknowledge the issue of epistemology and, relatedly, ontology. Epistemology addresses the nature of knowledge; ontology, the structure of reality or what is it that is known. The tension in science and other fields of knowledge is the separation between epistemology and ontology. There has been a longstanding assumption of an objectivist ontology, that the nature of reality exists independently of how we know it. However, the reality of human consciousness and experience raises the challenge of career theory to offer a good explanation of *qualia*, or the phenomenology of experience. These philosophical positions may seem quite removed from the reality of living lives and pursuing careers. However, they are central. Many career theories and social sciences generally share an objectivist ontology. As such, what aspects of knowledge about career are enhanced and what parts neglected?

Notwithstanding the plethora of career theories, it is interesting to speculate whether there is a theory that can explain in an integrated way how persons' lives are constructed, created, or constituted. Have we in the social sciences figured out how to talk about what we know or what we would like to know about the progress of our lives? Another important question about theory is whether and to what extent we are seeking explanations that can explain, predict, and control or does the theory speak to the interpretation of phenomenon, that is, how they are understood in the human context, including their meaning and significance. Can a theory do both successfully?

The argument to date suggests that we should address several issues/aspects in a theory of career. These include goals, culture, processes or how career is constructed, the influence or relation of the individual's career to other people and institutions. An approach must consider both stability and variability. An adequate theory of vocational behavior must be able to account for the goals toward which behavior is oriented. In many previous theories, accounting for goals has been more implicit than explicit. A theory also needs to be able to account for generativity, that is, how new behavior, actions, meaning and contexts are created (Seligman, Railton, Baumeister, & Sripada, 2013).

Finally, many of the earlier theories of career development were distinct from the practice of career counselling (Harmon, 1966). For some practitioners, career theory may have been irrelevant to counselling practice. Recent efforts, however, have made distinct efforts to increase the connection between career theory and career counselling practice (e.g., Pouyaud, 2016). Recent approaches to career theory have also emphasized a more agentic approach (e.g., Duarte & Cardoso, 2015; Evans, 2017). The question arises whether a common conceptual framework can speak to both career counselling and career development.

Complexity and Context

Two aspects of understanding career come to the fore as particularly challenging: its complexity and the context in which it occurs. The challenge for any theory is how to address both. Many career theories have, in efforts to be rigourous and scientific isolated specific parts of career such as personality traits that predict suitability for certain occupational groups. However, what would a more holistic and systemic perspective lead to? How would it help us understand career differently? There are challenges in pursing such a goal for career theory because even as we engage in it from a systems perspective, we, theorists, researchers, and practitioners are subject to the same tendency to reduce complexity to something that is manageable. The questions that need to be asked are, are we considering psychological, social, cultural and biological processes, and how are we taking these processes into account.

The complexity of career processes demands that we not move too quickly to a simple solution in the form of a theory. We should be wary of assuming everything can be explained by theory X. What we need is an approach that allows us to account for all the factors that we need to pay attention to. As career scientists, we tend to look at the social context and individual behavior in that context, although in the past we may have focused more on stable traits and abilities of the individual. The complexity of career suggests that our actions are based on the social and cultural contexts, in which we are embedded from the very beginning of our lives. Career theory needs to account for how new contexts are formed from our actions.

Previous theories have addressed context by specifying it. For example, Super's (1953) developmental approach to career specified the context at each stage of career development. More recent career theories do not specify the context to the same extent. One reason for not specifying context is that it is not always the same highly structured givens. It is not that the importance of context has diminished, but as Guichard and Pouyaud (2015) observed, it is much more fluid. It is particularly important for theories of career that they be explicitly linked to the environment. Hirschi (2018) took up the same theme in pointing to the silence of career theory in addressing the challenges of the fourth industrial revolution, including digitization, job polarization, and the gig economy.

The complexity and context in which careers are constructed also bring to the fore whether our approaches favour nomothetic or ideographic explanations, that is, whether career theories are oriented toward understanding and explaining what is common to all people or what is unique to individuals. When one considers "progress through life," then theories ought to adequately accommodate for the person-context interaction, and its dynamic and process-oriented characteristics. The actor and the context in which the actor acts should be linked. But it is more than saying a comprehensive career theory should address both person and context. Rather it is that they are linked, and the theory should reflect that linkage. Giddens (1976) captured this linkage by suggesting that human agency and social structures presuppose each other. The social context of career is dense with expectations that have been generated over millennia. At the same time, our expectations of "progress through life" allows each generation and cultural context to develop new sets of expectations through their own cultural practices (Kirmayer & Ramstead, 2017).

Meaning

The cognitive scientist, Popova (2014) observed, "We act in the world in no small measure because we expect our actions and intentions to be understood as meaningful, to be made sense of, by other people" (p. 2). Meaning is a particularly important aspect of career, especially as we look to the definition of career as the progress through life. This progress is representative of the meaning attributed to it. In addition, it is not simply the meaning the individual agent attributes to it, although he or she makes sense of their own progress through life. Rather the meaning has also to do with the culture and context in which social meaning attached to life has developed. It is here that language, cultural norms, symbols, technical artifacts, and customs have an important part to play, as Steiner and Stewart (2009) suggested. It was no longer just work, but the meaning of it, and that meaning is both intrinsic and extrinsic.

Not unrelated to the issue of meaning is narration. In recent years, narrative has become central to career, particularly to the career construction approach (Savickas, 2019). From the career construction perspective, narrative refers to a story one tells about oneself, but lies at the "intersection of self, context, and culture" (Savickas, p. 18). Identity is expressed in narratives. Narration is central to culturally mediated experience (Kirmayer & Ramstead, 2017, p. 405). Narration is less about making up my own story than it is about social practices of communication and conversation. Kirmayer and Ramstead identify a range of action that comprise and contribute to narratives including justifying action, positioning oneself, persuading others, and enjoining others to take action.

Prospection

Current evidence in neuroscience and cognitive psychology has identified prospection as an important cognitive process as one navigates the future (Gilbert & Wilson, 2007; Seligman et al., 2013). Specifically, prospection refers to "the act of thinking about the future" (Buckner & Carroll, 2007, p. 49). This view is well accepted in the career guidance literature, if not explicitly identified as prospection. Career guidance, one prominent function in the career field, is about planning one's future. A general principle of career guidance is to plan one's occupational future based on a current assessment of abilities and interests. Clearly this is an important step in the progress of planning one life.

Prospection is important to career and career guidance. It is also central to the action view elaborated in this chapter. For example, Herwig, Beisert, and Prinz (2013) approximate a definition of action as "body movements that depend on external and internal factors and are directed toward a prospective goal state" (p. 5).

Contextual Action Theory of Career

In this chapter, contextual action theory, as a broad conceptual explanation, is presented as the basis for understanding and defining career differently (Young, Domene, & Valach, 2015; Young & Valach, 2000, 2004). In this view, career is fully involved with, and reflective of, human action. By unpacking this approach, the basis for an innovative view of career, and by implication, for career counselling and career research, is proposed. It moves away from the longstanding reliance on personality, aptitude, development, cognition, or context as primary explanatory factors for occupational and life choices. The temporal dimension of human action, that is actions in the present as well as how they contribute to longer-term projects and career provide an important way in which people generally as well as career counselling clients in particular, can and do constitute the present and future. In addition, this conceptualization of human action shifts the focus away from the individual to the joint action between people, for example, as Prinz (2012) contended. Others have a significant place in individual human action and individuals in the actions of others.

By extension, we can say the same about career. Contextual action theory provides a framework for how this is realized.

One of the primary starting points for the contextual action theory of career is that as human beings we act, that is, we move with the intended effect of changing ourselves, the environment, or, more specifically, ourselves in relation to the environment in some way. We can also suggest that these human actions are the result of expectations that we have learned from our environment, and based on our experience. It is easy to recognize that work, career, occupation, progress in life, or whatever other term you wish to use, involve human action. The view presented in this chapter is that action is not just another term to use instead of behavior, cognition, construction, or process, although all are involved. Rather, human action is presented as a unit of social meaning and involves the participant's subjective experience and manifest behavior. It also includes the notions of intentionality and embodiment, which connect our consciousness to the interpersonal, social, and cultural worlds we inhabit. Action is the process that occurs between an actor and the environment. This assertion is central to understanding action. It also has implications for our understanding of career, the practice of career counselling, and how we conduct career-related research. Specifically, to address the issue of defining career, contextual action theory offers the following definition: "a superordinate construct that allows people to construct connections among actions, to account for effort, plans, goals, and consequences, to frame internal cognitions and emotions, and to use feedback and feedforward processes" (Young & Valach, 1996, p. 364).

Essentially, career represents a series of actions. It is something people do. Although occupational titles are one form of labeling career, for example, in the field of paid work, being a plumber, or in the field of unpaid work, being a family caregiver, are careers composed of actions. We, as cultural groups and individuals, make sense of, and identify them as careers. In the case of family caregiver, some people in Western societies may challenge the idea of family caregiver as a career, which points to how the career is constituted within cultures, societies, and social groups. However, family caregivers act in the moment; the individual caregivers and society may make sense of these actions across time and ascribe meaning to them by identifying them as having meaning in the medium- or long-term, that is, as projects and careers.

The first implication of contextual action theory is that it establishes a strong connection between action and career. In contextual action theory, career is conceptualized as a series of actions, both past and present actions, as well as those anticipated in the future. Project, the intermediate construct that we have found helpful in establishing the link between action and career, is the construction of meaning across actions in the shorter term. Thus, actions can contribute to projects and projects to careers.

However, it is not enough to simply assert that career is composed of human actions. Career is not simply made up of distinct actions as units of social meaning. Career is something more than these units—career is composed of units of social meaning that coalesce across longer periods of time to form superordinate groups of meaningful actions. We have identified these superordinate, coalesced or constituted meaning units as projects in the medium term and career in the long term. If we take the example of any person who has achieved much in their lives, one can identify a number of projects that have contributed to this achievement, all not necessarily successful in themselves. Similarly, those careers would have been made up of innumerable actions. The coalescing of units of social meaning is a complex and dynamic process that involves social groups, institutions, and culture.

Contextual action theory accounts for the complexity of human action. Consider, for example, the case of a young man from Indonesia who works in the sex-trade in a large North America city. There are many explanations for his actions in terms of conditions and events that may have led him to that occupation. Equally, there are many human actions that he engages in with others that represent meaningful goals, and which he constructs over time to be meaningful projects, and even a career. Ultimately, these projects and this career may be detrimental to his life. But it is not to say that he is not actively engaged in it. His occupation allows him to implement several different goals. For example, by being employed in the black market he can hide from government authorities who may wish to deport him to his country of origin. This occupation allows him to earn money, to associate with other young men in similar circumstances, to have housing with others. The complexity of this example allows us to propose a theory that includes action processes, the organization of action, as well as action systems identified above.

Action can also be seen as involving three processes that come together to constitute the action. These processes are manifest, subjective and social. These processes are not distinct entities of action. All three processes are represented in the action, and come together to form the action. Manifest behaviour refers to the aspects of the action that are observable. Subjective processes are those internal cognitive and emotional processes that accompany an action. In the case of joint action, these subjective processes may be shared. Social meaning refers to what the action signifies individually and socially.

Contextual action theory is also oriented toward understanding and framing how actions are organized. Specifically, actions are organized through behavioural elements, functional steps, and goals. We can readily observe that actions are composed of various behavioural elements, replying on skills, habits, internal and external resources. These behavioural elements contribute to actions. In the case of complex actions or series of actions in the form of projects or careers, these elements also rely on other people in the form of language, culture, institutions, time, and other resources to allow the action, project, or career to be engaged in. Functional steps are the contiguous elements one intentionally takes to reach one's goals. Goals represent that toward which an action is directed. Actions and their more complex representations in projects and careers are goal-directed, that is, they are oriented toward something, a goal. Elements, functional steps and goals are the means we use explicitly in the action-project research method, described in a subsequent chapter (Domene, Young, & Wilson, 2019).

Elsewhere we have proposed 29 characteristics, concepts, or constructs that contribute to the life enhancing career, identified by the level of how action is organized for each of the three systems of goal-directed action, that is, action, project, and career (Young & Valach, 2008). Thus, for example, we can hypothesize that meaningful goal-directed action is dependent in part on skills at the level of elements and relevant to a longer-term project at the level of meaning or goals. Consider, for example, a person's ability in expressing to his partner his desire to return to his country of origin for work opportunities when his partner wants to stay in the country to which they have immigrated. This action in the form of a conversation requires a certain skill and is relevant to what the person anticipates in his relationship with his partner and in his occupational future. Similarly, a second example suggests that a life-enhancing career can be postulated to allow for both predictability and novelty as functional processes. While the 29 components of the life-enhancing career are not exhaustive, they illustrate the detail and range of the contextual action theory of career. They also provide starting points for both researchers and practitioners in developing meaningful research questions or identifying challenges clients may face.

In this iteration of contextual action theory, joint action is emphasized, that is, the action that occurs between people. Many actions involve others. Indeed, there is considerable work in the career field focusing on joint actions in the form dialogues in the construction of career (e.g., Guichard, 2016). For example, Pouyaud, Bangali, Cohen-Scali, Robinet, and Guichard (2016) indicated how dialogues with the counsellor contributes to the construction of self. Similarly, Rapa, Diemer, and Bañales (2018) have shown that individual or collective critical action for social change influenced career expectancies and occupational attainment in marginalized youth. By establishing a link between action and the longer-term projects and career, we have moved career theory beyond a simple consideration of the individual to the social. In this view, career cannot simply be explained by individual cognitive processes that predict long-term progress-in-life outcomes. Rather, projects and careers depend on joint actions—actions that are embedded in socially constructed projects and career. Taken to the next step, our view is that the steering and regulation of action is a social as well as an individual process.

When we speak of joint action and project, of course, we are speaking in one sense of a specific activity, a mother and son talking about the son's future. But the substantial social connection is manifest more fully when we speak of career. It takes a society or culture to narrate or construct a career. Careers do not happen by themselves or solely within individuals. They are primarily social constructions, constructed in and by societies and cultures. Career is not simply a story that can be understood as a manifestation of a cognitive understanding or constructed through cognitive information processing. When we speak of career, we speak of one's engagement with society and culture.

Research Applications

Over several years, we have conducted career research using the action-project method, a qualitative method based on contextual action theory. This research as it pertains to the transition to adulthood including educational and occupational positions is reviewed in a later chapter (Domene et al., 2019). Our view is that this perspective and the corresponding action project research method (Young et al., 2005) lend themselves to addressing salient and underrepresented issues in the career literature. Among these topics are emotion, narrative, unconscious processes, intentionality, relationships, and culture (Young & Domene, 2012). These topics form the basis for a research agenda using contextual action theory. The important feature of the conceptualization and the method is that it begins with action which encompasses subjective, manifest and social processes. In addition, the method aligns with what action encompasses by accessing internal processes, manifest behaviour, and goals. It focuses on actual actions between individuals who are connected to each other by virtue of the topic of the research, and examines successive actions longitudinally.

This approach has been used to describe the career and project-related actions of partners in several different groups, for example, couples, parents and adolescents, parents themselves, and counsellors and clients. The specific contribution of these studies is that in them the researchers have been able to describe projects relevant people engage in together, including social meaning, internal and social processes, and manifest behaviours. It differs from survey research that has looked across populations for generalities and from qualitative research based on retrospective accounts. Here the action is the unit of analysis, and then on-going actions across time that form projects.

The method has been used in other cultural settings. For example, Khalifa, Alnuaim, Young, Marshall, and Popadiuk (2018) described the transition-to-adulthood projects, including educational, occupational and family plans between adult family members (parents, older siblings) and young adult children in Saudi Arabia. Marshall et al. (2011) identified the career development projects in Indigenous families in Canada. The method has been suggested for research in vocational psychology in other countries (Piccardo, Pizzorno, & Young, 2009) and in other disciplines (Marshall, Zaidman-Zait, Domene, & Young, 2012; Wall et al., 2016).

Counselling Applications

Career counselling is an important professional activity. Much career research and the theories on which it is based is ultimately oriented toward assisting clients with occupational and educational decision making or work adjustment concerns. Contextual action theory is particularly suited as a conceptual framework for career counselling for several reasons. First, counselling itself is an action. As such, there is no need to have different theories that address career behavior and career counselling. Secondly, contextual action theory provides a conceptual link between career counselling and mental health counselling (Valach & Young, 2017). This framework reflects the way that clients and counsellors experience and understand their own and others' lives as well as the basis for change in those lives.

Various approaches to career counselling have emphasized either social meaning, internal processes, or behaviour. For example, the recent attention to calling or vocation in career counselling attends to social meaning (e.g., Dik, Duffy,

& Eldridge, 2009). Watson's (2015) emotion-focussed therapy for career counselling addresses internal processes, while Sheward and Branch's (2012) cognitive-behavioural approach emphasizes both internal processes and behavior. In contrast, contextual action theory includes behavioural, internal and social processes. In this way, it provides a framework for clients and counsellors to see and act on the full range of action processes.

Contextual action theory provides a basis for how counsellors can be more explicit in identifying goals within counselling and in clients' lives more generally, and tying these goals to action (Young, Valach, & Domene, 2015). Five steps to using contextual action theory in career counselling are described in a later chapter of this text (Domene et al., 2019).

Conclusion

We began this chapter by raising five questions that are pertinent to proposing an innovative theory of career. First, what is the domain or phenomenon of career; how is it defined? Secondly, what is theory intended to do for career research and practice? Thirdly, how can career theory adequately accommodate the complexity of career and the variety of contexts in which it is embedded? Fourthly, where does meaning fit in career theory? Finally, how can career theory capture the person's navigation of the future?

Contextual action theory offers a comprehensive way of understanding career that is in line with recent developments in cognitive psychology and neuroscience and addresses many of the challenges that have arisen relative to career theory. The principal thesis is that careers (read *progress through life*) are constructed through the actions of people as they engage with their contexts and with each other. Contextual action theory addresses how people engage in action and how actions are constructed across time to form projects and career. For the purposes of career research and practice, it links concepts such as intentions, meaning, and identity.

As is evident in this chapter, action theory is not just about career as associated with occupational pursuits. At first blush, it may seem too broad and too encompassing a theory to be useful for career. But it is precisely by drawing on these significant theoretical developments in adjacent sciences that we can hope to address the important issues in career, link career with counselling practice and the lives of our clients and advance our discipline.

References

Arthur, M. B., Hall, D. T., & Lawrence, B. S. (1989). Generating new directions in career theory: The case for a transdisciplinary approach. In M. B. Arthur, D. T. Hall, & B. S. Lawrence (Eds.), *Handbook of career theory* (pp. 7–25). Cambridge: Cambridge University Press.

Blustein, D. L., Olle, C., Connors-Kellgren, A., & Diamonti, A. J. (2016). Decent work: A psychological perspective. *Frontiers in Psychology, 7*, Article ID 407.

Buckner, R. L., & Carroll, D. C. (2007). Self-projection and the brain. *Trends in Cognitive Sciences, 11*, 49–57. https://doi.org/10.1016/j.tics.2006.11.004.

Dik, B. J., Duffy, R. D., & Eldridge, B. M. (2009). Calling and vocation in career counseling: Recommendations for promoting meaningful work. *Professional Psychology: Research and Practice, 40*, 625–632. https://doi.org/10.1037/a0015547.

Domene, J. F., Young, R. A., & Wilson, C. L. L. (2019). Career counselling for emerging adults based on goal-directed action: An innovative approach to theory, research, and practice. In J. G. Maree (Ed.), *Innovating career counseling theory, research, and practice: In search of promoting inclusion and sustainable employment for all*. New York, NY: Springer.

Duarte, M. E., & Cardoso, P. (2015). The life design paradigm: From practice to theory. In L. Nota & J. Rossier (Eds.), *Handbook of life design: From practice to theory and from theory to practice* (pp. 41–59). Boston, MA: Hogrefe.

Evans, K. (2017). Bounded agency in professional lives. In M. Goller & S. Paloniemi (Eds.), *Agency at work: An agentic perspective on professional learning and development* (pp. 17–26). Cham, Switzerland: Springer International.

Gibson, J. J. (1979). *The ecological approach to visual perception*. Boston: Houghton-Mifflin.

Giddens, A. (1976). *New rules of sociological method: A positive critique of interpretive sociologies*. London: Hutchinson.

Gilbert, D., & Wilson, T. (2007). Prospection: Experiencing the future. *Science, 351*, 1351–1354. https://doi.org/10.1126/science.1144161.

Guichard, J. (2015). From vocational guidance to career counseling to life design dialogues. In L. Nota & J. Rossier (Eds.), *Handbook of life design: From practice to theory and from theory to practice* (pp. 11–25). Boston; MA: Hogrefe.

Guichard, J. (2016). Reflexivity in life design interventions: Comments on life and career design dialogues. *Journal of Vocational Behavior, 97*, 78–83. https://doi.org/10.1016/j.jvb.2016.08.001.

Guichard, J., & Pouyaud, J. (2015). Processes of identity construction in liquid modernity: Actions, emotions, identifications, and interpretations. In R. A. Young, J. F. Domene, & L. Valach (Eds.), *Counseling and action: Toward life-enhancing work, relationships, and identity* (pp. 91–114). New York: Springer Science + Business Media.

Harmon, L. W. (1966). A moving target: The widening gap between theory and practice. In M. L. Savickas & W. B. Walsh (Eds.), *Handbook of career counseling theory and practice* (pp. 37–44). Palo Alto, CA: Davies-Black.

Herwig, A., Beisert, M., & Prinz, W. (2013). Action science emerging: Introductions and leitmotifs. In W. Prinz, M. Beisert, & A. Herwig (Eds.), *Action science. Foundation of an emerging discipline* (pp. 1–33). Cambridge, MA: MIT Press.

Hirschi, A. (2018). The fourth industrial revolution: Issues and implications for career research and practice. *Career Development Quarterly, 66*, 192–204. https://doi.org/10.1002/cdq.12142.

Khalifa, H., Alnuaim, A. A., Young, R. A., Marshall, S. K., & Popadiuk, N. (2018). Crafting continuity and change in Saudi society: Joint parent-youth transition-to-adulthood projects. *Journal of Adolescence, 63*, 142–152. https://doi.org/10.1016/j.adolescence.2017.12.014.

Kirmayer, L. J., & Ramstead, M. J. D. (2017). Embodiment and enactment in cultural psychiatry. In C. Durt, T. Fuchs, & C. Tewes (Eds.), *Embodiment, enaction, and culture: Investigating the constitution of a shared world* (pp. 397–422). Cambridge, MA: MIT Press.

Marshall, S. K., Young, R. A., Stevens, A., Spence, W., Deyell, S., Easterbrook, A., & Brokenleg, M. (2011). Adolescent career development in urban-residing Aboriginal families in Canada. *Career Development Quarterly, 59*, 539–558. https://doi.org/10.1002/j.2161-0045.2011.tb00975.x.

Marshall, S., Zaidman-Zait, A., Domene, J. F., & Young, R. A. (2012). Qualitative Action-Project method in family research. *Journal of Family Theory & Review, 4*, 160–173. https://doi.org/10.1111/j.1756-2589.2012.00117.x.

McMahon, M. (2014). New trends in theory development in career psychology. In G. Arulmani, A. J. Bakshi, F. T. L. Leong, & T. Watts (Eds.), *Handbook of career development: International perspectives* (pp. 13–27). New York: Springer Science + Business Media.

Nota, L., & Rossier, J. (Eds.). (2015). *Handbook of life design: From practice to theory and from theory to practice*. Boston; MA: Hogrefe.

Parsons, F. (1909). *Choosing a vocation*. Boston, MA: Houghton-Mifflin.

Piccardo, C., Pizzorno, M. C., & Young, R. A. (2009). The action-project method and its applicability across a range of qualitative studies in vocational psychology. *Risorsa Uomo, 15,* 23–35.

Popova, Y. (2014). Narrativity and enaction: The social nature of literary narrative understanding. *Frontiers in Psychology, 5*(895), 1–14. https://doi.org/10.3389/fpsyg.2014.00895.

Pouyaud, J. (2016). For a psychosocial approach to decent work. *Frontiers in Psychology, 7*(422). https://doi.org/10.3389/fpsyg.2016.00422.

Pouyaud, J., Bangali, M., Cohen-Scali, V., Robinet, M. L., & Guichard, J. (2016). Exploring changes during life and career design dialogues. *Journal of Vocational Behavior, 97,* 3–12. https://doi.org/10.1016/j.jvb.2016.07.008.

Prinz, W. (2012). *Open minds: The social meaning of agency and intentionality*. Cambridge, MA: The MIT Press.

Rapa, M. A., Diemer, L. J., & Bañales, J. (2018). Critical action as a pathway to social mobility among marginalized youth. *Developmental Psychology, 54,* 127–137. https://doi.org/10.1037/dev0000414.

Savickas, M. L. (2019). Constructing self and identity. In M. L. Savickas (Ed.), *Career counseling* (2nd ed., pp. 15–36). Washington, DC: American Psychological Association.

Seligman, M. E. P., Railton, P., Baumeister, R. F., Sripada, C. (2013). Navigating into the future or driven by the past. *Perspectives on Psychological Science, 8,* 119–141. https://doi.org/10.1177/1745691612474317.

Sheward, S., & Branch, R. (2012). *Motivational career counselling and coaching: Cognitive and behavioural approaches*. London: Sage.

Steiner, P., & Stewart, J. (2009). From autonomy to heteronomy (and back): The enaction of social life. *Phenomenology and the Cognitive Sciences, 8,* 527–550. https://doi.org/10.1007/s11097-009-9139.

Super, D. E. (1953). The theory of vocational development. *American Psychologist, 8,* 185–190.

Valach, L., & Young, R. A. (2017). Action: A bridge between vocational and mental health counselling. *British Journal of Guidance and Counselling, 45,* 519–531. https://doi.org/10.1080/03069885.2017.1370628.

Wall, J. M., Law, A. K., Zhu, M., Munro, D., Parada, F., & Young, R. A. (2016). Understanding goal-directed action in emerging adulthood: Conceptualization and method. *Emerging Adulthood, 4,* 30–39. https://doi.org/10.1177/2167696815610695.

Watson, J. C. (2015). Emotion-focused psychotherapy: An alternative framework for career counseling. In R. A. Young, J. F. Domene, & L. Valach (Eds.), *Counseling and action: Toward life-enhancing work, relationships, and identity* (pp. 135–148). New York: Springer Science + Business Media.

Young, R. A., & Domene, J. F. (2012). Creating a research agenda in career counselling: The place of action theory. *British Journal of Guidance and Counselling, 40,* 15–30. https://doi.org/10.1080/03069885.2011.620603.

Young, R. A., Domene, J. F., & Valach, L. (2015). Counseling and action. In R. A. Young, J. F. Domene, & L. Valach (Eds.), *Counseling and action: Toward life-enhancing work, relationships, and identity* (pp. 1–10). New York: Springer Science + Business Media.

Young, R. A., & Valach, L. (1996). Interpretation and action in career counseling. In M. L. Savickas & M. B. Walsh (Eds.), *Handbook of career counseling theory and practice* (pp. 361–375). Palo Alto, CA: Davies-Black.

Young, R. A., & Valach, L. (2000). Reconceptualising career theory and research: An action-theoretical perspective. In R. A. Young & A. Collin (Eds.), *The future of career* (pp. 181–196). Cambridge: Cambridge University Press.

Young, R. A., & Valach, L. (2004). The construction of career through goal-directed action. *Journal of Vocational Behavior, 64,* 499–514. https://doi.org/10.1016/j.jvb.2003.12.012.

Young, R. A., & Valach, L. (2008). Action theory: An integrative paradigm for research and evaluation in career. In J. Athanasou & R. van Esbroeck (Eds.), *International handbook of career guidance* (pp. 643–658). New York, NJ: Springer-Science.

Young, R. A., Valach, L., & Collin, A. (2002). A contextual explanation of career. In D. Brown & Associates, *Career choice and development* (4th ed., pp. 206–250). San Francisco, CA: Jossey-Bass.

Young, R. A., Valach, L., & Domene, J. F. (2005). The action-project method in counseling psychology. *Journal of Counseling Psychology, 52,* 215–223. https://doi.org/10.1037/0022-0167.52.2.215.

Young, R. A., Valach, L., & Domene, J. F. (2015). Counseling processes and procedures. In R. A. Young, J. F. Domene, & L. Valach (Eds.), *Counseling and action: Toward life-enhancing work, relationships, and identity* (pp. 317–336). New York: Springer Science + Business Media.

Life-Design Counselling from an Innovative Career Counselling Perspective

Maria Eduarda Duarte, Maria Paula Paixão and José Tomás da Silva

Abstract Adopting a new career counselling perspective is an essential element in the continuous effort to innovate the life-design (LD) paradigm and make it sustainable in a dialogue together with other emerging counselling models and theories. This constant dialogue corresponds to the route traveled by seminal figures in the career counselling discipline and is currently best represented by a consistent effort to renovate assessment and intervention procedures and tools (particularly those promoting a holistic and dynamic view of the person-in-context). The discussion around employability is used as a platform for showing life-designing potential in this innovative agenda. In an effort to anticipate future challenges, the authors claim the advantage of adopting an integrated research agenda that is able to align converging epistemologies in career theory, assessment and practice in a both bottom-up (theory-building) and top-down (theory-driven) shared scientific endeavor.

Keywords Innovation · Life-design counselling (LDC) · Qualitative assessment · Career metaphors · Employability · Decent work agenda

Introduction

This chapter seeks to frame career counselling relative to what is considered as innovation. It also attempts to substantiate the notion that using stories is an innovation in career counselling, in other words, innovating through personalities telling a story to play out the idea's realities, and looking to integrate the story into and adapt it to the contexts in which they live. The emphasis is on upholding the notion that inno-

M. E. Duarte
Faculty of Psychology, University of Lisbon, Lisbon, Portugal
e-mail: maria.ec.duarte@gmail.com

M. P. Paixão (✉) · J. T. da Silva
Faculty of Psychology and Educational Sciences, University of Coimbra, Coimbra, Portugal
e-mail: mppaixao@fpce.uc.pt

J. T. da Silva
e-mail: jtsilva@fpce.uc.pt

J. G. Maree (ed.), *Handbook of Innovative Career Counselling*,
https://doi.org/10.1007/978-3-030-22799-9_3

vating in counselling is not to designate an operation of a *quantitative*, but rather of a *qualitative* nature, in the sense that the objective is to find the general set of relationships that defines the individual singularity in which nothing can be forgotten or ignored. Phrases such as *to innovate* and *innovation* appear to increasingly occupy the center of attention in the contemporary world and particularly in specialized career counselling literature.

But what are we talking about when we refer to life-design counselling (LDC) from an innovative career counselling perspective? In order to answer this question, we need to focus on the meaning of the word *innovation* as a platform that is used to highlight the main transformative moments in career counselling. This can be seen through the legacy of those who left their mark on the history of the topic, beginning with Frank Parsons and progressing through time until reaching the LD and other convergent contemporary paradigms.

Currently, both the constructivist and social constructionist epistemological lenses make a case for career interventions that need to incorporate a dynamic approach that goes beyond the traditional assumptions of stability and stages. This approach specifically encourages the development of adaptability competencies and identity resources that individuals need in order to do "imaginative thinking and the exploration of possible selves" (Savickas et al., 2009, p. 242). The centrality of qualitative career assessment, the innovative potential of career metaphors and the crucial role played by critical counselling processes (e.g., work alliance, innovative moments) also need to be integrated in the epistemological discussion encompassing career theory, research and practice.

Concerning research and practice, we strongly defend the idea that, in LDC, the main goal is not to guarantee employment for life (which is no longer feasible), but to help individuals construct their own lives in the social, economic and historical space in which they live by continuously ascribing new and useful meanings in the course of this construction process. Moreover, using the LDC paradigm (Savickas, 2015a), we try to support this idea based on the assumption that any analysis transpires from a learning process. A learning process, in turn, comes about through understanding, and understanding can only be achieved via the lenses of theoretical robust frameworks that take the individual-in-context into account.

We do not have a *crystal ball* to predict the future, but we have some tools and concepts that we can incorporate in the LD paradigm. Examples are the notion of decent work, the relevance of human needs 'nutrition' via innovative psychosocial interventions, and the effort to seek converging epistemologies in career theory, assessment and practice in a shared bottom-up (theory-building) and top-down (theory-driven) scientific endeavor.

All in all, we argue that innovating is a process not so much aligned with the idea of finding the right answers for contemporary complex problems, but rather with adopting an interrogative stance that continually searches for the best questions that promote and expand the critical and creative thinking that is needed to transform and move forward in the next decades.

Chapter Structure

Following the introduction, the first part of the chapter briefly discusses what innovating means in career counselling—by examining its etymological root as well as highlighting the pioneering work of some of its historical figures. The second part focuses on the LDC paradigm and the importance of adopting a storied approach to continuously innovate and expand the discipline's assessment and interventions tools within the career counselling process. The search for sustainable employability within LDC is discussed in the third part of the chapter. The fourth part tries to guess the next steps of LDC evolution by constructing new bridges with similar and promising paradigms, such as the psychology of working theory. Finally, in the conclusion, we underscore the importance of adopting a creative stance to make innovation possible.

Chapter Goals

The main goal of this chapter is to clarify and substantiate the idea of innovation from the LD paradigm perspective. It is argued that the methods and procedures that allow the adoption of a full storied approach and of an encompassing framework (that enables the articulation of employability with decent work goals) are the cornerstones of the future LDC agenda.

Innovation and Career counselling

What are we talking about when we refer to innovation or what is new? For the ancient Greeks, the *new* was the notion of recently ploughed land that had been prepared for planting. The Greek word was also a designation for *youth* and, by association, that which was *unexpected* or *out of the ordinary*. The Romans also adopted the phrase and adapted it, remaining faithful to *innovare*, or to renew. In this context, what matters is how such things are actually done, and how they function within the context of career counselling. The word *innovation* (and its cognates) brings with it a history littered with *realities*, such as those that Parsons (1909) noted early in the 20th century as the idea affirming itself symbolically as a radically human and social element. In this way, the act of innovating is seen as a story told by personalities who play out the idea's realities and who look to integrate it into the contexts in which they live and those that they strive to adapt to.

The individual, from a social and cultural point of view, is the result of the interaction of many diverse factors that surround him/her and with whom he/she must interact. This cultural and social production is indispensable for making sure that a discourse makes sense. Counselling is not constituted in a theoretical body for repetition, but rather for the articulation of differences and reading/explaining them in the context in which they occur. In that way, the counsellor is a *reader* who *reads* the counselee's narrative or discourse. That is, counselling is more of a process than a concept, more explicative than explorative or descriptive.

In order to establish a stronger bond between innovation and career counselling, one should take a brief look at the past. The first career counselling services originated at the beginning of the 20th century in a process that Parsons (1909) designated as 'vocational guidance.' In this particular field, this was perhaps the first act of innovation in the sense that it sought to aid individuals—particularly the younger generations—who lived through and felt the first results of the Industrial Revolution and experienced the need to choose a profession. A new context demanded new solutions and, most importantly, new ways of tackling the problems presented. However, the true act of innovation did not come about from one day to the next; a form of intervention that emerged from social work allowed for an embodiment, creating a new professional identity that Parsons in 1908 named the 'vocational counsellor' (Savickas, 2015a). Essentially, it was following World War II that the works of Ginzberg, Ginsburg, Axelrad, and Herma (1951), and later Super (1957), found their place into the history of vocational guidance, and the word *career* took on a notable conceptual role. The greater contribution is said to belong to Super for his developmental model of evaluation. It is here that we can identify a second instance of innovation involving movement from an emphasis on profession (Parsons, 1909) to an emphasis on the development of the career (Super, 1957, 1990).

The third innovation is a kind of 'moving through' until reaching the point of a study of the relationship between the individual, society and other individuals. It is a constructionist perspective, which is supported by the principle of a socially constructed reality. From this perspective, counselling is conceived as an encounter where an objective reality is consensually understood and re-recognized. Essentially, it can be said that the third innovation consists of the perception that the client of counselling is no longer an individual that is 'catalogued' through the use of measuring instruments calibrated to certain groups (age, gender, or socio-professional status), as was the case with the pioneering models. The individual is an active participant in the process of counselling and is through self-narration of the own life story capable of actively playing a part in the process: by giving it their own voice that is inevitably conditioned by the context in which they live and interacting with the changes that new technologies make available. This new paradigm is the natural heir of previous paradigms, and as such it introduced considerable shifts that are needed not only for the survival of such paradigms in their core function, but also for their improvement and their adaptation to new realities.

In career counselling, innovation can be seen as a theoretical reference that feeds off a dialogic relationship through which we can define arguments, order them, and later transform them into words that give meaning to the narrative of each. The role of the counsellor in this dialogic relationship involves the devolution, rather than the provision of the answer (or absence of an answer), thereby helping the counselee to find the most adequate words for the construction of the own discourse. In this way, the counsellor opens up a space in the relationship for the introduction of an individual discourse relative to a life story. The counsellor and the counselee are, therefore, two voices in dialogue. In fact, Savickas (2016) strongly defends the idea that LDC, as well as other postmodern constructivist and social constructionist approaches, should clearly promote reflexivity—a mindful and action-oriented reflection that helps individuals define new perspectives when facing transitions or turning points (Guichard, 2008). Reflexivity points out connections to the future that accrue with continuities from the past, thus projecting narrative information into the future that is capable of engaging counselees in the counselling process. According to Savickas (2016), it is important to engage counselees in dialogues that deconstruct and then reconstruct their career stories, and that construct meaning and form intentions. How? By transforming micro-narratives into a macro-narrative or life portrait that enables them to revise their career identity by setting realistic alternatives, new intentions and new action plans. Reflexivity is mainly required in novel situations and when substantial career transitions take place, in order to move the counselee to a new perspective.

Career Counselling as an Innovative Storied Perspective

The legacy of what 20th century theories of career guidance have achieved represents a big step in understanding individuality as rooted in a system. This legacy has allowed guidance and counselling to work with the theories of constructivism (Savickas, 2012) and social constructionism (Gergen, 2001). This more inclusive approach achieves a deeper understanding of the individual. The realities of the 21st century are obviously different from those that led to the conceptualization, development and implementation of the models and paradigms during most of the 20th century. In view of these realities, and in understanding career counselling in the 21st century, we must consider some new and varied aspects. One of these are the parameters that guide its application, such as examining the knowledge of new models and techniques and the working tools available. Thus, counselling can provide a richer supportive relationship in a way that better fits into a society where individuals are responsible for their particular career trajectories (Duarte, 2015a).

As recently argued by McMahon, Watson, and Lee (2018), qualitative career assessment is focused on stories and narratives that are shaped by rapidly changing macro-, meso- and micro-contexts. This approach is more closely aligned with constructivist and narrative approaches by having an idiographic nature and adopting a holistic (focusing on the individual) rather than a discrete (focusing on measures) approach. However, they underscore the fact that little attention has been paid to qualitative career assessment. They also make the case that the number of recent articles published on this topic has not increased in recent issues of the main journals when compared to issues published in the late 1990s or even the early 21st century. Let's not forget that Savickas's call to do so, both in career research and counselling, was made in 1993 (Savickas, 1993). Thus, the expected turn from scores (e.g., testing) to stories is only partial, and the authors present several motives to explain this fact (e.g., criteria of the editorial boards, lack of robustness of research on qualitative career assessment, and the strong and globally accepted quantitative tradition). This is one of the main reasons why McMahon et al. (2018) stress that research into qualitative assessment and its use in career counselling should be strengthened and expanded, and that it should provide more than just activities and processes (e.g., evidence of efficacy in specific groups of counselees, counsellors' competence to use it, and so on). Some examples of influential approaches that rely on qualitative assessment can nevertheless be cited: Peavy's socio-dynamic approach (1998); Cochran's narrative career counselling (1997); McMahon and Watson's storytelling model (2010); Maree's career construction model (2013); and action theory from Young et al. (2011).

McMahon and Watson (2015) boldly stated that while qualitative approaches to career assessment are all widely rooted in a learning, constructive and context-embedded enterprise, the specific procedures they rely on are anchored in different learning styles. These learning styles include auditory (with procedures such as structured, semi-structured or unstructured interviews); visual (with procedures like pattern identification, career genograms, collages, life-lines); and kinesthetic (with techniques such as career writing, card-sorts, and laddering). Utilizing appropriate methods based on learning styles can optimize the transformative potential of the counselling process.

Another example of qualitative career assessment can be derived from the construct of the career metaphor (Inkson, 2004). The incorporation of a career metaphor in the counselling context can be rather useful once it is rooted in theory, as it provides both an internal meaning and an external understanding. When used in an expanded rather than a restrictive way, it promotes new forms of thinking and acting on the topic of assessment in the counselling context. Additionally, it facilitates the use of innovative evaluation and intervention tools that foster the creation of purpose and meaning (Dik et al., 2015). Inkson (2004) contends that metaphors can undermine career thinking when they express powerful and culturally pervasive stereotypes. However, when alternative metaphors are jointly and creatively used, integrating complementary learning styles, they can provide both the counsellor and the counselee with a more inclusive and deeper understanding of career phenomena. For example, the legacy metaphor (career as an inheritance) can constrain the values and expectations of individuals coming from a low socio-economic status. However, the use of genograms (a visual procedure) and the analysis of early memories (a predominantly auditory tool), might help them feel empowered in their career construction efforts by enabling them to identify new or already existing (albeit not used) internal and external assets. The same thing happens with the matching metaphor (career as a fit), but LDC can extend *fit* across life contexts and temporal horizons, transforming jobs into callings (Dik et al., 2015). An example of a simultaneous and rather complex kinesthetic and auditory procedure is the job crafting technique, where counselees can shape their own experience to meet their work-related needs, thus promoting the alignment of a particular career path with a broader sense of purpose. The same reasoning can be extended to all the career metaphors discussed by Inkson (2004, 2006), where change in the discourse can be co-constructed via a coherent and creative set of procedures.

A further example of the use of qualitative career assessment in the LD paradigm (Savickas et al., 2009) is the procedures that result from career construction theory (Savickas, 2013). It is possible to assume innovation if one considers that the core ideas of the LD framework and career construction counselling facilitate its integration into psychotherapy. These core ideas include an emphasis on the individual as a constructor of contextual meanings via the use of life themes. Such meanings can be achieved by focusing counselees on their core themes to help them organize their self-experience (Cardoso, 2016).

According to Rossier, Ginevra, Bollmann, and Nota (2017), one aspect that is commonly found in the various dialogues between counselee and counsellor involves a tacit cooperation (work alliance): it is the ability to mutually understand and coordinate these dialogues. Another point in common is that it seems possible to identify an evident affinity between the procedural devices of the *discipline* (Caws, 1965). However, although allowing progress, this basic affinity between processes of understanding among different theories does not contribute to the definition of the concept of counselling per se (Duarte, 2015b). Indeed, this definition is seen through its instrumental character and, innovatively, it should affirm that knowledge informed by theory never coincides with the extensive area covered by the definition in question. There are always phenomena that escape definition, including the essence of individuals' career-life stories (Duarte, 2017). In that sense, and in contrast to a definition, theory provides what is needed for the discovery of career construction through life stories, namely through the reconstruction of one's narrative and the co-construction of an identity narrative. The LD paradigm does not take counselling to be a closed concept, but rather as one that is capable of integrating new elements (Duarte, 2017), as is the case with the use of the Innovative Moments Coding System, grounded in a narrative conception of the self (Cardoso, Silva, Gonçalves, & Duarte, 2014).

As for the future agenda of qualitative career assessment, McMahon et al. (2018) stress the need to attend to the following issues: (a) providing a clearer definition; (b) creating a rigorous research base and corresponding reporting (e.g., theoretical framework, methodological implications); (c) providing more detailed information about ethical considerations; (d) promoting their sound integration into the training of career counsellors; and (e) conducting research with diverse samples.

LDC in Search of Promoting Sustainable Employability

The information technology (IT) revolution, and the economic globalization of which it is part, have made it clear that corporations around the world are less and less likely to display a vested interest in supporting 30 year careers or providing permanent job arrangements for their employees. In fact, in the wake of the economic and technological changes in the labor market and the employment uncertainties that have erupted as a result, people have been forced to become self-directed in managing their careers as a way to foster readiness for the many expected and unexpected life-career transitions, as well as to increase their chances of employability. Because of these uncertain times, current career interventions need to incorporate a dynamic approach that goes beyond the traditional assumptions of stability and resemblance (e.g., Holland, 1997) and of career stages (e.g., Super, 1990). Counselling interventions need to specifically encourage the development of the adaptability competencies and identity resources needed by individuals. This dynamic model is not devised to guarantee employment for life (something that is no longer feasible for most people) but to help individuals construct their own lives in the social, economic and historical space in which they live.

Based on the perspective of constructivism (Savickas, 2011, 2012, 2015a, 2015b), LDC adheres to a contextualist philosophy of science and stresses the relevance of twin processes of designing and healing (Savickas, 2015b). It contrasts sharply with the previous 20th century paradigms of vocational counselling practice that were built on different perspectives and philosophies of theories and processes. However, the arrival of a new paradigm does not necessarily mean that the previous ones were wrong. It rather suggests that by themselves they are no longer wholly useful for the challenges facing the present world of work. Through that prism, prevalent career models are best viewed as "three developmental layers of acting, agency and authoring used by individuals in the construction of psychological individuation" (Savickas, 2013, p. 151).

LDC is essentially a manifestation of the broader narrative counselling type of psychological intervention. The LD paradigm proposes that the individual and the context are both resources and constraints that shape an individual's career trajectories and broader life (Rossier et al., 2017). The paradigm was created by an international team of career theorists and practitioners (Savickas et al., 2009) to address the challenges of the 21st century's volatile, uncertain, complex and ambiguous world of work (Savickas, 2015b). At the same time, it proposed a timely answer to the complex career-related needs and concerns of those individuals who hope to prosper and thrive in this 'brave new world'. LDC particularly, as an example of other constructionist and narrative intervention possibilities, seeks to encourage meaningful activities that further self-making, identity building and career construction (Savickas, 2012). It does so by moving from scores and stages to stories. As McAdams (1993) notes, the "stories we live by" represent rich narratives that include thoughts, needs, values, interests, feelings, meanings, experiences, trauma, and triumph, all of which are analyzed for underlying patterns and themes (Glavin, Haag, & Forbes, 2017).

The process of LDC entails assessment and counselling methods that consider the four keystone elements (i.e. life structure; development tasks; life patterns and themes; personality style) of career construction theory (CCT) (Savickas, 2013). Specifically, in terms of career counselling goals, the model highlights its "capacity for changing endings of the many people's life stories by fostering, in a preventive way, their adaptability, a broader activity base, goal-directed behaviour, and the narratability" (Nota et al., 2014, p. 255). In general, being a constructionist perspective,

LDC underscores "flexibility, employability, commitment, emotional intelligence, and lifelong learning" (Savickas, 2012, p. 14).

Life-Design Counselling and Employability

As previously mentioned, globalization, innovations in technology, and a *nomad* workforce are among the powerful variables that jointly create an unstable and unpredictable world of work for current decision makers. Worldwide, citizens are invited to reinterpret career not as a "lifetime commitment to any one employer, but as selling services and skills to a series of employers who need projects completed" (Savickas, 2011, p. 3). In sum, "considering the de-standardized, and individualized life courses that people now experience" (Savickas, 2015a, p. 136), they need to foster their *employability*, which includes preparing for possibilities and adapting to changes.

Career counsellors can help their clients to become more employable by encouraging their adaptability and narratability (Savickas, 2011). They usually do so within a career construction counselling framework beginning with a Career Construction Interview (CCI) (Savickas, 2011, 2015c). Based on a CCI assessment, the counsellor gathers rich information in the form of small stories on the client's life structure (comprising the roles that constitute one's life); career adaptability self-regulations (concerns, control, curiosity, and confidence); life patterns and themes (those that command, shape and define the client's self and forms of identity) (Guichard, 2009), and personality style (resemblances and reputation).

There is accumulated evidence that LDC is effective in promoting a person's adaptability and narratability. In fact, in the past decade, LDC for career construction has attracted increasing attention from researchers and practitioners on a global scale. For example, in a book recently edited by Maree (2017a), an internationally diverse group of scholars explored the rich links among several constructs included in the new lexicon of LDC, notably those of adaptability, employability and resilience (Savickas, 2015b). Even if it is easy to find strong evidence in those chapters on the hypothesized relationships among the three constructs, there is nevertheless a lack of studies addressing the *direct* impact of LDC methods and materials on an individual's prospects of employability.

Given the epistemological stance of social constructionism as the base of LDC, it should be noted that the bulk of the abovementioned research studies are qualitative in nature, typically following a case study type of research methodology (Yin, 2014). These studies offer many enlightening descriptions and rich comprehensive analyses of the processes underlying LDC, as well as their contribution to achieving relevant outcomes (e.g., adaptability, narratability, intentionality). Furthermore, these case studies have compiled evidence regarding the robustness of assumptions and theoretical principles underlying LDC, and their usefulness to different types of clients (Hughes, Gibbons, & Mynatt, 2013; Maree, 2014, 2015, 2016; Maree & Crous, 2012; Maree & Twigge, 2016), and evidence regarding specific cultural contexts and client goals (e.g., Rehfuss, Del Corso, Galvin, & Wykes, 2011). Moreover, other researchers using LDC or CCIs have begun to examine the role of therapeutic collaboration and its effect on narrative change and desired career outcomes (e.g., Cardoso et al., 2014; Cook & Maree, 2016; Di Fabio, 2016; Hartung & Vess, 2016; Pouyaud, Bangali, Cohen-Scali, Robinet, & Guichard, 2016; Reid, Bimrose, & Brown, 2016).

Life-Design Counselling and Achievement of Decent Work Goals

It should be kept in mind that LDC emphasizes that employability—"the ability to keep the job one has, or to get the job one wants" (Rothwell, 2015, p. 328)—is conceived as a capability and not as employment for life. Thus, promoting employability or helping clients acquire the strategic survival tools needed to cope and thrive in turbulent times, is an important goal for life-design career interventions (Maree, 2017a). Accordingly, employability (or "employment as an outcome") is basically a *means to an end*, not an end in itself. We assert that some vitality and reinvigoration of life design for the following decade can rest upon that seminal idea, already expounded in the initial LD proposal. In fact, since the beginning, LDC has strongly underscored the senselessness in compartmentalizing the 'work task' away from other life tasks (e.g., intimacy, social relationships). As such, policy makers, politicians and government officials must realize that contemporary citizens do not yearn exclusively for a way to earn their living (having a job/gainful employment), but rather for work that "provides individuals with ways to contribute meaningfully to the general social welfare of the community at large" (Taber & Briddick, 2011, p. 107) and that simultaneously offers opportunities for decent work (Maree, 2017a).

More recently, we have noted some initial and exciting collaboration between LDC tenets and other theoretical perspectives, particularly the psychology of working theory (PWT) (Blustein, 2006; Duffy, Blustein, Diemer, & Autin, 2016). Based on their common interest, the topic of Decent Work is addressed—a kind of work that promotes both individual and societal well-being (Briddick & Sensoy-Briddick, 2017). Nevertheless, ever since researchers started to address that agenda, societies have blatantly failed to create the necessary opportunities for decent work for all, to devise the strategies and programs that can improve the quality of life of all persons, or to alleviate poverty and eradicate rampant worldwide social inequities and injustices (Maree, 2017b).

Furthermore, we think that in the upcoming decade both scholars and practitioners should delve more deeply into studying the processes and uncovering the methods that can be put to good use in promoting the Decent Work Agenda (ILO, 1999), namely striking a balance between work and other life tasks for both female and male citizens across all age groups. Thus, when implementing LDC career interventions, career counsellors must begin by asking themselves how they can help their clients examine activities in life domains other than that of work. In so doing, they are contributing to an individual's self-construction and global well-being. Proponents of LDC pinpoint the need for counsellors to "develop personalized career counselling activities that make it possible to approach clients by giving them voice, respecting their uniqueness, establishing a counselling relationship, based on a working alliance where both client and counsellor actively participate" (Nota, Soresi, Ferrari, & Ginevra, 2014, p. 255).

Given that we live in information- and knowledge-based societies, to satisfy the demanding Decent Work Agenda, the potential of communication technologies must incorporate the 'basic mode of operations' (face-to-face individual counselling) and its traditional 'old proof' outreaching modalities (e.g., group counselling, self-directed interventions) in LDC. This is an important move towards expanding LDC's reach because, as Bridddick and Sensoy-Briddick (2012, p. 327) plainly put it, "there is a definitive need for low-cost, high-yield interventions and techniques or, in other words, affordable professional responses that can provide practitioners and their clients with a wealth of useful information". Perusal of the existing career literature reveals several promising works in that direction (see for example, Cardoso, Janeiro, & Duarte, 2018; Di Fabio & Maree, 2012; Hartung & Santilli, 2018; Nota, Santilli, & Soresi, 2016).

Finally, scholars, researchers and practitioners of different theoretical frameworks are invited to combine and coordinate efforts in the coming decades to address the pressing task of advocating and promoting sustainable employability and decent work for all. We agree with Briddick and Sensoy-Briddick (2017) who maintain that, together, the framework of LD interventions and the PWT offers solid bases for that mission. Both approaches show promise in going beyond the singular concern of making people more employable by addressing the important goal of promoting sustainable (decent) employability for all human beings.

Looking into the *Crystal Ball*: Some Thoughts on the Fourth Major Paradigm in Career Counselling

In 1937, American Delmore Schwartz wrote the short story entitled 'In Dreams Begin Responsibilities', and we agree with this sentiment because it reflects how new ideas about counselling roles are important to help people survive without losing their sense of individuality. In the current uncertain context where people are confronted with unforeseeable tasks, new demands and constraints, the focus must be not only on the individual, but also on the social, economic, and political spheres. In fact, postmodern epistemologies, like LDC, strongly support the fact that reality is constructed in social and cultural contexts, and multiple truths are dependent on diverse, albeit interrelated, micro- and macro-contextual systems.

As we have been arguing in this chapter, the rise of unemployment, underemployment and precarious work across the globe, as well as the crucial concerns regarding the future of work in a 'second machine age' (Blustein, Kenny, Di Fabio,

& Guichard, 2019) must be addressed from a psychosocial point of view. Such a new approach should be capable of highlighting the dimensions of work that nurture essential human needs (e.g. survival, social connections and self-determination). The nurturing of these universal needs must be closely aligned with adequate career practices and the corresponding assessment procedures that scaffold individuals in their responses to the main societal challenges confronting them.

Are we facing the second generation of the LD paradigm? Is this new generation of the LD paradigm built upon asking useful and meaningful questions, rather than giving more or less complex answers to a constantly evolving subject-context unit? Of course we think the answer to both questions is yes, because we believe that the LD paradigm is evolving into a new form where asking the right questions is the answer to help diverse pools of counselees facing future challenges in core life domains.

Our *crystal ball* seeks answers to questions such as the following: (1) From a theoretical, research and practical point of view, how can we strengthen the collaboration between the LD approach and more traditional (e.g., Super's Life-Span, Life-Space Theory) and emergent perspectives (e.g., Blustein's PWT) in order to create the greatest impact upon the career counselling field? (2) Which issues (of theory, research, practice) are the most practical to begin constructing the bridge between psychological and broader social and economic perspectives on career counselling, whose goal is to empower the counselee's self-construction processes? (3) What are the barriers to achieving integration and an innovating synthesis? (4) How can those barriers be overcome? (5) Who could start that process, where and how?

OECD (2012) contends that educational aims must be focused on providing successful educational outcomes for all learners, thus fostering equity—both in inclusion (ensuring that all learners reach at least the basic minimum level of skills) and fairness. Thus, personal and socio-economic circumstances such as gender, ethnic origin or family background are prevented from presenting obstacles to learning about, recognizing and fulfilling different learners' needs. Career counselling should be able to provide a meaningful framework that allows individuals from all backgrounds to make relevant career/life decisions, to survive and to even flourish in an era defined by flexible work and mobile (and often insecure) life pathways within contemporary liquid and globalized societies (Guichard, 2015). These aims clearly call for a thorough renovation of LDC's methods and materials. As an example of such a renovation, we emphasize the need to devise ICT tools and group-based interventions, to make them available in several community contexts, and to foster counselees' narratability competencies in a constructive dialogue with LDC trained practitioners.

In this second generation of the LD paradigm, we also conceive that individuals are proactive organisms with a natural tendency to optimize their own life contingencies towards increasing levels of coherence, synthesis and self-organization (a growth-oriented process). This process occurs at both the intrapersonal level (by bringing interests, preferences, and personal values into greater harmony to form a sense of autonomy or volition) and the interpersonal level (by forming the sense of belonging in the social network) (Cordeiro et al., 2018). Hence, optimal development or flourishment is achieved when career counselling is helpful in coherently and systematically affording supportive influences that help promote proactivity, integration, and well-being.

An integrated research agenda is needed, one that is able to align converging epistemologies in career theory, assessment and practice in a bottom-up (theory-building) as well as top-down (theory-driven) shared scientific endeavor. This would help bridge the gap between conceptual knowledge, assessment and counselling, while also incorporating co-culturally constructed diversity issues (e.g. gender, SES, sexual orientation, disability, age, etc.). The option to customize psychoeducational and counselling interventions seems evident (Savickas, 2016). While psychoeducational interventions (frequently with a promotional and universal emphasis) rely on reflection and involve a symbolic representation of experience and reflective self-examination, counselling interventions (often targeted and intensive) require reflexivity; that is, they envision career transitions from a new perspective and allow the revision of career identity.

Conclusion

Returning to the beginning of this chapter, to *innovate* can be seen as flexibility and a personal demand for the expression of just that, but it is often constrained by social and other kinds of pressure. Implicit expression requires an understanding of using a collective language (in the universal sense), a language that is understood by the interlocutor through the lens of the original meaning of the concept.

Essentially, to tackle *innovation* is positive, and it is just as well for career counselling that *new* theories exist, or current paradigms evolve. New paths for career interventions are opening in career counselling theories, both from a theoretical and practical point of view, thereby allowing for counselling to be understood as an interrogative process of critical thinking (Duarte, 2015b). Essentially, this interrogative process will be the new start of a new study of new problems that counselling will bring about. To this end, constructivist or constructionist approaches, or the theorization of narrative, will continue to pursue an end—without such approaches actually being that end—even if the focus is slightly different according to the specific post-modern point of view. For example, whereas constructivism focuses on meaning making and the construction of social and psychological worlds, the emphasis in social constructionism is on the contribution that social processes and interactions make to narrative construction.

It appears as if realities give a historic form to career counselling, because it is a specific field that deals with an actual reality. For example, the LD paradigm takes on the form of looking at things with enough consistency and coherency to construct itself with a specified, yet permanently transient truth, branded by time and in light of a certainty that will always be probabilistic. Diversifying the focus of counselling and the strategies used according to the counselees' needs, implies a mixture of forms to construct life trajectories, including working-life. These new forms must also acknowledge the dependencies between the individual and the labor market. The benefits of LDC rely precisely on this diversity of both trajectories and possibilities: customized dialogues that use different learning styles in career assessment will certainly address the specific needs of different counselees or of the same counselees at different moments in time. On the other hand, the emphasis on narratability can be used to empower counselees to construct a brighter future by expanding their skills portfolio.

So, everything is relative, even that *new* which we believe to be ours. It is not new, but simply the result of a different view. It has already been affirmed somewhere that artistic creators, in not being subject to the limitations (frames) of theoretical models, are capable of feeling something first, something that science only comes to understand later. That is the reason why we dare to use our *crystal ball*.

References

Blustein, D. L. (2006). *The psychology of working: A new perspective for career development, counseling, and public policy*. New York, NY: Routledge.

Blustein, D., Kenny, M., Di Fabio, A. M., & Guichard, J. (2019). Expanding the impact of the psychology of working: Engaging psychology in the struggle for decent work and human rights. *Journal of Career Assessment, 1,* 3–28. https://doi.org/10.1177/1069072718774002.

Briddick, W. C., & Sensoy-Briddick, H. (2012). The concept of role models in life design. *Cypriot Journal of Educational Sciences, 7,* 326–333.

Briddick, W. C., & Sensoy-Briddick, H. (2017). Paradigm and promise: Life design, psychology of working and decent work. In J. G. Maree (Ed.), *Psychology of Career Adaptability, Employability and Resilience* (pp. 317–327). Cham, Switzerland: Springer.

Cardoso, P. (2016). Integrating life-design counselling and psychotherapy: Possibilities and practices. *Career Development Quarterly, 64,* 49–63. https://doi.org/10.1002/cdq.12040.

Cardoso, P., Janeiro, I., & Duarte, M. E. (2018). Life-design counselling group intervention with Portuguese adolescents: A process and outcome study. *Journal of Career Development, 45,* 183–196. https://doi.org/10.1177/0894845316687668.

Cardoso, P., Silva, J., Gonçalves, M., & Duarte, M. E. (2014). Narrative innovation in Life-Design Counselling: The case of Ryan. *Journal of Vocational Behavior, 85,* 276–286. https://doi.org/10.1016/j.jvb.2014.08.001.

Caws, P. (1965). *The Philosophy of Science: A Systematic Account*. Princeton, NJ: Van Nostrand.

Cochran, L. (1997). *Career counseling. A narrative approach*. Thousand Oaks, CA: Sage.

Cook, A., & Maree, J. (2016). Efficacy of using career and self-construction to help learners manage career-related transitions. *South African Journal of Psychology, 36,* 1–10. https://doi.org/10.15700/saje.v36n1a1225.

Cordeiro, P., Paixão, M. P., Lens, W., Lacante, M., & Luyckx, K. (2018). Parenting styles, identity development and adjustment during career transitions: The mediating role of psychological needs. *Journal of Career Development, 1,* 83–97. https://doi.org/10.1177/0894845316672742.

Di Fabio, A. (2016). Life design and career counselling innovative outcomes. *The Career Development Quarterly, 64,* 35–48. https://doi.org/10.1002/cdq.12039.

Di Fabio, A., & Maree, J. G. (2012). Group-based life-design counselling in an Italian context. *Journal of Vocational Behavior, 80,* 100–107. https://doi.org/10.1016/j.jvb.2011.06.001.

Dik, B., Duffy, R., Allan, B., O'Donnell, M., Shim, Y., & Steger, M. (2015). Purpose and meaning in career development applications. *The Counseling Psychologist, 43,* 558–585. https://doi.org/10.1177/0011000014546872.

Duarte, M. E. (2015a). Some reflections on guidance and career counselling in the 21st century. In A. di Fabio & J-L. Bernaud (Eds.), *The Construction of the Identity in 21st Century* (pp 59–72). New York, NY: Nova Science.

Duarte, M. E. (2015b, May). Innovation in Career Counselling: Myths and Realities. Keynote presented at NICE Conference, Slovak University of Technology, Bratislava, Slovakia.

Duarte, M. E. (2017). Career counselling research-practice disparities: What we know and what we need to know. *South African Journal of Education, 37,* 1–7. https://doi.org/10.15700/saje.v37n4a1486.

Duffy, R. D., Blustein, D. L., Diemer, M. A., & Autin, K. L. (2016). The Psychology of Working Theory. *Journal of Counseling Psychology, 63,* 127–148. https://doi.org/10.1037/cou0000140.

Gergen, K. (2001). Psychological science in a postmodern context. *American Psychologist, 56,* 803–813.

Ginzberg, E., Ginsburg, S., Axelrad, S., & Herma, J. (1951). *Occupational Choice: An Approach to a General Theory*. New York, NY: Columbia University Press.

Glavin, K. W., Haag, R. A., & Forbes, L. K. (2017). Fostering career adaptability and resilience and promoting employability using life-design counselling. In J. G. Maree (Ed.), *Psychology of Career Adaptability, Employability and Resilience* (pp. 433–445). Cham, Switzerland: Springer. https://doi.org/10.1007/978-3-319-66954-0_25.

Guichard, J. (2008). Proposition d'un schéma d'entretien constructiviste de conseil en orientation pour des adolescents ou de jeunes adultes [Outline of a life-design counselling interview for adolescents and young adults]. *L'Orientation Scolaire et Professionnelle, 37,* 413–440. https://doi.org/10.4000/osp.1748.

Guichard, J. (2009). Self-constructing. *Journal of Vocational Behavior, 75,* 251–258. https://doi.org/10.1016/j.jvb.2009.03.004.

Guichard, J. (2015). From vocational guidance and career counseling to life-design dialogues. In L. Nota & J. Rossier (Eds.), *Handbook of Life Design: From Practice to Theory and from Theory to Practice*. Boston, MA: Hogrefe.

Hartung, P. J., & Santilli, S. (2018). My career story: Description and initial validity evidence. *Journal of Career Assessment, 26,* 308–321. https://doi.org/10.1177/1069072717692980.

Hartung, P. J., & Vess, L. (2016). Critical moments in career construction counseling. *Journal of Vocational Behavior, 97,* 31–39. https://doi.org/10.1016/j.jvb.2016.07.014.

Holland, J. L. (1997). *Making Vocational Choices* (3rd ed.). Odessa, FL, USA: Psychological Assessment Recourses.

Hughes, A. N., Gibbons, M. M., & Mynatt, B. (2013). Using narrative career counseling with the underprepared college student. *Career Development Quarterly, 61,* 40–49. https://doi.org/10.1002/j.2161-0045.2013.00034.x.

ILO (1999). *Decent Work: Report of the Director-General. International Labour Conference, 87th Session*. Geneva: International Labour Office. Retrieved from https://www.ilo.org/public/.

Inkson, K. (2004). Images of career: Nine key metaphors. *Journal of Vocational Behavior, 65*(1), 96–111. https://doi.org/10.1016/S0001-8791(03)00053-8.

Inkson, K. (2006). Protean and boundaryless careers as metaphors. *Journal of Vocational Behavior, 69,* 48–63. https://doi.org/10.1016/j.jvb.2005.09.004.

Maree, J. G. (2013). *Counselling for career construction*. Rotterdam, The Netherlands: Sense.

Maree, J. G. (2014). Career construction with a gay client: a case study. *British Journal of Guidance and Counselling, 42,* 436–449. https://doi.org/10.1080/03069885.2014.886670.

Maree, J. G. (2015). Career construction counseling: A thematic analysis of outcomes for four clients. *Journal of Vocational Behavior, 86,* 1–9. https://doi.org/10.1016/j.jvb.2014.10.001.

Maree, J. G. (2016). Career construction counseling with a mid-career black man. *Career Development Quarterly, 64,* 20–34. https://doi.org/10.1002/cdq.12038.

Maree, J. G. (Ed.). (2017a). *Psychology of Career Adaptability, Employability and Resilience*. Cham, Switzerland: Springer.

Maree, J. (2017b). Utilizing career adaptability and career resilience to promote employability and decent work and alleviate poverty. In J. G. Maree (Ed.), *Psychology of Career Adaptability, Employability and Resilience* (pp. 349–373). Cham, Switzerland: Springer.

Maree, J., & Crous, S. (2012). Life-design career counselling with an abandoned adolescent: A case study. *Journal of Psychology in Africa, 23,* 106–113. https://doi.org/10.1177/0081246314566785.

Maree, J. G., & Twigge, A. (2016). Career and self-construction of emergent adults: The value of life-designing. *Frontiers of Psychology, 6,* 1–12. https://doi.org/10.3389/fpsyg.2015.02041.

McAdams, D. P. (1993). *The Stories we Live by: Personal Myths and the Making of the Self.* New York, NY: Guilford Press.

McMahon, M., & Watson, M. (2010). Storytelling: moving from thin theories to thick and rich stories. In J. Maree (Ed.), *Career Counselling: Methods that Work.* Cape Town, South Africa: Juta.

McMahon, M., & Watson, M. (Eds.). (2015). *Career Assessment: Qualitative Approaches.* Rotterdam, The Netherlands: Sense.

McMahon, M., Watson, M., & Lee, M. (2018). Qualitative career counseling: A review and reconsideration. *Journal of Vocational Behavior.* https://doi.org/10.1016/j.jvb.2018.03.009.

Nota, L., Santilli, S., & Soresi, S. (2016). A life-design-based online career intervention for early adolescents: Description and initial analysis. *Career Development Quarterly, 64,* 4–19. https://doi.org/10.1002/cdq.12037.

Nota, L., Soresi, S., Ferrari, L., & Ginevra, M. C. (2014). Vocational designing and career counseling in Europe: Challenges and new horizons. *European Psychologist, 19,* 248–259. https://doi.org/10.1027/1016-9040/a000189.

OECD (2012). *Equity and Quality in Education: Supporting Disadvantaged Students and Schools.* OECD. https://doi.org/10.1787/9789264130852-en.

Parsons, F. (1909). *Choosing a Vocation.* Boston, MA: Houghton-Mifflin.

Peavy, R. (1998). *Socio-Dynamic counselling. A constructivist perspective.* Victoria, Australia: Trafford.

Pouyaud, J., Bangali, M., Cohen-Scali, V., Robinet, M. L., & Guichard, J. (2016). Exploring changes during life and career design dialogues. *Journal of Vocational Behavior, 97,* 3–12. https://doi.org/10.1016/j.jvb.2016.07.0080001-8791.

Rehfuss, M. C., Del Corso, J., Galvin, K., & Wykes, S. (2011). Impact of the Career Style Interview on individuals with career concerns. *Journal of Career Assessment, 19,* 405–419. https://doi.org/10.1177/1069072711409711.

Reid, H., Bimrose, J., & Brown, A. (2016). Prompting reflection and learning in career construction counseling. *Journal of Vocational Behavior, 97,* 51–59. https://doi.org/10.1016/j.jvb.2016.07.013.

Rossier, J., Ginevra, M., Bollmann, G., & Nota, L. (2017). The importance of career adaptability, career resilience, and employability in designing a successful life. In J. Maree (Ed.), *Psychology of Career Adaptability, Employability and Resilience* (pp. 65–82). Cham, Switzerland: Springer. https://doi.org/10.1007/978-3-319-66954-0_5.

Rothwell, A. T. (2015). Employability. In P. J. Hartung, M. L. Savickas, & W. B. Walsh (Eds.), *APA Handbook of Career Intervention* (Vol. 2, pp. 337–350). Washington, DC: APA Books.

Savickas, M. L. (1993). Career counseling in the postmodern era. *Journal of Cognitive Psychotherapy: An International Quarterly, 7,* 205–215. Retrieved from www.ingentaconnect.com/content/springer/jcogp/1993/00000007/00000003/art00006.

Savickas, M. L. (2011). *Career Counselling.* Washington, DC: American Psychological Association.

Savickas, M. L. (2012). Life Design: a paradigm for intervention in the 21st century. *Journal of Counseling and Development, 90,* 13–19. 10.1111/j.1556-6676.2012.00002.x.

Savickas, M. L. (2013). Career construction theory and practice. In R. W. Lent & S. D. Brown (Eds.), *Career Development and Counselling: Putting Theory and Research to Work* (2nd ed., pp. 147–183). Hoboken, NJ: Wiley.

Savickas, M. L. (2015a). Career counselling paradigms: Guiding, developing, and designing. In P. J. Hartung, M. L. Savickas, & W. B. Walsh (Eds.), *APA Handbook of Career Intervention* (Vol. 1, pp. 129–142). Washington, DC, USA: APA Books.

Savickas, M. (2015b). Life-designing with adults: Developmental individualization using biographical bricolage. In L. Nota & J. Rossier (Eds.), *Handbook of Life Design: From Practice to Theory and from Theory to Practice* (pp. 135–149). Boston, MA: Hogrefe.

Savickas, M. L. (2015c). *Life-design Counseling Manual.* Retrieved from http://www.vocopher.com.

Savickas, M. L. (2016). Reflection and reflexivity during life-design interventions: Comments on career construction counseling. *Journal of Vocational Behavior, 97,* 84–89. https://doi.org/10.1016/j.jvb.2016.09.001.

Savickas, M. L., Nota, L., Rossier, J., Dauwalder, J. P., Duarte, M. E., Guichard, J., … & van Vianen, A. E. M. (2009). Life designing: A paradigm for career construction in the 21st century. *Journal of Vocational Behavior, 75*, 239–250. https://doi.org/10.1016/jvb.2009.04.004.

Super, D. E. (1957). *The Psychology of Careers*. New York, NY, USA: Harper & Row.

Super, D. E. (1990). A life-span, life-space approach to career development. In D. Brown & L. Brooks (Eds.), *Career choice and development* (2nd ed., pp. 197–261). San Francisco, CA: Jossey-Bass.

Taber, B. J., & Briddick, W. C. (2011). Adlerian-based career counseling in an age of protean careers. *Journal of Individual Psychology, 67,* 107–121.

Yin, R. (2014). *Case Study Research Design and Methods* (5th ed.). Thousand Oaks, CA: Sage.

Young, R., Marshall, S., Valach, L., Domene, J., Graham, M., & Zaidman-Zait, A. (2011). *Transition to Adulthood: Action, Projects and Counselling*. New York, NY: Springer.

Sustainable Careers, Vulnerability, and Well-Being: Towards an Integrative Approach

Ieva Urbanaviciute, Felix Bühlmann and Jérôme Rossier

Abstract Career landscapes have changed over the recent decades with a de-standardization of career paths. Globalization, more flexible labor markets, and new ways of working are just a few of the many factors that erode the boundaries of a well-defined career path. Today, many workers are thus confronted by the vulnerability paradox, where diverse career opportunities and an emphasis on personal agency carry a share of uncertainty, inequity, and pressure to keep fit at all times. This chapter discusses the idea of sustainable careers as an antipode to occupational vulnerabilities in the modern world of work. Indeed, promoting sustainability in flexible and deregulated labor markets can be very difficult. However, this sustainability is necessary to promote employees' well-being. To elaborate these crucial challenges, we will develop an integrative theoretical approach encompassing both micro- and macro-level factors that may influence occupational trajectories and workplace experiences.

Keywords Occupational vulnerabilities · Sustainable careers · Well-being · Career development

I. Urbanaviciute · J. Rossier (✉)
Institute of Psychology, University of Lausanne, Lausanne, Switzerland
e-mail: jerome.rossier@unil.ch

I. Urbanaviciute
e-mail: ieva.urbanaviciute@unil.ch

I. Urbanaviciute · F. Bühlmann · J. Rossier
Swiss National Centre of Competence in Research LIVES, University of Lausanne, Lausanne, Switzerland
e-mail: felix.buhlmann@unil.ch

F. Bühlmann
Institute of Social Sciences, University of Lausanne, Lausanne, Switzerland

J. G. Maree (ed.), *Handbook of Innovative Career Counselling*,
https://doi.org/10.1007/978-3-030-22799-9_4

Chapter Structure

The chapter begins with an overview of issues and trends that characterize career development in the contemporary labor market, also defining the vulnerability paradox. We then discuss the role of contextual and personal factors that shape career trajectories and may play a role in determining workers' access to decent work and sustainable careers. To conclude, we present an integrative model that provides some insights into the micro- and macro-level actions that should be implemented to combat vulnerability and promote well-being.

Career Development in a Changing World of Work

Characteristics and Trends of the Modern Labor Market

Over the 20th century, labor markets in most developed countries have been characterized by an increase of the service sector and a concomitant decline of agricultural and—from the 1960s onwards—industrial sectors. This trend, in combination with the unprecedented economic boom of the post-war years led to labor market conditions that in hindsight became a historical exception: A large part of the European and North-American (male) population were employed in so-called *standard jobs*: full time, permanent, regular hours (9–5), with a single direct employer. Even though this situation still exists for a certain part of the workforce, since the 1970s this type of standard employment lost ground and has slowly been replaced by new atypical, flexible, or precarious forms of employment. In European countries, the share of employees with non-standard employments among the working age population typically varies between 10% and 40% (Hipp, Bernhardt, & Allmendinger, 2015). At the origin of this trend were demographic evolutions, such as the increase of female labor market participation, transformation of the welfare state and institutional and organizational adaptations to the macro-transformation of capitalism. The intensification of international exchanges of goods, services, and persons—globalization—and "the increasing role of financial motives, financial markets, financial actors and financial institutions in the operation of the domestic and international companies" (Epstein, 2005, p. 3)—financialization—have been identified as primary sources of this trend. To extract more value for their shareholders, firms began to concentrate on their core-business, outsourcing or displacing activities deemed as secondary, frequently restructuring the firms' organization, fighting against the influence of labor unions to create a more flexible work organization.

Precarization or Dualization?

According to Hipp et al. (2015), two theoretical (and mutually exclusive) "narratives" have been used to translate these macro-economic trends to the institutional level: Precariousness and dualization. The first hypothesis states that the precariousness of jobs and the percentage of insecure jobs has risen generally. Due to "rising economic competition and the associated deregulation of labor markets, the dismantling of social protection arrangements and the decline of the power of unions" (Hipp et al., 2015, p. 355; Kalleberg, 2009) the share of atypical—and often insecure jobs—such as jobs that are temporary, poorly paid, self-employed or part time would have increased over the years. The defenders of the polarization hypothesis argue that the labor market does not necessarily undergo a general dynamic of precarization, but that it is segmented between the protected workers at the core of the labor market and the precarious workers at the insecure margins. Also as a consequence of attempts of governments and unions to protect certain core segments of the work force, employers provide only flexible, insecure and poorly paid jobs for the employees at the margins (Hipp et al., 2015).

Socio-Economic Transformations and Lack of Job Security

On the level of institutions, two partially inter-dependent dynamics are at the root of these trends of precariousness and dualization. Private companies, facing increasingly competitive environments and pressure to increase shareholder value, undergo frequent restructuring, outsource domains and activities which do not belong to their core business, increase their internal or external flexibility[1] or the recourse on massive lay-offs. This has been made possible by new technologies and new ways of organizing the production process, but also by new forms of management (Gallie, White, Cheng, & Tomlinson, 1998). As a result, since the 1990s not only the unemployment rate, but also the share of atypical and often insecure jobs such as part-time employment, temporary employment or solo self-employment has risen in many European countries—even though differences in volume and combination of these forms of precarious employment differ among countries (Hipp et al., 2015). Insecure employment is more prevalent in certain sectors, such as construction, hospitality, wholesale, retail, and public services. There is also evidence that insecure jobs more frequently affect workers with a poor education and those at the margins of working age (young adults who enter the labor market and older workers before the transition to retirement). Concomitant to the increasing insecurity of working conditions, research has shown that the subjective feeling of insecurity has risen over time in many countries (Eurofound & EU-OSHA, 2014). This measure—for example in the

[1] External flexibility refers to changes in the volume of labor employed, often in the form of fixed-termed work contracts (temporary workers). Internal flexibility refers to the flexibility manifested by the employees of a firm at a certain point of time.

form of the perceived likelihood that one will lose one's job—certainly depends on objective vulnerability, but is not a perfect mirror of it. It can be mediated by the social environment of the individual or through media depictions of the labor market situation.

Pluralization of Career Paths

Increasing precariousness and the flexibility of the work organization has consequences on career paths—at least for certain social and occupational groups. The entry of an ever-higher share of women into the labor market, for instance, has contributed to a pluralization of career paths (Widmer & Ritschard, 2009). Recent studies in the United States show that job tenure since the 1980s goes in different directions for men and women (Hollister & Smith, 2014). While job tenure declines for men and never married women, it has increased for women with children (see also Gallie et al., 1998, for similar results in the British case). These empirical observations on job tenure contrasts certain accounts of so-called "boundaryless careers" (Arthur & Rousseau, 1996). Nevertheless, a recent German study on career complexity and career patterns argued that the complexity of careers has increased, in particular for the cohorts born until 1960 (but then slightly drops) (Biemann, Fasang, & Grunow, 2011). The de-standardization of the life course also implies a diversification of school-to-work or work transitions (Walther & Plug, 2006) and of career orientations that have become more protean (Sano, 2016).

Implications of the Changing Labor Market for Individual Career Development

Defining the "vulnerability paradox". As a consequence of the increasingly precarious and flexible labor markets, the concept of vulnerability in career development has become crucial. In broad terms, vulnerability in the occupational domain implies a restriction or constraint that impedes one's opportunities for career development, thereby having a negative impact on the quality of life. For instance, low socio-economic status (Landsbergis, Grzywacz, & LaMontagne, 2014), health issues (Schuring, Robroek, Otten, Arts, & Burdorf, 2013), a lack of work volition (Duffy, Blustein, Diemer, & Autin, 2016), and non-standard forms of employment (Rubery, Grimshaw, Keizer, & Johnson, 2018) may all be considered risks that can lead a person to a precarious situation. Individuals falling into these risk categories have less freedom of choice to construct and secure their careers in a desirable way, because they have lower access to the career development resources that are available to the less vulnerable part of the population. This may be also true for people in so-called traditional career paths that offer relatively few alternatives, thereby reducing the ways in which individual agency might manifest.

The modern multifaceted world of work seems to offer considerable career opportunities that could help counteract the vulnerabilities coming from the above-described risks. In light of this, the scientific literature increasingly refers to non-linear career paths (Lichtenstein & Mendenhall, 2002), as well as to protean (Hall, 2004) and self-directed careers (Park, 2009), all of which imply increased freedom to choose when, where, and how the career path is directed and shaped. Although career choices always result from the interplay between structures of opportunities (i.e., collective dimension) and individual strategies (i.e., individual dimension), this perspective also implies a shift of focus from a collective to a more individual way to manage career choices. We encounter a somewhat paradoxical situation here. With many options, the modern labor market is less stable and structured, so that the autonomy of choice may become a burden rather than an advantage if one is not well prepared. Given the numerous possible variations of individual career paths and dynamic changes in the world of work, workers are required to be particularly adaptable, able to capture new career opportunities, and keep their skills up to date. Hence, while a lack of structuring constraints in the occupational environment may be beneficial for autonomy, they can also become a vulnerability factor. The positive psychology literature points to what is called the paradox of choice: Choice is essential for autonomy to manifest, which in turn leads to higher well-being. Excessive, unconstrained choice, however, seems to have a paralyzing effect (see Schwartz, 2015). Taking career development as an example, we may thus refer to a paradox of vulnerability, whereby both a lack of options and too many options are equally strong risk factors for occupational vulnerabilities to occur. In the first case, one suffers from a too rigid career structure offering few alternatives, whereas in the second case structuring elements are lacking. The question is how we overcome these vulnerabilities and what may be the guiding principle in structuring non-linear career paths.

Sustainable careers. The concept of career sustainability (Van der Heijden & De Vos, 2015) seems to capture the complexities of modern careers, such as those depicted by the concept of vulnerability paradox. It offers a novel insight into the way the career paths can be structured to achieve positive outcomes. Sustainable careers denote the "sequence of career experiences reflected through a variety of patterns of continuity over time, thereby crossing several social spaces, characterized by individual agency, herewith providing meaning to the individual" (Van der Heijden & De Vos, 2015, p. 7). A recent theoretical model of sustainable careers (De Vos, Van der Heijden, & Akkermans, 2018) proposes three dimensions along which a (sustainable) career is built. These are the person, the context, and the time. The personal dimension refers to agency and self-determination in proactively developing one's career, the context refers to the multiple life domains that interact with and shape career choice, and the temporal dimension denotes a meaningful sequence of career episodes over the life course. Hence, we may identify two key categories of resources, a lack of which may develop into vulnerabilities. The first category entails personal resources (i.e., individual characteristics) to develop one's career in a proactive, adaptive, and meaningful way and includes such aspects as career competencies (Akkermans, Brenninkmeijer, Huibers, & Blonk, 2013) and career adaptability (Savickas & Porfeli, 2012). The second category refers to contextual resources or a lack of constraints (resources that reside in the environment) such as the compatibility between different life domains and opportunities within the work domain (De Vos, Van der Heijden, & Akkermans, 2018). The temporal dimension serves as an overarching facet of career sustainability providing the structure and meaning to the succession of career choices (which is seen as the individual career story) that results from the interplay between personal and contextual factors (see De Vos et al., 2018).

Sustainable career development seems to solve at least some of the problems posed by the vulnerability paradox described above by providing the tools for structuring one's career in the multifaceted world of work. However, the feasibility of sustainable career development is not unconditional. It strongly depends on macro-level factors in the labor market such as continuous access to decent work opportunities. These two concepts are extremely important in addressing the vulnerabilities of today's labor market, although they have been rarely discussed together. Only if the condition of decent work is satisfied can career sustainability be achieved (and in turn, engaging in sustainable career development practices may help one benefit from existing working conditions). For this reason, it is essential to understand what decent work refers to, before engaging in discussion of the interplay between personal and contextual factors for combating occupational vulnerabilities.

Decent work as a building block for career sustainability. The crucial importance of access to decent work for individuals' life development was emphasized by the United Nations (UN) *Declaration of Human Rights* in 1948 (UN General Assembly, 1948). Its article 23, al. 1 and 3, states "Everyone has the right to work [...] to just and favourable conditions of work and to protection against unemployment [...]. Everyone who works has the right to just and favourable remuneration ensuring [...] an existence worthy of human dignity [...]" (p. 75). In 1999, the concept of decent work was more precisely defined in the report of the Director-General to the International Labour Conference. This report is structured around four main priorities: Promoting human rights and work, promoting employment and fare retribution, strengthening social protection and security, and strengthening social dialogue.

> Decent work means productive work in which rights are protected, which generates an adequate income, with adequate social protection. It also means sufficient work, in the sense that all should have full access to income-earning opportunities. It marks the high road to economic and social development, a road in which employment, income and social protection can be achieved without compromising workers' rights and social standards. (ILO, 1999, p. 13)

In *the 2030 Agenda for Sustainable Development* of the UN (UN General Assembly, 2015), decent work was made one of 17 goals. Moreover, to promote sustainable careers, education and lifelong learning are key issues, mentioned in the 4th goal of this agenda.

Several new theories in the field of vocational psychology, such as the social cognitive model of career self-management (Lent & Brown, 2013), the life design paradigm (Savickas et al., 2009), the model of sustainable careers (De Vos et al., 2018), and the psychology of working theory (Duffy et al., 2016), posit that both contextual and individual factors have an impact on individual career paths and thus on an individual's life condition, including their ability to access decent work. The psychology of working theory in particular establishes a connection between (sustainable) career development and decent work. It stipulates that career development models: (1) must be adapted to emerging issues within the world of work, such as precarious new forms of employment and meaningfulness at work; (2) should focus on populations impeded from accessing decent work and find ways to reduce their barriers; and (3) should consider work in its various forms and within different cultural contexts. Decent work is at the core of the psychology of working theory, and leads to the satisfaction of three forms of human needs—survival, social connection, and self-determination (Blustein, 2006)—which in turn predict work fulfillment and general well-being. Access to decent work depends on economic and social factors, and is hindered for populations experiencing economic constraints or belonging to marginalized groups. However, the relationship between economic or social factors and decent work is partially mediated through psychosocial factors, such as work volition, both decent work and work volition having an impact on well-being (e.g., Masdonati, Schreiber, Marcionetti, & Rossier, 2019). When studying decent work and its implications for sustainable careers, it is thus important to consider both contextual antecedents and individual psychological factors that relate to well-being outcomes.

Contextual Antecedents and Personal Resources in Occupational Vulnerabilities

Understanding the Role of Contextual Factors

Notably, the conceptualization and implications concerning the role of contextual factors in occupational vulnerabilities vary across disciplines and research areas. Sociological literature proposes several hypotheses about how contextual mechanisms determine workers' vulnerabilities in career development. Hevenstone (2010) distinguishes three (not mutually exclusive) hypotheses that explain the vulnerable conditions of workers: the "free-market-seeking hypothesis", the "constrained individual choice" hypothesis, and the "entrepreneurial spirit" hypothesis.

According to the free-market seeking hypothesis, vulnerable conditions are mainly the result of employment strategies of firms. Engaging workers in insecure positions allows firms to "increase their external flexibility and to increase screening periods in an environment where it is difficult to sever employment relationships" (Hevenstone, 2010, p. 317; Kalleberg, 2009). The use of flexible employment would thus be higher in contexts or in countries where the core workforce is highly protected by the employment protection legislation. The constrained individual choice hypothesis argues that in weak economies or during slow economic conjuncture workers have greater incentives or are forced to accept flexible and insecure employment conditions. The entrepreneurial spirit thesis contends that in contexts, which promote individual risk taking and entrepreneurial spirit, workers are willing to take higher risk and to work in flexible contracts or start their own business.

Psychological literature tends to define contextual factors in a slightly different way, usually adopting a more "bottom-up" approach. Specifically, psychological theories of career choice and development tend to explain contextual aspects through the eyes of the individual, which adds to the understanding of the interplay between contextual factors and human agency, but may provide a too generalized view of the context. In this chapter, in line with recent psychological considerations on career development (Lent & Brown, 2013; McMahon & Patton, 2019; Savickas, 2013), decent work (Duffy et al., 2016), and the complexity of forces that contribute to career sustainability (De Vos et al., 2018), we consider it relevant to propose a distinction between *proximal* and *distal* contextual factors. Both types of contexts may determine the extent of occupational vulnerabilities and provide resources to deal with them. The proximal context refers to the immediate occupational environment and specifically to the psychosocial working conditions that are considered a primary source of work-related well-being. In this way, the proximal context has a narrow and momentary focus. The distal context, on the other hand, refers to the individual career development situation that has evolved over years and has been shaped by personal background and external forces in the world of work (e.g., changing labor markets). Hence, the distal context has a much broader focus, and it varies between employees with different occupational backgrounds and skills, affecting the way they make and interpret career choices.

Despite the fact that contextual determinants are widely acknowledged in the literature, research has rarely integrated this distinction into an empirical investigation. For instance, studies on labor market precariousness (e.g., Kalleberg, 2009) usually adopt a broad, distal perspective, whereas research on work-related vulnerabilities or well-being (e.g., Grebner, Semmer, & Elfering, 2005) mostly focuses on the proximal context. In this chapter, we propose a more integrative perspective on the different layers of occupational contexts. To better understand sustainable careers, it is particularly relevant to describe different forms of individual agency and how it manifests in proximal and distal contexts. To this end, the following section elaborates on recent advances in personal resources and their manifestations in career development. Specifically, we discuss three groups of resources that have been shown to be essential in occupational well-being and thus potentially contribute to promoting career sustainability and access to decent work.

Human Agency and Personal Resources in Sustainable Career Development

Self-determination. The concept of self-determination has been elaborated within the framework of self-determination theory (SDT, Ryan & Deci, 2000) and implies a relatively autonomous, purposeful action inspired by intrinsic motives. Several aspects are essential in understanding the nature of self-determined behaviors. First, any human action has an underlying motivation that can range from extrinsically controlled to autonomous behavior regulation (DeHaan & Ryan, 2014; Deci, Olafsen, & Ryan, 2017). Intrinsic or so-called self-determined motivation as well as autonomous forms of external behavior regulation (i.e., internalized regulation) form the strongest basis for thriving and well-being (Brown & Ryan, 2015). One of the pathways through which well-being is achieved and maintained goes through basic psychological-need satisfaction. SDT posits that intrinsically motivated behaviors are facilitated by the satisfaction of the three basic needs of autonomy, competence and relatedness, which in turn foster wellness (Brown & Ryan, 2015; Ryan & Deci, 2000). This theoretical framework also underscores the importance of the interaction between individual and environmental forces in basic need satisfaction. External environments may either promote or impede the satisfaction of basic needs, thereby providing favorable conditions or creating barriers to the individual's well-being. However, the theory also draws attention to individual differences that may help the person to make the most of the situation even if it is unfavorable.

We believe that SDT provides a promising framework for understanding sustainable work and career development. It offers a useful insight into how sustainable career outcomes (see De Vos et al., 2018) can be achieved by promoting autonomous work motivation and basic-need satisfaction at work. It can also be combined with the psychology of working theory (Duffy et al., 2016), which maintains that a combination of psychological and macro-level factors define decent work and thereby relate to the experience of fulfillment and well-being through the satisfaction of survival, social, and self-determination needs. In this way, SDT draws attention not only to the interplay of organizational and individual resources in preventing employee vulnerabilities, but also implies the role of individuals' functioning in the wider labor market in achieving sustainability and decent work.

To continue in this direction, we believe that understanding the role and the limits of self-determination within a wider career development perspective may help unravel important psychological mechanisms leading to employees' positive psychological functioning. For instance, it may be relevant to step beyond organizational boundaries and look how and under which conditions people are able to express autonomy and competence in the labor market, and maintain social connections in their working lives. From a broader perspective, sustainable career development implies not only positive experiences in a given workplace, but also a satisfactory succession of career transitions that help the person thrive as an employee. Hence, the question is how we facilitate self-determination in careers at the individual, institutional, and policy levels. In today's complex world of work, self-determined action of the individual is inevitably embedded in and constrained by a number of proximal (e.g., immediate work settings) and distal (e.g., opportunities in the labor market, personal career story) situations that need to be considered.

Psychological capital. Psychological capital is another excellent example of agency in the occupational domain. Drawing on the positive psychology framework, the model of psychological capital (Luthans, Youssef, & Avolio, 2007) identifies personal resources that help people manage the demands of the turbulent world of work, cope with stress, demonstrate positive vocational behaviors, and thereby achieve well-being. The term psychological capital denotes a positive psychological state of development, characterized by the four psychological resources of self-efficacy, optimism, hope, and resilience (Luthans et al., 2007). Notably, the theory puts an emphasis on state-like rather than trait-like characteristics. Unlike positive traits, which are characterized by relative stability over time, positive state-like capacities are more malleable and dynamic, and thus are open to change (Luthans & Youssef, 2007). Indeed, psychological capital can be developed through interventions (Luthans, Avey, & Patera, 2008) and have been shown to reduce negative workplace outcomes (Avey, Luthans, & Youssef, 2010), increasing employee well-being (Avey, Luthans, Smith, & Palmer, 2010).

While they constitute an overarching construct, psychological capital resources have been shown to contribute to positive work outcomes on their own as well. Self-efficacy is one of the best-explored aspects with ample meta-analytic evidence on its link to employee performance (Judge & Bono, 2001; Stajkovic & Luthans, 1998) and positive career development (Choi et al., 2012). Moreover, optimism defined as an attributional or explanatory style pertain to positive interpretation of the surrounding situations and events (Luthans et al., 2007). Furthermore, optimism has been recently incorporated into the models of employee engagement and has been treated as a personal resource helping to deal with job demands (e.g., Xanthopoulou, Bakker, Demerouti, & Schaufeli, 2007; Xanthopoulou, Bakker, & Fischbach, 2013). In turn, employee resilience refers to a personal resource of adapting to and recovering from stressful or adverse situations (Youssef & Luthans, 2007). It has been found to mitigate the negative consequences of stressful work situations, such as job insecurity (Shoss, Jiang, & Probst, 2018), to mediate the relationship between work stressors and strain (Crane & Searle, 2016), and contribute to work engagement (Cooke, Cooper, Bartram, Wang, & Mei, 2016). The last psychological-capital resource—hope—as conceptualized by Snyder (Snyder, 2002; Snyder, Irving, & Anderson, 1991), was found to relate to increased work performance (Peterson & Byron, 2008) and has also been identified as an important resource for proactive career development (Niles, 2011).

We believe that adding the career development perspective may provide a promising path for expanding research on psychological capital. Likewise, studies on sustainable careers and decent work may benefit from a closer examination of psychological-capital resources. Arguably, they are relevant not only in dealing with challenges within organizational boundaries, but may also constitute important personal strengths in managing occupational transitions and achieving sustainability in one's career in general. In this way, we may conceptualize psychological capital as not only a foundation of positive organizational behaviors, but rather as the basis for positive *vocational behaviors* that foster both work-related and overall well-being in the era of turbulent careers.

Career adaptability. Career adaptability is a well-known construct of personal resources in career development, also identified as a key resource for sustainable careers (De Vos et al., 2018). It is defined as a "psychosocial construct comprised of the resources an individual uses to respond to tasks and challenges of vocational development" (Johnston et al., 2013, p. 1). Specifically, this construct includes the resources of career *concern*, which refers to the ability to plan and to foster coping behaviors, career *control*, which refers to the ability to mobilize our subjectivity for career goals and projects, career *curiosity*, which facilitates adequate career choices through exploration, and career *confidence*, which has been associated with self-esteem and the ability to overcome career challenges. This set of career adaptability resources is related to the ability to develop intentions and to enact and narrate our careers (Savickas et al., 2009). It thus allows individuals to cope with changing circumstances, select acceptable environments, conciliate possible selves and the social environment, and adapt the context to their needs. In this way, career adaptability is similar to the notion of adaptation by accommodation and assimilation developed by Piaget (see Piaget & Inhelder, 1969).

Career construction theory (Savickas, 2002) describes adaptation as the result of a sequence that starts with adaptive readiness, mobilizing adaptive resources (i.e., career adaptability), and allowing expression of adapted responses, which together result in adaptation. Indeed, career adaptability as a self-regulation capacity can be activated and used to regulate the expression of adaptive responses, thereby contributing to peoples' self-directedness and career self-management (Rossier, 2015). These self-regulation capacities allow individuals (1) to manage their interrelations with the surrounding context, (2) to perceive the constraints and opportunities offered by the context and to take advantage of them, (3) to navigate in different areas of this context, and (4) to have an impact on the context. In line with these propositions, empirical evidence has confirmed that career adapt-abilities can be considered self-regulation processes that act as mediators between dispositions (or adaptive readiness) and career-related outcomes (Rudolph, Lavigne, & Zacher, 2017). For example, Rossier, Zecca, Stauffer, Maggiori, and Dauwalder (2012) have shown that career adaptability mediates the relationship between personality traits and work engagement. In addition, it may also buffer the negative impact of work-related strains (Maggiori, Johnston, Krings, Massoudi, & Rossier, 2013). We know that career adaptability can be trained (Koen, Klehe, & Van Vianen, 2012) and that an increase of career resources may lead to positive long-term developments by activating virtuous cycles (Fiori, Bollmann, & Rossier, 2015). Considering that career adaptability has been conceived as promoting career resilience and a tool for sustainable career development via marshaling personal and contextual resources, increasing the ability of people to use these resources may in turn facilitate access to decent work and decent life (Rossier, Ginevra, Bollmann, & Nota, 2017).

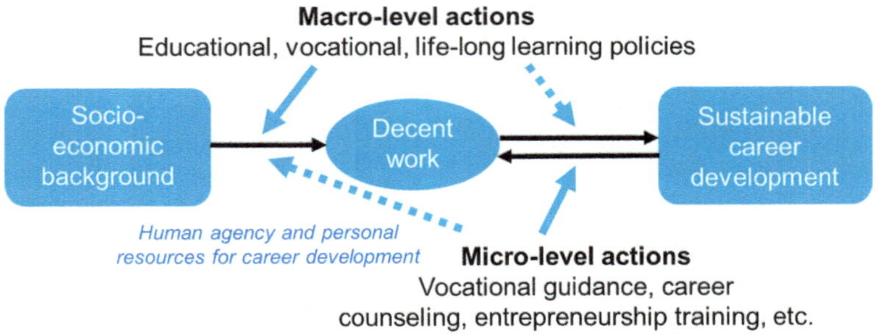

Fig. 1 Impact of macro- and micro-level actions on the relationship between socio-economic background, decent work, and sustainable career development

An Integrative Model for Sustainable Careers

To summarize the ideas of sustainable careers, contextual antecedents and personal resources, we hereby propose an integrative model that explains the pathways to sustainable career development, decent work, and well-being. A sustainable career implies that people benefit from favorable and secure conditions over time (Van der Heijden & De Vos, 2015), enjoy well-being at work, and profit from a higher overall life satisfaction. Decent working conditions (and a succession of decent jobs) are thus a prerequisite for a sustainable career and vice versa: sustainable career development may lead to more decent work experiences at the subjective level. Therefore, the management of work-to-work transitions is crucial. If contextual and personal resources cannot facilitate these transitions, they can potentially become situations of vulnerabilities.

To promote access to sustainable careers, it is important to promote access to decent work, and to secure work transitions. To do so, both macro-level actions for social protection and employment policies as well as micro-level actions aimed at supporting individual career paths should be developed. As illustrated in Fig. 1, the socio-economic context defines work opportunities under the regulation of the political context. For this reason, social policies that promote health and psychosocial well-being at work (by regulating working conditions, working hours, income levels, and the like) are crucial in achieving decent work and, in turn, in promoting sustainable career development. They directly influence the proximal context (e.g., by having implications on immediate working conditions) as well as the distal context (by influencing the individual situation in the labor market). In terms of labor market policies, it is particularly important that the protection of certain groups of workers does not contribute to exclusion or increased precariousness for other groups—so that men and women, younger and older workers, unqualified and highly qualified workers can all profit from decent working conditions.

The link between decent work and sustainable careers is then strengthened by personal resources and micro-level actions, such as career counselling and training opportunities. Individual agency and personal resources may have a crucial role here as they determine how working conditions are translated into further career development actions. We presume that the link between decent working conditions and sustainable career development is bilateral, which means that individual career behaviors and sustainable career construction practices may also predict where one ends up in terms of the working conditions (both objectively and subjectively defined). As suggested in the literature, one of the dimensions of sustainable career development is discovering the meaningfulness of work (De Vos et al., 2018). Equally, meaningfulness can stem from decent working conditions (Duffy, Autin, & Bott, 2015). Hence, one of the benefits of employing personal resources in the occupational domain may be that one is able to find and maintain the meaning of work despite turbulences in the career situation. This ability might be influenced by micro-level actions of vocational guidance and career counselling. These actions, for example, may strengthen individuals' career development opportunities by capitalizing on a variety of personal resources (including those mentioned in this chapter). In this way, micro-level actions may help to shape proximal career contexts by helping people achieve more satisfactory working conditions, and they certainly have an impact on how individual career trajectories evolve in the long run. In this case, the promotion of lifelong learning is also an important aspect to consider. If we want to ensure access to sustainable careers for all, we need these macro- and micro-actions to be within reach for everybody, especially for underserved and more vulnerable workers (Puertas, Cinamon, Neault, Pope, & Rossier, 2012). For these reasons, the development of specific career interventions for vulnerable and marginalized groups of workers is of prime importance (e.g., Di Fabio & Palazzeschi, 2016). However, we need to remember that everybody may face situations of precariousness or vulnerability. In this context, all actions taken to increase occupational safety and health culture in order to promote positive psychosocial work environment is certainly a step in the right direction.

Implications

The changes of the world of work and the de-standardization of life and career paths means that people have to manage an increasing number of unexpected situations and transitions. These changes also mean that macro- and micro-level actions have to be taken in order to counterbalance increased occupational precariousness and to help people manage their career transitions. This should be ensured for all across the entire life course, considering in particular the underserved population. For this reason, states should develop public policies to secure access to decent work, sustainable work, and decent lives for all. We need to promote social justice and contend with important social and economic inequalities. To help individuals manage their work transitions and careers, life-long learning should be promoted and career interventions provided for all, especially for the less privileged. It is important to facilitate access to vocational training, further education, or continuous education at all ages.

This would imply that these training or education options should propose flexible tracks to facilitate work, training, and family conciliation.

A sustainable career implies the benefits of secure and stable employment, including successive employments without major difficulties managing transitions, or being able to benefit from assistance to overcome career difficulties. This help can be provided by the proximal environment of a person but has also to be secured by social policies. These policies should guarantee that citizens benefit from unemployment insurance, have access to further education, and benefit from services such as career counselling to help them to manage career transitions. In a dynamic socio-economical market, public policies should promote the access to lifelong learning and career counselling for all. In addition to these factual aspects, work contributes to a person's overall view of him- or herself and of his or her environment. These services should for this reason also increase peoples' resources, agency, and their self-determination strategies. Societies should create favorable conditions to sustain the development of "human", "social", and "psychological capital".

Conclusion

The dynamic and unpredictable world of work can induce insecurity and precariousness, which according to the "vulnerability paradox", impacts both those who are constrained by structures and those who face too many career options. Engaging in sustainable career development may help solve some issues raised by this paradox and thereby promote occupational well-being. In order to do so, both micro- and macro-level actions are needed. We propose that sustainable career development is connected, by a feedback loop, with access to decent work. Macro-level actions, such as policy-making, ensure decent working conditions in socio-economic contexts, whereas micro-level actions, such as training and counselling, strengthen personal resources that are essential for achieving and making use of sustainability in one's working lives.

Acknowledgements The contribution of benefited from the support of the Swiss National Centre of Competence in Research LIVES—Overcoming vulnerability: Life course perspective, (grant number 51NF40-160590), and was partly done within the framework of a project on the professional integration of marginalized young adults (grant number 100014_156540) and of a project aiming at adapting and strengthening educational guidance and career counselling in West Africa (grant number IZ08Z0_177295), all financed by the Swiss National Science Foundation.

References

Akkermans, J., Brenninkmeijer, V., Huibers, M., & Blonk, R. W. B. (2013). Competencies for the contemporary career: Development and preliminary validation of the career competencies questionnaire. *Journal of Career Development, 40,* 245–267. https://doi.org/10.1177/0894845312467501.

Arthur, M. B., & Rousseau, D. M. (1996). *The boundaryless career: A new employment principle for a new organizational era*. New York, NY: Oxford University Press.

Avey, J. B., Luthans, F., Smith, R. M., & Palmer, N. F. (2010a). Impact of positive psychological capital on employee well-being over time. *Journal of Occupational Health Psychology, 15,* 17–28. https://doi.org/10.1037/a0016998.

Avey, J. B., Luthans, F., & Youssef, C. M. (2010b). The additive value of positive psychological capital in predicting work attitudes and behaviors. *Journal of Management, 36,* 430–452. https://doi.org/10.1177/0149206308329961.

Biemann, T., Fasang, A. E., & Grunow, D. (2011). Do economic globalization and industry growth destabilize careers? An analysis of career complexity and career patterns over time. *Organization Studies, 32,* 1639–1663. https://doi.org/10.1177/0170840611421246.

Blustein, D. L. (2006). *The psychology of working: A new perspective for career development, counseling, and public policy*. Mahwah, NJ: Lawrence Erlbaum Associates.

Brown, K. W., & Ryan, R. M. (2015). A self-determination theory perspective on fostering healthy self-regulation from within and without. In S. Joseph (Ed.), *Positive psychology in practice: Promoting human flourishing in work, health, education, and everyday life* (pp. 139–158). Hoboken, NJ: John Wiley & Sons Inc.

Choi, B. Y., Park, H., Yang, E., Lee, S. K., Lee, Y., & Lee, S. M. (2012). Understanding career decision self-efficacy: A meta-analytic approach. *Journal of Career Development, 39,* 443–460. https://doi.org/10.1177/0894845311398042.

Cooke, F. L., Cooper, B., Bartram, T., Wang, J., & Mei, H. (2016). Mapping the relationships between high-performance work systems, employee resilience and engagement: A study of the banking industry in China. *The International Journal of Human Resource Management*. Advance online publication. https://doi.org/10.1080/09585192.2015.1137618.

Crane, M. F., & Searle, B. J. (2016). Building resilience through exposure to stressors: The effects of challenges versus hindrances. *Journal of Occupational Health Psychology, 21,* 468–479. https://doi.org/10.1037/a0040064.

De Vos, A., Van der Heijden, B. I., & Akkermans, J. (2018). Sustainable careers: Towards a conceptual model. *Journal of Vocational Behavior*. Advance online publication. https://doi.org/10.1016/j.jvb.2018.06.011.

Deci, E. L., Olafsen, A. H., & Ryan, R. M. (2017). Self-determination theory in work organizations: The state of a science. *Annual Review of Organizational Psychology and Organizational Behavior, 4,* 19–43. https://doi.org/10.1146/annurev-orgpsych-032516-113108.

DeHaan, C. R., & Ryan, R. M. (2014). Symptoms of wellness: Happiness and eudaemonia from a self-determination theory perspective. In: K. M. Sheldon & R. E. Lucas (Eds.). *Stability of happiness: Theories and evidence on whether happiness can change* (pp. 37–55). London, UK: Academic Press. https://doi.org/10.1016/b978-0-12-411478-4.00003-5.

Di Fabio, A., & Palazzeschi, L. (2016). Marginalization and precariat: The challenge of intensifying life construction intervention. *Frontiers in Psychology, 7,* 444. https://doi.org/10.3389/fpsyg.2016.00444.

Duffy, R. D., Autin, K. L., & Bott, E. M. (2015). Work volition and job satisfaction: Examining the role of work meaning and person–environment fit. *The Career Development Quarterly, 63,* 126–140. https://doi.org/10.1002/cdq.12009.

Duffy, R. D., Blustein, D. L., Diemer, M. A., & Autin, K. L. (2016). The psychology of working theory. *Journal of Counseling Psychology, 63,* 127–148. https://doi.org/10.1037/cou0000140.

Epstein, G. A. (Ed.). (2005). *Financialization and the world economy*. Northampton, MA: Edward Elgar Publishing.

Eurofound and EU-OSHA. (2014). *Psychosocial risks in Europe: Prevalence and strategies for prevention*. Luxembourg: Publications Office of the European Union.

Fiori, M., Bollmann, G., & Rossier, J. (2015). Exploring the path through which career adaptability increases job satisfaction and lowers job stress: The role of affect. *Journal of Vocational Behavior, 91,* 113–121. https://doi.org/10.1016/j.jvb.2015.08.010.

Gallie, D., White, M., Cheng, Y., & Tomlinson, M. (1998). *Restructuring the employment relationship*. Oxford, UK: Oxford University Press.

Grebner, S., Semmer, N. K., & Elfering, A. (2005). Working conditions and three types of well-being: A longitudinal study with self-report and rating data. *Journal of Occupational Health Psychology, 10,* 31–43. https://doi.org/10.1037/1076-8998.10.1.31.

Hall, D. T. (2004). The protean career: A quarter-century journey. *Journal of Vocational Behavior, 65,* 1–13. https://doi.org/10.1016/j.jvb.2003.10.006.

Hevenstone, D. (2010). National context and atypical employment. *International Sociology, 25,* 315–347. https://doi.org/10.1177/0268580909360296.

Hipp, L., Bernhardt, J., & Allmendinger, J. (2015). Institutions and the prevalence of nonstandard employment. *Socio-Economic Review, 13,* 351–377. https://doi.org/10.1093/ser/mwv002.

Hollister, M. N., & Smith, K. E. (2014). Unmasking the conflicting trends in job tenure by gender in the United States, 1983–2008. *American Sociological Review, 79,* 159–181. https://doi.org/10.1177/0003122413514584.

ILO (1999). *Decent work: Report of the Director-General*. International Labour Conference, 87th Session, Geneva, Switzerland. Retrieved from https://www.ilo.org/public/libdoc/ilo/P/09605/09605(1999-87).pdf.

Johnston, C. S., Broonen, J.-P., Stauffer, S. D., Hamtiaux, A., Pouyaud, J., Zeccas, G., … Rossier, J. (2013). Validation of an adapted French form of the career adapt-abilities scale in four Francophone countries. *Journal of Vocational Behavior, 83*, 1–10. https://doi.org/10.1016/j.jvb.2013.02.002.

Judge, T. A., & Bono, J. E. (2001). Relationship of core self-evaluations traits—self-esteem, generalized self-efficacy, locus of control, and emotional stability—with job satisfaction and job performance: A meta-analysis. *Journal of Applied Psychology, 86,* 80–92. https://doi.org/10.1037/0021-9010.86.1.80.

Kalleberg, A. L. (2009). Precarious work, insecure workers: Employment relations in transition. *American Sociological Review, 74,* 1–22. https://doi.org/10.1177/000312240907400101.

Koen, J., Klehe, U.-C., & Van Vianen, A. E. M. (2012). Training career adaptability to facilitate a successful school-to-work transition. *Journal of Vocational Behavior, 81,* 395–408. https://doi.org/10.1016/j.jvb.2012.10.003.

Landsbergis, P. A., Grzywacz, J. G., & LaMontagne, A. D. (2014). Work organization, job insecurity, and occupational health disparities. *American Journal of Industrial Medicine, 57,* 495–515. https://doi.org/10.1002/ajim.22126.

Lent, R. W., & Brown, S. D. (2013). Social cognitive model of career self-management: Toward a unifying view of adaptive career behavior across the life span. *Journal of Counseling Psychology, 60,* 557–568. https://doi.org/10.1037/a0033446.

Lichtenstein, B. M. B., & Mendenhall, M. (2002). Non-linearity and response-ability: Emergent order in 21st-century careers. *Human Relations, 55,* 5–32. https://doi.org/10.1177/0018726702055001604.

Luthans, F., Avey, J. B., & Patera, J. L. (2008). Experimental analysis of a web-based training intervention to develop positive psychological capital. *Academy of Management Learning & Education, 7,* 209–221. https://doi.org/10.5465/amle.2008.32712618.

Luthans, F., & Youssef, C. M. (2007). Emerging positive organizational behavior. *Journal of Management, 33,* 321–349. https://doi.org/10.1177/0149206307300814.

Luthans, F., Youssef, C. M., & Avolio, B. J. (2007). *Psychological capital: Developing the human competitive edge*. Oxford, UK: Oxford University Press.

Maggiori, C., Johnston, C. S., Krings, F., Massoudi, K., & Rossier, J. (2013). The role of career adaptability and work conditions on general and professional well-being. *Journal of Vocational Behavior, 83,* 437–449. https://doi.org/10.1016/j.jvb.2013.07.001.

Masdonati, J., Schreiber, M., Marcionetti, J., & Rossier, J. (2019). Decent work in Switzerland: Context, conceptualization, and assessment. *Journal of Vocational Behavior, 110,* 12–27. https://doi.org/10.1016/j.jvb.2018.11.004.

McMahon, M., & Patton, W. (2019). The systems theory framework of career development: Accommodating context, complexity, and culture. In N. Arthur & M. McMahon (Eds.), *Contemporary theories of career development: International perspectives* (pp. 105–120). London, UK: Routledge.

Niles, S. G. (2011). Career flow: A hope-centered model of career development. *Journal of Employment Counseling, 48,* 173–175. https://doi.org/10.1002/j.2161-1920.2011.tb01107.x.

Park, Y. (2009). An integrative empirical approach to the predictors of self-directed career management. *Career Development International, 14,* 636–654. https://doi.org/10.1108/13620430911005690.

Peterson, S. J., & Byron, K. (2008). Exploring the role of hope in job performance: Results from four studies. *Journal of Organizational Behavior, 29,* 785–803. https://doi.org/10.1002/job.492.

Piaget, J., & Inhelder, B. (1969). *The psychology of child.* London, UK: Routledge & Kegan Paul.

Puertas, A., Cinamon, R. G., Neault, R., Pope, M., & Rossier, J. (2012). Group 4: Career development for diverse and underserved populations. In J. Trusty (Ed.), *The 2010 NCDA-IAEVG-SVP international symposium: Bridging international perspectives of career development* (pp. 33–46). Broken Arrow, OK: National Career Development Association.

Rossier, J. (2015). Career adaptability and life designing. In L. Nota & J. Rossier (Eds.), *Handbook of life design: From practice to theory and from theory to practice* (pp. 153–167). Göttingen, Germany: Hogrefe.

Rossier, J., Ginevra, M. C., Bollmann, G., & Nota, L. (2017). The importance of career adaptability, career resilience, and employability in designing a successful life. In K. Maree (Ed.), *Psychology of career adaptability, employability and resilience* (pp. 65–82). Cham, Switzerland: Springer International. https://doi.org/10.1007/978-3-319-66954-0_5.

Rossier, J., Zecca, G., Stauffer, S. D., Maggiori, C., & Dauwalder, J.-P. (2012). Career adapt-abilities scale in a French-speaking Swiss sample: Psychometric properties and relationships to personality and work engagement. *Journal of Vocational Behavior, 80,* 734–743. https://doi.org/10.1016/j.jvb.2012.01.004.

Rudolph, C. W., Lavigne, K. N., & Zacher, H. (2017). Career adaptability: A meta-analysis of relationships with measures of adaptivity, adapting responses, and adaptation results. *Journal of Vocational Behavior, 98,* 17–34. https://doi.org/10.1016/j.jvb.2016.09.002.

Rubery, J., Grimshaw, D., Keizer, A., & Johnson, M. (2018). Challenges and contradictions in the 'normalising' of precarious work. *Work, Employment & Society, 32,* 509–527. https://doi.org/10.1177/0950017017751790.

Ryan, R. M., & Deci, E. L. (2000). Self-determination theory and the facilitation of intrinsic motivation, social development, and well-being. *American Psychologist, 55,* 68–78. https://doi.org/10.1037/0003-066X.55.1.68.

Sano, Y. (2016). Diversification of regular employees' career orientations and the current status of careers and working styles. *Japan Labor Review, 13*(2), 46–69.

Savickas, M. L. (2002). Career construction: A developmental theory of vocational behavior. In D. Brown (Ed.), *Career choice and development* (pp. 149–205). San Francisco, CA: Jossey-Brass.

Savickas, M. L. (2013). Career construction theory and practice. In R. W. Lent & S. D. Brown (Eds.), *Career development and counselling: Putting theory and research into work* (2nd ed., pp. 147–183). Hoboken, NJ: Wiley.

Savickas, M. L., Nota, L., Rossier, J., Dauwalder, J.-P., Duarte, M. E., Guichard, J.,…van Vianen, A. E. M. (2009). Life designing: A paradigm for career construction in the 21st century. *Journal of Vocational Behavior*, *75*, 239–250. https://doi.org/10.1016/j.jvb.2009.04.004.

Savickas, M. L., & Porfeli, E. J. (2012). Career Adapt-Abilities Scale: Construction, reliability, and measurement equivalence across 13 countries. *Journal of Vocational Behavior, 80,* 661–673. https://doi.org/10.1016/j.jvb.2012.01.011.

Schuring, M., Robroek, S. J., Otten, F. W., Arts, C. H., & Burdorf, A. (2013). The effect of ill health and socioeconomic status on labor force exit and re-employment: A prospective study with ten years follow-up in the Netherlands. *Scandinavian Journal of Work, Environment & Health, 39,* 134–143. https://doi.org/10.5271/sjweh.332.

Schwartz, B. (2015). The paradox of choice. In S. Joseph (Ed.), *Positive psychology in practice: Promoting human flourishing in work, health, education, and everyday life* (pp. 121–138). Hoboken, NJ: John Wiley & Sons Inc.

Shoss, M. K., Jiang, L., & Probst, T. M. (2018). Bending without breaking: A two-study examination of employee resilience in the face of job insecurity. *Journal of Occupational Health Psychology, 23,* 112–126. https://doi.org/10.1037/ocp0000060.

Snyder, C. R. (2002). Hope theory: Rainbows in the mind. *Psychological Inquiry, 13,* 249–275. https://doi.org/10.1207/S15327965PLI1304_01.

Snyder, C. R., Irving, L., & Anderson, J. (1991). Hope and health: Measuring the will and the ways. In C. R. Snyder & D. R. Forsyth (Eds.), *Handbook of social and clinical psychology* (pp. 285–305). Elmsford, NY: Pergamon.

Stajkovic, A. D., & Luthans, F. (1998). Self-efficacy and work-related performance: A meta-analysis. *Psychological Bulletin, 124,* 240–261. https://doi.org/10.1037/0033-2909.124.2.240.

UN General Assembly (1948, December 10). *Universal Declaration of Human Rights*. 217 A (III). Retrieved from http://www.un.org/en/ga/search/view_doc.asp?symbol=A/RES/217(III).

UN General Assembly (2015, October 21). Transforming our world: the 2030 agenda for sustainable development, A/RES/70/1, Retrieved from https://www.refworld.org/docid/57b6e3e44.html.

Van der Heijden, B. I. J. M., & De Vos, A. (2015). Sustainable careers: Introductory chapter. In A. De Vos & B. I. J. M. Van Der Heijden (Eds.), *Handbook of research on sustainable careers* (pp. 1–19). Cheltenham, UK: Edward Elgar Publishing.

Walther, A., & Plug, W. (2006). Transitions from school to work in Europe: Destandardization and policy trends. *New Directions for Child and Adolescent Development, 2006*, 77–90. https://doi.org/10.1002/cd.170

Widmer, E. D., & Ritschard, G. (2009). The de-standardization of the life course: Are men and women equal? *Advances in Life Course Research, 14,* 28–39. https://doi.org/10.1016/j.alcr.2009.04.001.

Xanthopoulou, D., Bakker, A. B., Demerouti, E., & Schaufeli, W. B. (2007). The role of personal resources in the job demands-resources model. *International Journal of Stress Management, 14,* 121–141. https://doi.org/10.1037/1072-5245.14.2.121.

Xanthopoulou, D., Bakker, A. B., & Fischbach, A. (2013). Work engagement among employees facing emotional demands: The role of personal resources. *Journal of Personnel Psychology, 12,* 74–84. https://doi.org/10.1027/1866-5888/a000085.

Youssef, C. M., & Luthans, F. (2007). Positive organizational behavior in the workplace: The impact of hope, optimism, and resilience. Journal of Management, 33, 774-800. https://doi.org/10.1177/0149206307305562 .

Goal Facilitation Theory as Counselling Framework for Enhancing Employees' Career Adaptability and Thriving at Work

Melinde Coetzee

Abstract The chapter contributes to career counselling theory by introducing goal facilitation as a theoretical lens for understanding the direct and indirect links between the three concepts of organisational career instrumentality, career adaptability and thriving at work within the boundary conditions of individuals' life stage (age). The chapter draws on the experiences of (N = 606) white (56%) and black (44%) and male (54%) and female (46%) professional people (mean age = 37; SD = 11.08) employed across the globe (South Africa: 76%; Europe: 19%; Africa: 3%; Eastern countries: 2%). The interaction effect between low organisational career instrumentality and age in explaining low thriving at work was significantly stronger for the 25–39 years age group when compared with the mid-life aspirants (40–56 years). Moderated-mediation analysis showed that organisational career instrumentality positively explains thriving at work through career adaptability for the 30s transition candidates (25–39 years). The findings highlight organisational career instrumentality and career adaptability attitudes and behaviours as important mechanisms in career counselling intervention for understanding the dynamics between personal goal pursuit and state of thriving within the boundary conditions of clients' life stage. The chapter outlines implications for theory and provides guidelines for career counselling intervention.

Keywords Career adaptability · Career counselling · Goal facilitation · Life stage · Organisational career instrumentality · Thriving at work

In recent years, career counselling theory has been renovated to help clients construct and navigate meaningful lives within a more volatile, uncertain, complex and ambiguous (VUCA) work-life space (Guichard, 2016; Veldsman & Pauw, 2018). Modern career counselling intervention focuses on guiding clients toward developing the capacities that help them craft and sustain meaningful, self-directed careers that fulfil personal growth needs (Dahling & Lauricella, 2017). Part of this process involves preparing clients to remain open-minded in accepting and embracing

M. Coetzee (✉)
Department of Industrial and Organisational Psychology, University of South Africa, 392, Pretoria, Gauteng 0003, South Africa
e-mail: coetzm1@unisa.ac.za

J. G. Maree (ed.), *Handbook of Innovative Career Counselling*,
https://doi.org/10.1007/978-3-030-22799-9_5

change and take ownership of their employability instead of committing to a lifetime career in a single organisation (Maree & Twigge, 2016). Clients' increased willingness to engage in career self-construction through enhanced career adaptability (i.e., preparedness and readiness to cope with unpredictable career adjustments) helps to crystallise the meaning they strive to give to their lives (Bernaud, 2014; Maree & Twigge, 2016; Yuen & Yau, 2015). However, crafting a meaningful career in VUCA contexts has become more challenging with clients having to learn how to navigate a self-constructed career while also sustaining their employability, performance, health and wellbeing over time (Porath, Spreitzer, Gibson, & Garnett, 2012). To this end, the notion of psychological thriving has emerged as an important concept to consider in modern day career counselling intervention. Psychologically thriving clients are not merely surviving in stressful work-life spaces but rather are growing or perceive themselves to be on an upward life trajectory (Porath et al., 2012; Thomas & Hall, 2008). Although the notion of thriving is a valuable positive psychological contribution to modern career theory (Porath et al., 2012), research on the mechanisms explaining individuals' experiences of thriving is sparse, especially in the career counselling space.

The present chapter explores the role of goal facilitation (i.e., perceived instrumentality of the environment in enabling the achievement of personal goals: Fitzsimons & Shah, 2008) in explaining the link between organisational career instrumentality and thriving at work through career adaptability. Research among young secondary school adolescents (mean age: 14 years) by Yuen and Yau (2015) indicates links between career adaptability and presence of meaning in life and sense of well-being. Hirschi (2009) also found positive associations between career adaptability and working adults' positive development and psychological well-being. Goal orientation was also found to positively predict working adults' career adaptability and career optimism (Tolentino et al., 2014). A study by Doest, Maes, Gebhardt, and Koelwijn, (2006) found organisational instrumentality in personal goal facilitation to explain employees' job satisfaction and sense of well-being at work. Notwithstanding these studies pointing to links between individuals' goal orientation, career adaptability and sense of psychological well-being, the mechanisms explaining thriving at work are unclear. Moreover, understanding the role of age (life stage) in explaining individuals' sense of well-being across their careers is regarded as important but under-studied (Zacher & Schmitt, 2016).

The relationship dynamics between the concepts of organisational career instrumentality, career adaptability and thriving at work from a goal facilitation perspective have to date been neglected by career counselling research and frameworks that are interested in promoting employment and well-being sustainability in today's VUCA environment. In addition, age as a boundary condition for the relationship dynamics between the three constructs is also under-explored. The chapter contributes to career counselling theory by introducing goal facilitation as a theoretical lens in understanding the direct and indirect links between the three concepts of organisational instrumentality in career goal achievement, career adaptability and thriving at work within the boundary conditions of clients' life stage (age).

Theoretical Premise of Goal Facilitation Theory: Dynamics of Organisational Career Instrumentality, Career Adaptability and Thriving at Work

Goal facilitation theory posits that personal goals shape clients' day-to-day attitudes and behaviours because people are in constant pursuit of meaningful goals (Fitzsimons & Shah, 2008). People's careers and well-being are socially embedded and social environments are often considered instrumental to goal achievement. Individuals generate positive attitudes and behaviours relative to the advancement of important and meaningful goals in social environments (Xie, Zhou, Huang, & Xia, 2017). Meaningful life-career self-construction often involves looking at how social environments (for example, significant others, jobs, occupations, organisations) are instrumental in achieving important goals (Fitzsimons & Shah, 2008; Xie et al., 2017). The present study focused on the social context of the organisation within which the individual is pursuing the career as an important life goal and how individuals' experiences of the organisation's role in their career development influence their sense of thriving at work.

Organisational Instrumentality Toward Career Goal Achievement

Organisational instrumentality denotes the extent to which individuals feel that the organisation supports them in achieving their career goals, how positive and energised they feel about their career development in the organisation, and the clarity they have about their career within the particular organisation (Cardador, Dane, & Pratt, 2011; Coetzee, 2018). Goal facilitation theory (Labroo & Kim, 2009; Xie et al., 2017) posits that perceptions of organisational instrumentality are stronger when individuals have clear and accessible career goals than when they feel uncertain about their career development within the organisation. Research by Xie et al. (2017) also indicates positive links between meaningful goals from which individuals derive a sense of purpose and their perceptions of organisational instrumentality and support. Previous studies have demonstrated positive associations between perceived organisational career development support and career satisfaction, including organisational citizenship behaviours (Chen, 2011).

Perceived organisational support and instrumentality are mutually beneficial to employees and organisations. Research shows that employees who feel that the organisation values their contributions and cares about their well-being, and who have high levels of career satisfaction are more likely to strive toward achieving organisational goals than those who feel uncertain about the organisation's caring for and support of them (Chen, 2011). Investing in practices such as training and development, career growth opportunities and supervisor support practices was shown to enhance employees' perceptions of the organisation being instrumental in goal and personal potential fulfillment and caring about their well-being (Armstrong-Stassen & Ursel, 2009; Shanock & Eisenberger, 2006).

In the present study, the organisation's instrumentality in advancing individuals' career goals and full potential development was studied in relation to clients' career adaptability and thriving at work. The premise is made that instrumental career goal facilitation will link positively to higher levels of career adaptability and thriving at work, and that the link between organisational goal instrumentality and thriving at work through career adaptability will be stronger or lower for certain life stages. Understanding these relationship dynamics will inform career counselling intervention in the work context.

Career Adaptability

Career adaptability alludes to individuals' readiness to cope with the demands of work roles and adjustments required by changes in work and working conditions as indicated by certain career-related attitudes and behaviours (Yuen & Yau, 2015). These attitudes and behaviours reflect individuals' concerns about their career future (i.e.,. planfulness and optimism); their sense of ownership of and decisiveness about their career future (i.e., career control); their willingness to explore career opportunities and options (i.e., career curiosity); their anticipation of success in encountering challenges and overcoming obstacles (i.e., self-efficacious problem-solving or career confidence: Nilforooshan and Salimi, 2016; Savickas, 2005, 2013). A lack of these career adaptability attitudes and behaviours may be demonstrated in clients' indifference and pessimism about their career future (i.e., lack of clear career goals and plans), career indecision, unrealism about their careers and their potential, and career inhibition that thwarts actualising potential roles and achieving goals (Savickas, 2013). In line with goal facilitation theory, career concern (i.e., setting goals and planning future career moves) is seen as the most important dimension of career adaptability (Nilforooshan and Salimi, 2016). This perspective supports the premise that high levels of career adaptability will relate positively to positive states of thriving at work, especially when perceived organisational instrumentality is also high. Previous research has demonstrated positive links between career adaptability and work engagement, well-being, career success and job satisfaction (Fiori, Bollman, & Rossier, 2015; Maggiori, Johnston, Krings, Massoudi, & Rossier, 2013; Zacher, 2014).

Thriving at Work

Thriving at work alludes to the psychological state of continuous learning (i.e., having a psychological experience of personal growth, developing new knowledge, skills and capacities, and confidence) and vitality (i.e., feeling of being energised at and by work) that promote an overall sense of momentum and progress (Porath et al., 2012; Spreitzer, Porath, & Gibson, 2012). Thriving focuses on individuals seeking to develop their full potential as part of their sustained employability (Zhai, Wang, & Weadon, 2017). When experienced in concert, vitality and learning mutually enhance one another to form the overall experience of thriving or fulfilling one's potential (Porath et al., 2012). Being socially embedded, thriving is limited for example when one feels energised and alive while working but finds personal learning to be stagnant. Similarly, when one is learning but feels depleted, thriving suffers (Porath et al., 2012). Research studies indicate positive links between career development initiative and thriving outside of work, greater proactivity and better job performance (Paterson, Luthans, & Jeung, 2014; Porath et al., 2012; Prem, Ohly, Kubicek, & Korunka, 2017).

Thriving at work captures the affective (vitality) and cognitive (learning) components of individual growth and development in a work context, all of which are important for individuals to sustain their employability (Porath et al., 2012). Previous research has shown that perceived organisational support promotes heedful relating (i.e., being purposeful, careful, consistent in one's action) which in turn enables individual thriving (Abid, Zahra, & Ahmed, 2016). Similarly, in this study it was proposed that perceived organisational career instrumentality will enhance career adaptability and thriving at work.

Life Stage as Boundary Condition

Career counselling denotes the process of helping individuals make career-related decisions and effectively manage their careers over the life course, including developing the emotional resilience to cope with challenges that arise as their working lives progress (Kidd, 2007). From a developmental approach, clients are encouraged to move toward greater awareness of themselves and their situations and to develop decision-making skills relating to the respective developmental or life stage (Kidd, 2007). Career counselling intervention in the organisational context should therefore consider the role of age (life stage) when exploring the links between individuals' perceived organisational career instrumentality, career adaptability and thriving at work.

In this study, age (life stage) is conceived as a continuous variable and the labels of "30s transition candidates" (25–39 years: Mittal, 2017) and "mid-life aspirants" (40–56 years: Mittal, 2017) are used for descriptive purposes to refer to relatively higher and lower values of age, respectively. The 30s transition candidates have already entered the work world; they have started a career and are already involved in the challenges of sustaining their employability which, as part of their psychological thriving, generally involves striving for continuous personal growth and development and gaining experiences and capacities that will help them advance in their careers and develop to their full potential (Mittal, 2017). The mid-life aspirants have become masters in their field of occupation; they may be in a stage of wanting to change their career paths based on a sense of seeking the internal self as part of their growth and development (psychological thriving) instead of fulfilling the expectations of society. They may feel stagnated in their fields and may desire new challenges in their career-life to reach their full potential (Mittal, 2017).

Previous research has demonstrated that the patterns of interaction effects of work characteristics and age on occupational wellbeing are complex and differ for younger workers (18–39 years) and workers older than 40 years (Ng & Feldman, 2015; Zacher & Schmitt, 2016). The interaction patterns appear to depend on the specific work characteristics and occupational well-being indicator under consideration (Zacher & Schmitt, 2016). For example, job autonomy and feedback are more strongly positively related to job satisfaction among older than younger workers (Zacher & Schmitt, 2016) while positive links of job autonomy, skill variety and social support with job satisfaction are weaker among older than younger workers (Besen, Matz-Costa, Brown, Smyer, & Pitt-Catsouphes, 2013; Zacher & Schmitt, 2016).

Seen from the perspective of goal facilitation theory, it was proposed that the link between organisational career instrumentality and thriving at work through career adaptability will differ for the 30s transition candidates (25–39 years) and mid-life aspirants (40–56 years). This assumption alludes to the notion that the personal career goals and sense of thriving of clients in these two age groups will differ due to their respective unique life stage developmental needs. In other words, it was proposed that the nature of the link between organisational career instrumentality and thriving at work through career adaptability will be conditional upon the specific life stage (age group) and their unique career developmental needs.

Goal Facilitation as Career Counselling Framework

Goal facilitation theory has application value in solution-focused career counselling which can be a brief or long-term intervention (Looby, 2014). The solution-focused intervention abides by the counselling principles of attending ("How can I help?"), listening to what the client wants, reflecting (i.e., checking for understanding and building trust), encouraging (i.e., affirming and helping client to connect meaning), questioning (i.e., understanding and being curious about the client's perspective), silence (i.e., counsellor remaining neutral; client is seen as expert), identifying strengths and barriers from a systems perspective and facilitating hope. In solution-based counselling, client self-insight is developed by systematically answering and routinely revisiting the perennial question "What do I want to thrive in my career?'. This "miracle" question engenders hope which is facilitated by the client finding solutions or answers to thriving-related questions such as for example, "What are my life-career goals?; "What make me feel most alive?"; "What skills do I most enjoy using?" (Heslin & Turban, 2016; Looby, 2014).

Hope is created through goal formation; helping the client to recognise the process of identifying an ultimate career goal and establishing short-and long-term steps for achieving goals (Looby, 2014). As a co-construction effort, the counsellor assists the client in analysing adjustments to be made and what is needed systemically to support the achievement of the career goal. In the work context this would allude to the instrumentality of goal facilitation by means of organisational career development support practices and engaging in career adaptability activities (i.e., actively planning for one's future career moves; taking responsibility for building a career; exploring career options; and having confidence in one's ability to make wise career decisions: Nilforooshan & Salimi, 2016). Instrumentality embraces a systems approach throughout the process such as co-scanning with the client the current social environment for support and barriers that are impacting goal attainment (Looby, 2014). Research by Xie et al., (2017) indicates that organisational instrumentality in achieving meaningful goals explains the positive link between calling (sense of meaningfulness) and job satisfaction and positive work attitudes and behaviour. It is proposed that perceived organisational goal instrumentality will enhance important career adaptability attitudes and behaviours (i.e., career planning, decision-making, inquisitive exploring and efficacious problem-solving) that support the achievement of important career goals.

Building on goal facilitation theory, thriving is an emergent process (rather than a cumulative outcome) of career self-construction and goal achievement in a social context. The process of meaningful goal achievement involves an evolving sequence of work-life experiences over time (Heslin & Turban, 2016; Prem et al., 2017). Thriving is seen as an unfolding process of reflecting continuously on what the client really wants or desires in terms of their life and career over the life-span. Through goal facilitation techniques clients can learn how to identify gaps between their current and ideal emergent career, gain new perspectives on their current situation and concerns, and adjust their plans and goals as aspects of their career adaptability and thriving at work (Heslin & Turban, 2016). In practical terms, engaging goal facilitation techniques in a counselling intervention may encourage clients to engage in career adaptability behaviours, which in turn may further facilitate the adaptive function of thriving (i.e., the sense of one is moving forward).

The experience of thriving is shaped by the social context in which individuals are embedded (Porath et al., 2012). It is therefore proposed that as in the case of career adaptability, perceived organisational career instrumentality may also directly relate positively to clients' sense of thriving at work (i.e., enhanced feelings of vitality and learning or growing and developing). Organisational career instrumentality supported by career adaptability attitudes and behaviours may help clients feel that they are moving forward in their careers (i.e., experience feelings of thriving). However, the premise is also made that the indirect link between career instrumentality and thriving at work through higher levels of career adaptability will be conditional upon the life stage (age) of the client. The effect may be more positive for older than younger clients (Fig. 1).

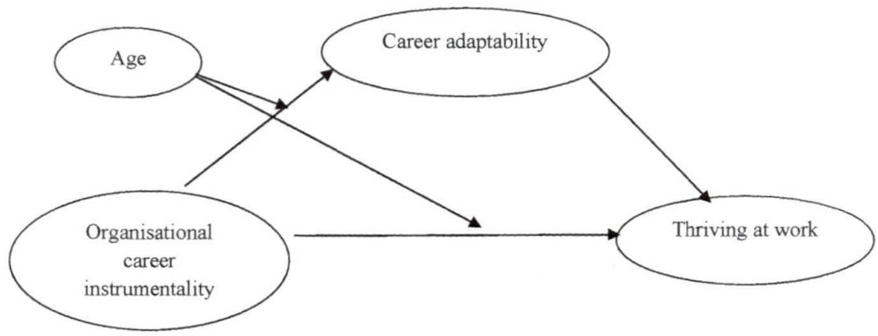

Fig. 1 Conceptual model of the research

Method

Participants

The convenience sample comprised (N = 606) white (56%) and black (44%) and male (54%) and female (46%) professional people (mean age = 37; SD = 11.08: 25–39 years: 64%; 40–56 years: 36%) employed across the globe (South Africa: 76%; Europe: 19%; Africa: 3%; Eastern countries: 2%). The participants were employed in managerial (38%), staff (30%) and professional business consultant (32%) positions in the services industry.

Measuring Instruments

Organisational career instrumentality (OCI). Based on the theory of Cardador et al., (2011), the items of the scale were developed by Coetzee (2018). The OCI comprises seven items construct (e.g. "I feel the organisation is supporting me in achieving my career goals") which measured an overall. Responses were measured on a 7-point Likert-type scale (1 = strongly disagree; 7 = strongly agree). The Cronbach alpha coefficient (internal consistency reliability) obtained for this study was high: 0.93.

Career adapt-ability scale (CAAS). The CAAS (Savickas & Porfeli, 2012) includes 24 items (e.g. "Planning how to achieve my goals") to measure the attitudes and behaviour of career concern, career curiosity, career control and career confidence. Responses were measured on a 5-point Likert-type scale (1 = not strong; 5 = strongest). In the present study the scale obtained a Cronbach alpha (internal consistency reliability) coefficient of 0.95.

Thriving at work scale (TWS). The TWS (Porath et al., 2012) includes 10 items measuring dimensions of vitality (e.g. "I feel alive and vital") and learning (e.g. "I find myself learning often"). Responses were measured on a 7-point Likert-type scale (1 = strongly disagree; 7 = strongly agree). In the present study the scale obtained a Cronbach alpha (internal consistency reliability) coefficient of 0.92.

Procedure

The research institution's online survey facilities were utilised to collect the data from the participants. The data were collected via the professional online social media site, LinkedIn.

Considerations of Ethics

Ethical clearance and permission to conduct the research were obtained from the management of the university. Participants were invited to voluntarily participate in the research study. The online questionnaire included an informed consent form. The privacy, anonymity and confidentiality of all the participants were ensured and honoured.

Statistical Analysis

A regression-based moderated-mediation analysis using the PROCESS version 2.13 for SPSS procedure developed by Hayes (2013) was performed to test the research model. The Preacher and Hayes (2008) bootstrapping procedure (bootstrap samples = 5000) was applied to test the proposed conditional indirect effects. Bootstrapping is a more stringent bias-correcting procedure which involves resampling and building a non-normal sampling distribution of the indirect effect from which confidence intervals can be constructed. This approach reduces the likelihood of Type I error (Preacher & Hayes, 2008; Hayes, 2015). The 95% lower and upper confidence interval levels (LLCI and ULCI) were used as threshold for examining the significance of direct and indirect effects. Following the guidelines of Shrout and Bolger (2002), LLCI and ULCI ranges that did not include zero provided evidence of significant direct and indirect effects.

Results

Measurement Model Validity

A confirmatory factor analysis (CFA) was conducted with SAS (2013) CALIS procedure to estimate the distinctiveness of the three latent variables. Maximum likelihood estimation was applied for the co-variance structure analysis. The results showed that the three-factor (organisational career instrumentality, career adaptability and thriving at work) distinguished well between the variables and that the measurement model had good data fit: Chi-square = 2960.79; df = 808; RMSEA = 0.06; SRMR = 0.06; CFI = 0.90; NFI = 0.90.

Descriptive Statistics and Bi-Variate Correlations

As shown in Table 1, the three construct variables (organisational career instrumentality, career adaptability and thriving at work) correlated positively and significantly ($r \geq 0.11$ to $r \leq 0.67$; $p \leq 0.01$; small to large practical effect). Age correlated with organisational career instrumentality and thriving at work, but not with career adaptability.

Testing Main and Interaction Effects

Table 2 shows that organisational career instrumentality had a significant positive main effect on career adaptability ($\beta = 0.04$, $p = 0.05$, bootstrap LLCI = 0.004; ULCI = 0.07) and thriving at work ($\beta = 0.50$, $p = 0.001$, bootstrap LLCI = 0.45; ULCI = 0.55). Age had neither a significant main effect on career adaptability not thriving at work. Career adaptability had a significant positive main effect on thriving at work ($\beta = 0.47$, $p = 0.001$, bootstrap LLCI = 0.36; ULCI = 0.58).

As shown in Table 2, the model for the interaction effect between organisational career instrumentality and age in predicting career adaptability explained 14% ($R^2 = 0.14$; $F = 2.83$; $p = 0.05$; moderate practical effect) of the variance. The interaction term between organisational career instrumentality and age was not significant.

The model for the interaction effect between organisational career instrumentality and age (life stage) in predicting thriving at work explained 51% ($R^2 = 0.51$; $F = 155.43$; $p = 0.0001$; large practical effect) of the variance. The interaction term between organisational career instrumentality and age was significant ($\beta = -0.12$, $p = 0.001$, bootstrap LLCI = −0.21; ULCI = −0.04).

Testing Conditional Direct and Indirect Effects: Age (Life Stage) as Boundary Condition

Table 2 shows that both age groups (25–39 years and 40–56 years) functioned as boundary conditions for the direct effect of organisational career instrumentality on thriving at work. As depicted in Fig. 2, the link between perceived low organisational career instrumentality and low thriving at work was significantly stronger for the 30s transition candidates (25–39 years) when compared with the mid-life aspirants (40–56 years).

Table 1 Descriptive statistics and internal consistency reliability coefficients

	Variable	Mean	SD	α	1	2	3	4
1	Age	–	–	–	–			
2	Organisational career instrumentality	4.61	1.72	0.93	0.10**	–		
3	Career adaptability	4.07	0.63	0.95	−0.05	0.11**	–	
4	Thriving at work	5.44	1.23	0.92	0.08*	0.67***	0.31***	–

Note N = 606. *$p \le 0.05$; ** $p \le 0.01$; *** $p \le 0.0001$

Table 2 Moderated-mediation effects of organisational career instrumentality and life stage in explaining career adaptability and thriving at work

Variables	Coefficient estimates		Bootstrap 95% CI	
	β	t	LLCI	ULCI
Model: Outcome—Career adaptability				
Constant	4.10	128.99***	4.04	4.16
Organisational career instrumentality (A)	0.04	2.16*	0.004	0.07
Age (B)	−0.06	−1.20	−0.17	0.04
Interaction term: AxB	0.01	0.21	−0.06	0.07
Model info				
$p = 2.83$*				
$R^2 = 0.14$				
Model: outcome—thriving at work				
Constant	3.50	14.84***	3.04	3.97
Organisational career instrumentality (A)	0.50	19.65***	0.45	0.55
Career adaptability	0.47	8.31***	0.36	0.58
Age (B)	0.10	1.40	−0.04	0.25
Interaction term: AxB	−0.12	−2.82**	−0.21	−0.04
Model info				
$Fp = 155.43$***				
$R^2 = 0.51$				
Conditional effects of organisational career instrumentality on thriving at work at the values of the age (life stage) groups				
25–39 years	0.50	19.65***	0.45	0.55
40–56 years	0.37	10.36***	0.30	0.44
Conditional indirect effect of organisational career instrumentality on thriving at work through career adaptability at the values of age (life stage) as moderator				
Mediating effects at values of age (moderator)	Effect β	Boot SE	LLCI	ULCI
25–39 years	0.02	0.01	0.003	0.04
40–56 years	0.02	0.01	−0.003	0.05

Note N = 606 *** $p \leq 0.001$; ** $p \leq 0.01$; * $p \leq 0.05$. *CI* Confidence interval. *LLCI* Lower level confidence interval. *ULCI* upper level confidence interval. *SE* Standard error

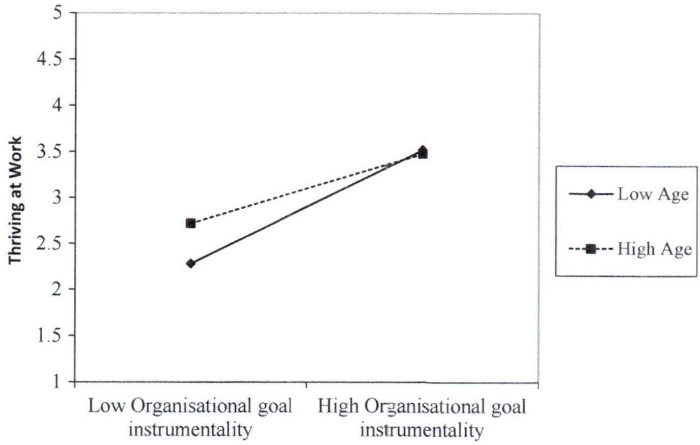

Fig. 2 Interaction effect: Organisational career instrumentality x age in explaining thriving at work levels. Low age: 25–39 years (30s transition candidates); High age: 40–56 years (mid-life aspirants)

Table 2 shows that only the age group 25–39 years functioned as boundary condition for the indirect effect of organisational career instrumentality through career adaptability on thriving at work ($\beta = 0.02$; bootstrap LLCI = 0.003; ULCI = 0.04). The mediating effect did not include zero, indicating a partial mediation effect of career adaptability in terms of the 30s transition candidates.

Discussion

The main aim of the chapter was to explore the direct and indirect links between perceived organisational career instrumentality, career adaptability and thriving at work within the boundary conditions of individuals' life stage (age) from a goal facilitation theory perspective. As expected, both organisational career instrumentality and career adaptability functioned as significant explanatory mechanisms of individuals' thriving at work. The finding is in agreement with the theoretical premise of goal facilitation theory that positive attitudes and behaviour are generated when individuals experience the advancement of meaningful and important goals in the social environment (Xie et al., 2017).

The study findings further suggest that perceived organisational instrumentality toward career goal achievement is stronger associated with thriving at work than with career adaptability. This finding could be ascribed to the notion that both organisational career instrumentality and thriving at work are socially embedded constructs (Porath et al., 2012; Xie et al., 2017) while career adaptability denotes important attitudes and behaviour for proactively adapting to changes influencing career development in the social environment (Nilforooshan and Salimi, 2016; Savickas, 2005).

Perceived organisational career instrumentality denotes positive feelings and beliefs about career development support toward career growth and goals (Cardador et al., 2011) which meaningfully tie in with feelings and cognitions about vitality and learning in the organisation (i.e., moving forward toward fulfilling one's potential in the organisation: Porath et al., 2012; Zhai et al., 2017). In this equation, the results showed that the link between perceived low organisational career instrumentality and low thriving at work was much stronger for the 30s transition candidates (25–39 years) when compared with the mid-life aspirants (40–56 years). Moreover, career adaptability functioned as mechanism in explaining the link between perceived organisational career instrumentality and thriving at work only for the 30s transition candidates. This finding could be ascribed to the 25–39 age group generally being more concerned than those in their mid-life stage about receiving organisational support in achieving goals toward advancing and growing in their careers. The 30s transition candidates generally have a strong desire to still make their mark in the world of work, sustain their employability, and gain the experiences that will help them advance in their careers (Mittal, 2017).

The findings appear to suggest that the development of career adaptability attitudes and behaviours may further enhance the link between perceptions of career advancement support and psychological thriving for individuals whose predominant career development goals may be to gain experiences and capacities that will help them become masters in their occupational field and sustain their employability. The lack of a mediating effect of career adaptability for the mid-life aspirants (40–56 years) may be attributed to the notion that this age group already have clear goals and encountered experiences that helped them to achieve important goals and master their occupational field. Their concerns may not revolve around career advancement in the organisation per se but rather intrinsic psychological growth and fulfilment through new challenges (Mittal, 2017).

The findings of the study must be interpreted with caution due to some limitations of the research design. First, although the sample included participants across the globe, the representativeness could be more expanded in the various countries, age, gender and race groups to increase the external validity of the findings. No generalisation can therefore be made and future replication studies are recommended in more representative samples. Second, the cross-sectional nature of the research design does not allow for cause-effect deductions but merely exploring the magnitude and direction of associations between the variables. Future longitudinal studies are recommended to study the conditional effect of age on the links between the construct variables.

Implications for Career Counselling Theory and Intervention

First, the findings demonstrated the unique role of personal goals and perceived instrumentality of the work context in achieving goals and fulfilling one's potential. In this regard, it may be useful for career counsellors to incorporate principles of goal facilitation theory in their career counselling intervention approach. Looby (2014) and Heslin and Turban (2016) assert that goal formation generates hope in clients while clear career goals and plans assist clients in moving forward in life. In the work context, career counsellors should consider the role of the organisation in supporting clients in their career development. Practices such as supervisor support through mentoring and coaching, career development plans, reviews and development planning including identifying further training and development and career advancement opportunities may enhance perceptions of organisational career instrumentality (Armstrong-Stassen & Ursel, 2009; Shanock & Eisenberger, 2006). The findings of the study suggest that such supportive practices may especially be relevant to the 30s transition candidates (25–39 years) to help them thrive at work (i.e., feel energised and experience personal growth and learning) with a sense of momentum and progress in their careers.

Second, the findings demonstrated the relevance of career adaptability for enhancing individuals' perceptions of the organisation being instrumental and supportive toward them thriving in their careers. The study shows that in this context, incorporating career adaptability in career counselling intervention is especially important for individuals in the 30s transition life stage. Individuals 25–39 years who perceive low organisational career instrumentality and experience low thriving may benefit from career intervention that help them develop career adaptability attitudes and behaviours (i.e., becoming concerned about their future as a worker by setting goals and plans; developing increased control over their career future by taking ownership; displaying a curiosity by exploring possible selves and future scenarios; and strengthening the confidence to pursue their aspirations and overcome challenges: Savickas, 2013).

Third, the findings corroborate previous research demonstrating that the conditional boundary effects of age in understanding the link between psychological constructs in a work context are often complex and patterns of interaction effects differ for younger and older workers because of unique life stage career developmental needs (Zacher & Schmitt, 2016). In the present study, the conditional effects of age need to be understood in the light of the psychological aspects measured by the three constructs of organisational career instrumentality, career adaptability and thriving at work. Practically, career counsellors need to take cognisance of life span development theory and acknowledge the role of age in career counselling intervention to ensure the relevance and appropriateness of their intervention approaches to various life stage groups. Building on goal facilitation theory, although clients of all ages pursue meaningful goals as an important part of psychological thriving, the nature and meaning of career goals with the concomitant career adaptability attitudes and behaviours may differ at various life stages.

Chapter Summary and Conclusion

The chapter introduced goal facilitation as a theoretical lens in understanding the direct and indirect links between the three concepts of organisational career instrumentality, career adaptability and thriving at work within the boundary conditions of individuals' life stage (age). Despite the research design limitations, the present study contributed valuable evidence-based insights in the boundary conditions of age in the work context when incorporating career goals, organisational career instrumentality, career adaptability and thriving at work in career counselling intervention. Career counsellors may draw from the study theory and findings to enrich their approaches toward career counselling intervention for modern day work contexts.

References

Abid, G., Zahra, I., & Ahmed, A. (2016). Promoting thriving at work and waning turnover intention: A relational perspective. *Future Business Journal, 2,* 127–137. https://doi.org/10.1016/j.fbj.2016.08.001.

Armstrong-Stassen, M., & Ursel, N. D. (2009). Perceived organizational support, career satisfaction, and the retention of older workers. *Journal of Occupational and Organizational Psychology, 82,* 201–220. https://doi.org/10.1348/096317908X288838.

Bernaud, J. L. (2014). Career counseling and life meaning: a new perspective of life designing for research and application. In A. Di Fabio & J. L. Bernaud (Eds.), *The Construction of the Identity in the 21st Century* (pp. 29–40). New York, NY: Nova Science.

Besen, E., Matz-Costa, C., Brown, M., Smyer, M. A., & Pitt-Catsouphes, M. (2013). Job characteristics, core self-evaluations, and job satisfaction: what's age got to do with it? *International Journal of Aging and Human Development, 76,* 269–295. https://doi.org/10.2190/AG.76.4.a.

Cardador, M. T., Dane, E., & Pratt, M. G. (2011). Linking calling orientations to organizational attachment via organizational instrumentality. *Journal of Vocational Behavior, 79,* 367–378. https://doi.org/10.1016/j/jvb.2011.03.009.

Chen, Y. (2011). Chinese knowledge employees' career values, perceived organisational support and career success. *Scientific Research, iBusiness, 3,* 274–282. https://doi.org/10.4236/ib.2011.33036.

Coetzee, M. (2018). *Organisational career instrumentality scale*. Department of Industrial and Organisational Psychology, University of South Africa. Pretoria: Unisa.

Dahling, J. J., & Lauricella, T. K. (2017). Linking job design to subjective career success: A test of self-determination theory. *Journal of Career Assessment, 25*(3), 371–388. https://doi.org/10.1177/1069072716639689.

Doest, L. T., Maes, S., Gebhardt, W. A., & Koelwijn, H. (2006). Personal goal facilitation through work: Implications for employee satisfaction and well-being. *Applied Psychology, 55,* 192–219. https://doi.org/10.1111/j.1464-0597.2006.00232.x.

Fiori, M., Bollman, G., & Rossier, J. (2015). Exploring the path through which career adaptability increases job satisfaction and lowers job stress: The role of affect. *Journal of Vocational Behavior, 91,* 113–121. https://doi.org/10.1016/j/jvb.2015.08.010.

Fitzsimons, G. M., & Shah, J. Y. (2008). How goal instrumentality shapes relationship evaluations. *Journal of Personality and Social Psychology, 95,* 319–337. https://doi.org/10.1037/0022-3514.95.2.319.

Guichard, J. (2016). Reflexivity in life design interventions: Comments on life and career design dialogues. *Journal of Vocational Behavior, 97,* 78–83. https://doi.org/10.1016/j/jvb.2016.08.001.

Hayes, A. F. (2013). *An introduction to mediation, moderation, and conditional process analysis: A regression-based approach*. New York, NY: Guilford Press.

Hayes, A. F. (2015). An index and test of linear moderated mediation. *Multivariate Behavioral Research, 50*(1), 1–22. https://doi.org/10.1080/00273171.2014.962683.

Heslin, P. A. & turban, D. B. (2016). Enabling career success as emergent process. *Organizational Dynamics, 45*, 155–164. http://dx.doi.org/10.1016/j.orgdyn.2016.07.001.

Hirschi, A. (2009). Career adaptability development in adolescence: Multiple predictors and effect on sense of power and life satisfaction. *Journal of Vocational Behavior, 74*, 145–155.

Kidd, J. M. (2007). Career counselling. In H. Gunz & M. Peiperl (Eds.), *Handbook of career studies* (pp. 97–113). London: Sage.

Labroo, A. A., & Kim, S. (2009). The “instrumentality” heuristic: Why meta-cognitive difficulty is desirable during goal pursuit. *Psychological Science, 20*, 127–134. https://doi.org/10.1111/j.1467-9280.2008.02264.

Locby, M. (2014). *Solution-focused career counseling*. Downloaded from the World Wide Web on 5 May 2018: https://www.ncda.org/aws/NCDA.

Maggiori, C., Johnston, C. S., Krings, F., Massoudi, K., & Rossier, J. (2013). The role of career adaptability and work conditions on general and professional well-being. *Journal of Vocational Behavior, 83*, 437–449. https://doi.org/10.1016/j/jvb.2013.07.001.

Maree, J. G., & Twigge, A. (2016). Career and self-construction of emerging adults: The value of life designing. *Frontiers in Psychology, 6*, 1–12. https://doi.org/10.3389/fpsyg.2016.02041.

Mittal, K. (2017). *Need for guidance for different age groups*. Downloaded from the World Wide Web on 5 May 2018: http://www.careerguide.com/blog/career-guidance-different-age

Ng, T. W. H., & Feldman, D. C. (2015). The moderating effects of age in the relationship of job autonomy to work outcomes. *Work Aging Retirement, 1*, 64–78. https://doi.org/10.1093/worker/wau003.

Nikrooshan, P., & Salimi, S. (2016). Career adaptability as mediator between personality and career engagement. *Journal of Vocational Behavior, 94*, 1–10. https://doi.org/10.1016/j/jvb.20.2016.02.010.

Paterson, T. A., Luthans, F., & Jeung, W. (2014). Thriving at work: Impact of psychological capital and supervisor support. *Journal of Organizational Behavior, 35*, 434–446. https://doi.org/10.1002/job.1907.

Porath, C., Spreitzer, G., Gibson, C., & Garnett, F. G. (2012). Thriving at work: Toward its measurement, construct validation, and theoretical refinement. *Journal of Organizational Behavior, 33*, 250–275. https://doi.org/10.1002/job.756.

Preacher, K. J., & Hayes, A. F. (2008). Asymptotic and resampling strategies for assessing and comparing indirect effects in multiple mediator models. *Behavior Research Methods, 40*(3), 879–891.

Prem, R., Ohly, S., Kubicek, B., & Korunka, C. (2017). Thriving on challenge stressors? Exploring time pressure and learning demands as antecedents of thriving at work. *Journal of Organizational Behavior, 38*(1), 108–123. https://doi.org/10.1002/job.2115.

SAS Institute. (2013). *What's new in SAS ®*. Cary, NC: SAS Institute Inc.

Savickas, M. L. (2005). The theory and practice of career construction. In S. D. Brown & R. W. Lent (Eds.), *Career development and counselling: Putting theory and research to work* (pp. 42–70). Hoboken, NJ: John Wiley & Sons.

Savickas, M. L. (2013). Career construction theory and practice. In R. W. Lent & S. D. Brown (Eds.), *Career development and counseling: Putting theory and research to work* (2nd ed., pp. 147–183). Hoboken, New Jersey: John Wiley & Sons.

Savickas, M. L., & Porfeli, E. J. (2012). Career adapt-abilities scale: construction, reliability, and measurement equivalence across 13 countries. *Journal of Vocational Behavior, 80*, 661–667.

Shanock, L. R., & Eisenberger, R. (2006). When supervisors feel supported: Relationship with subordinates' perceived supervisor support, perceived organisational support, and performance. *Journal of Applied Psychology, 91*(3), 689–695. https://doi.org/10.1037/0021-9010.91.3.689.

Shrout, P. E., & Bolger, N. (2002). Mediation in experimental and non-experimental studies: New procedures and recommendations. *Psychological Methods, 7*(4), 422–445.
Spreitzer, G. M., Porath, C. L., & Gibson, C. B. (2012). Toward human sustainability: How to enable more thriving at work. *Organizational Dynamics, 41,* 155–162. https://doi.org/10.1016/j.orgdyn.2012.01.009.
Thomas, S. P., & Hall, J. (2008). Life trajectories of female child abuse survivors thriving in adulthood. *Qualitative Health Research, 18,* 149–166.
Tolentino, L. R., Garcia, P. R. J. M., Lu, V. N., Restubog, S. L. D., Bordia, P., & Plewa, C. (2014). Career adaptation: The relation of career adaptability to goal orientation, proactive personality and career optimism. *Journal of Vocational Behavior, 84,* 39–48.
Veldsman, D. & Pauw, D. (2018). The relevance of the employee value proposition for retention in the VUCA world of work. In M. Coetzee, N. Ferreira, & I. L. Potgieter (Eds.), *Psychology of Retention: Theory, Research and Practice* (pp. in press). Dordrecht, the Netherlands: Springer.
Xie, B., Zhou, W., Huang, J. L., & Xia, M. (2017). Using goal facilitation theory to explain the relationships between calling and organization-directed citizenship behavior and job satisfaction. *Journal of Vocational Behavior, 100,* 78–87. https://doi.org/10.1016/j/jvb.2017.03.001.
Yuen, M., & Yau, J. (2015). Relation of career adaptability to meaning in life and connectedness among adolescents in Hong Kong. *Journal of Vocational Behavior, 91,* 147–156. https://doi.org/10.1016/j/jvb.2015.10.003.
Zacher, H. (2014). Career adaptability predicts subjective career success above and beyond personality traits and core self-evaluations. *Journal of Vocational Behavior, 84,* 21–30. https://doi.org/10.1016/j/jvb.2013.10.002.
Zacher, H., & Schmitt, A. (2016). Work characteristics and occupational well-being: The role of age. *Frontiers in Psychology, 7,* 1–7. https://doi.org/10.3389/fpsyg.2016.01411.
Zhai, Q., Wang, S., & Weadon, H. (2017). Thriving at work as mediator of the relationship between workplace support and life satisfaction. *Journal of Management and Organization, 62,* 1–17. https://doi.org/10.1017/jmo.2017.62.

Innovative Utilization of the Discrimination Model for Career-focused Counselling Supervision

Seth C. W. Hayden

Abstract Career-focused counselling supervision provides a venue in which elements of effective service delivery can be enhanced. Within career development services, Hoppin and Goodman (Clinical supervision of career development practitioners: Practical strategies National Career Development Association, Broken Arrow, OK. 2014) outlined the application of clinical supervision to career services professionals. Established approaches to clinical supervision such as the discrimination model (Bernard & Goodyear, in Counsellor Education and Supervision. 19 60–68, 1979, 1997) in which a career practitioner is assessed in three skills areas of intervention, conceptualization, and personalization (i.e. adapting his or her own personal style to counselling while being aware of personal issues). The supervisor shifts between the roles of consultant, counsellor, and teacher based on the development needs of the practitioner. This chapter contains information on the connection between career and mental health concerns as well as the manner in which supervision of career-focused counselling and more specifically the discrimination model can enhance career service delivery. Specific strategies grounded in this approach and a case study outlining its application are provided.

Keywords Career-focused counselling · Supervision of career services · Supervision · Discrimination model

Introduction

Innovative practices in career-focused counselling are not created in a vacuum. To support the ongoing development of career counsellors ensuring that they are responsive to the dynamic nature of the world of work, clinical supervision provides means in which to facilitate this process. Counselling supervision is an intervention in which to prepare, teach, and monitor the quality of counselling provided by supervisees (Evans, Wright, Murphy, & Maki, 2016). Supervision has been termed as unparalleled in its power and potential to prepare novice therapists for prac-

S. C. W. Hayden (✉)
Department of Counselling, Wake Forest University, Winston-Salem, NC, USA
e-mail: haydensc@wfu.edu

J. G. Maree (ed.), *Handbook of Innovative Career Counselling*,
https://doi.org/10.1007/978-3-030-22799-9_6

tice and assist more advanced therapists to further develop their treatment skills (Watkins, 2014). Watkins, Budge, and Callahan (2015) summarized empirical findings of several studies in which supervision was found to contribute to favorable supervisee outcomes such as increased sense of practitioner self-efficacy, enhanced self-awareness, enhanced treatment knowledge, enhanced skill acquisition, and utilization, and strengthening of the supervisee-client relationship.

In the United States, supervision is included in the National Career Development Association (NCDA) Multicultural Career Counselling Competencies (2009) emphasizing its importance within career counselling. In terms of competence, career practitioners who engage in supervision are tasked with gaining knowledge of and engaging in evidence-based supervision practice, pursuing education, and training related to counselling and supervision topics. This expands the context of supervision beyond administrative oversight of career service delivery to the level of a therapeutic intervention in need of sophisticated mechanisms to support career practitioner development. Regardless of the professional identity of the practitioner, engagement with a career practitioner can have a profound impact on both career and mental health dimensions (Osborn, Hayden, Sampson, & Peterson, 2016). Though there is attention on career-focused counselling supervision, more is needed to better understand ways in which to enhance counsellor development via supervision. Specifically, applying established clinical supervision models to career service delivery presents a foundational structure in which to effectively enhance career practitioners' engagement with clients.

Career-focused counselling supervision provides a venue in which elements of effective service delivery can be processed. Counselling supervision involves an intervention provided by a more senior career counsellor to a more junior-level practitioner with the aim of enhancing the quality of functioning of the more junior member and monitoring the quality of services administered (Bernard & Goodyear, 2014; Bronson, 2010). Within career development services, Hoppin and Goodman (2014) outlined the application of counselling supervision to career services practitioners (CSPs). Within the supervision of career services, common techniques include one-on-one and group supervision, role plays, and observations (Reid, 2010). NCDA has taken steps to support supervisors by offering specialized training for practitioners in a supervisory role, and in 2016 created a credential for supervisors of career-focused counselling with the aim of increasing competence in career-focused counselling supervision.

There has been attention in the professional literature devoted to supervision in relation to various aspect of career services. Counselling supervision has been indicated as a beneficial mechanism for enhancing the selection and implementation of career assessments (Hayden & Kronholz, 2014). Fostering intentionality in career assessment delivery within the context of counselling supervision has also been described (Hayden, 2018). In addition, Hilton, Brant, and Vess (2016) proposed the supervisee-centered outsider-witnessing career group supervision (SCOWCGS) model of career counselling group supervision which employs aspects of narrative therapy, outside-witnessing, and client centered supervision. SCOWCGS focuses on the co-constructed experience between the supervisee and client from the supervisees' perspective with the benefit being that counsellor trainees can practice their familiar micro skills and group work skills while layering on the conceptual framework of a supervision process. This prepares them to effectively engage in the process of group supervision.

Despite these efforts, there lacks developed information on a means in which to implement supervision theory within career services. Established approaches to clinical supervision such as the Discrimination Model (Bernard & Goodyear, 1979, 1997) offers a framework in which to utilize supervision as a means to facilitate CSPs' development. The application of this model in which the supervisor shifts between the roles of *consultant*, *counsellor*, and *teacher* based on the development needs of the practitioner who is assessed in three skills areas of *intervention*, *conceptualization*, and *personalization* (i.e. adapting his or her own personal style to counselling while being aware of personal issues) offers a framework to facilitate supervision. This framework lends to development in the utilization of various cognitive and narrative career theories. This chapter will discuss the connection between career-focused counselling and clinical supervision with specific attention on using the discrimination model to enhance career service delivery.

Complexity of Career Concerns

There is substantial evidence of the interconnection between career and mental health concerns contradicting the view that career-focused counselling is less involved in the interpersonal functioning of clients than mental health counselling, The Diagnostic and Statistical Manual of Mental Disorders (5th ed.; American Psychiatric Association, 2013) and the International Statistical Classification of Diseases and related health problems (11th ed.; World Health Organization, 2018) both include occupational-related difficulty within the criteria for diagnosing mental health concerns.

In addition, several specific connections between career development and depression (Rottinghaus, Jenkins, & Jantzer, 2009; Saunders, Peterson, Sampson, & Reardon, 2000; Etheridge & Peterson, 2012), psychological distress and family conflict (Constantine & Flores, 2006), and emotional and personality-oriented elements (Gati et al., 2011) have been empirically supported. A relationship between career interventions and mental health (e.g. Osborn, Hayden, Peterson, & Sampson, 2016) as well as career and mental health assessments (e.g. Dieringer, Lenz, Hayden, & Peterson, 2017; Dozier, Lenz, Freeman, 2016), has also been established further emphasizing the important of competent provision of career-focused counselling.

Supervision of Career Services

Though not extensive, there have been calls for implementation of clinical supervision of career practitioners (McMahon, 2003; McMahon & Patton, 2000). As mentioned, the National Career Development Association in the United States recent development of the Certified Clinical Supervisor of Career Counselling credential, the first of its kind to focus on clinical supervision competence in the realm of career counselling, further positioning career-focused counselling supervision as a critical element of practice. This has the potential to expand the emphasis devoted to the clinical supervision of career services. Even with these recent developments, career services are not viewed in a similar manner as other disciplines, as evidenced by the lack of attention to career-focused counselling within the clinical supervision literature.

The Systems Theory Framework has been proposed as a comprehensive theory that involves both those receiving services and the experience of the career practitioners (Patton & McMahon, 1999, 2006, 2014). The central elements of this learning perspective are (1) creating a learning environment, (2) the content of learning, and (3) a reflection on learning. The interactive process encompasses both the supervisor and supervisee within the process of career service provision.

The intersection of counselling supervision and career assessment delivery has received attention within the professional literature. Hayden and Kronholz (2014) discussed enhancing competence in the administration of career assessments via clinical supervision by using role plays, consistent engagement, and targeted interventions. Hayden (2018) discussed the fostering of intentionality in the administration of career assessments via clinical supervision with encouragement to utilize existing supervision theory to facilitate positive growth in this aspect of career services. Etheridge and Peterson (2010) found clinical supervision may facilitate mastery in the administration of career assessments by providing a venue in which to examine counsellor development in this component of career services.

Though this attention to clinical supervision within career counselling has enhanced our understanding of this resource for training CSPs, more specific information on the means in which to facilitate this process is warranted. Existing clinical supervision theory offers various frameworks in which to assist career counsellors in their development.

Hoppin and Goodman (2014) outlined the application of specific career development theories to career services supervision. Various theories and associated interventions were indicated to better inform the facilitation of the supervision of career-focused counselling. Though helpful, a detailed description of established approaches is warranted. A common approach is Bernard's Discrimination Model (1979, 1997), which has applicability in ensuring innovation in career counselling practice due to the structure of the model.

Discrimination Model

Bernard's Discrimination Model is often utilized in the supervision of counselling practice due to its simplicity in form, flexibility in adaptation, and empirical support across a variety of interdisciplinary domains (Timm, 2015). The model involves alternating roles of the supervisor (i.e. *teacher*, *counsellor*, *consultant*) and the foci of supervision (i.e. *intervention skills*, *conceptualization skills*, and *personalization skills*). The assuming of roles and the focus of supervision is adapted to the needs of the supervisee.

The supervisor as *teacher* is characterized by direction instruction, feedback, and evaluation to minimize confusion on the supervisee who may be confused by a less directive approach. The supervisor as *counsellor* facilitates reflection on aspects of the supervisee's experience. A supervisor in the *consultant* role acts as a resource while attempting to encourage supervisees to trust their own feelings, insights, and thoughts on their work (Luke & Bernard, 2006).

In terms of foci, *intervention skills* involve all observable behavior on the part of the practitioner that are specific to the counselling interaction. *Conceptualization skills* entail a counsellor's ability to select an appropriate intervention, to organize the experience of the client into an appropriate structure, and to establish process and outcome goals. Finally, *personalization skills* involve a counsellor's ability to use one's self in an appropriate therapeutic manner including interpersonal warmth, intrapersonal cohesion, and an ability to draw on the strengths of one's cultural characteristics (Bernard & Goodyear, 2014). The shifting between roles and foci are dependent on the developmental needs of the supervisee. A supervisor may also utilize multiple roles and foci within one supervision session as the supervisee's skills may be varied. For example, the supervisor may assume the role of *teacher* related to the provision of assessment feedback due to the supervisee being a novice in this process while serving as *consultant* related to a supervisee's facilitation of an intervention as the supervisee may be more competent in this area. A similar shift can occur in foci processed in supervision.

Given the ease in accessing this approach, its flexibility in structure, and skills focus, this model has utility in the supervision of career practitioners. The boundaries placed between the supervisory roles may prevent role ambiguity in which the supervisor struggles to define her or his responsibility in supervision (Nelson, Johnson, & Thorngren, 2000). The clarity in roles and the manner in which they are enacted is articulated within this approach offering direction in role induction within career-focused counselling supervision.

In addition, the Discrimination Model is amenable to several therapeutic orientations which is applicable to career-focused counselling given the myriad of career theories within the field (Bernard & Goodyear, 2014). Whether operating from cognitive perspectives such as Social Cognitive Career Theory (Lent, Brown, & Hackett, 1994, 2000) and Cognitive Information Processing Theory (Sampson, Reardon, Peterson, & Lenz, 2004) or a narrative lens such as Life Design (Savickas, 2012), the Discrimination Model can be instrumental in fostering competent service provision within the context of supervision from a variety of career-focused counselling approaches.

Career practitioners encounter a complex milieu of concerns and provide a wide range of services both within a singular interaction and across a given time period. From facilitating exploration of career options aligned with interests, values and skills, engaging clients in transferable skills exercises, and administering career assessments, the nature of performed tasks heightens the potential for an emotional and mental impact on those providing services. In addition, these professional duties include requisite skills in which ongoing development is needed to ensure competence in delivering career services for clients existing in a dynamic world of work. The Discrimination Model provides a working framework that allows for flexibility in responding to these complex tasks with supervisors shifting in role and focus based on the needs of the supervisee. It can also spark innovation by enabling the supervisor to provide instruction of current trends in the field of career counselling and also a supportive environment in which the supervisee can engage in creative practices in the provision of services.

The following are career-focused counselling supervision strategies grounded in the Discrimination Model with specific attention on fostering innovation in practice. Though not comprehensive in nature, they are intended to spur consideration of ways in which to utilize this approach to the betterment of supervisees' development as innovative career practitioners.

Supervision Strategies Grounded in the Discrimination Model

In working with supervisees to develop innovative strategies to assist their clients, several elements including implementing the Discrimination Model are beneficial to this process. Establishing a strong supervisory alliance, intentionality in fostering competence in areas of practice such as theoretical orientation adherence, ongoing monitoring of competency development, and encouraging innovation through practice are components of supervising career practitioners.

Establishing a Supervisory Alliance

The supervisory alliance has been indicated as primary in the effective facilitation of counsellor development (Watkins, 2014). Through the lens of the Discrimination Model (Bernard, 1979, 1997), an ability to function in the different roles of *consultant, counsellor,* and *teacher* while varying the foci of *conceptualization, intervention,* and *personalization* requires a relational connection between the supervisor and supervisee. As these roles and foci alternate based on need, a quality supervisory alliance informed by the needs of the supervisee is paramount.

An initial step in establishing this relationship within the context of the Discrimination Model is a supervisory professional disclosure (see Appendix). When initiating supervision, the supervisors discloses her/his professional background, career-focused counselling and supervision theoretical orientations, ways in which to communicate, and expectations of both parties. The supervisory professional disclosure statement ensures that an understanding of the roles and work that will transpire within the realm of supervision is established. In addition, a detailed presentation of the Discrimination Model is warranted as the content and tone of examining the career practitioner's work will change based on the various foci and roles being utilized. Time spent covering this information can establish a supervisory alliance which informs the nature of the interaction going forward. An invitation to revisit the professional disclosure statement at any point in supervision should be provided.

Intentionality in Fostering Competence

The Discrimination Model offers a tangible framework in which to enhance the competence of CSPs to effectively address the needs of those they serve. While the structure of the model is relatively simple, the implementation requires significant deliberation on the part of the supervisor. The alternating foci and roles based on the developmental needs of the career practitioner varies significantly both within and between sessions. A supervisee may exhibit an advanced ability in establishing a therapeutic alliance, but novice capability in delivering career assessments. Given this differentiation in aspects of career service delivery, a supervisor must be adept at shifting roles and foci based on the needs of the supervisee.

Awareness of the components of the Discrimination Model and designing supervisory interventions based on the approach contributes intentionality to the supervision process. Determining the appropriate role of *consultant, counsellor,* and *teacher* and utilizing effective practices for each enables the supervisor to appropriately support supervisee's development in the critical areas of career service delivery. In addition, identifying the manner in which foci (i.e. *conceptualization, intervention, personalization*) of the Discrimination Model is exhibited in the supervisee's work provides a structure to processing the myriad of tasks performed by CSPs. Categorizing topics of discussion within these foci while assuming appropriate roles offers the supervisor a means in which to construct targeted interventions to support development in these areas.

An additional aspect is a willingness on the part of the supervisor to discuss elements of intra and interpersonal reactions to supervisees' engagement with their clients. The Discrimination Model indicates the importance of this dimension via the *counsellor* role and *personalization* foci. Clear boundaries via role induction are needed to ensure the supervisor is not serving as the supervisee's personal counsellor. The supervisor indicating the potential for these discussions to occur within the context of the Discrimination Model both at the onset and at various points in supervision eliminates confusion by offering a theoretically-grounded rationale for these interactions. Supervisors' willingness to engage in these discussions has positive benefits for the supervisee as it provides as space in which to process personal reactions to their work including instances of challenges and successes which fosters competency development in *conceptualization* and *intervention*. Being intentional in structuring this aspect of supervision is essential.

Career Theory Utilization Within Supervision

Utilizing career theory within practice varies across practitioners and settings. CSPs indicated that career theory informs their work, but also a marginal level of integration of career theory in practice (Brown, 2002). Given this reality, the *teaching* and *consultant* roles offers a structure in which to examine the supervisee's identification with various career theories and the manner in which they can be utilized. A supervisor attuned to aspects of career theory is well-positioned to identify aspects of the supervisee's work that align with various career approaches. The foci of *conceptualization* and *intervention* through the lens of career theory provides a systematic method of examining the supervisee's development in these areas. In addition, *personalization* connects with the ability of a counsellor to use one's self, which in this case involves awareness of perceptions of aspects of personal functioning and the role of counselling to inform theoretical selection. A supervisor willing to explore these dimensions can assist supervisees in connecting their personal perceptions with specific career theories.

Ongoing attention within supervision to career theory utilization is imperative to supervisee development. Accessing career theory resources as well as directing supervisees to opportunities for growth models theoretically-grounded practice. Emphasis on this topic in supervision likely enhances the utlization of career theory in practice.

Ongoing Monitoring of Competency Development

Supervision plays a critical role in ongoing career-focused counselling competency development. Counselling supervision enables the supervisor to monitor the quality of counselling provided by supervisees (Evans et al., 2016). With this in mind, the Discrimination Model provides the means in which to continually enhance the competence of CSPs in the various skills and tasks inherent within delivering career services When working with supervisees, supervisors focusing on competence development as opposed to reporting of work encourages development of competency-focused practice. The roles and foci of the Discrimination Model enables ongoing teaching of new skills while consulting with supervisees to collectively problem-solving the career concerns of clients.

Career services are dynamic with new assessments, clinical considerations, and populations in need of support continually emerging over time. When utilizing this approach, empowering the supervisees to identify their own developmental needs as they arise encourages agency in their professional development.

Encouraging Innovation Through Supervision

The evolving world of work requires innovation within career-focused counselling. The diversity of occupational options as well as career development needs of various populations mandates that CSPs continually develop their skills in assisting those in need. Supervision, and more specifically, the Discrimination Model can enhance development of innovative interventions in career-focused counselling. A dynamic engagement in which various roles and foci are processed encourages the learning and implementation of new and relevant career interventions. The establishment of a strong supervisor alliance provides an environment in which authentic engagement between the supervisor and supervisee in which innovative interventions can be developed.

Both the supervisor and supervisee are responsible for ongoing professional development. As new theories and practices are discovered in the areas of *conceptualization* and *intervention*, both can serve in the roles of *teacher* and *consultant* sharing acquired knowledge with each other in the context of supervision. In addition, processing new strategies to assist clients when appropriate can avoid complacency in the practice of career-focused counselling. As CSPs progress from novice to experienced providers, there may be a tendency to rely on tried-and-true methods. Though these strategies may in fact be effective, a continual willingness to learn and develop new skills is essential.

Prior to using a new intervention, the supervisor can support the supervisee by serving as *teacher* and *consultant* processing the rationale for its use, the manner in which it is appropriate for the needs of the client, and anticipated outcomes. After innovative strategies are implemented, the supervisor may serve in the role of *counsellor* by providing an opportunity to process the supervisee's personal reaction to the implementation of the intervention. Validating the supervisee's innovative practice in serving clients encourages future engagement in a dynamic yet sound approach to career-focused counselling.

Conclusion

Counselling supervision of CSPs is a critical aspect of career services. Utilizing established approaches such as the Discrimination Model provides a framework in which to enhance the development of innovative career interventions. Operating in the roles of *consultant*, *counsellor*, and *teacher* coupled with attention on the foci of *conceptualization*, *intervention,* and *personalization* enables a supervisor to enhance competency development on the part of CSPs. Establishing a supervisory alliance, processing career theory utilization, monitoring ongoing competency development, and encouraging innovative practice within the context of the Discrimination Model can be implemented in career services supervision. By utilizing innovative interventions, CSPs are better equipped to respond to the needs of diverse clientele operating within a dynamic world of work.

Appendix

Supervision Professional Disclosure Statement

(Name)

Professional Experience

(Education)

I am looking forward to working with you in a supervisory relationship. This document is designed to present you with information regarding my background and the nature of supervision. Supervision is a professional relationship requiring all parties involved to fully understand the nature of this collaboration. This form will outline aspects of this collaboration.

I obtained a graduate degree in (discipline) from the (institution). I have experience working with (populations, topics, etc.). I am a (relevant certifications and licenses).

Supervision Services Offered/Models Used

In general, I subscribe to an integrated cognitive and relational approach to counselling. I adhere to this approach's emphasis on relationships and the manner in which these affect a person's experience. I view clients as existing in a cultural and social milieu, which affects their functioning and worldview. In addition, I also focus on the beliefs (feelings, thoughts, etc.) a person associates with various events in their life is another point of focus in my counselling.

In terms of career-focused counselling, I primarily subscribe to the tenants of (supervisor's career-focused counselling theory). This approach's focus on the (description of characteristics of the approach) which aligns with my view of the critical aspects of career development. While these concepts and ideas may characterize my counselling work, I understand that other theories and models offer benefits. I do not wish to unduly impose my counselling approach upon you as a supervisee. In relation to supervision, I adhere to tenants of the Discrimination Model. Counsellors are continually evolving and developing both personally and professionally. The process of counselling is a deeply personal interaction. While the goal is to assist clients/students with their issues, this process elicits feelings and issues for career-focused counsellors that may impede client/student progress. It is my view that having a functional understanding of one's self is an essential component of being an effective counsellor. Some level of introspection is an important aspect of being a counsellor. As your supervisor, I see my role as one to provide challenge and support while you look inside yourself in this way.

If we are to work together we will need to specify goals, methods, risks, and benefits of supervision, the approximate time commitment involved, and other aspects of your particular situation. Before going further, I expect us to agree on a plan to which we will both adhere. Periodically, we will evaluate our progress and redesign our goals if needed.

As with any powerful intervention, there are both benefits and risks associated with participating in clinical supervision. Risks might include fleeing strong anxiety upon being "evaluated" or experiencing uncomfortable levels of feelings such as anger, guilt, or sadness when working with your own issues which might affect your abilities to successfully function as a professional counsellor. If you are willing to take these risks, I believe that the benefits of personal and professional growth will far outweigh the fleeting discomfort.

Boundary Issues

It is important to remember that supervision and counselling are distinct activities, and that supervision does not include counselling for the supervisee. Although supervision is not counselling, it does involve self-discovery and, at times, self-confrontation. Because of this, supervision sometimes can feel like counselling to those who are used to a good bit of interpersonal distance. In supervision, we will address personal issues in terms of how they influence your professional work Should it seem that further attention to personal issues would be helpful, I will refer you elsewhere for that work.

There may be times when a discussion occurs in which we are colleagues as opposed to supervisor and supervisee. This experience of operating in a tight knit community will require us to clearly delineate our roles in various contexts. As your supervisor, I will not use information divulged in these various non-supervisory interactions in my evaluation of your clinical work.

Emergency Situations

Although it is unlikely, if an emergency situation arises in your clinical work in which you need direction and advice before our scheduled supervision, you should consult with me (contact information).

Ethical Standards

In conducting supervision, I adhere to the (relevant ethical codes and standards) and will supply you with a copy of all of these when appropriate. If, at any time, you are dissatisfied with my work, I would appreciate the opportunity to address the situation first

Supervisee Understanding

I have read this Professional Disclosure Statement. In addition, I have had the opportunity to meet with (supervisor's name), to ask questions, and to talk with him about both his and my expectations as we begin our supervisory relationship. I understand that as we continue to work together, I may have more questions. I am expected to raise these questions, and any other concerns I may have, with (supervisors name).

Supervisees Name (please print)

Supervisee's Signature Date

References

American Psychiatric Association. (2013). *Diagnostic and statistical manual of mental disorders* (5th ed.). Washington, DC: Author.

Bernard, J. M. (1979). Supervisor training: A discrimination model. *Counselor Education and Supervision, 19,* 60–68. https://doi.org/10.1002/j.1556-6978.1979.tb00906.x.

Bernard, J. M. (1997). The discrimination model. In C. E. Watkins, Jr. (Ed.), *Handbook of psychotherapy supervision* (pp. 310–327). New York, NY: Wiley.

Bernard, J. M., & Goodyear, R. K. (2014). *Fundamentals of clinical supervision* (5th ed.). Upper Saddle River, NJ: Merrill.

Bronson, K. M. (2010). Supervision of career counseling. In L. J. Bradley & N. Ladany (Eds.), *Counselor supervision: Principles, process, and practice* (4th ed., pp. 261–286). New York, NY: Taylor & Francis.

Brown, C. (2002). Career counseling practitioners: Reflections on theory, research, and practice. *Journal of Career Development, 29*(2), 109–127.

Constantine, M. G., & Flores, L. Y. (2006). Psychological distress, perceived family conflict, and career development issues in college students of color. *Journal of Career Assessment, 14,* 354–369.

Dieringer, D. D., Lenz, J. G., Hayden, S. C., & Peterson, G. W. (2017). The relation of negative career thoughts to depression and hopelessness. *Career Development Quarterly, 65,* 159–172. https://doi.org/10.1002/cdq.12089.

Dozier, V. C., Lenz, J. G., & Freeman, V. (2016). Using theory-based career assessments to connect career and mental health issues. *Career Planning and Adult Development Journal, 32*(1), 100–111.

Evans, A. M., Wright, S., Murphy, P., & Maki, J. (2016). Incorporating leadership models into counseling supervision: Recommendations to strengthen services. *Ideas and research you can use: VISTAS 2016*. Retrieved from https://www.counseling.org/docs/defaultsource/vistas/article_5124f227f16116603abcacff0000bee5e7.pdf?sfvrsn=4.

Etheridge, R. L., & Peterson, G. W. (2010). The measurement and development of competence in the use of career assessments. *Career Planning and Adult Development Journal, 25*(4), 14–28.

Gati, I., Gadassi, R., Saka, N., Hadadi, Y., Ansenberg, N., Friedmann, R., & Asulin-Peretz, L. (2011). Emotional and personality-related aspects of career decision-making difficulties: Facets of career indecisiveness. *Journal of Career Assessment, 19,* 3–20. https://doi.org/10.1177/1069072710382525.

Hayden, S. C. W. (2018). Fostering intentionality in career assessment utilization through counseling supervision. *Career Planning & Adult Development Journal, 33*(4), 90–97.

Hayden, S. C. W., & Kronholz, J. (2014). Integration of assessments in counseling: Developing competence within clinical supervision. *Career Planning & Adult Development Journal, 30*(4), 156–169.

Hilton, T. M. L., Brant, J., & Vess, L. (2016). Career counseling group supervision: A new approach in master's level counseling programs. *Career Planning and Adult Development Journal, 32*(1), 141.

Hoppin, J. M., & Goodman, J. (2014). *Clinical supervision of career development practitioners. Practical strategies*. Broken Arrow, OK: National Career Development Association.

Lent, R. W., Brown, S. D., & Hackett, G. (1994). Toward a unifying social cognitive theory of career and academic interest, choice, and performance. *Journal of Vocational Behavior, 45*(1), 79–122.
Lent, R. W., Brown, S. D., & Hackett, G. (2000). Contextual supports and barriers to career choice: A social cognitive analysis. *Journal of counseling psychology, 47*(1), 36–49.
Luke, M., & Bernard, J. M. (2006). The school counseling supervision model: An extension of the discrimination model. *Counselor Education and Supervision, 45*(4), 282–295.
Mcmahon, M. (2003). Supervision and career counsellors: A little-explored practice with an uncertain future. *British Journal of Guidance and Counselling, 31*(2), 177–187. https://doi.org/10.1080/0306988031000102351.
McMahon, M., & Patton, W. (2000). Career counsellors, support and lifelong learning: A case for clinical supervision. *International Journal for the Advancement of Counselling, 22,* 157–169.
National Career Development Association (2009). *Multicultural career counseling competencies.* Retrieved from https://www.ncda.org/aws/NCDA/pt/fli/12508/false.
Nelson, M. D., Johnson, P., & Thorngren, J. (2000). An integrated approach for supervising mental health counseling interns. *Journal of Mental Health Counseling, 22,* 45–59.
Osborn, D. S., Hayden, S. C. W., Peterson, G. W., & Sampson, J., Jr. (2016). The effect of brief staff-assisted career service delivery on drop-in clients. *Career Development Quarterly, 64*(2), 181–187. https://doi.org/10.1002/cdq.12050.
Patton, W., & McMahon, M. (1999). *Career development and systems theory: A new relationship.* Thomson Brooks/Cole Publishing Co.
Patton, W., & McMahon, M. (2006). The systems theory framework of career development and counseling: Connecting theory and practice. *International Journal for the Advancement of Counselling, 28*(2), 153–166.
Patton, W., & McMahon, M. (2014). *Career development and systems theory: Connecting theory and practice* (3rd ed.). Rotterdam, The Netherlands: Sense Publishers.
Reid, H. L. (2010). Supervision to enhance educational and guidance practice: A review. *International Journal of Education and Vocational Guidance, 10,* 191–205.
Rottinghaus, P. J., Jenkins, N., & Jantzer, A. M. (2009). Relation of depression and affectivity to career decision status and self-efficacy in college students. *Journal of Career Assessment, 17,* 271–285. https://doi.org/10.1177/1069072708330463.
Sampson, J. P., Reardon, R. C., Peterson, G. W., & Lenz, J. G. (2004). *Career counseling & services: A cognitive processing approach.* Belmont, CA: Brooks/Cole.
Saunders, D. E., Peterson, G. W., Sampson, J. P., Jr., & Reardon, R. C. (2000). Relation of depression and dysfunctional career thinking to career indecision. *Journal of Vocational Behavior, 56,* 288–298.
Savickas, M. L. (2012). Life design: A paradigm for career intervention in the 21st century. *Journal of Counseling & Development, 90*(1), 13–19. https://doi.org/10.1111/j.1556-6676.2012.00002.x.
Timm, M. (2015). Creating a preferred counselor identity in supervision: A new application of Bernard's discrimination model. *The Clinical Supervisor, 34*(1), 115–125.
Watkins, C. E., Jr. (2014). Psychotherapy supervision developments and innovations for the new millennium: Contributions from the cutting edge. *American Journal of Psychotherapy, 68*(2), 141–149.
Watkins, C. E., Jr., Budge, S. L., & Callahan, J. L. (2015). Common and specific factors converging in psychotherapy supervision: A supervisory extrapolation of the Wampold/Budge psychotherapy relationship model. *Journal of psychotherapy integration, 25*(3), 214.
World Health Organization. (2018). *International statistical classification of diseases and related health problems* (11th Revision). Retrieved from https://icd.who.int/browse11/l-m/en.

Career Counselling Interventions to Enhance Career Adaptabilities for Sustainable Employment

Brian J. Taber

Abstract Today's world of work consists of a number of changes and challenges that create uncertainty and insecurity in workers. Namely, the increasing sophistication and use of technology in the workplace, outsourcing of labor, and other modern business practices that emphasize a smaller workforce and increased efficiency can account for some of these insecurities. These factors have made lifetime employability a central issue in the lives of many workers. As a result, it is necessary to prepare people to deal with inevitable change and have the resources to effectively cope and maintain employment. Accordingly, to cope with the volatility in the world of work and the need for lifetime employability, it is proposed that the enhancement of career adaptabilities may provide the necessary foundation to successfully manage one's career in a fluid world of work. Career adaptabilities are rooted in career construction theory (Savickas in Career development and counselling: putting theory and practice to work. Wiley, Hoboken, pp. 147–186, 2013) and consists of four coping resources: concern, control, curiosity, and confidence. Concern refers to caring about one's vocational future; control refers to one's sense of agency; curiosity refers to one's initiative to learn about self and opportunities; and confidence refers to one's capacity to successfully face challenges and overcome obstacles. The coping behaviors exhibited by the dimensions of career adaptability help to explain factors related to how people may engage in activities such as career planning, networking, skill development, and job search behavior. Engagement in these activities improve the likelihood of maintaining employability. This chapter describes how career adaptabilities play a role in employability related behaviors and counselling interventions that enhance career adaptabilities.

Keywords Career adaptability · Career counselling · Employability

B. J. Taber (✉)
Oakland University, 2200 North Squirrel Road, Rochester, MI 48309, USA
e-mail: taber@oakland.edu

J. G. Maree (ed.), *Handbook of Innovative Career Counselling*,
https://doi.org/10.1007/978-3-030-22799-9_7

Introduction

Unfortunately, the prospect of involuntary job loss has become normative in today's world of work (Kalleberg, 2009). Those experiencing unemployment not only struggle with financial difficulties but may also experience accompanying psychological distress and impaired well-being (McKee-Ryan, Song, Wanberg, & Kinicki, 2005; Paul & Moser, 2009). Accordingly, it has become imperative that people are psychologically prepared to deal with such adverse transitions and attain re-employment as quickly as possible to offset both the psychological consequences and financial costs that come about with the loss of employment. To this end, career counselors not only need to be able to prepare clients with effective job search strategies, but also prepare clients to cope and have the necessary psycho-social resources to ensure that such methods are successfully implemented.

Given that struggles with continued employment have become part of the work lives for many, it is proposed that career adaptability provides a framework for intervention that can prepare people to manage their careers. Savickas (1997) introduced the psycho-social construct of career adaptability as a means of describing how people cope with the challenges, tasks, traumas, and transitions that people will encounter during the course of their careers.

Chapter Structure

The purpose of this chapter is to describe career adaptability, its significance in relation to employability, and how counselors can effectively intervene in areas where deficits exist. The chapter begins with a description and overview of the career adaptability dimensions of concern, control, curiosity, and confidence and their relevance in career development and management. The next section summarizes research regarding the influence of career adaptability dimensions on proactive career behaviors that play a role in employability. The final section provides guidelines for the assessment of career adaptability dimensions and counselling interventions for their enhancement.

Career Adaptability

Career adaptability is a key concept in career construction theory (Savickas, 2013) that pertains to the psycho-social resources that people possess to varying degrees to cope with current and future vocational development tasks, work traumas, and occupational transitions that people encounter during the course of their work lives. From a vocational development standpoint, adolescents and young adults contend with a number of socio-normative age-graded transitions as they prepare to enter the world of work. For example, emerging adults are expected to explore occupational options, select an occupation from a variety of fields that they deem appropriate, enter that occupation and progress in it until the next opportunity comes along (Super, 1990). During this process, they must adapt to the demands and challenges they face in this progression from exploration, selection, and implementation. Work traumas are unwanted and unforeseen distressing events that can occur in a person's work life. Events such as involuntary job loss due to downsizing, breeches in employment contracts, work place accidents and injuries can have a devastating impact on those that experience such events. These negative work events can exact a tremendous toll on one's capacity to cope with these adversities and move forward in their career. Occupational transitions encompass the movement from one position or occupation to another. Such transitions can be desired or unexpected. During the course of one's career a person may be promoted or demoted at their current place of employment or move on to work in another or similar position at a different organization. In either case, such transitions require the person to adapt to their new occupational situation and accompanying organizational culture and environment. Given the aforementioned mercurial conditions of the world of work, Savickas (2013) has identified four key resources that people may utilize as they adapt to changes regardless of their origin.

These resources are known collectively as career adaptabilities and encompass four dimensions of coping. The four dimensions include career concern, career control, career curiosity, and career confidence. Career concern reflects the degree of interest and involvement in one's vocational future. Having an orientation toward the future fosters an awareness that actions taken today affect tomorrow. Accordingly, being able to think about the future prepares one to plan and make choices that have both short- and long-term consequences. Failure to develop a sense of career concern can lead to indifference, apathy, and lack of planning. Career control reflects the processes that influence self-regulation. Specifically, control refers to the capacity to be conscientious, deliberate, and decisive. Having a sense of control fosters self-discipline and intentionality in choices and actions that impact one's career. Career curiosity denotes engagement in exploration and a desire to attain self-knowledge and occupational information. Such inquisitiveness leads to a better understanding of how one fits in the world of work and an examination of occupational alternatives. A lack of curiosity leads to unrealistic views of work and an imprecise view of self. Career confidence refers to the belief in one's ability to effectively pursue a course of action necessary to act upon vocational choices. Having confidence encourages one to try new things and build competencies. Lacking in confidence may lead to inhibition and avoidance of pursuing goals. Career adaptabilities play a significant role in the capacity to manage one's career and the trials that are inherent in the world of work. Of particular significance, is career adaptabilities' role in the facilitation of maintaining employment through proactive career behaviors.

Career Adaptability and Proactive Career Behaviors

Increasingly, people are called upon to manage their careers and take steps to ensure their continued employment (Gowan, 2014). Accordingly, workers today cannot afford to be passive in the governance of their work lives. Instead today's world of work requires proactive engagement in behaviors such as job skill development, setting goals, exploring options (Claes & Ruiz-Quintanilla, 1998), and when desired or necessary perform job search activities that lead to employment (Brown, Cober, Kane, Levy, & Shalhoop, 2006; Saks, 2005). The coping resources of career adaptability are an important factor that influence proactive career behaviors.

Career adaptabilities provide the resources for people to enact adaptive responses to the circumstances and problems that confront them (Savickas, 2013). With regards to sustainable employment, adaptive responses are reflected in the execution of proactive career behaviors. The performance of such behaviors leads to adaptive results such as employment and work goals. Connections between career adaptability and adaptive responses and results have largely affirmed the theoretically expected relationships and outcomes (Rudolph, Lavigne, & Zacher, 2017).

Research has demonstrated the connection between career adaptabilities and proactive career behaviors that facilitate employability. For instance, results from a study by de Guzman and Choi (2013) indicated that career adaptability dimensions are significantly related to the employability skills of communication, problem solving, and team work. The employability skills measured in this study are desirable by employers and transferable among a variety of occupations. Also, career adaptability dimensions have been found to be significant in the prediction skills that help people secure employment. In keeping with theoretically expected outcomes, Taber and Blankemeyer (2015) reported that concern incrementally predicted career planning and that confidence and curiosity mediated career skill development and career networking. Such skills are necessary to seek out, plan for, and secure career opportunities. Career adaptability dimensions have also been found to play a significant role in searching for work and securing employment. A longitudinal study conducted by Guan et al. (2013) indicated that those higher in career control were more likely to obtain a job after graduating from college. The study also showed that those higher in career concern had higher levels of job search self-efficacy and their career adaptability as a whole predicted a better fit between the person and the job. In a similar vein, Koen, Klehe, Van Vianen, Zikic, and Nauta (2010) performed a longitudinal investigation to see how career adaptability dimensions influence job search strategies and the job quality of unemployed job seekers. Results indicated that career adaptability dimensions were significant in preparing unemployed job seekers to use different search strategies. Career confidence was shown to predict quality of re-employment in terms of job satisfaction, sense of fit, and intention to stay with the new employer.

Even during times of unemployment, career adaptabilities may serve as a buffer against the deleterious effects on mental health and well-being that many experience (Paul & Moser, 2009). In a study with unemployed young adults, Konstam, Celen-

Demirtas, Tomek, and Sweeney (2015) reported that those having higher levels of career control and confidence reported higher levels of life satisfaction. Also, those higher in control reported more positive than negative emotions. Therefore, it appears that some dimensions of career adaptability have a positive impact on well-being during times when people are out of work. Given the importance of career adaptability dimensions in terms of their influence on factors that contribute to attainment of employment, counselors need to identify the areas that require interventions and techniques to enhance dimensions that need to be strengthened.

Career Counselling Interventions to Enhance Career Adaptability

The first step in counselling entails assessment. Accordingly, it is recommended that employment and career counselors assess the level of career adaptability to appraise clients' strengths and areas for enhancement. To facilitate this process, it is recommended that counselors use the *Career Adapt-Abilities Scale* (CAAS; Savickas & Porfeli, 2012). The CAAS is a 24-item scale that assesses the four dimensions of career adaptability. The items are grouped with six items per dimension, with *career concern* (items 1–6) encompassing the first group, *career control* (items 7–12) the next, followed by *career curiosity* (items 13–18), and finally *career confidence* (items 19–24). Both an online version and downloadable paper version are available through www.vocopher.com (Glavin & Savickas, 2010). A chapter by Glavin and Berger (2013) provides users with helpful scoring and interpretive guidelines for the *CAAS*. Those scoring in the lower end of any of the adaptability dimensions (i.e. 25th percentile or lower) require interventions to enhance the areas where they demonstrate the least strength. Based on the results from the *CAAS*, counselors can tailor their interventions based on the client's specific needs.

Counselling for Career Concern

Those with low levels of career concern may not give much thought about their career future and subsequently are prone to lack in preparedness and planning. To enhance career concern, Taber (2015) describes an intervention to increase future time perspective. Essentially, this technique begins by encouraging the client to reflect on their views of the past, present, and future. This progresses to getting the client to then think about the future and its possibilities. In order to accomplish this, the *Circles Test* (Cottle, 1967) is used to facilitate thinking about the different time perspectives. The client is provided with a writing implement and paper along with the following directions:

> Think of the past, present, and future as being in the shape of circles. Now arrange these circles in any way that best shows how you feel about the relationship of your past, present and future. You may use different size circles. When you have finished, label each circle to show which one is past, which one is present, and which one is the future. (Cottle, 1967, p. 60)

After the client has drawn their circles reflecting the past, present and future, the counselor turns toward exploration of the meaning of the different temporal zones with an emphasis on turning toward thinking about the future (Savickas, 1991). Questions that help with exploration are: (a) What were you thinking as you drew the circles? (b) What do their relative sizes mean to you? (c) Use three words to describe how you feel about your past, your present, and your future. (d) Describe a recent choice you have made and identify the time zone you focused on while making the decision. (e) How will your life be different in the future than it is today? The answers provide a means for the client to see how they think about time and subsequently how those views influence their choices and behaviors.

As the client describes each of the temporal zones, the counselor should try to solicit and reinforce any statements that pertain to the future. For example, if a client described a recent decision that focused on attaining immediate gratification, the counselor may want to engage the client in a conversation that examines the pros and cons of this approach and the implications for short-term and long-term decisions regarding their future career. By way of another example, if a client were to describe the past in negative terms, the counselor may want to focus on what can be done in the future to assure that such aversive events can be avoided moving forward. In so doing, the conversation can turn to what the client can do in order to ensure a more desirable future for themselves.

Examining the relative size of the circles to each other can also facilitate discussion about the future. For instance, if the past circle is larger than the others, the counselor can ask what it is from their past they would like to see continue in the future. Specifically, if there are any particular accomplishments in the past that the client values, a discussion could involve what was learned in the process of achieving those accomplishments. These lessons from the past can be used to create the future the client desires. There are occasions when client's preoccupation and focus on the past is the result of past failures and consequently, he or she may feel discouraged. In such cases, it may be necessary for the counselor to focus on helping the client attain a sense of hope (Snyder, 1994). When this occurs, the counselor can facilitate a discussion about unrealized goals the client may have had for themselves. For instance, a counselor may ask such things as (a) What made the goal difficult to attain? (b) What could have been done differently? (c) What lessons can be learned from goals that were not achieved? (d) If the same goal were attempted today, what would you do differently? The counselor looks for themes and patterns that emerge that relate to barriers and strengths. The discussion of past struggles and solutions can help the client to be better prepared and more confident in facing future obstacles in building their career. If the present circle is bigger relative to the others, the conversation can focus on what is happening in the present that is going well and what would it take to keep those good things going in the future. Also, the discussion can include what actions and decisions need to be taken today in order to ensure the work life they want for themselves in the future. If the client has a sense that they have a future, they are better situated to be able to plan for that future.

Assisting a client to plan for the future entails helping the client to think through the steps to get them from where they are today to where they want to be in the future. To accomplish this, the client is asked to draw a time line starting from the present to some desired end point such as employment. The path to that end point is contingent upon completing one step in order to go on to the next. For example, if a client's goal is to obtain employment, a plan may consist of the following: (a) conducting a job search (e.g. creating a Linkedin profile and using it for career networking, using internet job search websites, letting people they know that they are on the job market, attending career fairs), (b) identifying potential employers, (c) researching employers and identifying potential fit with the organization, (d) tailoring resume and cover letters for identified job opportunities, (e) practicing mock job interviews, (f) following up with thank you notes or e-mails with potential employers after completing job interviews. It is also important during the course of planning to discuss any potential obstacles that may occur. This can help to both normalize the idea that setbacks do happen as people pursue goals and also as a means to plan how to cope with obstacles when they occur. To that end, it is also helpful to discuss with the client how they can stay motivated to continue pursuing their employment goal.

Counselling for Career Control

Clients lacking in career control may be passive and indecisive when it comes to career decisions. Such clients may see luck, fate, or chance directing their vocational future. Such views are apparent when a client tends to blame others or perhaps believes that they "can't" achieve their goals, attributing it to external forces or circumstances. Accordingly, counselors can collaborate with a client to feel empowered and take charge of their career and act decisively. Connolly (1980) describes a counselling process model that assists clients in developing a more internal sense of control. The process consists of four strategies to aid in the development of control: facilitating awareness, facilitating responsibility, identifying the deficit, and using options counselling.

In order to facilitate awareness about how lack of a sense of internal control impacts the client, the counselor can focus on identifying and reflecting feelings associated with not being in control. As the client discusses their career problem, the counselor might pick up on feelings of powerlessness, helplessness, dejection, disappointment, and uncertainty. Helping the client make the connections between feelings and their view that the external world is in control of their work life facilitates awareness. In order to facilitate responsibility, the counselor can assist the client in making connections between feelings and behaviors that precipitate them. Using a "you feel… when you…" response format can help the client make the connections and personalize the behavior. For example, if a client has been unsuccessful in securing employment a counselor may respond to the accompanying feelings. The counselor may respond "you feel powerless when you apply for jobs and do not get a response". Once the connections are established, counselling then turns to identifying the deficit. Here, it is important to be specific about the skill deficit so that the client can see it as a behavior that is under their control. For example, a counselor may say "you feel helpless when you do not know how to conduct a successful job search". After the client has identified the behaviors and skills that they are able to control, the next step is to help them explore and consider options to remediate the problem. At this point, the counselor can engage the client in options counselling. To this end, the client is coached through a seven-step approach: (a) identify a goal, (b) determine there are options, (c) generate alternatives, (d) evaluate pros and cons of the alternatives, (e) select the best option, (f) implement that option—develop a plan to make it happen, and (g) evaluate the outcome. As a result of working through this final step, the client can now see that it is possible for them to take actions necessary to control work lives and become more decisive in the process.

Counselling for Career Curiosity

Those with a low sense of career curiosity are more apt to have an inaccurate view of themselves and the world of work. A deficiency in career curiosity may lead to a lack of focus in knowing what one wants or what options are available. Possessing a sense of curiosity initiates exploration with regards to seeking self-knowledge and occupational knowledge. Indeed, engagement in exploration is important for identity development (Flum & Blustein, 2000) and job search effectiveness (Werbel, 2000). The lack of career curiosity may reflect an absence of intrinsic motivation to engage in exploration activities (Blustein, 1988; Kiener, 2006). Motivational Interviewing techniques can help overcome this ambivalence regarding career exploration (Klonek, Wunderlich, Spurk, & Kauffeld, 2016; Stoltz & Young, 2013). The process of Motivational Interviewing is a client-centered approach that consists of seven components: (a) establishing a therapeutic relationship, (b) client assessment (c) developing discrepancies, (d) rolling with resistance, (e) addressing client self-efficacy, (f) establishing empathy, and (g) transition/termination. While a thorough discussion of Motivational Interviewing is beyond the scope of this chapter (see Miller & Rollnick, 2013), there are some key techniques that will be highlighted as important elements in resolving career exploration ambivalence.

Components in Motivational Interviewing that may prove useful in nullifying ambivalence reside in the context of establishing a therapeutic alliance, client assessment, and developing discrepancies. In building a therapeutic alliance, it is essential that the counselor evoke client change talk. Accordingly, the counselor engages the client in examining their readiness to begin career exploration. The counselor may pose questions such as "What would happen if learning about yourself and your career options became more important?", "What concerns do you have about exploring career options?", "What are some good things about not exploring career options?", and "What are some bad things about not exploring career options?" By evoking the client to think about career exploration, the client creates their own reasons for doing so rather than someone else telling them why they should. Client assessment from a Motivational Interview perspective may also be useful in getting clients to engage in exploration activities. Asking a client "On a scale from 1 to 10, with 1 being not ready to 10 most ready, how ready are you to engage in career exploration?" provides a sense of how prepared they are for exploration. This can be furthered explored with the client to gauge what would be necessary for them to increase the level of readiness. The counselor may follow up with questions such as "Why did you give yourself a 4 and not a zero?" or "You've given yourself a 4 on the scale. What would have to happen for it to move to a 10?" or "What keeps you from moving 4 to a 10?" Through the discussion of ratings, the client can examine their motivation and capacity for career exploration. Developing discrepancies can also serve a motivational technique for engagement in exploration. Discrepancies are simply having the client weigh the pros and cons of exploring and not exploring. The client articulates the advantages and disadvantages of both. For example, a client may say that the disadvantages of exploring are that "it is a waste of time" or "it really doesn't matter what job you take" or "luck more than anything determines where you work." On the other hand, they may say advantages are "maybe I can figure out what I'm good at and like" or "learn how to get a job that pays well" or "perhaps I can find a job where I don't have to worry about getting laid off." A dialogue about both sides of the issue can help the client to see from their own perspective what would be the best course of action. Once client curiosity has piqued and intrinsic motivation is strengthened, steps can be taken to begin the exploration process.

Career exploration can take different forms and be facilitated through a variety of methods. On a fundamental level, exploration is about clients learning more about themselves and potentially suitable work environments. Traditionally, counselors have used objective measures to assist clients' understanding of themselves in relation to work. For instance, career counselors may use interest inventories such as the *Self-Directed Search* (Holland & Messer, 2013) or the *Strong Interest Inventory* (Donnay et al., 2012) to appraise vocational interests with the purpose that clients may identify and explore potentially satisfying occupations. Counsellors may also use a variety of other objective assessments that appraise needs and values (Rounds & Jin, 2013) as well as work-related abilities (Metz & Jones, 2013). Ultimately, the goal is to identify traits and characteristics of the client and find complementary work that reinforces those characteristics. Information about the various occupational alternatives can be explored through resources such as the *Occupational Outlook Handbook* (https://www.bls.gov/ooh/) and *O*NET* (https://www.onetonline.org). When using such resources, it is important that the information be processed from the standpoint of how well the different occupations fit with career goals and lifestyle. Accordingly, a career counselor may want to furnish clients with a set of questions to help them think critically about the occupational information. Questions that may encourage thoughtful review of the information include: (a) What interests, needs, and values would be satisfied by this occupation? (b) What skills and training do you already have for this occupation? (c) What skills and training do you lack regarding this occupation? (d) What is the demand outlook for this occupation? (e) How does this job fit with your short-term employment goals? (f) How does this occupation fit with your long-term goals and desired lifestyle? (g) What other information do you need about yourself or this occupation to realistically evaluate its possibilities for you? (h) If you were to select this occupation, what immediate and future steps would you need to attain this goal? Through answering these questions, clients can evaluate the different occupational possibilities and select one that they believe will garner the most reward. Engaging in such a problem-solving exercise may have the added benefit of enhancing one's career confidence as well. Once clients have made a choice about an occupation or employment opportunity to pursue, they must have the confidence to execute the steps necessary for entry.

Counselling for Career Confidence

When clients lack in career confidence they may not feel that they have the capacity to attain their employment goal. Thus, lacking confidence becomes a psychological barrier to implementation of choice. Therefore, it is not just the career counselor's role to assist in exploration and decision making, but also assist in the building of confidence to facilitate the realization of that choice. Client career confidence can be influenced by the therapeutic working alliance (Savickas, 2005). The very nature of the therapeutic relationship between the client and the counselor enhances self-regard and self-acceptance. In the context of a collaborative and non-judgmental relationship, the client can feel safe to explore their issues around the lack of confidence in their capabilities as well as affirm their successes.

In this vein, it is helpful to explore their attributes and accomplishments and offer encouragement. The counselor may ask the client to describe their best personal qualities, accomplishments they are proud of, their best skills, challenges they have overcome, lessons from past mistakes that can be used in the future, and hoped for future accomplishments. Through the examination of these areas, the client may gain a sense that they are capable and competent in accomplishing future goals. In fostering encouragement and subsequently confidence, the focus of discussion should be on the client's strengths and success stories with emphasis on linking results to their actions. Clients may have a tendency to reflect more readily on shortcomings and things that have gone wrong in life. Therefore, it is also important that the counselor acknowledge and reinforce gains that the client has made during the course of counselling to solidify feelings of confidence. Recognition of when a client works hard towards achieving counselling goals demonstrates to them that they have the capacity for accomplishing what they desire and offers encouragement to continue (Sweeney, 2009). To augment encouragement, those lacking in confidence may be further assisted by seeking social/emotional support from those close to them as continued assurance and validation (Wong, 2015). When career confidence is successfully established, a sense of assuredness emerges that the client has the necessary capacity to confidently make decisions and enact their vocational choices.

Counselling Across Career Adaptability Dimensions

While some clients may have deficits in only one dimension of career adaptability others may have two or more. In which case as a rule of thumb it is helpful to think of the respective adaptabilities as being hierarchical in nature, that is to say, that one adaptability builds off another in a sequential fashion. According to Savickas (2013), career concern is the first and most important adaptability dimension, followed by career control, then career curiosity, and finally career confidence. In Career Construction Theory, it is posited that the career adaptable person is concerned about their vocational future, feels in control of that future, is curious about possible selves, and has the confidence to pursue career aspirations (Savickas, 2005). Therefore, from a counselling perspective it may be advantageous to first address the adaptabilities in the order in which they unfold. For example, if based on *CAAS* results, the client appears to be lacking in career control and career confidence, it is recommended that issues concerning control are addressed first. Before one can be confident, one must feel like they have a measure of control in life. Following the sequence of adaptabilities helps counselors formulate a treatment plan that uses one strength to build another.

Conclusion

Confronted with uncertainty and unpredictability in today's world of work requires that people have the necessary resources to cope with the inevitable changes and challenges to employment that ensue. Career adaptabilities are valuable psychosocial resources that can mitigate the negative consequences of these changes and set the stage to prepare people for what is necessary to maintain employment. Unfortunately, not all people will have developed career adaptabilities sufficiently to meet current demands in the world of work. This chapter describes practical interventions that can be used by career and employment counselors to help facilitate growth in the respective career adaptability dimensions. By turning career adaptability deficits into strengths, clients are better able to meet the challenges that they face in the quest to maintain lifetime employability.

References

Blustein, D. L. (1988). The relationship between motivational processes and career exploration. *Journal of Vocational Behavior, 32*, 345–357. http://dx.doi.org.huaryu.kl.oakland.edu/10.1016/0001-8791(88)90025-5.

Brown, D. J., Cober, R. T., Kane, K., Levy, P. E., & Shalhoop, J. (2006). Proactive personality and the successful job search: A field investigation with college graduates. *Journal of Applied Psychology, 91*, 717–726. http://dx.doi.org.huaryu.kl.oakland.edu/10.1037/0021-9010.91.3.717.

Claes, R., & Ruiz-Quintanilla, S. (1998). Influences of early career experiences, occupational group, and national culture on proactive career behavior. *Journal of Vocational Behavior, 52*, 357–378. http://dx.doi.org.huaryu.kl.oakland.edu/10.1006/jvbe.1997.1626.

Connolly, S. G. (1980). Changing expectancies: A counseling model based on locus of control. *Personnel & Guidance Journal, 59*, 176–180. http://dx.doi.org.huaryu.kl.oakland.edu/10.1002/j.2164-4918.1980.tb00525.x.

Cottle, T. J. (1967). The circles test: An investigation of temporal relatedness and dominance. *Journal of Projective Techniques and Personality Assessment, 31*, 58–71.

de Guzman, A. B., & Choi, K. O. (2013). The relations of employability skills to career adaptability among technical school students. *Journal of Vocational Behavior, 82*, 199–207. http://dx.doi.org.huaryu.kl.oakland.edu/10.1016/j.jvb.2013.01.009.

Donnay, D. A. C., Morris, M. L., Schaubhut, N. A., Thompson, R. C., Grutter, J., & Hammer, A. L. (2012). *Strong interest inventory*. Sunnyvale, CA: CPP Inc.

Flum, H., & Blustein, D. L. (2000). Reinvigorating the study of vocational exploration: A framework for research. *Journal of Vocational Behavior, 56*, 380–404. http://dx.doi.org.huaryu.kl.oakland.edu/10.1006/jvbe.2000.1721.

Glavin, K. W., & Berger, C., (2013). Assessing career adaptability using the career adapt-abilities scale. In A. Di Fabio & J. G. Maree (Eds.), *Psychology of career counseling: New challenges for a new era* (pp. 207–213). New York, NY: Nova Science Publishers.

Glavin, K. W., & Savickas, M. L. (2010). Vocopher: The career collaboratory. *Journal of Career Assessment, 18*, 345–354. http://dx.doi.org.huaryu.kl.oakland.edu/10.1177/1069072710374568.

Gowan, M. A. (2014). Moving from job loss to career management: The past, present, and future of involuntary job loss research. *Human Resource Management Review, 24*, 258–270. http://dx.doi.org.huaryu.kl.oakland.edu/10.1016/j.hrmr.2014.03.007.

Guan, Y., Deng, H., Sun, J., Wang, Y., Cai, Z., Ye, L. … Li, Y. (2013). Career adaptability, job search self-efficacy and outcomes: A three-wave investigation among Chinese university graduates. *Journal of Vocational Behavior, 83*, 561–570. http://dx.doi.org.huaryu.kl.oakland.edu/10.1016/j.jvb.2013.09.003.

Holland, J. L., & Messer, M. A. (2013). *Self-directed search* (5th ed.). Odessa, FL: Psychological Assessment Resources Inc.

Kalleberg, A. L. (2009). Precarious work, insecure workers: Employment relations in transition. *American Sociological Review, 74*, 1–22. http://dx.doi.org.huaryu.kl.oakland.edu/10.1177/000312240907400101.

Kiener, M. (2006). Decision making and motivation and its impact on career search behaviors: The role of self-regulation. *College Student Journal, 40*, 350–360.

Klonek, F. E., Wunderlich, E., Spurk, D., & Kauffeld, S. (2016). Career counseling meets motivational interviewing: A sequential analysis of dynamic counselor–client interactions. *Journal of Vocational Behavior, 94*, 28–38. http://dx.doi.org.huaryu.kl.oakland.edu/10.1016/j.jvb.2016.01.008.

Koen, J., Klehe, U., Van Vianen, A. E. M., Zikic, J., & Nauta, A. (2010). Job-search strategies and reemployment quality: The impact of career adaptability. *Journal of Vocational Behavior, 77*, 126–139. http://dx.doi.org.huaryu.kl.oakland.edu/10.1016/j.jvb.2010.02.004.

Konstam, V., Celen-Demirtas, S., Tomek, S., & Sweeney, K. (2015). Career adaptability and subjective well-being in unemployed emerging adults: A promising and cautionary tale. *Journal of Career Development, 42*, 463–477. http://dx.doi.org.huaryu.kl.oakland.edu/10.1177/0894845315575151.

McKee-Ryan, F., Song, Z., Wanberg, C. R., & Kinicki, A. J. (2005). Psychological and physical well-being during unemployment: A meta-analytic study. *Journal of Applied Psychology, 90*, 53–76. http://dx.doi.org.huaryu.kl.oakland.edu/10.1037/0021-9010.90.1.53.

Metz, A. J., & Jones, J. E. (2013). Ability and aptitude assessment in career counseling. In S. Brown & R. Lent (Eds.), *Career development and counseling: Putting theory and practice to work* (2nd ed., pp. 449–476). Hoboken, NJ: Wiley.

Miller, W. R., & Rollnick, S. (2013). *Motivational Interviewing: Helping people change* (3rd ed.). New York, NY: Guilford Press.

Paul, K. I., & Moser, K. (2009). Unemployment impairs mental health: Meta-analyses. *Journal of Vocational Behavior, 74*, 264–282. http://dx.doi.org.huaryu.kl.oakland.edu/10.1016/j.jvb.2009.01.001.

Rounds, J., & Jin, J. (2013). Nature, importance, and assessment of needs and values. In S. Brown & R. Lent (Eds.), *Career development and counseling: Putting theory and practice to work* (2nd ed., pp. 417–448). Hoboken, NJ: Wiley.

Rudolph, C. W., Lavigne, K. N., & Zacher, H. (2017). Career adaptability: A meta-analysis of relationships with measures of adaptivity, adapting responses, and adaptation results. *Journal of Vocational Behavior, 98*, 17–34. http://dx.doi.org.huaryu.kl.oakland.edu/10.1016/j.jvb.2016.09.002.

Saks, A. M. (2005). Job search success: A review and integration of the predictors, behaviors, and outcomes. In S. D. Brown & R. W. Lent (Eds.), *Career development and counseling: Putting theory and practice to work* (pp. 155–179). Hoboken, NJ: Wiley.

Savickas, M. L. (1991). Improving career time perspective. In D. Brown & L. Brooks (Eds.), *Career counseling techniques* (pp. 236–249). Needham Heights, MA: Allyn and Bacon.

Savickas, M. L. (1997). Career adaptability: An integrative construct for life-span, life-space theory. *The Career Development Quarterly, 45*, 247–259. http://dx.doi.org.huaryu.kl.oakland.edu/10.1002/j.2161-0045.1997.tb00469.x.

Savickas, M. L. (2005). The theory and practice of career construction. In S. D. Brown & R. W. Lent (Eds.), *Career development and counseling: Putting theory and practice to work* (pp. 42–70). Hoboken, NJ: Wiley.

Savickas, M. L. (2013). Career construction theory and practice. In S. Brown & R. Lent (Eds.), *Career development and counseling: Putting theory and practice to work* (2nd ed., pp. 147–186). Hoboken, NJ: Wiley.

Savickas, M. L., & Porfeli, E. J. (2012). Career adapt-abilities scale: Construction, reliability, and measurement equivalence across 13 countries. *Journal of Vocational Behavior, 80*, 661–673. http://dx.doi.org.huaryu.kl.oakland.edu/10.1016/j.jvb.2012.01.011.

Snyder, C. R. (1994). *The psychology of hope: You can get there from here*. New York, NY: Free Press.

Super, D. E. (1990). A life-span, life-space approach to career development. In *Career choice and development: Applying contemporary theories to practice* (2nd ed., pp. 197–261). San Francisco, CA: Jossey-Bass.

Stoltz, K. B., & Young, T. L. (2013). Applications of motivational interviewing in career counseling: Facilitating career transition. *Journal of Career Development, 40*, 329–346. http://dx.doi.org.huaryu.kl.oakland.edu/10.1177/0894845312455508.

Sweeney, T. J. (2009). *Adlerian counseling and psychotherapy: A practitioner's approach* (5th ed.). New York, NY: Routledge/Taylor & Francis Group.

Taber, B. J. (2015). Enhancing future time perspective and exploring occupational possible selves. In P. J. Hartung, M. L. Savickas, & W. B. Walsh (Eds.), *APA handbook of career intervention, volume 2: Applications* (pp. 101–111). Washington, DC: American Psychological Association.

Taber, B. J., & Blankemeyer, M. (2015). Future work self and career adaptability in the prediction of proactive career behaviors. *Journal of Vocational Behavior, 86*, 20–27. http://dx.doi.org.huaryu.kl.oakland.edu/10.1016/j.jvb.2014.10.005.

Werbel, J. D. (2000). Relationships among career exploration, job search intensity, and job search effectiveness in graduating college students. *Journal of Vocational Behavior, 57*, 379–394. http://dx.doi.org.huaryu.kl.oakland.edu/10.1006/jvbe.2000.1746.

Wong, Y. J. (2015). The psychology of encouragement: Theory, research, and applications. *The Counseling Psychologist, 43*, 178–216. http://dx.doi.org.huaryu.kl.oakland.edu/10.1177/0011000014545091.

Art Dialogues for Professional Communities: Theater and Play for Imagining and Developing the Good Life Within Organizations

Heidi S. C. A. Muijen, René Brohm and Stanske Lomans

Abstract Ever since ancient times, theater has served a political and educational function. We have brought theater into the workplace to explore the revitalization of political life, and to counterbalance instrumental approaches towards career innovation. Within the framework of Art Dialogue Methods (ADM) that we have developed over the years by using different kinds of art forms, we present an arts-based action research. Experiments with theater have alerted us to the potential of embodiment in art dialogues. We argue that theater in organizations takes transitional space not just as a means to readjust to a fixed social reality, but also to stimulate people to play around with organizational reality. Imagining and developing the good working life as a community can emerge from play and thereby provide community learning and an existential perspective for career counselling.

Keywords Artistic inquiry · Professional community · Business ethics · Theater counselling

Imagining Career Counselling

To see a World in a Grain of Sand.
And a Heaven in a Wild Flower.
Hold Infinity in the palm of your hand.
And Eternity in an hour. (Blake, 1984, p. 114)

H. S. C. A. Muijen (✉)
Thymia—Philosophical Counselling, Weesp, The Netherlands
e-mail: thymia@xs4all.nl

R. Brohm
De Nieuwe Kleren van de Wolf—Research Organization, Doorn, The Netherlands

S. Lomans
Berings & Lomans, Training and Storytelling Agency, Utrecht, The Netherlands

University of Applied Sciences Utrecht, Utrecht, The Netherlands

J. G. Maree (ed.), *Handbook of Innovative Career Counselling*,
https://doi.org/10.1007/978-3-030-22799-9_8

Crucial to career counselling today is that the fluidity of postmodern times be taken into consideration. We can no longer assume that worker capabilities and jobs are stable entities in the face of globalization, robotics, digitalization and persistent cost-reduction aims. We argue that many career theories do not adequately address today's age of uncertainty and wish to present an approach that fits fluid contexts.

Sociologists and philosophers have noticed a general fragmentation in society and lament the widespread loss of moral authorities (Bauman, 2006; Taylor, 2006). A lack of common social values has contributed to making the market logic dominant. However, sociological analyses (Giroux, 2018; Sennet, 2009) stress the need of finding a logic that counterbalances the so-called neoliberal spirit that approaches poverty, alienation and injustice in terms of individual choices and lifestyle. Modern answers are of no use in meeting postmodern challenges. How do we organize people's working lives in uncertain times?

Debates on career development have recurrently been criticized for following a typical enlightenment approach—firstly, for the latter's belief in an autonomous self, based on individualistic, voluntary assumptions, and secondly, for its rationalistic planning strategies (Draaisma, Meijers, & Kuijpers, 2018; Yuthas, Dillard, & Rogers, 2004). According to Savickas et al. (2010, p. 14) "… identity development is a lifelong process. An individual must repeatedly revise identity so as to adaptively integrate significant new experiences into the ongoing life story."

We understand the self as a co-creation in relationship with others, while avoiding the pitfall of the other extreme of determinism (Conyne & Cook, 2004). Similar to Gergen's (2009, p. 400) "I am linked therefore I am", we have argued for "Tango ergo sum" (Brohm & Muijen, 2010).

The second type of critique is aimed at the inadequacy of planned career approaches, already disclosed by its etymology: *career* originally meant a rush by a horse towards the finish. The suggested one-dimensional orientation in this metaphor towards a straightforward goal is clearly obsolete in a globalized world characterized by multiple cultures and rationalities in which generally accepted and socially embodied narratives do not exist anymore. Jobs have become fluid and careers are only loosely connected to self-identity. Rather than assuming a fixed and rational self, processes of identity formation (De Valverde, Sovet & Lubart, 2017) require in-depth explanation. Therefore, career planning itself has to be questioned fundamentally as it may actually add to existing processes of alienation and anomy (Durkheim, 1997).

Before designing models and acting on them, career counselors have to face questions like "Who is 'the person' that is supposed to learn? What is 'the world' in which one chooses a career? What is 'a career' when jobs change overnight?". To prepare citizens for the *cosmopolis* (Appiah, 2017; Toulmin, 1992), transformation is required. According to Draaisma et al. (2018, p. 12) "[a] focus on so-called 21st century skills becomes apparent, including critical analysis and problem solving, creativity and innovation, entrepreneurship, digital skills, communication, collaboration, social-cultural awareness, and self-regulation and reflection".

New directions point towards restoring relationships through (self-)narration and emphasize radical contextuality by substituting 'employability' for 'career guidance' (Maree, 2018) and creative identity formation (Busacca & Rehfuss, 2016; Lengelle &

Meijers, 2014). Closely connected to this development is a shift in attention from individual capabilities to intertwined processes. Some researchers emphasize relationality, while others accentuate group learning and collective sense-making (Conyne & Cook, 2004; Karwowski & Kaufman, 2017).

Although creativity has been recognized in constructivist, dialogical and narrative approaches towards career counselling, our stance is to apply its role more radically, following Mills (2000). This pivotal work makes a plea to suspend everyday beliefs to embody new positions with regard to larger socio-economic structures. More recently, the imagination has come to be seen as the conscious human equivalent of the code of life—our DNA (Harari, 2014). To reinvent social life, we have to trust our imagination. If we look for certainty, we never will find new ways. For imagination to expand from daydreaming to having an impact on citizens, professionals and organizations, we take dialogue as its crucial partner to reconsider daily routines and personal troubles in the light of public issues (Castoriadis, 2016; Muijen, Lengelle, Meijers, & Wardekker, 2018).

These considerations prompted us to develop Art Dialogue Methods (ADM) to stimulate creative processes by means of painting, philosophical board games and music—in teams as well as for personal development and organizational change (Muijen, 2001; Muijen & Brohm, 2017). In an arts-based action research we focussed on a dramaturgical approach. Therefore we ask:

How might theater help to revitalize the ethos of communities?

In Part I, we introduced the need for a political perspective on career counselling, while Part II deals with ADM as a means to rejuvenate the political power of play. In Part III, we present the methodology of action research into theater as politics and explain how we analyzed the process and results. In Part IV, we introduce the dramaturgical approach and highlight three modes of space by play-acting a central scene of Sophocles' play, *Antigone*. In Part V, we elaborate on the dynamics between these spatial modes by describing art dialogues. In Part VI, we present theater as part of the curriculum and in Part VII we conclude that another approach towards career guidance is required. Instead of training students and employees to plan their career individually as if it were a horse race, a shift in perspective is needed to sense-making as a community and making people's working lives meaningful.

Theater as (Inter)Cultural Heritage

Dramaturgical play is as old as the human race. Greek tragedy and comedy are said to have evolved from the religious cult, dedicated to chthonic god(esse)s of Euro-Asian origin. At Dionysian festivities, mythical figures like Maenads, Fauns and Satyrs were dancing and singing hymns, dedicated to the rejuvenation of life. Dramaturgical play developed, not just for religious purposes, but for political reasons as well.

The revival of Greek tragedy and comedy in classical French and English plays by authors like Molière and Shakespeare has contributed to developing the political power of theater. For example, the typical figure of the jester who is allowed to criticize the king symbolizes an emancipator motive of juxtaposing elements of the existing social order and giving a voice to the underdogs. As such, this figure is comparable to Antigone—according to its ancient Greek meaning her name (αντι- γονη) refers to countermovement (Hermsen, 2019, p. 76)—and to Anansi, known from oral traditions in the Caribbean area. Originally, the latter stories were transferred from Ghana during the era of European colonization (Addeah-Prempeh, 2019). Anansi embodies the wit of the scam and is comparable to the cunning fox in European narratives.

To develop ADM further, we have used theater as a rich (inter)cultural heritage. Rooted in a deeply layered understanding, we describe ADM by names that refer to these roots, such as *gnosis* (from *gnothi seauton*, 'know thyself', on the temple of Apollo). In order to understand the interwovenness of art and dialogue we need a method, very much according to the etymology of the words *meta* and *hodos*—*methodos*—as an in-depth exploration. A path (*hodos* = way) leads to insight (*meta* = what lies beyond) by means of different intelligences:

1. *Pathos* we still hear the etymology of pathos in words like empathy, sympathy, compassion, pathology. It was translated by the Romans as e-motion, literally being moved. We define pathos as the ability to give voice to anger, enthusiasm, grief and other emotions through sensitivity for others, relevant details and subtleties found in interaction.
2. *Mythos* refers to narrative imagination (Fry, 2018); the stories being told, myths about the creation of the world and about the quest for good (like in *Antigone*), as well as the very act of storytelling. Hereby, we find answers to existential questions that create order in the void that surrounds us.
3. *Logos* is deeper than common sense; broader than logical reasoning. It refers to dialogue as a way of understanding things; through words, images, or any kind of symbolic interaction (Langer, 1979). Dialogue is composed of the old-Greek *dia* (through an opening) and *logos*, referring to the (natural) principle of ordering the world. We see it as the synthesis of reflection on experiences, internal voices and coming to a mutual understanding (*logos*) in-between (*dia*) people.
4. *Ethos* precedes (moral) codes of conduct, and refers to pedagogical practices of building (good) character, communal habits and political (wise) actions. The etymology stresses the importance of transcending the individual scope of virtue and understanding ethics as relational qualities as a community, taking into account the inherent vulnerability of everyone who strives for the good life (Nussbaum, 2001).
5. *Phronèsis* the interplay of all intelligences results in collective wisdom embedded in good practices or *phronèsis*, which Aristotle understood as being both practical and ethical in nature (Eikeland, 2008). We see it as an emerging quality in (between) people and spaces, provoked through art and dialogue, inspired by Winnicott's transitional space (1972), Arendt's public space (1958), and Irigaray's in-between (2016). Despite differences between these theories, we have extracted a common theme: the art of establishing free interplay between various

voices and values within and between individuals. The idea of an indefinable space is similar to the mythological void or chaos from which the world is created, and to *chora* (χώρα), an old-Greek term designating the territory outside the *polis* (city state). In this sense, it is a non-place that refers, just as the middle voice in Plato's dialogues in Timaeus 48e4 (Derrida, 1993; Kisner, 2017), to neither being nor nonbeing. It rather designates an interval in-between, where all the forms were originally held, similar to a maternal womb.

Methodology: Arts-Based Action Research

We present a dramaturgical approach of ADM by reframing an arts-based action research project that was carried out in the nursing department of a Dutch university college (Lomans, 2018).

Music, dance, dramaturgical and art therapy, arts-based research and arts-based learning, phenomenology and hermeneutics all stem from ancient, narrative roots (Eisner, 2008; Gadamer, 1993; Habermas, 1984; McNiff, 1998) and use symbolic interaction as dialogical ways of sense-making. They share the idea of invocational and embodied aspects of knowledge to understand (social) situations and make them change. Dramaturgical play stimulates reflection by expressing internal voices and experiences, as well as a mutual understanding by voicing insights in-between people. We have borrowed from these traditions and developed ADM as developmental and research programs. By using different forms of art, we gained experience on how to stimulate multifaceted modes of understanding for exploring personal growth and professional development, complex social situations and organizational problems. In this way, art dialogues help to untangle complexity without reducing it to a single factor. At the same time, they initiate healing processes in a polyphonic way by using dialogues through diverse media, by means of play-acting, singing, dancing, imagining, moving, etc.

ADM helps to avoid the pitfall of rationalistic discourse that reduces the complexity of career development to an individual and organizational factor like career success. Neither the organization nor the individual alone can be held responsible for life's misfortune or success in career development. Instead, it is a matter of collective responsibility and of taking political action, thus developing ethos as a community.

Research Process

The reason for our research was the entrapment experienced by lecturers as shown in an internal report. Despite their positive feelings about teaching the nursing students, they were dissatisfied with the organizational rules that were curtailing their professional autonomy. The way in which the work was organized by means of disciplinary

ICT and 'Planning & Control' systems affected the quality of relationships and work experience (Shore & Wright, 2000).

Theater as a narrative response to their disempowerment was designed and executed as a way of individual and collective sense-making (2017–2018). It entailed three sessions with two groups of six lecturers collaboratively staging parts of *Antigone*. Their aim was to facilitate art dialogues on personal and professional experiences. The classic Greek tragedy shows the ethical appeal to maneuver between the laws of the gods (*logos*) and the laws of humans (*nomos*). Asking the lecturers to play the scene was meant to stimulate their reflection on a parallel clash between personal and professional values on the one hand and organizational norms on the other—thereby urging them to take action.

As the first analysis showed *that* the art dialogues had been meaningful, the question on *how* needed further elaboration. The first route was to focus on interactional dynamics through axial coding and thick descriptions of key moments. The second route involved new cycles of action research (2018–2019) aimed at broadening the scope towards performing actual organizational theater (Schreyögg, 2001) and enacting working-life scenes, while integrating emerging insights. These new cycles comprised eight meetings with twelve participants (lecturers and managers). The art dialogues were based on the participants' experiences as young nurses, and these resulted in four performances for colleagues. From 2018 to 2019 the focus shifted to involving students in the performance and including the performance in the curriculum.

We emphasize the importance of an elaborate dialogical setting to design the inquiry. It includes the choice of play, preparing participants to rehearse the text, directing the acting, assisting the reflections of participants (Schön, 1999) on their play-acting and role-taking, as well as a collaborative evaluation of the overall process, in order to find new meaning about who they want to be, both as individuals and as members of a community.

Data Analysis and Synthesis

The sessions were recorded on video, the ensuing dialogues were transcribed (95 pages with 282 quotations), and the jottings made during the session were developed into detailed field notes. The transcripts were coded and then processed by means of theme analysis, which resulted in the first research report (Lomans, 2018).

The next stage of the interpretation process involved recording the data. Following Strauss and Corbin (1997) for axial coding to analyze interactional dynamics, processes and change in terms of preconditions, contexts, interaction strategies and types of consequences (Fig. 1).

Central to an axial coding diagram is the phenomenon—in this case, the political act in its ambiguity as theatrical performance regarding a political situation and as a way to imagine political action. The etymology of politics—taking care of the *pólis*, the city state or community, with governance as only one of its aspects—points to

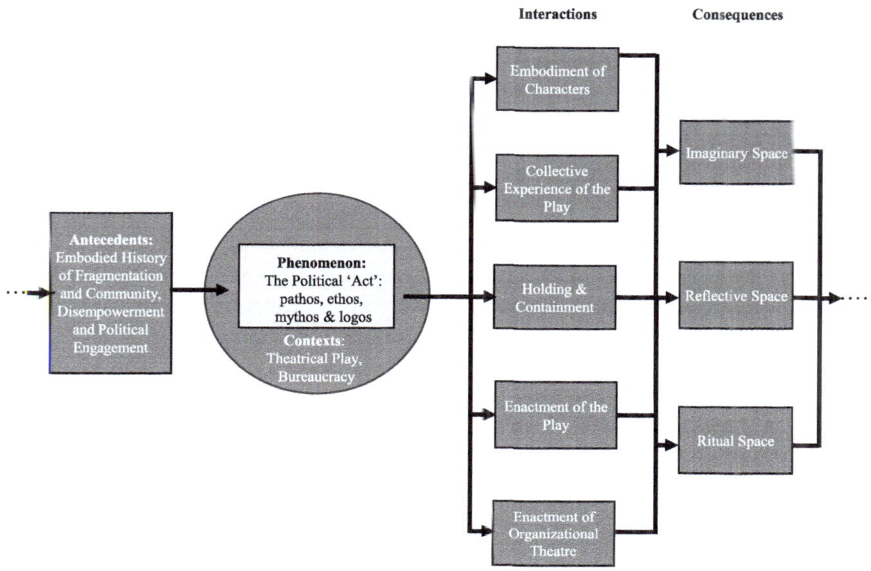

Fig. 1 Axial coding diagram

what we capture as the interplay between embodying characters (*pathos*) who reflect on playing through dialogues (*logos*), imagining (*mythos*) and (re-)positioning the self (*ethos*) in different roles. These roots are fundamental to empowerment in action research as well as in political theory (Arendt, 1958).

The antecedents to the phenomenon (the political act) consist of the participants' experiences that were validated in the orientation phase, as most of the participants reported recurrent feelings of being disempowered and frustrated by the organization (85 excerpts). It also became evident that, over time, participants felt reinvigorated and reconnected by engaging in play-acting, as they were beginning to sense new perspectives despite fatigue and heavy workloads (17 excerpts).

We identified the following five strategies with regard to interaction:

1. *Embodiment of Characters*:—Rehearsing the text according to directions of the theater counselor by imagining the implied context of the play. Participants typically reported on their uneasiness and joy in playing (20 excerpts).
2. *Collective Experience of Play*:—Stimulating participants to reflect on changes they experienced while playing (41 excerpts).
3. *Holding and Containment*:—Encouraging participants to express their feelings to each other and regarding the directions of the theater counselor (40 excerpts).
4. *Enactment of the Play*:—Play-acting *Antigone* and engaging in dialogues with participants on their role-taking (118 excerpts).
5. *Enactment of Organizational Theater*:—This was not a category of axial coding, but it facilitated the next stages of the action research.

Regarding the spatial consequences of these five interaction strategies, we discerned three main types. First: imaginary space, as participants experienced entering an alternative reality (112 excerpts). Second: reflective space, as participants engaged in exchanging ideas on how to act differently, individually, as well as collectively (122 excerpts). Third: ritual space, as participants showed new ways of role-taking (57 excerpts). As we reframed the action research from an ADM perspective, we do not base our conclusions on quantitative aspects of the analyses alone, as this would make *logos* dominant at the expense of the dynamics between *ethos*, *mythos*, *pathos* and theater *methodos*. Using all intelligences, we present an overview of the outcome, then provide an in-depth description of three example scenes and conclude by discussing their significance for transforming career guidance.

Results

While evaluating the process, the theater counselor witnessed developments among the participants on three levels:

The Lecturers Individually—Empowerment: "If you look at Geke now, she is much more powerful and credible. This power she can also use at other times."

The Team—Community Building: One of the participants who struggled terribly with the time pressures of her job: "Apparently I am not alone in this feeling, others are struggling as well." A lecturer remarked after seeing the performance: "It was such a beautiful reflection on […] what connects us."

The Students—Professional Guidance: Because of the enthusiastic response, the presentation became part of the 2019 curriculum, including art dialogues with the students about their internship experiences, thereby (career) guiding them to find their way as young professionals. Experiencing their teachers on stage, one of the students remarked: "… you were SO funny. Seeing you also made mistakes and had your moments when you just didn't know what to say, was very recognizable and supportive!"

Scene I: Antigone's Revolt

By securing a proper burial for her brother Polyneikes, Antigone acted against the decree of her uncle Creon, the new king of Thebe. Creon refused to bury Polyneikes as he had started a war, causing the loss of many lives and harm to the city. He therefore feared that giving Polyneikes a burial would lead to more upheaval. However, Polyneikes' right by birth to the throne indebted Creon morally.

This knot of interdependences served as a frame to perceive similar patterns in the lecturers' role-taking while feeling the urge to take a stance in the organization.

Art Dialogues

The theater counselor jotted down the following field notes:

> Merel, as Antigone, appears despondent. Especially as her articulation is colored with shame. I tell her that Antigone feels confident, she knows of no shame and is proud that she has buried her brother. I give her technical instructions, to stand firmly, look her opponent in the eyes and take time. Thus staying in the moment and really meeting him. When Merel follows these directions, her attitude and looks change. She acts proudly and in no way shamefully. One of her colleagues in the audience says: 'Now you sound powerful, it was really a NO!' Not in volume, but in intention. Other participants agree.

An essential component of theater as politics is reflection on playing. Sharing experiences and associations as a group turns the stage into a playing field for narratives. Therefore, it is important that emotions and conversations be voiced freely, without judgment or comments, as shown in the following transcript:

> Merel said: In the scene, I really feel like Antigone when she says, 'Everybody agrees with me, but no one will speak out.' In real life, in the organization, I might feel like Antigone. But then I realize that we as individuals 'cannot win the battle'.
>
> Lisa commented on her playing the character of Ismene, who persistently gave her stubborn sister Antigone a 'no' to her request to bury their brother together:
>
> Experiencing difficulty with saying 'no' is very similar to my own life. I find it so difficult to take a stance, it really costs me a lot of effort.
>
> Lisa experienced that in order to play Ismene's persistence in a convincing way, she had to develop a strong character not to give into Antigone's determination. It shows how playing a role requires awareness of the body and of one's internal dialogue. Participants were helped to become aware of nuances in their emotions as 21st century professionals, while at the same time they were connected with motives and personal struggles of the characters in the play.

From the first scene, we distilled three important theater ingredients, namely imaginary space, reflective space and ritual space.

Imaginary Space: The Sense of Playing

The first ingredient is the transition from everyday life to imaginary space, a place where one can visualize an alternative reality. A classic story like *Antigone* takes participants to another time and place in which the characters are not the modern type of manager, nurse or teacher, but kings, princesses, gods and warriors.

The art dialogues are characterized by two aspects:

1. Participants express having fun, excitement and surprise at embodying roles. This involves body awareness, learning how to use emotions and physical expression to really embody a character and to influence the dynamics on stage. Counselling on different levels simultaneously is needed so that participants feel their personal drive as well as the motives of the character in the play.

2. Participants express gratitude to the theater counselor for providing a safe holding environment (Winnicott, 1972). This concept originates primarily from parental nursing of the child, which later expanded to ever-widening circles of family, school and social life. As participants are vulnerable in this process it is of utmost importance that they feel safe to open up and establish bonds as a community, by encouraging them and giving comfort, while at the same time providing them with suggestions on how to create new routines and explore their identities: "*You are so positive in your feedback, I bought everything from you. You took me, step by step, out of my comfort zone. In this way, I learned something new.*"

This process was expanded as participants started to encourage one another.

Reflective Space: The Importance of Taking a Stance

Creating a reflective space is central to philosophical counselling. ADM adds invocative power to reflection and provokes embodiment to make the participants really feel the metaphorical meanings, wordplay and references to everyday life.

Organizing reflective space means inviting the participants to reflect on the scenes played—both on the what (content) and the how (process). Learning processes therefore take place on two levels: firstly, on the level of collaborative play-acting and storytelling, and secondly, on the content level of ethical dilemmas. Although the play is situated in a different cultural context, away from the contemporary situation, the participants recognize similar emotional frictions. Play-acting opens an imaginary space in which they re-enact felt dilemmas and existential themes, and reflect on their meaning. This urges them to take a stance, both on stage and in their working lives.

Antigone's quest to be a loving sister to her brother eventually meant making a choice that led to her death. Furthermore, Ismene's joy of living and her loyalty to Antigone clash. She cannot be a good sister and a good citizen while at the same time being true to her inner feelings. Creon's virtues of being a good king also clash with his being a good uncle. Then and now the question is: how to reconcile personal virtues with public obligations? Despite differences on a content level, the struggle itself is part of the human condition: how does one reconcile opposing values stemming from the different roles one has to play in life?

Reflective space gave participants the opportunity to explore different viewpoints and positions freely, not just in a cognitive way, but embodied by means of empathy, sympathy, antipathy.

For instance, in the dialogues, not everyone was negative about Creon's strict rule over Thebe and the need for law and order. Some sympathized with him because he wanted to keep stability and peace for the people, and they criticized Antigone's resistance: "*That brother did not even love her. [He was] Stubborn, irritating*", said a participant; and about Creon: "*I am not a manager but I always have sympathy for a certain orderliness and clarity: everyone benefits from it. […] There must be a captain on the ship.*"

Thus, reflective space invites participants to explore values, uncertainties and re-tell the story of their lives. At the same time, they recognize mutual struggles and ambiguities as professionals in the political context of the organization.

The art dialogues facilitated the sharing of disturbing experiences within the organization and stimulated collective storytelling that allowed the participants to criticize the social codes of the team and their relationship to management: thereby the *nomos* is being calibrated by the *(dia)-logos*. The story of Thebe and Creon's rule created a context in which they could reflect on their feeling of being oppressed as a professional team. They became conscious of the quality of the place they inhabit and how they worked together as a *polis*. The question to be answered was: Do they want to keep the status quo or create new ways as a community?

It is important to remember that the process does not happen in orderly or predictable steps. Rather, it is nonlinear and participants recurrently commute between imaginary and reflective space, which represents the threshold for entering ritual space.

Ritual Space: Fluid Reality

In the dialogues, substantial reflections were made on the transition of sense-making from play to everyday working life. Participants expressed a new understanding of the self and intentions for future action, both as individuals and collectively.

To comprehend this, we use the concept of ritual space, building on classical works from cultural anthropology and psychoanalysis (Turner, 1982; Winnicott, 1972). We especially embraced the idea that cultural experience, including play, is located in-between individuals and groups, nature and nurture. The liminal stage in rites of passage is the in-between when an old symbolic order fades away and a new reality is to be born; for example, the transition of members within communities from childhood to adulthood. Transitional objects are used that give people the necessary reorientation and comfort to enter another domain of life. From a psychoanalytic perspective, objects such as dolls and blankets help the baby make the transition from symbiosis with the mother to separation as an individual.

The theatrical setting consists of many transitional objects, for instance the text-book and the drama classroom, and it includes, in a more fundamental sense, the body, the felt-self, the positioning of the actors, the proximity of the audience. When participants engage in the dynamics between playing and reflecting, ritual space will emerge as a space in which self and others become intertwined and a community develops by shared sense-making. Our approach is to facilitate transitional processes in human life in general, linked to the view that, as soon as we have the courage to dismantle dominant discourses, reality is in essence fluid (Rizzuto, 2014).

Scene 2: Euridice and Creon

The scene showed the embodiment of Euridice, Creon's wife, as being a manipulative and calculating woman. Her power was not to be underestimated.

Art Dialogues

The theater counselor made the following remarks in her field notes:

> I try to let Eva embody the character of Euridice as the real ruler who manipulates her husband Creon completely. It is therefore important that Eva shows tranquility in her speech and checks whether her words actually have an impact on Creon.
>
> Bas, is playing the desperate and soft character of Creon as his natural 'color'. I therefore focus my feedback on Eva in particular. Gradually her playing improves. "I notice that speaking with a softer tone creates more contact", she says. This is confirmed by others. A colleague says: "Being quieter makes you much more convincing. I … even felt shivering."
>
> I ask Eva to stand upright and say: "Let Creon bow to you." Eva shows powerful energy. Cool and calculating instead of restless and desperate. I give her the assignment to stand behind Bas, to seduce him, to whisper the lyrics in his ear. From the side stage Merel says: "Good synergy, Eva, it is really beautiful." Eva laughs: "We are a beautiful couple, aren't we?" The scene gains more credibility and I say to Eva: "Now you are acting non-verbally, I see you listening and the words really do affect Bas."
>
> Gradually the participants grow in their ability to connect working life themes, like power and communication, with aspects of playing together.
>
> A participant notices: "At university, we also work very hard, […]trying to cope just like Creon and Antigone do, sticking to their point of view."
>
> For me, as Ismene, it [your conversation] is all about pride. It really moves me that you do not come closer together at all. Merel (playing Antigone) says: It is not pride, it is honesty! […]you really get disconnected[…], you are in your own monologue. … Just as in real life.
>
> Another participant remarks: "…to see what this means in the context of the organization, we'll have to explore together. […]There is no management against 'the others'. […]We have to do it together. At the same time, we are different and have to accept […]our different feelings on how we do things."

Back to reality, but which one? All the participants prioritized the meetings over many other pressing issues at work, even skipping other tasks in their agendas. One of them stated: "*I have learned now how much more powerful it is to do less. [….]I can especially enjoy this because I am part of a larger community.*"

As opponents in the play, participants developed insight into each other's motives and enhanced their communicative repertoire. In doing so, they discovered (unknown) aspects of themselves: "*I often stay in the background, as I am a bit of a contemplative type. Here on stage, the playing triggers and challenges me […]by really achieving something together. By having a shared mission, I could handle the whole world, that's how I felt when I left last week.*"

The art dialogues made them think about the core of their profession, its beauty, hardships and the (ethical) dilemmas.

In addition to counterplay, the feedback from the group helped participants to identify personal qualities and uncertainties in themselves. The way in which the audience reacted to the actors provided for even deeper reflection on their playing. The togetherness on and around the stage leads to the building of a community: the transition from a bunch of alienated and disempowered persons in disrupted organizational life to an ethos in which their bonds as professionals are restored.

A *communitas* had been developed, by getting attuned to one another. The interactions of the participants showed that as soon as people really listened and played, they were sincere in their responses and the playing was real. Thus, reality unfolded in its fluid quality!

Scene 3: Theater in the Curriculum

The initiative was born to create a presentation for nursing students to be performed during the lustrum of the University. The presentation would show dilemmas in their professional work, after which the lecturers would discuss ethical questions with the students.

There was a good response: nine lecturers and three managers, as well as some so-called training actors came forward. Now the playing was not based on an existing text like *Antigone*. The participants were invited to visualize their moments of pride and the dilemmas they experienced as young nurses. In the end, a number of collective themes were distilled: the friction of giving care under time pressure; how to do justice to the patient; is it (morally) justified to force people 'for their own good'? How does one cope with suffering, vulnerability, and power plays? Based on these and other themes, a number of scenes were orchestrated to create a performance. Careful consideration was given to what messages the presentation could convey to the students.

She Is Her Young Self Again!

The following emerged from the field notes: "*Laura tells the story of her first experiences as a young girl in a nursing house. She stands in the spotlight, in the middle of the stage, surrounded by her fellow players. Laura goes back in time to that very day. After many years of desk work, she is again a nurse with the nurses on the floor, showing how she felt then. She tells about the little clock she has received from her proud mother. When Laura rolls up her sleeves and puts on her trousers 'just like the girls', she is her young self again, uncertain and full of expectations.*

Her play is funny and moving at the same time. Then other participants transform into nurses and greet her enthusiastically. Suddenly we are actually in the nursing house. The nurses drink coffee and Laura is eager to begin her working day. The emergency bell rings. Laura cries out for joy: something is finally happening! The audience laughs when the nurses take action, in slow motion with music from a well-known medical soap. They give instructions, grab the emergency suitcase and move towards the patient, enlarging their actions and expressions. The audience is cheering and applauding. While performing in slow motion, colleagues laugh and shout their names outrageously."

Art Dialogues

On stage, the participants experienced being liberated from the disciplinary rules, protocols and hierarchical relationships of organizational life. One of the participants, Suus, said: "*Feeling vulnerable and […]very uncomfortable, until you think 'whatever'! Everyone is doing it! It gives you the feeling of being nude, really free to discover something. […]The fact that you don't feel restrained by thoughts going on in your head.*"

Linde remarked: "*I have the feeling that our lives are determined by the need to set goals, by being useful, by accomplishing all kinds of tasks. […]Playing makes me feel happy and gives joy. Indeed because it is not useful, you know, like when we played as kids, just for fun and not for tasks and obligations.*"

Another participant declared: "*I don't have the feeling we can make mistakes. You can do it differently, but that's okay!*"

Carnival and Recreating Reality

Reflecting on the second scene, Linde pointed to an important condition for creating free space: to let go of functional roles and useful activities, to be as spontaneous as a child. Playing is not for the sake of achieving a goal external to the play itself (Huizinga, 2008). Children play for the sake of playing. It needs trust and to let go "*Let's see where the playing will lead us.*"

After the third scene, the audience was invited to participate in the art dialogues and thus they became part of the playing. In this way, the *communitas* continued to develop and expand organically on and around the stage, with participants and spectators coming together in one carnival of play: "*To feel how the audience reacts! Everyone speaks in superlatives, embraces you and has enjoyed it.*"

Playing together resulted in feeling happy as a group and in becoming free in a way that is taboo according to normal codes of conduct, for example being seductive, manipulative, expressing anger. Acting gave very special energy; it caused fun and laughter, and at the same time everyone concentrated and listened attentively to one another.

The third scene especially showed that both participants and audience rediscovered the importance of taking care of the self with regard to their personal-professional values and sought an answer to the question: what do I need for the good life? (Foucault, 2005; Hadot, 2004). The team manager confessed: *"I have gotten to know these people in a totally different way. I'm used to having functional relationships with them, but in the rehearsals, I have seen everybody in a different role. I take these enriched images back to our daily work."*

Conclusion: The Good (Working) Life

The findings presented so far give a contextual and finely tuned answer to our central question: *How might theater help to revitalize the ethos of communities?*

Redefining Career Counselling

We conclude that ADM redefines career counselling. Theater as politics helps to raise awareness of the embodied roles that managers, professionals and students play within organizations, and it also experiments with ways of how to change them. As such, career guidance is about the adventurous art of role-taking, in-between being a pawn of organizational (societal) forces and the illusion of being the autonomous actor in control. It is in the eye of the other that one knows oneself. The postmodern answer to the ancient quest to know thyself (*gnothi seauton)* involves a multidimensional and poly-vocational view on the self as growing within communities. Therefore theater is more than intervention; it is politics in the sense of community building.

That said, ADM gives no roadmap. It is, however, a contextual and relational refined art of (re)directing interplay between different spaces and intelligences. This implies a huge advantage to planned career counselling programs in organizations. ADM literally sets the stage for transformative rituals and creates meaningful symbols, thereby counterbalancing fragmentary and accelerating forces (Hart, 2014). This implies shifting the perspective from career planning as a segregated part of individual life to a non-linear approach of lifelong learning as a community.

The craftsmanship of the theater counselor is crucial in guiding participants to really embody a character. Thus, existential experiences are reinforced by collective learning processes and vice versa: to know yourself by getting to know and acknowledging 'the other. Thereby, invoking an ethos for negotiating on organizational agreements. Therefore, theater as politics is an answer to postmodern challenges characterized by fluidity and alienation, in which individualistic and rationalistic approaches of career counselling have become obsolete.

Practical Implications for Career Counselling

ADM adds to career counselling by:

1. Expanding the individual orientation in existing programs to develop collective learning.
2. Changing the instrumental approaches of career counselors away from career guiding as a step-by-step procedure solving a practical problem towards an empowered, emancipatory way of sense-making as a professional community.
3. Shifting the predominant rational and verbal models to a non-linear dialogical and arts-based way of using all intelligences, to develop *phronesis*.
4. Redefining career counselling as a cultural praxis with a focus on healing horizontal and hierarchical relationships and making the working life meaningful as *communitas*. Since employees are hindered not just in their career, but in their professional life as a whole—by fragmentation, loss of control, feeling lonely, disempowered—we have to address these problems as interrelated phenomena. Therefore, we propose to embed career counselling in an overall ADM research-and-guidance process.

Reflections on Theater as Politics

As indicated earlier, the theater *methodos* integrates three modes of space:

In imaginary space, participants visualize issues (*mythos*), both by embodying (*pathos*) characters of a classic narrative (*Antigone*) and by telling the story of their lives.

In reflective space, there are cross-overs from classical to personal narratives, from playing on stage to empowered role-taking in everyday life (*ethos*). Thus, participants must find new words to give meaning (*logos*) to their working life by means of emplotment, "which makes the juxtaposing of events possible" (Hermans, 2001, p. 341), jumping back and forth between role-taking on stage and functional roles in their daily lives.

In ritual space, embodiment fuels the transition from 'as if' to real play and role-taking as a means "to live truthfully under imaginary circumstances" (Silverberg, 1997, p. 9). Thus, common ground is created for re-enactment as a constructive alternative to acting-out (Schaverien, 1994). The embodied processes of healing disruptions in and between people are conditional for developing both as a community and individually: to become who you really are, according to Nietzsche and other philosophers on the art of living.

Methodological Reflections

It is extremely important to let the imagination work unrestrainedly, as every association may be significant. It is also important to orchestrate different modes of consciousness and to acknowledge parallel processes on intrapersonal, interpersonal, team and organizational levels. Finally, it is essential to integrate these levels so that the quality of playing together as a community can emerge. As one of the participants reflected, "It is so special that from nothing we create something beautiful". The art dialogue dynamics will be lost if theater were to be limited in an instrumental framework of managerially set (educational) goals.

Theater as politics adds to the classical notion that emotional purification (catharsis) is enough by itself, as well as to the principle of pluralism as being predominantly a cognitive ability to switch perspectives. Through embodiment, participants learn to traverse back and forth between a theater perspective and a real-life perspective. In so doing, ADM enriches the psychodynamic principle that transitional space serves to help people find their way back to reality, as claimed by Winnicott (1972). Our research has shown how ritual space stimulates playing with fixed (organizational) roles.

An interesting philosophical implication of these enriched concepts is the deconstruction of metaphysical assumptions about reality itself. It challenges dominant ontological views, both from an idealistic stance (reality seen as a construction of subjects) and from materialistic perspectives (reality as determined by economic, cultural and social structures in organizations and society at large). Instead, the concept of fluid reality as a ritual space might be closer to the truth than the frozen realities that are recycled via dominant discourses.

References

Addeah-Prempeh, K. (2019). *An African storytelling production in an Asian setting*. Retrieved from https://questforwisdom.org/wijsheid/an-african-storytelling-production-in-an-asian-setting/.

Appiah, K. A. (2017). *Cosmopolitanisms*. New York City, NY: NYU Press.

Arendt, H. (1958). *The human condition* (2nd ed.) Chicago, IL: University of Chicago Press.

Bauman, Z. (2006). *Liquid modernity*. Cambridge, Malden, MA: Polity Press, Blackwell.

Blake, W. (1984). Auguries of innocence. In D. Herbert (Ed.), *Everyman's book of evergreen verse*. Rutland, VT: J.M. Dent & Sons Ltd., Charles E. Tuttle.

Brohm, R., & Muijen, H. (2010). Participatie en nabijheid als kwaliteiten van afstemming en samenwerking [Participation and proximity as qualities of coordination and cooperation]. *Filosofie, 20*(2), 50–55.

Busacca, L. A., & Rehfuss, M. C. (Eds.). (2016). *Postmodern career counselling: A handbook of culture, context, and cases*. Hoboken, NJ: Wiley.

Castoriadis, C. (2016). Radical imagination and the social instituting imaginary. In G. Robinson & J. F. Rundell (Eds.), *Rethinking Imagination* (pp. 136–154). London, UK: Routledge.

Conyne, R., & Cook, E. (2004). *Ecological counselling: An innovative approach to conceptualizing person-environment interaction*. Alexandria, VA: American Counselling Association.

Derrida, J. (1993). *Khôra*. Paris, France: Galilée.

De Valverde, J., Sovet, L., & Lubart, T. (2017). Self-construction and creative "life design". In M. Karwowski & J. C. Kaufman (Eds.), *The creative self: Effect of beliefs, self-efficacy, mindset, and identity* (pp. 99–115). Cambridge, MA: Academic Press.

Draaisma, A., Meijers, F., & Kuijpers, M. (2018). The development of strong career learning environments: The project 'career orientation and guidance' in Dutch vocational education. *Journal of Vocational Education & Training, 70*(1), 27–46. https://doi.org/10.1080/13636820.2017.1392995.

Durkheim, E. (1997). *The division of labour in society*. New York City, NY: Free Press.

Eikeland, O. (2008). *The ways of Aristotle: Aristotelian phronèsis, Aristotelian philosophy of dialogue, and action research*. Bern, Switzerland: Peter Lang.

Eisner, E. (2008). Art and knowledge. In J. G. Knowles & A. L. Cole (Eds.), *Handbook of the arts in qualitative research: Perspectives, methodologies, examples, and issues* (pp. 3–12). London, UK: Sage.

Foucault, M. (2005). *The hermeneutics of the subject: Lectures at the Collège de France 1981–1982* (Vol. 6). New York City, NY: Picador.

Fry, S. (2018). *Mythos: The Greek myths retold*. London, UK: Penguin Books.

Gadamer, H. G. (1993). *Wahrheit und Methode [Truth and method]*. Tübingen, Germany: Mohr Siebeck.

Gergen, K. J. (2009). *Relational being: Beyond self and community*. Oxford, UK: Oxford University Press.

Giroux, H. (2018). *Pedagogy and the politics of hope: Theory, culture, and schooling: A critical reader*. London, UK: Routledge.

Habermas, J. (1984). *The theory of communicative action*. Boston, MA: Beacon Press.

Hadot, P. (2004). *What is ancient philosophy?*. Cambridge, MA: Harvard University Press.

Han, B.-C. (2014). *The burnout society*. Palo Alto, CA: Stanford University Press.

Harari, Y. N. (2014). *Sapiens: A brief history of humankind*. New York City, NY: Random House.

Hermans, H. J. (2001). The construction of a personal position repertoire: Method and practice. *Culture & Psychology, 7*(3), 323–366.

Hermsen, J. J. (2019). *Het tij keren. Met Rosa Luxemburg en Hanah Arendt* [*Turn the tide. With Rosa Luxemburg and Hannah Arendt*. Amsterdam, Netherlands: Prometheus Nieuw Licht.

Huizinga, J. (2008). *Homo ludens. Proeve eener bepaling van het spel-element der cultuur* [*Homo ludens. A study on the play element of culture*]. Amsterdam, Netherlands: Amsterdam University Press/Athenaeum Boekhandel Canon.

Irigaray, L. (2016). *La Voie de I 'amour*. Sesto San Giovanni: Mimesis. [*The way of love*]. (2002). trans. Heidi Bostic and Stephen Pluháček London, UK: Continuum].

Karwowski, M., & Kaufman, J. C. (Eds.). (2017). *The creative self: Effect of beliefs, self-efficacy, mindset, and identity*. San Diego, CA: Elsevier Academic Press.

Kisner, W. (2017). The medial character of interdisciplinarity: Thinking in the middle voice. *Issues in Interdisciplinary Studies, 35*, 29–52.

Langer, S. (1979). *Philosophy in a new key. A study in the symbolism of reason, rite and art*. Cambridge, MA: Harvard University Press.

Lengelle, R., & Meijers, F. (2014). Narrative identity: Writing the self in career learning. *British Journal of Guidance and Counselling, 42*(1), 52–72. https://doi.org/10.1080/03069885.2013.816837.

Lomans, S. (2018). *Antigone: Theater als interventiepraktijk voor de ontwikkeling van positieve vrijheid van professionals ten aanzien van ervaren systeemdruk* [Antigone: *Theater as intervention for the development of positive freedom of professionals for experienced system pressure*]. (Unpublished Master's thesis). LESI & University of Humanistics, Utrecht.

Maree, J. G. (2018). Using life design counseling for career construction to facilitate sustainable employability and decent work in a developing country context. In V. Cohen-Scali et al. (Eds.), *Interventions in career design and education, Lifelong Learning Book Series 23* (pp. 195–215). Basel, Switzerland: Springer. https://doi.org/10.1007/978-3-319-91968-3_11.

McNiff, S. (1998). *Art-based research*. London, UK: Jessica Kingsley.

Muijen, H. S. C. A. (2001). *Metafoor tussen magie en methode. Narratief leren in organisaties en therapie [Metaphor between magic and method. Narrative learning in organizations and therapy]*. Kampen: Agora.
Mills, C. W. (2000). *The sociological imagination*. Oxford, UK: Oxford University Press.
Muijen, H. S. C. A., & Brohm, R. (2017). Art dialogue methods: Phronesis and its potential for restoring an embodied moral authority in local communities. *British Journal of Guidance & Counselling*. https://doi.org/10.1080/03069885.2017.1413170.
Muijen, H., Lengelle, R., Meijers, F., & Wardekker, W. (2018). The role of imagination in emergent career agency. *Australian Journal of Career Development, 27*(2), 88–98. https://doi.org/10.1177/1038416218777832.
Nussbaum, M. C. (2001). *The fragility of goodness: Luck and ethics in Greek tragedy and philosophy*. Cambridge, UK: Cambridge University Press.
Rizzuto, G. (2014). *Mediale levenskunst. Een interculturele polylog* [*Medial art of living. An intercultural polylog*]. Brussels, Belgium: ASP.
Savickas, M. L., Nota, L., Rossier, J., Dauwalder, J. P., Duarte, M. E., Guichard, J., et al. (2010). Life designing: A paradigm for career construction in the 21th century. *Journal of Vocational Behavior, 75,* 239–250. https://doi.org/10.1016/j.jvb.2009.04.004.
Schaverien, J. (1994). Images of art therapy. In T. Dalley (Ed.), *New developments in theory and practice*. London, UK: Routledge.
Schön, D. (1999). *The reflective practitioner. How professionals think in action*. London, UK: Routledge.
Schreyögg, G. (2001). Organizational theatre and organizational change. *Academy of Management Berlin*. Retrieved from http://www.diss.fuberlin.de/docs/servlets/MCRFileNodeServlet/FUDOCS_derivate_000000000150/13_2001.pdf.
Sennet, R. (2009). *The craftsman*. London, UK: Penguin.
Shore, C., & Wright, S. (2000). Coercive accountability: The rise of audit culture in higher education. In M. Strathern (Ed.), *Audit cultures: Anthropological studies in accountability, ethics and the academy* (pp. 57–89). London, UK: Routledge.
Silverberg, J. (1997). *The Sanford Meisner approach: Workbook two: Emotional Freedom*. Hanover, NH: Smith & Kraus.
Strauss, A., & Corbin, J. M. (1997). *Grounded theory in practice*. London, UK: Sage.
Taylor, C. (2006). *Sources of the self. The making of modern identity*. Cambridge, MA: Harvard University Press.
Toulmin, S. (1992). *Cosmopolis: The hidden agenda of modernity*. Chicago, IL: University of Chicago Press.
Turner, V. (1982). *From ritual to theatre: The seriousness of human play*. New York City, NY: Performing Arts Journal.
Winnicott, D. W. (1972). *Holding and interpretation*. London, UK: Hogarth.
Yuthas, K., Dillard, J. F., & Rogers, R. K. (2004). Beyond agency and structure: Triple-loop learning. *Journal of Business Ethics, 51,* 229–243. https://doi.org/10.1023/b:busi.0000033616.14852.82.

Advancing Innovative Career Counselling to Manage Transitions

Facilitating Career Transitions with Coping and Decision-Making Approaches

Yuliya Lipshits-Braziler and Itamar Gati

Abstract As the 21th-century world of work is rapidly changing, and career transitions have become more frequent, decision-making and coping skills can help individuals manage these transitions successfully. The aim of this chapter is to demonstrate ways of facilitating individuals' career transitions using a decision-theory viewpoint and coping-with- stress perspective. The first section of the chapter focuses on the features of career transitions. The second describes some ways in which the coping perspective could be applied to help understand and deal with career transitions. To highlight the advantages of using decision theory, the third section demonstrates the utility of the PIC model (Prescreening, In-depth exploration, and Choice; Gati & Asher in Contemporary models in vocational psychology Erlbaum, Mahwah, pp. 7–54, 2001a, Gati & Asher in Career Dev Q 50:140–157, 2001b) as a way of facilitating career transitions. The chapter concludes by exploring the implications of both decision-making and coping perspectives for career guidance and counselling.

Keywords Coping · Decision-making · Career transitions · Career counselling · Career assessment

Introduction

The 21th-century world of work is changing rapidly, presenting more career opportunities along with less job security (Hirschi, 2018). Current changes in the digitized and automated world of work are often called the fourth industrial revolution (Schwab, 2016). In this era, careers have become transient, "protean", and "boundaryless" (Arthur & Rousseau, 1996; Hall, 2004; Lent, 2013), and career transitions have become more frequent (Levin & Gati, 2014). These transitions could be voluntary or imposed, expected or sudden (Heppner & Scott, 2004), including job loss, retirement, change of occupational field, school-to-work transition, and the like.

Y. Lipshits-Braziler (✉) · I. Gati
Hebrew University of Jerusalem, Jerusalem, Israel
e-mail: yuliya.lipshits@mail.huji.ac.il

J. G. Maree (ed.), *Handbook of Innovative Career Counselling*,
https://doi.org/10.1007/978-3-030-22799-9_9

Making a career transition is often complex, demanding, and stress-evoking (Anderson, Goodman, & Schlossberg, 2012; Lipshits-Braziler, Braunstein-Bercovitz, & Kapach-Royf, 2018), and involves making a career decision. Many individuals report heightened levels of distress, confusion, and indecision during career transitions (Lipshits-Braziler et al., 2018; Saka & Gati, 2007). Facilitating these transitions is an important challenge for career counsellors. The effective use of decision-making and coping skills can help individuals navigate several career transitions over their lifetime (Gati, 2013; Lent & Brown, 2013; Lipshits-Braziler, 2018; Savickas, 2013).

Despite the recent growing interest in career transitions, there is insufficient research into the role of decision-making skills and adaptive coping behaviours during transitional periods. This chapter thus focuses on ways to facilitate individuals' career transitions, using a decision-theory-based viewpoint and a coping perspective. It also discusses the additional value of using assessments of the decision-making process and relying on the PIC (Prescreening, In-depth exploration, and Choice; Gati & Asher, 2001a, 2001b) model of career transitions. This is in line with the career-transition literature (e.g., Anderson et al., 2012; Barclay, 2015), which emphasizes the value of a theoretically-based framework as a guideline for structuring counselling interventions during transition phases.

Understanding Career Transitions

Individuals experience various transitions during their lives. Career transitions are influential events in people's lives as well as an important construct in career research and counselling (Chudzikowski, 2012). A transition can be defined as the internal psychological process individuals experience in adapting to an external change (Barclay, 2015). Transitions require individuals to change their assumptions and perceptions of themselves and the world, as well as their behaviour (Schlossberg, 2011).

Career transitions can be viewed as turning points in the course of one's working life (Sharf, 1997). Whereas many career transitions are fairly predictable, such as the school-to-work transition and retirement, others are situation-dependent and less predictable, such job loss (being fired or laid off), transfer, or demotion/promotion to another job. Transitions can be voluntary (e.g., quitting one job to find another) or involuntary (e.g., being fired due to downsizing; Hopson & Adams, 1977). Schlossberg (1981) also mentioned a non-event "transition"—an event that someone wishes would happen but never occurs (e.g., a promotion that never materializes). One important development in the career-transition literature is coming to view transition as a *process* rather than a single event or non-event (Kim, 2014).

The predictability of some transitions offers an opportunity for preparing individuals to cope with them in advance (Lent, 2013). In contrast, the low predictability and involuntary nature of other transitions explain why individuals might find them more difficult to cope with and experience anxiety, stress, feelings of sadness, loss, and difficulty letting go when going through such changes in their careers (Heppner &

Scott, 2004). A career transition often involves uncertainty and unease, even if it is a planned, positive change (e.g., from college to work; Barclay, 2015). In fact, positive change and growth may also derive from involuntary work changes (Sharf, 1997).

Career transitions have become much more frequent and normative in the modern career context (Chudzikowski, 2012), with its fluid, dynamic employment pattern. With the increasing frequency of career changes and moves, both within and between organizations, career transitions are seen as an adaptive developmental stage (Heppner & Scott, 2004), providing opportunities to develop new skills and competencies and thereby contributing to the person's employability (Chudzikowski, 2012). Regardless of the specific nature of the changes involved, transitions often have detrimental outcomes for the individual (even more than in the past). Viewing transitions as a decision-making process that the individual has to cope with is useful for facilitating them. Learning to cope during periods of transition can help minimize stress and develop self-efficacy and trust in one's ability to thrive.

Coping with Career Transitions

The transition model of Schlossberg (1981) and the transactional model of coping and stress (Lazarus & Folkman, 1984) are useful for understanding career transitions. According to these models, coping processes are central in a transition and include all the approaches individuals use to adjust to the particular set of transition demands. The transition model (Anderson et al., 2012; Schlossberg, 1981) explains the process and outcomes of a transition as the interaction of four sets of factors (the 4 S system): (1) *situation* (e.g., the person's perception of the particular transition), (2) *self* (e.g., the traits and psychological resources of the individual experiencing the transition), (3) *support* (e.g., the availability of various kinds of social support), and (4) *strategies* (e.g., information seeking, direct action, avoidance). Strategies for coping with a transition are a key element of the model, whereas the other three factors maybe seen as facilitating or impeding such coping. According to this model, it is important to discover the repertoire of coping strategies of those in transition. The model is not career-specific; it was developed as a counselling model for adults experiencing critical life events. However, it has been adopted in vocational psychology research and counselling (e.g., Barclay, 2015; Gysbers, Heppner, & Johnston, 2009; Heppner, 1998).

In Lazarus and Folkman's (1984) transactional model of coping and stress, coping is defined as an individual's response to specific external and/or internal demands encountered in stressful situations. In this model, appraisal has an important role in the way a person reacts, feels, and behaves. When faced with a stressor, a person first evaluates the potential threat (i.e., primary appraisal). For example, a career transition can be appraised as a loss, a harmful event, or a challenge. The perception of a threat triggers a secondary appraisal, whose function is to discover the coping options available to deal with it (Lazarus & Folkman, 1984; Skinner, Edge, Altman, & Sherwood, 2003). Situations perceived mainly as threatening prompt particular emotions and coping strategies, such as more anxiety and the greater use of escape, withdrawal, and support-seeking. Situations perceived mainly as challenging prompt different coping strategies, such as problem-solving (Skinner et al., 2003).

Coping strategies have often been described as problem-focused versus emotion-focused (Lazarus & Folkman, 1984), as engagement versus disengagement (Compas, Connor-Smith, Saltzman, Thomsen, & Wadsworth, 2001), as productive versus non-productive, and as support seeking (Frydenberg & Lewis, 1993). In a review of empirical studies of the association between coping and psychological outcomes, Compas et al. (2001) found that engagement (e.g., problem solving, information-seeking, problem-focused support, cognitive restructuring, and positive reappraisal of the stressor) was associated with better psychological adjustment, whereas disengagement (e.g., avoidance, social withdrawal, wishful thinking, and self-blame) was associated with poorer adjustment. However, these findings were not conclusive, as the nature of the adjustment appeared to be associated with the specific stressor. The construct of coping and the relative effectiveness of various coping strategies thus need to be evaluated for specific types of stressor, such as career transition. The use and effectiveness of coping strategies may also depend on the specific type of a career transition (e.g., school-to work, retirement, job loss, voluntary job change).

The Assessment of Coping with Career Transitions

Career assessments play a key role in helping individuals in their career decision-making process, but they need to be integrated into the overall career counselling process and cannot stand alone (Osborn, Finklea, & Belle, 2015). Career counsellors can use various assessments to help clients deal with career transitions. For example the counsellors can suggest that their clients fill out the Career Transitions Inventory (CTI; Heppner, Multon, & Johnston, 1994), which assesses the psychological resources and barriers that can enhance or inhibit career transitions. The CTI consists of five subscales: *readiness* (how motivated the person is to make the transition), *confidence* (one's sense of self-efficacy in being able to make a successful transition), *control* (how strongly one feel one can make one's own decisions), *perceived support* (how much support the person feels they get from friends and family), and *decision independence* (whether the person is making the decision primarily on the basis of their own needs or whether they are considering the needs and desires of others). According to Heppner (1998), the CTI is a tool for self-discovery and exploration, to help set up a dialog between the client and the counsellor. Counsellors can use it to help clients understand the psychological resources and hurdles affecting their ability to make a career transition, to overcome barriers and to maximize the strengths they bring to the transition process.

For individuals coping with a job loss, it could be beneficial to fill out the Coping with Job Loss Scale (CWJLS; Kinicki & Latack, 1990). This measure assesses five coping strategies, three for control-focused coping—*proactive search* (job-search activities), *nonwork organization* (focusing on non-job-search activities, such as saving money and keeping busy), and *positive self-assessment* (favourably evaluating one's skills and abilities)—and two for escape-focused coping: *distancing from job loss* (efforts to avoid the reality of the job loss or escape the situation) and *job devaluation* (reassessing the importance of other aspects of one's life). Interestingly, it was found that escape-focused coping leads to negative employment outcomes, while control-focused coping had no effect on the nature of one's reemployment (Kinicki, Prussia, & McKee-Ryan, 2000).

For young adults in transition from college to work, counsellors could suggest filling out the Strategies for Coping with Career Indecision during the College-to-Work Transition (SCCI-CWT) questionnaire (Lipshits-Braziler et al., 2018). The goal of this measure is to determine the individual's repertoire of coping strategies during the transition. The SCCI-CWT includes 14 strategies that belong to three main coping styles: Productive coping, Support-seeking, and Nonproductive coping.

The *productive coping style* includes six strategies that are postulated to facilitate coping with career indecision during the transition: instrumental information-seeking, emotional information-seeking (efforts to reduce the uncertainty involved in making the decision), systematic problem-solving, flexibility in the decision-making process and willingness to make compromises, accommodation (focusing on the positive aspects of the decision), and self-regulation. The *support-seeking coping style* comprises three strategies: instrumental help-seeking (seeking practical assistance), emotional help-seeking (seeking affective support), and delegation (shifting the responsibility for the decision to others). The *nonproductive coping style* consists of five strategies that are postulated as preventing coping with career indecision during the transition: escape (getting away from making the decision), helplessness (feelings of being unable to do anything to advance the decision), isolation (attempts to conceal difficulties from others and keep the associated worries to oneself), submission (focusing on the adverse features of career decision-making), and opposition (projecting the causes of one's difficulties onto others).

Lipshits-Braziler et al. (2018) found that greater utilization of productive coping strategies (in particular, optimistic and positive thinking about career transitions and self-regulation) was associated with positive career-related outcomes, such as a greater coping efficacy and higher levels of career choice satisfaction one year after graduation, as well as a more advanced career decision status. These results are consistent with the notion suggested by the social-cognitive model of career self-management (Lent & Brown, 2013), which claims that positive decisional outcomes (reduced decisional anxiety and increased decidedness) are consequences of adaptive behaviours; the findings are also consistent with the career construction model (Savickas, 2013), thus underlining the crucial role of available adaptive resources during career transition phases. Indeed, empirical evidence confirms that adaptive strategies help people deal with various types of stress-causing transitions, such as unemployment (Blustein, Kozan, & Connors-Kellgren, 2013) and retirement (Donaldson, Earl, & Muratore, 2010). Surprisingly, strategies such as information-seeking or problem-solving did not emerge as significant predictors of the choice-related outcomes (Lipshits-Braziler et al., 2018). In contrast, using nonproductive coping strategies (such as escape, helplessness, and ruminative thinking) was found to be negatively associated with good outcomes and positively associated with decisional distress (Lipshits-Braziler et al., 2018).

The assessment of clients' coping responses plays a critical role in advancing their self-awareness and self-knowledge and providing guidelines for interventions (Lipshits-Braziler, 2018). Career counsellors could discover a client's profile of coping strategies, which could help them tailor their counselling to that particular client's needs. The CTI, CWJLS, or SCCI-CWTQ could be administered before face-to-face counselling starts or at the very beginning. Administering the assessments before the first session can save in-session time for processing and discussing the results (Gati & Levin, 2015; Osborn et al., 2015). In preparation for the first session, the counsellor could send the clients a link to the online version of the questionnaires, and the results could be retrieved by the counsellor before the first session. Then, prior to or during the session, the counsellor could review the results of the assessments and verify the conclusions that emerged by discussing them with the client. In particular, career counsellors should help their clients gain a positive view about making a career transition and develop and employ adaptive coping strategies. Although many aspects of transitions may be beyond the client's control, individuals can gain some sense of control and move forward by taking charge of strengthening their resources, while acknowledging the aspects that are beyond their control (Peila-Shuster, 2016).

Decision-Making During Career Transitions

In today's world of work, empowering individuals as autonomous decision-makers is essential for successful career development (Gati, Levin, & Landman-Tal, 2019). This often involves helping individuals gain decision-making skills that can facilitate their transition decisions. Career transitions can be approached from a decision-theory aspect, which regards career choices as the outcome of a process. This section shows the importance of designing procedures for making better career-transition decisions throughout individuals' lives and demonstrates how the goal of making satisfying career choices during transitions can be better achieved if a systematic decision-making model is adopted. However, "elaborating career decision-making models to attend to issues of social justice represents the next critical challenge for career development theory and practice" (p. 44, Hartung & Blustein, 2002). Therefore this section also discusses social justice in implementing a decision-making model in career counselling. Social justice is often defined as equal opportunities for all members of society to engage in careers of their choice and reach their potential for satisfaction (Irving, 2005).

The decision-theory approach is applicable in situations with (a) an individual who has to choose a course of action out of a set of alternatives, (b) a set of objectives the individual seeks to achieve, and (c) a set of attributes and factors that the individual must take into account when evaluating and comparing the alternatives (Gati et al., 2019; Saka & Gati, 2007). These general features are present in most career transitions.

Decision theory has been regarded as a frame of reference for career decision-making for over fifty years (e.g., Gelatt, 1962; Katz, 1966). This perspective conceptualizes career choices in terms of the cognitive processes used to locate the career alternatives most compatible with the individual's preferences and capabilities. Career-decision making is a complex task: the number and variety of alternatives is often very large, and many attributes are required for adequately describing the potential alternatives and the individual's characteristics. Therefore, comparing the alternatives and evaluating their compatibility with the individual is a nontrivial task; indeed, many individuals report that they face difficulties in making career decisions (Amir & Gati, 2006; Gati et al., 2019). Social power relations may explicitly or implicitly bias individuals' career aspirations, which may lead to procrastination in career decision-making or to making less –than-optimal career decisions (Levin & Gati, 2015).

Decision-making during career transitions could be conceptualized with the PIC model (Gati & Asher, 2001a, 2001b), which tries to reduce the complexity of career decision-making by dividing the process into three distinct stages: Prescreening, In-depth exploration, and Choice. The PIC model could also be incorporated to address a social justice agenda. Individuals can begin the process at any of the stages of the model, according to their progress and status in the process. The model promotes a flexible decision process and encourages moving back and forth between stages to reflect on and update previous decisions. Research supporting the PIC model has been reviewed by Gati and his colleagues (Gati, 2013; Gati & Asher, 2001a; Gati & Levin, 2015; Gati et al., 2019).

Prescreening the Potential Alternatives

The goal of the prescreening stage is to deal with the overload of information in career decision making by helping the individual focus on the most relevant information. In certain career transitions the number of alternatives is small—for example, when the individual is working, without specific complains, but a friend tells her or him about a new job opening. In such cases she or he can skip prescreening and jump directly to the In-depth exploration stage. In other cases, however, when the number of alternatives to choose from is large (e.g., for a recent law school graduate), the first stage is to reduce the number of potential alternatives and find a manageable set of promising ones that deserve in-depth exploration. The method proposed for this process is *sequential elimination* (Gati, 1986; Gati & Asher, 2001a) using a wide variety of career-related aspects. The term *career-related aspects* (Gati, 1998 Gati & Gutentag, 2015) refers to all the relevant variables that can be used to describe both individuals (e.g., personal abilities, vocational interests, constraints such as disabilities) and career alternatives (e.g., income, length of training, flexibility of working hours, professional advancement). Such aspects are broader than vocational interests, and research has demonstrated that people tend to consider and compare career alternatives in terms of these aspects rather than only in terms of vocational interests

(Gati, 1998). This is done by focusing on one aspect at a time, beginning with the most important one, and comparing the individual's preferences in that aspect (e.g., not more an hour of travel to work) with the respective characteristics of the available jobs. Jobs that do not fit the individual's preferences in that aspect are eliminated. This process continues with the other aspects the individual considers relevant, in the order of their importance, until the number of remaining options is small and thus manageable (Gati, Kleiman, Saka, & Zakai, 2003). This method has many advantages. For example, Gadassi and Gati (2009) found that using career-aspect-based preferences and a sequential elimination model for prescreening can reduce gender bias in occupational choices.

One of the major challenges of career counselling is to help clients define their own preferences (Osipow, 1999). Unlike occupational information, which can be obtained by exploring the environment or from various occupational informational databases, clarifying one's career-related preferences requires intensive introspection, and rarely do individuals begin their career decision-making with a set of well-defined preferences (Gati et al., 2019). Biases can impact individuals' perceptions of the world of work as well as of their own preferences and abilities (Levin & Gati, 2015). Social stigmas and biases are among the influences of one's broader social setting are, and they can be a source of perceived and actual social constraints on an individual's career choice. Therefore, career counsellors need to understand the broader societal context in which clients' careers develop (Furbish, 2015) and their career preferences are shaped.

The sequential elimination model distinguishes among three facets of the individual's preferences: (a) the *importance* of the aspect (e.g., "likelihood of professional advancement"), (b) the level regarded as *optimal* (e.g., "very high"), and (c) additional, less desirable but still *acceptable* level(s), which represent the individual's willingness to compromise (e.g., "high" and "moderate").

Career alternatives are judged according to the individual's preferences in those career aspects that are the most important to the individual. This process is carried out, aspect by aspect, in the order of their relative importance to the individual. For each aspect, alternatives that are incompatible with the individual's preferences are eliminated. This sequential elimination process stops when the number of promising alternatives compatible with the individual's preferences is small. Thus, the outcome of the prescreening stage is a short list of promising alternatives worth further, in-depth exploration.

Stable preferences are essential for advancing in career decision-making (Gati & Gutentag, 2015), especially during the prescreening stage. Indeed, Gati and Gutentag (2015) found that young adults' aspect-based career preferences are quite stable over an interval of two years. Having cohesive—well-defined and focused—career preferences is an additional factor that leads to effective and efficient prescreening (Shimoni, Gutentag, & Gati, 2019). Cohesive career preferences are *differentiated*, *consistent*, and *coherent* (Gati & Ram, 2000). Differentiation refers to how much the individual's preferences differ in the various factors or aspects that are used to compare and evaluate the alternatives (i.e., their relative importance, the most preferred level, and the individual's willingness to compromise on particular aspects).

Consistency is the degree of similarity in an individual's pattern of preferences for related factors or aspects –aspects that frequently co-occur and co-vary in occupations and people's preferences (e.g., income and prestige or using analytical ability and length of training; Gati, Fassa, & Mayer, 1998). Coherence of preferences refers to how much the individual's preference pattern makes sense—with less willingness to compromise on more important aspects, a more extreme optimal level (e.g., "only teamwork") for the more important aspects and a less extreme one for the less important aspects.

Shimoni et al. (2019) operationalized these three aspect-based career preference cohesiveness indices—preference differentiation, consistency, and coherence—and an overall index for assessing preference cohesiveness, and tested them using the preferences of young adults deliberating about their future career. They found that those with greater career preference cohesiveness were more advanced in their career decision making process. Finally, they tested and found support for the two-week reliability and the two-year stability of career-preference cohesiveness.

To increase individuals' awareness of their aspect-related career preferences, counsellors can recommend that their clients fill out the *Career Preferences Questionnaire* (CPQ), embedded in a free, anonymous, self-help website aimed at helping people make better career decisions (www.CDDQ.org; for the English version see http://kivunim.huji.ac.il/eng-quest/pce.html retrieved May 27, 2019). The CPQ includes 31 aspects (or factors) considered relevant by many deliberating individuals and regarded as important by career counselling experts for distinguishing among occupations (Gati, 1998). The individuals are asked to report their preferences in each aspect. They are first asked to mark their most desirable (i.e., optimal) level (out of 5); for example, "only teamwork" (level 5). They then are asked to indicate additional acceptable level(s), for example "mainly teamwork" (level 4), reflecting their willingness to compromise. Finally, they are asked to rate the importance of each of the 31 aspects on a 7-point scale (1—*not important at all* to 7—*very important*). At the end, individuals received computerized personal feedback about their level of preference cohesiveness.

Clients can fill out the *CPQ* during the counselling session, or do this online before the session and send a copy of the results to their counsellor. Using online assessments during counselling also gives clients a contributory role and helps make them active partners (Gati & Asulin-Peretz, 2011). During the session the counsellor should review the results obtained from the *CPQ* and discuss the conclusions with the client. If the client's preferences are not cohesive, the counsellor should help the client explore and clarify his or her preferences. If the client's preferences are actually cohesive but he or she feels they are not, the counsellor should discuss this difference with the client. In addition, counsellors should be aware of clients' biased career preferences that may prevent them from choosing the career path best suited for them and reflect them to the clients. Counsellors could be advised to foster a critical consciousness in their clients, defined as critical reflection on systemic inequities combined with a commitment to address perceived injustices (Diemer, McWhirter, Ozer, & Rapa, 2015). When people are aware of the sociopolitical situation around them, it can become a catalyst for attaining critical consciousness, which opens the client to learning the skills of self-advocacy (Ibrahim & Heuer, 2016).

Counsellors should also recognize their own cultural and social identity, values, and worldview. Such recognition and self-reflection could help them provide ethically sound, culturally responsive, and social justice-oriented service for clients (Ibrahim & Heuer, 2016).

In-Depth Exploration of Promising Alternatives

The goal of the second stage of the PIC model is to pinpoint a few alternatives that are suitable for the individual in two ways: first, that the individual meets the job's requirements and, second, that the alternative fits the individual's preferences (Gati & Asher, 2001a). At this stage individuals can explore the jobs that were found promising during *prescreening*, focusing on one at a time, and collect more comprehensive information about each one.

The first fact that is important to verify is that the individual's previous training, expertise, and experience indeed match those of the job, including other specific requirements. The second fact to be verified is that the attributes of the alternative (e.g., a potential next job) indeed match the individual's preferences (e.g., less than an hour of commuting, salary above a certain amount). The desired outcome of this stage is a short list of suitable jobs.

Choice: Locating the Most Suitable Alternative

The in-depth exploration stage usually results in more than one alternative, so a third stage is required for identifying the most desirable job. It is important to be aware of the uncertainty involved in actualising the most preferred job (e.g., because the employer may prefer another applicant). It is therefore highly recommended that the individual finish the decision process by rank-ordering the suitable alternatives, so as to have a fall-back plan if obstacles emerge in actualising the most suitable one.

The choice stage involves a systematic comparison among the small number of alternatives under consideration, focusing on both the differences among them and the trade-offs between the advantages and disadvantages of each one (i.e., the compensation principle). One way to do this is by carrying out a systematic evaluation and comparison process, using a multi-attribute, comparison-based compensatory model, in which the gap between the individual's aspect-based preferences and the attributes of a particular job in the aspects used in the comparison is weighted by the relative importance of each aspect. The overall score of an alternative is the across-aspects sum of the products of the degree of fit between the individual's preferences and the attributes of the job, weighted by the aspect's importance.

To help individuals systematically compare the small number of alternatives on their short list, *Comparing and Choosing* (*C&C*), a decision-support module, was developed and embedded in a free self-help website that provides guidance designed to assist deliberating individuals in making better career decisions (www.cddq.org). C&C is an elaborated, refined, and upgraded version of Katz's (1966) decision table, guiding the deliberating individual through a structured sequence of steps. It guides them to perform a systematic comparison among a small set of career alternatives (2–4) to find the one that best fits the individual's preferred career description (for the English version see www.cddq.org/choice, retrieved May 27, 2019). Individuals are asked first to list the 2–4 career alternatives (majors, jobs, and the like) among which they are deliberating, and, if they are willing and able to do so—indicate the alternative that intuitively seems most suitable. They are then asked to list 3–12 factors, attributes, or aspects that are important to them for comparing the alternatives (an optional link to a list of 31 aspects considered relevant for comparing career options is given). Next, the individuals are asked to rate the relative importance of the attributes or aspects by assigning a number (weight) to each aspect, so that the total of the weights adds up to 100. They are then asked to report their optimal level for each aspect (e.g., to mark "only 4 years" for "length of training"). The participants are then asked to rate how well each career alternative is compatible with the level they reported as optimal for each aspect, using a five-point scale (varying from 0—*the alternative does not fit my preference in that aspect at all* to 4—*the alternative perfectly fits my optimal level in that aspect*). Next, the individuals are presented with the computed overall utility of each alternative (with a higher number indicating a better fit with their preferences). This number is the sum of the product of the relative importance of each aspect and its fit score (0–4), so that it can vary from 0 to 400. Finally, if the alternative selected intuitively as best is not the same as the one that emerged as best in the C&C, the individual will be asked to try and explain this inconsistency in their own words in an open text box. They will then be presented with the final summary of the whole procedure and the feedback. The outcome is an overall estimate of the utility of choosing each alternative, which reflects the degree of fit between the individual's preferences and his or her perception of the alternatives.

If it is reasonably probable that the alternative that emerged as best can be actualised, and the individual feels confident in this choice, then the process ends. If it is less probable that the most preferred alternative can be actualised, then the individual should also consider a second- or even third-best option. If the individual is not confident in choosing the option that emerged as best, he or she should go back to the in-depth exploration stage and collect additional relevant information. The outcome of the choice stage is the identification of the best alternative, or a rank-order of the best alternatives. In this way the C&C module can facilitate the transitions between a current job and a promising alternative or among several potential jobs, by helping compare and evaluate them systematically, and then comparing the outcome of the systematic comparison with the individual's intuition.

The PIC stages are the same for various career transitions, but there could be differences in the number of the promising alternatives at the end of Prescreening, the importance of certain career-aspects, and the time available for making a decision. For example, after an involuntary job loss, the individual's overall willingness to compromise by considering a larger range of acceptable levels within aspects may be greater. However, the aspect of economic security may be given greater importance, and the individual's willingness to compromise in this aspect may be less. If the individual feels a sense of urgency in finding an alternative job, his or her willingness to compromise may be greater. For a voluntary job change, when one of the alternatives is to stay on at the current job, the In-depth Exploration stage should focus on the distinctive differences between the current job and the alternatives.

Using Decision-Making and Coping Models in Career Counselling

Successfully managing and facilitating transitions is particularly important when considering today's world of work and the vast changes that have occurred in a fairly short time (Peila-Shuster, 2016), such as globalization, fast technological advancement, and changing organizational structures (Hirschi, 2018). In recent discussions of counselling for transitions (Anderson et al., 2012; Barclay, 2015) it has been emphasised that counselling for individuals who are undergoing career transitions should be structured around a theoretical framework. We propose integrating the principles of Schlossberg's Transition Model (2011) and Lazarus and Folkman's (1984) Transactional Coping Model with the PIC model (Gati & Asher, 2001a, 2001b) in career transition counselling.

According to the Transition and Transactional Coping Models, career counsellors should focus on understanding and assessing (a) how much clients are preoccupied with a specific career transition; (b) whether the timing of the transition is considered good or bad; (c) whether the transition is viewed as temporary or permanent; (d) how stressful this transition is for the client; (e) whether the client has a sense of control over the transition; (f) what coping resources are available; and (g) how clients organize their repertoire of coping responses. Assisting career clients in developing positive attitudes towards career transitions and making continual adjustments to ever-changing work environments are essential goals in career counselling (Stoltz & Young, 2012). Career counselling interventions that attempt to develop individual's coping skills should teach positive cognitive appraisal; that is, how to view career transitions as challenging rather than threatening. During the sessions counsellors should ask their clients how stressful they find the current career transition. Individuals with a high level of distress could benefit from discussions about its underlying causes and from learning the techniques for positive reappraisal and reinterpretation of career transitions in terms of challenge and mastery.

Moreover, it is important to pinpoint and deal with clients' dysfunctional beliefs about career decision-making during transitions. For example, a belief about the *criticality* of the decision, where the client views a career choice as a once-in-a-lifetime decision, it is more likely to prolong the process in an attempt to avoid making the wrong choice (Hechtlinger, Levin, & Gati, 2017). Another example of a dysfunctional belief is the *role of chance or fate* (Hechtlinger et al., 2017), where the client believes that chance or fate determines their career path and thus has no incentive to invest time and effort in the career decision-making process. Career counselors consider dysfunctional beliefs among the most severe career decision-making difficulties clients face and give them high priority in treatment (Gati, Amir, & Landman, 2010). However, young adults have less awareness of their dysfunctional beliefs than of other difficulties involved in career decision-making (Amir & Gati, 2006). Hence, eliciting clients' dysfunctional beliefs involving career decision making, helping them recognize that such beliefs are dysfunctional, and then challenging them are essential components of career counselling.

It is also important to train clients in career coping skills (both reducing nonproductive coping strategies and embracing productive ones). Career counsellors should also be aware of their own experience in coping with transitions (Sharf, 1997), and remember that individuals experience transitions differently. Career counsellors have a significant impact on the lives of their clients and therefore can and should use their influence to attempt to minimize social inequality (Levin & Gati, 2015). Career counsellors should be aware of their clients biased career preferences, and discuss these issues with them.

Career decision making is often defined as an ambiguous process due to the lack of clear criteria for optimal career choice, the lack of valid information, and the inconsistency in the process (Xu & Tracey, 2014). Individuals might lack motivation to initiate the career decision-making process if they find ambiguity anxiety-provoking (Xu & Tracey, 2017). Individuals who are tolerant with the inevitable ambiguity in making career decisions are less likely to have distorted career beliefs and get stuck in the outcome optimization process (Xu & Tracey, 2014). Ambivalence (i.e., holding two contrary positions) frequently occurs during career transitions—for example, simultaneously holding positive and negative attitudes toward the career change (Stoltz & Young, 2012). Motivation is a key component in the success of career transitions (Rochat, 2018), and Motivational Interviewing (MI) works directly to help clients resolve ambivalence and promote growth (Rochat, 2018; Stoltz & Young, 2012). MI is a client-centered method that aims at enhancing individuals' motivation and commitment to change by exploring and resolving ambivalence through eliciting and exploring their own motives to change (Miller & Rollnick, 2013). With this method, the counselor's role is not that of an expert but of a facilitator for the client in the process of coping and decision-making under ambivalence (Rochat, 2018). The key components of the MI are collaboration, acceptance, and empathy (see Rochat, 2018, and Stoltz & Young, 2012, for the application of various MI techniques to career counselling).

The *PIC* model can also reduce ambiguity and facilitate decisions during career transitions. The advantage of this model is that it divides the complex decision-making task into simple, sequential stages, taking into account people's limited information-processing capabilities (Gati & Asher, 2001a, 2001b; Gati & Tal, 2008; Saka & Gati, 2007). Interventions based on the *PIC* model have demonstrated their effectiveness in decreasing individuals' career decision-making difficulties (Gati, Saka, & Krausz, 2001), helping them advancing towards making a decision (Gati et al., 2003), and increasing the probability of greater occupational choice satisfaction six years afterwards (Gati, Gadassi, & Shemesh, 2006).

The role of career counsellors includes guiding clients through the stages of the decision-making process during career transitions, encouraging them to play an active and dominant role in each stage (Gati & Tal, 2008). During prescreening, career counsellors should help clients explicate their preferences (and their willingness to compromise, if needed), and attend to actual or perceived constraints. One role of career counsellors is encouraging their clients not to give up career alternatives due to socially constructed barriers (Levin & Gati, 2015). Social justice counselling includes understanding clients' cultural strengths, along with socially imposed challenges, and focusing on developing strengths, empowerment, and advocacy (Ibrahim & Heuer, 2016). The assessment of clients' preference cohesiveness can help career counsellors identify those in need of clarifying what they are looking for in their career (Shimoni et al., 2019).

During in-depth exploration, counsellors should direct clients to relevant sources of information, highlighting the quality of various sources in terms of accuracy and biases. During the choice stage counsellors can assist clients through the complex task of evaluating the suitable alternatives (Gati & Tal, 2008). Finally, counsellors can guide clients in exploring ways of increasing the likelihood of actualizing their most preferred alternative. The *PIC* model can serve as a framework for a dynamic counsellor-client dialogue as well as for monitoring the client's advancement in the process.

Future research should focus on studying the applicability of the PIC model among different ethnic and cultural groups, thus making it possible to investigate the influence of perceived or actual barriers that might limit various groups' range of considered career alternatives. Future research should also explore the associations between aspect-based career preference cohesiveness and work volition among disadvantaged groups. Future research should also try to discover the factors contributing to the cohesiveness of career preferences among different marginalized groups (on the basis of gender, ethnicity, age, disability, etc.) so as to promote social justice.

Conclusion

Decision-making and coping are important constructs in the Career Construction Theory of Adaptation (Savickas, 2013) and the Social Cognitive Model of Career Self-Management (Lent & Brown, 2013). Despite the recent growing interest in career transitions, there is insufficient research into the role of decision-making skills and adaptive coping activities during transition periods. This chapter has focused on ways of facilitating individuals' career transitions, using a decision-theory-based viewpoint and coping perspective. Based on these two theoretical frameworks, career counsellors can facilitate their clients' career transition by (a) addressing the difficulties and the distress involved in the transition; (b) reframing career transition as a positive challenge; (c) assessing individuals' career decision-making process; (d) instructing clients about how to make better career decisions; (e) enhancing the decision-making and coping skills required for an adaptive transition; and (f) guiding the individual through the process.

References

Amir, T., & Gati, I. (2006). Facets of career decision-making difficulties. *British Journal of Guidance and Counselling, 34,* 483–503. https://doi.org/10.1080/03069880600942608.

Anderson, M. L., Goodman, J., & Schlossberg, N. K. (2012). *Counseling adults in transition: Linking Schlossberg's theory with practice in a diverse world*. New York, NY: Springer.

Arthur, M. B., & Rousseau, D. M. (1996). *The boundaryless career: A new employment principle for a new organizational era*. Oxford, UK: Oxford University Press.

Barclay, S. R. (2015). Turning transition into triumph: Applying Schlossberg's transition model to career transition. In K. Maree & A. Di Fabio (Eds.), *Exploring new horizons in career counseling: Turning challenges into opportunities* (pp. 219–232). Rotterdam, The Netherlands: Sense Publishers.

Blustein, D. L., Kozan, S., & Connors-Kellgren, A. (2013). Unemployment and underemployment: A narrative analysis about loss. *Journal of Vocational Behavior, 82,* 256–265. https://doi.org/10.1016/j.jvb.2013.02.00.

Chudzikowski, K. (2012). Career transitions and career success in the new career era. *Journal of Vocational Behavior, 81,* 298–306. https://doi.org/10.1016/j.jvb.2011.10.005.

Compas, B. E., Connor-Smith, J. K., Saltzman, H., Thomsen, A. H., & Wadsworth, M. E. (2001). Coping with stress during childhood and adolescence: Problems, progress, and potential in theory and research. *Psychological Bulletin, 127,* 87–127. https://doi.org/10.1037/0033-2909.127.1.87.

Diemer, M. A., McWhirter, E., Ozer, E., & Rapa, L. J. (2015). Advances in the conceptualization and measurement of critical consciousness. *Urban Review, 47,* 809–823. https://doi.org/10.1007/s11256-015-0336-7.

Donaldson, T., Earl, J. K., & Muratore, A. M. (2010). Extending the integrated model of retirement adjustment: Incorporating mastery and retirement planning. *Journal of Vocational Behavior, 77,* 279–289. https://doi.org/10.1016/j.jvb.2010.03.003.

Frydenberg, E., & Lewis, R. (1993). *Adolescent coping scale*. Melbourne: Australian Council for Educational Research.

Furbish, D. S. (2015). Social justice: A seminal and enduring career counselling ideal. In K. Maree & A. Di Fabio (Eds.), *Exploring new horizons in career counseling: Turning challenges into opportunities* (pp. 281–296). Rotterdam, The Netherlands: Sense Publishers.

Gadassi, R., & Gati, I. (2009). The effect of gender stereotypes on explicit and implicit career preferences. *The Counseling Psychologist, 37,* 902–922. https://doi.org/10.1177/0011000009334093.

Gati, I. (1986). Making career decisions: A sequential elimination approach. *Journal of Counseling Psychology, 33,* 408–417. https://doi.org/10.1037/0022-0167.33.4.408.

Gati, I. (1998). Using career-related aspects to elicit preferences and characterize occupations for a better person-environment fit. *Journal of Vocational Behavior, 52,* 343–356. https://doi.org/10.1006/jvbe.1997.1623.

Gati, I. (2013). Advances in career decision making. In B. W. Walsh, M. L. Savickas, & P. J. Hartung (Eds.), *Handbook of vocational psychology* (pp. 183–215). New York, NY: Routledge.

Gati, I., Amir, T., & Landman, S. (2010). Career counsellors' perceptions of the severity of career decision-making difficulties. *British Journal of Guidance and Counselling, 38,* 393–408. https://doi.org/10.1080/03069885.2010.503700.

Gati, I., & Asher, I. (2001a). The PIC model for career decision making: Prescreening, in-depth exploration, and choice. In F. T. L. Leong & A. Barak (Eds.), *Contemporary models in vocational psychology* (pp. 7–54). Mahwah, NJ: Erlbaum.

Gati, I., & Asher, I. (2001b). Prescreening, in-depth exploration, and choice: From decision theory to career counseling practice. *Career Development Quarterly, 50,* 140–157.

Gati, I., & Asulin-Peretz, L. (2011). Internet-based self-help career assessments and interventions: Challenges and implications for evidence-based career counseling. *Journal of Career Assessment, 19,* 259–279. https://doi.org/10.1177/1069072710395533.

Gati, I., Fassa, N., & Mayer, Y. (1998). An aspect-based approach to person-environment fit: A comparison between the aspect structure derived from characteristics of occupations and that derived from counselees' preferences. *Journal of Vocational Behavior, 53,* 38–43. https://doi.org/10.1006/jvbe.1997.1609.

Gati, I., Gadassi, R., & Shemesh, N. (2006). The predictive validity of a computer-assisted career decision-making system: A six-year follow-up. *Journal of Vocational Behavior, 68,* 205–219. https://doi.org/10.1016/j.jvb.2005.08.002.

Gati, I., & Gutentag, T. (2015). The stability of aspect-based career preferences and of the recommended list of occupations derived from them. *Journal of Vocational Behavior, 87,* 11–21. https://doi.org/10.1016/j.jvb.2014.11.009.

Gati, I., Kleiman, T., Saka, N., & Zakai, A. (2003). Perceived benefits of using an internet-based interactive career planning system. *Journal of Vocational Behavior, 62,* 272–286. https://doi.org/10.1016/s0001-8791(02)00049-0.

Gati, I., Levin, N., & Landman-Tal, S. (2019). Decision-making models and career guidance. In J. A. Athanasou & H. N. Perera (Eds.), *International handbook of career guidance* (2nd ed.). Cham, Switzerland: Springer.

Gati, I., & Levin, N. (2015). Making better career decision. In P. J. Hartung, M. L. Savickas, & B. W. Walsh (Editors-in-Chief), *Handbook of career intervention: Vol. 2. Applications* (pp. 193–207). Washington, DC: American Psychological Association.

Gati, I., & Ram, G. (2000). Counselors' judgments of the quality of the prescreening stage of the career decision-making process. *Journal of Counseling Psychology, 47,* 414–428. https://doi.org/10.1037/0022-0167.47.4.414.

Gati, I., Saka, N., & Krausz, M. (2001). "Should I use a computer-assisted career guidance system?" It depends on where your career decision-making difficulties lie. *British Journal of Guidance and Counselling, 29,* 301–321. https://doi.org/10.1080/03069880124945.

Gati, I., & Tal, S. (2008). Prescreening, In-depth exploration, and Choice—The PIC model. In F T. L. Leong, B. W. Walsh, & P. J. Hartung (Eds.), *Encyclopedia of psychology, volume 4: Career counseling* (pp. 1605–1608). Thousand Oaks, CA: Sage.

Gelatt, H. B. (1962). Decision-making: A conceptual frame of reference for counseling. *Journal of Counseling Psychology, 9,* 240–245. https://doi.org/10.1037/h0046720.

Gysbers, N. C., Heppner, M. J., & Johnston, J. A. (2009). *Career counseling: Contexts, processes, and techniques*. Alexandria, VA: American Counseling Association.

Hall, D. T. (2004). The protean career: A quarter-century journey. *Journal of Vocational Behavior, 65,* 1–13. https://doi.org/10.1016/j.jvb.2003.10.006.

Hartung, P. J., & Blustein, D. L. (2002). Reason, intuition, and social justice: Elaborating on Parson s career decision-making model. *Journal of Counseling and Development, 80,* 41–47. https://doi.org/10.1002/j.1556-6678.2002.tb00164.x.

Heppner, M. J. (1998). The career transitions inventory: Measuring internal resources in adulthood. *Journal of Career Assessment, 6,* 135–145. https://doi.org/10.1177/106907279800600202.

Heppner, M. J., Multon, K. D., & Johnston, J. A. (1994). Assessing psychological resources during career transition: Development of the career transitions inventory. *Journal of Vocational Behavior, 44,* 55–74. https://doi.org/10.1006/jvbe.1994.1004.

Heppner, J. M., & Scott, A. B. (2004). Career transition. In J. H. Greenhaus & G. A. Callanan (Eds.), *Encyclopedia of career development* (pp. 156–158). Thousand Oaks, CA: Sage.
Hechtlinger, S., Levin, N., & Gati, I. (2017). Dysfunctional career decision-making beliefs: A multidimensional model and measure. *Journal of Career Assessment*. Advance online publication. https://doi.org/10.1177/1069072717748677.
Hirschi, A. (2018). The fourth industrial revolution: Issues and implications for career research and practice. *The Career Development Quarterly, 66*, 192–204. https://doi.org/10.1002/cdq.12142
Hopson, B., & Adams, J. D. (1977). Towards an understanding of transitions. In J. Adams, J. Hayes, & B. Hopson (Eds.), *Transition: Understanding and managing personal change* (pp. 1–19). Montclair, NJ: Allenheld & Osmun.
Ibrahim, F. A., & Heuer, J. R. (2016). *Cultural and social justice counselling: Client-specific interventions*. Cham, Switzerland: Springer International Publishing.
Irving, B. (2005). Social justice: A context for career education and guidance. In B. Irving & B. Malik (Eds.), *Critical reflections on career education and guidance* (pp. 10–24). Abingdon, UK: Routledge-Falmer.
Katz, M. R. (1966). A model of guidance for career decision making. *Vocational Guidance Quarterly, 15*, 2–10. https://doi.org/10.1002/j.2164-585x.1966.tb01148.x.
Kim, S. J. (2014). The career transition process: A qualitative exploration of Korean middle-aged workers in postretirement employment. *Adult Education Quarterly, 64*, 3–19. https://doi.org/10.1177/0741713613513491.
Kinicki, A. J., & Latack, J. C. (1990). Explication of the construct of coping with involuntary job loss. *Journal of Vocational Behavior, 36*, 339–360. https://doi.org/10.1016/0001-8791(90)90036-2.
Kinicki, A. J., Prussia, G. E., & McKee-Ryan, F. M. (2000). A panel study of coping with involuntary job loss. *Academy of Management Journal, 43*, 90–100. https://doi.org/10.2307/1556388.
Lazarus, R. S., & Folkman, S. (1984). *Stress, appraisal, and coping*. New York, NY: Springer.
Lent, R. W. (2013). Career-life preparedness: Revisiting career planning and adjustment in the new workplace. *The Career Development Quarterly, 61*, 2–14. https://doi.org/10.1002/j.2161-0045.2013.00031.x.
Lent, R. W., & Brown, S. D. (2013). Social cognitive model of career self-management: Toward a unifying view of adaptive career behavior across the life span. *Journal of Counseling Psychology, 60*, 557–568. https://doi.org/10.1037/a0033446.
Levin, N., & Gati, I. (2014). Facilitating the transition from school to work with a career decision-making approach: Process-related assessments and the PIC model. *Career Planning and Adult Development Journal, 30*, 127–143.
Levin, N., & Gati, I. (2015). Imagined and unconscious career barriers: A challenge for career decision making in the 21th century. In K. Maree & A. Di Fabio (Eds.), *Exploring new horizons in career counselling: Converting challenges into opportunities* (pp. 167–188). Rotterdam, The Netherlands: Sense Publishers.
Lipshits-Braziler, Y., Braunstein-Bercovitz, H., & Kapach-Royf, N. (2018). Strategies for coping with career indecision during the college-to-work transition: Concurrent and predictive validity. *Journal of Career Assessment*. Advance online publication. https://doi.org/10.1177/1069072718759983.
Lipshits-Braziler, Y. (2018). Coping with career indecision among young adults: Implications for career counseling. In V. Cohen-Scali, J. Rossier, & L. Nota (Eds.), *New perspectives on career counseling and guidance in Europe* (pp. 71–85). Cham, Switzerland: Springer International Publishing.
Miller, W. R., & Rollnick, S. (2013). *Motivational interviewing: Helping people change* (3rd ed.). New York, NY: Guilford Press.
Osborn, D., Finklea, J. T., & Belle, J. G. (2015). Integrating assessments into the career decision-making conversation. *Career Planning and Adult Development Journal, 30*, 144–155.
Osipow, S. H. (1999). Assessing career indecision. *Journal of Vocational Behavior, 55*, 147–154.

Peila-Shuster, J. J. (2016). Supporting student transitions: Integrating life design, career construction, happenstance, and hope. *South African Journal of Higher Education, 30*, 54–67. https://doi.org/10.20853/30-3-633.

Rochat, S. (2018). Examining motivational interviewing in career counselling from a motivational system theory perspective. *British Journal of Guidance & Counselling, 46*, 632–643, https://doi.org/10.1080/03069885.2018.1483005.

Saka, N., & Gati, I. (2007). Applying decision theory to facilitating adolescent career choices. In V. B. Skorikov & W. Patton (Eds.), *Career development in childhood and adolescence* (pp. 181–202). Rotterdam, the Netherlands: Sense Publishers.

Savickas, M. L. (2013). Career construction theory and practice. In S. D. Brown & R. W. Lent (Eds.), *Career development and counseling: Putting theory and research to work* (2nd ed., pp. 147–183). Hoboken, NJ: Wiley.

Schlossberg, N. K. (1981). A model for analyzing human adaptation to transition. *Counseling Psychologist, 9,* 2–18. https://doi.org/10.1177/001100008100900202.

Schlossberg, N. K. (2011). The challenge of change: The transition model and its applications. *Journal of Employment Counseling, 48,* 159–162. https://doi.org/10.1002/j.2161-1920.2011.tb01102.x.

Schwab, K. (2016). *The fourth industrial revolution*. New York, NY: Crown Business.

Sharf, R. S. (1997). *Applying career development theory to counseling* (pp. 237–259). Pacific Grove, CA: Brooks Cole.

Shimoni, A., Gutentag, T., & Gati, I. (2019). Assessing career preference cohesiveness. *Journal of Vocational Behavior, 112,* 51–63. https://doi.org/10.1016/j.jvb.2018.12.006.

Skinner, E. A., Edge, K., Altman, J., & Sherwood, H. (2003). Searching for the structure of coping: A review and critique of category systems for classifying ways of coping. *Psychological Bulletin, 129,* 216–269. https://doi.org/10.1037/0033-2909.129.2.216.

Stoltz, K. B., & Young, T. L. (2012). Applications of motivational interviewing in career counseling: Facilitating career transition. *Journal of Career Development, 40,* 329–346. https://doi.org/10.1177/0894845312455508.

Xu, H., & Tracey, T. J. G. (2014). The role of ambiguity tolerance in career decision making. *Journal of Vocational Behavior, 85*, 18–26. https://doi.org/10.1016/j.jvb.2014.04.001.

Xu, H., & Tracey, T. J. G. (2017). The reciprocal dynamic model of career decision ambiguity tolerance with career indecision: A longitudinal three-wave investigation. *Journal of Counseling Psychology, 64,* 538–549. https://doi.org/10.1037/cou0000220.

School to Work Transition of Non-college Bound Youth: An Integration of the Life Design Paradigm and the Psychology of Working Theory

Mary Beth Medvide, Saliha Kozan, David L. Blustein and Maureen E. Kenny

Abstract Young people, particularly those without a post-secondary education and marketable skills, encounter significant obstacles in their transition to the workforce. In an unstable world of work, it is crucial to provide youth with adequate vocational skills and adaptive psychosocial attributes (such as critical consciousness) to help them obtain decent work and adapt to the ever-changing work conditions while confronting the social injustices that impact their lives. In this chapter, we present an integrated framework for development of school-to-work transition programs based upon promising scholarship from the life design paradigm and the Psychology of Working Theory. We hope that the interventions built on this theoretical integration will inform more effective and humane educational, vocational, and public policies designed to foster access to decent and fulfilling work.

Keywords School to work transition · Life design · Psychology of working · Decent work

Introduction

The experience of working has changed significantly since scholars such as Super (1990) and Holland (1997) proposed how people find meaning in their work lives. Individuals now face uncertain economic futures and precarious work conditions (Blustein, Kenny, Di Fabio, & Guichard, 2019). In today's rapidly changing labor market and global economy, it is vital for workers to have flexible skill sets that equip them to adapt to technological advances and the growing competition for stable work. For workers with limited skills and no experience in post-secondary education, the experience of work is often unfulfilling, isolating, and demeaning (Blustein, Olle, Connors-Kellgren, & Diamonti, 2016). For this reason, programs that help young

M. B. Medvide (✉)
Suffolk University, 73 Tremont Street, Boston, MA 02108, USA
e-mail: mmedvide@suffolk.edu

S. Kozan · D. L. Blustein · M. E. Kenny
Boston College, 140 Commonwealth Avenue, Chestnut Hill, MA 02467, USA

J. G. Maree (ed.), *Handbook of Innovative Career Counselling*,
https://doi.org/10.1007/978-3-030-22799-9_10

people are necessary if they are to successfully transition from schools into the workforce.

Youth without higher education are at a significant disadvantage financially during their working lives and usually earn substantially less than peers with a post-secondary education (International Labor Organization [ILO], 2015). Moreover, unemployment among young people is a major global issue, and it is more pronounced for those youth without training and education that extends beyond secondary education (ILO, 2017). Considering this marked differential in earning potential across the lifespan, school-to-work transition programs, designed to prepare youth from disadvantaged communities for the transition directly into the workforce have the potential to assuage disparities and create a foundation for a meaningful work life in a changing labor market (Akkermans, Nykänen, & Vuori, 2015; Masdonati & Fournier, 2015).

School-to-work transition programs are especially important at a time when the deterioration of decent work is leading to an increasingly unstable and precarious workplace for young people entering the workforce (Blustein, in press; Blustein, Kenny, & Kozan, 2014). Decent work involves physically and psychologically safe work environments; access to adequate healthcare; fair and sufficient financial compensation; adequate rest and free time; and organizational values that complement one's family and social values (Duffy, Blustein, Diemer, & Autin, 2016). School-to-work transition programs need to reflect the changing economic and social conditions in which young people are constructing their identities and provide youth with the skills to adapt to a changing world of work (Masdonati & Fournier, 2015). While the school-to-work transition programs of the 20th century did well in helping many young people to learn about careers and develop goals for their initial employment upon graduation (Haase, Heckhausen, & Köller, 2008), these programs no longer reflect the nature of work young people are likely to encounter upon graduation. Accordingly, it is now important to identify the theoretical frameworks that can serve as a foundation for designing programs to prepare youth for social and economic challenges within workplaces and societies that are in flux (Akkermans et al., 2015).

Within the following sections, we first describe the current world of work for youth. Next, we provide an overview of the school-to-work transition literature. Finally, incorporating the life design paradigm (Savickas et al., 2009) and the Psychology of Working Theory (PWT; Blustein, 2006; Blustein et al., 2019; Duffy et al., 2016), we present a comprehensive framework that can inform school-to-work transition initiatives with the hope that a thoughtful integration of these perspectives can empower young people to overcome social injustices and foster their ability to adapt to a dynamic world of work.

The Current State of Work for Youth

Young people have unique strengths and challenges that shape their work lives. Moving from adolescence to adulthood, youth (i.e., individuals aged 15–24 years old) explore the world of work, develop vocational interests, and take steps towards reaching their goals (Kenny, 2013). While college students may achieve economic self-sufficiency through higher education and work or unpaid internship experiences, non-college bound youth, who often have fewer socioeconomic resources than those in post-secondary education, face pervasive work-related challenges earlier in their lives. Globalization and technological advancements have increased uncertainty about future among youth when making the transition from school to work (Mills & Blossfeld, 2009). In addition, the Great Recession of the early 21st century has disproportionately impacted youth globally even in the strongest economies such as the United States and European Union (Hoffman, 2015). In fact, the global financial crisis hit young people harder than any other groups (Carcillo, Fernández, Königs, & Minea, 2015).

It has become much harder for youth to secure employment and access decent work in the past decade. Although the global economy is recovering from the Great Recession, it has been a slow process with marginal improvements in youth employment (Organisation for Economic Co-operation and Development [OECD], 2016). With the decline in job opportunities, young people, especially those from disadvantaged backgrounds are unable to access starter jobs that would allow them to gain experience in the workforce and earn adequate income (Hoffman, 2015). Today's youth are more likely to be unemployed than adults, and the global youth unemployment rate is approximately 13%, which is three times as high as the adult unemployment rate globally. The employment outlook is grimmer in some regions of the world, such as North Africa, where nearly 30% of the youth are unemployed (ILO, 2017, 2018). More importantly, approximately one-third of youth unemployment is associated with long-term scarring effects that will impact future employment prospects, lifetime income, and well-being (Brada, Marelli, & Signorelli, 2014). Long-term unemployment increases the risk of being excluded from the workforce for young people (Bell & Blanchflower, 2011).

Another critical issue pertaining to the work lives of youth is the high number of young people who are not in education, employment, or training (NEET) Approximately one fifth of world's young people neither work nor attend school (ILO, 2017). In addition to its economic implications, this problem poses a significant challenge globally to many people as lack of work and structure in one's life might lead to social isolation and disengagement with negative consequences such as mental and physical health problems and crime (Carcillo et al., 2015). Youth from lower socioeconomic backgrounds, young women, migrant youth with limited language skills, and youth with health problems and lower educational attainment and skills are more likely to be NEET (OECD, 2016). Therefore, disadvantaged groups of youth deal with other forms of societal barriers that affect many domains of their lives including their transition from secondary-education to work. Without sufficient income and social resources, the NEET youth is at a significant risk of living in poverty.

By comparison, youth who can secure employment are likely to face barriers to quality work. Given their limited work experience, young people are more likely to have low-paid jobs with less security and social protection, and fewer opportunities for professional growth than older individuals. As such, working poverty is a more widespread problem among youth than adults in both the developed and developing world. Temporary jobs usually provide opportunities to gain training and work experience and, therefore, are usually perceived as a pathway to eventual job security and a sustainable income. However, youth with limited education, training, and skills are likely to get stuck in these jobs or quit employment because temporary jobs may fail to provide opportunities for skills development (OECD & ILO, 2014).

Furthermore, the mismatch between youth's skills and the labor market demands contributes to unemployment and indecent work (Brada et al., 2014). In an analysis of school-to-work transition in low- and middle-income countries, Sparreboom and Staneva (2014) reported more than half of the young population have skills that do not match job requirements. Specifically, the skills mismatch in higher income economies seems to be mainly related to over-education or over-qualification of the youth for available jobs and leads to prolonged periods of unemployment. In low-income economies, a lack of education and qualification is a more significant problem and increases the working poverty rate among young people with limited skills (Brewer, 2013).

In all these contexts, the mismatch between job requirements and education/training and the lack of decent work opportunities has long-term adverse effects on youths' successful transition into workforce, future work and economic prospects, and ability to contribute to their communities (Blustein et al., 2016). The challenges youth experience in today's workforce warrant well-organized and comprehensive efforts to assist them (Wood & Dahl, 2015). In addition, school-to-work transition programs that foster introspection about intrapersonal and interpersonal skills and the integration of school learning with developmentally appropriate, work-based experiences that prepare youth for the workforce are needed (Hoffman, 2015). In the following section, we provide an overview of the current literature on school-to-work transition and the need for more contemporary thinking in helping non-college bound youth to succeed.

School-to-Work Transition Programs

The initial development and goals of school-to-work transition programs have been influenced by the major historical and social events of the 20th century (Wood & Dahl, 2015). Events like World War II and the rise of the Information Age have impacted the types of work available to young people and the type preparation needed to enter the workforce. The beginning of the 20th century reflected a mix of skilled and unskilled work positions available to young people (Blustein, 2013). However, the changing labor market of the late 20th century and the 21st century has made it increasingly necessary for young people to have a skill set that could be expanded and refined once they have secured initial employment after graduation (Kenny, 2013). In the 21st century, counselors and researchers have responded to the social events and economic trends in refining the work-based interventions for young people to reflect the need for greater adaptability in finding employment and increased flexibility in responding to the developmental task of entering the workforce for the first time as a young adult (Pavlova, Lee, & Maclean, 2017).

The role of educational institutions in the school-to-work transition has varied historically and across countries. Kenny (2013) noted that international competition generated greater interest in school-to-work transition in the United States in the 1980s due to growing concerns that young people domestically were unequipped to enter the workforce when compared to international peers. This later led to legislation in the United States that paved the way for school-to-work transition programs as a supplement to education adolescents typically receive, although federal funding for such programs was ultimately cut (Kenny, 2013). European countries, including Finland and the Netherlands, have long made a conscious effort to prepare young people for entry into the workforce by including vocationally-based education tracks for adolescents (Akkermans et al., 2015). In addition, governments in other parts of the world, such as India and Hong Kong, have begun to infuse vocational elements into secondary education in recognition of the changing nature of work and shift in international labor markets (Pavlova et al., 2017). These trends suggest a growing recognition among educational institutions and governments that vocational interventions and information about the world of work are vital for young people preparing to enter the workforce.

It is common for school-to-work transition programs to provide adolescents with accurate information about the world of work and engage young people in discussion about their career goals (Wood & Dahl, 2015). In the case of apprenticeship programs, such as ones found in the German education system, adolescents are taught the requisite skills for their chosen vocation under the tutelage of experienced workers (Akkermans et al., 2015). While skill-building has historically been emphasized in school-to-work transition programs in the United States and elsewhere (Pavlova et al., 2017), the changing labor markets and the rise of precarious work conditions have created barriers for young people seeking employment without additional training or post-secondary education (Akkermans et al., 2015; Blustein et al., 2016).

Furthermore, goal-setting has consistently been a cornerstone of programs designed to help adolescents navigate the transition into the workforce (Haase et al., 2008; Kenny, 2013), but the way work has been introduced to young people through these programs has typically not included discussions of the precarious nature of work or socially constructed barriers to a meaningful work life (Diemer & Blustein, 2006; Kenny, 2013). Continued focus on goal-setting and exploration of career interests is developmentally appropriate and vital to young people (Wood & Dahl, 2015), but this is no longer sufficient for preparing them to enter the workforce. Akkermans and colleagues (2015) argued that young people who can successfully transition into the workforce show adaptation and resilience in the face of setbacks and the changing characteristics of the labor market. The question of how to help young people adapt and thrive as the world of work changes around them is necessary to answer if success can be an attainable reality. We present the life design paradigm in the next section as a framework to facilitate a successful transition into the workforce.

The Life Design Paradigm

Life design (Savickas et al., 2009; Savickas, 2012) is an emergent paradigm for exploring how people make sense of their work lives and respond to a dynamic and precarious world of work. It shares with career construction theory (Savickas, 2005) an emphasis on social constructionist tenets and the use of narrative-based intervention strategies (Savickas, 2012). Building on Savickas' (2005) earlier contributions, the life design paradigm assists clients in articulating, authoring, and acting upon their narrative descriptions of their work lives to respond to career-related developmental tasks or successfully navigate career transitions (Savickas et al., 2009). As an extension of Super's (1990) theoretical contributions, Savickas (2012) advocated for reflection of life themes that bridge personal and vocational domains to develop a cohesive life narrative and to achieve a sense of purpose in work. In the case of young adults entering the workforce after graduating from secondary education, the transition from the role of student to the role of worker is a developmental task that necessitates adaptability and reflection in addition to tangible skill development (Hoffman, 2015). Life design, with its emphasis on meaning and identity construction, is well-suited to assist young people in acting with intention and clarifying a sense of purpose during their transition into the workforce.

Life design builds upon selected theories of career development proposed in the 20th century with its focus on fostering meaningful and rewarding work lives and adopting a developmental, life-span view of the process of considering, exploring, implementing, and adjusting to career choices (Savickas, 2012). However, Savickas and colleagues (2009) also recognized the 20th century model of work and career was no longer the most responsive way to help individuals reach their career potential. For example, Super (1957, 1990) established the groundwork to consider career as a developmental process starting in childhood and continuing into retirement age. Super (1990) also established the understanding of work as one aspect of a multifaceted identity and a life domain where individuals can realize their self-concept. Super's (1957, 1990) theoretical contributions undergirded the 20th century concept of career as a stable and long-term commitment to a single employer. During this era, many individuals could expect a linear progression of a career in a single organization as they achieved developmental milestones within and outside of the workplace (Savickas, 2012).

This process was assumed to be the typical career trajectory and became influential in how work was viewed across the lifespan. As such, subsequent career development theories largely ignored the work lives of those with limited stability and volition to achieve such work-related progressions in status and pay (Blustein, 2006). These career theories were well-suited for individuals progressing through predictable steps of a career. However, these frameworks fall short of assisting individuals in uncertain times when such stability is unlikely to be realized despite the best efforts of motivated and committed workers (Savickas, 2012). In recognizing the shortcomings of these frameworks, Savickas and colleagues (2009) crafted the life design paradigm for working with individuals at various points in their academic and work lives. The life design paradigm proposes that individuals need to adapt to changing economic and social conditions and construct careers in the face of uncertainty and instability that typifies many work environments and contemporary societies (Masdonati & Fournier, 2015). With the emergence of this new reality for many workers, the life design paradigm was developed as an alternative for helping students and workers to respond to the unfolding of their careers in the face of uncertainty and instability (Savickas et al., 2009).

Identity and adaptability are at the core of the life design paradigm; interventions therefore help individuals to construct a sense of self that reflects their potential roles they may enact in the workplace and elsewhere in their lives (Savickas et al., 2009). Selecting and entering new work areas represent an ongoing development process young people are likely to repeat across the life course. The process of identity development, which was often understood as a development task of adolescence and young adulthood (Erikson, 1968), is now a continuing developmental process, as individuals need to construct, revise, and reconstruct the self through an ongoing, dynamic, and reflexive interaction with the changing social context (Savickas, 2005). Using a series of narrative exercises, individuals construct, deconstruct, and reconstruct their lives with the goal of coming to new understandings of themselves and the meanings they attribute to life events. These life events are not limited to the present; life design helps clients to connect their past to the future and to the possible selves that may emerge (Masdonati & Fournier, 2015). Through a strong working alliance with a vocational counselor/psychologist, individuals gain deeper understanding of their life themes, identity, and future goals. With a cohesive vision of the future in hand, individuals are prepared to adapt to the changing world of work and take steps towards their career goals (Savickas et al., 2009).

Research suggests that the life design paradigm can benefit adolescents to achieve developmental milestones in their career exploration and connect their present school tasks to future career goals (Masdonati & Fournier, 2015). For instance, a study of Italian middle school students found an online curriculum using life design was more successful in enhancing core aspects of career adaptability than a traditional career development intervention that focused primarily on providing students with information about the work options available to them upon graduating (Nota, Ginevra, Santilli, & Soresi, 2014). This suggests that life design interventions' focus on meaning-making and identity construction through stories and life themes can be beneficial for adolescents as they consider potential careers and explore the world of work.

These studies, although informative in establishing the potential of the life design paradigm as an intervention for young people currently enrolled in post-secondary education, do not fully explain the promise of this framework in helping youth who directly enter the workforce upon graduating from post-secondary education. Studies elsewhere, although not directly linked to life design, have reported that young people in transition from school to work need instrumental and relational support from teachers, career and school counselors, and family members to help them develop work-related goals and connect academic performance in the present to vocational decisions in the future (Kenny, Blustein, & Meerkins, 2018). Furthermore, providing instrumental and relational support through the counselling relationship can help young people gain awareness of the barriers they face and develop agentic action in moving forward in their work lives despite possible setbacks (Richardson, 2012). Such intentionality and agency can be achieved through life design interventions where clients and counselors co-construct coherent narratives that illuminate a sense of self and meaning-making through the experience of working (Savickas, 2012).

These scholarly contributions converge on the underlying tenets of life design and show a connection between Savickas' (2012) theoretical contributions and empirical studies on school-to-work transition (Masdonati & Fournier, 2015). Research on school-to-work transition has illuminated how young people optimally make sense of the barriers they face, utilize internal and external resources, and develop clarity in their interests within and outside of the workplace (Pavlova et al., 2017). This presents a picture of youth in flux at a time when work is precarious and economic conditions are uncertain (Blustein et al., 2016). The life design paradigm provides a framework for school-to-work transition interventions that aligns with seminal works by contemporary scholars within career development, such as Blustein (2006) and Richardson (2012), and builds upon work by Super (1990) that laid the initial groundwork for the school-to-work transition movement in the 20th century.

With research indicating work-bound youth benefit from informal support and structured career guidance as they articulate their work values and consider the options available to them (Masdonati & Fournier, 2015), life design is well-positioned to offer counselors a responsive way to help young people to adapt to a changing world of work and construct a meaningful work narrative. Despite the clear strengths of this framework, there are areas where integration with the PWT literature (Blustein, 2006, 2013; Duffy et al., 2016) can further enhance what is already a compelling and vital perspective for school-to-work transition among non-college-bound youth. In the next section, we will provide an overview of the contributions of PWT to the study of work in the current economic and social climate.

The Psychology of Working Theory

Although the world of work poses increasingly complex challenges for young people, many of the theoretical frameworks that guide research and practice around the school-to-work transition emerged across the latter half of the 20th century at a time when educational and work opportunities for many (but not all) young people were generally expanding. In the context of economic growth, the practice of career counselling and guidance focused largely on helping young people to make vocational choices that would be satisfying and provide a good fit with their interests and talents. Many theoretical concepts remain relevant in facilitating adaptive school-to-work transitions in the 21st century; yet, the realities of contemporary society require increased attention to the heightened instability of work, including the decline of decent work, and the importance of contextual factors that contribute to social and economic inequalities. In place of long-term employment, the labor market has experienced an increase in short-term, precarious work (Kalleberg & Vallas, 2017), which lacks the job security and employee benefits afforded by decent work (ILO, 2018). A growing body of research has documented the relationship between decent work and psychological well-being (e.g., Blustein et al., 2019; Kozan, Işık, & Blustein, 2019). In comparison with decent work, which has the potential to satisfy human psychological needs for belonging, identity, and self-determination (Blustein et al., 2019), underemployment and precarious work are often unfulfilling, isolating and demeaning (Kalleberg & Vallas, 2017). Additionally, economic inequality, which is dynamically related to social inequality, has been growing over the past 50 years in many regions of the world (Stiglitz, 2015). As access to the labor market becomes more competitive, those with less education and less social privilege and those who are targets of social oppression tend to fare worse in the competition for decent work. These individuals also tend to be the victims of increased prejudice due to blame for work scarcity (ILO, 2014, 2016).

In response to the decline in decent work and the growing inequalities in access to decent work, Blustein and colleagues have developed PWT (Blustein, 2006, 2013; Duffy et al., 2016). In a recent theoretical update of PWT, Blustein Kenny, Autin, and Duffy (in press) summarize the main tenets of this body of work as follows:

> The primary objective of PWT is to align current vocational research and practice with a social justice agenda promoting greater (a) inclusiveness within career development/vocational psychology and (b) equity in the distribution of resources that contribute to decent and dignified work for all (Blustein, 2006, 2013; Blustein et al., 2019; Duffy et al. 2016; Kenny et al., in press). In constructing this new approach to understanding and intervening in the work lives of people and communities, Blustein and colleagues have articulated several core assumptions underlying their framework. First, PWT assumes that work has the capacity to be an essential aspect of positive human functioning; specifically, we view access to decent, dignified, and stable work as a basic human right and integral to a person's capacity to survive, connect to others and the broader social world, and optimally to thrive in a life of meaning and purpose (Blustein et al., 2019). Secondly, PWT views work as inseparable from the context of the worker. That is, individuals' cultural background, family context, and social identities (e.g., racial, gender, social class identities) are thought to influence their experience within their work environment and vice versa. As such, PWT is largely focused on disparities in access to decent work across social contexts and identities (Blustein, 2006; Duffy et al., 2016). Third, the definition of work has been expanded to include unpaid work that encompasses caregiving work (Blustein, 2006). Finally, PWT assumes that the labor market of the twenty-first century will continue to undergo rapid change and seeks to describe the experiences of diverse groups of workers navigating this new occupational landscape (Blustein et al., 2019).

A recent linear model of the psychology of working perspective by Duffy et al. (2016) has generated significant interest in understanding the complex interplay of macro-level contextual factors and psychological factors in the prediction of life satisfaction and work fulfillment. The array of factors that are presented in the PWT model capture the core elements of the psychology of working perspective, including marginalization, economic constraints which frame the utility of work volition and career adaptability in the attainment of decent work. Optimally, access to decent work is then associated with the fulfillment of core human needs (need for survival, social connection/contribution, and self-determination) which would then foster work fulfillment and life satisfaction. Considerable empirical research has generated support for PWT (Blustein et al., 2019; Blustein et al., in press).

The influence of context in perpetuating and overcoming disparity has become more salient as work opportunities have diminished and as competition has increased. Blustein (2006) posited many people have always lacked choice or volition in deciding what they will do for a living and obtaining access to the labor market. Those without the economic and social resources to secure decent work or to pursue a career have often accepted whatever kind of work was available to meet their survival needs while also neglecting needs for self-determination and belonging in the workplace (Blustein, 2006). Furthermore, individuals who have been successful in advancing their careers have typically benefitted from economic and/or social support from friends, family members, their communities, and their connection to broader societal values (Kenny & Medvide, 2013).

The importance of relational support (e.g., warmth, acceptance, and respect for autonomy) and instrumental support (e.g., academic guidance and information-sharing) can foster awareness of socially constructed barriers as young people transition from school to work and foster self-efficacy to successfully confront prejudice and discrimination (Kenny, 2013). The negative impact of the socially constructed barriers and the costs of internalized social prejudices related to race, ethnicity, gender, religious affiliation, migrant status, disability status, sexual orientation and other "isms" has been well documented in recent research (Kenny & Medvide, 2013; Richardson, 2012). This mandates the need for greater attention to relational support and socially constructed barriers in school-to-work theory and practice.

The role of social and economic factors as key determinants of work and life outcomes mandates that young people and the adults who guide them need to be attentive to contextual constraints and supports and the means for responding effectively to seize opportunities and reduce barriers (Blustein et al., 2019). To some extent, this can be achieved through relationships where support is coupled with consciousness-building for the purpose of raising awareness and fostering agentic action (Blustein, 2013; Kenny, Blustein, Gutowski, & Meerkins, 2018; Richardson, 2012). Prilleltensky and Stead (2012) suggest that individuals need to consider not only how to adjust to the world of work, but how to transform society in ways that reduce oppressive policies and structures that limit choice and opportunity in accessing work. In sum, in response to the profound changes impacting the availability and access to decent work for all persons and especially marginalized groups, theoretical advances are needed to guide research and practice regarding the school-to-work transition that address concerns for individual and systemic change and for the deep impact of contextual assets and constraints in access to decent work and well-being. I the following section, we will present an integrated perspective that builds upon the strengths of the life design paradigm and PWT to provide responsive interventions for the vocational goals and career development of youth entering the workforce at an uncertain time economically and socially.

Integrating the Life-Design Paradigm and Psychology of Working Perspective

This chapter provides a rich opportunity for a synthesis of the life design paradigm and PWT, which can be more powerful when used together in developing ideas and interventions to foster the school to work transition for young people. As reflected earlier, life design counselling provides a narrative framework to foster career adaptability and support identity development. Another critical feature of the life design paradigm is its inclusive nature, which advocates for an integration of work and non-work contexts and roles to assist clients in developing meaning and purpose and enhancing a sense of coherence across life themes. Moreover, the use of narrative and social constructionist frameworks provides life design with a conceptual scaffolding that promotes an active and agentic stance on the part of clients and students. Each of these innovative characteristics of the life design paradigm can be integrated with PWT in important ways, with clear implications for the problems raised in this chapter. Following the aforementioned contributions of Prilleltensky and Stead (2012), PWT can enhance the challenge part of the adapt-challenge dialectic. In this section, we explore the adapt-challenge perspective in light of the challenges faced by youth entering an unstable, and often unwelcoming world of work.

Inherent in PWT is a focus on challenging systems and structures that sustain and support inequity and marginalization (Blustein, 2006, 2013). One of the key attributes within the PWT is critical consciousness (Diemer & Blustein, 2006; Freire, 1972). Critical consciousness refers to the capacity to read the world in a critical way in order to discern the root causes of social and economic systems. By reading the world, people would have knowledge, and hopefully the capacity, to challenge systems. The infusion of critical consciousness and liberation psychology into the fabric of PWT resulted in creating a set of ideas and theories that are focused on change, writ large (Blustein et al., in press; Kenny, Blustein, Gutowski et al., 2018). PWT is premised on the notion that work is the location of both dreams and disappointments, culminating in considerable inequity with respect to how people experience this essential part of life.

The life design paradigm is not explicit in its attention to systemic barriers, but Savickas and colleagues' (2009) framework for career counselling allows for an infusion of experiences with privilege and oppression into the construction of a sense of self and a reflection on life themes. Fostering critical consciousness is consistent with the goals of Savickas' (2012) approach to help clients to reauthor their life narratives and construct an identity as an agent in their own lives. According to Blustein (2006, 2013), reauthoring should not be limited to individualistic constructions of agency, but should also include attention to cultural factors that shape one's self-concept, attitudes toward vocations/working, and beliefs about their potential to engage in meaningful work.

Alongside this attention to the role of culture in how individuals construct their sense of self and understand the world of work is an intention to assist clients in constructing a life narrative in which agency is linked to action towards social change.

Savickas (2012) is resolute in the individuals' potential to achieve meaning in their work lives, and Blustein (2006, 2013) provides a perspective for enriching this proposition by articulating the role of socially constructed barriers in building a meaningful work life. The challenge in working with young people to foster critical consciousness lies both in helping them to rewrite their narratives to make sense of themselves as agents for social change and in reconstructing the counselling relationship to place questions of power and privilege in the forefront of interventions that are not explicit in their attention to critical consciousness. Critical consciousness may be helpful for young people so that they do not blame themselves for the impact of structural constrains in their lives, they may also feel powerless to effect structural change (Kenny, Blustein, Gutowski et al., 2018). The counselor can assist young people in understanding how and where they can push back against societal structures as individuals or as part of a collective effort and how they best navigate or circumvent those structures that cannot be altered in the short-term (Kenny, Blustein, Gutowski, et al. 2018, Kenny, Blustein, & Meerkins, 2018). Furthermore, as Blustein (2006) argued, it requires counselors to reconstruct their identities to make sense of their own role as activists and advocates.

As reflected in recent literature on life design counselling (Maree, 2017), scholars are now examining the use of these important new ideas for a growing diversity of client populations, such as individuals with disabling conditions (Ferrari, Sgaramella, Santilli, & Di Maggio, 2017) and clients from poor and vulnerable backgrounds (Maree, 2017). These contributions describe how counselors have expanded the life design paradigm to be applicable to individuals with less than optimal options in their lives. Indeed, the work by the life design scholars has embraced a thoughtful approach to expanding the impact of narratability and adaptability (Briddick & Sensoy-Briddick, 2017). Life design interventions do focus on helping clients to be active and agentic on their own behalf; the integration of PWT can expand the challenge aspect of the adaptability framework so that clients, counselors, and others interested in an adaptive school-to-work transition can take on systemic change.

We argue that the opportunity to design one's life should be part of the Decent Work Agenda, which is a formal initiative by the ILO to promote the infusion of human rights in advocacy efforts to improve working conditions globally (Blustein et al., 2019; ILO, 2008). So, how do counselors and educators consider challenging a neo-liberal system that does not value human beings as workers, but rather views people as commodities in a free-market economy? The first step is to label some of the prevailing policies about the school-to-work transition, which have not provided sufficient support and guidance, as unjust. Simply developing new programs and interventions is insufficient. We need to develop structures that will embrace young people entering the work force in order to provide them with training, education, and opportunities for critical reflection, critical consciousness, and the development of adaptive and marketable skills for the 21st century. Integrating the life design paradigm with PWT would suggest interventions at the individual, community, and systemic levels. One adaptation of life design using PWT might be to enhance the notion of adaptability so that it incorporates critical consciousness. In this manner, students and clients would no longer feel that they always have to adapt to a system that may, at times, leave them nothing but the crumbs of a viable work life. Moreover, the inclusive psychological practice aspect of the psychology of working, which would suggest integrative interventions focusing on personal and developmental goals in addition to work-based and career goals, can supplement the holistic features of life design.

From a community perspective, the life design paradigm and PWT can be used to inform the development of work-based learning and apprenticeship programs. Kenny, Blustein, Liang, Klein, and Etchie (2019) suggest that critical consciousness can be infused in career development education and work-based learning experiences. The life design literature would support the use of narrative methods of helping students to develop a path forward in their lives. In addition, the skill-building component of PWT would embrace the utility of enhancing both adaptability and challenge by helping students to develop their market-based skills and their skills in reading the world. From a systemic perspective, the integration of the life design paradigm and PWT would suggest that counselors and educators advocate for equitable schools, training programs, and occupational contexts, which would optimally radically change the context for both school and work.

The main challenges to a humane school-to-work transition are the lack of schools with sufficient resources and limited decent work opportunities available to these youth upon graduating. By developing policy-oriented research and building on the importance of self-determination and life design as human rights, our profession can, at the very minimum, be on the side of justice and decency. In addition to advocacy, the life design paradigm and PWT can inform the design of transition structures that support youth as they manage the move from school to work. This would be manifested by social and economic support for counselors and psychoeducational programs that help students navigate the transition between school and work. There is a particular need for systematic supports for youth who are not attached to schools, work, or training programs; therefore governments should support structured counselling and psychoeducation programs to provide youth without guidance and support.

Conclusion

The current economic state across the globe and the increased uncertainty young people face as they enter the workforce call for a new perspective on school-to-work transition. Although the career frameworks of the 20th century offer much in thinking about work and careers as a stable and predictable journey in one's life (Savickas et al., 2009), the 21st century has challenged researchers and counselors to infuse new ideas into how they define a meaningful work life and the strategies needed for young people to thrive within and outside of work settings (Blustein et al., 2019; Maree, 2017). Thus, an integration of the theoretical contributions of the life design paradigm (Savickas et al., 2009) and PWT (Blustein, 2006, 2013; Duffy et al., 2016) is warranted to help young people to transition into the workforce, adapt to uncertain and precarious conditions, and challenge inequities in their lives. By combining the strengths of these frameworks, counselors can implement responsive and timely interventions that move beyond skill development and training to foster critical consciousness, a sense of purpose and meaning, and connection to others so that young people can be successful in finding employment and achieving their vocational goals.

References

Akkermans, J., Nykänen, M., & Vuori, J. (2015). Practice makes perfect? Antecedents and consequences of an adaptive school-to-work transition. In J. Vuori, R. Blonk, & R. H. Price (Eds.), *Sustainable working lives: Managing work transitions and health throughout the life course* (pp. 65–86). New York, NY: Springer.

Bell, D. N. F., & Blanchflower, D. G. (2011). Young people and the Great Recession. *Oxford Review of Economic Policy, 27,* 241–267. https://doi.org/10.1093/oxrep/grr011.

Blustein, D. L. (2006). *The psychology of working: A new perspective for career development, counseling, and public policy*. New York, NY: Routledge.

Blustein, D. L. (Ed.). (2013). *The Oxford handbook of the psychology of working*. Oxford, England: Oxford University Press. https://doi.org/10.1093/oxfordhb/9780199758791.001.0001.

Blustein, D. L. (in press). *The importance of work in an age of uncertainty: The eroding work experience in America*. New York, NY: Oxford University Press.

Blustein, D. L., Kenny, M. E., Autin, K. L., & Duffy, R. D. (in press). The psychology of working in practice: A theory of change for a new era. *Career Development Quarterly*.

Blustein, D. L., Kenny, M. E., Di Fabio, A., & Guichard, J. (2019). Expanding the impact of the psychology of working: Engaging psychology in the struggle for decent work and human rights. *Journal of Career Assessment, 27,* 3–28.

Blustein, D. L., Kenny, M. E., & Kozan, S. (2014). Education and work as human birthrights: Eradicating poverty through knowledge, innovation, and collaboration. In UNDP (Ed.), *Barriers to and opportunities for poverty reduction: Prospects for private sector led-interventions*. Istanbul, Turkey: UNDP International Center for Private Sector in Development.

Blustein, D. L., Olle, C., Connors-Kellgren, A., & Diamonti, A. J. (2016). Decent work: A psychological perspective. *Frontiers in Psychology, 7,* 407. https://doi.org/10.3389/fpsyg.2016.00407.

Brada, J. C., Marelli, E., & Signorelli, M. (2014). Young people and the labor market: Key determinants and new evidence. *Comparative Economic Studies, 56,* 556–566. https://doi.org/10.1057/ces.2014.30.

Brewer, L. (2013). *Enhancing youth employability: What? why? and how? Guide to core work skills*. Geneva, Switzerland: ILO Skills and Employability Department. Retrieved from http://www.oitcinterfor.org/sites/default/files/file_publicacion/wcms_213452_0.pdf.

Briddick, W. C., & Sensoy-Briddick, H. (2017). Paradigm and promise: Life design, psychology of working, and decent work. In K. Maree (Ed.), *Psychology of career adaptability, employability and resilience* (pp. 317–328). Cham, Switzerland: Springer.

Carcillo, S., Fernández, R., Königs, S., & Minea, A. (2015). NEET youth in the aftermath of the crisis: Challenges and policies. *OECD social, employment and migration working papers*, 164. Paris, France: OECD Publishing. https://doi.org/10.1787/5js6363503f6-en.

Diemer, M. A., & Blustein, D. L. (2006). Critical consciousness and career development among urban youth. *Journal of Vocational Behavior, 68,* 220–232. https://doi.org/10.1016/j.jvb.2005.07.001.

Duffy, R. D., Blustein, D. L., Diemer, M. A., & Autin, K. L. (2016). The psychology of working theory. *Journal of Counseling Psychology, 63,* 127–148. https://doi.org/10.1037/cou0000140.

Erikson, E. (1968). *Identity, youth, and crisis*. New York, NY: W. W. Norton & Company.

Ferrari, L., Sgaramella, T. M., Santilli, S., & Di Maggio, I. (2017). Career adaptability and career resilience: The roadmap to work inclusion for individuals experiencing disability. In K. Maree (Ed.), *Psychology of career adaptability, employability, and resilience* (pp. 415–432). Cham, Switzerland: Springer.

Freire, P. (1972). *Pedagogy of the oppressed*. New York, NY: Penguin Books.

Haase, C. M., Heckhausen, J., & Köller, O. (2008). Goal engagement during the school-to-work transition: Beneficial for all, particularly for girls. *Journal of Research on Adolescence, 18*, 671–698. https://doi.org/10.1111/j.1532-7795.2008.00576.x.

Hoffman, N. (2015). *Let's get real: Deeper learning and the power of the workplace*. Boston, MA: Jobs for the Future.

Holland, J. L. (1997). *Making vocational choices: A theory of vocational personalities and work environments* (3rd ed.). Odessa, FL: Psychological Assessment Resources.

International Labor Organization. (2008). *ILO declaration on social justice for a fair globalization*. Retrieved from: http://www.ilo.org/wcmsp5/groups/public/---dgreports/---cabinet/documents/genericdocument/wcms_371208.pdf.

International Labor Organization [ILO]. (2014). *Global employment trends*. Retrieved from: http://www.ilo.org/wcmsp5/groups/public/---dgreports/---dcomm/---publ/documents/publication/wcms_234107.pdf.

International Labor Organization. (2015). *World employment social outlook: Trends 2015*. Retrieved from: http://www.ilo.org/wcmsp5/groups/public/---dgreports/---dcomm/---publ/documents/publication/wcms_337069.pdf.

International Labor Organization. (2016). *World employment and social outlook: Trends 2016*. Retrieved from: https://www.ilo.org/wcmsp5/groups/public/---dgreports/---dcomm/---publ/documents/publication/wcms_443480.pdf.

International Labor Organization. (2017). *Global employment trends for youth 2017: Paths to a better working future*. Retrieved from: https://www.ilo.org/wcmsp5/groups/public/---dgreports/---dcomm/---publ/documents/publication/wcms_598669.pdf.

International Labor Organization. (2018). *World employment and social outlook: Trends 2018*. Retrieved from: https://www.ilo.org/wcmsp5/groups/public/---dgreports/---dcomm/---publ/documents/publication/wcms_615594.pdf.

Kalleberg, A. L., & Vallas, S. P. (2017). Probing precarious work: Theory, research, and politics. In A. L. Kalleberg & S. Vallas (Eds.), *Precarious work (Research in the sociology of work* (Vol. 31, pp. 1–30). Bingley, England: Emerald.

Kenny, M. E. (2013). The promise of work as a component of educational reform. In D. L. Blustein (Ed.), *The Oxford handbook of the psychology of working* (pp. 273–291). New York, NY: Oxford University Press.

Kenny, M. E., Blustein, D. L., Gutowski, E., & Meerkins, T. (2018). Combatting marginalization and fostering critical consciousness for decent work. In V. Cohen-Scali, J. Pouyad, M. Podgorny, V. Dabrik-Podgorna, G. Alenson, J. L. Bernaud, I. Abdou Moumoula, & J. Guichard (Eds.), *Interventions in career design and education: Transformation for sustainable development and decent work* (pp. 55–73). Cham, Switzerland: Springer.

Kenny, M. E., Blustein, D. L., Liang, B., Klein, T., & Etchie, Q. (2019). Applying the psychology of working theory for transformative career education. *Journal of Career Development*. Advance online publication. https://doi.org/10.1177/0894845319827655.

Kenny, M. E., Blustein, D. L., & Meerkins, T. (2018b). Integrating relational perspectives in counseling. *The Career Development Quarterly, 66*, 135–138.

Kenny, M. E., & Medvide, M. B. (2013). Relational influences on career development. In S. D. Brown & R. W. Lent (Eds.), *Career development and counseling: Putting theory and research to work* (pp. 329–356). New York, NY: Wiley.

Kozan, S., Işık, E., & Blustein, D. L. (2019). Decent work and well-being among low-income Turkish employees: Testing the psychology of working theory. *Journal of Counseling Psychology, 66*, 317–327. https://doi.org/10.1037/cou0000342.

Maree, K. (2017). Utilizing career adaptability and career resilience to promote employability and decent work to alleviate poverty. In K. Maree (Ed.), *Psychology of career adaptability, employability, and resilience* (pp. 349–374). Cham, Switzerland: Springer.

Masdonati, J., & Fournier, G. (2015). Life design, young adults, and the school-to-work transition. In L. Nota & J. Rossier (Eds.), *Handbook of life design: From practice to theory and from theory to practice* (pp. 117–133). Boston, MA: Hogrefe Publishing.

Mills, M., & Blossfeld, H. P. (2009). Uncertain and unable to commit: A fourteen-country comparison of the impact of globalization on the early life course. In I. Schoon & R. K. Silbereisen (Eds.), *Transitions from school to work: Globalization, individualization, and patterns of diversity* (pp. 95–117). New York, NY: Cambridge University Press.

Nota, L., Ginevra, M., Santilli, S., & Soresi, S. (2014). Contemporary career construction: The role of career adaptability. In M. Coetzee (Ed.), *Psycho-social career meta-capacities: Dynamics of contemporary career development* (pp. 247–263). Cham, Switzerland: Springer.

Organisation for Economic Co-operation and Development. (2016). *Society at a glance 2016: OECD social indicators*. Paris, France: OECD Publishing. https://doi.org/10.1787/9789264261488-en.

Organisation for Economic Co-operation and Development, & International Labor Organization. (2014). *Promoting better labour market outcomes for youth*. Report on youth employment and apprenticeships prepared for the G20 Labour and Employment Ministerial Meeting, Melbourne Australia, 10–11 September. Retrieved from https://www.oecd.org/g20/topics/employment-and-social-policy/OECD-ILO-Youth-Apprenticeships-G20.pdf.

Pavlova, M., Lee, J. C. K., & Maclean, R. (2017). Complexities of school to work transitions. *Educational Research for Policy and Practice, 16*, 1–7. https://doi.org/10.1007/s10671-017-9211-5.

Prilleltensky, I., & Stead, G. B. (2012). Critical psychology and career development: Unpacking the adjust–challenge dilemma. *Journal of Career Development, 39*, 321–340. https://doi.org/10.1177/0894845310384403.

Richardson, M. S. (2012). Counseling for work and relationship. *The Counseling Psychologist, 40*, 190–242. https://doi.org/10.1177/0011000011406452.

Savickas, M. L. (2005). The theory and practice of career construction. In S. D. Brown & R. W. Lent (Eds.), *Career development and counseling: Putting theory and research to work* (pp. 42–70). Hoboken, NJ: John Wiley & Sons.

Savickas, M. L. (2012). Life design: A paradigm for career intervention in the 21st century. *Journal of Counseling & Development, 90*, 13–19. https://doi.org/10.1111/j.1556-6676.2012.00002.x.

Savickas, M. L., Nota, L., Rossier, J., Dauwalder, J., Duarte, M. E., Guichard, J. Van, et al. (2009). Life designing: A paradigm for career construction in the 21st century. *Journal of Vocational Behavior, 75*, 239–250. https://doi.org/10.1016/j.jvb.2009.04.004.

Sparreboom, T., & Staneva, A. (2014). *Is education the solution to decent work for youth in developing economies?: Identifying qualifications mismatch from 28 school-to-work transition surveys*, Work4Youth Publication Series, No. 23. Geneva, Switzerland: International Labor Office.

Stiglitz, J. (2015). *The great divide: Unequal societies and what we can do about them*. New York, NY: W. W. Norton.

Super, D. E. (1957). *The psychology of careers*. New York, NY: Harper & Row.

Super, D. E. (1990). A life span, life-space approach to career development. In D. Brown & L. Brooks (Eds.), *Career choice and development* (2nd ed., pp. 192–234). San Francisco, CA: Jossey-Bass.

Wood, C., & Dahl, H. (2015). Individualized career plans: Helping youths create successful school-to-work transitions. In P. J. Hartung, M. L. Savickas, & W. B. Walsh (Eds.), *APA handbook of career intervention* (Vol. 2, pp. 467–477)., Applications Washington, DC: American Psychological Association.

Innovating Career Counselling to Manage the Transitions to Bridge Employment and Retirement

Hannes Zacher, Rachel S. Rauvola and Cort W. Rudolph

Abstract In this chapter, we discuss innovative and successful approaches to career counselling for older workers who transition from their career job to bridge employment or retirement. Bridge employment refers to older workers' engagement in paid employment after leaving their career job, whereas retirement is the process of completely withdrawing from the labor force. After an introduction to the topic, we first review theoretical models and empirical evidence on predictors and outcomes of older workers' transitions from a career job to bridge employment or retirement. Next, we review research on career counselling in these contexts. Based on these insights, we conclude with implications for older workers, career counselors, organizations, and researchers.

Keywords Bridge employment · Retirement · Aging workforce · Older workers · Career transitions

Introduction

Due to demographic changes (e.g., low/decreasing birth rates, higher life expectancies, aging of baby boomers), the workforce in many countries is aging and becoming more age diverse (Chand & Tung, 2014; Kulik, Ryan, Harper, & George, 2014). These developments have significant implications for individuals, organizations, and society as a whole (Hertel & Zacher, 2018). For instance, governments are changing retirement policies, such that retirement entry ages are raised (e.g., from 65 to 67 years in Germany) or retirement entry is becoming more flexible and dependent on individuals' personal resources and preferences (Henkens et al., 2018; Peiró, Tordera, & Potočnik, 2013). Moreover, there is a growing awareness in organizations that negative age stereotypes can lead to disengagement among older workers and dis-

H. Zacher (✉)
Institute of Psychology, Leipzig University, Neumarkt 9-19, 04109 Leipzig, Germany
e-mail: hannes.zacher@uni-leipzig.de

R. S. Rauvola · C. W. Rudolph
Department of Psychology, Saint Louis University, St. Louis, MO, USA

J. G. Maree (ed.), *Handbook of Innovative Career Counselling*,
https://doi.org/10.1007/978-3-030-22799-9_11

crimination and, thus, need to be combated (Griffin, Bayl-Smith, & Hesketh, 2016; Von Hippel, Kalokerinos, Haanterä, & Zacher, 2018). Many of today's organizations do not know how to fill open positions with qualified younger workers and want to retain older workers as long as possible due to their valuable knowledge, experience, and judgment skills (Burmeister & Deller, 2016). At the same time, many older workers must (e.g., because they cannot afford to retire or need to support their families) or want (e.g., because they like their job, tasks, or coworkers) to work past traditional retirement ages (Mor-Barak, 1995; Oakman & Wells, 2016). In this chapter, we refer to "work" primarily as paid activities in the employment context, but of course a broader understanding of working also includes unpaid activities such as caregiving and volunteering.

Entering bridge employment (i.e., paid work after retiring from one's career job; Alcover, Topa, Parry, Fraccaroli, & Depolo, 2014) and retirement (i.e., transitioning from paid work to a complete and permanent withdrawal from the labor force; Wang, 2012) are major life transitions that can be experienced as stressful and to which individuals need to adjust (Hesketh, Griffin, & Loh, 2011; Schmitt, 2018; Wang, 2007). Indeed, Atchley (1972) noted that "retirement is perhaps the most crucial life change requiring a major adjustment of the older person" (p. 103). While today the transition from work to retirement at higher ages is a nearly universal phenomenon in developed countries and also many developing countries, retirement policies, practices, support systems, and expectations differ substantially across cultures (Peiró et al., 2013). Many older workers are able to cope with the transitions to bridge employment and retirement without external support other than help from their families and friends, whereas others may be in need of professional guidance (Jensen-Scott, 1993). The goal of this chapter is to discuss innovative and successful methods of career counselling for older workers who transition from their career job to bridge employment or from their career job or bridge employment to retirement.

Career counselling (sometimes also called career guidance) refers to a process in which trained professionals (i.e., career counselors) use communication-based techniques and provide expert advice to support their clients in making important career decisions and dealing with challenging career situations (Heppner & Heppner, 2003; Savickas, 2011). In addition to intervention characteristics (e.g., techniques, tools, approaches), the career counselling process involves the thoughts, feelings, and behaviors of the counselor and the client during counselling sessions. The career counselling process can be distinguished from its inputs (i.e., characteristics of the counselor and the client, such as demographics and personality; contextual characteristics, such as current job and family characteristics) and outcomes (i.e., immediate, intermediate, and distal changes, for instance in a client's attitudes, behaviors, and well-being; Heppner & Heppner, 2003). Accordingly, our focus in this chapter is on the individual and contextual antecedents (i.e., inputs) of innovative and successful career counselling in the contexts of bridge employment and retirement transitions, the characteristics of career counselling interventions (i.e., process), and the effects of career counselling on older workers' adjustment (i.e., outcomes such as health and well-being, attitudes, and behaviors).

The remainder of this chapter unfolds as follows. We first review theoretical models and empirical evidence on older workers' successful adjustment after transitioning from a career job to bridge employment or from a career job or bridge employment to retirement. Next, we review research on career counselling in these contexts. Based on these insights, we develop recommendations for career counselors, workers, organizations, and researchers in this area.

Transition to Bridge Employment

Bridge employment can be defined as working for pay, sometimes with reduced work hours and demands, between a major and longer-term career job and complete withdrawal from the labor force (Beehr & Bennett, 2015; Dropkin, Moline, Kim, & Gold, 2016). Bridge employment can be conceptualized from different theoretical perspectives, including bridge employment as a decision-making process, a distinct stage of career development, an adjustment process, and as a part of organizations' human resource management (Zhan & Wang, 2015). A number of theoretical models on bridge employment exist. For example, Beehr and Bennett (2015) developed a taxonomy of 16 types of bridge jobs and distinguished between individual, job/organizational, and societal predictors of bridge employment. They further suggested that engaging in bridge employment may affect older workers' personal and social identity, finances, social life, as well as health and well-being. They also argued that the transition to bridge employment involves a complex decision-making process that entails planning, intention formation, decisions and behavior, and adjustment. In another recently proposed model, Rudolph, De Lange, and Van der Heijden (2015) used life course, lifespan, and self-regulation perspectives to explain the psychological adjustment processes of bridge employees (e.g., sustaining work performance, well-being). These researchers proposed that adjustment to bridge employment results from the interplay of intrapersonal resources (e.g., self-efficacy) and the fit between contextual demands (e.g., socioeconomic demands) and resources (e.g., social support).

Empirical research on potential antecedents and outcomes of older workers' decision to engage in bridge employment has rapidly increased over the past two decades (e.g., Alcover et al., 2014; Griffin & Hesketh, 2008; Wang, Zhan, Liu, & Shultz, 2008). For example, an early study showed that excellent health, longer organizational tenure, as well as having a working spouse and dependent children contributed to the decision to accept bridge employment, whereas higher age and salary reduced the likelihood of bridge employment (Kim & Feldman, 2000). Furthermore, Kim and Feldman (2000) found that engaging in bridge employment was positively related to both retirement and life satisfaction. Another study showed consistently that, in comparison to full retirement, bridge employment participation predicted fewer major diseases and functional limitations, and better mental health (Zhan, Wang, Liu, & Shultz, 2009). As a final example, a study by Zhan, Wang, and Shi (2015) found that communal and generativity motives positively predicted engagement in bridge employment, independent of gender. In addition, status striving predicted bridge employment participation among older men, but not among older women. Consistent with the theoretical models described above, these findings illustrate that both individual and contextual characteristics impact on older workers' decision to engage in bridge employment, with significant implications for their psychological adjustment in this transition.

Transition to Retirement

Retirement refers to the process of transitioning from paid work (including bridge employment) or one's career job to a complete and permanent withdrawal from the labor force (Henkens et al., 2018; Wang, 2012). Similar to bridge employment, the retirement process can be understood from a decision making perspective, as an adjustment process, or as a distinct career development stage (Wang & Shi, 2014; Wang & Wanberg, 2017). Antecedents of retirement can be classified into individual (e.g., education, values), job/organizational (e.g. demanding work conditions), family (e.g., partner's retirement decisions), and socioeconomic context characteristics (e.g., health care coverage). Furthermore, outcomes of the retirement decision can be grouped into physical, psychosocial, and financial well-being or adjustment (Wang & Shi, 2014). Two important theoretical models of retirement include the temporal process model of retirement (including the phases of retirement planning, decision making, and adjustment; Shultz & Wang, 2011; Wang & Shultz, 2010) and the resource-based dynamic model of retirement adjustment. The latter model focuses on the role of individual and contextual resources and resource changes in predicting retirement adjustment (Wang, Henkens, & van Solinge, 2011).

Similar to bridge employment, research on the retirement process has rapidly grown over the past decade, with studies focusing particularly on the early stage of retirement planning (Earl, Bednall, & Muratore, 2015; Petkoska & Earl, 2009) and the later stage of retirement adjustment (Donaldson, Earl, & Muratore, 2010; Muratore & Earl, 2015). A meta-analysis on predictors and outcomes of retirement planning and the decision to retire found that retirement planning was weakly related to poor health, negative working conditions, and positive attitudes toward retirement, as well as lower work involvement and job satisfaction (Topa, Moriano, Depolo, Alcover, & Morales, 2009). Furthermore, the decision to retire was positively related to retirement planning and bridge employment, engagement in volunteer work, and retirement satisfaction.

With regard to adjustment to retirement, a longitudinal study found that retirees in the United States can be grouped into three distinct adjustment patterns. The first and largest group maintains high levels of well-being after the retirement transition, whereas retirees' well-being in the other two groups increases after the transition or follows a U-shaped pattern (Wang, 2007). Membership in the first group was predicted by having a bridge job, retirement planning, and by having a spouse who was not working. The "recovery pattern" (i.e., increases in well-being following the transition) could be predicted by high levels of physical demands, work stress, and low satisfaction in participants' career job. Membership in the group that followed a U-shape pattern in well-being could be predicted by health declines during the retirement transition, an unhappy marriage, and early retirement. Similar findings emerged in a study on older workers' adjustment to retirement conducted in Germany (Pinquart & Schindler, 2007). Consistent with research on bridge employment, these findings suggest that career counselling for workers who approach the retirement transition should not only take into account individual factors, but also social/family and work-related factors to help older workers prepare for retirement. Moreover, the findings suggest that career counselling interventions could be adapted to the specific characteristics and situations of clients (e.g., membership in one of the three groups identified in the studies described above) to achieve more successful outcomes.

Career Counselling Interventions in the Context of Bridge Employment and Retirement

Organizational programs and counselling for retirement are not new research topics, particularly not in the gerontological literature (e.g., Charles, 1971; Fillenbaum, 1971; Glamser & Dejong, 1975; Kalt & Kohn, 1975; Morrow, 1980). However, early studies in this area predominantly focused on interventions for older men from Western cultures. For example, an early study by Ash (1966) describes several effective techniques (e.g., several formal invitations to counselling sessions at ages 55, 60, 64, and 65) for encouraging male steel workers to think constructively about and plan early for retirement. Kremer and Harpaz (1982) reported that older male workers' intentions to participate in a preretirement counselling program were negatively influenced by a strong work orientation. Traditionally, preretirement programs and counselling interventions have focused mainly on older workers' financial resources for retirement and sometimes their health (Jacobs-Lawson & Hershey, 2005; Verwoerdt, 1970; Willett, 2008). More recently, however, organizational researchers and preretirement programs have addressed additional resources (Leung & Earl, 2012; Marcellini, Sensoli, Barbini, & Fioravanti, 1997; Muratore & Earl, 2015). For instance, a recent intervention study focused on psychological and social resources (e.g., optimism, self-efficacy, individual strengths, goals, social networks) as part of a resource-oriented group intervention to support older workers' retirement transition (Seiferling & Michel, 2017). Compared to a control group, program participants reported an increase in psychosocial resources which, in turn, led to greater intentions to master the retirement transition, less retirement anxiety, and fewer negative retirement expectations. In the spirit of this book's emphasis on innovating career counselling, in the following we describe two innovative approaches of career counselling for older workers transitioning to bridge employment or retirement. The first approach is based on the theory of work adjustment (Dawis & Lofquist, 1984; Harper & Shoffner, 2004; Lofquist & Dawis, 1969), whereas the second approach is based on an extension of life-span life-space theory (Chen, 2011b; Super, 1980). While there are other career development theories that have been adapted to the retirement context (e.g., life design perspective, Froidevaux, 2018; career transition theories, Schlossberg, 2003), we decided to focus on two of the most prominent theoretical frameworks of career development in this chapter.

Theory of Work Adjustment

The theory of work adjustment (Dawis & Lofquist, 1984) proposes that workers' personal satisfaction results from the correspondence or fit between their values and needs, on the one hand, and "reinforcers" (e.g., rewards, favorable work conditions) present in the work environment on the other hand. In addition, the better the fit between a workers' abilities and skills and the requirements and expectations of the work environment, the more likely they will perform their job well from the employer's perspective (called "satisfactoriness" in the theory of work adjustment). Dawis and Lofquist (1984) were the first to apply their theory to the case of career counselling for older workers in the retirement transition (see also Harper & Shoffner, 2004, for a detailed elaboration of this topic). The main goal of career counselling based on the theory of work adjustment is that retirees achieve levels of correspondence or fit between their individual abilities and needs, on the one hand, and environmental requirements and reinforcers, on the other hand, that are similar to their levels of fit before the retirement transition. To this end, career counselors and workers need to gain an understanding of important, possibly dynamic characteristics of the older individual (e.g., abilities, motives, personality). Moreover, they need to understand requirement and reinforcers in older adults' (work) environment that might be lost due to retirement (e.g., status, identity, rewards, social networks) and discuss how they could be meaningfully replaced once workers are retired (Harper & Shoffner, 2004). While Dawis and Lofquist (1984) focus on changes from a work environment to a non-work environment (e.g., family life, volunteering) after the retirement transition, their ideas also apply to the transition from a career job to bridge employment. If the postretirement environment cannot be selected or modified to fit the individual's current abilities and needs, the theory suggests that retirees, potentially with the help of a career counselor, need to accommodate for environmental losses (see also Baltes, 1997; Müller, De Lange, Weigl, Oxfart, & Van der Heijden, 2013). In sum, the theory of work adjustment suggests that career counselors should focus on the factors that contributed to older workers' preretirement satisfaction and satisfactoriness to support postretirement adjustment through improved ability utilization and personal needs satisfaction. A strength of the theory of work adjustment in this context is that it does not only focus on tasks, but also on other potential sources of worker and retiree (dis)satisfaction and satisfactoriness, such as social relationships and age discrimination (Harper & Shoffner, 2004).

A theoretical article by Hesketh et al. (2011) explicitly adapted the theory of work adjustment to the context of the retirement transition and retirement adjustment. This retirement transition and adjustment framework also focuses on dynamic intraindividual and environmental changes over time, and it embeds individual psychological decisions within a broader ecological context (e.g., family, groups, policies, culture). One the one hand, Hesketh and colleagues (2011) proposed that the fit between individuals' current abilities (e.g., cognitive, physical, social) and the abilities required (at home, at work, and in the community) leads to coping performance and adjustment (at home, at work, and in the community). This dynamic aspect of the framework suggests that, when individual and/or environmental changes lead to misfit, fit can be restored through the use of proactive behaviors (e.g., post-retirement work, seeking advice) and reactive adjustment behaviors (e.g., reduce activity, modify expectations). On the other hand, the fit between individuals' current needs and values (e.g., independence, activity, social relationships) and reinforcers supplied (e.g., finances, housing, healthcare) influences individuals' level of satisfaction. Again, in the case of misfit, fit can be restored through proactive and reactive environmental adjustment styles (e.g., job design, prevention of age discrimination, and other organizational interventions). The interplay between satisfaction and coping performance and adjustment, in turn, leads to positive aging (Hesketh et al., 2011), a concept related to successful and active aging at work (Zacher, 2015; Zacher, Kooij, & Beier, 2018; Zacher & Rudolph, 2017). Based on Hesketh et al.'s (2011) model, career counselling interventions should address workers' fit between individual abilities and environmental requirements, as well as fit between individual needs and environmental reinforcers. Moreover, they should focus on the proactive and reactive adjustment behaviors necessary to improve the fit between these individual and environmental aspects which, in turn, lead to improvements in individuals' satisfaction, coping performance, and positive aging. For example, counselors could discuss with older workers which age stereotypes they hold themselves and how these may impact their behavior, as well as how they could voice concerns against managerial and organizational age discrimination.

In a more recent paper, Hesketh, Griffin, Dawis, and Bayl-Smith (2015) extended their retirement transition framework by including additional variables that may play an important role in the retirement transition. Specifically, the researchers suggest that self-efficacy, personal and social identity, and stereotyping are likely to impact the perception of oneself and one's environment as well as dynamic adjustment behaviors and work styles. In addition, they argued that the dynamic process of adjusting behaviors and work styles is influenced by workers' subjective life expectancy, an age-related factor similar to occupational future time perspective (Rudolph, Kooij, Rauvola, & Zacher, 2018; Zacher & Frese, 2009). Importantly, Hesketh and colleagues (2015) emphasized the potential of their framework for use by individual workers in the retirement transition, as well as career counselors and organizations aiming to facilitate the adjustment processes of older workers. The updated retirement transition framework and associated empirical findings (see Griffin, Hesketh, & Loh, 2012) suggest that career counselling should particularly address the newly added variables, that is, older workers' self-efficacy beliefs, identification with life roles, age-based stereotypes, and subjective life expectancy. As these variables may be impacted by cultural differences (Marcus & Fritzsche, 2016; Minola, Criaco, &

Obschonka, 2016), counselors should also take older workers' cultural background into account.

Life-Career Re-engagement Framework

The second framework we describe here, the life-career re-engagement framework (Chen, 2011a, 2011b), is based on the well-established life-span life-space theory (Super, 1980; Super, Savickas, & Super, 1996). Life-span life-space theory focuses on different life and career stages, as well as the work and nonwork roles that individuals occupy across their lifespan. Specifically, the five developmental stages (with approximate age ranges) are growth (birth to 14 years), exploration (15–24 years), establishment (25–44 years), maintenance (45–65 years), and decline/disengagement (65 years and older). The five associated developmental tasks are called crystallization, specification, implementation, stabilization, and consolidation, respectively. Importantly, Super and colleagues (1996) suggested that these age ranges are based on historical norms that may change over time and that, as careers become more dynamic and flexible, people may go through these stages several times, independent of their age (i.e., people "re-cycle" through the stages). The work and nonwork roles outlined by life-span life-space theory include child, student, leisurite, citizen, worker, spouse/partner, homemaker, parent, and pensioner (Super, 1980). Thus, the theory adopts a developmental and role-based perspective (Super, 1984).

In a set of two papers, Chen (2011a, 2011b), extended Super's (1980) theory by developing a new conceptual framework of life-career re-engagement. The goal of this framework is to present an innovative counselling approach to help clients cope with the retirement transition. According to Chen (2011b), "counselling in this context can be considered a special helping intervention for life-career development aiming at helping clients to explore and to acquire a sense of renewed vocation in the retirement phase of their lives" (p. 25). Chen (2011b) questioned the appropriateness and topicality of the last stage in Super's model, originally called "decline" (Super, 1953) and later replaced with the term "disengagement" (Super et al., 1996), suggesting that older adults will withdraw from active functioning, for instance in paid worker roles. In this regard, Super's theory is similar to disengagement theory from the early gerontological literature, which suggests that, to age successfully, older adults should withdraw from active life roles (Cumming & Henry, 1961, see also Zacher & Rudolph, 2017, for a comparison of theories on successful aging). Chen (2011b) acknowledged that the retirement phase could or should also involve rest, relaxation, and leisure on the part of older adults, but that contemporary retirement experiences are more dynamic, entail much more complexity in decisions, and allow for a greater variety of activities.

Chen (2011b) outlined three key features of the life-career re-engagement framework. First, re-engagement involves a proactive approach to retirement, which means that individuals act in a self-initiated, future-oriented, and change-oriented way (Zacher & Kooij, 2017). Proactive retirees continue their life-career developmental tasks in retirement, making retirement the marker of the beginning of a new life-career developmental stage rather than the end of their career development. In other words, individuals experience a sense of vocation, meaning, creativity, and are engaged with activities that provide new fulfillment and enjoyment in their lives during the retirement phase (Chen, 2011b). They may even decide to go beyond their "comfort zone" and construct completely new career experiences (Savickas, 2005; Zacher & Griffin, 2015). Second, the framework requires continuous self-exploration and self-enhancement (Chen, 2011b). This is because the retirement experience is not static, but often experienced as a lengthy, diverse, and continuously evolving stage with great potential for personal change and transformation. Finally, part of the life-career re-engagement framework are life role interaction and integration (Chen, 2011b). This means that the roles of retirees are dynamic, open to change, complex, and multidimensional (e.g., worker, professional organization member, active volunteer, parent and/or grandparent, person of leisure). In sum, Chen (2011b) argued that the retirement phase can be a lengthy, yet revitalizing and unique experience of life-career development.

In the second, complementary article, Chen (2011a) discussed effective career counselling, guided by the life-career re-engagement framework, to promote older adults' retirement adjustment. The researcher argues that career counselors who work with retirees should not only possess relevant knowledge, skills, and abilities to counsel older adults, but also need to be very sensitive regarding the needs and retirement experiences of each individual client (see Zuehlsdorff & Baldwin, 1995). In particular, career counselors should consider three core factors while helping their clients develop new plans in the re-engagement phase (Chen, 2011a).

First, career counselling based on the life-career re-engagement concept requires that clients' financial resources are adequate to support a stable living in retirement (e.g., pension plan, retirement savings). Chen (2011a) acknowledges that re-engagement tasks may involve financial rewards; however, retirees should not depend on these earnings to pursue new goals in this life stage. Thus, career counselors should help their clients prioritize financial and non-monetary needs and expectations.

Second, similar to financial resources, clients' health should be good. Chen (2011a) argued that good physical and mental health are important requirements for planning and organizing a renewed and fulfilling retiree life. Career counselors should support their clients in developing a realistic view and flexible approach regarding activities that they are able to pursue, possibly after certain work- or nonwork-related accommodations have been made (Kensbock, Boehm, & Bourovoi, 2017), and activities that they cannot do or should avoid doing.

Finally, Chen (2011a) suggested that career counselors should take their clients' age and age-related characteristics (e.g., experience, future time perspective, age stereotypes) into account and help clients' deal with their age in a positive and constructive (i.e., not discriminatory), yet realistic (e.g., not overconfident) manner. Thus, on the one hand, clients should recognize the various gains in personal and contextual resources that come with age, such as increased experience and established social networks (Freund & Ebner, 2005). As noted by Chen (2011a), "Age should not, and will not, be a barrier, but an asset, in the re-engagement effort" (p. 35).

On the other hand, clients must become aware that age is accompanied by losses in certain psychological functions and resources, such as physical strength and fast information processing abilities (Salthouse, 2012). Thus, career counselling should help clients become aware of age-related limits and stereotypes, but also focus on age-related strengths for life-career development in the re-engagement stage (Chen, 2011a).

Subsequently, based on the life-career re-engagement framework, Chen (2011a) derived several broader recommendations for career counselling of individuals transitioning to retirement. First, career counselors should contextualize their clients' unique experiences, emphasizing that retirement adjustment is not only a normative developmental task for older adults, but a dynamic, complex, and in many respects idiosyncratic experience. While this experience is certainly shaped by the cultural, economic, social, and historical context in which individuals are embedded, it is important to be aware of the fact that there can be great interindividual differences and intraindividual plasticity (i.e., within-person modifiability over time) in workers' retirement experiences and adjustment (Zacher, Rudolph, & Baltes, 2019). Thus, career counselors should not simplify or overgeneralize an older adult's retirement situation and adjustment experiences and refrain from applying age-based stereotypes to their clients.

Second, career counselors need to help their clients negotiate a new or changing identity in the face of the transition from a work role to retirement (Chen, 2011a). As noted above in the context of the theory of work adjustment, a new role entails new environmental routines, requirements, and reinforcers (Dawis & Lofquist, 1984). Career counselors can help clients gain a better understanding of themselves in the retirement transition and learn to distance themselves from age-based stereotypes and unrealistic expectations. Moreover, career counselling can help clients see and interpret connections between their life and career roles in the past, present, and future. Based on a better self-understanding, career counselors can assist their clients transition to their new roles and identity better with the re-engagement stage.

Third, Chen (2011a) argued that the life-career re-engagement stage entails the development of new interests and, therefore, supports retirees' personal growth. Career counselors need to assist their clients in identifying, exploring, and possibly prioritizing new areas of interest that provide them with a sense of growth and meaningfulness. This process will be easier for some clients than for others, such as those who did not have time and opportunities to develop interests outside of their career job (Berg, Grant, & Johnson, 2010).

Finally, the entire process of life-career re-engagement represents a form of lifelong learning, with clients continuously accumulating new experiences guided by the career counselor (Chen, 2011a). Counselors should encourage clients to reflect on their past learning experiences and actively seek new opportunities to learn in the present and future. Importantly, career counselors should develop flexible learning goals and strategies taking clients' abilities, needs, and unique situation into account. Overall, the life-career re-engagement framework can guide career counselling and support individuals' adjustment in the retirement transition (Chen, 2011a, 2011b). However, it is important to keep in mind that this approach depends on cultural (e.g., national retirement policies and support systems), socioeconomic (e.g., adequate financial resources) and personal factors (e.g., openness to new experiences).

Implications, Recommendations, and Conclusions

The goal of this chapter was to describe and discuss innovative and successful methods of career counselling for older workers who transition from their career job to bridge employment or from their career job or bridge employment to retirement. In this final section of this chapter, we describe a number of implications for older workers, career counselors, organizations, and researchers based on the insights gained in previous sections.

With regard to older workers, our literature review clearly indicates that early retirement planning, not only with regard to (expected) finances and health, but also in terms of psychosocial resources, is an important predictor of successful adjustment in bridge employment and retirement. This includes the acquisition of important information regarding this new life stage (Jensen-Scott, 1993). Some older workers may be hesitant to participate in career counselling offered by their organizations. However, we encourage them to take advantage of this opportunity as career counselling and preretirement programs generally have been shown to be effective interventions. Based on the theory of work adjustment, older workers should consider which factors of their current work environment, including requirements and reinforcers, they would miss in bridge employment or retirement. Based on this analysis, they should select their later life engagements accordingly to optimize their personal satisfaction and satisfactoriness. The life-career re-engagement framework suggests that older workers should not perceive retirement as "decline" or "disengagement" but, rather, as a new stage that offers opportunities for reinvention and growth. Accordingly, Perry (1980) emphasized that successful adjustment to retirement depends not only on the existence of retirement plans and resources, but also positive attitudes toward retirement and a realistic picture of retirement. Older workers should distance themselves from negative age stereotypes and unrealistic expectations. The author argues that many people have access to counselling when they prepare for employment and when they work, and that there should also be access to counselors and guidance programs that address retirement.

For career counselors, our review of research on the transitions to bridge employment and retirement, as well as career counselling approaches to support older adults in these transitions, has a number of implications. First, in addition to improving their general counselling skills, career counselors should become familiar with theories and models in the areas of bridge employment and retirement (Lytle, Clancy, Foley, & Cotter, 2015). Knowledge about bridge employment and retirement will help career counselors become more sensitive to older adults' situation and experiences and learn to question prevalent negative age stereotypes (Zuehlsdorff & Baldwin, 1995). Counselors need to be aware and understand the factors (including personal, family, financial, and cultural) influencing older workers' bridge employment or retirement decisions in order to provide effective advice and support. This also includes the fact that for many older adults, the end of their working life constitutes a personal crisis and stressful situation, as their careers have been associated with valued, yet now threatened resources such as status, identity, money, and power (Hobfoll & Wells, 1998; Jensen-Scott, 1993). Moreover, when they were younger, workers may have been socialized in a culture that differs from the culture in which they plan to retire in terms of retirement-related policies, practices, as well as individual and societal expectations. In sum, career counselors should be aware of the unique and diverse motives of older workers intending to participate in bridge employment or to retire. This may include financial security, health care, or personal fulfillment (Lytle et al., 2015).

Career counselors should also consider a number of barriers for effective counselling with older adults. Specifically, older adults who are in most need of an intervention may be hard to reach, or there may be a lack of career-related opportunities for older adults. Additionally, it may be difficult to establish a counselling relationship with older or much older clients, and appropriate assessment instruments may not be available or not normed for an older age group (Jensen-Scott, 1993). Furthermore, older adults may also experience stereotype threat in assessment situations. Stereotype threat refers to an individuals' concerns that others believe stereotypes about one's age group, leading to anxiety and actual performance decrements (Finkelstein, King, & Voyles, 2015; von Hippel, Kalokerinos, & Henry, 2012). To address these issues, Jensen-Scott (1993) suggests that policy makers should start to educate adults early in life about the importance of retirement planning and career counselling. Moreover, career counselors should critically evaluate their own assumptions about aging and older age groups in order to combat negative effects of age stereotypes or generationalism (Rauvola, Rudolph, & Zacher, 2018; Staudinger, 2015). Career counselling training programs should include internships and other practical experiences, in which students interact with older adults to develop intergenerational competencies, reduce potential age-related biases, and learn relevant knowledge and skills to support older adults' continuous development (Henry, Zacher, & Desmette, 2015; Lytle et al., 2015).

Career counselors should be aware of older job seekers' particular vulnerability due to potentially limited opportunities in the labor market, reduced job search self-efficacy, and relatively lower job search intensity compared to younger adults (Zacher, 2013; Zacher & Bock, 2014). Career counselors can work with older job seekers to discuss their work histories and prioritize occupational goals, explore current abilities and skills that can be transferred to new jobs, and help them identify their strengths and areas for development (Lytle et al., 2015).

Last here, organizations facing increasingly older and age-diverse workforces, as well as problems recruiting highly qualified personnel, should invest resources into effective preretirement programs and counselling interventions to support older workers' bridge employment and retirement decision making. They should also find ways to encourage or reward middle-aged and older workers for participating in such interventions. A possible outcome of these interventions is that highly valued older workers remain employed for longer (Oakman & Wells, 2016). Organizations should also remind career counselors to consider not only personal, but also broader social (e.g., family, team), environmental, legal, and multicultural factors that may influence the decisions and adjustment of older workers (Lytle et al., 2015). Many organizations already treat age as an important dimension of diversity management and emphasize the lifelong nature of career development (Böhm & Dwertmann, 2015; Böhm, Kunze, & Bruch, 2014). Research suggests that diversity needs to be managed carefully to reap it benefits (e.g., exchange of different perspectives) and to minimize its disadvantages (e.g., age stereotypes) (Kearney & Gebert, 2009). Organizations could also collaborate with community service and adult education providers to ensure that their older employees can participate in retirement preparation programs and workshops (Lytle et al., 2015). At the same time, organizations should follow current retirement trends and options for older workers and the introduction of new laws and regulations relevant for the older members of the workforce. They should also be open to accommodate the unique and changing needs of older workers participating in bridge employment, such as disability accommodations, flexible work scheduling, and long-term leaves to caregiving responsibilities or chronic illness (Burch, Dugan, & Barnes-Farrell, 2018; Kensbock et al., 2017).

The processes (e.g., modes of delivery, procedures) of counselling for bridge employment and retirement planning are areas for future research as well as organizational application. Generally, more research is needed that adapts established career counselling and vocational behavior frameworks to the contexts of bridge employment and retirement. Although we have focused on theoretical extensions of the theory of work adjustment and life-span life-space theory, future research could adapt, for example, systemic and constructivist career theories (e.g., Arthur & McMahon, 2005; Savickas, 2013) to more exhaustively address challenges in the transitions faced by older workers. Furthermore, innovative approaches that integrate counselling with career sense-making (i.e., narrative reflection and insight on one's career history and future) have the potential to facilitate successful and identity-integrative bridge employment and retirement planning. London (1990) discusses the role of "career-end management" and the key role that career insight can play in such management. Specifically, career insight in this context can entail recognition of diminished work capabilities and interests, remaining work opportunities, post-work occupational activities, and desirable non-work activities. Through retirement workshops and other interventions, career insight and sense-making can be facilitated and promote "career continuity" across the end of one's working life (London, 1990) as well as retirement adjustment (Fuller & Redfering, 1976). This approach has been referred to as "narrative meaning making" and "intentional self-development" elsewhere in the literature (Bauer & McAdams, 2004), which are studied and leveraged around consequential transitions such as career changes like late-career job loss (Zikic & Richardson, 2007) and retirement (Jonsson, Kielhofner, & Borell, 1997; Simon & Osipow, 1996). Aside from the intraindividual well-being advantages, career sense-making and retirement planning interventions have also been shown to positively impact post-retirement career intentions (Muratore & Earl, 2015; Wöhrmann, Deller, & Wang, 2014). Technology could be leveraged by organizations here as well, through the use of innovative online retirement planning and sense-making templates, courses, news, and simulations (e.g., financial projections) as well as real-time access to expert counselors and advisors and other preretirement individuals (Dennis, 2002).

These resources should be tailored to specific late-career individuals, given trait- (e.g., proactive personality, time discounting) and demographic-based (e.g., gender) differences in retirement planning shown in the literature (Griffin, Loh, & Hesketh, 2012). Socioeconomic and health status, as well as the intersections between these and other identities (e.g., minority status), personal and contextual resources (e.g., financial literacy), and perceived norms around planning should play a central role in retirement planning and timing as well (Alessie, van Rooij, & Lusardi, 2011; Dennis, 2002; Griffin, Loh, et al., 2012; Noone, Alpass, & Stephens, 2010). Organizations must bear these considerations in mind when developing and implementing innovative career practices for pre-retirement adults.

Finally, further research is needed on the effectiveness of pre- and postretirement programs and counselling interventions (i.e., the "effects" of such initiatives), particularly interventions with older workers and retirees based on the theory of work adjustment and the retirement transition adjustment framework, as well as the life-career re-engagement framework. Why do older workers benefit from such interventions, and are there subgroups of older workers and retirees (e.g., those with adequate financial resources and in good health) that benefit more or less from them? How do interventions help older adults maximize the financial and psychological benefits of bridge employment or delayed retirement? What methods and forms of interventions are most effective, and for whom? Research should also examine why those older adults who may benefit the most from career counselling are least likely to participate.

In conclusion, the aging and increasingly age-diverse workforce requires innovative and successful approaches to career counselling of older adults transitioning to bridge employment and retirement. After a review of theories and empirical evidence on bridge employment and retirement, we presented two such approaches. Career counselling based on the theory of work adjustment and the life-career re-engagement framework are promising approaches to support older adults planning for bridge employment and retirement, their decision-making process, and the adjustment to new work and life roles. In addition to these psychological processes, career counselors are well advised to take into consideration (and adapt the counselling approach accordingly) important contextual factors, such as cultural background, socioeconomic status, and negative age stereotypes. To further improve our understanding of the role of counselling for the transitions from people's career jobs to bridge employment and retirement, future research could adapt additional established career development frameworks to these later-life contexts.

References

Alcover, C.-M., Topa, G., Parry, E., Fraccaroli, F., & Depolo, M. (2014). *Bridge employment: A research handbook*. London: Routledge.

Alessie, R., van Rooij, M., & Lusardi, A. (2011). Financial literacy and retirement preparation in the Netherlands. *Journal of Pension Economics & Finance, 10,* 527–545. https://doi.org/10.1017/S1474747211000461.

Arthur, N., & McMahon, M. (2005). Multicultural career counseling: Theoretical applications of the systems theory framework. *Career Development Quarterly, 53*(3), 208–222. https://doi.org/10.1002/j.2161-0045.2005.tb00991.x.

Ash, P. (1966). Pre-retirement counseling. *The Gerontologist, 6*(2), 97–99. https://doi.org/10.1093/geront/6.2.97.

Atchley, R. C. (1972). *The social force in later life*. Belmont, CA: Wadsworth.

Baltes, P. B. (1997). On the incomplete architecture of human ontogeny: Selection, optimization, and compensation as foundation of developmental theory. *American Psychologist, 52*(4), 366–380. https://doi.org/10.1037/0003-066X.52.4.366.

Bauer, J. J., & McAdams, D. P. (2004). Personal growth in adults' stories of life transitions. *Journal of Personality, 72,* 573–602. https://doi.org/10.1111/j.0022-3506.2004.00273.x.

Beehr, T. A., & Bennett, M. M. (2015). Working after retirement: Features of bridge employment and research directions. *Work, Aging and Retirement, 1*(1), 112–128. https://doi.org/10.1093/workar/wau007.

Berg, J. M., Grant, A. M., & Johnson, V. (2010). When callings are calling: Crafting work and leisure in pursuit of unanswered occupational callings. *Organization Science, 21*(5), 973–994. https://doi.org/10.1287/orsc.1090.0497.

Böhm, S. A., & Dwertmann, D. J. G. (2015). Forging a single-edged sword: Facilitating positive age and disability diversity effects in the workplace through leadership, positive climates, and HR practices. *Work, Aging and Retirement, 1*(1), 41–63. https://doi.org/10.1093/workar/wau008.

Böhm, S. A., Kunze, F., & Bruch, H. (2014). Spotlight on age-diversity climate: The impact of age-inclusive HR practices on firm-level outcomes. *Personnel Psychology, 67*(3), 667–704. https://doi.org/10.1111/peps.12047.

Burch, K. A., Dugan, A. G., & Barnes-Farrell, J. L. (2018). Understanding what eldercare means for employees and organizations: A review and recommendations for future research. *Work, Aging and Retirement*. https://doi.org/10.1093/workar/way011.

Burmeister, A., & Deller, J. (2016). Knowledge retention from older and retiring workers: What do we know, and where do we go from here? *Work, Aging and Retirement, 2*(2), 87–104. https://doi.org/10.1093/workar/waw002.

Chand, M., & Tung, R. L. (2014). The aging of the world's population and its effects on global business. *Academy of Management Perspectives, 28*(4), 409–429. https://doi.org/10.5465/amp.2012.0070.

Charles, D. C. (1971). Effect of participation in a pre-retirement program. *The Gerontologist, 11*(1), 24–28. https://doi.org/10.1093/geront/11.1_Part_1.24.

Chen, C. P. (2011a). Life-career re-engagement: A new conceptual framework for counselling people in retirement transition—Part 2. *Australian Journal of Career Development, 20*(2), 32–41. https://doi.org/10.1177/103841621102000205.

Chen, C. P. (2011b). Life-career re-engagement: A new conceptual framework for counselling people in retirement transition—Part I. *Australian Journal of Career Development, 20*(2), 25–31. https://doi.org/10.1177/103841621102000204.

Cumming, E., & Henry, W. E. (1961). *Growing old: The process of disengagement*. New York: Basic Books.

Dawis, R. V., & Lofquist, L. H. (1984). *A psychological theory of work adjustment*. Minneapolis, MN: University of Minnesota Press.

Dennis, H. (2002). The retirement planning specialty. *Generations, 26,* 55–60.

Donaldson, T., Earl, J. K., & Muratore, A. M. (2010). Extending the integrated model of retirement adjustment: Incorporating mastery and retirement planning. *Journal of Vocational Behavior, 77*(2), 279–289. https://doi.org/10.1016/j.jvb.2010.03.003.

Dropkin, J., Moline, J., Kim, H., & Gold, J. E. (2016). Blended work as a bridge between traditional workplace employment and retirement: A conceptual review. *Work, Aging and Retirement, 2*(4), 373–383. https://doi.org/10.1093/workar/waw017.

Earl, J. K., Bednall, T. C., & Muratore, A. M. (2015). A matter of time: Why some people plan for retirement and others do not. *Work, Aging and Retirement, 1*(2), 181–189. https://doi.org/10.1093/workar/wau005.

Fillenbaum, G. G. (1971). Retirement planning programs—At what age, and for whom? *The Gerontologist, 11*(1), 33–36. https://doi.org/10.1093/geront/11.1_Part_1.33.

Finkelstein, L. M., King, E. B., & Voyles, E. C. (2015). Age metastereotyping and cross-age workplace interactions: A meta view of age stereotypes at work. *Work, Aging and Retirement, 1*(1), 26–40. https://doi.org/10.1093/workar/wau002.

Freund, A. M., & Ebner, N. C. (2005). The aging self: Shifting from promoting gains to balancing losses. In W. Greve, K. Rothermund, & D. Wentura (Eds.), *The adaptive self: Personal continuity and intentional self-development* (pp. 185–202). Ashland, OH: Hogrefe & Huber Publishers.

Froidevaux, A. (2018). A life design perspective on the work to retirement transition. In V. Cohen-Scali, J. Rossier, & L. Nota (Eds.), *New perspectives on career counseling and guidance in Europe* (pp. 89–104). Cham, Switzerland: Springer.

Fuller, R. L., & Redfering, D. L. (1976). Effects of preretirement planning on the retirement adjustment of military personnel. *Work and Occupations, 3,* 479–487. https://doi.org/10.1177/009392857634005.

Glamser, F. D., & Dejong, G. F. (1975). The efficacy of preretirement preparation programs for industrial workers. *Journal of Gerontology, 30*(5), 595–600. https://doi.org/10.1093/geronj/30.5.595.

Griffin, B., Bayl-Smith, P., & Hesketh, B. (2016). The longitudinal effects of perceived age discrimination on the job satisfaction and work withdrawal of older employees. *Work, Aging and Retirement, 2*(4), 415–427. https://doi.org/10.1093/workar/waw014.

Griffin, B., & Hesketh, B. (2008). Post-retirement at work: The individual determinants of paid and volunteer work. *Journal of Occupational and Organizational Psychology, 81*(1), 101–121. https://doi.org/10.1348/096317907X202518.

Griffin, B., Hesketh, B., & Loh, V. (2012). The influence of subjective life expectancy on retirement transition and planning: A longitudinal study. *Journal of Vocational Behavior, 81*(2), 129–137. https://doi.org/10.1016/j.jvb.2012.05.005.

Griffin, B., Loh, D., & Hesketh, B. (2012). Using proactivity, time discounting, and the theory of planned behavior to identify predictors of retirement planning. *Educational Gerontology, 38,* 877–889. https://doi.org/10.1080/03601277.2012.660857.

Harper, M. C., & Shoffner, M. F. (2004). Counseling for continued career development after retirement: An application of the theory of work adjustment. *The Career Development Quarterly, 52*(3), 272–284. https://doi.org/10.1002/j.2161-0045.2004.tb00648.x.

Henkens, K., van Dalen, H., Ekerdt, D., Hershey, D., Hyde, M., Radl, J., et al. (2018). What we need to know about retirement: Pressing issues for the coming decade. *The Gerontologist, 58*(5), 805–812. https://doi.org/10.1093/geront/gnx095.

Henry, H., Zacher, H., & Desmette, D. (2015). Reducing age bias and turnover intentions by enhancing intergenerational contact quality in the workplace: The role of opportunities for generativity and development. *Work, Aging and Retirement, 1*(3), 243–253. https://doi.org/10.1093/workar/wav005.

Heppner, M. J., & Heppner, P. P. (2003). Identifying process variables in career counseling: A research agenda. *Journal of Vocational Behavior, 62*(3), 429–452. https://doi.org/10.1016/S0001-8791(02)00053-2.

Hertel, G., & Zacher, H. (2018). Managing the aging workforce. In D. S. Ones, N. Anderson, C. Viswesvaran, & H. K. Sinangil (Eds.), *The Sage handbook of industrial, work and organizational psychology* (2nd ed., Vol. 3, pp. 396–428). Thousand Oaks, CA: Sage.

Hesketh, B., Griffin, B., Dawis, R., & Bayl-Smith, P. (2015). Extensions to the dynamic aspects of the retirement transition and adjustment framework (RTAF): Adjustment behaviors, work styles, and identity. *Work, Aging and Retirement, 1*(1), 79–91. https://doi.org/10.1093/workar/wau004.

Hesketh, B., Griffin, B., & Loh, V. (2011). A future-oriented retirement transition adjustment framework. *Journal of Vocational Behavior, 79*(2), 303–314. https://doi.org/10.1016/j.jvb.2011.03.008.

Hobfoll, S. E., & Wells, J. D. (1998). Conservation of resources, stress, and aging: Why do some slide and some spring? In J. Lomranz (Ed.), *Handbook of aging and mental health: An integrative approach*. New York: Plenum Press.

Jacobs-Lawson, J. M., & Hershey, D. A. (2005). Influence of future time perspective, financial knowledge, and financial risk tolerance on retirement saving behaviors. *Financial Services Review, 14,* 331–344.

Jensen-Scott, R. L. (1993). Counseling to promote retirement adjustment. *The Career Development Quarterly, 41*(3), 257–267. https://doi.org/10.1002/j.2161-0045.1993.tb00376.x.

Jonsson, H., Kielhofner, G., & Borell, L. (1997). Anticipating retirement: The formation of narratives concerning an occupational transition. *The American Journal of Occupational Therapy, 51,* 49–56. https://doi.org/10.5014/ajot.51.1.49.

Kalt, N. C., & Kohn, M. H. (1975). Pre-retirement counseling: Characteristics of programs and preferences of retirees. *The Gerontologist, 15*(2), 179–181. https://doi.org/10.1093/geront/15.2.179.

Kearney, E., & Gebert, D. (2009). Managing diversity and enhancing team outcomes: The promise of transformational leadership. *Journal of Applied Psychology, 94*(1), 77–89. https://doi.org/10.1037/a0013077.

Kensbock, J. M., Boehm, S. A., & Bourovoi, K. (2017). Is there a downside of job accommodations? An employee perspective on individual change processes. *Frontiers in Psychology, 8,* 1536. https://doi.org/10.3389/fpsyg.2017.01536.

Kim, S., & Feldman, D. C. (2000). Working in retirement: The antecedents of bridge employment and its consequences for quality of life in retirement. *Academy of Management Journal, 43*(6), 1195–1210. https://doi.org/10.5465/1556345.

Kremer, Y., & Harpaz, I. (1982). Attitudes toward pre-retirement counselling: A path model *Journal of Organizational Behavior, 3*(3), 205–213. https://doi.org/10.1002/job.4030030302.

Kulik, C. T., Ryan, S., Harper, S., & George, G. (2014). From the editors: Aging populations and management. *Academy of Management Journal, 57*(4), 929–935. https://doi.org/10.5465/amj.2014.4004.

Leung, C. S., & Earl, J. K. (2012). Retirement resources inventory: Construction, factor structure and psychometric properties. *Journal of Vocational Behavior, 81*(2), 171–182. https://doi.org/10.1016/j.jvb.2012.06.005.

Lofquist, L. H., & Dawis, R. (1969). *Adjustment to work*. New York: Appleton-Century-Crofts.

London, M. (1990). Enhancing career motivation in late career. *Journal of Organizational Change Management, 3,* 58–71. https://doi.org/10.1108/09534819010001351.

Lytle, M. C., Clancy, M. E., Foley, P. F., & Cotter, E. W. (2015). Current trends in retirement: Implications for career counseling and vocational psychology. *Journal of Career Development, 42*(3), 170–184. https://doi.org/10.1177/0894845314545785.

Marcellini, F., Sensoli, C., Barbini, N., & Fioravanti, P (1997). Preparation for retirement: Problems and suggestions of retirees. *Educational Gerontology: An International Quarterly, 23*(4), 377–388. https://doi.org/10.1080/0360127970230406.

Marcus, J., & Fritzsche, B. A. (2016). The cultural anchors of age discrimination in the workplace: A multilevel framework. *Work, Aging and Retirement, 2*(2), 217–229. https://doi.org/10.1093/workar/waw007.

Minola, T., Criaco, G., & Obschonka, M. (2016). Age, culture, and self-employment motivation. *Small Business Economics, 46*(2), 187–213. https://doi.org/10.1007/s11187-015-9685-6.

Mor-Barak, M. E. (1995). The meaning of work for older adults seeking employment: The generativity factor. *International Journal of Aging and Human Development, 41*(4), 325–344. https://doi.org/10.2190/VGTG-EPK6-Q4BH-Q67Q.

Morrow, P. C. (1980). Retirement preparation: A preventive approach to counseling the elderly. *Counseling and Values, 24*(4), 236–246. https://doi.org/10.1002/j.2161-007X.1980.tb00879.x.

Müller, A., De Lange, A. H., Weigl, M., Oxfart, C., & Van der Heijden, B. (2013). Compensating losses in bridge employment? Examining relations between compensation strategies, health problems, and intention to remain at work. *Journal of Vocational Behavior, 83*(1), 68–77. https://doi.org/10.1016/j.jvb.2013.03.002.

Muratore, A. M., & Earl, J. K. (2015). Improving retirement outcomes: The role of resources, pre-retirement planning and transition characteristics. *Ageing & Society, 35*(10), 2100–2140. https://doi.org/10.1017/S0144686X14000841.

Noone, J., Alpass, F., & Stephens, C. (2010). Do men and women differ in their retirement planning? Testing a theoretical model of gendered pathways to retirement preparation. *Research on Aging, 32,* 715–738. https://doi.org/10.1177/0164027510383531.

Oakman, J., & Wells, Y. (2016). Working longer: What is the relationship between person–environment fit and retirement intentions? *Asia Pacific Journal of Human Resources, 54*(2), 207–229. https://doi.org/10.1111/1744-7941.12075.

Peiró, J. M., Tordera, N., & Potočnik, K. (2013). Retirement practices in different countries. In M. Wang (Ed.), *The Oxford handbook of retirement* (pp. 510–540). New York: Oxford University Press.

Perry, G. (1980). The need for retirement planning and counselling. *Canadian Journal of Counselling and Psychotherapy/Revue canadienne de counseling et de psychothérapie, 14*(2), 97–98.

Petkoska, J., & Earl, J. K. (2009). Understanding the influence of demographic and psychological variables on retirement planning. *Psychology and Aging, 24*(1), 245–251. https://doi.org/10.1037/a0014096.

Pinquart, M., & Schindler, I. (2007). Changes of life satisfaction in the transition to retirement: A latent-class approach. *Psychology and Aging, 22*(3), 442–455. https://doi.org/10.1037/0882-7974.22.3.442.

Rauvola, R. S., Rudolph, C. W., & Zacher, H. (2018). Generationalism: Problems and implications. *Organizational Dynamics*. https://doi.org/10.1016/j.orgdyn.2018.05.006.

Rudolph, C. W., De Lange, A. H., & Van der Heijden, B. (2015). Adjustment processes in bridge employment: Where we are and where we need to go. In P. M. Bal, D. T. A. M. Kooij, & D. Rousseau (Eds.), *Aging workers and the employee-employer relationship* (pp. 221–242). Cham, Switzerland: Springer.

Rudolph, C. W., Kooij, D. T. A. M., Rauvola, R. S., & Zacher, H. (2018). Occupational future time perspective: A meta-analysis of antencedents and outcomes. *Journal of Organizational Behavior 39*(2), 229–248. https://doi.org/10.1002/job.2264.

Salthouse, T. A. (2012). Consequences of age-related cognitive declines. *Annual Review of Psychology, 63,* 201–226. https://doi.org/10.1146/annurev-psych-120710-100328.

Savickas, M. L. (2005). The theory and practice of career construction. In S. D. Brown & R. W. Lent (Eds.), *Career development and counseling: Putting theory and research to work* (pp. 42–70). Hokoben, NJ: Wiley.

Savickas, M. L. (2011). *Career counseling*. Washington, DC: American Psychological Association.

Savickas, M. L. (2013). Career construction theory and practice. In R. W. Lent & S. D. Brown (Eds.), *Career development and counselling: Putting theory and research into work* (2nd ed., pp. 147–183). Hoboken, NJ: Wiley.

Schlossberg, N. K. (2003). *Retire smart, retire happy: Finding your true path in life*. Washington, DC: American Psychological Association.

Schmitt, A. (2018). Übergang in und Anpassung an den Ruhestand als Herausforderung aus psychologischer Perspektive [Transition into and adaptation to retirement as a challenge from a psychological perspective]. *Organisationsberatung, Supervision, Coaching, 25*(3), 337–347. https://doi.org/10.1007/s11613-018-0555-3.

Seiferling, N., & Michel, A. (2017). Building resources for retirement transition: Effects of a resource-oriented group intervention on retirement cognitions and emotions. *Work, Aging and Retirement, 3*(4), 325–342. https://doi.org/10.1093/workar/wax011.

Shultz, K. S., & Wang, M. (2011). Psychological perspectives on the changing nature of retirement. *American Psychologist, 66*(3), 170–179. https://doi.org/10.1037/a0022411.

Simon, J., & Osipow, S. H. (1996). Continuity of career: The vocational script in counseling older workers. *Career Development Quarterly, 45,* 152–162. https://doi.org/10.1002/j.2161-0045.1996.tb00265.x.

Staudinger, U. M. (2015). Images of aging: Outside and inside perspectives. *Annual Review of Gerontology and Geriatrics, 35*(1), 187–209. https://doi.org/10.1891/0198-8794.35.187.

Super, D. E. (1953). A theory of vocational development. *American Psychologist, 8,* 185–190. https://doi.org/10.1037/h0056046.

Super, D. E. (1980). A life-span, life-space approach to career development. *Journal of Vocational Behavior, 16*(3), 282–298. https://doi.org/10.1016/0001-8791(80)90056-1.

Super, D. E. (1984). Career and life development. In D. Brown & L. Brooks (Eds.), *Career choice and development* (pp. 192–234). San Francisco: Jossey-Bass.

Super, D. E., Savickas, M. L., & Super, C. M. (1996). The life span, life-space approach to careers. In D. Brown & L. Brooks (Eds.), *Career choice and development: Applying contemporary theories to practice* (3rd ed., pp. 121–178). San Francisco: Jossey-Bass.

Topa, G., Moriano, J. A., Depolo, M., Alcover, C. M., & Morales, J. F. (2009). Antecedents and consequences of retirement planning and decision-making: A meta-analysis and model. *Journal of Vocational Behavior, 75*(1), 38–55. https://doi.org/10.1016/j.jvb.2009.03.002.

Verwoerdt, A. (1970). The physician's role in retirement counseling. *The Gerontologist, 10*(1), 22–26. https://doi.org/10.1093/geront/10.1_Part_2.22.

Von Hippel, C., Kalokerinos, E. K., Haanterä, K., & Zacher, H. (2018). Age-based stereotype threat and work outcomes: Stress appraisals and rumination as mediators. *Psychology and Aging*. https://doi.org/10.1037/pag0000308.

von Hippel, C., Kalokerinos, E. K., & Henry, J. D. (2012). Stereotype threat among older employees: Relationships with job attitudes and turnover intentions. *Psychology and Aging, 28*(1), 17–27. https://doi.org/10.1037/a0029825.

Wang, M. (2007). Profiling retirees in the retirement transition and adjustment process: Examining the longitudinal change patterns of retirees' psychological well-being. *Journal of Applied Psychology, 92*(2), 455–474. https://doi.org/10.1037/0021-9010.92.2.455.

Wang, M. (2012). *The Oxford handbook of retirement*. New York, NY: Oxford University Press.

Wang, M., Henkens, K., & van Solinge, H. (2011). Retirement adjustment: A review of theoretical and empirical advancements. *American Psychologist, 66*(3), 204–2013. https://doi.org/10.1037/a0022414.

Wang, M., & Shi, J. (2014). Psychological research on retirement. *Annual Review of Psychology, 65,* 209–233. https://doi.org/10.1146/annurev-psych-010213-115131.

Wang, M., & Shultz, K. S. (2010). Employee retirement: A review and recommendations for future investigation. *Journal of Management, 36*(1), 172–206. https://doi.org/10.1177/0149206309347957.

Wang, M., & Wanberg, C. R. (2017). 100 years of applied psychology research on individual careers: From career management to retirement. *Journal of Applied Psychology*. https://doi.org/10.1037/apl0000143.

Wang, M., Zhan, Y., Liu, S., & Shultz, K. S. (2008). Antecedents of bridge employment: A longitudinal investigation. *Journal of Applied Psychology, 93*(4), 818–830. https://doi.org/10.1037/0021-9010.93.4.818.

Willett, M. (2008). A new model for retirement education and counseling. *Financial Services Review, 17*(2), 105–130.

Wöhrmann, A. M., Deller, J., & Wang, M. (2014). A mixed-method approach to post-retirement career planning. *Journal of Vocational Behavior, 84,* 307–317. https://doi.org/10.1016/j.jvb.2014.02.003.

Zacher, H. (2013). Older job seekers' job search intensity: The interplay of proactive personality, age, and occupational future time perspective. *Ageing & Society, 33*(7), 1139–1166. https://doi.org/10.1017/S0144686X12000451.
Zacher, H. (2015). Successful aging at work. *Work, Aging and Retirement, 1*(1), 4–25. https://doi.org/10.1093/workar/wau006.
Zacher, H., & Bock, A. (2014). Mature age job seekers: The role of proactivity. *Journal of Managerial Psychology, 29*(8), 1082–1097. https://doi.org/10.1108/JMP-05-2012-0158.
Zacher, H., & Frese, M. (2009). Remaining time and opportunities at work: Relationships between age, work characteristics, and occupational future time perspective. *Psychology and Aging, 24*(2), 487–493. https://doi.org/10.1037/a0015425.
Zacher, H., & Griffin, B. (2015). Older workers' age as a moderator of the relationship between career adaptability and job satisfaction. *Work, Aging and Retirement, 1*(2), 227–236. https://doi.org/10.1093/workar/wau009.
Zacher, H., & Kooij, D. T. A. M. (2017). Aging and proactivity. In S. K. Parker & U. K. Bindl (Eds.), *Proactivity at work: Making things happen in organizations* (pp. 258–294). New York: Routledge.
Zacher, H., Kooij, D. T. A. M., & Beier, M. E. (2018). Active aging at work: Contributing factors and implications for organizations. *Organizational Dynamics, 47*(1), 37–45. https://doi.org/10.1016/j.orgdyn.2017.08.001.
Zacher, H., & Rudolph, C. W. (2017). Successful aging at work and beyond: A review and critical perspective. In S. Profili, A. Sammarra, & L. Innocenti (Eds.), *Age diversity in the workplace: An organizational perspective* (pp. 35–64). Bingley, UK: Emerald.
Zacher, H., Rudolph, C. W., & Baltes, B. B. (2019). An invitation to lifespan thinking. In B. B. Baltes, C. W. Rudolph, & H. Zacher (Eds.), *Work across the lifespan*. New York: Academic press.
Zhan, Y., & Wang, M. (2015). Bridge employment: Conceptualizations and new directions for future research. In P. M. Bal, D. T. A. M. Kooij, & D. Rousseau (Eds.), *Aging workers and the employee-employer relationship* (pp. 203–220). Cham, Switzerland: Springer.
Zhan, Y., Wang, M., Liu, S., & Shultz, K. S. (2009). Bridge employment and retirees' health: A longitudinal investigation. *Journal of Occupational Health Psychology, 14*(4), 374–389. https://doi.org/10.1037/a0015285.
Zhan, Y., Wang, M., & Shi, J. (2015). Retirees' motivational orientations and bridge employment: Testing the moderating role of gender. *Journal of Applied Psychology, 100*(5), 1319–1331. https://doi.org/10.1037/a0038731.
Zikic, J., & Richardson, J. (2007). Unlocking the careers of business professionals following job loss: Sensemaking and career exploration of older workers. *Canadian Journal of Administrative Sciences, 24*(58–73). https://doi.org/10.1002/cjas.5.
Zuehlsdorff, H. W., & Baldwin, C. (1995). *Retirement counseling: Preparing for the "golden years"*. Nevada, USA: Educational Resources Information Center (ERIC).

Innovative Career Counselling Across the Life-Span

Maximizing Career Engagement Across a Lifetime of Transitions

Deirdre A. Pickerell and Roberta A. Neault

Abstract Across a lifespan, especially during times of significant workplace changes, increasingly interconnected global markets, and the rise of the gig economy, individuals experience many career-related transitions. These include, but are not limited to, such developmental milestone transitions as from secondary to post-secondary education, from school to work, and from work to retirement. Other common transitions include leaving for, and returning from, parental or maternity leave; returning to work after a significant illness or injury; navigating job losses; re-establishing careers post-immigration; and navigating promotions and growth opportunities. This chapter applies the Career Engagement model (Neault & Pickerell 2019; Pickerell & Neault, 2016) as a conceptual framework to support understanding and successfully navigating a myriad of career transitions. The Career Engagement model acknowledges a dynamic interaction between challenges and both individual and contextual capacity, recognizing that a mismatch between challenge and capacity can result in individuals becoming overwhelmed or feeling underutilized; both states, if allowed to progress without intervention, can result in disengagement. Through a review of career development and organizational development literature, and use of several case vignettes to illustrate how the Career Engagement model can be applied during different types of career transitions, this chapter offers practical tools to support the goal of this book, to promote inclusion and sustainable employment for all.

Keywords Career engagement · Career development · Transitions

Given the speed at which work is changing, impacted by such factors as advances in technology and the global economy, individuals can expect to make multiple transitions across their working lives. There is a complexity to each of these transitions as people juggle dynamic life roles and responsibilities and manage planned and unplanned gaps in paid employment. That the work individuals have prepared, and

D. A. Pickerell (✉) · R. A. Neault
Vancouver, Canada
e-mail: dpickerell@yorkvilleu.ca

R. A. Neault
e-mail: Roberta@lifestrategies.ca

J. G. Maree (ed.), *Handbook of Innovative Career Counselling*,
https://doi.org/10.1007/978-3-030-22799-9_12

perhaps trained extensively, for may not be in demand in the future adds to this complexity; keeping up with new ways of working will be exhilarating to some workers but overwhelming and discouraging to others.

The increasing prevalence of a "gig economy," seen by some as eroding more traditional work roles and structures, is further complicating career transitions (Callanan, Perri, & Tomkowicz, 2017; Lent, 2018). Grappling with the implications, career counsellors, educators, researchers, and policy makers are discussing "precarious" work and attempting to define and facilitate "good" or "decent" work (Callanan et al., 2017; Taylor, 2017). However, there is a risk that policies might disadvantage one group while trying to help another. For example, freelance workers in the USA make, on average $70,000 per annum (Reader, 2017); although their work fits within the gig category, most would not define it as precarious. Alternatively, there are many examples of massive layoffs within sectors that had been traditionally viewed as offering secure, stable, long-term employment (Carey, 2017; Healing, 2016). Perhaps it might be helpful to consider the quality and longevity of an individual's overall attachment to the workforce and other significant life roles (i.e., one's "career") than to discriminate between short-term gigs and longer-term employment relationships. A key role for career counsellors, therefore, could be to help clients identify and secure engaging and meaningful work, where they are valued regardless of the length of the contracts, and to effectively navigate the transitions from one position to the next.

In this chapter, we explore the changing context of work, the notion of decent or good work, the complexity of life and career transitions, and whether the concept of "engagement" is reserved only for the privileged or is a fundamental right for all. Using the Career Engagement model as a framework (Neault & Pickerell, 2011; 2019; Pickerell & Neault, 2016), we examine the dynamic interaction of individual and contextual influences on engagement, and shared individual, family, and organizational responsibilities for aligning challenge and capacity to maximize engagement. Case examples will be used to illustrate practical applications of the Career Engagement model in constructing careers that are sustainable across multiple life transitions within a constantly changing global workplace.

The first part of the chapter outlines several factors impacting today's worker, including the evolving nature of career and the rapidly changing world of work, which may result in many more life and work transitions than seen in the past. The second part explores the career engagement model. The work that influenced its development is introduced and links to career and organizational development theory are also discussed. The third part of the chapter uses six case studies to demonstrate how the Career Engagement model may be used as a conceptual framework for understanding factors contributing to feelings of being overwhelmed, underutilized, or both, and how interventions can be designed to return individuals to the zone of engagement. The chapter concludes with a reminder that a unique feature of the model is the directionality (i.e., that there are two routes to disengagement, through being underutilized or overwhelmed) and that understanding how someone became disengaged can inform appropriately targeted interventions to facilitate reengagement.

Rethinking Work and Life in Changing Contexts

Organizations and workers, and the professionals who support them, are facing environments not easily quantified or defined. How work is done, and even what work *is*, seems to be changing at an incredible pace. This has, perhaps inevitably, led to discussions about the future of work and what work may be good versus what work may be bad. These musings are done against a backdrop of lives and communities that seem to be constantly evolving, resulting in multiple transitions across a lifespan. In this section we briefly explore some of the factors impacting today's workers.

Numerous technological breakthroughs (e.g., robotics, 3D printing, biotech, quantum computing) are often considered to be the key characteristics of the fourth industrial revolution (a term coined by Schwab in 2016); it isn't simply advances in technology that separates this from previous industrial revolutions, but also advances in communication and the way billions of people are connected. Combined, these advancements are fundamentally changing how work is done and even how it is defined and conceptualized. In some cases, it has been hypothesized that this fourth industrial revolution, and the rise of digitization and automation, could replace work altogether. In one US report, it was estimated that close to half of all employment could be automated (Frey & Osborn, 2013). Bloom (2018) recently noted that "the conventional capitalistic 9-to-5 employment model has faded into a brave new economic reality of precarious labor and seemingly permanent economic insecurity" (para. 2); he went on to ask, "Does work as we know it have a future at all?" (para. 4).

Although various reports raise concerns regarding massive job losses, they may be somewhat misleading. Work is complex, comprising a wide range of specific tasks, some of which can be easily automated whereas others cannot. Further, ongoing advances are likely to create new work opportunities, many of which are beyond our imagination today. Demographic shifts will also continue to impact workplaces. As baby boomers retire, new "replacement" workers are in short supply in many sectors and jurisdictions; therefore, despite advances in automation, it's expected that unemployment rates will continue to decline (Samuelson, 2017). These trends are anticipated by some to result in a power shift that favours the worker, forcing employers to offer more generous compensation packages, improved working conditions, and greater opportunities to grow. Despite declining unemployment rates and a power shift favouring the worker, Deloitte's Human Captial Trends Survey (2018) has individuals recareering every 5 years, likely expanding the number of transitions individuals might normally expect.

Whether brought on by technological advances, the global economy, or demographic patterns, "the world of work has become faster paced, more diverse, and less predictable" (Lent, 2013, p. 2). These factors, and the continued growth of the gig economy (i.e., work on demand), automation, and job polarization have scholars, policy makers, and front-line practitioners trying to distinguish between what is good, or decent, and precarious work.

Defining good versus precarious work goes beyond the scope of this chapter; however, it is important to the broader discussion on how work is changing and whether those changes can be classified as good or bad. A key challenge facing all of those seeking to clearly define the two extremes of good versus precarious is that work can be a very personal experience, shaped by a wide range of factors. Some of these are external (e.g., pay and benefits, security, and safety). Others are more internal (e.g., opportunities for rewarding and fulfilling work and to help others). Life stage can also significantly impact whether a work role might be considered decent or precarious. Gig work, as just one example, may be good for a university student or retiree seeking to top up other sources of income, but be precarious for a single income family of five.

Despite recognizing the disparate opinions which exist around decent versus precarious work, the UK Government recently adopted the Quality of Jobs and Innovation Generated Employment Outcomes (QuInnE) framework which comprises six indicators: wages, employment quality, education and training, working conditions, work life balance, and consultative participation and collective representation (Taylor, 2017). The framework recognizes that, as they transition from role-to-role, individuals will need to identify both their priorities and their trade-offs, within their individual contexts. Similarly, Zizys (2014), in *Better Work*, outlined a set of practices that could be used to evaluate whether employers are creating good work; these include availability of, and investment in, worker training programs; engagement with educational system; and equitable compensation and benefit packages.

Although factors that contribute to work being considered good versus bad may be easily identified and measured, how these factors interact, and impact, quality of work is exceedingly difficult to quantify. Career counsellors, therefore, are encouraged to explore these factors within the context of their clients' individual realities. Assuming work in the gig economy is inherently precarious or that traditional unionized work environments are inherently good oversimplifies an incredibly complex topic. Further, it can also serve to disenfranchise individual worker experiences (e.g., a successful gig worker may take offense to his/her work being labelled as bad) and even discourage clients from exploring all options. Career counsellors have a critical role to play in helping clients to identify what work *works for them*, at any given stage, to navigate the increasingly complex world of work, and to maximize engagement across a series of planned and unplanned transitions over the course of their careers. Pryor and Bright (2011) related transition to movement or shifts, noting that "definitions in the field of human careers always come back to the acknowledgement of shift" (p. 5). A key challenge, however, that individuals, and the career counsellors they work with, must face is that humans tend to resist change and seek out stability and predictability. Yet, at this time, the only certainty and stability may be that "emerging career tasks for many people at all stages will be to secure and successfully handle multiple jobs from multiple employers at any given time in their career" (Hirschi, 2018, p. 200).

Career Engagement as Life Engagement

Career counselling for individuals and career development/management within corporate settings have evolved from a shared need—to prepare the future workforce and to help workers grow, stay productive, and transition effectively during times of change. However, as counsellor training is typically housed within a faculty of education or a psychology program, and organizational career development tends to fall under the umbrella of human resource management with training within the faculty of business, unfortunate silos have formed that separate the two related fields. The Career Engagement model was created, in part, to bridge those silos.

The Career Engagement model (see Fig. 1) comprises two main components—challenge (how challenging and meaningful work is) and capacity (individual and organizational/contextual skills, resources, and supports). Career engagement is realized by keeping these two components in relative balance. When challenge outweighs capacity, individuals move out of the zone of engagement to feeling overwhelmed; when capacity outweighs the challenge, individuals move out of the zone of engagement to feeling underutilized. If balance is not restored, individuals can become completely disengaged. The directionality (i.e., two routes to disengagement) is an important and unique component of the career engagement model.

The concept of career engagement was influenced by positive psychologists (e.g., Csikszentmihalyi's, 1997, notion of "flow"), educational psychologists (e.g., Vygotsky's, 1978, notion of the "zone of proximal development"), and work/organizational psychologists (e.g., Kahn & Heaphy's, 2014, notion of "personal engagement" and Warr's, 2017, "vitamin model").

Several career development theorists also influenced the Career Engagement model. For example, McMahon and Patton's (1995) Systems Theory Framework (STF) highlights the importance of context and environmental influences in understanding an individual's career journey. Krumboltz (2009) and Krumboltz and Levin (2010), acknowledged the impact of happenstance, recognizing that not all career issues (or solutions) reside solely within the control of the individual; Pryor and Bright's (2011) Chaos Theory of Careers similarly highlights the influence of change and chance on one's career trajectory. In their Hope-Action Theory, Niles, Amundson, and Yoon (2019) also emphasized the impact of environmental factors on careers.

Similar constructs have been examined within the organizational development literature. Much has been written on employee engagement in recent years (e.g., Neault & Pickerell, 2011; Schaufeli, 2015; Shuck, 2011). The job demands-resources (JD-R) theory (Bakker & Demerouti, as cited in Dicke, Stebner, Linninger, Kunter, & Leutner, 2018; Fletcher, Carter, & Lyubovnikova, 2018) has similarities to Csikszentmihalyi's flow theory; flow considers the intersection of challenge with an individual's skills and the JD-R theory considers a similar mapping of job demands to resources. The key difference between the two models is that "resources" in the JD-R theory includes both personal and external/organizational resources; similarly, Warr's (2017) vitamin model considers influences from both within the individual and the environment. This expansion, beyond individual skills (or other

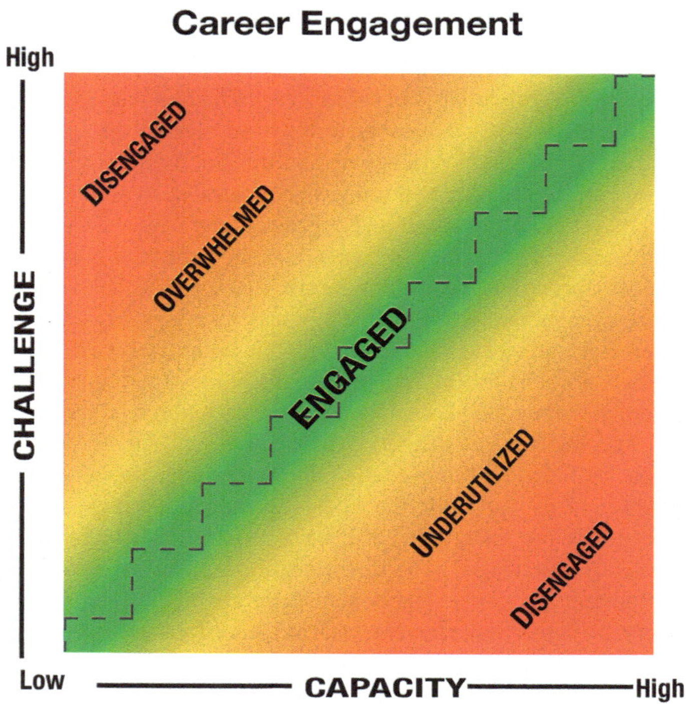

Fig. 1 The Career Engagement Model. *source*: Copyright 2011 by R. Neault and D. Pickerell, used with permission

personal characteristics) to a recognition of the impact of context and resources external to the individual, is an essential element of the Career Engagement model where the term "capacity" is used to represent such diverse influences as work-life balance, resources, work fit, work-life boundaries, supervisor support, alignment, and co-worker relationships (Neault & Pickerell, 2019; Pickerell & Neault, 2016).

In a factor analysis for one study using the Career Engagement model, "challenge" comprised both motivating and meaningful work (and not all work had both elements; Pickerell & Neault, 2016). Work can be motivating without being intrinsically challenging; Csikszentmihalyi (1997) demonstrated this in his research with assembly line employees—gamification can turn dull, monotonous work into a flow experience. However, according to Csikszentmihalyi (1997) a key to flow is having a clear purpose or goal (i.e., even assembly line employees understand how their role contributes to a larger goal). However, Graeber (2018), author of "Bullshit Jobs: A Theory," reported UK survey results revealing that 40% of workers felt that their jobs did not contribute in any meaningful way to their world. In interviews further exploring these results, Graeber found that work without meaning was linked to increased stress, workplace bullying, anxiety, and depression—and that, interestingly, all those issues disappeared when an opportunity to engage in meaningful work was presented.

From constructivist, constructionist, and life design perspectives, many authors (e.g., Peavy, 2004; Savickas, 2011) emphasize that careers are constructed and, therefore, can be reconstructed to make them more meaningful and satisfying. The Career Engagement model provides a useful framework for conceptualizing such reconstruction. The model illustrates two routes to disengagement—by becoming overwhelmed (too much challenge for the available capacity) or underutilized (too little challenge compared to capacity). By listening *for* the individual's story (as Savickas (2011) encourages career practitioners to do), the route to disengagement can be discerned; this, in turn, facilitates construction of a new path to engagement by re-aligning capacity and challenge. Realignment can be accomplished in several ways—reducing or increasing either challenge or capacity, and sometimes adjusting both.

Borrowing from Super's (1990) notion of the life-career rainbow, "career" in this model is intended to encompass the various life roles that intersect as one creates a life; as shifts in career engagement may occur even if there are no (or relatively minor) changes at work, this model has utility beyond the work role. For example, changes in one's physical or emotional health, relationships, financial security, family or community responsibilities, educational commitments, reputation, or any number of other influences can result in loss of engagement and becoming either overwhelmed or underutilized. In that sense, *career* engagement could be reconceptualized as *life* engagement, similar to Kahn's (1990) early focus on personal engagement. From this perspective, everyone has a life and, therefore, has the potential to be fully engaged; career engagement is not reserved for the privileged.

In fact, the model was designed to be inclusive; it has been used to conceptualize career interventions for individuals at extreme ends of the spectrum of cognitive ability, including a nuclear physicist and an individual who was non-verbal and profoundly developmentally delayed, as well as career, community, and school interventions for individuals from diverse cultures, socio-economic status, geographic regions, educational levels, and life stages. Career Engagement is designed to be aspirational (i.e., individuals aspire to be in the zone of engagement) and explanatory (i.e., individuals can identify when they move out of engagement, and reflect upon whether that shift was to feeling overwhelmed or underutilized). Specific examples of how career engagement provides a framework to conceptualize career concerns and design appropriate interventions will be explored in the following section.

Practical Implications for Career Counsellors

Career counsellors and coaches are dually impacted by the changing world of work; aside from managing their own careers amid complex changes, they play a critical role in helping others, both employed and unemployed, to identify sustainable work opportunities and to navigate career transitions. The case studies that follow highlight how the Career Engagement model can be used to support individuals during career transition.

School-to-School

Corrinne was excited to be accepted at her first-choice university, located in a major city over 1000 miles from the rural community that she'd lived in all through school. Based on her very high grades and impressive performance as an elite athlete, Corrinne had been awarded several generous scholarships; the largest one, though, was contingent on continued exemplary academic and athletic performance throughout her university career.

However, Corrinne got off to a rocky start in her first term. She found living in residence exhausting and wasn't able to sleep very well with so much constant noise. She also struggled to keep up with her reading and assignments in the midst of a grueling practice schedule. Ironically, surrounded by thousands of people—in residence, in her classes, and on her teams—she felt increasingly alone. She missed her friends, family, coaches, and teammates from home and was beginning to think that moving away to school had been the biggest mistake of her life! Noticing a change in Corrinne, her residence advisor suggested that Corrinne meet with a counsellor for help in adjusting to her new life at university.

Using the Career Engagement model as a conceptual framework, it appears that Corrinne is overwhelmed and, perhaps, on the verge of disengagement (in this case, considering giving up her scholarships and quitting school). The counsellor recognized that Corrinne was experiencing concurrent changes in challenge and capacity that, combined, were exacerbating her feelings of being out of control. As with any significant life changes, Corrinne was facing multiple challenges—new responsibilities, unfamiliar expectations, and a lack of routine were just a few. Also, for the first time, Corrinne, like many first-year university students, found herself surrounded by other bright students and accomplished athletes. Although she'd been the top student and athlete in her small-town school, she realized she'd need to work much harder to even achieve average grades in her courses or to maintain her place on the team. However, at the very time that she most needed to function at her highest capacity, Corrinne was struggling emotionally, relationally, and in terms of specific coping strategies.

The counsellor recognized that it would take a multi-faceted approach to help Corrinne successfully navigate her first term at university. Her most urgent need was to get sufficient sleep; the counsellor introduced some sleep hygiene strategies and explained the impact of sleep deprivation; this helped Corrinne to understand the importance of tackling this challenge of sleeplessness right away. The counsellor also recognized Corrinne's need for social support as a capacity-building strategy, both to combat Corrinne's loneliness and to offer an emotional outlet for her during this difficult transition. She normalized Corrinne's feelings and helped her to plan a couple of social opportunities within the next few days as well as to schedule daily online and phone check-ins with friends and family at home. The counsellor also helped Corrinne to explore what other immediate challenges she might be able to reduce. It became clear that creating a realistic study schedule was new to Corrinne; the counsellor referred her to a quick online course designed to help her set one up.

Both the counsellor and Corrinne recognized that it would take more than a quick fix to get Corrinne back to her previous level of engagement. However, by the end of their first session together, Corrinne was hopeful that she might be able to manage this transition and agreed to continue to work with the counsellor until she felt less overwhelmed.

Starting Over

Arash, his wife Masooma, and their five children were excited to finally be in their new home after spending the last 5 years in a refugee camp. Prior to fleeing Afghanistan, Arash was a heavy-duty mechanic and Masooma was a homemaker. Masooma does have dreams of working in the future, but recognizes she has an important role for now of attending to her family, getting her children settled in school, and taking English classes. Arash, however, wants to work immediately; he feels he has been out of work for far too long and wants to begin to provide for his family. Without better English skills though, he is not sure what kind of work he might be able to do. He visited a local employment centre for assistance; an appointment was booked for the following day with a case manager, to be facilitated by an interpreter.

Using the Career Engagement model as a guide, the case manager was able to determine that Arash was excited about working, but also a bit overwhelmed by all that he had to do and learn. Arash decided to focus on general labourer jobs at one of the big construction sites spread around the city, easily accessed by the city's transit system. He was referred to a resume coach, who with the support of an interpreter, worked with Arash to prepare a basic resume. Through the employment centre's refugee supports program, Arash was able to access a transit card and steel-toed boots to ensure he was work ready. As Arash was determined to get work immediately, he did not want to wait for referrals via the employment centre, even though those connections might provide more sustainable employment. Instead, aware that there were currently many job vacancies, Arash took an "apply for anything and everything" approach and, with the help of a friend he'd made at the employment centre found work within a few days at a site where many labourers spoke his language.

Within 3 months, however, Arash was back in the employment centre, having had multiple short term, cash-based jobs. He was a hard worker and didn't understand why he could not secure something more long term. The case manager, again with the help of an interpreter, referred Arash to a job developer on the team. Through the interpreter, the job developer explained that there were some local employers who were very committed to helping newcomers get relevant work experience and that there were some wage subsidy programs available that could help to top up Arash's pay to a fair rate for the type of work he would be doing. One of the programs had a very high success rate of participants being hired into full-time positions, with benefits, at the end of the program. Because Arash had in-demand skills as a mechanic, the job developer was confident that he would be a great fit for this program. Arash was excited to hear this and felt relieved that he might be able to soon be engaged in work that he'd find more challenging and interesting. An added bonus, from Arash's perspective, was that his English language learning would also be supported—the program would provide access to online training, supplemented with classes twice per week outside of work hours, either in the evenings or on the weekend.

Using the Career Engagement model, the job developer helped Arash to see that a haphazard, "anything will do" approach to job search was resulting in him feeling concurrently overwhelmed (at constantly starting over and wondering how long each job would last and where his next income would come from) and underutilized (always doing unskilled work and never having the opportunity to demonstrate other skills that he could offer). The program the job developer was recommending offered the needed supports to build Arash's capacity to meet bigger challenges; through a structured work-integrated learning plan, language supports, a wage subsidy, and a supportive employer and co-workers, Arash began his new job with an optimism that he hadn't felt for many, many years.

Parental Leave

Sam and Jasjit were delighted to finally be welcoming their first baby to the family. Both Sam and Jas were highly educated professionals—Sam, a contracts lawyer, and Jas, a research scientist. Although, ultimately, they planned to hire a nanny, they were looking forward to the first year of parenting and each intended to take a parental leave of 6 months away from work, with Jas taking the first 6 months off. The first couple of months went by in a blur, with sleepless nights, what seemed like constant feedings, and daily visits from friends and family members. However, by the third month, Jas was physically exhausted; feeling overwhelmed with never being caught up on laundry, cleaning, shopping, and other household tasks; and yet also feeling a bit resentful that Sam still had work to go to each day. Jas missed the intellectual stimulation from research meetings and data analysis and was craving a good conversation that wasn't solely about babies. Jas had been working with a career coach for the past couple of years and decided that it might be time to check back in to develop a plan for the remaining months at home.

Using the Career Engagement model as a framework, the coach helped Jas to unpack the complex emotions related to the early months of parenting and being away from work. Together, they first looked at factors related to feeling overwhelmed—both in terms of challenge and capacity. As new parents, Jas and Sam were both getting less sleep than they were used to; they were also anxious about ensuring their baby's safety and health, and meeting all of the important developmental milestones. An enjoyable part of the challenge, though, was the learning. As professionals, Jas and Sam both loved to learn and they were enjoying reading, listening to podcasts, and discovering answers to the questions that arose for them daily. The coach helped Jas realize, though, that this constant quest for new knowledge might be contributing to feeling overwhelmed, likening it to trying to complete a Ph.D. in parenting in just the first 2 months of their baby's life! Jas agreed to slow down a bit, allowing the knowledge to come at a more manageable pace and becoming more comfortable with simply not knowing. As a research scientist, Jas had learned to be patient; this skill could be transferred to parenting, too. However, Jas also decided to join a parenting group that could offer opportunities to learn from others and would also build in some additional social supports.

Jas and the coach then turned to Jas' concerns about being away from work and lack of a focus beyond the new baby. They discussed the importance of staying current and connected in Jas' area of research in order to ensure a smooth return to work when the baby was 6 months old. To increase challenge in this area, Jas decided to register for a self-paced online course and also to phone into the monthly project update meetings.

Jas' example illustrates how one can concurrently feel overwhelmed and underutilized. The directionality of the Career Engagement model facilitates addressing a variety of issues that may be contributing to experiences of disengagement. In this case, Jas was overwhelmed with all of the new responsibilities related to parenting but also feeling underutilized and disconnected from a highly valued professional role. Together, Jas and the coach were able to identify solutions to both of these concerns, co-constructing a pathway to bring Jas back into the zone of optimal engagement.

Returning to Work

Annika had been a police dispatcher for the past 10 years. Despite a sometimes chaotic and emotionally-charged environment, she loved helping people and had formed close relationships with the officers. She was passionate about what she saw as her dual responsibility of serving the public and protecting the members. After a series of traumatic calls, however, Annika began to experience panic attacks; when one of these occurred while on a call, it became clear that Annika could no longer perform her duties and she was put on stress leave. During her 8-month leave, Annika worked with a psychologist to help her process the situations she had faced and to develop better coping strategies. Although Annika worked hard throughout her recovery, and loved her job, it became clear that she could not return to work as a dispatcher. The potential for a scenario to trigger another attack, which in turn, could jeopardize the safety of the caller and attending officers, was too great. As such, Annika was forced to return to work in a different position. Unfortunately, the organization was not equipped to accommodate this change; a new role was not formally identified leaving Annika doing odd jobs, including reorganizing files, creating job aids/guides, and completing various administrative tasks. With no specific position, Annika also rarely knew where in the building she'd work from one day to the next; she "floated" from area to area. She was frustrated, angry, and feeling like she was being punished. She was contemplating legal action, and another stress leave, until she met with the new director of HR.

With a background in vocational rehabilitation, the director seemed to understand the challenges involved in returning to work after an illness, especially with no plan or supports in place. The director introduced Annika to the Career Engagement model, noting that, as a highly skilled professional, Annika was not used to performing the types of administrative tasks that she was being assigned. Further, with no context for the work, and no position to call her own, Annika could not see how her work contributed to the success of the organization; she had a strong desire to help and was used to making a difference in people's lives. As a result, she felt underutilized and, as time went on, completely disengaged.

Although Annika strongly believed she had the capacity to do more, as she learned more about career engagement she began to understand that disengagement outwardly appears the same, whether someone became disengaged through being overwhelmed or underutilized. Annika's supervisor, co-workers, and previous HR director saw her as frustrated, angry, and disinterested and assumed she was overwhelmed from being back at work so kept trying to make things easier. Their assumption was that Annika needed more time to build her capacity as she transitioned back into fulltime work.

Together, the HR director and Annika began to create a job that would help Annika return to the zone of engagement. They agreed the work needed to be challenging enough to make more effective use of Annika's skills and experience, while not being so demanding that it moved Annika out of feeling underutilized into being overwhelmed. They recognized this needed to be done incrementally as no one, including Annika, could confidently say what might be too much.

Annika's story demonstrates how important directionality is within the Career Engagement model. Understanding the route to disengagement, whether through being overwhelmed or underutilized, is critical to building strategies to return individuals to the zone of engagement.

Career Growth

Lars is in his mid thirties and has spent the last 8 years in marketing and promotions for a mid-sized agency. He loves his work, is highly skilled, and has enjoyed upward progression in his career. Until quite recently, he'd have reported being completely engaged in his work; however, feeling like he was reaching his peak where he was working, several months ago Lars decided to go out on his own. He had felt ready for the challenge of being a self-employed consultant and looked forward to building his business. Within 6 months, however, Lars was feeling completely overwhelmed and struggled to remember what a "good day at work" felt like. Before giving up and returning to full-time employment, Lars reached out to a career counsellor he'd worked with during graduate school.

The career counsellor used the Career Engagement model to explore what may have been happening since Lars transitioned to self-employment, explaining that although his skills, expertise, and knowledge had not changed, his work environment had which, in turn, can impact available resources. The first piece of the puzzle surfaced when Lars began to describe what tasks had been his primary focus over the past few months—almost all were administrative in nature. He'd incorporated his company, set-up business bank accounts, ordered business cards, and had a website built. All of these activities were largely outside of his skillset. Even though he hadn't thought they were overly challenging, his lack of capacity resulted in Lars being overwhelmed with business start-up activities. In addition, these activities had left little time to find potential contracts or to do the actual marketing tasks he loved.

As their discussions continued, another key item surfaced—isolation. Although Lars recognized he'd be working independently, he missed the team environment much more than he'd expected. Even picking corporate colours and finalizing a logo had become an issue … he had no one to ask and struggled to make decisions on his own. As a result, he had begun to fear that he couldn't possibly manage consultant work.

Noticing that Lars was seeing only the hindrances or challenges, the career counsellor encouraged Lars to make note of all he had accomplished. Other than daily or weekly management, his business was set-up and ready for clients. Over the course of his career, Lars had established strong working relationships with colleagues across his industry and, until recently, was an active member of his professional association. This helped Lars to recognize that, although his transition was more challenging than he'd anticipated, he was still committed to this phase of his career journey and was feeling more confident it would offer stable, and engaging, work.

The career counsellor encouraged Lars to consider how other self-employed professionals could support his business. From bookkeepers and virtual assistants to website designers, there were opportunities to contract out the work he found less engaging, allowing him to focus on the work he loved doing and supporting someone else's self-employment, or gig, endeavours. Lars also began to incorporate monthly networking meetings into his schedule and regular meet-ups with colleagues, helping to ensure he didn't feel so isolated.

On a brief check-in call, just 3 months later, Lars reported he was definitely back to being fully engaged in his career. He'd landed several small contracts, allowing him to begin to build his brand. Through his networking efforts, Lars had also partnered with another consultant, allowing them to bid on work that neither could manage independently. Lars was excited to report that they had just landed their first big contract!

Retirement

Antonio had been tracking the days until retirement for 3 full years, marking them off one by one on the calendar. He enjoyed contributing to the transition planning, training his replacement, and participating in a variety of retirement celebrations. The first 3 months after his retirement flew by as he caught up on long overdue tasks around the house, took his first extended vacation (3 glorious weeks!), and spent a special day individually with each of his seven grandchildren. This was what he had always imagined retirement to be!

However, then September came, Antonio's grandchildren were back in school, the backlog of household maintenance was finished, and friends had all returned to work after their summer vacations. Financially, Antonio had barely enough retirement income to meet his day-to-day needs and recognized that he needed to supplement his income to afford any extras; he certainly couldn't spend money at the rate he'd done on his once-in-a-lifetime vacation, for which he'd saved for 15 years. He began to feel lethargic, lonely, and generally disinterested in leaving his house. He stayed in bed longer, watched more TV, and stopped answering the phone when it rang during the day. At his annual check-up with his family physician, Antonio talked about how he'd been feeling and the doctor noticed a significant weight gain. The doctor was concerned about the possibility of depression and referred Antonio to a counsellor.

The counsellor used the Career Engagement model to help Antonio examine how the recent changes in his life might be contributing to him feeling disengaged. Most of the challenges that had kept Antonio engaged at work and during his first few months off had completely disappeared now, leaving a very big vacuum. Antonio's capacity, however, had changed very little in the past few months. He was bright, good with his hands, and generally enjoyed problem solving; however, without work and now that his home repairs had been completed, he had very few problems to solve. He had always been physically active but, ironically, now he was discovering that the less he did, the less he felt he had the energy to do. He found that extremely frustrating! He was bored watching TV all day but didn't know how else to spend his time. He was struggling to find a daily reason to get out of bed.

Together, Antonio and the counsellor used the Career Engagement model to examine how adjustments to challenge and/or capacity might help to move Antonio back to feeling engaged in his life and activities. They pinpointed Antonio's current position on the model as being underutilized—with high capacity but very low challenge. They suspected that he was getting close to becoming fully disengaged which is what the doctor had observed as potential symptoms of depression.

The counsellor engaged Antonio in activities to explore his interests, transferable skills, personality style, values, and what gives his life purpose and meaning. Antonio realized that what he'd looked forward to getting away from at work was the 9–5, 5 day per week commitment, with only 3 weeks of vacation. However, what he'd enjoyed at work was mentoring younger employees and sharing his acquired knowledge with them. He also realized that he missed some of the daily routine that had gotten him out of bed at a specific time with a focus for the day. Together the counsellor and Antonio brainstormed ways that he could build in more challenge and structure to his days, without becoming overly committed; Antonio recognized that, prior to his retirement, he'd been feeling overwhelmed at work, unable to keep up with his responsibilities, and frustrated that he had so little time available for family. He knew for sure that he didn't want to return to work full time—but part-time work would supplement his income, helping to ensure he could cover any unexpected expenses and allowing for the occasional night out.

Antonio recalled reading an ad for a new part-time role at his union's head office, serving as a mentor and liaison for new members, especially those who had recently immigrated. With his counsellor's encouragement, he agreed to follow up to find out more about the expectations for the role, ensuring that it would offer the flexibility he wanted to keep. The counsellor also encouraged Antonio to contact the volunteer centre in town; the website listed several interesting needs but one that really appealed to Antonio was driving seniors to medical appointments as this didn't result in any regularly scheduled long term commitments and, according to the posted information, his fuel costs would be covered.

Within just a few weeks, Antonio had found new purpose in his life and established a workable structure. A combination of part-time work, volunteer activities, and special "dates" scheduled with each of his grandchildren in the upcoming weeks had brought back enough challenge to fully engage him in life.

Cultural Considerations

In all cases, it is essential for counsellors, coaches, and career practitioners to take a culture-infused approach to their work (Arthur, 2019). For example, in working with Jas, the coach would need to examine personal beliefs about parenting, shared parental leave, and working parents and would also provide space to surface and support progress towards Jas' own parenting beliefs and values. With Arash, the employment counsellor would need to consider cultural family roles, the refugee experience, and also potential biases about language levels needed to function effectively at work. With Lars, it might be important to consider the counsellor's preconceived notions about self-employment and the gig economy, striving to ensure any bias, either for or against, didn't unduly influence their work.

Summary and Conclusion

As illustrated by the six case examples, the Career Engagement model helps counsellors, coaches, and their clients to better understand the importance of aligning challenge and capacity to maximize opportunities for engagement for all individuals. Such alignment is not static, especially during times of transition. It is also important to recognize that someone can be simultaneously overwhelmed and underutilized (e.g., overwhelmed in one role or task, underutilized in another). This is an interesting extension of the model, not fully explored in the original research. Finally, individuals who are completely disengaged, whether from becoming overwhelmed or feeling chronically underutilized, may outwardly appear the same (e.g., frustrated, angry, depressed, withdrawn, disinterested, lacking energy). However, interventions to return them to the zone of engagement will be different, depending on the route that led to disengagement. Although an exciting new project may re-engage someone who had been underutilized, it may exacerbate the disengagement of someone who was already overwhelmed. Similarly, offering additional time or resources to an individual who finds a project overwhelming may help to restore engagement; however, offering identical resources to an individual who is already feeling underutilized is likely to have the opposite effect, resulting in even less challenge and a deeper sense of not being needed at work.

Engagement is not reserved for the privileged. The Career Engagement model can help to unpack the individual and contextual/systemic factors that contribute to disengagement, informing individual and institutional, organizational, or policy changes that can contribute to inclusive and sustainable employment for all.

References

Arthur, N. (2019). Culture-infused career counselling: Connecting culture and social justice in career practices. In N. Arthur, R. Neault, & M. McMahon (Eds.), *Career theories and models at work: Ideas for practice*. Toronto, ON: CERIC.

Bloom, P. (2018, November). Creating the future of work today. *Futures of work*. Retrieved from https://futuresofwork.co.uk/2018/11/19/creating-the-future-of-work-today/.

Callanan, G. A., Perri, D. F., & Tomkowicz, S. M. (2017). Career management in uncertain times: Challenges and opportunities. *Career Development Quarterly, 65*(4), 353–365.

Carey, N. (2017, June 21). For thousands of U.S. auto workers, downturn is already here. *Reuters*. Retrieved from https://www.reuters.com/article/us-autos-workers-analysis/for-thousands-of-u-s-auto-workers-downturn-is-already-here-idUSKBN19C2R2.

Csikszentmihalyi, M. (1997). *Finding flow: The psychology of engagement with everyday life*. New York, NY: HarperCollins.

Deloitte Insights. (2018). *The rise of social enterprise: 2018 Deloitte global human capital trends*. Retrieved from: https://www2.deloitte.com/content/dam/Deloitte/at/Documents/human-capital/at-2018-deloitte-human-capital-trends.pdf.

Dicke, T., Stebner, F., Linninger, C., Kunter, M., & Leutner, D. (2018). A longitudinal study of teachers' occupational well-being: Applying the job demands-resources model. *Journal of Occupational Health Psychology, 23*(2), 262–277. https://doi.org/10.1037/ocp0000070.

Fletcher, L., Carter, M. R., & Lyubovnikova, J. (2018). Congruency of resources and demands and their effects on staff turnover within the English health care sector. *Journal of Occupational and Organizational Psychology, 91*(3), 688–696. https://doi.org/10.1111/joop.12214.

Frey, C. B., & Osborn, M. A. (2013). *The future of employment: How susceptible are jobs to computerisation.* Oxford: University of Oxford. Retrieved from https://www.oxfordmartin.ox.ac.uk/downloads/academic/The_Future_of_Employment.pdf.

Graeber, D. (2018, May 18). What's the point of pointless jobs? *Globe and Mail.* Retrieved from https://www.theglobeandmail.com/opinion/article-whats-the-point-of-pointless-jobs/.

Healing, D. (2016, November 29). Less hiring planned after 65% of oil and gas companies cut staff, survey finds. *Canadian Press*. Retrieved from http://calgaryherald.com/business/energy/less-hiring-planned-after-65-of-oil-and-gas-companies-cut-staff-survey-finds.

Hirschi, A. (2018). The fourth industrial revolution: Issues and implications for career research and practice. *Career Development Quarterly, 66*(3), 192–204.

Kahn, W. A. (1990). Psychological conditions of personal engagement and disengagement at work. *Academy of Management Journal, 33*(4), 692–724.

Kahn, W. A., & Heaphy, E. D. (2014). Relational context of personal engagement at work. In C. Truss, R. Delbridge, K. Alfes, A. Shantz, & E. Soane (Eds.), *Employee engagement in theory and practice* (pp. 82–96). London, England: Routledge.

Krumboltz, J. D. (2009). The happenstance learning theory. *Journal of Career Assessment, 17,* 135–154. https://doi.org/10.1177/1069072708328861.

Krumboltz, J. D., & Levin, A. S. (2010). *Luck is no accident: Making the most of happenstance in your life and career* (2nd ed.). Atascadero, CA: Impact Publishers.

Lent, R. W. (2013). Career-life preparedness: Revisiting career planning and adjustment in the new workplace. *Career Development Quarterly, 61*(2), 2–14. https://doi.org/10.1002/j.2161-0045.2013.0031.x.

Lent, R. W. (2018). Future of work in the digital world: Preparing for instability opportunity. *The Career Development Quarterly, 66*(3), 205–219. https://doi.org/10.1002/cdq.12143.

McMahon, M., & Patton, W. (1995). Development of a systems theory of career development. *Australian Journal of Career Development, 4,* 15–20.

Neault, R. A., & Pickerell, D. A. (2019). Career engagement: A conceptual model for aligning challenge and capacity. In N. Arthur, R. Neault, & M. McMahon (Eds.), *Career theories and models at work: Ideas for practice*. Toronto, ON: CERIC.

Neault, R. A., & Pickerell, D. A. (2011). Career engagement: Bridging career counseling and employee engagement. *Journal of Employment Counseling, 48*(4), 185–188.

Niles, S. G., Amundson, N., & Yoon, H. J. (2019). Hope-action theory: Creating and sustaining hope in career development. In N. Arthur, R. Neault, & M. McMahon (Eds.), *Career theories and models at work: Ideas for practice*. Toronto, ON: CERIC.

Peavy, R. V. (2004). *Sociodynamic counselling: A practical approach to meaning making*. Chagrin Falls, OH: Taos Institute.

Pickerell, D. A., & Neault, R. A. (2016). Examining the career engagement of Canadian career development practitioners. *Canadian Journal of Career Development, 15*(1), 4–14.

Pryor, R., & Bright, J. (2011). *The chaos theory of careers*. New York, NY: Routledge.

Reader, R. (2017). Freelancers are sick of being called "gig workers." *Fast Company*. Retrieved from: https://www.fastcompany.com/40481646/freelancers-are-sick-of-being-called-gig-workers.

Samuelson, R. J. (2017). *The looming labor 'shortage' isn't just a problem—it's also an opportunity*. Washington Post. Retrieved from: https://www.washingtonpost.com/opinions/the-looming-labor-shortage-isnt-just-a-problem–its-also-an-opportunity/2017/06/25/1c8c9572-5831-11e7-a204-ad706461fa4f_story.html.

Savickas, M. L. (2011). Constructing careers: Actor, agent, and author. *Journal of Employment Counseling, 48*(4), 179–181.

Schaufeli, W. B. (2015) Engaging leadership in the job demands-resources model. *Career Development International, 20*(5), 446–463. https://doi.org/10.1108/CDI-02-2015-0025.

Shuck, B. (2011). Integrative literature review: Four emerging perspectives of employee engagement: An integrative literature review. *Human Resource Development Review, 10*(3), 304–328. https://doi.org/10.1177/1534484311410840.

Super, D. E. (1990). A life-span, life-space approach to career development. In D. Brown & L. Brooks (Eds.), *Career choice and development* (2nd ed., pp. 197–261). San Francisco, CA: Jossey-Bass.

Taylor, M. (2017). *Good work: The Taylor review of modern working practices*. United Kingdom: UK Government, Department for Business, Energy & Industrial Strategy. Retrieved from: https://www.gov.uk/government/uploads/system/uploads/attachment_data/file/627671/good-work-taylor-review-modern-working-practices-rg.pdf.

Vygotsky, L. S. (1978). *Mind in society: The development of higher psychological processes*. In M. Cole, V. John-Steiner, S. Scribner, & E. Souberman (Eds.). Cambridge, MA: Harvard University Press.

Warr, P. B. (2017). Happiness and mental health: A framework of vitamins in the environment and mental processes in the person. In C. L. Cooper & J. C. Quick (Eds.), *The handbook of stress and health: A guide to research and practice* (pp. 57–74). London: Wiley-Blackwell.

Zizys, T. (2014). *Better work: The path to good jobs is through employers*. Toronto, ON: Metcalf Foundation. Retrieved from http://metcalffoundation.com/wp-content/uploads/2014/10/2014-10-02-Better-Work.pdf.

Innovation in Career-Related Learning: Starting Early in Primary Schools

Deirdre Hughes and Elnaz Kashefpakdel

Abstract Career development is a process that starts early in childhood. At the heart of this process is the need for robust evidence on how innovative career-related learning (CRL) in primary schools can strengthen the link between schooling and the world of work. Whilst there is a plethora of research into post-primary schooling, early childhood CRL is relatively under-researched. This chapter highlights pluralistic research into CRL in England's primary schools and lessons learned to inform teachers' continuous professional development. The first part of this chapter defines CRL and briefly focuses on findings from an international literature review. The second part draws upon qualitative research involving 17 primary schools in England utilising Interpretative Phenomenological Analysis. The third part extends the analysis through supplementary evidence gathered from key informants (n = 43) to aid the comparison of results and the development of effective CRL approaches. The fourth part of the chapter considers practical implications, including a theory of change (ToC) model designed to guide teachers' continuous professional development in CRL, followed by a short concluding section.

Keywords Aspirations · Career development · Career-related learning · Primary schooling · Continuous professional development

Introduction

> By making meaning of their explorations and experiences of the world through self-reflection and social interaction, children construct foundational stories about who they are and who they are becoming. (Ahn, 2011)

Globalisation and technological advancements are rapidly changing the world of work, as well as education systems (OECD, 2019). In recent years, while many devel-

---

D. Hughes (✉)
Exeter, England, UK
e-mail: deirdre.hughes3@btinternet.com

E. Kashefpakdel
London, UK

J. G. Maree (ed.), *Handbook of Innovative Career Counselling*,
https://doi.org/10.1007/978-3-030-22799-9_13

oped countries have gone through demographic transitions, with declining birth rates and an increase in the aging population, low-income countries in particular are experiencing an upswing in population growth (Wang, 2012). The latest World Migration Report (IOM, 2018) estimates that there are 244 million international migrants globally. For every migration statistic, there are children and families starting a new life in a new place—this does not take place in a social vacuum (Hughes, Akkok, Arlumani, & Zelloth, 2019). Across Europe, classrooms in primary schools are becoming more diverse (Ainscow, Dyson, Hopwood, & Thomson, 2016; Kaldi, Govaris, & Filippatou, 2018).

England has a relatively decentralised education system with many leadership and management decisions taken at a school level. There are almost 17,000 state primary schools in England (Institute for Government, 2018). In Britain, reports on social mobility have seldom mentioned primary schools, with sparse reference to the vital role that primary schools play in raising children's aspiration and broadening horizons (SMC, 2018). Recently the Department for Education (DfE) has invested £2 million to support careers-related learning (CRL) in primary schools. The Careers Strategy (DfE, 2017) highlights "there is no consistent approach across primary schools and limited evidence and best practice for schools to use when planning their activities" (p. 15). A strong appetite has emerged to learn more about what works so that children can develop positive attitudes about work from an early age. Pilot activities to test out new programmes (or expand the ones that work), including in challenging areas are now underway (CEC, 2019). There exists a gap in primary school teachers' continuous professional development (CPD), unlike arrangements already in place such as Careers and Employability Leadership Programmes in post-primary schools (Teach First, 2018; CEC, 2019).

The idea that schools can impact positively on student outcomes is a crucial driver in the rise of interest in school improvement research and practice (Day & Sammons, 2014, p. 5). Research findings indicate that holding biased assumptions and having narrow aspirations can, and does, go on to influence the academic effort children exert in certain lessons (Bandura, Barbaranelli, Caprara, & Pastorelli, 2001; Flouri and Pangouria, 2012; Gutman and Akerman, 2008), the subjects they choose to study (Archer and Dewitt, 2017; Kelly, 1989), and the jobs they end up pursuing (Akerlof and Kranton, 2000; Breen and Garcia-Penalosa, 2002). Research also shows early interventions can bring a lasting impact on children's development and perceptions of different occupations and of the subjects thus enabling access to them (Howard, Kimberly, Flanagan, Castine, & Walsh, 2015).

Much of teaching and learning in primary schools is anchored in the seminal work of major child development theorists (Erikson, 1985; Piaget, 1977) and learning theorists (e.g., Kolb, 1984; Vygotsky, 1978). But there is no consistency in the terminology and approach used when it comes to careers work in primary schools, despite childhood career development theorists (e.g., Gottfredson, 2005; Maree, 2015; McMahon & Watson, 2017; Savickas, 2013; Super, 1980, 1990) calling for more work to be done. Primary schools often provide opportunities by inviting employer representatives into school. Reading and number partner schemes, alongside enterprise education, have been familiar in the United States of America, mainland Europe, and the UK for many years (Millard, Menzies, & Baars, 2017; Torgerson, King, & Snowden, 2002). Contemporary literature on career development and its impact on young people's transitions to adulthood in post-primary schooling is well-researched (e.g., Meijers, Kuijpers, & Gundy, 2013; Schoon & Lyons-Amos 2017; Schoon & Silbereisen, 2009). In comparison, research examining early childhood career development is relatively under-developed (Crause, Watson, & McMahon, 2017). Yet, children often construct attachments and meanings to learning and work from an early age.

To address these challenges, it is important to highlight theoretical and practical perspectives, so that teachers and significant others can more fully understand what CRL activities and outcomes would be most impactful. Also, to consider how best to articulate this as part of a child's lifelong career development journey. Towards this end, this chapter emphasizes the importance of translating career development into CRL. This comprises early childhood activities in primary schools designed to give children from an early age a wide range of experiences of and exposure to education, transitions and the world of work. As a starting point, we adopt the simple notion that the effect of CRL experienced by children can be multiplied using encounters with people from different walks of life. These can and should take place both within and outside of the classroom. This is part of a lifelong learning and career development process. CRL is viewed through the lens of a literature review, an Interpretative Phenomenological Analysis (IPA) of a qualitative online survey of primary schools in England (n = 51), supplemented by in-depth findings of good/interesting policies and practices (n = 43) to aid the comparison of results and the development of effective CRL approaches. Finally, a Theory of Change (ToC) framework that can be applied in practice is outlined to help inform and support teachers' continuous professional development (CPD).

Outcomes from the Literature Review

To understand how children's career development translates into a primary school context, a literature search was conducted using Google Scholar, university and personal libraries to include both academic and so-called 'grey' literature. Table 1 below sets out the search strategy.

A modified search strategy was then adopted based on methodology applied within an earlier published international review of careers education, conducted by Hughes, Mann, Barnes, Baldauf, and Mc Keown (2016) and more recently Mann, Rehill, and Kashefpakdel (2018). Studies and other research papers were excluded if they related to examples of employability and/or career-related learning in secondary, further or higher education. Studies from outside of OECD countries were also not included. A total of 110 published articles including cross-sectional, longitudinal, quantitative and qualitative papers, along with intervention studies, and theoretical contributions were duly considered. Because differing methods arise from different epistemological positions (i.e. reductionist-positivist and phenomenological-interpretativist)

Table 1 Search strategy

Location	Time Period	Sample		Input		Outcome
OECD countries	2000 onwards	Primary	AND	Employer Employability	AND	Aspirations
		Primary School		Career(s)		Attainment
		Kindergarten		Career(s) learning		Achievement
		Children		Enterprise		Broadened Horizons Choices Cultural Capital Progression
		School		Employer engagement		Social mobility
				Multiculturalism Parents Stereotypes Teachers Workplace visits		Teamwork Transitions
				Employer visits		Knowledge
				World of work		Skills
				Workplace		Attitudes
				Work related learning		

combining these could be considered problematic. However, Goss and Mearns (1997) argue that the difference between qualitative and quantitative research does not mean we have to choose one or the other; they indicate the 'academic paradigm war' needs to move towards a truce and adopt a more pragmatic approach, which can yield more valuable research.

Why Is Career-Related Learning in Primary Schools Important?

Van der Heijden and De Vos (2015) define sustainable careers as "the sequence of an individual's different career experiences, reflected through a variety of patterns of continuity over time, crossing several social spaces, and characterized by individual agency, herewith providing meaning to the individual." (p. 7). This brings significant responsibility on the individual to learn, adapt and become resilient on a lifelong basis. In this context, children actively explore their worlds and begin to construct possibilities for their present and future selves (Cahill & Furey, 2017). These life stories include a sense of self (self-identity), roles, skills, and knowledge, and are shaped by everyday events and experiences.

The character of aspirations is strongly rooted in a young person's sense of what is 'reasonable' and 'natural' for 'people like me' to pursue (Chambers, Elnaz, Rehill, & Percy, 2018). Children enter schools with assumptions emerging out of their own day-to-day experiences. These are routinely shaped by role models and issues of gender, ethnicity and social class (Archer et al., 2012; Gottfredson 2002; Liu, McMahon, & Watson, 2015). From a review of research literature on gender and aspiration Gutman and Akerman (2008) argue such "naïve early understandings have already turned them [children] towards some possible futures and away from others" (p. 5). Many children often do not know enough about the world of work to have realistic ideas of what jobs exist, but they have absorbed enough to believe there is 'men's work' and 'women's work'. For example, Chambers et al. (2018) invited over 20,000 children aged 7–11 years old from the UK and internationally to draw and describe what they wanted to be when they grew up. Their free text descriptions were coded into one of 69 possible occupations. The results show by the age of seven it was clear that the jobs chosen reflected standard gendered ideas. Four times as many boys wanted to become engineers, as did girls. Twice as many boys as girls saw science as their chosen future, while girls were four times more likely than boys to want to be vets, and more than twice as likely to want to be doctors (p. 21).

Skorikov and Vondracek (2011) highlight childhood experiences are foundational in the construction of identity, observations of attitudes towards work within families, cultural stereotypes, and influence of the media can influence children's meaning of work and, in turn their occupational identities. According to Gottfredson (2002) the 'orientation of sex roles' occurs at the age of 6–8. At this age, she argues, children grasp the concept of a set of behaviours belonging to each sex and begin seeing jobs and future pathways as intrinsically gendered. By the age of age 9–13, this is where children begin to see their social value based on perceptions of social class and intelligence. Fundamentally, children have started to become more aware of potential constraints on their occupational choice. Care (2007) investigated young children's career development in the context of Gottfredson's stage theory. In a small-scale experiment, 84 children attending a kindergarten/early learning centre for four to five-year-old children exhibited gender stereotyping in their aspirations, with the clear majority nominating real occupational roles as opposed to fantasy ones. The pattern of aspirations support Gottfredson's proposals.

A review of best practice in parental engagement by Goodall and Vorhaus (2010) showed that parental engagement interventions are more likely to be effective if they are informed by a comprehensive 'needs analysis' and 'targeted' at particular groups of parents. Therefore, CRL interventions should be matched to the needs and profile of the families and parents they are aimed at, rather than providing 'one size fits all' support. Although parents seem to have the most prominent influence on children's career development, other family members—such as siblings and extended family—also have been shown to be an important influence (Schultheiss, Palma, Predragovich, & Glasscock, 2002). Liu et al. (2015) studied how parents influence children's career aspirations in mainland China from both the parents' and children's perspectives. Three superordinate themes were identified: responding positively to children's interests, emphasising education, and conveying career values.

Davis-Kean (2005) examined the influence of parent education and family income on child achievement. Although poverty was considered a major threat for child development, a closer look at the underlying mechanisms may help explain why so many poor children perform well in school despite restricted material resources. She argues if parents are successful in providing an emotionally stable and stimulating environment, the negative effects of financial restrictions can be minimized.

Schools and neighbourhood context also influence children's early attitudes and assumptions about the world of work. There are calls for greater efforts to broaden learners' science, technology, engineering and mathematics (STEM) aspirations to begin in primary schools (Archer & DeWitt, 2017). It is argued that there is a need to draw more readily on role models from local work places to challenge the stereotypical image of science careers as being 'only for the brainy' and for a limited cross section of society. By enriching their real-life experiences, learners can be encouraged to think again about the meanings and implications of what they are being taught in class (Mann & Dawkins, 2014). Through CRL schools can challenge the assumptions developed by children, allowing them to draw richer, more informed connections between education and ultimate economic and wider success in adult life (Knight, 2015, p. 76). This provides an opportunity for teachers and learners alike to have fun in the classroom linking subjects to possible jobs of the future. As Kelly (2004) has shown even very highly performing primary school pupils often struggle to see the meaning of academic learning, such as in Mathematics, to the real world.

Patton and McMahon (1997) found that career development is a concept understood by children from preschool. Given that children as young as five years can express occupational dreams (Phipps, 1995), and that career preferences are formed early (Poole & Low, 1985), it seems that valuable opportunities to influence the socialisation and career readiness of many children are being missed. Law (2010) suggests that children should be encouraged to sense and sift occupational information with a view of understanding it, which can provide a valuable foundation for a more extensive careers education later in post-primary schooling.

The prevailing historical view maintained that children's ideas about careers are unrealistic and likely to change and, therefore, not worth paying attention to (Gore et al., 2016). Yet, a body of literature continues to grow which demonstrates that children's ideas about careers are not only less 'magical' than thought previously, but also that the aspirations young people hold are often quite similar to those held in their teenage decision-making years (Auger et al., 2005; Care, Deans, & Brown, 2007). Recent research findings (Chambers et al., 2018; KidZania, 2017) reveal that the differences between children's career aspirations from childhood to early adulthood are marginal. Assumptions that children's career ambitions may be transitory may have dissuaded researchers from focusing on them in the past. From a UK policy perspective, Barnes and McGowan (2017) state:

> Education systems that require primary schools to teach career education—such as British Columbia and Ontario (Canada), the Czech Republic, Denmark, and, more recently, Croatia, Estonia, and Hungary—recognise that legislation by itself is not enough. Countries such as

New Zealand, some American states (e.g., Missouri and Georgia), England and Scotland that have voluntary guidelines and resources show take-up is often patchy (p. 173).

Types of Career-Related Learning

It is by no means a straightforward process to disentangle the unique contributions that different forms of CRL can be expected to have on children in primary schools. Despite their popularity, robust quasi-experimental or experimental studies looking at the impact of such provision on children are sparse. An exception is Huber, Sloof, and Praag (2012) who examined the impact of a five-day entrepreneurship education programme on primary school age Dutch participants. A total of 2751 learners were randomly allocated to control and intervention groups by class. The study found significant positive impact on the non-cognitive entrepreneurial skills of learners (e.g. risk-taking, creativity, self-efficacy). There exists an important research challenge around the issue of better understanding, and evidencing, the holistic impacts of CRL in primary school settings. The work described here represents an exploration of possible new directions. In a recent review of primary schools literature, Mann et al. (2018) developed a typology to help better understand careers work in primary education. Three areas are identified as:

- **Much of the work related to primary education is focused around educational outcomes for young people**—whether delivered through the provision of supplementary resource in the classroom (reading and number partners) or as a complementary mechanism to change learner attitudes about the value of education.
- **Provision is designed to enhance children's understanding of jobs and careers**—by challenging gender stereotyping or illustrating the uses of science in employment.
- **Enterprise education, engagement can be seen to offer means to secure additional learning outcomes to the usual diet of provision**—providing learners with the opportunity to explore and practice knowledge and skills (such as problem-solving and team working) demanded by the modern labour market.' (p. 26).

The more familiar form of skills development in British primary schools relates to enterprise education. This aims to provide the skills and tools that will help children succeed post-school, whatever they do (Enabling Enterprise, 2015). Millard, Menzies, and Baars (2017) argue that enterprise education can be approached in three ways including: (i) teaching about enterprise which helps developing learners' knowledge and understanding of issues such as how businesses work; (ii) teaching for enterprise which increases engagement with and interest in enterprise; and (iii) teaching through enterprise which is a more active learning process that helps young people develop an enterprise skill set by giving them experience of the wider world.

Technology-based learning activities can also support the child as a unique individual and encourage exploration, experimentation, risk taking, critical thinking, decision making and problem solving (Crause et al., 2017). For example, Chen et al. (2013) developed a platform Digital Learning Playground (DLP) to solve real-life problems supported by robots. The results indicated better learning performance, engagement, and enjoyment of the learners. Use of technology in conventional classrooms can help create an authentic learning environment. Where employer visits are not feasible, worksite simulation may be effective in helping children to expand their list of possible future career choices and to understand the ramifications of those decisions (Harkins, 2000).

Desired Outcomes from Career-Related Learning

Childhood proficiency in the skills of resilience, conscientiousness, self-awareness and motivation are found to be closely associated with educational attainment (Kautz, Heckman, Diris, Weel, & Borghans, 2014; Goodman, Joshi, Nasim, & Tyler, 2015). A series of quantitative longitudinal studies have drawn compelling relationships between school-age aspirations and both engagement in education and the achievement of adult economic outcomes (Flouri and Pangouria, 2012). Much of the work related to primary education is focused on children's educational outcomes. Moreover, US and Australian studies have found links between the nature of occupational aspirations of primary school age learners and later educational outcomes, with higher aspirations being positively related to higher levels of attainment and lower dropout rates (Knight, 2015, p. 76). Evidence from a longitudinal tracking study shows that learners who do not express STEM related aspirations at age 10 are unlikely to develop STEM aspirations by the age of 14. Consequently, they are less likely to pursue science subjects, achievement in which is related to higher adult earnings (Archer, 2014).

There is widespread agreement about the importance of connectedness and the benefits of actively developing intra-and inter-personal skills for healthy relationships and well-being (e.g., Cefai and Cavioni, 2014; Flouri and Panourgia, 2012; Payton et al., 2008; Roffey, 2010). This can lead to improved social and emotional skills. It also can enhance cultural understanding from an early age (Watson, McMahon, & Liu, 2015). These skills are sometimes captured by terms such as non-cognitive skills (non-academic skills), character, resilience and grit (e.g., Arthur, Kristjánsson, Walker, Sanderse, & Jones, 2015; DfE, 2019; OECD, 2018; Tough, 2016). Feinstein (2015) identifies key aspects of these social and behavioural capabilities including: self-perceptions, self-awareness and self-direction (including self-esteem and the belief that one's own actions can make a difference); motivation; self-control/self-regulation (generally characterised as greater impulse control and fewer behavioural problems); social skills, including relationship skills and communication skills; and resilience and coping (p. 6). Maree (2015) argues career counsellors should join forces with theorists and practitioners from different subject disciplines to determine how best to work collaboratively to promote resilience and wellbeing.

Analysis carried out by Goodman et al. (2015) on data from a major British Cohort Study (BCS) found these social and emotional skills and behaviours are important for future outcomes. Compared with cognitive ability they find that social and emotional skills matter similarly for socio-economic and labour market outcomes (such as higher income and wealth and being employed). Earlier analysis of data from the National Child Development Study in England also found that a combination of academic skills and social-emotional skills are associated with higher hourly wages and the likelihood of employment at age 42 (Carneiro, Crawford, & Goodman, 2007). Although these studies demonstrate a correlation between social-emotional skills and long-term outcomes, they cannot demonstrate causation, in part because there are many other factors that could have an effect on these outcomes (Gutman & Schoon, 2013).

Kirkman, Sanders, Emanuel, and Larkin (BIT, 2016) provide compelling evidence that children who take part in social action initiatives, such as volunteering, develop some of the most critical skills for employment and adulthood in the process. Using a number of randomized control trials (RCTs) and one pre-post comparison in England, the researchers compared the outcomes for children who took part in these funded initiatives against the outcomes of children who did not. They found that social action initiatives consistently improved children's levels of empathy, and their sense of community involvement. Many primary school teachers engage their students in everyday learning that could be described as CRL (Wade, Bergeron, White, Teeman, Sims, & Mehta, 2011). Different countries and even different states within countries resource and organise CRL in various ways. A major issue is how easily or otherwise CRL can be accommodated within the education system.

Qualitative Research and Methodologies

Online survey data collection from primary schools in England (n = 51) provides rich insight to barriers that primary schools have faced when designing and implementing CRL programmes and activities. IPA was used to analyze the initial findings. This is a variation of grounded theory in which the data are analyzed through emerging themes and categories—"There is no attempt to test a predetermined hypothesis—the aim is to explore flexibly and in detail, an area of concern" (Smith & Osborne, 2008, p. 55). From this, a purposeful sampling strategy was also used to develop case studies (n = 7) and to consult with expert key informants (n = 26) known to be active consumers of a range of CRL policies and practices. This was achieved by inviting the latter to attend an invitational discussion panel. There was no reward or coercion to take part in any aspect of the research.

Primary schools were asked in the online survey about the CRL activities, opportunities for training and challenges they face in the classroom. When asked about CRL leadership responsibilities, respondents highlighted that senior leaders (34%, n = 29), senior managers (31%, n = 29) and classroom teachers (28%, n = 29) in their schools accepted various levels of responsibility for delivering CRL. Further analysis showed that schools have invested in CRL in their primary school by organising a number of activities on a regular basis across the age groups. Parental engagement events, curriculum-linked activities and reading or number programmes using volunteers were the most common component of the respondents' CRL approaches. Findings indicated the respondents make CRL activities age-appropriate. For instance, 30% (n = 34) of the respondents organise workplace visits for children age 10, while only 4% (n = 2) offer such activities at age 5. Also, there was a strong indication that different activities can be effective. For instance 84% (n = 31) respondents indicated curriculum-linked activities are beneficial for making learning more relevant for real life and 81% (n = 31) reported this fosters self-efficacy and confidence. Some of the main underlining challenges they face when implementing CRL in their primary schools include: a lack of time (65%, n = 29) given demands in the curriculum, a lack of resources (65%, n = 29) such as financial and human resources, and local connectivity with employers and businesses (44%, n = 29). Most indicated that they would welcome further training on a range of subjects. 57% (n = 28) of the staff said they would benefit from training in how to integrate CRL into the curriculum and approximately 50% (n = 25) welcomed opportunities for understanding and monitoring the impact of CRL.

To aid the comparison of results and the development of effective CRL approaches, it is important to consider validity while designing the study and analysing the data. Lather (1986) challenges researchers to empower their participants using four validity tests to ensure the rigour of the work, calling for triangulation, construct validity, face validity, and catalytic validity (p. 67). Triangulation requires some discussion with participants. For construct validity, Lather uses the term 'systematized reflexivity' to explain the process of change that should happen when new theories or findings arise from the data. The iterative process lends itself to discovery. Researchers who wish to empower participants should always include participant checks throughout the process and the use of prompts makes those conversations much simpler (Guba & Lincoln, 1992). With face validity, case study participants and expert key informants (n = 43) were asked "When we discussed CRL in primary schools, I heard you say this…Is that correct and does it reflect your thinking?" Catalytic validity has been linked to democratic validity where study participants are seen as active collaborators and co-constructors of knowledge rather than as objects of research (Koro-Ljungberg, 2008, p. 986).

Building upon the survey findings, 17 primary schools were selected for in-depth case studies. These were mainly situated in England, with one exception. Only a third of the total schools were located within a major city. They represented Free School Meals (FSM) eligibility ranging from 2 to 50%. Most of the respondents (83.3%) held a position of 'Senior Leadership'. Telephone interviews lasting between 30 and 50 min. This allowed teachers to expand upon their earlier answers to the survey and provide any additional comments. In addition, further evidence was gathered from 26 key thought leaders from across England, including representatives from policy formation, teaching unions, employers and professional bodies, as well as academics and practitioners. The primary purpose was to validate interim findings and to identify any obvious gaps. Nine open-ended questions for consideration were sent prior to an expert panel discussion in London lasting two hours.

From this, it is noteworthy that the distribution of CRL roles in England's primary school is largely dependent on the size of the school and the capacity of senior leadership team. Moreover findings confirmed by the survey results and case studies suggest CRL is most effective when it is offered as part of a whole-school programme, delivered in line with the curriculum and supported by all staff, at all levels. Key informants agreed with this highlighting responsibility can often fall on a single member of staff that carries risks if the said member of staff retires or moves on from their role. In primary schools where the concept of CRL can be fluid and open to interpretation, the ability of a local senior leader(s) to prioritise and effectively communicate this activity to others is crucial. Case studies and further evidence from the key informants highlighted staff capacity issues and the ever-growing pressure on achieving set metrics. As a result, CRL in primary schools must be seen to contribute to, or sit alongside, the strategic vision, learning objectives and outcomes in subjects across the institution. It was argued this is best provided throughout the year with a whole menu of activities and programmes reinforcing and building on each other, rather than one off activities.

It is unsurprising that a number of teachers also expected some form of support and learning resources, topic ideas and lesson plans. In the case studies the most effective activities gave the children a chance to listen to people talk but also to ask questions. Teachers frequently stated that when organising CRL a key aim was developing children's non-academic skills such as: resilience, confidence and conversation skills.

> So, we looked at the national curriculum as it stands, and we wrote progression maps for every single subject separately. And then we focused on skill sets, and then within the skill sets we focused on the soft skills and built those back into the progression maps to show the staff how we were going to link that to the work that we were doing with Enabling Enterprise (Headteacher, London).

In the case studies, the majority stated they did not carry out any systematic evaluation of their CRL activities. However, some schools (29%, n = 5) noted they ask students and volunteers for anecdotal feedback to aid their decision-making about future activities. Findings suggest there is an appetite for further development work.

> I would be interested to see if anything we are doing is having an impact further down the line. Someone needs to develop some kind of tool or programme to help us do that. I would love to have something that would be quantifiable (Headteacher, East of England).

There was broad agreement amongst the key informants that deficiencies exist in the evidence-base when thinking about what 'good' schools provide. Schools must be aware of what CRL actually refers to, in order to understand what 'good' means in practice. Moreover, they reinforced the need to be cautious with the terms and definitions used in the primary phase. Specifically, that CRL in primary should not refer to careers guidance or careers advice in the same way that it may do in post-primary schooling. It was also highlighted most evaluations exploring CRL in primary do not explore what the students feel they need and what is effective. The difficult decision on exactly what to measure, and whether to measure at all, when evaluating CRL in the primary schooling phase is one that divided participants in this study.

Case studies and other key informants explored what would help teachers overcome some of the challenges they faced, or continue to face, when attempting to establish and/or deliver CRL activities in their school. Senior leaders highlighted either themselves or their curriculum teachers needed some form of CPD on current and future trends in the labour market. Many noted they do not have the confidence or experience to speak about vocational pathways.

> Most of the time teachers have been from school to university and then from university straight back to school, so often they don't have up to date information about careers and the routes available. So I guess an important piece of CPD could be around knowing about routes like higher apprenticeships and start letting children know about these from a younger age (Assistant Headteacher, West Midlands).

Evidence from empirical studies has consistently proved that schools make a difference and teachers have a much larger impact upon pupils' achievement than do schools (Reynolds & Teddlie, 2000; Willms, 2000). Therefore, CRL and professional development support for teachers is crucial when seeking to address the seismic changes taking place in the world of work and education (Kashefpakdel, Redhill & Hughes, 2018). This has a cascading effect on parents, employers, volunteers and, most importantly children themselves.

Implications for Teacher Training

Pedagogy is defined as 'the method and practice of teaching' (Oxford Dictionaries, n.d.). In other words, it is about how to teach. Studies on pedagogy therefore share the same vision—seeking the best way of teaching. Research on innovative CRL can put the spotlight on both teachers' understanding (internal) and their teaching processes and outcomes (external). Evidence shows also that positive impacts from CRL are greater when a consistent and whole school strategy is in place (Kashefpakdel, Rehill, & Hughes, 2019). Without effective CRL leadership and quality teaching and learning, pupil outcomes can be impeded. It is crucial to understand more holistically the influences on and processes of teaching CRL to improve children's education, social and economic outcomes.

There is a requirement to balance employer and volunteer engagement in primary schools alongside demand for teachers' continuous professional development (CPD) opportunities. Clearly, more work needs to be done to provide information, training and support for those involved including subject and cross-curricular activities, use of ICT and artificial intelligence (AI) and developing CRL action learning networks. Senior leaders often want to know how CRL can be embedded and what schools should be doing to facilitate this. A theory of change model (ToC) illustrated in Fig. 1, demonstrates key components of a teacher professional development programme (Kashefpakdel et al., 2019, pp. 84–85).

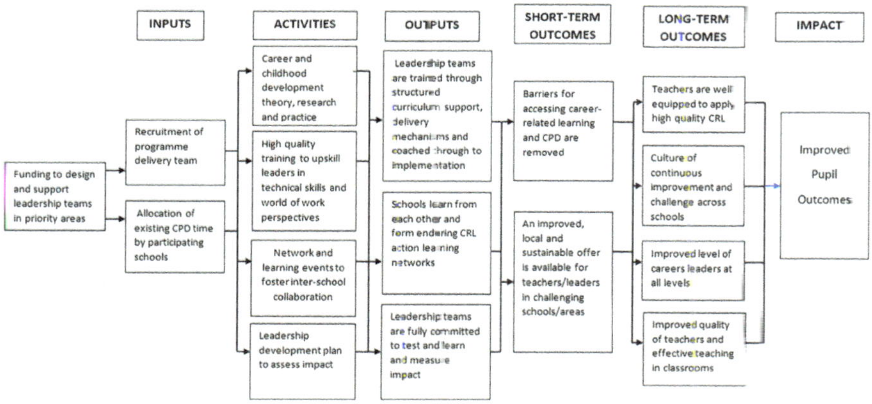

Fig. 1 Theory of change model

From the evidence a key obstacle to designing and delivering impactful CRL in England's primary schools is insufficient 'buy in' from the school leadership team. Therefore, both a 'top down' and 'bottom up' approach are essential for shared ownership of the process. The proposed ToC offers an outline framework for primary schools to critique and customize to meet their individual contextualized needs.

Conclusion

This pluralistic research underlines the importance of early years in shaping children's aspirations. The CRL approach challenges and further extends the philosophical bases of well-established primary school policies and practices. This study is not an exhaustive list of all literature on career development and CRL in primary schools. Our data is collected from a sample of primary schools, therefore, the results cannot be generalized across the whole country. The findings cannot, with any statistical validity, be extrapolated to a wider population. However, the study provides stimuli for action between teachers, employers and career development professionals.

Clearly there are some gaps in the existing body of research that merit closer attention by academics, teachers and career development professionals. For example, there is also scope to examine peer-to-peer influences on career aspirations and evidence-based strategies for improving parental engagement. More needs to be done to measure CRL impact using longitudinal studies and randomized control trials (RCTs) to complement qualitative studies. There is scope to investigate more fully a CRL impact measurement approach that can be piloted in differing contexts in both Western and Eastern cultures. All schools should develop innovative CRL policies, curriculum and practices that best suit their local circumstances. This provides impetus to building strong local employer, community partnerships, including closer working links with career development practitioners.

References

Ahn, J. (2011). Review of children's identity construction via narratives. *Creative Education, 2,* 415–417. https://doi.org/10.4236/ce.2011.25060.

Ainscow, M., Dyson, A., Hopwood, L., & Thomson, S. (2016). *Primary schools responding to diversity: Barriers and possibilities*. Cambridge: Cambridge Primary Research Trust.

Akerlof, G. A., & Kranton, R. E. (2000). Economics and identity. *Quarterly Journal of Economics, 115*(3), 715–753. https://doi.org/10.1162/003355300554881.

Archer, L. (2014). Conceptualising aspiration. In J. Stanley, A. Mann, & L. Archer (Eds.), *Understanding employer engagement in education: Theories and evidence* (pp. 23–35). London: Routledge.

Archer, L., DeWitt, J., Osborne, J., Dillon, J., Willis, B., & Wong, B. (2012). Science aspirations and family habitus: How families shape children's identification and engagement with science. *American Educational Research Journal, 49*(5), 881–908. https://doi.org/10.3102/0002831211433290.

Archer, L., & Dewitt, J. (2017). Participation in informal science learning experiences: The rich get richer? *International Journal of Science Education, Part B: Communication and Public Engagement, 7*(4), 356–373. https://doi.org/10.1080/21548455.2017.1360531.

Arthur, J., Kristjánsson, K., Walker, D., Sanderse, W., & Jones, C. (2015). *Character education in UK schools*. Birmingham: Jubilee Centre for Character and Virtues.

Auger, R. W., Blackhurst, A. E., & Wahl, K. H. (2005). The development of elementary aged children's career aspirations and expectations. *Professional School Counselling, 8*(4), 322–329.

Bandura, A., Barbaranelli, C., Caprara, G. V., & Pastorelli, C. (2001). Self-efficacy beliefs as shapers of children's aspirations and career trajectories. *Child Development, 72,* 187–206. https://doi.org/10.1111/1467-8624.00273.

Barnes, A., & McGowan, B. (2017). Targeted career exploration and development programmes. In M. McMahon & M. Watson (Eds.), *Career exploration and development in childhood: Perspectives from theory, practice and research* (pp. 172–185). Abingdon: Routledge.

Breen, R., & Garcia-Penalosa, C. (2002). Bayesian Learning and Gender Segregation. *Journal of Labor Economics, 20*(4), 899–922. https://doi.org/10.1086/342895.

Cahill, M., & Furey, E. (2017). *The early years: Career development for young children—A guide for educators*. Toronto: CERIC.

Care, E., Deans, J., & Brown, R. (2007). The realism and sex type of four- to five-year old children's occupational aspirations. *Journal of Early Childhood Research, 5*(2), 155–168. https://doi.org/10.1177/1476718x07076681.

Carneiro, P., Crawford, C., & Goodman, A. (2007). *The impact of early cognitive and non-cognitive skills on later outcomes*. London: Centre for the Economics of Education.

CEC. (2019). *Primary fund: Investing in career-related learning in primary schools*. London: Careers and Enterprise Company (CEC).

Cefai, C., & Cavioni, V. (2014). *Social and emotional education in primary school: Integrating theory and research into practice*. London: Springer.

Chambers, N., Elnaz, T. K., Rehill, J., & Percy, C. (2018). *Drawing the future: Exploring the career aspirations of primary school children from around the world*. London: Education and Employers.

Chen, G. D., Nurkhamid, Wang, C. Y., Yang, S. H., Lu, W. Y., & Chang, C. K. (2013). Digital learning playground: Supporting authentic learning experiences in the classroom. *Interactive Learning Environments, 21*(2), 172–183. https://doi.org/10.1080/10494820.2012.705856.

Crause, E., Watson, M., & McMahon, M. (2017). Career development learning in childhood: Theory, research, policy and practice. In M. McMahon & M. Watson (Eds.), *Career exploration and development in childhood: Perspectives from theory, practice and research* (pp. 186–198). Abingdon: Routledge.

Davis-Kean, P. E. (2005). The influence of parent education and family income on child achievement: The indirect role of parental expectations and the home environment. *Journal of Family Psychology, 19*(2), 294–304. https://doi.org/10.1037/0893-3200.19.2.294.

Day, C., & Sammons, P. (2014). *Successful school leadership*. Reading: Education Development Trust.

Department for Education. (2017). *Careers strategy: Making the most of everyone's skills and talents*. London: Department for Education (DfE).

Department for Education. (2019). *Education secretary sets out five foundations to build character, speech delivered at the church of England foundation for educational leadership conference*. London: Westminster.

Enabling Enterprise. (2015). *Primary schools: A complete approach to transforming students' enterprise skills*. London.

Erikson, E. H. (1985). *Childhood and society* (35th Anniversary Edition). New York: Norton.

Feinstein, L. (2015). *Social and emotional learning: Skills for life and work*. London: Early Intervention Foundation.

Teach First. (2018). *Evaluating the teach first careers leadership programme*. London: Teach First.

Flouri, E. & Panourgia, C. (2012). *Do primary school children's career aspirations matter? The relationship between family poverty, career aspirations and emotional and behavioural problems*. Working paper. London: Centre for Longitudinal Studies.

Goodall, J. & Vorhaus, J. (2010). *Review of best practice in parental engagement*. Research Report London: Department for Education.

Goodman, A., Joshi, H., Nasim, B., & Tyler, C. (2015). *Social and emotional skills in childhood and their long-term effects on adult life*. London: Early Intervention Foundation.

Gore, J., Holmes, K., M., Fray, L., McElduff, P., Weaver, N., & Wallington, C. (2016). Unpacking the career aspirations of Australian school students: Towards an evidence base for university equity initiatives in schools. *Higher Education Research and Development, 36*(7), 1383–1400. https://doi.org/10.1080/07294360.2017.1325847.

Goss, S., & Mearns, D. (1997). A call for pluralist epistemological understanding in the assessment and evaluation of counselling. *British Journal of Guidance and Counselling, 25*(2), 189–198.

Gottfredson, L. (2002). Gottfredson's theory of circumscription, compromise and self-creation. In D. Brown (Eds.), *Career choice and development* (pp. 85–148). San Francisco: Jossey-Bass.

Gottfredson, L. S. (2005). Implications of cognitive differences for schooling within diverse societies. In C. L. Frisby & C. R. Reynolds (Eds.), *Comprehensive handbook of multicultural school psychology* (pp. 517–554). New York: Wiley.

Guba, E. G., & Lincoln, Y. S. (1992). *Effective evaluation: Improving the usefulness of evaluation results through responsive and naturalistic approaches*. San Francisco: Jossey-Bass Publishers.

Gutman, L. M., & Akerman, R. (2008). *Determinants of aspirations*. London: Institute of Education Centre for Research on the Wider Benefits of Learning.

Gutman, L., & Schoon, I. (2013). *The impact of non-cognitive skills on outcomes for young people*. London: Education Endowment Foundation.

Harkins, M. A. (2000). Career education in primary grades: Building work-readiness through an experiential curriculum. *Childhood Education, 76,* 219–224. https://doi.org/10.1080/00094056.2000.10521166.

Howard, K. A., Kimberly, A. S., Flanagan, S., Castine, E., & Walsh, M. E. (2015). Perceived influences on the career choices of children and youth: An exploratory study. *International Journal for Educational and Vocational Guidance, 15*(2), 99–111. https://doi.org/10.1007/s10775-015-9298-2.

Huber, L. R., Sloof, R., & Praag, M. V. (2012). *The effect of early entrepreneurship education: Evidence from a randomized field experiment*. Bonn: Institute for the Study of Labor.

Hughes, D., Mann, A., Barnes, S.-A., Baldauf, B., & Mc Keown, R. (2016). *Careers education: International literature review*. London: Education Endowment Foundation.

Hughes, D., Akkok, F., Arlumani, G., & Zelloth, H. (2019). Migration: Theory, research and practice in guidance and counseling. *British Journal of Guidance and Counselling, International Symposium Series, Migration: Theory, research and practice in guidance and counselling, 47*(1), 1–5.

Institute for Government. (2018). *Working to make government more effective: Schools*. London: Institute for Government.

International Organisation of Migration. (2018). *World Migration Report 2018*. Switzerland: IOM, The UN Migration Agency, Geneva.

Kaldi, S., Govaris, C., & Filippatou, D. (2018). Teachers' views about pupil diversity in the primary school classroom. *Compare: A Journal of Comparative and International Education, 48*:1, 2–20. https://doi.org/10.1080/03057925.2017.1281101.

Kashefpakdel, K., Rehill, J., & Hughes, D. (2018). *What works? Career-related learning in primary schools*. London: Careers and Enterprise Company & Education and Employers.

Kashefpakdel, K., Rehill, J., & Hughes, D. (2019). *Career-related learning in primary: The role of primary teachers and schools in preparing children for the future*. London: Teach First & Education and Employers.

Kautz, T., Heckman, J. J., Diris, R., Weel, B., & Borghans, L. (2014). *Fostering and measuring skills: Improving cognitive and non-cognitive skills to promote lifetime success*. Germany: National Bureau of Economic Research.

Kelly, A. (1989). When I grow up I want to be a…: A longitudinal study of the development of career preferences. *British Journal of Guidance and Counselling, 17,* 179–200. https://doi.org/10.1080/03069888908258052.

Kelly, P. (2004). Children's experiences of mathematics. *Research in Mathematics Education, 6*(1), 37–57. https://doi.org/10.1080/14794800008520129.

KidZania. (2017). *Children can only aspire to what they know exists—Making role-play real play: Building a creative approach to social mobility*. London: KidZania and Havas Helia.

Kirkman, E., Sanders, M., Emanuel, N. & Larkin, C. (2016). *Does participating in social action boost the skills young people need to succeed in adult life? Evaluating youth social action: Final report*. London: Behavioural Insights Team.

Knight, J. L. (2015). Preparing elementary school counselors to promote career development: Recommendations for school counselor education programs. *Journal of Career Development, 42*(2), 75–85. https://doi.org/10.1177/0894845314533745.

Kolb, D. A. (1984). *Experiential learning: Experience as the source of learning and development* (Vol. 1). Englewood Cliffs, NJ: Prentice-Hall.

Koro-Ljungberg, M. (2008). Validity and validation in the making in the context of qualitative research. *Qualitative Health Research, 18*(7), 983–989.

Lather, P. (1986, September). Research as Praxis. *Harvard Educational Review, 56*(3), 257–278. https://doi.org/10.17763/haer.56.3.bj2h231877069482.

Law, B. (2010). *Building on what we know: Career-learning thinking for contemporary working life*. Cambridge.

Liu, J., McMahon, M., & Watson, M. (2015). Parental influence on mainland Chinese children's career aspirations: Child and parental perspectives. *International Journal for Educational and Vocational Guidance, 15*(2), 131–143. https://doi.org/10.1007/s10775-015-9291-9.

Mann, A. & Dawkins, J. (2014). *Employer engagement in education: Literature review*. Reading: CfBT Education Trust.

Mann, A., Rehill, J., & Kashefpakdel, E. T. (2018). *Employer engagement in education: Insights from international evidence for effective practice and future research*. London: Education Endowment Foundation.

Maree, K. (2015). Blending retrospect and prospect in order to convert challenges into opportunities in career counselling. In K. Maree & A. Di Fabio (Eds.), *Exploring new horizons in career counselling turning challenge into opportunities* (pp. 3–24). Sense: Rotterdam, The Netherlands.

McMahon, M., & Watson, M. (2017). Telling stories of childhood career development. In M. McMahon & M. Watson (Eds.), *Career exploration and development in childhood: Perspectives from theory, practice and research* (pp. 1–8). Abingdon: Routledge.

Meijers, F., Kuijpers, M., & Gundy, C. (2013). How do career competencies relate to career identity, motivation and quality of choice in Dutch prevocational and secondary vocational education? *International Journal for Vocational and Educational Guidance, 13*(1), 47–66.

Millard, W., Menzies, L., & Baars, S. (2017). *Enterprise skills: Teachability, measurability and next steps. A review of the evidence*. London: Enabling Enterprise.

OECD. (2018). *The future of education and skills: Education 2030*. Paris: Organisation for Economic Cooperation and Development Publishing.

OECD. (2019). *Envisioning the future of education and jobs: Trends, data and drawings*. Switzerland: World Economic Forum, Davos, Organisation for Economic Cooperation and Development Publishing.

Patton, W., & McMahon, M. (1997). Gender differences in children and adolescents' perceptions of influences on their career development. *School Counselor, 44,* 368–376.

Payton, J., Weissberg, R. P., Durlak, J. A., Dymnicki, A. B., Taylor, R. D., Schellinger, K. B., et al. (2008). *The positive impact of social and emotional learning for kindergarten to eighth-grade students: Findings from three scientific reviews*. Chicago: Collaborative for Academic, Social, and Emotional Learning.

Phipps, B. J. (1995). Career dreams of preadolescent students. *Journal of Career Development, 22*, 19–32. https://doi.org/10.1007/bf02247893.

Piaget, J. (1977). *Epistemology and psychology of functions*. Netherlands: Dordrecht, D. Reidel Publishing Company.

Poole, M. E., & Low, B. C. (1985). Career and marriage: Orientations of adolescent girls. *Australian Journal of Education, 29*(1), 36–46.

Reynolds, D., & Teddlie, C. (2000). The processes of school effectiveness. In C. Teddlie & D. Reynolds (Eds.), *The international handbook of school effectiveness research* (pp. 134–159). London: Falmer Press.

Roffey, S. (2010). Content and context for learning relationships: A cohesive framework for individual and whole school development. *Educational & Child Psychology, 27*(1), 156–167.

Savickas, M. L. (2013). Career construction theory and practice. In S. D. Brown & R. W. Lent (Eds.), *Career development and counseling handbook: Putting theory and research to work* (2nd ed., pp. 147–183). New York: Wiley.

Schoon, I., & Lyons-Amos, Mark. (2017). A socio-ecological model of agency: The role of structure and agency in shaping education and employment transitions in England. *Journal of Longitudinal and Lifecourse Studies*. https://doi.org/10.14301/llcs.v8i1.404.

Schoon, I. & Silbereisen, R. K. (2009). Conceptualising school-to-work transitions in context. In I. Schoon & R. K. Silbereisen (Eds.), *The Jacobs foundation series on adolescence. Transitions from school-to-work* (pp. 3–29). Cambridge: Cambridge University Press.

Schultheiss, D. E. P., Palma, T. V., Predragovich, K. S., & Glasscock, J. M. J. (2002). Relational influences on career paths: siblings in context. *Journal of Counseling Psychology, 49*(3), 302–310.

Skorikov, V. B., & Vondracek, F. W. (2011). Occupational Identity. In S. J. Schwartz, K. Luyckx, & V. L. Vignoles (Eds.), *Handbook of identity theory and research* (pp. 693–714). New York, NY, US: Springer Science and Business Media.

Social Mobility Commission. (2018). *Social mobility barometer 2018*. London: Social Mobility Commission.

Smith, J. A., & Osborne, M. (2008). Interpretative phenomenological analysis. In J. A. Smith (Ed.), *Qualitative psychology—A practical guide to research methods* (pp. 53–80). London: Sage.

Super, D. E. (1980). A life-span, life-space approach to career development. *Journal of Vocational Behaviour, 13,* 282–298. https://doi.org/10.1016/0001-8791(80)90056-1.

Super, D. E. (1990). A life-span, life-space approach to career development. In D. Brown, L. Brooks, and Associates (Eds.), *Career choice and development* (2nd ed., pp. 197–261). San Francisco: Jossey-Bass.

Torgerson, C. J., King, S. E., & Snowden, A. J. (2002). Do volunteers in schools help children learn to read? A systematic review of randomised controlled trials. *Educational Studies, 28*(4), 433–444. https://doi.org/10.1080/0305569022000042435.

Tough, P. (2016). *Helping children succeed: What works and why*. Mariner Books.

Van der Heijden, B., & De Vos, A. (2015). Sustainable careers: Introductory chapter. In A. De Vos & B. Van der Heijden (Eds.), *Handbook of research on sustainable careers* (pp. 1–19). Cheltehnam, UK: Edward Elgar Publishing.

Vygotsky, L. S. (1978). *Mind in society: The development of higher psychological processes*. Cambridge, MA: Harvard University Press.

Wade, P., Bergeron, C., White, K., Teeman, D., Sims, D., & Mehta, P. (2011). *Key stage 2 career-related learning pathfinder evaluation*. London: Department for Education.

Wang, Y. (2012). *Education in a changing world: Flexibility, skills, and employability*. Washington, DC: World Bank.

Watson, M., McMahon, M., & Liu, J. (2015). Parental influence on mainland Chinese children's career aspirations: Child and parental perspectives. *International Journal for Educational and Vocational Guidance, 15*(2), 131–143.

Willms, J. D. (2000). Monitoring school performance for standards-based reform. *Evaluation and Research in Education, 14*(3–4), 237–253.

Children's Career Development: The Building Blocks for Career Adaptability

Jacqueline J. Peila-Shuster, Laurie A. Carlson and Amy E. Huff

Abstract Today's world of exponential change, global connectedness, a deepening divide of "have" and "have-not," and constant uncertainty means that tomorrow's workers must be prepared to design their lives following indistinct and/or elusive maps while preparing for uncertain and insecure employment. This means that we can no longer wait to implement career development programming in high school and beyond, but instead must begin in early childhood to nurture children's career development and adaptability. Towards this end, the first part of the chapter provides information on the importance of understanding career development as a lifelong process beginning in childhood. The second part considers influences on childhood career development through the lens of an ecological model and the third section discusses career adaptability. The fourth part of the chapter provides practical implications using both the ecological model and the 4Cs of career adaptability as organizing frameworks and is followed by a short concluding section.

Keywords Childhood career development · Career adaptability · Career construction · Ecological model · Children's career development · Life design

Introduction

> The trouble with our times is that the future is not what it used to be.—Paul Valéry

Change is a fact of life. However, in today's world, change is occurring at an unprecedented rate and advances in technology are creating disruptive change or tipping points that "trigger sudden and significant change" (Butler, 2016, p. 399). This level of transformation is hard to grasp because rather than being linear, it is exponential and "is blurring the lines between the physical, digital, and biological spheres"

J. J. Peila-Shuster (✉) · L. A. Carlson
Colorado State University, Fort Collins, Colorado, USA
e-mail: Jackie.Peila-Shuster@colostate.edu

A. E. Huff
University of Colorado-Denver, Denver, Colorado, USA

J. G. Maree (ed.), *Handbook of Innovative Career Counselling*,
https://doi.org/10.1007/978-3-030-22799-9_14

(Schwab, 2016, para. 26). Schwab (2016), goes on to state that these changes will impact multiple aspects of living, from relationships to consumption patterns to career development. Accordingly, workers in these uncertain times have a future that is not what it used to be and must prepare for possibilities rather than just make plans (Savickas, 2013).

Bauman (2007) used the term liquid modernity to describe the constant mobility and changing nature of relationships, identities, and global economics in today's society. Individuals have fewer and more elusive social, organizational, and ideological frameworks that formerly guided and organized life trajectories and roles (Guichard, 2015). Given that adults are still learning to navigate this new landscape, today's children, more than ever before, will need to "find their own ways of *being* in this world" (Peila-Shuster, 2018, p. 452). This will require that they engage "in an ongoing process of designing their lives" (Guichard, 2015, p. 15).

To engage in this process, it is important to help children and the adults in their lives learn that career development is not an outcome, but instead a lifelong journey influenced by historical, cultural, societal, and global contexts beginning in early childhood. Furthermore, positive engagement with influential systems and subsystems in children's lives can allow for more holistic intervention frameworks that access allies, promote inclusive practices, engage support systems, and provide critical opportunities that are necessary for the development of career adaptability. Towards that end, this chapter emphasizes the importance of understanding career development as a lifelong process and provides information regarding influences on childhood career development through the lens of an ecological systems model. This is followed by information concerning career adaptability and suggestions for building career concern, control, curiosity, and confidence in children. Additionally, interventions that target various systems and subsystems that have significant influence on children's career development are proposed.

Career Development as a Lifelong Process

Accepting childhood as just a time of fantasy and play dismisses its importance as a time when children begin to develop their understandings, consciously or unconsciously, about the world of work (Porfeli, Hartung, & Vondracek, 2008). While children do not yet have the cognitive capacities to engage in deep, introspective reflexivity, they can commence the process of building their stories, or narratives, by accumulating a variety of experiences. These narratives are an avenue through which people "organize their lives, construct their identities, and make sense of their problems" (Savickas, 2015, p. 9). Thus, through imagination, exploration, and solving problems, children can learn to "construct a viable work future consistent with cultural imperatives reflected in family and community contexts" (Hartung, Porfeli, & Vondracek, 2008, p. 63).

Several career development theories have long held that career development begins in childhood (e.g., Ginzberg, Ginsburg, Axelrad, & Herma, 1951;

Gottfredson, 1981; Roe, 1956; Super, 1957). Furthermore, they convey the importance of the dynamic interaction between environment and career development and aspirations. Gottfredson (1981, 2002) suggested that limited or foreclosed occupational choice-making may occur because of unconscious, or barely conscious, processes influenced by beliefs regarding gender-stereotyped roles and social valuation/prestige attributed to various occupations. Social cognitive career theory (Lent, 2012; Lent, Brown, & Hackett, 2002) specifies that personal and environment influences can "serve to strengthen, weaken, or, in some cases, even override human agency in career development" (Lent, 2005, p. 102). Thus, innovative career counselling for children must seek to help children explore themselves and their world while also engaging and educating their families, schools, and communities in manners that promote inclusion, equity, and social justice.

Childhood Formative Experiences Influencing Career Development

While career development for children is not about career decision-making, childhood experiences set a strong foundation, positively or negatively, for later educational, career, and life choices. "It is the fusion of subjective (personal factors) and objective (environmental factors) experiences that strongly influence development during the formative years from early infancy to young adulthood" (Yohani, 2008, p. 311). This quote reflects the convictions of the authors of this chapter that environmental factors in children's lives can serve to promote career development or stifle it. Thus, viewing childhood career development through an ecological lens is imperative, and interventions at systems-levels may be highly influential.

Ecological Model

Because a child develops within the context of their environment, it is advantageous when addressing the career development needs of children that one considers the benefits of working from the Ecological Model (Schultheiss, 2008; VanderVen, 2006). Although many scholars contributed to the theory, Urie Bronfenbrenner articulated the Ecological Model in 1979 out of a need to more fully account for environmental context in the study of human behavior and learning (Derksen, 2010). Since then, his model evolved into a bioecological theory of human development which Bronfenbrenner continued to develop up until his death in 2005 (Tudge, Mokrova, Hatfield, & Karnik, 2009). It should be noted that the more mature form of his theory emphasized processes of human development through his Process-Person-Context-Time model (PPCT; Tudge et al., 2009). For the sake of this chapter, though, his initial ecological model is used as an organizing framework to appreciate the ecological systems enveloping childhood career development.

Microsystem. At the center of the ecological model lies the microsystem consisting of the individual themselves and their physical, intellectual, emotional, and spiritual interactions with those closest to them (Bronfenbrenner & Morris, 1998). These relationships include family, classmates, friends, teachers, child care providers, and others who have regular and significant contact with the child. The key to fully understanding the influence of the micro-systemic level is to recognize the phenomenological nature of it; that the character of what occurs in an individual's environment is second to how that person perceives the significance of aspects within the environment (Derksen, 2010). It is also critical that career practitioners understand the significant influence of biology within the model because such biological markers as cognitive functioning and physical abilities influence the interaction of the microsystem with the other levels over chronological time (Bronfenbrenner & Ceci, 1994).

School influences. According to Taveira, Oliveira, and Araújo (2016), research regarding childhood career development at the microsystem level has primarily encompassed family and school microsystems. However, none of the studies discussed in their meta-analysis appeared to involve school counselling interventions within these microsystems. Whiston, Tai, Rahardja, and Eder (2011) asserted that there is a dearth of information regarding school counselling interventions with youth, especially in regards to what specific programming or approaches work. They called for additional research with sound methodological approaches to be undertaken to identify "what works, with what students, and under what circumstances" (Whiston et al., 2011, p. 48). They made this call after conducting a meta-analysis on school counselling interventions at the elementary, middle, and high school levels using both published and unpublished studies. In their study, they found that school counselling interventions had a positive effect, especially regarding students' problem-solving abilities and decreasing discipline problems.

While the meta-analysis undertaken by Whiston et al. (2011) did not specifically address career development interventions, a meta-analysis of 67 studies on career intervention programs by Evans and Burck (1992) indicated a small positive effect size (.16) on student academic achievement. Furthermore, when they grouped the interventions with elementary students (16 studies), the effect size increased to .33. Gillies, McMahon, and Carroll (1998) also studied a career intervention when they evaluated a career education program for sixth-grade children in Australia. They found that compared to the control group, the intervention group better understood a range of career information sources they could use to learn about jobs and also had a better understanding of how their education connected to various occupations. In making these connections, the investigators suggested that the children were making some fairly mature cognitive links such as knowing that teamwork and being good problem-solvers were skills they were learning at school and would need in various occupations.

While Ferrari et al. (2015) did not study a career intervention, they did examine children's occupational knowledge in relation to career exploration and provided implications that are important for school-based interventions. They concluded that greater exploration equated to greater knowledge, but only for those occupational areas with which children had moderate experience, rather than areas in which they knew well or those in which they had very limited experience. Consequently, Ferrari et al. (2015) highlighted the role of contextualizing learning experiences regarding the world of work to encourage children to collect information about areas in which they have some knowledge and then link that new information with existing knowledge.

Family influences. Based on their review of the literature, Bryant, Zvonkovic, and Reynolds (2006) suggested that children tend to perceive that their parents' attitudes towards work are more negative than is actually the case, and that children are more aware of work's financial versus psychological rewards. Additionally, in a study of ninth grade students in the U.S., Lee and Porfeli (2015) found that students' perceptions of their parents' success in family life were aligned with their conceptualizations regarding work, whereas perceptions of parental success in work life was not a significant factor. This was an unexpected finding and the authors suggested that because youth observe their parents primarily in the home, this may serve as their gauge for their parents' functioning in the work domain as well. Furthermore, they found that the youth in this study who viewed work positively tended to be more engaged with their schoolwork.

Bryant et al. (2006) also concluded that middle childhood provides an important window in which satisfying parent-child activities can "serve as an important foundation for future vocational exploration" (p. 161). Satisfying activities may include play and exposure to the world of work. For example, in examining the life plan development of 13 young adult women about to graduate from college in a Northeast state in the United States, Zambrano-Varghese (2017) found that these women's plans began to develop at a very young age and included play experiences involving simulating life plans with toys, as well as being exposed to family members' careers and going to their places of employment. Additionally, while some of the young adult women in her study had negative and discouraging influences from significant people in their lives, and others had positive and encouraging influences, all had used these experiences to motivate them towards their life achievements.

In addition to providing play and exploration experiences, parental support and encouragement can also facilitate positive career development. Uusiautti and Määttä (2015) examined childhood experiences of top workers in Finland who had been awarded Employee of the Year. Their research suggested that parents had influenced their children's attitudes towards work more so than their career choices. Participants had indicated that their parents did not pressure them, and instead had assisted and encouraged them to think about their futures, make their own choices, and be open to opportunities.

Mesosystem. The mesosystem represents the interactions of two or more microsystemic factors and their influence on the individual (Bronfenbrenner & Morris, 1998). For example, this subsystem would include the relationship and interactions between a child's teachers and parents and how that influences the child. These varying parts of the child's microsystem may work together or in opposition to positively or negatively influence the child's development. It is also possible for one microsystem to mitigate the constraints from another system by providing resources to the child that are not available in their other microsystems (Bronfenbrenner & Ceci, 1994).

It appears that parents, teachers, and peers all play a role in childhood career development (Taveira et al., 2016). For example, familial support was found to be important in the development of agency in Italian youth and in career outcomes (Howard, Ferrari, Nota, Solberg, & Soresi, 2009). Furthermore, for girls in Italy, teachers and peers also played an important role in the development of agency (Howard et al., 2009). Additionally, for youth in the German federal state of Thuringia, positive parenting contributed to youth's career exploration as did schools that were considered to be accepting and open (Noack, Kracke, Gniewosz, & Dietrich, 2010). However, information regarding the influence on children's career development based on the **interactions** of varying microsystems (which constitutes the mesosystem) was not readily apparent.

Exosystem. The exosystem is comprised of elements that lie outside of children's everyday awareness but that touch them nonetheless (Bronfenbrenner & Morris, 1998). These elements can include the indirect influences from their parents' workplaces and other social institutions. The family context, according to Bryant, Zvonkovic, and Reynolds (2006), includes financial capital, social capital, genetics, family roles, culture, and family interface with work and other social institutions, to name a few. This family context, relevant throughout a child's development, provides a basis of parenting influences that includes assets as well as constraints that will continue to dynamically evolve as children also influence their parents (Bryant et al., 2006).

The importance of context from the exosystem cannot be understated as it will affect far more than the parent-child relationship. For example, "the challenges of having jobs with low socioeconomic status affect many of the parenting variables that lead to occupational knowledge, as well as problems with providing opportunities to explore vocations" (Bryant et al., 2006, p. 154). These parenting variables may include, but are not limited to, the financial and social capital necessary for out-of-school activities, or the difficulties involved in balancing long and demanding work hours with direct time spent with one's children.

Macrosystem. The macrosystem is the historical, political and cultural blanket that wraps around the child and the other systems in their world (Bronfenbrenner & Morris, 1998). As such, this influential system encompasses cultural and societal beliefs, the economy, governmental policies, etc., and while it may seem remote, it has great influence on children's career development. Thus, intervention approaches within this system often involve social and political advocacy (Palladino Schultheiss, 2005).

In summarizing two extensive literature reviews (see Hartung, Porfeli, & Vondracek, 2005; Watson & McMahon, 2005), some of the key results summarized by Porfeli et al. (2008) addressed the macrosystem:

- Career aspirations are relatively stable and become more so across the grade school years. These aspirations are influenced by gender-based occupational stereotypes throughout grade school and beyond.
- Career aspirations tend to be influenced by occupational stereotypes and a circumscription mechanism that channels girls away from math and science careers and boys away from female-dominated professions.
- Economically impoverished and African American and Hispanic children tend to maintain less prestigious career aspirations, and African American children exhibit a greater difference in the prestige of career aspirations and expectations, than do their wealthier Caucasian peers across the grade school years (p. 28).

These key results continue to be themes in more recent research. While untangling race, ethnicity, and socio-economic status has proven difficult in terms of their influence on individuals' career development (Howard et al., 2011), it is still apparent that these factors are highly influential. According to Diemer and Blustein (2007), racism, random violence, and poorly funded schools often encountered by urban youth can lead to a disconnect from their future occupational goals and aspirations. Howard et al. (2011) found that Native American adolescents aspired to less prestigious occupations requiring less education and yielding lower incomes. This was especially true for boys and for those from lower socioeconomic status backgrounds. In studying African-American children (third through sixth grades), Begg, Levitt, and Hayden (2017) found themes that indicated unrealistic expectations about future educational opportunities and career options with beliefs such as needing to be a famous performer or athlete to have enough money to avoid homelessness. Rural versus urban environments also influence child career development with work behaviors often ascribing to commonly accepted norms within each of these environments (Helwig, 2004; Schmitt-Wilson & Welsh, 2012).

A highly influential macrosytemic factor in childhood career development is gender norms and gendered work expectations (Helwig, 2004). Gender norms have been found to have impact upon the career development of both male and female students, although stronger influences were found for males (Lawson, Lee, Crouter, & McHale, 2018). Also, in regards to gender, Ferrari et al. (2015) found that being male predicted a higher perception of knowledge about Realistic occupations and being female predicted a higher perception of Social occupational knowledge (per Holland's codes; Holland, 1996) in fourth through seventh-grade Italian children. For Taiwanese kindergartners, Lee (2012) found that occupational aspirations were associated with the same-sex parent's or teacher's occupation. However, Lee also found that while boys tended to aspire to more masculine-type occupations, girls' aspirations were more evenly spread across neutral, feminine, and masculine occupations. Lawson, Crouter, and McHale (2015) suggested that gendered childhood socialization experiences around the age of 10 were associated with occupational attainment 15 years later, but were dependent upon sex of the child. They found that more traditional attitudes toward sex roles of mothers predicted gendered occupational attainment for sons, but not daughters, and that both sons and daughters who spent more time with their fathers secured more male-typed occupations. Vervecken and Hannover (2015) investigated the use of gender fair language to describe occupations with primary school-age children from Belgium and Germany. They found that compared to children whom the male occupations had been described using the generic masculine form, children presented with the linguistic pair form (feminine and masculine) had greater self-efficacy regarding traditionally masculine occupations and this effect was fully mediated by their perceptions that these occupations were not as difficult as suggested by traditional gender stereotypes.

Chronosystem. The chronosystem consists of the individual's development including interactions with the other systems over time (Bronfenbrenner & Morris, 1998). By incorporating the dimension of time, the influence of transitions, change, and constancy is recognized. One of the most prevalent experiences identified in literature related to the chronosystem is the multiple transitions that children make during their childhood (Taveira et al., 2016).

Career Adaptability and the 4 Cs

With the shift away from linear careers and the movement towards boundaryless careers (Porfeli & Vondracek, 2009), there is a greater need for subjective awareness through self-reflection and construction to develop skills for coping and adapting to changing conditions. Thus, what Super, Savickas, and Super (1996) proposed as career maturity has now been augmented by career adaptability which is defined as representing individuals' "resources for coping with current and anticipated tasks, transitions, traumas in their occupational roles that, to some degree large or small, alter their social integration" (Savickas & Porfeli, 2012, p. 662). Career adaptability is seen in an individual's readiness, skills, and resources in managing career development tasks; navigating transitions such as from school to work or high school to higher education; and the ability to cope with vocational traumas such as losing a job or industry changes (Savickas, 2005).

Of particular import for children is the development of the necessary elements, or building blocks, of career adaptability. Savickas (2013) determined these four dimensions (or four Cs) of career adaptability to be career concern, career control, career curiosity, and career confidence. Career concern is the recognition of the need to plan for the future (Savickas, 2013). This recognition can shape individuals' actions as they begin to see educational, vocational, and life experiences as opportunities to take steps towards goal achievement.

Career control refers to the development of the self-regulation that is necessary to engage in vocational tasks and transition processes (Savickas, 2013). While career control includes the recognition that one has control over their decisions and their future, it is not about the Western-value of independence in making these decisions. Instead career control consists of intrapersonal self-discipline and being conscientious, intentional, and decisive when engaged in career developmental tasks and transitions (Savickas, 2013). With the development of career control, there may be a greater possibility for individuals to take responsibility for their actions and persevere through roadblocks while adjusting and shifting decisions to adapt to changes.

Career curiosity is characterized by an inquisitiveness about one's own interests, others' experiences, and occupational alternatives, thus allowing for the exploration of possible selves and possible opportunities (Savickas, 2013). Curious individuals may be more likely to take opportunities to investigate their surroundings and seek out opportunities to grow (Rudolph, Lavigne, Katz, & Zacher, 2017).

Career confidence depicts self-efficacy in one's ability to learn new skills, navigate career problems or obstacles, pursue aspirations, execute action plans, and implement choices (Savickas, 2013; Savickas & Porfeli, 2012). Without career confidence, it can be difficult for an individual to keep growing forward as they will not believe in their abilities to navigate change and growth.

Developing career concern, control, curiosity, and confidence is important for all individuals. For children, these career adaptability building blocks are critical as they can lay an essential foundation for perceptions of opportunities and future choices. Furthermore, taking into account these elements of career adaptability can help expand perceptions of what career development can entail when working with children. For example, Briddick, Sensoy-Briddick, and Savickas (2018) utilized these constructs in developing a career curriculum for elementary-age students in Turkey. Through this curriculum, they sought to: (1) facilitate career concern through activities that bolstered children's exploration of themselves; (2) help children develop a sense of agency (and career control) and encourage excitement by engaging children in activities that raised their understanding of how they are active agents in their own lives; (3) stimulate curiosity about the world of work; (4) facilitate students' confidence in their developing abilities to help them cope with future challenges; and (5) connect what they were doing in school to future career dreams and possibilities.

Practical Implications for Career Adaptability Interventions

In this section, the authors provide practical implications for career practitioners, educators, parents, and others involved in children's lives. Building the career adaptabilities of career concern, curiosity, control, and confidence are directly discussed in terms of the microsystem and mesosystem. Because of their indirect, yet extensive, influences on the microsystem, the exo, macro, and chronosystems are addressed more broadly in terms of practical implications for career interventions that may assist with developing career adaptability.

Microsystem and Mesosystem

Directly engaging in career development within a child's microsystem provides multiple opportunities for developing career adaptability's four dimensions of career concern, career control, career curiosity, and career confidence. Possibilities are multiplied when interventions also involve other microsystem influences in children's lives including, but not limited to, interactions with parents and teachers.

Career concern. Implementing activities in children's homes, educational establishments, and community settings that encourage and engage children to think about their futures, and believe that they can attain a positive one, can be useful in fostering career concern. Children ages 4 and 5 have demonstrated the ability to mentally travel into the future and anticipate situations that can arise (Busby & Suddendorf, 2005). Thus, childhood relationships, experiences, and activities that promote appropriate risk-taking attitudes and provide an atmosphere safe and conducive for asking questions about the future provide a fertile ground for planting seeds to help children develop a positive future orientation and planful attitude, or career concern (Maree, 2018). Furthermore, this hopeful attitude regarding the future may be preventative given that Hartung et al. (2008) suggested when hope for the future is not nurtured, troublesome emotions and behaviors can emerge.

Career control. A sense of industry versus inferiority can be fostered by encouraging children's efforts to build or make things and complete chores (Erikson, 1968). Additionally, secure childhood relationships and positive experiences can help with the development of self-direction, autonomy, and self-reliance (Hartung et al., 2008). These attributes contribute towards building career control in that they facilitate skills in self-regulation and help children build their sense of control over their own actions, intentions, and decisions. Furthermore, helping children (in developmentally appropriate ways) to think about and make informed decisions, while also encouraging them to make their own decisions and choices, may further enhance their sense of control and thus build upon the skills needed for career control. This was seen in the previously mentioned study in which top workers in Finland indicated that their parents influenced them by encouraging them to think about their futures, make their own choices, and be open to opportunities (Uusiautti & Määttä, 2015).

Career curiosity. "Risk-taking and inquiring behaviours foster the child's development of a foundational sense of inquisitiveness and interest in the world of work," whereas inadequate career curiosity "limits exploration and prompts unrealism and unrealistic aspirations and expectations about the future" (Hartung et al., 2008, p. 70). Fortunately, children have a natural inquisitiveness and it is incumbent upon the adults and systems in their lives that it be nurtured and encouraged as they mature. Children's curiosity is more likely to be enhanced when adults minimize their control and accentuate the child's feelings of personal power and choice (Kashdan & Fincham, 2004). Thus, developing curiosity is assisted by the development of control. Because curious individuals tend to choose activities that will stretch them and are more willing to approach activities that have unclear outcomes (Kaczmarek et al., 2013), adults must let go and at times help children learn to fail forward (i.e., learn and grow from their mistakes). In developing or enhancing children's curiosity about the world of work, it may be useful to initially contextualize their experiences in ways that help them collect information about areas in which they know something and then link that new information with existing knowledge (Ferrari et al., 2015).

Career Confidence. Career confidence can be stimulated through the use of role playing, social modeling, and cognitive-behavioral interventions that are aimed at increasing self-efficacy beliefs (Hartung et al., 2008). Also, children who are exposed to work activities at home and at school are provided the opportunity to learn the "value of their 'work', develop self-belief, [and] develop an enhanced sense of self" (Maree, 2018, p. 439).

Drawing upon the work of Bandura (1977, 1986), career interventions that build career confidence can be targeted to utilize the four sources of self-efficacy—performance accomplishments, vicarious experiences, verbal persuasion, and physiological arousal. As children master goals and competencies ranging from tying their shoes to learning multiplication tables, adults can nurture their self-efficacy by praising and drawing upon these performance accomplishments to help children have the confidence to master new goals. Also, when faced with challenges and setbacks, helping children reframe them as learning opportunities can encourage a growth mindset (Dweck, 2015). This does not mean just valuing their efforts, but also includes accurately appraising the child's current level of achievement and then helping the child learn ways to improve.

Boosting children's career confidence through vicarious experiences, Bandura's (1977, 1986) second source of self-efficacy, occurs as important people and role models in children's lives exhibit appropriate behaviors and attitudes toward work and expose children to new opportunities to learn more about themselves and the world of work. Verbal persuasion, especially in the form of positive encouragement, can be important for children as they are at a developmental stage in which they may not yet have accurate self-appraisal skills and thus tend to depend upon trusted others to provide performance feedback (Bandura, 1994). Additionally, children tend to appraise their confidence about engaging in an action using cues from strong emotional reactions they have related to certain tasks or situations (Bandura, 1997; Usher, 2008). This notion is supported by Määttä and Järvelä (2013) who found that emotional and physiological states were the most powerful source of self-efficacy for the children ages 6–8 in their study. This contradicts Bandura's (1977) suggestion that performance accomplishments or mastery experiences are the most influential basis for building self-efficacy. It should be noted, though, that Määttä and Järvelä (2013) surmised that children may not have enough mastery experiences to call upon to help build self-efficacy, and thus they rely more on feelings and emotions

Additional considerations for micro and mesosystem interventions. The authors of this chapter propose that it is important to help children start learning the process of self-reflection as a precursor to the development of self-awareness, which underlies any aspect of self-growth, including the development of career concern, control, curiosity, and control. By nurturing a budding self-awareness, children can begin to construct their narrative even before developing the cognitive capacity to make meaning of it. Helping children reflect on and develop language around their likes, dislikes, interests, skills, and emerging values can facilitate the antecedents necessary for the life design goal of narratability which is the ability "to tell one's story clearly and coherently" (Hartung, 2015, p. 97). With this goal in mind, it is helpful to consider children's life career as a story with three main parts: (1) the lead character who represents who they are (and who they are becoming); (2) the educational and/or work setting that represents an environment where they will be most comfortable (which will continue to evolve); and (3) the story script which explains how each child can use work to implement a developing self-concept (Hartung, 2015). This also means that it is imperative to support children in gaining broader experiences, thus allowing for greater development of the self.

It is obvious that children's development of career concern, control, curiosity, and confidence involves multiple interactions with other children and adults within their micro and mesosystems. Thus, their emotional, educational, social, and career development requires the development of interpersonal and communication skills that facilitate honest, fair, helpful, and respectful interactions. Furthermore, given our diverse and global society, there is a need to successfully build and manage relationships and positively interact with diverse groups of people. Towards this end, children need help in developing conflict resolution and teamwork skills, as well as the ability to cope with outside pressures and influences (National Career Development Guidelines, n.d.). Those providing career interventions can utilize small groups to support children in the development of pro-social behaviors, especially since many critical dispositions such as cooperation, integrity, and respect for others are best taught in a social context and therefore lend themselves well to group or classroom interventions.

Additionally, school-wide and community activities can provide children with supportive audiences by bringing together parents, schools, community organizations, and businesses. Briddick et al. (2018) recommend events such as career fairs where parents, community organizations, and businesses collaborate; school-wide programs where children can exhibit their work from career development activities; and collaboration between high schools and elementary schools where high school students could, for example, take part in educating elementary students about their career aspirations.

Exosystem and Macrosystem

Career interventions focused in the microsystems and mesosystems cannot be disconnected from children's exosystems and macrosystems. It is imperative that career counsellors regularly examine exo and macrosystemic factors to uncover points of opportunity bias or systemic oppression which impacts future career possibilities for children. This also means that career counsellors must take care to consider the messages children have absorbed regarding their gender, social status, race, ethnicity, and other identities, as well as how they have been socialized regarding their place within societal hierarchies which can limit or foreclose career choices at an early age. For example, language can be powerful as seen with the study by Vervecken and Hannover (2015) where children's self-efficacy surrounding certain occupations was improved when they were presented with feminine and masculine linguistic pair forms. Also, while there may seem to be an inclination towards more egalitarian attitudes in some parts of the world, a recent study in the United States demonstrated that the gender-typing of children's playthings was still similar to what was observed over 40 years ago (MacPhee & Prendergast, 2018). Thus, gender stereotypes are present throughout children's lives and likely unconsciously absorbed.

To openly and critically consider the influences and messages to which children are consistently exposed, career counsellors may have unlearning to do in regards to their understanding about oppression, discrimination, and privilege (Anderson & Middleton, 2018). By engaging in critical consciousness (Freire, 1970), career professionals can heighten their sensitivity to, and awareness of, privilege and oppression and thus better see, hear, and understand spoken and unspoken messages pervading all environments and thus all children's lives. Critical consciousness is an ongoing process through which one must strive "to perceive the social, political, and economic contradictions, and to take action against the oppressive elements of reality" (Freire, 1970, p. 17). Career counsellors that engage in raising their awareness of their own socio-political position in relation to others can better act on that awareness to support and advocate for inclusive and socially-just career development programming and interventions.

Career counsellors must also actively work to deconstruct and mitigate oppressive messaging children encounter throughout their environments, and via individuals within those environments, that contribute to the restriction of career options. Visual ethnography is a useful method for appraising cultural climate (Banning, 1997; Banning & Bartels, 1997) through assessment of an environment's physical artefacts which are objects created from one's culture (Hormuth, 1990). These physical artefacts tend to uncover important and powerful statements about cultural beliefs and assumptions that are just below the level of consciousness (Kuh & Whitt, 1988). In evaluating these messages, one can gain knowledge regarding what children are learning from their environments, and through advocacy and education, can raise the critical consciousness of those involved in children's lives. "By auditing the physical spaces in which children spend their time…[children's] environments can be viewed with a broader lens that embraces perspectives regarding inclusion" (Peila-Shuster, 2015, p. 215). For suggestions on conducting a physical space appraisal, please see Peila-Shuster, Brantmeier, Kees, Anderson, and Aragon (2011).

Additionally, career interventions and support should extend beyond the individual child to include programs and resources for parents. In Wisconsin, United States, a work-based antipoverty program for low-income adults demonstrated positive effects on their children five years after program support ended (McLoyd, Kaplan, Purtell, & Huston, 2011). These positive effects included increased engagement of the children in career preparatory activities and lowered cynicism about the world of work. Programming for parents should also consider family success within the home, not just at work, since family functioning can be a contributor to the perceptions youth hold regarding work (Lee & Porfeli, 2015). Thus, education and interventions focused on parenting and family relationships may ultimately assist children's career development. Liu, McMahon, and Watson (2015) also suggested connecting formal career development programming in schools with informal family networks, inviting family members to be a part of career development activities, and providing information to parents to help them understand how they can assume positive roles in their children's career development. A career counsellor can foster this development by teaching important adults in children's lives how to have meaningful career conversations with young people, particularly around issues of ethnicity and culture (Pizzorno, Benozzo, Fina, Sabato, & Scopesi, 2014).

Career education for parents/caretakers, teachers, administrators and others involved in children's lives is crucial when considering today's rapid changes in an uncertain and global world. Shifting career trajectories, designing lives, and the need for career adaptability are often unfamiliar concepts. Furthermore, models and curriculums that teach outdated notions of the world of work and seek to only identify commonalities and fit between person and work environment are common. While the paradigms of career education and guidance are necessary and useful, they must be augmented with life designing (Savickas et al., 2009). Through life design interventions, individuals learn to author their own stories to find uniqueness, meaning, and purpose in their lives and to explore work as a potential vehicle for implementing their self-concepts.

Chronosystem

Throughout this chapter, the authors have contended that career development is a lifelong process and have provided recommendations for children's career development. With early intervention and facilitation, children can begin to develop the requisite knowledge and skills that will enhance their career adaptability and allow them to navigate uncertain times and uncharted journeys. Essential to this is imparting to children that their lives and the world are not stagnant and that their career paths will not be linear. Young children need to understand that career is a dynamic and complex experience woven into all other experiences over their lifetime. They will continue to evolve as will the systems and societies in which they live; hence, so must their life-careers. This concept is even more pertinent in today's reality where a global and ever-changing work economy requires the employee of tomorrow to be career adaptable.

Conclusion

While multiple theorists have maintained that childhood formative experiences and factors impact career development, much of the career development literature and research remains focused on adolescence and adulthood. This is concerning given that children are growing up in a world that is not what it once used to be. By engaging in and with the ecological systems in children's lives, adults can encourage and teach children ways to be planful for and hopeful about a future (career concern); help them develop a sense of agency in their lives (career control); nurture their sense of wonderment and possibility (career curiosity); and build their self-efficacy around managing life's twists and turns (career confidence). These intentional career development efforts can nurture, support, sustain, and prepare children for their futures, as well as create hope for our own future as a global society.

References

Anderson, S. K., & Middleton, V. A. (Eds.). (2018). *Explorations in diversity: Examining the complexities of privilege, discrimination, and oppression* (3rd ed.). New York, NY: Oxford.

Bandura, A. (1977). Self-efficacy: Toward a unifying theory of behavioral change. *Psychological Review, 84,* 191–215. https://doi.org/10.1037/0033-295X.84.2.191.

Bandura, A. (1986). *Social foundations of thought and action: A social cognitive theory.* Englewood Cliffs, NJ: Prentice Hall.

Bandura, A. (1994). Self-efficacy. In V. S. Ramachaudran (Ed.), *Encyclopedia of human behavior* (pp. 71–81). New York: NY: Academic Press.

Bandura, A. (1997). *Self-efficacy: The exercise of control*. New York, NY: Freeman.

Banning, J. H. (1997). Assessing the campus' ethical climate: A multidimensional approach. In J. Fried (Ed.), *Ethics for today's campus: New perspectives on education, student development, and institutional management* (pp. 95–105). San Francisco, CA: Jossey-Bass.

Banning, J. H., & Bartels, S. (1997). A taxonomy: Campus physical artifacts as communicators of campus multiculturalism. *NASPA Journal, 35*(1), 29–37.

Bauman, Z. (2007). *Liquid times: Living in an age of uncertainty*. Cambridge, UK: Polity Press.

Begg, N. A., Levitt, H. M., & Hayden, L. A. (2017). Understanding the school experience of African-American homeless children. *Journal of Constructivist Psychology, 30,* 235–254. https://doi.org/10.1080/10720537.2016.1183539.

Briddick, W. C., Sensoy-Briddick, H., & Savickas, S. (2018). Career construction materials: The story of a career development curriculum in a Turkish school. *Early Child Development and Care, 188,* 478–489. https://doi.org/10.1080/03004430.2017.1423483.

Bronfenbrenner, U. (1979). *The ecology of human development*. Cambridge, MA: Harvard University Press.

Bronfenbrenner, U., & Ceci, S. J. (1994). Nature-nurture reconceptualized in developmental perspective: A bioecological model. *Psychological Review, 101,* 568–586. https://doi.org/10.1037/0033-295X.101.4.568.

Bronfenbrenner, U., & Morris, P. (1998). The ecology of developmental processes. In R. M. Lerner (Ed.), *Theoretical models of human development* (5th ed., Vol. 1, pp. 993–1028). New York, NY: Wiley.

Bryant, B. K., Zvonkovic, A. M., & Reynolds, P. (2006). Parenting in relation to child and adolescent vocational development. *Journal of Vocational Behavior, 69,* 149–175. https://doi.org/10.1016/j.jvb.2006.02.004.

Busby, J., & Suddendorf, T. (2005). Recalling yesterday and predicting tomorrow. *Cognitive Development, 20,* 362–372. https://doi.org/10.1016/j.cogdev.2005.05.002.

Butler, D. (2016). Tomorrow's world. *Nature, 530,* 399. Retrieved from nature.com website: https://www.nature.com/polopoly_fs/1.19431!/menu/main/topColumns/topLeftColumn/pdf/530398a.pdf?origin=ppub.

Derksen, T. (2010). The influence of ecological theory in child and youth care: A review of the literature. *International Journal of Child, Youth, & Family Studies, 1*(3/4), 326–339. https://doi.org/10.18357/ijcyfs13/420102091.

Diemer, M. A., & Blustein, D. L. (2007). Vocational hope and vocational identity: Urban adolescents' career development. *Journal of Career Assessment, 15,* 98–118. https://doi.org/10.1177/1069072706294528.

Dweck, C. (2015, February 2). Carol Dweck revisits the 'growth mindset.' *Education Week*. Retrieved from https://www.edweek.org/ew/articles/2015/09/23/carol-dweck-revisits-the-growth-mindset.html.

Erikson, E. H. (1968). *Identity: Youth and crisis*. New York, NY: W. W. Norton.

Evans, J. H., Jr., & Burck, H. D. (1992). The effects of career education interventions on academic achievement: A meta-analysis. *Journal of Counseling & Development, 71,* 63–68. https://doi.org/10.1002/j.1556-6676.1992.tb02173.x.

Ferrari, L., Ginevra, M. C., Santilli, S., Nota, L., Sgaramella, T. M., & Soresi, S. (2015). Career exploration and occupational knowledge in Italian children. *International Journal of Education and Vocational Guidance, 15,* 113–130. https://doi.org/10.1007/s10775-015-9599-1.

Freire, P. (1970). *Pedagogy of the oppressed*. New York, NY: Continuum.

Gillies, R. M., McMahon, M. L., & Carroll, J. (1998). Evaluating a career education intervention in the upper elementary school. *Journal of Career Development, 24,* 267–287. https://doi.org/10.1177/089484539802400401.

Ginzberg, E., Ginsburg, S., Axelrad, S., & Herma, J. (1951). *Occupational choice: An approach to a general theory*. New York, NY: Columbia University Press.

Gottfredson, L. S. (1981). Circumscription and compromise: A developmental theory of occupational aspirations. *Journal of Counseling Psychology, 28,* 545–579. https://doi.org/10.1037/0022-0167.28.6.545.

Gottfredson, L. S. (2002). Gottfredson's theory of circumscription, compromise, and self-creation. In D. Brown & Associates (Eds.), *Career choice and development* (4th ed.). San Francisco, CA: Jossey-Bass.

Guichard, J. (2015). From vocational guidance and career counseling to life design dialogues. In L. Nota & J. Rossier (Eds.), *Handbook of life design: From practice to theory and from theory to practice* (pp. 11–25). Boston, MA: Hogrefe.

Hartung, P. J. (2015). Life design in childhood: Antecedents and advancement. In L. Nota & J. Rossier (Eds.), *Handbook of life design* (pp. 89–102). Boston, MA: Hogrefe.

Hartung, P. J., Porfeli, E. J., & Vondracek, F. W. (2005). Child vocational development: A review and reconsideration. *Journal of Vocational Behavior, 66,* 385–419.

Hartung, P. J., Porfeli, E. J., & Vondracek, F. W. (2008). Career adaptability in childhood. *The Career Development Quarterly, 57,* 63–74. https://doi.org/10.1002/j.2161-0045.2008.tb00166.x.

Helwig, A. A. (2004). A ten-year longitudinal study of the career development of students: Summary findings. *Journal of Counseling & Development, 82,* 49–57. https://doi.org/10.1002/j.1556-6678.2004.tb00285.x.

Holland, J. L. (1996). Exploring careers with a typology: What we have learned and some new directions. *American Psychologist, 51,* 397–406. https://doi.org/10.1037/0003-066X.51.4.397.

Hormuth, S. (1990). *The ecology of the self*. Cambridge, United Kingdom: Cambridge University Press.

Howard, K. A. S., Carlstrom, A. H., Katz, A. D., Chew, A. Y., Ray, G. C., Laine, L., et al. (2011). Career aspirations of youth: Untangling race/ethnicity, SES, and gender. *Journal of Vocational Behavior, 79,* 98–109. https://doi.org/10.1016/j.jvb.2010.12.002.

Howard, K. A. S., Ferrari, L., Nota, L., Solberg, V. S. H., & Soresi, S. (2009). The relation of cultural context and social relationships to career development in middle school. *Journal of Vocational Behavior, 75,* 100–108.

Kaczmarek, L. D., Kashdan, T. B., Kleiman, E. M., Baczkowski, B., Enko, J., Siebers, A., et al. (2013). Who self-initiates gratitude interventions in daily life? An examination of intentions, curiosity, depressive symptoms, and life satisfaction. *Personality and Individual Differences, 55,* 805–810. https://doi.org/10.1016/j.paid.2013.06.013.

Kashdan, T. B., & Fincham, F. D. (2004). Facilitating curiosity: A social and self-regulatory perspective for scientifically based interventions. In P. A. Linley & S. Joseph (Eds.), *Positive psychology in practice* (pp. 482–503). Hoboken, NJ: Wiley.

Kuh, G. D., & Whitt, E. J. (1988). *The invisible tapestry: Cultures in American colleges and universities* (ASHE-ERIC Higher Education Report No. 1). Retrieved from https://eric.ed.gov/?id=ED299934.

Lawson, K. M., Crouter, A. C., & McHale, S. M. (2015). Links between family gender socialization experiences in childhood and gendered occupational attainment in young adulthood. *Journal of Vocational Behavior, 90,* 26–35. https://doi.org/10.1016/j.jvb.2015.07.003.

Lawson, K. M., Lee, B., Crouter, A. C., & McHale, S. M. (2018). Correlates of gendered vocational development from middle childhood to young adulthood. *Journal of Vocational Behavior, 107,* 209–221. https://doi.org/10.1016/j.jvb.2018.05.002.

Lee, B., & Porfeli, E. J. (2015). Youths' socialization to work and school within the family. *International Journal for Educational and Vocational Guidance, 15,* 145–162. https://doi.org/10.1007/s10775-015-9302-x.

Lee, H.-C. (2012). What do you want to do when you grow up? Occupational aspirations of Taiwanese preschool children. *Social Behavior & Personality, 40,* 115–128. https://doi.org/10.2224/sbp.2012.40.1.115.

Lent, R. W. (2005). A social cognitive view of career development and counseling. In S. D. Brown & R. W. Lent (Eds.), *Career development and counseling: Putting theory and research to work*. Hoboken, NJ: Wiley.

Lent, R. W. (2012). Social cognitive career theory. In S. D. Brown & R. W. Lent (Eds.), *Career development and counseling: Putting theory and research to work* (2nd ed., pp. 115–146). Hoboken, NJ: Wiley.

Lent, R. W., Brown, S. D., & Hackett, G. (2002). Social cognitive career theory. In D. B. Associates (Ed.), *Career choice and development* (4th ed., pp. 255–311). San Francisco, CA: Jossey-Bass.

Liu, J., McMahon, M., & Watson, M. (2015). Parental influence on mainland Chinese children's career aspirations: child and parental perspectives. *International Journal for Educational and Vocational Guidance, 15,* 131–143. https://doi.org/10.1007/s10775-015-9291-9.

Määttä, E., & Järvelä, S. (2013). Involving children in reflective discussions about their perceived self efficacy and learning experiences. *International Journal of Early Years Education, 21,* 309–324. https://doi.org/10.1080/09669760.2013.867836.

MacPhee, D., & Prendergast, S. (2018). *Room for improvement: Girls' and boys' home environments are still gendered*. Sex Roles: Advance online publication. https://doi.org/10.1007/s11199-018-0936-2.

Maree, J. G. (2018). Promoting career development in the early years of a person's life through self- and career construction counselling (using an integrated qualitative + quantitative approach): A case study. *Early Child Development and Care, 188,* 437–451. https://doi.org/10.1080/03004430.2017.1365361.

McLoyd, V. C., Kaplan, R., Purtell, K. M., & Huston, A. C. (2011). Assessing the effects of a work-based antipoverty program for parents on youth's future orientation and employment experiences. *Child Development, 82*, 113–132. http://dx.doi.org/10.1111/j.1467-8624.2010.01544.x.

National Career Development Guidelines. (n.d.). Retrieved from http://acrn.ovae.org/ncdg.htm.

Noack, P., Kracke, B., Gniewosz, B., & Dietrich, J. (2010). Parental and school effects on students' occupational exploration: A longitudinal and multilevel analysis. *Journal of Vocational Behavior, 77,* 50–57. https://doi.org/10.1016/j.jvb.2010.02.006.

Palladino Schultheiss, D. E. (2005). Elementary career intervention programs: Social action initiatives. *Journal of Career Development, 31,* 185–194. https://doi.org/10.1177/089484530503100303.

Peila-Shuster, J. J. (2015). Career development for children: Addressing barriers, challenging perceptions, and building hope. In K. Maree & A. Di Fabio (Eds.), *Exploring new horizons in career counselling: Turning challenge into opportunities*. Sense: Rotterdam, The Netherlands.

Peila-Shuster, J. J. (2018). Fostering hope and career adaptability in children's career development. *Early Child Development and Care, 188,* 452–462. https://doi.org/10.1080/03004430.2017.1385610.

Peila-Shuster, J. J., Brantmeier, E. J., Kees, N., Anderson, S. K., & Aragon, A. (2011). Physical space appraisal. In M. Pope, J. S. Pangelinan, & A. D. Coker (Eds.), *Experiential activities for teaching multicultural competence in counseling* (pp. 70–71). Alexandria, VA: American Counseling Association.

Pizzorno, M. C., Benozzo, A., Fina, A., Sabato, S., & Scopesi, M. (2014). Parent-child career construction: A narrative study from a gender perspective. *Journal of Vocational Behavior, 84,* 420–430. https://doi.org/10.1016/j.jvb.2014.03.001.

Porfeli, E. J., Hartung, P. J., & Vondracek, F. W. (2008). Children's vocational development: A research rationale. *The Career Development Quarterly, 57,* 25–37. https://doi.org/10.1002/j.2161-0045.2008.tb00163.x.

Porfeli, E. J., & Vondracek, F. W. (2009). Career development, work, and occupational success. In M. C. Smith & T. G. Reio (Eds.), *Handbook of research on adult development and learning* (pp. 412–435). Mahwah, NJ: Erlbaum.

Roe, A. (1956). *The psychology of occupations*. New York, NY: Wiley.

Rudolph, C. W., Lavigne, K. N., Katz, I. M., & Zacher, H. (2017). Linking dimensions of career adaptability to adaptation results: A meta-analysis. *Journal of Vocational Behavior, 102,* 151–173. https://doi.org/10.1016/j.jvb.2017.06.003.

Savickas, M. L. (2005). The theory and practice of career construction. In S. D. Brown & R. W. Lent (Eds.), *Career development and counseling: Putting theory and research to work* (pp. 42–70). Hoboken, NJ: Wiley.

Savickas, M. L. (2013). Career construction theory and practice. In S. D. Brown & R. W. Lent (Eds.), *Career development and counseling: Putting theory and research to work* (2nd ed., pp. 147–183). Hoboken, NJ: Wiley.

Savickas, M. L. (2015). *Life-design counseling manual*. Publisher: Author.

Savickas, M. L., Nota, L., Rossier, J., Dauwalder, J.-P., Duarte, M. E., Guichard, J., et al. (2009). Life designing: A paradigm for career construction in the 21st century. *Journal of Vocational Behavior, 75,* 239–250. https://doi.org/10.1016/j.jvb.2009.04.004.

Savickas, M. L., & Porfeli, E. J. (2012). Career Adapt-Abilities Scale: Construction, reliability, and measurement equivalence across 13 countries. *Journal of Vocational Behavior, 80,* 661–673. https://doi.org/10.1016/j.jvb.2012.01.011.

Schmitt-Wilson, S., & Welsh, M. C. (2012). Vocational knowledge in rural children: A study of individual differences and predictors of occupational aspirations and expectations. *Learning and Individual Differences, 22,* 862–867. https://doi.org/10.1016/j.lindif.2012.06.003.

Schultheiss, D. E. P. (2008). Current status and future agenda for the theory, research, and practice of childhood career development. *The Career Development Quarterly, 57,* 7–24. https://doi.org/10.1002/j.2161-0045.2008.tb00162.x.

Schwab, K. (2016). The fourth industrial revolution: what it means, how to respond. Retrieved from World Economic Forum website: http://www.weforum.org/agenda/2016/01/the-fourth-industrial-revolution-what-it-means-and-how-to-respond.

Super, D. E. (1957). *The psychology of careers*. New York, NY: Harper.

Super, D. E., Savickas, M. L., & Super, C. M. (1996). The life-span, life-space approach to careers. In D. Brown & L. Brooks (Eds.), *Career choice and development: Applying contemporary theories to practice* (3rd ed., pp. 121–178). San Francisco, CA: Jossey-Bass.

Taveira, M. D. C., Oliveira, Í. M., & Araújo, A. M. (2016). Ecology of children's career development: A review of the literature. *Psicologia: Teoria e Pesquisa, 32,* 1–10. https://doi.org/10.1590/0102.3772e32411.

Tudge, J. R. H., Mokrova, I., Hatfield, B. E., & Karnik, R. B. (2009). Uses and misuses of Bronfenbrenner's bioecological theory of human development. *Journal of Family Theory & Review, 1,* 198–210. https://doi.org/10.1111/j.1756-2589.2009.00026.x.

Usher, E. L. (2008). Sources of middle school students' self-efficacy in mathematics: A qualitative investigation of student, teacher and parent perspectives. *American Educational Research Journal, 46,* 275–314. https://doi.org/10.3102/0002831208324517.

Uusiautti, S., & Määttä, K. (2015). *The psychology of becoming a successful worker: Research on the changing nature of achievement*. New York, NY: Routledge.

VanderVen, K. D. (2006). Chapter 10. Patterns of career development in child and youth care. *Child & Youth Services, 28*, 231–257. https://doi.org/10.1300/j024v28n01_04.

Vervecken, D., & Hannover, B. (2015). Yes I can! Effects of gender fair job descriptions on children's perceptions of job status, job difficulty, and vocational self-efficacy. *Social Psychology, 46*, 76–92. https://doi.org/10.1027/1864-9335/a000229.

Watson, M., & McMahon, M. (2005). Children's career development: A research review from a learning perspective. *Journal of Vocational Behavior, 67*, 119–132. https://doi.org/10.1016/j.jvb.2004.08.011.

Whiston, S. C., Tai, W. L., Rahardja, D., & Eder, K. (2011). School counseling outcome: A meta-analytic examination of interventions. *Journal of Counseling & Development, 89*, 37–55. https://doi.org/10.1002/j.1556-6678.2011.tb00059.x.

Yohani, S. C. (2008). Creating an ecology of hope: Arts-based interventions with refugee children. *Child and Adolescent Social Work Journal, 25*, 309–323. https://doi.org/10.1007/s10560-008-0129-x.

Zambrano-Varghese, C. (2017). Life plan development in young adult women: An exploration using grounded theory. *The Qualitative Report, 22*, 136–159. Retrieved from https://nsuworks.nova.edu/tqr/vol22/iss1/8.

Innovation Meets Need: Career Counselling and Youth Populations in Uncertain Times

William C. Briddick, Hande Sensoy-Briddick and Suzanne Savickas

Abstract According to the United Nations' Department of Economic and Social Affairs Population Division (UNDESAPD) the world's youth population between the ages 15–24 numbered 1.2 billion, approximately midway into the second decade of the 21st century (UNDESAPD, in Population Facts No. 2015/1: Youth population trends and sustainable development. United Nations, New York, 2015). The International Labor Organization (ILO) noted that the experiences of youth with employment and the world of work in the first decade of the 21st century were significantly impacted by the global economic crisis. The 13% youth unemployment rate that came between 2012 and 2014, as the crisis was stabilizing, reflected a more grim reality. Unemployed youth comprised 36.7% of the unemployed across the globe as of 2014 (ILO, in Global employment trends for youth 2015: Scaling up investments in decent jobs for youth. International Labour Office, Geneva, Switzerland, 2015). Scholars have recognized the delays experienced by youth populations as they seek to enter the world of work. As the second decade of this century approaches, the youth of the world are as in need now of career related services as ever before, if perhaps not more. The turn of the 21st century brought innovations within the field of career counselling in terms of theory, research, and practice. Particularly, life design (Savickas et al., in Journal of Vocational Behavior, 75(3):239–250, 2009; Savickas, in Journal of Counselling & Development, 90(1):13–19 2012, Savickas, in Life Design counselling manual. Rootstown, OH 2015) and career construction theory (Savickas, in Career choice and development. Jossey Bass, San Francisco, pp. 149–205, 2002; Savickas, in Career development and counselling: Putting theory and research to work. Wiley, Hoboken, NJ, pp. 42–70, 2005; Savickas, in Career development and counselling: Putting theory and research to work. Wiley, Hoboken, NJ, pp. 147–183, 2013) offer promising possibilities for working with youth populations.

W. C. Briddick (✉) · H. Sensoy-Briddick
Counselling and Human Development, College of Education and Human Sciences, South Dakota State University, 316 Wenona Hall, Brookings, SD 57007, USA
e-mail: chris.briddick@sdstate.edu

S. Savickas
Avenues of Counselling and Mediation, Medina and Fairlawn, OH, USA

J. G. Maree (ed.), *Handbook of Innovative Career Counselling*,
https://doi.org/10.1007/978-3-030-22799-9_15

Keywords Career construction · Life design · Career development · Youth populations

Introduction: Career Development and Career Counselling in the First Two Decades of the 21st Century

As we approach the close of the second decade of the 21st Century, it is worth noting the progress that has been made in strengthening the global presence of vocational guidance and related services, such as career development and career counselling. At the turn of the century, there was considerable interest in terms of changes in the world of work and the challenges ahead. In fact, before the arrival of the 21st Century itself, significant entities were weighing in on what to expect. In the United States, for instance, the United States Department of Labor (USDL) welcomed the new century with a publication entitled *Futurework, Trends and Challenges for Work in the 21st century* (USDL, 1999). More globally, the International Labor Organization met the new century focused on the availability of "decent work" for workers in the 21st century thus launching its Decent Work Agenda (ILO, 1999). Others would follow with the arrival of the new century, seeking to prepare us for changes in the world of work and careers (Collin & Young, 2000; Karoly & Panis, 2004).

More recently, the World Bank weighed in with a flagship report entitled *World Development Report 2019: The Changing Nature of Work* (World Bank, 2019). Jim Yong Kim, President of the World Bank Group, commented on the unique nature of this project. Kim noted the current growing global economy and the decreasing rate of poverty. He was quick to acknowledge that even with encouraging news there are challenges ahead, including those found in the world of work. Kim highlighted the need to avoid "simple and prescriptive solutions" focusing instead on the human capital aspects of the future of work (World Bank, 2019, p. vii).

He explained it as follows:

> Many jobs today, and many more in the near future, will require specific skills—a combination of technological know-how, problem-solving, and critical thinking—as well as soft skills such as perseverance, collaboration, and empathy. The days of staying in one job, or with one company, for decades are waning. In the gig economy, workers will likely have many gigs over the course of their careers, which means they will have to be lifelong learners. (p. vii)

The report itself arrives as the most distinct yet from the World Bank since it began publishing World Development Reports over 40 years ago. This status has been achieved as a result of posting the report online as it was being developed, encouraging feedback from readers around the world (World Bank, 2019, p. viii). The nature of work is indeed changing but so too is the manner in which we approach the changes.

Chapter Structure

The first part of the chapter introduces some of the new perspectives in career development and counselling that have arrived in the first two decades of the 21st Century including a brief discussion of career construction theory and the paradigm of life design. The second part of the chapter addresses the definition of youth as a population, as well as some of the unique challenges youth face as they approach and enter adulthood, including youth employment. The third part of the chapter opens an overview of life design counselling as a possible framework of intervention for addressing the needs of youth populations. The fourth part of the chapter describes two interventions, the Career Construction Interview (CCI) (Savickas, 2015) and My Career Story (Savickas & Hartung, 2012), a workbook designed to simulate the CCI, developed for working with both individuals and groups. The fifth part of the chapter provides a discussion that acknowledges difficult challenges while highlighting some of the encouraging efforts of scholars and practitioners including significant contributions from scholars in South Africa as well as the work of the Life Design Research Group and recent significant special issues within the professional literature that indicate a positive direction forward toward the future of the field. The chapter finishes up with a conclusion that connects the innovations of the origins of our profession to the innovations of the present day and the future.

New Arrivals in Career Development and Counselling

The new millennium brought with it new approaches in terms of theory and practice in career development and counselling. Our experiences of working and its personal meanings in our lives (Blustein, 2006; Duffy, Blustein, Diemer, & Autin, 2016) has received greater attention as has the relational aspects of our working lives (Blustein, 2011). Others have embraced the elements of chance and complexity in career development (Pryor & Bright, 2003, 2011; Krumboltz, 2009).

Career Construction Theory and the Paradigm of Life Design

Career construction theory (Savickas, 2002, 2005, 2013) has the distinction of not only being an innovation theoretically, but likewise is distinguished as being part of a larger paradigm, that being life design (Savickas et al. 2009; Savickas, 2012). Life design and career construction theory look more specifically at the self and how we construct ourselves and our careers. Savickas (2019) noted the need for something else among the traditional interventions of modernity's career guidance and high modernity's career education. Thus, Savickas underscores the significance of the arrival of post modernity's career counselling (p. 10). Savickas (2012, 2019) declared that the aim was not to replace existing interventions but rather to take a place beside them.

Who Are the Youth?

The Oxford English Dictionary defines youth as "the time when one is young; the early part or period of life; more specifically, the period from puberty till the attainment of full growth, between childhood and adult age" (Youth, 2018). The United Nations Educational, Scientific, and Cultural Organization (UNESCO) has suggested that "Youth' is best understood as a period of transition from the dependence of childhood to adulthood's independence and awareness of our interdependence as members of a community. Youth is a more fluid category than a fixed age-group" (UNESCO, n.d.). UNESCO's definition though recognizes an age range that includes when a person "may leave compulsory education, and the age at which he/she finds his/her first employment" (UNESCO, n.d.). It is likewise noted that the upper range of that period has been increasing over the years due to unemployment, as well as, the struggle of young people to be able to achieve their independence by establishing a life outside their family of origin. UNESCO settles on the UN definition of youth for regional and international activities of the organization, as the UN definition is one used to preserve statistical consistency. The UN definition of youth is the age range from 15 to 24 years of age. UNESCO becomes more flexible with its definition at the national level honoring an individual country's definition (UNESCO, n.d.). The Organization for Economic Co-operation and Development adheres to the age range of 15–24 years of age in describing youth particularly as it relates to employment and unemployment (OECD, 2018).

Within the aforementioned age range, a great deal transpires. Youth often finish their compulsory education and move in the direction of work, advanced training, or education. In many places the late teens to mid-20s comprises a time for young people to pursue a traditional four-year college or university education. Other young people might choose technical education or an apprenticeship, while others might choose another type of on the job training or perhaps work that requires no advanced preparation at all. In some instances, for a variety of reasons, young people might choose to or not be able to enter the world of work. The global economic crisis of 2007–2008 had lasting repercussions particularly for young people trying to get started in their training, education, and careers. However, the struggle for young people getting started in life and achieving their own sense of independence has been problematic for years.

Changing Times in Adulthood

Arnett (2000) provided an excellent means by which to conceptualize the life cycle of young people between the ages of 18 and 25, highlighting its distinction from adolescence or young adulthood. Emerging adulthood for Arnett described a period of time for young people who were not quite in adolescence anymore but not fully into what might be defined as adulthood yet. Still Arnett cautioned, "emerging adulthood exists only in cultures that allow young people a prolonged period of independent role exploration during the late teens and twenties" (Arnett, 2000, p. 469). Arnett highlighted the changes that took place in the last 50 years of the Twentieth Century that resulted in young people taking longer than previous generations to get married and start families, against the backdrop of increased activity in pursuing higher education. Arnett cited the upward shift in age for people getting married citing the US Census Bureau figures for the years 1970 and 1996. Between these years the median age for marriage for women increased from 21 in 1970 to 25 in 1996. For men the median age shifted from 23 to 27 during this same period (Arnett, 2000). By 2017, those figures had climbed once again with the median age at first marriage averaging 28.1 years for women and 29.9 years for men (United States Census Bureau, 2017). Arnett noted the median age of the birth of the first child reflected something similar. Looking at data between 1970 and 2000 when Arnett's article entitled *Emerging Adulthood: A Theory of Development From the Late Teens through the Twenties* was published, the mean age at first birth for women went from 21.4 years of age for women in 1970 to 24.9 years of age in 2000 (Matthews & Hamilton, 2002). Between 2000 and 2014 there was a 1.4 year increase in the mean age for first time mothers increasing from 24.9 in 2000 to 26.3 years of age in 2014 with a greater increase being observed in the latter half of this period (Matthews & Hamilton, 2016). Understanding the present state of first time parenting from a father's perspective is a bit more elusive, though a recent Stanford University study sheds some light. The mean paternal age in the US has indeed risen over the last 40 years with variations in terms of race, geography, and level of education. (Khandwala, Zhang, Lu, & Eisenberg, 2017, p. 2110). Essentially, men are waiting longer to become fathers while some continue fathering later in life. Across all levels of education, men are waiting longer to enter fatherhood, with the fathers earning college degrees being older on average at 33.3 years. Similar results have been found in countries such as Germany and England (Khandwala, Zhang, Lu, & Eisenberg, 2017).

Arnett's theory can help explain life for many young people around the globe but as with any theory, it has its limits. Arnett, Žukauskienė, and Sugimura (2014) discussed the implications for emerging adulthood in high-income countries, thus perhaps making it more applicable to some places more than others. Arnett et al., in this instance, provide an age range for emerging adulthood spanning ages 18–29. In our preparation of this particular chapter, we admit that we cannot account for or address every consideration in capturing the theoretical descriptions of youth or addressing every scenario facing youth with a single theoretical approach or intervention. Our contribution will likely be appropriate in some places more than others. Universal applicability may well be beyond the scope of the present contribution. For instance, in some places like India, the Middle East, and perhaps North Africa, young educated adults struggle with what has been described as *waithood* (Singerman, 2007). Singerman recognizing a similar term used by economists described *waithood* as:

> Economists speak of the phenomenon of "wait unemployment," or enduring long periods of unemployment, particularly by educated young people in countries with large public sectors, to secure a high paying 'permanent' position with good benefits. In a similar vein, many young people in Egypt and throughout the region experience "wait adulthood" or "waithood" as they negotiate their prolonged adolescence and remain single for long periods of time while trying to save money to marry. (p. 6)

Singerman acknowledged the dependent nature of this period where young people lack financial independence, noting that marriage is often financed by one's family. The significance of both family and societal values related to relationships and expectations of individuals and couples who are not yet married warrants serious consideration (Singerman, 2007, p. 6). Another demographic that might be outside the scope of our recommendations are youth who are not currently involved in education, employment, or some sort of training (NEET). However, the aforementioned considered, we will leave it to the reader's determination as to what might or might not be useful and adaptable to the work they are doing. Overall, it is our opinion, that life design and career construction theory has something to offer the aforementioned populations.

Youth Employment

In 2015, the world's youth population between the ages 15–24 numbered 1.2 billion. (UNDESA, 2015). A recent article in the *Wall Street Journal* (Duehren, 2018) noted the lowest youth summer unemployment rate for those 16–24 years old in over 50 years for the US. The unemployment rate was 9.2% for those seeking employment in 2018. It was indeed good news at first glance. Beyond the headline, however, were the realities that indicated, for some, the outlook was not quite as positive. For instance, after hitting a record low earlier in 2018, the unemployment rate for Black or African Americans rose again which resulted in a rather small 0.3% increase in unemployment among Black or African American youth from the previous year. The percentage of young people in America participating in the workforce was 60.6% in July, which has held steady since 2017 and represents the highest rate in almost 10 years as the participation rate has experienced a significant decline starting in 1989, a year when 77.5% of youth participated in the summer labor force. One expert noted that summer work opportunities are in competition with other possibilities such as unpaid internships and non-work related activities (Duehren, 2018, p. A2). The recent newspaper article provided excellent information for the US but certainly did not reflect the global realities of youth seeking employment.

In 2017, in spite of positive indicators of global economic conditions, the International Labor Organization (ILO) estimated an expected slight rise in the global unemployment rate to 13.1% for youth under the age of 25. The estimated number of youth unemployed worldwide was 70.9 million, a decrease from 2009 high of 76.7 million. The percentage itself does not reflect the extreme realities in places such as Northern Africa, where the unemployment rate for youth teeters near 30% (ILO, 2017). According to the Organization for Economic Co-operation and Development (OECD), as of 2017, 53.4% of the youth labor force in South Africa remained unemployed. The next closest country to South Africa, in terms of youth unemployment, is Greece where in 2017, 43.6% of its youth population remained unemployed (OECD, 2018). An ILO publication entitled *World Employment and Social Outlook: Trends 2018*, (ILO, 2018) still identified youth unemployment as a critical issue.

> The lack of employment opportunities for youth (i.e. those under 25 years of age) presents another major global challenge. Young people are much less likely to be employed than adults, with the global youth unemployment rate standing at 13 per cent, or three times higher than the adult rate of 4.3 percent. (p.2)

Life Design Counselling: Innovation and Meeting the Needs of Youth

Life design (Savickas et al., 2009; Savickas, 2012) emerged in first decade of the 21st century in response to a need for a new paradigm for career intervention based on the changes faced by workers at the turn of the new century. The world of work had become less predictable and permanent, more prone to temporary arrangements and uncertainty. The crisis in terms of both models and methods in career development recognized, life design emerged as a new paradigm for career intervention better suited and matched with the world of work in the new century. Given the unique challenges faced by youth populations in present day, life design provides an approach that seems well suited for the world of work encountered by young people at present, in addition to the more traditional models of career intervention of the 20th century. Savickas (2012) noted that the aim of life design is not to replace traditional paradigms of intervention but rather to take its place beside them thus enhancing a counsellors available options of intervention (p. 17). Thus, for youth populations there is hope and promise within life design for a world of work that has been described as VUCA or volatile, uncertain, complex, and ambiguous. Savickas et al. (2009) described the life design framework as being "life-long, holistic, contextual, and preventive", its interventions seeking to impact an individual's "adaptability, narratability, and activity" (p. 245). Adaptability (Savickas, 1997) is used in life design as a means of describing how clients can successfully anticipate and meet changes as they navigate the world of work via what Savickas et al. (2009) refer to as career construction theory's five Cs: concern, control, curiosity, confidence, and commitment. Concern should come to reflect a perspective that has hope and optimism. Control relates not only to self-regulation but implies being able to make the necessary adjustments across various settings, as well as one's capabilities of having some sense of control within a particular environment. Curiosity speaks to exploration of possibilities with regard to both self and opportunities. Confidence has to do with one's feelings about their ability to meet the challenges they might encounter in moving forward toward their goals and aspirations in life. Commitment addresses a broader focus beyond what one might have at a particular moment in terms of employment and rather includes one's ability to reflect upon their overall life projects and thus remaining committed to possibilities and action even in the face of uncertainty (Savickas et al., 2009, p. 245). Narratability is used to describe the story that clients are able to construct and tell as a result of the work of the client and counsellor. Life design uses narratability as a means of helping a client construct a story that can be seen as having coherence and continuity. Activity or meaningful action is essential in that it moves individuals beyond verbal discourse or talk and into acting or doing. By taking action and doing, the connection can be made in terms of the abilities one likes to use, as well as the interests one enjoys pursuing. Finally, intentionality is desired as a result of meaning making efforts, as it allows for a story that travels with the client, becoming a bridge of sorts between various jobs or positions one may hold across their career, as well as replacing certain long gone societal holding environments (Savickas et al., p. 246).

Savickas (2015) described the *Life Design Counselling Manual* as an application of career construction theory within life design counselling, citing the broader nature of life designing in general (pp. 5–6). Savickas drew distinctions between guidance and counselling, noting guidance's foundations in logical positivism and the significance of scores of inventories, compared to the use of stories within life design counselling that focus on the unique nature of the individual client (Savickas, 2015, pp. 7–9). Career construction theory used in life design counselling relies heavily on the relationship between the client and the counsellor working each based in their own expertise, the counsellor with their expertise in the career construction process and the client with their expertise rooted in the stories of their life. The expertise in one's own stories, however, is not enough to achieve success within the counselling process. Reflection upon one's own stories is essential, as is the act of sense-making (Savickas, 2015, pp. 10–14). Practitioners utilizing career construction theory understand that clients often show up when there is a transition afoot. In counselling, the client can share their transition narrative. From there, the counsellor can go about assisting the client in making sense of their story and how they might respond.

Intervention Model

The intervention model outlined by Savickas et al. (2009) itself is fairly straightforward in six steps:

1. The problem is defined and what the client hopes to achieve with the counsellor is identified.

2. The client and counsellor explore how the client currently views self in the present as well as how the client's self is organized and functions.
3. As a means of opening up perspectives, stories are used help make the implicit explicit and stories may well be reviewed, reorganized, revised, and revitalized.
4. The presenting problem is placed into the new story that has emerged, thus creating an opportunity for the client to explore new or anticipated identities.
5. Specific activities are identified that will assist the client in being able to test out or further realize the aforementioned identity possibilities.
6. Follow-up with the client both short and long term (pp. 246–247).

Savickas (2015) wrote more specifically with regard to client narratives:

> The process begins with addressing a client's tension by constructing micro-narratives that provide symbolic representations of concrete experience. This is followed by deconstruction of limiting ideas and false beliefs with attention concentrated on reflective observation and self-examination. The third step produces new intentions by reconstructing a macro-narrative with abstract conceptualizations that beget new realizations. Finally, client and counsellor co-construct an action plan that extends revisioning of the self through active experimentation in the real world. (pp. 9–10).

Useful Interventions

Two useful interventions rooted in the life design paradigm are the career construction interview (Savickas, 2015) and the *My Career Story* workbook (Savickas & Hartung, 2012). The first is an interview that is used with individual clients. The *My Career Story* workbook can be used individually as well as in a group setting for high school age populations and beyond. Savickas strategically chose the term useful in his first question of the Career Construction Interview (CCI) ("How may I be useful to you?") indicating that counsellors should be quite deliberate in doing so in recognition of the agency of the client. Using the word helpful might imply that the client is helpless rather than being there to use the counselling services made available to them (Savickas, 2015, p. 16).

The Career Construction Interview

The CCI is structured to solicit information about the client as a means of assisting them in identifying key information and life themes, as well as, addressing the current transition in their life. Upon gathering information about how the counsellor can be useful to the client, the interview's first question gathers information about early role models in the life of the client as a means of understanding the client's own construction of self. Next, is a question addressing the client's favorite magazines, television shows, and websites as a means of having an idea of the kind of environments and activities that capture the client's interest. This question now includes favorite video games given their current popularity. A third question solicits the client's current favorite story from a book or movie. What is important is not the central character but rather the story itself, as one's current favorite story often reflects a story or a script and client can perhaps utilize in crafting a desired outcome for their present transition (Savickas, 2015, pp. 31–33). The fourth question gathers a client's favorite saying or motto. What is significant here are favorite sayings or mottos a client has adopted as their own. It is important that in gathering mottos that the counsellor specifies favorite sayings that the client has selected, rather than those provided by others (i.e., parent, grandparent, etc.) as those selected by the client likely have a more unique, personal meaning. Mottos or favorite sayings reflect the best self-advice the client might have in trying situations, such as the transition they presently face (Savickas, 2015, pp. 33–34). The fifth question solicits three early recollections from the client. Savickas noted that early recollections serve as a "backstage" view of what is going on with the client in the present and serve as a means of having a better understanding of a client's pain or preoccupation (Savickas, 2015, p. 35).

The Career Construction Interview (Savickas 2015, 2019) has received considerable attention in the literature across the first two decades of the century and has witnessed a transformation from its earlier version as the Career Style Assessment to the Career Story Interview (CSI) and its most recent and present form as the Career Construction Interview (CCI). Contributions to the literature that provide a case study approach in using the CSI or the CCI are available (Barclay & Stoltz, 2016a, 2016b; Cardoso, 2016; Di Fabio, 2016; Hartung & Vess, 2016; Maree, 2013, 2014, 2016a, 2016b, 2017, 2018; Maree & Crous, 2012; Reid, Bimrose, & Brown, 2016; Taber & Briddick, 2011; Taber, Hartung, Briddick, Briddick, & Rehfuss, 2011; Savickas, 2005, 2011, 2013, 2019; Savickas & Lara, 2016). Savickas (2006, 2009) provides a total of three case studies across two resources that utilize video demonstrations of the CSI or CCI.

My Career Story

My Career Story (MCS) (Savickas & Hartung, 2012) is a workbook that can be used to assist individuals with authoring their own life stories. Hartung and Santelli (2018) noted that by design the MCS was meant to simulate the Career Construction Interview (p. 1). Hartung and Santelli provided an overview of the MCS workbook as well as preliminary findings on its validity. Findings and limitations considered, Hartung and Santelli noted that while more extensive research is needed, "the MCS workbook offers a promising theory-based, practical method for individuals and groups to use in constructing their life careers" (Hartung & Santelli, 2018, p. 318).

The authors of the MCS were quite deliberate in providing an overview for the user in terms of its purpose. Savickas and Hartung (2012) noted their intent in assisting those using MCS as they might be planning and making decisions about their career. Hartung and Santelli (2018) cited previous research (Brown & Ryan Crane, 2000; Brown et al., 2003) supporting the use of resources like workbooks as interventions for those seeking assistance with career planning and choice (p. 310). Savickas and Hartung (2012) recognized the significance of being able to explore and make decisions about one's career future with confidence and a sense of control. MCS lends itself to those facing some sort of transition in terms of their career path. While respecting the traditional matching model the MCS moves in the direction of something more meaningful, assisting the individual with the development of their life story while addressing the critical questions of "who" ("Who am I?"), "where" ("Where do I hope to fit into the world of work?"), and "how" ("How do I plan to go about doing that?") (p. 1). MCS is described as a resource for individuals groups, as well as educators working with high school and college populations. The workbook is broken down into three parts: Part I Telling My Story, Part II Hearing My Story, and Part III Enacting My Story.

Part I: Telling my story. Because the MCS workbook was designed to emulate the Career Construction Interview, it begins with an appeal to the individual completing the workbook to provide a brief description of just how they hope the MCS can be useful to them in the transition they are facing. Next, the MCS provides space for a list of occupations the individual has thought they might like to pursue in the past This is quite similar to the occupational daydreams solicited in the completion of Holland's *Self-Directed Search* (Holland & Messer, 2013). Four questions follow that are identical to those asked in the Career Construction Interview (CCI). The first question addresses role models. The individual is asked to recall who they admired growing up and what it was about them that they admired. During the CCI, the interviewer solicits role models as role models can be seen as an individual's first career choice, part of one's blueprint for self-construction (Savickas, 2015, p. 27). The CCI may offer an advantage over the MCS in that during the interview the interviewer can ask follow up questions regarding role models as well as ask the interviewee to reflect on similarities and differences between themselves and their role models as well as similarities and differences between their role models. The MCS format is certainly flexible enough that those using the resource with individuals or groups could provide additional instructions toward clarifying similarities and differences related to role models. The next question addresses an individual's favorite magazines and television shows. As mentioned previously, the MCS was introduced in 2012. Since that time, the CCI has come to include an expansion of this question to include references to an individual's favorite websites (Savickas, 2015) and more recently favorite video games have been considered as well. This question seeks to discover activities and environments of interest for the individual. The third question solicits an individual's favorite story whether it be one told in a book, movie, or by some other means. The individual is asked to briefly tell that story. The focus of this question is the story itself and not necessarily the main or favorite character of the story as what is significant for this question is the story or cultural script that maybe attractive to the individual as they are pondering how they would like their transition to be resolved. The final question solicits the individual's favorite saying or motto. More than one motto is permitted. An individual's favorite motto is seen as one's best self-advice. MCS does not solicit early recollections.

Part II: Hearing my story. Part II of MCS assembles a larger story from the pieces gathered in Part I. In this section, individuals can work on their definition of *self* as the lead character in their story. Next, they can identify the setting of their story or where they hope to be in regard to education or work. Finally, they can consider the script with a plot and theme, which helps them identify how they can utilize work in a way that best incorporates their unique self (Savickas & Hartung, 2012, p. 9). An analysis of self incorporates information related to role models leading to a description of the person they are becoming. An analysis of their favorite magazines and television shows follows, as a means of helping the individual understand the kinds of environments that interest them. A table is provided to assist the MCS user in being able understand the environments of their favorite magazines or television shows via Holland's R-I-A-S-E-C model. The individual's career story is summarized as Self, Setting, and Script along with a Success Formula. The MCS user is then instructed to return to page three of the workbook and rewrite their story related to the transition they face and the choices they might make based on what they now know regarding their best self-advice and their identified success formula. Essentially, this assists the individual in identifying their next steps for the road ahead (Savickas & Hartung, 2012, p. 14). The MCS then returns to the original list of occupations solicited on Page 4. The individual is instructed to reexamine the list of occupations they originally provided to see if any of those on the list now appear to be more attractive to them based on what they have learned via the MCS workbook. Additional information is provided on the O*NET system in the event the individual would like to further explore occupations. It should be noted that this section of MCS is likely adaptable to other occupational classification systems outside the US.

Part III: Enacting my story. This section of the workbook encourages the individual in terms of goal development for the next chapter of their story. The individual is then asked to consider what audiences they might choose to share their new story with as a means of clarifying it as well as making it more real. Finally, the individual is asked to consider what steps they might now pursue in taking action toward performing their story, small steps in moving toward their identified goals, which may include "trying out" an identified occupation (Savickas & Hartung, 2012, pp. 17–18).

Two of the present authors (Briddick and Sensoy-Briddick) have previously highlighted the utility of interventions such as the Career Construction Interview or its earlier version known as the Career Story Interview, as well as the *My Career Story* workbook (Briddick, & Sensoy-Briddick, 2012, 2017). In addition to MCS in English there are translations of it available in Portuguese, German, and French available on the Vocopher website at www.vocopher.com, where the CCI, MCS and the *Life Design Counselling Manual* can be downloaded as free resources.

Discussion

Challenges remain at present and on our voyage ahead. Time will tell if interventions within the paradigm of life design and career construction theory can effectively assist youth populations facing extreme rates of unemployment that results largely from a lack of available jobs or populations such as youth not in employment, education, or training (NEET). This maybe where the adaptability of the interventions prove key. As life design paradigm grew out of the internationalization movement within career development and counselling, recent international contributions offer hope.

Reid and West (2011) provide an excellent example in how they adapted career construction for use in the UK. In working with NEET youth Reid and West note the necessity of additional "intensive" assistance being available to address issues related to a youth's NEET status (Reid & West, 2011, p.181). Setlhare-Meltor and Wood (2016) provide an excellent case study utilizing life design in working with a client who had lived on the streets in his youth. More recently, Gerryts (2018) provided a study related to an intervention program she developed based in life design and career construction theory aimed at enhancing the employability of young adults from socio-economically challenged backgrounds in South Africa. With regard to waithood, an interesting study by McEvoy-Levy (2014) explored the narratives of Israeli and Palestinian children in waithood. While the article itself is not related to the professional literature of career development and counselling there are themes that emerged within these narratives related to career and the transition to adulthood. There are narratives of those who experience waithood awaiting our careful, undivided attention and intervention. Life-design and its interventions are assuredly up for the challenge.

How might life design and career construction be useful with youth populations including those described as NEET, in waithood, or perhaps even more vulnerable? Life design and career construction theory can be helpful for youth for the very reasons as it can be for anyone else. The paradigm and theory cannot create employment opportunities or speed up the wait until the conditions arrive that permit young people to begin their own careers and lives outside their families of origin. However, through discovering their stories, vulnerable youth (including disengaged youth) can benefit from three critical pieces of the career construction counselling process (Savickas, 2015) namely the relationship with the counsellor, reflecting on their own story and sense-making that comes as a result. Within some of the revisions of their story such youth can come to see themselves differently (identity) and thus perhaps this difference can help them move in the direction of preferred change. Counselors working with these populations will need to determine if career construction is appropriate for the clients they serve and perhaps what interventions might be most useful alone or as a part of a comprehensive career intervention program.

Setlhare-Meltor and Wood, along with academics like Gerryts, are a part of the emergence of life design and career construction in South Africa. This movement has largely been led by Kobus Maree, who has advanced life design and career construction via numerous contributions to the literature. In fact, Maree (2015) chronicled the research on the topic of life design and career construction in an article entitled *Research on life design in (South) Africa: A qualitative analysis*. His is a great example for others to follow in various places across the globe where scholars are seeking new possibilities for interventions perhaps not previously considered for vulnerable populations, who seem largely forgotten or ignored by society at large. Maree and others in South Africa answer the question as to whether or not life design and career construction has something to offer even the most vulnerable, marginalized populations with a resounding yes.

The Life Design Research Group will hopefully keep advancing both life design and career construction theory forward. It is worth noting two issues of key journals in recent years that have contributed significantly to the advance of life design and career construction theory and practice. Some of the aforementioned references to case studies applied to the use of the CCI can be found within these issues. The first was a special issue of the *Career Development Quarterly* that was published in March of 2016 and entitled *Special Issue: Advancing Career Intervention for Life Design* (Hartung, 2016). The second was special issue of the *Journal of Vocational Behavior* from December of 2016, which describes the efforts of the Life Design Research Group who met in Paris, France during the summer of 2014 at the Congress of the International Association for Applied Psychology (Savickas & Guichard, 2016). The editors of this issue note that it was during this meeting the group planned its third collaborative project noting that the first had been the development of the life design paradigm (Savickas, et al., 2009) while the second had been the development of the *Career Adapt-Abilities Scale* (Savickas & Porfeli, 2012). The third collaboration was to be a project entitled the *Symposium on Reflexivity in Life Design Interventions,* which was the research and writing that went into the eight articles that comprised the issue (Savickas & Guichard, 2016, pp. 1–2).

The two aforementioned special issues in the *Career Development Quarterly* and the *Journal of Vocational Behavior* were both critical and pivotal for the field and professional literature alike. Future efforts may want to consider special issues such as the Volume 64 2016 issue of the *Career Development Quarterly* guest edited by Weiqiao Fan and Frederick T. L. Leong and entitled *Special Issue: Career Development and Intervention in Chinese Contexts*. This issue and others like it can address career development and interventions within cultural contexts highlighting the historical trends as well as advances and innovations along the way. Most recently the *Journal of Vocational Behavior* published a special issue *entitled Career Construction Theory: Conceptual and Empirical Advancements* in April of 2019 (Rudolph, et al., 2019).

Conclusion

Frank Parsons, faced similar circumstances of uncertainty as modern practitioners face as he was getting the Vocation Bureau in Boston up and running while pulling together what would eventually become the foundational text of the vocational guidance movement, *Choosing a Vocation* (Parsons, 1909). Over a hundred years later, we are not only still using Parsons's original ideas but we have over time, advanced his original mission into a thriving field of service and study. While Parsons's work is still alive and well, over 100 years later, we have likewise innovated to meet the needs of our clients. The modern world of work and certain populations might lead some to conclude there are striking similarities between the era of Parsons and the present day. In short, young people are still in need of career related services to get started in their work life or career, individuals may find career related services lacking or nonexistent in their community, and the world of work is undergoing considerable change. It is our hope that by providing information on life design and its interventions, we offer a means to not only address some of the more traditional concerns but to likewise address some of the more modern concerns facing young people in their work and careers. As Savickas et al. (2009) noted:

> Individuals in the knowledge societies at the beginning of the 21st century must realize that career problems are only a piece of much broader concerns about how to live life in a postmodern world shaped by a global economy and supported by information technology. For instance, the issue of how to balance work-family activities and interactions is becoming salient in people's reflections about their competencies and aspirations. Managing interactions between different life domains has become a paramount concern for the many peripheral workers whose employment is contingent, free-lance, temporary, external, part-time, and casual. (p. 241)

What we have attempted to do is provide an example of a new paradigm and theory that has emerged in the early years of this century. Both can serve to empower youth via interventions as they move forward in their work or career. Knowledge of themselves and their stories can be useful in charting and navigating their journey ahead. A timeless quote by Frank Parsons in *Choosing a Vocation* might be useful to us today as scholars and practitioners, inspiring guidance for our own horizons and journeys. "It is better to sail with compass and chart than to drift into an occupation haphazard or by chance, proximity, or uninformed selection; and drift on through it without reaching any port worthy of the voyage" (Parsons, 1909, p. 101). May we keep this in mind as inspiration as we chart our personal and professional courses, seeking to serve the youth of our world on their voyage, while navigating our own.

References

Arnett, J. J. (2000). Emerging adulthood: A theory of development from the late teens through the twenties. *American Psychologist, 55,* 469–480.

Arnett, J. J., Zukauskiene, R., & Sugimura, K. (2014). The new life stage of emerging adulthood at ages 18-29 years: Implications for mental health. *Lancet Psychiatry, 1*(7), 569–576. https://doi.org/10.1016/s2215-0366(14)00080-7.

Barclay, S. R., & Stoltz, K. B. (2016a). The life design group: A case study vignette in group career construction counseling. *Journal of Student Affairs Research and Practice, 53*, 78–89. Retrieved from https://doi.org/10.1080/19496591.2016.1087859.

Barclay, S. R., & Stoltz, K. B. (2016b). The life-design group: A case study assessment. *Career Development Quarterly, 64,* 83–96. https://doi.org/10.1002/cdq.12043.

Blustein, D. L. (2006). *The psychology of working: A new perspective for career development, counseling, and public policy*. Mahwah, NJ: Erlbaum.

Blustein, D. L. (2011). A relational theory of working. *Journal of Vocational Behavior, 79*(1), 1–7. https://doi.org/10.1016/j.jvb.2010.10.004.

Briddick, W. C., & Sensoy-Briddick, H. (2012). The concept of role models in Life Design. *Cypriot Journal of Educational Sciences, 7*(4), 326–333.

Briddick, W. C., & Sensoy-Briddick, H. (2017). Paradigm and promise: Life-Design, Psychology of Working and decent work. In J. G. Maree (Ed.), *The psychology of career adaptability, employability, and resilience* (pp. 317–328). Dordrecht, The Netherlands: Springer Publishing.

Brown, S. D., & Ryan Krane, N. E. (2000). Four (or five) sessions and a cloud of dust: Old assumptions and new observations about career counseling. In S. D. Brown & R. W. Lent (Eds.), *Handbook of counseling psychology* (3rd ed., pp. 740–766). New York, NY: Wiley.

Brown, S. D., Ryan Krane, N. E., Brecheisen, J., Castelino, P., Budisin, I., Miller, M., & Edens, L. (2003). Critical ingredients of career choice interventions: More analyses and new hypotheses. *Journal of Vocational Behavior, 62*, 411–428. Retrieved from https://doi.org/10.1016/S0001-8791(02)00052-0.

Cardoso, P. (2016). Integrating life-design counseling and psychotherapy: Possibilities and practices. *Career Development Quarterly, 64,* 49–63. https://doi.org/10.1002/cdq.12040.

Collin, A., & Young, R. (Eds.). (2000). *The future of career*. Cambridge, England: Cambridge University Press.

Di Fabio, A. (2016). Life design and career counseling innovative outcomes. *Career Development Quarterly, 64,* 35–48. https://doi.org/10.1002/cdq.12039.

Duehren, A. (2018, August 17). Youth summer jobless rate at 50-year low. *Wall Street Journal*, p. A2.

Duffy, R. D., Blustein, D. L., Diemer, M. A., & Autin, K. L. (2016). The psychology of working theory. *Journal of Counseling Psychology, 63*(2), 127–148. https://doi.org/10.1037/cou0000140.

Fan, W., & Leong, F. T. L. (Eds.) (2016). Career development and intervention in Chinese contexts [Special issue]. *Career Development Quarterly, 64*(3).

Gerryts, E. W. (2018). *Enhancing the employability of young adults from socio-economically challenged contexts*. Unpublished dissertation, University of Pretoria, Pretoria, South Africa.

Hartung, P. J. (Ed.) (2016). Advancing career intervention for life design [Special issue]. *Career Development Quarterly, 64*(1).

Hartung, P. J., & Santelli, S. (2018). My Career Story: Description and initial validity evidence. *Journal of Career Assessment, 26*(2), 308–332. https://doi.org/10.1177/1069072717692980.

Hartung, P. J., & Vess, L. (2016). Critical moments in Career Construction Counseling. *Journal of Vocational Behavior, 97,* 31–39. https://doi.org/10.1016/j.jvb.2016.07.014.

Holland, J. L., & Messer, M. A. (2013). *Self-Directed Search (SDS) Form R: Assessment Booklet* (5th ed.). Lutz, FL: PAR.

ILO. (1999). *Decent work: Report of the director general, International Labour Conference, 87th Session*. Geneva: International Labour Office. Retrieved from http://www.ilo.org/public/english/standards/relm/ilc/ilc87/rep-i.htm.

ILO. (2015). *Global employment trends for youth 2015: Scaling up investments in decent jobs for youth*. Geneva, Switzerland: International Labour Office.

ILO. (2017). *Global employment trends for youth 2017: Paths to a better working future*. Geneva, Switzerland: International Labour Office.

ILO. (2018). *World employment and social outlook: Trends 2018*. Geneva, Switzerland: International Labour Office.

Karoly, L. A., & Panis, C. W. A. (2004). *The 21st century at work: Forces shaping the future workforce and workplace in the United States*. Santa Monica, CA: Rand Corporation.

Khandwala, Y. S., Zhang, C. A., Lu, Y., & Eisenberg, M. L. (2017). *Human Reproduction, 32*(10), 2110–2116. https://doi.org/10.1093/humrep/dex267.

Krumboltz, J. D. (2009). Happenstance learning theory. *Journal of Career Assessment, 17*, 135–154.

Maree, J. G. (2013). *Counselling for career construction connecting life themes to construct life portraits: Turning pain into hope*. Rotterdam, Netherlands: Sense Publishers.

Maree, J. G. (2014). Career construction with a gay client: A case study. *British Journal of Guidance and Counselling, 42*(4), 436–449. https://doi.org/10.1080/03069885.2014.886670.

Maree, J. G. (2015). Research on life design in (South) Africa: A qualitative analysis. *South African Journal of Psychology, 45*, 332–348. https://doi.org/10.1177/0081246314566785.

Maree, J. G. (2016a). Career Construction Counseling with a mid-career Black man. *Career Development Quarterly, 64*(1), 20–34. https://doi.org/10.1002/cdq.12038.
Maree, J. G. (2016b). How career construction counseling promotes reflection and reflexivity: Two case studies. *Journal of Vocational Behavior, 97,* 22–30. https://doi.org/10.1016/j.jvb.2016.07.009.
Maree, J. G. (2017). Mid-career construction counseling to instill spiritual awareness and allay fear. *South African Journal of Education, 37*(4), 1–10. Retrieved from https://doi.org/10.15700/saje.v37n4a1443.
Maree, J. G. (2018). Self- career construction counselling for a gifted young woman in search of meaning and purpose. *International Journal for Educational and Vocational Guidance*, 1–21. Retrieved from https://doi.org/10.1007/s10775-018-9377-2.
Maree, J. G., & Crous, S. (2012). Life Design career counselling with an abandoned adolescent: A case study. *Journal of Psychology in Africa, 22*(1), 106–113.
Mathews, T. J., & Hamilton, B. E. (2002). Mean age of mother, 1970–2000. *National Vital Statistics Reports, 51*(1), 1–13. Retrieved from https://www.ncbi.nlm.nih.gov/pubmed/12564162.
Mathews, T. J., & Hamilton, B. E. (2016). Mean age of mothers is on the rise: United States, 2000–2014. *NCHS Data Brief,* 23, 1–5. Retrieved October 15, 2018 from https://www.cdc.gov/nchs/data/databriefs/db232.htm.
McEvoy-Levy, S. (2014). Stuck in circulation: Children, 'waithood' and the conflict narratives of Israelis and Palestinians. *Children's Geographics, 12*(3), 312–326. https://doi.org/10.1080/14733285.2014929368.
OECD. (2018). *Employment rate by age group (indicator)*. https://doi.org/10.1787/084f32c7-en.
Parsons, F. (1909). *Choosing a vocation*. Boston, MA: Houghton Mifflin.
Parsons, F. (n.d.). *Youth and the world*. Unpublished manuscript, Frank Parsons papers. Manuscripts and Archives, Yale University Library.
Pryor, R. G., & Bright, J. (2003). The chaos theory of careers. *Australian Journal of Career Development, 12*(3), 12–20.
Pryor, R., & Bright, J. (2011). *The chaos theory of careers: A new perspective on working in the twenty-first century*. Hoboken, NJ: Taylor & Francis.
Reid, H., & West, L. (2011). Telling tales: Using narratives in career guidance. *Journal of Vocational Behavior, 78*, 174–183. https://doi.org/10.1016/jvb.2010.10.001
Reid, H., Brimrose, J., & Brown, A. (2016). Prompting reflection and learning in career construction counseling. *Journal of Vocational Behavior, 97*, 51–59. Retrieved from http://dx.doi.org/10.1016/j.jvb.2016.07.013.
Rudolph, C. W., Hannes, Z., & Hirschi, A. (Eds.). (2019). Career construction theory: Conceptual and empirical advancements [Special issue]. *Journal of Vocational Behavior*, (111).
Savickas, M. L. (1997). Career adaptability: An integrative construct for life-span, life-space theory. *Career Development Quarterly, 45*(3), 247–259.
Savickas, M. L. (2002). Career construction: A developmental theory of vocational behavior. In D. Brown & Associates (Eds.), *Career choice and development* (4th ed., pp. 149–205). San Francisco: Jossey Bass.
Savickas, M. L. (2005). The theory and practice of career construction. In S. D. Brown & R. W. Lent (Eds.), *Career development and counseling: Putting theory and research to work* (pp 42–70). Hoboken, NJ: Wiley.
Savickas, M. L. (2006). *Career counseling*. (Treatments for Specific Populations Video Series). Washington, DC: American Psychological Association.
Savickas, M. L. (2009). *Career counseling over time*. (Psychotherapy in Six Sessions Video Series). Washington, DC: American Psychological Association.
Savickas, M. L. (2011). *Career counseling*. Washington, DC: American Psychological Association.
Savickas, M. L. (2012). Life Design: A paradigm for career intervention in the 21st Century. *Journal of Counseling & Development, 90*(1), 13–19. https://doi.org/10.1111/j.1556-6676.2012.00002.x.

Savickas, M. L. (2013). Career construction theory and practice. In S. D. Brown & R. W. Lent (Eds.), *Career development and counseling: Putting theory and research to work* (2nd ed., pp. 147–183). Hoboken, NJ: Wiley.

Savickas, M. L. (2015). *Life Design counseling manual*. Rootstown, OH: (n.p.).

Savickas, M. L. (2019). *Career counseling* (2nd ed.). Washington, DC: American Psychological Association.

Savickas, M. L., & Guichard, J. (Eds.). 2016). Research on the Process of Narrative Career Counseling [Special issue]. *Journal of Vocational Behavior, 97*. Retrieved from http://dx.doi.org/10.1016/j.jvb.2016.07.015.

Savickas, M. L., & Hartung, P. J. (2012). *My career story: An autobiographical workbook for life-career success*. Retrieved from www.vocopher.com.

Savickas, M. L., Nota, L., Rossier, J., Dauwalder, J. P., Duarte, M. E., Guichard, J., … & van Vianen, A. E. M. (2009). Life designing: A paradigm for career construction in the 21st century. *Journal of Vocational Behavior, 75*(3), 239–250. https://doi.org/10.1016/j.jvb.2009.04.004.

Savickas, M. L., & Porfeli, E. J. (2012). Career adapt-abilities scale: Construction, reliability, and measurement equivalence across 13 countries. *Journal of Vocational Behavior, 80,* 66–673. Retrieved from https://doi.org/10.1016/j.jvb.2012.01.011.

Savickas, S., & Lara, T. (2016). Lee Richmond: A life designed to take the counseling profession to new places. *Career Development Quarterly, 64,* 75–82. https://doi.org/10.1002/cdq.12042.

Setlhare-Meltor, R, & Wood, L. (2016). Using life design with vulnerable youth, *Career Development Quarterly, 64* (1), 64–74. Retrieved from https://doi.org/10.1002/cdq.12041.

Singerman, D. (2007). The economic imperatives of marriage: Emerging practices and identities among youth in the Middle East. Technical Report 6, Brookings Institute and Dubai School of Government, Washington D.C.

Taber, B. J., & Briddick, W. C. (2011). Adlerian based career counseling in the age of Protean Careers. *Journal of Individual Psychology, 67*(2), 107–121.

Taber, B. J., Hartung, P. J., Briddick, H., Briddick, W. C., & Rehfuss, M. (2011). Career Style Interview: A contextualized approach to career counseling. *Career Development Quarterly, 59*(3), 274–287. https://doi.org/10.1002/j.2161-0045.2011.tb00069.x.

UNDESAPD. (May, 2015). *Population Facts No. 2015/1: Youth population trends and sustainable development.* New York: United Nations.

UNESCO. (n.d.). What do we mean by youth? Retrieved November 29, 2018, from http://www.unesco.org/new/en/social-and-human-sciences/themes/youth/youthdefinition.

United States Department of Labor. (1999). *Futurework, trends and challenges for work the 21st century*. Washington, DC: United States Department of Labor.

United States Census Bureau. (2017). American Community Survey 1-Year Estimates. Retrieved November 25, 2018 from https://factfinder.census.gov/faces/tableservices/jsf/pages/productview.xhtml?pid=ACS_12_1YR_B12007&prodType=table.

World Bank. (2019). *World Development Report 2019: The changing nature of work*. Washington, DC: World Bank. https://doi.org/10.1596/978-1-4648-1328-3.

Youth. (2018). In https://oed.com. Retrieved December 16, 2018 from http://www.oed.com.excelsior.sdstate.edi/view/Entry/232184?redirectedFrom=Youth#eid.

In Search of Addressing People's Career Adaptability and Career Identity Needs: Constructing the *Shaping Career Voices* Intervention

A. J. Albien

Abstract The inclusion of educational, cultural, economic, social and historical contexts in the development of career interventions can enhance adaptation to career-life transitions. In a South African context, interventions that promote career adaptability skills could enhance career adaptability competencies and bolster employability. This chapter reports on the designing and adapting a contextually grounded life-designing career intervention titled the *Shaping Career Voices* Intervention in the Kayamandi Township. A collaborative engagement process was undergone using focus group interviews and Delphi panel focus groups with community role players, including fieldworkers, teachers, principals, and Non-governmental Organisation members. A thematic analysis was conducted on the interview data using Career Construction Theory as a theoretical framework. Themes that emerged were used to create the content for the *Shaping Career Voices* Intervention Workbook. The development process contributed to career counselling practice and theory by demonstrating the incorporation of collaborative mechanisms in the practice of multicultural counselling with South African disadvantaged population groups to design contextually relevant career interventions in a non-western developing world context.

Keywords Multicultural career counselling · Career adaptability · Career-life transitions · Career identity · Life-designing career intervention · Contextually grounded interventions · South African disadvantaged youth · Sustainable employability

Introduction

South Africa, like many other nations, faces multiple challenges in creating work opportunities and reducing unemployment (Statistics South Africa, 2016). Contextual factors, such as unemployment, a weak national economy, and shifting entry requirements into occupations, constantly impact South African individuals and

A. J. Albien (✉)
Department of Psychology, Stellenbosch University, Stellenbosch, South Africa
e-mail: anouka@sun.ac.za

J. G. Maree (ed.), *Handbook of Innovative Career Counselling*,
https://doi.org/10.1007/978-3-030-22799-9_16

make career development processes inherently complex (Stead & Watson, 2017). Career psychologists can assist with the alleviation of pressing social problems by creating interventions that facilitate career decision-making processes among vulnerable and marginalised population groups. Career interventions can serve as vehicles to enable youth to transcend poverty as a long-term objective and can yield positive short-term effects on matters such as grades attained, school attendance, tertiary education enrolment, and employment outcomes (Perry & Smith, 2017).

This chapter contributes to research on career intervention development in a marginalised adolescent population group to improve career competencies that may need further development to facilitate employability. The present research was located in a peri-urban township called Kayamandi on the outskirts of Stellenbosch, South Africa. Previously this was a Black residential area during Apartheid, where migrant farm workers from the Eastern Cape were housed. A pejorative rural image of Kayamandi is projected, because it is surrounded by farmlands. The community is characterised by informal housing structures, limited municipality services, and high levels of crime, unemployment and poverty. Dominant occupations for residents in Kayamandi remain low-paying and have high turn-over rates, such as unskilled manual labour jobs or entrepreneurial jobs in the informal sector (Albien, 2013).

Chapter Structure

The first part of the chapter briefly discusses some of the challenges in creating work opportunities and reducing unemployment globally and in South Africa especially. In Part 2, the goals of the study are described. Part 3 speaks to the theoretical underpinnings of the *Shaping Career Voices* Intervention. Part 4 elaborates on the qualitative process that was undertaken in the creation, structure and adaptation of the career intervention. The design of the workbook is presented in Part 5 before the chapter is concluded.

Goals of the Chapter

The purpose of this research was to design and adapt the *Shaping Career Voices Intervention* as a qualitative, contextually relevant intervention. The intervention was partially guided by components of prior interventions developed for population groups without much access to volitional jobs (Blustein, Kozan, Connors-Kellgren, & Rand, 2015). Beneficial components included provided the following: occupational information in-session, individual attention within a group setting, opportunities to engage with occupational information in-session, examples of role modelling, written reflective exercises, and identification of existing support structures (Brown & McPartland, 2005). Outcomes that are more positive have been associated with the inclusion of these components in career interventions (Stead & Subich, 2017).

These components were collaboratively discussed with Kayamandi community role players to create a contextually relevant intervention and adaptations were based on their feedback in the design process.

Life Design Paradigm: Brief Theoretical Overview

The career intervention was theoretically grounded in a postmodern career counselling approach located within the life-designing paradigm to advocate subjective and contextually situated understandings of career behaviours (Maree, 2010a, 2010b). The importance of this approach in a South African context is because of the emphasis on the value of oral traditions and the contextual development of new meanings in career development to address complex issues in diverse cultural environments (Maree, Ebersöhn, & Molepo, 2006; Mkhize, 2015). The Life-design counselling model (Savickas et al., 2009) is informed by, and at the same time actualises, the career construction theory (CCT) (Savickas, 2011b) and self-construction theory (SCT) (Guichard, Pouyaud, De Calan, & Dumora, 2012). According to Savickas (2013), the key construct "adapt-abilities" is closely associated with Life design and comprises four dimensions. *Concern* involves a future orientation, *control* refers to self-regulation and responsibility for career decisions, *curiosity* describes career exploration activities, and *confidence* refers to self-efficacy and an individual's ability beliefs.

Questions have been raised by Watson (2013) if the basic tenets of the CCT are versatile enough to meet the needs of diverse cultural groups in developing world contexts, with particular reference to "non-career groups" (p. 6). This term specifically refers to underprivileged, underclass, disadvantaged, and non-normative population groups, whose career development has been undocumented. The CCT and by extension the Life-designing model have been found to be useful in unpacking and reformulating the subjective career meanings, contextual barriers, social and community expectations and career identity processes in Township youth to facilitate employability (Albien, 2018). In addition, McMahon, Watson, and Bimrose (2012) assessed the usefulness of career construction theory and uncovered a number of qualitative and quantitative indicators that supported the usefulness of this theoretical approach.

Furthermore, Life-design counselling models, such as the one described in this chapter, have been shown to enhance people's adaptability, narratability, intentionality, and activity (Savickas, 2011a). Three broad phases of the life-design counselling model informed the design of the present career intervention (Savickas, 2015): (1) encouraging people to tell small stories (constructions); (2) reconstruction of small stories into larger stories; and (3) co-construction of future stories. The intervention was built on the process of critical self-reflection of an individual's desired identity (Guichard et al., 2012), and included six stages based on the life-design intervention model of Savickas et al. (2009). The versatility and applicability of the life-design model has been documented across diverse settings, which includes developed and developing country contexts using both individual and group formats (Maree, 2017).

The facilitation and promotion of career life-design in group contexts is important, specifically in developing country contexts where one-on-one counselling is not accessible or affordable to the majority of the population. In disadvantaged contexts, group interventions have been shown to be an efficient format to enhance clients' career adaptability competencies (Di Fabio & Maree, 2012). Furthermore, various studies have indicated that life-design counselling helped clients to use their lived experiences and stories to develop the inner stability needed in a rapidly changing world-of-work (Maree, 2015a, 2015b). According to Maree (2017), career construction counselling, embedded in the Life-designing framework, offers "hope, especially to people in the poorest regions in South Africa, of escaping the cycle and trap of poverty and overcoming the barriers of poor education and the inability to find work" (p. 115).

Reflective Theoretical Underpinnings

Reflection is an important process in the Life-designing approach, however, often reflection is not deeply engaged with in career counselling. As a result, the reflective underpinnings of the career intervention presented here was created by using Schön's (2017) three reflection types. The first type is *reflection-on-action*, in which retrospective reflection is elicited after an event has passed, and was used in exercises that asked participants to think back to past events or experiences. Second, *reflection-in-action* is simultaneous, and can be compared to a running commentary in which an individual narrates thought processes during actions. The booklet used *reflection-in-action* by asking participants, in reflection text boxes, if they noticed/thought/learnt anything during the exercise. Third, *reflection-through-action* is the process of becoming aware of internalized or habituated sets of actions and thoughts. Additionally, reflection was also theorized according to Kolb's theoretical model (1984). *Reflection-in-action* is the first stage, which includes *concrete experience (CE)*, during which tacit knowledge is used to carry an experience forward. However, the reflection process is only initiated in the *reflection-on-action* type, which is mapped onto the *reflective observation (RO)* stage, and includes identifying the significance of an experience and/or questions triggered by the experience. In the *abstract conceptualization (AC)* stage, usable concepts or hypotheses are generated which can be compared to the *reflection-on-action* type. The next stage is the *active experimentation (AE)* stage of Kolb's (1984) cycle, where the implications of the generated concepts are tested. This stage links to *reflection-for-action*, when someone revisits earlier reflections in order to create a new plan or to confirm an understanding (Cowan, 1998; Moon 1999a, 1999b). These reflective theories informed the use of reflection exercises throughout the intervention, which extended the depth and range of reflective processes stipulated in the Life-designing approach.

Creation of the Shaping Career Voices Intervention

Each of the original career adaptability dimensions (i.e., concern, control, curiosity, confidence, and co-operation) are included in the intervention under discussion and were operationalized in terms of a number of specific exercises to facilitate reflection, self-awareness, and meaning-making (Savickas, 2005). These exercises were adapted from narrative therapy practices (Combs & Freedman, 2012; White & Epston, 1990), qualitative career counselling interviews (Bimrose & Hearne, 2012; McMahon, Watson, Chetty, & Hoelson, 2012), the career construction interview (Savickas, 2011b, 2012), case study approaches (Maree & Molepo, 2007; Maree et al., 2006) and established career interventions such as the *Career Interest Profile* (Maree, 2013). The end product was a mosaic of previous qualitative career counselling practices woven together by the perspectives of academics, field workers, Non-Governmental Organisations (NGOs) members, teachers, and principals. The inclusion of contextual role players allowed adaptations to be made to the career intervention that allowed the intervention to be culturally relevant and to address the contextually-bound challenges that existed and were specific to a South Africa Township context.

These contextual nuances were incorporated from a multitude of sources and perspectives. Information sources included: informal conversations with community members; individual and group interviews with Kayamandi role players; and Delphi panel focus group interviews with fieldworkers. Focus groups meetings were held with seven Kayamandi residents employed as fieldworkers, using the Delphi method to gain insight into prior career counselling experiences and needs in Kayamandi (Fletcher & Marchildon, 2014) to expedite the career intervention material development. The Delphi technique is a widely used and accepted method for gathering data from respondents within their domain of expertise to achieve a convergence of opinion. In this case, the opinions of individuals who were considered experts on the career difficulties that high school learners faced in the Kayamandi context were obtained (Hsu & Sandford, 2007). The fieldworkers (five females and two males) were at the time enrolled at higher education institutions or at further education and training colleges. Their ages ranged from 21 to 25 years old, which reflects an older normative age range (and provides an indication of the challenges faced in completing educational qualifications) in comparison to the typical middle-class undergraduate cohort, whose ages would range between 18 and 22 years old.

These experts were asked to voice adjustments they believed would be beneficial, such as the inclusion of examples, explanations, or instructions to aid understanding of the career assessments or career booklet exercises. The fieldworkers' recommendations allowed the contextual factors associated with being part of a marginalised population group to be incorporated, such as peer pressure and social comparison mechanisms. Furthermore, they became visible examples of success stories and became mentors (Matshabane, 2016) that provided access to available channels of information after the research process had ended. This was done in an attempt to pre-empt the pervading stereotype of 'parachute' research, where researchers leave no visible imprint on the community (London & MacDonald, 2014).

Additional community members and role player groups were consulted, including the principals of the two high schools, eight teachers from both high schools, and four management members of a Kayamandi-based NGO Vision Afrika, colloquially called Vision K, which undertook community development programmes, such as a variety of career-life skills afterschool workshops. The teachers' and principals' age range was between 33 and 54 years of age. They all had a higher education teaching qualification and had been teaching for a minimum of five and a maximum of 25 years. Both principals were male, and three of the teachers were male and five were female. Vision K staff members consisted of four Kayamandi youth, two males and two females (age range between 22 and 28), who had finished high school and were enrolled in part-time education courses. Below, we present a brief overview of the meetings held with Kayamandi role player groups and a summary of the suggestions that resulted from these meetings (see Table 1).

Engagement of Role Player Groups in the Development of the Career Intervention

Five meetings were held with the principals of the high schools in Kayamandi. Further meetings were conducted with eight teachers at the schools to create the intervention materials. Another four individuals, who belonged to the Vision K management team, were interviewed on four occasions during 2015 to garner insights for intervention materials (all participants signed informed consent forms). All information was documented in the form of written or voice notes. Many of the career intervention suggestions came from the team of fieldworkers, who were alumni of the two Kayamandi high schools. Discussions were held to determine what career development difficulties were experienced by adolescents, with the intention of developing useful exercises and activities that could instil a sense of agency in the participants. Once the career booklet had been created, another 12 meetings took place to assess the career booklet in terms of cultural relevance and practicality. There were four meetings held with fieldworkers and four meetings with teachers at each school. The principals and Vision K staff were not included due to time constraints. In total, 28 intervention content meetings were held in 2015 and 2016 before the final implementation of the career intervention. Specifically, 16 meetings were held before the creation of the career booklet. An overview of role player groups, their suggestions and the adapted exercises that were created is presented below in Table 1.

Many daunting obstacles were mentioned that township residents faced daily and these scenarios were discussed for use as case-study material for in-session examples. The fieldworkers were also critically involved in addressing linguistic concerns in the consent forms and assent forms. Decisions were made through a collaborative leadership approach, which acknowledged fieldworkers as experts in the Kayamandi context with access to localised knowledge (Matebeni, 2014).

Table 1 Process of intervention content construction

Groups	Suggestions	Exercise created
Teachers (T)	T.1. "You *need to find something that they can relate to, let them see I am not alone in being confused and scared*"	Nikiwe's case study was included. It was hoped that fieldworkers could also be role models/mentors
	T.2. "*They need to explore, often they have never even seen a pamphlet. They need to sit, absorb and get questions*"	The last session included pamphlets and answering of questions
	T.3. "*A positive voice must be encouraged, that one stands up for him/her. Saying no man, I can do this!*"	Mapping externalising conversations and the counter-story
	T.4. "*We need to talk about barriers, that are other voices, these kids face so many challenges*"	Putting the Voices of others into my story
	T.5. "*Role models. To pick the good role models and to know why you look up to that person. And it should not only be about money, clothes or we will lose them all to the tsotsis*"	Identifying the people who have shaped you
	T.6. "*They need to learn to plan step by step and know what they need to know*"	Actualising a career identity
	T.7. "They *need to learn to reflect where they came from, the decisions they made put them on a path and they can change that path at any time*"	Reflection exercises
Fieldworkers (F)	F.1. "*I like the idea of being the author of a story and the depending how you link events together you can either be a victim or a hero*"	Curiosity: Creating the plot of my career story
	F.2. "*We need to find a way to create a complex picture of all the small puzzle pieces that inform career choices, make them see all these small things link*"	Curiosity: Plotting my career story
	F.3. "*These kids they need perspective, they need to think about how others see them and how that compares to what they see. They really don't have much self-awareness*"	Co-operation: Johari's window
	F.4 "*And they have no clue what they like doing. It's always the same I like socialising and chatting on Facebook or WhatsApp. They need to think about what they like doing and how that links to skills that can be used in a job*"	Curiosity: Choosing my skills

(continued)

Table 1 (continued)

Groups	Suggestions	Exercise created
Principals (P)	P.1. "*Include exercises where they need to reflect on what others are telling them. They must be able to be critical and think this person is jealous and not being supportive*"	Control: Identifying positive and negative voices in my career story
	P.2. "*The one thing that worries me the most is that these kids have weak minds. They give up when it is too difficult to become that career. They listen to that voice inside that tells them they will fail no matter what they do*"	Confidence: Externalising conversations
Vision K (VK) management members	V.K.1. "*These kids they don't spend any time in the future, they are like grabbing anything that comes their way one moment to the next*"	Concern: The Future You
	V.K.2. "*Time is something that no one really thinks about. We need them to think this is what I did in the past, I learnt this lesson, now I do this thing differently, but in the future I must still learn to other things differently. That time connection is missing*"	Concern: My Career Voice: Past, present, and future career stories

Delphi panel meetings were all recorded, transcribed, and thematically analysed using Braun and Clarke's (2006) approach. In this approach the analytic process involved a progression from a description of the data based on patterns that indicated semantic content, to interpretation where the significance of these patterns was theoretically explored according to the CCT five career adaptability dimensions. The career intervention was structured for four sessions of two hours each, resulting in a total 20 h, which included eight hours' face-to-face time with 12 h of homework. The career intervention was broken up as follows: *Session 1* included the career concern dimension; *Session 2* included the career control and curiosity dimensions; *Session 3* included the career confidence and co-operation dimensions; and *Session 4* included pamphlets, consolidating a career identity and reflection questions.

Role Player Groups' Recommendations for the Career Intervention

In order to incorporate Kayamandi voices and reality-near experiences, the career workbook was critically discussed with the team of fieldworkers after feedback had been received from the teachers and principals. Three main categories of adaptations were discussed, namely the inclusion of the concept of co-operation, the use of Afrocentric imagery in the career booklet, and the narrative structure of the career intervention. In Table 2, the changes are listed that were suggested to improve the career booklet, as well as the ensuing adjustments that were made to the intervention.

The concept of co-operation was added to the intervention after many Delphi panel meetings with fieldworkers and school staff as an adaptation of the intervention to the Kayamandi context. These parties emphasized a huge community or social relational component that needed to be considered in developing career adaptability, which was supported by previous research conducted using the *CAAS-Iceland* (Einarsdóttir, Vilhjálmsdóttir, Smáradóttir, & Kjartansdóttir, 2015). The co-operation construct was included as an adaptation of the CCT to be contextually-relevant to the collectivistic amaXhosa sample (Stead & Watson, 2017). Thereby, the interconnectedness of social, contextual and cultural aspects was included, which resonates with non-western collectivistic worldviews (Holdstock, 2000), where co-operation with others to fulfil social obligations was paramount in the expression of a self-concept (Mkhize, 2015). Therefore, an examination of voices that influenced career decision-making was presented, to allow a reconciliation between individual ambition and Afrocentric duties in the creation of a coherent self-concept (Albien, 2013).

The use of African images in the workbook was considered but the main theme that emerged during discussions was that images of success were tied to Western notions of success and traditional African images often were not seen as desirable or prestigious enough. As a result, images were used that related to the content of the workbook and depicted people of diverse heritages. In addition, fieldworkers were apprehensive about the narrative structure of the career intervention because they were concerned that learners would not complete the intervention if the content seemed too unfamiliar as this would be associated with less value. Fieldworkers explained that a "testing and telling approach was expected" (Fieldworker 1: F.1). Learners had expectations of career counselling entailing a process in which they were told what they were good at and then matched with a corresponding career skill or trait. This misconception of the career counselling process was supported by previous research in the Kayamandi context (Albien & Naidoo, 2017).

Final Content of the Shaping Career Voices Intervention Workbook

The final version of the *Shaping Career Voices Intervention Booklet* (Albien, 2018) consisted of 19 pages with lined spaces to write down reflections. The final career booklet structure can be seen in Table 3, in which an overview is presented of the career dimension addressed, the associated workbook exercises, and the corresponding page numbers. Pamphlets of higher education institutions and colleges were provided in-session to facilitate career exploration. The intervention was facilitated by the fieldworkers and researcher as a team, thus creating a bilingual English and isiX-

Table 2 Process of career intervention redrafting

Groups	Suggested changes	Changes made
Teachers	T.1. "*You need lines for these kids to write on*"	Lined spaces were included
	T.2. "*You need to include fun things, like games or jokes*"	Fieldworkers included jokes and role playing
	T.3. "*They will get bored, make the instructions short*"	All text was reworked and shortened
	T.4. "*You should print this in an A5 booklet format so that they think it is not so much work, if they see it in an A4 format they will complain that it's too much writing*"	The booklet was printed in an A5 format
	T.5. "*You will have to check that they answer all the sections, they try to cheat and only fill out a few pages because they think you won't check*"	Each booklet was checked for completion
	T.6. "*You need to include pictures, they don't like pages of writing*"	Images were included on every page
	T.7. "*You need to give them career pamphlets to look at with you so you can help them fight that fear of not understanding*"	Career pamphlets were collected and included
	T.8. "*You need to make them choose three careers at the end. You know like plan a, plan b and plan c*"	This idea was included the whole way through
Fieldworkers	F.1. "*You will need to make these kids work to finish in time, we will have to explain the sections first and then give them time to work afterwards*"	This approach was followed and worked very well; however, there were also quiet times
	F.2. "*We will have to help them understand the externalising conversation using a role playing example*"	This was included and fieldworkers took turns using personal examples
	F.3. "*We will have to explain entry requirements and bursaries*"	This was included
	F.4. "*These reflection questions will need explaining because they are not used to reflecting*"	An explanation was given verbally about the value of thinking back to what was learned
	F.5. "*This plotting of events will confuse them, but they need to learn how a story is made, we need to give them examples*"	We used two examples of plotted stories in-session

hosa environment. Each team member was responsible for explaining demarcated sections of the booklet. Role playing scenarios were included and contextually-relevant examples were used to bring creativity and cultural-sensitivity into the relational space created. An introduction to narrative career counselling was provided in the beginning of the career booklet to explain how career adaptability could be facilitated. Thereafter, career adaptability was explained using a simple five Cs analogy, which included *concern*, *control*, *curiosity*, *confidence*, and co-*operation*.

The actual processes of reflexive construction, deconstruction, co-construction, and reconstruction were included and elucidated in the booklet. These constructive processes are theorised to form the cornerstone of the Life-designing approach and result in individuals' developing career adaptability competencies and designing subjectively successful lives (Savickas, 2011b). Meanings assigned to career-related experiences can result in a distinguishable plot as an implementation of the client's career identity into a work role (Savickas, 2013). CCT highlights the importance of the process of eliciting career-life stories to discover, examine and adapt central career-life themes to which individuals assign importance during their life-spans (Hartung, 2011). This was emphasised at the start of the intervention, where a narrative career counselling case study entitled Nikiwe's story was presented (Maree, 2010b).

The case study provided an example of how stories could stimulate reflection and help the participant re-author a new career-life narrative (Maree, 2017) In the case study, Nikiwe is described as a high school learner who turned to her teacher for help in facing career indecision and uncertainty. Life themes were described as "clues" to what career Nikiwe should choose. The narrative structure of the intervention was emphasized and compared to Nikiwe's dialogue with her teacher, with the aim of stimulating awareness of the presence and influence of common themes in an individual's career-life story. The participants were encouraged, throughout the career booklet, to reflect on how personal qualities, influential people and experiences could ultimately be interwoven to form their own unique career voice.

Career Adapt-Ability Section: Concern

The first section in the career booklet was *concern* and dealt with having a future orientation. The main exercise in this section was to write a newspaper story in third person about an ideal future self and reflect what choices would lead to this future self. The participants were requested to outline their achievements, describe the type of person they would like to be and the qualities they would like to be remembered for. A reflection box was added at the end of the section, in which participants were asked to reflect on what they learned in describing their future selves. The intention was to provide a space to include process-related reflections (Kolb, 1984; Moon, 1999b; Schön, 2017), which would help participants to identify life themes, goals, or values that were pertinent in shaping their career stories. The second exercise of the *concern* section was a table called *My Career Voice: Shaping my Career*

Table 3 Life-designing intervention structure

Adapt-ability dimension	Career question	Attitudes and beliefs	Competence	Career problem	Coping behaviours	Relationship perspective	Career intervention	Types of intervention
1. Concern	Do I have a future?	Planful	Planning	Indifference	Aware Involved Preparatory	Dependent	Orientation exercises	1. The Future You (p. 4) 2. My Career Voice: Past, present, and future career stories (p. 6)
2. Control	Who owns my future?	Decisive	Decision-making	Indecision	Assertive Disciplined Wilful	Independent	Decisional training	1. Identifying positive and negative voices in my career story (p. 7) 2. Putting the Voices of others into my story (p. 8)
3. Curiosity	What do I want to do with my future?	Inquisitive	Exploring	Unrealism	Experimenting Risk-taking Inquiring	Interdependent	Information-seeking activities	1. Identifying the people who have shaped you (p. 10) 2. Creating the plot of my career story (p. 11) 3. Choosing my skills (p. 12) 4. Plotting my career story (p. 13) 5. Career Pamphlets and fieldworker facilitated discussions in session (pp. 17–19)
4. Confidence	Can I do it?	Efficacious	Problem-solving	Inhibition	Persistent Striving Industrious	Equal	Self-esteem building	1. Externalising conversations (p. 14) 2. Mapping externalising conversations and the counter-story (p. 15)
5. Co-operation	Who is involved?	Collaborative Compromising	Negotiation	Indecision Foreclosure	Accommodating Interpersonally skilled Agreeable	Interdependent	Inter-relational and interpersonal skills training	1. Johari's window (p. 16) 2. Identifying positive and negative voices in my career story (p. 7) 3. Putting the Voices of others into my story (p. 8)

Adapted from Hartung (2007) (Reprinted with permission)

Story. This contained three columns, titled *past* (i.e., career decisions taken), *present* (i.e., current career actions), and *future* (i.e., career actions to be taken). Thereby participants could develop a time perspective by tying future career ideas identified to current decisions that they needed to make.

Career Adapt-Ability Section: Control

The next section, *control*, dealt with the responsibility that individuals needed to assume for constructing their own careers. This section was conceptually adapted for the township context from the *My Systems of Career Influences instrument* (*MSCI*: McMahon, Patton, & Watson, 2017) by examining participants' career voices at different levels. This included social (family, friends, teachers and culture) and societal-environmental (community and media) levels of influence. The *control section* was designed to develop critical thinking skills to help participants navigate various positive and negative influences in the township context. This exercise aimed to critically analyze the mixed-messages that were transferred between social groups in township contexts, which could lead to the perpetuation of career myths and dysfunctional and/or irrational career beliefs (Albien & Naidoo, 2017). Thereby, a subjective examination could occur of how career voices could affect the individual's behavior if control was not exerted in implementing his/her own career voice. The underlying belief was that individuals could adjust to different contexts, using self-regulatory strategies and that they could exert an influence on their context. This served to acknowledge contextual challenges but did not victimize or pathologize township youth in any way (Kapp et al., 2014). As a follow-up exercise, the second *Control* exercise was called *Putting the voices of others into my story*. Here the most meaningful career voices were transferred into the participant's current career journey using the same divisions again (family, friends, teachers, culture, community, and media) to discern which voices needed to be actively ignored. This left the career voices behind that were supportive and/or were able to provide information or mentorship. The section ended with a *reflection-in-action* exercise (Kolb, 1984; Moon, 1999a; Schōn, 2017) in which participants were asked what they would do in the future when negative voices were encountered.

Career Adapt-Ability Section: Curiosity

The third section, *curiosity*, included exploration activities to engage with the world-of-work. Participants were encouraged to explore possible selves in order to create a realistic career identity. The introduction, called *Voices of self: My story*, explained that narratives were created by linking specific events together over time, in a way that was uniquely meaningful to the individual. As a result, the individual became the author who choose the events to weave together that created a career-life story and that this story could be re-authored if steps were retraced or a different direction was taken. The *curiosity* section consisted of four parts. The first part was *Who has helped shape who you are*? (i.e., choosing three people whom the participants admired, but it was important that this choice was not based solely on materialistic indicators of success). Each fieldworker provided examples of their personal role models, with qualities listed that they valued as an example of the subjective integration of career and personal values (Savickas et al., 2009). The second part was *Creating the plot of my career story* where participants were encouraged to think about all the events, chance encounters, obstacles and people that had shaped their career story up until that point. A diagram was provided, in which participants had to fill in the boxes and then join the events by drawing a line to plot the order or sequence of events. Participants also had to write down a belief or meaning that connected these events. If participants wanted to, they could go back to their diagram to add skills and other relevant pieces of information or join the events differently as a way of re-authoring their experiences.

The third part was *Choosing my skills*. This section was based on the participants gaining self-awareness of their skills by looking at twelve categories of skills, namely mechanical, physical, manual finesse, analytical, creative, artistic, musical, social, persuasive, organizing, leadership, and academic skills (Bolles, 2009). Discussions were facilitated by fieldworkers about diverse skill sets that were visible in the informal and formal work sectors. Overlaps in skills for specific careers, the influence of self-identified skill sets on their current career ideas, and peer feedback that reflected additional skills not considered by the individual were discussed, using *reflection-in-action* (Schön, 2017). Lastly, the fourth part, *Plotting my career story*, required participants to integrate the identified skills, role models, and previous career events. This exercise allowed a re-authoring to occur, in which the individual questioned previous interpretations that linked events together to create a career-life story. The intervention highlighted that individuals needed to gain insight into the events, messages, reflections and meanings they were assigning importance to and as a result informed their self-concept and career identity (Morgan, 2000; Van der Merwe & Gobodo-Madikizela, 2009).

Career Adapt-Ability Section: Confidence

Confidence was the fourth dimension and is defined as the belief held by an individual about his/her capabilities, which has also been called self-efficacy (Bandura, 2006). Proactive career behavior has previously been linked to self-confidence, self-esteem, and self-efficacy in completing career-related career activities (Betz & Hackett, 1981; Lent, Brown, & Hackett, 2000). Most importantly, confidence also includes the ability to persist in pursuing aspirations and objectives in the face of obstacles and barriers. This career competency becomes essential when the township context is taken into consideration. The participants had faced extreme hardships compared to middle-class cohorts. Previous career interventions had not taken personal losses or traumas into consideration, when these often require a complete identify reformulation and extensive meaning-making processes that spill over into career development processes (Brown, 2015; Hartung & Taber, 2008). Therefore, an externalizing conversation approach was used (Morgan, 2000) in an overview called *Mapping externalizing conversations* (White, 1997, 1998), which allowed the participants to identify the greatest challenge (i.e., 'problem') currently faced in their career journey. The section ended with a summary that engaged the participants in the different types of reflection (*reflection-in-action*, *reflection-on-action*, *reflection-through-*action and *reflection-for-action*). Participants filled out a table that placed the 'problem' voice directly against a positive counter-story. In contrasting these two narratives, an understanding was generated about how meaning-making processes and subjective value was attached to both voices (Madigan, 2011; White & Epston, 1990).

Career Adapt-Ability Section: Co-operation

The last dimension was *co-operation*, which is described as beliefs held about working with others and collaboration. Johari's window (Luft, 1969) was used to indicate the hidden areas (skills or traits) that were unknown to the participants but were perceived by others. A four-quadrant window was filled out and called *My personalized Johari's window of my career story*. Johari's window has four equal cells, where *Cell 1* is known by the person and is known by others (i.e. an open area). *Cell 2* is a blind area, unknown by the person but known by others. *Cell 3* is a hidden area which includes what the person knows about him/herself that others do not know (i.e., the façade) (O'Toole, 2015). *Cell 4* is an unknown area that includes repressed feelings, fears, latent abilities, behaviours, experiences, etc. at both surface and deeper levels, which are unknown to the person and also unknown to others (Luft & Ingham, 1961a). Large unknown areas can be expected in individuals who lack experience, who are young or who lack self-belief. As a result, abilities that are under-estimated or untried through a lack of opportunity, encouragement, confidence or training can emerge through self-discovery, observation by others, collective or mutual discovery. However, the movement of unknown discovered knowledge into the hidden, blind or open area depends on the individual who discovered the information and what he/she does with it. A useful way to discover unknown abilities and reduce unknown areas is by providing opportunities to try new things with no great pressure to succeed. Information, which an individual is prepared to learn from others or experience, is incorporated in *Cell 2* (Luft & Ingham, 1961b). Participants' active engagement with and reflection on self-disclosure in the presence of others is incorporated in *Cell 3*. The model presumes that accurate self-awareness is a function of how much is known about the self and requires shifting information from *Cells 2*, *3*, and *4* into *Cell 1* (O'Toole, 2015). Therefore, the more an individual knows about him/herself, the more self-determination he/she will have in pursuing subjectively valued career actions.

Termination Section: Action Plan and Reflection

The section *Actualizing a career identity* was focused on helping participants to integrate snippets of information gained during the career intervention. The aim was to have three career choices at the end of the intervention. Pamphlets handed to participants included a range of training options such as Technical and Vocational Education and Training (TVET) colleges, universities, private further education and training institutions, learnerships, and internships. Questions and a checklist were incorporated in the career booklet to facilitate participants' career exploration activities. As a result, a safe space was created for engaging with difficult concepts (i.e. entry requirements). This session also created a holding space for disappointment if the minimum entry-level requirements were not met and a reformulation of career goals was needed. The last two pages of the career booklet included 12 reflection questions based on the reflective stages assigned to Kolb's Learning Cycle (Kolb, 1984; Moon, 1999a, 1999b; Schön, 2017). Evaluation questions assessed participants' reflections about what had meaningfully stood out during the intervention and if they had suggestions for improvements.

Conclusion

The present research confirms the usefulness of the life-design counselling approach in the (South) African (developing country) context through the creation of a career intervention that was specifically adapted to the Kayamandi context by including role player groups who were considered experts in the township context. Adaptations were included based on the suggestions that these role players made. Adaptations included: various reflection exercises based on different reflection process types; constructs based on collectivistic underpinnings that integrated the management of social mechanisms such as social comparison, and community and cultural expectations. These adaptations allowed the career construction theory, and by extension the life-designing approach, to be successfully used in a non-western, low-resource context. The most significant aspect of this career intervention was the positioning of the self and career identity of township learners within social webs and networks. Thereby, learners gained unique insights into their own personal process needed in making career decisions which was based on the integration of individual capabilities and values with social expectations and norms. This career identity reformulation was emphasized in narrative exercises that dealt with deconstructing critical social messages received from community members, in order to prevent individuals from internalising these negative voices, which were inherently associated with competition and jealousy in low-resource contexts. Therefore, self-and career construction counselling, as explained in this chapter, embedded in life-design counselling can be regarded as an effective means to promote people's career adaptability. We hope that even though South Africa faces challenges that are unique and extraordinary, the knowledge and practice that are constructed in South African contexts can and will be applied successfully in other contexts and cultures as well. More particularly, we hope that the career-intervention design process presented in this chapter will lead to the successful utilisation of these intervention materials with similar disenfranchised youth in other contexts and stimulate future research in this regard. The process that informed the design of the present intervention content and structure provides an innovative example of creating culturally sensitive career interventions that could contribute to promoting dialogues about social justice and decolonization of people in Global South (developing country contexts) especially (Sultana, 2014; Watson, 2010).

Acknowledgements I thank the students, teachers, non-governmental organisation representatives and fieldworkers of Kayamandi for participating in developing this contextually-relevant intervention. I also express our gratitude to the National Research Foundation (NRF) grant number AEMD160619172334, and the Stellenbosch University who funded this Ph.D. research (by awarding me a Postgraduate Merit Bursary). Deep appreciation is expressed for Prof. Maree's role in shaping this chapter according to his vast repertoire of narrative career counselling experience. Lastly, I thank Prof. Naidoo who supervised this Ph.D. research process for the insights that were gained by his influence throughout the research journey.

References

Albien, A. J. (2013). *Exploring grade 12 Kayamandi adolescents' career influences using the Systems Theory Framework of Career Development* (Master's thesis). Stellenbosch, South Africa: Stellenbosch University.

Albien, A. J. (2018). *A mixed-methods analysis of black adolescents' vocational identity status and career adaptability competencies in a South African township* (Doctoral dissertation). Stellenbosch, South Africa: Stellenbosch University.

Albien, A., & Naidoo, A. V. (2017). Deconstructing career myths and cultural stereotypes in a context of low resourced township communities. *South African Journal of Education, 37*(4), 1–12. https://doi.org/10.15700/saje.v37n4a1476.

Bandura, A. (2006). Guide for constructing self-efficacy scales. In F. Pajares & T. Urdan (Eds.), *Self-efficacy beliefs of adolescents* (pp. 307–337). Greenwich, CT: Information Age Publishing.

Betz, N. E., & Hackett, G. (1981). The relationship of career-related self-efficacy expectations to perceived career options in college women and men. *Journal of Counselling Psychology, 28*(5), 399–410. https://doi.org/10.1037/0022-0167.28.5.399.

Bimrose, J., & Hearne, L. (2012). Resilience and career adaptability: Qualitative studies of adult career counselling. *Journal of Vocational Behaviour, 8*(3), 338–344. https://doi.org/10.1016/j.jvb.2012.08.002.

Blustein, D. L., Kozan, S., Connors-Kellgren, A., & Rand, B. (2015). Social class and career intervention. In P. J. Hartung, M. L. Savickas, & W. B. Walsh (Eds.), *APA Handbook of career intervention: Foundations* (Vol. 1, pp. 243–257). Washington, DC: American Psychological Association.

Bolles, R. N. (2009). *What colour is your parachute? 2016: A practical manual for job-hunters and career-changers*. Berkeley, CA: Ten Speed Press.

Braun, V., & Clarke, V. (2006). Using thematic analysis in psychology. *Qualitative Research in Psychology, 3*(2), 77–101. https://doi.org/10.1191/1478088706qp063oa.

Brown, D. (2015). *Career information, career counselling and career development*. Pearson: University of North Carolina, Chapel Hill.
Brown, S. D., & McPartland, E. B. (2005). Career interventions: Current status and future directions. In W. B. Walsh & M. L. Savickas (Eds.), *Handbook of vocational psychology: Theory, research, and practice* (3rd ed., pp. 195–226). Mahwah, NJ: Lawrence Erlbaum Associates.
Combs, G., & Freedman, J. (2012). Narrative, poststructuralism, and social justice: Current practices in narrative therapy. *The Counselling Psychologist, 40*(7), 1033–1060. https://doi.org/10.1177/0011000012460662.
Cowan, N. (1998). *Attention and memory: An integrated framework*. Oxford, England: Oxford University Press.
Di Fabio, A., & Maree, J. G. (2012). Group-based life-design counselling in an Italian context. *Journal of Vocational Behaviour, 80*(1), 100–107. https://doi.org/10.1016/j.jvb.2011.06.001.
Einarsdóttir, S., Vilhjálmsdóttir, G., Smáradóttir, S. B., & Kjartansdóttir, G. B. (2015). A culture-sensitive approach in the development of the Career Adapt-Abilities Scale in Iceland: Theoretical and operational considerations. *Journal of Vocational Behaviour, 89*, 172–181. https://doi.org/10.1016/j.jvb.2015.06.006.
Fletcher, A., & Marchildon, G. (2014). Using the Delphi method for qualitative, participatory action research in health leadership. *International Journal of Qualitative Methods, 13*(1), 1–18. https://doi.org/10.1177/160940691401300101.
Guichard, J., Pouyaud, J., De Calan, C., & Dumora, B. (2012). Identity construction and career development interventions with emerging adults. *Journal of Vocational Behavior, 81*(1), 52–58. https://doi.org/10.1016/j.jvb.2012.04.004.
Hartung, P. J. (2007). Career construction: Principles and practice. In K. Maree (Ed.), *Shaping the story: A guide to facilitating narrative counselling* (pp. 103–120). Pretoria, South Africa: Van Schaik.
Hartung, P. J. (2011). Career construction: Principles and practice. In K. Maree (Ed.), *Shaping the story: A guide to facilitating narrative counselling* (pp. 103–120). Rotterdam, Netherlands: Sense.
Hartung, P. J., & Taber, B. J. (2008). Career construction and subjective well-being. *Journal of Career Assessment, 16*(1), 75–85. https://doi.org/10.1177/1069072707305772.
Holdstock, T. L. (2000). *Re-examining psychology: Critical perspectives and African insights*. London, UK: Routledge.
Hsu, C. C., & Sandford, B. A. (2007). The Delphi technique: Making sense of consensus. *Practical Assessment, Research & Evaluation, 12*(10), 1–8.
Kapp, R., Badenhorst, E., Bangeni, B., Craig, T. S., Van Rensburg, V. J., Le Roux, K., et al. (2014). Successful students' negotiation of township schooling in contemporary South Africa. *Perspectives in Education, 32*(3), 50–61.
Kolb, D. (1984). *The process of experiential learning*. Englewood Cliffs, NJ: Prentice Hall.
Lent, R. W., Brown, S. D., & Hackett, G. (2000). Contextual supports and barriers to career choice: A social cognitive analysis. *Journal of Counselling Psychology, 47*(1), 36–49. https://doi.org/10.1037//0022-0167.47.1.36.
London, L., & MacDonald, H. (2014). Transnational excursions: The ethics of northern anthropological investigations going south. In D. Posel & F. C. Ross (Eds.), *Ethical quandaries in social research* (pp. 93–110). Cape Town: Human Sciences Research Council Press.
Luft, J. (1969). *Of human interaction: The Johari model*. Palo Alto, CA: Mayfield.
Luft, J., & Ingham, H. (1961a). The Johari window. *Human Relations Training News, 5*(1), 6–7.
Luft, J., & Ingham, H. (1961b). The Johari Window: A graphic model of awareness in interpersonal relations. *Human Relations Training News, 5*(9), 6–7.
Madigan, S. (2011). *Narrative therapy*. Washington, DC: American Psychological Association.
Maree, J. G. (2010a). Editorial: Reassessing career counselling in Africa in the 21st century: Breathing new life into qualitative approaches. *Journal of Psychology in Africa, 20*(3), 353–358. https://doi.org/10.1080/14330237.2010.10820386.

Maree, J. G. (2010b). Brief overview of the advancement of postmodern approaches to career counselling. *Journal of Psychology in Africa, 20*(3), 361–368. https://doi.org/10.1080/14330237.2010.10820387.

Maree, J. G. (2013). Latest developments in career counselling in South Africa: Towards a positive approach. *South African Journal of Psychology, 43*(4), 409–421. https://doi.org/10.1177/0081246313504691.

Maree, J. G. (2015a). Research on life-design in (South) Africa: A qualitative analysis of outcomes of six case study participants. *South African Journal of Psychology, 45,* 332–348. https://doi.org/10.1177/0081246314566785.

Maree, J. G. (2015b). Poverty and life-designing. In L. Nota & J. Rossier (Eds.), *Handbook of the life-design paradigm: From practice to theory and from theory to practice* (pp. 233–248). Göttingen, Germany: Hogrefe.

Maree, J. G., & Molepo, J. M. (2007). Changing the approach to career counselling in a disadvantaged context: A case study. *Australian Journal of Career Development, 16*(3), 62–70. https://doi.org/10.1177/103841620701600312.

Maree, K. (2017). Utilizing career adaptability and career resilience to promote employability and decent work and alleviate poverty. In J. G. Maree (Ed.), *Psychology of career adaptability, employability and resilience* (pp. 349–373). New York: Springer.

Maree, K., Ebersöhn, L., & Molepo, M. (2006). Administering n career counselling in a diverse setting: Trimming the sails to the wind. *South African Journal of Education, 26*(1), 49–60.

Matebeni, S. (2014). My best participants' informed consent. In D. Posel & F. C. Ross (Eds.), *Ethical quandaries in social research* (pp. 125–139). Cape Town, South Africa: Human Sciences Research Council Press.

Matshabane, O. P. (2016). *Exploring the influence of role models on the career development process of school-going adolescents from a low-income community in South Africa* (Master's thesis). Stellenbosch, South Africa: Stellenbosch University.

McMahon, M. L., Patton, W., & Watson, M. (2017). *My system of career influences-MSCI (Adolescent): A qualitative career assessment reflection process*. Camberwell, VIC, Australia: Australian Academic Press.

McMahon, M., Watson, M., & Bimrose, J. (2012a). Career adaptability: A qualitative understanding from the stories of older women. *Journal of Vocational Behaviour, 80*(3), 762–768. https://doi.org/10.1016/j.jvb.2012.01.016.

McMahon, M., Watson, M., Chetty, C., & Hoelson, C. N. (2012b). Examining process constructs of narrative career counselling: An exploratory case study. *British Journal of Guidance and Counselling, 40*(2), 127–141. https://doi.org/10.1080/03069885.2011.646949.

Mkhize, N. (2015). Qualitative career assessment in African contexts. In M. McMahon & M. Watson (Eds.), *Career assessment: Qualitative approaches* (pp. 247–254). Rotterdam, Netherlands: Sense.

Moon, J. A. (1999a). *Learning journals: A handbook for academics, students and professional development*. London, UK: Routledge.

Moon, J. A. (1999b). *Reflection in learning and professional development*. Abingdon, Oxon: Routledge Falmer.

Morgan, A. (2000). *What is narrative therapy? An easy-to-read introduction*. Adelaide, Australia: Dulwich Centre Publications.

O'Toole, S. (2015). Indigenous mentoring and coaching. *Training & Development, 42*(5), 10–11.

Perry, J. C., & Smith, C. (2017). Career choice and poverty. In G. B. Stead & M. B. Watson (Eds.), *Career psychology in the South African context* (3rd ed., pp. 158–173). Pretoria: Van Schaik Publishers.

Savickas, M. L. (2005). The theory and practice of career construction. In S. D. Brown & R. W. Lent (Eds.), *Career development and counselling: Putting theory and research to work* (pp. 42–70). Hoboken, NJ: Wiley & Sons.

Savickas, M. L. (2011a). *Career counselling*. Washington, DC: American Psychological Association.

Savickas, M. L. (2011b). Constructing careers: Actor, agent, and author. *Journal of Employment Counselling, 48*(4), 179–181. https://doi.org/10.1002/j.2161-1920.2011.tb01109.x.
Savickas, M. L. (2012). Life-design: A paradigm for career intervention in the 21st century. *Journal of Counselling & Development, 90*(1), 13–19. https://doi.org/10.1111/j.1556-6676.2012.00002.x.
Savickas, M. L. (2013). The theory and practice of career construction. In S. D. Brown & R. W. Lent (Eds.), *Career development and counselling: Putting theory and research to work* (2nd ed., pp. 147–186). Hoboken, NJ: Wiley.
Savickas, M. L. (2015). *Life-design counselling manual*. Author: Publisher.
Savickas, M. L., Nota, L., Rossier, J., Dauwalder, J. P., Duarte, M. E., Guichard, J., et al. (2009). Life-designing: A paradigm for career construction in the 21st century. *Journal of Vocational Behaviour, 75*(3), 239–250. https://doi.org/10.1016/j.jvb.2009.04.004.
Schön, D. (2017). *The reflective practitioner: How professionals think in action*. London, UK: Routledge.
Statistics South Africa. (2016). *Mid-year population estimates: 2016*. Pretoria: Statistics South Africa.
Stead, G. B., & Subich, L. M. (2017). Career counselling practice. In G. B. Stead & M. B. Watson (Eds.), *Career psychology in the South African context* (3rd ed., pp. 119–136). Pretoria: Van Schaik Publishers.
Stead, G. B., & Watson, M. B. (2017). Indigenisation of career psychology in South Africa. In G. B. Stead & M. B. Watson (Eds.), *Career psychology in the South African context* (3rd ed., pp. 210–218). Pretoria: Van Schaik Publishers.
Sultana, R. G. (2014). Pessimism of the intellect, optimism of the will? Troubling the relationship between career guidance and social justice. *International Journal for Educational and Vocational Guidance, 14*(1), 5–19. https://doi.org/10.1007/s10775-013-9262-y.
Van der Merwe, C. N., & Gobodo-Madikizela, P. (2009). *Narrating our healing perspectives on working through trauma*. Newcastle, UK: Cambridge Scholars Publishing.
Watson, M. (2010). Career psychology in South Africa: Addressing and redressing social justice. *Australian Journal of Career Development, 19*(1), 24–29. https://doi.org/10.1177/103841621001900106.
Watson, M. (2013). Deconstruction, reconstruction, co-construction: Career construction theory in a developing world context. *Indian Journal of Career and Livelihood Planning, 2*(1), 3–14.
White, M. (1997). *Narratives of therapists' lives*. Adelaide, South Australia: Dulwich Centre Publications.
White, M. (1998). *Narrative therapy*. Adelaide, South Australia: Dulwich Centre.
White, M., & Epston, D. (1990). *Narrative means to therapeutic ends*. New York, NY: Norton.

Career Construction Counselling with Women Through a Feminist Lens

Jacqueline J. Peila-Shuster and Erica M. Hines

Abstract The purpose of this chapter is to consider the use of career construction counselling with women through a feminist counselling lens. To gain a clearer understanding of the significance of the topic, the first part of the chapter begins with an overview of the global gender gap, especially in relation to work. Additionally, the authors provide a case study to offer context and facilitate application of concepts throughout the chapter. The second part of the chapter provides information regarding various career barriers faced by women, and applies that information to the case study in an effort to sensitize readers to potential issues. The third part of the chapter attends to feminist counselling and the imperative to understand and honor intersectionality, and again applies this information to the case study. The fourth part integrates a feminist counselling lens with career construction for women and helps the reader consider implications regarding the case study, after which the chapter is concluded.

Keywords Career construction · Career counselling · Feminist counselling · Women's career issues · Women's career barriers

Introduction

While feminist theories are highly diverse and complex, there are two foundational themes of feminist counselling. The first is that the personal is political, which means that personal problems are connected to, and influenced by, the socio-political climate (Enns, 2004). This is aligned with the career construction theoretical principle that individuals construct their careers not solely based on the "self" but also within the context of their social world (Savickas, 2013a). Because career development intimately connects to, and is influenced by, socio-political (and oppressive) systems, it

J. J. Peila-Shuster (✉)
Colorado State University, Fort Collins, CO, USA
e-mail: Jackie.Peila-Shuster@colostate.edu

E. M. Hines
Community College of Aurora, Aurora, CO, USA

J. G. Maree (ed.), *Handbook of Innovative Career Counselling*,
https://doi.org/10.1007/978-3-030-22799-9_17

is understandable women would experience unique issues. The second theme of feminist counselling is that issues and symptoms are often coping mechanisms that have arisen in response to dealing with oppression (Enns, 2004). Since personal issues and career issues are rarely, if ever, separate, the coping mechanisms women may employ in dealing with oppression likely intertwine with career development issues. As such, it can be useful to address the career construction of women through a feminist lens that helps one to consider implicit bias and systemic oppression, especially during the deconstruction and co-construction processes of career construction counselling.

Global Gender Gap and Workforce Participation Trends

A broad overview of the global gender gap provides context for the significance of women's work issues in today's world. Based on current trends, the World Economic Forum (2017) calculated that the global gender gap could be closed in 100 years across 106 countries. This is an alarming trend compared to 83 years based on the previous year's report. The World Economic Forum contends economic and health gaps are the most challenging of the four gender gaps measured (economic participation and opportunity, educational attainment, health and survival, and political empowerment). Disappointingly, the economic gender gap has widened for two consecutive years and it stands at its lowest value (as measured by the Index) since 2008 resulting in estimates that it could take 217 years for it to close.

Closing the economic gender gap could result in substantially positive outcomes for the global community because "ensuring the healthy development and appropriate use of half of the world's total talent pool has a vast bearing on the growth, competitiveness and future-readiness of economies and businesses worldwide" (World Economic Forum, 2017, pp. 26–27). Indeed, according to the McKinsey Global Institute (2015), full global gender parity in the economy could equate to a US$28 trillion addition to the annual global Gross Domestic Product (GDP) in 2025 as compared to current conditions. The report further indicated that even if countries just matched the rate of improvement in gender parity in the best performing country in their region, it could add US$12 trillion in annual GDP.

However, while female labor force participation rates worldwide have increased in most countries since 1980, recent trends have shown that this global trend has only increased from 50.2 to 51.8%, and some estimates from the International Labor Organization (ILO) show that the global trend is negative (Ortiz-Ospina & Tzvetkova, 2017). According to Ortiz-Ospina and Tzvetkova (2017), this negative trend is primarily because of diminished workforce participation in some world regions, most notably in South and East Asia. Globally, the labor force participation ratio of females to males in 2016 was approximately 67.5%, meaning for every 100 males in the workforce, there were 67.5 females (The World Bank, 2017). This disparity is highly variable with some countries, such as Burundi or Mozambique having more females than males in the labor force, and others, such as Afghanistan or Algeria, having less than a 25% ratio of females to males in the workforce (The World Bank, 2017). This does not mean that women are working less, though.

Ortiz-Ospina and Tzvetkova (2017) delved deeply into ILO data and determined that women, more often than men, tend to work in the informal economy. They advised that this is an important point given that policies and laws tend to favor those working in the formal economy. Furthermore, given that informal workers "represent the majority of workers and enterprises in developing countries," (WIEGO, n.d., para. 2) one must also consider intersectionality and thus the multiple points of oppression many women encounter. Additionally, women spend more time that men on unpaid domestic care work (e.g., care of people, housework, and voluntary community work) all over the world, with the low end of the spectrum (Uganda) showing women working 18% more than men on these activities, and the high end (India) indicating they work 10 times more (Ortiz-Ospina & Tzvetkova, 2017). Obviously, multiple layers of complexity accompany women's participation rates in the workforce as a whole. Further, the individual perspectives of women, their cultural and contextual backgrounds, their points of privilege and of oppression, and the intertwining of these facets with career issues can complicate matters further.

Case Study: Introducing Julia

Following is a brief introduction to a case study referred to throughout this chapter. To maintain anonymity, Julia is a composite of a variety of individuals with whom the authors have had the fortune to work. It is our hope that she will help illuminate the information presented in this chapter in a realistic and useful manner.

Julia is a 34-year-old Latina in the United States who identifies as a woman of color, and is heterosexual and cisgender. She worked as a certified Physical Therapy Assistant (PTA) for approximately five years prior to having children. She had planned to return to school to earn her Doctor of Physical Therapy (DPT) and either return to the field as a registered physical therapist, or perhaps become a professor. However, upon having their first child, she and her husband decided she would stay home with the children while he continued to work full-time.

The children are now ages three and five and Julia is experiencing some confusion and anxiety regarding her life-career. She states that she loves her children, wants to be there for them, and does not want to "miss out on this time in their lives." However, she has found that being a full-time stay-at-home parent has not been as rewarding as she thought it would be. She misses her professional life as a PTA, and her dream of returning to school has continued. However, she reports that she feels pressure to stay home with the children.

Her husband has indicated that having a second income would be beneficial if Julia were to return to her job as a PTA, but she states he is not particularly supportive of her returning to school. Julia knows that if she were to return to work or school it would be an adjustment for both her and her husband in terms of renegotiating parenting and household labor roles. Additionally, both her parents and her husband's parents have questioned the wisdom of Julia returning to work, let alone school, until both children are in school for full days. However, they have stated that if she were to do so, they would be available to help with childcare because they do not want their grandchildren "raised by strangers." Julia feels shame about this idea, and is not sure how she would manage all of her roles and responsibilities at the level she thinks she should if she were to return to work or follow her dream of obtaining her DPT.

Career Barriers for Women

In a study with working professionals, Mate and Ryan (2015) found women, more than men, referred to overcoming barriers and building resilience, and they suggested that "women may require greater resilience than men over their careers" (p. 157). Women can encounter numerous barriers and obstacles in their career lives and providing a full literature review of those barriers is beyond the scope of this chapter. Instead, the authors have attempted to provide some recent studies as an overview of issues that are relatable to Julia's situation.

Julia's identity as a mother is obviously an issue in terms of her career and educational decisions. Career barriers present themselves for women with children since, typically, women are expected to be the primary childcare provider. Oh (2018) found in interviewing mothers in South Korea that while those who sought support for child care received it, they had to construct "a legitimate reason" (p. 494). According to Oh, this "deservingness" points to how maternal employment is negatively viewed, and thus mothers must make justifications for working. These mothers, overall, did not believe that they had an innate entitlement to work and receive support with childcare, and their interactions with husbands, parents, and parents-in-law were influential in the process of whether the mother determined her work was worthy of the support. Julia may think her career and educational goals are not worthy of the support she will need with parenting. Furthermore, it appears her husband, parents, and parents-in-law are influencing her thoughts and feelings.

While the South Korean mothers in the aforementioned study utilized their children's grandmothers for childcare, this is not an option for many mothers. Thus, the need to secure a job that allows for *caring security*, which "signifies the outcome of job conditions that assure continuity of safe and predictable care arrangements, including regular and smooth daily transfers of responsibility between parents and alternative care providers" (Carney & Junor, 2014, p. 466) can present another career obstacle for women. In fact, Carney and Junor (2014) found in their study using data from the Household, Income and Labour Dynamics of Australia (HILDA) survey (2001–2005) that there tended to be greater concentrations of mothers in occupations that allowed for a combination of both caring and career security.

Julia's family indicated they will provide childcare support, but they have done so in a way that has reinforced the idea that Julia is not a good mother if she obtains childcare outside of the family. Furthermore, it appears that Julia is expected to be the primary coordinator of childcare. Thus, options that provide the greatest opportunity for caring security may influence her decision to return to work or school.

Gender stereotypes and occupational segregation abound in the world of work and likely serve as gatekeepers to multiple opportunities, such as the STEM fields of computer science and engineering (Cheryan, Master, & Meltzoff, 2015). Gender stereotypes are not limited to the STEM fields, but are also evident in liberal arts. Buhr and Sideras (2015) found that students in International Relations courses tended to provide predictable gender-stereotyped lists of subfields in which they thought males or females would be more interested (e.g., human rights = female; military policy = male). However, their own interests did not necessarily follow their gender assumptions. The United Nations (2015) asserted that "occupational segregation of women and men continues to be deeply embedded in all [world] regions" (p. 87). Stereotypes also likely hold women back in their career progression with women being underrepresented in advanced degree programs, especially in science-related fields where women only constitute 30% of researchers worldwide (United Nations, 2015), and in senior level management positions where they comprised only 24% of senior roles worldwide in 2018 (Grant Thornton International Ltd., 2018, March).

Julia has long had a desire to return to school and obtain an advanced degree in the healthcare field. She has even had thoughts of becoming a professor at a university where she could not only teach others to become physical therapists, but where her research efforts could advance the field. It is possible that some of the pressures she is facing at home, and from society-at-large, are gender stereotypes regarding what she is supposed to be as a mother, especially a Latina mother. These stereotypes may have been at play when Julia made her original educational and career choices to become a physical therapy assistant (which typically requires a two-year associate's degree in the United States).

Equal pay for equal work also continues to be an obstacle facing women. For example, while occupations in the science, technology, engineering, and math (STEM) fields provide potentially higher-paying jobs, women continue to be underrepresented, constituting only 24% of those employed in STEM occupations in the United States in 2015 (Noonan, 2017, November). Furthermore, Noonan (2017, November) reported that while women in STEM jobs tend to earn 35% more than women in non-STEM jobs, and that the gender wage gap is smaller in STEM versus non-STEM jobs, the wage gap is still at 16%, meaning that for every dollar a man earns, a woman earns 84 cents. This gender pay gap extends beyond the United States with the United Kingdom and other mainland European countries reporting wage gaps averaging around 20% (Fleming, 2018).

While her husband is supportive of Julia's return to work, her overall pay as a physical therapy assistant is less than what she would earn if she obtained her DPT and became a physical therapist or a professor for a physical therapy program. Additionally, should Julia become a physical therapist, she would find that while the gender wage gap is smaller in this STEM field, according to statistics from the United States Census Bureau (2016) she would still possibly earn only 87.6% of what men earn as a physical therapist. Furthermore, given that Julia is Latina, it is reasonable to surmise she would earn even less given that Hispanic and Latina women average 62.1% of what White men earn overall (Bureau of Labor Statistics, 2019).

Another barrier for women's career-lives is overcoming gender-based work requests that can put them at a disadvantage in their careers. O'Meara, Kuvaeva, Nyunt, Waugaman, and Jackson (2017) found that male faculty at a set of 13 large research universities in the United States spent more than twice as much time on research than did women, whereas women spent more time than men on campus service, student advising, and teaching-related activities. These women faculty members also received more work requests overall, and for areas not related to research. Similarly, Pifer (2018) discovered that women faculty were connected with more for teaching-related purposes than for research purposes. Furthermore, El-Alayli, Hansen-Brown, and Ceynar (2018) found that female professors reported more requests from students for standard work demands such as office hour time, as well as for special favors such as being allowed to re-do an assignment, than did male professors. Should Julia realize her goal of becoming a professor at a university, these are potential obstacles to her future career and she would likely need good mentorship and strong allies to support her along her journey.

Fortunately, women have demonstrated adaptability in overcoming obstacles, as well as turning challenges into opportunities. McMahon, Watson, and Bimrose (2012) found evidence of career adaptability during transition periods as well as other aspects of their careers in women 45–65 years old from Australia, England, and South Africa. Similarly, Whiston, Feldwisch, Evans, Blackman, and Gilman (2015) reported that professional women over the age of 50 in the United States described themes regarding career adaptability within their current and future projected career-related tasks, transitions, and traumas. Additionally, Marine and Martínez Alemán (2018) found themes that suggested that women faculty from their study who had achieved tenure in higher education found it to be liberating and subsequently, "an opportunity to challenge traditional gender norms and discourse in the academy" (p. 229).

Feminist Counselling and Intersectionality

The complexity, diversity, and variations of feminist counselling are far beyond the scope of this chapter. Feminist counselling is not tied to a specific theoretical approach, nor a set of techniques, but it does have feminism at its foundation which "provides an umbrella framework, or a set of values for evaluating and orienting practice" (Enns, 2004, p. 8). Feminism seeks to end "all forms of domination, oppression, and privilege that intersect with sexism and gender bias, including (but not limited to) racism, classism, colonialism, heterosexism, ethnocentrism, white supremacy, ageism, and ableism" (Enns, 2004, p. 8). We, the authors of this chapter, assert that in defining feminism in this manner, multicultural career counselling competence is critical and brings intersectionality to the fore.

Intersectionality

To be multiculturally competent, career counsellors must look at all aspects which define their clients' experiences. Various identities resulting from one's "gender, race, ethnicity, social class, sexual orientation, physical ability, and religion/spirituality do not exist in separation for individuals, rather, these features are inherently intertwined" (Yakushko, Davidson, & Williams, 2009, p. 180). Since these features interconnect, it is critical to understand that one cannot extract gender from other components of one's identity, and that oppression and discrimination inextricably connect to this dynamic web. Intersectionality theory was first described by Kimberlé Crenshaw in 1989 and addressed primarily race and gender (specifically, Black women). Since then, intersectionality has grown to encompass more identities and is currently defined as "the complex, cumulative way in which the effects of multiple forms of discrimination (such as racism, sexism, and classism) combine, overlap, or intersect especially in the experiences of marginalized individuals or groups" (Merriam-Webster, n.d., para. 1). Thus, women who hold multiple minority identities have additional and more complex impediments they face which make it difficult to relate to dominant cultural norms, ideologies, and privileges, such as access to political power and material wealth (Yoon, 2016).

Further complicating matters is the understanding that an individual's self-concept is both a source of influence as well as acted upon by each of the ecological systems surrounding that individual (Yakushko et al., 2009). For example, career-related self-efficacy and outcome expectations are not only related to one's sense of identity as a scientist, as discovered in a study by Byars-Winston and Rogers (2019), but can also be shaped by privilege based on one's identity. More specifically, Thompson and Dahling (2012) found that gender and socioeconomic privilege predicted one's exposure to learning experiences, which subsequently helped shape self-efficacy and outcome expectations related to career. Additionally, Oh (2018) found that varying levels of education and socioeconomic status among South Korean women were related to differences regarding their *deservingness* to work. In other words, while all of the South Korean mother interviewees held commonalities of gender and motherhood, the kind of work and the status of their jobs contributed to whether they, and others, believed they deserved childcare support. According to Oh, results such as these reinforce the need for research to go beyond need and choice to explain how women of different SES backgrounds account for their work.

Each identity an individual holds is accompanied by varying levels of salience because people typically do not identify with all of their values equally and often are shaped by how various identities are oppressed or allowed to flourish (Yakushko et al., 2009). Additionally, individuals who identify more strongly with a particular group may perform behaviors that are consistent with the group's norm (Kelman, 2006), even if those norms may be inequitable. For example, after their study on tenured White women faculty over the age of 50 and born between 1946 and 1964, Marine and Martínez Alemán (2018) suggested that successful competition in the institution's reward system is determined by women faculty's adoption of the system's values, even those determined by feminist scholars to be inequitable. Furthermore, for those who hold an oppressed identity, the concern of fulfilling a negative stereotype of their racial or ethnic group (i.e., stereotype threat) may decrease the likelihood of them feeling that they fit in with a particular group (such as a professional group) (Ben-Zeev et al., 2017). Given that women who work within STEM fields already tend to be less likely than men to identify themselves as scientists (Williams & George-Jackson, 2014), the possibility of stereotype threat further influencing a culturally diverse woman to not identify with the scientific community is concerning. Indeed, Beasley and Fischer (2012) found that stereotype threat was a stronger predictor than academic preparation in terms of early departure of historically underrepresented students from STEM majors. Taken together, the results from these studies suggest that not only may it be more difficult for those from the non-majority group to identify with an occupational identity, but also, if they do, they may need to engage with group norms that continue systemic oppression.

In addition to salience of identities and group identification affecting women, the interaction of an individual's various identities within a range of ecological systems may influence one's identity to shift in order to adapt to various environments. These shifts occur since strengths in one culture may be seen as areas of deficit in other cultures (Grothaus, McAuliffe, & Craigen, 2012). Identity shifting, or identity negotiation (see Jackson, 2002; Shih, Young, & Bucher, 2013; Ting-Toomey, 2005), includes alterations to behaviors, such as changing one's speech or appearance, or suppressing certain behaviors or actions, to conform to norms within varying environments (Dickens & Chavez, 2018). It may be a conscious act (Dickens & Chavez, 2018; Jackson, 2002), or executed unconsciously and automatically, such as when changing one's thinking to better fit in with the dominant group (Jones & Shorter-Gooden, 2004). Identity shifting can be particularly present in Black women with Jones and Shorter-Gooden (2004) indicating that 58% of the women in their study reported changing their behaviors so they would be more accepted by White people. In their study on early-career college-educated Black women, Dickens and Chavez (2018) found themes in which the women worked to dismantle stereotypes and felt pressure to positively represent Black people in the workplace. These women wanted to make sure to separate themselves from prevailing stereotypes (Dickens & Chavez, 2018), which is reminiscent of the previously mentioned information regarding stereotype threat. Dickens and Chavez (2018) found that while there were benefits such as adaptability and relatability to peers, identity shifting also came with multiple costs and mixed feelings. Some of these women's sacrifices included distorted self-perception, especially as emerging professionals; removal of themselves from situations or remaining silent to avoid confrontation or future discrimination, thus opting for invisibility and assimilation to norms; and feelings of inauthenticity and perhaps betrayal of one's allegiance to the Black community.

Socio-political-historical context and the way it shapes the meaning of one's identities also demands attention when considering intersectionality. South African Indian women, in a study by Carrim and Nkomo (2016), had difficulties in overcoming the imposed passivity from both their Indian culture as well as the racialization processes of apartheid that had made up their early lives. Furthermore, similar to the

Black women in the study discussed in the previous paragraph, these women had to attend to cues from their White (and male) counterparts and assimilate to the workplace norms, while also experiencing discomfort and angst in not adhering to Indian cultural practices. Ultimately, these women "tried to construct hybrid identities [in their workplaces and their family/community spaces] that resisted the essentializing practices of each" (Carrim & Nkomo, 2016, p. 272).

Considerations regarding Julia. Julia has various intersecting identities, some of which provide her with points of privilege (e.g., cisgender and heterosexual), as well as points of oppression (e.g., ethnically diverse woman of color). It would be important for Julia's career counsellor to come alongside her to discover the salience of her varying identities within different aspects of her life. Together, Julia and her career counsellor can consider how the context she grew up in, and the one she currently lives in, has shaped who Julia is and how she interacts with the world. For instance, does Julia engage in identity shifting? How has she negotiated the worlds in which she lives, works, and plays?

Multiculturally responsive counsellors are also responsible for navigating their own biases and responses as well as respecting and engaging with Julia on how she, as the expert of her own story, views her situation and context in relation to her own culture. What does Julia consider to be points of oppression? How are those points of oppression exacerbated by her intersecting identities? Recognizing the unique characteristics of Julia in the context of her environment and within the constructs of her cultures, as well as how those are juxtaposed with her socio-political-historical context, is critical and will continue to be addressed in the following section regarding principles of feminist counselling.

Feminist Counselling

Feminist counselling seeks to raise consciousness surrounding social roles and systemic oppressive influences and link these societal influences to individuals' presenting issues (Popadiuk, 2015). According to Enns (2004), two primary themes categorize the varying assumptions held by feminist counsellors. The first is that the personal is political, which purports that personal problems are often related to the political and social climate in which the individual exists. The second theme is that individuals' problems or symptoms are not necessarily pathology, but instead are their means of coping and surviving in oppressive circumstances. The connection between individuals' inner selves and their outer worlds corroborate that the personal is political, and thus institutional changes must occur to match the personal changes that clients make (Enns, 2004). Whalen et al. (2004) recognized that while counselors can advocate with and for women and minorities, there are many environmental oppressors and it is a large task to combat each of them on a societal level since norms take time to adapt and modernize. They call for counsellors "to be concerned about arming people with effective skills to criticize and effect change in environments" (Whalen et al., 2004, p. 386); thus career counsellors may need to go beyond typical individual or small group counselling to engage in prevention, education, and advocacy work.

Along with the two primary themes of feminist counselling, Enns (2004) suggested there are core principles relating to the counselling relationship. Relationship principle one, according to Enns, purports that those aligning with feminist counselling do not believe that it is possible to practice values-free counselling. As such, she asserted that counsellors must clarify their values; understand how their values can affect clients; monitor themselves so they do not covertly influence clients; and actively seek to understand the worldviews, values, and experiences of diverse groups. Additionally, Whalen et al. (2004) called for counsellors to value clients' strengths with the understanding that strengths go beyond those traits historically valued in Western male culture such as autonomy, self-determination, and rationalism. Accordingly, career counsellors must broaden their lists of strengths to encompass "traits such as connectedness, intuition, expressiveness, and interdependence… traditionally associated with other cultural experiences" (Whalen et al., 2004, p. 380).

By focusing on client strengths, career counsellors "assume that the client is a capable, strong, healthy person who is currently experiencing a difficulty" (Whalen et al., 2004, p. 380); rather than pathologizing clients, they understand that clients are coping and surviving within the context of their world. This aligns with the second principle of feminist counselling in which counsellors believe that clients are competent and as such, their perspectives must be valued and affirmed, especially given that women's views of their own lives have historically been discounted by the mental health profession (Enns, 2004). Additionally, for far too long, culturally diverse individuals have had their "differences" equated with inferiority and pathology through the process of scientific racism and white supremacy (Sue & Sue, 2016). Counselors that focus on mental and physical health rather than pathology are said to value hygiology, and must challenge themselves to break out of their stereotypes and be inclusive of what optimal functioning may look like for other cultures and identities (Whalen et al., 2004). It is also critical that counsellors give heed to the importance of person-environment interactions by closely considering the multiple systems in which individuals live, with which they interact, and through which they are influenced. In understanding their clients' lens, counsellors can be better aware of environments and systems that reinforce stereotypes, perpetuate oppression, and shape various forms of interactions (Whalen et al., 2004).

By affirming clients as the expert on themselves, a more egalitarian relationship (relationship principle three) can be formed, but the feminist counsellor must be careful to not discount inherent power and role differences that exist in the counselling relationship (Enns, 2004). To mitigate this, Enns suggested that the feminist counsellor model to the client an awareness of power dynamics, as well as how to reduce power differentials and effectively navigate differing roles. Furthermore, in facilitating an egalitarian relationship, the counsellor must attend to the fourth principle guiding the feminist counselling relationship, which concerns the counselling contract and informed consent. Counselors that help clients understand their approach and why they make various choices facilitate a client-counsellor partnership (Enns, 2004). Clear goals allow for both counsellor and client to evaluate progress, and ongoing informed consent based in collaboration and information sharing can result in a greater likelihood of genuine autonomous consent (Brown, 1994; Enns, 2004). Ultimately, goals, processes, and outcomes of feminist counselling include valuing and affirming diversity; counselling for change, not adjustment; equality; balancing instrumental and relational strengths; helping clients find and use their own power; social change; and self-nurturance (Enns, 2004).

Considerations regarding Julia. In considering Julia, the feminist career counsellor with multicultural competencies would take the approach that Julia's issues are not the result of something being wrong with her, but instead, that her confusion and anxiety are in response to the oppressive systems and environments in which she lives. The career counsellor must gain additional insight into Julia's values and salient identities as well as her perspectives on her situation so as not to inadvertently make assumptions or impose the counsellor's values onto Julia. Juxtaposing these insights alongside the exploration of both overt and covert oppressive messaging she is receiving (and has received over her lifetime) could raise new understandings for Julia. Then, collaborating with Julia in an egalitarian relationship using culturally appropriate methods to facilitate the use of her strengths and resources can assist Julia in reclaiming her own power to move forward in the manner she deems most appropriate.

Career Construction Counselling with Women

From Matching to Managing to Meaning-Making

Vocational guidance, which involves matching people to jobs (albeit more complex than that), first dominated the field of career counselling and was followed by the paradigm of career education, which helps individuals develop attributes necessary to accomplish career developmental tasks and manage their career and life roles over the life span (Hartung, 2013; Savickas, 2012). While these two waves of career theories and interventions have guided the field of career counselling for much of its history, and continue to be important and useful, they are no longer enough (Savickas, 2013b). Today's world of rapid and constant change means that reference points that shape one's roles and routines, including those of one's work life, are fluid and uncertain, leaving individuals without frameworks of what would be considered a normal way of life (Guichard, 2015). In this era of liquid modernity (Bauman, 2007), the field of career development and counselling had to shift to keep up with societal demands that require individuals to find their own paths and ways of being that provide them with meaning.

> The intervention of [career] *counselling* [emphasis added] focuses clients' reflection on themes in their career story and then extends the themes into the future. It may recognize similarity, and it may promote readiness, yet counselling mainly uses reflexive process and

> thematic content to design a life. It is about uniqueness more than resemblance and emotion more than reasoning. (Savickas, 2013b, p. 653)

Traditional models of career development often lack consideration of sociocultural variables such as immigration status, impact of sex and racial discrimination, and educational barriers, which are critical to identities of women and minorities (Whalen et al., 2004). Additionally, societal values, customs, and norms provide implicit cues about appropriate and inappropriate career paths for women, thus creating a macro system that perpetuates stereotypes and myths about what it means to be a girl or woman at work (Cook, Heppner, & O'Brien, 2005). Furthermore, because "career education rests on a predictable trajectory of developmental tasks" and "relates to predictability, stability, and societal expectations" (Busacca & Rehfuss, 2017, p. 32), one cannot assume that career education is of equal value for all people since this so-called predictable trajectory is often more relevant to those with privilege. The shift towards career counselling to find uniqueness versus similarities may be especially useful for women as it honors their unique strengths and experiences rather than continually comparing them to a White male majority standard (Peila-Shuster, 2017).

Career Construction Counselling

Identity is not a stable entity, but instead involves how individuals think of the self in relation to their social roles (Savickas, 2012) and is a "fluid developmental resource that updates in context" (Pouyaud, 2015, p. 63). Savickas (2012) further noted that identity imposes meaning on vocational behavior and work activities. Similarly, Gibson (2004) suggested "each of us is unavoidably always in the process of choosing who to become in terms of the projects through which we bring an identity into being" (p. 179). These projects are elucidated through career construction counselling, which utilizes micronarratives to construct one's macro narrative (Savickas, 2013a). Narrative approaches to career counselling, such as career construction, assists clients to move away from thinking about themselves and their decisions in terms of roles or occupations and instead helps clients to understand themselves through a lens of meaning (Gibson, 2004). According to Yoon (2016), storytelling describes how individuals see the world and their various identities, and it uses specific language that resonates with them. Moreover, narrative approaches have similar processes and goals as feminist counselling in that they work towards helping clients attend to, deconstruct, and confront limiting cultural messages (Enns, 2017).

The process of career construction counselling involves the activities of construction, deconstruction, reconstruction, coconstruction, and action (Savickas, 2013a). [For step-by-step instructions regarding how to conduct the Career Construction Interview and reconstruct the client's responses into a macro narrative, please see the *Life Design Counselling Manual* by Savickas (2015).] In the construction phase, the career counsellor utilizes the Career Construction Interview (CCI) to elicit small stories (micronarratives) from clients that reveal how they have constructed their "self, identity, and career" (Savickas, 2013a, p. 168). Telling stories and expressing one's narrative reflects individual and social dynamics and can either constrain or expand the parameters through which an individual thinks (Yoon, 2016). Thus, during the CCI (and throughout the entire career counselling process), career counsellors should listen for, and work with the client to deconstruct discouraging and demoralizing ideas, beliefs, scripts, or incidents that often involve bias, oppression, and discrimination (Savickas, 2012, 2013a).

Gibson (2004) brought up an important point that there may be competing narratives regarding an individual's story. However, he went on to state that rather than determining the "right" interpretation, it is more important to consider the lens through which the story is viewed. This is where the deconstruction process of career construction counselling can be useful. By bringing unjust cultural and societal messages to conscious light and deconstructing them, women have the opportunity to choose the way in which they view their micronarratives, and thus how they reconstruct their macro narrative. Additionally, the CCI utilized in career construction counselling provides a sound structure to elicit stories and reconstruct them into a larger macro narrative, and it allows for greater assurance that the client remains the expert and the interpreter of their life, not the counsellor (Savickas, 2015).

It is important to keep in mind that while storytelling can be transformative, it also can be harmful if it serves to perpetuate dominant beliefs, assumptions, values, and emotions (Yoon, 2016). Thus, it is critical for career counsellors to move beyond the single storyline of a stereotype as they work with clients. To help with this, one must conduct the deconstruction process with the utmost care in following feminist and multicultural counselling practices such as honoring differing values and worldviews; not pathologizing client experiences, perspectives, or feelings; and valuing the client's characterization of optimal functioning.

Upon completing the interview, the career counsellor goes through the micronarratives elicited from the client to identify overarching themes by pulling together the client's own words and stories while taking the utmost care not to interpret. By identifying these overarching themes, the career counsellor is able to reconstruct a subjective macro narrative, or life portrait, regarding the client's identity (Savickas, 2012, 2013a) which "explains clients' past, orients them to the present, and guides them into the future" (Savickas, 2012, p. 16). Furthermore, the macro narrative highlights the client's career themes and how one has used, or can use, work as a way to shift from "preoccupation" to "occupation" as a way to become more whole (Savickas, 2012, 2013a). Additionally, as Maree (2013) so eloquently stated, it can facilitate client movement from "pain-filled to triumph-filled themes" (p. 4) and towards social contribution. Upon sharing the life portrait with the client, the career counsellor is attentive to the client's reactions and encourages further reflection and emotional engagement with the macro narrative as part of the coconstruction process (Savickas, 2012, 2013a). Together, the client and career counsellor modify the life portrait as appropriate and "craft a move in meaning with which to confront choices" (Savickas, 2012, p. 17). With this movement in meaning, action must ensue so that personal insights and intention translate into behaviors, which then can advance further self-creation and career constructing (Savickas, 2012, 2013a).

As suggested earlier, the reconstruction and coconstruction processes of career construction counselling can continue to involve deconstruction of limiting beliefs and oppressive messaging. The meaning making that can occur for the client through this reflexive process can lead to greater awareness of how stereotypes, oppression, and discrimination have affected life-career choices and circumstances. Clients can also begin to see how their methods of making meaning, coping, and surviving in oppressive circumstances can draw on their strengths to help them move forward into their future life design, hopefully with a broader and more hopeful perspective. Furthermore, this movement forward may include social contribution (Maree, 2013) in ways that include advocacy for social action and change, a goal of feminist counselling (Enns, 2004).

Career construction with Julia. Because Julia is a fictitious composite from a variety of clients, it would not be appropriate to fabricate her answers to the CCI. Thus, the authors have instead brought up points for readers to consider, especially concerning the deconstruction and coconstruction processes. For more thorough coverage of the questions in the CCI, and case samples, readers are referred to Maree (2014, 2016), Savickas (2013a, 2015), and Savickas and Lara (2016).

Tensions are likely to come up through Julia's early recollections and possibly her childhood role models. There may be themes indicating that Julia feels pulled between intersecting identities and conflicting values. What emotions come up for Julia as she describes her early recollections? How would others in her environment receive these emotions? What messages did she receive from others about her early childhood role models? Are there dynamic tensions between her role models? For example, she may have a role model that exhibits feminine qualities, but another role model that exhibits qualities more often attributed to men.

In considering Julia's favorite story as her script for moving forward, the career counsellor can pay attention to what that means to Julia based on her various identities and the potential barriers she will encounter. For example, Julia has already discussed issues surrounding motherhood, thus it may be useful to work with Julia to deconstruct the intensive motherhood ideology. This ideology requires the mother to be the central caregiver and devote copious amounts of time, energy, and material resources to her child (Hays, 1996). Additionally, Thompson and Dahling (2012) recommended exploration of experiences with resources and barriers that influence women's perceptions of the accessibility of various career options.

During the CCI, the feminist career counsellor is careful to attend to beliefs, feelings, and experiences that are possible indicators of oppression and when appropriate, explore those with the client. A strength of using narrative career counselling is that stressors individuals feel upon stepping outside of their cultural, familial, or societal expectations for a career can be identified and explored (Phipps, 2016). These tensions can provide fertile ground in raising new insights for Julia regarding social roles and systemic oppressive influences in her life. Ideally, she can see herself not as the problem, but instead as a strong woman who as coped with and survived oppressive circumstances. Julia can then use her story to reclaim her power and construct her life-career.

It is important to note that the feminist career counsellor must take care during this process not to impose any values onto Julia or try to be the expert. Instead, the career counsellor works to create space that acknowledges Julia as the expert and author of her own story. Taking back the power of their own identities can assist women in not feeling forced to adapt their identities to match that of societal norms regarding what a woman "should" be (Yakushko et al., 2009).

Conclusion

Utilizing career construction counselling through a feminist counselling lens can assist career counsellors in intentionally attending to personal, cultural, contextual, historical, and socio-political forces at work in women's lives. Feminist career counsellors can listen for messages regarding stereotypes, bias, discrimination, and oppression that impose barriers to individuals' journeys towards who they are becoming. This can be especially useful in career counselling women to raise their consciousness regarding how the personal is political and that some of their presenting issues may be coping mechanisms for dealing with oppression. In raising their critical consciousness (Freire, 1970), these women may reclaim their power, and in doing so, they can choose to actively master that which they have passively suffered.

References

Bauman, Z. (2007). *Liquid times: Living in an age of uncertainty*. Cambridge, United Kingdom: Polity Press.

Beasley, M. A., & Fischer, M. J. (2012). Why they leave: The impact of stereotype threat on the attrition of women and minorities from science, math and engineering majors. *Social Psychology of Education, 15,* 427–448. https://doi.org/10.1007/s11218-012-9185-3.

Ben-Zeev, A., Paluy, Y., Milless, K. L., Goldstein, E. J., Wallace, L., Márquez-Magaña, L., … Estrada, M. (2017). 'Speaking truth' protects underrepresented minorities' intellectual performance and safety in STEM. *Education Sciences, 65*, 65. https://doi.org/10.3390/educsci7020065.

Brown, L. S. (1994). *Subversive dialogues: Theory in feminist therapy*. New York, NY: Basic Books.

Buhr, R. L., & Sideras, N. (2015). Finding the invisible women: Gender stereotypes versus student interest in foreign policy and security subfields. *PS: Political Science & Politics, 48*, 473—477. https://doi.org/10.1017/s104909651500027x.

Bureau of Labor Statistics. (2019). Table 37: Median weekly earnings of full-time wage and salary workers by selected characteristics. *Labor Force Statistics from Current Population Survey*. Retrieved from https://www.bls.gov/cps/cpsaat37.htm.

Busacca, L. A., & Rehfuss, M. C. (2017). *Postmodern career counseling: A handbook of culture, context, and cases*. Alexandria, VA: American Counseling Association.

Byars-Winston, A., & Rogers, J. G. (2019). Testing intersectionality of race/ethnicity × gender in a social–cognitive career theory model with science identity. *Journal of Counseling Psychology, 66,* 30–44. https://doi.org/10.1037/cou0000309.

Carney, T., & Junor, A. (2014). How do occupational norms shape mothers' career and caring options? *Journal of Industrial Relations, 56,* 465–487. https://doi.org/10.1177/0022185614538442.

Carrim, N. M. H., & Nkomo, S. M. (2016). Wedding intersectionality theory and identity work in organizations: South African Indian women negotiating managerial identity. *Gender, Work and Organization, 23,* 262–277. https://doi.org/10.1111/gwao.12121.

Cheryan, S., Master, A., & Meltzoff, A. N. (2015). Cultural stereotypes as gatekeepers: Increasing girls' interest in computer science and engineering by diversifying stereotypes. *Frontiers in Psychology, 6*, Art. #49. https://doi.org/10.3389/fpsyg.2015.00049.

Cook, E. P., Heppner, M. J., & O'Brien, K. M. (2005). Multicultural and gender influences in women's career development: An ecological perspective. *Journal of Multicultural Counseling and Development, 33,* 165–189.

Crenshaw, K. (1989). Demarginalizing the intersection of race and sex: A black feminist critique of antidiscrimination doctrine, feminist theory and antiracist politics. *University of Chicago Legal Forum, 1989*(1), Article 8. Retrieved from https://chicagounbound.uchicago.edu/uclf/vol1989/iss1/8.

Dickens, D., & Chavez, E. (2018). Navigating the workplace: The costs and benefits of shifting identities at work among early career U.S. Black women. *Sex Roles, 78,* 760–774. https://doi.org/10.1007/s11199-017-0844-x.

El-Alayli, A., Hansen-Brown, A. A., & Ceynar, M. (2018). Dancing backwards in high heels: Female professors experience more work demands and special favor requests, particularly from academically entitled students. *Sex Roles, 79,* 136–150. https://doi.org/10.1007/s11199-017-0872-6.

Enns, C. Z. (2004). *Feminist theories and feminist psychotherapies: Origins, themes, and diversity*. New York, NY: Haworth.

Enns, C. Z. (2017). Contemporary adaptations of traditional approaches to counseling women. In M. Kopala & M. Keitel (Eds.), *Handbook of counseling women* (2nd ed., pp. 51–62). Thousand Oaks, CA: Sage.

Fleming, N. (2018, March). How the gender pay gap permeates science and engineering. *NewScientist*. Retrieved from https://jobs.newscientist.com/article/how-the-gender-pay-gap-permeates-science-and-engineering.

Freire, P. (1970). *Pedagogy of the oppressed*. New York, NY: Continuum.

Gibson, P. (2004). Where to from here? A narrative approach to career counseling. *Career Development International, 9,* 176–189. https://doi.org/10.1108/13620430410526201.

Grant Thornton International Ltd. (2018, March). *Women in business: beyond policy to progress*. Retrieved from https://www.grantthornton.global/globalassets/1.-member-firms/global/insights/women-in-business/grant-thornton-women-in-business-2018-report.pdf.

Grothaus, T. I. M., McAuliffe, G., & Craigen, L. (2012). Infusing cultural competence and advocacy into strength-based counseling. *The Journal of Humanistic Counseling, 51,* 51–65. https://doi.org/10.1002/j.2161-1939.2012.00005.x.

Guichard, J. (2015). From vocational guidance and career counseling to life design dialogues. In L. Nota & J. Rossier (Eds.), *Handbook of life design: From practice to theory and from theory to practice* (pp. 11–25). Boston, MA: Hogrefe.

Hartung, P. J. (2013). Career as story: Making the narrative turn. In W. B. Walsh, M. L. Savickas & P. J. Hartung (Eds.), *Handbook of vocational psychology* (4th ed., pp. 33–52). New York, NY: Routledge.

Hays, S. (1996). *The cultural contradictions of motherhood*. New Haven, CT: Yale University Press.

Jackson, R. L. (2002). Cultural contracts theory: Toward an understanding of identity negotiation. *Communication Quarterly, 50*(3–4), 359–367. https://doi.org/10.1080/01463370209385672.

Jones, C., & Shorter-Gooden, K. (2004). *Shifting: The double lives of Black women in America*. New York, NY: HarperCollins.

Kelman, H. C. (2006). Interests, relationships, identities: Three central issues for individuals and groups in negotiating their social environment. *Annual Review of Psychology, 57,* 1–26. https://doi.org/10.1146/annurev.psych.57.102904.190156.

Maree, J. G. (2013). *Counselling for career construction—Connecting life themes to construct life portraits: Turning pain into hope*. Rotterdam, The Netherlands: Sense.
Maree, J. G. (2014). Career construction with a Gay client: A case study. *British Journal of Guidance and Counselling, 42,* 436–449. https://doi.org/10.1080/03069885.2014.886670.
Maree, J. G. (2016). Career construction counseling with a mid-career Black man. *The Career Development Quarterly, 64,* 20–34. https://doi.org/10.1002/cdq.12038.
Marine, S. B., & Martínez Alemán, A. M. (2018). Women faculty, professional identity, and generational disposition. *The Review of Higher Education, 41,* 217–252. https://doi.org/10.1353/rhe.2018.0002.
Mate, S., & Ryan, M. (2015). Learning through work: How can a narrative approach to evaluation build students' capacity for resilience? *Asia-Pacific Journal of Cooperative Education [Special Issue], 16,* 153–161.
McKinsey Global Institute. (2015). *The power of parity: How advancing women's equality can add $12 trillion to global growth*. Retrieved from https://www.mckinsey.com/featured-insights/employment-and-growth/how-advancing-womens-equality-can-add-12-trillion-to-global-growth.
McMahon, M., Watson, M., & Bimrose, J. (2012). Career adaptability: A qualitative understanding from the stories of older women. *Journal of Vocational Behavior, 80,* 762–768. https://doi.org/10.1016/j.jvb.2012.01.016.
Merriam-Webster. (n.d.). *Intersectionality*. Retrieved from https://www.merriam-webster.com/dictionary/intersectionality#h1.
Noonan, R. (2017, November). *Women in STEM: 2017 update (ESA Issue Brief #06-17)* Retrieved from Economics and Statistics Administration, U.S. Department of Commerce: https://www.esa.gov/reports/women-stem-2017-update.
O'Meara, K., Kuvaeva, A., Nyunt, G., Waugaman, C., & Jackson, R. (2017). Asked more often: Gender differences in faculty workload in research universities and the work interactions that shape them. *American Educational Research Journal, 54,* 1154–1186. https://doi.org/10.3102/0002831217716767.
Oh, E. (2018). Who deserves to work? How women develop expectations of child care support in Korea. *Gender & Society, 32,* 493–515. https://doi.org/10.1177/0891243218772495.
Ortiz-Ospina, E., & Tzvetkova, S. (2017). *Working women: Key facts and trends in female labor force participation*. Retrieved from https://ourworldindata.org/female-labor-force-participation-key-facts.
Peila-Shuster, J. J. (2017). Women's career construction: Promoting employability through career adaptability and resilience. In K. Maree (Ed.), *Psychology of career adaptability, employability, and resilience* (pp. 283–297). Cham, Switzerland: Springer International.
Phipps, R. (2016). Culturally diverse women. In W. K. Killam, S. Degges-White, & R. Michel (Eds.), *Career counseling interventions: Practice with diverse clients* (pp. 129–145). New York, NY: Springer.
Pifer, M. J. (2018). His, hers, and ours: Gendered roles and resources in academic departments. *NASPA Journal About Women in Higher Education, 11,* 109–129. https://doi.org/10.1080/19407882.2018.1423573.
Popadiuk, N. E. (2015). Counseling women: Feminist perspective and contextual action theory. In R. A. Young, J. F. Domene, & L. Valach (Eds.), *Counseling and action: Toward life-enhancing work, relationships, and identity* (pp. 285–294). New York, NY: Springer.
Pouyaud, J. (2015). Vocational trajectories and people's multiple identities: A life design. In L. Nota & J. Rossier (Eds.), *Handbook of life design: From practice to theory and from theory to practice* (pp. 59–74). Boston, MA: Hofgrefe.
Savickas, M. L. (2012). Life design: A paradigm for career intervention in the 21st century. *Journal of Counseling and Development, 90,* 13–19. https://doi.org/10.1111/j.1556-6676.2012.00002.x.
Savickas, M. L. (2013a). Career construction theory and practice. In S. D. Brown & R. W. Lent (Eds.), *Career development and counseling: Putting theory and research to work* (2nd ed., pp. 147–183). Hoboken, NJ: Wiley.

Savickas, M. L. (2013b). The 2012 Leona Tyler Award address: Constructing careers-actors, agents, and authors. *Counseling Psychologist, 41,* 648–662. https://doi.org/10.1177/0011000012468339.

Savickas, M. L. (2015). *Life-design counseling manual*. Author: Publisher.

Savickas, S., & Lara, T. (2016). Lee Richmond: A life designed to take the counseling profession to new places. *The Career Development Quarterly, 64,* 75–82. https://doi.org/10.1002/cdq.12042.

Shih, M., Young, M. J., & Bucher, A. (2013). Working to reduce the effects of discrimination: Identity management strategies in organizations. *American Psychologist, 68,* 145–157. https://doi.org/10.1037/a0032250.

Sue, D. W., & Sue, D. (2016). *Counseling the culturally diverse: Theory and practice* (7th ed.). Hoboken, NJ: Wiley.

The World Bank. (2017). Ratio of female to male labor force participation rate (%) (modeled ILO estimate). Retrieved from https://data.worldbank.org/indicator/SL.TLF.CACT.FM.ZS.

Thompson, M. N., & Dahling, J. J. (2012). Perceived social status and learning experiences in social cognitive career theory. *Journal of Vocational Behavior, 80,* 351–361. https://doi.org/10.1016/j.jvb.2011.10.001.

Ting-Toomey, S. (2005). The matrix of face: An updated face-negotiation theory. In W. B. Gudykunsy (Ed.), *Theorizing about intercultural communication* (pp. 71–92). Thousand Oaks, CA: Sage.

U. S. Census Bureau. (2016). *Full-time, year-round workers and median earnings in the past 12 months by sex and detailed occupation: 2016*. Retrieved from https://www.census.gov/data/tables/time-series/demo/industry-occupation/median-earnings.html.

United Nations. (2015). *The world's women 2015: Trends and statistics*. New York, NY: United Nations, Department of Economic and Social Affairs, Statistics Division.

Whalen, M., Fowler-Lese, K. P., Barber, J. S., Williams, E. N., Judge, A. B., Nilsson, J. E., & Shibazaki, K. (2004). Counseling practice with feminist-multicultural perspectives. *Journal of Multicultural Counseling and Development, 32*, 379–389.

Whiston, S. C., Feldwisch, K. M., Evans, K. M., Blackman, C. S., & Gilman, L. (2015). Older professional women's views on work: A qualitative analysis. *The Career Development Quarterly, 63,* 98–112. https://doi.org/10.1002/cdq.12007.

WIEGO. (n.d.). *Women's economic empowerment*. Retrieved from http://www.wiego.org/wee.

Williams, M. M., & George-Jackson, C. (2014). Using and doing science: Gender, self-efficacy, and science identity of undergraduate students in STEM. *Journal of Women and Minorities in Science and Engineering, 20*, 99–126. https://doi.org/10.1615/jwomenminorscieneng.2014004477.

World Economic Forum. (2017). *The global gender gap report 2017*. Retrieved from https://www.weforum.org/reports/the-global-gender-gap-report-2017.

Yakushko, O., Davidson, M. M., & Williams, E. N. (2009). Identity salience model: A paradigm for integrating multiple identities in clinical practice. *Psychotherapy: Theory, Research, Practice Training, 46,* 180–192. https://doi.org/10.1037/a0016080.

Yoon, I. H. (2016). Trading stories: Middle-class white women teachers and the creation of collective narratives about students and families in a diverse elementary school. *Teachers College Record, 118*(2). Retrieved from http://www.tcrecord.org/Content.asp?ContentId=18232.

Innovating Career Counselling for Middle-Aged and Older Adults

Rachel S. Rauvola, Cort W. Rudolph and Hannes Zacher

Abstract In this chapter, we take a broad perspective in reviewing theory, empirical research, and practice applications on career counselling for middle-aged (i.e., approximately 40–60 years) and older adults (i.e., older than 60 years). To begin, we outline some of the key perspectives on career counselling and development across the lifespan, including career theories by Super (e.g., life-span life-space theory, developmental self-concept), Slocum (e.g., career plateau dynamics), and Savickas (e.g., career adaptability). After this theoretical overview, we provide a review of the literature on career development intervention strategies and programs for middle-aged and older adults. The focus here is on both individual and group-based career counselling strategies that are methodologically sound, and have bearing on middle-aged and older adult employee career issues in particular. To this point, the majority of these strategies and programs discussed are targeted toward improving employability across the lifespan, as well as supporting career transitions of particular applicability to older workers (e.g., retirement, workforce reentry). We then distill the findings from this review into a series of recommendations for future research and practice in career counselling and development interventions, which will ultimately support and sustain workers across the breadth of their careers and lives.

Keywords Mid-career · Late career · Aging workforce · Older workers · Career transitions · Retirement

As the population ages, so, too, does the workforce; as the nature of work becomes increasingly complex, so, too, does the need for innovative career interventions. In order to sustain careers, organizations, and global economies, it is imperative

---

Chapter 14 prepared for the book, *Innovating Career Counselling Theory, Research, and Practice: In Search of Promoting Inclusion and Sustainable Employment for All.*

R. S. Rauvola (✉) · C. W. Rudolph
Department of Psychology, Saint Louis University, Morrissey Hall 2753, St. Louis, MO 63108, USA
e-mail: shelly.rauvola@slu.edu

H. Zacher
Institute of Psychology, Leipzig University, Leipzig, Germany

J. G. Maree (ed.), *Handbook of Innovative Career Counselling*,
https://doi.org/10.1007/978-3-030-22799-9_18

that steps are taken to engage not only new entrants into the workforce but also middle-aged and older workers. These interventions are wide-ranging, including career stage-targeted counselling approaches; workforce retraining and adaptability programs; and knowledge sharing and mentoring. Unifying them, however, are the common goals of supporting the aging workforce and sustaining employment across the lifespan through age-inclusive organizational practices and policies.

The intersections between aging at work and career development interventions are nothing new (e.g., Robson, Hansson, Abalos, & Booth, 2006; Russell, 1991; Sterns & Miklos, 1995; Williams & Fox, 1995). Neither is the relevance of career counselling and development interventions for important work outcomes (e.g., mentoring and career satisfaction, Allen, Eby, Poteet, Lentz, & Lima, 2004) and for aging workers in particular (e.g., Cohen, 1991; Kooij, Jansen, Dikkers, & de Lange, 2010). The degree to which career development interventions for middle-aged and older adults, particularly contemporary and innovative interventions, are effective and worthwhile is underexplored, however. As such, this chapter synthesizes the literature on innovative career intervention approaches for middle-aged (i.e., 40–60 years old) and older adults (i.e., older than 60 years of age).

The first part of this chapter explores principles and concepts central to lifespan and life course approaches to the study of development and work. The second part discusses three lifespan-informed perspectives on careers (Super's (1980) life-span, life-space theory, Savickas' (1997) work on career adaptability, and Slocum, Cron, Hansen, & Rawlings's (1985) work on career plateaus (Slocum et al., 1985)) and their concepts relevant to mid-career and late-career individuals. The third part presents the results of a literature review on career development intervention strategies and programs for middle-aged and older adults, including individual and group-based strategies that are methodologically sound, career stage-relevant (i.e., mid-career, late career, and intracareer stages therein), and innovative. In the fourth part, we provide recommendations for research and practice in career counselling and development. We conclude with a brief recapitulation of the chapter in the fifth part.

Theoretical Perspectives on Career Counselling and Development Across the Lifespan

In order to ground our discussion of specific lifespan-informed theories relevant to career counselling and development, we first present an overview of the defining characteristics of lifespan and life course approaches to the study of development and work. Lifespan approaches view aging and development as dynamic, both continuous and discontinuous processes characterized by both gains and losses (e.g., Baltes, 1987). Rather than viewing development as relegated to early life and aging as a linear process of decline, lifespan theory presents these processes as lifelong as well as actively managed by individuals. Context also plays a role here, constraining and providing opportunities for goals and goal-related means (e.g., social resources), as well as generating a developmental "timeline" for socially expected behaviors and events (e.g., entry into the workforce, childbearing). A number of theories of lifespan development exist to account for such self-regulatory processes (e.g., dual-process model of assimilative and accommodative coping, Brandstädter & Renner, 1990; motivational theory of life-span development, Heckhausen, Wrosch, & Schulz, 2010; model of selection, optimization, and compensation, Baltes & Baltes, 1990; socioemotional selectivity theory, Carstensen, 1987, 1991) and are frequently applied to study work- and wellbeing-relevant outcomes. These theories have also been applied to specific developmental deadlines and transitions such as unemployment, retirement, and school-to-work transitions (e.g., Haase, Heckhausen, & Silbereisen, 2012; Körner, Reitzle, & Silbereisen, 2012; Kubicek, Korunka, Raymo, & Hoonakker, 2011).

This focus on transitions and contextualized "deadlines" is of primary importance in life course approaches to the study of development and work as well. Life course approaches, which have their roots in the field of sociology, account more for the historical embeddedness and socialization-based nature of development. Such approaches, including Salmela-Aro's (2009) "4-C" model of lifespan motivation and Elder's (1994, 1998) work on life course development, have been applied similarly to transitional life stages with a particular focus on work and non-work roles in context (e.g., Conger et al., 1990; Dietrich & Salmela-Aro, 2013; Elder & Clipp, 1989; Salmela-Aro, Nurmi, Saisto, & Halmesmäki, 2010).

Together, lifespan and life course perspectives are the basis for many predominant career theories, such as Super's (1957, 1980, 1990) life-span, life-space theory and Slocum and colleagues' work on career plateaus (Slocum et al., 1985; Slocum, Cron, & Yows, 1987; Stout, Slocum, & Cron, 1988). Indeed, the ties between the two theoretical traditions have been highlighted in recent lifespan and career literature (e.g., Nagy, Froidevaux, & Hirschi, 2019).

Theoretical concepts related to mid-career. Each of the three aforementioned theoretical perspectives has bearing on mid-career issues. First, undoubtedly the most ubiquitous career theory, Super's life-span, life-space theory presents an account of career trajectories across individuals' development. Super's work has taken on a number of different attributes along the way to its current form (e.g., the Life-Career Rainbow vs. the Archway model; Super, 1980, 1990; Super, Savickas, & Super, 1996). Over time, however, the fundamental propositions of Super's work remained much the same: that individuals occupy multiple roles over their lives, and that these roles and their surrounding environments exert different demands and hold different significance for individuals as they develop. In this way, Super's life-span, life-space theory shifts the focus of career theory and subsequent counselling or guidance programs onto the individual rather than the career to be chosen (Herr, 1997; Herr & Cramer, 1988). Importantly, Super uses the term *career* to refer to the "sequence of positions held during the course of a lifetime" in a particular life space (1980, p. 286). *Roles*, in contrast, refer more broadly to the positions in society that an individual occupies (e.g., spouse, parent, worker, retiree). Of most relevance to this chapter, an *occupational career* is a sequence of work-related positions held over the course of one's lifetime, and "worker" or "employee" is the primary role assumed in an occupational career.

As Super (1990) writes, his life-span, life-space approach to careers is not "integrated, comprehensive, and testable … but rather a 'segmental theory'", or a set of sub-theories joined together by learning concepts and career self-concept (p. 199). The foundational segments making up life-span, life-space theory comprise a number of career influences, ranging from fundamental environmental and personal attributes (i.e., geography, biography); external societal factors such as peers, the labor market, and family; and internal psychological factors such as personality, aptitudes, and values. These forces act upon individuals (and are acted upon by individuals) throughout developmental stages in constructing the self and various role self-concepts (e.g., role self-concepts associated with family, occupation, education, etc.). Super (1990) suggests that these components are joined together by learning, wherein individuals negotiate their interests amidst reactions to particular activities, ideas, and experiences. The idea of role self-concept is also integral to Super's work, and can be defined as a constellation of self-esteem, self-efficacy, and self-ascribed traits related to a given life role. Self-concept is produced by interactions between one's biopsychosocial composition and self- and other-feedback through learning experiences, and it is viewed as the ongoing product of development in different life areas (e.g., career development; Super, 1990). Super's theory is thus a theory of mutual interaction, negotiation, and adaptive coping across developmental life stages and roles.

There are five stages outlined by Super: growth, exploration, establishment, maintenance, and decline (later called "disengagement;" Super, 1990; Super et al., 1996). While (occupational) career stage will normatively correspond to particular ages (e.g., mid-career for middle-aged adults, late career for older adults), the stages outlined by Super occur multiple times over the course of one's career (i.e., intracareer stage cycles). The descriptions of each stage are thus vague approximations, as each individual is understood to experience decisions and transitions differently and thus reacts and adapts to circumstances uniquely (Super, 1980).

Importantly, these stages apply to each life role and associated self-concept; as such, an individual could be in the "exploration" stage of their civic role, while being in the "disengagement" stage of their career. While there may be a generally normative ordering of stage progressions within roles as one ages, such that more career exploration occurs at younger ages and more career disengagement occurs at older ages, these stages are entirely person-specific. Chronological age does not necessarily correspond to where one falls in these developmental stages in each life role. Moreover, these stages occur recurrently, or as Super refers to it, individuals "cycle" and "recycle" through these stages within particular roles such as their career (Super, 1980). For example, after maintenance of a particular vocational path for many years, and even the attainment of "career maturity" or "adaptation" relative to one's peers (i.e., stage-appropriate career decision-making capacity; Herr, 1997; Super & Knasel, 2007), an individual might experience a particular change in needs or values that prompt a new decision and re-entrance into career exploration. We bear the relevance of all five life stages in mind in our later discussion of innovative career counselling interventions, focusing on the career development tasks at each stage of greatest relevance to middle-aged and older adults.

Of most relevance to the midcareer stage, in the maintenance stage, commitment to and proficiency in one's career are sustained. These align with the developmental tasks of (up)holding, updating, and innovating. Thus, mid-career individuals are often concerned with retaining their occupational position and proficiencies, remaining current and up-to-date with respect to career field changes and advancements, and adapting so as to contribute innovatively in their roles (Cairo, Kritis, & Myers, 1996; Super, 1990). To this latter point, Savickas (1997) provides an important corollary to Super's life-span, life-space theory in the form of career construction and adaptability. Career construction theory is a developmentally-focused theory of vocational behavior that explains vocational choice and adjustment processes in terms of active individual engagement over the lifespan (i.e., in constructing one's career, adapting to internal and external changes, meaning-making; Savickas, 2005). As part of this theory, Savickas presents career adaptability as a replacement construct for career maturity, defining it as "the readiness to cope with the predictable tasks of preparing for and participating in the work role and with the unpredictable adjustments prompted by changes in work and working conditions" (1997, p. 254). Rather than focusing on the attainment of "maturity" as an end state, career construction and adaptability imply continued planfulness, exploration, anticipation of transitions, and decision-making in fitting the self with one's context. The study of career adaptability and adaptation outcomes has gained traction in recent years, and these constructs have been shown to relate to important work outcomes (e.g., job performance, work engagement; Rudolph, Lavigne, & Zacher, 2017; Rudolph, Lavigne, Katz, & Zacher, 2017).

Intersecting in many ways with the career stages offered by Super as well as the concept of adaptability elaborated upon by Savickas, the concept of career plateaus includes some of the scenarios in which individuals might reevaluate their career and decide on a new development plan, particularly in the mid-career stage. Although they were not the first to investigate this phenomenon, work by Slocum and colleagues furthers the theory surrounding when, why, and for whom career plateaus are most likely. In this literature, *career plateaus* can be sub-divided into hierarchical (or vertical, structural) and content (or horizontal) types. *Hierarchical career plateaus* refer to the point in an individual's career when "the likelihood of further hierarchical promotion is very low" (Slocum et al., 1985, p. 133). Plateauing does not necessarily bear a negative connotation, nor does it imply that an individual does not perform well enough to merit promotion; in fact, it is inevitable that some individuals plateau while others do not, given the structure of organizations and the limited promotion opportunities in them. Plateauing also entails a level of individual choice and self-selection out of promotion striving. When an individual decides to cease pursuing advancement within an organization, Slocum et al. (1987) refer to this as the process of personal plateauing: "although they may have the ability, they may have lost their desire to play the tournament mobility game" (p. 31; see also Ference, Stoner, & Warren, 1977). We consider both subjective (i.e., perceived) and objective (i.e., in terms of job level/status) hierarchical career plateaus simultaneously in this and later sections, although we acknowledge that their specific antecedents and outcomes may diverge (Tremblay & Roger, 1993). Additionally, as we adopt a lifespan perspective to careers herein, it important to consider the confluence of influences that may have bearing on individual career development. Indeed, past evidence supports the existence of interaction between the two types of plateaus (e.g., past objective career success and later subjective career success; Stumpf & Tymon, 2012).

We also note that while much of the literature is dedicated to investigating such hierarchical plateaus, content plateaus are also relevant to our discussion. *Content plateaus* entail mastery of job-relevant knowledge and skills, in the absence of forthcoming increases in responsibility or changes in job tasks. Thus, employees who experience content plateaus no longer feel challenged by their work tasks and responsibilities and have a low likelihood of content change (Allen, Russell, Poteet, & Dobbins, 1999; Hofstetter & Cohen, 2014). When content and hierarchical plateaus occur simultaneously, this is referred to as a *double plateau* (e.g., Allen et al., 1999; Xie, Lu, & Zhou, 2015). Given the similarity and overlap between content and hierarchical plateaus, we refer to them generally as "career plateaus" in the remainder of this section.

Much of the theory behind career plateauing suggests that plateaus are prompted by a variety of factors that are also part of Super's life-span, life-space theory. These include personal characteristics such as personality, motivation, needs, and self-perceptions; other-role demands from family, leisure, and other life spheres; and role (e.g., status) and organizational characteristics that promote maintaining stability and the status quo (Slocum et al., 1987). Each of these influences can promote plateauing through granting individuals a sense of purpose in their current role (e.g., "I need to stay in this role because I am needed and the only one who can do this job"), disincentivizing promotion seeking or acceptance (e.g., "Accepting a promotion would require relocating my family and that is not an option"), and/or creating a culture of reliability and constancy ("I'm content in my role and don't need anything to change"). As with Super's career stages, career plateauing can occur regardless of age, although research suggests that factors such as seniority, tenure, and organizational age-grading are often positively related to plateauing, and often starts to occur during mid-career stages (e.g., Allen et al., 1999; Lin, Chen, & Lai, 2018; Nicholson, 1993; Stout et al., 1988; Tremblay & Roger, 1993). To this point, plateaued employees, regardless of age, tend to engage in more continued maintenance, while non-plateaued employees engage in more exploration and establishment (Slocum et al., 1985).

Theoretical concepts related to late career. For those in later stages of their career, the theoretical concepts of most relevance to our discussion come from Super's work. Specifically, many late career individuals find themselves in the decline/disengagement stage of work, wherein time and resources devoted to a given career are slowly reduced and redirected, either to other areas of the life space (e.g., family, civic engagement) or to re-cycle through career development stages anew (e.g., return to an earlier stage in order to pursue a new career). The developmental tasks of decelerating (i.e., reducing engagement in work and work demands) and retirement planning are of most relevance at this stage. Specifically, individuals take steps to anticipate retirement in their jobs and personal lives, and they often pass responsibilities to other workers in their organization and/or become selective in taking on job activities (Cairo et al., 1996; Super, 1990). Plateauing occurs in later career stages as well and will thus be tended to in the intervention review.

Review of the Literature

In this section, we present the results of a literature review on career development intervention strategies and programs for middle-aged and older adults. Given space constraints, we focus on select contemporary interventions from the literature that display both innovation and methodological rigor, reporting on their main attributes and relevance to middle-aged and/or older employees. We organize these interventions according to relevant career stage(s) and discuss their central characteristics as they pertain to important career outcomes.

As noted above, the stages outlined by Super occur in "mini-cycles" across the lifespan; as such, the interventions we discuss are broadly relevant to individuals in mid- to late-career periods, but they are targeted at particular intracareer stages such as exploration and establishment that may occur within these periods. Thus, we discuss relevant interventions that are both age- (e.g., relevant to normative life stage considerations, workplace challenges) and stage-sensitive (e.g., relevant to particular career stage goals) that aim to improve work attitudes, behaviors, and wellbeing.

Mid-career. For employees in the middle of their career, a number of innovative counselling and development interventions are described in the literature. These employees, who are typically middle-aged (i.e., 40–60 years old), are presented with some distinct challenges at this point in their career. These challenges include, but are not limited to, changes in work motivation, attitudes, and priorities; career plateaus and feelings of stagnation; involuntary transitions and unemployment; and age discrimination combined with a lack of support for retraining (Eby & Buch, 1995; Kanfer & Ackerman, 2004; Yang, Johnson, & Niven, 2018). Although these challenges are not limited to mid-career individuals, the risks of self-blaming or diminished employability perceptions (i.e., "I'm too old to be a desirable employee") may be magnified among individuals who are farther along in their career (Stout et al., 1988). Fortunately, however, employee receptiveness and the potential to benefit from targeted career interventions may be magnified during the mid-career stage (Latack & Dozier, 1986). Indeed, if adequate support is provided to employees (i.e., in the form of development interventions and/or counselling), these factors can help produce a situation in which such transitions can be positive and growth-focused rather than negative and withdrawal-inducing (McCleese & Eby, 2006).

The interventions we identified in the literature that may be particularly useful to this end include retraining and adaptability interventions, as well as career counselling. We discuss each of these in turn as well as mention the considerations necessary for implementing such interventions (e.g., attunement to diverse populations, individual differences).

Retraining. A great deal of literature has been dedicated to studying the mechanisms and outcomes of mid-career *retraining*, the process of teaching individuals new and/or updated skills and knowledge that can facilitate their engagement in new job responsibilities or a new job altogether. We contend that retraining is relevant to mid-career individuals who are either seeking to maintain their current role proficiency (i.e., maintenance stage) through the developmental tasks of upholding and updating, or who are exploring new career or role opportunities following a career transition (i.e., exploration or establishment stages). Both approaches can help prevent hierarchical and/or content plateaus if they are of concern to an employee. Given the wide variety of conceivable retraining domains, interfaces, and topics across industries and job types, this section is devoted primarily to the literature on key attributes of retraining interventions that impact their effectiveness.

Although there are few solely retraining-focused interventions reported in the literature, retraining is noted by many as a key career development and work engagement strategy for mid-career employees (e.g., Avedon, 1996; De Vos, Dujardin, Gielens, & Meyers, 2016; Sterns & Dorsett, 1994). Despite this lack of empirical studies, there appears to be consensus about particular approaches and aspects of retraining programs that promote their effectiveness. Some interventions, as well as aggregated data across various industries and organizations, point toward these components. Much of this literature is dedicated to technology-relevant retraining, such as word processor use (Charness, Kelley, Bosman, & Mottram, 2001) and technology management (Wolf, London, Casey, & Pufahl, 1995). The former set of studies by Charness et al. (2001) had reasonable sample sizes ($N = 72$ for Study 1, $N = 48$ for Study 2) and employed a multi-day and multi-interface training program for a new word-processing application with an age-diverse sample. Among the variety of results reported, the most relevant to our discussion is the importance of prior experience on retraining effectiveness: compared to novices, older individuals with past experience using a word-processing application were able to offset (age-related) performance deficits on particular tasks (e.g., speed tasks). These results are attributed to knowledge transfer to occur in retraining as opposed to training contexts; this is to say that established knowledge, and even some motor skill experience, were able to facilitate the acquisition of new knowledge and skills in a related task environment (see also Singley & Anderson, 1989; see Sterns & Harrington, 2019; Wolfson, Cavanagh, & Kraiger, 2014 for age-focused reviews of other training considerations).

Leveraging skill and knowledge transfer in learning contexts, as well as existing experience and knowledge structures, is encouraged by others as key to the development, integration, and maintenance of sustainable work competencies (Daley, 1999; De Baets & Warmoes, 2012; De Vos et al., 2016). Whether or not past experience is in the same domain as the content of retraining, increasing opportunities for learning process or content transfer, as well as bolstering the perceived relevance and applicability of retraining for one's career, is of great importance (van der Heijden, 2002). Perceived transferability of knowledge and experience are key to adaptability as well (Brown, Bimrose, Barnes, & Hughes, 2012).

Wolf et al. (1995) investigated career experience as impactful for retraining effectiveness in a different form. The authors found experience, which they conceptualized as an index of age, number of past jobs, and career tenure, to be an important predictor of training behaviors (i.e., networking, career proactivity, and other reemployment-relevant behaviors) in a technology management retraining study with displaced engineers. This study ($N = 72$) found that the impact of past experience on training behaviors was contingent upon individuals' career motivation as well. For mid-career individuals (i.e., with medium levels of experience), higher motivation was related to lower levels of positive training behaviors; for late-career individuals (i.e., with high levels of experience), higher motivation was related to higher levels of positive training behaviors. Additionally, as Wolf et al. (1995) predicted, career experience was negatively associated with training outcomes (e.g., reemployment, salary adequacy) across the sample. The authors attribute these findings to individuals' entrenchment in particular career paths prior to entrance into the retraining program, suggesting that a combination of motivational and career-directive content (e.g., encouraging the exploration of novel career paths) are relevant in retraining interventions.

One way in which past experience likely impacts retraining intervention effectiveness is through increases in general and training-specific self-efficacy. These constructs have implications for the perceived expectancy (i.e., likelihood of success) of retraining participation and consequently impact choice to participate in training, motivation and engagement during training, and training outcomes (Maurer, Weiss, & Barbeite, 2003; Schmid, 2012; Sterns & Doverspike, 1988) Fittingly, self-efficacy is a core career transition variable in prevailing career assessment tools and models such as the Career Transitions Inventory (Heppner, Multon, & Johnston, 1994) alongside other factors such as motivation and perceived control. In light of the negative relationships of later career stage and age with general and training self-efficacy (e.g., Guthrie & Schwoerer, 1996; Rosen & Jerdee, 1990), considering self-efficacy (and related career transition variables) in retraining interventions for older workers is of particular importance. This is likely of greatest use for individuals re-entering exploration and establishment stages in their careers, as these individuals are often acquiring new skills and career knowledge rather than building upon existing career knowledge (i.e., which likely bolsters efficacy and control beliefs as well as motivation).

However, older workers' perceived need for retraining and the perceived utility of engaging in retraining can be quite low (e.g., Guthrie & Schwoerer, 1996; Larwood, Rodkin, & Judson, 2001; Schmid, 2012). This is likely due to the content, effort requirements, and expectancy associated with this training (Kanfer & Ackerman, 2004). Thus, use of continuous or regular training intervals to either update or expand employees' skills and knowledge may help lower barriers to training participation among middle-aged adults and recatalyze traditional "retraining" into a more innovative and adaptive approach suited for modern organizations (Hall & Mirvis, 1995; Larwood et al., 2001; Larwood, Ruben, Popoff, & Judson, 1997). Such an approach can also build a climate that is more supportive and facilitative of continued training and age-sensitive practices when combined with more informal resources such as perceived support (another key transition factor from the Career Transitions Inventory) and diversity in work tasks, roles, and teams (Luger, Anselmann, & Mulder, 2012). This also speaks to the need for tailored retraining interventions that address the specific needs of particular age and career stage populations (van der Heijden, 2002).

Individual differences are important to consider in designing retraining approaches. In a study by Heppner, Fuller, and Multon (1998), career transition self-efficacy was positively related to two of the Big Five personality factors (extraversion, openness) and negatively predicted by two other factors (neuroticism, agreeableness; Heppner et al., 1998). Thus, knowledge of individuals' personality characteristics could be relevant to the design and application of specific retraining interventions, particularly as these factors may intersect with other age-based shifts in training-relevant motivational and affective characteristics (e.g., desire to protect self-concept, positive affect-promoting motivational structures; Kanfer & Ackerman, 2004).

Additional considerations regarding mid-career employees include gender and other social identities. Berg, Hamman, Piszczek, and Ruhm (2015), for example, analyzed longitudinal data from a large stratified sample of German organizations and employees ($N = 759{,}931$ observations over three time points, with each individual appearing in the dataset up to three times) to examine the links between the provision of (re)training programs and employee retirement (Berg et al., 2015). Controlling for overall training participation in each organization, the authors found that female employees (and particularly low-wage female employees) working in organizations offering age-customized ("targeted") training opportunities as opposed to "standard" training (i.e., not tailored or sensitive to any age-relevant considerations) were less likely to retire. The authors link this lower likelihood of retirement to observable increases in women's wages and advancement in an organization's wage distribution. While similar results were found for male employees (particularly low-wage men) in organizations providing standard training programs, issues with available wage data made the causal interpretation of these results less clear for male employees. Overall, this would suggest that attention to individual differences such as gender and socioeconomic status are relevant considerations when developing and implementing retraining interventions. Employment behaviors, as well as career patterns and decisions, have reason to differ across demographics such as gender (e.g., due to differences in social context, role expectations, timing of labor force participation; Ollier-Malaterre & Foucreault, 2016; Shapiro & Mott, 1994). Taking a lifespan perspective thus brings attention to individual and contextual differences in career processes and the qualities of retraining interventions that will be most effective.

Adaptability interventions. Adaptability interventions can either be considered as a sub-type of retraining or a necessary adjunct to facilitating engagement in retraining (i.e., in line with self-efficacy and other important career transition competencies). We contend that these interventions are most relevant to mid-career individuals in establishment (i.e., gaining skills and stabilizing their career role) and maintenance (i.e., sustaining competence and engagement) stages, although due to their future-oriented and dynamic focus these interventions lend themselves to developmental tasks, career decision-making, and adaptability across intracareer stages. This area of the intervention literature can be considered as building "meta" career competencies. The competencies involve the "awareness an individual has about their competencies and the ability they have to control over, manage, and develop their competencies" (e.g., knowledge, reflexivity, metacognition, career visualization, self-awareness, etc.; De Vos et al., 2016, p. 101). In addition, they include the ability to consider one's "own strengths and weaknesses, to assess where [one's] skills are deficient, and to think over ways to improve [one's] value" (van der Heijden, 2002, p. 59). These competencies have been noted to be critical during transition periods and career decision points (e.g., job loss, defining new career projects, navigating plateaus), making them particularly relevant for mid-career individuals facing such scenarios in addition to age-related changes in engagement, motivation, abilities, needs, and values (De Vos et al., 2016). Adaptability can help mitigate knowledge and skill obsolescence (i.e., fostering upholding and updating) when accompanied by retraining as well (Super & Hall, 1978).

Generally speaking, the mid-career literature lacks thorough empirical study of career planning and adaptability interventions, and, when these interventions are reported, quantitative results are rare (van der Horst & Klehe, 2018). A recent study by Brown et al. (2012), however, provides some insights into the core components of adaptability necessary in interventions with mid-career individuals. This qualitative study used semi-structured interviews to explore career pathways, transitions, and career adaptabilities (e.g., career development and lifestyle orientations, tensions between individual and contextual constraints, self-reflexivity and learning) among 64 mid-career adults in Norway and the United Kingdom. Based on the resulting themes from these interviews, the authors recommended that organizational interventions focus on "opportunity structures" in particular contexts and times at work (i.e., provision of flexibility as well as structure in guiding career trajectories), such that formal and informal learning (i.e., "learning-while-working") are prioritized. Both the innovative and tailored approaches to retraining discussed above and the counselling interventions discussed next would seem to answer these calls.

Additionally, a recent study by van der Horst and Klehe (2018) describes a specific career adaptability intervention with mid-career employees. This study with 48 mid-career employees from a single organization (20 in the intervention group, 28 in the control group) utilized both structured group and computer-based interventions to improve career adaptability. The intervention first entailed the creation of an "ePortfolio", a system in which participants created a short personal profile with their CV as well as self-assessed personality and employability. After working on this platform, participants spent time interpreting their results, which was intended to help them enhance their self-awareness, sense of career control, as well as career confidence and self-efficacy. Next, in the half-day group event, individuals attended two presentations in addition to elective workshops centered around topics such as continuous career development, career planning and proactivity, and career-related self-efficacy. The speakers at this event were external coaches and experts, and the half-day concluded with a discussion of job change processes. Participants were assessed prior to the intervention and six months after the intervention to gauge changes in career adaptive responses. Results indicated that, compared to the control group, employees who participated in the intervention manifested significant increases in self-awareness, career decidedness, self- and environmental exploration, and career planning. Such positive findings are particularly compelling in light of the fact that this intervention was conducted during restructuring in the sample organization. However, as employment status or change were not reported across Times 1 or 2, it is unclear to what degree restructuring may have actually affected the employees who participated in this intervention. Nonetheless, this innovative approach would seem to bear future investigation and elaboration in career adaptability interventions for mid-career employees from different backgrounds and in different personal and organizational contexts.

Career counselling. Career counselling for mid-career success receives much more direct empirical attention in the literature; however, this literature does not consider implementation factors to the same degree as does the retraining literature. These approaches to career development involve generally one-on-one settings where a "counsellor" provides direct guidance to an employee regarding career stage-relevant issues, goal setting, and plan execution.

Just as with retraining, these approaches are applicable to mid-career individuals in a range of stages of their career process (e.g., exploration, establishment, maintenance) and who are faced with a variety of developmental tasks, although the content of the interventions will differ based on the concerns presented by individuals in these stages. For example, for individuals exploring new roles or career paths, guidance regarding the relative advantages and disadvantages of certain career changes, in light of individual and environmental factors as well as desired job characteristics (e.g., social interaction, flexibility, autonomy, engaging and challenging job content), would likely be of use. For individuals who are currently seeking to establish themselves in this new career, however, counselling might be most useful if it centers around skill cultivation and development, or how to best leverage contextual resources and social capital to stabilize one's new role. Finally, for individuals in the maintenance stage, counselling might address preventing or overcoming skill or knowledge obsolescence, and/or opportunities for finding balance between shifting personal priorities, motivation to work, and age-related gains and losses relevant to one's job (Sterns & Dorsett, 1994). These interventions can also be provided in certain contexts, such as around periods of personal/organizational uncertainty and transitions (e.g., mergers and acquisitions, job loss) to help mid-career employees mitigate and respond resiliently to career-related stress (Matteson & Ivancevich, 2008).

Much of the literature reporting empirical investigations of counselling interventions utilizes small sample sizes (or case study approaches) and thus it is difficult to draw more definite conclusions about intervention effectiveness. However, a few studies and reviews provide helpful information about counselling interventions. Bimrose and Hearne (2012), for instance, report on a review of four different qualitative counselling-relevant studies focused on resilience and career adaptability. One of the four studies involved participation in a career counselling intervention ($N = 50$ at Time 1, $N = 29$ by Time 2). Participants were interviewed over five years following the career development intervention, and this longitudinal data was analyzed to identify themes pertaining to intervention effectiveness and career outcomes (Bimrose & Barnes, 2008; Bimrose, Barnes, & Hughes, 2005). Although career outcomes were mixed, these were attributed by participants to factors external to their counselling and career plans (e.g., financial constraints, family commitments, labor market, health). Additionally, participants consistently identified effective counselling as containing the following elements: access to specialist information, reduced confusion and increased clarity, motivational/motivating orientation, focus on confidence and self-efficacy building, and structured opportunities for discussion and reflection (Bimrose et al., 2005; Bimrose & Barnes, 2008).

Interestingly, these authors also identified four types of career decision making styles in their longitudinal interviews, concluding that these styles have implications for the type of support that should be provided in counselling. Specifically, Bimrose and Barnes (2008) contrast a style-based counselling approach with prevailing rationalist views on career counselling. The latter practices entail assessment of individual abilities and interests on the one hand and jobs on the other hand, attempting to match abilities and interests with jobs in the most optimal way possible. Bimrose and Barnes (2008), however, contend that individuals do not always act in ideal or rational ways. Instead, transitions can be handled in a variety of ways (i.e., evaluative, strategic, aspirational, and opportunistic approaches) in light of different personal (e.g., motivational, affective) and contextual (e.g., situational, societal) factors. For instance, an employee may decide to remain in a job that does not maximize their ability usage but avoids seeking out retraining or relocation. Of course, formal assessments are still of great utility for early stages of this class of interventions, provided they are not the only tool used for assessing and developing plans for individuals in career counselling settings (see Guindon & Richmond, 2005, for a review of assessments and technology in career counselling; Perosa & Perosa, 1997, for a review of assessments with a focus on mid-career transitions).

While specific details of these styles are outside of the scope of this chapter, the recognition of idiosyncratic decision-making processes and unique cognitive, affective, and behavioral systems is key for effective, innovative, and lifespan-sensitive mid-career counselling interventions. This focus is similar to work on mid-career renewal counselling, in which Beijan and Salomone (1995) recommend that counselling be tailored not only to individuals' immediate vocational decisions but also to their past experiences, future expectations, and intersecting life domains. Indeed, the benefits of specific counselling approaches differ with respect to the types of ultimate career outcomes considered (e.g., objective compensation versus career satisfaction; Allen et al., 2004). On the other side of this equation, Chen (2003) describes some of the counsellor characteristics and assumptions that impact career development practice, specifically positivist versus constructivist approaches to careers conceptualizations (i.e., as self-realization, a set of ongoing growth experiences, or a context itself). Cognizance of these approaches and efforts to creatively integrate views on careers and counselling alongside employee characteristics, needs, and broader life considerations (e.g., life planning and development) seem to be the direction in which career counselling is moving (Guindon & Richmond, 2005). In fact, more integrative and nuanced approaches that are transparent, flexible, and encouraging can help build deeper levels of understanding, ownership, and relevant impact in mid-career individuals' careers and broader lives (Chen, 2003; Guindon & Richmond, 2005). These approaches can also reduce possible power dynamics and other role issues (e.g., continued marginalization of "token" employees) implied in certain counselling relationships (Carden, 1990). Many individuals studied in the career counselling literature fall into what the literature refers to as "special populations" (Guindon & Richmond, 2005, p. 98; e.g., physical or mental illness; "minority" status based on race, ethnicity, gender, education; economic disadvantage). Therefore, the effects of interventions can be compounded in already vulnerable mid-career individuals and, thus, counselling that is sensitive to these issues is of the utmost importance.

Late career. Individuals in their late career (i.e., typically 60 years or older) share many of the same issues and concerns as mid-career individuals. However, some additional intervention types and targets are of particular interest for this population. In examining the literature, we identified one specific areas of interest: knowledge transfer and mentoring interventions. The former intervention type addresses shifts in work values and motivation that have been well documented in the late career literature. Specifically, relatively older workers tend to prioritize generativity motives (i.e., the desire to contribute to the success of future "generations" through caring, "giving back"; Kanfer & Ackerman, 2004; Kooij, de Lange, Jansen, Kanfer, & Dikkers, 2011; Krumm, Grube, & Hertel, 2013). The motives can be satisfied through formal and informal "knowledge sharing" (also referred to as "knowledge exchange" or "knowledge transmission") and mentoring for this purpose (McAdams & de St. Aubin, 1998). We discuss this intervention in the following section, drawing upon the (limited) empirical literature that studies late-career adults. Unfortunately, given the limited literature in this area, we do not explore diverse populations and individual differences to the same degree as in the mid-career section; we do, however, return to this as a recommendation for future research.

Additionally, we wish to note that some may view the distinction between "intracareer stages" and "career stages" as losing significance and becoming synonymous as employees near retirement. This is based in the idea that individuals will likely not take on new occupational careers before or during retirement, and instead will "explore" and "establish" non-work roles and alternative vocational activities that may or may not be career-focused, per se (e.g., bridge employment, volunteering). However, the significance of bridge employment and its support for a number of individual motivations and characteristics (e.g., high career centrality), and contextual circumstances (e.g., need for health benefits, financial support) cannot be underestimated (Ulrich & Brott, 2005; Wang, Zhan, Liu, & Shultz, 2008).

Knowledge transfer and mentoring. As described above, knowledge transfer and knowledge-focused mentoring interventions address the generativity motives that are often of increased importance to older adults in and outside of work. Although they are distinct, we consider knowledge transfer and mentoring together given their relatedness and overlap in many intervention settings (e.g., knowledge sharing within mentoring relationships; Geisler, 2007). We contend that these interventions will be most beneficial for individuals in maintenance and disengagement (intra)career stages, because they will help to consolidate and focus careers on those aspects of most interest as well as ease the transition into retirement. Thus, they address the developmental tasks of decelerating (i.e., slowing work engagement, passing on knowledge and responsibilities) and retirement planning.

The number of intervention studies that look at these ideas in combination with older employees are in short supply, however. To this point, a recent meta-analysis by Ghosh and Reio (2013) underlined the positive outcomes of mentoring work for mentors themselves, including higher job satisfaction, organizational commitment, and job performance. Importantly, the authors suggest that these relationships are, in part, accounted for by gains in "satisfaction, meaning and purpose in [mentors'] lives, and a sense of accomplishment in finding an outlet for passing [on] accumulated knowledge and wisdom" (p. 108). The substantive evidence for this generativity-based explanation is lacking, however, and Ghosh and Reio conclude that the mentoring literature needs further longitudinal (i.e., to investigate the impact of mentoring over time and at particular junctures in one's career) and age-based consideration (i.e., to account for heterogeneity in mentoring–outcome relationships).

Still, knowledge sharing and mentoring are ripe areas for late career interventions (e.g., Lindbo & Shultz, 1998) and are core mechanisms for retaining valuable wisdom and experience in organizations (Gerpott, Lehmann-Willenbrock, & Voelpel, 2016; Joe & Yoong, 2006) and helping extend working lives. Indeed, findings from a study on mentoring and career plateau by Lentz and Allen (2009) suggests that mentoring experience moderates the relationship between job content plateauing and turnover intentions as well as job satisfaction. Specifically, this study found that the negative effects of job content plateaus on mentors' (as compared to non-mentors') turnover intentions and job satisfaction were mitigated by mentoring engagement. Lentz and Allen (2009) attribute these results to how mentoring can enrich individuals' jobs and help them cope with otherwise plateaued job content. In light of our earlier discussion of career plateaus and older employees, preventing the negative impact of career plateaus (and mitigating them through motivational and job content means) is an important goal. Knowledge sharing and mentoring may be beneficial to this end.

Innovative and cost-effective approaches to these interventions have emerged in recent years. Storytelling is increasingly used to support mentoring relationships and can even be integrated with a range of compelling technological platforms to facilitate formalized sharing, dialogue, and knowledge management (e.g., Gerpott et al., 2016; Savita, Hazwani, & Khalid, 2011). D'Abate and Alpert (2017) report on a qualitative study ($N = 39$) of an industry- and age-diverse (i.e., with nearly half of the sample between 51 and 60 years) sample of individuals in high-level management positions. This study focused in particular on the ways that storytelling in mentoring relationships can contribute to knowledge transfer and learning in such developmental relationships. The study's findings provide support for storytelling as a way of contributing to the career success of mentees (i.e., "younger generations" of the workforce) and broader organizational knowledge and history (i.e., "company folklore") of which mentors are aware and derive socioemotional benefit from. Similar conclusions about advantages of this approach were drawn by Furunes, Kaltveit, and Akerjordet (2018) in their qualitative study of nurses: older nurses reported knowledge sharing and mentoring, and being viewed as "resources" to less experienced peers, as work and continuance motivators (Furunes et al., 2018). Promoting storytelling in late career employees' formal and informal relationships with other employees may thus be a beneficial way of providing generativity opportunities to older adult employees and reinforce career identity (London, 1990).

Recommendations

Based on the strengths and weaknesses identified in this literature review, we have a number of recommendations for future research and practice in career counselling and development interventions for middle-aged and older adults.

Theoretical recommendations. Although career development theory, and specifically theory applicable across the lifespan, is well elaborated relative to its corresponding empirical literature, some recommendations are apparent. Namely, we recommend more cross-theoretical integration as well as explicit inclusion of contextual influences on career development in theory. Blustein (1997), for example, builds upon Super's work in his discussion of a "context-rich" perspective on career exploration. In this theoretical account, Blustein (1997) calls to broaden conceptions of career exploration and more directly consider different life roles and influences on career development (e.g., family, national context). We note this as a current shortcoming in the literature and its intervention foci. To accomplish this, more cross-theory collaboration is warranted, drawing on the perspectives from multiple "types" of career theories (e.g., Holland's congruence perspective, social learning, and work adjustment alongside the developmental theories reviewed herein; Osipow, 1990b).

Drawing on these different perspectives could help better represent contextual and personality-based influences on vocational choice and behavior, as well as processes of reinforcement and decision-making across the career lifespan. Through integration and contextual elaboration, more nuance around "when" individuals make career choices (e.g., enter a "mini-cycle"; reach a point of increased "decisional demand", Osipow, 1990a, p. 345; recognize an upcoming career developmental deadline, Heckhausen et al., 2010) could be provided in career theory. Creating more testable hypotheses around career "timing" and developmental influences would benefit the empirical and practical literature (e.g., helping to illuminate when and by what means interventions are most effective).

Empirical recommendations. Not surprisingly, the first empirical recommendation we have is to conduct more career development intervention studies targeted at middle-aged and older adult employees. To this point, as Sampson et al. (2014) highlight in their content analysis of the career development literature in 2013, "age" ranked 49th out of 50 in theory and research articles (with $n = 9$ and $n = 4$, respectively) and was unranked in practical articles. Insufficient attention and resources are directed toward these pursuits despite their great relevance for employee wellbeing and career outcomes. If we are to take the "practical sections" of theoretical and empirical papers seriously, the interventions discussed therein should be explored in the real world. The mid- and late-career principles and recommendations in work by such authors as Rosen and Jerdee (1990) and Greller and Simpson (1999), as well as lifespan work regarding organizational practices and policies by Truxillo, Cadiz, and Rineer (2017) and Zabel and Baltes (2015), are good starting points for developing new research questions and designing interventions.

In conducting these empirical studies, additional methodological considerations will be necessary as well. Specifically, we recommend that "best practices" in intervention studies be used, including appropriate sample sizes, randomized control groups, and thorough quantitative (in combination with qualitative) measurement at intentional and theory-driven time lags between baseline and follow-up time points (e.g., Cox, Karanika, Griffiths, & Houdmont, 2007; Murphy & Sauter, 2004; Nielsen, Taris, & Cox, 2010). These improvements will help more accurately and representatively estimate intervention impact (e.g., effect sizes). Pilot studies following similarly rigorous procedures will be useful in planning and revising larger-scale intervention studies as well (e.g., Hertzog, 2008; Lancaster, Dodd, & Williamson, 2004). Indeed, the use of pilot studies will also aid in considering the "level" of interventions (e.g., broad vs. specific population target, method of dissemination and intended level of change), their relevance for certain outcomes, and their efficacy and viability relative to other interventions, all of which warrant more representation in the career development literature (Wampold, Lichtenberg, & Waehler, 2002). Established "best practices" in work and aging research in particular will be important to combine with these efforts (Bohlmann, Rudolph, & Zacher, 2018).

We also recommend that greater diversity be represented in the sampling used for these interventions, as diverse workforce populations are and should be the target of contemporary, innovative career development interventions. In their review of the career development literature, Guindon and Richmond (2005) found a growing shift toward contextualized career development research and practice, as opposed to exclusive focus on majority groups while marginalizing minority individuals. In line with this, the methods, settings, and samples used in intervention studies should move toward accurate representation of relevant groups and contexts. As discussed earlier, distinct career challenges and strengths, as well as responsivity to interventions, occur for different identities. More of this research needs to be conducted among middle-aged and older adult employees to determine how identity-based differences may mirror or diverge from findings among young adults (e.g., career self-efficacy and gender, as in Sullivan & Mahalik, 2000). Thus, acknowledgement of diversity in designing, conducting, and evaluating intervention studies will prove valuable for innovating and optimizing contextualized, lifespan-informed approaches to career development.

Practical recommendations. Our primary and most obvious recommendations are to use the types of interventions described herein and draw from empirically sound studies elsewhere in selecting career development interventions. Aside from these, we also recommend that managers' and counsellors' intervention "toolbox" be expanded to include innovative age-sensitive interventions outside of the traditional "career development" space. These include work–life balance policies and practices (Darcy, McCarthy, Hill, & Grady, 2012), flexible work programs (Stirpe, Trullen, & Bonache, 2018), and work design and job crafting (Truxillo, Cadiz, Rineer, Zaniboni, & Fraccaroli, 2012) that could serve as adjuncts to other career development programming. Context, audience, and resources (e.g., technology) must all be considered in aligning and implementing these interventions. Finally, the effects of combined interventions and workplace characteristic/practices must be borne in mind to avoid any detrimental additive or multiplicative effects for employees of particular ages or career stages (e.g., negative impact of co-occurring high-performance work systems and flexible work programs on retention in Stirpe et al., 2018). Informing decision-making with theory and research on intervention attributes, as well as the interaction of these attributes with employees' values and preferences, will be important in tailoring the use of career development interventions in organizations.

Conclusion

Overall, the review of the career development literature reported herein suggests that more attention needs to be paid to the rigorous study of career counselling and development interventions for middle-aged and older adult employees. Although much theory regarding career stages, adaptability, and plateaus has been developed, its application in methodologically sound and innovative intervention studies has been limited. A range of career issues face modern employees in mid- to late-career stages, but limited space in the literature has been devoted to practical interventions for these populations. The importance of innovative career counselling and development across the lifespan cannot be understated. Only through well structured, theory- and research-informed practice can modern organizations hope to foster inclusion and sustained employability for their age-diverse workforce. The interventions and key practical considerations reviewed herein, alongside the recommendations outlined, should prove beneficial in guiding innovative, lifespan-informed career development research and practice to come.

References

Allen, T. D., Eby, L. T., Poteet, M. L., Lentz, E., & Lima, L. (2004). Career benefits associated with mentoring for protégés: A meta-analysis. *Journal of Applied Psychology, 89,* 127–136. https://doi.org/10.1037/0021-9010.89.1.127.

Allen, T. D., Russell, J. E. A., Poteet, M. L., & Dobbins, G. H. (1999). Learning and development factors related to perceptions of job content and hierarchical plateauing. *Journal of Organizational Behavior, 20,* 1113–1137. https://doi.org/10.1002/(sici)1099-1379(199912)20:7%3c1113:aid-job944%3e3.0.co;2-7.

Avedon, L. (1996). Issues of work transitions and training of older workers. In G. Taylor (Ed.), *Learning for the workplace: Nordic and Canadian perspectives* (pp. 35–42). Retrieved from https://files.eric.ed.gov/fulltext/ED430121.pdf.

Baltes, P. B. (1987). Theoretical propositions of life-span developmental psychology: On the dynamics between growth and decline. *Developmental Psychology, 23,* 611–626. https://doi.org/10.1037/0012-1649.23.5.611.

Baltes, P. B., & Baltes, M. M. (1990). Psychological perspectives on successful aging: The model of selective optimization with compensation. In P. B. Baltes & M. M. Baltes (Eds.), *Successful aging: Perspectives from the behavioral sciences* (pp. 1–34). New York: Cambridge University Press.

Beijan, D. V., & Salomone, P. R. (1995). Understanding midlife career renewal: Implications for counseling. *The Career Development Quarterly, 44,* 52–63. https://doi.org/10.1002/j.2161-0045.1995.tb00528.x.

Berg, P. B., Hamman, M. K., Piszczek, M., & Ruhm, C. J. (2015). The relationship between establishment training and the retention of older workers: Evidence from Germany. Institute for the Study of Labor (IZA), Discussion Paper No. 9508. Bonn, Germany.

Bimrose, J., & Barnes, S.-A. (2008). *Adult career progression & advancement: A five year study of the effectiveness of guidance.* Coventry, England: Warwick Institute for Employment Research. Retrieved from https://warwick.ac.uk/fac/soc/ier/publications/2008/eg_report_4_years_on_final.pdf.

Bimrose, J., Barnes, S.-A., & Hughes, D. (2005). *Effective guidance one year on: Evidence from longitudinal case studies in England.* Coventry, England: Warwick Institute for Employment Research. Retrieved from https://warwick.ac.uk/fac/soc/ier/publications/2005/egreportoct05.pdf.

Bimrose, J., & Hearne, L. (2012). Resilience and career adaptability: Qualitative studies of adult career counseling. *Journal of Vocational Behavior, 81,* 338–344. https://doi.org/10.1016/j.jvb.2012.08.002.

Blustein, D. L. (1997). A context-rich perspective of career exploration across the life roles. *The Career Development Quarterly, 45,* 260–274. https://doi.org/10.1002/j.2161-0045.1997.tb00470.x.

Bohlmann, C., Rudolph, C. W., & Zacher, H. (2018). Methodological recommendations to move research on work and aging forward. *Work, Aging and Retirement, 4,* 225–237. https://doi.org/10.1093/workar/wax023.

Brandstädter, J., & Renner, G. (1990). Tenacious goal pursuit and flexible goal adjustment: Explication and age-related analysis of assimilative and accommodative strategies of coping. *Psychology and Aging, 5,* 58–67. https://doi.org/10.1037/0882-7974.5.1.58.

Brown, A., Bimrose, J., Barnes, S.-A., & Hughes, D. (2012). The role of career adaptabilities for mid-career changers. *Journal of Vocational Behavior, 80,* 754–761. https://doi.org/10.1016/j.jvb.2012.01.003.

Cairo, P. C., Kritis, K. J., & Myers, R. M. (1996). Career assessment and the adult career concerns inventory. *Journal of Career Assessment, 4,* 189–204. https://doi.org/10.1177/106907279600400205.

Carden, A. D. (1990). Mentoring and adult career development; The evolution of a theory. *The Counseling Psychologist, 18,* 275–299. https://doi.org/10.1177/0011000090182011.

Carstensen, L. L. (1987). Age-related changes in social activity. In L. L. Carstensen & B. A. Edelstein (Eds.), *Handbook of clinical gerontology* (pp. 222–237). Elmsford, NY, USA: Pergamon Press.

Carstensen, L. L. (1991). Socioemotional selectivity theory: Social activity in life-span context. In K. W. Schaie (Ed.), *Annual review of gerontology & geriatrics* (vol. 11, pp. 195–217). Retrieved from Google Books.

Charness, N., Kelley, C. L., Bosman, E. A., & Mottram, M. (2001). Word-processing training and retraining: Effects of adult age, experience, and interface. *Psychology and Aging, 16,* 110–127. https://doi.org/10.1037/0882-7974.16.1.110.

Chen, C. P. (2003). Integrating perspectives in career development theory and practice. *The Career Development Quarterly, 51,* 203–216. https://doi.org/10.1002/j.2161-0045.2003.tb00602.x.

Cohen, A. (1991). Career stage as a moderator of the relationships between organizational commitment and its outcomes: A meta-analysis. *Journal of Occupational Psychology, 64,* 253–268. https://doi.org/10.1111/j.2044-8325.1991.tb00558.x.

Conger, R. D., Elder, G. H., Jr., Lorenz, F. O., Conger, K. J., Simons, R. L., Whitbeck, L. B., … Melby, J. N. (1990). Linking economic hardship to marital quality and instability. *Journal of Marriage and Family, 52*, 643–656. https://doi.org/10.2307/352931.

Cox, T., Karanika, M., Griffiths, A., & Houdmont, J. (2007). Evaluating organizational-level work stress interventions: Beyond traditional methods. *Work & Stress, 21,* 348–362. https://doi.org/10.1080/02678370701760757.

D'Abate, C. P., & Alpert, H. (2017). Storytelling in mentoring: An exploratory, qualitative study of facilitating learning in developmental interactions. *SAGE Open, 7,* 1–17. https://doi.org/10.1177/2158244017725554.

Daley, B. J. (1999). Novice to expert: An exploration of how professionals learn. *Adult Education Quarterly, 49,* 133–147. https://doi.org/10.1177/074171369904900401.

Darcy, C., McCarthy, A., Hill, J., & Grady, G. (2012). Work–life balance: One size fits all? An exploratory analysis of the differential effects of career stage. *European Management Journal, 30,* 111–120. https://doi.org/10.1016/j.emj.2011.11.001.

De Baets, S., & Warmoes, V. (2012). Learning later in life: The older workers' perspective. In *Working and ageing: The benefits of investing in an ageing workforce* (pp. 134–154). European Centre for the Development of Vocational Training. Retrieved from http://www.cedefop.europa.eu/files/3064_en.pdf.

De Vos, A., Dujardin, J.-M., Gielens, T., & Meyers, C. (2016). *Developing sustainable careers across the lifespan*. https://doi.org/10.1007/978-3-319-47741-1.

Dietrich, J., & Salmela-Aro, K. (2013). Parental involvement and adolescents' career goal pursuit during the post-school transition. *Journal of Adolescence, 36,* 121–128. https://doi.org/10.1016/j.adolescence.2012.10.009.

Eby, L. T., & Buch, K. (1995). Job loss as career growth: Responses to involuntary career transitions. *The Career Development Quarterly, 4,* 38–42. https://doi.org/10.1002/j.2161-0045.1995.tb00526.x.

Elder, G. H., Jr. (1994). Time, human agency, and social change: Perspectives on the life course. *Social Psychology Quarterly, 57,* 4–15. https://doi.org/10.2307/2786971.

Elder, G. H., Jr. (1998). The life course and human development. In W. Damon & R. Lerner (Eds.), *Handbook of child psychology: Vol. 1 Theoretical models of human development* (5th ed., pp. 939–991). New York, NY, USA: Wiley.

Elder, G. H., Jr., & Clipp, E. C. (1989). Combat experience and emotional health: Impairment and resilience in later life. *Journal of Personality, 57,* 311–341. https://doi.org/10.1111/j.1467-6494.1989.tb00485.x.

Ference, T. P., Stoner, J. A., & Warren, E. K. (1977). Managing the career plateau. *The Academy of Management Review, 2,* 602–612. https://doi.org/10.2307/257512.

Furunes, T., Kaltveit, A., & Akerjordet, K. (2018). Health-promoting leadership: A qualitative study from experienced nurses' perspective. *Journal of Clinical Nursing*. Advance online publication. https://doi.org/10.1111/jocn.14621.

Geisler, E. (2007). The metrics of knowledge: Mechanisms for preserving the value of managerial knowledge. *Business Horizons, 50,* 467–477. https://doi.org/10.1016/j.bushor.2007.07.001.

Gerpott, F. H., Lehmann-Willenbrock, N., & Voelpel, S. C. (2016). Intergenerational learning in organizations: A framework and discussion of opportunities. In A. Alexander-Stamatios, R. J. Burke, & C. L. Cooper (Eds.), *The aging workforce handbook: Individual, organizational, and societal challenges* (pp. 241–267). https://doi.org/10.1108/978-1-78635-448-820161010.

Ghosh, R., & Reio, T. G., Jr. (2013). Career benefits associated with mentoring for mentors: A meta-analysis. *Journal of Vocational Behavior, 83,* 106–116. https://doi.org/10.1016/j.jvb.2013.03.011.

Greller, M. M., & Simpson, S. (1999). In search of late career: A review of contemporary social science research applicable to the understanding of late career. *Human Resource Management Review, 9,* 309–347. https://doi.org/10.1016/s1053-4822(99)00023-6.

Guindon, M. H., & Richmond, L. J. (2005). Practice and research in career counseling and development–2004. *The Career Development Quarterly, 54,* 90–137. https://doi.org/10.1002/j.2161-0045.2005.tb00145.x.

Guthrie, J. P., & Schwoerer, C. E. (1996). Older dogs and new tricks: Career stage and self-assessed need for training. *Public Personnel Management, 25,* 59–72. https://doi.org/10.1177/009102609602500106.

Haase, C. M., Heckhausen, J., & Silbereisen, R. K. (2012). The interplay of occupational motivation and well-being during the transition from university to work. *Developmental Psychology, 48,* 1739–1751. https://doi.org/10.1037/a0026641.

Hall, D. T., & Mirvis, P. H. (1995). The new career contract: Developing the whole person at midlife and beyond. *Journal of Vocational Behavior, 47,* 269–289. https://doi.org/10.1006/jvbe.1995.0004.

Heckhausen, J., Wrosch, C., & Schulz, R. (2010). A motivational theory of life-span development. *Psychological Review, 117,* 32–60. https://doi.org/10.1037/a0017668.

Heppner, M. J., Fuller, B. E., & Multon, K. D. (1998). Adults in involuntary career transition: An analysis of the relationship between the psychological and career domains. *Journal of Career Assessment, 6,* 329–346. https://doi.org/10.1177/106907279800600304.

Heppner, M. J., Multon, K. D., & Johnston, J. A. (1994). Assessing psychological resources during career transition: Development of the career transitions inventory. *Journal of Vocational Behavior, 44,* 55–74. https://doi.org/10.1006/jvbe.1994.1004.

Herr, E. L. (1997). Super's life-span, life-space approach and its outlook for refinement. *The Career Development Quarterly, 45*, 238–246. https://doi.org/10.1002/j.2161-0045.1997.tb00468.x.

Herr, E. L., & Cramer, S. H. (1988). *Career guidance and counseling through the life span: Systematic approaches* (3rd ed.). New York, NY, USA: Harper Collins.

Hertzog, M. A. (2008). Considerations in determining sample size for pilot studies. *Research in Nursing & Health, 31*, 180–191. https://doi.org/10.1002/nur.20247.

Hofstetter, H., & Cohen, A. (2014). The mediating role of job content plateau on the relationship between work experience characteristics and early retirement and turnover intentions. *Personnel Review, 43,* 350–376. https://doi.org/10.1108/PR-03-2012-0054.

Joe, C., & Yoong, P. (2006). Harnessing the expert knowledge of older workers: Issues and challenges. *Journal of Information & Knowledge Management, 5,* 63–72. https://doi.org/10.1142/s0219649206001323.

Kanfer, R., & Ackerman, P. L. (2004). Aging, adult development, and work motivation. *Academy of Management Review, 29*, 440–458. https://doi.org/10.2307/20159053.

Kooij, D. T. A. M., Jansen, P. G. W., Dikkers, J. S. E., & de Lange, A. H. (2010). The influence of age on the associations between HR practices and both affective commitment and job satisfaction: A meta-analysis. *Journal of Organizational Behavior, 31,* 1111–1136. https://doi.org/10.1002/job.666.

Kooij, D. T. A. M., de Lange, A. H., Jansen, P. G. W., Kanfer, R., & Dikkers, J. S. E. (2011). Age and work-related motives: Results of a meta-analysis. *Journal of Organizational Behavior, 32,* 197–225. https://doi.org/10.1002/job.665.

Körner, A., Reitzle, M., & Silbereisen, R. K. (2012). Work-related demands and life satisfaction: The effects of engagement and disengagement among employed and long-term unemployed people. *Journal of Vocational Behavior, 80,* 187–196. https://doi.org/10.1016/j.jvb.2011.05.004.

Krumm, S., Grube, A., & Hertel, G. (2013). The Munster Work Value Measure. *Journal of Managerial Psychology, 28*, 532–560. https://doi.org/10.1108/jmp-07-2011-0023.

Kubicek, B., Korunka, C., Raymo, J. M., & Hoonakker, P. (2011). Psychological well-being in retirement: The effects of personal and gendered contextual resources. *Journal of Occupational Health Psychology, 16,* 230–246. https://doi.org/10.1037/a0022334.

Lancaster, G. A., Dodd, S., & Williamson, P. R. (2004). Design and analysis of pilot studies: Recommendations for good practice. *Journal of Evaluation in Clinical Practice, 10,* 307–312. https://doi.org/10.1111/j.2002.384.doc.x.

Larwood, L., Rodkin, S., & Judson, D. (2001). Retraining and the technological productivity paradox. *International Journal of Organization Theory and Behavior, 4,* 201–224. https://doi.org/10.1081/otb-100105402.

Larwood, L., Ruben, K., Popoff, C., & Judson, D. H. (1997). Aging, retirement, and interest in technological retraining: Predicting personal investment and withdrawal. *The Journal of High Technology Management Research, 8,* 277–300. https://doi.org/10.1016/s1047-8310(97)90007-9.

Latack, J. C., & Dozier, J. B. (1986). After the ax falls: Job loss as a career transition. *The Academy of Management Review, 11*, 375–392. https://doi.org/10.5465/amr.1986.4283254.

Lentz, E., & Allen, T. D. (2009). The role of mentoring others in the career plateauing phenomenon. *Group & Organization Management, 34*, 358–384. https://doi.org/10.1177/1059601109334027.

Lin, Y.-C., Chen, A. S.-Y., & Lai, Y.-T. (2018). Breach or bridge your career? Understanding the relationship between career plateau and internal employability. *Personnel Review, 47,* 986–1002. https://doi.org/10.1108/PR-04-2017-0101.

Lindbo, T. L., & Shultz, K. S. (1998). The role of organizational culture and mentoring in mature worker socialization toward retirement. *Public Productivity & Management Review, 22,* 49–59. https://doi.org/10.2307/3380589.

London, M. (1990). Enhancing career motivation in late career. *Journal of Organizational Change Management, 3*, 58–71. https://doi.org/10.1108/09534819010001351.

Luger, B., Anselmann, S., & Mulder, R. H. (2012). Characteristics of informal learning activities of older trainers at work. In *Working and ageing: The benefits of investing in an ageing workforce* (pp. 254–279). European Centre for the Development of Vocational Training. Retrieved from http://www.cedefop.europa.eu/files/3064_en.pdf.

Matteson, M. T., & Ivancevich, J. M. (2008). Merger and acquisition stress: Fear and uncertainty at mid-career. *Prevention in Human Services, 8*, 139–158. https://doi.org/10.1300/j293v08n01_10.

Maurer, T. J., Weiss, E. M., & Barbeite, F. G. (2003). A model of involvement in work-related learning and development activity: The effects of individual, situational, motivational, and age variables. *Journal of Applied Psychology, 88,* 707–724. https://doi.org/10.1037/0021-9010.88.4.707.

McAdams, D. P., & de St. Aubin, E. (Eds.). (1998). *Generativity and adult development: How and why we care for the next generation*. https://doi.org/10.1037/10288-000.

McCleese, C. S., & Eby, L. T. (2006). Reactions to job content plateaus: Examining role ambiguity and hierarchical plateaus as moderators. *The Career Development Quarterly, 55,* 64–76. https://doi.org/10.1002/j.2161-0045.2006.tb00005.x.

Murphy, L. R., & Sauter, S. L. (2004). Work organization interventions: State of knowledge and future directions. *Social and Preventive Medicine, 49,* 79–86. https://doi.org/10.1007/s00038-004-3085-z.

Nagy, N., Froidevaux, A., & Hirschi, A. (2019). Lifespan perspectives on careers and career development. In B. Baltes, C. W. Rudolph, & H. Zacher (Eds.), *Work across the lifespan*. New York, NY, USA: Academic Press.

Nicholson, N. (1993). Purgatory or place of safety? The managerial plateau and organizational agegrading. *Human Relations, 46*, 1369–1389. https://doi.org/10.1177/001872679304601201.

Nielsen, K., Taris, T. W., & Cox, T. (2010). The future of organizational interventions: Addressing the challenges of today's organizations. *Work & Stress, 24*, 219–233. https://doi.org/10.1080/02678373.2010.519176.

Ollier-Malaterre, A., & Foucreault, A. (2016). Cross-national work–life research: Cultural and structural impacts for individuals and organizations. *Journal of Management, 43,* 111–136. https://doi.org/10.1177/0149206316655873.

Osipow, S. (1990a). Careers: Research and personal. *The Counseling Psychologist, 18,* 338–347. https://doi.org/10.1177/0011000090182016.

Osipow, S. (1990b). Convergence in theories of career choice and development: Review and prospect. *Journal of Vocational Behavior, 36,* 122–131. https://doi.org/10.1016/0001-8791(90)90020-3.

Perosa, L. M., & Perosa, S. L. (1997). Assessments for use with mid-career changers. *Journal of Career Assessment, 5*, 151–165. https://doi.org/10.1177/106907279700500203.

Robson, S. M., Hansson, R. O., Abalos, A., & Booth, M. (2006). Successful aging: Criteria for aging well in the workplace. *Journal of Career Development, 33*, 156–177. https://doi.org/10.1177/0894845306292533.

Rosen, B., & Jerdee, T. H. (1990). Middle and late career problems: Causes, consequences, and research needs. *Human Resource Planning, 13,* 59–70. https://doi.org/10.1007/978-3-322-83820-9_22.

Rudolph, C. W., Lavigne, K. N., & Zacher, H. (2017a). Career adaptability: A meta-analysis of relationships with measures of adaptivity, adapting responses, and adaptation results. *Journal of Vocational Behavior, 98,* 17–34. https://doi.org/10.1016/j.jvb.2016.09.002.

Rudolph, C. W., Lavigne, K. N., Katz, I. M., & Zacher, H. (2017b). Linking dimensions of career adaptability to adaptation results: A meta-analysis. *Journal of Vocational Behavior, 102,* 151–173. https://doi.org/10.1016/j.jvb.2017.06.003.

Russell, J. E. A. (1991). Career development interventions in organizations. *Journal of Vocational Behavior, 38*, 237–287. https://doi.org/10.1016/0001-8791(91)90030-p.

Salmela-Aro, K. (2009). Personal goals and well-being during critical life transitions: The four C's–Channelling, choice, co-agency and compensation. *Advances in Life Course Research, 14,* 63–73. https://doi.org/10.1016/j.alcr.2009.03.003.

Salmela-Aro, K., Nurmi, J.-E., Saisto, T., & Halmesmäki, E. (2010). Spousal support for personal goals and relationship satisfaction among women during the transition to parenthood. *International Journal of Behavioral Development, 34,* 229–237. https://doi.org/10.1177/0165025409350956.

Sampson, J. P., Jr., Hou, P.-C., Kronholz, J. F., Dozier, V. C., McClain, M.-C., Buzzetta, M., … Kennelly, E. L. (2014). A content analysis of career development theory, research, and practice—2013. *The Career Development Quarterly, 62*, 290–326. https://doi.org/10.1002/j.2161-0045.2014.00085.x.

Savickas, M. L. (1997). Career adaptability: An integrative construct for life-span, life-space theory. *The Career Development Quarterly, 45,* 247–259. https://doi.org/10.1002/j.2161-0045.1997.tb00469.x.

Savickas, M. L. (2005). The theory and practice of career construction. In S. Brown & R. Lent (Eds.), *Career development and counseling: Putting theory and research to work* (pp. 42–70). New York, NY, USA: Wiley.

Savita, K. S., Hazwani, H., & Kalid, K. S. (2011). The development of a narrative management system: Storytelling in knowledge management. *International Journal of Computer, Electrical, Automation, Control and Information Engineering, 5*, 262–266. Retrieved from https://scholar.waset.org/1999.4/13860.

Schmid, K. (2012). Barriers to and benefits of further vocational training for older employees. In *Working and ageing: The benefits of investing in an ageing workforce* (pp. 106–133). European Centre for the Development of Vocational Training. Retrieved from http://www.cedefop.europa.eu/files/3064_en.pdf.

Shapiro, D., & Mott, F. L. (1994). Long-term employment and earnings of women in relation to employment behavior surrounding the first birth. *The Journal of Human Resources, 29,* 248–275. https://doi.org/10.2307/146098.

Singley, M. K., & Anderson, J. R. (1989). *The transfer of cognitive skill.* Cambridge, MA, USA: Harvard University Press.

Slocum, J. W., Jr., Cron, W. L., Hansen, R. W., & Rawlings, S. (1985). Business strategy and the management of plateaued employees. *The Academy of Management Journal, 28,* 133–154. https://doi.org/10.2307/256065.

Slocum, J. W., Jr., Cron, W. L., & Yows, L. C. (1987). Whose career is likely to plateau? *Business Horizons, 30,* 31–38. https://doi.org/10.1016/0007-6813(87)90006-1.

Sterns, H. L., & Dorsett, J. G. (1994). Career development: A life span issue. *Experimental Aging Research, 20,* 257–264. https://doi.org/10.1080/03610739408253975.

Sterns, H. L., & Doverspike, D. (1988). *Training and developing the older worker: Implications for human resource management. Fourteen steps in managing an ageing workforce*. Lexington, MA, USA: Lexington Books.

Sterns, H., & Harrington, A. K. (2019). Lifespan perspective on learning and training. In B. Baltes, C. W. Rudolph, & H. Zacher (Eds.), *Work across the lifespan*. New York, NY, USA: Academic Press.

Sterns, H. L., & Miklos, S. M. (1995). The aging worker in a changing environment: Organizational and individual issues. *Journal of Vocational Behavior, 47,* 248–268. https://doi.org/10.1006/jvbe.1995.0003.

Stirpe, L., Trullen, J., & Bonache, J. (2018). Retaining an ageing workforce: The effects of high-performance work systems and flexible work programmes. *Human Resources Management Journal*, 1–20. https://doi.org/10.1111/1748-8583.12205.

Stout, S. K., Slocum, J. W., Jr., & Cron, W. L. (1988). Dynamics of the career plateauing process. *Journal of Vocational Behavior, 32,* 74–91. https://doi.org/10.1016/0001-8791(88)90007-3.

Stumpf, S. A., & Tymon, W. G., Jr. (2012). The effects of objective career success on subsequent subjective career success. *Journal of Vocational Behavior, 81,* 345–353. https://doi.org/10.1016/j.jvb.2012.09.001.

Sullivan, K. R., & Mahalik, J. R. (2000). Increasing career self-efficacy for women: Evaluating a group intervention. *Journal of Counseling & Development, 78,* 54–62. https://doi.org/10.1002/j.1556-6676.2000.tb02560.x.

Super, D. E. (1957). *The psychology of careers: An introduction to vocational development.* Oxford, England: Harper & Bros.

Super, D. E. (1980). A life-span, life-space approach to career development. *Journal of Vocational Behavior, 16,* 282–296. https://doi.org/10.1016/0001-8791(80)90056-1.

Super, D. E. (1990). A life-span, life-space approach to career development. In D. Brown & L. Brooks (Eds.), *Career choice and development: Applying contemporary theories to practice* (pp. 197–261). San Francisco, CA, USA: Jossey-Bass.

Super, D. E., & Hall, D. T. (1978). Career development: Exploration and planning. *Annual Review of Psychology, 29,* 333–372. https://doi.org/10.1146/annurev.ps.29.020178.002001.

Super, D. E., & Knasel, E. G. (2007). Career development in adulthood: Some theoretical problems and a possible solution. *British Journal of Guidance and Counselling, 9,* 194–201. https://doi.org/10.1080/03069888108258214.

Super, D. E., Savickas, M. L., & Super, C. M. (1996). The life span, life-space approach to careers. In D. Brown & L. Brooks (Eds.), *Career choice and development: Applying contemporary theories to practice* (3rd ed., pp. 121–178). San Francisco, CA, USA: Jossey-Bass.

Tremblay, M., & Roger, A. (1993). Individual, familial, and organizational determinants of career plateaus: An empirical study of the determinants of objective and subjective career plateau in a population of Canadian managers. *Group and Organization Management, 18,* 411–435. https://doi.org/10.1177/1059601193184003.

Truxillo, D. M., Cadiz, D. M., & Rineer, J. R. (2017). The aging workforce: Implications for human resource management research and practice. In M. A. Hitt, S. E. Jackson, S. Carmona, L. Bierman, C. E. Shalley, & D. M. Wright (Eds.), *The Oxford handbook of strategy implementation.* https://doi.org/10.1093/oxfordhb/9780190650230.013.004.

Truxillo, D. M., Cadiz, D. M., Rineer, J. R., Zaniboni, S., & Fraccaroli, F. (2012). A lifespan perspective on job design: Fitting the job and the worker to promote job satisfaction, engagement, and performance. *Organizational Psychology Review, 2,* 340–360. https://doi.org/10.1177/2041386612454043.

Ulrich, L. B., & Brott, P. E. (2005). Older workers and bridge employment: Redefining retirement. *Journal of Employment Counseling, 42,* 159–170. https://doi.org/10.1002/j.2161-1920.2005.tb01087.x.

van der Heijden, B. I. J. M. (2002). Individual career initiatives and their influence upon professional expertise development throughout the career. *International Journal of Training and Development, 6,* 54–79. https://doi.org/10.1111/1468-2419.00150.

van der Horst, A. C., & Klehe, U.-C. (2018). Enhancing career adaptive responses among experienced employees: A mid-career intervention. Advance online publication. *Journal of Vocational Behavior*. https://doi.org/10.1016/j.jvb.2018.08.004.

Wampold, B. E., Lichtenberg, J. W., & Waehler, C. A. (2002). Principles of empirically supported interventions in counseling psychology. *The Counseling Psychologist, 30,* 197–217. https://doi.org/10.1177/0011000002302001.

Wang, M., Zhan, Y., Liu, S., & Shultz, K. S. (2008). Antecedents of bridge employment: A longitudinal investigation. *Journal of Applied Psychology, 93,* 818–830. https://doi.org/10.1037/0021-9010.93.4.818.

Williams, S. L., & Fox, C. J. (1995). Organizational approaches for managing mid-career personnel. *Public Personnel Management, 24,* 351–363. https://doi.org/10.1177/009102609502400307.

Wolf, G., London, M., Casey, J., & Pufahl, J. (1995). Career experience and motivation as predictors of training behaviors and outcomes for displaced engineers. *Journal of Vocational Behavior, 47,* 316–331. https://doi.org/10.1006/jvbe.1995.0006.

Wolfson, N. E., Cavanagh, T. M., & Kraiger, K. (2014). Older adults and technology-based instruction: Optimizing learning outcomes and transfer. *Academy of Management Learning & Education, 13,* 26–44. https://doi.org/10.5465/amle.2012.0056.

Xie, B., Lu, X., & Zhou, W. (2015). Does double plateau always lead to turnover intention? Evidence from China with Indigenous Career Plateau Scale. *Journal of Career Development, 42,* 540–553. https://doi.org/10.1177/0894845315580642.

Yang, W.-N., Johnson, S., & Niven, K. (2018). "That's not what I signed up for!" A longitudinal investigation of the impact of unmet expectation and age in the relation between career plateau and job attitudes. *Journal of Vocational Behavior, 107,* 71–85. https://doi.org/10.1016/j.jvb.2018.03.006.

Zabel, K. L., & Baltes, B. B. (2015). Workplace intervention effectiveness across the lifespan. In L. M. Finkelstein, D. M. Truxillo, F. Fraccaroli, & R. Kanfer (Eds.), *Facing the challenges of a multi-age workforce: A use-inspired approach* (pp. 209–229). New York, NY, USA: Routledge.

Innovative Career Counselling to Promote Social Justice

Coping with Uncertainty: Cultivating a Sense of Purpose Among Youth Through Innovations in Work-Based Learning Experiences

Maureen E. Kenny, Belle Liang, David L. Blustein, Lily Konowitz, Tera Meerkins, Allison White, Mary Beth Medvide, Xiaohe Gao and Anna Shuqom

Abstract Young people in many countries across the globe are facing increased competition for meaningful and decent work. In the context of rapid social and economic change, young people are often uncertain as to how to best prepare for their futures. Career development education (CDE) and work-based learning (WBL) can be instrumental in preparing youth for the future, but do not generally give attention to the rising inequity and uncertainty in the world of work that can undermine youth purpose and engagement in school and work preparation. In this chapter, we report on efforts to develop CDE/WBL drawing from PWT and life design perspectives, with an intentional focus on helping students to identify their sense of purpose and to foster personal and social agency in school and future planning. More specifically, we present the findings from interviews of twelve students enrolled in a summer CDE/WBL program, with a focus on offering opportunities to youth who may not otherwise have access to the career and workplace mentoring. We build on prior research examining the cultivation of youth purpose by exploring students' construction of purpose and their pathways to lives of purpose and meaning through CDE/WBL.

Keywords Career development education · Work-based learning · Psychology of working · Career uncertainty · Purpose

Introduction

Young people in many countries across the globe are facing increased competition for meaningful and decent work that offers adequate compensation, safe working

---

Coping with inequity and uncertainty: Cultivating youth purpose through innovations in work-based learning experiences.

M. E. Kenny (✉) · B. Liang · D. L. Blustein · L. Konowitz · T. Meerkins · A. White · M. B. Medvide · X. Gao · A. Shuqom
Boston College, Chestnut Hill, MA, USA
e-mail: kennym@bc.edu

J. G. Maree (ed.), *Handbook of Innovative Career Counselling*,
https://doi.org/10.1007/978-3-030-22799-9_19

conditions, and job stability or protection against unemployment (Katz & Kreuger, 2016). While access to decent work has been diminishing, precarious work, which tends to be short-term, project-based, and lacking in benefits and opportunities for skills development or advancement, has been on the rise (Kallenberg, 2009). While precarious work may be attractive to some young people by offering flexibility, evidence suggests that this instability has detrimental effects on physical, social and psychological well-being (Standing, 2014).

Young people are often uncertain as to how to best prepare for their futures given that the types of work available are shifting rapidly due in large measure to the impact of technology, globalization, and societal change (Kenny & Minor, 2015). Uncertainty and pessimism about the job market and future opportunities can serve to undermine students' long-term aspirations and engagement in their schooling as means to future success (Anant, Gassman-Pines, Fracis, & Gibson-Davis, 2011; Hill et al., 2018). More broadly, the uncertainty and anxiety aroused by changes in work and the world in general are leaving many youth without a clear sense of purpose and awareness of how to realize a life of meaning in the workplace (Dik, Byrne, & Steger, 2013; Di Fabio & Blustein, 2016).

Career development education (CDE), including school based curriculum and connecting activities, such as internships, job shadowing and work-based learning, have been designed to promote personal and social awareness, as well as career exploration and career decision making (Kenny, 2013). At the high school level, this approach has been successful in fostering career exploration, developing work readiness skills, promoting career decision-making self-efficacy, and raising career aspirations and outcome expectations (Ali, Yang, Button, & McCoy, 2012; Gamboa, Paixao, & Jesus, 2013; Kenny, 2013; Kenny, Blustein, Haase, Jackson, & Perry, 2006; McWhirter, Crothers, & Rasheed, 2000). While career development education (CDE), including work-based learning (WBL), can be helpful in preparing youth for the future, these approaches have generally not attended to the uncertainty in the world of work and in society more broadly, which is now serving to undermine youth purpose and work preparation (Kenny, 2013,2017; Nassar-McMillan, Taylor, & Conley, 2017; Whiston & Blustein, 2013). Consistent with the burgeoning literature on purpose and meaning in career development (e.g., Dik et al., 2013), we maintain that career development education (CDE) and work-based learning (WBL) could be instrumental in helping young people to develop an overarching sense of purpose, beyond decision-making or preparation for a specific career.

The goal of this chapter is to explore how CDE/WBL might serve as a pathway for promoting youth purpose and report on efforts to develop CDE/WBL with an intentional focus on helping students to identify their purpose and foster agency in school and future planning. These efforts are part of a broader initiative (Kenny, Blustein, Liang, Klein, & Etchie, 2019) to develop a transformative model of CDE drawing from Psychology of Working Theory (PWT; Blustein, 2006; Blustein, Kenny, Di Fabio, & Guichard, 2018; Duffy, Blustein, Diemer, & Autin, 2016). Another goal of this chapter is to provide a context for the integration of the youth purpose literature with parallel concepts within PWT, life design counselling and the broader career development literatures (Dik, Byrne, & Steger, 2013).

Theoretical Foundations

The Psychology of Working Theory (PWT; Blustein, 2006; Blustein et al., 2018; Duffy et al., 2016) was developed as an inclusive framework to guide career guidance interventions for all persons who work or want to work. Whereas career choice and career development interventions typically assume that persons have some degree of volition in their work options, PWT recognize that volition is limited for many persons as a function of social structures, economic resources and marginalization. Four core tenets of PWT are foundational to the CDE/WBL intervention described in this chapter, namely that (1) stable, dignified, and decent work has the capacity to connect people to others and optimally to a sense of meaning and purpose, (2) that experience in the work environment is influenced inevitably by one's context, including family background, social context, and cultural identity, (3) that the labor market will continue to undergo rapid change, and (4) that work includes both paid and unpaid roles, such as caregiving (Blustein, 2006; Blustein et al., 2018). Related to the first tenet, PWT articulates the importance of social contribution, which offers an important means for connecting with the social world (Blustein, 2006). In effect, the social contribution aspect of the PWT captures the sense of connection and meaning that people derive in being part of something that is bigger than themselves—contributing to the overall social and economic welfare of an organization, community, and society (Blustein, 2006).

Drawing from PWT, as well as Counselling for Work and Relationship (CWR: Richardson, 2012) and Career Construction for Life Design (Hartung & Vess, 2019; Savickas, 2005), the WBL program described in this chapter was designed to move students forward in school and future planning with attention to the four core tenets of the PWT framework. PWT acknowledges the perspective articulated in career construction theory and CWR that individuals need to develop the capacity for proactivity and the adaptability to cope with ongoing, unpredictable adjustments in work opportunities (Hartung & Vess, 2019; Savickas, 2005). Also consistent with these perspectives, the intervention encompasses a consideration of work and non-work roles and the promotion of a sense of work volition and career adaptability in relation to a radically changing world of work. The intervention seeks to help students refine their sense of purpose across work and non-work roles, increase their awareness of systemic and motivational barriers, and identify sources of support that can be accessed to navigate systemic barriers and effect personal and community change. This chapter focuses on youth purpose and personal and social agency in school and future planning as articulated by high school students participating in the WBL program.

Youth Purpose and Career Development Education

Although clarifying one's sense of purpose has been integral to considerations of self-awareness and career choice and CDE (Lent & Brown, 2013), the instability that characterizes the contemporary workforce requires that young people consider their purpose more broadly across work and non-work domains and consider the systemic obstacles that might impede their progress towards desired goals. *Youth purpose* has been defined by developmental scholars as a stable and generalized intention to accomplish something that is both meaningful to the self and of consequence to the world beyond the self (Damon, Menon, & Bronk, 2003). We believe that youth purpose is integral to a PWT informed model of CDE/WBL. Despite the current threats to youth purpose, research highlights its benefits in navigating developmental and contextual change, with higher levels of purpose being associated with cognitive, emotional, and behavioral engagement in school and work engagement, academic achievement, physical health, and psychological well-being among adolescents across varied ecological settings (Liang et al., 2017).

The literature on purpose within adolescent development and education has clear parallels with the career development tradition of fostering meaningful and rewarding options and life plans (Dik et al., 2013). Indeed, the concepts of purpose and meaning have been integrated thoughtfully into the career development literature, with relevant insights for this project (see Dik et al., 2013 for a review). Within the career development field, purpose has been defined as "people's identification of, and intention to pursue, particular highly valued, overarching life goals" (Steger & Dik, 2010, p. 133). Meaning refers to "the sense made of, and significance felt regarding, the nature of one's being and existence" (Steger, Frazier, Oishi, & Kaler, 2006, p. 81). Research has found that engaging in meaningful work that includes a social contribution component has been associated with greater levels of psychological adjustment. In addition, having a sense of meaningful work is associated with higher purpose, which can lead to better team functioning and greater vocational self-concept clarity (Steger, Dik, & Duffy, 2012). In career interventions with adults, Dik and Duffy (2015) suggest that counselors can assist clients in finding meaning in their work and lives by inviting them to identify their unique gifts and how these might be applied to help them to thrive in some areas of work and contribute either directly or indirectly to a set of social needs and to examine the alignment between their work and life goals.

Despite evidence supporting the benefits of purpose for youth, knowledge about ways to cultivate youth purpose, especially in the face of challenges in the world of work, is limited. Some research, however, has started to examine sources of youth purpose. Liang et al. (2017), for example, identified four major influences on the development of purpose among low-income high school youth enrolled in a program to promote college readiness. The four P's of purpose included People, such as parents, extended family members, teachers, and mentors who fostered youths' initial interest in a particular purpose and offered scaffolding support for their engagement in relevant activities. Students were also motivated to pursue their purpose because of its

Prosocial benefits to others, and because of their Propensity or possession of certain skills and character strengths that they perceived as relevant to their chosen purpose. Finally, Passion or students' interest and enjoyment in associated tasks was found to foster purpose. These findings have the potential to expand the limited knowledge on purpose development for youth. For example, efforts to cultivate purpose might be designed to offer mentoring and other experiences that enable youth to identify their own core values and to draw connections between these values and a long-term aspiration that it is personally meaningful.

In considering strategies for the promotion of youth purpose in CDE/WBL, we also find Richardson's (2012, 2015) notion of agentic action, which is informed by the CWR framework, to be helpful. Agentic action is an important construct in identifying and fostering mechanisms for individual and systemic change (Blustein, Kenny, Duffy, & Autin, in press). According to CWR, individuals co-construct lives of meaning through agentic action across their major life contexts, including work, school, and relationships. The role of the counselor from this perspective is to facilitate the development of agentic action so that individuals can take action in moving towards a life that is meaningful for them. As noted by Richardson (2015), the guideposts for career decision-making and the pathways to specific goals are unstable in a world of social and occupational uncertainty and inequality. Opportunities to engage in purposeful agentic actions across varied life contexts could be instrumental for constructing lives of personal or collective purpose in a shifting work and social landscape. Consistent with Richardson's (2012, 2015) perspective on agentic action, we maintain that CDE and WBL offer novel and relevant life experiences where young people can take action, reflect on the consequence of those actions, and adjust their goals or courses of action as needed based upon their experiences and reflections. Richardson (2012) notes furthermore that opportunities to engage in agentic action differ by social location, such that individuals' sense of purpose and life pathways are co-constructed in interaction with the opportunities and constraints in their lives. In this regard, CWR shares with PWT an emphasis on the primary role of social context. Following from this tenet, we maintain that CDE and WBL can guide young people in reflecting on the structural conditions that serve to expand and constrain the pathways in their lives and help them to consider how to navigate or to transform those structures through agentic action as individuals or in tandem with larger communities.

Scope and Nature of Our Study

The current study seeks to understand whether and how PWT-informed CDE/WBL can provide opportunities for engaging in agentic action that serves to cultivate youth purpose. More specifically, we interviewed twelve students enrolled in a summer CDE/WBL program designed for youth who would otherwise not have access to career and workplace mentoring. This study builds on the limited research examining the cultivation of youth purpose by exploring students' construction of purpose and their pathways to lives of purpose and meaning through CDE/WBL.

Program

The summer CDE/WBL program in which this study took places seeks to provide exposure to the world of work, opportunities for career exploration, and the development of 21st century work readiness skills. Students are matched with a local business organization for 10–15 h per week over a 6 week period and participate in a weekly 3 h workshop entailing reflection on experiences at the internship and engagement in activities directed towards the cultivation of purpose and skill building in communication, teamwork, cultural competence, critical awareness and problem solving. In recognition of the complex changes impacting the world of work, the workshops focused on enhancing the developmental competencies of youth for adapting to and navigating educational and work challenges, rather than focusing on career choice and decision-making. For example, students brainstormed solutions for common issues facing teens in their community (e.g. substance use) and learned about the most in-demand jobs today as compared to 20 years ago.

With regard to youth purpose, the workshops were designed to foster the four core components of purpose (propensity, passion, prosocial benefits, and people) through experiential group activities, individual reflection, and group sharing. Students were guided in identifying their core values, their strengths and their desired impact, with questions tailored for the WBL program (i.e., What are the core values of my internship setting? How can I live my core values at my internship? What problems do I see in the world? What impact do I want to have on my community? What positive impact can I make at my internship and in my career?), which were infused with relevant lessons pertaining to communication, teamwork, and critical thinking. Relational support was integrated through the assignment of a mentor in the workshop sessions and at the workplace. The workshops were developed and delivered by the youth services director in collaboration with university and community partners.

Although the community in which this program was implemented is relatively affluent, a significant percentage of the population also experiences economic hardship and insecurity. Eleven percent of students attending public schools in the city are living below the poverty line based on US criteria. The students participating in the program were diverse with regard to race and ethnicity (50% White, 33% Asian, 5% Black, 5% Latino), gender (44% male, 56% female), immigrant status (27% born outside the US), and family income (13% eligible for free or reduced lunch based on low family income).

Participants

Eight female and four male high school students between the ages of 15 and 19 (*M* = 16.5) were interviewed for this study. The students were entering tenth ($n = 2$), eleventh ($n = 3$), and twelfth ($n = 6$) grades in the fall, or had just graduated twelfth grade ($n = 1$). According to self-report, 41.7% ($n = 5$) identified as Asian/Asian-American, 16.7% ($n = 2$) as White, 8.3% as Black ($n = 1$), 8.3% ($n = 1$) as Latinx, and 25% ($n = 3$) as other, including Southwest Asia, Central Asian, and biracial. Twenty-five percent ($n = 3$) of students reported that they were born outside of the United States ($n = 3$) and 66.7% ($n = 8$) reported having at least one parent born outside of the US. Twenty-five percent ($n = 3$) of interviewees reported being eligible for free and reduced lunch. The demographic characteristics of the interview participants and description of their internship sites are presented in Table 1.

Protocol Development

A semi-structured interview was designed drawing from youth purpose research (Bronk, Menon, & Damon, 2004; Liang et al., 2016) to assess students' motivations for, and engagement in activities related to a long-term purpose or aspiration. Consistent with prior research on youth purpose (Bronk et al., 2004; Liang et al., 2016), participants were asked about their goals and dreams for the future in five and ten years. Because of our interest in learning about how the work-based learning experience relates to the development of purpose, students were also asked to reflect on how people and experiences within the internship and in their lives more broadly have influenced their aspirations and whether their goals have changed as result of the internship experience. In addition, students were asked about their personal qualities, skills, interests, and passions that make their aspirations a good fit, as well as any impact they hope to make. Students were then queried about possible challenges and barriers they might encounter and what motivates them to keep pursuing their goals when they confront barriers. Finally, students were asked about their plans and the steps they would need to take to reach their goals and dreams. (A copy of the interview is available from the first author).

Procedure

All students enrolled in the summer internship program were invited to participate in research assessing their perceptions of the program experience and of future work opportunities and barriers. Seventy-eight of the 95 students in the program turned in parental consent forms and completed a survey assessing their attitudes about school and work and their internship experience. Twelve students were also invited to

Table 1 Participant demographic data

Participant	Grade (entering)	Gender	Race/ethnicity	Birthplace	Parent Birthplace	Intern placement
Anna	10th	Female	Southwest Asian	US-born	Foreign-born	Health care
Ron	12th	Male	Central Asian	US-born	Foreign-born	STEM
Sarah	graduated	Female	White	US-born	US-born	STEM
Tania	12th	Female	Black	Foreign-born	US-born	Health care
Grace	12th	Female	Asian	US-born	Foreign-born	Human services
Alvin	12th	Male	Asian	Foreign-born	Foreign-born	STEM
Kisha	11th	Female	Biracial	US-born	US-born	Start up/small business
Fred	12th	Male	Asian	Foreign-born	Foreign-born	Social services
Joyce	12th	Female	Asian	US-born	Foreign-born	Education/historical
Milly	10th	Female	Asian	Foreign-born	Foreign-born	Health care
Ben	11th	Male	White	US-born	US-born	Human services
Mary	11th	Female	Latina	US-born	US-born	Start up/small business

participate in semi-structured interviews to provide in-depth insight into their future goals and experiences in the internship program. The interviews were conducted by three women, including two white doctoral students in counselling psychology and a South Asian master's student in mental health counselling.

Analysis of the Data

Once the interviews were transcribed, the data was analyzed following procedures of Consensual Qualitative Research (Hill, 2012). Two coding teams, drawn from masters and doctoral students and faculty in counselling psychology were involved in the data analysis. A doctoral student, who had served as a study interviewer performed the functions of auditor to review the coding procedure and offer feedback throughout the data analysis. Prior to beginning the analyses, team members acknowledged and discussed potential biases related to their own age, gender, educational level, social class, and race/ethnicity, their participation in other research and various phases of this program/research project, and their knowledge of related theory and research that might influence their perspective.

Interview coding followed three steps aligned with CQR: coding of domains, generating core ideas, and cross-analysis of domains and core ideas across interviews. Consistent with CQR methods, team members coded independently, met to review and discuss coding differences until consensus was reached. Once consensus was reached, the coding was reviewed by the auditor, with reviewer comments discussed by the coding teams.

Interview Findings

Six domains and 24 categories (See Table 2) emerged from the analysis. Consistent with the approach of Hill (2012), domains and categories that were expressed by all, or all but one of the participants (11 or 12 for our sample), were labeled as general, with those mentioned by at least half of the sample, but fewer than the criteria for general, labeled as typical (6–10 for this sample). Variant categories were those mentioned by 3–5 participants in this study, and categories mentioned by only one or two participants were excluded.

Future Planning

Future Planning captured students' thinking about their future plans and actions toward future goals. Students were largely focused on college attendance and professional careers and articulated a broad understanding of the intersection of work

Table 2 List of domains and categories

Domain	Category	Frequency
Future planning	Career/education goals	General
	Work-life aspirations	Typical
	Steps/mindsets	Typical
Challenges	Internship	Typical
	Academic challenges	Variant
	Internal challenges	Variant
	External challenges	Variant
Motivation	Passion	Typical
	Prosocial	Typical
	Personal utility	Typical
	Mastery	Typical
	Internal resources	Typical
	Influence of others	Typical
Caregiver messages/influence	Family legacy/story	Typical
	Value of Hard Work	Typical
	Learned a Specific Value or Skill	Typical
Propensity	Academic skills	Typical
	Character strengths	Typical
	Communication/interpersonal	Typical
	Service orientation	Variant

(continued)

Table 2 (continued)

Domain	Category	Frequency
Learning from internship	Clarification of career Interests or life goals	General
	Gained skills/knowledge	General
	Interaction with others	Typical
	Real world experience	Typical

and non-work activities. Ron, who aspires to a career in engineering, described the desired social impact of his career goals, "…because I don't want to grow up in a world where it's just pollution and CO_2 everywhere in the air, and you can't really breathe, and just best for sustainability, not depending on fossil fuels." Students typically articulated an awareness of specific actions or mindsets, such as studying, attending college, gathering knowledge, and determination that they deemed as important for reaching future goals.

Challenges

Students identified a range of past, present, or anticipated challenges or obstacles in their personal lives, at school, at the internship program, or in broader society. Grace described the social challenges that she encountered at her internship and how she overcame those:

> For me, I'm not a very social person, and because of that, at first it made me feel a little bit uncomfortable at first to interview and ask information from people, like from members. But once I talked to more people, got a little more comfortable, and I kind of learned how to keep up the conversation and get the information I need.

Fred identified an internal challenge that he experienced in the work setting and elsewhere, "If there was one challenge I faced I would have to say staying on task, and staying focused." Mary mentioned external challenges related to gender and ethnicity:

> I think being a woman in a business role, a management role would be tough. I think also being a Hispanic, being a minority would be tough. But I think if something's important to me, I don't think that a barrier is really going to stop me. I think I can always figure out a way to get around it. And I have a really big family and a lot of friends that can always help me through it.

Motivation

Students identified six sources of motivation related to their career or internship choice or in reference to a general goal or challenge. These included a sense of passion, prosocial benefits, personal utility, gaining mastery, the influence of others, and internal resources. Passion reflects students' expressed enjoyment, happiness, accomplishment or other intrinsically rewarding feelings as their incentive for pursuing certain goals or activities. Sarah explained, "This is what I'm passionate about and I want to just … get a job and work where you want to work." Prosocial reflected students' motivation to have a positive impact on others. Alvin, for example, spoke about the desire to benefit his country of origin though his future career, "Where I come from it's kind of poor country, so I would really like to try to help the country, the people in it. That makes me way more inspired to do environment stuff."

Some students also highlighted the personal or tangible benefits that they sought to gain in the internship program or through their future careers, such as money or prestige, while others described the desire to gain or master skills or knowledge, for their own sake. Internal resources reflected participants' perception that they could draw on internal resources to sustain motivation. Anna, for example, describes how past struggles "led me to have this eye-opening experience that to feel fulfilled and to do, really to have a purpose, I want to do things to benefit other people." Students also described their motivation as influenced by important others, such as family members, mentors or co-workers. Tania described how people in the internship served to shape her view on passion and how she might achieve social impact:

> I have this different view about medicine as a whole. Looking at the people at my [hospital internship], it's like they live as a family. Like, there's this holistic care they give to the patients and it's just captivating. And they have this connection among the coworkers, this connection they just live … And everything is towards the patient's care and I could just see the unity, and there's this one goal that everyone is trying to achieve. So that has kept me checked. Looking at it, it's like, 'Oh yeah, I really want to be that passionate.' I see those people, it's like a motivation for my own part It's like, you know what, I'm just gonna do this, because I admire this and I wanna be there someday, doing something like this.

Caregiver Influence and Messages

Students spoke about the influence of their caregivers with regard to the impact of family legacy and story, messages about the value of hard work, and learning a specific skill. Anna described the impact of her family story on her work attitudes:

> Really the main message I get from my family is just to do what you love and love what you do. It's cheesy but my dad, he came to this country when he was 17 years old. He escaped Persia and he's had, since he got to America, every job in the book and, as a kid, I watched him go from one to the next. But really what he always wanted to do is have a restaurant and that's what he ended up doing. And it's a pretty grueling job considering he works seven days a week and he's always there. But I've actually asked him, "Why do you do what you do?" Instead of getting a less grueling job and he said "Because I love what I do and it makes me happy so that's all that really matters to me." And I want to have that same mindset. That it doesn't really matter how hard it is, if it makes you happy. And that's the message I get from my family."

Joyce described several family lessons related to work life:

> Well, like from my family, I think I've learned that people in the workplace can be difficult, so I've learned how to kind of interact with people in a way that kind of minimizes the difficulties working with them. And I also think they both work odd jobs, but they seem to enjoy their jobs and they seem to have jobs where they're able to take time off, but then also, they're working a lot. But it seems like they enjoy their jobs. So, I think what I learned is that it's important to find a job that you enjoy but can also take a break from if you need to.

Propensity

Propensity refers to the presence of skills, strengths, and values that are perceived to be relevant for one's chosen purpose, including academic skills, character strengths, interpersonal skills, and service orientation. Mary, for example, was considering a career that would use math skills, because "I've always been good at math and I've always been good with things that you have directions on how to do them." Fred, felt that the summer internship had helped him to better understand his character strengths and weaknesses, stating:

> I've learned my strengths and weaknesses, like what I said about not being very good at focusing, so I know what to work on... One thing I confirmed about myself, I guess, is that I'm somewhat meticulous. I like to make sure things are done right, and sometimes I will double track entries to make sure that nothing is wrong."

With regard to service orientation, Joyce assessed the opportunity to help people as a source of joy related to her current internship and future career goals, explaining "I guess the impact I want to have is just to help people and help them help themselves, ... I feel like when I help people, I feel really good about myself. I feel like I've made a difference, like I've made someone happy or something, and I just really enjoy that feeling."

Learning from Internship

Students also described specific career related lessons gained through their internship and the accompanying workshops. These included enhanced understanding about one's interests, skills, likes and dislikes in the work environment and greater knowledge of work culture and the working world.

Joyce, explained how the internship helped her to clarify her career interests:

> Well, I think I always knew that I wanted to go into some science-based thing, but I think working here, or working at that site, really gave me a new idea of what I wanted to do. I didn't really think about doing public health or like health education before, but I guess it's put it into my brain, knowing that it's an option....I think this internship made me learn that I want to do something more in like helping people, not just like a random job, and I want to work in a place that's very collaborative and everyone's really friendly and kind of a small environment, and I definitely want to go into science and maybe health. It's just made me realize that I might be interested in public health and that type of thing.

Tania explained the benefits of the purpose activities that were included in the workshops:

> There was something about passion and purpose, why you do things. What are your drives? What are your challenges? So, it was like a reminder to me ... What do you want to do with your life? What are your weaknesses? How do you overcome this? So in this way some of the things we talked about. Like, we got to share with other people some of the challenges they face and how to tackle things, issues or troubles in real life when you're in the outside world.

> It's helpful because I have learned and I get to know some of those things and understand them better.

Ben describes how the internship experience helped him to develop authentic skills in a real world setting:

> So this definitely has given me an opportunity to just dive into the workspace and use those skills. It kind of flushed out the skills 100% because I didn't even realize those skills were even, I don't think in general I use that much of my organization unless I have schoolwork and that's just doing schoolwork. What about like managing files, and papers, and making sure to send an email by a certain time. How do I manage the time by the minute, by the hour? So it's definitely a lot more specific and I feel like that's going to help me out. … But also I figured out that I am very good at managing my time and managing my tasks So when I have four or five tasks in front of me I'm able to manage the time into increments and then say to myself I can do one task now, another task later. And once the first task is over, push it aside and focus on the second task.

Milly explained how her mentor had pushed her to learn, while Kisha described how she learned about teamwork through the internship.

> So, I learned that in a team setting, in this kind of team setting, I learned that I really liked it and really thrived in it, because it allowed me to work independently, but at the same time, I didn't feel like I was alone, like I had to do everything by myself."

Discussion of Findings

As part of our efforts to develop a transformative model of CDE, we sought to assess whether and how CDE and WBL might serve to foster youth purpose as an internal resource for navigating an uncertain work future. Our interviews with 12 youth who participated in a summer internship program described young peoples' experience of the summer program, their life contexts and pathways towards the future that reflect the theoretical foundations of the program and offer insights into the processes and factors that optimally cultivate youth purpose.

Theoretical Groundings

Consistent with PWT (Blustein, 2006; Duffy et al., 2016), CWR (Richardson, 2012) and career construction (Savickas, 2005) perspectives, students articulated their futures both in terms of work and non-work roles and emphasized the importance of relationships both within the workplace and across their lives more broadly. While some students saw the summer program and their future career choices as a means for accruing economic resources and social prestige, many were also motivated to master challenge, gain skills, and make a social contribution. In this way, the students largely embraced what Blustein (2006) has framed as an inclusive perspective on work, encompassing work and non-work roles and as satisfying needs for relationship, self-determination and social contribution, as well as financial need.

Consistent with the PWT and CWR, the program sought to expand critical awareness of social and systemic barriers that impede access to economic and social resources integral to work access and well-being. The interviews revealed how students' conceptualizations of their future pathways were shaped by contextual resources and constraints. With regard to resources, participants recognized social support garnered from family and from the internship context as valuable assets in overcoming barriers and facilitating progress along their chosen pathways. Some students expressed awareness of ways in which discriminatory practices based on race, ethnicity, and gender might pose obstacles. Student narratives highlight both the challenges and strengths of immigrant communities, with ethnic and cultural factors acknowledged as sources of pride and motivation.

Overall, students in this study articulated a strong sense of proactivity and work volition or the perceived ability to make occupational choices, despite the presence of obstacles (Duffy, Diemer, Perry, Laurenzi, & Torrey, 2012), which is conceptualized in PWT as an important psychological asset in the pathway to decent work. The level of agency expressed by participants in the context of challenge likely reflects their access to communities and families with educational assets, financial resources, and systems of social support. Relatedly, the program sought to heighten participant awareness of the availability of community resources to address barriers and to build relational supports within the program. The impact of economic constraints may emerge as a more dominant theme in communities where a greater percentage of students face economic challenges. Although the 6-week program did not offer opportunities for social action beyond the internship, the critical awareness fostered through the workshops could serve as a foundation for later social action at the personal or collective level.

Opportunities for Agentic Action

Drawing from Richardson's notion of agentic action (2012, 2015), the summer internship experience provided a context in which students could exert agentic action in testing-out their interests and skills in a real world setting. Most of the students entered the summer program expressing a future goal of attending college. For most, the summer internship provided an opportunity to further explore their interests, to identify their strengths, and to work on areas of identified weaknesses. Both the internship and the accompanying workshop were recognized by participants as providing opportunities to increase personal and social awareness and to build concrete knowledge and skills. The workshops additionally offered the opportunity to reflect on and make meaning of their workplace experiences in relation to their personal strengths and values and experiences grounded in their social location, many as first and second generation Americans. The internship experience served to further affirm, clarify or modify students' future direction and offer a pathway for next steps. In this way, the program enabled students, consistent with Richardson' (2015) notion of agentic action, to engage in exploring a relevant social context, to experience the effects of their actions, and to refine future steps on the basis of those experiences. In this way, the program can facilitate agentic action that serves as a basic process for the construction of lives of meaning (Richardson, 2015).

Cultivation of Youth Purpose

The four P's of purpose (Passion, Propensity, Prosocial and People) as identified by Liang et al. (2017) emerged in the students' descriptions of their internship experiences and in the ways in which the broader contexts of their lives interfaced with the summer internship experience to shape their goals and pathways towards the future. The students reported that the internship provided them with opportunities to further assess, refine and develop their passions and propensities. Students' discussion of their passions and propensities were closely linked in their narratives to their sense of purpose, their motivation in overcoming barriers, and their efforts in moving forward towards future goals. Students' expressed motivation and goals were often closely linked to an articulation of the prosocial benefits of their chosen goals either for their own communities or for society at large. Students' responses clearly conveyed their awareness and desire for purpose and impact, oftentimes related to some aspect of family or immigration history. Research suggests that adolescents who face marginalization may develop a sense of purpose in life directed at combating those systemic injustices that lead to marginalization (Sumner, Burrow, & Hill, 2018). In one study of low-income youth by Gutowski, White, Liang, Diamonti, & Berado (2017), the development of purpose for some youth was shaped by their desire to escape contextual constraints, such as financial strain or community violence, and by influence from important others who held high expectations.

People who are proximal to the students' relational spaces played an important role in shaping students' goals and sense of purpose. The importance of people emerged in students' description of the influences and messages received from their caretakers, the impact of others as a source of motivation, and the role of interaction with others, especially work mentors and co-workers, in fostering student learning from the internship. As in the Liang et al. (2017) study, the presence of persons, including family members, teachers, mentors, friends, and co-workers, offered affirmation and scaffolding for realizing one's purpose, including awareness of one's passions, talents, and desired impact on the world.

The importance of personal relationships is also a central feature of PWT and in Richardson's CWR (Richardson 2012). According to PWT (Blustein, 2006), for example, work is important as a source of purpose and meaning based, in part, on the relational connections and social contribution that are fulfilled through working. The role of people in the development of purpose that emerged in this study is also aligned with the identification of social support in the PWT as a factor that can serve to moderate the negative effects of marginalization and economic constraints. For these youth, people within their family and within the summer internship not only helped to foster purpose, but were viewed as supporting the development of work volition and progress along the pathway to decent work. In addition, meaning and purpose are reflected in the self-determination needs that working can optimally fulfill as manifested in the pursuit of engaging activities that are meaningful and authentic (Blustein, 2006).

Theoretical and Practical Implications

The student narratives suggest that work-based learning and career development education developed in alignment with the literature on youth purpose (Damon et al., 2003; Liang et al., 2017) and PWT, CWR, and career construction perspectives can engage youth in cultivating purpose. According to Dik et al. (2013), meaningful work arises from workplace activities that people find worthwhile or that foster or fulfill a sense of purpose. Purpose is one of the ways in which work activity can deliver personal and societal benefits by helping people to feel that they are contributing to the world in ways that they deem as important (Dik et al., 2013; Steger et al., 2012). Cultivating purpose may enable youth to pursue meaningful future work and overarching life goals, even when work is less stable and the traditional benefits of work (e.g., benefits and stability) are less available (cf Blustein et al., 2018). Baumeister and Vohs (2002) propose that purpose can lend structure to the present by linking current behaviors with future events to tell a coherent story, which can be important during times of uncertainty and rapid change. Although cross-sectional research documents the association of purpose with engagement, motivation, and personal investment both for youth and adults (Dik et al., 2013), more research is needed on the long-term benefits of purpose for sustaining youths' engagement and motivation in their future work and schooling.

Conclusions

This chapter describes our initial efforts in developing a transformative WBL model of CDE. In so doing we highlight the promise of youth purpose as a vital resource for guiding young people towards meaningful lives and work and in navigating the challenges of an uncertain future and inequitable social structures. Our interviews suggest that CDE and WBL, accompanied by reflective experiences, may offer a context for youth to exercise agentic action and reflection in developing a sense of purpose. Although the student narratives offer compelling insights into their perceptions of the work-based learning, career education experiences and sense of purpose, the immediate or long-term impact of these experiences is not clear. We hope that this chapter may serve as an impetus for further theoretical and program development and evaluation for career education that prepares youth for lives of meaning and purpose in a context of work uncertainty.

References

Ali, S. R., Yang, L. Y., Button, C. J., & McCoy, T. T. (2012). Career education programming in three diverse high schools: A critical psychology—case study research approach. *Journal of Career Development, 39*(4), 357–385.

Ananat, E. O., Gassman-Pines, A., Francis, D. V., & Gibson-Davis, C. M. (2011). *Children left behind: The effects of statewide job loss on student achievement (No. w17104)*. National Bureau of Economic Research.

Baumeister, R. F., & Vohs, K. D. (2002). The pursuit of meaningfulness in life. *Handbook of Positive Psychology, 1,* 608–618.

Blustein, D. L. (2006). *The psychology of working: A new perspective for career development, counseling and public policy*. NY: Routledge.

Blustein, D. L., Kenny, M. E., Di Fabio, A., & Guichard, J. (2018). Expanding the impact of the Psychology of Working: Engaging psychology in the struggle for decent work and human rights. *Journal of Career Assessment*. https://doi.org/10.1177/1069072718774002.

Blustein, D. L., Kenny, M. E., Duffy, R. D., & Autin, K. (in press). The Psychology of Working in practice: A theory of change for a new era. *The Career Development Quarterly.*

Bronk, K. C., Menon, J. L., & Damon, W. (2004). *Youth purpose: Conclusions from a working conference of leading scholars*. West Conshohocken, PA: John Templeton Foundation.

Damon, W., Menon, J., & Bronk, K. C. (2003). The Development of Purpose During Adolescence. *Applied Developmental Science, 7*(3), 119–128.

Di Fabio, A., & Blustein, D. L. (2016). From meaning of working to meaningful lives: The challenges of expanding decent work. *Frontiers in Psychology, 7,* 1119.

Dik, B. J., Byrne, Z. S., & Steger, M. F. (Eds.). (2013). Purpose and meaning in the workplace. Washington, DC: American Psychological Association. http://dx.doi.org/10.1037/14183-000.

Dik, B. J., & Duffy, R. D. (2015). Strategies for discerning and living a calling. In P. J. Hartung, M. L. Savickas, & W. B. Walsh (Eds.), *APA Handbook of career interventions* (Vol. 2, pp. 305–317)., Applications Washington, DC: American Psychological Association.

Duffy, R. D., Blustein, D. L., Diemer, M. A., & Autin, K. L. (2016). The psychology of working theory. *Journal of Counseling Psychology, 63,* 127–148. https://doi.org/10.1037/cou0000140.

Duffy, R. D., Diemer, M. A., Perry, J. C., Laurenzi, C., & Torrey, C. L. (2012). The construction and initial validation of the Work Volition Scale. *Journal of Vocational Behavior, 80*(2), 400–411.

Gamboa, V., Paixão, M. P., & de Jesus, S. N. (2013). Internship quality predicts career exploration of high school students. *Journal of Vocational Behavior, 83*(1), 78–87.

Gutowski, E., White, A., Liang, B., Diamonti, A. J., & Berado, D. (2017). How Stress Influences Purpose Development: The Importance of Social Support. *Journal of Adolescent Research, 33,* 074355841773775. https://doi.org/10.1177/0743558417737754.

Hartung, P. J., & Vess, L. (2019). Career construction for life design. In N. Arthur & M. McMahon (Eds.), *Contemporary theories of career development: International perspectives* (pp. 91–104). NY: Routledge, Taylor, & Francis.

Hill, C. E. (2012). *Consensual qualitative research: A practical resource for investigating social science phenomena*. American Psychological Association.

Hill, N. E., Liang, B., Bravo, D., Price, M., Polk, W., Parella, T., & Savitz-Romer, M. (2018). Adolescents' perceptions of the economy: Its association with academic engagement and the role of school-based and parental relationships. *Journal of Youth and Adolescence, 47,* 895–915.

Kalleberg, A. (2009). Precarious work, insecure workers: Employment relations in transition. *American Sociological Review, 74,* 1–22. https://doi.org/10.1177/000312240907400101.

Katz, L. F., & Krueger, A. B. (2016). The rise and nature of alternative work arrangements in the United States, 1995–2015. Retrieved from: https://krueger.princeton.edu/sites/default/files/akrueger/files/katz_krueger_cws_-_march_29_20165.pdf.

Kenny, M., Blustein, D., Liang, B., Klein, T., & Etchie, Q. (2019). Applying the psychology of working theory for transformative career education. *Journal of Career Development.* Advance online publication. https://doi.org/10.1177/08948453198276

Kenny, M. E. (2017). Preparing youth to meet the challenges of an uncertain future: A new direction of prevention. *Prevention and Health Promotion: Research, Social Action, Practice, and Training, 10*(2), 23–30.

Kenny, M. E. (2013). The promise of work as a component of educational reform. In D. Blustein (Ed), *Oxford Handbook of the Psychology of Working: An Inclusive Psychology for the 21st Century*. (pp. 273–291). NY: Oxford.

Kenny, M. E., Blustein, D. L., Haase, R. F., Jackson, J., & Perry, J. (2006). Setting the stage: Career development and the school engagement process. *Journal of Counseling Psychology, 53,* 272–279.

Kenny, M. E., & Minor, A. (2015). Developing self and resilience for an uncertain future: Positive youth development. In A. Di Fabio & Bernaud, J. L. (Eds). *The Construction of Identity in the 21st Century: A Fetschrift for Jean Guichard* (pp. 87–101). Hauppauge, NY: Nova Science.

Lent, R. W., & Brown, S. D. (2013). Social cognitive model of career self-management: Toward a unifying view of adaptive career behavior across the life span. *Journal of counseling psychology, 60*(4), 557.

Liang, B., White, A., Mousseau, A., Hasse, A., Knight, L., Berado, D., & Lund, T. (2017). The four P's of purpose among College Bound students: People, propensity, passion, and pro-social benefits. *Journal of Positive Psychology, 12*(3), 281–294. (http://dx.doi.org/10.1080/17439760.2016.1225118).

Liang, B., Lund, T. J., Mousseau, A. M. D., & Spencer, R. (2016). The mediating role of engagement in mentoring relationships and self-esteem among affluent adolescent girls. *Psychology in the Schools, 53*(8), 848–860.

McWhirter, E. H., Crothers, M., & Rasheed, S. (2000). The effects of high school career education on social–cognitive variables. *Journal of Counseling Psychology, 47*(3), 330.

Nassar-McMillan, S. C., Taylor, J., & Conley, A. H. (2017). Promising career and workforce development programs and services in middle and high school settings. In V. S, Solberg & S. R. Ali (Eds.), *The handbook of career and workforce development: research, practice, and policy* (147–162), New York: Routledge, Taylor and Francis.

Richardson, M. S. (2012). Counseling for work and relationships. *The Counseling Psychologist., 40,* 190–242. https://doi.org/10.1177/0011000011406452.

Richardson, M. S. (2105). Agentic action in context. In R. A. Young et al. (Eds.) *Counseling and action* (pp. 51–68). New York: Springer.

Savickas, M. L. (2005). The theory and practice of career construction. In S. Brown & R. W. Lent (Eds.), *Career development and counseling: Putting theory and research to work* (Vol. 1, pp. 42–70). New York: John Wiley.

Standing, G. (2014). Understanding the precariat through labour and work. *Development and Change, 45*(5), 963–980.

Steger, M. F., Dik, B. J., & Duffy, R. D. (2012). Measuring meaningful work: The Work and Meaning Inventory (WAMI). *Journal of Career Assessment, 20,* 322–337. https://doi.org/10.1177/1069072711436160.

Steger, M. F., & Dik, B. J. (2010). Work as meaning. In P. A. Linley, S. Harrington, & N. Page (Eds.), *Oxford handbook of positive psychology and work* (pp. 131–142). Oxford, England: Oxford University Press.

Steger, M. F., Frazier, P., Oishi, S., & Kaler, M. (2006). The meaning in life questionnaire: Assessing the presence of and search for meaning in life. *Journal of Counseling Psychology, 53,* 80–93.

Sumner, R., Burrow, A. L., & Hill, P. (2018). The development of purpose in life among adolescents who experience marginalization: Potential opportunities and obstacles. *American Psychologist, 73,* 740–7521.

Whiston, S. C, & Blustein, D. L. (2013). The impact of career interventions: Preparing our citizens for the 21st century jobs. (Research Report). National Career Development Association (www.ncda.org) and the Society for Vocational Psychology (www.div17.org/vocpsych/)

Teacher Exclusion in Post-apartheid Schools: On Being Competently (Un)Qualified to Teach

Nuraan Davids and Yusef Waghid

Abstract Commonly, debates on educational inclusion/exclusion in South Africa are centred on learner and student experiences. While current calls for decolonisation and decoloniality have encompassed demands for broader racial representation among academics in higher education, the particular solitary and isolationary experiences of minority group teachers have slipped below the radar, and remain largely unnoticed, and hence, unrecorded. The encounters and confrontations of minority group teachers embody a specific complexity which brings into disrepute professional competence because of racial identity. In other words, minority group teachers are deemed as less competent on the basis of their disconnection from the majority group teachers. This means that while a teacher might have a qualification to teach, he or she is not *qualified* to teach because of *who* he or she is. In this regard, the interest and concern of this chapter is threefold. What are the implications for conceptions of social justice, if teachers experience pedagogical undermining and estrangement as practices of exclusion? Secondly, how might innovative career counselling assist in cultivating pedagogies and ways of being that move towards openness and inclusion? And thirdly, how can career innovation be extended beyond normative parameters of advancement, and instead be reconceived as an enactment of social justice? Our argument is in defence of teacher inclusion: teachers are included when they are recognised for the responsible acts they perform in expediting student learning. In our case, responsibility is conceptually and pragmatically linked to cultivating decoloniality, evoking student potentialities, and acting responsibly and ethically.

Keywords Teacher exclusion · Professional competence · Social justice · Career counselling · Decoloniality

---

N. Davids (✉) · Y. Waghid
Stellenbosch University, Cape Town, South Africa
e-mail: nur@sun.ac.za

J. G. Maree (ed.), *Handbook of Innovative Career Counselling*,
https://doi.org/10.1007/978-3-030-22799-9_20

Introduction

Discussions and debates around learner inclusion in South Africa's recently desegregated schools have mostly focused on the experiences of learners as they navigate their way through unfamiliar academic, social, cultural, and linguistic landscapes. In turn, much of the controversies surrounding practices of exclusion, marginalisation and discrimination—whether in terms of race, culture, religion, special needs, or sexuality—have centred on learners (Francis, 2017; Msibi, 2012; Meier & Hartell, 2009; Soudien & Sayed, 2004). Very little, if any, attention has been given to the particular experiences of teachers, as they, too, enter unfamiliar spaces of desegregated staff rooms. Presumably, the assumptions are that teachers are not at the same level of risk of exclusion and isolation as learners; that the standards and frameworks informing notions of teacher professionalism would preclude any unfair treatment of teachers; that educational leaders and teachers alike would simply know and be better than to treat professional colleagues with anything less than dignity. The truth, however, is somewhat different. On the one hand, teachers and learners from historically disadvantaged schools in post-apartheid South Africa often share common reasons for migrating to historically advantaged (white) schools—namely, better-resourced schools, smaller classes, safer school environments, and in the case of teachers, the possibility of a higher SGB-supplemented salary. On the other hand, however, not only have the shifts in teacher composition and numbers been significantly less than that of learners (Hofmeyr, 2000), but the teaching community is much less socially integrated (Soudien, 2004).

That schools in post-apartheid South Africa remain largely disparate spaces in terms of meaningful practices of belonging and participation for both learners and teachers, hold serious implications for the promotion and cultivation of social justice. While much of the attention has centred on the experiences of exclusion and isolation of learners, part of the solution in addressing the displacement and misrecognition of learners resides in looking at teacher compositions, not only in terms of external representation, but in terms of internal participation. It is imperative that learners not only encounter good teaching and safe spaces of engagement, but also points of resonance and reflection in terms of who teaches them. This is certainly not to say that 'white' learners should be taught by 'white' teachers, or that 'black' learners should be taught by 'black' teachers. What we are arguing for is that in terms of cultivating diverse notions of citizenship, coupled with nurturing the potentialities of all learners, they (learners) have to witness and experience that diversity within their learning contexts. In turn, pre-service educator programmes ought to place renewed emphasis on career preparation in terms of creating spaces for conversational engagements and deliberations in relation to particularities of histories and lived experiences. In this sense, regard for the other—which is at the core of social justice—is embedded in teaching theories, so that these might be made visible not only in their teaching, but in how they recognise and celebrate differences among their learners. In sum, unless pre-service (and in-service teachers) are exposed to different narratives and divergent perspectives as a natural way of the world, they will not be adequately prepared for a career, which is fundamentally shaped through diverse ways of thinking, being and acting. The more diverse these encounters, the greater the knowledge spectrum, and the deeper the types of engagement. Maintaining a Eurocentric or Afrikaner-centric character of school (as is the case in post-apartheid historically advantaged South African schools) not only denies role models to students from diverse identities, but also denies self-understanding to White teachers (Pinar, Reynolds, Slattery, & Taubman, 2000).

We commence this chapter by considering understandings of 'competence'—both in terms of policy, and in practice, by paying particular attention to the experiences of minority group teachers. Minority group teachers refer to teachers, who constitute the minority in terms of race, culture, religion, language, accent, sexuality, and ethnicity (Davids & Waghid, 2015). We look at how these teachers are excluded through a language of 'competence', and how, even when they are included in particular schools, they continue to experience pedagogical undermining by principals, colleagues, parents and learners.

Notions of 'Competence' and Minority Group Teachers

It is argued, states Carr (1993: 254), that schools and society need teachers who are not just knowledgeable or well-informed about education, but whose knowledge and understanding is expressed or exhibited in their abilities—teachers, in short, who are competent by virtue of the intelligent application of their knowledge and understanding in effective practice. Current competency analyses of professionalism, explains Carr (1993: 258), are inclined to focus on generic competences—that is, effective teaching skills of planning, organisation, communication, classroom management. And, although, as Carr (1993) continues, competence is presumed as a matter of achieving standards within a given practice or career, understandings of competence are complex, because they adopt different meanings in different contexts of discourse. As Hiebert and Neault (2014: 691) explain, the components that contribute to being a competent professional vary from one country to another; the language used to describe these factors also varies, which often creates a barrier to international cooperation and collaboration. In turn, they continue, there are differences in the philosophical approach used to develop competency frameworks. While some approaches are based on the belief that a framework should focus on the competencies required to deliver quality career services regardless of the primary professional affiliation of the person providing services, other approaches, state Hiebert and Neault (2014: 698), are based on the belief that a framework should focus on the competencies that are unique to career practitioners and are not likely to be part of the competency set of other professional groups.

To Carr (1993: 260), the problem with a notion of a generic competence is precisely that it confuses or misconstrues the idea of a capacity. He contends that one cannot set out to construe those highly important and rightly valued professional competences—that is, practical skills, aptitudes and abilities which are required by teachers for the successful pursuit of their craft—in terms of an inventory of discretely specifiable causally effective powers without descent into an essentially reductive quasi-behaviourist caricature of professional competence in the more substantial capacity sense. At best, states Carr (1993: 176), competence models and benchmark standards should be regarded as identifying no more than highly general categories of professional aim, value, responsibility and/or expertise for teacher development. He is adamant that any interpretation of such codes and models as either lists of directives to be followed in a spirit of blind obedience or behaviourally measurable skills, however, is professionally debilitating and ought to be resisted (Carr, 2006: 176)

Educational reform in post-apartheid South Africa has followed similar generic and problematic adaptations of what is construed as a 'competent' teacher. The 'Norms and Standards for Educators' (NSE) (DoE, 2000) uses an outcomes-based approach to teacher education and provides detailed descriptions of what a competent educator should be able to demonstrate. In terms of this policy, norms are understood as competencies, while standards are linked to the qualifications for the development of teachers. The emphasis of the NSE (DoE, 2000) is on performance in schools, classrooms and management, and support services of the schooling system. The policy identifies seven roles that a teacher should be able to perform, and describes in detail the knowledge, skills and values that are necessary to perform the roles successfully (DoE, 2000):

- Learning mediator—mediate learning in a manner that is sensitive to the diverse needs of learners, including those with barriers to learning, construct learning environments that are appropriately contextualised and inspirational, and communicate effectively, showing recognition of and respect for the differences of others.
- Interpreter and designer of learning programmes and materials—understand and interpret provided learning programmes, design original learning programmes, identify the requirements for a specific context of learning and select, and prepare suitable textual and visual resources for learning.
- Leader, administrator and manager—make decisions appropriate to the level, manage learning in the classroom, carry out classroom administrative duties efficiently and participate in school decision-making structures in ways that are democratic.
- Scholar, researcher and lifelong learner—achieve ongoing personal, academic, occupational and professional growth through pursuing reflective study and research in his or her learning area, in broader professional and educational matters, and in other related fields.
- Community, citizenship and pastoral role—practise and promote a critical, committed and ethical attitude towards developing a sense of respect and responsibility towards others. Uphold the constitution and promote democratic values and practices in schools and society. Develop supportive relationships with parents and other key persons and organisations based on a critical understanding of community and environmental development issues.
- Assessor—understand that assessment is an essential feature of the teaching and learning process and know how to integrate it into this process.

- Learning area, subject, discipline and phase specialist—be well grounded in the knowledge, skills, values, principles, methods and procedures relevant to the discipline, subject, learning area, phase of study, or professional or occupational practice.

According to Harley, Barasa, Bertram, Mattson, and Timm (2000: 291), each of the above seven roles is defined in terms of foundational, practical and reflexive competences. In terms of the NSE (DoE, 2000), while foundational competence is a demonstrated understanding of the knowledge and thinking which underpins actions taken, practical competence is the demonstrated ability, in an authentic context, to consider a range of possibilities for action, and perform the action chosen. The ability to integrate the above two competences in order to reflect more critically on both is referred to as reflexive competence, which develops the ability to adapt to change and unforeseen circumstances, and explain the reasons behind these adaptations (DoE, 2000). As a policy document, the NSE (DoE, 2000) identifies a competent, professional teacher as one who is able to integrate a complex set of roles with a social, economic and moral responsibility. As Parker and Adler (2005: 60) assert, the NSE (DoE, 2000) projects an official policy image of a desired or 'ideal' competent teacher and his or her learners, rather than a constructed reality based in practice. In addition to homogenising conceptions of teacher professionalism and teacher identities, the NSE conceives of competence as a particular set of preconceived techniques and functions. In other words, teacher competency is conceived as that which is immediately tangible, and hence, measurable. Missing from these generic conceptions of teacher competence are any ideas of values, ethics and teacher identity.

In post-apartheid's recently desegregated schools, (mis)construed ideas of 'competence' are deliberately used as practices of exclusion and exclusivism. While learners from historically marginalised racial, cultural and ethnic groups are excluded through structures of exorbitant school fees, feeder areas, and language, teachers from these same groups are kept at bay—both externally and internally—through a language of 'competence' (Jansen, 2004) and 'standards' (Soudien & Sayed, 2004). Subreenduth (2013: 591) maintains that in South Africa, there is no demise of race—just a displacement of its meaning. As Jansen (2004) explains, the refusal or avoidance of historically white schools to appoint black teachers is justified by profound racialized and dichotomised conceptions of white competence and black incompetence. On a very explicit level, black, coloured and Indian teachers are deemed not to possess the same level of competencies and capabilities as white teachers, and are therefore not appointed at historically white schools. Incoming black teachers, explains Jansen (2007: 30), 'are already framed in ways that disempower them, and the same nurturing and accommodation that is so readily made for novice white teachers seldom apply to novice black teachers'.

It is common, therefore, to find that even where the learner demographics have shifted entirely from a predominantly white to pluralist and diverse learner body, this diversity is not evident in the teaching staff. The exclusion of diverse teacher identities is by no means limited to historically white schools. Coloured and black schools, which have also seen significant patterns of learner diversity seldom, if ever, appoint black teachers (Simelane, 2018; Makhetha, 2017).

Yet, external forms of exclusion are seemingly easier to manage through frameworks of employment equity—at least, in principle. Of greater concern is the complexity of the less obvious practices of internal exclusion. As both Young (2000) and Biesta (2009) argue, inclusion does not necessarily imply full participation and regard. Teachers from historically marginalised groups might find themselves as part of a particular school staff, but their presence does not equate to participation or deliberative engagement with the practices of that particular educational space (see Biesta, 2009). In this sense, practices of inclusion are not necessarily diametrically opposed to exclusion. One such example involves a 'black' teacher, who was appointed at a 'coloured' school as a teacher of Mathematics, but was only allowed to teach Mathematical Literacy—on the basis that she required 'mentoring'. Four years after being appointed, she was still teaching only Mathematical Literacy (Davids & Waghid, 2015). More importantly, practices of exclusion, justified through a language of 'competence' and 'standards' are not only defined by race. Instead, what one witnesses are intersections of identity constructions, which, in turn, are used to feed into more intricate forms of marginalisation, othering, and rendering of 'incompetent'.

Notions of 'competence' are evidently also connected to constructions and stereotypes of language, accent, religion, culture, nationality, ethnicity, as well as sexuality. One such case involves a South African 'Indian' teacher, who had taught Accounting at an Indian school for ten years before applying for the position of Head of Department (HOD) at a former White school in 2011. He was eager to advance his career, had just completed a BEd (Hons) degree, and was proud of his new appointment. His initial pride soon turned into humiliation, as he realised that although he was appointed as the HOD of Accounting, the departmental meetings were arranged and managed by a 'more senior' teacher. In addition, the 'more senior teacher' also had the responsibility of moderating all examination question papers, because he had yet to understand the 'ethos' of the school (Davids & Waghid, 2015). He was assigned to teach only grades 9 and 10, even though he had previously taught grades 11 and 12. To worsen matters, he was inundated with requests from parents that their children be moved to other classes. In a meeting to discuss this, the principal had reassured him that it was not his teaching that was a problem, but his accent, and that perhaps he could try to change that. The confidence, which he had always enjoyed as a teacher was replaced by deep feelings of insecurity and doubt in his abilities to teach (Davids & Waghid, 2015). We are reminded of Hargreaves's (1998: 845) conception of teaching as an emotional practice; that the bond teachers have with their learners is the central influence with regard to their choice of method, teaching context and practice. The teacher's decision to leave—after only ten months at the school—was made when the principal asked him whether he would be taking leave to celebrate Eid (a Muslim festival day). The principal had seemingly failed to realise that he was in fact not Muslim, but a practising Hindu—raising all sorts of questions about essentialized constructions and conceptions of identity and cultural orientation (Davids & Waghid, 2015).

Another case centres on parents' unease that their children would be taught by a 'black' lesbian. In this instance, the specific contention was not only that the teacher was a black lesbian, but that her lifestyle choice would somehow be used to legitimise homosexuality. The teacher, therefore, could not be trusted to competently teach learners about sexuality, as presumably her identity as a lesbian precluded her from doing so (Bhana, 2012). In all the examples cited in this discussion is a clear resistance to difference, diversity and otherness, disguised in an exclusive language of competence. The associated perils with the ongoing external and internal exclusion of teachers from minority groups extend beyond parameters of integrated and inclusive schooling. At stake here are deeply needed discussions on what we understand as the role and responsibility of education to be in relation to the cultivation of a peacefully co-existing democratic society. What renders a lesbian teacher incompetent to teach learners about sexuality? What informs the implicit normative assumption that a heterosexual teacher might be more competent to fulfil this role?

In the ensuing discussion we look at the implications for conceptions of social justice, if teachers experience pedagogical undermining and estrangement as practices of exclusion.

Pedagogical Undermining of Teachers: Implications for Social Justice

Career development scholars and practitioners, such as Hansen (2003), Tang (2003), as well as Evans, Kincade, Marbley and Seem (2005) are in agreement that career counselling needs to do more to serve diverse populations, and reconsider the foundational necessity for social justice. To Lee and Hipolito-Delgado (2007: xiv), social justice is understood as the full participation of all people in the life of a society—particularly those who have been systematically excluded on the basis of race or ethnicity, gender, age, physical or mental disability, education, sexual orientation, socioeconomic status, or other characteristics. According to Ratts (2009), career counselling ought to be mindful not only of patterns of marginalisation in relation to particular groups, but need to focus on social advocacy as an advancement for equity. This mindfulness includes being alert to potential barriers and obstacles, which might hinder access, and the development of professionals (Butler, 2012). Within the South African context, the terrain of obstacles and barriers are as complex, as they are intersectional. While racism remains the most common signifier of exclusion, many teachers are also subjected to forms of marginalisation and discrimination on the basis of religion, culture, ethnicity, language, accent, sexuality, and class.

That understandings about competence remain trapped in a language of technicist skills and functions—as evident in the NSE (DoE, 2000)—means a stifling not only of what teaching ought to yield, but indeed, what type of career counselling is necessary for the development of teacher professionalism. In any context, competent teachers and teaching have to be considered in relation to societal needs and expectations. And because these needs and expectations are constantly shifting, our ideas about teaching and education have to be equally fluid—from understandings of historical context and influence, to political and socio-economic demands. Evident from the preceding discussion is not only a distorted understanding of 'competence', but a privileging of particular norms (racial, cultural, religious, linguistic, sexual), which renders any other enactments or ways of being as other, and therefore, 'incompetent'. Leaning or depending on notions of 'competence' have particular implications. On the one hand, this dependency undermines what it means to teach, because it conceives of teaching not only as a pre-determined skill, but also as one ascribed to a pre-determined 'teacher'. Such conceptions serve not only to undermine ideas of professional development, but legitimise teacher and teaching stagnancy. For this reason, we are drawn to Harris's (1997) argument that competence-based teacher education ultimately leads to teachers' de-professionalisation and de-skilling. On the other hand, when teachers are conceived as incompetent on the basis of who they are, rather than on their knowledge and skills, we are left with complex issues and patterns of 'misrecognition' (Taylor, 1994: 25), and 'repeated negations of identity' (Bhabha, 1994: 46).

Seemingly, ideas of teacher stagnancy, as well as negations of identity are equally problematic for the purposes of education. In this regard, Carr (1993: 265) argues:

> The knowledge and understanding which should properly inform the professional consciousness of the competent teacher is thus primarily neither the knowledge that of scientific theory nor the knowledge how of routine craft skills - even though it draws on the one and informs the other - but a kind of moral wisdom or judgement which is rooted in rational reflection about educational policies and practices and what is ethically, as well as instrumentally, appropriate to achieve them. Above all, then, the source from which professional competence in what I have called the capacity sense springs is a thorough initiation into the diverse modes of rational discourse, the plurality of voices, in which the character and quality of educational goods are discussed and evaluated. This also implies an introduction to questions about what is of educational value in curriculum terms, what constitutes just and equal educational access, what counts as morally acceptable (and not just technically efficient) pedagogy, and about the wider social and political aspects of human flourishing in which any talk of educationally improving people (often against their wishes) must be implicated.

Presumably—if we look at post-apartheid educational reform—'a commitment to the common good' (DoE, 1997: 8), implies a socially just agenda, and point of departure. What type of career counselling is necessary to recognise both implicit and explicit barriers to teacher professionalism? What is the role of career counselling in ensuring that who teachers are can safely be brought into diverse contexts, without being at the risk of languages of 'competence'? How can schools contribute to a common or public good when embedded practices, misconstrued as 'competence', are specifically geared at undermining the pedagogical worth of minority group teachers? How can teachers ensure that learners are open to difference and that which is unfamiliar, when schools choose to remain closed to certain groups of teachers? What are the implications for social justice when schools remain shut off from the society of which it claims to be a part?

For starters, when learners only encounter one kind of teacher, their world not only becomes smaller, but their perspective and scope is narrowed. In other words, the greater the diversity, the greater the chances of encountering the unknown—not only in terms of identity, as in *who* teachers are, but also in terms of how the world is experienced differently by different people, from different perspectives. In this way, encountering difference is a gateway not only to engaging with, and from different perspectives, but it also provides an avenue through which to encounter the legacies of social injustice, perpetuated through apartheid. In this regard, confronting the poor representation of diversity in what is supposedly desegregated schools extends way beyond meeting equity frameworks. There is both a profound irony and disturbance in recognising that the very systems and spaces (schools), which are meant to provide socially just opportunities for learners, perpetuate unjust practices of exclusion in relation to minority group teachers. Post-apartheid education policies and acts are replete with inferences and references to the teacher as an advocate for fairness, inclusion, and social justice—with the assumption, of course, that teachers themselves are indeed socially just. Teachers, by virtue of their privilege of teaching, have an important role to play in disrupting notions and practices of prejudice and discrimination. Most importantly, teachers have a critical role to play in restoring the humanity, which apartheid stripped away. In the same way, they have a moral responsibility to ensure that learners recognise that differences exist, and that these differences should not be used as a basis for discrimination, exclusion, or humiliation. At the core, therefore, of what it means to be socially just, is to understand and practice what it means to be human. This means that when teachers, principals and parents declare certain teachers as 'incompetent', based on who they are – 'black', 'coloured', 'indian', homosexual, Muslim, Hindu, and so on – they are not acting in a manner, which is socially unjust, they are acting inhumanely, by humiliating the humanity of another. As Smith (1999: 26) reminds us, colonised people are 'compelled to define what it means to be human because there is a deep understanding of what it has meant to be considered not fully human, to be *savage*.' The ongoing marginalisation and pedagogical undermining of teachers is not limited to mere exclusion of particular identities, narratives, and life experiences. Firstly, when minority group teachers are excluded, they are precluded from accessing a particular space and its resources—physically, in the form of external inclusion, and internally, in the form of engaging and allowing their voices to give shape to educational discourses and debates. Secondly, for as long as particular groups of teachers are marginalised in particular schools, the life histories and experiences of these groups will continue to be misrecognised and negated. As a result, the real risk remains that not only are learners only exposed to one idea of who and what a teacher is, but they are also constrained in relation to their own ideas and hopes of what is possible for themselves. In this regard, career counsellors, as pointed out by Ratts, Singh, Nassar-McMillan, Butler, and McCullough (2016), have realised the need to adopt a more contextual approach to working with professionals and communities, recognizing that individuals are part of a larger ecosystem. Understanding these contexts is becoming increasingly important—not only for individuals from historically marginalized backgrounds, but also for those, who occupy spaces of privilege, whether in terms of race, gender, sexuality, class or religion. According to Ratts et al. (2016: 33), an understanding of intersectional ties and the influence of discrimination, marginalisation and oppression on well-being requires a commitment to exploring individuals and their social environment. They assert that when a contextual lens is applied to human development issues, counselors begin to realize that a multilevel approach—that is, both individual counselling and social justice advocacy - is necessary.

Thus far, we have provided insights into how teachers from minority groups are excluded on the basis of 'competence' and 'standards'. We have brought into contestation normative constructions of what constitutes 'the teacher'. In turn, we have raised awareness of the implications for social justice should certain groups of teachers continue to be excluded—whether externally or internally. In the concluding section of this chapter, we turn our attention to how career counselling might assist in cultivating pedagogies and ways of being that move towards openness and inclusion. We also consider how career innovation can be extended beyond normative parameters of advancement, and instead be reconceived as an enactment of social justice.

Career Counselling in Cultivating Pedagogies that Move Towards Openness and Inclusion

In taking cognisance of the intersectionality of marginalisation and exclusion, our point of departure is that counselling is not an action whereby someone, say a teacher, does something for another—that is, a learner. Career counselling, which is interested in establishing and cultivating climates of openness and inclusion, is as interested in the individual, as it is in the environment in which the individual finds him or herself. A teacher, therefore, does not practice in isolation from either of the environments of teaching (as a professional identity), or learning (in relation to learners). As Ratts et al. (2016: 34) maintains, while certain situations call for individual counselling, other situations may require interventions that take place in the community of the school, for example. Stated differently, on the one hand, it might be necessary to make sense of an individual teacher's own experiences of exclusion and marginalisation, and of his or her perceptions of the world. On the other hand, as has been illustrated in the first half of this chapter, it might be necessary to work with an entire school staff and community in order to address the challenges and difficulties of the individual. A recent incident at a Cape Town school involved a group of parents setting up a whats'app chat group, in which they questioned the qualifications and competency of a newly appointed Black African teacher. To limit counselling to the teacher in this matter will not address the broader climate of unwarranted suspicion, or quite blatantly, as was later confirmed, racial prejudice. Being able to balance individual counselling with social justice advocacy, state Ratts et al. (2016), is important to avoiding burnout and to developing clear boundaries.

Following on the above, we posit that counselling is a human encounter on the basis of which, for example, a teacher engages *with* learners. That is, counselling is not something that a teacher does for learners and then they react in specific ways, but counselling is an encounter in which a teacher and learners engage with one another to the extent that both parties are active learners in the interdependent human activity. Each of them – the teacher (counsellor) and the learner (counselee) brings their own identities, life experiences, expectations and narratives into the human encounter of counselling. The greater the differences of perspectives they encounter in and through the other, the richer the counselling. By implication, our understanding of the relationship between a teacher and a learner is one of counsellor engaging with counselee to the extent whereby they are interdependently shaped by the encounter. In other words, both the counsellor and counselee are constituted by the encounter of counselling and in such a way they make sense of one another's perspectives or points of view. It is not that the counselee is guided by the counsellor but instead, the encounter engenders mutually engaging action whereby both parties are guided by one another's reasons for engagement. The latter view of counselling immediately takes issue with a practice of counselling depicted as one person doing something for others.

Our justification for arguing in defence of enacting counselling *with* one another—that is, counsellor and counselee—is guided by an understanding that when people are included in an encounter they are more prone to learn with one another. Learning *with* one another is different from learning *from* one another and learning *of* one another. Learning *from*, and learning *of* one another conceives learning as an activity, which someone does for someone else as if the other is incapable of learning with another. Conceptions such as these—that is learning *from* and learning *of*—implies a pedagogical gap between the teacher and learner, which runs the risk of excluding the learner from fully engaging with and within the counselling encounter. Our understanding of learning with, and by implication experiencing counselling with others, is premised on an understanding of a notion of inclusive democratic action whereby the action is guided by a willingness of people in doing things for themselves and with others rather than always being told by others how to think and act. The implication of such a Rancierean view of inclusive democracy is based on a view that learners or counselees can also think and do things for themselves (Rancieré, 1991). And, when learners do things for themselves, they can be said to act with an equal intelligence in the sense that they are speaking beings who can make up their minds for themselves and disrupt inclusively democratic encounters.

The benefit of looking at the practice of counselling as an encounter constituted by what a counsellor and counselees bring to the encounter is one that Rancieré (1991) would purport as being more inclusive and by implication, open. The openness of an inclusive encounter is enhanced by the willingness and recognition of both counsellor and counselee to come to speech and to shape the act of counselling. To be open is tantamount to speaking one's mind. And, speaking one's mind in a Rancierean way is most likely to be realised when counsellor and counselee are not merely included in an encounter but more poignantly when they recognise one another's equal ability to articulate their points of view. Hence, our view of counselling is tantamount to teachers and students engaging evocatively in a pedagogic encounter whereby they learn with one another.

Our next move is to advance a view that career innovation ought to be extended beyond normative parameters of advancement, and instead be reconceived as an enactment of social justice. Our argument is in defence of teacher inclusion and by implication, learner inclusion: teachers are included when they are recognised for the responsible acts they perform in expediting student learning. And, as we have argued for in the earlier section of this chapter, learner learning is achievable on the basis of teachers and students engaging in pedagogic encounters with one another. We shall now show as to how counselling and its concomitant link to pedagogic encounters ought to be enacted in ways that advance socially just human action. We now argue that responsibility is conceptually and pragmatically linked to cultivating decoloniality, evoking student potentialities, and acting responsibly and ethically, as teachers as counsellors, engage with learners as counselees to do things with one another.

Career Counselling as a Socially Just Pedagogic Encounter: A Move Towards Decoloniality

Considering that career counselling as espoused above is constituted by pedagogic encounters through which teachers and learners engage with one another and in turn, are guided by the deliberative decisions that ensue from such encounters, our next task is to show how such human actions enhance social justice. We have already alluded to the idea that equality ought to be a central feature of what it means to act with social justice. That is when humans act with equality the possibility is always there that they would act in the interests of what is socially just. Our view of social justice is premised on Benhabib's (1996) notion that humans act justly in the interest of their societal structures and happenings if they frame their actions along the lines of deliberative iterations. The point is, when people act in a spirit of social justice they do so with deliberations and iterations. Put differently, their democratic actions or encounters are attuned to deliberative iterations. This implies that humans do not merely articulate their views and listen to what others have to say about their claims. In addition, human encounters become constituted by talking back. That is, articulations and listening are insufficient conditions for deliberative actions. Such actions also need to be iterative in the sense that people are allowed to talk back and shape the encounters. When spaces are cultivated in which people are encouraged to talk back, and bring their own stories and experiences into encounters, the possibility of exclusion diminishes. And, when they do so, they have in mind acting with social justice. Moreover, acting in a socially just way would encourage people to act with a sense of responsibility and responsiveness. Thus when career counselling is constituted by counsellors' acts of deliberative iterations such an encounter is not only informed by what counsellors and counselees deliberate on over and over again. But rather, counselling would also be directly geared to make counsellors and counselees act responsibly and responsively. And, when they act responsibility and responsively, they would have come to understand that their encounters are ethically-driven purposive human actions. Not only do they steer clear of instrumental action such as doing things to please others for utilitarian purposes, but their human encounters – their counselling actions – are directed to bring about change in their societies' impoverished situations. By implication, they deliberate iteratively about the vulnerable situations that confront their communities and in turn endeavour to take a stand, for instance, to work towards the cultivation of decoloniality.

We are attracted to the view that decoloniality is an act of transformation in which a case is made for undermining exclusive thoughts and practices bequeathed to us by an oppressive and aggressive form of colonisation (Achebe, 1989). And, when counsellors and counselees take a stand, they act deliberatively and iteratively in defence of decoloniality, and hence, in offence to any form of injustice or unjust practices. Coloniality undermines any forms of inclusiveness, openness, and democratic action on the basis that humans were taught they should not speak and do things for themselves. Coloniality is not only preserved in policies, structures and language. As Giroux (1992: 19) brings to our attention, coloniality is as evident in the forms of privilege that benefit males, whiteness, and property as well as those conditions that have disabled others to speak in places where those who are privileged by virtue of the legacy of colonial power assume authority and the conditions for human agency.

Our defence of decoloniality stems from our democratically informed stance that teachers and students should engage deliberatively and iteratively. Like social justice, decoloniality is concerned with identifying and disrupting the structures that perpetuate oppression while also working to shed light on those perspectives that have been devalued by hegemonic systems of knowledge and power. This is why Mignolo (2007: 159) refers to decoloniality as 'a redemptive and liberatory epistemology that seeks to de-link from the tyranny of abstract universals'. Like social justice, which is intent upon inclusion and openness, decoloniality is centred on rehumanizing the world—that is, to see all people as humans; and secondly, to discard forms of hierarchy that impose superiority between one human being and another. Re-humanising the world means the dismantling of preconceived ideas of the other, erasing superficial constructions of power; it means being open to that which is not yet known. Only then, the possibility to think differently about counselling and by implication, teacher-and-teacher, teacher-and-student, as well as teacher-and-community engagement would be much more enhanced.

In sum, we have argued for a position of socially just action whereby humans are provoked to do things with one another. In the main our view of career counselling emanates from the afore-mentioned claim that counsellors and counselees act deliberatively and iteratively in democratic encounters as they endeavour to cultivate socially just human relations. Only then, would it be possible to tackle major dystopias such as remnants of colonialism that seemed to have permeated our educational curricula, and which associate teaching with normative constructions of 'competence', as opposed to recognising that learning is enhanced through the inclusion of diverse and broader perspectives.

References

Achebe, C. (1989). *Hopes and impediments: Ssys*. New York: Anchor Books.

Benhabib, S. (1996). Towards a deliberative model of democratic legitimacy. In S. Benhabib (Ed.), *Democracy and difference: Contesting the boundaries of the political* (pp. 67–94). Princeton, NJ: Princeton University Press.

Bhabha, H. K. (1994). *The location of culture*. London: Routledge.

Bhana, D. (2012). Understanding and addressing homophobia in schools: a view from teachers. *South African Journal of Education, 32,* 307–318.

Biesta, G. (2009). Sporadic democracy: Education, democracy, and the question of inclusion. In M. Katz, S. Verducci, & G. Biesta (Eds.), *Education, democracy, and the moral life* (pp. 101–112). Washington, DC: Springer.

Butler, S. K. (2012). Issues of social justice and career development. *Career Planning & Adult Development Journal, 28*(1), 140–151.

Carr, D. (1993). Question of Competence. *British Journal of Educational Studies, 41*(3), 253–271.

Carr, D. (2000). *Professionalism and ethics in teaching*. London and New York: Routledge.

Carr, D. (2006). Professional and personal values and virtues in education and training. *Oxford Review of Education, 32*(2), 171–183.

Davids, N., & Waghid, Y. (2015). The invisible silence of race: On exploring some experiences of minority group teachers at South African schools. *Power and Education, 7*(2), 155–168.

Department of Education (DoE). (1995). *White Paper on education and training*. Pretoria: Government Printer.

Department of Education (DoE). (1997). *White Paper on higher education*. Pretoria: Government Printer.

Department of Education (DoE). (2000). *The norms and standards for educators*) Pretoria: Government Printer).

Evans, K. M., Kincade, E. A., Marbley, A. F., & Seem, S. R. (2005). Feminism and feminist therapy: Lessons from the past and hopes for the future. *Journal of Counseling & Development, 83*, 269–277.

Francis, D. (2017). Homophobia and sexuality diversity in South African schools: A review. *Journal of LGBT youth, 14*(4), 359–379.

Giroux, H. (1992). Postcolonial ruptures and democratic possibilities: Multiculturalism as anti-racist pedagogy. *Cultural Critique, 21,* 5–39.

Hansen, L. S. (2003). Career counselors as advocates and change agents for equality. *The Career Development Quarterly, 52,* 43–53.

Hargreaves, A. (1998). The emotional practice of teaching. *Teaching and Teacher Education, 14*(8), 835–854.

Harley, K., Barasa, F., Bertram, C., Mattson, E., & Timm, H. (2000). The real and the ideal: Teachers' roles and their competences in South African policy and practice. *International Journal of Educational Development, 20,* 287–304.

Harris, A. (1997). The deprofessionalization and deskilling of teachers. In K. Watson, C. Modgil, & S. Mogdil (Eds.), *Teachers, teacher education and training* (pp. 57–65). London: Cassell.

Hiebert, B., & Neault, R. (2014). Career counselor competencies and standards: Differences and similarities across Countries. In G. Arulmani, A. Bakshi, F. Leong & A. Watts (Eds.) *Handbook of career development. International and cultural psychology* (pp. 689–707). New York: Springer.

Hofmeyr, J. (2000). The Emerging School Landscape in Post-apartheid South Africa. Available at: http://www.sun.ac.za/afrikaans/management/institutional-forum/Pages/default.aspx/Taakgroepe/iptg/hofmeyr.pdf. Accessed May 4, 2014.

Jansen, J. D. (2004). Race and education after ten years. *Perspectives in Education, 22*(4), 117–128.

Jansen, J. D. (2007). Learning and leading in a globalized world: The lessons from South Africa. In T. Townsend & R. Bates (Eds.), *Handbook of teacher education: Globalization, standards and professionalism in times of change* (pp. 25–40). Dordrecht: Springer.

Lee, C. C. & Hipolito-Delgado, C. P. (2007). Introduction: Counselors as agents of social justice. In C. C. Lee (Ed.), *Counseling for social justice* (2nd ed.) (Alexandria, VA: American Counseling Association) pp. xiii–xxviii.

Makhetha, T. (2017) School racism row: Parents don't want a black principal. *IOL*, 25 July. Available online at: https://www.iol.co.za/news/south-africa/gauteng/school-racism-row-parents-dont-want-a-black-principal-10458915.

Meier, C., & Hartell, C. (2009). Handling cultural diversity in education in South Africa. *SA-eDUC Journal Special Edition in Education and Ethnicity, 6*(2), 180–192.

Mignolo, W. D. (2007). Introduction: Coloniality of power and de-colonial thinking. *Cultural Studies, 21*(2–3), 159.

Msibi, T. (2012). I'm used to it now: Experiences of homophobia among queer youth in South African township schools. *Gender and Education, 24*(5), 515–533.

Parker, D., & Adler, J. (2005). Constraint or catalyst? The regulation of teacher education in South Africa. *Journal of Education, 36,* 59–78.

Pinar, W. F., Reynolds, W. M., Slattery, P., & Taubman, P. M. (2000). *Understanding curriculum: An introduction to the study of historical and contemporary curriculum discourses*. New York: Peter Lang.

Rancieré, J. (1991). *The Ignorant School Master: Five Lessons in Intellectual Emancipation* (K. Ross, Trans.). Stanford: Stanford University Press.

Ratts, M. (2009). Social justice counseling: Toward the development of a fifth force among counseling paradigms. *The Journal of Humanistic Counseling, 48*(2), 160–172.

Ratts, M., Singh, A., Nassar-McMillan, S., Butler, S. K., & McCullough, J. R. (2016). Multicultural and social justice counseling competencies: Guidelines for the counseling profession. *Journal of Multicultural Counseling and Development, 44,* 28–48.

Simelane, B. C. (2018). Another Gauteng school embroiled in a principal appointment row. Available online at: https://www.dailymaverick.co.za/article/2017-12-05-another-gauteng-school-embroiled-in-a-principal-appointment-row/#.WsoO4ohuZPY.

Smith, L. T. (1999). *Decolonizing methodologies: Research and indigenous people*. London: Zed Books.

Soudien, C. (2004). Constituting the class: An analysis of the process of integration in South African schools. In L. Chisholm (Ed.), *Changing class: Education and social change in post-apartheid South Africa* (pp. 89–114). Cape Town: HSRC Press.

Soudien, C., & Sayed, Y. (2004). A new racial state? *Exclusion and inclusion in education policy and practice in South Africa, Perspectives in Education, 22*(4), 101–115.

Subreenduth, S. (2013). Theorizing social justice ambiguities in an era of neoliberalism: The case of post apartheid South Africa. *Educational Theory, 63*(6), 581–599.

Tang, M. (2003). Career counseling in the future: Constructing, collaborating, advocating. *The Career Development Quarterly, 52*, 61–69.

Taylor, C. (1994). The politics of recognition. In C. Taylor & A. Gutmann (Eds.), *Multiculturalism: Examining the politics of recognition* (pp. 25–74). New Jersey: Princeton University Press.

Young, I. M. (2000). *Inclusion and democracy*. Oxford: Oxford University Press.

Innovative Career Counselling in Special Populations

People with Refugee Backgrounds: Innovating Career Research and Practice Through Systems and Narrative Approaches

Mary McMahon, Mark Watson and Peyman Abkhezr

Abstract International migration is a daunting experience. The challenge of international migration for people with refugee backgrounds is further compounded by the often protracted migration process that may transcend the borders of several countries as well as by the trauma that stimulated their initial departure from their home country. In addition, for people with refugee backgrounds the challenge of beginning again in a culturally and linguistically unfamiliar host country is immense. The focus of this chapter is on people with refugee backgrounds who have been resettled. International migration, especially that of people with refugee backgrounds, also challenges host countries to find appropriate mechanisms to ensure safe and successful transitions. In the current climate of rapid societal change and high levels of international migration, career counselling seems to be in an ideal position to provide support for people with refugee backgrounds in resettlement countries. Indeed, career counselling was founded as a discipline at a time of great societal change and has always been underpinned by social justice values. However, career counselling is beset by challenges such as its western middle-class origins, its potential to lose touch with its social justice values, and its continued emphasis on individualised, psychological interventions. The complexity of the transition and resettlement of people with refugee backgrounds may be clearly understood from the perspective of systems theory and may be illustrated by systems mapping which facilitates the depiction of the recursive interplay of multiple influences. Systems mapping may be incorporated in narrative career counselling. In this regard, narrative career counselling has a role to play by eliciting the systemic stories of people with refugee backgrounds to

---

M. McMahon (✉)
School of Education, The University of Queensland, Brisbane Q4072, Australia
e-mail: marylmcmahon@uq.edu.au

M. Watson
School of Behavioural and Lifestyle Sciences, Nelson Mandela University, Port Elizabeth 6001, South Africa
e-mail: Mark.Watson@mandela.ac.za

P. Abkhezr
Faculty of Education, School of Early Childhood and Inclusive Education, Queensland University of Technology, Kelvin Grove 4059, Queensland, Australia
e-mail: p.abkhezr@qut.edu.au

J. G. Maree (ed.), *Handbook of Innovative Career Counselling*,
https://doi.org/10.1007/978-3-030-22799-9_21

better understand their career development and in facilitating inclusive and sustainable employment. Narrative career counselling promises more inclusive approaches although, to date, the evidence base is limited. The focus of this chapter is on an innovative response offered by systems and narrative approaches to career counselling and research in better understanding and responding to the career needs of people with refugee backgrounds in resettlement countries.

Keywords People with refugee backgrounds · Refugees · Migration · Career counselling · Systems approaches · Narrative approaches

Introduction

> but things were different here. Things have become more complicated than I expected.

These are the words of Ahmad, a 20 year-old man with a refugee background who arrived in his resettlement country full of hopes and dreams and subsequently found that achieving these was more challenging than he expected. Ahmad is just one of the millions of people worldwide facing the dilemma of resettlement in a country vastly different from their home countries.

In the context of this chapter, people with refugee backgrounds are considered as "forcibly displaced individuals" (United Nations High Commissioner for Refugees [UNHCR], 2014, p. 6) who have been resettled and live outside their home country. For more than a decade the world has witnessed an increasing trend of forcibly displaced people that has been described as "the largest displacement of refugees in modern history" (Newman, Bimrose, Nielsen, & Zacher, 2018a, p. 1). War, persecution, conflict and extreme violence are forcing people to move either within their own country of origin or to seek asylum from accessible countries that offer safe temporary shelter. The United Nations High Commissioner for Refugees (UNHCR) indicated that in 2018 over 68.5 million people have been forcibly displaced (UNHCR, 2018a), many of whom seek resettlement in other countries. Of these, the UNHCR offices in the Middle East and Africa hold over 65% of the global submissions for resettlement each year (UNHCR, 2018a).

At the time of writing, of the population of displaced people internationally, over 1.4 million are in urgent need for resettlement (UNHCR, 2018a). However, only a small proportion of these people is successfully resettled each year. For example, it is projected that in 2019 fewer than one hundred thousand of these people will be granted permanent resettlement in other countries through the UNHCR resettlement program (UNHCR, 2018a).

The UNHCR resettlement program is the only active resettlement program worldwide and aims to establish solutions for the protection and resettlement of the world's most vulnerable refugees. Countries such as Turkey, Lebanon, Iran, Uganda, and Cameroon have continually hosted a large number of refugees over the past few decades and 37 economically developed countries (e.g., United States of America,

Canada, Australia) in collaboration with the UNHCR have agreed to share the responsibility for protecting refugees and solution building for the refugee crisis through this resettlement program.

Despite the global demand for resettlement, only between 10 and 15% of this need is met each year through the UNHCR resettlement program and even then some of those referred for resettlement are rejected by the potential host countries (UNHCR, 2018a). For example, in 2016, out of nearly 170,000 referrals sent to participating countries, over 162,000 were accepted and resettled by the host countries. The remainder of those in urgent need for resettlement must continue living in their temporary and often difficult, underprivileged circumstances either in transitory countries or refugee camps where access to food, health care, housing, education and employment is limited (Centre for Multicultural Youth, 2014).

In 2017 the number of refugees resettled in the participating host countries dramatically dropped to only 75,200 people due to an overall reduction in the 37 participating host countries' willingness to accept and resettle refugees (UNHCR, 2018b). Not all participating host countries accept an equal number of referrals. Some of these countries only accept a few cases each year through the resettlement program. For instance, in 2017 the largest numbers of resettlements were made through the United States of America (USA; 26,782), followed by the United Kingdom (9218), Sweden (5955), France (5207), Canada (4118), Germany (3867) and Australia (3775) (UNHCR, 2018b). Of these refugees in urgent need of resettlement, it was predicted that in 2017 over one million would be children and young people (UNHCR, 2016). Some of these young refugees have lived either their whole or most of their lives in camps or in a state of uncertainty and confusion about their final destination in transition countries.

As far as the resettlement program is concerned, the migration journey of people with refugee backgrounds occurs primarily from the "global south" to the "global north", terms used to refer to either non-Organisation for Economic Cooperation and Development (OECD) and OECD countries respectively or simply as an alternative designation for respectively referring to economically developing and economically developed countries. The majority of refugee movement occurs within the global south (Munck, 2008). In the context of this chapter, the term *people with refugee backgrounds* refers to those who move across the south-north divide.

People with refugee backgrounds who move from economically developing to economically developed countries face various challenges in their migration and resettlement process. Most people who are resettled through the UNHCR resettlement program are those who have experienced a protracted migration journey and have spent years in transitory situations before they arrive in their final country of resettlement. Such transitioning through various locations and waiting for final resettlement exposes people with refugee backgrounds to a diverse range of cultural and contextual influences in their countries of origin, transition and resettlement (Abkhezr, McMahon, Glasheen, & Campbell, 2018). Among the resettlement challenges facing people with refugee backgrounds are employment, career development and education.

The world of work of the economically developed countries is undergoing dramatic shifts in the twenty first century and may appear even more complex and unpredictable to people with refugee backgrounds who come from economically developing countries characterised by agrarian or industrial economies. Pursuing a subjectively preferred field of education or finding and maintaining employment within the complex post-industrial context of the global north may pose challenges for many people with refugee backgrounds after resettlement. Yet, finding stable employment as quickly as possible is important to reduce welfare dependency and enhance the educational and health outcomes of the children of resettled refugees (Newman et al., 2018a).

This chapter considers the migration journeys experienced by people with refugee backgrounds. In relation to this population, the authors use the term '*people with refugee backgrounds*' in preference to the more stereotypical, limiting, and exclusive label of 'refugees'. The chapter begins by considering the challenges of the migration journey and resettlement through a case study. Subsequently, the chapter considers career counselling and research in relation to its foundation in social justice and the inclusion of this population through successful resettlement and integration. The innovative contribution of narrative and systems approaches to career counselling and research are considered in terms of people with refugee backgrounds.

Case Study

So far this chapter has presented a range of facts and international statistics about people with refugee backgrounds. The reality, however, of moving from academic discussion to the actual life experience of a person with refugee background reveals the intensity, complexity, and interrelatedness of a myriad of systemic influences that profoundly impact the resettlement process. This is highlighted in the following case study of Ahmad.

I was a top student with excellent marks in school before we had to leave. I was always encouraged by my parents to study and become an engineer. My uncle was an engineer and he had a good life. But after we moved out of our hometown things changed. My father wasn't there with us. He couldn't! We had to separate. Also there was no such thing as school. So I didn't go to school at all for about two years. Then there were a couple of places where they helped people like us but we were from different countries and most of us didn't know any English. So we had to spend our time in those places just learning English. Our finances didn't let us do much beyond the help that was offered for free by some NGO or charity organisations. Two years before we arrived in Australia I managed to attend a small school consistently. I got to complete year 8 and 9 there. I was planning to continue school and get my high school completion certificate when we arrived in Australia, but things were different here. Things have become more complicated than I expected.

The previous excerpt is from the fictional case study of Ahmad, a young 20 year-old man from Iraq who left his country of birth at age 11 with his mother and two younger sisters. Subsequent to their departure they lived in two transitory countries. His father, who was forced to take a different path, joined them a year before they arrived in Australia. Throughout the years of their protracted displacement and waiting for a decision about their status from the United Nations High Commissioner for Refugees (UNHCR), he and his family repeatedly talked about future plans related to his education, work and life in a country such as the USA or Australia. After arriving in Australia, Ahmad realised that to attend university and achieve his dream of studying engineering he needed to learn more English, complete secondary school, or get a qualification from another institution (such as a technical college) related to his intended university course with a high GPA or maybe gain some related work experience in order to meet the university entry requirements. Additionally, as a male, his cultural responsibility, along with his father, was to provide for his family. However, finding a job and maintaining work also proved to be difficult for him and his father. Despite this, both Ahmad and his father found work as cleaners by using contacts in their newly developing networks and as a result, the family, who initially lived in public and community housing arrangements, were able to move into their own rental house.

Ahmad felt both proud of contributing to this milestone in his family's resettlement and encouraged that he could also achieve his career goals if he works hard. He believes that he must achieve his long-held dreams in order to feel happy with his life. Ahmad wants his parents to feel proud of him as the eldest child in the family since they have supported him in the face of challenges. He wants to be able to support them when they get older and are unable to work anymore. Ahmad's story is similar to that told by many people with refugee backgrounds who are trying to construct their lives and careers in new countries which may be vastly different from their country of origin.

The Migration Journey of Ahmad

Ahmad's migration journey, of which successful resettlement is a critical part, cannot be over simplified and is best understood holistically. The literature on migration provides several ways of considering the migration journey and its impact on people with refugee backgrounds. One such understanding is that the migration journey occurs as four stages of pre-migration, migration, resettlement, and living in the host country (Pierce & Gibbons, 2012).

The pre-migration stage concerns the often traumatic circumstances that stimulate people to leave their homes in search of safety and a better life which leads to the next stage, migration. The migration process is often protracted and difficult and sees people leaving behind all that they are familiar with, including sometimes, family members, friends and social networks. Survival during this stage is not certain and may involve traversing other countries, often on foot, to reach refugee camps. The migration stage may last several years during which the resettlement stage may begin.

Resettlement involves applying and being assessed for refugee status in a prolonged process of people establishing the legitimacy of their refugee status while all the time hoping that it will be granted and starting a new life in a resettlement country will be possible. Moving to a resettlement country signals the end of the resettlement stage and the beginning of the fourth stage of living in the host country. The excitement of resettlement which is sometimes initially supported by government programs and agencies, may soon become dampened by the realities of living in the host countries such as language, cultural norms, limited support networks, meeting basic needs, and securing education and basic employment (Pierce & Gibbons, 2012).

There may be inherent problems, however, in providing sequential, linear models which portray people with refugee backgrounds homogeneously rather than as a heterogenous population whose experiences of the migration journey may be highly varied and personal. For example, the gender, race and class dimensions of the migration journey are far from homogeneous (Munck, 2008). Further, some people with refugee backgrounds reject dominant western discourses associated with such models (Abkhezr, McMahon, & Rossouw 2015; Hutchinson & Dorsett, 2012) that emanate primarily from the global north (Munck, 2008). Ahmad's migration journey from the global south to resettlement in the global north may be considered at different levels. At one level, linear stage models offer some generic insight into Ahmad's migration journey; at another level, his personal journey needs to be recognised as deeply personal and contextually embedded. The diverse factors evident in Ahmad's migration journey may be understood from the perspective of systems theory.

Systems Theory and Systems Mapping

Recognising the complexity of organisms, Ludwig von Bertalanffy (1968), a biologist, proposed general systems theory as a way to comprehensively understand any organism. Each part of an organism needs to be considered in the context of the whole (i.e., the system) and the whole is best understood as a collection of interacting parts (the sub-systems). Von Bertalanffy's emphasis on interaction between parts is illustrative of the dynamic and complex nature of systems. Moreover, von Bertalanffy emphasised open systems which interact with their environment as living systems such as plants and animals do. Thus, humans are also recognised as open systems comprised of many sub-systems (e.g., the skeletal system, the respiratory system and the nervous system) that interact with their environments.

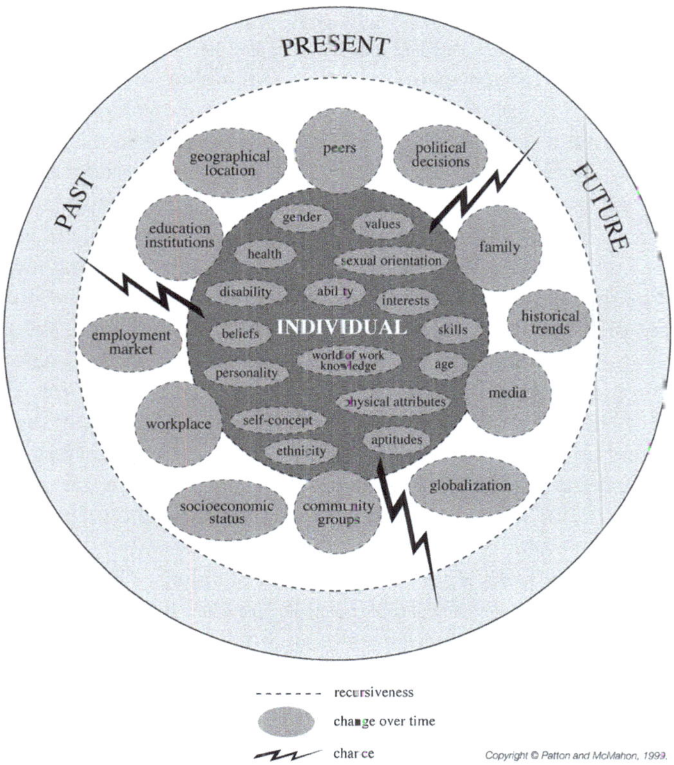

Fig. 1 The systems theory framework of career development. Copyright (C) Patton & McMahon (1999)

Subsequent to von Bertalanffy's seminal work, systems theory has been applied in several fields including business, engineering, and philosophy and is evident in common use terms such as computer systems, transport systems and education systems (McMahon & Patton, 2018). Systems theory has also been applied directly in career development through the work of Patton and McMahon (1999, 2014) and Vondracek, Ford, and Porfeli (2014) and is reflected in other career theories that recognise the influence of a broad range of factors on career development [e.g., Super's (1990) lifespan life-space theory and the chaos theory of careers (Pryor & Bright, 2011)].

The focus in this chapter is on the Systems Theory Framework of career development (STF; Patton & McMahon, 1999, 2014) because it not only provides a theoretical account of career development from a systems perspective but it also demonstrates the application of systems mapping to provide a holistic visualisation of career development. In essence, the STF (see Fig. 1) is a map of influences and interrelationships (McMahon & Patton, 2017, 2018) that emphasises the "individual in context" (McMahon, Watson, & Patton, 2014, p. 30) nature of career development.

The STF is a systems map of the contextual influences on an individual's career development; the term 'influence' signifies interaction between the influences and the individual or other influences in the system (McMahon & Patton, in press). The systems map of the STF (see Fig. 1) locates at its centre the individual system which incorporates a range of intrapersonal influences including psychological (e.g., self-concept, values, interests and personality), biological (e.g., gender and ethnicity), and physical (e.g., skills and ability) influences. Intersecting the individual system are the influences of the social system including family, peers, education institutions, community groups, media, and workplaces. The individual system and the social system live within the context of a broader environmental-societal system that includes the influences of political decisions, historical trends, globalisation, socioeconomic status, employment markets and geographic location. The dynamic nature of these influences is represented by the process influences of change over time, chance, and recursiveness. All three of the systems of influence are located with the context of past, present and future time. Change over time may be incremental (e.g., aging) or it may be sudden and unpredictable (e.g., a natural event such as a fire or a man-made event such as a political coup). Recursiveness represents the ongoing interaction within and between systems that influence the individual.

Systems maps may facilitate meaningful understanding (Flood, 2010) of a situation such as a career decision or transition. In the case of Ahmad, a systems map could assist him to holistically understand the complex influences on his migration process and his education and work decisions. Moreover, a systems map drawn by Ahmad could assist a career counsellor to better understand Ahmad's context of his career decision making. In practice, a systems map stimulates individuals to tell stories about the degree and nature of the systemic influences on their career development and provides a conceptual and practical map (McMahon & Patton, 2017) for both clients and career counsellors. Indeed, making meaning of a systems map is facilitated by storytelling which is fundamental to narrative career counselling.

Narrative Career Counselling

The history of career theory and career counselling models is an evolving story of responding to a changing world of work and a diversifying clientele. A major evolution occurred in the second half of the last century that saw the emergence of constructivist approaches in career psychology. The underlying philosophy of these approaches moved career psychology from its predominant focus on objectivity and predictability to a greater focus on context and understanding individual career development in terms of the individual's subjective perceptions and experiences.

Narrative career counselling is embedded in this increasing influence of constructivism on career psychology. A narrative approach to career counselling makes intuitive sense. McMahon (2018) points out, for instance, that telling stories has always been central to human behaviour and that people's lives consist of multiple stories that they tell and indeed retell. It is in the telling of these stories that people are able to reflect on where they have been, where they are and who they are becoming. This storytelling process can assist people in developing an integrated narrative identity (McAdams & McLean, 2013). A goal of narrative counselling is to provide the space for a client to voice their perceptions and feelings about their career development, and to ascribe a subjective understanding of how they see themselves. This encourages a client to be an active agent in their career development.

In recent times a wide variety of narrative approaches have been proposed. Indeed, McMahon (2018) suggests that narrative career counselling is multidirectional. Whatever the narrative approach adopted, there is general consensus in the literature that narrative career counselling is well-suited for working with people of refugee background (Abkhezr & McMahon, 2017). For instance, Abkhezr et al. (2018) argue that narrative career counselling would assist career counsellors in moving away from more traditional career counselling approaches to one that provides people with refugee background with "a space for the exploration of various culturally and contextually shaped voices present in the lives of participants" (p. 18). These authors refer also to the suitability of a narrative career counselling process for finding lost and silenced voices, while Abkhezr and McMahon (2017) argue further that narrative career counselling provides people of refugee background an opportunity to create cohesive and meaningful stories of their migration experience. Importantly, Pierce and Gibbons (2012) suggest that a narrative career counselling approach may help redress the "culture of disbelief" (p. 117) experienced by people of refugee background when the stories they tell as part of the resettlement stage are questioned by others. The latter authors also suggest that the narrative career counselling process may help people of refugee background.

In any recently emerging career counselling approach challenges arise that need to be addressed. So it is with narrative career counselling. Several authors describe potential challenges. McMahon (2018) points to the fact that narrative approaches have been more philosophical than practical to date, that they can be abstract, that they may focus more on understanding than meaningful action steps, that they can take too long, and that they may focus more on personal than career counselling issues for which career counsellors may not have sufficient training. Pierce and Gibbons (2012) argue further that narrative career counselling approaches may suggest a more activist role than career counsellors are prepared to commit to.

Despite these challenges, narrative career counselling can be considered as a model that "transcends information and advice" and "draws on constructivist, narrative, reflexive and critical approaches" in career psychology (Reid & West, 2016, p. 4). Narrative career counselling is a potential form of assistance for people with refugee backgrounds such as Ahmad who are considering their career options in their Western countries of resettlement. To be of use and assistance to people with refugee backgrounds, narrative career counselling raises sensitivity among career counsellors to issues of social justice and advocacy (Arthur, 2013) and reminds them that cultural, contextual and psychosocial sensibilities are linked to creativity and innovation in practice (Reid & West, 2016). Thus, it is possible that narrative career counselling could be beneficial to Ahmad.

The Migration Journey of Ahmad: Integrating Systems Mapping and Narrative Career Counselling

Ahmad's journey of migration and resettlement is one of complexity and disruption to most aspects of his life. Narrative career counselling may be used as a stimulus for storytelling and making meaning of the disrupted career development of a person with refugee background. Systems mapping can complement narrative career counselling by providing a visual stimulus for reflection and meaning making. Examples of systems mapping are already present in the narrative career counselling literature. For example, Peavy (1998) employed life-space mapping as a means of stimulating meaning making in a sociodynamic approach to counselling. Indeed, Slowik (2014) proposes life-space mapping as an innovative method in career counselling people with refugee backgrounds that assists them to analyse their migration journey and value their biographical and formal, non-formal and informal experiences for constructing their careers.

A further example of systems mapping already present in the narrative career counselling literature is the qualitative career assessment instrument based on the STF (Patton & McMahon, 2014), My System of Career Influences (MSCI; McMahon, Patton, & Watson, 2013, 2017), which guides users through the construction of a systems of influence diagram. Systems mapping affords clients the opportunity of presenting their personal influences in a systems map. Systems maps are holistic diagrams of a particular topic (Király, Köves, Pataki, & Kiss, 2016) such as career development. The MSCI has been used with diverse clients including young people with disadvantaged backgrounds (Albien & Naidoo, 2017; McMahon, Watson, Foxcroft, & Dullabh, 2008) to reflect on and tell stories about their personal circumstances and their futures.

Career counselling clients such as Ahmad could draw systems maps related to their career development and to their educational and career decision making (see Fig. 2). The examples of systems mapping in the narrative career counselling literature suggest that career counsellors provide support, guidance and some structure for clients in the drawing of their systems maps. Systems maps may be regarded as a stepping off point for a narrative conversation about the influences depicted in the map.

Ahmad's map (depicted in Fig. 2) could stimulate storytelling about his previous education and achievements. It also demonstrates the recursive link between the ability he displayed in his school results in his home country, his broken education over several years and the challenge for him in his resettlement country of gaining the education he aspires to. A rich conversation could be stimulated about the impact of the migration journey on Ahmad which is evident in his comment 'Leaving my country changed everything'. Stories of hope and strength could also be elicited from Ahmad's map through his comment 'I am hardworking'. The cultural stories told by Ahmad could reveal a recursive relationship with his stories of his parents, their expectations of him, and his responsibilities towards them. Stories could also emerge as Ahmad talks about the 'people I know' and the recursive link between his

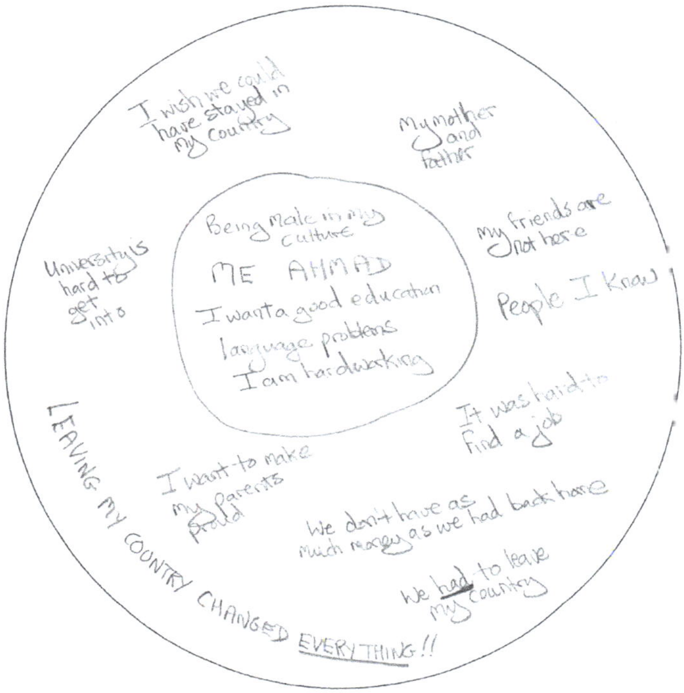

Fig. 2 Ahmad's systems map

past, present and future. For example, he is living in his resettlement country with his parents and has few social networks. Despite this Ahmad has used his newly found networks to find work as a cleaner and is proud of this achievement that has helped his family to move into a rental home. Thus, a story of strength and resilience emerges through the systems map and could provide a foundation for future career planning and decision making.

Importantly, systems mapping and its associated storytelling promotes a sense of agency in clients as the career counsellor becomes a facilitator of a process who encourages clients to actively participate. As evident in this brief example, a systems map can provide a rich source of information from which stories can be told, meaning can be made, and futures can be constructed. Together, systems mapping and narrative career counselling may contribute an innovative approach to career counselling people with refugee backgrounds about their educational and career decisions.

Innovating Practice

In combining systems mapping with narrative career counselling innovations for practice are offered in relation to working with people with refugee backgrounds. First, systems mapping in combination with narrative career counselling may assist people with refugee backgrounds to move from dominant migrant scripts towards constructing connected and coherent stories that move towards a more positive self. Second, stories that have been forgotten or less often told during the migration journey may be identified through the process of systems mapping and scaffolded in the supportive process of narrative career counselling. Third, systems mapping may sensitise narrative career counsellors to the socio-cultural history of people with refugee backgrounds. For example, Abkhezr, McMahon and Rossouw (2015) emphasise several suggestions for career counsellors working with people with refugee backgrounds, specifically: (1) view refugee career development as a personal-cultural phenomenon for each individual, (2) consider that there are macro-level and contextual influences beyond the individual's control that call for advocacy, social action and lobbying, and (3) recognise the heterogeneity of refugees and consider how individuals make sense of their cultural, contextual and relational factors. Integrating systems mapping and narrative career counselling may enable the realisation of these suggestions.

Fourth, clients are afforded a greater sense of agency through the drawing of their maps and the telling of their stories. Moreover, through the process of being assessed for refugee status, people with refugee backgrounds have repeatedly told stories that scripted, positioned, and disempowered them. Systems mapping and narrative career counselling provide people with refugee backgrounds the time and space to reposition themselves by writing the script of their preferred stories and choosing the stories they tell rather than telling the stories often expected of them during the assessment process. Fifth, from the perspective of systems mapping, the narrative career counsellor enters the system of influences of clients from refugee backgrounds (McMahon & Patton, in press; Patton & McMahon, 2014). Thus, it would be important for narrative career counsellors to recognise the unique cultural backgrounds of clients and their previous experiences of interviews, education and work. There would be a need to clarify the nature of the narrative career counselling and systems mapping process (Abkhezr & McMahon, 2017). By entering the system of influences of clients with refugee backgrounds, career counsellors may experience "compassion fatigue" (Lanfranchi & Akinsulure-Smith, 2018, p. 382) for which self-care and supervision may be important. Despite the potential contributions of systems mapping and narrative career counselling, further research is needed to better understand these processes and their integration.

Innovating Research

Narrative career counselling has been widely advocated and has intrinsic appeal. To date, however, its evidence base is limited (McMahon, 2018) as is the evidence base in career counselling for systems mapping. Both present rich opportunities for research that can build on extant research. For example, research on systems mapping has been conducted on populations who are disadvantaged (Albien & Naidoo, 2017; McMahon et al., 2008; Slowik, 2014). This body of research employs soft systems methodologies, specifically participatory systems mapping, which are qualitative, interpretative and participative and encourage participants to think systemically and consider their future career directions. In addition, the little researched topic of the boundary between narrative research and career counselling with people with refugee backgrounds has been explored (Abkhezr, McMahon, Campbell, & Glasheen, in press).

There has also been a special issue of the Journal of Vocational Behavior that focused on qualitative research of the process of narrative career counselling (Savickas & Guichard, 2016). Career research has long been criticised for its limited research on people from disadvantaged backgrounds and it is encouraging to note that a special issue of the Journal of Vocational Behavior (Newman, Bimrose, Nielsen, & Zacher, 2018b) focused on how refugees seek work and the challenges of navigating their careers. Further, the special issue suggested five future directions for research including the need to: (1) move beyond exploratory research, (2) confirm the empirical viability of proposed conceptual models, (3) test qualitative research results on larger refugee populations, (4) conduct more longitudinal research, and (5) place a greater emphasis on gender issues for people with refugee backgrounds. In addition, Pierce and Gibbons (2012) recommend further research to explore which qualitative storytelling techniques work best with different refugees. It is interesting to note that over a decade ago, McMahon and Watson (2007) developed a systems map for encouraging reflection and critical analysis of career research.

Conclusion

The case study of Ahmad illustrates the reality of what policy makers and other professionals such as career counsellors experience when they try to facilitate successful integration of people with refugee backgrounds in the resettlement country. Narrative career counselling and systems mapping have the potential to be part of the solution for the successful integration of people with refugee backgrounds in their resettlement countries. Systems mapping provides an innovative mechanism for integrating systems theory and narrative career counselling in order to promote inclusion and sustainable employment for people with refugee backgrounds.

References

Abkhezr, P., & McMahon, M. (2017). Narrative career counselling for people with refugee backgrounds. *International Journal for the Advancement of Counselling, 39,* 99–111. https://doi.org/10.1007/s10447-017-9285-z.

Abkhezr, P., McMahon, M., Campbell, M., & Glasheen, K. (In press). Exploring the boundary between narrative research and narrative intervention: Implications of participating in narrative inquiry for young people with refugee backgrounds. *Narrative Inquiry.*

Abkhezr, P., McMahon, M., Glasheen, K., & Campbell, M. (2018). Finding voice through narrative storytelling: An exploration of the career development of young African females with refugee backgrounds. *Journal of Vocational Behavior, 105,* 17–30. https://doi.org/10.1016/j.jvb.2017.09.007.

Abkhezr, P., McMahon, M., & Rossouw, P. (2015). Youth with refugee backgrounds in Australia: Contextual and practical considerations for career counsellors. *Australian Journal of Career Development, 24,* 71–80. https://doi.org/10.1177/1038416215584406.

Albien, A. J., & Naidoo, A. V. (2017). Deconstructing career maps and cultural stereotypes in a context of low resourced township communities. *South African Journal of Education, 37*(4), 1–12. https://doi.org/10.15700/saje.v37n4a1476.

Arthur, N. (2013). Social justice and career guidance in the age of talent. *International Journal for Educational and Vocational Guidance, 14,* 47–60. https://doi.org/10.1007/s10775-013-9255-x.

Centre for Multicultural Youth. (2014). *Migrant & refugee young people negotiating adolescence in Australia.* Carlton, Australia: Centre for Multicultural Youth.

Flood, R. L. (2010). The relationship of 'Systems Thinking' to action research. *Systemic Practice and Action Research, 23,* 269–284. https://doi.org/10.1007/s11213-010-9169-1.

Hutchinson, M., & Dorsett, P. (2012). What does the literature say about resilience in refugee people? Implications for practice. *Journal of Social Inclusion, 3*(2), 55–78.

Király, G., Köves, A., Pataki, G., & Kiss, G. (2016). Assessing the participatory potential of systems mapping. *Systems Research and Behavioral Science, 33,* 496–514. https://doi.org/10.1002/sres.2374.

Lanfranchi, M., & Akinsulure-Smith, A. M. (2018). The role of mental health counselors in international human rights: Reflections on counseling services with urban refugees at the Refugee Law Project in Kampala, Uganda. *The International Journal for the Advancement of Counselling, 40,* 365–386. https://doi.org/10.1007/s10447-018-9331-5.

McAdams, D. P., & McLean, K. C. (2013). Narrative identity. *Current Directions in Psychological Science, 22,* 233–238. https://doi.org/10.1177/0963721413475622.

McMahon, M. (2018). Narrative career counselling: A tension between, potential, popular appeal, and proof. *Australian Journal of Career Development, 27,* 57–64. https://doi.org/10.1177/1038416218785537.

McMahon, M., & Patton, W. (2017). The Systems Theory Framework A conceptual and practical map for career counselling. In M. McMahon (Ed.), *Career counselling: Constructivist approaches* (pp. 123–126). London: Routledge.

McMahon, M., & Patton, W. (2018). Systemic thinking in career development theory: Contributions of the Systems Theory Framework. *British Journal of Guidance and Counselling, 46,* 229–240. https://doi.org/10.1080/03069885.2018.1428941.

McMahon, M., & Patton, W. (in press). The Systems Theory Framework: A systems map for career theory, research and practice. In J. Athanasou & H. Perera (Eds.), *International handbook of career guidance.* Dordrecht, The Netherlands: Springer.

McMahon, M., Patton, W., & Watson, M. (2017). *The My System of Career Influences (MSCI—Adolescent) Facilitators' Guide.* Brisbane, Australia: Australian Academic Press.

McMahon, M., & Watson, M. (2007). An analytical framework for career research in the postmodern era. *International Journal for Educational and Vocational Guidance, 7,* 169–179. https://doi.org/10.1007/s10775-007-9126-4.

McMahon, M., Watson, M., Foxcroft, C., & Dullabh, A. (2008). South African adolescents' career development through the lens of the Systems Theory Framework: An exploratory study. *Journal of Psychology in Africa, 18,* 531–538. https://doi.org/10.1080/14330237.2008.10820232.

McMahon, M., Watson, M., & Patton, W. (2013). *The My System of Career Influences Adult Version (MSCI Adult): A reflection process*. Brisbane, Australia: Australian Academic Press.

McMahon, M., Watson, M., & Patton, W. (2014) Context-resonant systems perspectives in career theory. In G. Arulmani, A. Bakshi, F. Leong, & T. Watts (Eds.), *Handbook of career development: International Perspectives* (pp. 29–42). New York: Springer.

Munck, R. (2008). Globalisation, governance and migration: An introduction. *Third World Quarterly, 29*(7), 1227–1246. https://doi.org/10.1080/01436590802386252.

Newman, A., Bimrose, J., Nielsen, I., & Zacher, H. (2018a). Vocational behavior of refugees: How do refugees seek employment, overcome work-related challenges, and navigate their careers? *Journal of Vocational Behavior, 105,* 1–5. https://doi.org/10.1016/j.jvb.2018.01.007.

Newman, A., Bimrose, J., Nielsen, I. & Zacher, H. (Eds.). (2018b). Vocational behavior of refugees: How do refugees seek employment, overcome work-related challenges, and navigate their careers? [Special issue] *Journal of Vocational Behavior, 105*.

Patton, W., & McMahon, M. (1999). *Career development and systems theory: A new relationship*. Pacific Grove, CA: Brooks/Cole.

Patton, W., & McMahon, M. (2014). *Career development and systems theory: Connecting theory and practice*. Rotterdam, The Netherlands: Sense.

Peavy, R. V. (1998). *Sociodynamic counselling: A constructivist perspective*. Victoria, Canada: Trafford.

Pierce, L. M., & Gibbons, M. M. (2012). An ever-changing meaning: A career constructivist application to working with African refugees. *Journal of Humanistic Counseling, 51,* 114–127. https://doi.org/10.1002/j.2161-1939.2012.00009.x.

Pryor, R., & Bright, J. (2011). *The chaos theory of careers: A new perspective on working in the 21st century*. Hoboken, NJ: Taylor & Francis.

Reid, H., & West, L. (2016). Negotiating professional and personal biographies in a liquid world Creating space for reflexive innovation in career counselling. *British Journal of Guidance and Counselling, 44,* 562–575. https://doi.org/10.1080/03069885.2016.1145014.

Savickas, M. L., & Guichard, J. (Eds.), (2016). Research on the process of narrative career counseling [Special issue]. *Journal of Vocational Behavior, 97*.

Slowik, A. (2014). 'Life space mapping' as an innovative method in career counselling for refugees, asylum seekers and migrants. *Procedia—Social and Behavioural Sciences, 114*, 80–85. https://doi.org/10.1016/j.sbspro.2013.12.661.

Super, D. E. (1990). A life-span life-space approach to career development. In D. Brown & L. Brooks (Eds.), *Career choice and development: Applying contemporary theories to practice* (2nd ed., pp. 197–261). San Francisco, CA: Jossey-Bass.

United Nations High Commissioner for Refugees (UNHCR). (2014). *War's Human Cost: UNHCR global trends 2013*. Geneva, Switzerland: Author.

United Nations High Commissioner for Refugees (UNHCR). (2016). *UNHCR projected global resettlement needs 2017*. Geneva, Switzerland: Division of International Protection United Nations High Commissioner for Refugees.

United Nations High Commissioner for Refugees (UNHCR). (2018a). *UNHCR global appeal 2018-2019*. Geneva, Switzerland: Division of International Protection United Nations High Commissioner for Refugees.

United Nations High Commissioner for Refugees (UNHCR). (2018b). *UNHCR projected global resettlement needs 2019*. Geneva, Switzerland: Division of International Protection United Nations High Commissioner for Refugees.

von Bertalanffy, L. (1968). *General system theory*. New York: George Braziller.

Vondracek, F. W., Ford, D. H., & Porfeli, E. J. (2014). *A living systems theory of vocational behavior and development*. Rotterdam, The Netherlands: Sense.

A Framework for Career Reconstruction Following Personal Injury and Disability

James A. Athanasou and Harsha N. Perera

Abstract Obtaining a new job or finding a new career is of prime importance for many seriously injured adults from motor vehicle injuries, workplace accidents or other personal injuries (e.g., medical negligence, public liability). The huge number of such cases world-wide calls for career, vocational rehabilitation or employment counsellors to heighten their awareness of the specific issues related to adult personal injury and disability. At the outset, the general situation in Australia is used as an example of the problems in education and workforce participation of those with disabilities. Issues of lower than average educational achievement, the impact on employment participation and the extent of discrimination are outlined. With this background in mind, the present state of career counselling for personal injury and disability is reviewed and a framework for a career counselling approach is proposed that (a) addresses the existential needs of the person and (b) builds upon their pre-injury vocational identity in order to adapt. A career construction outlook that promotes adaptability and resilience is proposed as a basis for working with personal injury in those who are moving back to the world of work.

Keywords Personal injury · Disability · Career development · Career construction theory · Return-to-work

When an accident or injury occurs in mid-life there are myriad interwoven personal, social, health or vocational consequences. Firstly, a person's recovery may be complete or incomplete. Then there is the transition from hospital to everyday life that needs to be managed for those who will have a long-term restriction (Frank 2018; National Center for Injury Prevention and Control, 1999, p. 2). Amongst these transitions is the issue of return to work or maintaining a source of economic sustain-

J. A. Athanasou (✉)
Discipline of Rehabilitation Counselling, Faculty of Health Sciences, The University of Sydney, 75 East Street, Lidcombe, NSW 2141, Australia
e-mail: james.athanasou@sydney.edu.au; athanasou@gmail.com

H. N. Perera
College of Education, University of Nevada Las Vegas, 4505 Maryland Pkwy, Box 453003, Las Vegas, NV 89154-3003, USA
e-mail: Harsha.Perera@unlv.edu

J. G. Maree (ed.), *Handbook of Innovative Career Counselling*,
https://doi.org/10.1007/978-3-030-22799-9_22

ability. The desire to work is a reasonable aspiration for any person, but, in Australia in 2015, there were over 2.14 million people with a disability, of whom only 54% were in the labor force (Australian Bureau of Statistics, 2017). This chapter covers the context within which career counselling approaches in vocational rehabilitation can assist those people recovering from such a personal injury. The nature of acquired disabilities is defined and their effect on career development is documented briefly. Approaches that are existential in nature are described as essential for the reconstruction of a career. The use of a narrative approach to career intervention in traumatic brain injury is offered as one example in addressing the issue of how to help people reconstruct their career and life following a personal injury. The approach is essentially idiosyncratic as "no two people will have exactly the same symptoms" (Power & Hershenson, 2003, p. 1021).

The sheer volume of personal injuries is not acknowledged widely in careers fields. In Australia in 2013–2014, 531,800 persons experienced a work-related injury in the last 12 months. This was around 4.25% of the 12.5 million who had worked at some time in the last year (Australian Bureau of Statistics [ABS], 2014). For road vehicle traffic crashes, there were 32,775 seriously injured in 2010 in Australia (Australian Institute of Health and Welfare, 2015, p. 12). Injury, of course, is a worldwide phenomenon but one whose extent is vastly underestimated in the careers field. For example, the World Health Organization *Global Status Report on Road Safety, 2015* indicated that "up to 50 million people incur nonfatal injuries each year as a result of road traffic crashes, while there are additional indirect health consequences that are associated with this growing epidemic" (2015, p. x).

The personal injury of interest in this chapter is one which results in a disability. In the *Survey of Disability, Ageing and Carers* (Australia Bureau of Statistics, 2013), a disability is defined formally as a limitation, restriction or impairment, which has lasted, or is likely to last, for at least six months and restricts everyday activities. Typically, this is associated with a medical diagnosis.

Disabilities are wide-ranging and cover the following: loss of sight (not corrected by glasses or contact lenses); loss of hearing where communication is restricted, or an aid to assist with, or substitute for, hearing is used; speech difficulties; shortness of breath or breathing difficulties causing restriction; chronic or recurrent pain or discomfort causing restriction; blackouts, seizures, or loss of consciousness; difficulty learning or understanding; incomplete use of arms or fingers; difficulty gripping or holding things; incomplete use of feet or legs; nervous or emotional condition causing restriction; restriction in physical activities or in doing physical work; disfigurement or deformity; mental illness or condition requiring help or supervision; long-term effects of head injury, stroke or other brain damage causing restriction; receiving treatment or medication for any other long-term conditions or ailments and still being restricted; or any other long-term conditions resulting in a restriction (Australia Bureau of Statistics, 2013). Parenthetically, it would be truly amazing if any career theory were able to cope with such a diverse range of conditions.

The special toll that disabilities take on education and workforce participation was outlined by Athanasou, Murphy, and Mpofu (2019). They utilised the official Survey of Disability Ageing and Carers in Australia to summarize the educational disadvantages and vocational inequalities for the 4.29 million people with disabilities in Australia of whom 2.16 million were aged 15–64 years. Amongst people with a disability, there is a decidedly lower rate of school completion (41.1% with a reported disability vs. 62.8% with no reported disability). Distinctly fewer persons with a disability obtain degrees (17.0% with a reported disability vs. 30.1% with no reported disability). Median income is markedly reduced ($465 per week with a reported disability vs. $950 per week with no reported disability). Labour force participation is significantly lower (53.4% with a reported disability vs. 88.2% with no reported disability), and the unemployment rate in 2015 was 10.0% for those with a disability and almost twice that of those without a disability (5.3%). Alternate duties were provided in only 2% of cases and workplace accommodations made only in 4% of instances. Supported employment was available in only 2.2% of cases.

Of course, employment with a disability has never been easy for the majority of people. The focus of this chapter, however, is the disability from a personal injury that occurs in mid-life. For such a person, there has been a lived-awareness of what it means to have a non-disabled life. Following injury, the contrast can be stark and unexpected. Career counselling can play a pivotal role in such issues of transition in dealing with what the philosopher Karl Jaspers called "boundary situations" (i.e., momentous occasions in life).

There are issues of what sort of work can be done and which career options are suitable. While these questions share some features of career choice at an earlier stage of career development, the added complication is that an injured adult normally had already constructed some sort of career pathway. One's personal, social and vocational life is upturned. Moreover, the luxury of time to adjust may not be available when one has dependent children or other financial obligations that were previously satisfied through employment.

In an ideal world, the injured person would return to the same employer in the same job. Other alternatives include (a) the same employer in a different job; (b) a different employer in a different job; (c) a return to work but not being able to continue; and (d) never returning to work. Amongst 461 patients with compensable injuries it was reported:

> At the time of assessment only 23% had returned to work. Just on 30% of the patients 151 had not worked and some 48% had returned to work but were now not working. Of those who were working, only 14% returned to the same employer in the same job; 37% were in a different job with the same employer; and the majority (49%) were with a different employer in different job (Athanasou, 2017a, 2017b, p. 4)

These categories included self-employment, which occurs only in around 2–3% of cases based on vocational rehabilitation data from the United States (Yamamoto & Alverson, 2018, p. 270). In any event, all these different employment outcomes constitute widely different pathways within which career counselling can navigate. Accordingly, there is a role for career counselling and it behoves all health professionals "… to see work as an outcome of their interventions, and that this needs to be thought about from the beginning of a health episode …" (Frank, 2018, p 3).

Career and Personal Counselling

Amidst others, Krumboltz, Foley, and Cotter (2013) have advocated that 'the distinction between career and personal counselling is artificial and unnecessary" (p. 15). Career counselling, however, does not feature widely in approaches to the return to work of persons with an injury. For instance, Tokar and Kaut (2018) examined decent work amongst 320 workers with Chiari malformation (a cranial malformation in the base of the skull where the cerebellum extends into the spinal canal) and commented on "the limited applicability of traditional career choice and development theories to individuals with chronic health conditions" (p. 127). Libeson, Downing, Ross, and Ponsford (2018) made no reference at all to career counselling when they reported the experience of return to work of 15 individuals with traumatic brain injury who underwent a rehabilitation program. After a follow-up from 1 to 8 years' post-injury (mean = 4.5 years), nine had returned to their pre-injury work, three had moved to a new employer and three were not working. Factors that were identified as influencing return to work include the following: (a) pre-injury employment including employer loyalty; (b) personal client factors (motivation, family and social support, readiness for return to work); (c) injury-related client factors (cognitive and mood problems, physical injuries); (d) work factors (employer support, work modifications, nature of the job, financial incentives); and (e) rehabilitation factors (return to work program, role of the occupational therapist, work preparation, client involvement).

Career and personal counselling following injury is considered a valuable component in achieving the tangible outcome of return-to-work or a non-vocational adjustment. Although a five-year follow-up of 11,585 Finnish workers after a severe occupational injury reported that 81% were able to work (Kulmala, Luoma, & Koskinen, 2018), not all were able to resume their pre-injury career. Amongst 81,062 workers in British Columbia, the likelihood of return to work following a musculoskeletal injury (the most common type of injury) varied from 70% for torso fractures to 88% for back sprains and strains McLeod, Reiff, Maas, & Bultmann, 2018). Return to work, however, is a complex phenomenon and varies according to functional independence, age, sex, marital status, hospital length but also the type of pre-injury occupation. From a study of 1341 persons with head injury, return to work was lowest (32%) for the 398 in manual labor and highest for the 192 in professional or managerial occupations (Walker, Marwitz, Kreutzer, Hart, & Novack, 2006). In discussing return-to-work following injury and disability, an essential consideration in counselling is considered to be (a) resolution of existential issues then (b) the maintenance of adaptability and resilience.

Acquired disability does not feature at all in major career counselling approaches. Indeed, Athanasou (2014, p. 178) noted that the term "disability" is not even listed in the index of many major career works. Disability, however, has started to make an appearance in some specific theories such as the INCOME approach of Hershenson (2005) as well as in meta-theories such as the Systems Theory Framework (Patton & McMahon, 2006) or the Psychology of Working Framework (Blustein, Kenna Gill, & De Voy, 2008) and Psychology of Working Theory (Duffy, Blustein, Diemer,

& Autin, 2016). Blustein et al. (2008, pp. 302–303), for instance, offered a case example of a 45-year-old male receiving treatment for post-traumatic stress disorder and depression following a motor vehicle accident. This case focused on (a) the symptoms of depression and its relation to being unemployed, (b) exploring strengths and assets, (c) an interest assessment, (d) an assessment of transferable skills, and (e) assisting him to find a job.

While this approach has useful aspects, it does impinge on the role of psychiatry and it does not acknowledge openly that the issue of work, jobs, occupations or career is really his response to the world-at-large. *Ceteris paribus*, it is an expression of himself, a statement about his identity, goals or purpose in life. Even before applying the trait-factor or person-environment or work-adjustment guidance or job-seeking approaches (Athanasou, 2017a, 2017b)—which are extremely relevant for career decision-making following personal injury—there is a need for an approach that resolves the existential anguish of these new *Grenzsituationen* (border situations; i.e., an injury in one's life) (Salamum, 2006, p. 4).

Life and Career Reconstruction

An Existential Approach

In an existential approach, the patient[1] is led to the idea that he or she alone is responsible for creating their life and the purpose for which it operates. This is not an easy notion for some to grasp. It flies against the experiences of a lifetime in which operant, instrumental and classical conditioning to circumstances dull one's sensitivity to meaning. Cohen (2003) advocated the adoption of an existential focus and referred to the work of Frankl who "clearly demonstrated how important the construct of meaning is to vocational choice" (p. 209). Cohen advocated three techniques to promote an existential analysis as follow:

(a) the use of guided imagery, an intervention that asks people to close their eyes and imagine themselves in a career. This experience is then explored, analyzed and evaluated (Cohen, 2003, p. 201; Skovholt, Morgan, & Negron-Cunningham, 1989);
(b) using personal narratives to allow patients to describe their life and its future potential in order to construct a way ahead (Cohen 2003, pp. 201–202);
(c) a Socratic dialogue involving propositions and questions to provoke thinking (Cohen 2003, p. 206).

The aim is to evaluate one's goals and to achieve personal integrity and to live a life that is in accordance with values. It is recognized that the existential approach is

[1]The first author [JA] works within a medical setting where "patient" and not "client" is the appropriate term.

inherently philosophical and psychodynamic. It is not amenable to standard empirical evaluations such as randomized control trials. It is also not a prescriptive approach where an intervention is applied in a standardized fashion.

The Role of Narrative

Autobiography, however, is one key ingredient for any existential analysis. Whilst some patients are able to do this for themselves, for others it is developed through the interview. As Del Corso and Rehfuss (2011) indicated, narrative is used: "… to capture an individual's subjective life experience as a story. Through narrative individuals share who they are and what matters to them" (p. 334). The meaning attributed to personal experiences is unraveled and the focus is on the patient's own personal goals. The individual can be given the opportunity to articulate their history and experience. This can become the building block for the future.

While the past embodied the essence of who they were, it might now be far from adequate to cope with a changed future. To ensure adjustment, a new narrative must be added to manage what lies ahead. In short, personal injury requires that the new and the old narrative must be joined so that a rough map for the future can be drawn. For this reason, a departure might need to be made from behaviors that prevailed in the past. In many instances, even a cursory history shows that stability had not yet been achieved at the time of injury. This is especially the case with younger males who are more prone to personal injury than females (Urdry, 1998).

Adaptation and Resilience

Injuries demand adaptation and resilience to almost every aspect of functioning from health, through to ability to perform daily living activities, self-satisfaction, personal relationships, financial needs or conditions of living. As a result, an overall lowered quality of life has been reported in 254 Australian patients with compensable injuries (Athanasou, 2015). Using the World Health Organization's 8-item *EUROHIS Quality of Life Scale* it was indicated that "The ratings on every one of the eight indicators were below those of a cross-cultural sample across 10 countries in Europe ($n = 4849$). The average of 2.70 was also well below that for a non-depressed sample in Australia ($n = 192$, $M = 3.30$)" (p. 22). Within the model that is proposed, the reaction to an injury may be framed in terms of a resilient reaction and a process of adaptation to the changed social environment. The counsellor helps someone to formulate new schemas of attitudes, beliefs and actions relevant to the process of adjusting to injury.

Adaptation and Adaptability Aspects of adaptation that have as their basis a willingness to respond to changing conditions have been set out in the context of careers (Savickas & Porfeli, 2012). The potential to traverse workplace changes positively is the hallmark of career adaptability (Bimrose & Hearne, 2012, p. 339). At this point, the active engagement of the counsellor is psychodynamic and entails (a) developing an active as opposed to a passive concern for the future, (b) the promotion of self-discipline, (c) reinforcing a search for possibilities, and (d) maintaining the necessary confidence. The career adaptability envisaged by Savickas is extended to a type of life adaptability and resolving one's existential situation. In order to achieve this adaptation, one's life needs to be re-arranged. Through self-examination, the tragedy and experience of injury needs to be given meaning and resilience is developed (Savickas, 2013).

Resilience Resilience is consistent with the findings that "adversity, no less than prosperity, can change us for the better" (Affleck & Tennen, 1996, p. 900). They noted that this change can occur through cognitive adaptations such as adaptive beliefs (e.g., benefit-finding) or improved coping strategies (e.g., benefit-reminding) and pointed to examples from medical adversity (e.g., spinal cord injury). There are multiple channels for developing resilience or adaptation. It is not intended to be prescriptive, but one approach is through narrative or autobiography to provide that foundation.

Adaptivity The willingness to respond to changing situations may also be influenced by a person's adaptivity (Savickas, 1997, 2002). Adaptivity, also referred to as adaptive readiness, is a dispositional trait reflecting the flexibility and willingness to change that is evoked to proactively meet career challenges, work traumas, and unfamiliar tasks (Perera & McIlveen, 2017; Savickas & Porfeli, 2012). Several dispositional constructs have been used in the scientific literature to reflect adaptivity. These include proactive personality (Tolentino et al., 2014), locus of control (Zacher, 2016), core self-evaluation (Zacher, 2014), as well as combination of the five-factor personality traits (Perera & McIlveen, 2017). Such adaptivity dispositions may constitute an important part of an individual's pre-injury vocational identity that fosters adaptation to changing condition post-injury.

Career Construction Theory Accordingly, a personal engagement with the patient becomes more important than routine vocational assessments. To this end, Career Construction Theory (Savickas, 2005, 2013) gives recognition to how work becomes important in one's life history—over time, one constructs one's social and vocational identity (Savickas, 2005). A Career Construction approach focuses on how each patient has positioned work in their life. Narrative is integral to a career construction approach, but it is recognized that the life-story is highly subjective and subject to many influences (e.g., excusing failures, presenting oneself in a positive manner, suppression of emotions, lack of insight, memory problems, desire for coherence or structure). Nevertheless, recurrent topics and obvious precedents will surface in a narrative that (a) reflect archetypes or (b) form schemas or (c) represent basic patterns of responding. The following section outlines how some aspects of this framework may be applied to personal injury and uses the example of traumatic brain injury. The final section of this chapter provides examples (traumatic brain injury) and considers the application of innovative techniques with specific injuries.

Traumatic Brain Injury

Mortality from traumatic brain injury is around 5 per 100,000 in the US (Thurman & Guerrero, 1999) but for those who recover, even a mild traumatic brain injury does not leave one unscathed. Almost invariably, it results in permanent disabilities with varying cognitive, physical and psychosocial deficits. Cognitive effects range from attention, concentration, awareness, memory, judgement, aphasia through to other language or communication deficits. Physical effects can be widespread including hemianopia, auditory loss, balance, hemiplegia, diabetes, loss of smell, headaches or fatigue. Psychosocial factors range from anxiety, depression, impulsive behavior, promiscuity, or inappropriate responses. No claim is made that this list is exhaustive.

From a return to work perspective, an earlier report on return-to-work rates following acquired brain injury in Australia and New Zealand indicated that they varied from 29 to 64% with a median of 46% and for 23 international studies the return-to-work rates varied from 19 to 88% (median also 46%). When the results of all Australia and New Zealand varied studies were combined to form a total of 1010 subjects then the overall return-to-work rate was 44% (Athanasou, 2003). Looking to some of the most recent 2017 studies, the return to work rates vary but they are generally low: (a) for 293 veterans with traumatic brain injury at one-year follow up it was 21% (Dillahunt-Aspillaga et al., 2017); (b) for a sample of 133 adult patients in Paris at four years follow-up it was 38% (Ruet et al., 2017); (c) and these return-to-work outcomes fluctuated from 12% at 3 months, to 57% at two years and 43% at 10 years for a small sample of 109 patients (Grauwmeijer, Hellenbrok, Haitsma, & Ribbers, 2017). The most common factors perceived to assist those who return to work have been found to be "support of family and friends (92%) and of treatment providers (80%), and employers who provided accommodations (76%)" (Colantonio et al., 2016). Return to work post-severe traumatic brain injury is frequently unstable and workers often experience difficulties. As expected, thinking and concentrating and fatigue were the most common barriers to employment (Ruet et al., 2017).

Fadyl and McPherson (2009) reviewed approaches to vocational rehabilitation (20 quantitative articles; 3 qualitative articles) that were grouped as program-based skills job training, individual placement through supported employment or case coordinated rehabilitation. They concluded that their success was restricted (Fadyl & McPherson, 2009, p. 204). Moreover, established psychosocial interventions, such as cognitive behavior therapy, peer-mentoring, or motivational interviewing were not considered effective in maintaining increases in coping over time for persons with traumatic brain injury (Mueller et al., 2018).

Instead, Nochi (2000) used self-narratives with those who seemingly were able to cope with their injury. This covered background, rehabilitation, plans for the future, thoughts, feelings and specific events. Five categories emerged as important for those who felt at ease with their situation as follows: (a) the self, better than others (comparison with others who were worse off); (b) the grown self (the positive contribution of an injury to one's life, for example, insight); (c) the recovering self (restoring the previous self); (d) the self, living here and now (restoring self-worth by focusing on progress or improvement without contrasting to others); and (e) the protesting self (learning what to do as individuals or to change the world). An example of narrative reconstruction was provided by Nochi as a person who "… may want to have a narrative where he is still the breadwinner of the family, although he has already lost his job" (2000, p. 1802). It was considered that a narrative approach would help if it occurred earlier in the traumatic brain injury experience and that it may be transferable to other disabilities. There is also evidence from a study of self-efficacy and self-awareness in 81 clients with traumatic brain injury across eight regions of Florida that the services need to be customized for the individual (Dillahunt-Aspillaga et al., 2015, p. 10).

Notwithstanding this observation, some limitations of interventions that have been mentioned elsewhere (Power & Hershenson, 2003, p. 1028) include the following: (a) the need for the effects of the traumatic brain injury to stabilize and this may take anywhere up to two years; and (b) having the cognitive skills to devise life or career plans or evaluate options may be lacking or inhibited. Indeed, it is recognized that not all persons with traumatic brain injury have the capacity to work in a competitive labor market or even a disability employment service. Finally, a career construction approach does not overlook the contribution of programs such as supported employment or placement counselling but operates in conjunction with vocational rehabilitation. The penultimate section outlines an overarching framework that has been adopted for career counselling following personal injury and disability.

Framework for Personal Injury and Vocational Counselling

The elements of the framework are straightforward and for practical purposes divided into a medical stage focused on recovery followed by a vocational rehabilitation stage that is focused on life reconstruction. The stages may interact and may follow a recursive sequence. The key elements of the return-to-work sequence are presented schematically in Fig. 1.

The initial focus of the medical stage is survival. For instance, in motor accidents in Australia in 2010 there were 25.8% who seriously injured with a threat to life (Australian Institute of Health and Welfare, 2015, p. 12). Once the recovery sequence stabilizes, medical or allied health practitioners would focus first on the activities of daily living. Possibly they may deal with career issues, such as the potential for return to work in passing but mainly the role of the medical professional would be to certify work incapacity for compensation purposes. The rehabilitation stage of the framework invokes counselling and guidance with the aim of developing adaptability and resilience. For many patients, resilience and adaptation may be achieved without support or through a variety of existential approaches such as narrative counselling, purpose-in-life approaches, paradoxical intention, guided imagery, or Socratic questioning to name but a few. As adaptability and resilience are addressed then the issues of vocational or non-vocational adjustment can come into focus and in particular, return-to-work services provided. The center-piece of this framework is counselling

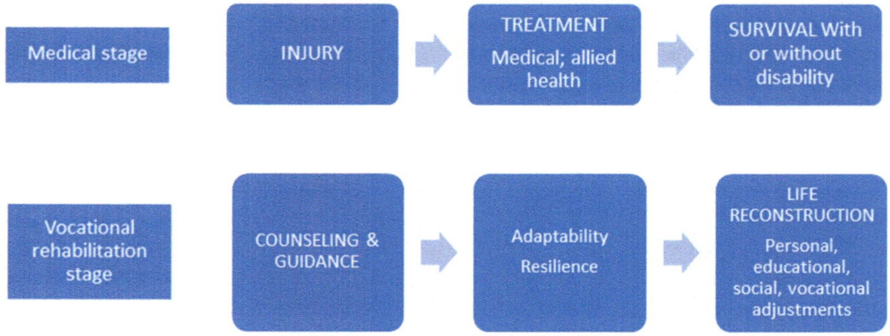

Fig. 1 An overall framework for personal injury and vocational counselling

for adaptability/resilience and the life-career reconstruction through narrative—this forms the central thesis of this chapter.

Concluding Comments

An innovative approach might then be based within the ambit of existential approaches and Career Construction Theory (CCT; Savickas, 2005, 2013). Whilst narrative is a central component of CCT, access to counselling is almost non-existent for the close to half a million Australians undergoing serious injury each year that requires hospitalization.

The focus of narratives in a career-construction approach is to give meaning to life—their past life but also to their future possibilities. This is consistent with the acceptance of loss theory of Dembo, Leviton, and Wright (1975). A reformed story may substitute for dysfunctional thoughts and overcome the depreciation of the self. Patients who have undergone injury, however, encounter myriad health professionals often for very limited periods of time, or even on a single occasion. Even vocational rehabilitation counselling is a type of mandated step-by-step process of assessment, report writing and recommendation for placement and some return to work activities. Nevertheless, an interpretative process can be stimulated by narratives and questions that focus on a purpose in life. Regrettably, this might only be able to occur in practice on a once-only or limited basis in interaction with various professionals and for this reason a brief-focused intervention is not capable of evaluation in a formal sense. For instance, in the author's (JA) medico-legal practice, patients are seen only once for an hour and a half for a mandated vocational assessment. No claim is made for the therapeutic efficacy of this brief narrative approach other than the anecdotal reports of satisfaction and change. It is recognized that this is hardly enough to justify large-scale implementation, but such clinical insights are a starting point in reformulating vocational rehabilitation counselling of persons who have undergone personal injury.

An existential approach to narrative sits well within the framework of a Career Construction Theory and can be applied informally by doctors and allied health professionals throughout the process of recovery. It allows the patient time to construct, deconstruct, reconstruct and plan through stimulating thought processes. Using short narrative scenarios enables the individual to give voice to their concerns and to find (i.e., construct) ways to address them. This is achieved by promoting active adaptation rather than passive adjustment.

References

Affleck, G., & Tennen, H. (1996). Construing benefits from adversity: Adaptational significance and dispositional underpinnings. *Journal of Personality, 64*(4), 899–922.

Athanasou, J. A. (2003). Acquired brain injury and return to work in Australia and New Zealand. *Australian Journal of Career Development, 12*(1), 58–65.

Athanasou, J. A. (2015). Compensable injury and quality of life. *Australian Journal of Rehabilitation Counselling, 21*(1), 18–28. https://doi.org/10.1017/jrc.2015.4.

Athanasou, J. A. (2017a). A vocational rehabilitation index and return to work after compensable occupational injuries in Australia. *Australian Journal of Rehabilitation Counselling, 23*(2), 1–11. https://doi.org/10.1017/jrc.2017.8.

Athanasou, J. A. (2017b). *Promoting career development after personal injury*. Rotterdam: Sense Publishers.

Athanasou, J. A., Murphy, G. C., & Mpofu, E. (2019). The impact of disabilities on earning or learning in Australia and the implications for career development. *Australian Journal of Career Development*. https://doi.org/10.1177/1038416218772062.

Australian Bureau of Statistics. (2013). *Disability, ageing and carers, Australia*. Catalogue No. 4430.0, November 2013. Canberra: Author.

Australian Bureau of Statistics. (2014). *Work-related injuries, Australia*. Catalogue No. 6324.0. July 2014 to June 2014. Canberra: Author.

Australian Bureau of Statistics. (2017). *Disability, ageing and carers, Australia: Summary of findings, 2015*. Catalogue No. 44300DO020_2015. Canberra: Author.

Australian Institute of Health and Welfare. (2015). *Trends in serious injury due to road vehicle traffic crashes, Australia 2001 to 2010. Injury research and statistics series no. 89*. Catalogue No. INJCAT 165. Canberra: Author.

Bimrose, J., & Hearne, L. (2012). Resilience and career adaptability: Qualitative studies of adult career counseling. *Journal of Vocational Behavior, 81,* 338–344.

Blustein, D. L., Kenna, A., Gill, N., & DeVoy, J. E. (2008). The psychology of working: A new framework for counseling practice and public policy. *The Career Development Quarterly, 56*(4), 294–308.

Cohen, B. N. (2003). Applying existential theory and intervention to career decision-making. *Journal of Career Development, 29*(3), 195–209.

Colantonio, A., Salehi, S., Kristman, V., Cassidy, J. D., Carter, A., Vartanian, O., et al. (2016). Return to work after work-related traumatic brain injury. *NeuroRehabilitation, 30;39*(3), 389–399.

Del Corso, J., & Rehfuss, M. C. (2011). The role of narrative in career construction theory. *Journal of Vocational Behavior, 79,* 334–339.

Dembo, T., Leviton, G. L., & Wright, B. A. (1975). Adjustment to misfortune: A problem of social-psychological rehabilitation. *Rehabilitation Psychology, 22,* 1–100.

Dillahunt-Aspillaga, C., Jorgensen-Smith, T., Ehlke, S., Hanson, A., Sosinski, M., & Gonzalez, C. M. (2015). Disability adjustment and vocational guidance counseling for individuals with traumatic brain injury. *Journal of Applied Rehabilitation Counseling, 46*(1), 3–13.

Dillahunt-Aspillaga, C., Nakase-Richardson, R., Hart, T., Powell-Cope, G., et al. (2017). Predictors of employment outcomes in veterans with traumatic brain injury: A VA traumatic brain injury model systems study. *Journal of Head Trauma Rehabilitation, 32*(4), 271–282.

Duffy, R. D., Blustein, D. L., Diemer, M. A., & Autin, K. L. (2016). The psychology of working theory. *Journal of Counseling Psychology, 63,* 127–148. https://doi.org/10.1037/cou0000140.

Fadyl, J. K., & McPherson, K. M. (2009). Approaches to vocational rehabilitation after traumatic brain injury: A review of the evidence. *Journal of Head Trauma Rehabilitation, 24*(3), 195–212.

Frank, A. (2018). Navigating the heath-work interface—Vocational rehabilitation in the UK. *Occupational Medicine, 68,* 2–4.

Grauwmeijer, E., Hellenbrok, K. M. H., Haitsma, I. K., & Ribbers, G. M. (2017). Employment outcomes ten years after moderate to severe traumatic brain injury: A prospective cohort study. *Journal of Neurotrauma, 34*(17), 2575–2581.

Hershenson, D. B. (2005). INCOME: A culturally inclusive and disability-sensitive framework for organizing career development concepts and interventions. *The Career Development Quarterly, 54*(2), 150–161.

Krumboltz, J. D., Foley, P. F., & Cotter, E. W. (2013). Applying the happenstance learning theory to involuntary career transitions. *The Career Development Quarterly, 61*(1), 15–26.

Kulmala, J., Luoma, A., & koskinen, L. (2018). Able or unable to work? Life trajectory after severe occupational injury. *Disability & Rehabilitation*. https://doi.org/10.1080/09638288.2018.1464603.

Libeson, L., Downing, M., Ross, P., & Ponsford, J. (2018). The experience of return to work in individuals with traumatic brain injury (TBI): A qualitative study. *Neuropsychological Rehabilitation*. https://doi.org/10.1080/09602011.2018.1470987.

McLeod, C. B., Reiff, E., Maas, E., & Bultmann, U. (2018). Identifying return-to-work trajectories using sequence analysis in a cohort of workers with work-related musculoskeletal disorders. *Scandinavian Journal of Work, Environmental and Health, 44*(2), 147–155.

Mueller, C., Wesenberg, S., Nestmann, F., Stubbs, B., Paul, B., & Raymont, V. (2018). Interventions to enhance coping after traumatic brain injury: A systematic review. *International Journal of Therapy and Rehabilitation, 25*(3), 107–119. https://doi.org/10.12968/ijtr.2018.25.3.107.

National Center for Injury Prevention and Control. (1999). *Traumatic brain injury in the United States: A report to Congress*. Washington: U.S. Department of Health and Human Services.

Nochi, M. (2000). Reconstructing self-narratives in coping with traumatic brain injury. *Social Science and Medicine, 51,* 1795–1804.

Patton, W. & McMahon, M. M. (2006). *Career development and systems theory. Connecting theory and practice* (2nd ed.). Rotterdam: Sense Publishers.

Perera, H. N., & McIlveen, P. (2017). Profiles of career adaptivity and their relations with adaptability, adapting, and adaptation. *Journal of Vocational Behavior, 98,* 70–84 https://doi.org/10.1016/j.jvb.2016.10.001.

Power, P. W., & Hershenson, D. B. (2003). Work adjustment and readjustment of persons with mid-career onset traumatic brain injury. *Brian Injury, 17*(12), 1021–1034.

Ruet, A., Jourdan, C., Baven, E., Darnoux, E., Sahridj, D., Ghout, I., et al. (2017). Employment outcome four years after a severe traumatic brain injury: Results of the Paris severe traumatic brain injury study. *Disability Rehabilitation, 18,* 1-8.

Salamum, K. (2006). Karl Jasper's conceptions of the meaning of life. *Existenz, 1*(1–2), 1–8.

Savickas, M. L. (1997). Career adaptability: An integrative construct for Life-Span, Life-Space Theory. *The Career Development Quarterly*, *45*(3), 247–259. https://doi.org/10.1002/j.2161-0045.1997.tb00469.x.

Savickas, M. L. (2002). A promise fulfilled. *Australian Journal of Career Development*, *11*(3), 7–8. https://doi.org/10.1177/103841620201100302.

Savickas, M. L. (2005). The theory and practice of career construction. In S. D. Brown & R. W. Lent (Eds.), *Career development and counseling: Putting theory and research to work* (pp. 42–70). Hoboken, NJ, US: Wiley.

Savickas, M. L. (2013). Career construction theory and practice. In R. W. Lent & S. D. Brown (Eds.), *Career development and counseling: Putting theory and research to work* (2nd ed., pp. 147–183). Hoboken, N J: Wiley.

Savickas, M. L., & Porfeli, E. J. (2012). Career adapt-abilities scale: Construction, reliability, and measurement equivalence across 13 countries. *Journal of Vocational Behavior, 80*(3), 661–673. http://dx.doi.org/10.1016.j.jvb.2012.01.011.

Skovholt, T. M., Morgan, J. I., & Negrion-Cunningham, H. (1989). Mental imagery in career counseling and life planning: A review of research and intervention methods. *Journal of Counseling and Development, 67*(5), 287–292. https://doi.org/10.1002/j.1556-6676.1989.tb02504.x.

Thurman, D., & Guerrero, J. (1999). Trends in hospitalization associated with traumatic brain injury. *Journal of the American Medical Association, 282,* 954–957.

Tokar, D. M., & Kaut, K. P. (2018). Predictors of decent work among workers with Chiari malformation: An empirical test of the psychology of working theory. *Journal of Vocational Behavior, 106,* 126–137. https://doi.org/10.1016/j.jvb.2018.01.002.

Tolentino, L. R., Garcia, P. R. J. M., Lu, V. N. & Restubog, S. L. D., Bordia, P., & Plewa, C. (2014). Career adaptation: The relation of adaptability to goal orientation, proactive personality, and career optimism. *Journal of Vocational Behavior, 84*, 39– 48. https://doi.org/10.1016/j.jvb.2013.11.004.

Udry, J. R. (1998). Why are males injured more than females? *Injury Prevention, 4,* 94–95.

Walker, W. C., Marwitz, J. M., Kreutzer, J. S., Haart, T., & Novack, T. A. (2006). Occupational categories and return to work after traumatic brain injury: A multicenter study. *Archives of Physical Medicine and Rehabilitation, 87,* 1576–1582.

World Health Organization. (2015). *Global status report on road safety 2015*. Geneva Author.

Yamamoto, S. H., & Alverson, C. Y. (2018). Vocational rehabilitation and self-employment of people with disabilities: Factors of successful outcomes. *Journal of Vocational Rehabilitation, 48,* 269–283.

Zacher, H. (2014). Individual difference predictors of change in career adaptability over time. *Journal of Vocational Behavior*, *84*(2), 188–198. https://doi.org/10.1016/j.jvb.2014.01.001.

Zacher, H. (2016). Within-person relationships between daily individual and job characteristics and daily manifestations of career adaptability. *Journal of Vocational Behavior*, *92*(1), 105–115. https://doi.org/10.1016/j.jvb.2015.11.013.

A Career Education Approach Based on Group Dialogues to Help Adolescents and Emerging Adults in Their Self Construction

Valérie Cohen-Scali and Jacques Pouyaud

Abstract In the current context of globalization, most individuals need to develop multiple social affiliations and are involved in varied work situations which are more precarious and changing than in the past. Emerging adults have the main task of self-constructing (Cohen-Scali & Guichard, in L'Orientation Scolaire et Professionnaire 3:315–320, 2008) while taking into account the effects of their actions on others and on the environment (Cohen-Scali et al., in Interventions in career design and education: transformation for sustainable development and decent work. Springer, New York, 2018). This chapter aims to contribute to an approach to work identity construction based on social interactions and more specifically on group dialogues from a Life and Career Design perspective.

Keywords Work identity · Social interactions · Group dialogues · Self-construction

Chapter Structure

The first part of the chapter discusses the key role played by reflexivity in the self-construction of young people in today's context of globalization. The second part focuses on the role played by dialogues in developing this reflexivity. The third part presents a group career intervention based on the Dialogues for Life and Career Designing (DLCD) approach aiming at promoting reflexivity through group dialogues with adolescents and emerging adults.

V. Cohen-Scali (✉)
Conservatoire National des Arts et Métiers, Center of Research on Work and Development, Hesam Université, Paris, France
e-mail: valerie.cohenscali@lecnam.net

J. Pouyaud
Laboratory of Psychology (EA 4139), University of Bordeaux, Bordeaux, France

J. G. Maree (ed.), *Handbook of Innovative Career Counselling*,
https://doi.org/10.1007/978-3-030-22799-9_23

Introduction

Rapid changes in society (whether these concern technological changes impacting the world of work or climate changes and population growth) give rise to a growing feeling of uncertainty in individuals (Cohen-Scali et al., 2018; Guichard, Drabik-Podgórna, & Podgórny, 2016). For young people such new challenges render career construction particularly complex and risky (Cohen-Scali, 2015). For example, in France young people are becoming increasingly worried (Béduwé & Dupray, 2018) when entering the labor market: in 2010, 28% said they were worried after three years of work experience compared with 16% in the same situation in 2001. This is especially the case for young people who are unemployed or inactive. Because of these changes career counsellors and professionals in vocational career psychology and education have to implement new forms of interventions focused more on reflecting on meaning of life.

The paradigm of Life Design (Nota & Rossier, 2015) provides new leads for researchers and professionals in designing interventions better adapted to the changes affecting society. According to the Life Design epistemology, individuals change as they develop social interactions in different environments and as they engage in activities that confer meaning to their situation and behaviors (Savickas, 2015). This paradigm underscores the fact that each individual is unique and so is the manner in which she/he evolves. Thus, traditional interventions using standardized methods of appraisal (tests correlating behaviors with standards) are no longer relevant. Career education and counselling interventions therefore become frameworks for intervention enabling a customized approach taking the biological and social ecosystem of each individual into account. In the current socioeconomic context, life and career design interventions are aimed at developing reflexivity as a critical way of appraising the individual's personal and social experience. Such reflexivity is needed for constructing the identity (Guichard, 2009) and in changing the life model (Curie, Hajjar, Marquié, & Roques, 1990) of individuals. The reflexivity of critical consciousness (Blustein, 2006) or critical reflexivity (Mcllveen, 2015) are founded on the capacity to produce renewed inner dialogues making it possible to envisage changes in activities and the identification of new personal perspectives and new positions within the social context. However, counselling interventions based on dialogues are conducted most of the time within the framework of counsellor-client dyads and are rarely on the basis of dialogic interactions between members of a group.

This chapter seeks to highlight the importance of Life Design interventions for encouraging individual and group dialogic interactions by increasing the reflexive capacities of individuals. In the first part of the chapter, the central role played by reflexivity in the self-construction of young people will be evoked. The second part of the article will focus on the role played by dialogues in developing this reflexivity. We will then propose a project for a group intervention based on the Dialogues for Life and Career Designing (DLCD) approach (Guichard, Bangali, Cohen-Scali, Pouyaud, & Robinet, 2017) aimed at promoting reflexivity through group dialogues with adolescents and emerging adults.

Self-construction in Life Design: Mobilizing the Reflexivity Processes

The Life Design paradigm is rooted in career counselling constructivist approaches. These postmodern approaches consider that the individual constructs her/his own reality through social interactions, seeking to confer meaning to her/his experiences and then using these to interpret the situations encountered (Watson & McMahon, 2011). While 'constructivist' approaches underline the role of action, the 'constructionist' perspectives stress the importance of language and social interaction as a tool for human development. Life Design counselling interventions make massive use of language and narration to change self-perceptions. Language makes it possible to increase reflexivity, self-awareness and self-development. Critical consciousness is deployed through the opportunities provided in Life Design interventions of thinking of oneself as a social subject with social and cultural affiliations.

Career counselling should be built on self-construction processes through narratives. On the basis of Ricoeur's works (1992), the narrative identity is a construct enabling action "to be transformed into experience" through a division between idem-identity and ipse-identity (Pouyaud, 2015, p. 61). The language, according to Ricoeur, makes it possible to take a distanced view of a life experience, which is indispensable for self-construction.

The Life Design paradigm considers individuals as actors in the construction of the meaning of their experiences. Objectives set for career counselling interventions concern changing identity through developing reflexive capacities (Savickas et al., 2009). Archer (2011) defines reflexivity as "the regular exercise of mental ability, shared by all normal people, to consider themselves in relation to their (social) context and vice versa. The imperative of engaging in reflexive deliberations (which may also involve interpersonal as well as intrasubjective exchanges) derives, quite simply, from the absence of social guidelines indicating what to do in novel situations" (Archer, 2011, p. 2). For Archer, transformation of self is possible through inner conversation and implies that the engaged and innovative "I" is capable of controlling a more inert and consistent "self" (Archer, 2011). Reflexive individuals are therefore prepared for change because they are able to make a critical appraisal of their aptitudes in the light of their experiences, their capacities and their values.

On the basis of an empirical study, Archer observes three types of reflexive individuals depending on the positions adopted in society. She identifies the *communicative reflexives*, who produce reflections closely connected to their everyday interactions and conversations, internalize others in their inner dialogues, and through their reflexivity reinforce their integration within the social world. A second group is the *autonomous reflexives*. They develop reflections independently from their social interactions, are more isolated, and focus on the actions to engage in rather than on developing inner deliberations. Another group is the *meta-reflexives* who are able to critically review their reflections. They focus on their concerns and direct their inner conversation towards self-development. For Archer, certain situations can lead people to suspending their reflexivity. These persons are named *fractured reflexives*:

they simply react to what happens to them. To her view, each profile also has certain characteristics in terms of career design. Fractured reflexives are uncertain regarding their career and find activities of fleeting interest. Meta-reflexives seek jobs in the non-profit sector motivated by social engagement. Autonomous-reflexives expect, above all, material rewards from work and focus on salary. Communicative reflexives pay particular attention to feedback from people close to them and their families in their career choices and sometimes take jobs recommended by their family.

This variability in reflexive experiences should no doubt be taken into account in defining Life and Career Design interventions. The global objective of Life and Career Design interventions is to help individuals become meta-reflexives, with prospect development and decent work perspectives in planning their future (Guichard et al., 2016). These interventions define a set of goals aimed at encouraging reflexivity through exploratory activities, dialogue or narration. The prime objective of these interventions is to develop adaptability by helping individuals express their different experiences and develop greater flexibility and the capacity to anticipate change. Another objective is to develop abilities to work out self-narratives. This consists of using dialogue in counselling to enable the persons to build a relevant picture of their life, consistent with their past (Savickas, 2011). It also helps them to map their subjective identity forms (Guichard, 2009). Narratives involve a co-construction of subjective identify forms that takes into account how the client relates to the contexts of her/his life and to the individuals in these contexts: «*Subjective Identity form is the way a given individual sees himself or herself and others in a particular context as well as relates to others and the objects in the context* (Savickas et al., 2009, p. 245). The construction of this representation of the self requires mobilizing certain types of reflection such as those identified by Dumora (1990) in her work with secondary school students. The reflexivity practiced by the students to reflect on their life design is based on several processes which occur simultaneously during their schooling.

Blustein (2006) uses the term "critical consciousness" which is an important skill to develop in clients to help them strengthen their capabilities and thus reduce inequalities. Critical consciousness consists in focusing reflexivity on the outside world. It leads to considering oneself as a member of a society, and to becoming aware of one's capacity for individual and collective action in order to improve one's situation. Critical consciousness can also help clients promote decent work, quality of life at work, and the protection of the environment (Guichard et al., 2016). Critical consciousness can combine with the processes of personalization or self-creation, identified by Malrieu (2003). Personalization takes place at several levels which coexist and have to be reconciled. The first level concerns activities which the individual must conduct within her/his inner circle. The individual must choose these activities, organize them, carry out projects and associate these projects with affiliations. These activities can sometimes come into conflict. Such conflicts generate a feeling or originality, of uniqueness of self. At the second level the person becomes aware of the importance of others and of social structures, in carrying out and coordinating her/his activities. The individual realizes that her/his choices and decisions are predetermined and this leads her/him to perceive herself/himself as a historical subject. At the same time, she/he can take a distanced view of her/his determinations, and these perceptions increase the feeling of self-fulfillment. The third level in the personalization process involves the individual's actions. This construction of meaning concerns the person, society and the relationship between the two. To achieve this, the individual produces a series of value judgments on the basis of which she/he can make decisions. For Malrieu (2003), the person must resolve conflicts and choose between many different demands. This third level involves adjusting behaviors through critical consciousness. Malrieu defines personalization as a complex dialectic which consists of discovering, negotiating and reexamining social norms. The person can become aware of the processes of influence, engagement and distancing to which she/he is subjected and associate them within original or innovative behavior patterns (Malrieu, 2003).

The Role of Career Counselling Dialogues in the Development of Reflexivity for Self-construction

According to the socio-constructivist approach to life design counselling, identity and individual development are co-constructed in social actions and interactions occurring in a given context (Gergen, 1999). The relations can be described as "human associations characterized by ongoing connections and emotional bonds" (Richardson, 2012, p. 203). Individuals are interdependent and engaged in various relational contexts among which work is one of the most important.

Dialogues in these relational contexts can contribute to self-construction. These dialogues make it possible to experiment with one's personal identity in three ways (Harré & van Langenhove, 1999). They enable the client to develop her/his agency during dialogues in which she/he can claim responsibility for certain actions. At the same time, these dialogues enable the construction of social representations of the world that surrounds the person. They help in appraising events and their contributions to the client's biography. They also enable the development of intentionality. As agents, individuals co-construct perceptions of self which inform intentional action (Mascolo, Fischer, & Neimeyer, 1999). The dialogues facilitate the construction of meaning and its evolution (Richardson, 2012). Meaning is constructed through the presence of signs in a given context. For Josephs, Valsimer, and Surgam (1999), understanding a sign implies immediately understanding its opposite—the counter-sign. Dialogues can reveal new interpretations of sign and counter-sign structures. Signs can be gradually extended to imply other signs, or can reconstruct themselves and evolve towards a higher degree of complexity (Josephs et al., 1999). For Savickas (2005), relationships make it possible to construct meaning and mattering, as an interpersonal process by which individuals learn from their activities and successes via cultural discourses and sharing their experiences with others. Relationships make it possible to re-signify the client's own experiences and this new meaning emerges through narration.

Narrative Identity: A Dialogue Centered on Past Personal Experience

Many narrative-based interventions are built on the works of Ricoeur and McAdams. Ricoeur (1992) focuses on mythical narratives in which he sees the expression of human problems and conceives hermeneutics as the central process for the construction of beliefs in modern society. Thus, any narrative is necessarily linked to the person who hears it. This person will only understand the narrative if she/he feels involved and is able to take part in constructing its meaning. Hermeneutics makes it possible to understand a story by interpreting it. All stories include setting a plot in the form of a human action represented as a myth. For Ricoeur (1998), the plot is set in three phases by the actor. The first one, Mimesis 1, is a symbolic pre-understanding of human action. The second one is mimesis 2, the poetic plotting of this action. Regarding the third, Mimesis 3, the reader or listener reconfigures the narrative she/he applies to the plot of her/his existence. Identity is described as a tension between two poles: the idem-identity is the fact that we can feel ourselves to be identical and recognizable throughout time. The second pole is ipse-identity, which corresponds to maintaining the self (self-constancy). Both poles are activated during life stories and combine in an innovative narrative employment (Ricoeur, 1992).

Building on Erikson's work, McAdams (1993) associates the identity that develops in late adolescence with an "integrated life history" in which identity is considered as a self narrative. Adolescents thus develop an embryonic version of their lives, a schematic life story. Life history is a psychosocial construct that depends on culture and in which each person is the co-author of her/his life in relation to the cultural and social context. McAdams (1999) has conducted semi-structured interviews with clients who were asked to talk about their life as if it were recounted in the form of a book. Each chapter must have its own specific plot. The person was invited to describe particularly important scenes or episodes in their lives and are then asked to imagine what the next chapters of the book might be. At the end, the person must identify the theme that embodies the entire story, like a sort of embedded metaphor. This process of reflecting on the past is the principle means by which narrative identity is constructed (Bluck & Habermas 2000; Savickas, 2011).

> An identity narrative tells a life history that revises identity over time without losing its essential meaning. It tells a story about self, a narrative of becoming oneself in response to the continuous changes that occur during the life course. (Savickas, 2011, p. 21).

The development of life history in the life design counselling practices proposed by Savickas (2011) is not limited to a narrative. It involves certain attitudes and interventions on the part of the practitioner and requires that a dialogue be established. The counsellor must see the story as a means by which the client can pursue a quest that will lead to her/him undertaking actions contemplated during the intervention. It is also recommended the interviewee be asked questions so she/he may detail certain elements of her/his story. The counsellor encourages the person to make connections between these narrated elements and her/his current concerns and to then identify those elements which are consistent with the story and in continuity with it. The relationship established between the client and the counsellor requires a commitment (creating a bond through a working alliance), interaction (facilitating the development of the narrative) and encouragement (an empathic and supportive attitude). The practitioner listens and takes note of the client's micro-narratives in response to her/his questions. She/he then tries to identify a consistent theme running through these micro-scripts to place them within the broader narrative and help the client create a self-portrait. For the clients, to reflect on and tell their stories fosters an understanding of their self in their professional lives and allows them to fully identify with the roles they seek to adopt in the future.

Life Design Counselling Dialogues for Building and Reconsidering the Principal Dimensions of One's Subjective Identity

The approach using Life Design counselling dialogues (Guichard et al., 2017) involves certain central concepts: identity cognitive frame, dynamic system of identity forms, and dual and trine forms of reflexivity. The concept of «identity cognitive frame» (Guichard, 2001) has been construed on the basis of the definition of "cognitive frame" (Barsalou, 1992) as a structure for organizing and processing—in long-term memory—information about a set of phenomena forming a whole. Information making an "identity cognitive frame" is about the different personal characteristics of—socially formed—categories of individuals. This information—corresponding to the "identity supply" (Dubar, 1998) of a society—is organized in memory and reactivated in a singular way by each individual: these processes being a function of all his/her experiences refer to some "habitus" (Bourdieu & Wacquant, 1992).

To act and interact in each of their everyday situations, individuals activate the identity cognitive frame (s) relevant in this situation. This activation—that triggers adaptation and updating of the concerned identity cognitive frame (s)—manifested itself in the form of a certain individual's behavior, of certain ideas that come to his/her mind, of affects he/she feels, of some words that he/she expresses, etc.: this set is defined as a "subjective identity form" (SIF) corresponding to the underlying "identity cognitive frame". While identity cognitive frames—as information's organizing and processing in memory—are non-conscious by definition, individuals can become aware of their subjective identity forms. The Life Designing Dialogues are aimed specifically at working out such an awareness.

This approach to subjective identity (or self-identity) describes it as a "dynamic system of subjective identity forms". Some subjective identity forms in people's SIF systems may be more important than others at some point in their life. A subjective identity form is central to the SIF system when a person hopes to achieve something very important for her/him, when she/he experiences positive affects that matter to her/him, and when other subjective identify forms in the person's SIF system make sense in relation to it. This main SIF can also relate to a project that is important to the person. In such a case, it is an expected subjective identity form (ESIF). Subjective identity forms which include such expectations of self-fulfillment are central to the organization of the dynamic system of subjective identity forms at a given point in time.

Being dynamic, a person's subjective identity form system (SIFS) is not immutable. Two interacting factors play a role in the transformation of the SIFS. The first is the transformation of the cognitive frames in long-term memory, according to the interactions within the society contexts which play the role of "identity suppliers". The second factor refers to all the changes and experiences that mark the course of a person's life and the way in which she/he feels and interprets them. Two forms of reflexivity play a role in the changes of a person's SIF system. Dual reflexivity, a mode of relating to oneself in which the person sees herself/himself in terms of an ideal she/he wishes to attain. It inspires the person to carry out certain activities in order to attain this ideal. Dual reflexivity is a stabilizing factor in the SIF system. The other form of reflexivity is trine reflexivity in which reflection takes the form of a continuous dialogue involving three positions. In this dialogue "I" says "something" to "you" ("you" being another person or myself, "you" understands "something" about the "something" that "I" has stated [From Peirce, "you" can be called an *interpretant* (Murphey, 1993)]. Based on this *interpretant*, "you" answers "something" to "I" who then produces a new *interpretant*. In each exchange, there is a gap between what is said and what is understood. This process creates a polyphony of resonances between the different evoked "you positions" that inspires new affects, ideas and representations.

The contexts of daily life play a very special and important role in the development of self-reflexivity, as highlighted in the "model of the system of activities" (Curie et al., 1990). It is even more so during the Life Design Counselling Dialogues. Such dialogues indeed activate these two forms of reflexivity—and more particularly the trine one—in the counselees' minds. These dialogues are aimed at helping individuals to express expectations about their futures as manifested either within one or another of their subjective identity forms or by the (emotional and cognitive) relationships between certain aspects of some of their subjective identity forms. To this end, during these dialogues (Guichard et al., 2017), counselees are encouraged to narrate their past and present experiences to the counsellor. The narration of each of these experiences opens up the possibility of conferring many new potential meanings to them and triggers affects in the person. The dialogue also makes it possible for connections and distinctions to be made between the different experiences. Reflexivity is greatly stimulated during life design counselling dialogues through the support provided by the counsellor.

The Activity System Model: An Approach for Studying and Stimulating the Reflections of Young People in School-to-Work Transition

Life design counselling dialogues are based on narrating and explaining activities and experiences. The activity system model is founded on the notion that emphasizes the active role of subjects in the self-construction process. This model makes it possible to understand the dynamics between the different activities of individuals, which are explored and possibly reviewed during life design counselling dialogues. The activity system approach is a modeling of Malrieu's active socialization and personalization approaches (Curie et al., 1990; Malrieu, 2003). This model refers to how individuals engage with their environment through the meaning they give to their daily activities. This meaning comes out through the regulation of actions in each sphere of life and of relationships between these different spheres. Life design counselling dialogues are a way of developing a meta-reflexivity to explore this system and its regulations.

According to this model, individuals play a creative role in their environment, through the meaning they give to their actions and the choices and trade-offs they make. In this model, the individual's activities are grouped under four life domains (family, career, personal and community). These life domains are considered to be relatively autonomous subsystems of a more global system. The individuals are likely to perceive relationships of resources or constraints in the activities, whether or not these activities belong to the same life domain. The model is based on the idea that in order to understand the behaviors of individuals in given situations it is necessary to consider the interactions of these behaviors between themselves and with the other "life domains". The purpose of this model is to describe the principles of organization and coordination of activities conducted by the subjects in their different life domains and to analyze the processes of construction and transformation during the life design counselling dialogues (Pouyaud, 2015). The individuals' perception of themselves as an agent in a given context is therefore apprehended through the system of perceived relationships between activities and life domains. The individuals give meaning to the involvement in their life contexts, to their behaviors and choices. These choices and decisions in the construction of the individual are attempts to resolve conflicts perceived at a micro level (time dedicated to competing activities) and at a macro level (socialization conflicts).

Conversations, Group Dialogues and Self-construction

Group conversations and dialogues do not replace one-to-one counselling interventions which can be more in-depth, involve several sessions and focus on an individual's specific life design problem. Group dialogues should therefore be used to complement one-to-one interventions. These can have several objectives. They can prepare young people to engage in more effective one-to-one support because they make it possible to discuss similar situations encountered by others and thus enrich their knowledge of different experiences. Group interactions concerning career experiences make it possible to conceive new intentions of actions and develop new perspectives. It is an educational activity of co-construction based on the unique experiences of group members.

The Benefits of Group Conversations for Developing Reflexivity

Such a perspective can be based on research conducted on the effects of family interactions on self-construction. Based on Piaget's assimilation/accommodation approach for modeling identity construction, McLean (2016) emphasizes the role of collective family narratives in the construction of individual identities. She designs interventions in which all family members were asked to narrate some of their funniest or happiest shared memories or memories reflecting a major change in their life. A few months later, she met the same young people individually and asked them to share family memories as well as a personal memory that was important to them (McLean, 2005). It showed that some young people define themselves more in relation to family stories, while others evoke truly personal stories or family stories that they review entirely. She observed differences between those who produce few reflexive comments about such memories and others who develop many reflexive comments. Mc Lean shows that narratives in families construct the identity of each member (a process referred to as "narrative ecology"). Shared consensual stories thus constitute an ecological narrative space. The role of conversations between parents and teenagers about career intentions and career plans was identified by Young and colleagues (Young et al., 1997; Young, Ball, Valach, Turkel, & Wong, 2003). "The conversations parents and adolescents have together about careers are joint actions because they are not specified entirely by the individual intentions or actions of either person but are determined by what happens between them" (Young, et al., 1997, p. 73). The study of the conversations showed that joint actions are mentioned and specific intentions for actions are produced. They allow the co-construction of career design projects through the expression of intentions followed by the implementation of new actions.

In the field of career management, Borge, Butterfield, and Lalande (2013) studied career conversations between managers and employees. They showed that these career-related dialogues, which concern engagement, problems of absenteeism, intentions regarding withdrawal or training, benefited managers and employees. Managers get to know employees better and become more aware of their problems. Employees feel listened to and identify career prospects.

As observed by Di Fabio and Maree (2012), group interventions for career counselling have been poorly developed. Participants often experience career interventions collectively, but these interventions are not designed to take into account interactions as dialogues helping constructing the self. Thomsen considers career guidance as a collective phenomenon. Empirical studies, show that in collective career guidance sessions that promote social and verbal interactions, participants are willing to establish links with community issues, to become aware of their possibilities for taking collective action and develop their role in society (Thomsen, 2012).

In ethics education classes, collective dialogues have been used to develop self-awareness or the ability to take into account the attitude of others towards oneself (Mead, 1934/2006). For example, philosophical conversations appear to contribute to the moral education of individuals because they make it possible to practice reflexivity, empathy and logical reasoning (Habermas, 2001). These group conversations develop debating and listening skills. They make it possible to become a competent moral thinker, a competent reflexive speaker and listener. Noddings (2002) believes that in order to develop an ethical sense in young people, it is important that they should have conversations that address major existential themes such as birth, death, love, luck and quality of life. Issues that are addressed in popular stories, legends, myths and religions as well as in many contemporary films or works of fiction. For Noddings (2002) "Again, the object is not simply to provide students with more information, although expanded conversation will certainly do that. Instead, the object is to arouse sensibilities, to get students to think and feel beyond the facts, to reach for what all this means for their own life and the lives of others" (Noddings, 2002, p. 137). Noddings also encourages ordinary conversations between students and teachers because they provide a rich learning environment. With such conversations, students learn many important things for their self-development and their awareness of ethical and moral issues. For example, they learn to listen to others, to express and defend their ideas, to respond without offending others, and to reflect on what others say to them. "These conversations are essential to moral life (…) we learn through them how to meet and treat one another" (Noddings, 2002, p. 146).

Group Intervention for the Co-construction of a Socio-ecological Space and the Development of Career Education

Career design interventions based on interactions and conversations between group members are poorly developed. They require knowledge in social psychology and a facilitator to manage group dynamics. Beauvois stresses that the group is a space or a means by which certain processes that intervene in social life can emerge (Mugny, Oberlé, & Beauvois, 1995). For Johnson and Johnson (2006), the main features of the group are interpersonal interactions, interdependence, common goals, a sense of affiliation, motivation, relationships structured by a series of roles and norms, and mutual interpersonal influences. The purpose of training-groups (T-groups) and action research based on Lewin's work is to enable people to learn through social interactions. "In a training group, participants have the task of building a group that will meet the requirements of each of its members for them to be able to develop. Group members have the opportunity to learn about themselves, about interpersonal relationships, about groups, and about broader social systems" (De Vissher, 2001). Groups share an experience in the here and now that creates bonds between the members. This is a process of relatedness (De Vissher, 2001) that involves establishing a bond between a person and a system or sub-system which she/he belongs to. For Pagès (1968), the group is a structure where relatedness (or solidarity) is learned and where un-relatedness—associated with anxiety—may be experienced.

The group is made up of people who develop interactions and inter-influences, what Lewin (1947) refers to as the field of the group. It is a space where forces that bring about change are distributed. The action of modifying the group field is conducted in three stages:

- Unfreezing: disruption of immobility through information, feedback, and elucidation
- Moving: displacing tensions, readjustment of relationships, reconstruction of meaning
- Refreezing: stabilization of a new situation which is satisfactory for the group and identification of possibilities for applying lessons learned to new situations.

The continuous experience of interaction is the privileged locus and instrument for change at group, interpersonal and intra-individual levels (De Vissher, 2001). Group experience should make it possible to broaden the scope of the experiences, roles and values of each member of the group and promote the emergence of a participatory society.

In the following section a proposal for a group intervention is presented. It is a career education intervention based on a socio-ecological perspective, aimed at fostering interactions in the form of dialogues between participants. Carried out in a classroom or training group context, this proposed intervention is intended to facilitate reflection on career design and social participation. It can be combined with individual counselling interventions. It involves developing a collective life design approach based on the idea that self-construction can be facilitated and made more efficient through comparing one's experiences with those of others. This comparison not only broadens the scope of experiences but also offers a continuous social validation of the intentions expressed by each individual.

Collective Interventions Based on Group Dialogues in Life and Career Design

This fourth section focuses on career counselling dialogues using group interactions for the development of reflexivity and of a more flexible form of identity (Young et al., 1997). The intervention is based on the T-group and action research operating modes. It is founded on the notion that each participant can learn about herself/himself and develop her/his reflexivity, critical thinking and critical consciousness through interactions with others. It is also founded on the model of life and career design counselling dialogues which, until now, has only been applied to counsellor-counselee dialogues (Guichard et al., 2017). The main assumption is that group dialogues will trigger a development—in each participant's mind—of some of their identity cognitive frames and possibly a construction of new ones. The group should share its experience by translating it into a form that is understandable to all the participants. Putting the experience into words may accelerate and enrich the process of trine reflexivity and thus accelerate a change or reorganization of identity. We believe that this activity, developed in the classroom, for example, could raise questions about the self and about counselling which would encourage more requests for one-to-one interviews. This would make it possible to reactivate a dialogical process possibly more focused on certain specific activities.

Organisation:

	Task and instructions from the facilitator
This intervention should be carried out in a class of adolescents or emerging adults (aged 12–22). It requires the participation of facilitators (psychologists, counsellors, teachers) trained in psychosocial interventions	The facilitators organize the class into groups of 8–10 people. One facilitator is required per group of 8–10 participants. Each participant must have a notepad and a pen. At each stage the facilitator should give instructions, and note the group's consensual responses. Large sheets of paper and felt pens are needed. The entire procedure can be performed in one day

Step 1 group session: Task of identifying common expectations.

The first step consists of group discussions on two themes: (1) How do participants see the transition they should face soon and the decisions they have to make? How could this group's activities be useful for their coping with this transition? And (2): How do they see work. Participants are invited to express themselves freely in response to stimulus-based questions. The facilitator ensures all participants express themselves and encourages interaction. She/he notes down the consensual answers to the questions asked. The facilitator uses group facilitation and semi-structured interview techniques.

Step 1:

	Task and instructions from the facilitator	
Theme 1: Perception of the transition and expectations about this group's activities (or other activities) for coping with it:	Representations of the transition they will soon face. Each group collectively provides answers to the following questions: *How do you view the transition you should face soon? What kinds of decisions will you have to make? Do you think this transition could impact on your future life? Which impacts?*	The facilitator writes down the group's answers

(continued)

(continued)

	Task and instructions from the facilitator	
– Expectations about this group's activities (and other forms of support) for coping with this transition	Each group discusses and gives answers to the following questions: "*What are your expectations as regards this group's activities for coping with this transition? Which questions would you like to have answers to? How would you like to be supported for making the best possible decisions?*"	
Theme 2: Work Representations of work	Each group must collectively provide three answers to the question "*When we talk about work, what does it make you think of? What comes to mind?*"	One participant must report the consensual answers
Expectations regarding work	Each group must discuss and provide answers to the question "*What are your expectations regarding work? Which questions would you like to answer about work?*"	

Step 2: Elicitation of dimensions of identity forms common to the members of the group and particular to one or some of them.

As previously explained, identity cognitive frames are memorizing-structures and processes in the individuals' minds that refer to the different personal characteristics of—socially formed—categories of people. These frames constitute the cognitive foundation of (1) both their perceptions of self, their behaviors and (inter)actions in the different contexts in which they act, interact and engage and (2) of their perceptions of other people, of their anticipations about these other people's behaviors, and about most current elements in any of these contexts. When a person thinks of herself/himself in connection with a cognitive identity frame (e.g. as a physician), she/he activates in her/his mind a series of long-term memory structures related to her/his actual experience as a patient, a hospital intern or the grandchild of a doctor. The individual therefore has a personal perception of what it means to be a doctor, which is not the same as that of another individual (Guichard et al., 2017).

As already mentioned, such a set of perceptions of self (linked to some affects), behaviors, and anticipations about other people and elements generally present in a context has been named a "subjective identity form". A SIF is both an activation and updating of an identity cognitive frame for both an understanding of the current context.

Step 2:

	Task and instructions from the facilitator	
On the occasion of this workshop second step, participants are asked to explicit—and discuss—the major characteristics of some SIF— corresponding to their lives' most important domains—as much as they can make them public	Depending of the available time, facilitator can focus on either a single domain or activity or some or all of them. He/she gives the following instruction: "*Please answer each of the 5 following questions by coming up with at least a consensual answer and some answers peculiar to some members of your sub-group:* – *When you think about yourself at (high) school, what's your favorite activity?* – *Why do you like it?* – *Is there something that you hate at (high) school?* – *What are your expectations as regards your future based on your (high)-school experience?* – *How would you describes yourself as a (high)-school student?*" Then, same set of questions is asked again, about another life domain (sports, family, friendship …)	These domains are defined with reference to the activity system model (Curie et al., 1990). This means that participants—forming subgroups of 3–4—are asked to describe their daily activities in different life domains. • School/university activities: during classes, home work, informal working time, etc. • Activities with family/friends • Leisure activities • Work activities

The facilitator collects the answers. The answers are written up on large sheets of paper that make the "*Catalogue of the Public Identity Forms*" of the group participants. This catalogue may be structured as a map with some Public Identity Forms appearing as more central (as displaying some important expectations shared by many group members) than others.

Step 3: Towards a mapping of the Subjective Identity Forms System of each group member.

Each participant is asked to think about and design his/her system of subjective identity forms in relationship to the public identity forms' catalogue of the current group.

Step 3:

	Task and instructions from the facilitator	
First, a general discussion is organized about this catalogue	Each participant is invited to react and comment this common outcome: "*What do they think of it? According to this catalogue, what seems very important in most participants' current lives? What appears to be generally of minor importance? Does it seem to be some consensus among the group members? What are the major differences between them?*"	

(continued)

(continued)

	Task and instructions from the facilitator	
Secondly, participants are asked to consider the catalogue in relationship to their personal views on themselves	They are asked to think privately—during a short period of time—of the following questions before exposing their answers to the group: "*Do they find in this catalogue certain characteristics that describe well some aspects of the view they have of themselves? Which ones? What differentiates them most from the catalogue? In which way do they fit into it? How would they like to evolve in relation to the contexts described in the catalogue?*"	The facilitator invites all the group members to make helping comments on the answers given by each participant, which he/she notes down
Thirdly, participants are asked to draw a picture of their system of Subjective Identity Forms	Two steps: (1) their current System of SIF: "me today", (2) their expected System of SIF: "me, as I need to be for achieving what matters to me". In both cases, they are invited to make clear distinctions between the SIF they consider central (as encompassing some major expectations about themselves) and the more peripheral ones	
Participants who agree display the 2 diagrams of their SIF's system	Participants get to know the displayed diagrams. Informal exchanges then takes place with the diagrams' authors. No participant is forced to display his/her diagrams	Facilitator says that each diagrams' author will take them home. They will be able to supplement or modify them based on ideas that came to their mind or on points they did not want to expose publicly

Step 4: Evaluation of changes inspired by the approach.

Step 4:

	Task and instructions from the facilitator
The group comes together for a last activity involving the answers given in the workshop's first step	The facilitator comes back to the answers about the participants' expectations as regards this group's activities for coping with this transition and about work. He/she asks the following questions: *Have some answers been provided? What are they? Which questions remain unanswered and which new questions are raised? How can they be answered? What comments do you have regarding the approach?*

Finally, participants are given the possibility of having one-to-one sessions with a counsellor to help them put discussed changes into practice.

Conclusion

In the current context of globalization, individuals feel the need to develop multiple social affiliations. At the same time they are experiencing work situations that are more precarious and changing than in the past. Career counselling interventions are now attempting to use the perspective of decent work as a framework for engaging individual and collective action for social justice and sustainable human development. However, current forms of career counselling, even the most recent (Savickas et al., 2009), are often criticized for being focused solely on the individual. The constructionist-constructivist framework and the life Design interventions presented in this chapter are intended to address this issue with a more social and collective approach to life design and decent work. In the life design approach, self-construction is the main task individuals are required to undertake to address the challenges of the 21st century. Life and career design counselling methods are intended to help individuals give meaning and direction to their lives by putting into words their personal values and standards. The main goal in this approach to counselling is to foster "reflexivity" in individuals with regard to their activities in their various spheres of life. More precisely, life and career design dialogues (Guichard, 2009) aim to help clients identify desirable future prospects, both personal and professional, that may give meaning to their lives, and to specify the means to achieve them (Savickas et al., 2009). We think that a collective version of life design counselling using group dialogues should more effectively introduce the decent work perspective into the life design paradigm. This approach using group dialogues as a way of fostering individual and collective reflexivity for social justice and change needs to be experimented with. What can be expected from these collective interventions? We believe that they can open up new perspectives in personal, social and professional terms as well as foster new skills in using social interactions to clarify certain situations. They are also expected to help increase adaptability in individuals and encourage them to attach more importance to their career and life design. In accordance with the work of R. Young (Young, Domene, & Valash, 2015; Young et al., 1997), we expect to observe an increase in the number of planned project-related actions and enhanced self-narrative skills or biographying in clients (Delory-Momberger, 2014). Group interactions focused on current and future activities can also be a part of life and career design education. Confronted with the narrative of the other group members, participants are called on to participate by drawing from their own experiences and biographical resources. These biographical interactions in the group should allow the enhancement of the identity, and of the emotional and cognitive resources of each member. This experience is made possible when there are a minimum number of shared experiences between the members of the group, who can then feel they share a common fate.

Acknowledgement The authors thank Pr. Jean Guichard for his reading and suggestions.

References

Archer, M. (2011). *The reflexive imperative in late modernity*. New York: Cambridge University Press.

Barsalou, L. W. (1992). *Cognitive psychology: An overview for cognitive scientists*. Hillsdale, NJ: Lawrence Erlbaum Associates.

Béduwé, C., & Dupray, A. (2018). Perceived job insecurity in early careers: A tale of two French cohorts. CEREQ *Training and Employment*. Retrieved from file:///Users/jacquespouyaud/Downloads/Training133.pdf.

Borge, W. A., Butterfield, L. D., & Lalande, V. (2013). Career conversations in small-to-medium-sized businesses: A competitive advantage. *Canadian Journal of Counselling and Psychotherapy, 2*, 169–187.

Bourdieu, P., & Wacquant, L. (1992). *An invitation to reflexive sociology*. Chicago, IL: The University of Chicago Press.

Bluck, S., & Habermas, T. (2000). The life story schema. *Motivation and Emotion, 24*(2), 121–147. https://doi.org/10.1023/A:1005615331901.

Blustein, D. (2006). *The psychology of working. A new perspective for career development, counseling and public policy*. Mahwah, NJ: Lawrence Erlbaum Associates.

Cohen-Scali, V. (2015). School-to-work transition and the model "To make oneself self". In A. M. Di Fabio & J. L. Bernaud (Eds.), *The construction of the identity on 21st century* (pp. 171–187). New York: Nova Publishers.

Cohen-Scali, V., & Guichard, J. (2008). Introduction: Identités et orientations [Identities and guidance]. *L'Orientation Scolaire et Professionnaire, 3*, 315–320. https://doi.org/10.4000/osp.1714.

Cohen-Scali, V., Pouyaud, J., Podgorny, M., Drabik-Podgorna, V., Aisenson, G., Bernaud, J. L., et al. (Eds.). (2018). *Interventions in career design and education: Transformation for sustainable development and decent work*. New York: Springer.

Curie, J., Hajjar, V., Marquié, H., & Roques, M. (1990). Proposition méthodologique pour la description du système des activités [Methodological proposal for the description of the system of activities]. *Le Travail Humain, 53*, 103–118.

Delory-Momberger, C. (2014). *De la recherche biograhique en education. fondements, méthodes, pratiques* [Biographical research in education. fundamentals, methods, practices]. Paris: Teraèdre.

De Vissher, P. (2001). *La dynamique des groupes d'hier à aujourd'hui* [Group dynamics from the past to the present day]. Paris: Presses Universitaires de France.

Di Fabio, A., & Maree, G. K. (2012). Group-based life design counseling in an italian context. *Journal of Vocational Behavior, 80*, 100–107. https://doi.org/10.1016/j.jvb.2011.06.001.

Dubar, C. (1998). *La socialisation. Construction des identités sociales et professionnelles (2ème édition revue)* [Socialization: The construction of social and professional identities, 2nd ed.]. Paris: Armand Colin.

Dumora, B. (1990). La dynamique vocationnelle chez les adolescents de collège: continuité et ruptures [Vocational dynamics in middle school adolescents: Continuity and disruptions]. *L'Orientation Scolaire et Professionnelle, 2*, 111–127.

Gergen, J. K. (1999). *An invitation to social construction*. London, UK: Sage Publications.

Guichard, J. (2001). Adolescents' scholastic fields, identity frames and forms and future projects. In J. E. Nurmi (Ed.), *Navigating through adolescence: European perspectives* (pp. 279–306). New York: Routledge Falmer.

Guichard, J. (2009). Self-constructing. *Journal of Vocational Behavior, 75*, 251–258. https://doi.org/10.1016/j.jvb.2009.03.004.

Guichard, J., Bangali, M., Cohen-Scali, V., Pouyaud, J., & Robinet, M. L. (2017). *Concevoir et orienter sa vie: les dialogues de conseil en life design* [Designing and guiding one's life: Life design counseling dialogues]. Paris: Qui plus est.

Guichard, J., Drabik-Podgórna, V., & Podgorny, M. (Eds.). (2016). *Counseling and dialogue for sustainable human development*. Torun, Poland: University of Wroclaw.

Harré, R., & van Langenhove, L. (1999). *Positioning theory*. Oxford, UK: Blackwell Publishers.

Habermas, J. (2001). *La théorie de l'agir commucationnel* [The theory of communicative action, Vol. 1]. Paris: Fayard.

Johnson, D. H., & Johnson, F. P. (Eds.). (2006). *Joining together: Group theory and group skills* (9th ed.). Boston, MA: Pearson Allyn and Bacon.

Josephs, I. E., Valsiner, J., & Surgam, S. E. (1999). The process of meaning construction. In J. Brandtstädter & R. M. Lerner (Eds.), *Action & development. Theory and research through the life span* (pp. 257–282). Thousand Oaks, CA: Sages Publications.

Lewin, K. (1947). Frontiers in group dynamics: Concept, method and reality in social science; social equilibria and social change. *Human Relations, 1,* 5–41. https://doi.org/10.1177/001872674700100103.

Malrieu, P. (2003). *La construction du sens dans les dires autobiographiques* [The construction of meaning in autobiographical narratives]. Toulouse: Eres.

Mascolo, M. F., Fischer, K. W., & Neimeyer, R. A. (1999). The dynamic codevelopment of intentionality, self, and social relations. In J. Brandtstädter & R. M. Lerner (Eds.), *Action & development. Theory and research through the life span* (pp. 133–168). Thousand Oaks, CA: Sages Publications.

McAdams, D. P. (1993). *The stories we live by: Personal Myths and the making of the self*. New York: William Morrow.

McAdams, D. P. (1999). Personal narratives and the life story. In L. Pervin & O. John (Eds.), *Handbook of personality. Theory and research* (2nd ed., pp. 478–500). New York: Guilford Press.

McLean, K. C. (2005). Late adolescent identity development: Narrative meaning-making and the memory telling. *Developmental Psychology, 41,* 683–691. http://psycnet.apa.org/doi/10.1037/0012-1649.41.4.683.

McLean, K. C. (2016). *The co-authored self. Family stories and the construction of personal identity*. New York: Oxford University Press.

McIlveen, P. (2015). Affective research approach to professional competencies for life design. In L. Nota & J. Rossier (Eds.), *Handbook of life design. From practice to theory and from theory to practice* (pp. 269–282). Göttingen: Hogrefe.

Mead, G. H. (1934/2006). *Mind, self, society*. Chicago, IL: The University of Chicago Press.

Mugny, G., Oberlé, D., & Beauvois, J. L. (1995). *Relations humaines, groupes et influence sociale* [Human relations, groups and social influence]. Grenoble, France: Presses universitaires de Grenoble.

Murphey, M. G. (1993). *The development of Peirce's philosophy*. Cambridge, MA: Harvard University Press.

Noddings, N. (2002). *Educating moral people*. New York, NJ: Teachers College Press.

Nota, L., & Rossier, J. (Eds.). (2015). *Handbook of life design. From practice to theory and from theory to practice*. Göttingen, Germany: Hogrefe.

Pouyaud, J. (2015). Vocational trajectories and people's multiple identities: A life design. In L. Nota & J. Rossier (Eds.), *Handbook of life design. From practice to theory and from theory to practice* (pp. 59–75). Göttingen, GE: Hogrefe.

Pagès, M. (1968). *La vie affective des groupes*. [The emotional life of groups]. Paris: Dunod.

Richardson, M. S. (2012). Counseling for work and relationship. *The Counseling Psychologist, 40*(2), 190–242. https://doi.org/10.1177/0011000011406452.

Ricoeur, P. (1992). *Oneself as another*. Chicago, IL: University of Chicago Press.

Ricoeur, P. (1998). *Time and narrative* (Vol. 3). Chicago, IL: University of Chicago Press.

Savickas, M. L. (2005). The theory and practice of career construction. In S. D. Brown & R. W. Lent (Eds.), *Career development and counseling. Putting theory and research to work* (pp. 42–70). Hoboken, NJ: Wiley.

Savickas, M. L. (2011). *Career counseling*. Washington, DC: American Psychological Association.

Savickas, M. L. (2015). Life designing with adults—Developmental individualization using biographical bricolage. In L. Nota & J. Rossier (Eds.), *Handbook of life design. From practice to theory and from theory to practice* (pp. 135–150). Göttingen, Germany: Hogrefe.

Savickas, M. L., Nota, L., Rossier, J., Dauwalder, J. P., Duarte, M. E., Guichard, J., et al. (2009). Life designing: A paradigm for career construction in the 21st century. *Journal of Vocational Behavior, 75,* 239–250. https://doi.org/10.1016/j.jvb.2009.04.004.

Thomsen, R. (2012). *Career guidance in communities*. Aarhus: Aarhus University Press.

Watson, M., & McMahon, M. (2011). The narrative of constructivism and career counseling. In M. Watson & M. McMahon (Eds.), *Career counseling and constructivism. Elaboration of constructs* (pp. 1–13). New York, NJ: Nova Science Publishers.

Young, R. A., Ball, J., Valach, L., Turkel, H., & Wong, W. S. (2003). The family career development project in Chinese Canadian family. *Journal of Vocational Behavior, 62,* 287–304. https://doi.org/10.1016/S0001-8791(02)00022-2.

Young, R. A., Domene, J., & Valach, L. (Eds.). (2015). *Counseling and action. Toward life-enhancing work, relationships and identity*. New York, NJ: Springer.

Young, R. A., Valach, L., Paseluiko, M. A., Dover, C., Matthes, G. E., Paproski, D. L., et al. (1997). The joint action of parents and adolescents in conversation about career. *The Career Development Quarterly, 46,* 72–86.

Enhancing the Employability of Young Adults from Socio-economically Challenged Contexts: Theoretical Overview

Erna W. Gerryts and Jacobus G. Maree

Abstract The effect of unemployment is devastating to the health and well-being of individuals, families, and communities, as well as to the economy of countries. To alleviate some of the effects of unemployment, it seems key to enhance the employability of people (those from socio-economically challenged backgrounds especially). We begin this chapter by discussing generally the occupational world and current trends that bring about global changes. This is followed by explication of the chapter structure and the goals of the study. Next, we shift our attention to an elaboration of the changing world of work and developing country contexts, focussing on the South African situation specifically. The importance and desirability of becoming employable is explicated, after which the theory of employability is deliberated from three perspectives to obtain a holistic view of the construct and to inform adaptability-related intervention. Since we regard acquiring career adaptability as a key aspect that promotes employability, literature on how to develop career adaptability is explored next. Given the idiosyncratic occupational dilemmas disadvantaged people in young adulthood in particular face, and the influence of poverty experienced in this developmental stage, the emphasis then shifts to a discussion of some keys for employability counselling intervention for this population in particular before the chapter is concluded.

Keywords Employability · Career adaptability · Young adults · Employability counselling · Unemployment · Socio-economically challenged

Introduction

> Lifetime employability instead of lifetime employment is put forward as the new protection in the labour market. (Forrier & Sels, 2003)

E. W. Gerryts (✉) · J. G. Maree
Department of Educational Psychology, University of Pretoria, Pretoria, South Africa
e-mail: gerryts.erna@gmail.com

J. G. Maree
e-mail: kobus.maree@up.ac.za

J. G. Maree (ed.), *Handbook of Innovative Career Counselling*,
https://doi.org/10.1007/978-3-030-22799-9_24

Unemployment and, especially, lack of employability have a direct negative impact on the global economy, as well as on the health and well-being of individuals, families, and communities. Employability, in its broadest sense, implies the relationship between two forces, the one being the world of work, and the other the person/individual/job-seeker. The world of work globally has challenges especially in deficient socio-economic circumstances but it also offers opportunities in this specific time and age we live in. The job-seeker on the other hand has a specific culture, life stage and life role, unique individual characteristics, and relationships within his/her family. His or her autobiographical story relates to multiple unique developmental opportunities that can be used as a means to design a future life and career. Possibilities must be explored to enhance the employability of people (from the perspective of this chapter, people from socio-economically challenged backgrounds specifically).

Chapter Structure

The first part of the chapter discusses briefly some aspects of the transformed world of work globally. The second part deals with the goals of this chapter, after which part three focusses on the impact of change on developing country contexts such as South Africa. In part four, the meaning and importance of promoting employability and its link with career adaptability are discussed. The dire situation of young adults in a disadvantaged cultural context (in the current case, South Africa) especially is elaborated. Part five shifts the attention to a discussion of some keys for employability counselling intervention for this population, after which the chapter is concluded.

Goals of the Chapter

The chapter relates to the situation in South African contexts with young adults facing socio-economic deprivation. The overall goal of the chapter is to reflect on how the employability of young adults from socio-economically challenged contexts can be enhanced. The emphasis is on the individual level (keeping in mind what is offered, suggested, and required from other perspectives) and on young adults who study at skills training organisations that want to develop workplace readiness knowledge and skills. We are interested in establishing how these individuals can be influenced and motivated to become more adaptable in order to change their own situation with regard to employability specifically.

Transformed World of Work Globally

Deloitte (2016) and the World Economic Forum (2016) identified four major global drivers that force institutions and companies across the world to stay relevant, namely demographic upheaval, digital technology, an even faster pace of change, and new social contracts between companies and workers.

Demographics of Workers

The demographics of employees in corporate companies have changed (Bimrose, 2010). Workers are both younger and older, and they are more diverse than before. Millennials, who currently make up more than half of the workforce globally, have a substantial impact on the workplace, have high expectations about values in the workplace, want to make a positive difference in society, expect continuing learning and growth opportunities, want to be remunerated to be able to retire comfortably, often do not stay for long at one company, and are loyal to their own values (Deloitte, 2016). Baby boomers are often working into their 70s and 80s and must adapt to being supervised by young managers (whom they often mentor and coach) (Deloitte, 2016).

Employees are more diverse and require company cultures to be inclusive to focus on shared beliefs for the business. The spectrum of diversity includes race, ethnicity, gender, sexual orientation, socio-economic status (SES), age, physical abilities, and religious and political belief (Patrick, 2013). Therefore, conscious practices must be put in place to enhance understanding among employees and between employees and employers.

Digital Revolution

In 2016, humankind was almost entirely connected although there is inequality regarding bandwidth, price, and efficiency of the service in different areas of the world (Castells, 2015). The Fourth Industrial Revolution (Schwab, 2016) has the potential to change irreversibly the basics of the way in which we live and work. Industries and organisations in all countries experience forms of digital disruption caused by the need to digitise their production systems and transform not only product offerings, but also the way they manage their business. Another technological innovation that is part of the Fourth Industrial Revolution is the Internet of Things (IoT) (Deloitte, 2016). Through Artificial Intelligence (AI), things and digital objects are connected to the internet and become active participants in business processes (Eloff, Eloff, Dlamini, & Zielinski, 2009). This is already seen in robotics, nanotechnology, 3D printing, genetics, and biotechnology. Everyday objects will as early as 2020 have network connectivity (Schwab, 2016), thus allowing them to send and receive data. The ultimate goal for the IoT is to translate into the Internet of Services

(IoS), which is defined as "the vision for next-generation services provided over the Internet" (Eloff et al., 2009), and therefore companies need to generate innovative service-based business models. This will introduce another futuristic dimension into the world of work that will inevitably change jobs.

The Pace of Change

Parallel to changed demographics and the digital revolution, the rate of change is increasing (Deloitte, 2016). Businesses and companies need agility in the way they manage and work to be able to adapt to the fast pace of change. Business model innovators such as *Uber* and *Airbnb* put pressure on companies to reposition themselves to meet business challenges that are new to what and in what way they have been operating before.

New Agreements Between Companies and Workers Generally, more than a third of workers around the globe are contract and part-time workers in corporate companies (Deloitte, 2016). Employees are often reluctant to join a company and climb their career ladder in that same company (Savickas, 2013). There seems to be less loyalty between employees and employers, but an openness to a variety of ways in how to employ people. The Fourth Industrial Revolution predicts great hope for prosperity and future job creation, but many jobs will be taken over by robots/devices and certain jobs will undergo major changes or simply cease to exist. The way products and services are utilised will be changed. This needs proactive adaptation by companies, governments, societies and individuals. How and where people work will lead to challenges for management and governing practices (Schwab & Samans, 2016).

The Changing World of Work and Developing Country Contexts: Focus on South Africa

South Africa is one of the most unequal societies in the world (Maree, 2013a) and has a Gini coefficient of between 0.66 and 0.70 (World Bank, 2016). It is the only African economy that belongs to the G20 forum. Despite this, the growing population of unemployed youth is a matter of serious concern (WEF, 2016) in South Africa—as in the rest of Africa. The total population of South Africa is close to 58 million, and people under the age of 25 years make up ca 48% of this figure (WEF, 2016). The majority of South Africans do not take personal responsibility for their careers (Maree, 2015).

Unemployment and Poverty

South Africa is in the top 10 countries on global unemployment rankings worldwide. The unwieldy part is the effect it has had on the youth of South Africa over generations, creating a cycle of hopelessness that becomes part of families over years. One of these symptoms is the fact that 12 million mothers/caregivers receive a social government grant (Ferreira, 2015) of R 400,00 (ca USD27) per month for support (until the child is 18 years old)-to care for children, some of whom are part of child-headed households. Sixteen million South Africans live on social government grants.

Skills Shortage

Poverty adds to the skills shortage in South Africa. People often do not have the funds to skill themselves so as to stand a chance to find suitable employment. On the other hand, organisations are often unable to fill certain positions because of the lack of skills of available workers. Companies report a lack of industry-specific qualifications/certifications in skills trades. The root of the dilemma lies in the inadequacy of education of the workforce (Business Tech., 2015; Kruger, 2016). South Africa has a major shortage specifically in technical skills (Steyn, 2015). Many students who are enrolled in tertiary institutions in South Africa are studying in fields that are irrelevant to the needs of business (Kruger, 2016). Business needs for science, technology, engineering, and maths (STEM) skills are not met sufficiently and this leaves companies unable to fill crucial posts.

Education

Cross-national assessments of educational achievement portray the South African education system as the worst among participating middle-income countries, performing worse than many low-income African countries (Spaull, 2013). Quality of schooling has been a major area of concern since 1994 and still carries remnants from the apartheid regime when government spent as much as nine times more on schooling for Caucasian than on education for other cultures (Van Niekerk, 2012). The general climate in the South African school system is often one of inertia, low teacher morale, and a lack of accountability.

Career Counselling in South Africa

Historically and today still, career counselling finds itself in a similar situation to the situation in Education. Maree (2009, p. 437) comments on and advocates for promoting South African career counselling, as "the majority of black persons are still not receiving adequate career counselling" in South Africa. Many students exit school and enter tertiary institutions without having been exposed to any career counselling whatsoever. South Africa does not have enough counsellors and psychologists to service the need of our diverse cultural population. Moreover, generally speaking, relatively privileged counsellors facilitate career counselling in contexts that differ from their own. This kind of intervention may 'silence' clients during career facilitation (Maree, 2013b). Likewise, assessment methods and practices are contentious issues in the South African context. In the current South Africa, traditional career assessment methods and career counselling are still used pre-dominantly. Drawing on contemporary approaches to career counselling is not common practice. Career counsellors often maintain that an integrative quantitative-qualitative approach to career counselling is too time-consuming, expensive, and more suited to individual, Western and North American (career) counselling settings (Maree, 2015).

What Does Employability Entail?

Employability can best be described as a multi-dimensional concept (Fugate & Kinicki, 2008; Guilbert, Bernaud, Gouvernet, & Rossier, 2016). By exploring several definitions, we came under the impression of its wide range. Scholars employ different lenses to grasp the complex mosaic (Forrier & Sels, 2003) that employability encompasses. Reference is often made to a demand-side and a supply-side of employability (Jonck & Minnaar, 2017; Sin & Neave, 2014). The supply-side is constituted by higher education institutions/organisations and students/individuals (what they offer), while the demand-side involves the views of employers and industry on what a person needs to be employable. Guilbert et al. (2016, p. 69) support the importance of implementing a "systemic integrative approach to and a wider interpretation of employability". Adopting this proposition, we explore employability from three perspectives: Education, industry (the employer), and the person (individual).

Educational Perspective

The educational perspective on employability has evolved over the last two decades. The concept developed gradually as contributors became more aware that employability assets need to be developed at tertiary level for graduates to function optimally in industry and that it is likely that non-traditional career 'paths' and ways to obtain employment will become the norm (Sin & Neave, 2014). These authors warn that higher or tertiary education is only one of the factors—along with personal and external factors—that makes for employability. A qualification does not ensure employment. It is quite possible to be employable but not be in employment (Brown, Hesketh, & William, 2003; Sin & Neave, 2014) or to have a degree but struggle to find employment. Employability designates graduate potential to obtain and function in a job (Sin & Neave, 2014; Yorke, 2006) but also comprises actual job acquisition (Yorke, 2006). Higher education increases people's employability, but more than tertiary education is needed to be employable. In the world of work today, with protean and boundaryless careers, employment contracts give less job security than previously and yet employers are the main suppliers and decision makers for jobs and career development opportunities.

Educational Theories on Employability Higher education practitioners have explored employability since the late nineties (Dearing, 1997; Hillage & Pollard, 1998). Their conclusion then was that employability is a lifelong process that involves four elements (Cole & Tibby, 2013): (1) employability assets, namely knowledge, skills, and attitudes; (2) deployment, which requires career management skills, and the skills to search for a job; (3) presentation, namely ability to apply for a job such as writing a CV and acquiring interview techniques; and (4) personal circumstances such as family responsibilities and external factors that have an impact on employability assets to enter the labour market. These elements clearly portray individual components as well as systemic components. Cole and Tibby (2013) view employability as the joint responsibility of everybody at a tertiary institution and insist that students should be committed to lifelong learning. Bowden, Hart, King, Trigwell, and Watts (2000) argued that part of being employable—over and above the preparation of students for the labour market—is that students also need to be developed as responsible citizens.

An educational perspective on employability occupies itself with preparing and developing students to be able to find employment. An industry perspective busies itself with recruiting the best people to benefit the organisation. There is often disharmony between these two perspectives. What companies need from tertiary education training is often different from what is offered to students. As markets evolve and the world of work changes, higher education institutions often do not adapt fast enough to accommodate these shifting labour market needs. Between what industry wants from employees and what the education system offers lies the individual perspective—young adults, graduates, or employees who try to start making a living amidst ever-changing and unpredictable economic and political situations.

The employer (industry)-perspective on employability will be discussed in the next section, after which the employee (individual) perspective will be addressed.

Industry (Employer) Perspective

Employability and Employment Hogan, Chamorro-Premusic, and Kaiser (2013) claim that there is consensus among employers regarding the general qualities they seek in employees. "From the employers' perspective, the single-most important characteristic determining employability is interpersonal skill or social competence" (Hogan et al., 2013, p. 8). Equally important is the ability to work in a team (Chen, Kanfer, DeShon, Mathieu, & Kozlovski, 2009). The mode of work today is less formal and less structured with less routine, and requires working with co-workers from different cultural, educational, and technical backgrounds (Hogan et al., 2013). Another important factor that is valued from employers' side for recruitment involves self-presentation skills such as attitude, gesticulation, use of personal space, facial features and eye interaction are needed in interviews and meetings (Hogan et al., 2013; Warhurst & Nickson, 2001).

It is important for employees to be able to adapt and to some sense be compliant to a new environment. The antithesis of employability (unemployability) would then be a combination of irritability, rudeness, social insensitivity, and incompetence (O'Boyle, Forsyth, & Banks, McDaniel, 2012) which is not what employers want from potential employees. Perceptions of employers about factors they see as important for candidates/possible employees to make a positive contribution to their company would determine employability (Hogan et al., 2013). These perceptions are quite straightforward: Would the person fit into the organisation socially? Is he/she capable? Is he/she willing to work hard? What is the nature of the relationship between the characteristics of the person and the specific organizational context/culture of the firm?

Employability and Talent Management Within Companies 'Talent' relates to employers' view (CIPD, 2016) on the employability transaction between organisations and workers. In human resource circles, talent management is recognised as the "process of attracting, developing, and retaining people" (p. 7). The term can easily be misunderstood from different contexts. From a business or industry viewpoint, talent refers to the added value talented people bring to make themselves useful for the business. Bridgestock (2009) rightly emphasises the individual responsibility of employees to acquire skills to manage themselves and to personally navigate their careers by being curious about new learning and career opportunities. Exploring new prospects would create opportunities to expand professional relationships and motivate employees to stay relevant and marketable. To *remain* employable within a company, individuals attempt to meet the expectations of their employer, which can be divergent from their individual career journey (CIPD, 2016). Employees can easily lose sight of their personal career focus in a job where they are remunerated well and then stop navigating their personal career ambitions.

Individual Perspective

Theory on employability is often approached from a person perspective. Wedekind and Mutereko (2016) refer to employability as the ability to retain work and grow in an occupational pathway. According to Wedekind and Mutereko (2016), the 'person' perspective of the concept of employability shifts the emphasis away from work as being security to placing autonomy in the hands of the individual. This perspective emphasises the individual's contribution to his/her own employability situation. Sin and Neave (2014) allude to employability as a multi-faceted characteristic of an individual, striving to obtain the skills and attributes he/she deems necessary in the job market. Rothwell, Herbert, and Rothwell (2008, p. 2) define employability as the "perceived ability to attain sustainable employment appropriate to one's qualification level". Fugate, Kinicki, and Ashforth (2004) accentuate individual adaptability as a distinguished dimension that is part of being employable.

Employability and Its Link with Adaptability in Individuals Fugate et al. (2004) consider employability as a psycho-social construct with individual characteristics that grow *adaptive* cognition, behaviour, and affect: Seen from this perspective, *improvement of people's adaptability would promote their employability*. Employability from a person perspective predisposes individuals to improve their situation proactively (consciously adapt to given situations), rather than to wait for others to improve their situation. Fugate et al. (2004) and Koen (2013) distinguish between three component dimensions of employability, namely career identity, adaptability, and social and human capital. Each of these dimensions comprises different skills, knowledge' and behaviours. Jointly, they create the competency to find and keep a job. Whereas Fugate et al. (2004) initially referred to adaptability as readiness to cope and the willingness to explore personal career possibilities, they later on (Fugate & Kinicki, 2008) describe employability as a *disposition* in employees or potential employees. Adaptability seems to be the vehicle that drives an individual's employability competence. Individuals who are employable pro-actively pursue their occupational interests and experience better job satisfaction, which then influence their performance (Crant, 2000; Fugate & Kinicki, 2008).

Intervention to enhance people's employability ought to influence as many as possible of the factors that were discussed in this chapter. Researchers (Coetzee, Ferreira, & Potgieter, 2015; Fugate et al., 2004; Koen, 2013; Savickas, 2005) repeatedly emphasise the influence of *career* adaptability for the development of employability specifically. The construct of career adaptability and the means to develop employability skills in individuals (by employing career adaptability knowledge and skills) are therefore explored in the next section.

Career Adaptability

Career adaptability positively relates to employability capacities (Coetzee et al., 2015) and can also be seen as the preparation to instil employability (Koen, 2013). In an attempt to positively influence their employability skills, young adults from disadvantaged backgrounds especially should therefore be exposed to career adaptability skills and concepts in a planned intervention.

Although career adaptability is one concept, the two words will first be explored independently, after which the full concept be described.

The Future of Career

In the contemporary industrialised society, careers have become less "predictable, sequential, and ascendant" (Vondracek, Ford, & Porfeli, 2014, p. 3). Many authors have shed light on the different terms used to describe careers in the 21st century workplace (see, e.g. Maree, 2017; Savickas, 2013). These terms reveal that the concept of 'career' has become much wider than the totality of work one does over a life time. Work plays an increasingly central and dynamic role in people's lives, with the result that career has become a lifestyle concept (Niles & Harris-Bowlsbey, 2009). Super (1976) used to view career as the course of events constituting a life, whereas Herr, Cramer, and Niles (2004) described career as the total constellation of roles played over the course of a lifetime. A career emerges from the constant interplay between the person and the environment (Niles & Harris-Bowlsbey, 2009). Career is also a determinant of social status (Super, 1976) and self-concept (Super, 1981). Super (1976) linked personal and situational factors in his career development theory. Certain life-roles (e.g. being a student or a parent) play out in certain theatres (e.g. home, community, or school). For the purposes of this chapter, a job is regarded as a group of positions doing similar tasks, an occupation is regarded as a group of related jobs, and a career comprises a series of positions occupied by an individual during their life course (M. L. Savickas, personal communication, July 12, 2014).

Adaptability

Savickas (1997, p. 194) refers to adaptability as "the quality of being able to change, without great difficulty, to fit new or changed circumstances". Individuals are considered adaptable when they act in an appropriate manner in a specific situation (Maree, 2010).

Career Adaptability

While people's characters may become stable over time, the environment and context are constantly changing, which requires the individual to continually choose and adjust (Niles & Harris-Bowlsbey, 2009). Super (1976) reflected on "career decision making readiness" (p. 44) of adults in the workplace where changing occupational opportunities and changes in life-roles required new career decisions (Niles & Harris-Bowlsbey, 2009). The term 'career maturity' was used to evaluate adult individuals' readiness to make career decisions. However, since career maturity has an embedded evaluative component (Savickas, 2013) and implies that maturity should be reached, the cyclic and on-going nature of adaptability is undermined. Therefore, Savickas (1997) argues that "career adaptability should replace career maturity as the critical construct in the career developmental perspective" (p. 247).

Career adaptability has become a key construct (Savickas, 2005) in vocational psychology to assist individuals to navigate work transitions and manage their careers. All definitions of career adaptability embrace one concept, namely "abilities for adjusting to changing work environments" (Stoltz, 2015, p. 266). Career adaptability and employability both involve the self, identity and (coping) resources that deal with change and transition. Career adaptability and employability seem to be the result of the narrative of individuals who developed and improved their probability to thrive.

Development of Career Adaptability Savickas (2008) formulated core questions for each of the four constructs (or C's) of career adaptability, namely: Do I have a future? (Career concern); Who owns my future? (Career control); What do I want to do with my future? (Career curiosity); and Can I do it? (Career confidence). These questions verbalise something of the dilemmas that individuals have to deal with when confronted with unexpected choices, traumas or transitions. Each of the constructs portrays a certain attitude and belief.

Del Corso (2013) theorises about possible reasons for the absence of the four career adapt-abilities.

Career concern seems absent when individuals have alternatives (back-up plan) to employment such as financial support from government; possible family or illegal activities that serve their needs better than full-time employment; or having adopted a short-term focus. The same applies when they struggle with mental illness or experience trauma, or if they experience difficulty to think about upcoming change, for instance, a new job, retirement, or retrenchment.

Career control is probably absent when the system of influence within which the individual functions is not supportive. Family members (parents, spouses, and influential members in the community) in a rigid, constricted, or fused family system, and employers that make things 'difficult' for employees, hinder the individual to pursue his/her own career goals. Constraining psychological influences such as self-defeating thoughts, external locus of control, or mental impairments may also obstruct the individual in exerting control over work situations. Unreasonable employers can also hinder career control in individuals who occupy some form of employment.

Career curiosity is affected when individuals struggle to build a cohesive self as they move through various jobs, tasks, responsibilities and work roles. Their identity feels fragmented and they feel confused about who they really are.

Career confidence suffers due to mistaken beliefs within an individual's 'private logic' about his/her social roles, self-worth, gender, race, or age. These false beliefs about themselves limit individuals to formulate and implement career goals. Low levels of career confidence would influence their response to stressors in the work environment (Del Corso, 2013). These pointers (suggested by Del Corso, 2013) should be at the core of the intervention to influence employability in people.

Given the idiosyncratic occupational adaptability, and employability dilemmas people in young adulthood face, and the influence of poverty experienced in this particular developmental stage, the emphasis now shifts to a discussion of the unique career counselling situation of this population in particular before the chapter is concluded.

Young Adulthood

Young adulthood, according to Erikson's (1968) theory, is seen as the ages between 19 and 40 years and deals mostly with identity regarding intimate relationships (Sokol, 2009). Living, working, and conducting our career counselling research in a developing country context, we are routinely and predominantly introduced to and work among young adults between the ages of 18 and 42 who are not in employment, education, or training ('NEETs') (Creamer, 2013) (Gerryts, 2018; Maree, 2018; Maree, Gerryts, Fletcher, & Jordaan, in press; Maree & Twigge, 2015; Twigge, 2016). We have a shared and sincere interest in the well-being of this population—specifically those that are unemployed and come from socio-economically disadvantaged, resource-scarce backgrounds. Their main aim mostly is to complete some skills training programme and find a job with the assistance of the organisation where they studied.

Traditionally, adulthood was associated with five milestones focusing on completion of school, leaving home, entering the workforce, getting married, and becoming a parent (Settersten & Ray, 2010). However, young adults in industrialised societies and developing countries visualise work and life from a dramatically different perspective than 40–50 years ago and they do not regard adulthood in the same way. In the 21st century, individuals reach adulthood at an individual pace and some never achieve all five milestones, because they deliberately decide not to marry or to have children. In fact, young adults postpone and/or reach these markers sometimes entirely out of order. Many never commit to a monogamous relationship or they leave school to start working and go back to study long after they became financially secure (Henig, 2010). These years of 'wandering' are also referred to as the *Odyssey years* (Brooks, 2007), due to the improvised nature in which young people try to make sense of their lives.

Arnett (2000) proposed a development period called emerging adulthood to describe similar social tasks as set out by Erikson's stages of adolescence and young adulthood in young people from industrialised countries. What emerging adults themselves want from life is a job that pays well, a job that is personally meaningful, and to have a lasting bond with a partner. Emerging adults view adulthood as individualistic character qualities rather than reaching certain milestones. Their subjective sense of adulthood, according to a variety of studies (Arnett, 1997, 1998; Sheer, Unger, & Brown, 1994), are accepting responsibility for the self and making independent decisions. A more tangible criterion applied by emerging adults regarding attaining adulthood is becoming financially independent (Arnett, 2000). The stage of emerging adulthood leaves many talented young people hesitant and sometimes disillusioned to decide and enter a set-out career journey because of the high perceived workforce and societal demands. Identity development is not completed in adolescence but spans into young adulthood (and beyond) (Kroger, 2007; Sokol, 2009). Meaningful occupational decisions are especially imminent in young adulthood, though—a time to develop and consolidate goals, particularly in the areas of career and family (Vaillant & Milofsky, 1980). Young or emerging adults currently take much time to explore their identity in terms of a career and they need support to endure career instability.

In the next section, we explore young adulthood from a non-Western, African, and disadvantaged perspective.

Emerging Adulthood in a Disadvantaged Cultural Context: Focus on South Africa

Arnett (2004) realised that conceptions about the passage to adulthood are different in minority groups in the United States of America (USA) (for instance, African Americans, Latinos, and Asians Americans). Collectivistic values and traditional gender-specific roles are alive in these minority groups, namely that men should be the providers for the family from a young age and women should be at home, caring for the children and running the household. Lower Socio-Economic Status (SES) would force adolescents to take up responsibility for the family earlier than in the case of affluent families. This situation results in young adults taking up adult roles earlier than in cases where they were not forced by circumstances to take up family roles of responsibility (Arnett, 2004).

In the next paragraphs, these concepts are explored from a South African perspective.

In South Africa, urbanisation, housing problems, political factors, and economic underdevelopment, combined with (often extreme) poverty, significantly changed family structures in disadvantaged contexts. Common family types found in these contexts (black African families in particular) are absent-spouse, single-parent, child-headed, and siblings-families (children or young people raising their siblings)

(Department of Social Welfare & Development, 2012). Black South African families share a number of characteristics despite ethnical differences, such as that their children are important, they have strong family ties, being married has implications, and a happy family life is important (Viljoen, 1994). Polygamy and *lobola* (significant payment given by the groom to the family of the bride) are traditions that are seen to prevent divorce and marital disintegration. Traditionally, children are not encouraged to leave the home, but to contribute to the household income. The sons are encouraged to stay with the parents even if they are married if there is sufficient space for all. Once the home is physically too small for the whole family, the eldest brother and his family will leave the parents' home to start their own home. The youngest brother is traditionally bound to look after the parents when they are old, and he would stay in the house of the parents. This support system in black communities is based upon regulations, values, as well as socialisation patterns created through feelings of social responsibility and reciprocal support (Nzimande, 1996) traditionally practised in rural areas. The main purpose is the maintenance of the group's character throughout the extended family.

Emerging Adulthood and Socio-economic Status (SES)

SES is associated with social standing and is measured by combining educational level, income, and occupation (APA, 2007). High social class is associated with privilege, power, and control. Studies of SES often reveal inequities in the access to and distribution of resources (APA, 2007). Students from socio-economically disadvantaged backgrounds all over the world attain poorer academic outcomes (Martin, Mullis, Foy, & Stanco, 2012; Sandoval-Hernandez & Cortes, 2012) than their wealthy peers (Erberber, Stephens, Mamedova, Ferguson, & Kroeger, 2015). Coming from a background of low socio-economic status (SES) is pervasive among black South African young adults (that comprise the overwhelming majority of our research participants), who increasingly experience tremendous pressure to study and become educated to be able to support families who have been poverty stricken for generations. Young adults who are educated and have a job are obliged to support the members of the family who are unemployed. Students who receive bursaries to study often use their bursary money to support the family at home, rather than to use the grant for rent or living cost while they are studying. Young black South African women often become mothers at a young age without being married, which results in many single mothers being dependent on the government's social grants and relying on their own mothers to care for their babies.

Enhancing the Employability of Young Adults from Socio-economically Challenged Contexts: Keys for Intervention

Career counselling researchers and practitioners must be extremely sensitive to and observant of the dominating and devastating effect that poverty mostly has on counsellees. Moreover, counsellors should carefully note specific cultural nuances (Pope, 2015) when dealing with these counsellees. Culturally appropriate intervention is needed that relate to how and what to do when counsellors encounter counsellees who are substantially 'different' to themselves. In his *Career Counselling with Underserved Populations model (CCUP)*, Pope (2015) provides practitioners with 13 keys for career intervention in research. Below, we briefly explain how these keys can be operationalised to promote the employability of young adults from socio-economically disadvantaged contexts.

First, it is essential to be frank about one's possible personal cultural biases (which could be perceived by counsellees as not being authentic).

Second, counsellors need to know how identity development works to effectively deal with different 'cultures'. Counsellors need to be cognisant of their own identity development as a member of a specific culture group but also acknowledge that we all are a product of many 'cultures'. Apart from for instance being part of a nationality or a gender group, and having specific beliefs, counsellees are in a certain development stage (Erikson, 1968). Demonstrating sensitivity and compassion that is congruent with that stage is essential.

According to the third key, specific issues are related to a certain culture (e.g. counsellees' prevailing level of socio-economic disadvantage).

The fourth key involves addressing issues of discrimination and assisting counsellees to deal with it before the actual discrimination occurs.

Fifth, it should be noted that some racial and ethnic cultures who value group survival, interdependency, and collectiveness over individual survival, have a strong appeal for group counselling.

Sixth, Pope (2015) refers to the important role that family plays in collectivist cultures. Key decisions such as getting married or choosing a career would almost always be decided in consultation with the extended family. When coming from a collectivist culture, counsellees are often unaware of the significant role the extended family plays within their context, due to their subjective involvement in the family of origin.

Seventh, the matter of dual-career counsellees should be acknowledged and considered.

Eighth, it is pivotal to use culturally sensitive career assessments.

The ninth key that counsellors need to know is how to help counsellees overcome internalised negative stereotypes. Pope (2015) suggests that counsellors use culturally appropriate self-esteem interventions such as self-talk (self-narration).

'Coming-out' issues comprise the tenth key. This aspect pertains to sexual and gender issues.

The eleventh key in the CCUP model for counsellors is to obtain knowledge and create awareness about stereotypical jobs/occupations for certain 'cultures'.

The twelfth key involves the important role of the atmosphere that would be created in the intervention with regard to differences. A supportive atmosphere towards cultural (and other!) differences would enhance trust and willingness to cooperate and learn. This could be very useful to counsellees who had never had the opportunity to receive career counselling of any nature.

The last key comprises the provision of positive social justice advocacy (promoting change by championing the rights of counsellees that are not afforded due respect and dignity).

These points should remind counsellors again to be sensitive to the dominating mindset and practices of a Westernised approach to career counselling, which is often implemented exclusively through assessments and beliefs.

Conclusion

In this chapter, we reflected on how the employability of young adults from lower socio-economic contexts can be enhanced. Globally, young people nowadays take longer to settle, find work, and to start families than in previous generations. This phenomenon is referred to as the *Odyssey years* (Brooks, 2007) and a new life stage called *young* or *emerging adulthood* (Arnett, 2000) has developed. Disadvantaged young adults are in a particularly challenging position because of their poor financial means and the fact that so many of them are relatively unemployable. Poverty obstructs their career identity formation and promotes stereotypical mindsets that do not only hinder their career development, but also locks many of these young people in destructive mindsets that influence them negatively personally and impede their employability development.

Our literature overview revealed that well-developed career adaptability skills should translate into employability attributes. These attributes include attitude, self-efficacy, self-esteem and confidence, pro-activity, and communication skills. We therefore focus on a theoretical overview of how these young adults' career adaptability can be enhanced. These guidelines are broadly based on key points of the CCUP (*Career Counselling with Undeserved Populations*) model of Pope (2015). Applying these points practically during career counselling with young adults can uncover counsellees' strengths and areas for development while they narrate their career-life stories and elicit advice from within and, ultimately, bolster their employability.

References

American Psychological Association (APA). (2007). Report of the APA task force on socioeconomic status. Retrieved from https://www.apa.org/pi/ses/resources/publications/task-force-2006.pdf.

Arnett, J. J. (1997). Young people's conceptions of the transition to adulthood. *Youth & Society, 29*, 1–23.

Arnett, J. J. (1998). Learning to stand alone: The contemporary American transition to adulthood in cultural and historical context. *Human Development, 41*, 295–315.

Arnett, J. J. (2000). Emerging adulthood. A theory of development from the late teens through the twenties. *American Psychologist, 55*(5), 469–480.

Arnett, J. J. (2004). *Emerging adulthood: The winding road from the late teens through the twenties*. New York: Oxford University Press.

Bimrose, J. (2010). Adapting in a changing world: Dealing with repeated career transitions. In K. Maree (Ed.), *Career counselling: Methods that work* (pp. 118–127). Cape Town, South Africa: Juta.

Bowden, J., Hart, G., King, B., Trigwell, K., & Watts, O. (2000). *Generic capabilities of ATN university graduates*. Retrieved from http://www.clt.uts.edu.au/ATN.grad.cap.project.index.html.

Bridgestock, R. (2009). The graduate attributes we've overlooked: Enhancing graduate employability through career management skills. *Higher Education Research & Development, 28*(1), 31–44.

Brooks, D. (2007, October 9). The odyssey years. *The New York Times*. Retrieved from http://www.caroddoapclasses.com/sitebuildercontent/sitebuilderfiles/theodysseyyearsarticle.pdf.

Brown, P., Hesketh, A., & William, S. (2003). Employability is a knowledge-driven economy. *Journal of Education and Work, 16*(2), 107–126.

Business Tech. (2015). 2015 Crimes stats for South Africa: Everything you need to know. Retrieved from https://businesstech.co.za/news/government/99648/2015-crime-stats-for-south-africa-everything-you-need-to-know/.

Castells, M. (2015). *The impact of the internet on society: A global perspective*. Open Mind. Retrieved from https://www.bbvaopenmind.com/en/article/the-impact-of-the-internet-on-society-a-global-perspective/?fullscreen=true.

Chartered Institute of Personnel and Development (CIPD). (2016). *Attitudes to employability and talent, Research report, September 2016. Chartered Institute of Personnel and Development* London, England: The Broadway.

Chen, G., Kanfer, R., DeShon, R. P., Mathieu, J. E., & Kozlovski, S. W. J. (2009). The motivating potential of teams: A test and extension of Chen and Kanfer's (2006) model. *Organisational Behavior and Human Decision Processes, 110*, 45–55.

Coetzee, M., Ferreira, N., & Potgieter, I. L. (2015). Assessing employability capacities and career adaptability in a sample of human resource professionals. *SA Journal of Human Resource Management, 13*(1), 1–9. https://doi.org/10.4102/sajhrm.v13i1.682.

Cole, D., & Tibby, M. (2013). *Defining and developing your approach to employability, a framework for higher education institutions*. York, England: The Higher Education Academy.

Crant, J. M. (2000). Proactive behavior in organizations. *Journal of Management, 26*, 435–462.

Creamer, R. (2013). *'NEETs crisis' emerging as SA's most urgent challenge*. Retrieved from http://www.engineeringnews.co.za/article/neets-crisis-emerging-as-sas-most-urgent-challenge-2013-06-25/rep_id:4136.

Dearing, R. (1997). *Higher education in the learning society*. Report of the National Committee of Enquiry into Higher Education. London, England: HMSO.

Del Corso, J. J. (2013). The theory of career adaptability. In A. Di Fabio & J. G. Maree (Eds.), *Psychology of career counselling: New challenges for a new era* (pp. 117–130). Hauppauge, NY: NOVA.

Deloitte. (2016). *The 2016 Deloitte Millennium survey*. Retrieved from https://www2.deloitte.com/global/en/pages/about-deloitte/articles/millennialsurvey.html.

Department of Social Welfare & Development, Government of South Africa. (2012, October). *White paper on families in South Africa*. Retrieved from http://www.dsd.gov.za/index.php?option=com_docman&task=cat_view&gid=33&Itemid=39.

Eloff, J. H. P., Eloff, M. M., Dlamini, M. T., & Zielinski, M. P. (2009). *Internet of people, things and services-the convergence of security, trust and privacy.* Retrieved from http://researchspace.csir.co.za/dspace/bitstream/10204/4409/1/Eloff_2009.pdf.

Erberber, E., Stephens, M., Mamedova, S., Ferguson, S., & Kroeger, T. (2015, March). Socioeconomically disadvantaged students who are academically successful: Examining academic resilience cross nationally. *IEA's Policy Brief Series, No. 5*, Amsterdam, IEA. http://www.iea.nl/policy_briefs.html.

Erikson, E. H. (1968). *Identity, youth, and crises*. New York: Norton.

Ferreira, L. (2015). Factsheet: Social grants in South Africa—Separating myth from reality. *African Check.* Retrieved from https://africacheck.org/factsheets/separating-myth-from-reality-a-guide-to-social-grants-in-south-africa/.

Forrier, A., & Sels, L. (2003). The concept employability: A complex mosaic. *International Journal of Resources Development and Management, 3*(2), 102–124.

Fugate, M., & Kinicki, A. M. (2008). A dispositional approach to employability: Development of a measure and test of implications for employee reactions to organizational change. *Journal of Occupational and Organizational Psychology, 81*(3), 503–527.

Fugate, M., Kinicki, A. J., & Ashforth, B. E. (2004). Employability: A psycho-social construct, its dimensions, and applications. *Journal of Vocational Behavior, 65,* 14–38.

Gerryts, E. W. (2018). *Enhancing the employability of young adults from socio-economically challenged contexts* (Ph.D. thesis). Pretoria, South Africa: University of Pretoria.

Guilbert, R., Bernaud, J., Gouvernet, B., & Rossier, J. (2016). Employability: Review and research prospects. *International Journal for Educational and Vocational Guidance, 16*(1), 69–89.

Henig, R. M. (2010, August 18). What is it about 20-somethings? Why are so many people in their 20's taking so long to grow up? *The New York Times*. Reprints. Retrieved from http://www.nytimes.com/2010/08/22/magazine.

Herr, E. L., Cramer, S. H., & Niles, S. G. (2004). Career guidance and counselling through the lifespan—Systematic approaches (6th ed.). *Canadian Journal of Counselling and Psychotherapy/Revue Counselling de Counselling et de psychothérapie, 38*(2). Retrieved from http://cjc.synergiesprairies.ca/cjc/index.php/rcc/article/view/830.

Hillage, J., & Pollard, E. (1998). *Employability: Developing a framework for policy analysis.* Research Brief No. 85. London, England: Department for Education and Employment.

Hogan, R., Chamorro-Premusic, T., & Kaiser, R. B. (2013). Employability and career success: Bridging the gap between theory and reality. *Industrial and Organisational Psychology, 6*(1), 3–16.

Jonck, P., & Minnaar, R. (2017). Employability skills indicators as perceived by employers in the Free State Province of South Africa. In A. Goujon, M. Haller, & B. Muller Kmet (Eds.), *Higher education in Africa: Challenges for development, mobility and cooperation* (pp. 107–129). Newcastle, England: Cambridge Scholars Publishing.

Koen, J. (2013). *Prepare and pursue: Routes to suitable (re-)employment* (Ph.D. thesis). Amsterdam, The Netherlands: University of Amsterdam. Retrieved from http://hdl.handle.net/11245/2.120347.

Kroger, J. (2007). *Identity development: Adolescence through adulthood*. Thousand Oaks, CA: SAGE Publications.

Kruger, N. (2016). South Africa has a skills shortage: How so we fix it? *World Economic Forum.* Retrieved from https://www.weforum.org/agenda/2016/05/south-africa-skills-shortage-how-do-we-fix-it/.

Maree, J. G. (2009). Career counselling in the 21st century: South African institutions of higher education at the crossroads. *South African Journal of Higher Education, 23,* 436–458.

Maree, J. G. (2010). Career story interviewing using the three anecdotes technique. *Journal of Psychology in Africa, 20,* 369–380.

Maree, J. G. (2013a). Latest developments in career counselling in South Africa: Towards a positive approach. *South African Journal of Psychology, 43*(4), 409–421.

Maree, J. G. (2013b). *Counselling for career construction: Connecting life themes to construct life portraits: Turning pain into hope*. Rotterdam, The Netherlands: Sense.

Maree, J. G. (2015). Poverty and life design. In L. Nota & J. Rossier (Eds.), *Handbook of life design: From practice to theory and from theory to practice* (pp. 233–248). Toronto, Canada: Hogrefe.

Maree, J. G. (2017). Life design counselling. In G. Stead & M. Watson (Eds.), *Career psychology* (3rd ed., pp. 105–118). Pretoria, South Africa: Van Schaik.

Maree, J. G. (2018). Self- and career construction counseling for a gifted young woman in search of meaning and purpose. *International Journal for Educational and Vocational Guidance*. https://doi.org/10.1007/s1077.

Maree, J. G., Gerryts, E. W., Fletcher, L., & Jordaan, J. (in press). Using career counselling with life design principles to improve the career adaptability and employability of disadvantaged young adults. *Journal for Psychology in Africa, …*

Maree, J. G., & Twigge, A. (2015). Career and self-construction of emerging adults: The value of Life Designing. *Frontiers in Psychology, 6,* 2041. https://doi.org/10.3389/fpsyg.2015.02041.

Martin, M. O., Mullis, I. V. S., Foy, P., & Stanco, G. M. (2012). *TIMSS 2011 international results in science.* Chestnut Hill, MA: TIMSS & PIRLS International Study Center, Boston College.

Niles, S. P., & Harris-Bowlsbey, J. (2009). *Career development interventions in the 21st century* (3rd ed.). Upper saddle River, NJ: Pearson Education.

Nzimande, S. V. (1996). Family structure and support systems in black communities. In L. C. Gerdes (Ed.), *Marriage and family life in South Africa: Research priorities* (pp. 28–47). Pretoria, South Africa: Human Sciences Research Council.

O'Boyle, E. H., Forsyth, D. R., Banks, G. C., & McDaniel, M. A. (2012). A meta-analysis of the dark triad and work outcomes: A social exchange perspective. *Journal of Applied Psychology, 97,* 557–579.

Patrick, H. A. (2013). Managing workplace diversity: Issues and challenges. *Sage Open, 2*(3), 346–351.

Pope, M. (2015). Career counselling with underserved populations. In K. Maree & A. Di Fabio (Eds.), *Exploring new horizons in career counselling* (pp. 297–312). Rotterdam, The Netherlands: Sense.

Rothwell, A., Herbert, I., & Rothwell, F. (2008). Self-perceived employability: Construction and initial validation of a scale for university students. *Journal of Vocational Behavior, 73,* 1–12. https://doi.org/10.1016/j.jvb.2007.12.001.

Sandoval-Hernandez, A., & Cortes, D. (2012). *Factors and conditions that promote academic resilience: A cross-country perspective.* Paper presented at the annual meeting of the 55th Annual Conference of the Comparative and International Education Society, Caribe Hilton, San Juan, Puerto Rico.

Savickas, M. L. (1997). Career adaptability: An integrative construct for life-span, life-space theory. *The Career Development Quarterly, 45,* 247–259.

Savickas, M. L. (2005). The theory and practice of career construction. In S. D. Brown & R. W. Lent (Eds.), *Career development and counselling* (pp. 42–70). Hoboken, NJ: Wiley.

Savickas, M. L. (2008, December). *Life-design international research group: Career adaptability project*. Paper presented at Humboldt Universitat, Berlin, Germany.

Savickas, M. L. (2013). The theory and practice of career construction. In S. D. Brown, & R. W. Lent (Eds.), *Career development and counseling: Putting theory and research to work* (2nd ed., pp. 147–186). Hoboken, NJ: Wiley.

Schwab, K. (2016). The Fourth Industrial Revolution: What it means, how to respond. *World Economic Forum.* Retrieved from: https://www.weforum.org/agenda/2016/01/the-fourth-industrial-revolution-what-it-means-and-how-to-respond/.

Schwab, K., & Samans, R. (2016). The future of jobs. Employment, skills and workforce strategy for the Fourth Industrial Revolution. *World Economic Forum.* Retrieved from http://www.nmi.is/media/338436/the_global_competitiveness_report_2016-2017.pdf.

Settersten, R. A., Jr., & Ray, B. (2010). What's going on with young people today? The long and twisting path to adulthood. *The Future of Children, 20*(1), 19–41.

Sheer, S. D., Unger, D. G., & Brown, M. (1994, February). *Adolescents becoming adults: Attributes for adulthood.* Poster presented at the Biennial Meeting of the Society for Research on Adolescence, San Diego, CA.

Sin, C., & Neave, G. (2014). Employability deconstructed: Perceptions of Bologna stakeholders. *Studies in Higher Education, 41*(8), 1447–1462.

Sokol, J. T. (2009). Identity development throughout the lifetime: An examination of Eriksonian theory. *Graduate Journal of Counseling Psychology, 1*(2), 139–147.

Spaull, N. (2013). South Africa's Education Crisis: The quality of education in South Africa 1994-201. *Centre for Development & Enterprise.* Retrieved from http://www.section27.org.za/wp-content/uploads/2013/10/Spaull-2013-CDE-report-South-Africas-Education-Crisis.pdf.

Steyn, L. (2015). SA's skills deficit has a negative effect on employment. *Mail & Guardian 18 May 2015.* Retrieved from http://mg.co.za/article/2015-05-18-sas-skills-deficit-has-a-negative-effect-on-employment.

Stoltz, K. B. (2015). Counselling toward career adaptability. The change of a new era. In K. Maree & A. Di Fabio (Eds.), *Exploring new horizons in career counselling* (pp. 263–277). Rotterdam, The Netherlands: Sense.

Super, D. E. (1976). *Career education and the meaning of work.* Washington, DC: Office of Education.

Super, D. E. (1981). A developmental theory: Implementing a self-concept. In D. H. Montross & C. J. Shinkman (Eds.), *Career development in the 1980's: Theory and practice* (pp. 28–42). Springfield, IL: Thomas.

The World Bank. (2016). *The World Bank in South Africa.* Retrieved from http://www.worldbank.org/en/country/southafrica/overview.

Twigge, A. (2016). *Verkenning van die waarde van lewensontwerpberading ten opsigte van self-konstruksie by die ontluikende volwassene* [Exploring the value of life design counselling in the self-construction of the emerging adult] (Doctoral thesis). Pretoria, South Africa: University of Pretoria.

Vaillant, G. E., & Milofsky, E. (1980). Natural history of male psychological health: IX. Empirical evidence for Erikson's model of the life cycle. *American Journal of Psychiatry, 137,* 1348–1359.

Van Niekerk, P. (2012). Past and present ideologies in South African schooling: Towards a framework of ethics. *Acta Academica, 44*(4), 134–162.

Viljoen, S. (1994). *Strengths and weaknesses in the family life of black South Africans.* Pretoria, South Africa: Human Sciences Research Council.

Vondracek, F. W., Ford, D. H., & Porfeli, E. J. (2014). *A living systems theory of vocational behaviour and development.* Rotterdam, The Netherlands: Sense.

Warhurst, C., & Nickson, D. (2001). *Looking good, sounding right: Style counselling and the aesthetics of the new economy.* London, England: Industrial Society.

Wedekind, V., & Mutereko, S. (2016). Work integrated learning for engineering qualifications. *Journal of Education and Work, 29*(8), 902–912.

World Economic Forum Report 2016. (2016). *Human capital report.* Retrieved from http://reports.weforum.org/human-capital-report-016/economies/#economy=ZAF.

Yorke, M. (2006). Employability in higher education: What it is—What it is not. *York: Higher Education Academy Online.* Retrieved from: http://www.employability.ed.ac.uk/documents/Staff/HEA-Employability_in_HE.pdf.

Enhancing the Employability of Unskilled and Unemployed Young Adults: Practical Guidelines

Jacobus G. Maree and Erna W. Gerryts

Abstract A great need exists to enhance the employability and develop the (career) adaptability of (unskilled and) unemployed young adults (UUYA). In this chapter, we examine interventions that may address this need. We begin the chapter by highlighting key aspects of employability counselling and discussing the life- and career counselling-based principles and employability literature on which the intervention is based. Next, we focus on an overview of the intervention itself. This is followed by a detailed description and elaboration of each activity (mentioned in the intervention plan), after which the chapter is concluded.

Keywords Adaptability · Employability · Unskilled · Unemployed · Young adults · Career counselling · Life design

Introduction: Employability Counselling

As mentioned elsewhere, we believe that the kind of intervention elaborated in this chapter alludes to 'employability counselling' (Maree, 2016a; Maree & Di Fabio, 2015).[1] We argue in favour of assisting people to change and become adaptable in the current unpredictable world of work (Maree, 2009). Earlier, Human Resources Development Canada (HRDC) (1998) coined the phrase 'employment counselling' to refer to "a set of interventions designed to help clients identify and resolve issues which must be faced in making and carrying out employment-related decisions" (Busque, 1995, n. p.). In the context of this chapter, their definition seems to provide some substance to the concept of 'employability counselling'. HRDC (1998) developed the following four-dimensional employability framework as a basis for

[1] Actual research (based on the intervention described and proposed in the current chapter) yielded very promising outcomes (Gerryts, 2018; Maree, Gerryts, Fletcher, 7 Jordaan, in press) and inspired this chapter.

J. G. Maree (✉) · E. W. Gerryts
Department of Educational Psychology, University of Pretoria, Pretoria, South Africa
e-mail: kobus.maree@up.ac.za

J. G. Maree (ed.), *Handbook of Innovative Career Counselling*,
https://doi.org/10.1007/978-3-030-22799-9_25

understanding the different issues pertaining to employability (Amundson, 2003; Patsula, 1992).

a. Career exploration alludes to exploring, analysing, and subsequently choosing a career or job.
b. Skill enhancement refers to training or preparing for a certain job. This includes acquiring the skills needed to execute a certain job as well as more generic skills, for instance, literacy, interpersonal, and self-management skills.
c. Job search enhancement denotes identifying job vacancies, being contracted by employers, applying for jobs, how one behaves during a job interview, as well as the actual act of getting appointed. Moreover, this term alludes to the integration or re-integration of unemployed people into the workplace.
d. Job/work maintenance refers to adopting the attitudes needed to remain employed and be successful in the workplace.

These dimensions relate strongly to 'traditional' career guidance and development across the life-span and buttresses the mistaken belief that offering career counselling predominantly implies helping people choose careers and associated fields of study. Using this lens, employability counselling alludes to career counselling and includes a focus on specific competencies that would empower people to conduct thorough job analysis and searching for specific jobs in addition to being able to adapt to changes in the market. This lens also associates with the necessary shift in what is expected from them by the job market to retain their employment and their marketability (sought after in the occupational world). From our perspective, though, what is needed currently is employability counselling. This includes drawing on Life design related interventions (based on self- and career construction counselling principles; see Tables 1 and 2) to help people become more employable, career resilient, and career adaptable.

Chapter Structure

The first part of the chapter examines briefly some aspects of employability counselling. Then, the chapter structure and the goals of the chapter are explained briefly. Three distinguishable models of intervention are highlighted and an overview of the proposed intervention is explicated. Next, employability-enhancing strategies are explicated. Each activity is elaborated and illustrated in detail, after which the chapter is concluded.

Chapter Goals

The primary goal of the chapter is to present a practical intervention strategy to address the need to develop the (career) adaptability of (unskilled and) unemployed

Table 1 Integrative career counselling framework (Duarte, 2017; Hartung & Santili, 2018; Savickas, 2010, 2015b)

Paradigm	Vocational guidance	Career development	Life design
Perspective	Positivism	Humanism	Constructionism
Focus is on	Resemblance	Career and how client develops career over time	Reflection, reflexivity, addressing the life-designing needs of insecure workers with unstable jobs
Application	Guide, advise	Educate, coach	Design, heal
Client regarded as	Social actor	Motivated agent	Autobiographical author
Aim of intervention	Enhance self-knowledge; compose an identity narrative and career story; increase information about opportunities and conditions for success; and match client to collective profiles of people	Assess development status; orient client to developmental tasks (challenges); identify resources needed; and develop the attitudes, beliefs and competencies needed to master developmental tasks appropriate to life stages	Construct career by selecting and organising incidents and episodes from the micro-narratives to craft an identity narrative and career-life story, and then help client make meaning of these stories; reconstruct micro- and meso-stories into an identity narrative; and co-construct the next chapter in the client's life

Compiled from Duarte (2017) and Savickas (2015a, 2015b)

young adults (UUYA) in order to bolster their employability. We propose and illustrate a number of career counselling techniques and strategies to ground the intervention.

The next section deals with the career counselling strategies that are recommended to ground the intervention.

Career Counselling Strategies

Career counselling is usually based on three distinguishable models of intervention (Savickas, 2010, 2015a). The *Vocational guidance* model focuses on individual differences, lends itself to increasing self-knowledge and occupational knowledge, and attempts to match the self to an occupation. *Career development* interventions focus on the individuals' status of development and aim to enhance attitudes, beliefs,

Table 2 Relationship between career counselling waves, interventions, and theoretical underpinnings (compiled from Duarte, 2017; Savickas, 2015a, 2015b)

Career counselling wave	Theoretical underpinning	Associated intervention (Duarte, 2017; Guichard, 2005, 2009; Savickas, 2011, 2015a, 2015b, 2019)	Example: demonstrative questions
Vocational guidance	Differential	Provide information; matching	Which career will 'fit' my personality?
Career guidance/education	Developmental	Provide psycho-educational, and psychosocial information	a. How should I conduct job analysis? b. How do I go about improving my interpersonal relationships?
Life design and career counselling	Storied (psychodynamic)	Help client identify key life themes, reflect and draw on his/her reflexivity	a. What are my key life themes? b. Help me find a career that will enable me to make meaning and find a sense of meaning in life

and skills to develop themselves further. *Life design* interventions focus on career construction by using personal narratives to co-construct the client's future. Table 1 presents these models of intervention in more detail (Savickas, 2010).

The link between and progression from vocational guidance to life design is illustrated in Table 2 as is the relationship between the career counselling waves, interventions, and theoretical underpinnings.

The following should be noted, though. If counsellees have never been exposed to vocational guidance, career development, or life design counselling at school, intervention should first accommodate their idiosyncratic vocational guidance related needs. Often, in such instances, these counsellees want to find jobs and to be employed urgently. Furthermore, at present, the vast majority of career counsellors in our (developing country) context only focus on vocational guidance and career development. However, ideally, interventions should contain fragments from all three intervention models to prepare and equip participants adequately to meet the rapidly changing demands of the workplace.

The research conducted that implemented the intervention strategy advocated in this chapter on employability enhancing interventions involved young adult participants between the ages of 18 and 42 (Gerryts, 2018). These participants were from different rural and urban areas in South Africa. The common denominators between the participants were that they are from socio-economically challenged contexts and did not have access to tertiary studies.

Overview of the Intervention

A mixed methods research design is proposed (drawing on scores and stories) with particularly strong emphasis on qualitative methods. Mahoney (2003) McMahon and Patton (2006), Patton (2011), and Schultheiss (2005) maintain that when career counselling based on self- and career construction principles is implemented, and qualitative methods are emphasised, assessment and counselling processes are inextricably inter-linked and counsellees become more self-aware in the process.

Most assessments that are proposed as part of the intervention advocated in this chapter are informal and qualitative. These assessments are idiographic (not statistically compared to norms) and idiosyncratic (individualistic) in nature. The focus is on meaning making and eliciting and understanding the unique subjective experiences of each participant, rather than making generalised infernal about individuals compared to a population and the 'normal curve'. The aim is to explore and uncover instead of 'telling' counsellees what to do. The *Career Adapt-Abilities Scale* (*CAAS*) (Maree, 2012; Savickas & Porfeli, 2012) and the *Career Decision-Making Difficulties Questionnaire (CDDQ)* (Gati, Krausz, & Osipow, 1996) that are proposed for purposes of pre- and post-testing can be administered twice or even thrice to assess the effectiveness of the intervention quantitatively, in conjunction with qualitative assessment strategies to assess the effect of the intervention qualitatively.

The intervention should fit a group situation (activities should be organised for group settings). The intervention can run over six weeks to three months (or longer) and can take place in a number of periods of one hour (or longer) each, on one or two different days of the week or, for instance, on a bi-weekly basis. The number of contact sessions is flexible. As mentioned in Chapter "Enhancing the Employability of Young Adults from Socio-economically Challenged Contexts: Theoretical Overview", interventions must aim to be culturally appropriate and avoid discrimination against diversity and culture in any form (see Chapter "Enhancing the Employability of Young Adults from Socio-economically Challenged Contexts: Theoretical Overview").

Based on the career intervention models presented in Table 1, counsellees need enhanced self-knowledge and occupational knowledge to know where they will 'fit' (*vocational guidance*). They also need conducive attitudes that will assist them to develop themselves and conquer any self-limiting beliefs that may have hampered them or be hampering them due to challenging personal circumstances. Apart from attitude, counsellees need to act, nurture their dreams by working hard, and enthusiastically take responsibility for their personal career in the future (*career education*). These issues form part of the counselling process and need to be effectively dealt with or processed during sessions to empower counsellees. Assisting counsellees in the development of these important characteristics will enhance the success of the counselling process. Personal narratives are used to inform counsellees about how to take the next steps towards building and constructing themselves and their future career (facets of *life design*) (Hartung & Santili, 2018). Table 3 depicts the link between the models of career intervention and the intervention itself.

Table 3 Link between proposed career counselling techniques and the three career intervention models (see the next section)

Career intervention models (Savickas, 2010; 2015b)		
Vocational guidance	**Career development**	**Life design**
↓	↓	↓
Career counselling techniques that were used in the intervention		
Body map Career construction genogram (CCG) (Di Fabio, 2010) Career adaptability lecture *CIP* Part 2, 3	*CAAS* Career adaptability lecture Career story narratives	*CIP* Part 4 (career story narratives) One-minute presentation about future career (‘*end in mind*’)

Activities that can serve to promote *vocational guidance* as part of the intervention are body mapping, the CCG, a lecture on career adaptability and Part 2 and 3 of the *CIP* (Maree, 2016b). Part 2 of the *CIP* lists career categories that enable participants to select fields of interest and occupations in those categories that interest them. Part 3 of the *CIP* constitutes a reflection based on Part 2, as participants are required to say which specific career they will currently choose and why, as well as which career they will not pursue and why.

Aspects of the intervention that address areas of *career development* (second career intervention model) are the administering of the *CAAS* (Maree, 2012; Savickas & Porfeli, 2012), an introductory lecture on career adaptability, the rap[2] based on habits, and the participants’ career story narratives. Activities that are in keeping with the *life design* intervention model include Part 4 of the *CIP,* which contains open-ended questions that facilitate and enhance career story-telling. A one-minute speech that every participant delivers at the end (second-last meeting) of the intervention, serves as an introduction/presentation of themselves and gives participants the opportunity to formulate their dreams and plans for their future career.

Next, we explain how we arrived at employing specific techniques advocated in this chapter. Aspects of employability that are addressed in the intervention are discussed specifically.

[2] See Fig. 1, where ‘rap’ is explained.

Table 4 Employability-enhancing techniques and strategies

1. Self-efficacy, self-esteem and confidence
2. Positive attitude
3. Proactive attitude
4. Lifelong learning awareness
5. Interpersonal skills (rewarding to deal with)
6. (Self-motivated) work ethic—do more than what is required
7. Adaptability
8. Communication skills
9. Network/connections (socially and professionally)
10. Realisation of the importance of acquiring relevant qualifications and work-related experience

Employability-Enhancing Techniques and Strategies

Some conclusions drawn from the literature review on employability (Gerryts, 2018) regarding what an intervention of the kind alluded to in this chapter could involve to influence people's employability and career adaptability positively, are summarised in Table 4.

We expect an intervention of this kind to affect the first eight aspects of the employability enhancing techniques and strategies directly (The last two aspects are crucially important and would be influenced indirectly by embarking on such an intervention.) In Table 5 we indicate what activities we believe might influence specific employability aspects.

Table 5 graphically demonstrates our belief (premised on our literature research overview and evidenced by our research findings (Gerryts, 2018; Maree, Gerryts, Fletcher, & Jordaan, 2019) that people's

a. self-efficacy, self-esteem (sense of self), and confidence levels can be influenced positively by most of the activities in the intervention;
b. attitudes can be influenced positively through the *rap* (that should form part of every contact session);
c. awareness of the need for lifelong learning can be enhanced by what participants learn by means of the career construction genogram and a brief discussion on career adaptability;
d. interpersonal skills can be improved by participating in the activities dealing with interview skills and participation in group work-based activities;
e. work ethic is likely to be influenced positively by executing certain follow-up activities (homework) and by attending contact sessions;
f. adaptability is likely to be promoted by the self-awareness that would result from the interactive discussions on career adaptability and by their involvement in the *CAAS* assessment and intervention;

Table 5 Link between aspects of employability and different activities embedded in the interventions

Employability aspects	Intervention techniques to enhance employability aspects
• Self-efficacy, self-esteem, and confidence	Body map
• Attitude, proactivity	Career construction genogram
• Lifelong learning awareness	Presentation skills and recording
• Interpersonal skills	Interview skills
• Work ethic – do more than what is required	Career adaptability lecture
• Adaptability	Group work
• Communication skills	Reflections
	7 Habits (rap)
	CAAS
	CIP

g. communication skills will be influenced positively by their enhanced presentation skills and interview skills, by participating in the *CIP* intervention (Maree, 2016c) and by reflecting on activities and their subsequent reflexivity; and ultimately;
h. employability is bolstered in the process.

Perspective

Our explanation of why the actual activities that are recommended to facilitate the intervention was premised on and attempts to integrate Savickas's (2013) career intervention framework with the employability theory framework assembled from the literature review. The latter sheds light on what would be necessary in this kind of intervention (labelled employability counselling intervention). Our research has also shown that while it is theoretically possible to distinguish between career counselling and employability counselling, the two forms of counselling and intervention share many overlapping areas and principles.

Next, we focus on details of the intervention we advocate. Each activity is discussed in detail.

Actual Employability Counselling Intervention Proposed

An outline of the different sessions of the intervention that are proposed in the current chapter are explicated in Table 6. Also included are the outcomes we achieved during our previous intervention (Gerryts, 2018)

A detailed description of each activity (mentioned in the intervention plan) is discussed next.

'Seven-Habits' Rap

To create a sense of cohesion within the group, the second author of this chapter wrote a rap song (see Fig. 1) based on Covey's (2004) conceptualisation of the seven habits of highly effective people. The words were meant to persuade and inculcate a positive attitude in participants throughout the intervention and to serve as an ice-breaker in the first session.

The inspiration to write the rap came from the books *The leader in me* (Covey, 2008) and *The 6 most important decisions you'll ever make* (Covey, 2006). Since rap is a genre that is familiar in African cultures and used to present the voice of the black inner-city youth in New York (Clark, 2007), the second author of this chapter decided to present the seven habits in a rap style (a kind of music genre originates from inner city street cultures).

The seven-habits rap was recited at the beginning of every session to facilitate students' easy recall of its principles and message. After a while, participants initiated the 'song' themselves at the start of each session. The rap's words and rhythm (used during the intervention) appear in Fig. 1.

Biographical Form

A biographical form (BF) (information sheet) to elicit first-hand information about the participants (see Addendum 1). (People interested in implementing the intervention model advocated here may wish to include or exclude as many of the questions as they think fit.)

The *Career Adapt-Abilities Scale* (*CAAS*)
The *CAAS* (Savickas & Porfeli, 2012) assesses psychosocial resources for managing occupational transitions, developmental tasks and work traumas (Savickas, 2005).

The *Career Decision-Making Difficulties Questionnaire (CDDQ)* (Gati et al., 1996; Gati & Saka, 2001)
The *CDDQ* can be used to evaluate clients' decision-making difficulties.

Table 6 The suggested intervention and outcomes achieved previously

Session	Content	Activities	Outcomes that influenced employability during actual research
1	Introduction Interactive discussion on current challenges in the world of work and the need for career adaptability	'Seven habits' rap (see Fig. 1) Biographical information form to be completed Pre-test: *CAAS* and *CDDQ*	The rap served as an ice-breaker and attitude influencer Participants were introduced to challenges of the current world of work, got to know what career adaptability is, how the scoring for *CAAS* worked, and why they needed to improve their adaptability
2	Self-awareness, self-esteem, and confidence contents	Body-map technique	Enhanced self-awareness Exploration and recognition of personal strengths
3	Family influences	Career construction genogram (CCG) Group discussion	Uncovering of the role family played in individual careers
4	Exploring of career interests	Completion of the *Career Interest Profile* (*CIP*) (Maree, 2016b)	Participants completed the *CIP* (Maree, 2016b)
5	Career interest	Group discussions on career interest categories and related occupations and portrayed in the *CIP* (Maree, 2016b) (Part 2, 3)	Participants gained knowledge and personal awareness in regard to their career interest fields and shared the information with their small groups
6	Career stories/narratives	Worksheet: role models Facilitated group discussions on their responses to Part 4 of the *CIP*	Career story-telling Participants shared their aspirations ("What do I aspire to?") with their small groups followed by a group discussion to facilitate career exploration
7	Career stories/narratives	Participants completed an identity statement envisaged during previous sessions on the *CIP*	Participants reflected on and formulated their life-scripts, for instance, My ideal work setting, I want to keep myself busy with … and elicited self-advice from within in a facilitated environment

(continued)

Table 6 (continued)

Session	Content	Activities	Outcomes that influenced employability during actual research
8	Communication skills	General guidelines on presentation skills and interview techniques	A group discussion on physical presentation: What to wear, non-verbal communication, projection of voice, etcetera, was beneficial to participants. Examples that were used enabled participants to critically different presentations and its effect
9	Interview skills	Interview simulation	Participants were given the opportunity to mimic interview situations to prepare themselves for real-life interviews
10	Communication: One-minute speech recordings	Recordings of presentations (one-minute speeches)	Participants prepared a one-minute speech and were given the opportunity to present themselves and what they aspired to in front of a 'live' audience
11	Communication: One-minute speech playback and receiving feedback	Speeches were played back in class over two sessions Participants critiqued themselves	Participants got the opportunity to see themselves while they presented; they got the opportunity to give feedback to fellow students on their impressions about their speeches
12	Conclusion Post-tests: *CAAS* and *CDDQ*	Students watched recordings of themselves and their fellow classmates	Participants reflected on the influence of the different activities and their presentations on their self-confidence and self-efficacy

Fig. 1 Rap based on *The seven habits of highly effective people* (Covey, 2004)

Interactive Discussion: Introduction and the Need for Career Adaptability

The introductory discussion on career adaptability and the need to become employable started with an overview about the road to adulthood, what is expected of adults traditionally, and how the African concept of emerging adulthood differs from the Western concept. The constantly changing world of work and the need to be adaptable were addressed next. The analogy of the bamboo that bends and therefore lasts longer than the oak tree that resists (stays firm) in times of storms was used as a metaphor to demonstrate the need to be adaptable in the today's working world. Career adaptability was then defined and the constructs and scoring on the *CAAS* were explained. The reasons for low scores in some cases were explained and demonstrated with practical examples to assist participants in understanding these concepts.

Body-Map Technique

The aim of the body-map technique is to facilitate a process whereby people can look at themselves from a new perspective—both physically and characteristically. Body mapping is an innovation that was developed from the *Memory Box Project* in Cape Town, South Africa (Gastaldo, Magalhães, Carrasco, & Davy, 2012; Vasquez, 2004). The University of Cape Town launched this project in 2001 as part of its *AIDS and Society Research Unit*. The aim with the *Memory Box project* was to assist people living with HIV&AIDS in telling their life-stories in alternative ways (Vasquez, 2004). A *body map* is a life-size human body image (Gastaldo et al., 2012), a physical profile of an individual's body on paper (see Addendum 2 for an example of a body map). The process of creating a body map by using art-based techniques "visually represents aspects of people's lives, their bodies and the world they live in" (Gastaldo et al., 2012, p. 5). *Body mapping* (as well as other narrative techniques) is a way to empower those who are sometimes stigmatized and isolated (Vasquez, 2004) to open up and allow others to enter their world and experience how it is to live in their own bodies (Cornwall & Welbourn, 2002). In a medical context, the use of body maps is therapeutic and encourages well-being. Together with the drawing of body maps come the stories people tell about their own body map. Personal narratives create both self-awareness and awareness of others, and they recognise and identify vulnerabilities and strengths in each other (Skultans, 2000).

In practice, every participant receives a sheet of paper (the same quality as newspaper but clear and not printed on); big enough for an average human body to fit onto the full paper. Participants assist one another to draw the body map. Every other person draws the outline of their fellow participant's body on the paper while the other lies down on the paper, stretched out on the floor. Outer dimensions of each participant are drawn, and every person works on his/her own image on paper. Completed drawings are stuck onto the classroom walls in a way that offers every participant a clear view of his/her own body map (by viewing the self on the same life-size height). Each participant then uses another colour and writes strictly only positive comments with regard to his/her personal body features on the body map adding positive comments based on their appearance. Positive comments on the map regarding other strengths (emotionally, psychologically, and spiritually) of which they are aware in themselves are included, too. Participants then walk around, observing the body maps of their fellow participants and give 'compliments' or 'gifts' (strengths they observed) by writing them in the corner of the person's body map. All comments

Table 7 Uses of body mapping (Solomon, 2002)

Type of use		Purpose: to …
1.	Therapeutic	Develop fresh insights, find new directions, explore identity and social relationships
2.	Treatment information and support	Educate people about physiology and medication
3.	Research	Yield data that can be followed up/supported with feedback from participants (e.g. interviews or writing)
4.	Advocacy	Promote a cause because they communicate feelings, thoughts and ideas
5.	Inter-generational dialogue	Help people of different generations to talk to each other (the process can be used with children, caregivers, parents, and guardians, to build trust and understanding)
6.	Team building	Build positive group relationships and help people in the group appreciate their differences
7.	Art making	Teach art, drawing, colour, and composition as well as help people to open up to their own creativity
8.	Biographical	Show and tell people's life stories (autobiographies)

must be constructive, complimentary, and uplifting. This exercise is done under strict supervision to ensure that students only focus on strengths within one another and in the self.

All participants are allowed to take their body map home and are invited to write a reflection about the body-map exercise. They also have to write about what they appreciate or not from participating in the exercise and whether this experience has brought them any insights.

Table 7 summarises possible uses of body maps.

The aim and purpose of using body maps as part of this kind of intervention can be found in number 1 (therapeutic), number 3 (research), and number 8 (biographical). First, we select the body-map technique to enhance participants' self-awareness as well as their self-confidence and self-esteem as they focus on personal strengths. Second, this exercise is meant to teach participants to focus on what is positive and to embrace an attitude conducive to the realisation of possibilities. Third, the technique is selected to share with fellow participants and tell their own stories to make themselves heard. Participants are encouraged to take a picture (with their mobile phones) of their personal body maps and to write a reflection based on their experience of drawing and sharing their body maps.

Career Construction Genogram (CCG)

A genogram (Bowen, 1978) is a structural family map that represents at least three generations of a family and outlines the structure and emotional processes of the family (Bitter, 2009) on one page. It is also a qualitative method to explore family structure and is often used in family therapy. The CCG is a further development of Bowen's genogram applied in career development counselling contexts. It encourages clients to tell and re-tell their stories (Maree, 2018a) as part of a process to design their future lives. The CCG is also a reflective activity that provides insight into the family system. The method to draw a genogram is explained to participants, after which they have to draw a genogram of their own family on A3-sized paper. They indicate the present or past job/career held by every person in their family and are asked to indicate with which family members they had good relationships. After the exercise in class, participants are requested to write a reflection on what they had learned about themselves by reflecting on their family members and their careers.

According to Chope and Van Velsor (2010, p. 95), the "family background, history, support, conflicts, nurturing, exposure to new ideas or protection from them" dynamically influence career interests and choice. An example of this is a 17-year-old boy who is the middle child between two brothers, both with autistic disorders. The youngest brother's impairment is so severe that he cannot speak at all. The oldest brother severely isolates and has no friends while at university—to the extent that he speaks to no-one outside his family circle. This family situation will always have an impact on this (middle child) young man, who wants to become a medical doctor. It is not surprising that his only aim is to minimise pain in others and in this process, he forgets his own needs by not demanding anything from his parents but only trying to support them the moment he walks into their home.

To emphasise the important influence that family can have on career development, we briefly explore in the following paragraphs who and what a family is, the influence of family resources in career development, and the influence of family relationships on career.

Role of Family in Career Development

Vocational development already starts in childhood (Maree, 2018b). The family structure, different roles assigned to family members, their value systems, and the attitudes members acquire by being part of a family are some aspects that need to be explored in career development (Palos & Drobot, 2010). The influence of families on interest development and career decision making constitutes an integral part of career exploration (Chope & Van Velsor, 2010). Who the family is, where they are situated, what they do within as well as outside the household, and how they approach life in general, directly influence vocational development in children and emerging adults. If the family is integral to career development, *what* is a family and *who* is family?

The Influence of Family Resources on Career Development

Other significant factors around family that contribute to vocational development are the 'capital' or resources owned by the family (Palos & Drobot, 2010). Children from affluent families are in a more favourable situation than children who come from socio-economically deprived situations. For example, the children in a family that goes on overseas holidays and frequently travels in their own country are much better informed about cultures, currencies, technology, different opportunities, and diverse races than a family who stays in an informal settlement in a remote part of a country with no internet connection and struggling to make ends meet.

Relationships with Family Members

The nature of the relationship and interactions that developed between parents and children establish a basis for the vocational exploring process (Palos & Drobot, 2010). Family relationships are related to the development of careers and to employability. Career counselling theorists and practitioners link attachment and parental style to vocational development (Chope & Van Velsor, 2010) and to possible problematic issues in the workplace.

A relational perspective explores the interactions between parents and children (and extended family members) and is fundamental to the vocation-exploring process (Palos & Drobot, 2010). Open communication and support offered, as well as trust between a parent and a child can influence career-exploring activities, career aspirations, future plans, and the perception of experience barriers that occur in the process of choosing a career (Palos & Drobot, 2010). A healthy and caring relationship with one family member (even in dire circumstances) can bring hope, promote self-worth, bolster interest, and pave the way for a young adult to a productive life ahead.

In the next paragraphs, we discuss the exploring of career interests as part of the proposed intervention.

Career Interest

As previously mentioned, most of the participants in our research and outreach projects have never had career counselling before. This means they were not exposed to an opportunity to express their career interests in a structured or organised way. Some of the participants were not even aware that one can participate in career interest assessments. For this intervention, the demonstrated success of the *Career Interest Profile (CIP)* (Maree, 2016b) in multi-cultural contexts are advocated here.

Career Interest Profile (CIP)

Everyone has a painful story to share and if one finds a career that they are more passionate about, they are able to heal others, and at the same time heal themselves (Kobus Maree quoted by Good Work Foundation, 2017).

The *Career Interest Profile (CIP)* (Maree, 2016b) was initially established as a narrative career counselling assessment that could be successfully used with all culture groups in the South African context. Today, the *CIP* is also used in different countries because of its success in servicing people in multi-cultural contexts (Di Fabio & Maree, 2013). The *CIP* is not restricted to a certain age group and it resembles what Savickas (1994) proposed and advocated for counselling approaches to be successful, namely that clients would accept an approach that fits the spirit of their current age. The *CIP* has the goal to stimulate clients to tell and reflect on their career and life stories (Maree, 2013).

There are 'objective' and 'subjective' parts to the *CIP* that enable a researcher to collect 'objective' (scores) and 'subjective' data (stories). The objective part lists 19 career categories and asks participants to rank the career categories in order of preference or dislike, based on their feelings and actions (Maree, 2010). In the intervention, participants were asked to only select and rank the first five career categories that they preferred.

The subjective part extracted small personal narratives from the individual, for example, strengths, challenges, what he/she enjoyed or did not enjoy doing, role models, favourite stories, TV shows, websites, personal mottoes and favourite quotations, biggest successes and failures up to now, etc. The subjective data was rich in meaning making and provided good opportunities for promoting reflective discussion between client and counsellor. The objective and subjective data on interest repeatedly reflected on confirmed one another and assisted clients and counsellors in co-constructing career-life themes to that might help clients make "well-informed and appropriate career decisions" (Maree, 2011, p. 181).

The administering, feedback, and group discussions relating to the *CIP* normally take up three sessions of the intervention. In the first session, Part 3 is completed (Career category preferences/dislikes) and discussed in small groups of three to four members each. The remaining sessions (as indicated in the programme) are utilised to discuss role models and short personal narratives, and to write a personal life script.

Our rationale for using the *CIP* is our extensive and successful experience in practice and the findings in previous research (see e.g. Di Fabio & Maree, 2013; Gerryts, 2013; Maree, 2018a, 2018b), which has shown the *CIP* to be an assessment instrument and intervention mechanism that enables researchers to elicit useful and practical information that can be organized to assist clients. Regrettably, traditional career assessment and guidance still constitute the dominant way in which career counselling is conducted in South Africa. Use of the *CIP* promotes the implementation of an integrative quantitative and qualitative (career construction-based) approach to career counselling (Maree, 2016b); an approach that we embrace and that we believe is essential for any career counsellor.

Communication Skills

Both interview and presentation skills were prioritised and selected as oral communication skills sets that needed to be part of the intervention programme. Interview and communications skills expose and prepare participants for situations in which they would find themselves before being appointed in jobs/positions. Both these skills (being prepared for interview situations and introducing/presenting yourself in front of others) can be viewed as recruitment training for people who are not employed. From the literature study in Chapter "Enhancing the Employability of Young Adults from Socio-economically Challenged Contexts: Theoretical Overview" regarding the perspective that industry holds on what is perceived as employability, interpersonal skills, and emotional-social competence (Hogan, Chamorro-Premusic, & Kaiser, 2013) emerged as priorities. Communication and recruitment skills are part of career development, which is defined by Watts (2003) as the lifelong process of managing the progression in learning and work.

Both interview and presentation skills require participants to be self-confident and to sell themselves and their skills in conversational settings. To prepare participants for the recruitment process, they need to know what to expect of an interview situation, how to dress appropriately, what typical questions they could expect, and to be prepared to answer those questions confidently. These skills will be used throughout their careers.

Participants are also exposed to simulated interview situations, which are discussed in the next section.

Interview Skills: Simulated Interviews

This facet of the intervention programme starts with a group discussion on interview situations. Topics such as being on time, how to dress appropriately for an interview, listening attentively to what is being asked, non-verbal language, eye contact with panel members, and how to introduce yourself, were discussed. Next, a list of possible interview questions is handed to every participant, after they are divided into groups of four to five individuals (depending on the size of the group). An interview situation is subsequently simulated. The furniture in the room is arranged to mimic an interview setting. Every participant gets an opportunity to be the interviewee, while the others in the small group act as panel members and pick five questions from the list between them to ask the interviewee. As the group rotates, everybody has an opportunity to be interviewed. Then the group gets together, reflectively discusses what happened during the interviews, and share possible learnings from their experiences. Participants are encouraged to give constructive feedback to improve each other's listening and responses.

Presentation Skills: One-Minute Speech

This section of the intervention programme aims to assist participants in presenting themselves to significant people whom they may meet in future situations. They are put in a situation where they can practise how to introduce themselves and talk about their future dreams and careers. This module concludes the intervention.

All participants are expected to give a one-minute prepared introductory speech about themselves. By this time students have been through the intervention and are expected to be more self-aware and know more about their strengths, interests, career goals/dreams, and how they planned to get there (realise their dreams). All participants get an opportunity to introduce themselves (who they are), what they are currently busy with and what they see as the end goal of their career (their career dream). These presentations are video-recorded and played back to them in front of their group in the concluding contact session. In the concluding contact session, participants are asked to 'critique' their own short presentation once it has been played back to them. They also have to tell the rest of their group what they feel proud of and where they want to improve. The rest of the class are invited to give constructive feedback to each participant.

Possible Aspects that Can Be Added to the Intervention

Some aspects did not form part of the specific intervention under discussion that may add value in employability counselling. These include written communication skills such as the skill to write a professional curriculum vitae (CV). This could take the form of an assignment and could be followed by a facilitated session to help participants improve their written CV. Another aspect that could enhance employability counselling would be to assist participants to analyse their social-digital footprint which can be perceived as a person's living novel in real life; especially for people in the millennial age group who grew up with the internet. Employers and employees use available online information to assess the reputation of potential companies and job-seekers. Employers progressively explore social media profiles (e.g. Facebook or LinkedIn) of potential employees to determine culture fit (Smartt, 2018) with their companies. 'People analytic' techniques (Burgess, 2018) will probably be standard procedure in recruitment in the new future. Participants should therefore be aware of the influence their social media postings have on their reputation for employability. Participants can critically explore the impression prospective employers may arrive at once they are aware and critically observant of their digital footprint. Participants can then consciously manage (and enhance) these perceptions and postings with their emerging career in mind.

Conclusion

In this chapter, we purposefully focus on a population that is not privileged. We make a conscious attempt to achieve a sound balance between "science" and "art" (creating a practical training module) to widen the usefulness of the chapter for career counselling researchers, theorists, and practitioners. We propose a practical life design-based intervention strategy (and associated techniques) to address the huge need to develop the (career) adaptability and enhance the employability of (unskilled and) unemployed young adults (UUYA). Based on life- and career counselling-based principles and linked with employability literature, the life design intervention comprises of 12 sessions (this number is flexible, though). Our research seems to suggest that the intervention works particularly well with (unskilled and) unemployed young adults (UUYA) in a seriously disadvantaged African setting (Maree et al., in press).

Addendum 1—Biographical Form (BF)

Name & surname

……………………………………………………………………………………………………

………….

Male ………… Female ………… Age …………………………… Birthdate

……………………………………..

a. Can you tell me a little about your life before you started at ………? (What did you do?)

b. What type of education do you have?

c. What kind of work experience do you have?

d. Do you receive unemployment benefits from government?

e. What prompted you to apply *for this programme*?

f. How did you hear about this programme?

Addendum 2—Example of a Body Map

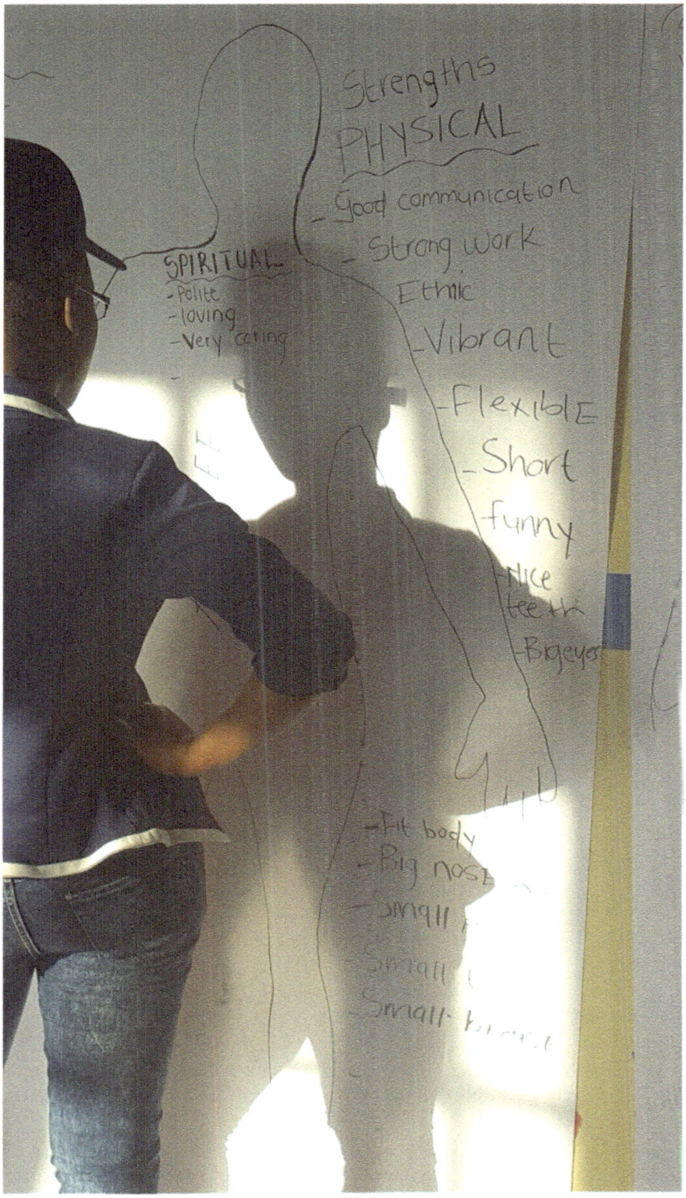

References

Amundson, N. E. (2003, November 17–18). Career development: Employability dimensions. *Food for Thought*, (1), 1–3. Retrieved from http://sks.karabuk.edu.tr/kariyer/belgeler/CAREER_DEVELOPMENT.pdf.

Bitter, J. R. (2009). *Theory and practice of family therapy and counselling*. Belmont, CA: Brooks/Cole.

Bowen, M. (1978). *Family therapy in clinical practice*. New York, NY: Aronson.

Burgess, M. (2018). *Check your digital footprint before recruiters do. Careerone*. Retrieved from https://www.careerone.com.au/watercoolertalk/job-hunting/job-interview/clean-up-your-digital-footprint-before-recruiters.

Busque, G. (1995). Measurement model for employment counselling. *ERIC Digest*. Retrieved from https://www.ericdigests.org/1998-2/model.htm.

Chope, R. C., & Van Velsor, P. (2010). The role of the family in career interest development. In K. Maree (Ed.), *Career counselling methods that work* (pp. 95–100). Cape Town, South Africa: Juta.

Clark, M. K. (2007). *Africa: The rise of African hip hop. All Africa*. Retrieved from http://allafrica.com/stories/200710011449.html.

Cornwall, A., & Welbourn, A. (2002). *Realizing rights. Transforming approaches to sexual & productive well-being*. New York, NY: Zed Books.

Covey, S. (2006). *The 6 most important decisions you'll ever make: A guide for teens*. Greenwich, CT: Touchstone.

Covey, S. R. (2004). *The 7 habits of highly effective people. Powerful lessons in personal change*. London, England: Simon & Schuster.

Covey, S. R. (2008). *The leader in me*. London, England: Simon & Schuster.

Di Fabio, A. (2010). Life designing in the 21st century: Using a new, strengthened career genogram. *Journal of Psychology in Africa, 20*, 381–384.

Di Fabio, A., & Maree, J. G. (Eds.). (2013). *Psychology of career counselling: New challenges for a new era. Festschrift in honour of Prof. Mark Savickas*. New York, NY: Nova Science.

Duarte, M. E. (2017). Career counselling research-practice disparities: What we know and what we need to know [Special issue]. *South African Journal of Education, 37*(4). https://doi.org/10.15700/saje.v37n4a1486.

Gastaldo, D., Magalhães, L., Carrasco, C., & Davy, C. (2012). *Body-map storytelling as research: Methodological considerations for telling the stories of undocumented workers through body mapping*. Retrieved from http://www.migrationhealth.ca/undocumented-workers-ontario/body-mapping.

Gati, I., Krausz, M., & Osipow, S. H. (1996). A taxonomy of difficulties in career decision making. *Journal of Counseling Psychology, 43*(4), 510–526.

Gati, I., & Saka, N. (2001). High school students' career-related decision-making difficulties. *Journal of Counseling and Development, 7*(3), 331–340.

Gerryts, E. W. (2013). *Using a narrative approach to develop the sense of self of a young engineer* (Masters' dissertation). Pretoria, South Africa: University of Pretoria.

Gerryts, E. W. (2018). *Enhancing the employability of young adults from socio-economically challenged contexts* (Ph.D. thesis). Pretoria, South Africa: University of Pretoria.

Good work Foundation. (2017). *Professor of education has a dream for South-Africa*. Retrieved from http://www.goodworkfoundation.org/professor-of-education-has-a-dream-for-south-africa/.

Guichard, J. (2005). Life-long self-construction. *International Journal for Educational and Vocational Guidance, 5*, 111–124.

Guichard, J. (2009). Self-constructing. *Journal of Vocational Behavior, 75*, 251–258.

Hartung, P. J., & Santili, S. (2018). My career story: Description and initial validity evidence. *Journal of Career Assessment, 26*, 308–321.

Hogan, R., Chamorro-Premusic, T., & Kaiser, R. B. (2013). Employability and career success: Bridging the gap between theory and reality. *Industrial and Organisational Psychology, 6*, 3–16.

Human Resources Development Canada (HRDC). (1998). *Evaluation of the transition jobs fund phase 1: Final report*. Ottawa, Canada: Human Resources Development Canada.
Mahoney, M. J. (2003). *Constructivist psychotherapy: A practical guide*. New York, NY: Guilford Press.
Maree, J. G. (2009). Career counselling in the 21st century: South African institutions of higher education at the crossroads. *South African Journal of Higher Education, 23,* 436–458.
Maree, J. G. (2010). Career story interviewing using the three anecdotes technique. *Journal of Psychology in Africa, 20,* 369–380.
Maree, J. G. (2011). Career counselling in South Africa institutions of higher learning in the 21st century: Re-discovering the potential of qualitative approaches. *South African Journal of Higher Education, 25*(4), 1–11.
Maree, J. G. (2012). Career adapt-abilities scale-South African form: Psychometric properties and construct validity. *Journal of Vocational Behaviour, 80*(3), 730–733.
Maree, J. G. (2013). *Counselling for career construction: Connecting life themes to construct life portraits: Turning pain into hope*. Rotterdam, The Netherlands: Sense.
Maree, J. G. (2016a). *Career Interest Profile (CIP) version 5*. Pinegowrie, South Africa: JvR Psychometrics.
Maree, J. G. (2016b, July). Why career counselling is more valuable now than ever before. *The Conversation, Edition Africa.*
Maree, J. G. (2016c, August). What lessons can we learn on the topic from the 2015 Florence conference? Career and Life Design interventions for sustainable development and decent work. Retrieved from http://www.kobusmaree.org/wp-content/uploads/2016/06/1.JGMareeDecentWork.Wroclaw.RoundTable.20160606.1145-1315.Mon1_.pdf.
Maree, J. G. (2018a). Innovative career construction counselling for a creative adolescent. *British Journal of Guidance and Counselling*. https://doi.org/10.1080/03069885.2018.1504202.
Maree, J. G. (2018b). Promoting career development in the early years of a person's life through self- and career construction counselling. *Early Child Development and Care, 188*(4), 425–436.
Maree, J. G., & Di Fabio, A. (2015). *Exploring new horizons in career counselling: Turning challenge into opportunities*. Rotterdam, The Netherlands: Sense.
Maree, J. G., Gerryts, E. W., Fletcher, L., & Jordaan, J. (2019). Using career counselling with life design principles to improve the career adaptability and employability of disadvantaged young adults. *Journal for Psychology in Africa, 29*(2), 110–120.
McMahon, M., & Patton, W. (Eds.). (2006). *Career counselling: Constructivist approaches*. London, London: Routledge.
Palos, R., & Drobot, L. (2010). The impact of family influence on the career choice of adolescents. *Procedia social and Behavioral Sciences, 2*(2), 3407–3411.
Patsula, P. (1992). *The assessment component of employment counselling*. Ottawa, Canada: Human Resource Development Canada.
Patton, W (2011). Theoretical underpinnings and practical application of constructivist approaches to career counselling. In K. Maree (Ed.), *Shaping the story. A guide to facilitate narrative career counselling* (pp. 121–131). Pretoria, South Africa: Van Schaik.
Savickas, M. L. (1994). Overview of career development. In M. L. Savickas & R. W. Lent (Eds.), *Convergence in career development theories* (pp. 139–154). Palo Alto, CA: CPP Books.
Savickas, M. L. (2005). The theory and practice of career construction. In S. D. Brown & R. W. Lent (Eds.), *Career development and counselling* (pp. 42–70). Hoboken, NJ: Wiley.
Savickas, M. L. (2010, July). *Life designing: Framework and introduction*. Paper presented at the 27th International Congres of Applied Psychology, Melbourne, Australia.
Savickas, M. L. (2011). *Career counseling*. Washington, DC: American Psychological Association.
Savickas, M. L. (2013). The theory and practice of career construction. In S. D. Brown & R. W. Lent (Eds.), *Career development and counseling: Putting theory and research to work* (2nd ed., pp. 147–186). Hoboken, NJ: Wiley.
Savickas, M. L. (2015a). *Life design counseling manual*. Retrieved from http://www.vocopher.com/.

Savickas, M. L. (2015b). Career counseling paradigms: Guiding, developing, and designing. In P. J. Hartung, M. L. Savickas, & W. B. Walsh (Eds.), *APA handbook of career intervention: Vol. 1. Foundations* (pp. 129–142). Washington, DC: APA Press.

Savickas, M. L. (2019). *Career counseling* (2nd ed.). Washington, DC: American Psychological Association.

Savickas, M. L., & Porfeli, E. J. (2012). *Career adapt-abilities scale*. Retrieved from http://www.vocopher.com/ms/caas/CAAS%20master.pdf.

Schultheiss, D. E. P. (2005). Qualitative relational career assessment: A constructivist paradigm. *Journal of Career Assessment, 13*(4), 381–394.

Skultans, V. (2000). Narrative, illness and the body. *Anthropology and Medicine, 7*(1), 5–13.

Smartt, N. (2018). Know your job candidate's digital footprint. *North Bay Business Journal*. Retrieved from https://www.northbaybusinessjournal.com/opinion/8282291-181/employment-recruiting-digital-networking?artslide=2&slide=GAL.

Solomon, J. (2002). "*Living with X*": *A body mapping journey in time of HIV and AIDS. Facilitator's Guide*. Psychosocial Wellbeing Series. Johannesburg: REPSSI. Retrieved from http://www.repssi.org/index.php?option=com_content&view=article&id=46&Itemid=37.

Vasquez, G. (2004). *Body perceptions of HIV and AIDS: The Memory Box Project*. CSSR working Paper, No. 64. South Africa: Centre for Social Science Research, University of Cape Town. Retrieved from http://www.uct.ac.za/depts/cssr/pubs.html.

Watts, T. (2003). *Why career development matters*. Retrieved from https://career.ibu.edu.ba/assets/userfiles/career/why_career_development_matters.pdf.

Innovative Career Counselling Assessment

Figure Piloting Innovation: Integrating the Career Adapt-Abilities Scale—UK into Practice

Jenny Bimrose and Gill Frigerio

Abstract Implementation of new theories that are rigorous and research-based into practice is challenging. It requires a willingness to take risks, both on the part of the individual practitioner, but also the employing organization. Funding mechanisms that reward a focus on placement into sustainable employment can operate as powerful inhibitors of innovatory practices that focus on holistic approaches to professional practice. The Career Adapt-Ability Scale International (CAAS-I), a scale developed to integrate vocational psychology with constructivist approaches is one such example of a theoretically informed innovation currently available. Here, validation and implementation of the scale adapted for the UK context into higher education, then a professional association are discussed, together with lessons learned regarding the implementation of innovatory practice.

Keywords Career adapt-ability scale-UK · Innovation · Risk-taking · Organizational contexts

Introduction

Whilst effective innovation is critical for the long term credibility, viability and sustainability of the career counselling profession, the implementation of new theories underpinned by high quality and rigorous research that can be integrated into practice is challenging (Sampson, Bullock-Yowell, Dozier, Osborn, & Lenz, 2017). It requires a willingness to take risks, at least during the experimental phase of implementation. In this chapter it is argued that commitment beyond the level of the individual counsellor practitioner is also required; this should extend to the organizational context and sometimes beyond. Without meaningful management support and encouragement, changing practice at the level of the individual practitioner is likely to be difficult—perhaps especially for organizations in receipt of public funding with high levels of accountability around targets that typically measure successful

---

J. Bimrose (✉) · G. Frigerio
The University of Warwick, Coventry, UK
e-mail: Jenny.Bimrose@warwick.ac.uk

J. G. Maree (ed.), *Handbook of Innovative Career Counselling*,
https://doi.org/10.1007/978-3-030-22799-9_26

placement into employment or training. Where practitioners are self-employed, the risk of experimenting with new approaches is, of course, magnified.

The Career Adapt-Ability Scale International (CAAS-I), a scale developed to integrate vocational psychology with constructivist approaches (Savickas, 1997) is one particular example of a theoretically informed innovation currently available to practitioners. The scale comprises four scales, each with six items. The four scales measure: concern (relating to the extent to which an individual is focused on preparing for their future); control (relating to the extent of self-discipline exercised); curiosity (indicating the extent to which information and opportunities are explored); and confidence (meaning how barriers are approached), as psychosocial resources for managing career transitions and development (Savickas & Porfeli, 2012). It was produced as an international measure from a collaboration amongst researchers, with members of the original research team translating it and amending it for their own countries (Leong & Walsh, 2012). Its use in practice is for identifying individual strengths relevant to building their careers, with individuals measuring their strengths across a five point scale (from strongest to not strong). It also identifies areas that are not so strong, to be worked upon. It is not, therefore, a tool that was developed in one country to be used in others, but one that was developed internationally and developed further in different country contexts. In line with the constraints indicated above, the career adaptability scale, together with the concepts underpinning it, was validated in the UK in 2014. First, it was piloted in several higher education practice context with students. This particular context in the UK, with its ongoing preoccupation with the employability agenda, represented an appropriate test bed for innovation in this domain. Five UK universities piloted the scale in 2015, providing a wide demographic in the study population. A sixth pilot developed and began the trialing of an online version of CAAS-UK. The six pilots explored the use of the concepts and scale in relation to work placements; mature learners; the targeting of interventions towards particular student groups; exploring its potential as a vehicle for institutional change, as well as an online resource.

Second, a professional membership association used the tool and concepts for career development support services. The Chartered Accountants' Benevolent Association (CABA) in the UK, a charity supporting the well-being of chartered accountants and their families (https://www.caba.org.uk), provided an interesting contrast with the higher education pilots since the end users comprised a mature and highly qualified group of professionals and their family members, who were at a very different stage of their career trajectory, compared with the students in higher education. After a feasibility study in 2016, an online version of the CAAI was launched for the CABA membership in 2017.

Learning from these two phases of innovations in practice is shared in this chapter, with a clear indication of the conditions required to ensure that innovation in the career field is successful. These include stable staffing levels and long term service improvement plans, commitment from a wide range of organisational stakeholders, and theoretically rigorous training from staff involved to facilitate the incorporation of new theories into their everyday practice, and resources. Understanding that extends beyond the counselling room and includes online resources and promotional activities ensure service users also appreciate the innovations from which they benefit.

The first part of this chapter presents a summary of how the Career Adapt-Abilities Scale was developed in the UK. It goes on to reflect on the challenges to the integration of theory and research into practice. Next, the chapter outlines the method used to guide the piloting of the tool in a higher education context, the results from the pilots and ponders the operational difficulties encountered during the pilots. This is followed by a similarly structured account of the piloting of the tool in a professional association for accountants. A discussion and conclusion complete the chapter.

Theoretical Orientation

The theoretical lens of the chapter reflects that which informed the development of the original Career Adapt-Abilities Scale. Specifically, career construction theory, which adopts a contextual and cultural position on social adaptation, arguing that human development can be understood as an attempt to integrate the person with the environment (Savickas & Porfeli, 2012). Importantly, an occupation is regarded as an important means of social integration and sustenance, with individuals having to constantly adapt and accommodate to survive in volatile labour markets.

The Career Adapt-Abilities Scale UK

The origin of the Career Adapt-Abilities Scale is well documented (Savickas & Porfeli, 2012). A cross-disciplinary, international team of academics from 18 countries initially collaborated to produce an operational definition of career resources or adapt-abilities, followed by the development of the Career Adapt-Abilities Scale-International Form 2.0 (CAAS International). This served as the basis for further research in 13 countries (Porfeli & Savickas, 2012). The majority of the research studies undertaken by the original research group adopted a quantitative focus, since their primary purpose was to validate the inventory in different countries, with care taken to establish cross-cultural validity. However, two research groups followed different methodologies, producing qualitative descriptors (Bimrose, Barnes, Brown, & Hughes, 2011; Brown, Bimrose, Barnes, & Hughes, 2012; McMahon, Watson, & Bimrose, 2012). As a consequence, a contextualized version of the career adaptability scale for use in the United Kingdom (UK) was not validated until 2014. Following the successful validation of this tool, it was piloted in two contrasting operational contexts; higher education in the UK and a professional association.

Integration of Theory and Practice

A meta-analysis of career choice interventions recently concluded that: "counsellor support was associated with the largest effect sizes" (Whiston, Li, Goodrich Mitts, & Wright, 2017, p. 182). This represents strong testimony to the pivotal importance of the counsellor's role. A related, but separate, set of arguments relate to the integration of theory, research and practice. While it may seem obvious that these three domains should be integrated in practice, it appears that the reality is different: 'theories, research and practice need to be better integrated so they can address the practical issues facing the global labor force (Ali & Brown, 2017, p. 73). Given the explosion into research based on CAAS-International, with the evolution of the tool rooted in theoretical constructivism, what seems to be currently largely absent are reports of attempts by counsellors to integrate it into practice. Ali and Brown (2017) argue that integration implies "bidirectional relationships between each of these concepts" (p. 73) that are not linear but iterative. They also argue that integrating research and practice to ensure effective and efficacious practice requires "a publicly engaged approach to research and scholarship…that focuses on collaboration with and benefits to communities external to the university" (Ali & Brown, 2017, p. 74). A key impediment to achieving greater integration into practice is the existent difficulty in communication among theorists, researchers, and practitioners (Sampson et al., 2017, p. 190). Examples of suggested strategies to address this difficulty includes: undertaking research that integrates theory and practice; creating resources that integrate theory and research; and "communicating and collaborating more regularly with practitioners who are not typically involved in creating theory and conducting research" (p. 192). With this in mind, pilot projects were undertaken by members of the same research team who carried out the CAAS-UK validation study that address this communication challenge.

Innovation in Higher Education Contexts

This section details the process of the higher education pilots, which aimed to investigate the feasibility of applying the concept of career adapt-ability and the scale into career education and employability activities of universities across the UK (Wright & Frigerio, 2015). It was expected that the pilot evaluations would identify factors which would impact the use of the CAAS-UK in UK careers guidance practice.

Methodology

The need for scientific studies that promote new knowledge, accessible to counsellors, is ongoing (Subich, 2001), in addition to the need to place a higher value on researcher-practitioners as legitimate contributors to this new knowledge (Sampson et al., 2017). Reflecting these arguments, five university careers services and one higher education charity participated in six pilots, in response to a general call for expressions of interest. Research-practitioners from participating services were asked to specify their own objectives for the pilot. The objectives, methodology and results are fully reported elsewhere (Wright & Frigerio, 2015). Hard copy and electronic pdf forms of the CAAS-UK were provided to the lead researcher-practitioners, along with briefing notes and support from the research team throughout the duration of the pilots. Each career service designed pilot activities for specific groups of students in line with their particular career service provision. For example, one service embedded the pilot within a specific programme of study, whereas as another made it a feature of their support to students returning from placement. All student participants in their respective institutions were given an information sheet which introduced the concept of career adapt-ability, described the pilot study, explained its voluntary nature and made explicit that there was no link to their course of study, or higher education more generally. Anonymity was assured via assigned participant numbers.

Schultheiss (2017) argues that theorists and researchers be paired with practitioners at joint conferences or 'interprofessional meetings' (p. 171), to facilitate greater collaboration. In line with this recommendation, lead research-practitioners were invited to attend a one day symposium to report results and share experiences (Wright & Frigerio, 2015). These were collated and analysed by the research team to identify constraining and enabling factors for the use of the CAAS-UK in practice.

Results

Selected results are considered in this section. Lead career professionals who collected data in their employing institutions, representing all six pilot sites, reported on pilot experiences at the one day symposium according to a framework provided by the core researchers for the study. These were collated and analysed by the author team to identify constraining and enabling factors for the use of the CAAS-UK in practice, discussed below.

Operational Difficulties in Using an Innovative Model

Careers professionals' motivations for participating in the pilots varied and included an innate desire to innovate, an interest in solutions to address challenges of the changing practice context, a general interest in research or a response to the interest or encouragement of a manager. None of the services had particularly identified career adaptability as a new theoretical basis for their service independently of the work of the team who conducted the validating study. Moreover, combined with their pressured professional roles, a lack of protected time for the study, operational difficulties in reaching student participants within particular timeframes and a lack of familiarity with underpinning concepts and processes meant that this interest was sometimes frustrated since they did not necessarily have the optimal amount of time and knowledge needed to carry out the study.

Student Response Reported by Lead Careers Professionals

Patterns in the scores of individuals who had completed the CAAS-UK emerged clearly in the pilots, for example, the mean scores from the postgraduate sample were slightly lower overall than those from the mostly undergraduate sample in study one reported above. Student participants had some difficulty in grasping the underlying concepts, seen as contrasting with the dominant employability narrative and common expectations of more didactic, matching based approaches. For student participants who were asked to complete reflective diaries independently based on feedback delivered by email, responses were too low to draw conclusions, but 75% of the online participants reported that their scores were useful to them to some extent, and 83% reported the feedback and advice on future action as being useful to some extent.

Integration with Career Counselling Interventions

When used with a discussion of the concepts involved, reported patterns provided a valuable basis for a career counselling intervention. The evaluation of these pilots also revealed the need for a full briefing in the underlying concepts and their origins for the career counselling and development practitioners, before they attempted to integrate it into their practice. However, for time pressured career counsellors, this represents a significant investment in continuing professional development, which may not always be possible.

Contribution to Career Development Learning

It was also found that moderated use of the scale as a reflective tool can be an effective means to facilitate an individual's reflection on their learning. Career adapt-ability concepts fit well into support programs designed to help students learn from work experience and to the experience of coping with transitions between university and work contexts. As indicated above, the scale was made available in an online environment in one of the pilots. Scores from the CAAS-UK online and the accompanying signposting to action that was included in the online version were generally experienced as useful by student participants. Perhaps unsurprisingly, it became evident from participant feedback that the online version required significant amendment to make it more user friendly and the concepts required more explanation than was possible in this limited pilot (Wright & Frigerio, 2015).

Institution Wide Benefits

Findings from all six pilots suggest that, as well as providing a constructive and valued activity for students as part of careers support services, career adapt-ability offers a promising framework for structuring conversations and debates between career counsellors and administrative/senior management colleagues. The development of the competencies embedded in the career adapt-abilities scale represents an outcome that may help to reconcile conflicting perspectives that may be evident between those who fund and manage careers services, compared with professionals delivering services to clients. For example, trend data for the CAAS-UK collected over a number of years may show useful patterns in student perceptions of their adapt-abilities over their course of study, which could inform career development planning at an institutional level (Wright & Frigerio 2015).

Limitations

The nature of the pilots meant that no rigorous evaluations were carried out. However, the pilots provide powerful insights into the need to pay careful attention to the operational contexts in which innovation is implemented. There were limitations in all areas of the reported studies. In the first study, due to possible variation in the data collection methods, the degree of standardization necessary for optimal use of psychometric testing was not possible. Each higher education institution, however, was supplied with a script and instructions for data collection to ensure consistency as far as this was practically possible. It should also be noted that the sample did not exactly mirror the overall UK student population, being slightly skewed towards female and slightly older overall.

Further limitations exist with the pilot studies carried out in higher education institutions. These pilots were undertaken within a very short time scale, due to the need to adhere to academic timetabling and funding conditions. Findings are, therefore, indicative rather than conclusive. Additionally, because of the tight timescale available to carry out the pilots, evaluations were based on immediate responses rather than longer term reflections or outcomes.

Additional research is indicated. A longitudinal study over at least two academic years might be particularly useful in permitting longer term evaluation of the potential of the CAAS-UK in developing career adapt-ability in UK students. Careful exploration of student perceptions of any benefits from initiatives designed to develop career adapt-ability would also add to the body of knowledge. In addition, a mapping of career adapt-ability on to the strategic priorities of the service would provide a more secure basis for evaluation. Given that service accountabilities are often focused on adaptive outcomes of post-education placement, distinct measures are needed to capture the development of adapt-ability resources and the pursuit of adaptive responses amongst service users (Johnston, 2018).

Innovation in a Professional Association Context

This section presents and discusses the integration of an online version of the CAAS-UK in a professional membership organisation in the UK. The overall purpose of the study was to explore the feasibility of modifying the language of the psychometrically validated Career Adapt-Ability Inventory for the UK (CAAI UK) in partnership with CABA (Chartered Accountants' Benevolent Association), with the intention of providing the tool as part of a membership offer to the Institute of Chartered Accountants in England and Wales (ICAEW), through CABA. The inventory was validated in 2013 with a representative sample of students in higher education, with confirmatory factor analysis supporting the validity of the model and strong correlations with a number of related factors demonstrating good convergent validity for the instrument. Before, however, using it as the basis of intervention by CABA for the membership of ICAEW, it was necessary to investigate the extent to which the perceptions and understandings of the concepts central to the currently validated version of the CAAI UK are relevant to the membership of above named professional bodies for the accountancy profession.

Methodology

The overall aim of the feasibility study for CABA was to test the viability of the CAAI UK scale as part of a membership offer. The methodology for the pilot study comprised three distinct, but overlapping, phases as follows: a critical review of the outcomes of the pilots of the CAAI UK higher education context to identify the most appropriate methodology for use in the CABA context; the use of cognitive interviewing as a robust research methodology to test out the 24 item scale of the CAAI UK; development of an analytical paper that reviewed the outcomes of the cognitive interviewing and identified potential development routes, including an online version, in discussion with CABA.

Twenty respondents took part in the study, through the use of cognitive interviewing. These respondents were recruited to the research investigation by CABA, using their website. For the first phase of interviews, 10 respondents who had participated in some form of continuing professional development (CPD) offered by CABA were selected from a list of 41 volunteers who responded to the request to express an interest. In the second phase of interviews, 10 respondents who had not participated in CPD offered by CABA were selected from a list of 13 volunteers. In order to secure responses from as varied a population range as possible, an equal number of men and women were selected, with equal numbers also selected from the two age ranges 36–49 and 50–64. Volunteers were emailed, inviting them to participate. Attachments to the email provided a description of the project and a consent form as well as the pro-forma listing the 24 questions from the CAAI-UK. With the shorter list of volunteers, the scope to ensure balance between males/females and with age range was more restricted, with seven females and three males participating.

Results

The pilot evaluation found that the CAAI-UK, validated with students, would be relevant for the professional membership, provided a small number of amendments were made to some questions. Certain themes emerged from the data that had general significance to the research inquiry, rather than specifically relating to the questions under scrutiny. These relate to the characteristics of the career adapt-ability framework itself as well as the experience of using an assessment tool, and are discussed below.

Different Perspective of Adult Professionals

During the research inquiry, it became evident that these adult professionals brought a different perspective from students in higher education. A significant number of the respondents in this study had already suffered redundancy (with some having experienced redundancy more than once), or were facing the prospect imminently. Some were attempting to return to employment after a career break (whether this was chosen to provide child care, or enforced, through ill health), and finding this very challenging, in terms of the demands of employers advertising vacancies. Others were balancing career development with family transitions and others were getting close to retirement and wanting to plan for a phased exit. Newer entrants were grappling with the prospect of the lack of job security extending over the foreseeable future and sometimes the lack of stimulation in their current roles.

Challenge to an Holistic Approach to Career Development

Perhaps because of the varied collective experience of employment in the accountancy sector, there was much more criticism forthcoming of both the language of the inventory and the concepts expressed. In particular, many found it difficult to grasp the concept of an holistic approach to career development and preparation. For respondents, a clear separation between work and private life seemed to exist.

'Career' related solely to paid employment and conversation during interviews was dominated by a sense of clear objective job success criteria involving (mainly vertical) progression. Many respondents struggled with the concept of career development being intertwined with other aspects of their personal life. Typically, 'career in accountancy' was viewed in traditional, hierarchical terms and seen as quite separate from other life domains. This runs contrary to the assumptions underpinning career adapt-ability, which sees and defines career broadly as a basis for individuals to explore what gives life meaning. It follows that some questions were therefore interpreted as vague and therefore difficult to comprehend.

Challenge to the Concept of Lifelong Learning

This view of work being separate from the rest of life was further endorsed by a high level of dissatisfaction with the question focusing on awareness of the education and career choices that existed. Many felt that this question was irrelevant to them because education was something for a younger age group and that their educational choices were now, in reality, severely constrained. The centrality of lifelong learning, with empowerment and autonomy as key concepts for career adapt-ability and resilience in a volatile labour market, seemed not to be embedded in the consciousness of respondents.

Professional Identity as a Mediating Variable

The shared experiences of the accountancy profession over a number of years (in some cases, over decades) provoked, perhaps unsurprisingly, responses that reflected the clear professional identity of members. For example, there seemed to be an irritation with an inventory that attempted to soften the impact of some questions. One respondent criticised the 'softly, softly' approach reflected in the five point scale for self-assessment. The verbal indications, ranging from 'not strong', through 'somewhat strong' should be amended to a numerical value. This is what accountants are about—'tell it how it is!' was the mandate.

A significant feature of working with respondents at varying ages and stages, in contrast with the higher education pilots, was the variability in response to the concepts of career adapt-ability. All interviewees for this study had significant working experience, with models of career development learned from experience as a result. One respondent expressed strong views about the construction of the inventory and how this could be rendered more effective for online use, by providing further detailed explanation for each question. This is consistent with the difficulties some students in the HEI pilots had with the conceptual understanding and perceived relevance of career adapt-ability.

Integration into Practice

Indications from the feasibility study were that the use of the inventory, modified for the membership of the professional association, needed to be embedded in a broader programme of career support. Consequently, an online version of the tool, with slight language modifications, was made open access on the CABA website from January, 2017. In the first year, 670 users completed the inventory. By July, 2018, the number of users completing the inventory is 836. This has been achieved without any specific marketing or promotion. The decision was made to give the inventory a 'soft launch', with the resource featuring in campaigns, alongside other offers to membership. Currently, the level of usage has settled to approximately 30 completions per month. Each September, CABA runs a promotion of services to members and last year, the tool was added to this annual event. Last September (2017), as part of this event, an offer was made for a session with a career coach for everyone who completed the tool. Initially, this was an offer for the first 50 who completed. In the event, over 80 completed, so all of these members were also offered a session with a career coach.

Career coaches have embraced the tool as a resource that is useful for structuring a coaching intervention. No particular training has been provided for coaches, who have taken to it 'intuitively', though all coaches were introduced to it when it was launched. Those coaches with an HR and/or careers background have found it a particularly useful resource.

One coach has embraced the tool to the extent that she has developed a two hour workshop around the inventory for women returners, which ran in 2017 with 12 participants. In 2018, a seminar to student accountants with 130 attendees was delivered. In the same year, three workshops in Australia were run with general membership and one group of unemployed, with 23 attendees in total. Further workshops were being offered with business for a general membership group.

CABA intends to continue to offer the tool as a resource—the inventory now features in their literature to members. It has proved to be maintenance free with no plans to enhance the attractiveness of the technical features, because it delivers what is needed as it currently exists.

Follow up of members who have completed the inventory, to evaluate the extent to which CAAI has assisted or supported career development would be too difficult—and it is too early to make any realistic assessments.

Discussion

The UK HE context represented a suitable test bed for piloting the validated CAAS-UK. The six pilot evaluation reported here, including an online version, showed that career adapt-ability and the CAAS-UK shows promise in terms of its' potential for use in developing the career adapt-abilities, or readiness and resources of higher education students to negotiate successfully the challenges and transitions of life and work. It also highlights some areas for further research into CAAS scores in different groups of people (e.g. age differences; differences between schools of study; cultural differences etc.). The pilot findings also add weight to the assertions of those who suggest that career adaptability can be developed in individuals (e.g. Savickas, 2013; Zacher, 2014). Further research is needed to explore how the concepts and the scale can best be used as part of an institution's career and employability provision, involving longer time periods to accommodate the annual academic cycle. The professional development needs of practitioners in relation to new theoretical concepts also requires consideration. The pilot evaluation of an online version of the CAAS-UK has provided encouragement for developing this method of making the inventory more widely accessible. The research undertaken so far on an online version could be used as a basis for refining and improving effective accessibility for the scale.

The research into the applicability of the CAAS-UK for membership of a professional association was also highly instructive. Once again, minor language modifications were found to be necessary to ensure that the target audience of primarily qualified and experienced professional was able to understand the concepts presented in the questions. Having achieved these slight modifications, the amended version was presented online, as the most effective and efficient medium for the purposes intended. The resource has been embedded into the services to members, with promotion of its use being undertaken from the organisational centre, on an annual basis. While the inventory is available online for completion on an open access basis, its use is also being integrated into other service provision (like workshops for particular groups) when and where this is deemed to be appropriate.

Conclusion

A key challenge for the career adapt-ability scale is to achieve successful integration into career counselling practice, on an international basis. The pilot evaluations carried out in the UK in two contrasting operational contexts, higher education and a professional association, that are discussed in this chapter, provide insights into the processes of implementation for this new instrument into practice, though clearly further research and evaluation is needed, with a longitudinal perspective likely to provide a rich source of learning. The online version indicates the potential of the instrument for wider access to large audiences and the exemplar of the professional association's use of the tool is testimony to its usefulness in practice, provided that it is made available within a context that provides explanation and follow up support. The manner in which the professional association espoused the tool, making it a mainstream resource within its continuing professional development offer to members, demonstrates the utility and power of the tool for users in labour market transitions.

Acknowledgements The pilots in higher education were funded by an external body (Higher Education Academy), with a full account of methodology, findings and implications available in an open access report (Wright & Frigerio, 2015).
The feasibility study and subsequent implementation into practice of the CAAI as an online tool received funding support from CABA. CABA has given its full support to the publication of this chapter.

References

Ali, S. R., & Brown, S. D. (2017). Integration of theory, research, and practice: Using our tools to address challenging times. In J. P. Sampson, E. Bullock-Yowell, V. C. Dozier, D. S. Osborn, & J. G. Lenz (Eds.), *Integrating theory, research, and practice in vocational psychology: Current status and future directions*. Tallahassee, FL: Florida State University. http://doi.org/10.17125/svp2016.ch6.

Bimrose, J., Barnes, S-A., Brown, A. & Hughes, D. (2011). *The role of career adaptability in skills supply*. Evidence Report 35. Wath-upon-Dearne, London: UK Commission for Employment and Skills. Retrieved from: https://warwick.ac.uk/fac/soc/ier/publications/2011/bimrose_ca_main.pdf.

Brown, A., Bimrose, J., Barnes, S.-A., & Hughes, D. (2012). The role of career adaptabilities for mid-career changers. *Journal of Vocational Behavior, 80,* 754–761.

Johnston, C. S. (2018). A systematic review of the career adaptability literature and future outlook. *Journal of Career Assessment, 26*(1), 3–30.

Leong, F. T. L., & Walsh, W. B. (2012). Guest editors' introduction to the special issue. *Journal of Vocational Behavior, 80,* 659–660.

McMahon, M., Watson, M., & Bimrose, J. (2012). Carer adaptability: A qualitative understanding from the stories of older women. *Journal of Vocational Behavior, 80,* 762–768. https://doi.org/10.1016/j.jvb.2012.01.016.

Porfeli, E. J., & Savickas, M. L. (2012). Career adapt-abilities scale-USA form: Psychometric properties and relation to vocational identity. *Journal of Vocational Behavior, 80,* 748–753.

Sampson, J. P., Bullock-Yowell, E., Dozier, V. C., Osborn, D. S., & Lenz, J. G. (Eds.). (2017). *Integrating theory, research, and practice in vocational psychology: Current status and future directions*. Tallahassee, FL: Florida State University. Retrieved from http://journals.fcla.edu/svp2016/.

Savickas, M. L. (1997). Career adaptability: An integrative construct for life-span life-space theory. *The Career Development Quarterly, 45,* 247–259.

Savickas, M. L. (2013). Career construction theory and practice. In R. W. Lent & S. D. Brown (Eds.). *Career development and counseling: Putting theory and research to work* (2nd ed., pp. 147–183). Hoboken, NJ: Wiley.

Savickas, M. L., & Porfeli, E. J. (2012). Career adapt-abilities scale: Construction, reliability, and measurement equivalence across 13 countries. *Journal of Vocational Behavior, 80,* 661–673.

Schultheiss, D. E. (2017). Integrating theory, research, and practice in vocational psychology: Perspectives of a Journal of Vocational Behavior Editorial Board Member. In J. P. Sampson, E. Bullock-Yowell, V. C. Dozier, D. S. Osborn, & J. G. Lenz (Eds.), *Integrating theory, research, and practice in vocational psychology: Current status and future directions* (pp. 166–174). Tallahassee, FL: Florida State University. Retrieved from http://journals.fcla.edu/svp2016/article/view/90530.

Subich, L. (2001). Dynamic forces in the growth and change of vocational psychology. *Journal of Vocational Behavior, 59,* 235–242. https://doi.org/10.1006/jvbe.2001.1829.

Whiston, S. C., Li, Y., Goodrich Mitts, N., & Wright, L. (2017). Effectiveness of career choice interventions: A meta-analytic replication and extension. *Journal of Vocational Behavior, 100,* 175–184.

Wright, T. & Frigerio, G. (2015) *The career adapt-ability pilots project*. York: The Higher Education Academy. https://www.heacademy.ac.uk/sites/default/files/resources/CareerAdapt-abilityPilotsProject_0.pdf/. Accessed 17/04/17.

Zacher, H. (2014). Career adaptability predicts subjective career success above and beyond personality traits and core self-evaluations. *Journal of Vocational Behavior, 84*, 21–30. https://doi.org/10.1016/j.jvb.2013.10.002.

Using Interests and Holland's Model of Vocational Personality Types in Career Counselling: Some Thoughts and Research Findings

Brandon Morgan, Anthony V. Naidoo, Carolina Henn and Stephan Rabie

Abstract Interests are often used in career counselling and Holland's model of vocational personality types is often implicitly or explicitly the vehicle used to explain interest scores. In this chapter we set out to investigate interests and the applicability of Holland's model of vocational personality types in career counselling. We start with a definition of interests and then present some thoughts on the measurement of interests. This includes a discussion of the spherical structure of interests and the general interest factor. We then present some findings on the propositions made in Holland's model of vocational personality types and show that these propositions continue to be relevant in career counselling. In the last section of this chapter, we briefly discuss the three waves in career counselling and then provide some thoughts on using interests and Holland's model of vocational personality types in career counselling.

Keywords Interests · Holland's model of vocational personality types · Career counselling

---

B. Morgan (✉) · C. Henn
Department of Industrial Psychology and People Management, University of Johannesburg, Johannesburg, South Africa
e-mail: bmorgan@uj.ac.za

C. Henn
e-mail: carolinah@uj.ac.za

A. V. Naidoo
Department of Psychology, Stellenbosch University, Stellenbosch, South Africa
e-mail: avnaidoo@sun.ac.za

S. Rabie
Department of Global Health, Stellenbosch University, Stellenbosch, South Africa
e-mail: srabie@sun.ac.za

J. G. Maree (ed.), *Handbook of Innovative Career Counselling*,
https://doi.org/10.1007/978-3-030-22799-9_27

Introduction

Many career theories or models position interests as (important) determinants of occupational selection (Hansen & Wiernik, 2018). It therefore comes as no surprise that counsellors often use interest scores in career counselling. These scores can be used in many different ways to facilitate the counselling process. One way that interests are used is by interpreting these scores against the backdrop of Holland's model of vocational personality types (hereafter referred to as Holland's model). Holland's model remains popular because of its practical applicability and the ease with which it can be used in counselling settings (Hansen & Wiernik, 2018; Nauta, 2010, 2013). However, does research support the predictions made in Holland's model? In this chapter, we set out to explore this question.

The first part of the chapter provides a definition of interests and then makes a distinction between manifest and inventoried interests. The second part discusses the measurement of interests using interest inventories and considers how technological advancements might influence interest measurement. The third part of this chapter provides an overview of Holland's model of vocational personality types and discusses some findings on the theoretical predictions made by the model. It also includes a brief discussion of the Things-People and Data-Ideas dimensions and the general interest factor. The fourth section provides a concise summary of three waves in career counselling. In the fifth and last section we provide some thoughts on using Holland's model of vocational personality types in (qualitative) career counselling. Before proceeding, we need to highlight a caution. In needing to keep the chapter as short and useful as possible, we have tried to be succinct. This comes at a price; in summarising large amounts of information, some details may have been omitted. We therefore encourage readers to peruse the sources we have cited in this chapter and critically engage with the material we have presented.

Defining Interests

What are interests? This is not an easy question to answer as there are many different definitions in the literature. A common definition offered by Strong (1943, 1955) is that interests reflect movement *toward* or *away from* some activity that a person *likes* or *dislikes* (only the very basic elements of Strong's more comprehensive definition are presented here). Interests have also been defined as a *preference* for activities (Crites, 1999; Hansen & Wiernik, 2018) and an expression of personality (Holland, 1997) or self-concept (Bordin, 1943; Hartung, 2007). The reader is referred to Hansen (1984) and Hogan and Blake (1999) for a more complete overview. For Rounds and Su (2014, p. 860), interests are "traitlike *preferences* for activities, contexts in which activities occur, and outcomes associated with preferred activities that motivate goal-orientated behaviors and orient individuals toward certain environments" (emphasis added). In their definition, interests are viewed as relatively stable traits, although states can be integrated into the definition (Hansen & Wiernik, 2018; Su, 2018).

A few words on the motivational component of interests are needed. For Rounds and Su (2014), interests influence three motivational processes, namely direction, vigour, and persistence (also see Nye, Su, Rounds, & Drasgow, 2012; Su, 2018). These processes, in turn, affect behavioural outcomes (Rounds & Su, 2014). Savickas (1995, p. 191) also views interests as a motivational construct and writes that interest "symbolizes the relationship between an individual and the world". In his view, interests guide movement and "are the bridge across which needs and goals seek gratification" (p. 191). From this perspective, interests are viewed as less stable and more subjective than proposed in the trait view (Hartung, 2007; Savickas, 1995). How, then, can we define interests? Based on Hansen's (1984) review and our reading of the literature, we define interests in this chapter as outward-directed preferences for some activity or activities (Crites, 1999; Hansen & Wiernik, 2018; Rounds & Su, 2014) which are related to personality and self-concept (Hartung, 2007; Holland, 1997) and which motivate behaviour (Rounds & Su, 2014; Savickas, 1995).

Manifest and Inventoried Interests

A distinction also needs to be made between expressed interests, manifest interests, inventoried interests, tested interests, and experimental interests (Crites, 1999; Super & Crites, 1962). The first three, which represent the most common way of measuring interests, are concerned with verbal expression of interest for an activity or occupation, actual participation in an activity or occupation, and self-reported interest scores obtained from interest inventories (Super & Crites, 1962). Interests, at least in our experience, are often measured using interest inventories. Expressed and manifest interests, however, should not be ignored in practice. Savickas (2015), for example, avers that manifest interests should be preferred (in individual counselling) because they have better predictive validity than inventoried interests (e.g., Cairo, 1982). With respect to different ways in which interests can be measured, Holland (1997) wrote that there are advantages and disadvantages to using different approaches and that the counselling situation should dictate the way in which interests are measured.

Measuring Career Interests Using Interest Inventories

Interest inventory items typically measure preference (e.g., dislike or like) for some activity or object or for some occupation or field of study (Harmon, 1999; Rounds & Su, 2014). The difference between these two formats is the focus either on activities or objects (e.g., *teach people life-skills*) or on job titles (e.g., *schoolteacher*). Activity items tend to be more concrete whereas occupational titles tend to be more abstract (Tracey, 2009 cited in IMC SED, 2014). Consider an occupation such as *fitter and turner*. Not all clients may have knowledge about activities performed in this occupation or even what the occupation is. An activity such as *fix machines in a factory*, in contrast, is less ambiguous. Providing clients with definitions and/or common activities performed in each occupation may therefore be useful in career counselling; not only to reduce ambiguity but also to facilitate career discussion and exploration (Maree & Taylor, 2016). O*Net Online (https://www.onetonline.org/) has many resources that can be used in this regard (but keep in mind that O*Net primarily reflects occupations in the United States). It is particularly important that items are easily understood when using an interest inventory with adolescents or children (e.g., Tracey & Ward, 1998).

Counsellors should also ensure that the item content is context-appropriate. According to Einarsdóttir, Rounds, and Su (2010, p. 362), "[o]ccupations develop in a cultural context and are influenced by historical, political, and ecological factors". Geographic, economic, and cultural differences can therefore influence how people perceive, interpret, and endorse interest items (Einarsdóttir et al., 2010; Glosenberg, Tracey, Behrend, Blustein, & Foster, 2019; Morgan & de Bruin, 2018). Savickas (2013), for example, writes that interests are self-constructed strategies that are constructed in a cultural context. With respect to interest inventories, this means that imported interest inventories might contain items that fail to capture relevant occupations or activities or even contain occupations or activities that are irrelevant in a specific context (Einarsdóttir et al., 2010; Fouad, 1999; Glosenberg et al., 2019; Leong, Austin, Sekaran, & Komarraju, 1998). Counsellors therefore need to carefully consider items in interest inventories before using them in practice.

Technological Advancements and the Measurement of Career Interests

Counsellors can also not ignore the changing world of work when using interest inventories. Hirschi (2018) writes that the Fourth Industrial Revolution is changing how people work and might bring about new occupations that do not yet exist. New ways of working include, for example, remote offices, flexible working hours, and independent work (Manyika et al., 2016). Interest inventories need to have items that reflect these new ways of working and counsellors must investigate the extent to which items are aligned with current and future occupations. Technological changes may also impact on how interests are measured. Renninger and Hidi (2011) discuss some interesting alternatives to measuring interests, such as behavioural measures and neuroscientific methods.

Multimedia and the internet could also be considered as alternative ways to present interest items or even career counselling as a whole (Gore & Leuwerke, 2000; Staples & Luzzo, 1999). Šverko, Babarović, and Međugorac (2014) have shown, for example, that online pictures presented alongside occupational descriptions can be used in interest inventories allowing for better contextualisation of the items. There is also evidence that online career counselling increases career exploration behaviours (Dozier, Sampson, & Reardon, 2013). An advantage of using computers when measuring interests is that a response time to each item can be obtained. Tracey and Tao (2018) showed that there was a curvilinear relationship between response time and item response. That is, the more an activity is liked or disliked, the quicker a person responds to it. This is a potentially useful source of information because it allows the counsellor to investigate and discuss item response length with the client, particularly if unusual patterns are detected. Discrepancies between response time and item response could also be discussed (Tracey & Tao, 2018).

Capturing Affective Responses

Interest inventory items usually use a lexical response format (e.g., dislike and like) to obtain interest preference scores. This approach, according to Tracey and Tao (2018), might not adequately capture the cognitive and emotional components inherent in responses to these items, as it has been found that responses to interest items elicit an emotional response (Phan, Amrhein, Rounds, & Lewis, 2019; Phan & Rounds, 2018; Tracey & Tao, 2018). It also appears that there is an affective duality, i.e., both positive and negative emotions, inherent in responses to interest inventories (Phan & Rounds, 2018). To better capture this emotional component and help contextualise interests, Phan et al. (2019) suggest that a bipolar *emojis* response format be used in interest inventories. Phan and Rounds (2018), in turn, have shown that adapted semantic-differential scales with affect anchors can be used to obtain positive and negative scores. This allows counsellors to discuss with their clients activities or occupational titles that elicit positive emotions, negative emotions, or both positive and negative emotions.

Holland's Model of Vocational Personality Types

In the sections above, we defined interests and briefly discussed some considerations when measuring interests. We now turn our attention to Holland's model of vocational personality types. To keep this chapter succinct, we have decided to focus more on some research findings on the model propositions rather than on the model itself. The reader is referred to Holland (1997) and Nauta (2013) for a more detailed discussion of Holland's model.

Key Assumptions

Holland's model consists of four key assumptions: (a) there are six personality and (b) environment types (although factors is probably a better term to use; see Tracey & Rounds, 1993); (c) people search for and enter occupations that match their interests; and (d) a person's behaviour results from the interaction of his or her interest profile and the interest profile of the environment (Holland, 1997).

Six personality and environment types. Holland (1997) believed that the interest space could be divided into six broad interests: Realistic, Investigative, Artistic, Social, Enterprising, and Conventional (RIASEC). These interest types are associated with different values, skills, beliefs, and interests (Savickas, 2015) and are a useful starting point for career counselling. Holland (1997) used the three highest interest scores to form a three-letter code (e.g., REC, SIA, etc.). As Nauta (2013) points out, there are 720 possible three letter codes that can be formed from the six interest types. There is no reason, though, for counsellors to only measure these six interest types. Tracey (2002), for example, uses eight interest types instead of the six RIASEC interest types. Indeed, Tracey and Rounds (1995) have shown that the interest space can be divided into any number of interests depending on the needs of the counselling situation.

The Realistic interest, for example, could be divided into more specific interests such as *physical activity*, *engineering*, and *skilled trades*. These narrower interests are often referred to as basic interests (Rounds, 1995) and allow for greater specificity in measurement (Su, 2018). Using basic interests in combination with Holland's six interest types provides potentially more information for discussion during the counselling process and allows the counsellor and client to move between different levels of measurement abstraction. It is important, though, to use basic interests that represent the whole interest space (i.e., all six of Holland's interest types). The counselling situation should also be kept in mind when deciding what level of measurement abstraction to use (Harmon, 1999; Tracey & Rounds, 1995). Using more than six interest types might, for example, be difficult to discuss in some settings, although the basic interests do tend to be more concrete and therefore have more easily understood labels.

Environments attract people with similar interest profiles. The assumption that people in occupations have similar interest profiles (i.e., homogeneity) is fundamental to using interests in career counselling (Nye, Perlus, & Rounds, 2018). It is assumed, for example, that people who have a strong (relative) Investigative interest gravitate toward scientific-like occupations. The available evidence partially supports this idea (Fouad, 1999; Nauta, 2010). That is, people in the same occupation tend to have similar interest profiles. There is evidence, however, that occupations differ in homogeneity (Nye et al., 2018) and that there might be environments within environments (Holland, 1997). It is also not clear how occupational changes associated with the Fourth Industrial Revolution might impact on this assumption. Environment homogeneity has implications for how interest scores are interpreted and should not be ignored. Nye et al. (2018), for example, recommend that counsellors consider different permutations of interest scores (e.g., SIA, ISA, AIS, etc.) when discussing results with clients rather than using the Holland three-point code as is (but consider differentiation too—discussed in the next section). Counsellors should also discuss the relative importance that clients place on interest scores in occupational or educational selection before measuring interests because there might be other factors that explain more variance in this selection (Matjie & Coetzee, 2018; Tracey & Gupta, 2008).

Secondary Assumptions

There are five secondary assumptions that complement the first four assumptions: (a) calculus, (b) congruence, (c) consistency, (d) differentiation, and (e) identity (Holland, 1997). In this section, we briefly discuss and present research evidence for these assumptions.

Calculus. The calculus assumption is concerned with the structure of the six interest or environment types (Holland, 1997). Broadly, there are three competing models used to explain the structure of interests: (a) dimensional models, (b) classification models, and (c) spatial models (Rounds & Day, 1999). The reader is referred to Rounds and Day (1999) for a detailed description of these models. Holland's model can be considered a spatial model. He asserted that "the distances among the types or environments are inversely proportional to the theoretical relationships between them" (Holland, 1997, p. 5). This model is often described as Holland's hexagon. In this model, the ordering of the six interest types (i.e., RIASEC) matters because this ordering represents the theoretical similarity of the interest types (Darcy & Tracey, 2007; Holland, 1997). Studies investigating the structural validity of Holland's model typically search for RIASEC ordering and the circular structure of these interest types in correlation matrices (Tracey, 2000). Failure to find this ordering and circular structure invalidates Holland's model in that context (assuming multiple studies with large sample sizes) and may, for example, indicate contextual differences in the way people view the relationships between interests (Tracey & Gupta, 2008) or even that it is not the correct interest model (Gati, 1979). This would mean that the model and interest inventories that measure the model cannot be interpreted in the same way (Rounds & Day, 1999).

Does Holland's model show the same structure across different countries? Rounds and Tracey (1996) conducted a large-scale meta-analysis to investigate this question They found that Holland's model fit well in the United States but that the fit outside of the United States was less than satisfactory. Interestingly, they found that the fit of Holland's model in other Western countries (e.g., Canada) was also worse than the United States. Their results certainly cast doubt on the cross-cultural transportability of Holland's model. More recent studies (e.g., Atitsogbe, Moumoula, Rochat, Antonietti, & Rossier, 2018; Glosenberg et al., 2019) have shown that Holland's model does tend to fare relatively well in other countries but that model fit is moderated by economic development (Glosenberg et al., 2019). These mixed findings mean that the circular model might not be the best representation of the interest structure outside of the United States (Glosenberg et al., 2019; Rounds & Tracey, 1996). Practitioners should therefore ensure that there is validity evidence for the circular structure of interests in a particular context before using Holland based measures in practice (Glosenberg et al., 2019). In the sections that follow, we discuss the spherical model of interests and the general interest dimension, although it must be kept in mind that they are not directly part of the calculus assumption.

Things-People, Data-Ideas, and Prestige. Prediger (1982) found that unrotated principal components analysis of RIASEC correlation matrices produced three orthogonal dimensions. The first was a general interest dimension and the second and third were called the Things-People and Data-Ideas dimensions. The Things-People and Data-Ideas dimensions reduce Holland's hexagon to two orthogonal bipolar dimensions (see Glosenberg et al., 2019; Tay, Su, & Rounds, 2011 for criticisms and cautions of this model). Scores on these two dimensions can be obtained through a weighted linear combination of RIASEC scale scores with weights derived from the RIASEC hexagonal coordinates. A client's interest profile can be projected into Holland's hexagon using Things-People and Data-Ideas dimension scores. Tracey and Rounds (1996) suggested that a Prestige dimension be added to the Things-People and Data-Ideas dimensions, resulting in a spherical interest structure. Sodano and Tracey (2008) believe that this dimension reflects a combination of ability and effort whereas Tracey (2016) writes that it is "the general difficulty, training, knowledge, and education required of the various activities" (p. 13). Readers are referred to the Personal Globe Inventory (Tracey, 2002) for more information on the spherical interest model and interests used in this model.

General interest. Responses to interest inventory items produce a relatively large general interest factor (unless a forced choice response format is used; Wee, 2016). Conceptually, the general interest factor can be viewed as profile elevation, i.e., a person's total or mean score across all scales (Nagy, Marsh, Lüdtke, & Trautwein, 2009). However, its interpretation is less clear. Tracey (2012) suggests that there are three possible interpretations: (a) it is a nuisance variable that shifts profiles up and down but has no substantive meaning, (b) it is a bias and should be controlled, or (c) it has substantive meaning and should be interpreted. With respect to the latter, the general interest appears to represent interest flexibility (Darcy & Tracey, 2003) or positive affect and outlook (Tracey, 2012). It should not, however, be used to indicate interest strength (Darcy & Tracey, 2003; Prediger, 1988). That is, interest rank ordering (i.e., interest profiles) should be interpreted instead of absolute interest strength (Prediger, 1988; Tracey, 2012).

Congruence. The congruence assumption (essentially person-environment fit) states that the match or fit between a person's interests and the predominant interest types in the environment should have predictable outcomes and that it is beneficial for people to work in such matching environments (Furnham, 2001; Holland, 1997). If this match does not lead to predictable outcomes, then using interests in career counselling would not matter (Tracey & Robbins, 2006). Early research on congruence produced mixed or even negative results (Spokane, 1985; Spokane, Meir, & Catalano, 2000; Tinsley, 2000), calling its usefulness into question. More recent meta-analyses (e.g., Nye et al., 2012; Nye, Su, Rounds, & Drasgow, 2017; Van Iddekinge, Roth, Putka, & Lanivich, 2011) have, however, been more supportive of the congruence hypothesis. The reader is referred to Wilkins and Tracey (2014) and Su (2018) for a summary of congruence-outcome relationships. In brief, there is some evidence that congruence is related to, for example, occupational and education persistence and performance (Nye et al., 2012), job satisfaction (Dik, Strife, & Hansen, 2010), and intended and actual turnover (Van Iddekinge et al., 2011).

Most research tends to investigate the direct effect between some congruence index and some outcome. Tracey (2007) and Wilkins and Tracey (2014), however, suggest that there might be moderators of congruence-outcome measures that change the strength and/or direction of these relationships. There is evidence, for example, that environmental homogeneity (Tracey, Allen, & Robbins, 2012), interest flexibility (Tracey & Robbins, 2006; Tracey et al., 2012), and interest consistency (Tracey, Wille, Durr, & de Fruyt, 2014) moderate congruence-outcome relationships. Cross-cultural or national differences, or even differences within people, should also be considered as potential moderators (Glosenberg et al., 2019; Leong et al., 1998; Wilkins & Tracey, 2014). It would be problematic to assume that congruence-outcome relationships are universal and that congruence can be applied equally across different contexts (or clients) without any evidence to support this claim. For counsellors, this means that congruence does seem to matter but that it might matter more for some people or occupations than for others (Nauta, 2013).

Differentiation. The differentiation assumption is concerned with how well-defined an interest profile (or an environment) is (Holland, 1997). Holland (1997) believed that some people have a narrow set of interests (high differentiation), whereas other people have broader interest profiles (low differentiation). In his view, differentiation is associated with choosing an occupation and ease of occupational selection (Nauta, 2013). Holland calculated differentiation as the difference between the largest RIASEC score and the smallest RIASEC score (with scores on a common metric). The larger this difference, the more differentiated the profile. Alternatively, differentiation can be thought of as the standard deviation (variance) of scores in an interest profile (see Atitsogbe et al., 2018) or as the circular standard deviation (variance) when RIASEC scores are transformed into polar coordinates (Tracey & Robbins, 2006). With respect to the latter, differentiation is profile amplitude, i.e., the vector length (Tracey et al., 2014). The structural summary method can be used to obtain this differentiation score (as well as direction of the vector projection and consistency of profile scores). Gurtman and Pincus (2003) provide a non-technical primer on calculating and interpreting the structural summary method parameters in counselling settings.

Holland (1997) believed that people with greater differentiation should have more predictable career behaviours than people with less differentiation. There is, however, limited support for the differentiation hypothesis (Nauta, 2010). Research has found, for example, that differentiation is unrelated to difficulties with career decision making (Atitsogbe et al., 2018) and career maturity (Černja, Babarović, & Šverko, 2017). Jaensch, Hirschi, and Spurk (2016), in contrast, found that differentiation was positively related to career decidedness and career engagement. Tracey et al. (2014)

found that differentiation was positively related to educational and occupational congruence but not to educational and occupational certainty. They also found that differentiation was unrelated to career and life satisfaction. Differentiation did, however, moderate the congruence-occupational stability relationship, with participants who scored lower on differentiation having no linear relationship between congruence and occupational stability and those who scored higher on differentiation having a positive linear relationship between congruence and occupational stability (Tracey et al., 2014).

Consistency. The consistency assumption is intimately connected with the calculus assumption. This assumption proposes that interest types that are closer together on the hexagon should have more in common than interest types that are spaced further apart. Applied to clients (or environments), it means that interest profiles with dominant scores that are closer to each other on the hexagon should lead to more predictable behaviour (Holland, 1997) and that people with more consistent interest types should find it easier to select an occupation (Nauta, 2013). Holland (1997) used the hexagon structure to categorise consistency as high, middle, or low. More sophisticated approaches to calculating consistency are given by Tracey et al. (2014) and Atitsogbe et al. (2018). Research on the consistency assumption has produced mixed findings. There is some evidence that consistency is related to occupational choice (O'Neill, Magoon, & Tracey, 1978), career satisfaction (Pesier & Meir, 1978), educational and occupational congruence (Tracey et al., 2014), and career indecision (Atitsogbe et al., 2018). Other studies have found though that consistency is unrelated to career satisfaction (Tracey et al., 2014) and career choice preparedness (Hirschi & Läge, 2007). It also appears that consistency moderates the relationship between congruence and occupational stability with those who scored lower on consistency showing a positive relationship between congruence and occupational stability (Tracey et al., 2014).

Identity. The identity assumption refers to the influence of a person's identity on their selection of a career path (Holland, 1997) and is closely related to consistency and differentiation (Nauta, 2013). Holland (1997) believed that people differ in interest clarity. It is thought that this clarity is related to career aspirations and achievement and career path certainty (Holland, 1997). There is, however, limited research on this hypothesis. Some research has found that identity is related to career choice preparedness (Hirschi & Läge, 2007) and career decision-making self-efficacy (Nauta & Khan, 2007). These results suggest that identity might be used as a measure of career choice preparedness in career counselling (Nauta & Khan, 2007).

The Three Waves in Career Counselling

In the sections that follow, we summarise the major shifts that have occurred in career counselling. We then provide some thoughts on using interests and Holland's model in (qualitative) career counselling. The three dominant approaches in career counselling have been (a) the trait-factor approach, (b) the human lifespan development approach, and (c) the life design and/or postmodern (e.g., narrative) approach (Hartung, 2010). In the trait-factor approach, a battery of suitable psychometric tests is administered to a client and scores are used as an objective measurement of the client's personal or self-characteristics (Savickas, 1992). The counsellor would then proceed to logically connect (or match) this self-knowledge with the knowledge of work (Hartung, 2010). The second approach, based on the work of Super, considered individual development and shifted career counselling from the aforementioned objective approach to a more subjective and meaning-making approach (Hartung, 2010; Savickas, 1996; Super, 1990). In this approach, psychometric tests and qualitative assessment of life themes are used to work within the context of the client's life. The importance of different life roles is highlighted and career stage concerns are explored through various qualitative techniques (Hartung, 2010; McMahon & Watson, 2010; Perry, 2010).

The life design approach is related to career construction theory (Savickas, 2002). In life design counselling, counsellors place emphasis on helping clients to construe the patterns, themes, and meanings inherent in their emerging life-career stories and experiences (Savickas, 2002) and enhancing their reflective career consciousness. While possibly better suited to clients who lack a sense of vocational identity and are low in confidence about their career direction and decision-making ability (Maree, 2007a; Savickas, 2002), this approach accommodates melding together both interest scores (e.g., manifest interests) and personal stories in a comprehensive assessment and counselling intervention (Hartung, 2007). It must be kept in mind, though, that career construction has a somewhat different view of interests. Savickas (2013), for example, writes that Holland's six RIASEC interests are self-constructing strategies that reflect reputation. The life design approach offers clients a way to consider the meaning of work and other roles in their experiences, and how they can use these role domains to meaningfully develop their own career stories, contribute to society, and match themselves to suitable educational and work environments (Hartung, 2010). The reader is referred to Savickas (2015) for a detailed overview of life design counselling.

Using Interests and Holland's Model with Qualitative Career Counselling

We believe that career counselling cannot be a linear process where a counsellor merely administers and scores an interest inventory (or other assessment) and then *gives* recommendations to the client based on these scores (Savickas et al., 2009). Such a process is insufficient and indeed incomplete, offering a limited perspective on the career counselling process; one that does not serve the client's best interests (see Maree, 2007b). Rather, career counselling should be a non-linear recursive process in which both the counsellor and client are actively engaged in constructing meaning (McIlveen & Patton, 2007). This means that counsellors and clients should examine and re-examine interest profiles in light of all other sources of information. This information may include, for example, the clients' knowledge base, their exposure to the world of work, their unique background, and their current context (Chope & Consoli, 2007; Holland, 1997; Shepard & Marshall, 2000). It must also be kept in mind that selecting a career or field of study is not always based completely on interests and that focusing solely on interest scores (or other assessment results) can easily cause the counsellor to miss other important information (Blomerus, 2016; Glosenberg et al., 2019).

Interests tell us something about clients' self-constructed strategies (Savickas, 2013), their identity or self-concept (Hartung, 2007; Hogan & Blake, 1999), and their personality style, and can be measured using an interest inventory (i.e., inventoried interests), through verbal expression (i.e., expressed interests), or even through actual participation in activities (i.e., manifest interests). Specific ways in which interests could be gauged are, for example, asking the client about school subjects that were enjoyed, school activities that were engaged in, past and present hobbies and pastimes, and favoured entertainment (Hartung, 2007; Savickas, 2015). Discussion and exploration of interests are important and counsellors should not ignore manifest and expressed interests (Reardon & Lenz, 1999). Although Savickas (2015) prefers manifest interests, inventoried interests can be useful. Counsellors could, for example, gauge convergence (or divergence) of these different sources of interest profiles (Holland, 1997) and explore personal meanings that clients ascribed to these profiles. This, in turn, can help broaden career exploration (Cairo, 1982; Spokane & Decker, 1999). Keep in mind that inventoried interests should not be treated as objective realities but rather used to discuss clients' career stories (Savickas, 1995, 2013). What inventoried interests can more easily provide compared to expressed and manifest interests are relative standing on the general interest dimension and differentiation and consistency scores.

Holland's model might lend itself well to this non-linear career counselling process, particularly because it is able to organise interest information into a format that is easier for the client to understand (Holland, 1997). However, there must first be validity evidence for the RIASEC circular ordering model before using Holland's model in practice (Glosenberg et al., 2019). This model should therefore not be imposed on clients (Morgan & de Bruin, 2018) but rather seen as one potential tool that can be used to facilitate career counselling. McMahon and Watson (2012) have recently developed a qualitative structured interview that can be used to discuss and reflect on Holland interest codes. This interview can assist clients to contextualise interest scores and consider how their context shapes their career path (McMahon, Watson, & Zietsman, 2018). Readers are referred to McMahon et al. (2018) for examples of integrating interest scores with narrative career approaches.

Holland's model allows counsellors to locate (or project) the client broadly within the interest space. It is also possible to locate careers in the RIASEC space alongside clients' projections. The RIASEC model and the client's location in the model alongside occupation projections (e.g., congruence) could then be used for discussion (see Prediger, 1981). Clients could further be encouraged to find out more about careers close to their projection and comment on what they *like* or *dislike* about these careers (see Nauta, 2013). Instruction of the RIASEC map itself (i.e., career education) might also help, such as discussing the different interest types and exploring occupations related to each interest type (Tracey, 2008). Using basic interests alongside RIASEC interests could help narrow down clients' interests. It might emerge, for example, that a client has a general people orientation (e.g., a high score on Social relative to other scores), but that his or her interests gravitate more strongly toward Artistic aspects of this dimension, and the performing arts in particular. Using the three-letter Holland code might hide these nuances in interest profiles. As such, interest scores, when combined with qualitative techniques, can be used as a point of departure for counsellors to collaboratively explore clients' career potential.

Counsellors are also encouraged not to ignore profile elevation (general interest), differentiation, and consistency when using Holland's model (Bullock & Reardon, 2005; Gati & Blumberg, 1991). For more thoughts on using these aspects see Bullock and Reardon (2005) and Nauta (2013). Briefly, counsellors are encouraged to explore the meaning of these scores with clients (Bullock & Reardon, 2005) and what these scores may imply for occupational selection and outcomes. An undifferentiated profile may, for example, require counsellors to consider different permutations of a three-letter Holland code (Nauta, 2013), i.e., consider the dependence of these interests. In summary, we recommend that interest scores and Holland's model be used in conjunction with other postmodern counselling approaches and that counsellors make use of the rich information provided by Holland's model as supplementary information rather than simply obtaining a three-letter Holland code and using it to make career (matching) suggestions.

Conclusion

In this chapter, we presented some thoughts and findings on interest measurement and Holland's model of vocational personality types. In addition, we provided some reflections on using interests and Holland's model in (qualitative) career counselling. In summary, we believe that interest scores and Holland's model can have value in career counselling but that these should not be used in isolation of other information. In particular, we have argued that there is merit to using these different sources of information alongside postmodern career counselling approaches to facilitate the career counselling process. At the same time, though, there is a definite need for more research on the usefulness and applicability of Holland's model, especially within the changing world of work.

References

Atitsogbe, K. A., Moumoula, I. A., Rochat, S., Antonietti, J.-P., & Rossier, J. (2018). Vocational interests and career indecision in Switzerland and Burkina Faso: Cross-cultural similarities and differences. *Journal of Vocational Behavior, 107,* 126–140. https://doi.org/10.1016/j.jvb.2018.04.002.

Blomerus, L. (2016). *The career constructions of and influences on career choices of adolescents in a low-income school* (Unpublished doctoral dissertation). Stellenbosch University, Stellenbosch, South Africa.

Bordin, E. S. (1943). A theory of vocational interests as dynamic phenomena. *Educational and Psychological Measurement, 3,* 46–62. https://doi.org/10.1177/001316444300300105.

Bullock, E. E., & Reardon, R. C. (2005). Using profile elevation to increase the usefulness of the self-directed search and other inventories. *The Career Development Quarterly, 54*(2), 175–183. https://doi.org/10.1002/j.2161-0045.2005.tb00149.x.

Cairo, P. C. (1982). Measured interests versus expressed interests as predictors of long-term occupational membership. *Journal of Vocational Behavior, 20,* 343–353. https://doi.org/10.1016/0001-8791(82)90021-5.

Černja, I., Babarović, T., & Šverko, I. (2017). Could differentiation and consistency of interests serve as career maturity indicators of elementary school children? *Društvena Istraživanja: Časopis Za Opća Društvena Pitanja, 26,* 41–58. https://doi.org/10.5559/di.26.1.03.

Chope, R. C., & Consoli, A. J. (2007). A storied approach to multicultural career counselling. In K. Maree (Ed.), *Shaping the story: A guide to facilitating narrative counselling* (pp. 87–100). Pretoria, South Africa: Van Schaik.

Crites, J. O. (1999). Operational definitions of vocational interests. In M. L. Savickas & A. R. Spokane (Eds.), *Vocational interests: Meaning, measurement, and counseling use* (pp. 163–170). Palo Alto, CA: Davies-Black.

Darcy, M., & Tracey, T. J. G. (2003). Integrating abilities and interests in career choice: Maximal versus typical assessment. *Journal of Career Assessment, 11*(2), 219–237. https://doi.org/10.1177/1069072703011002007.

Darcy, M. U. A., & Tracey, T. J. G. (2007). Circumplex structure of Holland's RIASEC interests across gender and time. *Journal of Counseling Psychology, 54,* 17–31. https://doi.org/10.1037/0022-0167.54.1.17.

Dik, B. J., Strife, S. R., & Hansen, J.-I. C. (2010). The flip side of Holland type congruence: Incongruence and job satisfaction. *The Career Development Quarterly, 58*(4), 352–358. https://doi.org/10.1002/j.2161-0045.2010.tb00183.x.

Dozier, C. V., Sampson, J. P., & Reardon, R. C. (2013). Using two different Self-Directed Search (SDS) interpretative materials: Implications for career assessment. *Professional Counselor, 3*(2), 67–72.

Einarsdóttir, S., Rounds, J., & Su, R. (2010). Holland in Iceland revisited: An emic approach to evaluating U. S. vocational interest models. *Journal of Counseling Psychology, 57*(3), 361–367. https://doi.org/10.1037/a0019685.

Fouad, N. A. (1999). Validity evidence for interest inventories. In M. L. Savickas & A. R. Spokane (Eds.), *Vocational interests: Meaning, measurement, and counseling use* (pp. 193–210). Palo Alto, CA: Davies-Black.

Furnham, A. (2001). Vocational preference and P-O fit: Reflections on Holland's theory of vocational choice. *Applied Psychology, 50,* 5–29. https://doi.org/10.1111/1464-0597.00046.

Gati, I. (1979). A hierarchical model for the structure of vocational interests. *Journal of Vocational Behavior, 15,* 90–106. https://doi.org/10.1016/0001-8791(79)90021-6.

Gati, I., & Blumberg, D. (1991). Computer versus counselor interpretation of interest inventories: The case of the self-directed search. *Journal of Counseling Psychology, 38*(3), 350–366. https://doi.org/10.1037/0022-0167.38.3.350.

Glosenberg, A., Tracey, T. J. G., Behrend, T. S., Blustein, D. L., & Foster, L. L. (2019). Person-vocation fit across the world of work: Evaluating the generalizability of the circular model of vocational interests and social cognitive career theory across 74 countries. *Journal of Vocational Behavior, 112*, 92–108. https://doi.org/10.1016/j.jvb.2019.01.002.

Gore, P. A., Jr., & Leuwerke, W. C. (2000). Information technology for career assessment on the internet. *Journal of Career Assessment, 8*, 3–19. https://doi.org/10.1177/106907270000800102.

Gurtman, M. B., & Pincus, A. L. (2003). The circumplex model: Methods and research applications. In J. A. Schinka & W. F. Velicer (Eds.), *Handbook of psychology: Research methods in psychology* (Vol. 2, pp. 407–428). New York: Wiley.

Hansen, J.-I. C. (1984). The measurement of vocational interests: Issues and future directions. In S. D. Brown & R. W. Lent (Eds.), *Handbook of counseling psychology* (pp. 99–136). Australia: Wiley.

Hansen, J.-I. C., & Wiernik, B. M. (2018). Work preferences: Vocational interests and values. In D. S. Ones, N. Anderson, C. Viswesvaran, & H. K. Sinangil (Eds.), *The SAGE handbook of industrial, work & organizational psychology* (2nd ed., Vol. 1, pp. 408–448). Thousand Oaks, CA: SAGE.

Harmon, L. W. (1999). Measuring interests: Approaches and issues. In M. L. Savickas & A. R. Spokane (Eds.), *Vocational interests: Meaning, measurement, and counseling use* (pp. 171–192). Palo Alto, CA: Davies-Black.

Hartung, P. J. (2007). Career construction: Principles and practice. In K. Maree (Ed.) *Shaping the story: A guide to facilitating narrative counselling* (pp. 103–120). Hatfield, Pretoria: van Schaik Publishers.

Hartung, P. J. (2010). Career assessment: Using scores and stories in life designing. In K. Maree (Ed.), *Career counselling: methods that work* (pp. 1–10). Lansdowne, South Africa: Juta.

Hirschi, A. (2018). The fourth industrial revolution: Issues and implications for career research and practice. *The Career Development Quarterly, 66*(3), 192–204. https://doi.org/10.1002/cdq.12142.

Hirschi, A., & Läge, D. (2007). Holland's secondary constructs of vocational interests and career choice readiness of secondary students. *Journal of Individual Differences, 28*(4), 205–218. https://doi.org/10.1027/1614-0001.28.4.205.

Hogan, R., & Blake, R. (1999). John Holland's vocational typology and personality theory. *Journal of Vocational Behavior, 55*, 41–56. https://doi.org/10.1006/jvbe.1999.1696.

Holland, J. L. (1997). *Making vocational choices: A theory of vocational personalities and work environments* (3rd ed.). Lutz, FL: Psychological Assessment Resources Inc.

[IMC SED]. (2014, October 1). *Innovations in career assessment* [Video File]. Retrieved from https://www.youtube.com/watch?v=cxvMCweEcdA&t=1625s.

Jaensch, V. K., Hirschi, A., & Spurk, D. (2016). Relationships of vocational interest congruence, differentiation, and elevation to career preparedness among university students. *Zeitschrift für Arbeits- und Organisationspsychologie, 60*, 79–89. https://doi.org/10.1026/0932-4089/a000210.

Leong, F. T. L., Austin, J. T., Sekaran, U., & Komarraju, M. (1998). An evaluation of the cross-cultural validity of Holland's theory: Career choices by workers in India. *Journal of Vocational Behavior, 52*, 441–455. https://doi.org/10.1006/jvbe.1997.1637.

Manyika, J., Lund, S., Bughin, J., Robinson, K., Mischke, J., & Mahajan, D. (2016). *Independent work: Choice, necessity, and the gig economy*. New York: McKinsey Global Institute. Retrieved from https://www.mckinsey.com/featured-insights/employment-and-growth/independent-work-choice-necessity-and-the-gig-economy.

Maree, K. (Ed.). (2007a). *Shaping the story: A guide to facilitating narrative counselling* Hatfield, Pretoria: Van Schaik Publishers.

Maree, K. (2007b). First steps in developing an interest inventory to facilitate narrative counselling. In K. Maree (Ed.), *Shaping the story: A guide to facilitating narrative counselling* (pp. 176–205). Hatfield, Pretoria: Van Schaik Publishers.

Maree, K., & Taylor, N. (2016). *Maree Career Matrix manual*. Johannesburg, South Africa: JvR Psychometrics.

Matjie, T., & Coetzee, M. (2018). Exploring the links between gender, dwelling, and career orientations of African emerging adults. *Journal of Psychology in Africa, 28,* 303–309. https://doi.org/10.1080/14330237.2018.1501896.

McIlveen, P., & Patton, W. (2007). Narrative career counselling: Theory and exemplars of practice. *Australian Psychologist, 42*(3), 226–235.

McMahon, M., & Watson, M. (2010). Story telling: Moving from thin stories to thick and rich stories. In K. Maree (Ed.), *Career counselling: Methods that work* (pp. 53–63). Lansdowne, South Africa: Juta.

McMahon, M., & Watson, M. (2012). Telling stories of career assessment. *Journal of Career Assessment, 20*(4), 440–451. https://doi.org/10.1177/1069072712448999.

McMahon, M., Watson, M., & Zietsman, L. (2018). Adults changing careers through university education: Making meaning of quantitative career assessment scores through an integrative structured interview. *SA Journal of Industrial Psychology, 44*. https://doi.org/10.4102/sajip.v44i0.1487.

Morgan, B., & de Bruin, G. P. (2018). Structural validity of Holland's circumplex model of vocational personality types in Africa. *Journal of Career Assessment, 26*(2), 275–290. https://doi.org/10.1177/1069072717692747.

Nagy, G., Marsh, H. W., Lüdtke, O., & Trautwein, U. (2009). Representing the circles in our minds: Confirmatory factor analysis of circumplex structures and profiles. In T. Teo & M. S. Khine (Eds.), *Structural equation modeling in educational research: Concepts and applications* (pp. 287–315). Rotterdam: Sense Publishers.

Nauta, M. M. (2010). The development, evolution, and status of Holland's theory of vocational personalities: Reflections and future directions for counselling psychology. *Journal of Counseling Psychology, 57,* 11–22. https://doi.org/10.1037/a0018213.

Nauta, M. M. (2013). Holland's theory of vocational choice and adjustment. In S. D. Brown & R. W. Lent (Eds.), *Career development and counseling: Putting theory and research to work* (2nd ed., pp. 55–82). Hoboken, NJ: Wiley.

Nauta, M. M., & Kahn, J. H. (2007). Identity status, consistency and differentiation of interests, and career decision self-efficacy. *Journal of Career Assessment, 15,* 55–65. https://doi.org/10.1177/1069072705283786.

Nye, C. D., Perlus, J., & Rounds, J. (2018). Do ornithologists flock together? Examining the homogeneity of interests in occupations. *Journal of Vocational Behavior, 107,* 195–208. https://doi.org/10.1016/j.jvb.2018.04.004.

Nye, C. D., Su, R., Rounds, J., & Drasgow, F. (2012). Vocational interests and performance: A quantitative summary of over 60 years of research. *Perspectives on Psychological Science, 7*(4), 384–403. https://doi.org/10.1177/1745691612449021.

Nye, C. D., Su, R., Rounds, J., & Drasgow, F. (2017). Interest congruence and performance: Revisiting recent meta-analytic findings. *Journal of Vocational Behavior, 98,* 138–151. https://doi.org/10.1016/j.jvb.2016.11.002.

O'Neil, J. M., Magoon, T. M., & Tracey, T. J. (1978). Status of Holland's investigative personality types and their consistency levels seven years later. *Journal of Counseling Psychology, 25*(6), 530–535. https://doi.org/10.1037/0022-0167.25.6.530.

Perry, J. C. (2010). Using the best of both worlds: Not a question of one or the other. In K. Maree (Ed.), *Career counselling: Methods that work* (pp. 11–23). Lansdowne, South Africa: Juta.

Pesier, C., & Meir, E. I. (1978). Congruency, consistency, and differentiation of vocational interests as predictors of vocational satisfaction and preference stability. *Journal of Vocational Behavior, 12*(3), 270–278. https://doi.org/10.1016/0001-8791(78)90015-5.

Phan, W. M. J., Amrhein, R., Rounds, J., & Lewis, P. (2019). Contextualizing interest scales with emojis: Implications for measurement and validity. *Journal of Career Assessment, 27,* 114–133. https://doi.org/10.1177/1069072717748647.

Phan, W. M. J., & Rounds, J. (2018). Examining the duality of Holland's RIASEC types: Implications for measurement and congruence. *Journal of Vocational Behavior, 106,* 22–36. https://doi.org/10.1016/j.jvb.2017.11.011.

Prediger, D. J. (1981). Mapping occupations and interests: A graphic aid for vocational guidance and research. *The Career Development Quarterly, 30,* 21–36. https://doi.org/10.1002/j.2164-585X.1981.tb01072.x.

Prediger, D. J. (1982). Dimensions underlying Holland's hexagon: Missing link between interests and occupations? *Journal of Vocational Behavior, 21*(3), 259–287. https://doi.org/10.1016/0001-8791(82)90036-7.

Prediger, D. J. (1988). Is interest profile level relevant to career counseling? *Journal of Counseling Psychology, 45*(2), 204–211.

Reardon, R. C., & Lenz, J. G. (1999). Holland's theory and career assessment. *Journal of Vocational Behavior, 55,* 102–113. https://doi.org/10.1006/jvbe.1999.1700.

Renninger, K. A., & Hidi, S. (2011). Revisiting the conceptualization, measurement, and generation of interest. *Educational Psychologist, 46*(3), 168–184. https://doi.org/10.1080/00461520.2011.587723.

Rounds, J., & Day, S. X. (1999). Describing, evaluating, and creating vocational interest structures. In M. L. Savickas & A. R. Spokane (Eds.), *Vocational interests: Their meaning, measurement and use in counseling* (pp. 103–133). Palo Alto, CA: Davies-Black.

Rounds, J., & Su, R. (2014). The nature and power of interests. *Current Directions in Psychological Science, 23*(2), 98–103. https://doi.org/10.1177/0963721414522812.

Rounds, J., & Tracey, T. J. G. (1996). Cross-cultural structural equivalence of RIASEC models and measures. *Journal of Counseling Psychology, 43*(3), 310–329.

Rounds, J. B. (1995). Vocational interests: Evaluation of structural hypotheses. In D. Lubinski & R. V. Dawis (Eds.), *Assessing individual differences in human behavior: New concepts, methods, and findings* (pp. 177–232). Palo Alto, CA: Consulting Psychologists Press.

Savickas, M. L. (1992). New directions in career assessment. In D. H. Montoss & C. J. Shinkman (Eds.), *Career development: Theory and practice* (pp. 336–355). Springfield, IL: C.C. Thomas. Palo Alto, CA: Davies-Black Publishing.

Savickas, M. L. (1995). Examining the personal meaning of inventoried interests during career counseling. *Journal of Career Assessment, 3*(2), 188–201. https://doi.org/10.1177/106907279500300206.

Savickas, M. L. (1996). A framework for linking career theory and practice. In M. L. Savickas & W. B. Walsh (Eds.), *Handbook of career counseling theory and practice* (pp. 191–208). Palo Alto, CA: Davies-Black Publishing.

Savickas, M. L. (2002). Career construction: A developmental theory of vocational behavior. In D. Brown (Ed.), *Career choice and development* (4th ed., pp. 149–205). San Francisco, CA: Jossey-Bass.

Savickas, M. L. (2013). Career construction theory and practice. In S. D. Brown & R. W. Lent (Eds.), *Career development and counseling: Putting theory and research to work* (2nd ed., pp. 147–185). Hoboken, NJ: Wiley.

Savickas, M. L. (2015). *Life-design counseling manual.* Retrieved from https://dwd.wisconsin.gov/youthapprenticeship/pdf/2017_forum/eidsmoe/manual_LifeDesignCounseling.pdf.

Savickas, M. L., Nota, L., Rossier, J., Dauwalder, J., Duarte, M. E., Guichard, J., et al. (2009). Life design: A paradigm for career construction in the 21st century. *Journal of Vocational Behavior, 75*(3), 239–250. https://doi.org/10.1016/j.jvb.2009.04.004.

Shepard, B., & Marshall, A. (2000). Career development and planning issues for rural adolescent girls. *Canadian Journal of Counselling, 34*(3), 155–171.

Sodano, S. M., & Tracey, T. J. G. (2008). Prestige in interest activity assessment. *Journal of Vocational Behavior, 73*(2), 310–317. https://doi.org/10.1016/j.jvb.2008.07.002.

Spokane, A. R. (1985). A review of research on person-environment congruence in Holland's theory of careers. *Journal of Vocational Behavior, 26*(3), 306–343. https://doi.org/10.1016/0001-8791(85)90009-0.

Spokane, A. R., & Decker, A. R. (1999). Expressed and measured interests. In M. L. Savickas & A. R. Spokane (Eds.), *Vocational interests: Meaning, measurement, and counseling use* (pp. 211–234). Palo Alto, CA: Davies-Black.

Spokane, A. R., Meir, E., & Catalano, M. (2000). Person-environment congruence and Holland's theory: A review and reconsideration. *Journal of Vocational Behavior, 57*(2), 137–187. https://doi.org/10.1006/jvbe.2000.1771.

Staples, J. G., & Luzzo, D. A. (1999). *Measurement comparability of paper-and-pencil and multimedia vocational assessments.* Iowa City, IA: ACT Research Report Series 99-1.

Strong, E. K., Jr. (1943). *Vocational interests of men and women*. Palo Alto, CA: Stanford University Press.

Strong, E. K., Jr. (1955). *Vocational interests eighteen years after college*. Minneapolis, MN: University of Minnesota Press.

Su, R. (2018). The three faces of interests: An integrative review of interest research in vocational, organizational, and educational psychology. *Journal of Vocational Behavior*. Advance online publication. https://doi.org/10.1016/j.jvb.2018.10.016.

Super, D. E. (1990). Career and life development. In D. Brown & L. Brooks (Eds.), *Career choice and development* (2nd ed., pp. 192–234). San Francisco, CA: Jossey-Bass.

Super, D. E., & Crites, J. O. (1962). *Appraising vocational fitness* (Rev ed.). New York, NY: Harper Collins.

Šverko, I., Babarović, T., & Međugorac, V. (2014). Pictorial assessment of interests: Development and evaluation of pictorial and descriptive interest inventory. *Journal of Vocational Behavior, 84,* 356–366. https://doi.org/10.1016/j.jvb.2014.02.008.

Tay, L., Su, R., & Rounds, J. (2011). People-things and data-ideas: Bipolar dimensions? *Journal of Counseling Psychology, 58*(3), 424–440. https://doi.org/10.1037/a0023488.

Tinsley, H. E. A. (2000). The congruence myth: An analysis of the efficacy of the person-environment fit model. *Journal of Vocational Behavior, 56*(2), 147–179. https://doi.org/10.1006/jvbe.1999.1727.

Tracey, T. J. G. (2000). Analysis of circumplex models. In H. E. A. Tinsley & S. D. Brown (Eds.), *Handbook of applied multivariate statistics and mathematical modeling* (pp. 641–664). San Diego, CA: Academic Press.

Tracey, T. J. G. (2002). Personal Globe Inventory: Measurement of the spherical model of interests and competence beliefs. *Journal of Vocational Behavior, 60,* 113–172. https://doi.org/10.1006/vbe.2001.1817.

Tracey, T. J. G. (2007). Moderators of the interest congruence-occupational outcome relation. *International Journal for Educational and Vocational Guidance, 7,* 37–45. https://doi.org/10.1007/s10775-006-9111-3.

Tracey, T. J. G. (2008). Adherence to RIASEC structure as a key career decision construct. *Journal of Counseling Psychology, 55*(2), 146–157. https://doi.org/10.1037/0022-0167.55.2.146.

Tracey, T. J. G. (2012). Problems with single interest scales: Implications of the general factor. *Journal of Vocational Behavior, 82*(3), 378–384. https://doi.org/10.1016/j.jvb.2012.10.001.

Tracey, T. J. G. (2016). *Personal Globe Inventory PGI, PGI-Short, and PGI-Mini manual version 1.4.* Retrieved from https://pgi.asu.edu/sites/default/files/PGI%20Manual%20v1.4.pdf.

Tracey, T. J. G., Allen, J., & Robbins, S. B. (2012). Moderation of the relation between person-environment congruence and academic success: Environmental constraint, personal flexibility and method. *Journal of Vocational Behavior, 80,* 38–49. https://doi.org/10.1016/j.jvb.2011.03.005.

Tracey, T. J. G., & Gupta, S. (2008). Interest assessment in an international context. In J. A. Athanasou & R. Van Esbroeck (Eds.), *International handbook of career guidance* (pp. 525–537). Dordrecht: Springer.

Tracey, T. J. G., & Robbins, S. B. (2006). The interest-major congruence and college success relation: A longitudinal study. *Journal of Vocational Behavior, 69,* 64–89. https://doi.org/10.1016/j.jvb.2005.11.003.

Tracey, T. J., & Rounds, J. B. (1993). Evaluating Holland's and Gati's vocational-interest models: A structural meta-analysis. *Psychological Bulletin, 113*(2), 229–246.

Tracey, T. J. G., & Rounds, J. (1995). The arbitrary nature of Holland's RIASEC types: A concentric-circles structure. *Journal of Counseling Psychology, 42*(4), 431–439. https://doi.org/10.1037/0022-0167.42.4.431.

Tracey, T. J. G., & Rounds, J. (1996). The spherical representation of vocational interests. *Journal of Vocational Behavior, 48,* 3–41.

Tracey, T. J. G., & Tao, C. (2018). Response latency in interest assessment: An added tool? *Journal of Vocational Behavior, 108,* 121–131. https://doi.org/10.1016/j.jvb.2018.07.001.

Tracey, T. J. G., & Ward, C. C. (1998). The structure of children's interests and competence perceptions. *Journal of Counseling Psychology, 45*(3), 290–303.

Tracey, T. J. G., Wille, B., Durr, M. R., & De Fruyt, F. (2014). An enhanced examination of Holland's consistency and differentiation hypotheses. *Journal of Vocational Behavior, 84*(3), 237–247. https://doi.org/10.1016/j.jvb.2014.01.008.

Van Iddekinge, C. H., Roth, P. L., Putka, D. J., & Lanivich, S. E. (2011). Are you interested? A meta-analysis of relations between vocational interests and employee performance and turnover. *Journal of Applied Psychology, 96*(6), 1167–1194. https://doi.org/10.1037/a0024343.

Wee, J. M. C. (2016). *Deciphering the general factor in interest measures: Response style or attitude* (Unpublished master's thesis). University of Illinois at Urbana-Champaign, Chicago, United States of America.

Wilkins, K. G., & Tracey, T. J. G. (2014). Person environment fit and vocational outcomes. In M. Coetzee (Ed.), *Psycho-social career meta-capacities: Dynamics of contemporary career development* (pp. 123–138). Cham, Switzerland: Springer International Publishing.

Sustainable Career Cards Sort (SCCS): Linking Career Choices to the World Needs

Shékina Rochat and Jonas Masdonati

Abstract Recently, there has been a call for career counselling interventions that promote the construction of a more humane sustainable world. In fact, contemporary world is facing collateral crises at various levels, and career counsellors should be able to help their clients to make career choices that are in accordance with ethical principles and tackle these emergencies. This is likely to contribute both to help solving these crises and to allow career clients to find meaning in their work. The aim of this chapter is to propose a career counselling intervention that help counselees to design their career pathway in ways that can contribute to a fair and sustainable human and global development. The chapter presents the development and the initial validation of the Sustainable Career Cards Sort (SCCS), an innovative cards sort tool aiming at connecting the clients' current career concerns with those of the world. The suggested intervention comprises reflective activities on pictures representing the most important world's crises. Implications for research and practice are discussed.

Keywords Sustainable career cards sort · Sustainable development · Meaning · UN goals · Career intervention

Sustainable Career Cards Sort (SCCS): Linking Career Choices to the World Needs

In the last decades, there has been a global increasing awareness on the growing crises that our contemporary world is facing, both at the environmental, human and societal levels (e.g., ILO, 2001; UN, 2015). On September 25, 2015, all the Heads of States and Governments present at the United Nations General Assembly adopted the resolution "Transforming our world: The 2030 agenda for global action" (UN, 2015). This agenda consists of 17 sustainable development goals and 169 targets that are aimed at directing actions to preserve the humanity and the planet (See Table 1

S. Rochat (✉)
Vaud State Office of Career Counselling, Rue de la Borde 3d, 1004 Lausanne, Switzerland
e-mail: shekina.rochat@vd.ch

J. Masdonati
Institute of Psychology, University of Lausanne, Lausanne, Switzerland

J. G. Maree (ed.), *Handbook of Innovative Career Counselling*,
https://doi.org/10.1007/978-3-030-22799-9_28

Table 1 UN's (2015) goals

Goals	
1	Ending poverty in all its forms
2	Ending hunger, improving nutrition and promoting sustainable agriculture
3	Ensuring healthy lives and promoting well-being
4	Ensuring inclusive and equitable quality education at all ages
5	Achieving gender equality and empowering all women and girls
6	Ensuring availability of water and sanitation for all
7	Ensuring access to sustainable energy for all
8	Promoting sustainable economic growth and decent work for all
9	Promoting sustainable industrialization and fostering innovation
10	Reducing the inequalities within and among countries
11	Building inclusive, safe, sustainable and resilient cities
12	Ensuring sustainable production and consumption
13	Combatting climate change and its impacts
14	Protecting the oceans, seas and marine resources
15	Protecting the terrestrial ecosystem
16	Promoting peaceful and inclusive societies, providing access to justice and inclusive institution for all
17	Revitalizing the global partnership for sustainable development

for a summary of these goals, and UN (2015) for a complete list of the targets). The urge to meet these world's need emphasize the importance to develop career counselling interventions that help individuals to design their career paths in ways that take into account and possibly contribute to sustainable and fair human and global development (Guichard, 2013, 2016, 2018). In fact, the ethical standards of psychologists emphasized their responsibility in helping constructing a better world where "peace, liberty, responsibility, humanity and morality prevail" (International Association of Applied Psychology, 2008). More specifically, Fouad, Gerstein and Toporek (2006) emphasized that social justice was at the core of the emergence of vocational counselling psychology, until the field became more concerned by issues of counselling psychologists' identity and of positioning the career practitioners on the economic market. Today's crises highlight the need to refocus on ways that career counselling can help address these issues.

The goal of this chapter is to introduce a qualitative assessment tool, the Sustainable Career Card Sort (SCCS), aiming at sensitizing career clients to the ways their life and career could contribute to serve the world needs. The first part of the chapter briefly reviews the rationale for promoting humane, faire and sustainable career decision-making as well as its potential impact on the meaning people derived from their work and their lives. The second part of this chapter introduces the SCCS and presents its validation procedure. The third part discusses the validity of the proposed intervention and its possible implications for research and practice.

Linking Career Choices to the World Needs

Recently, the development of the Psychology of Working Framework (PWF; e.g., Blustein, 2001, 2006) and of the Psychology of Working Theory (PWT; Duffy, Blustein, Diemer, & Autin, 2016) and subsequent research contributed to increase the concerns on social justice in career counselling by highlighting the impact of social class, discrimination, marginalization and barriers on the satisfaction and well-being at work. These advancements thus contributed to meet the counselling psychology's urge upon which it is "critical that more counselling psychologists develop a sophisticated understanding of social justice, social action, and advocacy" (Fouad et al., 2006, p. 2). These frameworks and theories have mostly focused on urging practitioners to put their best efforts in contributing to ameliorate the access to decent work (e.g., Blustein, Kenny, Di Fabio, & Guichard, 2018; Di Fabio & Maree, 2016; Duffy et al., 2016; Guichard, 2013, 2018; Massoudi et al., in press). In psychological terms, such a decent work has been defined as work that

> helps all workers attain a sense of self-respect and dignity, experience freedom and security in the workplace, and (as far as possible) is afforded the opportunity to choose and execute productive, meaningful and fulfilling work that will enable them to construct themselves adequately and without restrictions and make social contribution. (Di Fabio & Maree, 2016, p. 26)

Focusing on the process of securing a decent job seems to be a worthy goal for career counsellors to promote social justice, as "access to work was viewed as a major vehicle to social equity" (Fouad et al., 2006, p. 3). However, as suggested by Guichard (2016), "work must be examined in relation to far broader issues, such as how it impacts the planet and what kind of human beings and what world it contributes to constructing" (p. 186). Consequently, Guichard (2018) recently broadened this scope in emphasizing that career counselling interventions should imperatively and actively encourage every citizen of the world to reflect on how their career can contribute to a more humane, fair, and sustainable global development—that is, actively contributing to solve the world's need, such as listed by the UN (2015). Such an endeavor is posited as critical to help construct a better world for all. However, it is also likely that encouraging clients to consider how their career can contribute to fulfill the world's need can foster meaningfulness and a sense of purpose work and life—where meaning is comprised as "the sense made of, and significance felt regarding, the nature of one's being and existence" (Steger, Frazier, Oishi, & Kaler, 2006, p. 81) and purpose as "people's identification of, and intention to pursue, particular highly valued, overarching life goals" (Steger & Dik, 2010, p. 133). Thus, Dik and Duffy (2009) suggested that fostering meaning in people's work through career counselling interventions may contribute to promote social justice.

According to Ford and Smith (2007), meaning derive from the achievement of personal objectives that help people seeing themselves and their accomplishments as contributing to something greater. Steger, Dik, and Duffy (2012) identified three different levels of meaningful work according to the degree to which work is perceived as more than simply executing a task: work perceived has having (1) a goal in the organization, (2) a meaning in one's personal life, and (3) the potential to contributing to the common good. In fact, Steger (2016) stated that a core way to achieve meaning at work is to seeking the ways through which our work can contribute to a greater common good—that is, to enlarge one's self concern to include larger interests. However, Guichard (2013) highlighted that, if some people tend to consider the consequences of their career choice for the humanity and for distant others, most of them only take into consideration the implications that their career choice may have for their "near and dear". This is unfortunate considering that the desire to have a positive impact on the common good is consistently related to the experience of meaningful work (Grant, 2007).

Therefore, we believe that, by strongly encouraging people to link their talents to the perceived world needs, career counselling is likely to help them become employable and find sustainable and meaningful work. This has important implication, because meaningful work has been positively related to a wide range of positive outcomes both in terms of personal well-being and work satisfaction (see Steger, 2016, for a review). More broadly, altruism—comprised as attempts to benefiting someone else without expecting material rewards—toward family, friends, community and the humanity in general has been found to contributing to meaning in life (Xi et al., 2016). Especially, Xi and colleagues found that compared to altruism toward family, friends and community, altruism toward the humanity in general appear to be the most important predictor of meaning in life. Similarly, Jung and Heppner (2017) found that work mattering at the societal level (i.e., perception that one's work matter to the society) correlated stronger with meaning in work than work mattering at the interpersonal level (i.e., perception that one's work matter to our co-worker). Therefore, there is a strong interest in encouraging people to consider how their career can serve the greater good, both at the individual and societal levels.

A Call for Interventions

Due to the importance of the possible outcomes of finding meaning in one's career, Dik et al. (2015) encouraged career counsellors to stimulate their clients "to focus not only on personal fit when choosing a career but social fit as well" (p. 18). To achieve that goal, Dik and Duffy (2009) suggested to ask the client to answer several questions related to what is important for them in their life and what can be their purpose in life prior to help them connecting these aspects with their current or future work role. However, Guichard (2018) highlighted that we need to go beyond narrative and evocative interventions in order to help people understand how their career can contribute to the greater good.

More specifically, Kosine, Steger, and Duncan (2008) designed a purpose-centered intervention "Make Your Work Matter" to foster students' recognition of how their career can contribute to the greater good for the society. The intervention consisted of three modules: (a) a semi-structured interview conducted by the student with a trustworthy adult about the role of work in life, (b) a card sort assessment of personal values, and (c) a game to illustrate how each occupation contribute to the good of the society. This intervention was tested by Dik, Steger, Gibson, and Peisner (2011) in a pilot study conducted among eight-grade students. Results showed that students who participated in this intervention demonstrated greater improvement in their career development attitudes compared to their counterparts in the control group, but that no improvements were found regarding their sense of purpose, calling or prosocial attitudes. Therefore, new types of interventions are needed in order to help people perceive how their career development can contribute to meet the world's need.

Recently, Guichard (2018) suggested two interventions to meet the broader goal of achieving a universal human, sustainable, and fair development. The first intervention focuses on helping people and institutions implementing work and exchange systems with the lightest ecological impact. The second intervention consists of helping people contributing to the development of global humane activities. More precisely, Guichard (2018) highlighted potential guidelines for a group intervention among young people that consist first of an introduction on the current labor market that aim at fostering awareness on the importance for each human being to have access to a decent and humane work. Second, the intervention aims at fostering a reflection on (1) the possible ways to achieve goals such as those stated by the UN through work activities, (2) which of these activities they would like to take part in, (3) the talents they have to develop in order to achieve it, and (4) the ways to do so. In this chapter, we propose to develop and operationalize this later intervention through the development of the Sustainable Career Card Sort (SCCS), a card sort depicting the world's needs, based on the UN goals for sustainable development. Careers are here considered as sustainable when individuals' career decisions take into account ethical dimensions and their impacts on the greater good, particularly on global needs and the world urgencies. In this view, our acceptation of sustainable career differs from that of De Vos, Van der Heijden, and Akkermans (2018) who insists on sustainability in terms of continuity through time and work experiences.

The Sustainable Career Card Sort (SCCS)

"Where your talents and the needs of the world cross; there lies your vocation" said Aristotle. In this section, we propose a new career counselling intervention specifically designed to help the people link their talents and preferences to the world's needs. To do so, we propose to combine an assessment of the career clients' strengths with an assessment of the world's needs they would like to contribute to. To assess the clients' strengths, we rely on Dik et al. (2015) suggestion to use inventories such as the VIA strengths inventory (Peterson, Park, & Seligman, 2005) or the Clifton's StrengthsQuest/StrengthsFinder (Clifton, Anderson, & Schreiner, 2006) to promote a sense of meaning in clients' work. In fact, Littman-Ovadia and Steger (2010) suggested that cultivating one's character strengths at work consisted of a good way to facilitate meaning at work. To help the clients identifying which of the world's needs they would like to contribute to, we developed the Sustainable Career Card Sort (SCCS).

Card sorts appeared as a judicious way to identify to which broader goals the career clients would like to contribute to the greater good. In fact, this type of qualitative assessment has been repeatedly emphasized as an interesting method to foster an active role of the client in the processes of collecting and interpreting information in career counselling. Additionally, it offers immediate feedback to the client and the counsellor and is easily adaptable to the specific characteristics of the client (Chope, 2015; Gysbers, Heppner, & Johnston, 2014; Osborn, Kronholz, & Finklea, 2015; Stead & Davis, 2015). Beyond all these characteristics, card sorts appeared to be especially of high relevance due to their accessibility to all types of populations, including the marginalized one (Slaney & Mackinnon-Slaney, 1990, in Osborn et al., 2015). Moreover, Bellier-Teichmann (2017) emphasized that the use of images in card sorts is generally well appreciated by clients who found it original, concrete and funnier than simple text.

The SCCS is based on graphic illustrations of the UN's (2015) goals for sustainable development. It consists of 19 cards, each of them representing a goal. The intervention involves four stages. In a first stage participants are asked to sort the cards into three different categories ("not at all", "somewhat", and "totally") according to the degree to which they are sensitive to this goal. A blank card can also be added to represent a goal that is perceived as very relevant to the client but that is missing in the stack. In a second stage, participants are asked to make a ranking of the goals that they considered as "totally" sensitive, which allows identifying those to which they would like to contribute the most. In the third stage, counselees are encouraged to reflect on how they would like to contribute to these goals, and on how they think that their career choice can help them pursuing this direction. In the final stage, the career counsellor inquires how the client thinks his or her unique set of strengths can be put in action to contribute to this goal, both through their career choice and in their daily life.

The next section describes the procedure we followed to select the relevant items and graphic content for the SCCS.

Method

Validation Procedure

The validation procedure consisted of three steps: (1) identifying and selecting the goals, (2) identifying the relevant pictures, and (3) selecting the best pictures. The 17-UN goals and their 169 related sub targets were reviewed by the first author of this chapter in order to identify a limited number of goals to be addressed in the SCCS. This process resulted in the selection of 19 objectives. Nine of the UN goals were took as such (i.e., goals 1, 4, 6, 7, 12, 13, 14, 15), while five where split (2, 3, 8, 11, 16) to form distinct goals, and some of them were grouped together (5 and 10, second parts of goal 2 and 10). Finally, the part related to innovation on the goal 9 and the goal 17 were removed, since we consider that they consist of more of specific ways to achieve the other goals. In addition, "promoting a decent migration" (one of the targets of UN goal 10 "reducing the inequalities within and among countries") was added as a goal in itself, as we considered it as being a salient current concern and deserving therefore an explicit place in the SCCS. Table 2 displays the final selection of the 19 goals that constitute the SCCS. This final selection was submitted to the second author in order to reach consensus.

Once the goals composing the SCCS selected, possible illustrations were retrieved on the Internet. For each goal, two pictures were selected: one that represented the current (negative) state of the concern, and one that represented the desired (positive)

Table 2 Final selection of the 19 SCCS goals and rating for the corresponding image

SCCS goals		Positive image		Negative image		Image selected
		Ind. rating (%)	Group rating	Ind. rating (%)	Group rating	
1	Ending poverty	17.24	0	89.66	8	N
2	Ending hunger and improving nutrition	68.97	0	75.86	9	N
3	Allowing everyone to be healthy	89.66	2	79.31	9	N
4	Promoting well-being for all	82.76	8	48.28	1	P
5	Ensuring quality education for everyone	96.55	7	96.55	4	P
6	Reducing inequalities of all kinds	65.52	2	55.17	6	N
7	Ensuring availability of water sanitation for all	93.10	2	82.76	7	N
8	Ensuring access to sustainable energy for all	58.62	8	37.93	1	P
9	Promoting decent work for all	44.83	3	20.69	3	P[†]
10	Promoting sustainable economic growth	17.24	7	48.28	2	P
11	Promoting sustainable agriculture and industrialization	68.97	9	79.31	1	P
12	Building inclusive, safe, sustainable and resilient cities and communities	51.72	7	13.79	1	P
13	Ensuring sustainable production and consumption	58.62	5	37.93	4	P
14	Combatting climate change and its impacts	62.07	1	75.86	8	N
15	Protecting the oceans, seas and marine resources	93.10	0	96.55	9	N
16	Protecting the terrestrial ecosystem	96.55	3	62.07	6	N

(continued)

Table 2 (continued)

SCCS goals		Positive image		Negative image		Image selected
		Ind. rating (%)	Group rating	Ind. rating (%)	Group rating	
17	Promoting peace and combatting against all forms of violence	68.97	5	68.97	5	P*
18	Providing access to justice and inclusive institution for all	72.41	9	20.69	0	P
19	Promoting decent migration	44.83	1	96.55	8	N

Note Rates and percentage = number of students who spontaneously attributed the image to the goal at hand; image selected = image selected in the consensus; *N* = negative image; P = positive image; † = image selected based on individual ratings as no consensus could have been found among groups; * = images selected based on the discriminant power of the study, as neither group exercise nor ratings allowed to make a choice. Some groups rated both or neither images

state. For example, the goal 15 "Protecting the oceans, seas and marine resources" was illustrated both by polluted waters and by clean marine ecosystem. That led to total of 38 pictures. The relevance of the selection was then tested with a sample of 29 students completing a Master degree in career counselling psychology in a Swiss university (M_{age} = 28.24, *SD* = 6.95, 86.21% women). This procedure comprised two exercises lasting 45 and was carried out by the two authors of the study during a compulsory career counselling psychology class. In the first exercise, each student received a list comprising the 19-goals and was asked to read them carefully. After that, the 38 illustrations were randomly numbered displayed on a screen. The students were asked to indicate which pictures were most likely to illustrate each one of the 19 goals on the list (multiple responses were accepted). In the second exercise, the students were divided into nine groups of three to four participants. Each group received a leaflet displaying the 19 goals and the two images (positive and negative) that were initially selected to illustrate each of them. The groups were asked to reach a consensus about which image (positive or negative) appeared to be the most appropriate to illustrate each goal. The students also had the opportunity to comment on their choice.

At the end of the procedure, the authors of the study solicited the students' reactions regarding the two exercises and explained them the finality of this picture selection. The selected images were then forwarded to a graphic designer, in order to conceive flat design illustrations for each card. Instructions on how to use this card sort was then defined.

Analysis

Individual attributions of each picture to the different goals were computed for analyzing the outcomes of the first exercise. Group consensus for the best picture (positive or negative) were also computed and served as a basis for determining the positive or negative content of the image illustrating the goal at hand. When no consensus was found among groups, the authors referred to individual ratings in order to select the most appropriate image. Discriminating power of the images was also computed so to choose the more adequate type of image when neither group consensus nor individual ratings were able to help selecting an image. This power was estimated by dividing the numbers of correct individual ratings for one goal with the total number of ratings for the image.

Results

Individual Ratings

Percentage of individual ratings of the image showed a convergence between students and authors attribution of the images to a specific goal (positive images: $M = 62.42$, $SD = 27.00$; negative images: $M = 65.88$, $SD = 23.83$), demonstrating a relative validity for the assumed associations. Table 2 shows the ratio of students who associated the same images to the specific goals as the authors did. Results show that some images were attributed to various goals, sometimes due to the inclusiveness of the goals themselves. For example, the images showing poor households (negative image for the goal 12 "Building inclusive, safe, sustainable and resilient cities and communities") or working children (negative image for the goal 9 "Promoting decent work for all") were mostly attributed to the broader goal 1 "Ending poverty" (with respectively 26 and 19 ratings for this category).

Group Consensus

Results from the second exercise allowed to choose the content nature (positive or negative) of the images best representing the SCCS goals. The students considered that nine of the goals were best represented by an image displaying the current negative state, and that eight were best represented by a representation of the positive desired state. Interestingly, the chosen type of image did not always match the degree of spontaneous association referred in the first exercise. For example, individuals were more likely to associate the positive image to the goal 3 "Allowing everyone to be healthy" rather than the negative one, while the groups decided that the negative image represented best this objective.

Groups were not able to reach a consensus for the goals 9 "Promoting decent work for all" and 17 "Promoting peace and combatting against all forms of violence". As in the first exercise more students spontaneously attributed the positive image to the goal of "Promoting decent work for all," the positive type of content was kept. However, as in their comments, three groups of students indicated that neither images fitted the concept well for this goal, the image content was refined for the flat design support. The students' individual rating did not help to discriminate the positive or negative content for the goal "Promoting peace and combatting against all forms of violence" as they were equally rated in the first exercise. Therefore, we considered the discrimination power of these images. It appeared that the negative image was more attributed to other goals (ratio of 51.28%) than the positive one (66.67%). Consequently, we opted for the positive content to illustrate this goal. Among the selected images, 10 display a positive content for the goal that should be achieved and 9 a negative content reflecting the current state of the situation.

The selected images were then forwarded to a graphical designer with additional information. Especially, the images' content for the images 9, 10 and 12 was refined in order to better illustrate these concepts, as the individuals' ratings for these was quite low. Figure 1 display some examples of the final flat design images.

Fig. 1 Sample of the graphical illustrations for the selected goals

Discussion

This chapter intended to introduce a qualitative assessment tool, the SCCS, aiming to sensitize career clients to the ways their life and career could take into account and possibly contribute to serve the world's needs. In order to proceed to an initial validation of the tool, based on the UN 2030 agenda for global action (UN, 2015) we first identified 19 objectives for a sustainable world. Then, we submitted 38 positive or negative illustrations of these objectives to career counselling students, which led to the selection of the picture that best represents each goal. The final kit of cards consists of 19 items and one optional blank card—so as to add specific absent objectives. Nine of the selected goals were found to be better illustrated through a depiction of the current negative state of situation while ten appeared to be best represented by the hopeful positive state of situation for the future. The SCCS can then be used in career counselling through a four-stage intervention, asking the counselee to class each card according to its degree of subjective importance, to rank the most salient cards, and to reflect on how she or he can contribute to this goal, and especially regarding his or her personal forces.

Through this activity, our hope is that this kind of assessment serves both individuals living a more meaningful life and the goals for better world to be achieved. The card sort format seems particularly relevant to reach all kind of counselees, even the marginalized and underrepresented one and to help them identify how they can benefit the society and to derive meaning. In fact, a study conducted by Allan, Autin and Duffy (2014) among employed adults found that, regardless of their social class, most of the participants mentioned helping others and contributing to the greater good as the main source of meaning in their work.

In fact, even individuals in accomplishing apparently undesirable jobs for physical, social or moral reasons might still be able to secure and sustain a positive identity by reframing the meaning associated to their job, adjusting the weight attributed to the desirable and undesirable part of the job, or focusing on the non-stigmatized features of the job and its social implications (Ashforth & Kreiner, 1999, 2003). By asking the people to what extent they can contribute to the selected objective through their daily life, we also wanted to emphasize that work is not the only way to serve others and that "this goal can be pursued within any life role" (Dik & Duffy, 2009, p. 428). However, one may wonder if reflecting on how one's choice can contribute to sustainable development may be more difficult for people who cannot freely choose their occupation or for people whose job only serves a survival function.

However, these results are limited by the small size of the sample and its nature as the participants were university students, and not unemployed or marginalized people. Also, it appeared that we did not take into consideration the students' cultural background, which may have impacted the selection of the images. Moreover, the validation of the tool is only at its initial stage: the SCCS has not yet been systematically tested in a real career counselling setting, and additional information is needed in order to carefully address all the intervention stages, and mainly to find the best inputs for the discussion on the sorting exercise (i.e. how to link meaningful world issues with personal career issues).

Implications for Research

The above-mentioned limits suggest that the relevance of the SCCS and its efficiency to promote a sense of meaning among career clients should be tested in a multidisciplinary perspective. In fact, McMahon, Watson and Lee (2018) highlighted the need to provide a stronger evidence-based for qualitative career assessments. More precisely, they suggested that:

> qualitative career assessment researchers (a) underpin their research with a theoretical framework that inform the research aims, research questions and methodology; (b) carefully consider the characteristics of the research sample; (c) employ research models that are culturally valid for the population being researched; (d) ensure research rigor by explicitly applying criteria for reliability and validity in quantitative research or trust-worthiness in qualitative research; and (e) consider ethical issues related to the research and, where appropriate, obtain ethical approval to conduct the research.

As the proposed intervention is innovating, well-documented case studies appears as a judicious way to start assessing its impact in career counselling (Stead et al., 2012). This could be done through recording the intervention and administrating questionnaires on meaning in life and on mattering—such as the Work and Meaning Inventory (WAMI; Steger et al., 2012) and the Work Mattering Scale (WMS; Jung & Heppner, 2017)—prior and after the completion of the intervention, as well as three months later. Participants' characteristics would have to be described in a detailed way so as to have a better understanding of the personal and demographic factors that can influence his or her understanding of these concepts (Dik & Shimizu, 2018). Moreover, Gysbers et al. (2014) highlighted that the efficiency of card sorts strongly depends on the career counsellor's abilities to lead the clients to new insights and ideas. Therefore, the career counsellor's educational and professional background would also have to be documented.

Implications for Practice

We believe that the SCCS may be a useful tool to complement the traditional forms of career assessment, in order to fuel career clients with the sense that their upcoming career can be a way to consider and possibly serve the world needs. In fact, Dik and Duffy (2009) highlighted that "the desire to find a job that has meaning and purpose can be an important component in the career decision-making process" (p. 432). However, this type of intervention may also be useful for career changers and those who are searching for more meaning in their current work. Standard career counselling interventions usually comprise three main stages: (1) clarifying the person's needs and goals; (2) investigating the person's life path, interests, abilities, values and personality traits, and encouraging information seeking; (3) reasoning about the options, decision-making and planning (Masdonati, Massoudi, & Rossier, 2009). The SCCS can be useful at each of these stages. In the first stage, it can be introduced as a way to help clarifying the goals the person is trying to achieve through career counselling, and to suggest a connection between his/her needs and the world's ones. It can also be presented as part of the investigation step, for example as a complement to the assessment of personal values and interests. Finally, it can also be used during the third stage of counselling, as an additional criteria for decision-making or to reinforce the meaningfulness of a career choice.

However, practitioners should pay attention to present the world's needs as challenges and not as threats. In fact, Post (2005) reveals that altruistic behaviors and emotions are associated with high levels of well-being, health and longevity as long as people are not submerged by the helping tasks. In this sense, it is worth noting that people who developed the habit to think at issues as challenges instead of threats are more likely to think and act in productive way and to diminish negative stress (Drach-Zahavy & Erez, 2002; Ford & Smith, 2007). Therefore, it is important to help people developing a sense of trust in their capacities to progress toward a goal (Ford & Smith, 2007). This is why the proposed intervention suggests combining the use of the SCCS with a strengths-based assessment such as the VIA-Strengths inventory (Peterson et al., 2005). Last but not least, it appears that the suggested intervention is also likely to develop a sense of meaning for the career counsellors themselves as they can perceive their job not only as a way to match people with preferable occupations, but as a way to match talents with the world's needs, and thus contributing to the personal well-being of the person they encounter and to that of the world they live in. In fact, Dik and Duffy (2009) suggested that adopting a social justice framework may help counselling psychologist to see their own work as a calling.

Conclusion

The current world is facing some great challenges that need to be tackled as soon as possible. In this chapter, we attempted to provide career counsellor with a new intervention tool, the SCCS, aiming at helping clients connecting their talents to the world needs so that they can contribute to foster decent and sustainable humanity for all. Future studies should focus on the efficacy of this tool to foster a sense of meaning in a multicultural way.

References

Allan, B. A., Autin, K. L., & Duffy, R. D. (2014). Examining social work meaning within the psychology of working framework. *Journal of Career Assessment, 22,* 543–561. https://doi.org/10.1177/1069072713514811.

Ashforth, B. E., & Kreiner, G. E. (2003). Profane or profound? Finding meaning in dirty work. In B. J. Dik, Z. S. Byrne, & M. F. Steger (Eds.), *Purpose and meaning in the workplace* (pp. 127–149). Washington, DC: American Psychological Association. https://doi.org/10.1037/14183-007.

Ashforth, B. E., & Kreiner, G. E. (1999). "How can you do it?": Dirty work and the challenge of constructing a positive identity. *Academy of Management Review, 24,* 413–434. https://doi.org/10.2307/259134.

Bellier-Teichmann, T. (2017). *Evaluer les difficultés, les besoins et les ressources chez les patients souffrant de troubles psychiques: une approche centrée sur le rétablissement* [Assessing difficulties, needs and resources in patients with mental disorders: A recovery-focused approach]. Doctoral dissertation, University of Lausanne, Lausanne, Swizerland.

Blustein, D. L. (2001). Extending the reach of vocational psychology: Toward an inclusive and integrated psychology of working. *Journal of Vocational Behavior, 59,* 171–182. https://doi.org/10.1006/jvbe.2001.1823.

Blustein, D. L. (2006). *The psychology of working: A new perspective for career development, counseling, and public policy*. Mahwah, NJ: Lawrence Erlbaum Associates.

Blustein, D. L., Kenny, M. E., Di Fabio, A., & Guichard, J. (2018). Expanding the Impact of the psychology of working: Engaging psychology in the struggle for decent work and human rights. *Journal of Career Assessment*. https://doi.org/10.1177/1069072718774002.

Chope, R. C. (2015). Card sorts, sentence completions, and other qualitative assessments. In P. J. Hartung, M. L. Savickas, & W. B. Walsh (Eds.), *APA handbook of career intervention* (Vol. 2, pp. 71–84). Applications Washington, DC: American Psychological Association.

Clifton, D. O., Anderson, E. C., & Schreiner, L. A. (2006). *StrengthsQuest: Discover and develop your strengths in academics, career, and beyond*. New York, NY: Gallup Press.

De Vos, A., Van der Heijden, B. I. J. M., & Akkermans, J. (in press, 2018). Sustainable careers: Toward a conceptual model. *Journal of Vocational Behavior.* https://doi.org/10.1016/j.jvb.2018.06.011.

Di Fabio, A., & Maree, J. G. (2016). Using a transdisciplinary interpretive lens to broaden reflections on alleviating poverty and promoting decent work. *Frontiers in Psychology, 7*. https://doi.org/10.3389/fpsyg.2016.00503.

Dik, B. J., & Duffy, R. D. (2009). Calling and vocation at work: Definitions and prospects for research and practice. *The Counseling Psychologist, 37,* 424–450. https://doi.org/10.1177/0011000008316430.

Dik, B. J., Duffy, R. D., Allan, B. A., O'Donell, M. B., Shim, Y., & Steger, M. F. (2015). Purpose and meaning in career development: Applications. *The Counseling Psychologist, 43,* 558–585. https://doi.org/10.1177/0011000014546872.

Dik, B. J., & Shimizu, A. B. (2018). Multiple meanings of calling: Next steps for studying an evolving construct. *Journal of Career Assessment*. https://doi.org/10.1177/1069072717748676.

Dik, B. J., Steger, M. F., Gibson, A., & Peisner, W. (2011). Make Your Work Matter: Development and pilot evaluation of a purpose-centered career education intervention. *New Directions for Youth Development, 132,* 59–73. https://doi.org/10.1002/yd.428.

Drach-Zahavy, A., & Erez, M. (2002). Challenge versus threat effects on the goal-performance relationship. *Organizational Behavior and Human Decision Processes, 88,* 667–682. https://doi.org/10.1016/S0749-5978(02)00004-3.

Duffy, R. D., Blustein, D. L., Diemer, M. A., & Autin, K. L. (2016). The psychology of working theory. *Journal of Counseling Psychology, 63,* 127–148. https://doi.org/10.1037/cou0000140.

Fouad, N. A., Gerstein, L. H., & Toporek, R. L. (2006). Social justice and counseling psychology in context. In R. L. Toporek, L. H. Gerstein, N. A. Fouad, G. Roysicar, & T. Israel (Eds.), *Handbook of social justice in counseling psychology: Leadership, vision, and action* (pp. 1–16). London, UK: Sage Publications.

Ford, M. E., & Smith, P. R. (2007). Thriving with a social purpose: An integrative approach to the development of optimal human functioning. *Educational Psychologist, 42,* 153–171. https://doi.org/10.1080/00461520701416280.

Grant, A. M. (2007). Relational job design and the motivation to make a prosocial difference. *Academy of Management Review, 32,* 293–417. https://doi.org/10.5465/amr.2007.24351328.

Guichard, J. (2013). *Career education, education, and dialogues for a fair and sustainable human development.* Paper presented at the Inaugural conference of the UNESCO Chair of Life Long Guidance and Counseling, November 26, 2013, University of Wroclaw, Poland.

Guichard, J. (2016). Life- and working-design interventions for constructing a sustainable humane world. *Studia Parodoznawcze/Journal of Counsellogy, 5,* 179–190.

Guichard, J. (2018). Quelles interventions d'accompagnement à l'orientation pour contribuer à un développement mondial, humain, equitable et durable?

Gysbers, N. C., Heppner, M. J., & Johnston, J. A. (2014). Gathering client information using an occupational card sort. In N. C. Gysbers, M. J. Heppner, & J. A. Johnston (Eds.), *Career counseling: Contexts, processes, and techniques* (4th ed., pp. 209–222). Alexandria, VA: ACA.

International Association of Applied Psychology. (2008). *Universal declaration of ethical principles for psychologists.* Retrieved from: http://www.iupsys.net/about/governance/universal-declaration-of-ethical-principles-for-psychologists.html#preamble.

International Labour Office (ILO). (2001). *Reducing the decent work deficit. International conference 89th session 2001 (Report to the Director General).* Geneva, Switzerland: International Labour Office.

Jung, A.-K., & Heppner, M. J. (2017). Development and validation of the Work Mattering Scale (WMS). *Journal of Career Assessment, 25,* 467–483. https://doi.org/10.1177/1069072715599412.

Kosine, N., Steger, M. F., & Duncan, S. (2008). Purpose-centered career development: A comprehensive model. *Professional School Counseling, 12,* 133–136. https://doi.org/10.5330/PSC.n.2010-12.133.

Littman-Ovadia, H., & Steger, M. F. (2010). Character strengths and well-being among volunteers and employees: Towards an integrative model. *Journal of Positive Psychology, 5,* 419–430. https://doi.org/10.1080/17439760.2010.516765.

Masdonati, J., Massoudi, K., & Rossier, J. (2009). Effectiveness of career counseling and the impact of the working alliance. *Journal of Career Development, 36,* 183–203. https://doi.org/10.1177/0894845309340798.

Massoudi, K., Abessolo, M., Amenyona Atitsogbe, K., Banet, E., Bollmann, G., Dauwalder, J.-P. … Rossier, J. (in press). A value-centered approach of decent work. In V. Cohen-Scali et al. (Eds.), *Life-and-career designing for sustainable development and decent work.* New York, NY: Springer.

McMahon, M., Watson, M., & Lee, M. C. Y. (2018). Qualitative career assessment: A review and reconsideration. *Journal of Vocational Behavior.* https://doi.org/10.1016/j.jvb.2018.03.009.

Osborn, D. S., Kronholz, J. F., & Finklea, J. T. (2015). Card sorts. In M. McMahon & M. Watson (Eds.), *Career assessment: Qualitative approaches* (pp. 81–88). Boston, MA: Sense Publishers.

Peterson, C., Park, N., & Seligman, M. E. P. (2005). Assessment of character strengths. In G. P. Koocher, J. C. Norcross, & S. Hill (Eds.), *Psychologists' desk reference* (2nd ed., pp. 93–98). New York, NY: Oxford University Press.

Post, S. G. (2005). Altruism, happiness, and health: It's good to be good. *International Journal of Behavioral Medicine, 12,* 66–77. https://doi.org/10.1207/s15327558ijbm1202_4.

Slaney, R. B., & Mackinnon-Slaney, F. (1990). The use of vocational card sorts in career counseling. In E. C. Watkins & V. Campbell (Eds.), *Testing in counseling practice* (pp. 317–371). Hillsdale, NJ: Erlbaum.

Stead, G. B., & Davis, B. L. (2015). Qualitative career assessment: Research evidence. In M. McMahon & M. Watson (Eds.), *Career assessment: Qualitative approaches* (pp. 21–30). Boston, MA: Sense Publishers.

Stead, G. B., Perry, J. C., Munka, L. M., Bonnett, H. R., Shiban, A. P., & Care, E. (2012). Qualitative research in career development: Content analysis from 1990 to 2009. *International Journal for Educational and Vocational Guidance, 12,* 105–122. https://doi.org/10.1007/S10775-011-9196-1.

Steger, M. F. (2016). Creating meaning and purpose at work. In L. G. Oades, M. F. Steger, A. Delle Fave, & J. Passmore (Eds.), *The Wiley Blackwell handbook of the psychology of positivity and strengths-based approaches at work* (pp. 60–81). Hoboken, NJ: Wiley.

Steger, M. F., & Dik, B. J. (2010). Work as meaning. In P. A. Linley, S. Harrington, & N. Page (Eds.), *Oxford handbook of positive psychology and work* (pp. 131–142). Oxford, UK: Oxford University Press.

Steger, M. F., Dik, B. J., & Duffy, R. D. (2012). Measuring meaningful work: The Work and Meaning inventory (WAMI). *Journal of Career Assessment, 20,* 322–337. https://doi.org/10.1177/1069072711436160.

Steger, M. F., Frazier, P., Oishi, S., & Kaler, M. (2006). The Meaning in Life Questionnaire: Assessing the presence of and search for meaning in life. *Journal of Counseling Psychology, 53,* 80–93. https://doi.org/10.1037/0022-0167.53.1.80.

UN (2015). *Transforming our world: The 2030 Agenda for sustainable development.* Retrieved from https://sustainabledevelopment.un.org/post2015/transformingourworld.

Xi, J., Lee, M., LeSuer, W., Barr, P., Newton, K., & Poloma, M. (2016). Altruism and existential well-being. *Applied Research in Quality of Life, 12,* 67–88. https://doi.org/10.1007/s11482-016-9453-z.

Innovative Career Counselling Interventions

Drawing on the Innovative Moments Model to Explain and Foster Career Construction Counselling

Paulo Cardoso, Miguel M. Gonçalves and Mark L. Savickas

Abstract Career Construction Counselling (CCC) is a narrative intervention that supports individuals in the elaboration of narrative identity and career construction. CCC theory, research, and practice has benefited from the Innovative Moments Model (IMM) to explain client change. Similar to CCC, the IMM is grounded on a narrative conception of human functioning, in which psychological difficulties arise from problematic self-narratives that constrain meaning-making. Change occurs when clients challenge problematic self-narratives and construct new meanings that lead to new ways of behaving, thinking, or feeling. These novelties are termed innovative moments. The integration of IMM into the study of CCC has provided empirical evidence about the processes of client change throughout this intervention. Findings show that the transformation of a client's self-narrative is associated with the aims of each session that involve a movement from a focus on structuring the past to an increased engagement in projecting the future. Moreover, results suggest the possibility of using IMs as process markers to guide counsellors in facilitating client change during counselling sessions. This chapter explains the contribution of IMM to CCC theory, research, and practice; describes the IM framework; reviews CCC process research using the IMM; and finally discusses research implications for CCC theory and practice are discussed.

Keywords Career construction counselling · Innovative moments · Client change · Career research · Narrative change · Life design

P. Cardoso (✉)
Department of Psychology, CEFAGE, University of Évora, Évora, Portugal
e-mail: pmscar@gmail.com

M. M. Gonçalves
School of Psychology, University of Minho, Braga, Portugal

M. L. Savickas
Northeast Ohio Medical University, Rootstown, USA

J. G. Maree (ed.), *Handbook of Innovative Career Counselling*,
https://doi.org/10.1007/978-3-030-22799-9_29

Drawing on the Innovative Moments Model to Explain and Foster Career Construction Counselling

Career Construction Counselling (CCC; Savickas, 2011, 2019) focuses on individuals' narratives to encourage the autobiographical author to reflexively transform life themes and extend their occupational plots by identifying fitting settings, possible scripts, and future scenarios. CCC aims to move clients beyond the reflection involved in guidance and education to a reflexivity that enables them to actively master what they passively suffer. CCC discourse proposes that *reflection* within one's current perspective can lead to small, first-order changes; whereas *reflexivity* brings a new perspective that can lead to transformative second-order change (Fraser & Solovey, 2007).

The CCC model developed by theorizing successful practices. Evidence resulting from practice, client feedback, and case analysis allowed improvement of the CCC model and the development of manuals for guiding practitioners (Savickas, 2015; Savickas & Hartung, 2012). Research has shown that CCC yields good outcomes in individual (Cardoso, Gonçalves, Duarte, Silva, & Alves, 2016; Cardoso, Silva, Gonçalves & Duarte, 2014a, 2014b; Rehfuss, Del Corso, Galvin & Wykes, 2011) and group interventions (Barclay & Stoltz, 2015; Cardoso, Janeiro, & Duarte, 2017; Di Fabio & Maree, 2011; Obi, 2015). Moreover, research also suggests that change is related to a client's level of development (Cardoso et al., 2017), the quality of collaboration (Cardoso et al., 2017; Taveira, Ribeiro, Cardoso, & Silva, 2017) and the complexity of a client's problem (Cardoso et al., 2014a, 2014b). Finally, research has allowed the description of how client change occurs during the intervention (Cardoso et al., 2014a, 2014b, 2016).

Two factors have contributed to the development of research on CCC. On one hand, the development of CCC manuals (Savickas, 2015; Savickas & Hartung, 2012) allowed the conditions to ensure greater control of the intervention procedures and, therefore, enhance the internal validity of research findings'. On the other hand, the integration of the IM framework (Gonçalves, Matos, & Santos, 2009) into CCC allowed the construction of conceptual and assessment tools, such as the Innovative Moments Coding System (Gonçalves, Ribeiro, Mendes, Matos & Santos, 2011) and the Return to Problem Coding System (Gonçalves, Ribeiro, Stiles et al., 2011), that made possible the analysis and description of client change. This knowledge has been fundamental for theory and practice. What we now know about CCC effectiveness, its determinants and how change evolves during the intervention enriches CCC theory. This knowledge also facilitates the use of markers for guiding practice and improving counsellors' skills.

The purpose of this chapter is to present the contribution of the Innovative Moments Model (IMM; Gonçalves et al., 2009) for CCC theory, research and practice. We begin by presenting the Innovative Moments framework. Then the CCC model is described, followed by the presentation of the typical sequence of client change. In the closing section we suggest how to use the knowledge on client change to evoke and expand innovative moments.

Clients Change from the Innovative Moments Perspective

The IMM was developed in the context of psychotherapy process and outcome research and later applied to vocational counselling by using a series of systematic case studies (Cardoso et al., 2014a, 2014b, 2016). The main assumption of this model is that human beings shape important meanings in their lives and identities by authoring narratives (Bruner, 1990; McAdams, 1999; White, 2007). These life narratives are a non-representative sample of the persons' autobiographical memories (Singer, Blagov, Berry, & Oost, 2013). The way these autobiographical memories connect to the self shapes personal identity (Habermas & Bluck, 2000; McAdams 1993; Smorti & Fioretti, 2016). It is assumed that memories unrelated to the self tend to be disregarded, while memories attuned to the person are easily integrated in the person identity (Pasupathi, Mansour, & Brubaker, 2007). This constructive process, which first crystallizes around end of adolescence (Habermas & Bluck, 2000), remains a life-long task. In psychopathology, life narratives tend to be dysfunctional (see Neimeyer, Herrero, & Botella, 2006 on several types of narrative construction disorders), often lacking flexibility and becoming too rigid When this occurs, individuals face what White and Epston (1990) termed a problem-saturated life narrative, in which the identity of the person is somehow "colonized" by the problematic contents. Thus, memories and events akin to the problematic content are easily adjusted to the self, validating the dysfunctional self-concept, while events with meanings incongruent with the self are treated as trivial, or just ignored. When meanings discrepant from the problem-saturated narrative emerge, unique outcomes occur (White & Epston, 1990). In these moments the person thinks, behaves, relates, or feels differently from what could be expected based on the rigid narrative identity. Innovative moments (IMs) are the empirical operationalization of these exceptions and novelties.

Studies on IM development in psychotherapy allow the identification of seven different types of innovation, organized into three developmental levels (see Gonçalves et al., 2017, Table 1).

Level 1 IMs occur when clients differentiate themselves from the problematic pattern (or the problem-saturated narrative). Using examples from career counselling cases (Cardoso, 2014a, 2014b, 2016), these level 1 IMs can emerge in a form of specific actions (e.g. "I took those tests, passed them all, and did great on all of them", Action 1 IM), as reflections of meaning (e.g. "But it just terrifies me to think about it, because I'm just afraid that it'll suck", Reflection 1 IM), or as rejections of the previous problematic meaning-making, or people who may support it (e.g. "I'm not an accountant. I'm not an investment banker, I'm not an engineer, right?", Protest 1 IM).

Level 2 IMs contain more than just a differentiation from the problematic pattern in that the new meanings center on how the change could be expanded. Usually, this emerges in two possible forms: a contrasting self or a change process. A contrasting self occurs when the client narrates a positive contrast between a problematic self-facet and a new adaptive facet. To follow the previous example, a client may state

Table 1 Examples of innovative moments

IMs level	Subtype	Definition	Examples
Level 1 IMs (creating distance from the problem)	Action 1	Performed and intended actions to overcome the problem	C: This weekend I was able to talk to my husband about the possibility of leaving my job
	Reflection 1	New understandings of the problem	C: I realized that changing my job wouldn't necessarily leave my family in a helpless situation
	Protest 1	Objecting to the problem and its assumptions	C: I've had enough of worrying about the others. What about my life, my plans, where do they fit?
Level 2 IMs (centered on the change)	Action 2	Generalization into the future and other life dimensions of good outcomes (performed or projected actions)	CC: The implementation of the new career plans is changing your way of living? C: Yes, yes. I am starting to see that I can't forget about myself, not only at work but also in other dimensions of my own life. Before I just did tried to answer to everbody's needs but now I am making time to do things that I really enjoy, that actually make me feel alive
	Reflection 2	Contrasting the self (what changed?) OR Transformation process (how/why change occurred?)	C: Yes, these sessions have helped me to see my indecision otherwise. That makes me feel good, makes me believe that I will be able to solve the problem
	Protest 2	Assertiveness and empowerment	C: Now it's time to fight for myself, of choosing what I feel is the best for me. I also want to be happy, feel fulfilled, just be me
Level 3 IMs (consolidating change)	Reconceptualization	Meta-positions where the self is repositioned outside the problematic experience and also understands the processes involved in this transformation	C: Not knowing which direction to take, or which decisions and choices to make to find myself… It made me feel confused, without peace. Now it's different. To know where we are, what we want and the career we want to embrace gives us peace and tranquility

Adapted with permission from Montesano, Oliveira, and Gonçalves (2017) that "Now I am more decided than before" (Reflection 2). A change process refers to the identification of what has been allowing the person to make a significant change. Following the previous example, it could be "I've learned a lot about my interests" (Reflection 2 IM). Level 2 IMs, may also occur as reflections (e.g. ' I've kind of realized that I have to do some other job first if I want to go into that industry", Reflection 2 IM), as protest that empower positioning of the self (e.g. "I'm in charge of my own actions", Protest 2 IM), or as actions that envision the change process in the future (e.g. "It was… something I always wanted, to study abroad… an experience for a few months, to stay there for a few months", Action 2 IM).

Eventually, level 3 IMs occur when a client articulates a contrasting self with a change process, that is, the two components of level 2 IMs. Continuing with the examples from previous career counselling case studies, a level 3 IM could be: "I knew before that I wanted something related to Biology, but I had not searched. And I knew it was more Biology because I liked the area more. Because it was something that I really wanted to do, but now I actually like it, I have been looking into jobs, those that Marine Biology leads to, and one of them was working at a zoo, and so". Previously, this type of IM was termed reconceptualization (Gonçalves & Ribeiro, 2012), and important developmental functions were associated with this type of IM. This IM involves a contrast between the past problematic self with an emergent adaptive one, which allows the person to solve their ambivalence on change, by favoring the last. Moreover, in describing the change process, the person reports an agentic role in which the client constructs the change and not something that happens to her or him. Finally, this IM bridges the past with the present and the future in a meaningful way. Although there is no research on this topic, we believe level 3 IMs are probably similar to what McAdams (2001) referred to as redemptive sequences, in which a narrative turns a negative event in people lives into something positive.

Finally, research on psychotherapy has shown that level 1 IMs are typical of the initial phase of successful psychotherapy and gradually pave the way to level 2 IMs, with level 3 IMs emerging after mid-treatment (Gonçalves, Ribeiro, Mendes, et al., 2011). Poor outcome cases usually have a higher presence of level 1 IMs, but level 2 and 3 IMs do not emerge or have a residual presence.

Career Construction Counselling

CCC and IMM share a narrative perspective. In this epistemological matrix, career is conceptualized as the macronarrative that organizes self-experience across the life span. CCC interventions aims at rewriting life narratives to change perspective and facilitate the construction of career plans that contribute to the process of self-organization as they provide meaning to life (Kelly, 1955).

In CCC, constructing career plans involves a process that evolves across three phases (Savickas, 2011). In the first phase, the main career counselling tasks are to support the formulation of career problems and the exploration of career constructs such as needs, interests, and values. After problem formulation, counsellors use the

Career Construction Interview (CCI; Savickas, 2011a), a semi-structured interview that evokes self-making and career constructing episodes through the exploration of the following five topics: (1) role models to explore possible selves; (2) magazines, television shows, and websites to indicate manifest interests in work environments and activities; (3) current favorite story from a book or movie to explore plans to script the career transition; (4) quotes or mottos to examine self-advice; and (5) early recollections to provide perspective on concerns related to the career transition (Savickas, 2015). The second counselling task in this phase, is to evoke and explore career constructs including needs, interest, or aptitudes.

The second phase involves two main tasks: reconstruction of a career portrait and career plans elaboration. To facilitate career portrait reconstruction, client and counsellor deepen the exploration of life episodes to identify life themes, that is, the identification of the core problem or set of problems in life as well as the means the clients finds to achieve the solution (Csikszetmihalyi & Beattie, 1979). In a narrative approach to career counselling the identification of life themes that link events and experience across the career enables clients to rewrite their macronarrative. In vocational behavior, this process is revealed in the relationships between needs, interests, and goals. Indeed, life themes emerge in such relationship where needs are expressions of core issues structured early in life (past), while career goals reveal the proposed solutions to such problems through using the work role (future). In turn, interests represent tools the client uses (present) to pursue goals and, thereby, satisfy needs. Thus, helping clients develop awareness of the relationship between their needs, interests, and career plans is critical for rewriting a narrative identity (McAdams, 1993) that links the past, the present and the future with continuity and coherence. As clients projects the self into the future through career plans the second task of this phase is achieved.

The third phase involves the tasks of reviewing actions intended to implement career plans, encouraging career construction, and promoting reflection on changes achieved and the factors underpinning such changes. In this way, counsellors foster clients' reflexivity concerning the change process by positioning clients as observers of their own path to construct a comprehensive self-narrative.

Drawing on the Innovative Moments Model

To Research Client Change

The trans-theoretical nature of IMM with its narrative conception of change facilitates the contribution of this framework to CCC theory, research, and practice. The integration of IMM into CCC began by using the Innovative Moments Coding System (IMCS; Gonçalves et al., 2011) to analyze and describe IMs evolution in case studies intensively analyzed (Cardoso et al., 2014a, 2014b, 2016). Findings showed a pattern of narrative transformation characterized by gradual increase of narrative novelty, that is IMs, throughout the intervention. In phase I, Level 1 IMs predominate in that, Reflection 1 IMs occur with higher frequency yet Action 1 and Protest 1 also occur to a lesser extent. In phase II, Level 1 IMs still occur but, gradually, Level 2 MIs become more salient, suggesting the importance of Level 1 narrative elaboration to sustain the emergence of more complex novelty in the narratives. Among Level 2 IMs, Reflection 2 IMs occur in higher proportion relative to Protest 2 and Action 2. In phase 3, Level 2 IMs remain the most frequent narrative innovation while the proportion of Level 1 IMs remains high. In this intervention phase, Level 3 IMs emerges when counsellors invite clients to describe the changes they have achieved and the processes underlying these changes.

In short, findings reveal a pattern of clients' change evolving from level 1 IMs to higher levels of narrative elaboration (Level 2 and 3). Level 1 IMs presence throughout all the intervention also suggests the importance of this type of narrative elaboration to sustain the emergence of higher levels of narrative novelty. Moreover, results revealed a parallel between the evolution of IMs and the counselling tasks of each CCC phase and, therefore, underlying counsellors' role as facilitators of client change.

To Describe Client Change

Despite its exploratory nature, the case studies analyzed intensively from the IMM perspective were important for the development of theory on client change during CCC. Indeed, the empirical evidence from these cases, other case studies (Cardoso, 2012; Cardoso, Savickas, & Gonçalves, in press; Savickas, 2016a, b), and our own experience as counsellors allowed the elaboration of a model that describes clients' general progression in CCC from the perspective of IMs (Fig. 1).

The model depicts a parallel between the sequence of career counselling tasks and the evolution of IMs throughout the intervention. Clients' progress is characterized by a particular level and certain types of IMs within each of the three intervention phases. In the first phase, counselling tasks related to problem formulation and to exploration of career constructs in the clients' life episodes evoke Level 1 IMs (Action 1, Reflection 1 and Protest 1). Indeed, the support of career problems formulation prompts Reflection 1 IMs as this counselling task involves exploring the career issue's causes and consequences and encouraging new perspectives on career problems.

In this phase, the prevalence of Reflection 1 IMs also results from initial exploration of clients' needs, goals, interests or aptitudes, as revealed in Vanda's words when life episodes on manifest interests were evoked:

Vanda—*Marine Biology, which is something I like a lot. Because I like sea animals a lot, it's something I like a lot* (Reflection 1).

Occasionally, Action 1 IMs occur when clients refer to past attempts to manage career construction difficulties. Protest 1 IMs may also emerge when clients express the first critical positions in relation to the problem or the people who support it. In the following example Ryan criticizes colleagues' attitudes relative to work:

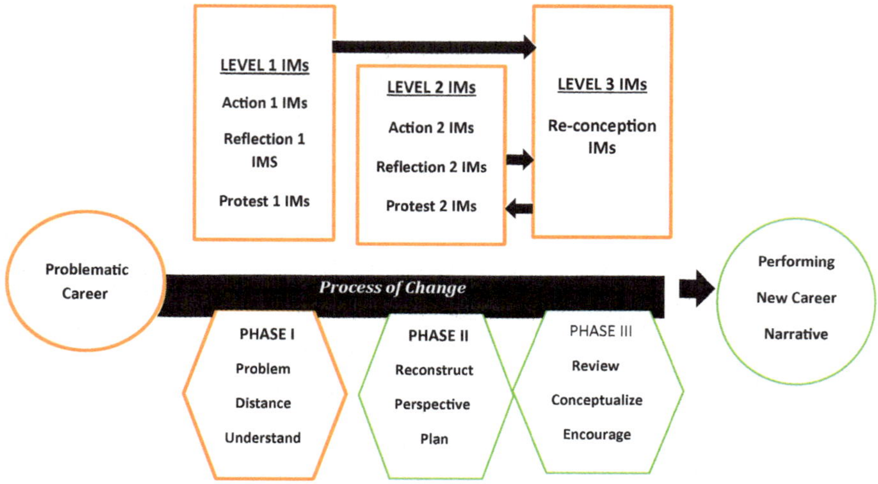

Fig. 1 Procedures and tasks in the Construction of Career Change

Right, exactly, and I can't help it. And then they don't like when you talk and it's like, hey, I get my work done, you know, I do my job. I've, you know, I've worked my way up fairly quickly (Protest 1).

In the second phase, Level 1 IMs still occur and create a solid ground necessary to sustain the emergence of Level 2 IMs. The resolution of counselling tasks related to career portrait reconstruction and the elaboration of career plans may also explain the increasing proportion of Level 2 IMs. In fact, the focus on the construction of a continuous and coherent self-narrative facilitate the emergence of Reflection 2 IMs, such as the elaboration of a new self-representations, references to adaptive thoughts (e.g. Michael - "If I see a lack of direction, then I'll go ahead and just say I'll take it and do the best that I can", Reflection 2) and feelings of well-being as consequences of change. At the end of phase II, clients design the first sketches of new career plans (Action 2 IMs) or may express Protest 2 IMs to affirm career plans as they reposition themselves toward the problem. The words of Michael illustrate the emergence of a new position towards the problem: "Why would I bother? That's my life, you know (Protest 2)".

Finally, in CCC third phase, Level 1 IMs and Level 2 IMs are still present, prompted by the tasks of reviewing actions intended to implement career plans and encouraging career construction. In fact, these counselling task resolutions imply the continuous elaboration of career problems causes and consequences, the expression of adaptive thoughts or references to intentions to fight the problem (Reflection 1 IMs). Emerging in lower proportion may be critiques against the problem or people who support it (Protest 1). These counselling tasks also allow a continuous elaboration of self-representation as well as references to self-worth or feelings of well-being resulting from changes achieved (Reflection 2). Positions of assertiveness and empowerment (Protest 2) also occur, strengthening the personal agency needed to face the challenges of career plans implementation. At the end of the third phase, Level 3 IMs emerge as clients reconceptualize change in a dialogue about the changes achieved and the factors underpinnings such changes. In the following example Maria refers her understanding about how to overcome ambivalence in career and in other life domains:

Maria—*To know where we are, what we want and the career we want to embrace gives us peace and tranquility. It is not just the career, though, because relationships involve hard work, too…it is the importance of knowing which direction things must take. It makes me feel uncomfortable, not knowing which direction to take, or which decisions and choices to make to find myself. I don't want to stray from myself, I don't. There are so many contingencies that can separate us from ourselves* (Reconceptualization IM).

As mentioned, level 3 IMs evocation aims to strength an integrated representation of the change process in which clients emerge as authors of their own change, not just actors in it. This fosters a sense of personal agency and authority which is important in dealing with the challenges involved in implementing career plans.

To Facilitate Client Change

The sequential model of client change, showing the parallel between counselling tasks and client's narrative transformation, may be used as a heuristic for guiding process-oriented interventions. This practice focuses on meaning (re)construction in which counsellors take into account intervention process markers to decide what to say or do moment-by-moment in the session (Montesano, Oliveira & Gonçalves, 2017). On the one hand, IMs work as markers for expanding and reinforcing client change throughout the intervention (Cardoso et al., 2014a). On the other hand, counsellors may refer to the pattern of IMs evolution to adjust the intervention to a client's level of narrative change. Next, we draw on process-oriented methods to describe practical implications resulting from our knowledge about the sequence of client change.

Evoking and Expanding IMs

As noted, process-oriented interventions could be implemented by using IMs as markers for evoking and expanding client change. In that sense, counsellors may use three different kinds of dialogue (Montesano et al., 2017): (1) identifying and evaluating the effects of IMs, (2) highlighting and contrasting self-positions, and (3) fostering a meta-perspective of change. Next, we will make a detailed characterization of these types of dialogues in which narrative means will be emphasized since they belong to our intervention repertoire. However, the dynamic and flexible nature of CCC facilitates the integration of tools from other approaches to maximize the intervention efficacy (Cardoso, 2016).

Identifying and Evaluating the Effects of IMs

The goal of this type of conversation is to facilitate the identification and description of as many IMs as possible. In that sense, whenever an IM arises counsellors should ask questions, offer reflections, or give feedback that has the client stay with and explore the innovation. For example, counsellors may use exploratory reflections (e.g., "This means that you realized you also like creative activities?") or emphatic inferences (e.g. "Yeah, you become more self-confident, and this had an impact on your occupational identity") to invite a client to deepen and extend self-experience elaboration. Other possibilities include the use of experience-near approaches to explore emotions contained in life-story episodes. By facilitating the symbolization of emotional experience counsellors promote clients' awareness of their needs, which is fundamental to revealing self-positions usually silenced or to identify life themes (Cardoso, 2012). With this aim, counsellors begin by evoking the emotion in life episodes (e.g. "What did you feel during this episode?") followed by questions inviting the client to symbolize the emotion evoked (e.g. "If that emotion spoke what would it say?").

Highlighting Contrasting Self-positions

In this type of conversation, the counsellor aims to bring to the foreground competing self-positions, and therefore, give voice to potential new self-narratives. Thus, this type of conversation is recommended "when change is flourishing but still weak" (Montesano et al., 2017, p. 91) or when the self-narrative is dominated by a single problem hindering the emergence of new self-positions. In these circumstances, highlighting contrasting self-positions is a way of making a client aware of a new self-narrative, which is relevant both to begin the rupture with rigid functioning and to increase motivation to change. The process begins by pointing out the juxtaposition between different self-positions or voices, followed by the exploration of each position.

In CCC, contrasting self-positions could be evoked throughout the intervention. However, a privileged moment occurs when role models are evoked because this topic easily allows exploration of the contrast between the ideal-self and the actual-self, the former evoked by the role- models. The following vignette illustrates the first step of this conversation in which the counsellor makes the client aware of the contrasting positions between ideal-self versus actual-self:

Con—*Over time, there are characteristics of your role models that remain the same. To me it is like a pattern revealing the person you want to become, an ideal that you are looking for. Does it make sense to you?*

In the second step, counsellors explore each contrasting-position to facilitate clients' analysis and differentiation of self-experience. In this process Level 2 IMs may be evoked and expanded, including new self-representations (Reflection 2) and positions of assertiveness and empowerment (Protest 2). The following example illustrates the emergence of Level 2 IMs resulting from the exploration of contrasting self-positions:

Client— *Yes, it makes lot of sense. In all my role models I admire their strength …Yes, I realize that my sense of vulnerability makes me seek that strength, the will to win …* (Reflection 2).

As the analysis of ideal-self evolve expressions of Protest 2 may emerge:

Client—*I feel stronger now, not that vulnerable person. I want to be believe in myself* (Protest 2).

Conversation highlighting contrasting self-positions also may occur when counsellors explore temporal markers using now and "as-if" questions or analyze differences between past and present and/or present and future. For example, the analysis of early recollections is also a privileged moment to work on contrasting self-positions. Indeed, by inviting clients to describe three early recollections counsellors evoke expressions of the client's main life problem and a possible solution to that problem throughout career construction (Savickas, 2015). After the analysis of early recollection meanings (past) counsellors may evoke the link between themes underlying such episodes and present self-experiences (e.g. "Nowadays, how is this life theme is revealed?"). The counsellor explains to the client that the early recollections reveal the perspective that the client is taking on the present problem. This analysis of the perspective of the problem and possible solutions in the present deepens the knowledge of problem causes and consequences (expansion of Reflection 1 IMs) and expands the self-narrative (expansion of Reflection 2 IMs). Most importantly, it enables the counsellor to understand a client's current perspective (usually passive endurance) and suggest possible new perspectives (usually active mastery) that foster change. The CCC model considers change in perspective as a critical goal.

Highlighting contrasting self-positions also prompts intensifying critiques against the problem (Protest 1IM) and positions of assertiveness in which clients affirm their rights and needs (Protest 2 IM). Usually, protest is directed against a dominant position (internal or external) that hinders the resolution of non-dominant needs and goals. Thus, to expand protest and reinforce the awareness of the emergent self-position, the counsellor begins by asking the client to intensify the protest (e.g. "Say it louder" or "Do it again"). Next, to explore and expand the emergent non-dominant position, counsellors invite to express their needs and goals to an the dominant self-position who supports the problem (e.g. "Tell the other side/person what do you need/want?").

Promoting a Meta-Perspective of Change

This type of conversation aims to foster clients' distancing from the immediacy of self-experience (Montesano et al., 2017) by placing them as an observer of their experiences, identifying and analyzing patterns and singularities, and linking personal experiences. The reflexivity implicit in this process allows higher-order narrative elaboration such as the integration of emergent self-representations into a more comprehensive self-narrative.

A meta-perspective of change could be evoked by using reflexive questions to facilitate the identification and analysis of patterns and singularities (e.g. "Throughout your life how the need to fight and win has been revealed?") or to links personal experiences (e.g. "What is the relation between the characteristics of the people you admire and your early recollections?"). Another strategy uses writing exercises, as proposed in the autobiographical workbook, *My Career Story* (Savickas & Hartung, 2012), in which clients are invited to rewrite their life story after elaborating on life story episodes. Indeed, the process of writing literally places the client in the double position of actor ("Me) and narrator ("I") of self-experience (James, 1890), a distancing position fundamental for clients to gain perspective on self-experience and rewriting life story.

Another type of a dialogue that fosters a meta-perspective of change involves facilitating a reflexive positioning that unifies well-developed positions and connects them to new forms of being (Gonçalves & Ribeiro, 2012). The first moment involves the exploration of contrasts between "how I was then and how I am now" which enables a client to describe the transformation process. In a second moment, counsellor may invite a client to explore the processes underlying this transformation (e.g. "What contributed to the changes you have described?").

The use of this counselling dialogue is based on empirical evidence in psychotherapy showing an association between level 3 IMs and positive counselling outcomes (Fernandez-Navarro et al., 2018). This level of narrative elaboration seems to sustain change and develop personal agency (Gonçalves & Ribeiro, 2012). Research on individuals' daily change (Meira, Gonçalves, Salgado & Cunha, 2009) also reinforces the idea that inviting clients to talk about their change at the end of CCC intervention leads them to produce level 3 IMs. Thus, we recommend that counsellors attempt to evoke level 3 IMs at the conclusion of counselling if they have not emerged spontaneously (Cardoso, 2012; Cardoso et al., 2016).

Adjusting the Intervention to Client's Level of Narrative Change

Understanding the sequence of client change can guide counsellors in adjusting the intervention to a client's level of narrative change. Indeed, the three types of conversations described above occur throughout CCC. However their prevalence evolves according to the IMM of change. Obviously, counsellors should avoid facing clients with counselling tasks for which they are not prepared.

During the first phase of CCC, Level 1 IMs [Action 1, Reflection 1 and Protest 1 IMs] should prevail because identifying and evaluating the problem is fundamental to deepen understanding of the problem's causes and consequences. The increasing proportion of Level 1 IMs sustains the elaboration of Level 2 IMs during the next phases of the intervention. In the second phase, the identification and evaluation of IMs is still important, however, as Level 2 IMs gain in preponderance, conversation highlighting contrasting self-positions also should increase to promote the emergence and differentiation of new self-positions as well as to favor the exploration of self-experience in different life story moments and situations.

As clients' self-experience becomes more differentiated and its understanding is deepened (e.g., clear understanding of career problems causes and consequences, increasing expressions of a new self-narrative and empowerment) it is important to evoke conversations promoting a meta-perspective of change, that is, conversations favoring the integration of life episodes/experiences into a continuous and coherent macronarrative about personal characteristics, manifest interests, and future career plans. Habermas and Bluck (2000) refer to this process as autobiographical reasoning, that is, the construction of a sense of self from autobiographical memories. Thus, during phase 2 and phase 3, counsellors introduce this type of dialogue when clients have reached a level of narrative elaboration that allows higher-order narrative processes, such as linking personal experiences in different moments and situations (Reflection 2), facilitating the awareness of life themes in different moments across life story (Reflection 2), or projecting the self into the future by constructing new career plans (Action 2). Narrative coherence and continuity could be reinforced at the end of the intervention by evoking Level 3 IMs. Besides adding narrative continuity and coherence, re-conceptualizing change also allows a new self-experience in the counselling process. In fact, the possibility of elaborating on what changed and how change occurred positions clients as agents of their own change, which contrasts with the initial position of greater passivity. In short, process-oriented interventions place counsellors as facilitators of a change in which their clients learn they are the authors not just actors.

Conclusion

The insights provided by the Innovative Moments narrative model of change processes extends and enriches the Career Construction model of counselling tasks and procedures in at least three ways. First, the IMM, and its operationalization in coding manuals, enables researchers to truly study the micro-processes involved in successful career counselling, not just career construction dialogues. Second, the IMM offers educators and supervisors a practical tool for helping counsellors learn and practice highly effective procedures that they may use to foster the processes of change in their clients. And third, counsellors themselves may use the IMM to self-monitor their own procedures and client processes in the moment-to-moment dynamics of each counselling session. Being aware of narrative evolution markers, counsellors are able to adjust the dialogue to the levels of change achieved while challenging clients to go further in the change process.

References

Barclay, S. R., & Stoltz, K. B. (2015). The Life-Design group: A case study assessment. *Career Development Quarterly, 64,* 83–96. https://doi.org/10.1002/cdq.12043.

Bruner, J. (1990). *Acts of meaning*. Cambridge, MA: Harvard University Press.

Cardoso, P. (2012). Maladaptive repetition and career construction. *Journal of Vocational Behavior, 81*(3), 364–369. https://doi.org/10.1016/j.jvb.2012.09.003.

Cardoso, P. (2016). Integrating life-design counseling and psychotherapy: Possibilities and practices. *The Career Development Quarterly, 64*(1), 49–63. https://doi.org/10.1002/cdq.12040.

Cardoso, P., Gonçalves, M. M., Duarte, M. E., Silva, J., & Alves, D. (2016). Life design counseling process and outcome: A case study with an adolescent. *Journal of Vocational Behavior, 93,* 58–66. https://doi.org/10.1016/j.jvb.2016.01.002.

Cardoso, P., Janeiro, I., & Duarte, M. (2017). Life Design Counseling group intervention with Portuguese adolescents: A process and outcome study. *Journal of Career Development, 44,* 1–14. https://doi.org/10.1177/0894845316687668.

Cardoso, P., Savickas, M. L., & Gonçalves, M. M. (in press). Innovative moments in career construction counseling: Proposal for an integrative model. *Career Development Quarterly, 69*(3).

Cardoso, P., Silva, J., Gonçalves, M. M., & Duarte, M. E. (2014a). Innovative moments in Career Construction Counseling. *Journal of Vocational Behavior, 84,* 11–20. https://doi.org/10.1016/j.jvb.2013.10.001.

Cardoso, P., Silva, J., Gonçalves, M. M., & Duarte, M. E. (2014b). Narrative innovation in Life Design Counseling: The case of Ryan. *Journal of Vocational Behavior, 85,* 276–286. https://doi.org/10.1016/j.jvb.2014.08.001.

Csikszetmihalyi, M., & Beattie, O. V. (1979). Life themes: A theoretical and empirical exploration of their origins and effects. *Journal of Humanistic Psychology, 19*, 45–63.

Di Fabio, A., & Maree, J. G. (2011). Group-based life design counseling in an Italian context. *Journal of Vocational Behavior, 80,* 100–107.

Fernandez-Navarro, P. et al. (2018). Reconceptualization innovative moments as a predictor of symptomatology improvement in treatment for depression. *Clinical Psychology & Psychotherapy,* 1–9.

Fraser, J. S., & Solovey, A. D. (2007). Second-order change: The golden thread that unifies effective treatments. Washington, DC: American Psychological Association.

Gonçalves, M. M., Matos, M., & Santos, A. (2009). Narrative therapy and the nature of "innovative moments" in the construction of change. *Journal of Constructivist Psychology, 22,* 1–23. https://doi.org/10.1080/10720530802500748.

Gonçalves, M. M., & Ribeiro, A. P. (2012). Therapeutic change, innovative moments and the reconceptualization of the self: A dialogical account. *International Journal of Dialogical Science, 1,* 81–98.

Gonçalves, M. M., Ribeiro, A. P., Mendes, I., Alves, D., Silva, J., Rosa, C., et al. (2017). Three narrative-based coding systems: Innovative moments, ambivalence and ambivalence resolution. *Psychotherapy Research, 27*(3), 270–282.

Gonçalves, M. M., Ribeiro, A., Mendes, I., Matos, M., & Santos, A. (2011). Tracking novelties in psychotherapy process research: The innovative moments coding system. *Psychotherapy Research, 21,* 497–509.

Gonçalves, M. M., Ribeiro, A. P., Stiles, W. B., Conde, T., Matos, M., Martins, C., et al. (2011). The role of mutual in-feeding in maintaining problematic self narratives: Exploring one path to therapeutic failure. *Psychotherapy Research, 21*(1), 27–40. https://doi.org/10.1080/10503307.2010.507789.

Habermas, T., & Bluck, S. (2000). Getting a life: The emergence of the life story in adolescence. *Psychological Bulletin, 126,* 748–769.

Kelly, G. (1955). *The psychology of personal constructs*. New York: Norton.

McAdams, D. P. (1993). *The stories we live by: Personal myths and the making of the self.* New York: William Morrow.

McAdams, D. P. (1999). Personal narratives and the life story. In O. John, R. W. Robins, & L. A. Pervin (Eds.), *Handbook of personality: Theory and research* (2nd ed., pp. 478–500). New York, NY: Guilford Press.

McAdams, D. P. (2001). The psychology of life stories. *Review of General Psychology, 5*(2), 100–122. https://doi.org/10.1037//1089-2680.5.2.100.

Meira, L., Gonçalves, M. M., Salgado, J., & Cunha, C. (2009). Everyday life change: Contribution to the understanding of daily human change. In M. Todman (Ed.), *Self-regulation and social competence: Psychological studies in identity, achievement and work–family dynamics* (pp. 145–154). Athens: ATINER.

Montesano, A., Oliveira, J. T., & Gonçalves, M. M. (2017). How do self-narratives change during psychotherapy? A review of innovative moments research. *Journal of Systemic Therapies, 36*(3), 81–96.

Neimeyer, R. A., Herrero, O., & Botella, L. (2006). Chaos to coherence: Psychotherapeutic integration of traumatic loss. *Journal of Constructivist Psychology, 19*(2), 127–145.

Obi, O. P. (2015). Constructionist career counseling of undergraduate students: An experimental evaluation. *Journal of Vocational Behavior, 88* 215–219. https://doi.org/10.1016/j.jvb.2015.03.009.

Pasupathi, M., Mansour, E., & Brubaker, J. R. (2007). Developing a life story: Constructing relations between self and experience in autobiographical narratives. *Human Development, 50*(2–3), 85–110.

Rehfuss, M. C., Del Corso, J., Glavin, K., & Wykes, S. (2011). Impact of the Career Style Interview on individuals with career concerns. *Journal of Career Assessment, 19,* 405–419. https://doi.org/10.1177/1069072711409711.

Savickas, M. L. (2011). *Career counseling*. Washington, DC: American Psychological Association.

Savickas, M. L. (2015). *Life-design counseling manual*. Vocopher.com.

Savickas, M. L. (2016a). Examining the personal meaning of inventoried interests during career counseling. *Journal of Career Assessment, 3*(2), 188–201.

Savickas, M. L. (2016b). Reflection and reflexivity during life-design interventions: Comments on career construction counseling. *Journal of Vocational Behavior, 97*, 84–89.

Savickas, M. L. (2019). *Career counseling* (2nd ed.). Washington, DC: American Psychological Association.

Savickas, M. L., & Hartung, P. J. (2012). *My career story*. Vocopher.com.

Singer, J. A., Blagov, P., Berry, M., & Oost, K. M. (2013). Self-defining memories, scripts, and the life story: Narrative identity in personality and psychotherapy. *Journal of Personality, 81*(6), 569–582.

Smorti, A., & Fioretti, C. (2016). Why narrating changes memory: A contribution to an integrative model of memory and narrative processes. *Integrative Psychological and Behavioral Science, 50*(2), 296–319.

Taveira, M. C., Ribeiro, E., Cardoso, & Silva, F. (2017). The therapeutic collaboration in life design counselling: The case of Ryan. *South African journal of Education, 37*(4), 1–12.

White, M. (2007). *Maps of narrative practice*. New York, NY: Norton.

White, M., & Epston, D. (1990). *Narrative means to therapeutic ends*. New York, NY: Norton.

Poetic Reflexivity and the Birth of Career Writing: An Autoethnographic Love Story

Reinekke Lengelle and Frans Meijers

> *Coherence is an achievement, not a given. This is the work of self-narrative: to make a life that seems to be falling apart come together again, by retelling and 'restoryin' the events of one's life.*
>
> Bochner (1997, p. 429)

Abstract The intention of this chapter is to show how autoethnographic research might promote reflexivity among career professionals. We aim to answer the question: can writing one's own life and career story assist career practitioners and researchers in identifying patterns, idiosyncrasies, vulnerabilities that will make them more aware of the elements that are fundamental to career construction and that have been mentioned in a variety of disparate places in the existing career literature? What interested us as career researchers and co-creators of the narrative approach *Career Writing* in considering the innovative intention of this book, was how writing our own career story could deepen our professional reflexivity and might also help others to do so.

[1] Career Writing is a narrative career identity formation approach where people use creative, expressive, and reflective writing to develop a new story about who they are and where they are going. In the method those writing work actively with life themes. The approach is founded on a model of identity development by Meijers and Lengelle (2012). For a full overview see, Lengelle (2014) and Lengelle and Meijers (2015).

Frans Meijers—Deceased

R. Lengelle (✉)
Athabasca University, Athabasca, Canada
e-mail: reinekke@athabascau.ca

R. Lengelle · F. Meijers
The Hague University of Applied Sciences, Hague, Netherlands

J. G. Maree (ed.), *Handbook of Innovative Career Counselling*,
https://doi.org/10.1007/978-3-030-22799-9_30

Introduction

The intention of this chapter is to show how autoethnographic research may be an innovative way to promote reflexivity among career professionals. What interested us as career researchers and co-creators of the narrative approach *Career Writing*[1] was how writing our own career story could deepen our professional reflexivity and might inspire others to do so. In this context we define reflexivity as a "doubling of the self" (see Hunt & Sampson, 2002, p. 4) where as a multi-voiced person, able to express and at the same time observe myriad selves, "we are both inside and outside ourselves simultaneously and able to switch back and forth fluidly and playfully from one position to the other, giving ourselves up to the experience of "self as other" whilst also retaining a grounding in our familiar sense of self" (see Bolton, 2010, p. 4, in Lengelle, 2014). The idea of using a writing process to promote professional development is not new (Bolton, 2010; Hunt & Sampson, 2002) and in our own work on the development of career identity we show how creative, expressive and reflective writing can promote the internal (with one's self) and external (with others) dialogue which drives career-identity formation (Lengelle, 2014; Meijers & Lengelle, 2012). In autoethnography researchers do this dynamic work "simultaneously, moving inward and outward and inward again, from epiphany, aesthetic moment, or intuition into an "interpretive community," the group of researchers who also write about our topics and whose conversations we want to join" (Adams, Holman-Jones, & Ellis, 2015, p. 49).

This chapter—true to autoethnographic principles—combines the story of our own career development through time with elements and interpretations from the existing career literature. We aim to respond here to questions such as, "what has shaped me and led me to the career I now have?" and in our case, "how was Career Writing born: what made our careers as poet/writing teacher and educator/researcher come together and shape a method and approach to life that is more than the sum of its parts?"

In the process of peer-review of this chapter, a colleague asked whether the use of our stories only—and then from two highly-educated academics—may make this work less applicable or too elitist for career professionals in general. In response, we argue that it is precisely this approach to our stories that can reach others: we make ourselves accessible and vulnerable; we draw back the curtain of educational level and status and show how we have struggled, wondered, dealt with our preoccupations and acknowledge the influence of happenstance. This exploration is about what patterns we might discern and how identifying experiences and their meanings (and the different voices/selves within the self that factor into career-identity formation—for a fuller description of career identity, see Meijers & Lengelle, 2012) that will serve us as we assist others in shaping their careers and identities through reflexive practices.

Chapter Structure

The chapter begins with a description of why career professionals might consider writing their own career story and discerning patterns of influence for themselves via autoethnography. It then describes the motivation for this research method and continues with the individual stories of each author as well as how their stories come together and resulted in the development of the narrative method Career Writing. Subsequently five important elements for discerning what contributes to "career choice" are listed: painful life experiences, personal/family/cultural history and influences, chance/fate, talents/aptitudes and dialogue linking the aforementioned elements. The chapter ends with the news of one of the authors being terminally ill and this portion of the personal narrative reads like a festschrift. The conclusion of the chapter emphasizes the use of this type of reflexive narrative activity for promoting personal and professional development.

Context and Motivation

In current career literature, scholars speak of career counsellors' needing to facilitate the development of "poetic creativity…necessary to help turn scattered stories and emotions into experiential vignettes that reflect the students' efforts to get a life." (Savickas, 2010, p. 16). We also know from training teachers responsible for career counselling in higher education ourselves that once these professionals have a taste of their own poetic creativity through Career Writing, they become thirsty to invest in further professional development (Lengelle, 2014) and are less likely to reduce career learning to a set of "skills" and compulsory reflection exercises that frequently bore and irritate students and might in fact lead to a decline in reflection (Meijers & Mittendorff, 2017).

In the same way that the majority (84%) of therapists go into therapy as part of their personal and professional development, though only a minority are required to do so in their graduate programs (13% in North America) (Pope & Tabachnick, 1994), career professionals may benefit for similar reasons. The self-examination and exercising of emotions involved in reflexive journeys such as we're suggesting may help, as happens in therapy, professionals cultivate (1) more empathy, (2) an ability to better anticipate unstated feelings, (3) an understanding of the dangers and potentials of transference, and (4) ways to de-stigmatize the need for help—one "calibrates the instrument" in working with others (Reidbord, 2011).

We have argued recently too that imagination is a vital part of developing career agency, where agency is not a fixed characteristic or aimed for destination, but an emergent quality that requires playfulness and dialogue to arise in an ongoing way (Muijen, Lengelle, Meijers, & Wardekker, 2018). Such learning processes differ fundamentally from matching paradigms, psychometric testing, or insights gleaned from personality-type models. The results of such categorization and mapping traits and talents are scarcely grist for the mill of narrative self-exploration.

As narrative career practitioners and researchers, we behold each person's evolving story (i.e. identity) as a complex landscape of idiosyncratic voices, where some voices have been squelched, others may be screaming at one another, some are blocked or muddy, and some have been dominating mightily. In our work, as alluded to above, the self is conceptualized as a dynamic multiplicity of voices. This idea we borrow from Dialogical Self Theory (for a detailed overview see Hermans & Hermans-Konopka, 2010)—here selves, or so-called "I-positions", may limit and confuse our ability to develop and "decide" but they can also be creatively played with and observed and move us forward in an ongoing dance of integration (Lengelle, 2016b). This myriad of positions that make up this dynamic and multi-dimensional "self" can be constructed, viewed, integrated and reorganized in the form of an evolving narrative.

We propose that it is also beneficial to deliberately narrate our own lives and serve our students and clients better because when we write about ourselves honestly, we experience how vulnerable we are as we tell of our particular pain and unearth life themes and can empathizes with our clients and students. We can also see in what ways random events and chance have played a part in our life and career choices; as we make note of this, we often experience firsthand—and hopefully with some humour—how irrational the nature of choice-making is.

Our motivation for writing autoethnographically and encouraging others to do the same is at once intended to create of identity something 'coherent' (as the Bochner quote at the start of this chapter suggests) while paradoxically respecting the 'incoherence' inherent in 'self stories'. We may hope ultimately to befriend our humanity with some compassion and notice our often illogical paths and yearnings. In doing so we will likely be able work more effectively with the paradoxical writings and tellings of those we aim to be useful to.

Method

Autoethnography involves the writing of lived experience in order to shed light on cultural, social, and even political dynamics (Hesse-Biber & Leavy, 2006). It is a "research method that allows the author to write in a highly personalized style, drawing on his or her experience to extend understanding about a societal phenomenon" (Wall, 2006, p. 146). It has been previously used in careers' research to explain the construction of career assessment and counselling procedures as well as to explore how self, theory and practice came together (McIlveen, 2007, p. 301). In doing scholarship with the aim of "producing meaningful, accessible, and evocative research grounded in personal experience…" (Ellis, Adams, & Bochner, 2011, p. 274) autoethnography seeks to identify archetypically human patterns, without generalizing in a quantitative way.

We decided on autoethnography for several additional reasons, first because the method parallels narrative learning processes we mean to facilitate with students and clients through Career Writing, stimulating the internal and external dialogue as described to above. Second, we wanted to engage readers. Academic reading can sometimes feel impenetrable to practitioners and "…the academic self is frequently cut off from the ordinary, experiential self" (Bochner, 1997, p. 421). Third, we also wanted to walk the talk of vulnerability in the process of taking a step in our own reflexivity as career researchers and trainers. We each tell our own story first and then how our work came together.

The Story of Reinekke

When I was in my early twenties, one of my first writing teachers at the University of Alberta, Eunice Scarfe, asked our group of 15 women writers if any of us had lost a parent young or had emigrated. I said yes on both counts. My father had left our family after we came to Canada when I was five. Eunice went on to explain that if we had suffered some form of exile early in life, we were more likely to become writers. Perhaps her theory was based on anecdotal evidence, but it got me thinking; you might say it was my first experience in realizing that perhaps my urge to write stories and poems and keep a journal were attempts at meaning making. I note that this notion strongly resembles the ideas of career researcher Mark Savickas who says that our preoccupations are often at the source of our occupations because people attempt to "actively master what they have passively suffered" (1997, p. 11). In a similar vein, American career coach and author Barbara Sher, from her many years of practical experience, has described career *drive* as a combination of pain + talent (Sher, 2013). Perhaps my pain was a split family, being an immigrant kid, and my talent was connecting (and writing)—looking back, I believe I was driven to forge new connections; words became a powerful resource.

I was raised with two sisters and a brother and am the third child. The fictional stories I wrote as a kid were frequently about big, happy families, but also, themes of being orphaned and displaced were common. My first name was unfamiliar in Canada and few could pronounce it. I also had short hair and many kids mistook me for a boy; I wore my brother's hand-me-downs—brown corduroy pants and green t-shirts—which didn't help. My peers teased me about my name and this too made it difficult to truly feel 'landed' as an immigrant. Affected by feelings of being a stranger in a strange land and being pained at times by a sense of not belonging and yearning for connection, my vocation may have grown in part out of this predicament. That, along with a talent for writing, and coming from a family of eager learners and storytellers with a tradition of pursuing university education set me on my path of writing and healing. Indeed, my career path and vocation are not surprising—not nearly as unpredictable as the unique result of being poet, teacher, and researcher might suggest.

As part of the immigration experience, I was also confronted with two languages in a very formative period of my life. I recall being about six and sitting in a classroom where I was asked to complete a test but was completely unable to do so because of my lack of familiarity with English at the time. An adult saw my dilemma and came to my rescue, telling my story for me, and getting me put appropriately back in kindergarten where I could play with other children and, in that playful space, learn English. In reflecting on this now, I'm quite moved by the compassion this stranger showed me and this may have been a seed in my draw and propensity to be a vulnerable teacher: recognizing the vulnerability in my students and facilitating them always with this in mind (MacRorie, 1974).

In that kindergarten class we would paint and our teacher would write on the back of the paintings what we told her they meant. It was empowering that someone was listening and took those words seriously and even wrote them down. In a similar vein my mother encouraged us to paint and she also wrote down titles and meanings on the back of our canvasses. These were some of my first conscious experiences of feeling heard, reflecting on a creative work, and belonging in a safe and imaginative learning space. Interestingly, the visceral and embodied also played a part in my kindergarten classroom, with a most memorable day dedicated to textures—we put our hands in buckets of jello, pushed our fingertips into a bowl full of wet marbles, sat with our feet in white flour, a soft place I remember not wanting to leave.

What I am driven to do is to help people heal, through writing/storytelling, so they too may regain a sense of belonging or connection—with themselves firstly, and then in their families, at work and in their communities. I want to do this in the context of providing a "soft" place, even if hard truths are articulated and tears are shed. Creative challenges and compassion in the learning space are my mottos for good educational practice.

That said, the story of my vocational interests and aptitudes would not be complete without a story about my parents. My father, who I developed a close relationship with in my teens and into adulthood, emphasized the need for personal development and handed me a copy of Alice Miller's *Drama of the Gifted Child* (Miller, 1981) when I was 15. He wanted me to read it so we could discuss it at length and he also insisted that I speak up and challenge him in his arguments. When I went to live with him at 16, he literally said to me, "I want you to speak up when you don't agree with me; I never want you to think to yourself, 'the asshole is home again'". He also sent me to a psychologist in my early twenties, saying, "next to a university degree, a driver's license, and typing diploma, you must do this, because it will save you a lot of time in life." This set the tone for our rich conversations that continued until his death in 2013. It is noteworthy that in writing this section, I had to stop to cry, feeling both grief and gratitude; I sense vocations cannot be unravelled without such vulnerability and an acknowledgement of the help we have received from others.

I also had the great fortune of having a caring stepfather who helped me with schoolwork. He firmly believed in my writing and had been a teacher and school principal. He often said, "editors are a dime a dozen but truly creative people are rare; keep writing". He also cautioned without discouraging me, "writing is the longest apprenticeship in the world" and he constantly corrected our grammar as we spoke, even interrupting joke-telling to make sure we got the words right. I smile as I remember this and note that both my fathers loved to educate. My step-father ran a vocational college in Northern Alberta, Canada for the majority of his career and the core messages I took from both him and my biological father were that education was important, but that formal education wasn't enough for personal development, and that men support a woman's (i.e. daughter's) success and accomplishments as a matter of course.

My mother worked for the government and did her civil servant job like an entrepreneur. She always had great intuition about which clients she should go see in her role as liaison between the provincial government and private land donors to expand provincial parkland. Her bosses, she reported, were frequently caught between the discomfort of not being able to control her while having to acknowledge that she got very good results. She is a natural networker, a woman who trusts strong gut feelings, embodies and offers creative thinking as she continues to read and study into her senior years. She is also a painter and I always feel that my creativity in writing, if somehow inherited, is from her. She also has a fierce survival savvy, born in WWII in Amsterdam where she and her mother went hungry and were witness to war crimes.

As a young mother of four and a divorcee, my mother arrived in Canada in her mid-thirties, got herself employed and went on with life in determined fashion. She didn't hide her sorrow, nor was she overpowered by it. I remember camping trips and creative projects (e.g. building a picnic table together on which she painted a large abstract leaf), and her overall joie de vivre. From her I have absorbed a can-do attitude as she modeled initiative taking and independence. My mother also had a critical voice and there was no doubt about what she expected in the way of respect and good behaviour. This made me sensitive to the power of language to both harm and heal. One of my sisters and I now study non-violent communication (Rosenberg, 2015) which has many parallels with my work of healing through writing; as siblings with the same parents, my sister and I realize our child selves at times still feel fragile and we can be overly self-critical.

I began teaching creative writing shortly after completing my MA degree (in Pedagogy from Leiden University, The Netherlands). I had just returned to Canada at age 25 and instead of getting the good-enough job to start earning money, I went to the local college and university extension department to launch writing courses. It took me years to earn a living wage, but a consultant friend had advised me after graduation that one shouldn't 'bury a rock' (i.e. one's dream) because, he said, "rocks always come up; the frost pushes them to the surface anyway; might as well get on with it without delay." His rock metaphor helped me stay on course with uncompromising enthusiasm and focus.

In the years that followed, I taught more and more writing courses and was hired as a writer-in-residence for our city's university hospital. In the meantime, I also married and had two daughters. Working from home became important and I developed online writing courses, this time for Canada's online university (Athabasca University).

By the time my work began to merge with Frans', I had more than a decade of teaching and writing behind me and a job as a visiting graduate professor. However, what I noticed was that I wanted to be able to describe better what was happening in the "black box of writing and healing;" I was ready to embark on scholarly work to become a better professional, both through research and theory building. I remember that around 2006 I was invited by the University of Alberta to speak to Ph.D. students about writing and personal development. I drew my model on the whiteboard and spoke of going from a first to a second story (for overview see, Meijers & Lengelle, 2012). When someone asked me what learning process was at the heart of this movement, I could not answer. I knew the learning process intuitively, I had exercises to help people move through it, but I could not name or describe what occurred in what I called the "transformational space." It was time for conceptual and professional expansion.

The Story of Frans

I am the son of a small town blacksmith and my mother founded and ran a household supplies store beside the blacksmith shop. My parents only completed primary school because they had to go to work early to earn a living. Born in 1950, I grew up in a very homogenous environment; everyone in our small Dutch town was Roman Catholic and white and there was a consensus about how to live, how to behave. Rituals accompanied every stage of life. This kind of environment would ordinarily lead to a secure and predictable future with no great need to reflect about life's meaning and direction. However, although I grew up living most of my childhood within a ten-kilometer radius of our family home and in a recent biography project still referred to myself as a "small-town boy," *times were a changing* as I grew up (with a wink to Bob Dylan). This change began with the opportunity to pursue education beyond the vocational level, unlike most of my family including my siblings.

This wonderful opportunity for expansion, however, was also very disorienting and frequently put me in situations where I had to figure out what the rules of engagement were. In the psychological reports that were made about me in my childhood school years, I was described as a boy who had an above average intelligence, came across as somewhat rigid and formal in his beliefs, and had a tendency to be passive and socially awkward though independent. These assessments also revealed that outwardly I appeared at times unemotional but this wasn't the real state of affairs.

For many years I referred to myself as a chameleon and like Reinekke, I too felt like a stranger in a strange land. However, my exile had to do with class and education, and expressed itself in a fear of becoming disoriented or lost and striving for recognition in the academic and professional world I became part of. When I entered university to study the sociology of education, I realized the problem of children like me in higher education was not that it was only personally disorienting, but that their success was often determined and complicated by a host of other barriers. The birth of my calling happened as a combination of my own unresolved pain and disorientation, and the liberating conceptual understanding that grew in me about the struggle of children from working-class backgrounds. This struggle was real and ubiquitous. The desire to make educational success easier and school more meaningful for children like myself was the start of my life's work. That my calling has everything to do with themes surrounding orientation and identity and my own life questions is truly no coincidence.

When I entered university, in the late sixties, there was also an historical movement across Western Europe and the United States to challenge the status quo and push back against the establishment. Bob Dylan's song, "The times they are a-changing," was my favourite for many years. The repressive rule-bound culture of the fifties was being systematically broken down as the post-war generation that was reaching adulthood rebelled and questioned established practices, rules and institutions. I grew my hair long, was part of a band, and participated actively in student movements and demonstrations. My focus was primarily on educational reform. I was also a draft dodger and began my academic career early when my proposal for Ph.D. research was approved. That said, at the time very few Dutch academics were publishing in English (i.e. internationally) and I did not always find the mentoring I required as a young academic in the departments where I worked. As someone from a working class background, I also did not know how to ask or reach out to become part of important networks that might have benefitted me. As a result, I often felt that I was working in isolation and this later drove me to establish my own networks and research groups.

The other inheritance from my working class background, despite my parents' hard-working, practical and loving way, was a lack of emotional awareness. Emotions were there, but no one spoke about them. Having emotions was considered "not done" and this has had a lasting impact on my personal and professional life. A stark example of growing up without acknowledging feelings was when I was 18 and my father died without as much as a conversation about his illness or overt expressions of love. This left me with unresolved grief that showed up years later and for which I sought counselling.

It was then that I began to get an inkling that I was spending a lot of my time in my head. In order to gain a sense of control over my life, I strove to rationally understand and explain everything that was happening to me and as a result I became conceptually strong, without fully realizing that I was lacking connection and an affective knowledge of myself and others. This, I believe, is part of the reason I didn't so much "choose" things in life, but rather I followed the random opportunities that came my way and reacted to them.

As a result of these beginnings, my personal development did not keep up with my professional progress. I had a conflict with one of my early bosses that I was not successful in resolving properly or to my satisfaction. I had friends and a stable home life but had not learned to emotionally invest or identify some of the internal conflicts that were holding me back. Although I came across as jovial and engaged, the place I most experienced a sense of meaning and connection was in the long hours of working alone and later, in conversations with a few cherished colleagues. Waking up to my limitations began in part when I had a heart attack in my early fifties.

It was a shock to be confronted with my mortality. I realized I could have died and left my then teenaged daughters without a father. I had the wherewithal to request a conversation with the hospital psychologist when I was in the ICU and when I asked him what I should learn from the experience, he wisely replied, "it is not what you *should*, or even what you *can* learn from it, but what you *want* to learn from it." These words have often returned and become a kind of life motto. Over the years they have provided a thread of continuity in my career and personal life; this way of responding to whatever life challenge appears is ingrained. Along with the development of more emotional awareness, this motto allows me to be more "response-able" for my life without condemning myself or blaming my background or my lot in life. I liken these words to having a "growth mindset" before that concept was coined by Dweck (2006).

What Mezirow (2009) called the disorienting dilemma and Savickas (2011) calls the preoccupation or life theme, I see as inroads to create our own wisdom out of pain, and that is what I realize I've done and am now doing. When I have been asked to speak about career counselling in the 21st century at schools and for business, I have often caught myself saying, "wisdom is the ability to see the pain behind the things" which is an concept I first heard in the work of Ofman (2013). This is also what is at the heart of the *Career Writing*—the starting point of learning is to identity and be with the painful challenge of a boundary experience (Meijers & Lengelle, 2012).

Reinekke and I started working together at a point when I realized that careers work needed more creative approaches. The overly rational focus in guidance that showed up in information provision and career competencies started to irritate and dissatisfy me greatly. In 2002, a colleague and I wrote an article about the role of emotions in decision-making (Meijers & Wardekker, 2002)—this was a precursor to the work that would follow. In 2007 Reinekke and I began developing our ideas around career-identity development as a learning process that is both cognitive and affective. I see that creativity is a way to access and integrate both. In the beginning, however, I did not fully realize how important it would be for me to develop myself emotionally and make my own personal development a priority. Doing so has enriched my life on many levels and without this learning I would not be able to speak of career and identity development as I do now.

Our Work Together

In 2007 we both went to the *National Association of Poetry Therapy* (NAPT) conference in Portland, Oregon. Reinekke was a NAPT member and Frans was looking for more creative ways to approach career guidance. He was familiar with narrative approaches and intuited that this was likely the direction to go into seek more integrative and effective career learning methods in education. Reinekke was teaching the graduate course, *Writing the Self,* and other writing courses for personal development and was looking for ways to professionalize her work further (e.g. research and theory-building).

It would seem at first that describing what became our mutual career is merely a coming together of ideas and fixing skill gaps, but our sharing and blending and creating a new intellectual project (i.e. *Career Writing*) became more than the sum of its parts. In terms of the Dialogical Self Theory (DST), we might speak of two I-positions forming a third position or hybrid position, where the gains made are qualitatively different and represent a meta-level integration (Hermans & Hermans-Konopka, 2010; Lengelle, 2016a). As Frans likes to say, "for us, one plus one equals three".

The encounter of Frans's I-position as "skilled conceptual thinker" and Reinekke's "skilled creative and therapeutic writing facilitator and poet" did not only mean our melding resulted in a "creative writing facilitator with a good conceptual understanding" or "a social scientist who had become creative." The confluence of our preoccupations and the ways in which we had each tried to cope with them, made the merging of our work and lives both more tension-filled and in the end, more fruitful. We became meaningfully better at what we thought we already did so well!

The birth of our narrative method *Career Writing* meant that we'd created something qualitatively different, something neither of us could have envisioned before. In order to achieve this, we had to both 'fall in love' with what the other had already had a lifetime of practice at and re-examine things we thought we already had down pat. Reinekke learned to love academic reading and sharpen her conceptual thinking, which improved her abilities as a poet. Frans learned to love personal development and hone his intentions to learn about relationships; his theories that had always had an academic rigour now also breathed with life.

We determined and affirmed that the motor for identity and career learning is the internal and external dialogue one has about experiences—that this is indeed what makes identity formation (e.g. career learning) possible. In order to integrate the boundary experience of our meeting, we embarked on a new dialogue, both with each other and with ourselves. Put in DST terms, Frans's tendency to disconnect and avoid feelings and Reinekke's need to connect and have her feelings met with compassion, created tension and *a decentering movement* that felt like an attack on both our default identity narratives. We could no longer do more of what we had been doing (too well) and our encounters in many ways created more pain than we had previously experienced on a conscious level. The visceral metaphor we use to acknowledge this is: our wounds became visible and we poked harshly into the other's hurt with the way in which we each had learned to cope with our own.

Upon reflection and in conversation with each other during this writing project, we realized we have surprisingly similar life themes or preoccupations (i.e. feeling like a stranger in a strange land). Reinekke as exiled stranger and immigrant aware of her social status as a child of divorced parents and a misfit regarding language, clothes, and her name. Frans as exiled stranger with regards to class and milieu. We indeed realized looking at our individual stories and in the way we trigger each other that we both work within the tension of wondering if we measure up. We are both pre-occupied with filling that gap in ourselves and we want to help others do the same. It is no surprise then that our meeting immediately increased our opportunities for doing this work better and expanding it, yet the development of our mutual calling and joint work and personal life would also greatly amplify the struggles we each experienced in relation to our life themes (i.e. preoccupations).

On a basic level the other's mere presence meant we were being asked to, "please give up the safety mechanisms that you have taken a lifetime to cultivate and which have worked for you, and please do so promptly. I need you to do this, so I will be okay." Our meeting and interaction led to a boundary experience, a term we use in the identity-learning theory for Career Writing (Meijers & Lengelle, 2012). Indeed, we were made to question previous identifications and bonds and embark on a journey of identity learning. Our old stories and ways of being would not and did not suffice to bring our work and personal lives together.

On the other hand, our similar handicap (i.e. both feeling like a stranger in a strange land) and the vocations that we had each pursued and created to cope simultaneously produced a centering movement (Hermans & DiMaggio, 2007). We were committed to the same thing (i.e. personal development) and our identities grew stronger and we gained confidence in both our work and in our personal lives. The magnetic pull that would birth our new calling and partner relationship was a complex mixture of experiencing and dialoguing about our pain and developing talents—again, the combination of the latter two elements are at the heart of our drive (Sher, 2013).

To conclude our story, we propose that our joint career was born out of mutual sources of pain resulting in similar ambitions but opposite and yet complementary ways of coping. The simple (i.e. one plus one is two) equation is that Frans' commitment to conceptual thinking and academic work gave status and professionalization opportunities to Reinekke, allowing her to feel like less of a stranger in her professional life and context. At the same time, Reinekke's creative and affective approach to teaching and learning, gave Frans' work more depth and allowed him to see that for his professional development, personal growth is a prerequisite; he began to feel less like a stranger in his personal life. However, the more complex equation or "third position" or "hybrid position" (i.e. the gains we had not predicted and meant one plus one was indeed three) was that Frans's professional success deepened and came alive (which for instance resulted in us both gaining international recognition) and Reinekke noted unexpected but important improvements in work and personal relationships.

Results and Discussion

After writing these stories and checking with each other and two additional colleagues about their content, composition, and emerging themes, we talked about what could be gleaned from our stories. As is the intention of autoethnographic work, we used them as material for our self-reflection and to identity patterns that might offer others insight as well.

We identified four key elements in our stories that appear in the career literature and a fifth (i.e. dialogue) tying them together in the process of meaning-making.

1. **Pain**. In our stories, we confirmed that "we try to actively master what we have passively suffered" as Savickas claims (Savickas, 1997, p. 11). In both our cases, what troubled us motivated us too. Our joint calling is also where both our preoccupations met. Indeed, one might say *Career Writing* is a method that

helps people to reconnect with themselves and others in creative ways in the pursuit of meaningful career learning. It is noteworthy that what had made us suffer and had made us compensate for that suffering has made us strong in ways that were ultimately imbalanced—we had taken our coping to exaggerated and dysfunctional levels. For instance, Reinekke tended to worry and obsess over personal dynamics and Frans tended to blanket feelings with conceptual musings. In our work together and in service of others, we became keenly aware that our work should for instance not be cause for rumination (Lengelle, Luken & Meijers, 2016) and that the emergence of agency requires a safe holding space of imaginative development that does not limit itself to the cognitive realm (Muijen et al., 2018).

2. **History**. Our family and cultural patterns influenced what was expected, what was possible, and what should be questioned. We are both influenced by hard-working Calvinist Dutch culture that our parents also passed on to us, but also by the more jovial and forgiving Catholic background of Frans's parents and Reinekke's mother. We also had additional powerful influences that allowed us to break away from traditional norms. Frans was influenced greatly by the societal shift in the 1960s and Reinekke was influenced by her emancipated mother and a father who asked her to engage in critical dialogues early on and encouraged her to question his (white male) authority. The outcome of these histories was two conscientious, autonomy-focused individuals who were ready to take each other on to break down established dysfunctional patterns on both personal and institutional levels.
3. **Chance/fate**. Conversations with many of our friends and colleagues over the years confirm what researchers like Pryor and Bright say in their book Chaos Theory of Careers (2001): we are all influenced by the random events, chance meetings, and the luck we have in our lives. No one can tell of a calling or career without saying something like, "And then I happened to run into so and so…" or "A position opened up, just as I was about to give up on that." These random events include our own meeting, as well as running into particular teachers or books at crucial times in our lives, the fluke of the generation we were born into (i.e. different political and social environments) and the influence of current economic realities (e.g. equal opportunity; precarious labour). Of course 'chance' alone does not determine opportunity, how we respond to those opportunities is what ultimately matters.
4. **Talents/aptitudes**. whether inborn or a gift of socialization, we concede that particular talents and aptitudes (and lack thereof) have also influenced the development of our careers. Reinekke developed a knack for writing at a very early age and is socially outgoing. Frans is entrepreneurial like his parents and learned early on that he was a good speaker with a penchant for keeping audiences interested in his messages while also making them laugh. We are both blessed with enough brains to write and do research, and with enough love for people to teach and engage with others, build networks, and rejoice in another's success. Conversely, neither of us is a science or math whiz, which may explain our preference for qualitative research and our destiny of ending up in the social sciences. Though

talents are emphasized in career guidance literature, they do not give people a sense of direction or provide meaning, but they do limit and enhance people's ability to make particular choices (Savickas, 2011). Once people have established an inkling of their route or sense of direction, talents are useful and invaluable tools to live out and enact a vocation. If Sher's equation, pain plus talent is drive, the talent is the cart and the pain is the living, breathing heartbeat of the horse that pulls it in a particular direction.

5. **Dialogue**. the process of meaning making through dialogue ties the previous four elements together. It is through both the internal dialogue (conversation we have with ourselves) and the external dialogue (conversation we have with others) (Lengelle, 2016a) that we begin to integrate the parts of the 'self' that make up identity stories we can use to live by and adjust as needed. That is why a process like autoethnography is useful to promote reflexivity: it is a way of engaging the dialogue about experience that brings disparate career influences together meaningfully.

The conscious integration of pain, cultural and family history, chance, and talent happens when we can reflect upon and find the language to articulate connections. It is not about constructing the 'truth' but rather to put together meaningfully a story of how we have become and what we would like to become good at. To use a metaphor: if one's pain, history, fate, and talents are the materials to construct a calling or career, dialogue becomes the blueprint for building.

An Unexpected Chapter

And they lived happily ever after.... or rather, stories (i.e. career narratives) must change as society changes and as our own lives do. This became starkly clear in April 2018 when Frans was diagnosed with a terminal ureter cancer with an estimated life expectancy of less than a year. For Frans this means the premature ending of his life and work; for Reinekke this means losing both spouse and primary work partner.

The fact that career identities are always changing has been brought home to us more powerfully than ever and meant that this chapter was not complete after the initial draft was done. We are in the process of a fundamental re-narration and we hope this chapter will give others courage to contemplate, explore their (career) stories and cultivate the precious internal and external dialogue that has made (and still makes) our own career learning possible and immensely rewarding.

Feedback on this chapter by our colleague Kat McNichol who has a detailed understanding of autoethnographic and career writing helped us ask a number of new questions as we begin to re-narrate our story and respond to the new circumstances. She asked us (1) "Reinekke, what insight have you gained knowing Frans is dying? What direction do you see your work going in? What will your calling become? What do you want it to become?" and (2) "Frans—what do you want your legacy to be? What do you want to leave Reinekke with for the future when it comes to your work, your shared calling? Is there a baton that you see her carrying forward? Or, if you feel like you don't want to burden her with your baton, then what are you hoping for? How would you sum up your calling and life work in light of your diagnosis?"

Reinekke

My personal insight before and even more so in the wake of Frans's diagnoses is that there is always an opportunity for learning, here and now, not in an imagined future. In any transition period when one's life is uncertain, there is wisdom in staying close to feelings while also observing what is happening and using words to make meaning. I have written 50 new poems in the last six months in the wake of the news and Frans helped me edit a book of Dutch poems and reflections that included a chapter on the first month of his diagnosis. Perhaps one might say, "as long as one is creating from a place of connection, even if the process involves loss and grief" we are restor(y)ing our lives.

I am also reminded how crucial empathy is in everything we teach and learn; everyone is going to be confronted by difficulty and sudden life changes. In my interactions with others, I operate from the fundamental intention to "create no pressure" and hope for the same in return. This does mean that a challenge will arise for me when I have an unmet need or someone else does, and that need cannot be welcomed in some way. In wrestling kindly with these kinds of 'problems' in my own life, I learn how to be useful to others and stay humble.

The direction I see my work going is further along the same lines. When I say "lines" I mean the directions in which what I call my "warm inner compass" points. I have always followed this, but now do so with more equanimity and openness. I want to continue to bring career writing (and in broader terms "writing the self") to people—both to individuals and to communities. This actually means I want to "bring people home to themselves" in a way that makes for healthier interactions.

Frans

In response to the questions about what I see for Reinekke and the future of work, I first want to say, I don't have a baton to pass on. Everyone has to find out their own baton. In that sense there is no inheritance that Reinekke should feel defined by or obliged to pursue. I want her to follow her own heart—that is what will always bring the most happiness and intrinsic motivation for learning. As a teacher in heart and soul, I would encourage Reinekke and all professionals in our field to keep developing new things, do research, and continue to ensure there are theoretical foundations for the work and methods developed. Every beautiful method is doomed to be misused without the proper theoretical understanding.

I am deeply saddened that my life and work is cut short. I would have liked to do this work for another ten years and watch Reinekke continue her career, with me in a more supporting role. My career yearnings have been realized in some fundamental ways in our years together. In as early as the late nineties I was writing about identity and narrative in a way that would in part seed the work Reinekke and I took on and developed and that came alive as I became more emotionally alive. This fundamental step in my own learning, this internal and external dialogue that now welcomes emotions, allows me to accept this process of living while dying.

Reflections on the Method and Research

The issue frequently brought up when critiquing autoethnographic research is that it's too personal and that too few participants are involved to draw conclusions from the work. The viewpoints articulated are after all subjective. That said, the results of this method are not intended to be quantifiable generalizations but rather archetypal patterns—in this way, one might say that the personal can say something about the other too.

We drew from personal experience but we did so as two researchers and career practitioners who have worked with thousands of people in seminars and writing courses. We also made use of research by other narrative career counsellors who successfully work with clients in a similarly self-explorative way. That said, it would be valuable to see if creating an autoethnographic writing seminar for career practitioners and researchers might yield additional and poignant insights; this may be one of Reinekke's future projects.

Conclusion

The question as to whether autoethnographic research can improve professional reflexivity among career professionals is of course not definitively answered. What we aimed to do was to show what it contributed to our own reflexivity and inspire others to do the same. When we embarked on this chapter, we did not know that the five elements that we listed would emerge so clearly; they emerged as we wrote; our lived experience clearly resonated with earlier readings we had absorbed.

Before this writing we had intuited that the *one-plus-one is three* metaphor applied to us, but only by writing our stories were we able to articulate what that meant specifically. We also did not, in earlier drafts, anticipate that our lives would change so drastically in one year and this chapter gave us a chance to have a kind of life and career review: we are left with a sense of gratitude. Career Writing is the 'child' that was born of our devotion to work and each other. And this autoethnographic reflection reminds us that in putting the pen to the page in reflection allows us to make meaning and give direction to our lives.

Final Note

Frans died peacefully on November 16, 2018. Reinekke made the final edits to the chapter based on generous peer-reviewer feedback. The work described here continues, as does the self-reflexive processes that fuel identity learning and career progress.

References

Adams, T., Holman-Jones, S., & Ellis, C. (2015). *Autoethnography: Understanding qualitative research*. Oxford: Oxford University Press.

Bochner, A. (1997). It's about time: Narrative and the divided self. *Qualitative Review*, 418–438.

Bolton, G. (2010). *Reflective practice: Writing & professional development* (3rd ed.). London: Sage Pulications.

Dweck, C. S. (2006). *Mindset the new psychology of success*. New York, NY: Random House.

Ellis, C., Adams, T. E., & Bochner, A. P. (2011). Autoethnography: An overview. *Historical Social Research/Historische Sozialforschung*, 273–290.

Hermans, H. J. M., & DiMaggio, G. (2007). Self, identity and globalization in times of uncertainty: A dialogical analysis. *Review of General Psychology, 11*(1), 31–61.

Hermans, H. J. M., & Hermans-Konopka, A. (2010). *Dialogical self theory. Positioning and counter-positioning in a globalizing society.* Cambridge, UK: Cambridge University Press.

Hesse-Biber, S. N., & Leavy, P. (2006). *The practice of qualitative research*. Thousand Oaks, CA: Sage Publications.

Hunt, C., & Sampson, F. (Eds.). (2002). *The self on the page: Theory and practice of creative writing in personal development*. London: Jessica Kingsley Publishers.

Lengelle, R. (2014). *Career writing: Creative, expressive, and reflective approaches to narrative and dialogical career guidance* (Published doctoral dissertation). Tilburg, The Netherlands: Tilburg University.

Lengelle, R. (2016a). What a career coach can learn from a playwright: Expressive dialogues for identity development. In. H. J. M. Hermans (Ed.), *Stimulating a dialogical self: Groups, teams, cultures, and organizations* (pp. 37–53). New York, NY: Springer.

Lengelle, R. (2016b). *Jezelf Schrijven*. Oud-Turnhout/'s-Hertogenbosch: Gompel & Svacina.

Lengelle, R., Luken, T., & Meijers, F. (2016). Is self-reflection dangerous? Preventing rumination in career learning. *Australian Journal of Career Development, 25*(3), 99–109.

Lengelle, R., & Meijers, F. (2015). Career writing: Creative, expressive, and reflective approaches to narrative career learning and guidance. *The Canadian Journal of Career Development/Revue canadienne de développement de carrière, 14,* 19–31.

MacRorie, K. (1974). *A vulnerable teacher*. Rochelle Park, NJ: Hayden Book Company.

McIlveen, P. (2007). The genuine scientist-practitioner in vocational psychology: An autoethnography. *Qualitative Research in Psychology, 4*(4), 295–311.

Meijers, F., & Lengelle, R. (2012). Narratives at work: The development of career identity. *British Journal of Guidance and Counselling, 40*(2), 157–176.

Meijers, F. & Mittendorff, K. (red.). (2017). *Zelfreflectie in het hoger onderwijs [Self reflection in higher education]*. Antwerpen-Apeldoorn: Garant.

Meijers, F., & Wardekker, W. (2002). Career learning in a changing world: The role of emotions. *International Journal for the Advancement of Counselling, 24*(3), 149–167.

Mezirow, J. (2009). A critical theory of adult learning and education. *Adult Education, 32*(1), 3–24.

Miller, A. (1981). *The drama of the gifted child: How narcissistic parents form and deform the emotional lives of their talented children*. New York, NY: Basic.

Muijen, H., Lengelle, R., Meijers, F., & Wardekker, W. (2018). The role of imagination in emergent career agency. *Australian Journal of Career Development, 27*(2), 88–98.

Ofman, D. (2013). *Bezieling en kwaliteit in organisaties [Inspiration and quality in organizations]*. Utrecht, the Netherlands: Servire.

Pope, K. S., & Tabachnick, B. G., (1994) Therapists as patients: A national survey of psychologists' experiences, problems, and beliefs. *Professional Psychology: Research and Practice, 25*(3), 247–258.

Pryor, R. G. L., & Bright, J. E. H. (2001). *The chaos theory of careers: A new perspective on working in the 21st century*. New York, NY: Routledge.

Reidbord, S. (2011, September 18). Therapy for therapists: should therapists have therapy themselves? *Psychology Today*. Retrieved from www.psychologytoday.com/us/blog/sacramento-street-psychiatry/201109/therapy-therapists.

Rosenberg, M. (2015). *Non-violent communication* (3rd ed.). Encitas, USA: Puddle Dancer Press.

Savickas, M. (2010). Career Studies as self-making and life design. *NICEC, 23*, 15–17.

Savickas, M. (2011). *Career counselling*. Washington, D.C.: APA.

Savickas, M. L. (1997). Career adaptability: An integrative construct for life-span, life-space theory. *The Career Development Quarterly, 45*(3), 247–259.

Sher, B. (2013). *It's only too late if you don't start now: How to create your second life at any age*. New York: Dell.

Wall, S. (2006). An autoethnography on learning about autoethnography. *International journal of qualitative methods, 5*(2), 146–160.

Career Counselling for Emerging Adults Based on Goal-Directed Action: An Innovative Approach to Theory, Research, and Practice

José F. Domene, Richard A. Young and Cassidy Wilson

Abstract In this chapter, we discuss the ways in which Contextual Action Theory can be used to understand career development during emerging adulthood, and to address career concerns that commonly arise during this phase of life. After providing a brief introduction the theory, we describe career development processes that are central to emerging adulthood, focusing on exploration and initial engagement with the world of work, identity formation, and changes and characteristics of emerging adults' social relationships. We then describe existing studies that have applied Contextual Action Theory to understanding these developmental processes. Finally, we delineate an approach to career counselling that is grounded within Contextual Action Theory, focusing on the central tasks of this career counselling model, as well as novel interventions that can be used to address emerging adults' career concerns and to facilitate their broader transition to adulthood.

Keywords Contextual action theory · Action project method · Emerging adulthood · Young adult · Career development · Career counselling

Career Counselling for Emerging Adults Based on Goal-Directed Action: An Innovative Approach to Theory, Research, and Practice

Although the concept remains contested in the scholarly literature, there is a growing body of research suggesting the existence of a distinct developmental period occurring between adolescence and full adulthood, known as emerging adulthood (Arnett,

J. F. Domene (✉)
University of Calgary, Calgary, Canada
e-mail: jfdomene@ucalgary.ca

R. A. Young
University of British Columbia, Vancouver, Canada

C. Wilson
University of New Brunswick, Fredericton, Canada

J. G. Maree (ed.), *Handbook of Innovative Career Counselling*,
https://doi.org/10.1007/978-3-030-22799-9_31

2000, 2004, 2016). As Arnett explains, emerging adulthood is a time of transition in many aspects of young people's lives as they shift from adolescent attitudes, roles and responsibilities, to full adulthood. It is also a pivotal time of life for providing career-related support and counselling, assisting people undergoing a multitude of transitions with formulating goals and plans for their future life, and with achieving those goals and plans. In light of this opportunity, in this chapter we discuss an innovative approach to career counselling for emerging adults.

Chapter Goals

In writing this chapter, we have two primary goals. First, we hope to provide the reader with a broad understanding of one specific approach to understanding and researching career development during emerging adulthood: Contextual Action Theory (CAT). Second, we intend to demonstrate how that approach can be applied in the context of working with career concerns that are prevalent during emerging adulthood.

Chapter Structure

We set the stage for our discussion by providing a brief introduction to CAT, a framework for understanding human experience through the lens of goal-directed action, and by highlighting three central developmental processes of emerging adulthood that are salient to career counselling with this population. We proceed to introduce the research methodology that has grown out of the theory, and discuss the existing body of research examining the process of transitioning to adulthood using the framework of CAT. Finally, we present an emerging model of career counselling for this population, grounded in both the propositions of the theory, and the growing research evidence about the contextual, goal-directed, action-oriented nature of career development in emerging adulthood.

Introduction to Contextual Action Theory

Although goal-directed action has most often been conceptualized in the field as an outcome or consequence of counselling, we argue that it is also central to the process of counselling (Young, Domene, & Valach, 2015). In making this argument, we draw on von Cranach, Ochsenbein, and Valach's (1986) conceptualization of human action as intentional, conscious (though not always rational) behaviour that is influenced by and influences one's social context. Building on this definition of action, we have proposed a specific theoretical framework for understanding action as it relates to human development across life domains, including the domain of work:

CAT. CAT has been described in greater detail in Chap. A Contextual Action Theory of Career of this volume and elsewhere (Valach, Young, & Lynam, 2002; Young & Domene, 2018; Young et al., 2010). However, an overview of key tenets within the theory will facilitate our discussion of how emerging adults' career concerns can be conceptualized from a CAT perspective. The theory also recognizes that, in daily life, people typically engage in actions with others; that is, family members, friends, co-workers, and counsellors, rather than in isolation. Therefore, CAT researchers and practitioners tend to focus on joint actions; that is, actions involving multiple individuals working together. By emphasizing joint action, CAT connects people's goals to their social context.

As we describe in previous works (Valach et al., 2002; Young & Domene, 2018; Young et al., 2010), CAT proposes that action is organized according to varying degrees of complexity. At its simplest, action is organized in terms of elements, which are the basic behavioural units involved in an action and include such things as asking questions, providing explanations, and expressing disagreement within a counselling session. Action is also organized in terms of somewhat more complex functional steps, which are a series of elements that, together, are intended to achieve a goal. For example, as part of the goal of excelling in a job interview, a job applicant may engage in steps such as studying a company's mission/vision statement, researching the company online, and practice answering questions with a friend. The goals towards which actions are directed form the most complex way in which action is understood to be organized within CAT. Goals are the intentions or purposes that drive people's actions. Simultaneously, goals also provide actions with meaning, and link specific actions with the broader social context. Examples of goals that might emerge out of an initial career counselling session might include helping a young person to better understand themselves and the world of work, or achieving a successful transition from school into full-time, long-term employment.

In conjunction with this framework for action organization, we have proposed the existence of three simultaneously present perspectives for understanding action (Valach et al., 2002; Young & Domene, 2018; Young et al., 2010). Action can be perceived in terms of people's externally observable behaviors, their manifest behavior. However, within CAT, action encompasses more than behavior alone. A second perspective from which action can be perceived is internal processes; that is, the cognitions and emotions that accompany manifest behavior when people engage in action, and serve to steer and regulate that action. Finally, action can also be perceived in terms of social context, which encompasses the meanings of actions that emerge when people explain or interpret those actions to others. To fully understand an action, it is important to consider not only the external behavior, but also the mental and social aspects of that action.

It is also important to consider the time-frame over which goals can be achieved, which in CAT is represented in the interconnected concepts of action, project, and career (Valach et al., 2002; Young & Domene, 2018; Young et al., 2010). "Action" is defined as occurring within a span of seconds, minutes or hours. Thus, the kinds of goals that can be achieved with a single action are short-term in nature. To address goal-directed actions over a somewhat longer time-period, the theory proposes the concept of a "project". Projects occur when actions directed towards achieving a particular goal take place over days, weeks, or months. Most of the goals that clients and career counsellors work on together fall within the time-frame of projects. However, CAT also recognizes that some goals have no pre-defined end point, but instead are pursued over the course of years or even a lifetime. The theory uses the concept of "career" to describe these long-term goals. Importantly, this definition of career encompasses long-term goals in any area of life, not just goals related to work or employment.

Career-Related Developmental Processes of Emerging Adulthood

In their discussion of career counselling with emerging adults, Domene, Landine, and Stewart (2015a) identify three central developmental processes that are likely to be salient to career counselling with this population. Specifically, they describe emerging adults' (a) educational and occupational exploration and initial engagement; (b) identity formation and its implications for work; and (c) experience of change in their close social relationships. These developmental processes are important for career counsellors to understand in order to work with this population, and can be understood from the framework of goal-directed action (Young et al., 2011).

Exploration and Initial Engagement

In industrialized societies with extended periods of emerging adulthood, this is the period of life where people consider different possibilities for their future work and pursue career goals through education, and initial entry into the workforce. However, there is substantial variability in how this process of exploration and initial engagement unfolds for different individuals. Domene et al. (2015a) noted that, although some emerging adults successfully engage in career exploration, complete their education and transition smoothly into the workforce, this ideal progression is only one of the career development trajectories that can occur. Other emerging adults may remain uncertain in their career choice well into emerging adulthood (Arnett, 2004; Konstam & Lehmann, 2011), complete their career exploration but struggle with completing the educational requirements of their chosen occupation (Courtney & Hook, 2016; Mortimer, Zimmer-Gembeck, Holmes, & Shanahan, 2002), or know what occupation they wish to enter and successfully complete their education, but then experience substantial difficulty in making the transition into full-time, long-term employment (Blustein, Olle, Connors-Kellgren, & Diamonti, 2016; Frank, Frenette, & Morissette, 2015). In the 21st Century, increasing numbers of emerging adults have found themselves unemployed or underemployed after leaving school, to the point that the label "NEET" (not in education, employment or training) has become part of the lexicon of our profession.

The problems that many emerging adults experience with their initial exploration and engagement with the labour market can have deleterious effects on many aspects of these individuals' lives. The most direct is that, without employment as a means to generate income, these young people are at increased risk of poverty or reliance on government assistance. Indirectly, problems with completing the exploration and initial engagement process also hinder individuals' transition to independent living, or lead to multiple unsuccessful attempts to leave the family home (Arundel & Ronald, 2016; Horowitz & Bromnick, 2007). Difficulties that emerging adults experience with this developmental process have also been associated with negative psychological outcomes, including decreased sense of well-being and increased symptoms of anxiety and depression (Domene, Arim, & Law, 2017; Keller, Samuel, Bergman, & Semmer, 2014; Symonds, Dietrich, Chow, & Salmela-Aro, 2016). Conversely, the process of exploration and initial engagement can be supported by key members of emerging adults' social contexts, such as their parents and romantic partners (Young et al., 2011).

Identity Formation

The process of forming a clear identity is a central task of transitioning from adolescence to adulthood (Arnett, 2004; Boardman, 2017; Petersen, Marcia, & Carpendale, 2004) and, consequently, is particularly salient for emerging adults. As Petersen and colleagues (2004) explained, identity can be conceptualized as a personality process that develops over time and is experienced as "feelings of both continuity and discontinuity with one's past that give meaningfulness to one's present and a direction to one's future" (p. 114). From this explanation, it is evident that identity formation and career development are intertwined in substantive ways. Indeed, the development of a vocational or professional identity is a central part of the identity formation process across many cultures (Porfeli, Lee, Vondracek, & Weigold, 2011). In addition, this vocational/career identity formation process may be connected to the previously described educational/occupational exploration and engagement processes, although these connections have not been well studied (Grosemans, Hannes, Neyens, & Kyndt, 2018). Regardless of the nature of the connection, a more established sense of identity is associated with positive career development outcomes (Domene et al., 2015a).

Social Relationships

Emerging adulthood is characterized by numerous changes in the nature of young people's social relationships (Domene et al., 2015a). One such change occurs in emerging adults' relationships with their parents, which typically involves emerging adults becoming more functionally and psychologically independent over time, as they learn to interact with their parents as adults rather than as children (Booth, Brown, Landale, Manning, & McHale, 2012). There is a growing body of research indicating that parents influence their children's career development into emerging adulthood (Shulman, et al., 2015; Whiston & Keller, 2004), particularly in families from cultures with family-centered values (Fisher & Padmawidjaja, 1999; Mao, 2017). Nonetheless, as the nature of individuals' relationships with their parents change through emerging adulthood, it is likely that the ways in which parents influence and work with those individuals in the pursuit of their career-related goals also changes. Consequently, attending to the changing relationships between an emerging adult client and his or her parents may be important in career counselling with that individual.

Another characteristic of social relationships in emerging adulthood is the establishment of longer-term romantic relationships (Domene et al., 2015a; Young et al., 2011). These relationships tend to be more exclusive, intimate, and committed than romantic relationships at earlier stages of life, but at the same time more varied and featuring a wider range of patterns of relationships engagement than later in life (Arnett, 2004; Shulman & Connolly, 2016). Moreover, these longer-term romantic relationships are connected to career development in several important ways during emerging adulthood: (a) progression in one tends to be associated with progression in the other, while problems in one area can spill over into the other; (b) romantic relationships have been found to be a meaningful source of support and direction during the transition to work; and (c) many emerging adults experience concerns about work-life balance, more specifically, the balance between work and relationship goals.

Relationships with non-romantic peers and friends also change during emerging adulthood (Domene et al., 2015a). For many individuals, friendship networks expand as they enter into post-secondary institutions, and enter more fully into the world of work (Arnett, 2015). These peers can serve as an important source of information, emotional and instrumental support. For example, Young et al. (2015) found that emerging adults and their friends pursue goals together, related to such things as maintaining their friendships in the midst of change; constructing their past, present, and future identities; and engaging in exploration related to their future education and occupation. Similarly, Young, Marshall, and Murray (2017) described numerous characteristics of future-oriented conversations that emerging adult friends have with each other, suggesting that peer relationships can be important in young people's planning for and problem-solving around their future careers.

The existing literature indicates that the changes in people's significant social relationships during emerging adulthood have important implications for their career development. Moreover, as we discuss in the subsequent section, research conducted within a CAT framework reveals that emerging adults engage in joint actions with both parents and romantic partners to pursue goals related to their future careers.

Applying Contextual Action Theory to Researching Emerging Adult Career Development

A growing body of research has explored these and other developmental processes of emerging adulthood from the perspective of CAT. These studies share a common methodology, the Action-Project Method (APM), which was developed specifically to explore goal-directed action in terms of the organization and perspectives of action proposed by CAT (Young, Valach, & Domene, 2005). Moreover, we have argued that APM is particularly well suited for studying developmental processes during emerging adulthood (Wall et al., 2016), in part due to the capacity of the method to access both internal processes, including identity formation processes, and the social contexts of human development. We believe that an explanation of this method is beneficial for understanding the existing body of CAT research on emerging adulthood career development.

Defining Characteristics of the Action-Project Method

The APM is a systematic, naturalistic qualitative method for exploring goal-directed joint action in daily life. It combines a constructivist epistemology with a relativist ontology that derives directly from the propositions of CAT (Domene & Young, 2008; Young & Valach, 2004; Young, Valach, & Collin, 1996). The research method has developed alongside CAT, and includes variants addressing longitudinal research questions (Wall et al., 2016), dyadic and family-wide interactions (Marshall, Zaidman-Zait, Domene, & Young, 2012), systematic qualitative comparisons (Domene & Young, 2008) and sample sizes that range from a few cases to 20 or 30 dyads. Despite the existence of these variations, there are four defining characteristics of the APM.

The first defining characteristic is that the unit of analysis in the APM is action, rather than underlying psychological traits (Young et al., 1996, 2005). The APM was developed to systematically assess and explore joint actions, projects, and career occurring between two or more individuals. This dyadic and family focus is a second defining characteristic of the method (Marshall et al., 2012, Young et al., 2005). In combination, these two characteristics lead to the method being particularly well suited for exploring processes (e.g., counselling process, the process of transitioning to adulthood) rather than outcomes, as well as for exploring action as it occurs in daily life (i.e., action within social context).

Thirdly, the APM is also defined by a distinct set of data collection procedures designed to capture all three perspectives of action proposed by CAT (Wall et al., 2016; Young et al., 2005). Specifically, data collection includes (a) direct, video-recorded observation of pairs/groups of participants' *manifest behavior* in a conversation with each other; (b) a "self-confrontation procedure," in which participants review the video-recording to facilitate reflection about the *internal processes* accompanying their manifest behavior; and (c) the construction of *social meaning* between pairs/groups of participants (during the conversation), and between participants and researchers (during the self-confrontation).

Finally, the APM is defined by the characteristics of its data analysis process, in which "discussion to reach consensus while incorporating multiple sources of information forms the heart of the analysis process" (Domene & Young, 2008, p. 62). APM data analysis is always carried out by multiple researchers inductively examining the data sources, and discussing possible interpretations together to reach agreement regarding the most appropriate interpretation. This inductive examination and discussion is informed by the content of the data, the levels of action organization theorized by CAT (i.e., elements, functional steps, goals/intentions), and the researchers' pre-existing knowledge of the phenomenon being studied. The quality of the analysis process is also supported by a range of procedures to promote rigour and trustworthiness, which are described in Domene and Young (2008) and Young et al. (2005).

CAT Research on Emerging Adult Career Development

The existing body of CAT research on the career development of emerging adults needs to be understood not only in terms of the procedures of the APM, but also in the context of the modern world and the challenges it presents for career. Parada and Young (2013) contend that young people who are currently transitioning to adulthood, including entering the workforce, are facing a much different context than previous generations. They are becoming adults in circumstances that have not been experienced before; circumstances that reflect substantial changes in society. For example, among many authors who have addressed this issue, Bauman (2001) spoke of the "inherently dynamic aspects of modernity" (p. 67), and Sennett (1998) used the term "flexible capitalism" to account for changes in the work in Western societies such that a sense of identity and security can no longer be expected, as they were formerly. Similarly, the impact of technological change and the digital economy on the world of work has been characterized by some as a "fourth industrial revolution" (Caruso, 2018, p. 379). These issues of complexity and change are incorporated in CAT through the acknowledgement of the dynamic, and multidimensional nature of human action.

It is in this context that, with our colleagues, we have conducted a range of studies exploring aspects of emerging adult career development, some of which has been framed within the larger issue of transition to adulthood. To elaborate, we were interested in the goal-directed actions and projects of young people as they engaged in this period of transition to adulthood, including but not limited to the transition to work. At the same time, we did not want to direct or limit a priori what actions research participants would engage in relative to their transition. In each of the studies described below, participants were recruited because they identified aspects of the transition to adulthood to be of interest or concern. This research was also conducted within the theoretical framework of CAT and utilized the APM, described above.

Counsellor-client dyads. To address the question of how counsellors and emerging adult clients jointly construct and engage in goal-directed projects pertinent to the transition to adulthood, we examined the counselling that occurred between professional counsellors and youth who sought assistance with their transition to adulthood (Young et al., 2011). Twelve counselling dyads, involving 37 counselling session were examined using the APM. The primary projects that emerged from this study were building relationships, and identity formation. Identity is the larger framework in which career was situated in these projects. Educational and vocational issues were the starting point of many of the counselling relationships. It is particularly important that the counsellor was able to provide the relational context in which this goal-directed behavior was realized.

Friends. The question of how emerging adults construct the transition to adulthood as goal-directed projects jointly with friends, was addressed in a subsequent study (Young et al., 2015). Fifteen young adult friendship dyads were studied over a 9-month period, using videotaped conversations, the self-confrontation procedure, and telephone monitoring. Their joint projects were grouped broadly as negotiating and maintaining friendship, constructing identity, and promoting career. These projects allowed participants to be intimate and reciprocal with each other, provide support, share emotion, and exercise judgement. The findings illustrate the crucial role relationships play in the construction of identity, and its connection to educational and occupational goals during emerging adulthood.

Romantic partners. In a study focusing on how couples who self-identified as being in a committed relationship take action toward future work and life together, 18 young adult dyads provided data regarding their joint projects over a 6-8-month period. The joint projects that emerged in this study were explicitly about pursing educational and work futures and balancing priorities and their future lives together, with different couples taking a variety of different goal-directed actions in pursuit of those projects (Domene et al., 2012). This study confirmed career development as a joint project with high priority for committed couples in emerging adulthood. Indeed, the authors concluded the career development of the young adults in these relationships belonged to both parties.

Families. The contextualized and dynamic nature of joint, goal directed actions and projects in the career development of emerging adults was evident when examining these processes in Saudi Arabia (the preceding studies described in this section were carried out in Canada). Khalifa, Alnuaim, Young, Marshall, and Popadiuk (2018) investigated the joint transition to adulthood projects of 14 parent-emerging adult dyads in Saudi Arabia. Three kinds of joint projects emerged: (a) negotiating educational and career futures, (b) promoting gender roles and marriage, and (c) shaping independence. However, these projects were part of a higher level goal that represented the context in which they were embedded. Specifically, the researchers identified this higher level goal as crafting generational change and continuity. The projects that these young people engaged in with their parents manifested "tensions between the desire to preserve traditions and local identities, and new ways for youth to engage in adult work and marriage" (Khalifa et al., 2018, p. 146). Moreover, these tensions were not only between the emerging adult negotiating for change while the parent sought continuity, but between these individuals and society as a whole.

Emerging adults with developmental disabilities. Two studies have been undertaken to address emerging adults transitioning from secondary school to the world of further education, work, or non-work in the context of developmental disabilities. Marshall and colleagues (Marshall et al. 2018) revealed that both relationship and planning-for-the-future goals were present in all the parent-youth projects in this study. Importantly from a career perspective, planning for future was a distinct, and essential part of these projects. These projects addressed internal resources (i.e., emotional regulation in the face of changes) and external resources (i.e., availability of and information about post-high school training opportunities). The adults in these projects also signaled a degree of self-determination by expressing desires, withholding information, and directing the conversation in some instances.

Parents and other familial caregivers also engaged in joint projects between themselves relative to the transition of individuals with developmental disabilities (Young et al., 2018). These projects were broadly identified as equipping the emerging adult for adult life, connecting for personal support, and managing day-to-day while planning for the future. For example, equipping the young person for life as an adult included employment equipping projects such as finding training programs, or job opportunities. Other parents were challenged by the current situation such that their projects revolved around managing the day-to-day challenges of their son or daughter making this transition. For these families, planning for the future, both the young person's and their own, was a secondary issue.

A Contextual Action Theory Approach to Career Counselling

Career counselling can be conceptualized as goal-directed action occurring between clients and counsellors, where the focus is on the actions and goals of clients related to their future life and work. Thus, CAT can be a particularly relevant framework for career counselling practice. It informs career counselling in three specific ways, which are described in the remainder of this chapter. First, it provides a broad framework for understanding processes within counselling, as well as processes that clients participate in their own lives, irrespective of the counselling approach or career theory that the practitioner follows. Secondly, we have identified five broad, process steps to be used with CAT in counselling. Finally, the specific method we have used in our research, that is, the APM, also has applications to counselling. Each of these represents a way of applying CAT in career counselling to emerging adults.

Taking a Goal-Directed Perspective

First, as we have explained, people understand their own and others behavior as goal-directed. Whether or not career counsellors follow an explicit goal-directed theoretical orientation, they can readily understand that counselling is a goal-directed activity with its own a series of goals and sub-goals. Moreover, the joint action between counsellor and client suggests that their joint goals are negotiated, often tacitly. In addition, most clients want to change something about themselves and their lives as they move forward, often framed as reaching for or achieving some anticipated state. Both the goals within counselling and client goals in their lives outside of counselling are reflected in what the client and counsellor are doing. Both client and counsellor are acting in light of these goals. It is likely that some of these goals are obvious to both the counsellor and client, others may be less discernable, and different goals may be implicitly assumed by each party. Indeed, one of the helpful aspects of counselling is to facilitate making these goals more apparent and understandable. However, even when goals are made explicit, there may be a tendency—tacit or otherwise—on the parts of both counsellor and client to explain, understand, or justify them in terms of past, seemingly causal factors. Indeed, the counsellor may want to help the client address these factors to facilitate the realization of future goals.

Taking the perspective of CAT in counselling allows the counsellor to shift away from looking at the client's career situation as being primarily caused by the past, and allows the counsellor to focus on how the client is navigating the future in the context of their life history. This view has been referred to as prospection; that is, constructing, encoding, and remembering the future (Gilbert & Wilson, 2007; Seligman, Railton, Baumeister, & Sripada, 2013). Addressing future behavior in a goal-directed manner is often the implicit or explicit content of career counselling with emerging adults.

This orientation to the future has been explored in cognitive psychology (Stewart, Gapenne, & DiPaolo, 2010) and includes reference to cognitive systems and motor processes. Seligman and colleagues (2013) maintain that prospection is a central organizing feature of perception, cognition, affect, memory, motivation, and action. Others have identified the neurological basis for the organization of goal-directed actions (e.g., Rizzolatti, Cattaneo, Fabbri-Destro, & Rozzi, 2014) Consistent with several other contemporary theories of career development (Arthur & McMahon, 2018), CAT's emphasis on goal-directed action represents a considerable departure from the relatively stable personality or vocational interests that served as the primary focus of career counselling in much of the 20th century. Implementing this approach not only requires counsellors to be attuned to the client's orientation to the future, but importantly, how the client's actions and projects in the present are related to the future.

The Major Counselling Tasks

Taking a goal-directed perspective in career counselling can be augmented considerably by the five major counselling tasks that are informed by CAT (Domene & Young, 2019; Domene, Valach, & Young, 2015b; Young & Valach, 2016; Young, Valach, & Domene, 2015). These tasks overlap with many other approaches to career counselling, but nevertheless are important to review here. First, we recognize that the overall counselling process is to create and maintain a working alliance with the client. The second task is to link what the client is discussing in counselling to their daily life. The third task is to assist the client identify systems and levels of actions, projects, and career. The fourth task is to deal with emotions. Finally, the counsellor and client have to address suboptimal, actions, projects and career. These tasks are not listed here in a sequential order; instead, they permeate counselling.

Engaging in a working alliance. The notion of the working alliance in counselling encapsulates much of what has been said heretofore in this chapter. The working alliance is the joint action of the client and counsellor. Moreover, it is the joint action through which and because of which other actions occur. The counsellor and client join each other to articulate certain goals and to work together to reach them. The working alliance involves attentiveness and empathy on the part of the counsellor and the client, directly and immediately experienced by both. Each brings to the counselling relationship their own cultural and interpersonal skills and attitudes. Each also actively negotiate their joining; their working alliance. We understand the working alliance to be at the core of effective CAT-informed career counselling.

Linking to daily life. Narrative is the means through which clients can provide a link between their present, past and future actions and the counselling process. Narrative refers to facilitating the client's telling of an extensive story about their life. The process of narrative construction in career counselling engages the counsellor as the facilitator of its telling: to be aware of emotion and identity issues, but not to use it as a data gathering source. Within CAT-informed career counselling, narratives are invariably constructed around goals, both in the telling and the told. They provide the basis for continuity from the past to the present, and from the past and the present to the future in the client's life. Narratives can provide counsellors with insight into a client's life, and the people, places, and other life contexts that are important to them. As a function of gaining this greater comprehension through listening to a client's narrative, the importance of different client goals may be better understood.

Identifying actions and projects. In this chapter and elsewhere, we have presented the details of our understanding of action by identifying the systems of action, that is, actions, projects, and career, and the levels of action, that is, goals, functional steps, and elements. This framework for understanding the complexity of action can be used directly in the counselling process. Specifically, the counsellor may be able to assist the client to identify either systems of action, or levels of action that are highlighted or challenged in both their narrative and the counselling process. The purpose is not diagnostic; it is to assist the client in identifying specific aspects of goal-directed actions that are strengths, and those that are challenges.

Attending to emotion. Some practitioners may believe that emotion has a less prominent place in the career counselling of emerging adults than in other counselling domains, or with clients at other life stages. CAT holds that emotion is both a critical motivating factor, and an important outcome of action. This is even more the case when actions across time are constructed as projects and careers. Therefore, it is important that career counsellors recognize and address emotion. The narrative, described earlier, is one place where the connection between emotion and action is evident. It can point to the specific emotions that are at play in the client's past actions. The emotions evident in past actions, may be emotions that energize or impede current career-related actions and projects. Thus, addressing them in counselling is vital. Similarly, how emotions are expressed in the ways clients represent their prospective thinking may be indicative of their motivation for future actions or the expected outcomes of them. That is, the more emotionally invested a client is in their goals for the future, the higher the likelihood of that client taking actions in their lives outside of counselling, towards achieving that goal.

Addressing sub-optimal actions, projects, and careers. Career counselling with emerging adults is often about the client's future, to what the client aspires to be, and the steps needed to realize that future. At the same time, present or past projects that are sub-optimal may interfere directly with the realization of that future. To be effective, career counselling should include a focus on working through, modifying, or changing sub-optimal actions and projects. In fact, it is common for clients to seek counselling specifically because they are engaged in sub-optimal projects. For some emerging adults, to seek counselling about their future is the acceptable way for them to address larger, more troubling projects in which they are engaged. Space in the counselling process has to be provided for the narrative about a detrimental project to emerge. Recognizing the connections between the client's sub-optimal, and optimal projects is one means of addressing this issue. Another is to recognize the strengths within detrimental projects that the client may use for optimal projects they are pursuing. Identifying these strengths, even within a problematic project can work to empower clients and offer them new perspectives and more functional internal processing; for example, beliefs about themselves, in the career counselling process.

Specific Strategies

Several specific counselling strategies have arisen from our use of the action-project research method described in this chapter. These include the use of the self-confrontation procedure, and the action-project procedure as an intervention, which includes several aspects that can be used separately in counselling.

The self-confrontation procedure. When used in clinical practice, the self-confrontation procedure refers to the playing back of the video recording of a counselling interaction with the client, immediately or very soon after the session itself is completed (Popadiuk, Young, & Valach, 2008; Valach, Michel, Dey, & Young,

2002; Young, Valach, Dillabough, Dover, & Matthes, 1994). Briefly, in this procedure, the video of a 10–15 min segment of the counselling session is reviewed by the client and counsellor. The video is stopped at one-two minute intervals, at the completion of a meaning unit. The client then has the opportunity to respond to the counsellor's question, "What were you thinking and feeling at the moment of the conversation?" The purpose of the self-confrontation procedure is assist the client to identify cognitions, and affect that they may have experienced during the session. Any part of a career counselling session in which the client is providing a narrative is particularly appropriate for a subsequent self-confrontation procedure. In this case, it would allow the narrative to be provided in the session without extensive counsellor interruption. Our use of the self-confrontation procedure has provided clients with the opportunity to articulate thoughts and feelings they may have had during the session which were not expressed at that time. It also can give clients a greater sense of agency as developers of the narrative, and, by extension, of their lives. It reinforces the value of being able to tell their story and providing connection of actions across time, that is, in constructing their projects and careers. For some clients, this facilitates a shift from an external to an internal locus of control. Although existing use of the self-confrontation procedure in counselling has not focused on emerging adult career concerns, we anticipate that the same principles that make the self-confrontation procedure useful in other counselling contexts will apply to career counselling with emerging adult clients.

The APM as an intervention. We are currently in the process of adapting, and researching the APM for counselling practice with emerging adults. Specifically, all the parts of the APM are being used as a novel supportive intervention for young people who are newcomers to Canada making both the transition to adulthood, and the transition to a new country. The intervention is intended to assist these emerging adults to identify, and engage in their goal-directed projects pertinent to educational, occupational, and other life tasks. Within CAT, human behaviour is goal-directed, and can be supported and enhanced from this perspective. Therefore, this supportive intervention focuses on, but is not limited to, the transition-related, joint goal-directed actions and projects that young adult newcomers undertake, pertinent to the transition to adulthood. As with the APM as a research method, this supportive intervention focuses on a pertinent joint project between the young person and another significant person in their social environment, for example, colleagues from work or school, family members, friends, immigrant support workers, romantic partners, roommates, and teachers.

Our novel supportive intervention is based on facilitating the goal-directed projects of emerging adults by helping them identify their projects with significant others in their social context related to career, employment, education, and other life roles over two session. The project is then supported through the counsellor's telephone monitoring for a period of three months. The innovative aspects of this support program include identifying and working with the significant other person, engaging in joint conversations that are observed and contribute to the identification of the dyad's joint project, and the identification of ways in which the project can be enhanced. In addition, part of the intervention allows the clients to participate in the self-confrontation procedure that enhances the goals identified above. Preliminary evidence emerging from research we are currently conducting on this intervention suggests that some clients find this short-term intervention to be beneficial in supporting their transition into adulthood and into a new country (Silva et al., 2018).

Conclusion

Elsewhere, Young and Domene (2012) have proposed a research agenda for career counselling, including with emerging adults, based on CAT and the APM. Specifically, we have argued that focusing on actions, and the longer-term and more complex projects and career, researchers can address aspects that are particularly important in career counselling, and career processes generally. These include emotion (see Young, Paseluikho, & Valach, 1997); attention and language (see Young & Valach, 2016); narrative, unconscious processes (see Dyer et al., 2010); as well as relational and cultural contexts (see Young et al., 2011). We hope that the arguments and evidence presented in this chapter have demonstrated that CAT, as a theory centered on goal-directed action, can serve not only as a framework for conducting innovative career-related research with emerging adults, but also as a guide for innovative, context-sensitive career counselling practice with this population.

References

Arnett, J. J. (2000). Emerging adulthood: A theory of development from the late teens through the twenties. *American Psychologist, 55,* 469–480. https://doi.org/10.1037/0003-066X.55.5.469.

Arnett, J. J. (2004). *Emerging adulthood: The winding road from the late teens through the twenties*. New York, NY: Oxford University Press.

Arnett, J. J. (2015). Socialization in emerging adulthood: From the family to the wider world, from socialization to self-socialization. In J. E. Grusec & P. D. Hastings (Eds.), *Handbook of socialization: Theory and research* (pp. 85–108). New York, NY: Guilford Press.

Arnett, J. J. (2016). Emerging adults in Europe: Common themes, diverse paths, and future directions. In R. Zukauskiene (Ed.), *Emerging adulthood in a European context* (pp. 205–215). New York, NY: Routledge.

Arundel, R., & Ronald, R. (2016). Parental co-residence, shared living and emerging adulthood in Europe: Semi-dependent housing across welfare regime and housing system contexts. *Journal of Youth Studies, 19,* 885–905. https://doi.org/10.1080/13676261.2015.1112884.

Arthur, N., & McMahon, M. (2018). *Contemporary theories of career development: International perspectives*. London, United Kingdom: Routledge.

Bauman, Z. (2001). *The individualized society*. Cambridge, United Kingdom: Polity Press.

Blustein, D. L., Olle, C., Connors-Kellgren, A., & Diamonti, A. J. (2016). Decent work: A psychological perspective. *Frontiers in Psychology, 7,* 1–10. https://doi.org/10.3389/fpsyg.2016.00407.

Boardman, L. (2017). An experiential exploration of identity during emerging adulthood: The impact of growth experiences on emerging adulthood characteristics. In J. D. Sinnott (Ed.), *Identity flexibility during adulthood: Perspectives in adult development* (pp. 71–81). Cham, Switzerland: Springer.

Booth, A., Brown, S. L., Landale, N. S., Manning, W. D., & McHale, S. M. (2012). *Early adulthood in a family context*. New York, NY: Springer.

Caruso, L. (2018). Digital innovation and the fourth industrial revolution: Epochal social changes? *AI & SOCIETY, 33,* 379–392. https://doi.org/10.1007/s00146-017-0736-1.

Courtney, M. E., & Hook, J. L. (2016). The potential educational benefits of extending foster care to young adults: Findings from a natural experiment. *Children and Youth Services Review, 72,* 124–132. https://doi.org/10.1016/j.childyouth.2016.09.030.

Domene, J. F., Arim, R. G., & Law, D. (2017). Change in depression symptoms through emerging adulthood: Disentangling the roles of employment status and employment satisfaction. *Emerging Adulthood, 5,* 406–416. https://doi.org/10.1177/2167696817700262.

Domene, J. F., Landine, J., & Stewart, J. (2015a). Emerging adult career transitions. In P. J. Hartung, M. L. Savickas, & W. B. Walsh (Eds.), *APA handbook of career intervention* (Vol. 2, pp. 479–494). Washington, DC: American Psychological Association.

Domene, J. F., Nee, J. J., Cavanaugh, A. K., McLelland, S., Stewart, B., Stephenson, M., et al. (2012). Young adult couples transitioning to work: The intersection of career and relationship. *Journal of Vocational Behavior, 81,* 17–25. https://doi.org/10.1016/j.jvb.2012.03.005.

Domene, J. F., Valach, L., & Young, R. A. (2015b). Action in counseling: A contextual action theory perspective. In R. A. Young, J. F. Domene, & L. Valach (Eds.), *Counseling and action: Toward life-enhancing work, relationships and identity* (pp. 151–166). New York, NY: Springer.

Domene, J. F., & Young, R. A. (2008). Expanding the action project method to encompass comparative analyses. *International Journal of Qualitative Methods, 7,* 54–80. http://ejournals.library.ualberta.ca/index.php/IJQM/index.

Domene, J. F. & Young, R. A. (2019). Career counselling using contextual action theory: Key concepts for practice. In N. Arthur, R. Neault, & M. McMahon (Eds.), *Career theories and models at work: Ideas for practice* (pp. 115–124). Toronto, ON: CERIC.

Dyer, B., Pizzorno, M. C., Qu, K., Valach, L., Marshall, S. K., & Young, R. A. (2010). Unconscious processes in career counselling: An action theoretical perspective. *British Journal of Guidance and Counselling, 38,* 343–362. https://doi.org/10.1080/03069885.2010.482395.

Fisher, T. A., & Padmawidjaja, I. (1999). Parental influences on career development perceived by African American and Mexican American college students. *Journal of Multicultural Counseling and Development, 27,* 136–152. https://doi.org/10.1002/j.2161-1912.1999.tb00220.x.

Frank, K., Frenette, M., & Morissette, R. (2015). *Labour market outcomes of young postsecondary graduates, 2005 to 2012* (Economic Insights. Statistics Canada Catalogue number 11–626-X). Retrieved from http://www.statcan.gc.ca/pub/11-626-x/11-626-x2015050-eng.pdf

Gilbert, D., & Wilson, T. (2007). Prospection: Experiencing the future. *Science, 351,* 1351–1354. https://doi.org/10.1126/science.1144161.

Grosemans, I., Hannes, K., Neyens, J., & Kyndt, E. (2018). Emerging adults embarking on their careers: Job and identity explorations in the transition to work. *Youth & Society*. Advanced online publication. https://doi.org/10.1177/0044118X18772695.

Horowitz, A. D., & Bromnick, R. D. (2007). "Contestable Adulthood": Variability and disparity in markers for negotiating the transition to adulthood. *Youth & Society, 39,* 209–231. https://doi.org/10.1177/0044118X06296692.

Keller, A. C., Samuel, R., Bergman, M. M., & Semmer, K. K. (Eds.). (2014). *Psychological, educational, and sociological perspectives on success and well-being in career development*. Dordrecht, The Netherlands: Springer.

Khalifa, H., Alnuaim, A. A., Young, R. A., Marshall, S. K., & Popadiuk, N. (2018). Crafting continuity and change in Saudi society: Joint parent-youth transition-to-adulthood projects. *Journal of Adolescence, 63,* 142–152. https://doi.org/10.1016/j.adolescence.2017.12.014.

Konstam, V., & Lehmann, I. S. (2011). Emerging adults at work and at play: Leisure, work engagement, and career indecision. *Journal of Career Assessment, 19*, 151–164. https://doi.org/10.1177/1069072710385546.

Mao, C. H. (2017). Paternal and maternal support and Taiwanese college students' indecision: Gender differences. *Australia Journal of Career Development, 26*, 103–112. https://doi.org/10.1177/1038416217725768.

Marshall, S. K., Stainton, T., Wall, J. M., Zhu, M., Murray, J., Wu, S., et al. (2018). Transition to adulthood as a joint parent-youth project for young persons with intellectual and developmental disabilities. *Intellectual and Development Disabilities, 56,* 263–277. https://doi.org/10.1352/1934-9556-56.5.263.

Marshall, S. K., Zaidman-Zait, A., Domene, J. F., & Young, R. A. (2012). Qualitative action-project method in family research. *Journal of Family Theory & Review, 4,* 160–173. https://doi.org/10.1111/j.1756-2589.2012.00117.x.

Mortimer, J. T., Zimmer-Gembeck, M. J., Holmes, M., & Shanahan, M. J. (2002). The process of occupational decision making: Patterns during the transition to adulthood. *Journal of Vocational Behavior, 61,* 439–465. https://doi.org/10.1006/jvbe.2002.1885.

Petersen, D. M., Marcia, J. E., & Carpendale, J. I. (2004). Identity: Does thinking make it so? In C. Lightfoot, M. Chandler, & C. Lalonde (Eds.), *Changing conceptions of psychological life* (pp. 113–126). Mahwah, NJ: Lawrence Erbaum.

Popadiuk, N., Young, R. A., & Valach, L. (2008). Clinician perspectives of the therapeutic use of the self-confrontation procedure with suicidal clients. *Journal of Mental Health Counseling, 30,* 13–30. https://doi.org/10.17744/mehc.30.1.h37l81l71u4986n0.

Porfeli, E. J., Lee, B., Vondracek, F. W., & Weigold, I. K. (2011). A multidimensional measure of vocational identity status. *Journal of Adolescence, 34,* 853–871. https://doi.org/10.1016/j.adolescence.2011.02.001.

Parada, F., & Young, R. A. (2013). Youth work transitions: A review with implications for counselling and career practice. *Canadian Journal of Counselling and Psychotherapy, 47,* 196–222. Retrieved from https://cjc-rcc.ucalgary.ca/cjc/index.php/rcc/issue/archive.

Rizzolatti, G., Cattaneo, L., Fabbri-Destro, M., & Rozzi, S. (2014). Cortical mechanisms underlying the organization of goal-directed actions and mirror neuron-based action understanding. *Physiological Reviews, 94,* 655–706. https://doi.org/10.1152/physrev.00009.2013.

Seligman, M. E. P., Railton, P., Baumeister, R. F., & Sripada, C. (2013). Navigating into the future or driven by the past. *Perspectives on Psychological Science*, *8*(2), 119–141. https://doi.org/10.1177/1745691612474317.

Sennett, R. (1998). *The corrosion of character: The personal consequences of work in the new capitalism.* W. W. Norton & Company: New York, NY.

Silva, V., Chevalier, M., Chiang, M., MacKenzie, M., Kesha Pradhan, K., Record-Lemon, R., & Young, R. A. (2018). *Advocating for newcomers to Canada through goal-directed project support.* Poster presented at the 2018 Canadian Counselling Psychology Conference, Calgary, AB.

Shulman, S., Barr, T., Livneh, Y., Nurmi, J.-E., Vasalampi, K., & Pratt, M. (2015). Career pursuit pathways among emerging adult men and women: Psychosocial correlates and precursors. *International Journal of Behavioral Development, 39,* 9–19. https://doi.org/10.1177/0165025414533222.

Shulman, S., & Connolly, J. (2016). The challenge of romantic relationships in emerging adulthood. In J. J. Arnett & J. J. Arnett (Eds.), *The Oxford handbook of emerging adulthood* (pp. 230–244). New York, NY: Oxford University Press.

Stewart, J., Gapenne, O., & Di Paolo, E. A. (2010). Introduction. In J. Stewart, O. Gapenne & E. A. Di Paolo (Eds.), *Enaction: Toward a new paradigm for cognitive science* (pp. vii–xvii).

Symonds, J., Dietrich, J., Chow, & Salmela-Aro, K. (2016). Mental health improves after transition from comprehensive school to vocational education or employment in England: A national cohort study. *Developmental Psychology, 52*, 652–665. https://doi.org/10.1037/a0040118.

Valach, L., Michel, K., Dey, P., & Young, R. A. (2002a). Self-confrontation interview with suicide attempters. *Counselling Psychology Quarterly, 15,* 1–22. https://doi.org/10.1080/09515070110101487.

Valach, L., Young, R. A., & Lynam, M. J. (2002b). *Action theory: A primer for applied research in the social sciences*. Westport, CT: Praeger Publishers.

von Cranach, M., Ochsenbein, G., & Valach, L. (1986). The group as a self-active system: Outline of a theory of group action. *European Journal of Social psychology, 16,* 193–229. https://doi.org/10.1002/ejsp.2420160302.

Wall, J. M., Law, A. K., Zhu, M., Munro, D., Parada, F., & Young, R. A. (2016). Understanding goal-directed action in emerging adulthood: Conceptualization and method. *Emerging Adulthood, 4,* 30–39. https://doi.org/10.1177/2167696815610695.

Whiston, S. C., & Keller, B. K. (2004). The influences of the family of origin on career development: A review and analysis. *The Counseling Psychologist, 32,* 493–568. https://doi.org/10.1177/0011000004265660.

Young, R. A., & Domene, J. F. (2012). Creating a research agenda in career counselling: The place of action theory. *British Journal of Guidance and Counselling, 40,* 15–30. https://doi.org/10.1080/03069885.2011.620603.

Young, R. A., & Domene, J. F. (2018). Contextual action theory: Concepts, processes, and examples. Manuscript accepted for publication in N. Arthur & M. McMahon (Eds.). *Contemporary theories of career development: International perspectives* (pp. 78–90). London, United Kingdom: Routledge.

Young, R. A., Domene, J. F., & Valach, L. (2015a). Counseling and Action. In R. A. Young, J. F. Domene, & L. Valach (Eds.), *Counseling and action: Toward life-enhancing work, relationships, and identity* (pp. 1–10). New York, NY: Springer.

Young, R. A., Marshall, S. K., Foulkes, K., Haber, C., Lee, C. S. M., Penner, C., et al. (2011a). Counseling for the transition to adulthood as joint, goal-directed action. *Journal of Vocational Behavior, 79,* 325–333. https://doi.org/10.1016/j.jvb.2011.02.005.

Young, R. A., Marshall, S. K., & Murray, J. (2017). Prospective content in the friendship conversations of young adults. *Journal of Adolescence, 54,* 9–17. https://doi.org/10.1016/j.adolescence.2016.11.001.

Young, R. A., Marshall, S. K., Stainton, T., Wall, J., Curle, D., Zhu, M., et al. (2018). The transition to adulthood of young adults with IDD: Parents' joint projects. *Journal of Applied Research in Intellectual Disabilities, 31,* 224–233. https://doi.org/10.1111/jar.12395.

Young, R. A., Marshall, S. K., Valach, L., Domene, J., Graham, M. D., & Zaidman-Zait, A. (2011b). *Transition to adulthood: Action, projects, and counseling*. New York, NY: Springer.

Young, R. A., Marshall, S. K., Wilson, L. J., Green, A. R., Klubben, L., Parada, F., et al. (2015b). Transition to adulthood as a peer project. *Emerging Adulthood, 3,* 166–178. https://doi.org/10.1177/2167696814559304.

Young, R. A., Paseluikho, M., & Valach, L. (1997). Emotion in the construction of career in conversations between parents and adolescents. *Journal of Counseling and Development, 76,* 36–44. https://doi.org/10.1002/j.1556-6676.1997.tb02374.x.

Young, R. A., & Valach, L. (2004). The construction of career through goal-directed action. *Journal of Vocational Behavior, 64,* 499–514. https://doi.org/10.1016/j.jvb.2003.12.012.

Young, R. A., & Valach, L. (2016). Action and language: Contextual action theory in counselling. *Revue Psychologie Française, 61,* 31–42. https://doi.org/10.1016/j.psfr.2013.03.001.

Young, R. A., Valach, L., & Collin, A. (1996). A contextualist explanation of career. In D. Brown, L. Brooks, & M. J. Lynam (Eds.), *Career choice and development* (3rd ed., pp. 477–512). San Francisco, CA: Jossey-Bass.

Young, R. A., Valach, L., Dillabough, J., Dover, C., & Matthes, G. (1994). Career research from an action perspective: The self-confrontation procedure. *Career Development Quarterly, 43,* 185–196. https://doi.org/10.1002/j.2161-0045.1994.tb00857.x.

Young, R. A., Valach, L., & Domene, J. F. (2005). The action-project method in counseling psychology. *Journal of Counseling Psychology, 52,* 215–223. https://doi.org/10.1037/0022-0167.52.2.215.

Young, R. A., Valach, L., & Domene, J. F. (2015c). Counseling processes and procedures. In R. A. Young, J. F. Domene, & L. Valach (Eds.), *Counseling and action: Toward life-enhancing work, relationships, and identity* (pp. 317–336). New York: Springer.

Young, R. A., Valach, L., Marshall, S. K., Domene, J. F., Graham, M. D., & Zaidman-Zait, A. (2010). *Transition to adulthood: Action, projects and counseling*. New York, NY: Springer.

Postmodernising Career Counselling in a Deep Rural Context

Jacobus G. Maree

Abstract Society's collective response to the effect of sweeping changes in the occupational world on people living in poverty has been inadequate as has been its ability to turn global changes and challenges into prospects for sustainable decent work for all people, especially those in disadvantaged contexts. Moreover, little if any innovation in career counselling has been witnessed in these contexts. This chapter examines the value of an innovative strategy aimed at postmodernising the approach to and practice of career counselling in a deep rural part of South Africa. First, I briefly cover the effect of global changes in the workplace on people's career-lives. Next, I discuss some aspects of a postmodern approach that draws on life design counselling with respect to self- and career counselling theory, research, and practice. This is followed by a brief discussion of the background to a research project aimed at postmodernising career counselling in a deep rural area of South Africa during a three-phase project (2016–2018), after which I elaborate on the research approach followed as well as the key elements of the intervention used in this project. The research findings are presented and discussed before the way forward is mapped out and the chapter concluded.

Keywords Sustainable decent work · Resource scarce environment · Postmodernising career counselling · Life design · Self- and career construction counselling · Group-based career counselling

Introduction

Work contexts are changing rapidly and becoming more unpredictable, and work patterns are following suit. This is confirmed by Hirschi (in press) and Rudolph, Zacher, and Hirschi (2019) who state that "*heterogeneous career patterns have resulted from changes in the nature of work, organizational structures, psychological contracts, workforce demographics, as well as broader economic factors*" and add that "*[r]ecent*

J. G. Maree (✉)
Department of Educational Psychology, University of Pretoria, Pretoria, South Africa
e-mail: kobus.maree@up.ac.za

J. G. Maree (ed.), *Handbook of Innovative Career Counselling*,
https://doi.org/10.1007/978-3-030-22799-9_32

theoretical advances have suggested that in this changing career environment, people need to construct their own meaning of working" (p. 2). Those of us working in the field of career counselling are constantly challenged to rethink what we do and respond in a manner that updates and innovates career counselling theory, practical intervention, and research endeavours. This is consistent with Graham, Hjorth, and Lehdonvirta's (2017) view that "*in much of the world, un- and under-employment is a major social and economic concern for policy-makers, for people with jobs, and for people looking for jobs*" (ILO, 2017, p. 1).

Globally, unemployment is steadily increasing—in vulnerable, disadvantaged contexts in particular. The situation of poor, rural people is deteriorating as job opportunities become scarcer. Learners who have failed to achieve sufficiently well at school to qualify for acceptance into fields of study at tertiary education institutions are at a major disadvantage. Unless they find a way to access training and become employable, their chances of escaping their depressing circumstances are extremely limited. Exacerbating their situation is the fact that very few of these learners have ever received career counselling. In addition, a positivist approach to career counselling is generally offered to the few that do somehow manage to access this service—a service that is mostly characterised by the use of career counselling inventories that can be largely irrelevant in the contexts in which these learners find themselves.

Seen from the perspective outlined above, the need for cutting-edge career counselling for all people is more pressing today than at any comparable stage in human history. It should be the collective goal of all career counsellors, society, and communities to help workers, prospective workers, and unemployed people rekindle their sense of meaning, purpose, and hope in the contemporary, ever-shifting occupational landscape. Many authors, including Chiaradonna (2017), Savickas (2015a), and Maree (2018a), believe that helping people find employment can no longer be regarded as the main aim of career counselling. At a time when occupational contexts are changing rapidly, when many jobs are disappearing, and when new jobs are emerging that require new skills, more than anything else, people today need to become adaptable, career resilient, and employable. Likewise, to an increasing extent, changing occupational contexts are compelling workers to merge their work and life roles and to understand that continued employability will depend largely on people's capacity to learn and develop throughout their lives and to boost their sense of self-awareness as well as their career agility (Lozanov, 2018). From the perspective of this chapter, it is clear that many workers in global south countries ('peripheral' workers) are at great risk of losing their jobs (Guichard, 2013; ILO, 2017). Often living alongside each other in mushrooming informal settlements (frequently colloquially and denigratingly referred to as squatter camps), these workers struggle to find employment while their families mostly live in squalor and extreme poverty. The general inability to create opportunities for sustainable work for such people is a serious indictment of society's lack of capacity or will to solve this problem, which could easily lead to social and political instability and turmoil. To improve the situation, it seems essential to innovate the practice and theory of career counselling constantly and substantially to enable it to stay abreast of fundamental changes brought about and further envisaged by the advent of the 4th Industrial Revolution in particular.

As much has already been written on life design and related issues (see e.g. Maree, 2015a, 2018a), only a brief summary of these issues is given below.

Chapter Structure

The first part provides the background to the research reported on in the chapter. In the second part, the postmodernising of career counselling with regard to life design counselling-related principles is elaborated. The third part covers the background to and the methodology of a three-phase project aimed at postmodernising career counselling in a disadvantaged, deep rural developing country context. Part four talks to the intervention details of the three phases of the project, and, in the fifth part, the findings are presented and discussed before the chapter is concluded.

Chapter Goals

The goal of the chapter is twofold. First, details of a theoretical intervention strategy aimed at postmodernising career counselling with regard to life design counselling-related principles will be elaborated. Second, the implementation of the proposed strategy aimed at postmodernising career counselling in a disadvantaged, deep rural developing country context will be presented and examined.

Postmodernising Career Counselling

According to Maree (2019), storied career counselling (Cochran, 2011) and career construction counselling (Savickas, 2002a, 2002b) are linked to postmodernist approaches, while life design counselling (Savickas et al., 2009) augments the matching (differential) and developmental paradigms that prevailed in the 20th century. Postmodernism represents an assortment of related theories and approaches (Watson, McMahon, Mkhize, Schweitzer, & Mpofu, 2011) that developed from the conviction that the 'reality' created by different people differs in terms of personal, historical, and cultural histories and contexts (Hergenhahn, 2005). Postmodernism holds that people are much more than the 'total' of their scores on tests (Taber, Hartung, Briddick, Briddick, & Rehfuss, 2011) and that drawing on quantitative approaches in relative isolation does not take into account people's uniqueness (Duffy & Dik, 2009).

As I explain in the next section, the approach to career counselling that is advocated in the three-phase project elaborated on later in this chapter is founded on and aims to promote the ideal of postmodernising career counselling.

Life Design Counselling Principles

Life design counselling, which relates to personal and interpersonal relationships as well as career construction principles, is a more inclusive intervention than life and career construction counselling. Career counsellors who administer life design counselling elicit, draw on, and integrate

a. quantitative (i.e., people's scores on interest inventories) as well as
b. qualitative information in respect of
    i. the stages where they make their sense of self and identity known, and
    ii. their multiple micro career-life stories in order to relate career construction theory to the life design counselling discourse.

Career counselling practitioners often draw on the following three distinct intervention models in their work (Savickas, 2010, 2015b).

a. *Vocational guidance*, which highlights individual differences between people and strives to enhance their self- and work-related knowledge. A match is sought between people's selves and certain occupations.
b. *Career development*, which focuses on people's developmental status and aims to improve people's attitudes, beliefs, and competencies (ABCs) to promote further development.
c. *Life design* interventions, which revolve around self- and career construction and draw on people's personal stories to co-construct and sometimes reconstruct people's career-lives and map out their futures.

Table 1 illustrates the progress from vocational guidance to career development and, eventually, to life design; it also shows the association between the three kinds of career counselling interventions and their theoretical underpinnings.

The perspectives discussed in this chapter indicate that career counselling styles differ from context to context. However, traditional (person-environment fit) career counselling still predominates globally. In Africa, especially, very few career counsellors have been trained in the newer paradigms or have embraced newer ideas such as self- and career construction and life design. Furthermore, many people seek career counselling without ever having received vocational guidance, career development, or life design counselling at all. In such instances, career counsellors are obliged to attend to their career counselling needs first and foremost, which often is to access some form of employment urgently. Moreover, the overwhelming majority of career counsellors in the contexts referred to in this chapter almost exclusively provide only vocational guidance and career guidance or education. To help counsellees meet the demands of the changing workplace, all career counselling interventions should be aimed at integrating the three different but related intervention models discussed above.

Table 1 Progression from vocational guidance to career development and life design (compiled from Duarte, 2017; Savickas, 2015a, 2015b)

Theoretical underpinning	Associated intervention (Duarte, 2017; Guichard, 2005, 2009; McAdams, 2013; Savickas, 2011a, 2011b, 2015a, 2015b,2019)	Question(s) signifying expected outcome
Differential	Tries to find the 'best fit; provides information; matching	Which career will 'fit' my personality?
Developmental	Provides Psycho-educational and psychosocial information	a. How should I conduct job analysis? b. How should I go about improving my interpersonal relationships?
Storied (psychodynamic)	Helps clients identify key life themes and reflect and draw on their reflexivity	a. What are my key life themes? b. How should I go about to find a career that will enable me to make meaning and find a sense of purpose and hope in life?

Career Construction Theory (CCT; Savickas, 2005, 2001)

Career construction counselling (CCC) endeavours to enable people to use their autobiographies or career-life stories as a compass to guide their career journeys. Action and forward movement are key elements of CCC where the aim is to construct an 'autobiographical bridge' between a painful past, the current present, and the imminent future. Construction, deconstruction, reconstruction, and co-construction of career-life stories are key elements in equipping counsellees with the skills to face an insecure and unpredictable future often characterised by numerous transitions in people's personal and career-lives. Hurtful memories and a painful past are revisited, examined, reframed, and interpreted from a different and hope-orientated perspective. In eliciting these painful stories, people are helped to listen to (hear) themselves and identify their key life themes (Savickas, 2011a, 2011b, 2019).

Self-construction Theory (SCT; Guichard, 2005, 2009)

Closely associated with CCT theory and practice, Guichard's (2009) self-construction theory (SCT) comprises the narration of people's stories and connecting them to practicable future career-life projects. This includes reconstructing career-life identities, which, especially today, are in a heightened state of flux. Self-construction counselling endeavours to enhance the attainment of more robust, integrated, and trustworthy career-life identities that promote meaning-making and living purposeful lives. The latter is demonstrated by positive responses to questions such as "Who am I?", "Where am I?", "Where am I going?", "Why do I work?", and "What meaning does my life have?" (Guichard, 2005).

Career Adaptability

Career adaptability manifests in matters such as responsible career choice making, the capacity to navigate career-related transitions, and the ability to manage work-life traumas in unpredictable and uncertain work environments (Del Corso, 2013; Hartung, 2011, 2015; Savickas, 2015b).

The following four dimensions of career adaptability relate to key career-related questions, attitudes, beliefs, and competencies.

a. People who display Career Concern respond positively to the question, "Do I have a future?" and work actively work towards realising that future.
b. People who display Career Control respond positively to the question, "Who owns my future?" and are in control of their future.
c. People who display Career Curiosity possess sufficient self- and career knowledge to respond positively to the question, "What do I want to do with my future?" and enter the world of work.
d. People who display Career Confidence demonstrate sufficient levels of self-efficacy to answer the question, "Can I do it?" positively and can deal with perceived and real difficulties in achieving career goals.

Career adaptability seems to be the vehicle that drives people's employability. Employable people proactively pursue their occupational interests and experience greater job satisfaction, which, in turn, influences their work performance (Crant, 2000; Fugate & Kinicki, 2008).

In the next section, I report on a research strategy to postmodernise career counselling in a deep rural context during a three-phase project (2016–2018), followed by a discussion of the research findings and mapping put the way forward. I begin by explicating the background of the project.

The Good Work Foundation (GWF) Education Model for Rural Africa

Towards the end of 2015, Dr. Jopie de Beer, MD of JvR Psychometrics (the only official Multi-Health Systems (MHS) training institution and test distributor in sub-Saharan Africa) introduced me to Ms. Kate Groch: CEO: Good Work Foundation, Ms. Mo Groch: Head of Leadership and Staff Development of the GWF, and Ms. Mercyful Mathebula-Lekhuleni: Bridging Year Student and Career Support of the GWF. Dr. De Beer—aware of my deep involvement with community outreach and related projects aimed at promoting sustainable, decent work for people across the

Photograph 1 The author, Ms. Mo Groch, and some of her staff members at the Good Work Foundation

diversity spectrum—had recommended that I meet with Ms. Groch to discuss the *Career Interest Profile* (*CIP*, ver. 4; Maree, 2015b). The GWF had started using this qualitative assessment instrument a year or two earlier in career counselling work with young people in desperately poor rural communities in the five GWF centres across South Africa. They were keen to find out more about the rationale for the *CIP*, its development, as well as about the move towards integrating qualitative and quantitative approaches with current developments in the field of career counselling. I visited the GWF in Hazyview early in 2016 (Photograph 1)[1] to see the interventions that were being conducted there.

Mo Groch's introductory comment revealed her passion for the work the GWF was doing: "The realm of rural education has many challenges but great opportunities. The opportunities make it a very exciting space to be working in." It soon became clear to me that the GWF (under Kate and Mo Groch's inspiring leadership) was already putting life and career construction theory as well as life design theory into practice in an exemplary manner. In collaboration with strategic partners, the GWF offers basic literacy training and career-related education to school-aged and adult learners (Photograph 2). The GWF's career training academies provide career-related skills courses and digital literacy training for adult learners (Photograph 3). Adult learners (roughly 90% of whom are recent school-leavers) use the 12-month course as a bridging year that offers them a 'second chance' by laying the foundation for English and digital literacy and enabling them to become more employable and eligible for further studies, which further bolsters their employability. Before the course, these learners lacked the adaptability and the skills needed to make them employable. As a result, they were unable either to find employment or enrol at

[1]Written informed assent and consent were obtained from all the participants, and permission was granted for the anonymous publication of the findings (including the photographs).

Photograph 2 Training facilities at the Good Work Foundation

a tertiary training institution. Consequently, their prospects of finding sustainable decent work were extremely slim before they attended the course.

Against this background, I now reflect on an ongoing project that commenced in the deep rural area under discussion in 2016 and that examines the usefulness of life design-based intervention in a typical developing country context.

Using an Adapted Action Research Approach to Postmodernising Career Counselling in a Rural Area

In all the project phases discussed here, an adapted action research paradigm was used (Wong, 2011). As explained elsewhere (Maree, 2017a, 2017b), my aim was less on achieving 'generalizable' outcomes and more on assessing the extent of change that was achieved with the intervention (Ferrance, 2000). I was also curious to find out how change was brought about by action research of the kind explained here and to create awareness and promote action that would lead to social change (Greenwood & Levin, 2000). Lastly, I tried to promote (social) transformation, emancipation, change, satisfactory development, and felt empowerment in the participants (Creswell & Creswell, 2017; Wink, 2005).

Photograph 3 Digital tree of knowledge (made entirely from discarded computer parts) where staff and learners meet to discuss important matters. This 'tree' contains power points, a sound system, a USB, etc

The adapted action research approach (Wong, 2011) comprised three cycles of intervention per year to promote reflection, reflexivity, and action (forward movement). Notwithstanding the fact that I commenced the intervention from an established base (life design-related intervention), I constantly endeavoured to improve the intervention based on the lessons that were learned (Elias et al., 1997) to meet the unique needs of the research participants and context. Each new cycle was carefully planned, based on what had occurred during previous phases of the project (Maree, 2014, 2018a). Lastly, while I believe that substantial progress has been made in customising the life design approach (designed elsewhere in the world) to meet the idiosyncratic career counselling needs of people in the kind of rural context referred to here, more research in diverse contexts is needed before we can claim that definitive outcomes have been achieved. The envisaged next cycle (to take place in 2019) should bring us closer to a degree of certainty in this regard.

The need to follow an adapted action research approach stemmed from the fact that career counselling innovations such as self- and career construction counselling and life design (Guichard, 2009; Savickas, 2015b) are not routinely applied in African contexts, least of all in deep rural areas. These kinds of interventions were designed primarily for use in one-on-one situations in developed country contexts. In typical global south (developing country) contexts, the overwhelming request is for group-based career counselling. Although the need is to assess and administer career counselling to large numbers of people, there is little evidence to confirm the reliability and validity of postmodern kinds of approaches in developing countries.

Goals of the Project

The overall goal of the research was to postmodernise career counselling in a poor rural region by helping the participants elicit and reflect on their micro-career-life stories and draw on these reflections to uncover strengths in themselves and deal with areas for growth in a way that would strengthen their adaptability and promote their employability. The end goal was to help them find sustainable decent work and, in doing so, contribute to sustainable development in this region.

Participants. All the participants were from a resource-scarce, deep rural region of South Africa. All of them had left school and had failed to find employment or to enrol successfully for tertiary study. These (adult) participants were selected (2016, 2017, and 2018 intake) to participate in a life design-based counselling project on the basis of

i. their willingness to participate,
ii. their inability to pay for a career counselling service, and
iii. their inability to find any form of decent work or to be accepted for further study on account of their poor marks at the end of Grade 12 and/or their inability to pay for tertiary tuition.

Intervention Details

First Phase (2016). In 2016, in addition to the intervention with the participants, I demonstrated the basic elements of life design intervention to Mo and her colleagues. More particularly, I informed them how I used the *CIP* (Maree, 2015b) to show how life- and career construction can help people across the diversity spectrum construct themselves and chart their careers, become employable, regain a sense of meaning, purpose, and hope, design successful lives, and make social contributions. The participants' feedback, and especially their progress, was promising. It also augured well for the further use of the intervention strategy, which was specifically designed for replication in similar contexts. Towards the end of the year, Mo and I decided that I would return in 2017 on three different occasions and interact with the learners myself.

Second Phase (2017). In 2017, I first visited the GWF's Hazyview centre in February. To start off with, the *Career Adapt-Abilities Scale-South Africa* (*CAAS-SA*) (Maree, 2012) was administered pre-test. The participants were then asked what they

Photograph 4 Career construction counselling administered in group format

hoped to gain from the sessions, and their responses were video-recorded. This was followed by an interactive discussion on changes in the world of work, the need for career counselling, the need to become adaptable and employable, and the importance of establishing a sound sense of self. The participants were shown video clips reflecting changes in the world of work, after which the *CIP* (Ver. 5, 2017a, 2017b) was administered in group format (Photograph 4) and the outcomes discussed in smaller groups facilitated by me and GWF staff members (Photographs 5 and 6). The session ended by recommending several fields of study and requesting the participants to do a thorough job analysis that was based on a brief presentation on the topic and using a job analysis questionnaire tailored to suit their particular needs (Maree, 2011).

I returned to the GWF at the beginning of June, 2017. The participants were invited to share questions, concerns, challenges, and so forth regarding issues that may have arisen after their job analysis in small groups and to revisit their vision and mission statements. All the participants then shared their revised vision and mission statements with the whole group while being videotaped (Photograph 6). Once again, all the group members were invited to provide inputs. Following this, the participants were requested to finalise their applications for further study, learnerships, and so forth and report back during the concluding session. The session ended with the re-administration of the *CAAS-SA*. In September 2017, I returned to the GWF for the last time. The participants were given the opportunity to see themselves during

Photograph 5 Participants 'working' in small groups

their presentations and encouraged to provide feedback to fellow participants on their impressions of their presentations. All the participants were allowed to discuss their plans for 2018 and recount their vision, mission, and identity statements. This session, too, ended by administering the *CAAS-SA* (Maree, 2012) (Post-test 2) for a third time and by asking the participants for written feedback not only on how they experienced the third session but also on the three sessions as a whole (Table 2).

Phase 3 (2018). In 2018, I replicated the 2017 intervention with a number of modifications:

a. The intervention was completed over four days (two days per session). The third session was devoted to training the trainers at the various campuses of the GWF.
b. Appropriately qualified staff members and volunteers assisted me in facilitating the smooth running of this phase of the project (involving 31 students).
c. I also administered the *Career Decision-making Difficulty Questionnaire* (*CDDQ*; Gati, 2011; Gati, Krausz, & Osipow, 1996; Gati & Levin, 2014; Gati & Saka, 2011a, 2011b) as a pre-test and as a post-test (in addition to the *CAAS-SA*). In addition, I administered the *CIP* (Ver. 6; Maree, 2018b).

Photograph 6 Participant's sharing his revised vision and mission statements with the whole group

Brief Discussion of Findings

Quantitative findings: *CAAS* outcomes. Although the small sample sizes preclude any generalisation of the results, a number of trends nonetheless emerged from the research that are worth noting and call for further investigation.

First, a practically meaningful improvement was noted in the participants' overall career adaptability as well as in their Curiosity, Concern, and (in the case of the men) Control and Confidence scores. The women's Confidence and Control scores consistently showed no improvement. Contextualising these findings seems straightforward: the research context under discussion is a male-dominated community in which only a handful of women ever succeed in accessing tertiary training institutions or finding sustainable work. The women are by and large still expected to be subservient to men, to raise the children, and to do the household chores while the men are expected to find employment to provide for the family. The women's depressing circumstances to a large extent seemed to have negatively influenced their Confidence (belief) that they were capable of realising their career-related dreams and their sense of being in Control of their situation.

Table 2 Outline of the life design-based intervention

Steps	Intervention goal(s) (Savickas et al., 2009)	Intervention to promote achievement of the intervention outcomes
General	Addressing participants' career counselling needs	Helping participants elicit and reflect on their micro-career-life stories and draw on these reflections to choose careers, make-meaning, promote a sense of purpose, and inspire hope
Step 1	Establishing a working relationship	Holding group discussions to help participants get to know each other and complete Part 1 (biographical details) of the *CIP*
Step 2	Exploring participants' subjective sense of self Facilitating critical self-reflection and reflexivity	Completing Parts 2 (career category preferences), 3 (six career-choice questions), and 4 (15 career-life story narrative questions) of the *CIP* and discussing participants' responses to questions on their strengths, areas for growth, etc. Participants reflected on their reflections to bring about reflexivity
Step 3	Objectifying stories to open up new perspectives	Helping participants draft their identity statements and life story titles and headings. (Re)constructing life stories in terms of past and present chapters
Step 4	Contextualising challenging areas in new stories Reconfirming participants' ability to construct their identities	Reviewing 'problems' and regarding them as opportunities Identifying and reconfirming strengths as well as areas for growth and problem-solving competencies
Step 5	Constructing identities Devising plans to help participants deal with challenges Sharing 'new' stories with compassionate audience	Revisiting favourite quotations to elicit inner advice Juxtaposing painful past and inspiring future stories as well as 'faulty' beliefs (cognitions) and inspiring decisions
Step 6	Conducting follow-up	Conducting regular follow-ups

Quantitative findings: *CDDQ* outcomes (Gati, 2011a, 2011b). The participants' post-test results revealed statistically and practically meaningful improvement in the dimension Lack of Information with subdimensions Lack of Information about the Decision-Making Process, Lack of Information about the Self, and Lack of Information about Ways of Obtaining Information. However, it became clear that changes to the current intervention were needed to target their unsatisfactory Readiness to choose a career. In other words, the participants (the men and the women alike) showed a lack of willingness to make a decision, a distorted perception of the career decision-making process (including irrational expectations and dysfunctional thoughts about careers), and inconsistent information challenges. The participants believed they had contradictory information about themselves or about the careers they considered occupations. Moreover, they showed internal confusion as well as external conflict (the gap between their career preferences and the preferences voiced by significant others or contradictions between the opinions of significant others).

Qualitative Findings

A number of themes emerged inductively that tended to confirm the quantitative themes listed above, some of which are listed below (substantiating comments appear between brackets).

Theme 1: Eagerness to seize every opportunity that comes along: "*Now I know that there are many doors that I can knock on*".
Theme 2: Clarity of career focus: "*I have a better idea of what I want to do with my life.*"
Theme 3: Improved sense of self and identity: "*The sessions have helped me understand who I am.*"
Theme 4: Profound sense of feeling hamstrung and confused (this theme emerged from the women's narratives only): "*At the GWF everybody tries to 'empower' me; when I get home, the reality of the situation 'hits' me and I feel depressed again.*"
Theme 5: Value of being allowed to listen to oneself: "*It was amazing to be allowed to hear myself speaking; to listen to my own 'voice'.*"
Theme 6: Opening up of possibilities coupled with lack of confidence: "*A world of possibilities; a beacon of hope has been opened but huge barriers continue to exist 'outside'.*"
Theme 7: Deep desire to move forward: "*Even while I know that my parents are unemployed and I have little support or encouragement.*"
Theme 8: The support of the group as a buttress and inspires action: "*The help and support of everybody in the group gives me hope.*"

The research confirmed the quantitative findings discussed above. While the women in general experienced the intervention as positive and inspiring, they repeatedly voiced their frustrations that factors beyond their control were impeding their self- and career construction and thus their life designing. Moreover, their feedback strengthened the perception that the women, like those living in poverty (in seriously disadvantaged, resource-scarce environments in particular) and minorities, '*gragamba*' ('*kirigamba*') ('*makwerekwere*') (slang for 'foreigners'), seemed curiously 'lost' in a kind of intersectionality interface: While unemployment is an issue of grave concern, the women gave clear evidence that their particular needs were not being addressed in their communities (as a separate matter), as can be seen in the following comments: ('Pearl', 23 years old): "*There is no support for my dreams in our township*" and ('Precious' 26 years old): "*The intervention gave me so much hope … But I can only become happy when I leave this place forever*".

Follow-up

Follow-up confirmed the success of the intervention, especially in the case of the men. Virtually all the men participating in the research reported finding work, obtaining a learnership, or being accepted into a field of study at a tertiary training institution. However, while a number of the women, too, reported similar outcomes, the dire situation of the women generally in the area continues to impede their progress. For many reasons beyond their control, many women simply cannot find employment or find a way to leave their area to study and further develop themselves. This situation remains a source of great concern to all stakeholders.

Sequel

Based on the lessons learned during the first three phases of the project, as well as the need for the constant innovation and ongoing sustainability of the programme, my role in 2019 will be limited to that of researcher and advisor only. Assessments will take place on three occasions: in February, June, and September 2019. The life design programme will be revamped to include 17 themes to guide the intervention throughout the year: "Who am I?", "My values", "Careers out there", "My self-awareness", "My social-emotional intelligence", "My career-life story", "My career interests", "My CV", "My budget", Online communication", "Designing a plan for success", "Networking", "Learning to learn", "Life skills", "Work skills", "My interviews", and "Prepare my starting point". The programme will be spread over a number of weeks to meet the needs of participants identified by the results of the *CDDQ* in particular. The intervention will form a part of the Good Work Foundation's (GWF) year-long Bridging Year Academy (BYA) course for young, disadvantaged, unemployed rural South Africans (also see Maree and Gerryts, in press).

The research again confirmed that the social context co-determines whether and how vocational guidance, career guidance (career education), or career counselling (life design) is applied (Maree, in press). The need for ongoing contextualising of career counselling theory and practice (instruments and intervention) was also re-affirmed. Eliciting and considering the inputs of the research participants and other stakeholders during each phase of the intervention emerged as a key element in ensuring the trustworthiness of the intervention. Input from stakeholders from different socioeconomic strata was used to ensure appropriate co-contextualisation. Drawing on the inseparable twin actions of innovating and contextualising career counselling paradigms can help promote the aim of postmodernising career counselling, which is to better meet the idiosyncratic needs of people from diverse contexts, individually and collectively.

Conclusion

It seems fair to conclude that life design intervention—based on the principles of self- and career construction counselling—can be applied successfully in African (developing country) contexts to postmodernise career counselling. However, this requires ongoing contextualising of career counselling theory and practice. In this regard, the present research highlighted the feasibility and importance of designing novel career-counselling interventions and related instruments that 'work' in contexts that differ from those in which the interventions and instruments were initially designed.

The research also confirmed the value of postmodernising career counselling intervention in developing countries and showed furthermore that the nature of such intervention need not differ substantially from related intervention in developed countries. By eliciting and examining the career-life stories of research participants in the manner described in this chapter, researcher-counsellors can determine what works and what does not work in everyday situations and tailor interventions to meet the specific needs of different research groups in their particular contexts. Research and intervention can in this way promote Goal 8 of the UN Agenda (UN, 2016, p. 1): "*Promote sustained, inclusive, and sustainable economic growth, full and productive employment and decent work for all.*"

No financial support was received for this project.

References

Chiaradonna, A. (2017). *Staying relevant: Managing yourself and your career*. Retrieved from https://register.gotowebinar.com/register/3598727376762693l5?utm_source=Sailthruandutm_medium=emailandutm_campaign=Insights%20-%2017-05-28%20-%20Guestandutm_content=Aandutm_term=Insights%20-%20Guest%20-%20Smart%20List%20v3.

Cochran, L. (2011). The promise of narrative career counseling. In K. Maree (Ed.), *Shaping the story—A guide to facilitating narrative career counselling* (pp. 7–19). Rotterdam, The Netherlands: Sense.

Crant, J. M. (2000). Proactive behavior in organizations. *Journal of Management, 26*, 435–462.

Creswell, J. W., & Creswell, J. D. (2017). *Research design: Qualitative, quantitative, and mixed-methods approaches*. Thousand Oaks CA: Sage publications.

Del Corso, J. J. (2013). The theory of career adaptability. In A. Di Fabio & J. G. Maree (Eds.) *Psychology of career counselling: New challenges for a new era* (pp. 117–130). Hauppauge, NY: NOVA.

Duarte, M. E. (2017). *Sustainable decent work*. Invited public lecture at University of Pretoria. Pretoria: Pretoria University.

Duffy, R. D., & Dik, B. J. (2009). Beyond the self: External influences in the career development process. *The Career Development Quarterly, 58*, 29–43.

Elias, M. J., Zins, J. E., Weissberg, R. P., Frey, K. S., Greenberg, M. T., Haynes, N. M., et al. (1997). *Promoting social and emotional learning: Guidelines for educators*. Alexandria, VA: Association for Supervision and Curriculum Development.

Ferrance, E. (2000). *Themes in education: Action research*. The Education Alliance, Brown University. Retrieved from http://www.alliance.brown.edu/pubs/themes_ed/act_research.pdf.

Fugate, M., & Kinicki, A. M. (2008). A dispositional approach to employability: Development of a measure and test of implications for employee reactions to organizational change. *Journal of Occupational and Organizational Psychology, 81*(3), 503–527.

Gati, I. (2011). *Career decision-making difficulties questionnaire* (*CDDQ*): Abridged professional manual. Retrieved from http://kivunim.huji.ac.il/cddq/CDDQ-Manual-3-2011.doc.

Gati, I., & Saka, N. (2011a). Internet-based versus paper-and-pencil assessment: Measuring career decision-making difficulties. *Journal of Career Assessment, 9*, 397–416. https://doi.org/10.1177/106907270100900406.

Gati, I., & Saka, N. (2011b). High school students' career-related decision-making difficulties. *Journal of Counseling and Development, 7*(3), 331–340.

Gati, I., Krausz, M., & Osipow, S. H. (1996). A taxonomy of difficulties in career decision making. *Journal of Counseling Psychology, 43*(4), 510–526.

Gati, I., & Levin, N. (2014). Counseling for career decision-making difficulties: Measures and methods. *Career Development Quarterly, 62*(2), 98–113. https://doi.org/10.1002/j.2161-0045.2014.00073.x.

Graham, M., Hjorth, I., & Lehdonvirta, V. (2017). Digital labour and development: impacts of global digital labour platforms and the gig economy on worker livelihoods. *Transfer, 23*(2), 135–162. https://doi.org/10.1177/1024258916687250).

Greenwood, D. J., & Levin, M. (2000). Reconstructing the relationships and society through action research. In N. K. Denzin & Y. S. Lincoln (Eds.), *Handbook of qualitative research* (pp. 85–106). San Francisco, CA: Sage.

Guichard, J. (2005). Life-long self-construction. *International Journal for Educational and Vocational Guidance, 5*, 111–124.

Guichard, J. (2009). Self-constructing. *Journal of Vocational Behavior, 75*, 251–258.

Guichard, J. (2013, September). *Which paradigm for career and life designing interventions contributing to the sustainable development of a fairer world during the 21st century*? Inaugural conference at the IAEVG International Conference, Montpellier, France.

Hartung, P. J. (2011). Career construction: Principles and practice. In K. Maree (Ed.), *Shaping the story: A guide to facilitating narrative counselling* (pp. 103–120). Rotterdam, The Netherlands: Sense.

Hartung, P. J. (2015). Life design in childhood: Antecedents and advancement. In L. Nota & J. Rossier (Eds.), *Handbook of life design: From practice to theory, and from theory to practice* (pp. 89–101). Göttingen: Hogrefe.

Hergenhahn, B. R. (2005). *An introduction to the history of psychology* (5th ed.). Belmont, CA: Thomson Wadsworth.

Hirschi, A. (in press). The fourth industrial revolution: Issues and implications for career research and practice. *The Career Development Quarterly.*

International Labor Organization (ILO). (2017). *World employment social outlook: Trends 2017*. Geneva, Switzerland: International Labor Office.

Lozanov, L. (2018). *The six Cs of career agility*. Retrieved from https://www.tek-experts.com/the-six-cs-of-career-agility/.

Maree, J. G. (2011). Career counselling in South Africa institutions of higher learning in the 21st century: Re-discovering the potential of qualitative approaches. *South African Journal of Higher Education, 26*(3), 661–669.

Maree, J. G. (2012). Career adapt-abilities scale-South African form: Psychometric properties and construct validity. *Journal of Vocational Behaviour, 80*(3), 730–733.

Maree, J. G. (2013). *Counselling for career construction: Connecting life themes to construct life portraits: Turning pain into hope*. Rotterdam, The Netherlands: Sense.

Maree, J. G. (2014). Creating a sense of hope: The essence of career construction for life designing in a developing country context. In M. Pope, L. Y. Flores, & J. Rottinghaus (Eds.), *The role of values in careers* (pp. 213–232). Charlotte, NC: Information Age Publishing.

Maree, J. G. (2015a). Research on life design in (South) Africa: A qualitative analysis. *South African Journal of Psychology, 45*, 332–348.

Maree, J. G. (2015b). *The Career Interest Profile (Version 4)*. Randburg, SA: JvR Psychometrics.

Maree, J. G. (2017a). *The career interest profile (CIP) (Version 5): Obtaining, qualitatively, a profile of personal career-life themes and interests*. Randburg, South Africa: JvR Psychometrics.

Maree, J. G. (2017b). *Career interest profile (Version 5)*. Randburg, South Africa: JvR Psychometrics.

Maree, J. G. (2018a). Promoting career development in the early years of a person's life through self- and career construction counselling. *Early Child Development and Care, 188*(4), 425–436.

Maree, J. G. (2018b). *The career interest profile (Version 5)*. Randburg, SA: JvR Psychometrics.

Maree, J. G. (2019). Applying the narrative approach in career counselling and related research. In A. Fynn, S. Laher, & S. Fynn (Eds.), *Research methods in South Africa: Theory and applications* (pp. …). Johannesburg, South Africa: Wits University Press.

Maree, J. G. (in press). Contextualisation as a determining factor for career counselling throughout the world. In J. A Athanasou & H. N. Perera (Eds), *International handbook of career guidance* (2nd ed.) (pp. …). New York, NY: Springer.

McAdams, D. P. (2013). The psychological self as actor, agent, and author. *Perspectives on Psychological Science, 8*(3), 272–295.

Rudolph, C. W., Zacher, H., & Hirschi, A. (2019). Editorial. Empirical developments in career construction theory. *Journal of Vocational Behavior*. https://doi.org/10.1016/j.jvb.2018.08.006 (Online first publication).

Savickas, M. L. (2001). Toward a comprehensive theory of career development: Disposition, concerns and narratives. In F. T. L. Leong & A. Barak (Eds.), *Contemporary models in vocational psychology: A volume in honor of Samuel H. Osipow* (pp. 295–320). Mahwah, NJ: Lawrence Erlbaum.

Savickas, M. L. (2002a). Career construction: a developmental theory of vocational behavior. In D. Brown (Ed.), *Career choice and development* (4th ed., pp. 149–205). San Francisco, CA: Jossey-Bass.

Savickas, M. L. (2002b). Reinvigorating the study of careers. *Journal of Vocational Behavior, 61*, 381–385.

Savickas, M. L. (2005). The theory and practice of career construction. In S. D. Brown, R. W. Lent (Eds.), *Career development and counselling* (pp. 42–70). Hoboken, NJ: Wiley.

Savickas, M. L. (2010). Foreword: Best practices in career intervention. In K. Maree (Ed.), *Career counselling: Methods that work* (pp. xi–xii). Cape Town, South Africa: Juta & Company.

Savickas, M. L. (2011a). *Career counseling*. Washington, DC: American Psychological Association.

Savickas, M. L. (2011b). New questions for vocational psychology: premises, paradigms, and practices. *Journal of Career Assessment*. https://doi.org/10.1177/1069072710395532.

Savickas, M. L. (2015a). Career counselling paradigms: Guiding, developing, and designing. In P. Hartung, M. Savickas, & W. Walsh (Eds.), *The APA handbook of career intervention* (Vol. 1) (pp. 129–143). Washington, DC: APA Books.

Savickas, M. L. (2015b). *Life-design counselling manual*. Rootstown, OH: (n.p.).

Savickas, M. L. (2019). *Career counselling* (2nd ed.). Washington, DC: American Psychological Association.

Savickas, M., Nota, L., Rossier, J., Dauwalder, J.-P., Duarte, M. E., Guichard, J., et al. (2009). Life designing: A paradigm for career construction in the 21st century. *Journal of Vocational Behavior, 75*(3), 239–250.

Taber, B. J., Hartung, P. J., Briddick, H., Briddick, W. C., & Rehfuss, M. C. (2011). Career style interview: A contextualized approach to career counseling. *The Career Development Quarterly, 59*, 274–287.

United Nations (UN) (2016). *Transforming our world: The 2030 Agenda for sustainable development*. Retrieved from https://sustainabledevelopment.un.org/post2015/transformingourworld.

Watson, M., McMahon, M., Mkhize, N., Schweitzer, R. D., & Mpofu, E. (2011). Career counseling people of African ancestry. In E. Mpofu (Ed.), *Counselling people of African ancestry* (pp. 281–293). New York, NY: Cambridge University Press.

Wink, J. (2005). *Critical pedagogy*. Boston, MA: Allyn & Bacon.
Wong, M. W. Y. (2011). Adapted action research as an instructional strategy in a music teacher education programme in Hong Kong. *Music Education Research, 13*(1), 107–120.

A Socio-constructionist Career Counselling Model Grounded in the Intersectionality of Gender, Class and Race/Ethnicity

Marcelo Afonso Ribeiro and Maria Celeste Couceiro Gama de Almeida

Abstract This chapter discusses a proposed model of socio-constructionist career counselling (CC) grounded in the intersectionality of gender, class, and race/ethnicity. It further covers the case study of a 30-year-old lower socioeconomic status (SES), unemployed Black woman, who received CC in Brazil. The model is based on the life design paradigm, the psychology of working theory (PWT), and Latin American critical theories, and its two basic principles are intercultural dialogue and hybridism. It is grounded on four basic theoretical underpinnings (relational ontology, career as a working life project and working life trajectory, narratability, and the counselee as a subject of rights) and seven basic technical underpinnings (counsellor acting as an intermediary, focus on the process, counselling as a successive process of co-construction, diatopical hermeneutics, discursive validation, critical consciousness, and communitarian strategies). The limitations and potentialities of the proposed CC model are also discussed.

Keywords Social constructionism · Career counselling · Vulnerability · Intersectionality · Latin America

Introduction

Several authors have emphasized the importance of intersectionality factors in career counselling (CC) practices (e.g., Blustein, 2011; Duarte, 2015; Duffy, Blustein, Diemer, & Autin, 2016; Rascován, 2005), but most of them do not address

The chapter was based on a career counselling case study held by Maria Celeste C. G. Almeida and supervised by Marcelo A. Ribeiro. It has been supported by CNPq—Conselho Nacional de Desenvolvimento Científico e Tecnológico, Brasil (National Council for Scientific and Technological Development-Brazil) by means of a regular research grant (304599/2018-2).

M. A. Ribeiro (✉) · M. C. C. G. de Almeida
University of São Paulo, São Paulo, SP, Brazil
e-mail: marcelopsi@usp.br

M. C. C. G. de Almeida
e-mail: mcelestegalmeida@gmail.com

J. G. Maree (ed.), *Handbook of Innovative Career Counselling*,
https://doi.org/10.1007/978-3-030-22799-9_33

intersectionality in CC in a direct and practical manner. Duffy et al. (2016) give intersectionality a key role in the CC process but have as yet not come forward with practical proposals.

Intersectionality can be described as a transdisciplinary theory aimed at capturing the complexity of identities and social inequalities through an integrated approach grounded in the interconnectedness of social class, gender, and race/ethnicity (Crenshaw, 1989/2018). According to Cole (2009): "[i]ntersectionality makes plain that gender, race, class, and sexuality simultaneously affect the perceptions, experiences, and opportunities of everyone living in a society stratified along these dimensions" (p. 179).

This chapter discusses how intersectionality can be included theoretically and practically in CC practices by considering a proposal developed and evaluated by a university CC service in Brazil. The proposal seeks to contribute to the advancement of studies in CC and social justice on the basis of a case study dealing with the issues and dilemmas of a lower socioeconomic status (SES) Black woman living in a country with high unemployment and informality (International Labour Organization—ILO, 2017).

Intersectionality can be considered a key factor in CC since "the awareness of social place, gender and skin color attributes at work fosters the person's ability to place himself/herself as a subject of his/her educational and professional future" (Silva, Paiva, & Ribeiro, 2016, p. 50).

The first part of the chapter argues that intersectionality factors should feature prominently in CC. The second part presents a proposal model for CC grounded in intersectionality. The third part deals with the case study of a lower SES, 30-year-old Black woman who received CC. The last part makes some recommendations for including intersectionality in CC.

A Proposed CC Model Grounded in Intersectionality

The proposal for a socio-constructionist CC model grounded in intersectionality reflects the epistemology of the global North (psychology of working theory, PWT, and the life design paradigm) with contextualized theories from the global South (pedagogy of the oppressed, critical vocational psychology, and human rights perspective).

Key Concepts

This proposal is based on two key principles: *intercultural dialogue* and *hybridism.*[1] *Intercultural dialogue* is informed by the idea that the production of knowledge is

[1]We have put the theoretical and technical underpinnings in italics every time they have appeared in the text to highlight them.

always built on the relationship of all the social actors involved in a given context (e.g. counsellor and counselee in CC practices), without the one carrying more weight than the other (Santos, 2014). Thus, intercultural dialogue "can be offered by someone from a different cultural group than those who it is done with" (Silva et al., 2016, p. 49). It therefore has to be "forged *with* others, not *for* others" (Freire, 1970, p. 32). *Hybridism,* on the other hand, is characterized by the idea that the world is built on the reproduction of knowledge and on ways of being and acting. However, new links between existing ways of being and acting may emerge and create *hybrids* or *monsters*. While *hybrids* are integrated into the social order of things, the term *monster* denotes a lack of a recognized social place (Latour, 1993).

Theoretical and Technical Framework

We propose four theoretical principles for CC: *relational ontology* (Blustein, 2011; McNamee, 2012), the *concept of career as working life project and working life trajectory* (Ribeiro, 2016), *narratability* (Savickas et al., 2009), and recognizing the *counselee as a subject of rights, choices, and discourses* (Ayres et al., 2006; Bohoslavsky, 1983; Duffy et al., 2016; Rascován, 2005). We go on to list seven technical principles for CC as the basis for the proposed model. First, the counsellor should act as an *intermediary* (Lehman, Ribeiro, Uvaldo, & Silva, 2015). Second, counselling should *focus on the process* rather than on a predefined plan (Bohoslavsky, 1983; Savickas et al., 2009). Third, counselling should be understood as a *successive process of co-construction* (Duarte, 2015). Fourth, the counsellor should use a *diatopical hermeneutics* (Santos, 2014). Fifth, the counsellor should use a *communitarian strategy* (Rascován, 2005). Sixth, a *discursive validation* should be provided (Winslade, 2005). And, finally, a *critical consciousness* should be improved as proposed by Freire (1970) in the educational field and integrated in the CC field as proposed by Duffy et al. (2016). These principles will be explained in greater detail as they occur throughout the text.

Practicalities of the CC Intervention

In operational terms, the proposed CC will be conducted individually (face-to-face) over nine one-hour meetings, with a proposed follow-up meeting four months later. These meetings will be divided into three stages: firstly, a focus on psychosocial issues and life project construction; secondly, an intermediary moment of transition; and, finally, action plan construction. The CC practice will be based on narrative construction, identification of social discourses into these narratives, deconstruction of both narratives and social discourses, and the reconstruction of a narrative that takes into account the intersectionality issues in career construction. The main tools will be speech and project construction, which will help chart a way for expanding dialogue, negotiating meanings, and integrating differences.

For a preliminary overview of the proposed model, see Ribeiro (2016, 2018a, 2018b) and Silva et al. (2016), where intersectionality is briefly touched upon. This chapter builds on the publications of the above authors by adding two new components. Firstly, it introduces the proposed CC model with intersectionality as the key factor; and, secondly, it shows practical application of the model on the basis of a case study of a lower SES 30-year-old Black woman who received CC.

The Case of Mary: Female, Black, Poor, and Unemployed

Case Study: Method of Analysis

An exploratory and descriptive case study was conducted with the aim of linking the data to propositions and assessing the effectiveness and relevance of the proposed CC practice. The case study data were analyzed by identifying a set of casual links based on the initial theoretical statement. The underlying principles were tested enabling us to draw some preliminary conclusions about the proposed CC and the inclusion of intersectionality in CC practices.

Because the principles are so closely linked, it is not possible to discuss them separately. We therefore elected to deal with them jointly on the basis of four 'scenes' selected from the CC process by means of which we could analyze the theoretical and technical features involved, as well as the counselee's achievements. A scene can be described as the relational dynamics in different daily life situations into a scenario (context in which the scene occurs) and developed by a script (the way lived situations occur) (Paiva, 2005).

We used the *class habitus* concept of Bourdieu (1977) as a basis for understanding social class, Butler's (1990) gender analysis for understanding gender issues, and Delgado and Stefancic (2017) critical race theory (CRT) for understanding race and ethnicity issues. These three theoretical models/proposals have social construction as a key axis, which is consistent with our main epistemological framework, namely a social constructionist perspective (McNamee, 2012).

CC Setting and Context

The CC process is part of a university CC service offered at one of the most eminent universities in Latin America with a tradition of assisting middle and high-SES youths choose an appropriate profession and also of assisting adults in their career transitions. Although the traditional target population of this well-known CC service has been higher SES people, a different population segment—mainly lower SES and unskilled people, usually without a profession or defined working activity—has also requested the service as a way of enhancing their working lives. Intersectionality is important for this group's career construction and has led to the development of different kinds of CC interventions.

Participants—The Counsellor and the Counselee

The counsellor was a 60-year-old, middle-SES White woman with a college degree, and, as stated previously, the counselee was a 30-year-old, lower SES Black woman who was unemployed at the time of the CC process. Her working history consisted of several discontinuous and informal jobs as well as periods of unemployment, which is common in a large part of the Brazilian population (Antunes, 2015). The only exception to this working trajectory pattern was a job in a logistics company where she worked successfully in her field of expertise (quality management); however, she was dismissed without any clear reasons being given. Here it is important to mention that the woman presented herself in traditional African dress, including hairstyle, underlining her identity as a Black woman. The counselee will henceforth be referred to as Mary (a pseudonym). She readily gave her informed consent to the publication of the case study.

Four Scenes from the CC Process

Scene 1—Issues Arising from the First Meetings

The first scene of the first meeting in the CC process was marked by the counsellor asking Mary why she had sought CC, and Mary replied as follows:

> I am unemployed, and I want to know what my true vocation is and what I like to do. The situation is very difficult. I have tried to get a job, but I achieved nothing. Thus, I have tried to sell, because some say when you are unemployed, the more accessible job is selling. However, I am unable to sell.[2]

Based on a *relational ontology* (Blustein, 2011; McNamee, 2012), Mary's request arose from collaboration between the parties involved in the CC process (counsellor and counselee). And, through the lens of intersectionality, we can recognize the power relations between two different *class habitus* people in this first scene: the counsellor's *class habitus* (White middle-class woman with college degree working at a recognized university) and the counselee's *class habitus* (lower SES, unemployed Black woman). The counsellor is thus socially more powerful than the counselee.

[2]The responses of the participants are verbatim with only very light editing in order to preserve the authenticity of the responses.

The counsellor did not have a preconceived view (e.g. regarding what it means to be unemployed) and always asked Mary about the meanings she assigned to her experiences. The counsellor also introduced her own meanings in the CC setting in order to position herself and clarifying differences between her and Mary's ideas. This focused attention on the influences of intersectionality in the narrative constructions of both people and assisted in the narrative deconstruction and reconstruction process, which was a key element in the proposed CC model.

In a sense, Mary has attempted to meet both *class habitus* patterns in her initial request, when she said: "*I am unemployed, and I want to know what my true vocation is and what I like to do.*"

Being no longer unemployed is the issue linked to Mary's *class habitus*, while finding her true calling and what she would like to do seems to represent the counsellor's *class habitus*. According to Bourdieu's (1977) theory, this scene established a relationship power field of domination and subordination between the counsellor and the counselee. The field is an outcome of the interaction between the *class habitus* and *capital* (*social, cultural and economic*) of both parties involved in the relationship resulting in a hierarchical relationship. In the first CC scene, we can hypothesize that Mary referred to "*finding her true calling*" only because she has felt subordinated to the counsellor's *class habitus*. In general, middle-class people seek self-realization in their career projects and in finding their "true calling" or vocation (Duffy, Autin, England, Douglass, & Gensmer, 2018; Savickas, 2000). The counsellor should therefore focus first of all on the power field established at the beginning of the counselling process in order to embed intersectionality as a key feature of the proposed CC practice.

Intercultural dialogue (Santos, 2014) serves as a basis for the CC intervention through the *intermediary* position of the counsellor (Lehman et al., 2015) and through *diatopical hermeneutics* (Santos, 2014). The *intercultural dialogue* principle stresses the incompleteness of all knowledge as well as the need for dialogue among all the social actors involved in a relationship in a given context. The *diatopical hermeneutics* principle recognizes that both knowledges from a specific relationship should be considered valid with no hierarchical link between them. In the case of CC, the counsellor has the scientific and technical knowledge, and the counselee has the everyday life knowledge, both knowledges being considered on an equal basis. And, finally, the counsellor should act as an *intermediary* to ensure that the CC is not a distinctively personal process, but s/he should include social and communitarian elements and resources in its strategies (e.g. encouraging conversations with people of the same age and social condition who live in the same neighborhood as the counselee). This is one of the cornerstones of a CC grounded in intersectionality since it embeds people from the same community and context of the counselee into the counselling process so that they can actively participate in the counselee's career construction.

Mary continued by saying that the "*situation is very difficult. I have tried to get a job, but I achieved nothing. Thus, I have tried to sell, because some say when you are unemployed, the more accessible job is selling. However, I am unable to sell.*"

She presented one possible type of work based on her *class habitus* (work in sales), which is a typical type mentioned by people with the same *class habitus* as Mary.[3]

Mary (the counselee) seemed to be unaware of the place she occupied in the social power relations, which subjected her to the established discourse from her *class habitus* and has turned her personal narrative into a reproduction of this *class habitus*. Later, we will explain what was done to make her gradually become aware of this issue and to realize its importance in constructing her career. As indicated by the life design paradigm, this attitude of reproducing the established discourse of its *class habitus* can be understood as a *saturated narrative* on a single life theme, which can be defined as a narrative dominated by distorted and disempowering assumptions as well as monological and rigid meaning-making processes. A *life theme* can be described as a core issue or a set of core issues in a person's life history that the person wishes to solve and the means s/he finds to achieve a solution (Cardoso, 2012).

Mary went on to say, "*some say when you are unemployed, the more accessible job is selling*", which seems to be a *class habitus* assumption taken as an accept assumption, as though there is no other way. This transforms the idea of lack of power arising from Mary's *class habitus* into a *saturated narrative*.

According to the life design paradigm (Savickas et al., 2009), *intentionality* is a key factor in constructing working projects. Mary's narrative seems to reflect her difficulty in being in touch with her *intentionality* and in being aware of her *class habitus*, and she handled this difficulty by establishing a *saturated narrative*.

The precarious work and social conditions evidenced by Mary's current unemployment situation, as well as her discontinuous and unstable working trajectory, seem to be the primary triggering factor for her first narratives and for causing her suffering and psychosocial vulnerability. This can be seen as a psychosocial phenomenon, since the suffering has a twofold dimension: the psychological dimension represented by a lack of *self-determination*, and the social class dimension represented by the *social humiliation*.

Duffy et al. (2016) define *self-determination* as the "experience of being engaged in activities that are intrinsically or extrinsically motivating in a meaningful and self-regulated fashion" (p. 139). And, for Gonçalves Filho (1998), *social humiliation* is simultaneously a political and psychological phenomenon understood as a "form of anguish generated by the social inequalities conundrum" (p. 15).

It is therefore necessary to recognize the impossibility of planning something different regarding working life to what Mary's *class habitus* has appeared to establish. Nevertheless, Mary did not fully identify with what her *class habitus* seemed to establish and really wanted more than that thus expressing a movement/desire to go beyond the boundaries of her *class habitus*, as can be seen in her own words: "*However, I am unable to sell.*"

Seen through the lens of a more traditional understanding, "*be[ing] unable to sell*" could suggest a competence requiring further development. However, from an

[3]In this regard, Antunes (2015) and ILO (2017) highlighted that people with a similar socioeconomic profile to Mary's in Brazil have job opportunities only in the service sector, mainly in sales or telemarketing.

intersectional point of view, it could be interpreted as a resistance strategy in addition to a growing desire for social mobility. Thus, "*be[ing] unable to sell*" could mean both disability and resistance.

This has posed a dilemma for the counsellor who had two options: either co-constructing a regulatory strategy or an emancipatory one. On the one hand, if she decided to propose a regulatory strategy, she would highlight Mary's competences and seek to enhance her adaptability to the working world, as is commonly the case in practices addressed to adults. If she decided to propose an emancipatory strategy, on the other hand, she would recognize Mary as a *subject of rights, choices, and discourses* (Ayres et al., 2006; Bohoslavsky, 1983; Duffy et al., 2016).

By adopting *diatopical hermeneutics* (Santos, 2014) and an *intermediary* position (Lehman et al., 2015), the counsellor and counselee could co-construct strategies and narratives. These co-constructions aimed at enhancing Mary's psychosocial competence to tell a story—her *narratability* (Savickas et al., 2009)—and better understand the working opportunities in her specific context and her position in the societal power relations—her *critical consciousness* (Freire, 1970). The counsellor also helped Mary think about how to transcend her situation through alternative working outlets different from selling, for instance.

These alternative working outlets could emerge as *hybrids* or *monsters* (Latour, 1993); however, the main aim of CC should be the co-construction of *hybrids*. This cannot rest with the counsellor alone but requires communitarian support and joint action with the counselee's community. This is why the proposed CC interventions are based on *communitarian strategies* (Rascován, 2005).

Because of the assumption that the counsellor and counselee have different power positions in the CC setting and because of the aim to include intersectionality in the CC process, the counsellor asked Mary to explain everything from her own perspective and also gradually revealed the predominant social discourses and how they influenced Mary's decisions and actions causing her to remain in a subservient position. The counsellor then asked Mary about her recurrent and saturated unemployment narrative in an attempt to deconstruct it:

> You told me about several jobs you have done, including last week about the venture you are working. But, at the same time, you always say you are not working, you are unemployed. How do you see that? Is not the venture a job? What is a job for you?

Scene 2—Who Is Mary? and What Does She Want Out of Life?

Mary said that until the age of 28, she "*was some kind of a plastic doll... without even being aware of it and lifeless... what I have to say is more of the same*"; however, from 28 years old onwards, she began saying, "*I am looking for help, because I am in turmoil*", She explained this crisis by pointing out that "*I don't think I had had literacy for life, now I realize this*", concluding that "*I never had a dream*", because "*the world is Hollywoodian, but life is hard.*"

Mary appeared to be suffering from the dictates of her *class habitus* ("*what I have to say is more of the same*") and by a lack of awareness of her position in the world ("*I was some kind of a plastic doll… without even being aware of it and lifeless*"). She thus produced a *saturated narrative* (Cardoso, 2012) and a low *critical consciousness* about her situation (Duffy et al., 2016).

When Mary said: "*I am looking for help, because I am in turmoil*", she implied that her narratives no longer have made sense (psychosocial dimension) and that something had been missing or should be different (social class dimension). Nonetheless, she apparently had no idea about what this feeling meant (low *critical consciousness*), even if she stated that getting out of unemployment was the main reason for seeking professional assistance (social dimension).

Mary seemed to gain awareness from understanding socially determined limits, as expressed in her words: "*The world is Hollywoodian, but life is hard.*" At this point, the counsellor asked her: "*Are you telling me there are two different worlds and yours is a world of difficulties, not a glamour one?*"

The social discourse that dominate Mary's life is very heartening and, in some sense, idealized ("*The world is Hollywoodian*"), but daily living can be hard depending on one's social class position ("*but life is hard.*"). This led Mary to say, "*I don't think I had had literacy for life, now I realize this*", that is, she could not see the harshness of living and the social limits posed by her difficult living conditions. That is why she was in crisis and has talked about the trauma experienced by her:

> The word 'trauma' has a deep connection with my relationship with people, mainly regarding to my place in the working world. I'm not yet decided what may be my place at work; I'm not even sure I'll be able to do this one day.

This leads us to wonder whether this is a psychological or social class issue, what her place would be in this world, and what she would be allowed to do in this world. She said, "*I have never had a dream*", as she had never felt authorized to do anything outside her *class habitus*. This experience was built into her relationship with the counsellor, generating a *saturated narrative* (Cardoso, 2012). She gave a good example which seemed to explain her saturated narrative by saying that "*it was like I had been walking aimlessly*" (without thinking, changing or having consciousness).

We might speculate how she could transcend her *class habitus* and do something differently. Mary said that her recent dream include an image of Venus (she wanted to be recognized and admired); however, "*it seems that something is missing, I need to be part of the gears, like in Chaplin's movie 'Modern Times'* (she needs to be part of the world)." At this point, the counsellor asked her: "*Why can't you be part of the gears? Why can't you dream?*"

This induces Mary to talk about the limitations placed on her by her *class habitus*, which had led her to construct only a discontinuous working trajectory defined by a lack of projects ("*it was like I had been walking aimlessly*"), and to believe she would never be able to enjoy the better job opportunities in the working world: "*I need to be part of the gears, like in Chaplin's movie 'Modern Times.'*"

Mary suspected that she needed to change from the world she had been living into another world in order to achieve something different: "*I dream of working in another state, another country, it would be different, it could be, maybe, even in an office*." In other words, she seemed to know that she needed to transcend what had been established by her *class habitus* and accordingly sought CC at a recognized university to assist her in her project to be part of the working world 'gears' from which she has been excluded up until that moment. The CC's objectives was therefore to help Mary transcend what had been established by her *class habitus*.

Our CC Proposal

Scene 3—Mary's Working Trajectory Narrative and Her Only Meaningful Job Story

Mary's working trajectory was marked by discontinuity, transitory periods of work, and largely unspecified work. This trajectory included informal works of all kinds, mainly in sales or distributing leaflets in the streets as well as other low-level employments. These jobs were taken because they were all that was available rather than because of any personal interest, with the single exception of a job in an enterprise in her area of expertise, which lasted about two years. She said she had experienced fulfilment and happiness in this job.

Mary stated that she could easily get jobs by networking with people from the same *class habitus* but that she was not interested in these kinds of jobs. This is probably why she had been unsuccessful and had remained only for a short period of time in each one.

Mary had rejected what had been offered to her and had failed to go beyond her *class habitus*. She had looked for a better job, but it did not turn out as she thought it would. We can hypothesize that this was due to laziness, inefficiency, or lack of interest in this kind of jobs, possibly indicating a form of social class resistance. It is important to draw attention that this is a good example of how intersectionality helps CC to think different from usual, as previously stated.

Nonetheless, Mary was in doubt: "*I could do much better than this. I don't know why I do not do. Am I lazy?*" This prompted us to question why she had not been able to work at a job she liked. We can hypothesize that she failed to understand the social and cultural determinants of her life, resulting largely from her *class habitus*. The jobs she could get were not the ones she considered as work, and she did not know what could be done to resolve her situation: "*I would do nothing again that I have already done. That's not what I want, but I also don't know what I want to do.*"

Mary seemed to know what she did not want; but she also could not figure out what she wanted, nor how to change. Thus, she resigned herself and said that the only way out was to adapt: "*I must seize this opportunity, even it is not the perfect one for me.*"

At that moment, Mary had a low *critical consciousness* (Duffy et al., 2016) and did not see herself capable of changing or as a *subject of rights, choices, and discourses* (Ayres et al., 2006; Bohoslavsky, 1983). Our view was that she could not change her life while she remained unaware of the reasons why she did not have access to interesting job opportunities.

> Nobody has ever taught what life looks like. I've always been very naive. I knew nothing about evil. This harmed me a lot and I remained at a standstill. I was not able to bounce back, and I got lost.

The *class habitus* leads people to reproduce ways of living and thinking without questioning, what makes complicated to identify ways of changing life. What needs to be stressed is the importance of *intercultural dialogue* (Santos, 2014) with someone from another *class habitus* in order to improve the possibilities of transcendence. This is one of the key points of our CC proposal.

Mary reported that jobs opportunities never seemed intended for her: "*They are for those already there*". And she was not there—she was not one of 'them' due to her different *class habitus*, which she perceived as lower than the socially optimal level. She summed up her life as "*ordinary and inexpressive*", which was not acceptable to her and which was why she sought CC. She felt something was not working properly but that she could change. Her main issue was a lack of clarity, mainly due to her low *critical consciousness* about what exactly was going wrong and how to change (Duffy et al., 2016).

Mary described in some detail her unique, successful, and positive working experience in a good job in a private company where, using her expertise, she felt happy and fulfilled. But then she was suddenly dismissed without any explanation.

She said she had been harassed at work mainly because of the way she dressed, which emphasized her blackness. She was annoyed, but she did not complain, as she felt nothing would be done to prevent it or protect her.

> I have usually read more than ten emails each day saying: "Take a look her hair, take a look at her dreadlocks". This happened all the time. They kept exchanging e-mails and talking about me. They added a photo of a monkey with lipstick on exactly the same day I went to work with makeup and lipstick, and plenty of other things as well.

Mary worked hard in this specific job and wanted to make a career in the company, but then she was suddenly dismissed ostensibly. The company claimed that she was disorganized and unproductive. "*I deluded myself… I constructed a big castle, but I have not been supported. I was not recognized, but undervalued and despised.*" When Mary started in the job, she was humiliated and later dismissed presumably for being a Black woman, although she did not say so at any time. She knew she was being discriminated against as a result of racial prejudice, but she had a low *critical consciousness* (Duffy et al., 2016) about the discrimination or avoided developing a consciousness in order not to be subjected to this kind of prejudice. This was most likely a self-defense strategy. However, she also mentioned a Black woman CEO of a Brazilian company as an example of what a Black woman could achieve.

A lower SES Black woman in Mary's job did not make sense to a society ruled by prejudice, which could illustrate the racial and social prejudice she suffered. In terms of the *hybridism* proposed by Latour (1993), Mary was a *monster* to be eliminated, not a *hybrid*, since the position she held would more commonly be occupied by a

White middle-class person. In her case, Mary's competence and good performance was trumped by the gender, social class, and racial discrimination that seemed to have prevailed. Nevertheless, she was unable to realize this and, instead, felt guilty about her failure. This indicates that social class, gender, and race/ethnicity are socially constructed as stated respectively by Bourdieu (1977), Butler (1990), and Delgado and Stefancic (2017).

Her condition as a Black woman thus arose as a factor that has seemed to hamper new opportunities in the working world: "*It is not an issue for me, I know what I can achieve, but the other does not know, that's why they deny what I am.*" Yet others saw only her gender, her skin color, and the way she gets dressed. She felt as though "*she was building a house on sand. I make things right, but it seems that something is missing*". She considered ways of dealing with the problem: "*I think studying, improving and doing my best… the other is the other, there is nothing I can do about that.*"

A key issue that must be tackled here is Mary wanting to find a possible solution to her problem through personal effort, but her life history had shown that this had never been sufficient. She seemed not to know what she should do to change this picture.

Mary had repeated in different ways the same *saturated narrative* (Cardoso, 2012) based on a single life theme constructed at the beginning of the CC. The same old narrative was that she got jobs, but she did not like them, and she could not understand why she kept repeating this pattern. In general, she had accepted some responsibility for the consequences, but she did not know how to break free from this narrative.

In our current CC proposal, the person concerned will gradually deconstruct and reconstruct his/her narrative in a *process of co-construction* as advocated in the life design paradigm (Duarte, 2015; Savickas et al., 2009) through *intercultural dialogue* and *diatopical hermeneutics* (Santos, 2014). This process or strategy has three distinct aims. First, it aims to achieve narrative reconstruction and *narratability* development (Savickas et al., 2009) where the counselee can tell a meaningful life story that includes the intersectionality of gender, class, and race/ethnicity. Secondly, it seeks to enhance *critical consciousness* (Duffy et al., 2016). And, thirdly, it aims to foster a *discursive validation* (Winslade, 2005) where the working trajectory and project can have a new focus and generate new alternatives based on *hybrids* (Latour, 1993). Examples are given below of how this can be achieved based on three scenes from the CC process.

In the first scene, the counsellor has asked Mary to compile a list of what she would like to do at work. However, she produced a list of what she would not like to do, which is what she had been doing for years. This indicates that she knows what she does not want, but she is not yet able to project what she wants, or she thinks things cannot be different. Her *critical consciousness* (Duffy et al., 2016) may thus increase, mainly through her awareness of her place in the power relations in the world.

In the second scene, the counsellor asked Mary to remake the list by talking to people close to her, thereby including the communitarian dimension in the CC process. This also heightened Mary's awareness of the difficulties caused by the intersectionality of gender, class, and race/ethnicity and strengthened the counsellor's *intermediary* position by linking the CC process to the Mary's life narrative (Lehman et al., 2015) and to her home community experiences, thereby defining CC as a *communitarian strategy* (Rascován, 2005).

In the third scene, the counsellor asked Mary to search for people close to her and living in the same kind of context, but who had succeeded in doing things differently and had enhanced their lives rather than choosing a Black woman CEO of a Brazilian company as her model.

This strategy validated the trajectory of the Black female CEO as a *hybrid* (Latour, 1993)—seen as something unusual but socially accepted. However, Mary had to find examples from her own close context and avoid idealized ones since she was a poor Black woman.

Thus, rather than assist counselees in an individualized construction process, CC should facilitate and support their connection with the working world and career possibilities that can be co-constructed through joint action with the community in which the counselees wish to construct their careers (Rascován, 2005).

The *intermediary* position supports the *hybrid interventions* rationale according to which knowledge is built on the relationship of all the social actors involved in a given context (Santos, 2014), and the counsellor/counselee relationship extends to all counselee relationships with the world. This is necessary since the counsellor is not part of the counselee's world, and the counselee needs to make use of the resources of his/her home community to *co-construct meaningful working life projects* (Duarte, 2015).

The main objective is to avoid searching for an idealized job or getting an unwanted one but rather to find a desired and real job. At this stage in the CC process, analysis and intervention grounded in intersectionality is crucial.

Scene 4—Conclusions

In the final scene, the counsellor recalled the CC process up to that point and analyzed the Mary's report about a job interview she had a few days previously in order to activate a closing strategy known as *discursive validation* (Winslade, 2005). In this strategy, *critical consciousness* (Duffy et al., 2016) regarding the intersectionality of gender, class, and race/ethnicity is fostered and an attempt is made also to construct working projects that take intersectionality into account without being completely subject to it but, rather, transcend it.

The counsellor has asked Mary: "*Do you believe that you will remain getting jobs you don't wish, or will it be possible to do it differently being a Black woman, as the Black CEO previously mentioned by you?*" According to Latour (1993), Mary could remain a *monster* without a recognized social place or she could transcend this status and become a *hybrid* with a legitimized social place.

Mary said that she had several attributes that could clearly distinguish her in the working world, including education, health, intelligence, willpower, and ability. She was looking for a job that she could really enjoy every day, that offered the prospect of financial reward, and that would give her recognition as a worker. Mary was searching for a job different to that determined by her *class habitus*, which tended to reduce all working activity to merely meeting survival needs. This dimension is one of the three fundamental human needs listed by Duffy et al. (2016), but the need for social connection and the need for self-determination are still lacking. Mary's apparent wish for a clearly-recognized place with power and autonomy was beyond her *class habitus* and was hampered by her being a Black woman.

According to Arulmani (2011), most people do not have a career but, rather, 'livelihood planning' where recognition, power, and self-determination are not factors in their working trajectories. Nevertheless, Mary wanted more, but she did not know if it would be possible to get it. The central dialogue about her desire to transcend her *class habitus* is encapsulated below.

Counsellor	"*What does it take to achieve a work you wish, with financial returns and in which you feel important?*"
Mary	"*I do not have a clear answer.*"
Counsellor	"*What do you think you need to get the job you want?*"
Mary	"*With a little more knowledge and known persons, things could be easier. But I do not have.*"

Mary drew attention to her lack of academic qualified training due to the fact she had not attended a socially valued college. Her low-qualified network of relationships was large and efficient, but it always offered her the same type of work, which can be explained in terms of *class habitus* reproduction (Bourdieu, 1977).

Counsellor	"*What do you think you need to pull out from the place you are into and move beyond?*"
Mary	"*Accept any job that is offered.*"

At this point, Mary said that the way out for her working project would be to comply with her *class habitus* and abandon any attempt to do something different in her life and possibly become a *hybrid* (Latour, 1993). This induced the counsellor to activated *discursive validation* (Winslade, 2005) by saying:

> They say that you are lazy and disorganized, but you are always called to come to work by your network of relationships. However, you want more, and it is really hard to get a job. Even more so for a Black woman.

Mary	"*Are you asserting that?*"
Counsellor	"*Yes, I am.*"
Mary	"*Thank you, thank you very much for your words.*"

The counsellor thus provided a *discursive validation* for Mary's working trajectory by stating that being a woman, Black and poor had compromised her working projects and have led her to the same type of work throughout her whole life. In agreeing with the counsellor and thanking her, Mary seemed to better understand the determinants of her life trajectory, what provides probable evidence of Mary's *critical consciousness* growth.

This could have been said at the outset, but it needed the CC process to help Mary think clearly and logically and enhance her *critical consciousness* (Duffy et al., 2016) regarding her wish to construct working projects beyond her *class habitus* (Bourdieu, 1977). Thus, Mary could critically understand something she had experienced throughout her life, but could not make sense of, that is, the psychosocial disadvantages resulting from the intersectionality of gender, class, and race/ethnicity.

Counsellor	*"How do you see yourself as a Black woman?"*
Mary	*"We need to face prejudice. That's it. People are extremely prejudiced, although this does not bother me. I know about my competences, but the others do not. So, they deny what I really am."* (This statement is further evidence of Mary's *critical consciousness* growth)

Mary expressed her final assessment of the CC process as follows:

> It was really good. It helped me a lot. Things became clear and I understood a little bit for about my life. I thank you very much for that. I will keep for life for following what you have said. I liked it very much.

We hope that this case study has made the CC proposal outlined here more comprehensible.

Conclusion

This chapter showed that CC may not change the world, but it can help counselees better understand the world they live in when seeking to construct their careers. It can also help them recognize and validate what they do as work and assist them to move beyond a devalued subservient position. Embedding intersectionality in CC settings is a way to improve this process since it helps make people aware of the social position they occupy regarding gender, race/ethnicity, and social class and devise strategies to transcend this position. *Discursive validation*, the *co-construction process*, *diatopical hermeneutics*, *critical consciousness* enhancement and *communitarian strategies* are key elements for doing so.

Although it was designed for the Brazil, the CC proposed here suggests a way of theoretically and technically dealing with social justice issues by including intersectionality in global CC settings. Its theories or practices allow it to be applied to any context in either the global South or the global North. The proposed theoretical-technical framework should be deconstructed and reconstructed in accordance with the population and context where it is applied.

References

Antunes, R. (2015). The new morphology of the working class in contemporary Brazil. *Socialist Register, 51*, 178–198.

Arulmani, G. (2011). Striking the right note: The cultural preparedness approach to developing resonant career guidance programmes. *International Journal for Educational and Vocational Guidance, 11*, 79–93. https://doi.org/10.1007/s10775-011-9199-y.

Ayres, J. R. C. M., Paiva, V., França Jr., I., Gravato, N., Lacerda, R., Negra, M. D., … Silva, M. H. (2006). Vulnerability, human rights, and comprehensive health care needs of young people living with HIV/AIDS. *American Journal of Public Health, 96*(6), 1001–1006. https://doi.org/10.2105/ajph.2004.060905.

Blustein, D. L. (2011). A relational theory of working. *Journal of Vocational Behavior, 79*(1), 1–17. https://doi.org/10.1016/j.jvb.2010.10.004.

Bohoslavsky, R. (1983). *Vocacional: Teoria, técnica e ideologia [The vocational: Theory, technique and ideology]*. São Paulo, Brazil: Cortez.

Bourdieu, P. (1977). *Outline of a theory of practice*. Cambridge, England: Cambridge University Press.

Butler, J. (1990). *Gender trouble*. London, England: Routledge.

Cardoso, P. (2012). Maladaptive repetition and career construction. *Journal of Vocational Behavior, 81*(3), 364–369. https://doi.org/10.1016/j.jvb.2012.09.003.

Cole, E. R. (2009). Intersectionality and research in psychology. *American Psychologist, 64,* 170–180. https://doi.org/10.1037/a0014564.

Crenshaw, K. (1989/2018). Demarginalizing the intersection of race and sex (1989). In K. T. Bartlett & R. Kennedy (Eds.), *Feminist legal theory* (pp. 57–80). New York, NY: Routledge.

Delgado, R., & Stefancic, J. (2017). *Critical race theory: An introduction*. New York, NY: New York University Press.

Duarte, M. E. (2015). Some reflections on guidance and career counselling in the 21st century. In A. Di Fabio & J.-L. Bernaud (Eds.), *The construction of the identity in 21st century* (pp. 59–72). New York, NY: Nova.

Duffy, R. D., Autin, K. L., England, J. W., Douglass, R. P., & Gensmer, N. P. (2018). Examining the effects of contextual variables on living a calling over time. *Journal of Vocational Behavior, 107,* 141–152. https://doi.org/10.1016/j.jvb.2018.04.003.

Duffy, R. D., Blustein, D. L., Diemer, M. A., & Autin, K. L. (2016). The Psychology of Working Theory. *Journal of Counseling Psychology, 63*(2), 127–148. https://doi.org/10.1037/cou0000140.

Freire, P. (1970). *Pedagogy of the oppressed*. New York, NY: Continuum.

Gonçalves Filho, J. M. (1998). Humilhação Social—Um problema político em psicologia [Social humiliation—A political problem into psychology]. *Revista Psicologia USP, 9*(2), 11–67. https://doi.org/10.1590/S0103-65641998000200002.

International Labour Organization. (2017). *World employment and social outlook: Trends 2017*. Geneva, Switzerland: International Labour Organization.

Latour, B. (1993). *We have never been modern*. Cambridge, MA: Harvard University Press.

Lehman, Y. P., Ribeiro, M. A., Uvaldo, M. C. C., & Silva, F. F. (2015). A psychodynamic approach on group career counseling. *International Journal for Educational and Vocational Guidance, 15*(1), 23–36. https://doi.org/10.1007/s10775-014-9276-0.

McNamee, S. (2012). From social construction to relational construction: Practices from the edge. *Psychological Studies, 57*(2), 150–156. https://doi.org/10.1007/s12646-011-0125-7.

Paiva, V. (2005). Analysing sexual experiences through 'scenes'. *Sex Education, 5*(4), 345–358. https://doi.org/10.1080/14681810500278295.

Rascován, S. (2005). *Orientación vocacional: Una perspectiva crítica [Career counselling: A critical perspective]*. Buenos Aires, Argentina: Paidós.

Ribeiro, M. A. (2016). Career counseling for people in psychosocial situations of vulnerability and flexicurity: A social constructionist proposal. In T. V. Martin (Ed.), *Career development: Theories, practices and challenges* (pp. 79–110). New York, NY: Nova.

Ribeiro, M. A. (2018a). Comprensiones híbridas y diálogo intercultural [Hybrid understanding and intercultural dialogue]. *Revista Mexicana de Orientación Educativa, 15*(34), 1–21.

Ribeiro, M. A. (2018b). Towards diversified ways to promote decent working trajectories: A life and career design proposal for informal workers. In V. Cohen-Scali, J. Pouyaud, M. Podgórny, V. Drabik-Podgórna, G. Aisenson, J.-L. Bernaud, I. Abdou Moumoula, & J. Guichard (Eds.), *Interventions in career design and education: Transformation for sustainable development and decent work* (pp. 180–201). New York, NY: Springer.

Santos, B. S. (2014). *Epistemologies of the south: Justice against epistemicide*. Boulder, CO: Paradigm.

Savickas, M. (2000). Renovating the psychology of careers for the twenty-first century. In R. A. Young & A. Collin (Eds.), *The future of career* (pp. 53–68). Cambridge, England: Cambridge University Press.

Savickas, M. L., Nota, L., Rossier, J., Dauwalder, J. P., Duarte, M. E., Guichard, J., … van Vianen, A. E. M. (2009). Life designing: A paradigm for career construction in the 21st century. *Journal of Vocational Behavior*, *75*, 239–250. https://doi.org/10.1016/j.jvb.2009.04.004.

Silva, F. F., Paiva, V., & Ribeiro, M. A. (2016). Career construction and reduction of psychosocial vulnerability: Intercultural career guidance based on Southern epistemologies. *Journal of the National Institute for Career Education and Counselling, 36,* 46–53. https://doi.org/10.20856/jnicec.3606.

Winslade, J. (2005). Utilising discursive positioning in counseling. *British Journal for Guidance and Counselling, 33*(3), 351–364. https://doi.org/10.1080/03069880500179541.

Psychotherapy Lessons that Inform Career Counselling

Steven I. Pfeiffer and Renata Muniz Prado

Abstract This chapter introduces the reader to principles found to be efficacious in the practice of mental health-based psychotherapy, and their application to career counselling. Drawing upon the clinical psychotherapy research literature, and personal experience as therapists, the authors discuss two factors that have been found to each play a statistically significant and clinically beneficial role in the research literature on effective psychotherapy: the psychotherapy relationship and progress monitoring. We propose that these two factors in effective psychotherapy may have application and relevance to the practice of career counselling. The chapter also briefly discusses the use of the Internet in counselling, including ethical considerations.

Keywords Psychotherapy · Career counselling · Therapeutic alliance · Progress monitoring · Ethics and counselling

Introduction: Principles in Evidence-Based Psychotherapy

When first invited to contribute a chapter to this handbook, the first author's initial reaction was one of reluctance and even considerable trepidation; although a well-published academic clinician, he is anything but an authority on vocational psychology or career counselling. His 40-year career has focused on the social and emotional needs of high ability children and youth, what happens psychiatrically when things go awry, and the efficacy of psychotherapy as one tool to ameliorate psychological problems and promote well-being and optimal mental health (Pfeiffer, 2018). Career counselling has not been on his professional radar screen! However, after some soul searching and deliberation with the second author, a Brazilian psychologist who completed a post-doctoral fellowship at Florida State University with

S. I. Pfeiffer (✉)
Florida State University, Tallahassee, USA
e-mail: spfeiffer@fsu.edu

R. M. Prado
Universidade de Brasília, Brasília, Brazil

J. G. Maree (ed.), *Handbook of Innovative Career Counselling*,
https://doi.org/10.1007/978-3-030-22799-9_34

the first author, we both reflected on a paper that the first author had written some thirty-five years ago at the invitation of a medical colleague. The paper sought to make a connection between effective counselling skills—as applied by accomplished psychotherapists, and the "bedside manner" of skilled physicians (Pfeiffer, 1986). This chapter essentially builds upon this earlier paper, arguing that what makes psychotherapy uniquely effective may have relevance and even important application to effective career counselling.

We need to start by defining some terms. First, let's discuss what we mean by psychotherapy. Counselling or psychotherapy is a collaborative enterprise in which clients (often called patients) and therapists negotiate ways of working together on mutually agreed-upon therapeutic goals to foster positive outcomes (American Psychological Association [APA] Presidential Task Force on Evidence-Based Practice, 2006). Psychotherapy is viewed as a prescriptive, creative, and personal—even intimate, way of working with clients [or patients] to assist them in modifying, changing, reducing or eliminating factors that interfere with their otherwise effective living and quality of life (Corsini & Auerbach, 1998). Psychotherapy often is an intimate and creative process that provides what is called "corrective emotional experiences," allowing clients to think, feel and act in ways that they may have avoided in the past. It can also be a means of enhancing a client's functioning with the goal of optimizing mental health, subjective well-being, and even existential meaning in life (Frank & Frank, 1993; Frankl, 1959; London, 1986; Pfeiffer, 2018).

Before we begin discussing two salient and highly valued components of evidence-based psychotherapy,[1] and their possible relevance to career counselling, we start with a very brief overview of career development and career counselling. We will then explore the main thesis of our chapter; namely that findings from what makes psychotherapy effective may have possible application to career counselling.

Goals of the Chapter

This chapter introduces the reader to principles found to be efficacious in the practice of mental health-based psychotherapy, and their application to career counselling. Drawing upon the clinical psychotherapy research literature, and personal experience as therapists, the authors discuss two factors that have been found to each play a statistically significant and clinically beneficial role in the research literature on effective psychotherapy: the psychotherapy relationship and progress monitoring. We propose that these two factors in effective psychotherapy may have application and relevance to the practice of career counselling. The chapter also briefly discusses the use of the Internet in counselling, including ethical considerations.

[1]Because of space limitations, we limited our discussion to two evidence-based components of mental health psychotherapy. The reader should recognize that there are other, important elements that help make psychotherapy effective (for example, the judicious application of specific psychotherapeutic techniques).

An Overview on Career Development and Career Counselling

As pointed on the Guidelines for Integrating the Role of Work and Career into Professional Psychology Practice (American Psychological Association, n.d.), work and career have a central role in the lives of individuals, therefore vocational well-being impacts emotional well-being (Blustein, 2008). The accomplishment of career goals is one of the career counselling purposes which involves a collaborative and supportive relationship that affords many different positive outcomes over the life span. Career counselling focuses on behavioral outcomes in the world of work, including career choice, work satisfaction, career adaptability, an awareness of internal and external factors that continue throughout the lifetime. This ongoing, complex process, or career development, is defined as "the total constellation of economic, sociological, psychological, educational, physical, and chance factors that combine to shape one's career" (Sears, 1982, p. 139).

Smith and Wood (2018) conceptualize career development as all-encompassing, a focus on an individual's total experience with their career, beginning in childhood with the early knowledge of self, and leading to career decision-making throughout life, the experience of work, and ultimately, retirement. Accordingly, these authors view career development as including both all those formal and informal experiences that constitute and impact one's world-view of work and what work means in a person's live. Zunker (2016) lists key issues career counsellors must be aware of, working in the 21st century, which include: lifelong learning, counselling in a culturally diverse society, the effective use of information, globalization and economic restructuring. Empirical studies of career development provide the basis for career interventions. Theories and research guide an evidence-based practice, and also help create reliable and useful measures fundamental to career assessment.

Career counsellors assist clients to explore, pursue and attain their career goals. A handbook on career counselling proposed by UNESCO in 2002 states that the career counselling process consists of four elements: (a) helping individuals to gain greater self-awareness in areas such as interests, values, abilities, and personality style, (b) connecting to resources so that they can become more knowledgeable about jobs and occupations, (c) engaging in the decision-making process in order to choose a career path that is well suited, and (d) assisting individuals to be active managers of their career paths (including managing career transitions and balancing various life roles) as well as becoming lifelong learners in the sense of professional development over the lifespan.

Maree (2017, 2018) reinforces the changes in the world of work must affect career counselling practices. Therefore, the use of a qualitative and quantitative approach integrating subjective and objective information is effective, especially with minority groups. Assessments are an important resource for counsellors working with career services. Career-related assessment provides information on interests, skills, and abilities; academic achievement; personality style; career beliefs, readiness, or maturity variables. Although not every counselling process uses testing, standardized assessment results help to delineate intervention strategies that would best meet clients' subjective and special needs. The outcome and information provided should empower clients to make the best decisions, have more confidence and control on their career trajectory, but also point out areas that need attention and have intersections with career development, such as mental health issues (Osborn & Zunker, 2016).

Career development, as a scholarly field, and career counselling, as a practice field, are committed to understanding work behavior and to effectively and ethically applying this knowledge to practices that will enrich clients' lives (Brown & Lent, 2013; Sampson, 2017). Certainly, it can be expected that the career counselling process will frequently address mental health and quality of life aspects in a variety of circumstances, such as job transition, job loss impact, and changing career goals. These events might interfere with other life roles and influence emotional experiences, including anxiety, stress, confusion, and frustration (Dozier, Lenz, & Freeman, 2016).

Current approaches to career counselling that focus on the whole person advise the need to integrate in career development practice, and view as dynamically synergistic, both career and personal concerns (Zunker, 2016). Clients may need assistance in navigating their life career trajectory; and personality, values, or lifestyle preferences are relevant variables that must be considered. With this rationale in mind, interrelating these two dimensions—one's career and personal world, clients will be better served by professionals skilled in personal counselling and psychotherapy. "Effective counselling, regardless of the title or specialized training of the counsellor, requires a systems perspective where clients are viewed as whole individuals. Problems should not be viewed in isolation" (Sampson, 2007, p. 2).

Evidence-Based Practice of Psychotherapy: A Common Factors Perspective

Psychotherapy researchers have long sought to determine both *how* and *why* psychotherapy works. The research has been wide-ranging, focusing on studying specific techniques (such as reciprocal inhibition, hypnosis, dream interpretation, mindfulness training, systematic desensitization, and Eye Movement Desensitization Reprocessing [EMDR], to name just a few techniques), extra-therapeutic factors such as level of social support, and client motivation to change, and the special therapeutic relationship between the counsellor and client—called 'common factors' (such as therapist empathy, therapeutic alliance, and client hopefulness).

While psychotherapy researchers have shed considerable light on our understanding of "what makes psychotherapy work," it is important that we not forget what Nobel Prize winner Kandel (1998) reminds us about recent advances in the clinical neurosciences informing psychotherapy. Kandel proposed that "all mental processes, even the most complex psychological processes (as those in psychotherapy), derive from operations of the brain" (p. 460). Kandel admonished clinicians that "insofar as psychotherapy or counselling is effective… it presumably does so through learning, by producing changes in the gene expression that alter the strength of synaptic connections" (p. 460). Although we won't elaborate further in this chapter on the rich and growing body of evidence from clinical neuroscience which helps us understand why, and when, psychotherapy works, we readily acknowledge that experience transforms the brain, cognitive, and emotional processes work in partnership at a physiological level, and finally, that psychotherapy activates and stimulates the neural substrates of the brain that can lead to real behavioral change. Okay, enough on how advances in neuroscience can help guide our understanding of psychotherapy.

A debate has existed within the psychotherapy research community for a long time about whether specific therapeutic techniques (often called therapeutic 'ingredients') or the therapeutic relationship (as mentioned above, often called 'common factors') is the active element or factor that produces the real benefits obtained when psychotherapy is effective. Our position—based on our careful review of the research literature and based on our first-hand experience as psychotherapists, is that *both* techniques *and* the common factors found in the therapeutic relationship are real and important when psychotherapy works. In this chapter, we will focus on what is uniquely special about the therapeutic relationship. We want the reader to appreciate that there are a large number of specific techniques, when judiciously applied for specific problems or psychiatric disorders that are quite helpful with proven scientific value. However, in this chapter we restrict our discussion to what is known about the power of the common factors in psychotherapy—those found in the therapeutic relationship. We focus on common factors because we believe that they have relevance and application to career counselling.

When clients are asked what they find most helpful in their psychotherapy, and when one examines the research on what specific factors predicts effective psychological treatment, the likely answer is: the psychotherapy relationship, the 'healing alliance' between the client and the therapist (Norcross & Lambert, 2018). There exists considerable research on the many facets that make up the therapy relationship. We have decided to focus on just a few facets, which will highlight—we hope—the power of the healing alliance, the common factors across all psychotherapies that make counselling effective. Gelso and Carter (1985, 1994) operationally defined the therapeutic relationship as the feelings and attitudes that the psychotherapist and the client have toward one another, and the manner in which these are expressed. Of course, this rather generic definition leaves open the potential to include almost everything under the *therapeutic sun*. It harkens back to the first author's early work with primary care physicians on what constitutes effective *bedside manner* (Pfeiffer, 1986). Of course, when effective, the therapeutic relationship does not exist apart from what the clinician does in terms of method and planned interventions. As mentioned above, the psychotherapy field has distinguished between relationships and techniques. In reality, what one does and how one does it are complementary, synergistic, and inseparable. In other words, our position is that the value and impact of a treatment method or protocol is inextricably linked to the relational and interpersonal context of the counselling setting in which it is applied with the client. Relational elements, such as therapist humor, self-doubt/humility, timing, and deliberate practice all play a role in successful counselling. However, meta-analyses of these relationship elements have not yielded large effect sizes, at least when primarily defined when examining distal post-treatment outcomes (Norcross & Lambert, 2018)—a topic that we cover in a subsequent section of this chapter.

Quantitative meta-analyses on psychotherapy outcome research has indicated, however, a group of common factors that do contribute to client success, factors that consistently yield large effect sizes across multiple studies. For example, Elliott, Bohart, Watson, and Murphy (2018) conducted a meta-analysis of 82 studies that investigated the association between psychotherapist empathy and client success at the end of counselling. Their meta-analysis, consisting of over 6000 client research participants, yielded a weighted mean r of .28. This is a medium effect size. The corresponding d was .58 (large effect size). A d of .58 is quite impressive. This number translates into more joyful and better adjusted clients; in other words, these 82 studies confirm that clients who work with more empathic therapists tend to progress more in treatment, evidence greater improvement, and less relapse following the conclusion of treatment.

Common factors that have been investigated in the psychotherapy research literature include: the therapeutic alliance, collaboration between therapist and client, therapist empathy, collecting and delivering client feedback, genuineness of the therapist, goal consensus, emotional expression, cultivating positive expectations, managing counter-transference, and self-disclosure and immediacy. For each of these common factors, at least ten independent research studies have been conducted with no fewer than 1000 client research participants. Norcross and Lambert (2018) summarized the meta-analytic associations between these relationship (common factors) components and psychotherapy outcomes in a special issue of the journal, *Psychotherapy*, aptly entitled, "Psychotherapy relationships that work." Their summary of the meta-analytic associations concluded that alliance, collaboration, goal consensus, empathy, positive regard and affirmation, and collecting and delivering client feedback were "demonstrably effective." They concluded, in addition, that: congruence/genuineness, emotional expression, cultivating positive expectations, and managing counter-transference were "probably effective," based on the extant meta-analytic research. This is profound and compelling findings, in that the meta-analytic studies that they aggregated on these different common factors included from 10 to over 300 independent studies, with 1318 to over 30,000 client research participants!

What is the big-picture take-away from these research findings? We find three highly pertinent conclusions, with implications for career counselling.

- First, practitioners providing mental health-related psychotherapy *and* career counselling are encouraged to pay particular attention to nurturing and supporting the therapeutic relationship as one primary aim of their treatment. This is particularly true for cultivating the therapeutic alliance between clinician and client; creating a sense of collaboration and goal consensus—an attitude of "we are in this together as a team," and establishing agreed-upon, mutually shared goals. Therapist empathy—understanding what the client is experiencing or trying to express in counselling or psychotherapy—is a highly powerful common factor in all effective counselling.

- Second, practitioners are encouraged to routinely monitor clients' satisfaction with the counselling relationship, comfort with the planned efforts, and response to treatment. This is as true in career counselling as in mental health psychotherapy. A next section of the chapter provides more detail on this very point about progress monitoring—monitoring of *both* the quality of the therapeutic relationship and the headway and improvement toward shared treatment goals. Progress monitoring sends a powerful message to the client that the clinician genuinely cares about them and their work together, and it also provides the therapist with real-time feedback on how counselling is evolving, including whether adjustments need to be made.
- Third, practitioners need to be open to the possibility that their work with one or more clients may not be characterized by a strong working alliance. Not every client is equally easy or pleasant to work with! And yet the quality of the alliance has consistently correlated with psychotherapy outcome; stronger alliances being associated with better therapeutic outcomes (Horvath, Del Re, Flückiger, & Symonds, 2011; Zilcha-Mano, 2017).

Next, we turn to the topic of progress monitoring and outcome assessment. This is one of the factors that a systematic review of the meta-analytic outcome literature indicates correlates with successful outcomes in counselling. In fact, a recent meta-analysis of routine outcome monitoring of 24 independent studies by Lambert, Whipple, and Kleinstäuber (2018) concluded that routine outcome monitoring is correlated with improved outcomes—it contributes to psychotherapy relationships that work! Professional bodies such as the American Psychological Association (American Psychological Association Presidential Task Force on Evidence-Based Practice, 2006) has recommended that routine outcome monitoring be a part of effective psychological services.

The Importance of Progress Monitoring and Feedback

Now that we have provided an overview on career development and counselling, and made what, we hope, is a compelling case for the efficacy and power of 'common factors' in mental health psychotherapy, we discuss in a bit more detail the important factor in the efficacy of successful psychotherapy: the value of progress monitoring and measuring outcomes. The first author began writing on the importance of outcome monitoring over twenty-five years ago, in a series of invited essays for *Perspectives on Outcomes* (Pfeiffer, 1998a, 1998b). It seems intuitive and logical that implementing reliable outcome monitoring protocols that gauges the effectiveness of planned psychotherapeutic efforts are essential to best clinical practice (Pfeiffer & Shott, 1996). Progress monitoring and outcome assessment specifically quantify, in reliable and in real-time, the short- and longer-term impact of therapeutic services.

An example from the medical-surgical field may help illustrate this very point. Assume that a patient is admitted to an emergency room with an acute myocardial infarction (i.e., a heart attack). The attending physician determines that the patient requires specific medication to alleviate the immediate chest pain, bed rest, a change of diet, increase in exercise and elimination of smoking to stabilize his precipitous medical condition and lastly a surgical procedure to restore blockage of two arteries adjacent to the heart. To be considered a successful treatment, the cardiac team requires both short-term and longer-term favorable outcomes for the patient.

In this example, the short-term outcome is obviously the alleviation of the acute and painful chest pain that initially brought the patient to the emergency room. The longer-term outcome—as much a measure of the success of the cardiac team's intervention as the short-term outcome—is the discharged patient's return to a normal quality of life with no more likelihood than any other male his age, race/ethnicity, or demographic profile of experiencing a second acute myocardial infarction.

The combined impact of the surgery, nutritional counselling, physical therapy consultations, and physician's admonition regarding smoking and adopting a healthier lifestyle will all be put 'to the test' when the hospital contacts the patient six-months and one-year following his initial hospitalization to measure his adherence to the prescribed treatment by the cardiac team. These follow-up contacts (i.e., the 6-month and one-year follow-ups) assess the longer-term impact of the cardiac program's planned efforts, and are every bit as important as the successful short-term outcome promoted by the cardiac team. Both the immediate and the longer-range outcomes speak to the quality of care, efficacy, and value that the cardiac team provided to the patient (Pfeiffer, 1998a, 1998b).

We believe that the same logic applied to the above medical-surgical example can, and should, be equally embraced by and applied to the behavioral healthcare field—including the practice of psychotherapy and career counselling. Clients, family members, insurance companies and other funding sources, tax payers, and various other constituent groups and stakeholders all expect mental health psychotherapy and career counselling services to have what the first author calls 'holding power.' In other words, it makes very little sense—from a financial, ethical, or allocation of human resources perspective—to provide intensive, often highly personal and even 'intrusive,' and typically expensive psychotherapy and career counselling services if the client only accrues very short-term benefits.

There is another, related but somewhat distinct benefit to routine outcome monitoring of psychotherapy, and career counselling. There is a subtle but pernicious self-assessment bias among all physicians and psychotherapists. The general perception of healthcare providers is that their own success rate approaches 85% (i.e., their clinical judgment is that almost all of their clients improve as a result of their efforts on their behalf). Each clinician also believes that their own clients experience better outcomes than their fellow clinicians' clients, a fascinating finding that holds true not only for physicians and psychotherapists, but across many professions and craftsmen (Walfish, McAlister, O'Donnel, & Lambert, 2012). Practitioners rarely note worsening in their client's record. In other words, psychotherapists, and very likely career counsellors, are biased toward the positive, and are optimistic about the potential for change that their therapeutic work brings to bear on their clients (Lambert, 2017; Pfeiffer, 1998a).

The reality is that not all psychotherapy is universally effective or helpful. The same is very likely true for career counselling. In a number of well-controlled psychotherapy outcome research studies, a majority of treated clients improve (depending upon a host of factors, such as severity and chronicity, initial age of inset of the dysfunction, social and familial factors). But not *all* clients improve, and a small percent—perhaps 8%, actually worsen (Lambert, 2017). What this means is that routine outcome monitoring, with real-time feedback, is critically important to alert clinicians to lack of progress, and even potential treatment failures (Pfeiffer, 1998a, 1998b; Pfeiffer, 2015). Feedback is critically valuable in mental health psychotherapy and medicine, and we suspect, in career counselling, as well, because timely feedback reinforces and improves human performance. Measuring, monitoring, and providing ongoing feedback during the course of psychotherapy, even short-term counselling and career counselling, improves outcomes (Lambert, 2017). Objective outcome assessment data corroborates a clinicians' subjective impressions of success (or lack thereof). And timely outcome assessment data can help adjust a clinician's planned efforts if the data is not as favorable as expected. Ongoing, real-time feedback using reliable outcome assessment data enables a psychotherapist and career counsellor to be exquisitely attuned and responsive to the client. It provides opportunities for the clinician to make adjustments during the course of the counselling.

Electronic technologies can serve a facilitative role in monitoring client improvement and measuring outcomes. A number of recent research studies, in fact, have demonstrated the cost-effectiveness and clinical value of self-rated and clinician-rated electronic outcome monitoring measures (Lambert, 2017; McAlpine, McCreedy, & Alang, 2018; Murphy et al., 2011). There are a number of clinical, ethical, and practical issues to consider when implementing a client monitoring and outcome protocol. A few concerns include protecting and limiting access to the outcome data, coding the data to protect the identity and confidentiality of the clients, ensuring that the measures are reliable and valid for their specific, intended purposes, and determining *a priori* just how much change is enough to warrant client improvement (Pfeiffer, 1998a, 1998b). We recommend that solo and clinicians in group practice, as well as agencies and large-scale healthcare organizations, consult with an outcome measurement expert before setting up a routine monitoring outcome system. There are enough small details to "drive the clinician batty" without the sound advice of an expert. We next turn to internet-based assessment and counselling, a topic related to the above discussion on electronic routine outcome monitoring.

Internet-Based Assessment and Counselling

The rise in popularity and use of internet-assisted modes of communication resulted in the potential for new delivery methods of mental health services, as online counselling. E-therapy, telepsychology, tele-mental health, are other names of this new service modality in the digital era. Many studies and a few meta-analysis reviews pointed online counselling can be as effective as face-to-face sessions (Anderson & Titov, 2014; Barak, 2010). Despite empirical evidence and the important role information and communication technology has in our society, the long-term implications of distance counselling are unknown, and many clinicians remain unfamiliar or uncomfortable with the potential of online delivery service. Moreover, the use of online services demands a professional ethical behavior where security, privacy, and confidentiality are mandatory concerns that will ensure 'best practice' principles. This section explores some challenges, opportunities, and ethical issues online practitioners have within this chosen service, as discussed by Kraus, Stricker, and Speyer (2010); Goss, Anthony, Stretch, and Nagel (2016) and others.

Technology facilitates reaching clients who are limited by geographic location, financial constraint or medical condition, to gain access to counselling services. Also, shy or socially phobic clients who are uncomfortable with face-to-face interaction can often benefit from this less intimate arrangement. Internet-facilitated counselling is offered in a multiplicity of modes and contexts, some examples are text-based counselling, video or audio calls, asynchronous communication through email, synchronous through chat or instant messaging. Videoconferencing is the most popular platform because it is real time and most similar to in-person encounters, as the psychotherapist and client can see and hear each other simultaneously. Usually synchronous sessions are recommended because the clinician is able to observe nonverbal cues and subtle messages that otherwise could be missed using other e-technology.

Of course, text-based *e*-therapy is dependent on the client's writing abilities. An advantage is that the therapists' thoughts are more objective, visible, concrete and permanent. In asynchronous communication, unlike verbal conversation, the time delay affords the benefit of providing more time to reflect in a deliberate way on the choice of wording and phrasing. Taping has the advantage of reinforcing insights and important discussion points during the construction of a personal narrative; in addition, clinicians can help clients express themselves through writing—often a valuable adjunct to mental health psychotherapy. Therefore, it is important to verify in the beginning of the process the client's preference, comfort level, and skills in writing, reading and typing. Questions proposed by Suler (2010) help to assess the suitability for a text-based psychotherapy: "What do reading and writing mean to the person? What needs do these activities fulfill? Are there any known physical or cognitive problems that will limit the ability to read and write?" (p. 24).

Online practitioners must be aware that the use of words influences the quality of text relationship; poor writing may result in misunderstanding. Compared with face-to-face psychotherapy, text-based communications can create issues such as: loss of cues (silence or other meta-communication), anonymity, disinhibition, or "log off'" when the client feels in distress. The lack of cues, without seeing the client's facial expression, tone of voice or body-language, can lead to ambiguity, misinterpretation, and increase the 'projection' of the clinicians' own expectations—all impacting transference and counter-transference (Kraus, Stricker, & Speyer, 2010). Despite best-practices and ethical standards, as the Guidelines for the Practice of Telepsychology, recommends the establishment of client identity for safety and avoid dual relationship, anonymity may be reasonable under some circumstance as well. Disinhibition is one of the effects of asynchronicity and "invisibility" over the text-based online counselling, as people feel more comfortable to self-disclosure and to discuss problems.

Barak (2010) notes that internet-based assessment might be useful for psychotherapists and counsellors; Barak suggests that clients can be administered various types of psychological and vocational tests through the web, including personality inventories, career-interest questionnaires, or intellectual ability tests. While administering online instruments or guiding clients to complete the tests by themselves, clinicians perceived clear benefits, including real-time feedback to the clients. Other efficient uses include having clients compete mental-health screening scales while waiting for their session or evaluating a client's readiness for online counselling.

It is apparent that online-assessment is a new and burgeoning component of counselling practice, with obvious advantages. What is perhaps less apparent are the unintended and not fully considered ethical and legal and privacy risks with its use and implantation in psychotherapy and career counselling practices (Anderson & Titov, 2014).

Some Ethical Considerations in Online Counselling and Psychotherapy

Ethical standards related to online health and career service can be found at the Guidelines for the Practice of Telepsychology (Join Task Force for the Development of Telepsychology Guidelines for Psychologists, 2013), American Counselling Association Code of Ethics (2014) and 2015 NCDA Code of Ethics (National Career Development Association, 2015). Space limits our discussion to only a few issues. Those documents offer helpful guidance and recommendations; this is clearly an evolving and dynamic area of counselling practice, and professionals must be cognizant of applicable law and regulations and ethics that govern online practice.

Confidentiality

When planning to initiate a distance counselling relationship, practitioners must inform their clients of the likely benefits and potential limitations and risks of technology. The practitioner needs to be able to protect the client's personal data and confidential information. It is necessary to apply security measures to protect data and information from inappropriate and unintended breaches. The use of encryption is nonnegotiable, and therapists must be aware of the legal implications of the platform they are using. Procedures to ensure data storage and transmission must be used in a manner that facilitates protection and appropriate disposal. Of course, it is imperative to use a secure, robust password, with a secure back-up system in place.

Informed Consent

The Guidelines for the Practice of Telepsychology reminds the practitioner that informed consent between therapist and client is imperative, even whether using distance counselling, social media or technology. There are unique issues that must be addressed in the consent process as pointed by the Code of Ethics from ACA (2014): "distance counselling credentials, physical location of practice, and contact information; risks and benefits of engaging in the use of distance counselling technology, and/or social media; possibility of technology failure and alternate methods of service delivery; anticipated response time; emergency procedures to follow when the counsellor is not available; time zone differences; cultural and/or language differences that may affect delivery of services; possible denial of insurance benefits; and social media policy" (p. 17).

Evidence-Based Assessment (EBA)

The scope of EBA ethics is twofold, including both the process through which assessment is conducted, and the tests and measures utilized for the evaluation (Hunsley & Mash, 2007; Pfeiffer, 1998a, 1998b). Assessment in psychotherapy—and in career counselling—is inherently a decision-making process fraught with biases and potential errors that plague clinical decision-making. For example, practitioners are subject to cognitive heuristics and biases such as confirmatory bias. Confirmatory bias is preferentially seeking evidence or data consistent with an initial hypothesis or conceptualization of the client's situation or problem at the cost or risk of not considering emerging, new or contradictory information (Garb, 2005). See our earlier discussion on this very topic when explaining the importance of ongoing progress monitoring and outcome assessment. The practitioner needs to be cognizant of a number of potential assessment and diagnostic 'land-mines,' and intentionally seek not only corroborative but potentially contradictory data to ensure a fair and objective and clinically meaningful assessment.

A related component of this pernicious ethical issue in clinical assessment is the importance of using standardized instruments with documented reliability and validity. And also, the availability of local norms, when appropriate. This may sound like a simple solution for the practitioner, but it really isn't. The practitioner needs to identify tools of established reliability and validity metrics designed for the specific population and task that they are intended, measures that are readily available, free or inexpensive, brief, and easy for the client to complete (Pfeiffer, 1998a, 1998b). The challenge becomes greater in low resource mental health and career counselling settings; identifying which measures to use in the public sector is further complicated by the sheer volume of diagnostic and assessment tests available to select from, high workload, low financial resources, limited time, and the intense demands for resources (Nunno, 2006).

Digital Mediums and Ethical Issues

In order to have a successful online presence and practice, professionals need to reflect on the goals and objectives for using these tools. As mentioned already, practitioners need to be familiar with the new field using e-technology in clinical practice, be well-versed with the regulations and standards for practice within their profession and understand the strengths and limitations of using e-technology. For example, when maintaining a professional website or an internet page that offers distance counselling services, it is important to have accessibility to persons with disabilities, or translation capabilities. Therapists must ensure that electronic links are working and professionally appropriate, as well as provide links to relevant licensure and professional certification boards. When using public media, therapists must avoid disclosing confidential information, and make sure that the client's preferences and privacy for social media is fully respected and paramount.

Emerging technologies have an important potential role in marketing and delivering much-needed mental health psychotherapy and career counselling services. Mental health professionals must be vigilant and exquisitely cautious in respecting ethical standards and guidelines relevant to the use of e-technology. Some obvious issues include: boundaries between private and professional lives; online data security that could be accessed, copied, forwarded or shared; presenting partial information (intentional bias); out-of-date information; or digital exclusion of groups, must be considered and counsellors play a key role in helping individuals and clients evaluate, use, and contribute to social media information. Periodic training is imperative to become knowledgeable about these new resources (Kettunen & Makela, 2018; Sampson et al. 2018).

The Ethical Principles of Psychologists and Code of Conduct (APA, 2017), the Guidelines for the Practice of Telepsychology (Join Task Force for the Development of Telepsychology Guidelines for Psychologists, 2013) and the National Career Development Association Code of Ethics (2015) offers important information to assist clinicians and counsellors who aim to create and maintain a virtual professional presence: (a) separate professional from personal presence on social media to clearly distinguish between both kinds of digital presence; (b) only post or provide information within the scope of your professional competence and qualifications; (c) act judiciously to protect the privacy, confidentiality and reputation of clients, colleagues, organizations, and others; (d) respect privacy of client's virtual presence and avoids searching their social media information; (e) provide fair and equitable treatment to all clients, an example is to have an alternate service delivery method for the ones who lack technical knowledge; (f) respect copyright, trademark, fair use laws, and original sources, as when others' content is posted sources are clearly identified with links to original materials; (g) educating clients about the role of social media in the career development process and job search, promoting an understanding of the benefits and risks of it.

Concluding Comments

We have covered a great deal of territory in this chapter. Perhaps more than we initially intended to initially discuss! We hope that the reader has found our discussion on common factors in psychotherapy valuable. And we hope that the reader has grasped the underlying message intended by our writing this chapter: many of the things that have been shown to be helpful in psychotherapy can be applied to career counselling. The components of the therapeutic relationship, often called the common factors in psychotherapy, are one such group of relational elements that, we contend, may apply with equal relevance in successful career counselling. Many contend that so much of what occurs in career counselling mirrors the processes found in effective psychotherapy. We agree. We hope that practitioners within the career counselling field consider the importance of creating a sense of collaboration and goal consensus—an attitude of "we are in this together as a team," and establishing agreed-upon, mutually shared goals. We hope that career counsellors also recognize and appreciate the value of empathy in their work—understanding what the client who is seeking career guidance is experiencing or trying to express.

We also have argued that routine progress monitoring and outcome assessment, shown to be correlated with positive outcomes in psychotherapy, may hold similar value in career counselling. We think it should. Future research will hopefully confirm this belief. Finally, we have discussed online counselling, its uses and some cautionary notes. It is apparent that the *e*-train has already left the counselling station, and that it is our collective responsibility and obligation to ensure that we apply this new technology in a thoughtful, compassionate, ethical, legal manner. And that researchers evaluate its efficacy and cost-effectiveness across both mental health psychotherapy and career counselling.

References

American Counselling Association. (2014). 2014 *ACA code of ethics*. Retrieved from https://www.counseling.org/resources/aca-code-of-ethics.pdf.

American Psychological Association. (n.d.). *Professional practice guidelines for integrating the role of work and career into psychological practice*. Retrieved from https://www.apa.org/about/policy/work-career-practice.pdf.

American Psychological Association. (2017). *Ethical principles of psychologists and code of conduct*. Retrieved from https://www.apa.org/images/ethics-code-2017_tcm7-218783.pdf.

American Psychological Association Presidential Task Force on Evidence-Based Practice. (2006). Evidence-based practice in psychology. *American Psychologist, 61*(4), 271–285. http://dx doi.org/10.1037/0003-066X.61.4.271.

Anderson, G., & Titov, N. (2014). Advantages and limitations of internet-based interventions for common mental disorders. *World Psychiatry, 13*(1), 4–11. https://doi.org/10.1002/wps.20083.

Barak, A. (2010). Internet-supported psychological testing and assessment. In R. Krauss, G. Stricker, & C. Speyer (Eds.), *Online counseling: A handbook for mental health professionals* (2nd ed., pp. 225–255). San Diego, CA: Elsevier.

Blustein, D. L. (2008). The role of work in psychological health and well-being: A conceptual, historical, and public policy perspective. *American Psychologist, 63*(4), 228–240. https://doi.org/10.1037/0003-066X.63.4.228.

Brown, S. D., & Lent, R. W. (2013). *Career development and counseling: Putting theory and research to work* (2nd ed.). Hoboken, NJ: John Wiley & Sons.

Corsini, R. J., & Auerbach, A. J. (1998). *Concise encyclopedia of psychology*. New York: Wiley.

Dozier, C., Lenz, J., & Freeman, V. (2016). Using theory-based career assessments to connect career and mental health issues. *Career Planning and Adult Development Journal, 32*(1) 100–111.

Elliott, R., Bohart, A. C., Watson, J. C., & Murphy, D. (2018). Therapist empathy and client outcome: An updated meta-analysis. *Psychotherapy, 55*(4), 399–410. https://doi.org/10.1037/pst0000175.

Frank, J. D., & Frank, J. B. (1993). *Persuasion and healing: A comprehensive study of psychotherapy*. Baltimore, MD: Johns Hopkins University Press.

Frankl, V. E. (1959). *Man's search for meaning*. Boston, MA: Boston Press.

Garb, H. N. (2005). Clinical judgment and decision making. *Annual Review of Clinical Psychology, 1,* 67–89. https://doi.org/10.1146/annurev.clinpsy.1.102803.143810.

Gelso, C. J., & Carter, J. A. (1985). The relationship in counseling and psychotherapy: Components, consequences, and theoretical antecedents. *The Counseling Psychologist, 13*(2), 155–243. https://doi.org/10.1177/0011000085132001.

Gelso, C. J., & Carter, J. A. (1994). Components of the psychotherapy relationship: Their interaction and unfolding during treatment. *Journal of Counseling Psychology, 41*(3), 296–306. https://doi.org/10.1037/0022-0167.41.3.296.

Goss, S., Anthony, K., Stretch, L. S., & Nagel, D. M. (2016). *Technology in mental health: Applications in practice, supervision, and training* (2nd ed.). Springfield, IL: Charles C. Thomas.

Horvath, A. O., Del Re, A. C., Flückiger, C., & Symonds, D. (2011). Alliance in individual psychotherapy. *Psychotherapy: Theory, Research, & Practice, 48*(1), 9–16. http://dx.doi.org/10.1037/a0022186.

Hunsley, J., & Mash, E. J. (2007). Evidence-based assessment. *Annual Review of Clinical Psychology, 3,* 29–51. https://doi.org/10.1146/annurev.clinpsy.3.022806.091419.

Join Task Force for the Development of Telepsychology Guidelines for Psychologists. (2013). Guidelines for the practice of telepsychology. *American Psychologist, 68*(9), 791–800. http://dx.doi.org/10.1037/a0035001.

Kandel, E. R. (1998). A new intellectual framework for psychiatry. *American Journal of Psychiatry, 155*(4), 457–469. https://doi.org/10.1176/ajp.155.4.457.

Kettunen, J., & Makela, J. P. (2018). Practioners' conception of ethical practice in social networking in career services. *International Journal for Educational and Vocational Guidance*. Advance online publication. http://dx.doi.org/10.1007/s10775-018-9383-4.

Krauss, R., Stricker, G., & Speyer, C. (2010). *Online counseling: A handbook for mental health professionals* (2nd ed.). San Diego, CA: Elsevier.

Lambert, M. J. (2017). Implementing routine outcome monitoring (ROM) in clinical practice. *Journal of Health Service Psychology, 43,* 55–59.

Lambert, M. J., Whipple, J. L., & Kleinstäuber, M. (2018). Collecting and delivering progress feedback: A meta-analysis of routine outcome monitoring. *Psychotherapy, 55*(4), 520–537. https://doi.org/10.1037/pst0000167.

London, P. (1986). *The modes and morals of psychotherapy* (2nd ed.). London, England: Taylor & Francis.

Maree, J. G. (2017). Mid-career construction counseling to instill spiritual answers and allay fears. *South African Journal of Education, 37*(4), 1–10. http://dx.doi.org/10.15700/saje.v37n4a1443.

Maree, J. G. (2018). *Self and career construction counseling for a gifted young woman in search of meaning and purpose*. International Journal for Education and Vocational Guidance: Advance online publication. https://doi.org/10.1007/s10775-018-9377-2.

McAlpine, D. D., McCreedy, E., & Alang, S. (2018). The meaning and predictive value of self-rated mental health among persons with a mental health problem. *Journal of Health and Social Behavior, 59*(2), 200–214. https://doi.org/10.1177/0022146518755485.

Murphy, J. M., Masek, B., Babcock, R., Jellinek, M., Gold, J., Drubner, S., et al. (2011). Measuring outcomes in outpatient child psychiatry: The contribution of electronic technologies and parent report. *Clinical Child Psychology and Psychiatry, 16*(1), 146–160. https://doi.org/10.1177/1359104509352895.

National Career Development Association. (2015). 2015 NCDA code of ethics. Retrieved from https://www.ncda.org/aws/NCDA/asset_manager/get_file/3395.

Norcross, J. C., & Lambert, M. J. (2018). Psychotherapy relationships that work III. *Psychotherapy, 55*(4), 303–315. https://doi.org/10.1037/pst0000193.

Nunno, M. A. (2006). The effects of the ARC organizational intervention on caseworker turnover, climate, and culture in children's service systems: Commentary. *Child Abuse and Neglect, 30*(8), 849–854. https://doi.org/10.1016/j.chiabu.2006.03.001.

Osborn, D. S., & Zunker, V. G. (2016). *Using assessment results for career development* (9th ed.). Boston, MA: Cengage Learning.

Pfeiffer, S. I. (1986). Brief office counseling and the primary care physician. *Southern Medical Journal, 79,* 721–722.

Pfeiffer, S. I. (1998a). Improving treatment outcome: Incorporating multiple perspectives. In P. Meadowcroft (Ed.), *Perspectives on outcomes* (pp. 28–32). Pittsburgh, PA: Corporation for Standards & Outcomes.

Pfeiffer, S. I. (1998b). Measuring improvement in a client's social skills. In G. E. Driggs (Ed.), *Perspectives on outcomes* (pp. 28–31). Pittsburgh, PA: Corporation for Standards & Outcomes.

Pfeiffer, S. I. (2015). *Essentials of gifted assessment*. Hoboken, NJ: Wiley.

Pfeiffer, S. I. (2018). Strengths of the heart helps explain optimal mental health among youth. *Austin Child & Adolescent Psychiatry, 3*(1), 1–2.

Pfeiffer, S. I., & Shott, S. (1996). Treatment outcomes assessment: Conceptual. In C. Stout (Ed.), *The complete guide to managed behavioral healthcare* (pp. 1–11). NY: John Wiley.

Sampson, J. P. (2007). *Client problems and counseling services: Integrating career, mental health, and marriage and family*. Unpublished manuscript, Florida State University, Tallahassee, Florida.

Sampson, J. P. (2017). A Cognitive Information Processing Theory for career choice: Challenges and opportunities for integrating theory, research, and practice. In J. P. Sampson, E. Bullock-Yowell, V. C. Dozier, D. S. Osborn, & J. G. Lenz (Eds.), *Integrating theory, research, and practice in vocational psychology: Current status and future directions.* (pp. 62–72). Retrieved from https://files.eric.ed.gov/fulltext/ED575010.pdf.

Sampson, J. P., Jr., Osborn, D. S., Kettunen, J., Hou, P. C., Miller, A. K., & Makela, J. (2018). The validity of social media-based career information. *The Career Development, 66*(2), 121–134. https://doi.org/10.1002/cdq.12127.

Sears, S. J. (1982). A definition of career guidance terms: A national vocational guidance association perspective. *Vocational Guidance Quarterly, 31*(2), 137–143. https://doi.org/10.1002/j.2164-585X.1982.tb01305.x.

Smith, C. K., & Wood, S. M. (2018). Career counseling for the gifted and talented: A life span development approach. In S. I. Pfeiffer (Ed.), *Handbook of giftedness in children: Psychoeducational theory, research and best practices* (2nd ed., pp. 315–334). New York, NY: Springer.

Suler, J. (2010). The psychology of text relationships. In R. Krauss, G. Stricker, & C. Speyer (Eds.), *Online counseling: A handbook for mental health professionals* (2nd ed., pp. 25–53). San Diego, CA: Elsevier.

United Nations Educational, Scientific and Cultural Organization [UNESCO]. (2002). *Handbook on career counselling: A practical manual for developing, implementing and assessing career counselling services in higher education setting*. Paris, France: UNESCO.

Walfish, S., McAlister, B., O'Donnell, P., & Lambert, M. J. (2012). An investigation of self- assessment bias in mental health providers. *Psychological Reports, 110*(2), 639–644.

Zilcha-Mano, S. (2017). Is the alliance really therapeutic? Revisiting this question in light of recent methodological advances. *American Psychologist, 72*(4), 311–325. https://doi.org/10.1037/a0040435.

Zunker, V. G. (2016). *Career counseling: A holistic approach* (9th ed.). Boston, MA: Cengage Learning.

Career Counselling with Soul

Spencer G. Niles and Daniel Guttierez

Abstract As the world of work continues changing and evolving so must career counsellors. Previous approaches to career counselling have focused on decision-making and standardized assessments, but today's worker is searching for work that is meaningful and gives them hope. In this chapter, we discuss career counselling with soul, an approach to career counselling rooted in helping clients clarify their authentic self and explore how to live authentically in the workplace. We also discuss the role of meaning and hope in work, identify the tenets of the action hope model, and present strategies for self-clarity, self-reflection, and implementing career counselling with soul.

Keywords Career · Soul · Meaning

Introduction

Predicting the future of career counselling poses a daunting task to anyone tempted to try it. Yet, we view that task as necessary for advancing the career development field. In part, this is because traditional and more standardized career intervention strategies, which rely heavily on standardized assessments and counsellor control, no longer hold dominance within our field. Such interventions envision a world-of-work that no longer exists. They emphasize a narrow skillset oriented to the content of career decision-making and minimize the acquisition of the knowledge, skills, and awareness requisite for 21st century careers in which change is a growing constant and career self-management is a common expectation (Niles & Harris-Bowlsbey, 2017). Such developments suggest an increased need for workers to be adaptable, savvy relative to navigating work, and able to sustain a sense of hope for the future (Niles, Amundson, & Neault, 2011). Thus, more recent approaches to career intervention emphasize narratives, active engagement, and action-oriented hope. These models provide exciting lenses for viewing what is necessary to help clients create careers

S. G. Niles · D. Guttierez (✉)
College of William & Mary, School of Education, 8795, Williamsburg, VA 23188, USA
e-mail: dgutierrez@wm.edu

J. G. Maree (ed.), *Handbook of Innovative Career Counselling*,
https://doi.org/10.1007/978-3-030-22799-9_35

within a fluid work world offering little job security regardless of how competent one is or how hard one works.

In addition to the evolving world of work, the worker has changed over the years as well. Upwards of 70% of individuals want jobs that they see as meaningful regardless of financial gains (LinkedIn, 2017). It can be argued that all generations want meaningful work, but the expansion of multimedia and computer technology makes this generation the most globally connected, giving them easy access to the plights of the world and leading them on a quest to find a social cause to rally behind. The worker of today *prioritizes* work that gives them a purpose, connects them to others, and makes them happy. However, many new to the world of work find themselves unsuccessful at finding such jobs, and uncertain about what the future holds.

The current career contexts workers experience requires more current career interventions. Job satisfaction represents one indicator of this. Job satisfaction is an attitudinal construct reflecting the degree to which people like their jobs and is positively related to employee health and job performance (Spector, 1997 as cited in O'Leary, Wharton & Quinlan, 2009: 222–223). Although findings vary across studies and nations, the level of job dissatisfaction among workers globally is noteworthy, and this fact has implications for career counselling practice. According to the Conference Board Job Satisfaction Survey (2014), less than half of United States (US) workers are satisfied with their jobs. This finding has been consistent across the past eight years of this survey. In 2013, 47.7% of workers in the US were satisfied with their jobs, well below the historically high level of 61.1% in 1987. In a study investigating job satisfaction among Turkish university faculty and staff, Eroglu, Coban, and Irmis (2014) found high levels of job dissatisfaction among the 400 university personnel who participated in their study. Research from the United Kingdom conducted by the Chartered Institute of Personal Development (2016) found that almost one in four workers were looking to leave their jobs. The level of job satisfaction reported by workers in this study was a two-year low in job satisfaction.

Higher levels of job dissatisfaction are often associated with poor mental health, which also has adverse outcomes for workers. According to the Harvard Mental Health Letter (2010), researchers who analyzed employee responses to a World Health Organization (WHO) questionnaire found that workers with depression reported on average 27 lost work days per year—nine of them because of sick days or other time taken out of work, and another 18 reflecting lost productivity. Moreover, workers with depression are more likely than others to lose their jobs and to change jobs frequently (Harvard Mental Health Letter, 2010). According to the WHO, depression, and anxiety significantly impact the economy and have an estimated cost to the global economy at around 1 trillion US$ per year in lost productivity.

Chapter Structure

This chapter begins with a brief discussion of the world of work and traditional methods of career counselling. The second part of this chapter describes the case for meaningful work or rather the desire for workers to do work that gives them a sense of purpose and the influence meaning has on job satisfaction. The third part of the chapter describes a new approach to career counselling that emphasizes self-clarity, empowering the authentic self, and action-oriented hope. The chapter concludes with a brief description of strategies to aid in soul-focused career counselling.

The Case for Meaningful Work

The declining level of job satisfaction connects back to the notion of workers' searching for meaningful work. Researchers found that job satisfaction is positively associated with meaning at work and mediated by job happiness. In other words, workers with a higher sense of meaning in their work are happier workers, and that results in higher levels of reported job satisfaction (Golparvar & Abedini, 2014). Spirituality at work, which researchers defined as a positive state of value and feelings of excitement from work, is positively associated with meaning at work and ultimately contributes to job satisfaction as well (Golparvar & Abedini, 2014). We consider these concepts of valuing and finding meaning to be core conditions to your authentic self. Thus, as these studies point out, the condition of one's authentic self or soul can significantly alter the trajectory of job satisfaction.

To get a closer look at how meaning at work relates to job happiness, Niessen, Sonnetag, and Sach (2012) asked 121 employees working in social services to complete a battery of surveys three times a day. Findings from this study demonstrated that workers who started their day believing work was meaningful were more likely to experience thriving by the end of the day. Thriving was described as encompassing the "positive experience of human growth, reflected by the experience of vitality and learning" (p. 469). Thriving fuels individuals at work improving performance, and helping them grow (Niessen, Sonnetag, & Sach, 2012). Implications of this study include that meaning at work fluctuates in individuals throughout work days and if managers are able to somehow facilitate or induce that sense of positive meaning on a daily basis, they will improve employee work outcomes.

The idea that positive emotion and meaningful experiences can facilitate growth and improved functioning is at the heart of positive psychology (Seligman, 2004). One of the core theories in positive psychology is the broaden-and-build model (Fredrickson, 2001). Essentially, this model suggests that positive emotions incite in individuals an upward spiral that increases their creative problem-solving skills, broadening their outlook on potential solutions and helping them build upon their existing resources to increase growth (Fredrickson, 2001). Fredrickson (2001) theorized that by inducing experiences that evoke love, joy, contentment, and interest, you increase the likelihood that someone will expand their intellectual resources, become more psychologically resilient, have improved wellbeing, and decrease their negative affect. Fredrickson (1998, 2009) believed that the need for positive emotion was coded into the universal human experience as a survival mechanism that provided early ancestors with the resources and creative thinking needed to find solutions for their dangerous surroundings. Moreover, Fredrickson (2000) argued that positive emotion helps individuals discover a meaningful life, which then produces more positive emotion. If this broaden-and-build theory is accurate, then human beings are hardwired to search for meaning and positive meaningful experiences are a critical part of human functioning and work performance.

However, the idea that meaning in life is associated with human functioning far pre-dates the positive psychology movement. Holocaust survivor and pioneering psychotherapist, Viktor Frankl believed that the primary source of human motivation was the will to meaning—the innate human drive to discover meaning in life (Frankl, 1984). While suffering the atrocities of several concentration camps, Frankl (1984) noticed that the main difference between those who endured and those who entered despair was their ability to hold on to a meaning for life. He quoted Nietzsche (Frankl, 1984) when he said, “if you give [people] a *why*, [they will] be able to deal with anyh*ow*.” He witnessed survivors who would lose grip on their meaning for life and quickly enter a deep despair, while others would remain resilient and cling to a positive attitude, and in some cases be found going hut to hut comforting others and giving away their last piece of bread.

Frankl 1984 believed that by finding meaning in life’s everyday moments one could rise above despair, depression, anxiety, and even unavoidable suffering. How does one find meaning? Frankl suggest three paths: (a) by experiencing or encountering something or someone self-transcendent; (b) by the attitude we take towards are suffering; and (c) through creating a work or doing a deed. Our focus in this chapter is the third pathway—work. Working is a method of finding meaning in life. However, not just any work will do. Frankl was referring to self-transcendent work or work that emits from the soul’s quest for meaning. Instead of pursuing money or societal expectations for success, Frankl encourages us to search for an opportunity to create something, experience something, and keep an attitude of hope in the face of difficult life circumstances while recognizing that success will be a byproduct of that quest for meaning.

When one takes people’s meaning away from their work (and life) they begin to spiral downward towards dissatisfaction (Frankl, 1984). Moreover, many of us struggle with the existential vacuum, a constant state of emptiness and frustration that is rooted in a lack of meaning in life. This can also be described as a spirit-soul disconnection. Discovering meaning in life connects us to our souls and shapes our outlook on life (Frankl, 1984, 2014). The search for meaning is our primary motivator in life (Frankl, 1984) and fosters are ability to cope with difficulties (Folkman, 2008) and make sense of trauma (Tedeschi & Calhoun, 1996). Therefore, when meaning is missing from someone’s life and work they find themselves in a sense of void, which is why it makes complete sense that today’s worker would prioritize meaningful work. But, how do career counsellors help their clients connect with work that is meaningful for them?

Towards a New Approach to Career Counselling

A starting place is considering how career practitioners approach career counselling. Traditional career intervention approaches seek to fix the problem (typically the need to make a career decision) and ignore the evolving contextualized development of those seeking career assistance. The need to develop skills to respond (rather than react) to constant change within a lived context that continually shapes each person's evolving self suggests an increased demand for workers to be more adaptable, savvier relative to navigating work, and more able to create as well as sustain a sense of hope for the future. Fortunately, more recent approaches to career intervention emphasize narratives (Savickas, 2009), active engagement (Amundson, 2009) in career construction, and the importance of action-oriented hope (Niles, In, & Amundson, 2014). Such models provide new lenses for viewing what is necessary to facilitate career creation within a fluid work world offering little job security regardless of how competent one is or how hard one works.

Uncertainty regarding one's work future gives rise to new coping challenges. Questions arise such as "How do I prepare for a job that might not exist in ten years? What do I do when how hard I work ultimately does not matter but is required for me to maintain my job in the meantime? What is my value as a worker when my work is contingent upon factors far beyond my control? How do I plan a future for my family in the current context?" Freud noted that coping with ambiguity can be unsettling to most and overwhelming to many thereby giving rise to the need for career counsellors competent in addressing the challenges workers experience.

A positive element within such challenges is that to address them constructively, we must consider core questions regarding our existence and our essence. As we clarify what is essential, we move closer to finding what some refer to as our "authentic self." Others use words like "soul" and "true self" to describe the same. Indeed, many of us would not engage in such deep self-exploration were we not confronted by the challenges we experience in our career development—so within these challenges are great opportunities.

This chapter draws upon the current context to propose career counselling strategies that help others to consider their careers from deep self-reflection to foster clarification and articulation of the essential and necessary elements of oneself. These characteristics must be manifested within one's life structure to experience a sense of purpose in one's life. Moreover, this level of self-understanding is crucial for having the capacity for coping effectively with the uncertainty and ambiguity inherent in the world-of-work.

The Intent of Soul-Focused Career Counselling

Career counsellors using soul-focused career counselling seek to empower people to use the essential questions about who they are to clarify a level of purpose and meaning that transcends workplace challenges. Each person represents a unique constellation of experiences, talents, history, and contexts. The fact that each person is unique in history is one thing that we commonly share. Clarifying that uniqueness represents one of life's most essential tasks. That said, soul clarification is a process rather than an outcome. As Donald Super (1964) noted, the "self evolves over time making choice and adjustment continuous processes."

Furthermore, work evolves over time making choosing and adjusting continuous requirements. These two basic and intersecting facts elevate developmental aspects of career and prioritize the need for career practitioners to engage their clients in a learning process that highlights essential competencies for developing awareness and acquiring the capacity to translate awareness into direction—and, then to be able to engage in these processes across time the person adapts to evolutionary developments in the self and contextual influences. From this perspective, the over-reliance on standardized assessment and traditional approaches positioning the practitioner as the expert and the client as dependent upon the practitioner's expertise are limited substitutes for more comprehensive strategies in which clients learn competencies that can be applied across the lifespan to maximize their soul-spirit connection.

Soul-Focused Career Counselling

If the focus on soul-focused career counselling is to empower clients to learn how to clarify their authentic self, then a significant dimension within this process becomes facilitating the implementation of one's authentic self in the world, especially the workplace. We define this as the soul-spirit connection. Like "soul", spirit can be interpreted in various ways. We highlight the understanding of spirit as the manifestation of one's soul in the world. When there is a robust soul-spirit connection, then the probability of a positive work experience increases as one is authentically engaged in their work.

Hope-Action Theory identifies essential competencies that provide a foundation for soul-focused career construction. These competencies are: (a) hope, (b) self-reflection, (c) self-clarity, (d) visioning, (e) goal-setting/planning, (f) implementing, and (g) adapting (Niles, Amundson, & Neault, 2011). These competencies reflect the integration of three models into one. Bandura's (2001) human agency theory, Snyder's (2002) hope theory, and Douglas Hall's (1996) protean career theory constitute the theoretical basis for Hope-Action Theory.

Human agency relates to being vigilant regarding self-examination; engaging in the process of envisioning future events and the likely results of one's actions before setting plans; purposefully developing and carrying out action plans; and implementing and monitoring the achievement of goals (Bandura, 2001). According to Snyder (2002), having goals and believing in one's capacity to identify and implement strategies for goal achievement constitute the essential elements of hope. Here we distinguish between hope that is merely wishful thinking and action-oriented hope (the perspective that incorporates taking steps with confidence and motivation toward goal achievement). Adaptability and self-identity are central to protean career theory (Hall, 1996), which emphasizes the non-linearity of career development. Collectively, these three theoretical perspectives provide the basis to the competencies necessary for soul-focused career construction.

Niles, Yoon, Amundson, and Balin (2010) provided empirical support for the seven-factor structure of the Hope-Action Theory, which consists of hope, self-reflection, self-clarity, visioning, goal-setting/planning, implementing, and adapting. Specifically, using the *Hope-Action Inventory* (*HAI*) to measure these seven competencies, Niles et al. conducted confirmatory factor analysis with a sample of 382 U. S. postsecondary students. The overall goodness-of-fit indices strongly supported the seven-factor model (RMSEA = 0.0 RMR = 0.045, NNFI = 1.00, CFI = 1 00, and GFI = 0.98). Additionally, the overall score of the Hope-Action Inventory positively correlated with vocational identity ($r = 0.45$), supporting the positive role that action-oriented hope-centered career competencies play in adaptive career development (Niles et al., 2010).

The HAI has 28 items; sample items for each construct are as follows:

- **Hope**: I am hopeful when I consider my future.
- **Self-Reflection**: I think about things that have happened to me.
- **Self-Clarity**: I can list at least five things that I am good at.
- **Visioning**: I often imagine possible future events in my life.
- **Goal Setting and Planning**: I make a plan before taking action.
- **Implementing**: I take action once I have clear goals..
- **Adapting**: I change my plans when needed in order to reach my goals.

Response options are based on a four-point Likert scale (1 = *definitely false* to 4 = *definitely true*). When the *HAI* is completed, a profile is presented indicating the user's scores on the seven scales. Using this profile helps the career counsellor understand user strengths as well as areas for strengthening. For instance, low scores on hope, self-reflection. and self-clarity indicate the need for specific interventions that will bolster hope, teach, and encourage self-reflection activities with an eye toward developing self-clarity. Likewise, a profile that is high in self-clarity but low in self-reflection and implementing indicates the need for teaching the importance of self-reflection and encouraging engagement in self-reflective activities. This profile also suggest the need to be cautious in accepting the user's self-clarity as it is difficult to develop self-clarity without engaging in self-reflection. This latter profile also indicates the need for support when the user takes action as career choices are implemented. In these ways, the *HAI* provides very useful data to career counsellors and clients relative to targeting specific competencies in the career counselling process.

Action-Oriented Hope. Without action-oriented hope, there is no reason to expect someone to engage in career self-management. This type of hope involves "envisioning a meaningful goal and believing that positive outcomes are likely to occur should specific actions be taken" (Niles, Yoon, Balin, & Amundson, 2010, p. 102). Action-oriented hope empowers an individual to look for possibilities even in the face of adversity and to engage actively in career behaviors. Snyder (2002) described it as demonstrating "the perceived capability to derive pathways to desired goals and motivate oneself via agency thinking to use those pathways" (p. 249). Therefore, Snyder's three components of hope are: (a) agency thinking, (b) pathways thinking, and (c) goals. Goals create the direction one seeks to move toward. Pathways thinking describes the strategies one can use to achieve those goals. Agency thinking indicates the degree to which a person is both motivated to implement those strategies and confident that the strategies can be implemented successfully. Collectively these three components comprise action-oriented hope.

We advocate being intentional with clients relative to assessing their level of action-oriented hope for each activity within the career counselling process. Specifically, career counsellors need to address the following three questions that correspond to each component of action-oriented hope theory for every career counselling activity: "Does the client understand the goal of the activity? Does the client know how to achieve the goal (i.e., pathways)? Can and will the client take the necessary steps to achieve the goal (i.e., agency thinking)?" For example, in engaging in assessment activities, we suggest that career counsellors discuss with clients how self-assessment is an essential activity for achieving self-clarity (i.e., assessment represents a strategy to achieve the meaningful goal of self-clarity). We then discuss strategies for engaging in self-assessment (formal and/or informal self-assessment) to achieve self-clarity, then once a specific plan is collaboratively determined as appropriate for achieving the goal of self-clarity, we advocate asking the client whether the strategy is something that the client feels that he or she can do and will do. If the answer to any of those questions is not affirmative, then the career counsellor must address that particular issue directly (e.g., clarifying the goal, refining the strategies, addressing cognitive beliefs regarding agency thinking related to the strategies identified for goal achievement). Researchers note the importance of action-oriented hope in career development. For example, Yoon et al. (2013) found that hope predicts student engagement and vocational identity among post-secondary school students in the US and Canada. Another study found that graduate students with higher hope were less likely to procrastinate on academic tasks (Alexander & Onwuegbuzie, 2007). Hope enables people to believe that they can carry out specific steps towards their goals (Snyder, 2002). Hope is a crucial factor that drives individuals to engage in other hope-centered activities.

Self-reflection. Self-reflection refers to the capacity to examine one's beliefs, thoughts, behaviors, feelings, and circumstances (Niles, Amundson, & Neault, 2011). Self-reflection involves engaging in the soul-focused consideration of questions such as: "What matters to me? What do I like? What do I want my life to be like? What skills do I enjoy using? What opportunities are possible? What gives me joy?" The list of potential self-reflections is endless and determined by what emerges from the individual's context and situation. Self-reflection involves intentionally considering the dynamic interaction between the person and the person's environment. Reflecting upon how these interactions shape the person's understanding of their uniqueness and authentic self.

Self-reflection is the cornerstone to soul-focused career counselling. Activities such as meditation, yoga, journal writing, poetry writing and reading, playing music all create opportunities for deep self-reflection. For example, the career counsellor can provide a poem that stimulates the client to engage in self-reflection relative to how the content of the poem can be applied to the client's life. As another example, the career counsellor can encourage the client to create a mural using photographs of those people whom have been particularly influential teachers or "soul teachers" in the client's life. The client can then discuss what each person has helped the client learn about him or herself and how that learning is relevant to who the client is today. Finally, the client can be encouraged to focus on "soul places" or sacred spaces they have experienced in their lives. For instance, a client may have a sacred place where they vacation each summer, a favorite spot where they have lived, and a particular place they visited as a tourist where they felt particularly alive. Each of these could be described as "soul places" because they represent particular locations where the client has experience sacred moments in which they connected with their authentic self. Using the same approach as with "soul teachers", the client can develop a mural of photographs of their soul places. Once assembled, the client can be encouraged to share why they view each location as a soul place. The career counsellor can reinforce with the client the key client characteristics revealed when the client shares why each soul place is sacred to them.

The emphasis in self-reflection is on "human being" rather than "human doing," which is to say that self-reflective activities highlight the importance of listening to oneself rather than engaging in accomplishment oriented goal related behaviors. Regular and intentional engagement in self-reflection activities fosters the development of self-reflective insights that serve as an essential foundation for self-clarity.

Self-clarity. Because regular engagement in self-reflection leads to soul-focused self-clarity, these two dimensions are intertwined (Niles, Amundson, & Neault, 2011). Self-clarity emerges as individuals develop answers to deep questions emerge from self-reflection. It is a process that demands individuals to continually engage in self-reflection to maintain self-clarity. People are required to integrate new information that they obtain by interacting with their environments throughout their lives. Action-oriented hope propels individuals to make constant effort to assimilate new information with their self-knowledge. The process of developing self-clarity is akin to developing a photograph before digital photography. That is, self-reflection can be likened to entering the photographer's darkroom to do the work that produces a clear and unique image (self-clarity). An ancient Greek maxim emphasized that "knowing thyself" is the foundation of living life wisely, noting the importance of self-clarity.

There are many different career counselling strategies for attaining self-clarity. Some are traditional such as when the career counsellor engages the client in the use of a standardized assessment instrument. Others are less traditional such as when the client engages in completing the "My Life as a Book" exercise (Niles & Harris-Bowlsbey, 2017). In this activity, the client is asked to consider her life as if it were a book and to give her book, or her life, a title. Then, the client is asked to divide her life into chapters, giving each chapter of her life a title. The identification of key learnings from each chapter is a key part of this step in the activity. That is, the client is encouraged to consider what she learned (whether it is actually accurate or not) from each chapter of her life. These learnings can then be examined for whether they are helpful today. For example, a client may have learned that women cannot do particular types of work when, in fact, they can. Such dysfunctional beliefs can be challenged and reframed into more useful beliefs such as "women can do any work." The next step in the "My Life as a Book" activity is to identify the future chapter of one's life that one has yet to live but feels as though she must live for her book, or her life, to be complete. For instance, the client may want to eventually be a parent. Considering how this life role could be fitted into one's life structure provides useful forethought for future decisions. Finally, the client is encouraged to write a dedication for their book, or their life. Such information can provide useful insights to further enhances one's self-clarity. Amundson (2009) has outlined some additional dynamic strategies that help broaden perspective and challenge negative personal assumptions.

Visioning, Goal setting, Implementing and Adapting. Merging soul-focused self-awareness with career possibilities requires visioning, goal setting, implementing plans, and adapting plans based on newly acquired information about oneself and one's situation. Blending self-awareness and career awareness provides the springboard for envisioning future possibilities and identifying desired future outcomes (visioning). Visioning emphasizes possibility thinking before probability thinking (Pryor, Amundson, & Bright, 2008). Possibility thinking draws upon self-awareness without the influence of specific contextual factors (e.g., financial resources, job availability, family commitments). Possibility thinking highlights the individual's dreams, desires, and passions. Probability thinking, by contrast, factors in the likelihood of a particular career choice occurring by emphasizing standardized assessment data to determine probability-based future predictions of successful performance in particular occupational options. Merging both approaches, possibility and probability thinking, is important in visioning.

Thus, visioning begins with brainstorming the range of options possible and then considers what is probably within the scope of possibilities. Options identified as desirable and probable are then selected for greater exploration to gain in-depth information about those options and to determine whether they continue to be desirable (goal setting). Goal setting requires identifying specific action steps that must be taken to achieve the goal identified. Goal setting involves identifying pathways for moving from the present situation to the future possibility. Once goals are established then plans are created for reaching the goals. "Next steps" provide the road map for taking action or implementing preferred options.

Implementing indicates taking action steps that align with established goals and plans. Career development practitioners working with clients engaged in implementation may assume the role of coach. In this role, they provide clients with encouragement, support, and guidance. As actions are taken toward goal attainment, new information is obtained that must be considered in light of whether the current direction is appropriate (adapting). Thus, action focuses on learning not the traditional definition of succeeding or failing. What do you learn about yourself and the world as a result of the actions you have implemented?

This process leads naturally into self-reflection directed toward self-clarity, which will, in turn, lead to an evaluation as to whether or not the current course of action needs to be revised. "Personal flexibility" is essential for openness to modifying goals. Personal flexibility refers to the capacity to "change with change and to be able to adapt to it, to be able to take on new roles required, and to relinquish roles that are no longer relevant" (Herr, Cramer, & Niles, 2004, p. 127).

Taken together, the constant interaction between the person and the environment calls for vigilance about maintaining soul-focused self-clarity. It also demands efforts to maintain awareness of how the evolving self informs career goals and plans as well as the flexibility to respond in an adaptive way to the change in self and/or one's work environment. Hope enables individuals to engage in these tasks in any situation. Therefore, career practitioners should attend to the client's level of hope for coping effectively with each of these career tasks to sustain positive momentum and adaptability (Niles, Amundson, & Neault, 2011).

Chapter Summary

In this chapter we focus on the need to go deeper in career counselling to help the client connect with his or her authentic self. Each client is unique in all of human history- past, present, and future. In this way, all clients are universally connected. A key to career counselling with soul is helping clients embrace this basic fact as they work to clarify and articulate their uniqueness. A major goal of career counselling is to help clients identify and use their uniqueness in the world. In an existential sense, there is an awesome responsibility in this that is shared by every person. Because we are each unique, it can be argued that we each have a unique purpose to serve in the world. Finding one's purpose and then giving it away to the world is critical.

To guide clients in this process, we recommend infusing the Hope-Action Theory with interventions focused on helping clients (re)connect with their soul or their authentic selves and then to connect their authentic selves with opportunities that enable them to expressed their uniqueness in the world. In this way, career counselling with soul seeks to foster a strong soul-spirit connection. When there is a soul-spirit disconnect, a variety of maladies can arise for the client. Developing depression, addictions, "numbing out," experiencing elevated interpersonal conflicts, increases in suicidal ideation are all examples of the deleterious effects of a soul-spirit disconnect.

Conclusion

Career counselling with soul highlights creativity and curiosity in the career intervention process as career counsellors provide meaningful opportunities to help clients reconnect with their authentic selves and then use what they learn as a result to envision career possibilities that maximize their opportunities for a soul-spirit connection. We contend that many people yearn for this sort of meaningful experience in their lives. Career counselling provides an ideal context for helping clients identify opportunities for this sort of meaningful expression in the various life roles that clients play in their lives. Career counsellors who are mindful of the importance of helping clients experience a soul-spirit connection highlight subjective meaning making processes as they collaboratively assist their clients to translate experiences into soul-focused career decisions.

References

Alexander, E. S., & Onwuegbuzie, A. J. (2007). Academic procrastination and the role of hope as a coping strategy. *Personality and Individual Differences, 42,* 1301–1310.

Amundson, N. E. (2009). *Active engagement: The being and doing of career counselling* (3rd ed.). Richmond, BC: Ergon Communications.

Bandura, A. (2001). Social cognitive theory: An agentic perspective. *Annual Review of Psychology, 52,* 1–26.

Clarke, A., Amundson, N. E., Niles, S. G, & Yoon, H. J. (in press, October). Action-oriented hope: An agent of change for internationally educated professionals. *Journal of Employment Counseling.*

Donald Super, E. (1964). A Development approach to vocational guidance: Recent theory and results. *Vocational Guidance Quarterly, 13*(1), 1–10.

Eroglu, S. G., Coban, H., & Irmis, A. (2014). Research on job dissatisfaction of the university staff. European *Journal on Research in Education* 2, 185–192.

Folkman, S. (2008). The case for positive emotions in the stress process. *Anxiety Stress and Coping, 21*(1), 3–14.

Frankl, V. E. (1984). *Man's search for meaning: An introduction to logotherapy* (3rd ed.). New York, NY: Simon & Schuster.

Fredrickson, B. L. (1998). What good are positive emotions? *Review of General Psychology, 2*(3), 300–319.

Fredrickson, B. L. (2000). Extracting meaning from past affective experiences: The importance of peaks, ends, and specific emotions. *Cognition and Emotion, 14*(4), 577–606.

Fredrickson, B. L. (2001). The role of positive emotions in positive psychology: The broaden-and-build theory of positive emotions. *American Psychologist, 56*(3), 218–226.

Fredrickson, B. (2009). *Positivity*. New York, NY: Harmony.

Golparvar, M., & Abedini, H. (2014). A comprehensive study on the relationship between meaning and spirituality at work with job happiness, positive affect and job satisfaction. *Management Science Letters, 4*(2), 255–268.

Hall, D. T. (1996). Protean careers of the 21st century. *The Academy of Management Executive, 10,* 8–16.

Herr, E. L., Cramer, S. H., & Niles, S. G. (2004). *Career guidance and counseling through the lifespan* (6th ed.). Boston, MA: Allyn & Bacon.

LinkedIn. (2017). *Purpose at work: The 2016 global report.* Retrieved from https://business.linkedin.com/content/dam/me/business/en-us/talent-solutions/resources/pdfs/purpose-at-work-global-report.pdf.

Niessen, C., Sonnentag, S., & Sach, F. (2012). Thriving at work—A diary study. *Journal of Organizational Behavior, 33*(4), 468–487.

Niles, S. G., & Harris-Bowlsbey, J. G. (2017). Career development interventions (5th ed.). Columbus, OH: Pearson.

Niles, S., Amundson, N., & Neault, R. (2011). *Career flow: A hope-centered approach to career development*. Boston, MA: Pearson.

Niles, S. G., Yoon, H. J., Balin, E., & Amundson, N. E. (2010). Using a hope-centered model of career development in challenging times. *Turkish Guidance and Counselling Journal, 4,* 101–108.

Niles, S. G., Yoon, H. J., & Amundson, N. E. (2010a). *The Hope-Centered Career Inventory* [Online assessment]. Retrieved from http://mycareerflow.com.
Niles, S. G., In, H. & Amundson, N. E. (2014). Using an action oriented hope-centered model of career development. *Journal of Asia Pacific Counseling, 4*, 1–13.
O'Leary, P., Wharton, N., & Quinlan, T. (2009). Job satisfaction of psysicians in Russia. *International Journal of Health Care Quality Assurance, 23*, 221–231.
Pryor, R. G., Amundson, N. E., & Bright, J. E. H. (2008). Probabilities and possibilities: The strategic counseling implications of the chaos theory of careers. *The Career Development Quarterly, 56*, 309–318.
Savickas, M. L. (2009). Career-style counseling. In T. J. Sweeney (Ed.), *Adlerian counseling and psychotherapy: A practitioner's approach* (5th ed., pp. 183–207). New York, NY: Routledge.
Seligman, M. E. (2004). *Authentic happiness: Using the new positive psychology to realize your potential for lasting fulfillment*. New York, NY: Simon and Schuster.
Snyder, C. R. (2002). Hope theory: Rainbows in the mind. *Psychological Inquiry, 13*, 249–275. 10.1207S15327965PLI1304_01.
Spector, P. (1997). *Job satisfaction: Application, assessment, causes and consequences*. Thousand Oaks, CA Sage Publications.
Tedeschi, R. G., & Calhoun, L. G. (1996). The Posttraumatic Growth Inventory: Measuring the positive legacy of trauma. *Journal of Traumatic Stress, 9*(3), 455–471.
Yoon, H. J., In, H., Niles, S. G., Amundson, N. E. (2015). The effects of hope on student engagement, academic performance, and vocational identity. *The Canadian Journal of Career Development, 14*, 31–41.

Intrapreneurial Self-Capital as an Innovating Construct for Promoting Inclusion and Sustainable Employment: A Case Study of an Italian University Student

Annamaria Di Fabio

Abstract Intrapreneurial Self-Capital (ISC) (Di Fabio, 2014) is a promising career construct of the 21st century. It is a core of individual intrapreneurial resources that allow people to deal with frequent changes and transitions by producing innovative solutions when faced with constraints imposed by the environment. This chapter introduces the ISC construct, scale and training and also offers a brief review of the empirical research on ISC. Furthermore the chapter delineates how ISC can contribute to promoting inclusion and sustainable employment with reference to the sustainability of one's personal career/life project. The contribution also presents a case study which briefly describes the application of the ISC training with a final-year postgraduate student at the University of Florence. The Life Adaptability Qualitative Assessment (LAQuA) was administered before and after the training to detect qualitative, meaningful changes in the participant's narratives about career adaptability plus quantitative changes in employability and life project reflexivity. The results underscore ISC as a key resource and also offer new research and intervention perspectives for inclusion and sustainable employment for all.

Keywords Intrapreneurial Self-Capital · Inclusion · Sustainable employment · Sustainable career/life project · Case study · Psychology of sustainability and sustainable development

Chapter Structure The first part of the chapter presents the ISC construct, scale and training and also offers a brief review of the empirical research on ISC. The second part introduces how ISC can contribute to promoting inclusion and sustainable employment referring to the sustainability of one's personal career/life project. The third part presents a case study which briefly describes the application of the ISC training with a final-year postgraduate student at the University of Florence and the fourth part is a short discussion of the observations resulting in the case study. The last part delineates the conclusion of the chapter.

A. Di Fabio (✉)
Department of Education Languages, Intercultures, Literatures and Psychology, University of Florence, Florence, Italy
e-mail: adifabio@psico.unifi.it

J. G. Maree (ed.), *Handbook of Innovative Career Counselling*,
https://doi.org/10.1007/978-3-030-22799-9_36

Introduction

The complexity of the current world of work (Blustein, Kenny, Di Fabio, & Guichard, 2019; Di Fabio & Bernaud, 2014, 2018; Di Fabio & Maree, 2013, 2016; Guichard, 2009, 2016; Maree, 2007, 2013, 2016, 2017, 2018; Di Fabio & Maree, 2013, 2015, 2018; Savickas, 2011) calls for new resources to face the multiple challenges and continuous changes that put at risk the well-being of individuals (Di Fabio & Kenny, 2016b, 2018; Peiró & Rodriguez, 2008). Particularly young people in transition to world of work feel uncertainty for their future and have doubts about their resources to become future workers, about the real feasibility of their career and life project and the impact they can have on the society at large (Di Fabio, Kenny, & Claudius, 2016). They are unsure about the opportunities their academic studies open for the possibility of career construction (Peiró, Sora, & Caballer, 2012).

This framework highlights the importance of developing new career constructs and relative measures and trainings from a primary preventive perspective (Di Fabio & Kenny, 2015, 2016a, Hage et al., 2007; Kenny & Hage, 2009) to increase the individual's resources to navigate the current scenario promoting inclusion and sustainable employment as well as in the new framework of the psychology of sustainability and sustainable development (Di Fabio, 2017a, 2017b; Di Fabio & Rosen, 2018). Intrapreneurial Self-Capital (ISC) (Di Fabio, 2014) is thus configured as an innovative career construct for the 21st century. A scale to measure it (Di Fabio, 2014) and a training to enhance it (Di Fabio & van Esbroeck, 2016) were also developed. ISC also offers a promising resource in relation to sustainable employment with reference to the sustainability of one's personal career/life project (Di Fabio, 2019; Di Fabio & Kenny, 2016b; Maree & Di Fabio, 2018).

Intrapreneurial Self-Capital

ISC (Di Fabio, 2014) is a core of individual intrapreneurial resources that allows people to deal with frequent changes and transitions by producing innovative solutions when faced with constraints imposed by the environment to turn these constraints into resources. ISC is a higher-order construct comprising the following seven specific constructs: (1) core self-evaluation as positive judgment of oneself in terms of self-esteem, self-efficacy, locus of control and absence of pessimism (Judge, Erez, Bono, & Thorensen, 2003; (2) hardiness, with its three dimensions: commitment, control and challenge (Maddi, 1990); (3) creative self-efficacy as the perceived ability to solve problems creatively (Tierney & Farmer, 2002); (4) resilience, as the perceived ability to cope with adversity adaptively (Tugade & Fredrickson, 2004); (5) goal mastery, as the perceived ability to continuously develop one's own skills (Midgley et al., 2000); (6) decisiveness, as the perceived ability to make decisions timeously in any life context (Frost & Shows, 1993) and (7) vigilance, as the careful searching for relevant and consistent information (Mann, Burnett, Radford, & Ford, 1997).

To detect ISC, the Intrapreneurial Self-Capital Scale (ISCS) (Di Fabio, 2014) was developed. The ISCS is composed of 28 items. Examples of items include 'I am able to deal with most of my problems' for core self-evaluation; 'Working committed to the maximum really pays off in the end' for the commitment dimension of hardiness; 'Planning in advance can help avoid most future problems' for the control dimension of hardiness; 'Changes in routine are attractive to me' for the challenge dimension of hardiness; 'I'm able to solve problems creatively' for creative self-efficacy; 'I'm able to achieve objectives despite obstacles' for resilience; 'One of my goals is to acquire new skills' for goal mastery; 'I spend a lot of time to decide even for very simple things' for decisiveness (reverse score); 'Before deciding I try to clear my mind about my goals' for vigilance. The items have a response format on a five-point Likert scale ranging from 1 = *strongly agree* to 5 = *strongly disagree*. A higher-order structure with a single second-order factor was found through second-order confirmatory factor analysis with a Cronbach's alpha coefficient of 0.86. The predictive validity of ISC was supported by a positive relationship between ISC and academic performance in terms of grade point average (Di Fabio, 2014). Furthermore the positive association of ISC with perceived employability (Rothwell, Herbert, & Rothwell, 2007) and career decision self-efficacy (Betz & Taylor, 2000) and the inverse relation of ISC with career decision-making difficulties (Gati, Krausz, & Osipow, 1996) supported the concurrent validity of the scale (Di Fabio, 2014).

Intrapreneurial Self-Capital Training

From a primary preventive perspective (Di Fabio & Kenny, 2015, 2016a; Di Fabio & Kenny, 2016b; Hage et al., 2007; Kenny & Hage, 2009), the relevance of increasing the individual's resources is highlighted (Di Fabio & Blustein, 2010; Di Fabio & Kenny, 2012a, 2012b, 2016b, 2018; Di Fabio & Palazzeschi, 2015, 2016 Di Fabio & Saklofske, 2014a, 2014b, 2018). ISC is configured as a positive strength (Di Fabio, 2014), and the Intrapreneurial Self-Capital training (ISC training) (Di Fabio & Van Esbroeck, 2016) was developed to enhance this core of intrapreneurial resources. This training's first session includes the exercise 'The book of my life story' to promote reflection on one's whole life. This exercise also comprises reflection on 'The future chapter of my life story'. The next three sessions entail the elements of ISC as follows: the second session covers positive self-concept and hardiness; the third session concerns creative self-efficacy and resilience; and the fourth session regards goal mastery, decisiveness and vigilance. The exercises within each session have the following three levels: the first level promotes reflection for the self-evaluation of each ISC element, the second level encourages the recognition of specific positive aspects in relation to each ISC element and the third level recognizes aspects within past, present and future chapter/s in the individual's life story to positively clarify the elements of ISC. Furthermore specific exercises to enhance each specific element are given to the participants. The fifth session regards a validation to outline new authorship in constructing the next chapter in one's own individual life. Personal strategies to obtain awareness and improvement of one's individual intrapreneurial resources are taken into consideration to reach greater awareness. The ISC training has two formats: a short version (five sessions of four hours each, weekly) and a long version (five sessions of eight hours each, weekly). The long version of the training includes specific supplementary exercises for each component of ISC in addition to those in the shorter version (Di Fabio, 2014; Di Fabio & Van Esbroeck, 2016). The exercises in the ISC training are administered in written form to enhance self-reflection on one's own intrapreneurial skills. ISC can be administered to different targets—including early on, to young people who are facing transitions, such as that from the university to the world of work (Di Fabio, 2014), facilitating the recognition and reflection on one's individual intrapreneurial strengths for successfully constructing one's career and next life steps (Di Fabio & Van Esbroeck, 2016). The ISC training can be applied both individually and in a group modality using the methodology of the power of the audience (Di Fabio & Maree, 2012). According to this methodology, the members are positioned in a circle and speak in turn with the psychologist facilitator one at a time. Therefore, the group participants engage as individuals in a one-to-one intervention session, but at the same time they have the possibility to reflect more in-depth on themselves by listening to the stimuli offered by the other participants in the intervention.

Research on Intrapreneurial Self-Capital

ISC (Di Fabio, 2014) is a relatively new construct. In the literature some interesting studies can be found that have examined this promising career construct in relation to different outcomes.

In 2016 Di Fabio and Gori examined, with 141 Italian white-collar workers, the contribution of ISC as a mediator in the relationship between emotional stability (low neuroticism) and flourishing, finding a strong contribution. This result underscored that the innovative construct of ISC seems to contribute to adaptive outcomes, such as flourishing as eudaemonic well-being in terms of optimal human functioning, ranging from positive relationships, to feelings of competence, to having meaning and purpose in life (Diener et al., 2010).

This contribution led to an in-depth study into the relationships of ISC with different aspects of well-being (Di Fabio & Gori, 2016a, 2016b). A following study (Di Fabio, Palazzeschi, & Bucci, 2017) examined the relationships between ISC and well-being (both hedonic and eudaemonic well-being), controlling for the effect of personality traits (Big Five Model). As a measure of hedonic well-being satisfaction with life was considered (Diener, Emmons, Larsen, & Griffin, 1985; Di Fabio & Gori, 2016a, 2016b), and as a measure of eudaemonic well-being flourishing was used (Diener et al., 2010; Di Fabio, 2016a). Hierarchical regression analyses showed that ISC explained a percentage of incremental variance beyond that explained by personality traits in relation to both life satisfaction and flourishing. These results indicated that ISC is relevant for both hedonic and eudaemonic well-being.

Following this line of research Di Fabio and Kenny (2018) extended the previous studies analyzing the relationship between ISC and both hedonic and eudaemonic well-being, controlling for the effects of personality traits (Big Five Model) in 563 Italian university students. In this study, with respect to the previous study (Di Fabio et al., 2017), additional measures of both hedonic and eudaemonic well-being were used. In the study by Di Fabio and Kenny (2018) for hedonic well-being, in addition to life satisfaction (the cognitive aspect of hedonic well-being), positive and negative affects (the affective aspects of hedonic well-being) (Watson, Clark, & Tellegen, 1988) were also considered. For eudaemonic well-being, in addition to flourishing meaning in life (Morgan & Farsides, 2009) was also included. Hierarchical regressions analyses showed that ISC explained a percentage of incremental variance beyond that accounted for by personality traits in relation to both hedonic and eudaemonic well-being, particularly in relation to eudaemonic well-being in terms of flourishing. These results support the fact that ISC may be a new, positive, promising resource for promoting both hedonic and eudaemonic well-being.

A more recent study (Di Fabio, Palazzeschi, Bucci, Duradoni, Pesce, & Burgassi, in press) examined the contribution of ISC in relation to both perceived employability (Fugate & Kinicki, 2008) and career decision-making self-efficacy (Betz, Klein, & Taylor, 1996; Betz & Taylor, 2000), controlling for the effects of personality traits in Italian workers. Hierarchical regression analyses showed that ISC explained a percentage of incremental variance beyond that accounted for by personality traits in relation to both perceived employability and career decision-making self-efficacy. The results suggest that ISC offers a promising resource for enhancing employability and career decision-making self-efficacy for workers in the 21st century in a framework of sustainability of career and life project (Di Fabio, 2019; Maree & Di Fabio, 2018) in the liquid and unpredictable scenario that is the 21st century.

Intrapreneurial Self-Capital for Inclusion and Sustainable Employment in the Framework of the Psychology of Sustainability and Sustainable Development

A new perspective in the framework of the psychology of sustainability and sustainable development (Di Fabio, 2017a, 2017b; Di Fabio & Rosen, 2018) considers ISC a key resource to promote inclusion and sustainable employment, referring to the sustainability of one's personal career/life project.

The psychology of sustainability and sustainable development (Di Fabio, 2017a, 2017b; Di Fabio & Rosen, 2018) constitutes a new research area in the field of sustainability science. It addresses sustainability issues by introducing psychological contributions and enhancing its trans-disciplinary perspective. The concept of sustainability is considered not only in relation to the ecological, social and economic environment but also with respect to the psychological environment, aiming at improving the quality of life for each individual with and in the environments

(Di Fabio & Rosen, 2018; Di Fabio & Tsuda, 2018). The psychology of sustainability and sustainable development goes beyond the traditional perspective centred on the three 'Es' of economy, equity and ecology (Brundtland Report, 'Our Common Future', 1987; Harris, 2003) based on remediating exploitation and depletion to prevent irreparable alteration. This perspective introduces a framework focused not only on using increasingly smaller quantities of resources but also on regenerating resources and on keywords such as promotion, enrichment, growth and flexible change (Di Fabio, 2017a, 2017b). There is a shift in the focus from pressure to opportunity/challenge, from using a small amount of resources to regenerating resources, from a negative vision of problems to a positive vision of problems and from damage/threat to opportunity/change. The psychology of sustainability and sustainable development creates a new axis for psychological reflection on what is truly sustainable for individuals considering a meaningful construction with coherence, direction, significance and belonging (Di Fabio, 2017b; Schnell, Höge, & Pollet, 2013). Sustainability and sustainable development is anchored to authentic meanings for individuals, further highlighting the importance of connections, meaning and purpose (Di Fabio & Blustein, 2016), psychological respect, care and connectedness (Di Fabio, 2016b; Di Fabio & Rosen, 2018).

In this framework the career/life project is especially sustainable when it is anchored to the construction of a life full of authentic connection and meaning (Di Fabio, 2017a, 2017b; Di Fabio & Blustein, 2016), becoming really decent when aspects of self-determination and meaning (Duffy et al., 2017; Di Fabio & Kenny, 2018) are included. In this framework ISC can be considered as a resource for inclusion and sustainable employment. Inclusion calls for positive relationships, and ISC is a fundamental variable in terms of positive, life-long self-management in the preventive Positive Self Relational Management (PS&RM) (Di Fabio & Kenny, 2016a, 2016b) model. This model underscores the importance of positive preventive resources, such as ISC, for positive relational management and well-being to promote decent work and decent life (Di Fabio & Kenny, 2016a, 2016b, 2018, 2019), enhancing the importance of positive relationships and the inclusion of others for well-being—considered one of the main sustainable development goals in the 2030 Agenda of the United Nations (2018). For individuals, having positive resources, such as ISC, associated to different aspects of well-being in terms of hedonic well-being but especially eudaemonic well-being in regard to finding meaning in life and flourishing (Di Fabio et al., 2017; Di Fabio & Kenny, 2018) is important to construct for more sustainable career/life projects (Mare & Di Fabio, 2018).

Case Study

This chapter describes a case study regarding the application of the ISC training with a final-year male postgraduate law student at the University of Florence, who was concerned about how to develop his future career path. For this reason he choose to participate in an ISC training at the career services of the University of Florence. ISC training aims to support individuals to identify and enhance their personal strengths in terms of intrapreneurial characteristics for sustainable employability and employment. In particular, the case study describes the application of the ISC training in helping the participant to discover his personal intrapreneurial resources and facilitating self-awareness for constructing future career and life projects (Di Fabio, 2014; Di Fabio & Van Esbroeck, 2016). This case study permits an analysis of the process of enhancing the personal strengths of a young individual in an uncertain condition being in transition to the world of work. The Life Adaptability Qualitative Assessment (LAQuA) (Di Fabio, 2015) was administered before and after the training to detect meaningful qualitative changes in the participant's narratives about career adaptability plus quantitative changes in employability (Di Fabio & Maree, 2013) and life project reflexivity (Di Fabio, Maree, & Kenny, 2018).

The study examined the following three questions:

- How was the ISC training applied to the case of an Italian male university law student who is concluding his university (master's degree) path?
- How did ISC help the participant to increase awareness of his personal intrapreneurial resources and to identify more clearly the objectives for his professional and personal life?
- How did ISC increase the perceived employability of the Italian male university law student after the intervention?

Materials and Methods

Participant and Context Lorenzo (a pseudonym), who participated in the study, was 27 years old and concluding his university (master's degree) path in Law at the University of Florence in Italy. He was very concerned about his future career, and he was uncertain about his personal resources. He asked to participate in the ISC training at the career service centre at the School of Psychology of the University of Florence. He required this intervention because he wanted to potentiate his strengths as he was insecure about his resources and potentialities.

Qualitative Assessment Instrument

Life Adaptability Qualitative Assessment (LAQuA) The LAQuA (Di Fabio, 2015) is a qualitative instrument aiming at evaluating the effectiveness of the post-modern career and life interventions. LAQuA was developed for qualitatively assessing career adaptability, evaluating change or lack of change in the individual's life narratives before and after the intervention. Twelve written questions are included in the LAQuA, with three questions for each dimension (Concern, Control, Curiosity and Confidence) of the *Career Adapt-Abilities Inventory—International Version 2.0* (Savickas & Porfeli, 2012). Following are the 12 written questions of the LAQuA:

Concern: 1a) What does it mean to you to be oriented toward your future? 1b) Do you think you are oriented toward your future? 1c) Why?
Control: 2a) What does it mean to you to take responsibility for your future? 2b) Do you think you do take responsibility for your future? 2c) Why?
Curiosity: 3a) What does it mean to you to be curious about your own future? 3b) Do you think you are curious about your future? 3c) Why?
Confidence: 4a) What does it mean to you to have confidence in your own ability to build your future? 4b) Do you think you have confidence in your ability to build your future? 4c) Why?

The narratives generated by the individual before and after the intervention as answers to the 12 questions are compared. The comparison and evaluation of the narratives were carried out using the 24 qualitative indicators related to each of the four dimensions of career adaptability (Concern, Control, Curiosity and Confidence) (Di Fabio, 2015).

The 24 qualitative descriptors are used for the LAQuA coding system, structured in five qualitative analysis change categories that permit the detection of changes or lack thereof for each dimension of career adaptability at different levels of reflexivity (Increased Reflexivity, Revised Reflexivity, Open Reflexivity, Enhanced Reflexivity and No Change) (Di Fabio, 2015). The LAQuA is, therefore, an instrument that allows the careful detection of change or lack of change in narratives before and after intervention, specifically for the four career adaptability dimensions (Concern, Control, Curiosity and Confidence) and with a distinction of change into different levels of reflexivity.

Quantitative Assessment Instruments

Self-Perceived Employability for Students Scale (SPES) To measure self-perceived employability, the Italian version (Di Fabio & Palazzeschi, 2013) of the SPES (Rothwell, Herbert, & Rothwell, 2007) was used. The questionnaire is composed of 16 items and uses a five-point Likert scale (1 = *strongly disagree*, 2 = *disagree*, 3 = *neither agree nor disagree*, 4 = *agree*, 5 = *strongly agree*). Examples of items include 'The skills and abilities that I possess are what employers are looking for' and 'I feel I could get any job so long as my skills and experience are reasonably relevant'. The scale is unidimensional, with a Cronbach's alpha of 0.75 (Di Fabio & Palazzeschi, 2013).

Life Project Reflexivity Scale (LPRS) To detect life project reflexivity, the LPRS (Di Fabio et al., 2018) was developed. The LPRS is composed of 15 items, with a response format on a five-point Likert scale from 1 = *strongly disagree* to 5 = *strongly agree.* The scale has three dimensions: Clarity/Projectuality (example of item: 'The projects for my future life are clearly defined'), Authenticity (example of item: 'The projects for my future life are full of meaning for me') and Acquiescence (example of item: 'The projects for my future life are more anchored by the values of the society in which I live than my most authentic values'). The Cronbach's alpha coefficients for the three dimensions were $\alpha = 0.89$ for Clarity/Projectuality, $\alpha = 0.86$ Authenticity, $\alpha = 0.83$ for Acquiescence and $\alpha = 0.86$ for LPRS in total.

Procedure

The LAQuA, SPES and LPRS were administered before and after the ISC training by a psychologist qualified in the administration of this instrument. Three independent, trained judges compared the participant's responses to the LAQuA written questions generated by the client before and after the intervention. An interrater reliability analysis using the kappa statistic was carried out to evaluate the level of consistency among the judges.

The study was conducted according to the requirements of privacy and informed consent in Italian law, and the participant's anonymity was guaranteed.

Lorenzo participated in the ISC training's (Di Fabio, 2014; Di Fabio & Van Esbroeck, 2016) long version of five weekly one-day sessions (eight hours a session) in a group setting, based on the power of audience framework (Di Fabio & Maree, 2012).

Rigour of the Study

It is essential to guarantee the trustworthiness of the study results using different strategies in relation to the data collection and analysis process: credibility, confirmability, transferability and dependability (Maree, 2012). The credibility of data regards 'factors such as the significance of results and their credibility for participants and readers' (Maree, 2012, p. 141). Credibility in the present case study was guaranteed by external confirmation of the results by submitting the documentation to other researchers. Confirmability concerns 'the objectivity of the data and the absence of research errors. Results can be regarded as confirmable when they are derived from the participants and the research conditions rather than from the (subjective) opinion of the researcher' (Maree, 2012, p. 142). External researchers, who assessed whether the methods and procedures of the study had been described in enough detail to permit verification, granted confirmability. Transferability is relative to 'the extent to which the results can be "exported" and generalised to other contexts' (Maree, 2012, p. 142). Transferability in the present case study was obtained through the comprehensive presentation of the participant's personal situation and the techniques applied to stimulate the narratives. Specific information was also provided on the context of the case to permit other researchers to evaluate the applicability of the results to other contexts. It is fundamental to affirm that this study attempted to give a comprehensive description of the participant's situation without any effort at generalization. Dependability regards 'the stability and consistency of the research process and methods over time and influences the degree of control in a study' (Maree, 2012, p. 141). Dependability was guaranteed through the independent judgement of the participant's FCA and LAQuA by three expert judges.

Results

The level of reflexivity in all the four dimensions of adaptability (Concern, Control, Confidence and Curiosity) of the narratives produced by Lorenzo through the LAQuA administered before and after the intervention are given below.

Lorenzo's answer to the first LAQuA question before the ISC training was: '*To me, to be oriented toward my future means having awareness that today's choices will shape my future* (qualitative descriptor: Predicting); and after the ISC training it was: '*To me, to be oriented toward my future means to think now about my future because I am aware that today's choices will shape my future. It is important to me to understand what I would like really to do professionally because I have to decide now on what I have to invest in because all my future steps depend on this choice. I'm considering doing the internship to become a lawyer but only to use my competences for people in difficulty as a lawyer, for example, in the service of a humanitarian organization*' (identical qualitative descriptor Predicting but more in-depth reflexivity: Aware Increased reflexivity: in the narratives produced after the ISC training, there were identical descriptors, but they were described with more in-depth reflexivity).

Lorenzo's answer to the second LAQuA question before the ISC training was: '*To me, to take responsibility for my future means being responsible for choosing something I really believe in*' (qualitative descriptor: Honest); and after the ISC training it was: '*To me, to take responsibility for my future means doing what's right for me, what I really want, what is it meaningful for me. My parents always wanted me to be a lawyer, but if I finally choose this option it will be because it is really meaningful for me*' (identical qualitative descriptor but more in-depth reflexivity: Honest). '*I think that it is also important to make decisions by myself without being influenced by others*' (new, different qualitative descriptor: Autonomous) [new, different qualitative descriptor: Autonomous; Enhanced reflexivity (E): in the narratives produced after the ISC training, there is an identical descriptor/s but described with more in-depth reflexivity plus a new, different descriptor/s].

Lorenzo's answer to the third LAQuA question before the ISC training was: '*To me, to be curious about my future means to look for opportunities to grow as a person*' (qualitative descriptor: Developing); and after the ISC training it was: '*To be curious about my future means to try to grow as a person*' (identical qualitative descriptor: Developing); '*During the intervention, reflecting on myself and on my resources, I thought that being curious about my future could mean becoming curious about new opportunities or about different perspectives regarding the same opportunity. For example, regarding the possibility of becoming a lawyer, I would like to understand what a lawyer really does and in which fields it is possible to operate*' [new, different qualitative descriptor: Searching; Open reflexivity (O): in the narratives produced after the ISC training, there is an identical descriptor/s—with the same level of reflexivity in presenting the descriptor—plus a new, different descriptor/s].

Lorenzo's answer to the fourth LAQuA question before the ISC training was: '*To me, to have confidence in my own abilities to build my future means to be aware of having the resources to overcome obstacles*' (qualitative descriptor: Resilient); and after the ISC training it was: '*To me, to have confidence in my own abilities to build my future means to be able to work up to my ability. The intervention permitted me to have a greater awareness of my ability and resources, for example, in terms of my relational competences and my sensitivity towards others, and I think that I can construct my future on them*' [new, different qualitative descriptor: Capable; Revised reflexivity R: in the narratives produced after the ISC training, the previous descriptor/s has disappeared, and a new, different descriptor/s has appeared].

The quantitative evaluation found that the administration of the SPES and LPRS before and after the interventions showed an increase both in perceived employability (from 36 to 64) and in dimensions of life project reflexivity (in Clarity/Projectuality from 11 to 21; in Authenticity from 13 to 22; in Acquiescence from 20 to 10).

Discussion

The case study presented in this chapter shows the value of the ISC training (Di Fabio, 2014) in supporting individuals to identify and enhance their personal strengths in terms of intrapreneurial characteristics for sustainable employability and employment. In the current scenario, taking place in the 21st century, the development of a sustainable career/personal project is essential (Di Fabio, 2017a). A project is sustainable when it develops present aims without compromising future goals (Di Fabio, 2017a). A project is also sustainable when it is strongly rooted in a meaningful construction (Di Fabio, 2017a; Schnell et al., 2013) and thus linked to authentic meaning for the individual (Di Fabio & Blustein, 2016) and meaningful construction (Di Fabio & Blustein, 2016).

In this case study, the changes in the participant could be recognized through analyses of the narratives before and after the intervention via use of the LAQuA (Di Fabio, 2015). The LAQuA analysis showed changes in the participant's reflexivity regarding adaptability in the narratives before and after the intervention. The level of reflexivity in all the four dimensions of adaptability (Concern, Control, Confidence and Curiosity) appears to have increased. In relation to Concern, Lorenzo underscored the importance of thinking in the present moment regarding one's own future because today's choices will shape one's future. In relation to Control, the participant highlighted the significance of taking responsibility for your own future by doing what is right for you, what the you really want, what is it meaningful to you. In relation to Curiosity, the participant realized the importance of becoming curious about new opportunities or about different perspectives regarding the same opportunity. Lorenzo identified employment as sustainable when it is truly meaningful for him and permits him to realize himself. Furthermore, from a quantitative perspective, there was an increase in Lorenzo's perceived employability after the intervention, suggesting the potentialities of the ISC training in enhancing the employability of participants. Also an increase in life project reflexivity—in particular an increase in Clarity/Projectuality and in Authenticity and a decrease in Acquiescence—emerged, highlighting that the ISC training seems to also facilitate the enhancement of processes of reflexivity for constructing personal and professional projects.

The trustworthiness and credibility of the study were verified, but a limitation could be the subjective interpretation of the judges rating the study. A follow-up session six weeks after the intervention showed that Lorenzo had graduated in Law and started his internship in a non-profit association. Nonetheless a follow-up assessment six to 12 months after the intervention would be useful to further confirm the results achieved in this case study.

Conclusion

Despite the above limitations, the case study indicated the value of ISC interventions for enhancing inclusion and sustainable employment. The results thus underscored ISC as a key resource for inclusion and sustainable employment. Sustainable development calls for the sustainability of an individual's career/life project. Such a project is sustainable (Mare & Di Fabio, 2018) if it expresses meaningfulness as coherence, direction, significance and belonging (Bernaud, 2013, 2015, 2018; Di Fabio, 2017a, 2017b; Bernaud & Di Fabio, in press; Schnell et al., 2013), highlighting the value of the passage from the paradigm of motivation to the paradigm of meaning (Di Fabio & Blustein, 2016) and paying attention to the construction of a sustainable career/life project deeply associated to the authentic individual's meaningfulness.

References

Bernaud, J. L. (2013). Career counseling and life meaning: A new perspective life designing for research and applications. In A. Di Fabio & K. Maree (Eds.), *Psychology of career counseling: New challenges for a new era* (pp. 19–39). New York, NY: Nova Science Publishers.

Bernaud, J.-L. (2015). *Psychologie de L'accompagnement: Concepts et Outils pour Développer le Sens de la vie et du Travail*. Paris, France: Dunod.

Bernaud, J.-L. (2018). *Introduction à la psychologie existentielle*. Paris, France: Dunod.

Betz, N. E., Klein, K. L., & Taylor, K. M. (1996). Evaluation of a short form of the career decision-making self-efficacy scale. *Journal of Career Assessment, 4,* 47–57.

Betz, N. E., & Taylor, K. M. (2000). *Manual for the career decision making self-efficacy scale (CDMSES) and CDMSES–Short Form*. Unpublished manuscript, Ohio State University, Columbus, OH.

Blustein, D. L., Kenny, M. E., Di Fabio, A., & Guichard, J. (2019). Expanding the impact of the psychology of working: Engaging psychology in the struggle for decent work and human rights. *Journal of Career Assessment*. https://doi.org/10.1177/1069072718774002.

Brundtland Report (1987). *Our common future*. New York, NY: Butterworth.

Diener, E. D., Emmons, R. A., Larsen, R. J., & Griffin, S. (1985). The satisfaction with life scale. *Journal of Personality Assessment, 49*(1), 71–75.

Diener, E., Wirtz, D., Tov, W., Kim-Prieto, C., Choi, D. W., Oishi, S., et al. (2010). New well-being measures: Short scales to assess flourishing and positive and negative feelings. *Social Indicators Research, 97*(2), 143–156.

Di Fabio, A. (2014). Intrapreneurial self-capital: A new construct for the 21st century. *Journal of Employment Counseling, 51,* 98–111. https://doi.org/10.1002/j.2161-1920.2014.00045.x.

Di Fabio, A. (2015). Life adaptability qualitative assessment (LAQuA): A narrative instrument for evaluating counseling intervention effectiveness. In J. G. Maree & A. Di Fabio (Eds.), *Exploring new horizons in career counselling: Turning challenges into opportunities* (pp. 43–62). Rotterdam, The Netherlands: Sense Publishers.

Di Fabio, A. (2016a). *Flourishing scale*: Primo contributo alla validazione della versione italiana [*Flourishing Scale*: First contribution to the validation of the Italian version] *Counseling. Giornale Italiano di Ricerca e Applicazioni, 9*(1). https://doi.org/10.14605/cs911606.

Di Fabio, A. (2016b). Positive relational management for healthy organizations: Psychometric properties of a new scale for prevention for workers. In G. Giorgi, M. Shoss, & A. Di Fabio (Eds.), From organizational welfare to business success: Higher performance in healthy organizational environments. Research Topic in *Frontiers in Psychology. Organizational Psychology, 7,* 1523. https://doi.org/10.3389/fpsyg.2016.01523.

Di Fabio, A. (2017a). The psychology of sustainability and sustainable development for well-being in organizations. In G. Arcangeli, G. Giorgi, N. Mucci, J.-L. Bernaud, & A. Di Fabio (Eds.), Emerging and re-emerging organizational features, work transitions and occupational risk factors: The good, the bad, the right. An interdisciplinary perspective. Research Topic in *Frontiers in Psychology. Organizational Psychology, 8*, 1534. https://doi.org/10.3389/fpsyg.2017.01534.

Di Fabio, A. (2017b). Positive healthy organizations: Promoting well-being, meaningfulness, and sustainability in organizations. In G. Arcangeli, G. Giorgi, N. Mucci, J.-L. Bernaud, & A. Di Fabio (Eds.), Emerging and re-emerging organizational features, work transitions and occupational risk factors: The good, the bad, the right. An interdisciplinary perspective. Research Topic in *Frontiers in Psychology. Organizational Psychology, 8*, 1938. https://doi.org/10.3389/fpsyg.2017.01938.

Di Fabio, A. (2019). The challenge of sustainability in the construction and managing of personal project for a decent work and a decent life: Psychological contributions. In V. Cohen-Scali, J. Pouyaud, V. Drabik-Podgorna, M. Podgorni, G. Aisenson, J. Luc Bernaud, I. Moumoula, & J. Guichard (Eds.), *Life-and career designing for sustainable development and decent work* (pp. 173–194). Switzerland: Springer.

Di Fabio, A., & Bernaud, J.-L. (Eds.). (2014). *The construction of the identity in 21st century: A festschrift for jean guichard*. New York, NY: Nova Science Publishers.

Di Fabio, A., & Bernaud, J.-L. (Eds.). (2018). *Narrative interventions in post-modern guidance and career counseling: Innovative qualitative approaches, accountability, and case studies*. Switzerland: Springer.

Di Fabio, A., & Blustein, D. L. (2010). Emotional intelligence and decisional conflict styles: Some empirical evidence among Italian high school students. *Journal of Career Assessment, 18*(1), 71–81. https://doi.org/10.1177/1069072709350904.

Di Fabio, A., & Blustein, D. L. (Eds). (2016). *From meaning of working to meaningful lives: The challenges of expanding decent work*. Lausanne: Frontiers Media. https://doi.org/10.3389/978-2-88919-970-9.

Di Fabio, A., & Gori, A. (2016a). Measuring adolescent life satisfaction: Psychometric properties of the satisfaction with life scale in a sample of italian adolescents and young adults. *Journal of Psychoeducational Assessment, 34*(5), 501–506. https://doi.org/10.1177/0734282915621223.

Di Fabio, A., & Gori, A. (2016b). Neuroticism and flourishing in white collars workers: From self-esteem to intrapreneurial self-capital for adaptive outcomes. In A. Di Fabio (Ed.), *Neuroticism: Characteristics, impact on job performance and health outcomes* (pp. 129–146). New York: Nova Science Publishers.

Di Fabio, A., & Kenny, M. E. (2012a). Emotional intelligence and perceived social support among Italian high school students. *Journal of Career Development, 39,* 461–475. https://doi.org/10.1177/0894845311421005.

Di Fabio, A., & Kenny, M. E. (2012b). The contribution of emotional intelligence to decisional styles among Italian high school students. *Journal of Career Assessment, 20,* 404–414. https://doi.org/10.1177/1069072712448893.

Di Fabio, A., & Kenny, M. E. (2015). The contributions of emotional intelligence and social support for adaptive career progress among Italian youth. *Journal of Career Development, 42,* 48–59. https://doi.org/10.1177/0894845314533420.

Di Fabio, A., & Kenny, M. E. (2016a). From decent work to decent lives: Positive self and relational management (PS&RM) in the twenty-first century. In A. Di Fabio & D. L. Blustein (Eds.), From meaning of working to meaningful lives: The challenges of expanding decent work. Research Topic in *Frontiers in Psychology. Section Organizational Psychology*, *7*, 361. https://doi.org/10.3389/fpsyg.2016.00361.

Di Fabio, A., & Kenny, M. E. (2016b). Promoting well-being: The contribution of emotional intelligence. In G. Giorgi, M. Shoss, & A. Di Fabio (Eds.), From organizational welfare to business success: Higher performance in healthy organizational environments. Research Topic in *Frontiers in Psychology. Organizational Psychology*, *7*, 1182. https://doi.org/10.3389/fpsyg.2016.01182.

Di Fabio, A., & Kenny, M. E. (2018). Intrapreneurial self-capital: A key resource for promoting well-being in a shifting work landscape. In A. Di Fabio (Ed.), Psychology of sustainability and sustainable development. Special Issue in *Sustainability* MDPI, *10*(9), 3035. https://doi.org/10.3390/su10093035.

Di Fabio, A., & Kenny, M. E. (2019). Decent work in Italy: Context, conceptualization, and assessment. *Journal of Vocational Behavior, 110,* 131–143.

Di Fabio, A., Kenny, M. E., & Claudius, M. (2016). Preventing distress and promoting psychological well-being in uncertain times through career management intervention. In M. Israelashvili & J. L. Romano (Eds.), *The Cambridge handbook of international prevention science* (pp. 233–254). Cambridge: Cambridge University Press.

Di Fabio, A., Kenny, M. E., & Claudius, M. (2017a). Preventing distress and promoting psychological well-being in uncertain times through career management intervention. In M. Israelashvili & J. L. Romano (Eds.), *The Cambridge handbook of international prevention science* (pp. 233–254). Cambridge: Cambridge University Press.

Di Fabio, A., & Maree, J. G. (2012). Group-based life design counseling in an Italian context. *Journal of Vocational Behavior, 80,* 100–107. https://doi.org/10.1016/j.jvb.2011.06.001.

Di Fabio, A., & Maree, J. G. (Eds.). (2013). *Psychology of career counseling: New challenges for a new era. Festschrift in honour of Prof. Mark Savickas*. New York, NY: Nova Science Publishers.

Di Fabio, A., & Maree, J. G. (2016). Using a transdisciplinary interpretive lens to broaden reflections on alleviating poverty and promoting decent work. In A. Di Fabio & D. L. Blustein (Eds.), From meaning of working to meaningful lives: The challenges of expanding decent work. Research Topic in *Frontiers in Psychology. Section Organizational Psychology*, *7*, 503. https://doi.org/10.3389/fpsyg.2016.00503.

Di Fabio, A., Maree, J. G., & Kenny, M. E. (2018). Development of the life project reflexivity scale: A new career intervention inventory. *Journal of Career Assessment*, 1–13. https://doi.org/10.1177/1069072718758065.

Di Fabio, A., & Palazzeschi, L. (2013). *Self-perceived Employability for students*: Un primo contributo alla validazione italiana [*Self-perceived Employability for students*: A first contribution to Italian validation]. *Counseling. Giornale Italiano di Ricerca e Applicazioni, 6,* 97–105.

Di Fabio, A., & Palazzeschi, L. (2015). Hedonic and eudaimonic well-being: The role of resilience beyond fluid intelligence and personality traits. *Frontiers in Psychology, Section Developmental Psychology, 6,* 1367. https://doi.org/10.3389/fpsyg.2015.01367.

Di Fabio, A., & Palazzeschi, L. (2016). Marginalization and precariat: The challenge of intensifying life construction intervention. In A. Di Fabio & D. L. Blustein (Eds.), From meaning of working to meaningful lives: The challenges of expanding decent work. Research Topic in *Frontiers in Psychology. Section Organizational Psychology, 7,* 444. https://doi.org/10.3389/fpsyg.2016.

Di Fabio, A., Palazzeschi, L., & Bucci, O. (2017). In an unpredictable and changing environment: Intrapreneurial self-capital as a key resource for life satisfaction and flourishing. In G. Arcangeli, G. Giorgi, N. Mucci, J.-L. Bernaud, & A. Di Fabio (Eds.), Emerging and re-emerging organizational features, work transitions and occupational risk factors: The good, the bad, the right. An interdisciplinary perspective. Research Topic in *Frontiers in Psychology. Organizational Psychology, 8,* 1819. https://doi.org/10.3389/fpsyg.2017.01819.

Di Fabio, A., Palazzeschi, L., Bucci, O., Duradoni, M., Pesce, E., & Burgassi, C. (in press). The contribution of intrapreneurial self-capital beyond personality traits in employability and career decision-making self-efficacy: A key resource for sustainable career and life project. In A. Di Fabio (Eds.), *Positive psychology for healthy organizations: the challenge of primary prevention in a cross-cultural perspective.* New York, NY: Nova Science Publishers.

Di Fabio, A., & Rosen, M. A. (2018). Opening the black box of psychological processes in the science of sustainable development: A new frontier. *European Journal of Sustainable Development Research,* 2(4), *47.* doi https://doi.org/10.20897/ejosdr/3933.

Di Fabio, A., & Saklofske, D. H. (2014a). Comparing ability and self-report trait emotional intelligence, fluid intelligence, and personality traits in career decision. *Personality and Individual Differences, 64,* 174–178. https://doi.org/10.1016/j.paid.2014.02.024.

Di Fabio, A., & Saklofske, D. H. (2014b). Promoting individual resources: The challenge of trait emotional intelligence. *Personality and Individual Differences, 65,* 19–23. https://doi.org/10.1016/j.paid.2014.01.026.

Di Fabio, A., & Saklofske, D. H. (2018). The contributions of personality and emotional intelligence to resiliency. *Personality and Individual Differences, 123,* 140–144. https://doi.org/10.1016/j.paid.2017.11.012.

Di Fabio, A. & Tsuda, A. (2018). The psychology of harmony and harmonization: Advancing the perspectives for the psychology of sustainability and sustainable development. In A. Di Fabio (Ed.), Psychology of sustainability and sustainable development. Special Issue in *Sustainability MDPI, 10,* 4726. https://doi.org/10.3390/su10124726.

Di Fabio, A., & Van Esbroeck, R. (2016). Intrapreneurial self-capital: A concept fitting a life-designing intervention. *Counseling. Giornale Italiano di Ricerca e Applicazioni, 9*(2). https://doi.org/10.14605/cs921611.

Duffy, R. D., Allan, B. A., England, J. W., Blustein, D. L., Autin, K. L., Douglass, R. P.,… & Santos, E. J. (2017). The development and initial validation of the Decent Work Scale. *Journal of Counseling Psychology, 64*(2), 206–221. https://doi.org/10.1037/cou0000191.

Frost, R. O., & Shows, D. L. (1993). The nature and measurement of compulsive indecisiveness. *Behavior Research and Therapy, 31,* 683–692.

Fugate, M., & Kinicki, A. J. (2008). A dispositional approach to employability: Development of a measure and test of implications for employee reactions to organizational change. *Journal of Occupational and Organizational Psychology. 81,* 503–527.

Gati, I., Krausz, M., & Osipow, S. H. (1996). A taxonomy of difficulties in career decision making. *Journal of Counseling Psychology, 43,* 510–526.

Guichard, J. (2009). Self-constructing. *Journal of Vocational Behavior, 75,* 251–258.

Guichard, J. (2016). Reflexivity in life design interventions: Comments on life and career design dialogues. *Journal of Vocational Behavior, 97* 78–83.

Hage, S. M., Romano, J. L., Conyne, R. K., Kenny, M., Matthews, C., Schwartz, J. P., et al. (2007). Best practice guidelines on prevention practice, research, training, and social advocacy for psychologists. *The Counseling Psychologist, 35,* 493–566.
Harris, J. M. (2003). Sustainability and sustainable development. *International Society for Ecological Economics, 1*(1), 1–12.
Judge, T. A., Erez, A., Bono, J. E., & Thoresen, C. J. (2003). The core self-evaluations scale: Development of a measure. *Personnel Psychology, 56,* 303–331.
Kenny, M. E., & Hage, S. M. (2009). The next frontier: Prevention as an instrument of social justice. *The Journal of Primary Prevention, 30,* 1–10.
Midgley, C., Maehr, M. L., Hruda, L. Z., Anderman, E., Anderman, L., Freeman, K. E., ... & Urdan, T. (2000). *Manual for the patterns of adaptive learning scales*. Retrieved from University of Michigan website. http://www.umich.edu/~pals/PALS%202000_V13Word97.pdf.
Maddi, S. R. (1990). Issues and interventions in stress mastery. In H. S. Friedman (Ed.), *Personality and disease* (pp. 121–154). New York: Wiley.
Mann, L., Burnett, P., Radford, M., & Ford, S. (1997). The Melbourne decision making questionnaire: An instrument for measuring patterns for coping with decisional conflict. *Journal of Behavioral Decision Making, 10,* 1–19.
Maree, J. G. (Ed.). (2007). *Shaping the story: A guide to facilitating narrative career counseling*. Pretoria, South Africa: Van Schaik.
Maree, J. G. (Ed.). (2012). *Complete your thesis or dissertation successfully: Practical guidelines*. Cape Town, South Africa: Juta.
Maree, J. G. (2013). *Counselling for career construction: Connecting life themes to construct life portraits: Turning pain into hope*. Rotterdam, The Netherlands: Sense.
Maree, J. G. (2016). Career construction counseling with a mid-career black male. *Career Development Quarterly, 64,* 20–35. https://doi.org/10.1002/cdq.12038.
Maree, J. G. (Ed.). (2017). *Psychology of career adaptability, employability, and resilience* (pp. 107–123). New York: Springer.
Maree, J. G. (2018). Contextualisation as a determining factor for career counseling throughout the world. In J. A. Athanasou & H. N. Perera (Eds.), *International handbook of career guidance* (2nd ed.). New York: Springer.
Maree, J. G., & Di Fabio, A. (Eds.). (2015). *Exploring new horizons in career counselling: Turning challenges into opportunities*. Rotterdam, The Netherlands: Sense Publishers.
Maree, J. G. & Di Fabio, A. (2018). Integrating personal and career counseling to promote sustainable development and change. *Psychology of Sustainability and Sustainable Development. Special Issue in Sustainability MDPI, 10*(11), 4176. https://doi.org/10.3390/su10114176.
Morgan, J., & Farsides, T. (2009). Measuring meaning in life. *Journal of Happiness Studies, 10*(2), 197–214. https://doi.org/10.1007/s10902-007-9075-0.
Peiró, J. M., & Rodríguez, I. (2008). Work stress, leadership and organizational health. *Papeles del Psicólogo, 29,* 68–82.
Peiró, J. M., Sora, B., & Caballer, A. (2012). Job insecurity in the younger Spanish workforce: Causes and consequences. *Journal of Vocational Behavior, 80*(2), 444–453.
Rothwell, A., Herbert, I., & Rothwell, F. (2007). Self-perceived employability: Construction and initial validation of a scale for university students. *Journal of Vocational Behavior, 73,* 1–12.
Savickas, M. L. (2011). *Career counseling*. Washington, DC: American Psychological Association.
Savickas, M. L., & Porfeli, E. J. (2012). Career adapt-abilities scale: Construction, reliability, and measurement equivalence across 13 countries. *Journal of Vocational Behavior, 80,* 661–673.
Schnell, T., Höge, T., & Pollet, E. (2013). Predicting meaning in work: Theory, data, implications. *Journal of Positive Psychology, 8,* 543–554. https://doi.org/10.1080/17439760.2013.830763.
Tierney, P., & Farmer, S. M. (2002). Creative self-efficacy: Its potential antecedents and relationship to creative performance. *Academy of Management Journal, 45,* 1137–1148.
Tugade, M. M., & Fredrickson, B. L. (2004). Resilient individuals use positive emotions to bounce back from negative emotional experiences. *Journal of Personality and Social Psychology, 86,* 320–333.

United Nations. (2018). *Sustainable development goals: 17 goals to transform our world*. Retrieved from https://www.un.org/sustainabledevelopment/development-agenda/.

Watson, D., Clark, L. A., & Tellegen, A. (1988). Development and validation of brief measures of positive and negative affect: The PANAS scales. *Journal of Personality and Social Psychology, 54*(6), 1063–1070.

A Group-based Career Guidance Intervention for South African High School Learners from Low-income Communities

Anthony V. Naidoo, Michelle Visser, Marietha de Wet, Stephan Rabie, Izanette van Schalkwyk, Michèle Boonzaier, Gideon de Bruin, Liezel Shirley and Caitlin Venter

Abstract This chapter describes the design, implementation and evaluation of a group-based career guidance and counselling intervention with learners attending resource-constrained high schools in South Africa. In the South African education system, the Grade 9 level represents a crucial milestone in that learners are required to make decisions about their choice of school subjects for the final phase of their schooling (Grades 10 to 12). Indications are that in the prevailing absence of career guidance services in many public schools and with the challenges faced in their home and community contexts, many learners are making uninformed, trial-and-error, and haphazard decisions about their school subject choices that may compromise their future career options. Drawing from literature that argues for a contextual understanding of structural conditions and social justice concerns that may limit or compromise career exploration and decision-making, we describe an integrated career guidance intervention to combine quantitative and qualitative methodologies with a group-based approach to assist learners to engage with proactive career planning. The career guidance intervention incorporates the following components:

- Individual career interest assessment using the *South African Career Interest Inventory*
- Career guidance workshops aiding learners to explore their personal career attributes using quantitative and qualitative data
- Integration of emerging information into a career life design matrix to inform subject choice
- Identification and mitigation of barriers and challenges that may impede or limit career aspirations
- Development of an action plan to motivate learners to pursue their career goals.

A. V. Naidoo (✉) · I. van Schalkwyk · L. Shirley · C. Venter
Department of Psychology, Stellenbosch University, Stellenbosch, South Africa
e-mail: avnaidoo@sun.ac.za

M. Visser · M. de Wet · M. Boonzaier · G. de Bruin
Department of Industrial Psychology, Stellenbosch University, Stellenbosch, South Africa

S. Rabie
Department of Global Health, Stellenbosch University, Stellenbosch, South Africa

J. G. Maree (ed.), *Handbook of Innovative Career Counselling*,
https://doi.org/10.1007/978-3-030-22799-9_37

The intervention seeks to harness both quantitative and qualitative career assessment processes to help learners initiate a life design approach to their career development, to align their school subject choice (for Grades 10 to 12) with their career aspirations.

Keywords Career guidance · Group-based intervention · Adolescent career transition · Social justice · Developing countries

Introduction

There are indications that children in developed countries, where career education and guidance services are in place, are engaging in the dynamic process of career exploration—exploring the world of work, examining the self, and understanding how these two are related—from an earlier age (Hirschi, Niles, & Akos, 2010). Evidence suggests that from an early age, children are able to use their interests, abilities, values and beliefs to guide how and what they learn, and to formulate their occupational goals in relation to the world-of-work (Hartung, Porfeli, & Vondracek, 2005). A different reality is emerging from developing countries where political and economic conditions present a more challenging developmental press for young adolescents influencing their career preparation and aspirations (Stead & Watson, 1998).

With career counselling in South Africa being available primarily to people who can afford to pay for the service (Naidoo, Pretorius, & Nicholas, 2017), the importance of career guidance and counselling at secondary school level cannot be underestimated, and the integration of career education into the curriculum of all learners from pre-school to school-leaving age has been strongly advocated (Akhurst & Mkhize, 2006). In this chapter, we describe the design, implementation and evaluation of a group-based career guidance and counselling intervention with learners attending resource-constrained high schools in South Africa. The intervention sought to expose Grade 9 learners to both quantitative and qualitative career assessment processes to help initiate a proactive life design approach to their career development to align their choice of school subject (for Grades 10 to 12) with their career aspirations.

Chapter Structure

In the first part of the chapter we examine the status of career guidance specifically pertinent to the school context. We examine the dominant discourses underpinning career guidance before elucidating the macro-environmental context of career guidance in South African schools. The Career Guidance (CG) intervention is then presented with accompanying quantitative and qualitative assessment results. In this chapter the term *learners* refers to individuals attending high school as used in the South African context.

The Status of Career Guidance

Sultana (2017) asserts that CG continues to feature high on the international public policy agenda. This resurgence is stimulated in part by the severe economic downturn, and by resultant policy steers from such supranational and transnational entities such as the Organization for Economic Co-operation and Development, the World Bank, and the European Union. Watts and Sultana (2004) broadly define CG as a range of services to assist an individual or groups of individuals to make educational, training and occupational choices and to manage their careers in various educational and occupational environments. These services may be face-to-face or distal (including helplines and web-based services) and may include career information, assessment and self-assessment tools, counselling interviews, career education and career management programmes, taster programmes, work search programmes, and transition services.

There is growing recognition of the importance of career education and guidance in schools, not only in helping young people to make the immediate choices that confront them but also in laying the foundations for lifelong learning and lifelong career development. This is evident, for example, in the inclusion of career education in the curriculum, incorporating career awareness, career exploration, and the development of career management skills (Watts & Sultana, 2004).

In developing countries such as South Africa, the pressing nature of the personal and behavioural problems of many students may result in guidance counsellors spending much of their time on these problems at the expense of focusing on helping students in relation to their educational and vocational choices. There is an increasing risk of career education and guidance in schools becoming marginalised (Flederman, 2009).

Discourses About Career Guidance

Undergirding the definitional characteristics of CG (Watts & Sultana, 2004) is the question of how CG is construed and implemented. Sultana (2017) draws on a typology articulated by Habermas (1971) to identify three fundamental discourses about CG. Each discourse serves to organize or construct our thoughts and actions in particular ways. What we actually do in the real world, the way we organize our services and how we interact with others reveal particular ways of construing the world and valuing specific aspects over others. Different discourses function as lenses that incline us to consider certain social practices as problems, to articulate such 'problems' in particular ways, and to prefer one set of solutions for them over another (Sultana, 2017).

One of the dominant discourses of CG is referred to by Sultana (2017) as a 'technocratic' or 'social efficiency' approach. With the main concern here being to ensure a smoother relationship between the supply and demand of skills for the benefit of the economy, the role of the career guidance consultant is to help individuals identify their skills profile and to match this as closely as possible with the presumed needs of the labour market. This 'social efficiency model' is premised on the smooth functioning of the economy, and while it values the aspiring of individuals, it is equally quick to exhort clients and citizens to be realistic, to adapt to the prevailing employment market, and to take on what is available. In this discourse, there is little space for critiquing the way the economy works, or little recognition of the way in which the skills components of many jobs have been diluted, or how temporary work, short-term contracts and overall job insecurity might generate profits for the organization but provide very little if any opportunity for personal growth and fulfilment (Sultana, 2017).

A second foundational discourse that serves to guide career guidance practices Sultana (2017) refers to as 'developmentalist', 'hermeneutic', or 'humanist'. In this approach, the personal growth and fulfilment of the individual are foregrounded, to support the self-discovery and flourishing of his/her capacities and aspirations. In this approach, the notion of 'choice' is paramount, as is that of constructing identity through a satisfying integration in the different arenas and roles of the life rainbow (Super, 1990) that include but go beyond paid employment. The central focus here is to facilitate self-exploration and self-construction, or, as it is now referred to, 'life design' (Savickas, 2012).

A third approach to career guidance Sultana (2017) terms 'social reconstructionist' or 'emancipatory'. Whereas the previous two discourses tend to endorse liberal notions of the individual who is seen to be a rational actor who exercises choices in relation to economic and or personal priorities, emancipatory discourses are more social and communitarian in their scope, and committed to questioning the status quo rather than encouraging people to fit in. This approach is preoccupied with developing the knowledge that leads to freedom—where, rather than remaining insulated from critiques which are outside their immediate frame of reference, individuals are enabled to decode the way in which the economy and labour market functioning undermine the development and fulfilment of whole groups of citizens. Implicit in this approach is a critical engagement with the way work is organized in contemporary society, where the accumulation of capital in the hands of a few has severe negative repercussions at national, regional, and even planetary levels (Sultana, 2017).

The goal of the CG practitioner would therefore be to 'conscientise' individuals and groups in the Freirian sense (Freire, 1970) as to the source of their troubles, which, while experienced as on a personal level, emanate from the structural arrangements in place. Conscientisation is typically accompanied by social mobilisation and advocacy initiatives that ensure that unjust structures are challenged in the hope that they are ultimately, transformed (Silva, Paiva, & Ribeiro, 2016).

In a middle-income country such as South Africa that is struggling with contending developmental challenges, the social justice imperative for career guidance is of particular relevance. In the next section, we discuss some of the environmental press conditions impacting CG at school level in South Africa.

The South African Macro-Environmental Context

Democratic South Africa continues to face burgeoning challenges to its educational system, which are affecting the quality of education, the levels of high school attrition, and the resulting growth in unemployment. Concerns have been expressed about the poor school pass rates and levels of national numeracy and literacy. School attrition has reached alarming proportions: approximately 60% of first graders will ultimately drop out rather than complete Grade 12 and only 12% of high school graduates will be eligible to pursue higher education (Department of Basic Education, Republic of South Africa, 2015). One consistent finding is that dropping out of school results in poorer psychological, physical, social, and economic health for the school dropout (Lamb, 2011).

School attrition also impacts employability. In the third quarter of 2018, unemployment rates were 27.5%, with the majority of the unemployment burden shouldered by youth (Statistics South Africa, 2018). The normative developmental expectation for youth to transition from adolescence to adulthood, consolidate a personal and social identity whilst considering work and other social roles may be an impossible mission within these contexts of adversity. For many youth, identity formation and work role transitioning may be under threat because of the interplay of adverse structural conditions that undermine this process (Blustein, 2013; Dube-Addae, 2019). The study-career-work nexus appears daunting for many South African high school students.

With the political transition in 1994, one of the serious casualties in the higher education system was the differential access to career guidance. Prior to 1994, only the historically white schools had full-time trained guidance teachers with no career guidance provided in black schools (Watts, 1980). When the country entered the political transitional period, the role of the guidance teacher was abandoned due to shifting priorities and virtually no guidance was offered in schools (Naidoo et al., 2017). With new policy developments, CG has been included as a part of the Life Orientation (LO) curriculum from Grade R to Grade 12 since 2002. While impressive in its scope, several limitations to effective CG have been identified: the LO curriculum is limited to two hours a week with CG comprising only one-quarter of the curriculum in Grades 10–12; LO teachers often have other competing teaching assignments and many have no background or training in CG; classes are typical large and in excess of 40 learners; schools in rural and township settings may also not have access to adequate resources and ICT facilities (Flederman, 2009). In such low-resourced communities, CG has become marginalised (Watts & Sultana, 2004) and ineffective (Flederman, 2009), and may obscure social justice concerns (Fickling, 2015).

These structural constraints represent formidable barriers for many Grade 9 learners who are expected to make important decisions about their choice of school subjects for the final phase of their schooling (Grades 10 to 12). Indications are that in the prevailing absence of career guidance services in many public schools and the challenges faced in their homes and community contexts, many learners are left unaided making decisions about their school subject choices that may severely constrain their career development trajectory, and stymie their future career options (Akhurst & Mkhize, 2006).

As noted by Savickas (2001, p. 302), these macro-environmental variables operate through a social opportunity structure that "too often assigns developmental pathways based on gender, race, and ethnicity". The interaction and intersection between clients' cultural contexts (for example, gender and race) and large environmental variables (for example, patriarchy, social class, geographical location) may result in differential career development experiences (Sultana, 2017), and, therefore, necessitate alternative interventions.

Innovative Techniques and Approaches

In South Africa, several career researchers (Albien & Naidoo, 2018; Alexander, Seabi, & Bischoff, 2010; Maree, 2006; Stead & Watson, 2006) contend that the post-modern (culturally relevant) career counselling discipline needs to reflect innovative methods, techniques and structures to ensure effective and culturally relevant career counselling. Maree and Beck (2004) have called for career counselling to shift from an objective approach to an interpretative process using new and creative ways of assessment. They aver for the career counsellor to be facilitators rather than prescriptive experts, and learners should be able to speak, act, think and choose for themselves. Learners must be assisted to construct their own meaning in the career exploration process, and to take responsibility for their own choices and development.

Similarly, Morgan, Naidoo, Henn, and Rabie (Chapter 27 in this volume) contend that career counselling should not be a linear process with the counsellor merely administering and scoring an interest inventory and then providing recommendations to the learner based on these scores. Instead, career counselling should be a recursive process in which both the counsellor and learner are actively engaged in constructing meaning (Maree, 2018; McIlveen & Patton, 2007) factoring in the realities of the learner's family and community contexts (Albien & Naidoo, 2017).

In a recent article, Maree (2018) recommended the integrated use of qualitative assessment instruments and techniques in conjunction with "traditional" quantitative assessment instruments as the test-and-tell positivist approach on its own often falls short of either bringing about change in people's career-lives, accommodating subjective client data or capturing and assessing qualitative changes in people's self-narratives (Rehfuss, 2009). Maree (2018) suggests that the integrative strategy can be successfully implemented to help clients transition from career indecision, rediscover a sense of agency, purpose and meaning, gain confidence in eliciting their career-life story and draw on their own advice (under the guidance of a career counsellor). Several researchers and practitioners have acknowledged the need to re-establish the rigour and efficiency of career counselling interventions, especially when an integrative, qualitative + quantitative approach is used (Blustein, Kenna, Gill, & DeVoy, 2008; Hartung, 2011; Savickas, 2015).

Added to Maree's (2018) advocacy for post-modern career counselling practice to reflect innovative methods, techniques and structures, is the need (and the social justice imperative) (Lee & Hipolito-Delgado, 2007; Toporek, Lewis, & Crethar, 2009) to harness effective group-based career guidance (GBCG) as a methodology. There is increasing evidence, although not always explicitly stated, that GBCG interventions may be effective in achieving career behavioural outcomes in the school context, particularly in disadvantaged communities (see Akhurst & Mkhize, 2006; Albien, 2018; Dube-Addae, 2019; Maree & Beck, 2004; Maree, Cook, & Fletcher, 2018; Maree & Molepo, 2004; Miles & Naidoo, 2017). Peer support and learning from peers have also been identified as important career guidance enablers (Albien & Naidoo, 2018).

Moreover, Pyle and Hayden (2015) describe how purposefully designed group career guidance interventions may be used to deliver relevant information on matters related to educational, career, social and/or personal development, and offer individuals the opportunity to synthesise and relate the information to the context of their own personal situation. When properly constructed, there is less concern with the delivery of factual information and more with assisting the learner in developing insights and knowledge of self and the world from within her/his own unique frame of reference (Maree, 2018). Tolbert (as cited in Pyle, 1986) lists the following core elements of group career guidance: (1) career planning and decision-making require input about occupations; (2) accurate data about self (abilities, interests and values) are needed; and (3) the process offers opportunities to explore personal meaning, identify and examine subjective aspects of the self, get feedback from others, and try out roles.

Rationale for the Intervention

The Grade 9 year in the South African educational environment represents a crucial career transition (Watson & Stead, 1990). Learners are required to make decisions about their choice of school subjects for the final phase of their schooling (Grades 10 to 12). Indications are that with the prevailing dearth of CG services in many public schools and the absence of parental support and impoverished community contexts (Albien & Naidoo, 2018), many learners are left to make uninformed, trial-and-error, and random subject-choice decisions (Akhurst & Mkhize, 2006; Stead & Watson, 1998) that may later limit access to certain tertiary study options. Inadequate support at school may contribute to poor academic achievement, which, in turn limits career opportunities for learners (Maree, 2006).

Very few schools in the country have access to the services of trained career counsellors, despite Cosser and du Toit's (2002, p. 93) assertion that 'career guidance, in whatever form … has a positive effect on intention to enter higher education'. This significantly impacts proactive career planning and decision-making and underscores the need not only to improve the quality of career counselling in schools where this facility is available, but, more importantly, to initiate CG and counselling services in schools where these services are lacking (Maree & Molepo, 2004). Further, Savickas (1999) contends that individuals who recognize and acknowledge the importance of making career choices, and who understand the consequences of these choices, manage work-related challenges more effectively. Studies now emphasise that career management strategies for adolescents should aim specifically at helping them become more planful, adaptive (Savickas, 1999), proactive (Claes & Ruiz-Quintanilla, 1998) and more resilient to cope with predictable and unpredictable career adjustments and transitions, whether they are self-determined or not (Blustein, 2013; Savickas et al., 2009).

The intervention described and reported on in this chapter evolved in response to the challenges outlined above and from research findings from a career development project (Albien & Naidoo, 2018; Dube-Addae, 2019) initiated at two of the schools included in the intervention. It constitutes a response to the question of whether more meaningful career guidance programmes can be designed and implemented in low-resourced schools in partnership with other organizations and tertiary institutions.

Goals of the Study

The primary goal of the study was to design a group-based career guidance intervention to assist learners in making informed career decisions regarding their choice of school subjects. More particularly, we explored the extent to which an integrated group approach combining quantitative and qualitative career strategies can help learners manage career transitions (Maree, 2018). We were interested in not only the quantitative impact of the intervention on their career development but also in their subjective impressions of the intervention.

Procedure

The principals and LO teachers of eight schools in low-income communities in the Cape Winelands district, a peri-urban region about 60 km east of Cape Town, were invited to participate in the project. Given the LO objective for Grade 9 learners to receive assistance with choosing their school subjects, the schools consented to allocating 10 to 12 h of their LO classes for the intervention which were organized into three $\times$ 4 h workshops (see Table 1 for an overview of the intervention sessions). The LO teachers were included in the intervention to facilitate logistical planning, capacitation, and for continuity of the CG themes into the school's LO curriculum.

The CG intervention incorporated the following components:

- Assessment of objective career interests using the *South African Career Interest Inventory* (Morgan, 2014, Morgan, de Bruin, & de Bruin, 2015);
- Facilitation of two CG workshops to aid learners to explore their personal career attributes using quantitative and qualitative data and integrating or merging of the

information into a career life design matrix to inform subject choice (see *Career Flower* discussed in a later section);
- Discussion of barriers and challenges that may impede or limit career aspirations;
- Designing an action plan to motive learners to pursue their career goals.

A career booklet was designed for the intervention by Psychology and Industrial Psychology students as part of their academic module requirements. The booklet provided spaces for the Grade 9 learners to insert their personal information; the booklet also provided pertinent information about career resources, bursaries institutions for higher learning, and other career-related services and learnerships, internships, apprenticeships and bursary applications. The students received training to facilitate the intervention in teams of three per Grade 9 class.

Participants

Across the eight high schools participating in the intervention, all thiry two Grade 9 classes (1098 learners) were included. The sample mean age was 15 years (SD = 1.02), and was distributed relatively equally across gender, comprising 613 females (55.8%) and 485 males (54.2%). Sixty percent of the sample was Afrikaans-speaking, 30 percent isiXhosa-speaking, and 7 percent English-speaking. All the learners were conversant in English (at least as a second language). Most of the present study's participants came from a lower socioeconomic background, with 20.95% (n = 230) of parents or caregivers unemployed, 45.08% (n = 495) of caregivers employed in unskilled labour, and 19.13% (n = 210) of caregivers employed in skilled labour.

Data Gathering Instruments

We used four instruments to gather data pertinent to the goals of the study.

The South African Career Interest Inventory (***SACII***; Morgan, 2014). The SACII is a measure of career interests, and is an operationalisation of Holland's (1997) vocational personality theory in the South African context (Morgan et al., 2015). To provide a detailed analysis of an individual's interest structure, the *SACII* consists of 142 items across six scales—namely Realistic, Investigative, Artistic, Social, Enterprising and Conventional. The *SACII* has demonstrated promising psychometric properties in the South African context to date, with sufficient reliability coefficients reported in a number of studies with diverse samples (Morgan et al., 2015; Rabie & Naidoo, 2019). In particular, Rabie (2017) demonstrated the *SACII* to be a reliable and valid measure of vocational interests in a sample of adolescent secondary school learners in the same region as the current study.

My Career Flower (Naidoo, 2011). The *My Career Flower* depicted in Fig. 1 is a flexible heuristic tool designed and adapted to be used with high school learners

Table 1 Overview of the Intervention Programme

Session	Process	Intended Outcomes
1. Overview, Ethics & Pre-test	- Participants are introduced to the purpose of the study.	Participants are motivated to become fully involved in the intervention.
	- Assent forms are completed.	
	- *Career Maturity Inventory* is completed.	The *CMI* pre-test data are obtained to determine initial career adaptability status.
	- *South African Career Interest Inventory* is completed.	The *SACII* is scored to obtain the three highest measured interest scores of the participants for use in the next session.
2. Completing the My *Career Flower*	- Participants receives their own CG booklet and fill in their own subjective information for each of the petals of the *My Career Flower*. Favourite school subjects; hobbies/sports; role models; dream jobs, and challenges or barriers are filled in.	The aim of this activity is help participants begin to construct their subjective career stories and manifest interests.
	- The *SACII* scores are transferred to indicate the participants' top three inventoried interests.	
	- Facilitators assist participants to complete the *My Career Flower*.	The *SACII* scores provide the participants with an objective measure of their interests. These inventoried interests can be compared with their subjective information and with other resources. in the manual to identify career clusters associated with the participant's profile.
3. *My Career Flower* synthesis	- The facilitators process each petal with the participants and use participant examples to illustrate significance of particular career attributes in the participant's narrative.	Participants are given the opportunity to reflect on their own objective and subjective information and make sense of their own lives.

(continued)

Table 1 (continued)

Session	Process	Intended Outcomes
	- Participants are encouraged to weave or develop their own career narrative from the information they have presented.	
	- The career information is collated and career options are considered linked to objective and subjective interests. Appropriate school subjects are identified and selected.	By listening to the narratives of their peers, learners are also exposed to other career perspectives and information thus expanding their knowledge of the world of work.
	- Participants develop an action plan to gain more information about their career options.	Participants are motivated to assume agency to explore and plan their career pathway.
4. Post-test and Evaluation	- Participants complete the *CMI* post-test and evaluation questionnaire.	Data is obtained to assess the intervention quantitatively and qualitatively.
		Learners are referred to the university for further information or for individual career counselling.

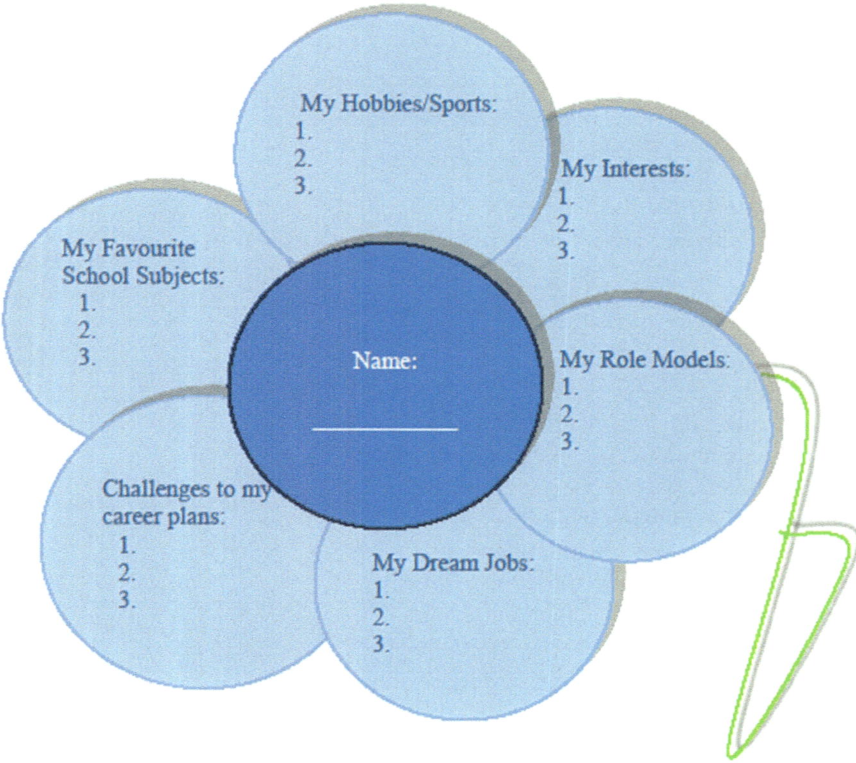

Fig. 1 My career flower-exploring my career plans. Adapted from Naidoo (2011)

either individually or in a group or workshop setting to facilitate career exploration and self-awareness (Naidoo, 2011). It is based on the premise that there are objective and subjective attributes that can be identified and synthesised in exploring and constructing an individual's career life narrative (Savickas, 2015) and in making well-informed career decisions (Maree, 2018). As part of this intervention, participants were asked to fill in the petals on the *My Career Flower* to indicate their favourite school subjects, hobbies, talents or sport preferences, interests, their role models, dream jobs, and the obstacles standing in the way of their career aspiration. For the career interest petal, participants used the top three interest scores from the *SACII* assessment that been conducted in the previous session.

The career counsellor's facilitation of the discussion of the participants' responses to the respective career attributes is crucial to allow participants the opportunity to reflect and make sense of their own inputs on the *My Career Flower*, discover connecting and diverging themes emerging from their responses, and begin to synthesise their own career narrative. There is also the benefit of gaining additional perspectives and insights from their peers' career life narratives (Albien & Naidoo, 2018).

This process allows the participants to link their subjective (qualitative) career attributes with their measured career interests and participants can be guided to make informed decisions (Maree, 2018) regarding the selection of subjects for the last phase of their high school. Participants were encouraged to reflect on the vocational implications of their selections with the view to longer-term career planning.

The Career Maturity Index Form C (***CMI-C***). The *CMI-C*, used as the pre-test–post-test measure in the study, is a measure of career choice readiness that includes theoretically relevant and practical content scales for diagnostic work within school populations (Savickas & Porfeli, 2011). The *CMI-C* has 24 items that measure career choice readiness across four subscales, namely: Concern, Curiosity, Confidence, and Consultation (Savickas & Porfeli, 2011). The Concern, Curiosity, and Confidence subscales combine to create a composite Total Score, signifying an individual's level of career adaptability and readiness to make an occupational choice. The initial validation study of the *CMI-C* demonstrated sufficient reliability across the five scales and was found to provide an accurate representation of an individual's readiness to make occupational choices (Savickas & Porfeli, 2011). The *CMI-C* has been used as a measure of career-choice readiness in diverse samples (Janeiro, Mota, & Ribas, 2014) and was found to have acceptable reliability coefficients, signifying the cross-cultural applicability of the *CMI-C*.

Evaluation Form. A 12 item evaluation form was used with a 5 point Likert scale assessing the participants' feedback on the workshop. Three open-ended questions assessed what participants considered to be the favourite part of the intervention, the least useful aspect that can be improved, and what the participant learned about himself/herself.

Ethical Considerations

Ethical clearance for the study was obtained from Stellenbosch University's Research Ethical Committee as well as the Western Cape Department of Education. Permission was obtained from eight schools in the Stellenbosch district. All the principals and LO departmental heads were involved in the planning and implementation of the intervention. Caregiver consent was sought and written informed assent was obtained from the learners. Counselling services were made available to participants after the intervention.

Results

The quantitative results for the pre- and post-intervention effects, as measured by the *CMI-C*, are summarised in Table 2. We used one-way repeated measures ANOVA to test the effect of the intervention.

At the end of the second and third workshop, all of the participants completed self-report evaluation forms to assess the organization, facilitation, and content of the workshop. The large majority (81.1%) of the participants gave the intervention a

Table 2 One-way ANOVA results for the pre-post intervention effect analysis

Subscales	Pre-$\bar{x}$	Post-$\bar{x}$	Wilk's lambda	*df*	*F*	*p*	η
Total score	8.05	8.97	.967	773	26.261	.000	.033
Concern	3.05	2.78	.983	773	13.596	.000	.017
Curiosity	2.51	2.97	.962	773	30.337	.000	.038
Confidence	2.50	3.22	.915	773	71.394	.000	.085
Consultation	2.02	4.10	.390	773	1208.851	.000	.610

Note N = 774

rating of 1 (the best possible score), with .3% of the sample a rating of 5 (the lowest possible score). More importantly, the sample's self-reported sense of readiness to make future career choices (i.e., choosing subjects at school, deciding on a career path) improved from 42.3% of the learners at the pre-test to 67.0% at the post-test. Learners attributed these improvements to their expanding knowledge about potential career and study choices and the various career trajectories available to them, as well as the motivational and study skills they were exposed to, and the discussion about overcoming the barriers they were facing.

Discussion

Overall, the quantitative results confirm the intervention to significantly enhance early adolescents' career adaptability and ability to engage in the career decision-making process. In resource-constrained communities, access to career-related resources and information and opportunities to engage in discussion about career planning is often limited, impeding young individuals' ability to engage actively in career exploration. Our results suggest that disadvantaged secondary learners' career adaptability can be advanced significantly by providing group-based activities that encourage learners to integrate objective and subjective interests and career attributes with their career plans. In linking their personal objective and subjective career interest data learners enhance their self-awareness and gain confidence in their career decision-making (Maree, 2018; McIlveen & Patton, 2007; Morgan, Naidoo, Hein, & Rabie, in press).

Participants were encouraged to reflect on the vocational implications of their selections with the view to longer-term career planning (Watts & Sultana, 2004). Access to career information and resources and career guidance services need to be regarded as sine qua non for an improved education dispensation for all South African high school learners. Collaboration of schools with universities and community organizations is needed (Ebersöhn & Mbetse, 2003) to attain this emancipatory goal, given limited state resources.

Regarding the regression observed in the Concern subscale, which measures the extent to which individuals are involved in their career decision-making process, Savickas and Porfeli (2011) posit that this involvement is determined by how imminent the career development task is. The most important developmental task for the Grade 9 learners is choosing their senior phase school subjects—a task that is imminent. However, the items of the *CMI-C* Concern subscale are related to choosing an occupation (not subjects)—something that may be a distant thought for Grade 9 learners. Thus, the observed regressive intervention effect could be an item-level error reflection as these items may be regarded by this sample and age group as being not applicable to their context.

The significant finding with the Curiosity subscale may reflect the exposure to a variety of career options and information surfacing in the intervention activities and from the group discussions. This may stimulate learners' exploration of the study-career-work nexus and information-seeking behaviour about occupations and their requirements. These results are supported by the qualitative findings of learners actively engaging with teachers and community members about their occupations (Shirley, 2018; Venter, 2018).

The improvement in the Confidence subscale score is significant. We contend that many learners, who have learnt to adapt to the challenging structural and social conditions in their community contexts (Albien & Naidoo, 2018), may not have an optimistic outlook on their future, and subsequently may have their sense of self-efficacy and agency severely undermined, impacting on their confidence to make an informed career/subject decision. However, as the intervention focuses on promoting self-exploration, agency, and also engages directly with self-identified barriers that participants identify in the *My Career Flower* (many of the barriers identified pertained to constrained financial resources in the family), these discussions potentially open up ideas about overcoming external hurdles and identifying resources (Ebersöhn & Mbetse, 2003) by, for example, accessing bursaries, applying for learnerships, internships and volunteer training opportunities with the Sector Education and Training Authorities. The learners may have gained confidence in their ability to (re)consider career goals they may have initially eliminated and thus are able to reassess their career decisions and realistic occupation choices.

The improved scores on the Consultation subscale may indicate that the intervention (which relied on peer group discussion) may have created awareness of the different resources learners have available to inform their career decisions. Moreover, they can discuss their options, based on the information provided in the intervention, with their peers, family members, school teachers, mentors/role models, and even community members involved in the occupations they're contemplating. Here Savickas and Porfeli (2011) argue for considering cultural frameworks at play when interpreting scores on this scale. In particular, the consultation scale score reflects a continuum of family career conversations from "do as we advise" to "it is up to you." This illustrates the individualistic vs communal family dynamics tension that may manifest in South African family structures (Albien & Naidoo, 2018; Stead & Watson, 2006). The higher scores may reflect that salience of the family and the peer group (i.e., interdependent relational style) may be at play here.

Benefits of the Intervention

The major benefit of the intervention was that the entire Grade 9 learner population at eight schools located in low-resourced communities received an 8 h group-based career assessment and guidance programne designed to assist the learners with aligning their required subject choice selection for the final phase of high school with their career plans. The intervention combined quantitative and qualitative methods to link the assessment of inventoried interests with learners' manifest interests and subjective career attributes depicted on their personalised *My Career Flower*. The personalised booklets can continue to be used as a career resource in designing their career action plans for the final phase of their secondary education.

The intervention provided the Grade 9 learners with a novel opportunity to engage with an imminent career transition. According to Savickas and Porfeli (2011), such an encounter provides individuals with the opportunity to engage in reflection and consultation and acquire knowledge, ideas and opportunities that they can use to shape their future. Many participants stated that they felt inspired to engage actively in career consultation as a direct consequence of the workshops (Shirley, 2018).

Limitations of the Study

There were several limitations that impacted the study. Ethical and logistical considerations precluded the use of a quasi-experimental, pre-test post-test comparison group design. This should be considered in a single school setting where it would be feasible to expose the control group to the intervention at a later stage. As the study was conducted as eight different schools by different teams of facilitators using the same materials and process, there was inevitable variability in the intervention that could not be controlled for. For example, there were no electricity plugs in some classrooms, ruling out the use of the data projector. Facilitators improvised and used their laptops to share the workshop information.

Although the facilitation teams had members who were bilingual in English and Afrikaans, there were not sufficient facilitators conversant in isiXhosa and this may have limited the level of discussion in some schools. The career booklet was available only in English which may have been a disadvantage to some of the participants.

Recommendations for Future Research

In addition to the implicit recommendations identified in the previous section to improve the research design, the following recommendations are made with a view to enhancing the outcomes of future intervention:

- The intervention should be redesigned to be presented over a longer period (one session per week for eight weeks) and to fit into the LO 40-min class period.
- Small group activity should be used in the larger classes.
- The intervention should be supported by the opportunity for referral for individual career counselling for the learners. At some schools, parents also requested a parent information session to enable them to support their children with subject choice decision-making and preparation for post-school planning.
- An improved mixed-method research design can be applied to assess the impact of the intervention at the end of the Grade 9 school year and longitudinally in the Grade 12 year.

Conclusion

The results of the study confirm the need to engage young adolescent learners at an early stage in the career exploration process. Rather than using CG to focus mainly on educational decisions viewed as ends in themselves, learners are encouraged to focus rather on the vocational implications of their decision and on longer-term career planning (Watts & Sultana, 2004). The study confirms that learners from resource-constrained communities can benefit significantly from innovative and creative career interventions that harness and integrate both objective and subjective career information, and use group-based activities that allow space for both collective and individual reflection and for designing an action plan. The integration of emerging information into a career life design process such as the *My Career Flower* (Naidoo, 2011), *Career Matrix* (Maree & Taylor, 2016), or *My System of Career Influences* (McMahon, Watson, & Patton, 2005) can provide Grade 9 learners with resources that can assist them make informed decisions about their subject choice in line with their evolving career narrative and plans. As advocated by Albien and Naidoo (2017), crucial in contextualising the career process is an active engagement with identified barriers, myths and concerns that constitute the lived reality of the high school participants.

Acknowledgements We acknowledge funding received from the Rupert Educational Foundation and Stellenbosch University to implement this intervention research in the eight schools. We are grateful to the principals and LO teachers who graciously accommodated our project amidst their busy schedules. We are also express appreciation to the Grade 9 participants in the project.
Lastly, we acknowledge that this project would not have been accomplished without the generous offer of time and energy of the "Power Moms" volunteers from Delft, the 2018 postgraduate students and volunteers in the Psychology Department and Industrial Psychology Department at Stellenbosch University, and for the coordinating lecturers, Marietha de Wet and Stephan Rabie.

Disclosure statement No potential conflict of interest was reported by the authors.

References

Akhurst, J., & Mkhize, N. (2006). Career education in South Africa. In G. B. Stead & M. B. Watson (Eds.), *Career psychology in the South African context* (2nd ed., pp. 139–151). Pretoria, South Africa: Van Schaik Publishers.

Albien, A. (2018). *A mixed methods analysis of black adolescents' vocational identity status and career adaptability competencies in a South African township* (Unpublished doctoral dissertation). Stellenbosch University, Stellenbosch, South Africa.

Albien, A. J., & Naidoo, A. V. (2017). Deconstructing career myths and cultural stereotypes in a context of low resourced township communities. *South African Journal of Education, 37*(4), 1–12. https://doi.org/10.15700/saje.v37n4a1476.

Albien, A. J., & Naidoo, A. V. (2018). Barriers and enablers for career development among marginalized South African youth. In V. Cohen-Scali, J. Rossier, & L. Nota (Eds.), *New perspectives on career counseling and guidance in Europe* (pp. 147–164). Cham, Switzerland: Springer.

Alexander, D., Seabi, J., & Bischoff, D. (2010). Efficacy of a post-modern group career assessment intervention of disadvantaged high school learners. *Journal of Psychology in Africa, 20*(3), 497–500.

Blustein, D. (2013). The psychology of working: A new perspective for career development, counseling, and public policy. In D. Blustein (Ed.), *The Oxford handbook of the psychology of working* (pp. 1–27). New York, NY, US: Oxford University Press.

Blustein, D. L., Kenna, A. C., Gill, N., & DeVoy, J. E. (2008). The psychology of working: A new framework for counseling practice and public policy. *The Career Development Quarterly, 56*(4), 294–308.

Claes, R., & Ruiz-Quintanilla, S. A. (1998). Influences of early career experiences, occupational group, and national culture on proactive career behavior. *Journal of Vocational Behavior, 52*(3), 357–378.

Cosser, M., & Du Toit, J. (2002). *From school to higher education? Factors affecting the choices of grade 12 learners* (Vol. 1). Pretoria, South Africa: HSRC Press.

Department of Basic Education. (2015). *Annual report 2014/15*. Pretoria, South Africa: Government Services.

Dube-Addae, T. (2019). *Narrative identities: Voices of the unemployed youth in a low-income community in South Africa* (Unpublished doctoral dissertation). Stellenbosch University, Stellenbosch, South Africa.

Ebersöhn, L., & Mbetse, D. J. (2003). Exploring community strategies to career education in terms of the asset-based approach: Expanding existing career theory and models of intervention. *South African Journal of Education, 23*(4), 323–327.

Fickling, M. (2015). *Career counselors' perspectives on social justice advocacy* (Unpublished doctoral dissertation). University of North Carolina, Greensboro, United States of America.

Flederman, P. (2009). A career advice helpline: A case study from South Africa. *International Journal of Education Vocational Guidance, 11*, 111–123.

Freire, P. (1970). *Pedagogy of the oppressed*. New York, NY: Herder and Herder.

Habermas, J. (1971). *Knowledge and human interest*. Boston, MA: Beacon Press.

Hartung, P. J. (2011). Barrier or benefit? Emotion in life-career design. *Journal of Career Assessment, 19*(3), 296–305. https://doi.org/10.1177/1069072710395536.

Hartung, P. J., Porfeli, E. J., & Vondracek, F. W. (2005). Child vocational development: A review and reconsideration. *Journal of Vocational Behavior, 66*(3), 385–419. https://doi.org/10.1016/j.jvb.2004.05.006.

Hirschi, A., Niles, S. G., & Akos, P. (2010). Engagement in adolescent career preparation: Social support, personality and the development of choice decidedness and congruence. *Journal of Adolescence, 34*(1), 173–182. https://doi.org/10.1016/j.adolescence.2009.12.009.

Holland, J. L. (1997). *Making vocational choices: A theory of vocational personalities and work environments*. Odessa, FL: Psychological Assessment Resources.

Janeiro, I. N., Mota, L. P., & Ribas, A. M. (2014). Effects of two types of career interventions on students with different career coping styles. *Journal of Vocational Behavior, 85*(1), 115–124. https://doi.org/10.1016/j.jvb.2014.05.006.

Lamb, S. (2011). School dropout and completion: An international perspective. In S. Lamb, E. Markussen, R. Teese, N. Sandberg, & J. Polesel (Eds.), *School dropout and completion: International comparative studies in theory and policy* (pp. 21–72). Dordrecht, The Netherlands: Springer.

Lee, C. C., & Hipolito-Delgado, C. (2007). Counselors as agents of social justice. In C. C. Lee (Ed.), *Counseling for social justice* (pp. xiii–xxviii). Alexandria, VA: American Counseling Association.

Maree, J. G. (2006). Current issues in South African career counselling and availability of teachers in science and technology. *Psychological Reports, 98,* 151–152.

Maree, J. G. (2018). Advancing career counselling research and practice using a novel quantitative + qualitative approach to elicit clients' advice from within. *South African Journal of Higher Education, 32*(4), 149–170. https://doi.org/10.20853/32-4-2558.

Maree, J. G., & Beck, G. (2004). Using various approaches in career counselling for traditionally disadvantaged (and other) learners: Some limitations of a new frontier. *South African Journal of Education, 24*(1), 80–87.

Maree, J. G., Cook, A. V., & Fletcher, L. (2018). Assessment of the value of group-based counselling for career construction. *International Journal of Adolescence and Youth, 23*(1), 118–132. https://doi.org/10.1080/02673843.2017.1309324.

Maree, J. G., & Molepo, J. M. (2004). Facilitating post-modern career counselling in the Limpopo province of South Africa: A rocky ride to hope. *Australian Journal of Career Development, 13*(3), 47–54. https://doi.org/10.1177/103841620401300310.

Maree, J. G., & Taylor, N. (2016). Development of the Maree Career Matrix: A new interest inventory. *South African Journal of Psychology, 46*(4), 462–476.

McIlveen, P., & Patton, W. (2007). Dialogical self: Author and narrator of career life themes. *International Journal for Educational and Vocational Guidance, 7*(1), 67–80. https://doi.org/10.1007/s10775-007-9116-6.

McMahon, M., Watson, M., & Patton, W. (2005). Developing a qualitative career assessment process: The my system of career influences reflection activity. *Journal of Career Assessment, 13,* 476–490.

Miles, J., & Naidoo, A. V. (2017). The impact of a career intervention programme on South African Grade 11 learners' career decision-making self-efficacy. *South African Journal of Psychology, 47*(2), 209–221.

Morgan, B. (2014). *Towards the development and evaluation of the South African Career Interest Inventory* (Unpublished doctoral dissertation). University of Johannesburg, Johannesburg, South Africa.

Morgan, B., de Bruin, G. P., & de Bruin, K. (2015). Constructing Holland's hexagon in South Africa: Development and initial validation of the South African Career Interest Inventory. *Journal of Career Assessment, 23*(3), 493–511.

Morgan, B., Naidoo, A. V., Hein, C., & Rabie, S. (in press). Using interests and Holland's model of vocational personality types in career counselling: Some thoughts and research findings. In J. G. Maree (Ed.), *Handbook of innovative career counselling* (pp. xx–xx). New York, NY: Springer.

Naidoo, A. V. (2011). *Career flower—Enhancing vocational self-awareness. Career development group activity* (Unpublished manuscript). Psychology Department, Stellenbosch University, Stellenbosch, South Africa.

Naidoo, A. V., Pretorius, T. B., & Nicholas, L. (2017). The emergence of career psychology in South Africa: A socio-historical perspective. In G. B. Stead & M. B. Watson (Eds.), *Career psychology in the South African context* (3rd ed., pp. 1–20). Pretoria, South Africa: J. L. van Schaik.

Pyle, K. R. (1986). *Group career counseling: Principles and practices*. Ann Arbor, Michigan: ERIC Clearinghouse on Counseling and Personnel.

Pyle, K. R., & Hayden, S. C. (2015). *Group career counseling: Practices and principles* (2nd ed.). Broken Arrow, OK: National Career Development Association.

Rabie, S. (2017). *A translation and psychometric investigation of the South African Career Interest Inventory across gender and race among secondary school learners* (Unpublished doctoral dissertation). Stellenbosch University, Stellenbosch, South Africa.

Rabie, S., & Naidoo, A. V. (2019). Validating the adaptation of the first career measure in isiXhosa: The South African Career Interest Inventory—isiXhosa version. *South African Journal of Psychology, 49*(1), 109–121. https://doi.org/10.1177/0081246318772419.

Rehfuss, M. C. (2009). The future career autobiography: A narrative measure of career intervention effectiveness. *The Career Development Quarterly, 58*(1), 82–90. https://doi.org/10.1002/j.2161-0045.2009.tb00177.x.

Savickas, M. L. (1999). The transition from school to work: A developmental perspective. *The Career Development Quarterly, 47*(4), 326–336.

Savickas, M. L. (2001). Toward a comprehensive theory of career development: Disposition, concerns and narratives. In F. T. L. Leong & A. Barak (Eds.), *Contemporary models in vocational psychology: A volume in honor of Samuel H. Osipow* (pp. 295–320). Mahwah, NJ: Lawrence Erlbaum.

Savickas, M. L. (2012). Life design: A paradigm for career intervention in the 21st century. *Journal of Counseling & Development, 90,* 13–19.

Savickas, M. L. (2015). Career counseling paradigms: Guiding, developing, and designing. In P. J. Hartung, M. L. Savickas, & W. Walsh (Eds.), *APA handbook of career intervention* (Vol. 1, pp. 129–143). Washington, DC: American Psychological Association.

Savickas, M. L., Nota, L., Rossier, J., Dauwalder, J. P., Duarte, M. E., Guichard, J., et al. (2009). Life designing: A paradigm for career construction in the 21st century. *Journal of Vocational Behavior, 75*(3), 239–250.

Savickas, M. L., & Porfeli, E. J. (2011). Revision of the Career Maturity Inventory: The adaptability form. *Journal of Career Assessment, 19*(4), 355–374. https://doi.org/10.1177/1069072711409342.

Shirley, L. (2018). *An evaluation of a career intervention's effectiveness in improving career maturity among Grade 9 secondary school learners in Delft* (Unpublished honours thesis). Stellenbosch University, Stellenbosch, South Africa.

Silva, F. F. D., Paiva, V., & Ribeiro, M. A. (2016). Career construction and reduction of psychosocial vulnerability: Intercultural career guidance based on Southern epistemologies. *Journal of the National Institute for Career Education and Counselling, 36*(1), 46–53.

Statistics South Africa. (2018). *Quarterly labour force survey* (*Quarter* 2). Retrieved from http://www.statsgov.za/.

Stead, G. B., & Watson, M. B. (1998). Career research in South Africa: Challenges for the future. *Journal of Vocational Behavior, 52*(3), 289–299. https://doi.org/10.1006/jvbe.1997.1627.

Stead, G. B., & Watson, M. B. (2006). Indigenisation of career psychology in South Africa. In G. B. Stead & M. B. Watson (Eds.), *Career psychology in the South African context* (pp. 181–190). Pretoria, South Africa: J. L. van Schaik.

Sultana, R. (2017). Anchoring career guidance in the Mediterranean? In search of southern perspectives. In R. Sultana (Ed.), *Career guidance and livelihood planning across the Mediterranean* (pp. 3–18). Rotterdam, The Netherlands: Sense Publishers.

Super, D. E. (1990). A life-span, life-space approach to career development. In D. Brown & L. Brooks (Eds.), *Career choice and development: Applying contemporary theories to practice* (pp. 197–261). San Francisco, CA: Jossey-Bass.

Toporek, R. L., Lewis, J. A., & Crethar, H. C. (2009). Promoting systemic change through the ACA advocacy competencies. *Journal of Counseling & Development, 87*(3), 260–268.

Venter, C. (2018). *Perceived career barriers among Grade 9 secondary school learners in a South African disadvantaged community: A qualitative study* (Unpublished honours thesis). Stellenbosch University, Stellenbosch, South Africa.

Watson, M. B., & Stead, G. B. (1990). Work-role salience of South African adolescent. *Journal of Vocational Behavior, 36*(3), 249–257.
Watts, A. G. (1980). Career guidance under apartheid. *International Journal for the Advancement of Counselling, 3*(1), 3–27.
Watts, A. G., & Sultana, R. G. (2004). Career guidance policies in 37 countries: Contrasts and common themes. *International Journal for Educational and Vocational Guidance, 4*(2–3), 105–122.

Turning Water into Wine: An Innovative Way of Overcoming Stress Through Poetry

Esther M. Wafula

Abstract An individual's career cannot be separated from other aspects of their life. Experiences like the sudden loss of a loved one or other unexpected events or transitions can lead to a sense of overwhelming stress and disempowerment and these emotions don't disappear at the workplace. Yet such challenging experiences can be leveraged for personal and professional development. This chapter explores the utility of poetry writing to facilitate healing and growth in the context of unexpected life and career related transitions. Through autoethnographic inquiry, the author describes how writing poetry helped her overcome the stress arising from various losses and unexpected life and career transitions in her own life. The author tracks her progress along four career learning stages, the broadening of her I-positions based on Dialogical Self Theory, and the evolution of her metaphors toward a more hopeful self-narrative. The chapter demonstrates the value of therapeutic writing for self-healing and growth from a disempowered first story to a more empowered second story. Implications for counselling practice and suggestions for further research are discussed.

Keywords Autoethnography · Healing and growth · Poetry therapy · Therapeutic writing · Career writing · Career transitions · Stress

Introduction

The anxiety and uncertainty resulting from insecure employment, work traumas, and even regular career transitions, are increasingly accepted realities of the 21st century (Blustein, 2017; Callanan, Perri, & Tomkowicz, 2017; Kalleberg, 2009; Maree, 2013; Pisarik, Rowell, & Thompson, 2017). To thrive in this new reality individuals are required to develop adaptability and resilience in order to be more employable (Maree, 2017). While much of contemporary career literature is focused on developing cognitive adaptability, relatively few authors have paid attention to the emotional

E. M. Wafula (✉)
Nairobi, Kenya
e-mail: ewafula@sefidconsult.com

J. G. Maree (ed.), *Handbook of Innovative Career Counselling*,
https://doi.org/10.1007/978-3-030-22799-9_38

dynamics involved. However, an individual's career cannot be separated from other aspects of their life outside the workplace, such as the sudden loss of a loved one or other unexpected events and transitions. In addition, emotional distress and mental health factors can complicate career decision making (Dieringer, Lenz, Hayden, & Peterson, 2017). Frequent career transitions, related traumas and/or difficulties in other life domains can be so overwhelming that they become a "boundary experience" (Lengelle, 2014, p. 25) which challenges an individual's identity to move forward with confidence. Often, involuntary transitions, like job losses for example, involve readjustments of personal and career identity, emotional upheaval and bewilderment (Borgen, 1997). Thus, the need for more holistic counselling approaches that take both the personal and the career domains into account (Chen, 2001; Zunker, 2016); enhance self-awareness (Amundson, 1995; Brown & Brimrose, 2015); and foster resilience, are warranted, enabling individuals to face the destabilizing events in their lives with more adaptability (Maree, 2017).

The usefulness of narrative approaches in postmodern career counselling has been recognized by many writers including Brott (2001), Chen (2001), Maree (2013), Rehfuss (2013), Maree (2015), Yost, Yoder, Chung, and Voetmann (2015) and Busacca (2017). Career writing (Lengelle, 2014), which employs creative, expressive and reflective writing (including poetry) is one such approach. It facilitates in-depth self-exploration and the construction of career identities through a self-directed dialogical learning process, thereby developing what Lengelle, Meijers and Bonnar call "a warm inner compass" (2018, p. 185). Through a stronger connection with oneself, this warm inner compass equips a client with the tools to navigate the broader world of work, make meaning of career transitions, and even consider such changes as opportunities rather than setbacks or failures (Meijers & Lengelle, 2012).

Chapter Structure

The purpose of this chapter is to illustrate the potential of therapeutic writing to facilitate the kind of holistic learning and transformation that 21st century career counselling clients need. The chapter begins by providing a rationale for the autoethnographic method, my motivations for the study and why I use autobiographical poems as data. The second section tracks my healing journey through analysis of my poems using an analytical framework developed by Lengelle, Meijers, and Hughes (2016). The final section offers some implications for practice and suggestions for further research.

Why Autoethnography?

While acknowledging the value of traditional research methods such as interviews and surveys, some scholars have advocated for the expansion of what can be considered valid research (Denzin & Lincoln, 2000). Bond (2002) notes that traditional research methods often exclude important dimensions of what it means to be human by privileging thinking and analysis over experience, and its related actions and emotions. Autoethnography is one approach that enables researchers to convey the richness and depth of human experience. Autoethnographies have been defined as "highly personalized accounts that draw upon the experiences of the author/researcher for the purposes of extending sociological understanding" (Sparkes, 2000, p. 21). Autoethnography considers the researcher's subjectivity a legitimate lens through which social and cultural phenomena can be viewed (Meekums, 2008). Gallardo, Furman, and Kulkarni (2009) highlight different benefits of using autoethnography as research, including its usefulness in understanding private and taboo topics. Siddique (2011) contends that autoethnography can make valuable contributions to counselling and psychotherapy research. Finally, Richardson and St. Pierre (2018) view autoethnography as valuable not only as a source of research, but also as a process that can facilitate healing for the researcher.

Motivation for the Study

I decided to write an autoethnography after I noticed that writing poetry had facilitated my own healing following several unexpected losses and transitions in my career and life. I embarked on a retrospective study to find out how poetry made such healing possible and whether those mechanisms could be replicated with career counselling clients.

Methodology

To deepen the reader's understanding of how I overcame stress through poetry, I will analyze my poems through the approach developed by Lengelle et al. (2016) to track clients' progress during creative writing interventions. The three constituent parts of the approach are described briefly below to clarify the source and theoretical underpinnings of the method.

I. **Law's** (2010) **career learning stages**: These are four learning stages—sensing, sifting, focusing, and understanding—that demonstrate progression from the initial disempowered story to a new more hopeful story. The *sensing* stage involves gathering information and impressions (including sensory information) about how things are regarding work, role and self. In the *sifting* stage, one sorts through the information gathered in the first stage, e.g. through making comparisons, into more identifiable patterns or themes that may guide action. The *focusing* stage involves defragmentation of varying points of view by bringing together themes that arose during the preceding two stages. Finally, the *understanding* stage occurs when the individual has developed the capacity to identify the causes and likely effects of particular challenges in specific situations. The learning process is not linear. Hence overlaps and some regressions may be noted between the learning stages (Lengelle, 2014).

II. **Dialogical Self Theory**: This theory conceptualizes the self as a "dynamic multiplicity of *I*-positions or voices in the landscape of the mind" (Hermans & Hermans-Konopka, 2010, p. 31, italic in the original). These voices or "I-positions" point to things that are 'important to us' (i.e. salient in some way). For instance, "I-as capable professional" or "I-as vulnerable after loss". As more I-positions are welcomed into the conversation, promoter positions and meta-positions develop. Promoter positions are actionable positions, characterized by considerable openness toward the future, integrating new and already existing personal positions into a more adaptive self. A meta-position on the other hand is characterized by self-reflection, self-skepticism and disengagement from one's immediate emotional position. A meta-position provides "a helicopter view" (Hermans, 2018, p. 11) that facilitates decision-making and liberty from rigid and maladaptive patterns. Dialogical Self Theory also distinguishes between the centralizing and decentering movements involved in the dialogical process. Centralizing movements aim at establishing unity and continuity in the multiplicity of positions, while the direction of decentering movements is away from the self's hypothetical center through disruption of the existing order and integration (Hermans & Hermans-Konopka, 2010).

III. **The three metaphors of transformation**: These were identified by Lengelle et al. (2016) as a result of analyzing metaphors that consistently emerged during a healing journey facilitated through poetry (see also McClocklin & Lengelle, 2018). *Thread* metaphors appear early in a counselling intervention and continue throughout the narrative. They are expanded upon and revisited often as a client integrates the events and memories from their past, linking them to the present and imagined future. *Nudging* metaphors urge one forward step by step from a 'first' disempowered, dysfunctional, loss-or-suffering infused narrative toward a 'second' more empowered, hopeful and life-giving story. *Crystallizing* metaphors appear near the end of the intervention or healing process and tend to articulate a solution through personal insight or advice to the self.

My Data

The data for this chapter consists of autobiographical poems I wrote between 2016 and 2018 as part of my personal journals. Despite a life-long love for poetry reading and writing, I had written virtually no poems for nearly a decade until I resumed writing in 2016. The importance of poetry writing as a means of expression and personal healing was brought home to me in 2017. At my deepest point of despair, I felt I could no longer handle the stress I was under and decided to end my life. Suicidal thoughts had hovered over my mind for several months. Then, one day in

August 2017, I came so close to taking my life that I wrote a suicide note, in the form of a poem titled *Epilogue*. Much of the poem contained what I considered last words to my loved ones. However, before I could complete it, I wrote another poem titled *I have just written the Epilogue*. This follow-up poem was a small but important step away from the emotional cliff-edge past which I may never have returned. In subsequent days and months, I wrote many poems, each helping lift my despair. By early 2018, my spirit was lighter and more hopeful. Upon reflection, I realised that through poetry, I had documented my descent into "the valley of the shadow of death" (Biblica, 1984, Psalm 23: 4) and my subsequent exit from that valley to a place of greater emotional health and self-awareness.

Background to the Autobiographical Poems

Some events that occurred between 2008 and 2017 help explain the angst that informed the poems presented in this chapter. In mid-2008, I delivered twin boys, but lost one at birth. I wept on that bittersweet day, but had to quickly move on to care for my surviving son. I had no opportunity to grieve for Daniel, my deceased son. That grief was part of the deeply buried pain I addressed in several poems I wrote almost a decade after Daniel's passing. Between 2010 and 2014, my family and I made three international relocations, two of which were unanticipated. This involved 3 job changes for me, the final one being the most challenging as I abruptly transitioned from an employee to an independent consultant—or one of the "peripheral workers" that Guichard (2009, p. 252) talks about. In mid-2013, David, my surviving son was diagnosed with autism. Soon thereafter, my husband and I lost a family business we had invested in for many years, resulting in a period of financial strain for my family. By August 2016, I felt overwhelmed, as evidenced by the poem *My back's against the wall*—the first poem I wrote in 2016. Between 2016 and 2017, I also experienced severe back pain which required medical attention and weeks of physiotherapy. Despite these symptoms of distress, I felt too embarrassed to admit the challenges I was facing to others, and therefore did not seek counselling.

I now realize that the losses and transitions mentioned above were, individually and collectively, boundary experiences for me. According to Lengelle & Meijers (2009), a boundary experience is "an experience whereby an individual encounters the boundaries of his or her existing self-concept and cannot cope with a situation and its exigencies" (p. 58). Such experiences can challenge, diminish or destroy one's sense of identity and impair their confidence. Despite encountering various boundary experiences for almost a decade, I had not allowed myself to truly face my pain. This was not an intentional strategy. I thought I was handling the challenges well by recovering quickly after the painful events. I failed to realize that I was simply burying pain that would bear the fruit of despair later on.

Analysis of the Autobiographical Poems

In this chapter, I will analyze nine of the poems I wrote between 2016 and 2018. The selected poems, presented here in full or in part, illustrate my inner journey through and out of emotional turmoil. Based on Lengelle et al.'s (2016) framework, I will track my inner journey through the parallel movements across the career learning stages (Law as cited in Lengelle & Meijers, 2009), the broadening of my I-positions (Hermans & Hermans-Konopka, 2010) and the evolution of my metaphors (Lengelle et al., 2016).

My Progress Through the Career Learning Stages

Here, I present the specific poems that reflect my progression along Law's (2010) career learning stages of sensing, sifting, focusing and understanding.

The sensing stage. Lengelle (2014) posits that therapeutic writing in the context of a boundary experience helps one explore, describe and write down emotions during the sensing stage. Individuals "open up to what is happening inside", which facilitates awareness of their feelings as they happen in the body (Lengelle, 2014, p. 27). Meijers (2002) contends that the fear and uncertainty characteristic of periods of growth and development should neither be avoided nor be controlled prematurely. It is wiser to make room for one's feelings in an accepting, non-judgemental way, because feelings trigger us and focus our attention, which in turn can lead to learning (Lengelle, 2014). This allows initial symbols and sensory metaphors, with the potential to restructure life stories to emerge along with the expression and expansion of various I-Positions (Lengelle, 2014).

Below is the first poem I wrote after my re-engagement with poetry. It exemplifies my sensing stage especially in its references to various bodily sensations:

My back's against the wall

My back's against the wall
I have fallen off my high horse
I can smell and taste the dust
My eyes squint
In an effort to see
My ears perk up
In an effort to hear

Who are you?
What do you want from me?
Why have you pursued me this far
On the road to my Damascus?

Two other poems are relevant here. I wrote *Epilogue,*[1] intending it to be my suicide note. Soon thereafter, I wrote *I have just written the epilogue* as a reflection upon it. These two poems helped me notice, accept and describe the emotions I felt at my darkest hour without judgement.

Epilogue

One never knows
How far their tether goes
One never knows
The day, or night
On which the end may come…

One does not expect
Their tether to end
On a bright Tuesday morning
At the height of summer.

But mine has….

There is an urgency
As if each breath is borrowed

Shall I leave a note?
No, maybe I should leave notes
Notes of thanks and apology
I don't expect them to understand
But at least I should not burden them
With endless whys.

So,
With the precious breaths still left
I determine who I will write to.

Melua[2] asked-
If all your dreams were on fire
Which one would you save?
She also asked-
When it comes down to the wire
Should I be afraid?

Well,
All my dreams

[1]Only the parenthetical stanzas of the *Epilogue* poem are presented in this chapter. I have omitted the stanzas in which I expressed the intended final words to my loved ones because those must remain private.

[2]This is in reference to Katie Melua's song: *Dreams On Fire*, whose lyrics are available on: http://katiemelua.com/tracks/dreams-on-fire/.

And more
Much more
Is on fire…

So
This is it.
No wing,
No prayer
It is
Farewell….

When I wrote *Epilogue* the urgency and finality of that moment elicited the most essential information about the emotional crisis I was in, while writing the poem provided a safe container for those feelings. Acknowledging my sense of loss and disillusionment through this poem validated my pain to myself and launched my healing journey.

I have just written the epilogue

I have just written
The epilogue.
I think I remembered
Everyone I needed to.

It is quite telling
That neither my boss
Nor my banker
Made the list

It is equally telling
That neither my books
Nor my pearls
Deserved my final tears

When it came down to it
Every precious minute
I spent remembering my loves
Requited and unrequited,
Those who cherished and those who trampled
Each of them a bead
On this multi-colored necklace I have strung.

So,
What more
Is there to do
Except to acquiesce?

The poem *I have just written the epilogue* afforded me a crucial reflective stance that helped me disengage from the immediate emotional upheaval in order to consider my situation more soberly. As a result, I did not acquiesce to the urge to end my life.

The sifting stage. At the sifting stage, the individual sorts through their initial anguish without feeling overwhelmed. Consequently, they can reflect on and expand upon the metaphors that may have emerged. More I-positions are also expressed at this stage, but not in a chaotic manner. Decentering movements (Hermans & Hermans-Konopka, 2010) prompt the person to imagine broader possibilities and outcomes than what they might previously have considered.

Below are two poems that facilitated my inner journey during the sifting stage:

Will you speak?

I am a late bloomer just like Moses
But at least he had his burning bush.
As I wander here, in these dark, howling places
I can't help but wonder- did I already squander
All my sacred moments?

Was I too busy minding the mundane
To hear your voice in the silence?
Was I too busy counting losses
To notice the grace
With which the dew falls?

Now my feet are shorn
And my heart stripped bare
I am ready to listen
But-
Will you speak?

Let us suppose

Let us suppose 2018
Was the year I turned 18
Without losing the benefit
Of twenty years' experience-

Who would I embrace
Who would I eschew?
Which cups would I drink
Which ones would I let pass?
Which stories would I tell
Which ones would I repress?

What lores would I hold sacred
Which ones would I scorn?

What books would I read
Which ones would I avoid?
What jackets would I wear
Which ones would I discard?

What scars would I hide
Which ones would I don with pride?
Which loves lost would I grieve
Which ones would I let lie?
What paths would I take
Which ones would I make?

Let us suppose 2018
Was the year I turned 18
Without losing the benefit
Of twenty years' experience-

What version of me
Would you know?

The emergence of comparisons, analogies, personal constructs and concepts are evident in these poems. In *Will you speak?* I compared myself to the biblical figure of Moses. In other poems not presented here, I compared myself to Sisyphus in Greek mythology, and also wrote of discarding "vicarious wisdom" and "borrowed epiphanies". These personal constructs also exemplified decentering movements (Hermans & Hermans-Konopka, 2010) prompting me to imagine new possibilities and outcomes for my life. In *Let us suppose* I acknowledged that life presents many choices and opportunities to imagine different versions of myself. I started to consider, among other things, the possibility of making new paths rather than simply taking those that were already in place.

The focusing stage. At the focusing stage, salient material that emerged in the sensing and sifting stages is deepened, broadened and shaped into insights. The key task here is the formulation of one's distinct points of view after evaluating culturally supplied perspectives, and deciding which ones to agree or disagree with (Law, 2010).

During my focusing stage, I formulated some viewpoints that helped me transition from my first disempowered story to a more empowered second story. This transformation is noticeable in the following poems:

Nothing prepares you

Nothing prepares you
For the day the morning light
No longer shimmers
Across the water
To melt away the darkness.

Nothing prepares you
For that lonesome place
Of songless winds
In fields
Devoid of flowers.

Nothing surprises you
More
Than the animating doubt
That lights the way
Out of the abyss.

What dawns
More gradually
Are the hitherto self-evident truths
You jettison
As you dance with paradox.

Poetry in four parts

Part I
Poetry is the wheel
On which I cast, mold, and trim myself.

The kiln
In which I burn the vase
Of its ambivalence.

The pot
In which I boil down my days
Distilling myths and haunting doubts
For some salient drops of truth.

Part II
Poetry is a basket
In which I gather precocious flowers and fallen leaves.

The crucible
In which my hopes deferred and private joys
Cohere into signature perfumes.

A tear stained jar
That bears
The costly ointment
Of my devotion…

Positive engagement with uncertainty is evident in the poem *Nothing prepares you* where I wrote of dancing with paradox. The poem *Poetry in four parts* demonstrates the centralizing and integrative movements through which I tried to "string together feelings, ideas and life themes" (Lengelle, 2014, p. 28) that had emerged from the sensing and sifting stages. This is exemplified by the lines: "…Distilling myths and haunting doubts/For some salient drops of truth" and by words like "gather" and "cohere". The coalition of positions that emerged for me at this stage were: I-as dancing with paradox (as opposed to I-as certain), and I-as surrendered (as opposed to I-as striving).

The understanding stage. Finally, the insights gained in the focusing stage are consolidated into a second story in the understanding stage. This involves formulation of a "personal theory" (Lengelle & Meijers, 2009, p. 64) or an "explanatory hypothesis" (Law, 2010, p. 19) about what has happened so far in one's life. The individual notices what the first story they have been telling themselves is, and how they need to develop a more empowering second story. The second story, which is similar to a quest rather than a restitution narrative (Smith & Sparkes, 2004), begins to emerge, and the individual describes feelings of wholeness and relief (Lengelle, 2014). The emerging second story is also characterized by a growth mindset (Dweck, 2007) which embraces reality more readily by assuming that the challenges we face are not failures but rather signs of learning that needs to take place.

My progression to the understanding stage is illustrated in the poems: *What if?* and *Some Poems*.

What if?

What if
I believed
I was destined to be here?

That I am an answer
To my mother's and my grand-mother's prayers?

That I am needed
And have something to contribute?

What if
I acknowledged
The elephant in the room?
That some un-relinquished autobiographies
Rob today of salient beauty?

That some cherished maps only obscure
And will never lead me into the light?

What if
I blessed
Everything
That knocked me down?

Knowing
The ground
On which I fall

May well
Be a tomb
For what in me must die

But is also
A womb
For what in me should live?

What if
I really
Showed up for my life?

Some poems

Part II

Some poems
By an alchemy
You can't quite decipher
Call forth the numinous
And you, discerning the moment
Of transient wonder
Halt your chariot
And surrender
To the baptism that feels like dying

But is the serendipitous
Happenstance
That redefines you
Into a genuine truth seeker
From the jaded traveler
Who honors no sages
The reluctant pilgrim
Who worships for expedience
At the shrines of gods
You neither love nor trust.

Part III

Some poems
Are the stirred pools
In which you digest
Your crippling fears

And gather the courage
To reclaim your name
To bear the burden
Of embodying your voice
Muted too long
By the clamor
Of this or the other dogma.

Some poems
Like Pegasus
Carry you aloft
Across the threshold
Of an existence
That seemed once
So ordinary
But is now
Imbued with meaning
And you
With newfound zeal become
Its lifelong devotee.

My emerging second story is articulated in lines such as "I am destined to be here.../I have something to contribute". Clarity about what caused some of my emotional problems also emerged in lines like "...some un-relinquished autobiographies/Rob today of salient beauty" and "...some cherished maps only obscure". Law (2010) suggested that people can be helped to gain understanding through reflection on their own as well as on other people's biographies. In *Some Poems*, I reflected on two biblical stories of transformation: the baptism of the Ethiopian eunuch (Acts 8: 26–39) and the healing of a crippled man at the pool of Bethesda (John 5: 1–13). These two stories provided rich layers of meaning and contributed to the emergence of the quest narrative and growth mindset with which I now engage my life.

Broadening of I-Positions and Development of Meta- and Promoter Positions

According to Lengelle et al. (2016), progress along the learning stages also involves the broadening of one's I-positions and the development of meta-and promoter positions. Previously marginalized positions such as I-as-emotions-needing-attention or I-as-listener are granted voice. Promoter positions, characterised by openness toward the future and self-innovation emerge and "reorganize the self toward a higher level of development" (Hermans & Hermans-Konopka, 2010, p. 228). Meta-positions, likened to a helicopter view, also emerge, allowing the individual some self-skepticism and distance from the immediate emotional position, in order to make executive decisions from a broader point of view (Hermans, 2018). Lengelle et al. (2016) argue that these developments in I, meta and promoter positions are facilitated by metaphors which "form a bridge from emotions to new understandings" (p. 61).

Various metaphors emerged in my poems during my journey from emotional turmoil to emotional health. In the sensing stage, my metaphors relayed a sense of struggle, defeat, disillusionment and loss. For example, "My back's against the wall", "Fallen off my high horse"; "end of the tether", "dreams on fire". These metaphors gave voice to I-positions I had silenced for too long. My metaphors in the sifting stage were less raw but still expressed the ambiguity, incoherence and questioning expected in an "ante-narrative" (Lengelle, 2014, p. 28). These include "my feet are shorn" and "my heart stripped bare". They also signalled the developing openness to a new story, as indicated by "I am ready to listen" in *Will you speak?* My metaphors in the focusing stage suggested centralizing movements and emerging coherence through references to making pottery, boiling, flower gathering, and perfumery in *Poetry in four parts.* The emergence of a promoter position is exemplified by the metaphor "dancing with paradox". Finally, the metaphors in the understanding stage were more positive and conveyed my commitment to the emerging quest narrative (Smith & Sparkes, 2004). Metaphors relating to I-as-pilgrim and I-as-a-genuine-truth-seeker represented the emerging meta-positions that helped me reflect on my life from an objective distance.

The Thread, Nudging and Crystallizing Metaphors

Lengelle et al. (2016) argue that different types of metaphors play different roles in bridging emotions and cognitions. These are: the *Thread* metaphor; *Nudging* metaphors and the *Crystallizing* metaphor. The thread metaphor that emerged early and reappeared consistently throughout my learning process was that of journey or pilgrimage. It showed up in the first poem: *My back's against the wall* in the words "On the road to my Damascus". It also appeared indirectly in reference to my being a "jaded traveller" and "reluctant pilgrim" in *Some poems*. It is notable that both my first and last poems in this series described unexpected, transformative encounters along the journey. However, in the first poem—*My back's against the wall*—the encounter seems humbling: the Divine has brought me low, I am left disoriented and tasting defeat. In the last poem—*Some poems*—the encounter is also unexpected and transformative. This time, however, instead of being thrown off my horse, I halt the chariot and surrender to the experience willingly. These two poems act like book-ends to the learning process described in this chapter.

My nudging metaphors included references to "the edge of things", "end of the tether" and "threshold". These metaphors signalled the fact that I was on the cusp of something new, and helped me stay open to whatever lessons would come. Another nudging metaphor related to the idea of encountering the numinous. This appeared indirectly in reference to the "burning bush" in *Will you speak?*; as "epiphanies" in *Vicarious wisdom*; as "alchemy" in *The summons* (the latter two poems are not presented in this chapter); and as "the numinous" in *Some poems*. The "burning" metaphor deserves further comment. In *Will you speak?* I decried my lack of a "burning bush". However, the burning metaphor reappeared in *Epilogue*, as "Dreams on fire". I now believe that my longed for "burning bush" may have come disguised as "Dreams on fire".

Finally, my solution articulating metaphor (the crystallizing metaphor) emerged in *Some Poems*. The advice I gave myself about how to live going forward stated the need to: "digest your crippling fears/And gather the courage/To reclaim your name/To bear the burden/Of embodying your voice." Writing this autoethnography, which has required significant self-disclosure, is one of the steps I have taken to honour this advice.

Implications for Practice

One of Richardson and St.Pierre's (2018) criteria for judging autoethnography is its impact on the emotions and the intellect. Since the emotional impact of an autoethnography is best determined by the reader, I will only comment on the intellectual impact of this chapter in the form of implications for counselling practice and suggestions for further research.

Therapeutic Writing in Career Counselling: Opportunities and Risks

This chapter demonstrates the power of poetry writing to facilitate engagement with the challenging circumstances in one's life, including unanticipated career transitions. Writing poetry helped me articulate painful feelings I had buried for too long following accumulated losses and unplanned transitions. The metaphors emerging in my poems facilitated a much-needed change in my self-narrative. They conveyed symbolically not only the deficit-laden perspective in my first story, but also possible new ways I could inhabit the world in my new self-narrative. Consequently, I am now able to function better in my personal and professional domains, by being more cognitively alert, emotionally and physically healthy and having a more positive affect at home and at work. My self-awareness was greatly enhanced in the process and with it my proactivity in responding to difficult life and career situations. This use of poetry, as spontaneous as it seemed in my case, is not new or unique to me.

Since its use by healers in ancient societies, poetry therapy has gradually gained currency, as evidenced by the establishment of a National Association for Poetry Therapy in 1980 (NAPT, n.d.) and the publication of numerous books on the subject (Mazza, 2017). Poetry therapy is currently widespread across disciplines, nations, populations, problem areas and settings (Fox, 1997; Chavis & Weisberger, 2003; Samuels & Lane, 2013; Gold, 2014; Mazza, 2017). The growing popularity of poetry in counselling contexts is mainly due to its evocative power to facilitate healing and personal growth through metaphor, emotion and sensation—all closely related to right-brain image processing (Samuels & Lane, 2013). Furthermore, poetry provides a safe container because it is often less literal than prose—it allows clients to face their concerns in a more abstract way. Poetry also limits word use, which helps clients distil salient themes (Lengelle, 2014) and focus on what really matters to them

Various approaches exist to guide practitioners using poetry in different contexts. Mazza's RES model is one of the most well-established approaches. It consists of the receptive or prescriptive component where other people's poems are offered to the client for reference, the expressive or creative component where the client´s own writing is used, and the symbolic or ceremonial component that employs metaphors, rituals and storytelling (Mazza, 2017). While acknowledging the usefulness of Mazza's RES model, I found Lengelle and Meijers' transformation-through-writing model (2009) a more comprehensive heuristic tool when analysing how and why poetry writing facilitated my own healing. This model demystifies why writing heals by explaining what happens as one progresses through the "transformational space" between their disempowered first story and their empowered second story (Lengelle & Meijers, 2009, p. 59). First, writing fosters the detachment and development of an observer stance that enables clients to break their identification with their first stories and the victim mindset. Secondly, writing personally relevant material activates the internal and external dialogue necessary for a fuller, more honest engagement with one's story. Moreover, the process enhances a client's capacity to do their own internal work, to notice and attend to the insights that arise, and to discuss them with their career counsellor, should they wish to.

However, some risks must be considered when using therapeutic writing with clients. Some clients may experience distress when writing about traumatic experiences they have had in the past (Pennebaker & Smyth, 2016), at least in the short term. Other drawbacks of expressive writing include over-intellectualizing, rumination and substituting writing for action (Pennebaker & Smyth, 2016). Some clients enrolling for therapeutic writing programs may also present serious mental health concerns such as severe levels of depression or be at risk of self-harm. It is therefore crucial for counsellors to clearly communicate the scope of concerns that can be addressed through therapeutic writing programs, and require their clients to seek specialized mental health services when necessary. Therapeutic writing practitioners should also establish detailed procedures to guide referral of clients for specialized counselling services if needed.

The Value of Analytical Frameworks

This chapter used the analytical approach proposed by Lengelle et al. (2016). The three-narrative type model of restitution, chaos and quest narratives developed by

Frank (1997) is another useful conceptual framework that counsellors and researchers could adopt to analyze client stories and poetry. Such frameworks "help us to see the complexity and messiness of lived experience afresh and to generate new insight and practice" (Bond, 2002, p. 133). By providing some objective distance between oneself, their written material, and the emotions writing invokes, such analytical frameworks can also enhance one's "helicopter view" or meta-position (Hermans, 2018, p. 11). From that perspective, one can develop self-compassion and critical insight into such things as a tendency to avoid grief, for instance. It also creates a foundation for allowing new decisions to emerge organically.

The Important Role of Metaphors in Therapeutic Writing and Career Counselling

The significance of metaphors in counselling contexts has been highlighted by many researchers including Fox (1989), Wickman, Daniels, White, and Fesmire (1999), Lyddon, Clay, and Sparks (2001), Inkson and Amundson (2002), Inkson (2003), Robert and Kelly (2010), Sharoff (2013), Amundson (2015) and Muijen, Lengelle, Meijers, and Wardekker (2018). Metaphors can lead to personal transformation by promoting awareness, insight and deeper understanding of oneself (Sharoff, 2013). Barner (2011) contends that metaphors can help a client "make sense of their own career narratives" (p. 91), by helping uncover their implicit assumptions about themselves, their world, and the future they envision. Lengelle et al. (2016) discovered that metaphors help clients access their personal wisdom by creating bridges between their struggles, challenging feelings and new understandings, helping them articulate "new stories of identity" (p. 66).

The Crucial Role of Emotions in Facilitating Personal Healing and Development

The experience I have described in this chapter demonstrates that emotions are a double-edged sword. Lingering, unprocessed emotions can be poisonous. However, when attended to carefully and intentionally, emotions are invaluable guides on the path to personal healing and growth. As Greenberg (2002) argues, enduring change often occurs when individuals move from an intellectual understanding of themselves, to an emotional experience of themselves. And, enlisting deep and even painful emotions is often necessary in therapy to promote the most profound changes. In therapeutic writing, emotions play a critical role by triggering attention which in turn triggers learning (Lengelle, 2014). Similarly, Hoggan, Mälkki and Finnegan (2016) contend that emotions are "more than mere addenda to the learning process or barriers to rational thought; they can instigate the learning process and lead to more holistic ways of knowing and being" (p. 55). Counsellors should therefore help their clients open up to their emotions without trying to control them prematurely (Meijers 2002).

Suggestions for Further Research

Future studies could employ the retrospective approach like I did, making research subjects the archeologists of their own past (Shapiro, 2004). Other studies could investigate the utility of therapeutic writing in real-time, exploring different experiences in the career and life domains of individuals in a variety of settings. The effectiveness of creative, expressive and reflective writing (including poetry) to facilitate professional reflexivity has been demonstrated in various studies (e.g. Lengelle, Meijers, Poell, & Post, 2014; Lengelle et al., 2016, 2018). However, further research on poetry's specific effects when used in career writing could be expanded upon.

Autoethnography provides opportunities for the exploration of a wide range of topics, including those often marginalized or considered taboo. Although other African scholars have written autoethnographies before, these are relatively few and far between compared to those from other parts of the world (Ngunjiri, 2014; Brock-Utne, 2016). There is therefore room for more African scholars to use the autoethnographic method in their research. Collaborative autoethnography could also enrich our understanding of various topics of interest, within the African context and beyond (Ngunjiri, Hernandez & Chang, 2010).

Conclusion

People are bound to experience a variety of destabilizing events, losses and transitions in the course of their lives. The 21st century career landscape is particularly insecure and complex. Yet, responding to these and other personal challenges that may affect one's career agency are considered an individual's responsibility. When faced with personal and professional boundary experiences, individuals can feel disoriented and disempowered. However, as demonstrated in this chapter, writing can be employed to powerful effect to facilitate learning and transformation during transitions in the personal and professional domains. My experience has specifically illustrated poetry's inherent power to facilitate personal healing and transformation. Poetry helped me overcome stress at a dark time in my life thereby turning my "water" into "wine". With this in mind, I hope that this chapter will encourage more counsellors to adopt therapeutic writing, including poetry therapy, as key tools in their therapeutic (and career-learning) toolboxes.

References

Amundson, N. E. (1995). An interactive model of career decision making. *Journal of Employment Counselling, 32*(1), 11–21. https://doi.org/10.1002/j.2161-1920.1995.tb00420.x.

Amundson, N. E. (2015). Using metaphor in career intervention. In P. J. Hartung, M. L. Savickas, & W. B. Walsh (Eds.), *APA handbook of career intervention: Volume 2. Applications* (pp. 293–304). Washington, DC: American Psychological Association.

Barner, R. W. (2011). Applying visual metaphors to career transitions. *Journal of Career Development, 38*(1), 89–106. https://doi.org/10.1177/0894845309359287.

Biblica. (1984). *The Holy Bible: New International Version*. Colorado Springs, CO: Biblica Inc.

Blustein, D. L. (2017). Epilogue. In *Psychology of career adaptability, employability and resilience* (p. 450). https://doi.org/10.1007/978-3-319-66954-0.

Bond, T. (2002). Naked narrative: Real research? *Counselling and Psychotherapy Research, 2*(2), 133–138. https://doi.org/10.1080/14733140212331384907.

Borgen, W. A. (1997). People caught in changing career opportunities: A counselling process. *Journal of Employment Counselling, 34*(3), 133–143. https://doi.org/10.1002/j.2161-1920.1997.tb00990.x.

Brock-Utne, B. (2016). Research in Africa using an autoethnographical approach. *World Studies in Education, 17*(2), 5–16. https://doi.org/10.7459/wse/17.2.02.

Brott, P. E. (2001). The storied approach: A postmodern perspective for career counseling. *The Career Development Quarterly, 49*(4), 304–313. https://doi.org/10.1002/j.2161-0045.2001.tb00958.x.

Brown, A., & Brimrose, J. (2015). Identity development. In P. J. Hartung, M. L. Savickas, & W. B. Walsh (Eds.), *APA handbook of career intervention: Volume 2. Applications* (pp. 241–254). Washington, DC: American Psychological Association.

Busacca, L. A. (2017). Career counseling in postmodern times: Emergence and narrative conceptions. In L. A. Busacca & M. C. Rehfuss (Eds.), *Postmodern career counseling: A handbook of culture, context, and cases* (pp. 23–36). Alexandria, VA: American counseling association.

Callanan, G. A., Perri, D. F., & Tomkowicz, S. M. (2017). Career management in uncertain times: Challenges and opportunities. *The Career Development Quarterly, 65*(4), 353–365. https://doi.org/10.1002/cdq.12113.

Chavis, G. G., & Weisberger, L. L. (2003). *The healing fountain: Poetry therapy for life's journey*. St. Cloud, MN: North Star Press of St. Cloud Inc.

Chen, C. P. (2001). Career counselling as life career integration. *Journal of Vocational Education & Training, 53*(4), 523–542. https://doi.org/10.1080/13636820100200175.

Denzin, N. K., & Lincoln, Y. S. (2000). *Handbook of qualitative research* (2nd ed.). Thousand Oaks, CA: Sage.

Dieringer, D. D., Lenz, J. G., Hayden, S. C., & Peterson, G. W. (2017). The relation of negative career thoughts to depression and hopelessness. *The Career Development Quarterly, 65*(2), 159–172. https://doi.org/10.1002/cdq.12089.

Dweck, C. (2007). *Mindset: The new psychology of success* (2nd ed.). New York, NY: Ballantine Books.

Fox, R. (1989). What is meta for? *Clinical Social Work Journal, 17*(3), 233–244. https://doi.org/10.1007/bf00755347.

Fox, J. (1997). *Poetic medicine: The healing art of poem-making*. New York, NY: Jeremy P. Tarcher/Putnam.

Frank, A. W. (1997). *The wounded storyteller: Body, illness, and ethics*. Chicago, IL: University of Chicago Press.

Gallardo, H. L., Furman, R., & Kulkarni, S. (2009). Explorations of depression: Poetry and narrative in autoethnographic qualitative research. *Qualitative Social Work: Research and Practice, 8*(3), 287–304. https://doi.org/10.1177/1473325009337837.

Gold, R. (2014). *Writing with at-risk youth: The Pongo teen writing method*. Lanham, MD: Rowman & Littlefield Education.

Greenberg, L. S. (2002). *Emotion-focused therapy: Coaching clients to work through their feelings*. Washington, DC: American Psychological Association.

Guichard, J. (2009). Self-constructing. *Journal of Vocational Behavior, 75*(3), 251–258. https://doi.org/10.1016/j.jvb.2009.03.004.

Hermans, H. J. (2018). *Society in the self: A theory of identity in democracy*. New York, NY: Oxford University Press.

Hermans, H. J., & Hermans-Konopka, A. (2010). *Dialogical self theory: Positioning and counter-positioning in a globalizing society*. Cambridge, United Kingdom: Cambridge University Press.

Hoggan, C., Mälkki, K., & Finnegan, F. (2016). Developing the theory of perspective transformation: Continuity, intersubjectivity and emancipatory praxis. *Adult Education Quarterly, 67*(1), 48–64. https://doi.org/10.1177/0741713616674076.

Inkson, K. (2003). Images of career: Nine key metaphors. *Journal of Vocational Behavior, 65*(1), 96–111. https://doi.org/10.1016/s0001-8791(03)00053-8.

Inkson, K., & Amundson, N. E. (2002). Career metaphors and their application in theory and counselling practice. *Journal of Employment Counselling, 39*(3), 98–108. https://doi.org/10.1002/j.2161-1920.2002.tb00841.x.

Kalleberg, A. L. (2009). Precarious work, insecure workers: Employment relations in transition. *American Sociological Review, 74*(1), 1–22. https://doi.org/10.1177/000312240907400101.

Law, B. (2010). *A career learning theory*. Retrieved from http://www.hihohiho.com/newthinking/crlrnoriginal.pdf.

Lengelle, R. (2014). *Career writing: Creative, expressive and reflective approaches to narrative and dialogical career guidance*. Unpublished doctoral dissertation, University of Tilburg, Tilburg, The Netherlands.

Lengelle, R., & Meijers, F. (2009). Mystery to mastery: An exploration of what happens in the black box of writing and healing. *Journal of Poetry Therapy, 22*(2), 57–75. https://doi.org/10.1080/08893670903072935.

Lengelle, R., Meijers, F., & Bonnar, C. (2018). Poetic creativity: The career writing method for professional reflexivity in the 21st century. In N. Arthur, R. Neault, & M. McMahon (Eds.), *Career theories and models at work: Ideas for practice* (pp. 183–193). Toronto, Canada: Canadian Education and Research Institute for Counselling (CERIC).

Lengelle, R., Meijers, F., & Hughes, D. (2016). Creative writing for life design: Reflexivity, metaphor and change processes through narrative. *Journal of Vocational Behavior, 97*, 60–67. https://doi.org/10.1016/j.jvb.2016.07.012.

Lengelle, R., Meijers, F., Poell, R., & Post, M. (2014). Career writing: Creative, expressive and reflective approaches to narrative identity formation in students in higher education. *Journal of Vocational Behavior, 85*(1), 75–84. https://doi.org/10.1016/j.jvb.2014.05.001.

Lyddon, W. J., Clay, A. L., & Sparks, C. L. (2001). Metaphor and change in counselling. *Journal of Counselling & Development, 79*(3), 269–274. https://doi.org/10.1002/j.1556-6676.2001.tb01971.x.

Maree, J. G. (2013). *Counselling for career construction: Connecting life themes to construct life portraits: Turning pain into hope*. Rotterdam, The Netherlands: Sense.

Maree, J. G. (2015). Life themes and narratives. In P. J. Hartung, M. L. Savickas, & W. B. Walsh (Eds.), *APA handbook of career intervention. Volume 2. Applications* (pp. 225–239). Washington, DC: American Psychological Association.

Maree, K. (2017). The psychology of career adaptability, career resilience, and employability: A broad overview. In *Psychology of career adaptability, employability and resilience* (pp. 3–11). https://doi.org/10.1007/978-3-319-66954-0.

Mazza, N. (2017). *Poetry therapy: Theory and practice* (2nd ed.). London, United Kingdom: Routledge.

McClocklin, P. A., & Lengelle, R. (2018). Cures for the heart: A poetic approach to healing after loss. *British Journal of Guidance and Counselling, 46*(3), 326–339. https://doi.org/10.1080/03069885.2017.1381665.

Meekums, B. (2008). Embodied narratives in becoming a counselling trainer: An autoethnographic study. *British Journal of Guidance and Counselling, 36*(3), 287–301. https://doi.org/10.1080/03069880802088952.

Meijers, F. (2002). Career learning in a changing world: The role of emotions. *International Journal for the Advancement of Counselling, 24*(3), 149–167. Retrieved from https://pdfs.semanticscholar.org/6ad4/ae0b3c0b370442e8c5d24ce179aaf25386af.pdf.

Meijers, F., & Lengelle, R. (2012). Narratives at work: The development of career identity. *British Journal of Guidance and Counselling, 40*(2), 157–176. https://doi.org/10.1080/03069885.2012.665159.

Melua, K. (2016, October). *Dreams on fire*. Retrieved July 21, 2018, from http://katiemelua.com/tracks/dreams-on-fire/.

Muijen, H., Lengelle, R., Meijers, F., & Wardekker, W. (2018). The role of imagination in emergent career agency. *Australian Journal of Career Development, 27*(2), 88–98. https://doi.org/10.1177/1038416218777832.

NAPT. (n.d.). History of NAPT—National Association for Poetry Therapy. Retrieved February 25, 2018, from https://poetrytherapy.org/index.php/about-napt/history-of-napt/.

Ngunjiri, F. W. (2014, January). *Voice and representation: Collaborative autoethnography as method for studying African leadership and management realities*. Paper presented at 2nd Biennial Conference—Africa Academy of Management, Gaborone, Botswana.

Ngunjiri, F. W., Hernandez, K. C., & Chang, H. (2010). Living autoethnography: Connecting life and research. *Journal of Research Practice, 6*(1). Retrieved from http://jrp.icaap.org/index.php/jrp/article/view/241/186.

Pennebaker, J. W., & Smyth, J. M. (2016). *Opening up by writing it down: How expressive writing improves health and eases emotional pain* (3rd ed.). New York, NY: Guilford Publications.

Pisarik, C. T., Rowell, P. C., & Thompson, L. K. (2017). A phenomenological study of career anxiety among college students. *The Career Development Quarterly, 65*(4), 339–352. https://doi.org/10.1002/cdq.12112.

Rehfuss, M. C. (2013). The role of narratives in career counseling: Career as story. In A. Di Fabio & J. G. Maree (Eds.), *Psychology of career counseling: New challenges for a new era* (pp. 61–68). New York, NY: Nova Science Publishers.

Richardson, L., & Pierre, E. A. (2018). Writing: A method of inquiry. In N. K. Denzin & Y. S. Lincoln (Eds.), *The SAGE handbook of qualitative research* (5th ed., pp. 1410–1444). Thousand Oaks, CA: Sage.

Robert, T., & Kelly, V. A. (2010). Metaphor as an instrument for orchestrating change in counselor training and the counselling process. *Journal of Counselling & Development, 88*(2), 182–188. https://doi.org/10.1002/j.1556-6678.2010.tb00007.x.

Samuels, M., & Lane, M. R. (2013). *Healing with the arts: A 12-week program to heal yourself and your community*. New York, NY: Beyond Words Publishing Inc.

Shapiro, J. (2004). Can poetry be data? Potential relationships between poetry and research. *Families, Systems, & Health, 22*(2), 171–177. https://doi.org/10.1037/1091-7527.22.2.171.

Sharoff, L. (2013). Creative power of metaphorical expression. *Journal of Holistic Nursing, 31*(1), 6–18. https://doi.org/10.1177/0898010112461948.

Siddique, S. (2011). Being in-between: The relevance of ethnography and auto-ethnography for psychotherapy research. *Counselling and Psychotherapy Research, 11*(4), 310–316. https://doi.org/10.1080/14733145.2010.533779.

Smith, B., & Sparkes, A. (2004). Men, sport, and spinal cord injury: An analysis of metaphors and narrative types. *Disability & Society, 19*(6), 613–626. https://doi.org/10.1080/0968759042000252533.

Sparkes, A. C. (2000). Autoethnography and narratives of self: Reflections on criteria in action. *Sociology of Sport Journal, 17,* 21–43.

Wickman, S. A., Daniels, M. H., White, L. J., & Fesmire, S. A. (1999). A "Primer" in conceptual metaphor for counselors. *Journal of Counselling & Development, 77*(4), 389–394. https://doi.org/10.1002/j.1556-6676.1999.tb02464.x.

Yost, P. R., Yoder, M. P., Chung, H. H., & Voetmann, K. R. (2015). Narratives at work: Story arcs, themes, voice, and lessons that shape organizational life. *Consulting Psychology Journal: Practice and Research, 67*(3), 163–188. https://doi.org/10.1037/cpb0000043.

Zunker, V. G. (2016). *Career counselling: A holistic approach* (9th ed.). Boston, MA: Cengage Learning.

Innovating Towards Career Learning Environments: Changes in Teachers' Role Perception Regarding Career Guidance

Aniek Draaisma, Frans Meijers and Marinka Kuijpers

Abstract To realise a career learning environment for students that is more focused on careers and 'life-long learning', as opposed to concentrating primarily on gaining a diploma, teachers are increasingly supposed to approach their students dialogically in Dutch vocational education. A change in attitude and behaviour, however, is only sustainable if a change in the teachers' own role perception is established. In this chapter, the aims and design of the COG/SVE project and the results of previous studies regarding the project is explained, as well as the methods used for the current longitudinal qualitative study. Interviews were conducted with 47 selected teachers participating in the project 4 times over a period of 3 years. The results of the study show that considerable development was achieved by many of the teachers from being primarily diploma focused to being primarily career focused. However, within the schools represented in our study, the change patterns of the individual teachers differed. The changes on the level of the organisation, as initiated by the innovation project, therefore appeared to exert different influences on the individual change processes of the teachers. We conclude that a change in role perception is a collective matter in communication and team learning, but it seems to require individual support and guidance. Thus, our recommendation is to support collective learning as well as the needs of individual members of teams of teachers in a dialogical manner.

Keywords School-based career learning · Career dialogues · Teachers' role perception

A. Draaisma (✉) · M. Kuijpers
Welten Institute, Open University, Heerlen, The Netherlands
e-mail: info@aniekdraaisma.nl

F. Meijers
Research Group Pedagogy of Career Development, The Hague University of Applied Sciences, The Hague, The Netherlands

J. G. Maree (ed.), *Handbook of Innovative Career Counselling*,
https://doi.org/10.1007/978-3-030-22799-9_39

Introduction

Students in vocational education in the Netherlands, as in the rest of Western Europe, depend on the career counselling services that schools provide, since delivery by external services has mostly been eliminated (Hooley, Watts, & Andrews, 2015; Hughes, Meijers, & Kuijpers, 2015; Meijers, 2001). Therefore, the responsibility for guiding students regarding their career paths generally lies with teachers (Oomen, Van den Dungen, Pijls, & Egelie, 2012). Teachers tend to find this role quite difficult, as they are generally used to talking *to* their students rather than with them (Mittendorff, 2010; Winters, 2012), while conceptions of adequate teaching are increasingly focused on guiding and facilitating the students in their personal and professional development in a dialogical manner (Beijaard, Verloop, & Vermunt, 2000; Den Boer & Hoeve, 2017; Geijsel & Meijers, 2005).

To promote contemporary career guidance for students, the innovation project 'Career Orientation and Guidance in Secondary Vocational Education' (COG/SVE) was developed and has been implemented in the Netherlands since 2010. The project aims to reform teachers' approach to their students through a career-focused and dialogical attitude. Previous research concerning the effects of the COG/SVE training programme on the form and content of career dialogues has shown that teachers ask more career-oriented questions and that more career-oriented responses are given by students after participating in the off-the-job and on-the-job parts of the programme (Kuijpers & Meijers, 2017). However, before teachers become focused on career guidance and approach their students in a more dialogical way, they need to embrace a different view of their teaching role. Only after such a new view has been adopted successfully can sustainable changes in individual behaviour and the routines of teacher teams be expected (Den Boer & Hoeve, 2017; Hoekstra, Brekelmans, Beijaard, & Korthagen, 2009). Research concentrating on transforming the role perceptions of teachers is to a large extent lacking, although knowledge about these processes is required to realise a culture change in education.

The aim of this chapter is to provide an in-depth description of the cultural changes initiated by the project at the level of individual teachers in school organisations, focusing on their role perception. In the first part, we explain the aims and design of the COG/SVE project and the results of previous studies regarding the project. Secondly, we provide an overview of the existing literature on teachers as career guides and (changing) teachers' role perception more generally. We thirdly discuss the aim of the longitudinal qualitative study and the methods used for data collection and analyses. Fourthly, by discussing the results and stating the conclusion, this chapter offers an insight into the change process regarding the perception of their role as a teacher and explores the factors that contribute to a possibly different view of their teaching role.

COG/SVE Innovation Project

Most schools embrace the idea of developing the different skills that are needed to meet the demands of today's labour market, such as the ability to show flexibility and the possession of career management skills (Lengelle, Meijers, & Van der Heijden, 2017; Schulz, 2008). However, they mostly do so without the recognition that such skills require a different learning environment from that in which the focus was on traditional technical competencies (Smith & Comyn, 2004). Therefore, in 2010, the Dutch Ministry of Education financed the national five-year innovation project 'Career Orientation and Guidance in Secondary Vocational Education' (COG/SVE). This project was developed to encourage vocational educational institutions to initiate the creation of a strong career learning environment for their students.

Central to this career learning environment is dialogue with the students, in which meaning is attached to concrete experiences with work and self-regulated learning is developed (Kuijpers, Meijers, & Gundy, 2011; Meijers, Kuijpers, & Gundy, 2013). A career learning environment should be practice based and offer students a growing say in the choices that they make to develop their ability to give direction to their career. This learning environment differs considerably from a traditional environment by not focusing primarily on information transfer and not being geared towards a standard learning route (Den Boer & Hoeve, 2017).

In Dutch education the focus of teachers in their behaviour towards students is merely on academic performance and not on dialogues with students or on their experiences with work (Kuijpers & Meijers, 2017; Meijers & Kuijpers, 2014; Winters, 2012). Realising this career learning environment is therefore a change process that requires innovation to implement sustainable change in the culture and structure and consequently in the attitudes and behaviour of teachers (Fullan, 2007). As teachers' professional development is regarded as crucial for educational change (Lieberman & Pointer Mace, 2008), a training programme on conducting career dialogues with students was the starting point of the transformation towards a dialogical career learning environment.

The training programme consisted of both off-the-job and on-the-job phases, because an off-the-job training programme for teachers had proved to be insufficient to achieve significant changes in career dialogues (Meijers & Kuijpers, 2014). In combination with individual coaching and team coaching on the job, however, the programme was effective in improving guidance conversations (Kuijpers & Meijers, 2017). In the off-the-job phase, which took a total of two days with periods of two to four weeks between them, the emphasis was on explaining the theory and putting the theory into practice in career conversations. In the on-the-job phase, the emphasis was on the translation of the training to the teachers' own school environment. From each participating school, two (or in some cases more) teachers received an extended training programme to become a *school coach*; they were trained to train their own colleagues in improving their career dialogues with students. All the other teachers took part in a four-session in-school training programme (two individual and two team sessions) with their school coaches, using video-recorded guidance conversations, role-playing activities, and recent theoretical insights concerning career development. The teachers were taught to encourage the students to develop their career competencies by conducting career dialogues that were reflective and activating in form and aimed at the development of a career identity and career-oriented actions in content (Kuijpers & Meijers, 2017).

Previous studies on the COG/SVE innovation project focused on the collective learning of teacher teams and on the role of the team leaders and other managers regarding changing the learning environment of the students (see Draaisma, Meijers, & Kuijpers, 2017, 2018a, 2018b). It was found that ongoing communication between the different levels of the organisation (teachers, middle managers, and higher managers) as an aspect of developing a vision and policy seemed advisable to ensure full support from all involved. Determining the direction of the learning process together exerted a positive influence on the outcomes of educational reform. Furthermore, clear policy and direction and collective learning are required to establish changes in the learning environment of students.

Teachers as Career Guides: Changing Their Role Perception

The development of a career identity takes place by means of meaningful real-life (work) experiences and individual conversations about these experiences (Kuijpers et al., 2011; Meijers & Lengelle, 2012, 2016). During these conversations, teachers are required to adopt a guiding role and ask purposeful questions that will allow students to draw their own conclusions instead of transmitting information or controlling the situation. This new teacher behaviour of guiding instead of directing, and asking questions instead of talking, excludes giving advice and is instead based on reflections on prior experiences to learn from them for future experiences by uncovering personal motivations (Den Boer & Hoeve, 2017; Lodders & Meijers, 2017; Winters et al., 2013). Valuable conversations can take place during scheduled career conversations, but short conversations can also occur during classes or breaks, if situations are considered meaningful for the student.

The research by Winters (2012) showed that, when teachers develop a dialogical rather than a monological conversation style, students respond with more reflective answers. However, it also showed that, most of the time, teachers talk *to* instead of *with* students during career dialogues. Consequently, the focus of school-based career guidance is still mainly on helping students to further their academic achievement and not on helping them to construct their career aspirations and prepare for their work roles and career competencies after the completion of their education.

Changing the attitudes of teachers towards their students from primarily knowledge transfer to a focus on ongoing career development requires substantial changes in their daily practice and therefore a change in their role perception. Den Boer and Hoeve (2017) argued that, for educational change to occur, a change in the routines of teachers and their teams is fundamental. Routines are patterns of behaviour that supply stability; changing routines generates chaos and uncertainty and can therefore be experienced as undesirable. Based on Nelson and Winter (1982), it has been argued that collective routines involve different roles, describing what individual group members do and why. From a cultural approach, the routines and roles involved are part of the organisational culture, as they are the outcome of organisational norms and values and direct behaviour and attitudes. Peterson and Spencer (1991, p. 142) described the organisational culture as 'the deeply embedded patterns of organisational behaviour and the shared values, assumptions, beliefs, or ideolcgies that members have about their organization and its work'. Changing the organisational culture of a school or teacher team therefore means changing these deeply embedded patterns (Blood & Thorsborne, 2005).

The beliefs that teachers hold about education and being a good teacher have been argued to influence their actual behaviour in the classroom (Assen, Meijers, Otting, & Poell, 2016; Korthagen, 2004; Pajares, 1992). Therefore, teachers' perception of their own role as a teaching professional plays an essential part in students' learning environment and schools' culture. Teachers' role perception refers to the self-description of teachers and is the answer to questions such as 'What does it mean to call oneself a teacher?', 'How do I see myself as a teacher?', and 'What kind of teacher do I want to be?' (Korthagen, 2004; Van Lankveld et al., 2017). Role perception includes task perception too (Kelchtermans, 2009).

Teachers' role perception is part of their professional identity, which is seen as a dynamic process, negotiated through experiences, consisting of multiple sub-identities, and difficult to separate from the non-professional self (Beauchamp & Thomas, 2009; Beijaard et al., 2000; Beijaard, Meijer, & Verloop, 2004; Vloet, 2015). Like teachers' professional identity, role perception implies both a person and a context, as it is as much about what teachers find to be important in their profession as it is about the conceptions and expectations of others about the profession (Beauchamp & Thomas, 2009; Beijaard et al., 2004). Research concentrating on transforming certain aspects of professional identity, such as roles and responsibilities, with a focus on external influences is to a large extent lacking (Trede, Macklin, & Bridges, 2012).

Aim and Research Questions

In this chapter, we aim to answer the following research question: *To what extent have the role perceptions of teachers participating in a national project regarding career learning changed since its start, and to what extent are these changes influenced by changes on the school organisational level?* Based on the aforementioned literature and previous studies regarding the project (see Draaisma et al., 2017, 2018a, 2018b), it is probable that the perceptions of the teachers concerning their role in education are an essential part of the targeted reculturing of the organisations. Therefore, we expected them to be influenced by school organisational factors, such as the collective learning of teacher teams, the middle and higher management involved, and the development of a clear policy for career learning. Furthermore, we anticipated learning from their individual experiences to understand the general dynamics occurring during reculturing and providing recommendations for future innovation.

This research comprised a longitudinal qualitative study, designed to investigate the extent to which the COG/SVE project has provided an impulse for changes in teachers' role perception and to explore explanations for these developments.

Method

The measurement occasions of this longitudinal study took place from October 2013 to June 2016. In this section, the sample is described as well as the selection procedure of the sample, when and in what way the data were collected, and how these were analysed.

Sample and Selection

As part of the COG/SVE project, 2 central training days were organised for 238 teachers from 20 of the 34 participating schools during the period from September to December 2013. The schools were spread throughout the Netherlands and included inner-city schools as well as schools in rural regions. The teachers from the 14 other schools received their training at a different time and were therefore not included in this study.

In October 2013, at the start of their first training day, 238 participating teachers completed a questionnaire on their personal motivation and aspirations regarding the project and on the existence of their school's policy and vision concerning COG. Teachers with contrasting scores on the questionnaire were approached personally to provide the maximum variation in sampling (Miles, Huberman, & Saldaña, 2014) and to avoid distorted results. Eventually, 50 selected teachers from 18 different schools agreed to participate in 2013. During our longitudinal study, three teachers who were interviewed in 2013 were excluded from the sample due to their lack of willingness to participate in later measurements or having left the school as a teacher. Of the 47 participating teachers, 30 were female, 41 taught specific subjects, and 6 worked exclusively as student guides or career counsellors. All the teachers took part on a voluntary and anonymous basis.

Data Collection

We interviewed the selected teachers four times over a period of three years. The first interviews took place from October 2013 to January 2014, during or just after the second off-the-job training day. Forty-four interviews were recorded with a video camera, one interview was conducted via Skype (and recorded), one interview was conducted through a non-recorded telephone conversation, and one teacher answered the questions in writing.

The second interview took place approximately six months later and the third a year after the second interview. Respectively thirty-seven and thirty-eight interviews were conducted through non-recorded telephone conversations. Notes were taken during the interviews, and these were processed immediately afterwards into interview reports. During both measurements, seven interviews were conducted face to face, recorded with a video camera, and transcribed verbatim to provide multiple in-depth interviews as additions to the shorter telephone conversations. Respectively three and two teachers did not respond to our requests regarding this measurement.

The fourth and last interview took place another year later, in April to June 2016. Forty-one interviews were conducted face to face and recorded with either a video camera or an audio device to enable verbatim transcription of the interviews. Six interviews were conducted through a non-recorded telephone conversation, processed immediately afterwards into interview reports, and member checked by the teachers.

The interviews conducted with the 47 teachers were semi-structured. The researchers monitored a list of topics that had to be covered during each measurement. The emphasis of the interviews was on the teachers' perspective concerning COG in the school and their role in providing this for their students. Furthermore, we discussed the changes experienced since the start of the project in the daily practice of the teachers as well as the changes at the organisational level, at the team level, and at the student level. The teachers also described their experiences of conducting career dialogues with the students. All the face-to-face interviews took between 20 and 75 min, with an average of approximately 45 min. All the telephone interviews took approximately 15 min.

Analyses

We first analysed the interviews with the forty-seven teachers who participated in all four measurements. We scored each interview on three different aspects of the teachers' role perception, if possible, to determine whether any developments in the aspects were observable. The emphasis of our study was on the first and last measurements to elicit the total development during the project. We identified segments in the interviews that indicated the teachers' views of what 'being a (good) teacher' meant regarding career guidance and what the teachers thought the corresponding tasks of 'being a (good) teacher' were.

Focusing on the role perception of a dialogical career guide, the scoring scales developed were as follows: *diploma focused to career focused*, *monological to dialogical*, and *directing to guiding*. The scales were developed by means of the described literature as well as a pilot of four interviews with five teachers that were scored by different authors. During this development process, regular meetings between the authors were held to adjust the scales until they were clearly distinctive. Each interview received one score per scale, from one (mostly diploma focused, monological, or directing) to four (mostly career focused, dialogical, or guiding; see Appendix 1 for the categories related to each score).

After the scoring of measurement 4, an indication of the development since measurement 1 on each aspect per teacher was given (− = 1 score down, . = same score, + = 1 score up, ++ = 2 scores up). In this way, we were able to construct an overview of the changes observed in the 47 teachers' role perception, focusing on career guidance. We made a distinction between 'regular' teachers and teachers who were also school coaches, meaning that they had received extended training to train the teachers of their school in COG. During and after the phase of analysis, regular meetings between the authors were held to discuss the methods, procedure, and findings.

To investigate whether the observed changes were influenced by the school organisational changes initiated by the COG/SVE project, we thereafter clustered the developments of the teachers and school coaches of the same schools.

Results

Changes in Role Perception

To answer the research question concerning the extent to which the role perception of teachers participating in the COG/SVE project had changed since the start of the project, we constructed Table 1, as explained in the Method section. The scores of the individual teachers in Table 1 generally show a linear development between all four measurements. Therefore, we focus on the results of the first and last measurements.

As can be seen, 20 out of 30 'regular' teachers scored 2 (*more diploma focused, less career focused*) at measurement 1 and only 6 (20%) scored higher than 2 (*more career focused* and *mostly career focused*) at the same point. This means that, during measurement 1, most teachers were predominantly diploma focused and less career focused. For the school coaches, 9 out of 17 (53%) scored 3 or 4 in measurement 1, which means that they were *more career focused, less diploma focused*, or *mostly career focused*. For the other two scales, the differences between the 'regular' teachers and the school coaches were rather small. Furthermore, in measurement 1, the 47 teachers typically scored higher on the *monological to dialogical* and *directing to guiding* scales than on the *diploma-focused to career-focused* scale. On the *monological to dialogical* and *directing to guiding* scales, the teachers and school coaches mostly scored 3, *more dialogical* and *more guiding* (respectively 19 and 26) in measurement 1. Most (27) teachers and school coaches scored 2 (*more diploma focused*) and 12 scored 3 (*more career focused*) on the *diploma-focused to career-focused* scale in measurement 1. This shows that the teachers already perceived their behaviour as 'high' for a dialogical and guiding educational attitude immediately

Table 1 Development of career focused, dialogical and guiding perception of teachers' role over 4 measurements

	Career focused			Dialogical			Guiding		
	M1	M4	Development	M1	M4	Development	M1	M4	Development
Teacher									
1	2	2	.		3	.	3	3	.
2	2	2	.	3	3	.	3	3	.
3		3	.	3	3	.	3	4	+
4	2	3	+		2	.	3	3	.
5	2	2	.	3	3	.	3	3	.
6	1	3	++		2	.	2	3	+
7	2	3	+	2	4	++	2	3	+
8	2	3	+	3	2	–	2	2	.
9	2	3	+	3	3	.	4	4	.
10	2	2	.	2	2	.	3	2	–
11	1	3	++	1	2	+	2	3	+
12	2	2	.	2		.	3	3	.
13	2	1	–		2	.			
14	2			2			2		
15	2	2	.		2				
16	2	3	+	3	3	.	3	3	.
17	3	3	.	2	3	+	3	3	.
18	2	3	+	2		.	2	3	+
19	3			4	4	.	3	3	.
20				3			3	3	.
21	2	2	.	3	2	–	2	3	+
22	2	2	.		2		3	2	–
23	3		.				3		.
24	2	3	+	3	3	.	3	3	.
25	2	3	+	3	3	.	2	3	+
26	3	3	.	2	3	+			
27	3	3	.	2	2	.	3		.
28	2	4	++		4	+	3	4	+
29	2	2	.	2	3	+	3	3	.
30	3	2	–	3	2	–	3		
School coach									
31p	3	4	+	3	4	+	4	4	.
32	4	4	.	4	4	.	4	4	.

(continued)

Table 1 (continued)

	Career focused			Dialogical			Guiding		
	M1	M4	Development	M1	M4	Development	M1	M4	Development
33p	2	2	.	2			2		
34	2	2	.	2	2	.		3	.
35	2	3	+	3	3	.		3	.
36p	3	4	+					3	.
37	2	3	+	2	3	+			
38					3	.			
39	3	3	.	3	3	.	3	3	.
40	4	4	.			.	3	4	+
41p	3	4	+	3	3	.	3		+
42	2	2	.	3	2	–	3	3	.
43	2	3	+	3		.	3	3	.
44	3	3	.	3	3	.	3	3	.
45	2		++	2	3	+	3		.
46	4	4	.	3	3	.	3	4	+
47	3	4	+			.	2	3	+

p = also project manager, n = non response, empty = no scoring possible due to the content of the interview
− = 1 score down, . = same score, + = 1 score up, ++ = 2 scores up

after or on the first day of the training programme but relatively low on being career focused.

Furthermore, Table 1 shows the most considerable development for the *diploma-focused to career-focused* scale, indicating visible development among the teachers' own perception from being diploma focused towards being more career focused. In all, 19 of the 47 teachers ('regular' teachers as well as school coaches) showed an increase in scores on this scale, with 4 of them scoring 2 points higher than during measurement 1. Of all the teachers, 22 scored the same during the first and last measurements. For the *monological to dialogical* scale, most teachers (27) also showed no change between the first and the last measurement. The scores of 9 teachers increased between the first and the last measurement: considerably fewer than those with increasing scores on the *diploma-focused to career-focused* scale. Finally, for the *directing to guiding* scale, 12 teachers showed an increase for the last measurement compared with the first and 25 teachers scored the same in both measurements. For all 3 scales, the scores of only a few teachers (respectively 2, 4, and 2) declined.

To conclude, the scores showed that many teachers were considerably more *diploma focused* at measurement 1, the starting situation, than at measurement 4, when they scored higher for being *career focused*. The school coaches started with higher scores than the 'regular' teachers at measurement 1. Furthermore, the *diploma-focused to career-focused* scale experienced the most considerable development, with 19 of the 47 teachers showing an increase. For the *monological to dialogical* and *directing to guiding* scales, most teachers showed no change between the first and the last measurement.

School-Specific Stimulating Factors

To address possible explanations for the different patterns in changing role perception in greater depth, we clustered the teachers and school coaches of the 18 different schools. In this way, we were able to explore the potential change patterns within the same schools (see Table 2) to investigate the extent of the influence of school organisational factors.

Table 2 Teachers' development in role perception, clustered per school

	Teacher	School coach	Development career focused	Development dialogical	Development guiding
School					
1					
	1		.	.	.
	4		+	.	.
	6		+	.	+
		31p	+	+	.
2					
	2		.	.	.
		33p	.		
3					
	3		.	.	+
	5		.	.	.
		32	.	.	.
4					
	7		+	++	+
5					
	8		+	–	.
	9		+	.	.
	11		++	+	+
	12		.	.	.
	13		–	.	

(continued)

Table 2 (continued)

	Teacher	School coach	Development career focused	Development dialogical	Development guiding
6					
	10		.	.	–
		34	.	.	.
7					
	14				
8					
	15		.		
	16		+	.	.
	17		.	+	.
		36p	+		.
9					
	18		+	.	+
		38		.	
10					
	19			.	.
	20				.
		39	.	.	.
		43	+	.	.
11					
	21		.	–	+
	22		.		–
		44	.	.	.
12					
	23		.		.
	24		+	.	.
13					
	25		+	.	+
14					
	26		.	+	
	27		.	.	.
	28		++	+	+
		47	+	.	+
15					
	29		.	+	.
	30		–	–	

(continued)

Table 2 (continued)

	Teacher	School coach	Development career focused	Development dialogical	Development guiding
		39	.	.	.
		45	++	+	.
		46	.	.	+
16					
		35	+	.	.
		37	+	+	
17					
		40	.	.	+
		42	.	–	.
18					
		41p	+	.	+

p = also project manager, n = non response, empty = no scoring possible due to the content of the interview
– = 1 score down, . = same score, + = 1 score up

The clustered scores per school showed that, within the schools, the change patterns of the individual teachers and school coaches are in many cases not comparable. The scores for the scales *diploma focused to career focused*, *monological to dialogical*, and *directing to guiding* for teachers and school coaches in the same schools did not show the same development, even though their organisational factors were the same. Therefore, based on the interviews with the 47 teachers, it appears that the factors of influence differ for individual teachers and that the changes observed in teachers' role perception might be influenced but are not determined by school-specific organisational factors.

Discussion of the Results

With this study, we aimed to answer the research question: *To what extent have the role perceptions of teachers participating in a national project regarding career learning changed since its start, and to what extent are these changes influenced by changes on the school organisational level?* The results showed that many teachers were more diploma focused at measurement 1, the starting situation, but they scored higher on being career focused at the last measurement. Less development was shown on the *monological to dialogical* and *directing to guiding* scales through the following measurements. This can be explained by the positions that the teachers held within their organisations: all the teachers except six taught subjects in classes, but, although the COG/SVE project requested complete teacher teams to participate in the training programme, most schools sent groups of teachers who were already active in some form of student guidance, such as mentorship and work placement supervision. The initial high scores related to a dialogical and guiding perception of their role as a (good) teacher showed that the form of their approach to students did not develop substantially, although the content of their communication with students became more career focused than in the first measurements.

It appeared that the school coaches generally scored higher than the 'regular' teachers in measurement 1 and the last measurement for all three scales. At the first measurement point, this could be explained by their probable prior affinity with (career) guidance and in the second measurement also by the extended training that the school coaches received to train teams of teachers in conducting career dialogues. The school coaches received not only more information and practice than the other teachers but also guidance in actively processing this information and integrating practice into their own COG training. This indicates that extended training, such as that provided by school coach training, is beneficial to changes in teachers' role perception.

To investigate whether these changes can be explained by school organisational changes initiated by the COG/SVE project, we clustered the developments of the teachers of the same schools. However, within the schools represented in our study, the change patterns of the individual teachers and school coaches of the same schools differed. The organisational changes that were stimulated by the COG/SVE project did lead to a development in being more career focused at the level of individual teachers. The ways in which these organisational changes were interpreted and internalised by the teachers, however, were dissimilar.

This research showed that individual changes are stimulated by the COG/SVE project and that these changes differ for teachers of the same schools. A possible explanation for this finding could be a lack of individual support by team leaders and other middle managers, which was detected in earlier research on the COG/SVE project (Draaisma et al., 2017, 2018a, 2018b). Changing established roles is challenging (Den Boer & Hoeve, 2017), as a change of behaviour can cause uncertainty. It could therefore require a form of guidance that is open and safe, one in which vulnerability is allowed. Furthermore, motivation for learning and developing is present within individuals, as long as their basic psychological needs for autonomy, feelings of competence, and social relatedness are satisfied (Deci & Ryan, 2008). It is possible that the lack of individual support of teachers during the change process led to an absence of this satisfaction.

Based on our findings and the aforementioned literature, it is expected that through dialogues changes in the organisational culture of the schools can be experienced, as reculturing is a process of co-creating new meanings in situations of ambiguity and uncertainty in a dialogical manner (Fullan, 2007; Geijsel, Meijers, & Wardekker, 2007). Individual learning requires reflection, which takes place in internal and external dialogues (Schellhammer, 2018). After making the new knowledge and skills of the individual explicit through dialogic reflection, this knowledge can be shared with other members of the collective. In this way, not only are dialogue and reflection awarded to students; rather, by maintaining the principles of COG throughout the organisation, a dialogic career learning environment can also be established in the work environment of teachers.

Limitations and Future Research

This study was exploratory in nature, as, to our knowledge, research on transforming the role perception of teachers regarding career guidance has not been conducted previously. Therefore, our frame of analysis was developed for this study. Although we have discussed the categories in relation to our data thoroughly and consider that our analysis sets out the rather abstract concept of role perception regarding dialogical career guides accurately, it would be advisable to advance a framework for future research. As we scored the interviews within the framework by looking for segments that expressed the categories formulated, we recommend quantifying the categories by means of the example statements in Appendix 1. In this way, quantitative research on measuring role perception regarding career guidance can be developed.

Furthermore, the teacher interviews that we analysed in determining role perception were all self-reported and therefore subjective. Previous research has shown that teachers evaluate their student-centred attitudes more highly than their students do (Meijers, Kuijpers, & Bakker, 2006) and than is apparent from observations (Assen et al., 2016). Taking this into consideration by drawing conclusions based on the behaviour originating from the role perception of teachers is recommended.

We found that fostering changes in teachers' role perception can be viewed mainly as an individual process in interaction with the environment as opposed to focusing primarily on collective learning processes. To gain more insights into this individual process and the way in which it can be guided or supported by others, we recommend conducting future research on the interplay between the individual, the collective, and the context. The perspective of professional identity learning is a valuable addition to the role perception perspective, as professional and personal identity learning includes other roles, tasks, and personality traits of teachers (Assen et al., 2016; Trede et al., 2012; Vloet, 2015). Further research in this area could help to define the—as yet—ambiguous concept of professional identity and the external influences on its formation and transformation processes. Furthermore, future research could determine the ways in which changes in the role perception of teachers is related to changes in their actual behaviour towards students, both individually and in the collective routines and practices of teacher teams.

Conclusion

In this study, we provided a description of the changed perceptions of the participants' roles as teachers by conducting interviews with the teachers on four different measurements, discussing their perspective on teaching in the initiated career learning environment for their students. It showed the consequences of the changes in the work environment of teachers, brought about by the project, on the level of the individual teachers. This research indicated that individual changes are stimulated by the COG/SVE project but that these changes differ for teachers of the same schools. The results showed that most teachers were considerably more career focused at the fourth measurement than they were at the start. Teachers who received extended training to become a school coach generally scored higher than the 'regular' teachers during the first and last measurements on being career focused as well as on being more guiding than directing and being more dialogical than monological. However, different change patterns for individual teachers and for school coaches of the same schools or even teacher teams were found, even though the same organisational factors mostly applied to the entire school. The changes in role perceptions of the individual teachers therefore seemed to be stimulated in different ways.

By means of the study described in this chapter, a more complete understanding of teachers' role perception and the (conditions of the) role-changing process was formulated. This contributes to more effective programmes for developing professionalism and individual guidance in the context of educational reform, as it provides an analytic lens for teacher role development and for sense making by teachers themselves in times of uncertainty and change. Finally, implementing educational innovation is a collective matter through team learning, but it requires support and guidance for each individual to address his or her own process of change.

Appendix 1: Scales of Role Perception for Analysing Teacher Interviews

Diploma focused to career focused

1. **Mostly diploma focused**. *The only purpose of our education is to obtain the diploma, because the students have already chosen their course. I try to keep them in and help them through their courses. Conversations with students are about diplomas, grades, and study skills.*
2. **More diploma focused, less career focused**. *COG is a method and consists mainly of choosing further education and preventing students from dropping out. Students have already chosen their course, but, if that choice proves to be wrong, I'll help them find something else. I keep an eye on the students' possibilities and keep them realistic.*
3. **More career focused, less diploma focused**. *I need to pay attention to the students' career, and switching is fine if that is better for the student. I give students classroom assignments in preparation for their career and continue with what they take from the pre-education regarding career orientation. I talk with them about their work placements.*
4. **Mostly career focused**. *I am a COG guide. I prepare students for lifelong learning and their future. Career guiding is an important task of secondary*

vocational education, and my job is to help students to develop and reflect on their career skills and to maintain their dreams. We are failing our students if we do not do this.

Monological to dialogical

1. **Mostly monological**. *I inform students about further education and about the student himself (what he can do or does). Conversations with students should be short and effective, using certain conversational techniques. If students are doing well, they do not need dialogues with me.*
2. **More monological, less dialogical**. *I work with my students in groups on COG assignments, in which they talk to each other about their careers. I conduct one-to-one conversations with students who are not doing well, not with the students who are doing well.*
3. **More dialogical, less monological**. *I can help students reflect and develop by asking questions about their qualities and motives. For these conversations, I wish to take time, which is not always possible. Sometimes I give group assignments on COG, but I also want to conduct one-to-one career conversations with all students, including the ones who are doing well.*
4. **Mostly dialogical**. *I conduct dialogues with students as often as possible, also during and between classes, and I am an equal conversation partner. I listen to students and take them seriously. I pay as much attention to students who are doing well as to those who are not and try to conduct an (individual) dialogue with students in group lessons.*

Directing to guiding

1. **Mostly directing**. *I direct students in their career and conduct conversations with students to lead them towards a different course if that is more suitable. Students often do not know what they want and can do, and I mostly do. Students who are doing well do not need guidance.*
2. **More directing, less guiding**. *I try to show students the right direction, and I advise on their career. I can make them more aware of what they want and can do.*
3. **More guiding, less directing**. *I want to motivate students for the next challenge, activate them, and make them think. I find guidance interesting, and I look at the individual students. I ask what they are going to do themselves and what steps they are going to take. I can help them learn and reflect by developing career competencies.*
4. **Mostly guiding**. *I am a guide, as every good teacher is. I listen to students, follow their development, offer support where necessary, and help them take their own steps. Education is about what the students want, not about what the school/teacher/government wants.*

References

Assen, J., Meijers, F., Otting, H., & Poell, R. (2016). Explaining discrepancies between teacher beliefs and teacher interventions in a problem-based learning environment: A mixed methods study. *Teaching and Teacher Education, 60,* 12–23.

Beauchamp, C., & Thomas, L. (2009). Understanding teacher identity: An overview of issues in the literature and implications for teacher education. *Cambridge Journal of Education, 39,* 175–189.

Beijaard, D., Meijer, P., & Verloop, N. (2004). Reconsidering research on teachers' professional identity. *Teaching and Teacher Education, 20,* 107–128.

Beijaard, D., Verloop, N., & Vermunt, J. (2000). Teachers' perceptions of professional identity: An exploratory study from a personal knowledge perspective. *Teaching and Teacher Education, 16,* 749–764.

Blood, P., & Thorsborne, M. (2005, March). *The challenge of culture change: Embedding restorative practice in schools.* Paper presented at the Sixth International Conference on Conferencing, Circles and other Restorative Practices: Building a Global Alliance for Restorative Practices and Family Empowerment, Sydney, Australia. Retrieved from http://www.thorsborne.com.au/conference_papers/Challenge_of_Culture_Change.pdf.

Deci, E., & Ryan, R. (2008). Self-determination theory: A macrotheory of human motivation, development, and health. *Canadian Psychology/Psychologie Canadienne, 49,* 182.

Den Boer, P., & Hoeve, A. (2017). A routine perspective on implementing reflective career conversations in education. *British Journal of Guidance and Counselling, 45,* 178–187.

Draaisma, A., Meijers, F., & Kuijpers, M. (2017). Towards a strong career learning environment: Results from a Dutch longitudinal study. *British Journal of Guidance and Counselling, 45,* 165–177.

Draaisma, A., Meijers, F., & Kuijpers, M. (2018a). Process description of a dialogue-focused intervention to improve career guidance policy in three schools. *Australian Journal of Career Development, 27,* 40–53.

Draaisma, A., Meijers, F., & Kuijpers, M. (2018b). The development of strong career learning environments: The project 'Career Orientation and Guidance' in Dutch vocational education. *Journal of Vocational Education and Training., 70,* 27–46.

Fullan, M. (2007). *The new meaning of educational change*. New York, NY: Teachers College Press.

Geijsel, F., & Meijers, F. (2005). Identity learning: The core process of educational change. *Educational Studies, 31,* 419–430.

Geijsel, F., Meijers, F., & Wardekker, W. (2007). Leading the process of reculturing: Roles and actions of school leaders. *The Australian Educational Researcher, 34,* 135–161.

Hoekstra, A., Brekelmans, M., Beijaard, D., & Korthagen, F. (2009). Experienced teachers' informal learning: Learning activities and changes in behavior and cognition. *Teaching and Teacher Education, 25,* 663–673.

Hooley, T., Watts, A., & Andrews, D. (2015). *Teachers and careers: The role of school teachers in delivering career and employability learning*. Derby, United Kingdom: The International Centre for Guidance Studies, University of Derby.

Hughes, D., Meijers, F., & Kuijpers, M. (2015). Testing times: Careers market policies and practices in England and the Netherlands. *British Journal of Guidance and Counselling, 43,* 183–201.

Kelchtermans, G. (2009). Who I am in how I teach is the message: Self-understanding, vulnerability and reflection. *Teachers and Teaching: Theory and Practice, 15,* 257–272.

Korthagen, F. (2004). In search of the essence of a good teacher: Towards a more holistic approach in teacher education. *Teaching and Teacher Education, 20,* 77–97.

Kuijpers, M., & Meijers, F. (2017). Professionalising teachers in career dialogue: Effect study. *British Journal of Guidance and Counselling, 45,* 83–96.

Kuijpers, M., Meijers, F., & Gundy, C. (2011). The relationship between learning environment and career competencies of students in vocational education. *Journal of Vocational Behavior, 78,* 21–30.

Lengelle, R., Meijers, F., & Van der Heijden, B. (2017). The foundations of career resilience. In K. Maree (Ed.), *Psychology of career adaptability, employability and resilience* (pp. 29–47). New York, NY: Springer.

Lieberman, A., & Pointer Mace, D. (2008). Teacher learning: The key to educational reform. *Journal of Teacher Education, 59,* 226–234.

Lodders, N., & Meijers, F. (2017). Collective learning, transformational leadership and new forms of careers guidance in universities. *British Journal of Guidance & Counselling, 45,* 532–546.

Meijers, F. (2001). The effects of the marketisation of career guidance services in The Netherlands. *International Journal for the Advancement of Counselling, 23,* 131–149.

Meijers, F., Kuijpers, M., & Bakker, J. (2006). Over leerloopbanen en loopbaanleren. Loopbaancompetenties in het (v)mbo [About learning careers and career learning. Career competencies in vocational education]. Driebergen: Het Platform BeroepsOnderwijs.

Meijers, F., & Kuijpers, M. (2014). Career learning and career learning environment in Dutch higher education. *Journal of Applied Research in Higher Education, 6,* 295–313.

Meijers, F., Kuijpers, M., & Gundy, C. (2013). The relation between career competencies, career identity, motivation and quality of choice. *International Journal for Educational and Vocational Guidance, 13,* 47–66.

Meijers, F., & Lengelle, R. (2012). Narratives at work: The development of career identity. *British Journal of Guidance and Counselling, 40,* 157–176.

Meijers, F., & Lengelle, R. (2016). Reflective career dialogues. *South African Journal of Higher Education, 30,* 21–35.

Miles, M., Huberman, A., & Saldaña, J. (2014). *Qualitative data analysis: A methods sourcebook.* Thousand Oaks, CA: Sage.

Mittendorff, K. (2010). *Career conversations in senior secondary vocational education* (Doctoral dissertation). Eindhoven University of Technology, Eindhoven, The Netherlands. Retrieved from https://pure.tue.nl/ws/files/3197781/201010118.pdf.

Nelson, R., & Winter, S. (1982). *An evolutionary theory of economic change.* Cambridge, MA: Belknap Press of Harvard University Press.

Oomen, A., Van den Dungen, M., Pijls, T., & Egelie, J. (2012). *Career development in the Netherlands: State of play.* 's- Hertogenbosch, The Netherlands: Euroguidance Netherlands.

Pajares, M. (1992). Teachers' beliefs and educational research: Cleaning up a messy construct. *Review of Educational Research, 62,* 307–332.

Peterson, M., & Spencer, M. (1991). Understanding academic culture and climate. In M. Peterson (Ed.), *ASHE reader on organization and governance* (pp. 140–155). Needham Heights, MA: Simon & Schuster.

Schellhammer, B. (2018). Dialogical self as a prerequisite for intercultural adult education. *Journal of Constructivist Psychology, 31,* 6–21.

Schulz, B. (2008). The importance of soft skills: Education beyond academic knowledge. *NAWA Journal of Language and Communication, 2,* 146–154.

Smith, E., & Comyn, P. (2004). The development of employability skills in novice workers through employment. In *Generic skills in vocational education and training: Research readings* (pp. 95–108). Retrieved from http://files.eric.ed.gov/fulltext/ED493988.pdf.

Trede, F., Macklin, R., & Bridges, D. (2012). Professional identity development: A review of the higher education literature. *Studies in Higher Education, 37,* 365–384.

Van Lankveld, T., Schoonenboom, J., Kusurkar, R., Volman, M., Beishuizen, J., & Croiset, G. (2017). Integrating the teaching role into one's identity: A qualitative study of beginning undergraduate medical teachers. *Advances in Health Sciences Education, 22,* 601–622.

Vloet, K. (2015). *Professionele identiteitsontwikkeling van leraren als dialogisch proces. Een narratieve studie in een masteropleiding in speciale onderwijszorg en loopbaanbegeleiding van leerlingen* [Teachers' professional identity development as dialogical process. A narrative study in a Master course in Special Educational Needs and career guidance of students] (Doctoral dissertation). Universiteit voor Humanistiek, Utrecht, The Netherlands. Retrieved from https://core.ac.uk/download/pdf/53106356.pdf.

Winters, A. (2012). *Career learning in vocational education: Guiding conversations for career development* (Doctoral dissertation). Katholieke Universiteit Leuven, Leuven, Belgium. Retrieved from https://core.ac.uk/download/pdf/34536259.pdf.

Winters, A., Meijers, F., Harlaar, M., Strik, A., Baert, H., & Kuijpers, M. (2013). The narrative quality of career conversations in vocational education. *Journal of Constructivist Psychology, 26,* 115–126.

Using Technology to Promote Innovation in Career Counselling

Innovating Career Development Through Technology via a Cognitive Information Processing Theory Lens

Debra Sue Osborn

Abstract Today's technologies offer a wide array of venues through which career development can be facilitated. Both traditional technologies such as computer-assisted career guidance programs and trendy technologies such as phone apps provide new ways to help with constructing one's self-knowledge, learning about the world of work, fostering decision making skills, or managing dysfunctional career thinking. Social media has expanded the ways in which people learn about themselves and the world of work by actively connecting individuals with shared interests and passions. Opportunities to learn new skills are a video click away, as are free tests to identify one's personality and "perfect" career options. While the quantity of online information and resources is overwhelming, often the quality of these resources is questionable. When individuals are relying on these sources to inform and ultimately make career/life decisions, career practitioners have an ethical and moral obligation to help them evaluate the robustness of these instruments and information sources. Cognitive Information Processing theory (Sampson et al. in Career counselling and services: a cognitive information processing approach. Brooks/Cole, Pacific Grove, 2004) identifies four essential elements for designing and constructing a satisfying career. In this chapter, we will be using these four elements as an organizational framework for describing how today's technologies can be used in innovative ways to build competency in each of these areas. In addition, this chapter will address how career practitioners can help their clients navigate and evaluate the quality of online resources.

Chapter Structure

The aim of this chapter is to identify innovative approaches to career development through the use of technology. To help provide a structure to the various technological resources, a theoretical framework is provided. Thus, the first part of this chapter will focus on how one theory, i.e., Cognitive Information Processing (CIP) theory, is

D. S. Osborn (✉)
Florida State University, Tallahassee, USA
e-mail: dosborn@fsu.edu

J. G. Maree (ed.), *Handbook of Innovative Career Counselling*,
https://doi.org/10.1007/978-3-030-22799-9_40

used with traditional resources to enhance career construction. The second part of this chapter applies innovative technological approaches to the essential elements identified by CIP. The third section acknowledges and identifies potential ethical issues associated with the use of technology and career development. The fourth section discusses how technology can be used in innovative ways with career counselling theory, practice and research, with the final section identifying key areas for future research focused on technological innovations within the field of career counselling.

Constructing Careers via Cognitive Information Processing Theory

Cognitive Information Processing theory (CIP; Sampson, Reardon, Peterson, & Lenz, 2004), a career theory that has existed for over four decades, provides a clear pathway for helping individuals construct their careers. A primary aim of CIP theory is to help individuals increase their capability to make informed, thoughtful career decisions by examining key areas involved in career decision making and by working through a career decision-making process. The basic model of CIP identifies four essential elements that a person applies when constructing a career decision, pictured in the form of a pyramid of information processing (See Fig. 1). At the foundational level are self and options knowledge. Self-knowledge is comprised of everything central to an individual. In the past, this mainly included one's interests, values and skills, but today, this would include all elements that comprise a person's knowledge about self, so might include multiple identities of culture, religion, calling, gender, disability, socio-economic status, sexual orientation, political views, and so forth. Self-knowledge develops over time and may flex and change as one interacts with and adapts to their environment (Savickas, 2005). Traditional career interventions focused on building self-knowledge would be interest inventories, aptitude tests, autobiographies, card sorts, and the like.

Options knowledge includes knowledge about specific occupations such as work tasks, training paths, salaries, and also includes general information about the world of work, such as employment trends. Options knowledge can be expanded to include any path an individual is considering, such as educational and training possibilities, types of work (e.g., part time, full time, contract, entrepreneurial), and possible ways for constructing work in a person's life (e.g., how to balance work with other life roles and demands). One builds options knowledge through interfacing with information, people, and experiencing work and life. Thus, options knowledge may be biased, depending on the source and how the individual codes and inputs the information being received. Traditional career interventions aimed at building options knowledge would include providing the client with career and educational/training information and perhaps a way to organize career information, such as a table that allows for comparing options.

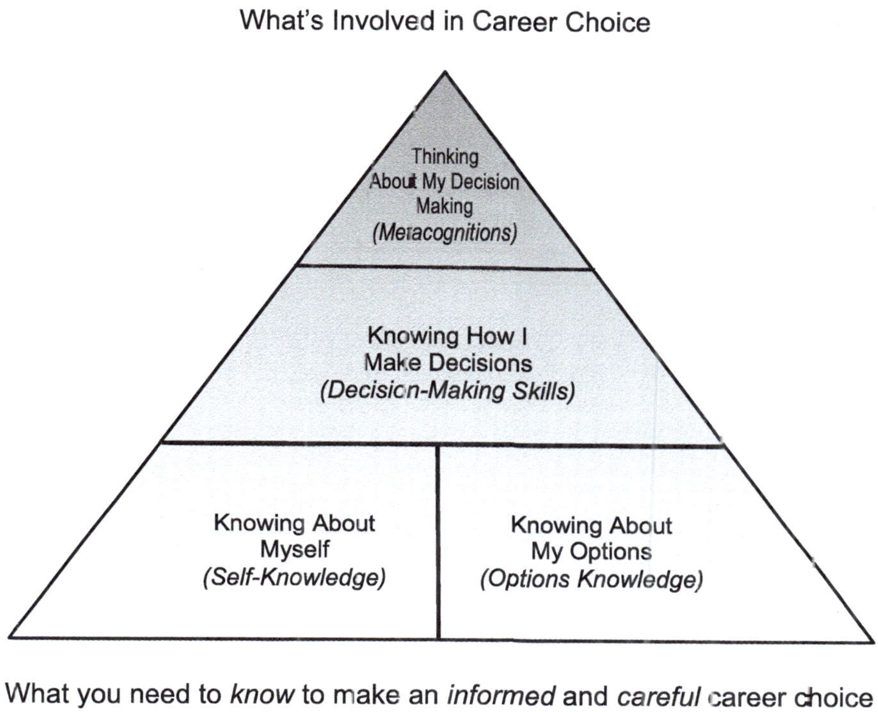

Fig. 1 Client version of the pyramid of information processing domains. Adapted from Sampson, Peterson, Lenz, and Reardon (1992)

If the foundational domains constitute the "knowing" aspect of constructing one's career, the middle domain represents the "doing" aspect, i.e., where and how the construction takes place. In the center of the pyramid is a cyclical decision-making model, called the CASVE (pronounced Cuh-Sah-Vay) Cycle (See Fig. 2). ***Communication*** is the first stage and is the moment at which a person becomes aware that there is a gap between where they are and where they want to be in terms of their career. This awareness could emerge internally (e.g., anxious feelings, somatic issues) or externally (e.g., others asking questions, requirements to make a field of study decision). ***Analysis*** occurs as a person considers, explores and prioritizes their self and options knowledge. This might involve the use of formal or informal assessments or career information from various sources. As one culminates this information, they also begin the often-simultaneous process of ***Synthesis-Elaboration*** or expanding and ***Synthesis-Crystallization*** narrowing of their options. Prioritizing a first choice and backup option is the goal of the next stage, ***Valuing***, often resulting from consideration of the costs and benefits of each option to the individual, their significant others, and society. In the ***Execution*** stage, a person tries out their first choice, whether through volunteering, taking a class, or through employment. As they interact with their first choice, they move back to the ***Communication (Revisited)*** stage where

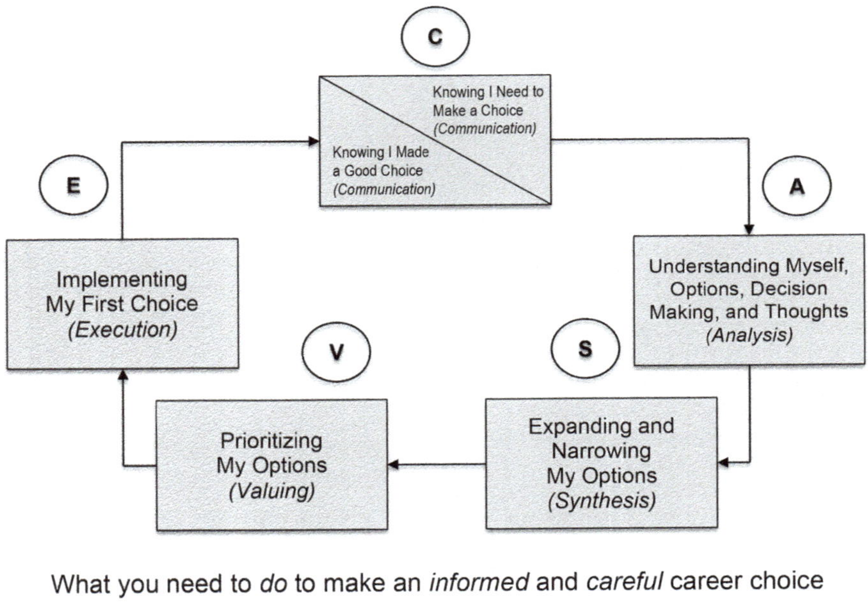

Fig. 2 A guide to good decision making: the CASVE cycle. Adapted from Sampson et al. (1992)

they evaluate their choice in light of internal and external cues and to determine the state of the gap. If the gap still remains, a person might consider their backup option or further analysis of self and options. Traditional career interventions aimed at enhancing career decision making might be decision making guides, such as the Guide to Good Decision Making (Sampson et al., 1992) or goal setting activities.

At the apex of the pyramid is the executive processing domain, which houses awareness and monitoring of self-talk. Negative self-talk has been predictive of career indecision (Bullock-Yowell, Peterson, Reardon, Leierer, & Reed, 2011; Kleiman et al., 2004), and can impact a person's capability to explore, build and engage in the other domains (Sampson et al., 2004). In addition, negative or dysfunctional career thinking such as "I can never make good decisions" or "I am not good at anything" has been linked to mental health concerns (Bullock-Yowell et al., 2011; Dieringer, Lenz, Hayden, & Peterson, 2017; Edralin, 2018; Finklea, 2016). These thoughts impact how an individual sees self and options, and when faulty begin to impede the decision-making process. It is at this time that they must be addressed. Traditional career interventions aimed at reducing negative or dysfunctional beliefs include identifying negative thoughts through inventories such as the Career Thoughts Inventory (CTI; Sampson, Peterson, Lenz, Reardon, & Saunders, 1996a) cognitive restructuring or disputing irrational beliefs (Bernard, 2009) or workbook activities, such as those in the CTI Workbook (Sampson, Peterson, Lenz, Reardon, & Saunders, 1996b).

These four elements (i.e., self-knowledge, options knowledge, decision making, and executive processing or self-talk) interact and impact each other. For example, one likely evaluates occupational information through the lens of self-knowledge. A person preferring to work with people will likely evaluate occupational information for the amount of time that occupation allows for social interactions. Negative self-talk impacts the way a person views themselves, their options, as well as their capability as a career decision maker. Thus, if negative self-talk is present, CIP recommends a career practitioner address and correct these thoughts prior to intervening with an assessment, information, or decision-making activities. If the metaphor of constructing a house is applied to constructing a career, dysfunctional career thoughts would be like ongoing rain that can weaken the foundation. The work of building the foundation of self and options knowledge is made that much more difficult when negative thoughts rain down and interfere. Only when the deluge of negative thoughts ceases can the foundation shore up to the point that solid, reliable construction can continue. While traditional tools can be used to enhance each component and at each step in the career decision-making process, the next section will examine how technology might provide further enhance the components and steps.

Innovative Approaches for Using Technology in Career Decision Making

Self Knowledge

Technological approaches for enhancing have traditionally included computer-assisted career guidance programs (CACGs; Betz & Turner, 2011) like *SIGI3* (sigi3.org) or *Focus* (focus2career.com), and standardized assessments such as the *Self-Directed Search* (*SDS*; Holland & Messer, 2013) the *Campbell Interest and Skill Survey* (*CISS*; Campbell, 1992), and the *Maree Career Matrix* (2016) many of which are available online. Technology can also be infused with constructivist approaches to building self-knowledge in innovative ways, such as through having individuals share their favorite YouTube videos that have meaning for them, or to use personal media to create their own digital narrative (Glavin, Smal, & Vandermeeren, 2008). The *Maree Career Matrix* (Maree, 2016) is an online assessment that offers an integrated theoretical approach (i.e., RIASEC, developmental and social learning) in assessing interests and confidence towards specific careers. Another constructivist assessment that has an online option is the *Career Interest Profile* (Mareee, 2017), which employs a narrative approach with open-ended questions that address several components of self-knowledge, such as biological details and family influences, reasons related to a person's career choices, an individual's preferences and dislikes, and several questions designed to obtain the career story narrative. Other technologically-based non-standardized approaches to exploring and constructing self-knowledge might include image or videos an individual posts on social media sites such as Pinterest, Instagram, or Facebook. For example, I was working with a client whose Facebook profile and the majority of photos posted were of him fishing, hunting, playing banjo, or guitar and singing. His RIASEC type was clearly in the Realistic and Artistic areas. Career practitioners who prefer non-standardized approaches such as collages or card sorts or clay or artwork, can help clients create a record of these via digital pictures that can be stored electronically or printed and kept in a file.

Options Knowledge

Perhaps the most commonly used technologies for providing career information in the United States are O*NET (onetonline.org), and the online Occupational Outlook Handbook (bls.gov/ooh). In the United Kingdom, online career information tools include prospects.ac.uk and jobs profiles through the National Career Service (nationalcareersservice.direct.gov.uk/job-profiles/home). Company websites provide information not only about the company, but also sometimes provide job descriptions that can be helpful at the career planning stages, in that an individual can proactively decide to include experiences such as volunteer work or a course on a specific topic that relates directly to the required or desired qualifications. Similarly, an individual can conduct an online search for a position with the word "resume" on it to see what others have included as experiences and training and use that as a guide.

Apps such as Glassdoor combine company and current job posting information with social media, where individuals post about their experiences with a company, ranging from interview questions asked to pros and cons of working there. Of course, the information presented is personally biased to the individual posting. The same is true for other sources of career information that have a social element, such as personal blogs, Twitter feeds, and the like. Sampson, Osborn, Kettunen, Hou, and Miller (2018) identified concerns about the validity of socially-constructed career information and potential types of bias that might be present. A key ethical concern is when individuals use invalid career information as a main basis for their career decision-making.

The gaming industry also provides users with opportunities to learn about work. Sims4: Get to Work allows players to experience being a doctor, scientist, detective or owner of a retail business. Webkinz is an interactive virtual world where children work at different jobs to earn "kinzcash" that enables them to purchase food, furnishings, and other items for a virtual stuffed animal that mirrors the one they purchased in the real world. Apps such as Happy Chef2 and Cooking Mama teach cooking skills, and sites such as agame.com provide simulation games for surgery, cooking, bartending, management, and the like.

With respect to career information, career development professionals are required to "assist clients in determining the validity and reliability of information found on websites and in other technology applications" (NCDA Code of Ethics, 2015, p. 17). Thus, part of the career practitioner's role should include teaching individuals how to evaluate the validity of career information, regardless of the form in which it is presented. This is a vital component of a career practitioner's role, in that individuals are often relying on career information and assessments we are using to make life decisions that may require years of training. Because a career practitioner will not always be by the side of a client, and due to the ease with which individuals can access information, teaching clients how to evaluate the credibility of career resources will hopefully extend that discernment of what is quality beyond the career session. Sampson et al. (2018) proposed four key elements of career information validity, including comprehensiveness, accuracy, relevancy and that it is understandable. In addition, they also noted the following areas of "information invalidity" (p. 127) that practitioners can review with clients, including bias (intentional or unintentional, popularity, or similarity), limited range of experience, outdated information, and lack of context being provided. A career practitioner can model how to evaluate career information, websites, or apps in real time with clients, as they access online resources together. Alternatively, a career practitioner could post a brief video on how to evaluate information or online resources, or create a checklist.

Decision Making Skills

Different technological instruments can be used at each stage of the decision-making process. As an example, consider the CASVE Cycle described earlier. For the *Communication* stage, an individual might engage with a mood tracker about their career decision, or journal about internal and external influencers. CACGs and online career information, among other tools outlined earlier can be used for exploring and building upon self and options knowledge in the *Analysis* stage. Brainstorming and mind-mapping apps and programs can be used in the *Synthesis* stage to expand and narrow options. Apps for comparing pros and cons can be used in the *Valuing* stage, but so could a simple table created as a fillable form. For *Execution*, list generators or reminder tools on smart phones or other devices can be used to outline next steps.

CACGs often have a decision-making component. For example, *SIGI3* has a section called "Analysis" that focuses on deciding. *FOCUS2* has a "Take Action Plan" section. Online career assessments resulting in a list of occupational matches often provide recommendations of next steps in the decision-making process that include strategies for learning options of interest. Beyond CACGs, there appears to be very few technology-based tools focused specifically on walking clients through the process of career decision making. Gati and Osipow's (2001–2014; cddq.org) *Career Decision Making Difficulties Questionnaire* was designed to identify barriers an individual might be facing with their career concern, and provides some potential next steps towards addressing those barriers.

General decision making and goal setting apps might be also be useful. For example, FYI Decision allows individuals to input the decision they are making, such as "choosing a career," and then add in self-constructed variables that are important to them (such as salary, training, related to interests or values). They then weight each of those variables on how important each is. Following this step, they add in the options they are considering, and then rate each of the options on each of the variables they identified. Following this, results are generated that show how each of the options compare to their weighted variables, and identify the "best choice" in relation to those weighted preferences. A pdf report can then be generated from that analysis.

While apps such as these can be useful, they are not based on career theory or models, such as the Guide to Good Decision-Making exercise (Sampson et al., 1992) that walks individuals through the CASVE Cycle. While an interactive version of the guide does not exist, the document can be converted into a writeable PDF to allow individuals to complete it electronically. In addition, if a client saves the document in the cloud, with tool such as Google drive, Dropbox, or Evernote, they can access it at different times in various locations, even editing and building upon it with their career practitioner. Having career theory-based decision-making apps or interactive websites is a present need within our field.

Self-talk

Apps devoted to helping individuals manage self-talk, engage in cognitive restructuring, and build self-esteem are ampler than those for other areas of career decision making. Some of these might be seen in the form of anxiety management, mindfulness, thought stopping, or wellness. Cognitive behavior therapy-based apps, such as Woebot guide users through challenging and altering negative cognitions. It appears that technological instruments focused on cognitive restructuring are increasing (Berry & Lai, 2014). Others (Osborn, Kronholz, Finklea, & Cantonis, 2014) suggest meditation, mindfulness, and journaling tools as other technological resources that can aid in addressing negative metacognitions. Clients can also use social media sites such as P*interest and Instagram, or online stickies such as padlet.com, to create boards or stories for self-affirmation. Today's techknowledgeable client can create their own meme's or gifs with encouraging mantras, or use a reminder app to send positive affirmations throughout the day. These could be using existing pictures of celebrities, or could be created using pictures of important people in the client's life paired with some encouraging words. Alternatively, a client might need to rely less on others' encouragement and more on their own. In that case, the client might create memes with their own pictures and self-created encouragements.

Innovation Is Not Without Risks

Technology offers multiple opportunities for fantastic innovation with career service delivery. However, career practitioners must be aware of the potential shortcomings and ethical considerations that are present with using technology and innovative approaches with clients and always act in accordance with standard ethical guidelines stipulated by national Ethics Committees. Some of these include security of information, client confidentiality, privacy, client readiness, access issues to the technologies, time required to train a client to use the technology, and evidence for using an untested, new intervention (Osborn et al., 2014). Career practitioners are also encouraged to not only evaluate online assessments and career information sources, but to teach their clients to do the same (Sampson et al., 2018). Professional organizations such as the National Career Development Association have provided ethical guidelines that address these and other issues.

Using Technology to Innovate Career Counselling Theory, Practice, and Research

Throughout this chapter, one career theory, *Cognitive Information Processing theory* (Sampson et al., 2004) has been used as an example of how technology can interface with theory and practice. Applications to other theories, such as RIASEC (Holland, 1997) are also possible. For constructivist and narrative approaches (Savickas, 2005), technologies described in the self-knowledge section can be applied in similar ways. For example, the *Career Interest Profile* (Maree, 2017) is an example of an online assessment that utilizes a narrative approach for helping individuals describe their career stories. Narrative approaches particularly lend themselves well to journaling and visual (image and video) programs and apps. These tools also provide a platform for individuals to tell personal stories of marginalization and create personal agency stories, a key assumption of Psychology of Working (Blustein, 2006; Duffy, Blustein, Diemer, & Austin, 2016) as well as a way to infuse culture (Arthur, 2017) and other influences a person is experiencing (Patton & McMahon, 2006) into the career conversation. They also provide a way to document experiences with happenstance (Krumboltz, 2009) and chaos (Pryor & Bright, 2003) and begin to identify themes. The technological resources provided for building options knowledge could also be applied to Super's (1980) *Exploration* stage. In addition, virtual reality and augmented reality provide additional avenues for individuals to experience tasks associated with specific occupations. Apps focusing on self-esteem, cognitive restructuring and self-efficacy can also apply to the beliefs portion of *Social Cognitive* career theory (Brown & Lent, 2005), as well as the self-observed generalizations in *Learning theory* (Krumboltz, 1996).

Practitioners already use these resources, such as apps, online career information, and social media sites in creative ways for their expediency and convenience, and also because clients are familiar and comfortable with them. Technology can make our interventions richer. What used to be a hand-written career autobiography can now include fewer words and more visual representations and symbols. Written out cognitive reframes can be transformed into verbal, self-recorded video mantras that are sent throughout the day. Shared applications and cloud capabilities allow clients and career practitioners to share files and access them from more than one location, thus reducing the likelihood of losing treatment plans, key websites, assessment results and increasing the potential for personal agency as well as ongoing collaboration and continued support as a person constructs not only their current career plan but creates a repository for their personal career history, their present career considerations, and their future plans. In addition, online provision of services, whether through a static website that provides career information and career guides or through synchronous chat options allows practitioners to extend their services and increase access to career services for all.

Recommendations for Further Research

Actual empirical research on the use of current technology to enhance career development is lagging behind the rapid, ongoing, expansive emergence of programs, apps, and tools and their efficacy for career service delivery. We have some evidence, although slightly dated and more general in nature, on the benefits of computer-assisted career guidance programs for informing career decisions (Niles & Garis, 1990; Osborn, Peterson, Sampson, & Reardon, 2003). More current studies on the validity and reliability of assessments embedded in these systems, as well as what types of career concerns or client characteristics are best served by specific aspects of CACGs are needed to help practitioners use these tools with higher precision. Comparison studies of traditional interventions such as decision-making guides or writing out cognitive reframes and apps focused on these activities are needed. Exploring how socially constructed career information impacts career decision-making among various groups is another avenue for research. The impact of virtual and augmented reality occupational experiences on career interest, exploration and commitment has yet to be explored. Understanding the benefits and drawbacks of providing career services virtually, as well as which interventions and which clients might be most favorable is yet another area that we must examine to ensure we are providing best practices. The research landscape for exploring the technology-career development interface is as vast and expansive as the emerging technologies themselves.

Conclusion

Integrating technology into career service delivery used to be limited to stand-alone CACGs or links to national career information and company websites. Advances in technologies continue to create innovative opportunities for career practitioners to enhance and extend career services for their clients. Coupled with these opportunities is the caution to ensure client safety and confidentiality. Given the time and expense that accompanies one's decision to pursue a specific career, we hold the responsibility to ensure that the tools we use with clients are valid and reliable, and that we use them in ways that have been shown to be beneficial for those whom we serve.

References

Arthur, N. (2017). Constructivist approaches to career counseling: A culture-infused approach. In M. McMahon (Ed.), *Career counseling: Constructivist approaches* (2nd ed., pp. 54–64). New York, NY: Routledge.

Bernard, M. E. (2009). Dispute irrational beliefs and teach rational beliefs: An interview with Albert Ellis. *Journal of Rational-Emotive & Cognitive Behavior Therapy, 27*, 66–76

Berry, R. R., & Lai, B. (2014). The emerging cognitive-behavioral therapy for anxious youth. *Rational Emotive & Cognitive Behavior Therapy, 32*, 57–66. https://doi.org/10.1007/s10942-014-0184-5.

Betz, N. E., & Turner, B. M. (2011). Using item response theory and adaptive testing in online career assessment. *Journal of Career Assessment, 19*, 274–286. https://doi.org/10.1177/1069072710395534.

Blustein, D. (2006). *The psychology of working: A new perspective for career development, counselling, and public policy*. New York, NY: Routledge.

Brown, S. D., & Lent, R. W. (2005). *Career development and counseling: Putting theory and research to work*. New York: Wiley.

Bullock-Yowell, E., Peterson, G. W., Reardon, R. C., Leierer, S. J., & Reed, C. A. (2011). Relationships among career and life stress, negative career thoughts, and career decision state: A cognitive information processing perspective. *The Career Development Quarterly, 59*, 302–314.

Campbell, D. (1992). *Campbell interest and skill survey*. London: Pearson.

Dieringer, D. D., Lenz, J. G., Hayden, S. C. W., & Peterson, G. W. (2017). The relation of negative career thoughts to depression and hopelessness. *Career Development Quarterly, 65*, 159–172. https://doi.org/10.1002/cdq.12089.

Duffy, R. D., Blustein, D. L., Diemer, M. A., & Austin, K. L. (2016). The psychology of working theory. *Journal of Counseling Psychology, 63*, 127–148. https://doi.org/10.1037/cou0000140.

Edralin, C. (2018). *The relationships among personality factors, negative career thoughts, and profile elevation* (Unpublished doctoral dissertation). Florida State University, Tallahassee, FL.

Finklea, T. J. (2016). *The connection between psychopathology and dysfunctional career thoughts* (Unpublished doctoral dissertation). Florida State University, Tallahassee, Florida. Retrieved from: http://diginole.lib.fsu.edu/islandora/search/finklea?type=edismax.

Gati, I., & Osipow, S. (2001–2014). *CDDQ.org*. Retrieved from http://kivunim.huji.ac.il/cddq/.

Glavin, K., Smal, P., & Vandermeeren, N. (2008). Integrating career counseling and technology. *Career Planning and Adult Development Journal, 25*, 160–176.

Holland, J. L. (1997). *Making vocational choices*. Odessa, FL: Psychological Assessment Resources.

Holland, J. L., & Messer, M. A. (2013). *Self-Directed Search® 2013 Fifth Edition (SDS)® professional manual*. Lutz, FL: PAR.

Kleiman, T., Gati, I., Peterson, G., Sampson, J., Reardon, R., & Lenz, J. (2004). Dysfunctional thinking and difficulties in career decision making. *Journal of Career Assessment, 12*, 312–331. https://doi.org/10.1177/1069072704266673.

Krumboltz, J. D. (1996). A learning theory of career counseling. In M. L. Savickas & W. B. Walsh (Eds.), *Handbook of career counseling theory and practice* (pp. 55–80). Palo Alto, CA, USA: Davies-Black Publishing.

Krumboltz, J. D. (2009). The happenstance learning theory. *Journal of Career Assessment, 17*, 135–154. https://doi.org/10.1177/1069072708328861.

Maree, J. G. (2016). *The Maree Career Matrix*. Randburg: JvR Psychometrics.

Mareee, J. G. (2017). *The career interest profile (version 6)*. Randburg, South Africa: JvR Psychometrics.

National Career Development Association. (2015). *NCDA Code of Ethics*. Retrieved from https://www.ncda.org/aws/NCDA/asset_manager/get_file/3395.

Niles, S., & Garis, J. W. (1990). The effects of a career planning course and a computer-assisted career guidance program (SIGI PLUS) on undecided university students. *Journal of Career Development, 16,* 237–248.

Osborn, D. S., Kronholz, J. F., Finklea, J. T., & Cantonis, A. M. (2014). Technology-savvy career counselling. *Canadian Psychology, 55*(4), 258–265. Retrieved from http://fsu.digital.flvc.org/islandora/object/fsu%3A543799. https://doi.org/10.1037/a0038160.

Osborn, D. S., Peterson, G. W., Sampson, J. P., Jr., & Reardon, R. C. (2003). Client anticipations about computer-assisted career guidance outcomes. *The Career Development Quarterly, 51,* 356–367. https://doi.org/10.1002/j.2161-0045.2003.tb00616.x. Retrieved from http://search.proquest.com/docview/219544152?accountid_4840.

Patton, W., & McMahon, M. (2006). The systems theory framework of career development and counseling: Connecting theory and practice. *International Journal for the Advancement of Counseling, 28,* 153–166.

Pryor, R., & Bright, J. (2003). The chaos theory of careers. *Australian Journal of Career Development, 48,* 89–91. https://doi.org/10.1177/103841620301200304.

Sampson, J. P., Jr., Osborn, D. S., Kettunen, J., Hou, P.-C., & Miller, A. K. (2018). The validity of socially-constructed career information. *Career Development Quarterly, 66,* 121–134. https://doi.org/10.1002/cdq.12127.

Sampson, J. P., Jr., Peterson, G. W., Lenz, J. G., & Reardon, R. C. (1992). A cognitive approach to career services: Translating concepts into practice. *The Career Development Quarterly, 41,* 67–74.

Sampson, J. P., Jr., Peterson, G. W., Lenz, J. G., Reardon, R. C., & Saunders, D. E. (1996a). *Career Thoughts Inventory*. Odessa, FL: Psychological Assessment Resources.

Sampson, J. P., Peterson, G. W., Lenz, J. G., Reardon, R. C., & Saunders, D. E. (1996b). *Improving your career thoughts: A workbook for the Career Thoughts Inventory*. Odessa, FL: Psychological Assessment Resources.

Sampson, J. P., Jr., Reardon, R. C., Peterson, G. W., & Lenz, J. G. (2004). *Career counseling and services: A cognitive information processing approach*. Pacific Grove, CA: Brooks/Cole.

Savickas, M. L. (2005). The theory and practice of career construction. In R. W. Lent & S. D. Brown (Eds.), *Career development and counseling: Putting theory and research to work* (pp. 42–70). Hoboken, NJ: Wiley.

Super, D. E. (1980). A life-span, life-space approach to career development. *Journal of Vocational Behavior, 13,* 282–298.

Epilogue

As I read through the breadth and depth of the forty chapters in this timely handbook, it is hard not to be at once both moved and challenged—moved at the extraordinary commitment and passion of every one of the authors, each one devoting their intellectual and practical expertise to supporting career development both for individual clients and for the scientific field in changing times; and challenged by the seemingly insurmountable nature of these changes. Nevertheless in reading through the book the energy of each of the authors is felt, and the attendant vitality, creativity—and innovation—in the field of career counselling is abundantly evident. This book is a credit to its tireless editor Professor Kobus Maree for this bringing together of such a global record of innovative career counselling.

This *Handbook of Innovative Career Counselling* is set within the conversation about increasing insecurity and precariousness of work, invoking vulnerability for individuals and challenging traditional assumptions of decent work and sustainable career development. Paradoxically, this complexity prompts people to look for simplicity in answers and approaches. The book's chapter authors acknowledge the shortcomings of current career planning approaches and emphasize the need for career counselling to respond to the complexity, diversity, fluidity and unpredictability in the current world of work. As Muijen, Brohm, van de Wolf and Lomans noted, "Modern answers are of no use in meeting postmodern challenges" (current volume).

This book demonstrates that the discipline of career development has embraced this challenge as authors write from theoretical, research and practice perspectives to deliver examples of innovative thinking and practice. As Hartung (current volume) noted, complex problems have prompted "contemporary perspectives on career to better account for the dynamic, non-linear, contextualized, diverse, and uniquely patterned nature of human work life within a rapidly changing and tumultuous global work environment".

There are three key themes within the book which I want to emphasize in this epilogue. These themes include first, the importance of internationalization; second, the ongoing challenge of integration, both within the field (e.g., theory, research and

J. G. Maree (ed.), *Handbook of Innovative Career Counselling*,
https://doi.org/10.1007/978-3-030-22799-9

practice), and in relation to integration with other disciplines; and third, the challenge to continue to be innovative across all aspects of career development. While space does not permit a reference to all chapters in the book, I reiterate the innovative and scholarly contribution made by each author. This book sets the field of career development alight and challenges us all to continue to share and learn aspects of our work to not only maintain credibility and relevance for our clients but to ensure the advancement of our discipline into the future.

Internationalization

Hartung (current volume) emphasized that "In many places around the world career counselling grows more unified by internationalizing itself". This process of sharing and learning about our practice globally was accelerated at the beginning of the 21st century through the work of the OECD, the World Bank and European Commission and the program of international reviews of career guidance services across thirty-seven countries (OECD, 2004; Watts & Fretwell, 2004; Sultana, 2004). This international activity significantly increased what was known about the policy and delivery of career guidance and spawned a number of international symposia in Ottawa in 1999 (Hiebert & Bezanson, 2000); Vancouver in 2001 (Bezanson & O'Reilly, 2002); and Toronto in 2003 (OECD/European Commission, 2004). The International Centre for Career Development and Public Policy (ICCDPP) was established in 2004, with a key set of goals as follows:

- To provide information and advice on how to develop and improve national and regional policies and systems for career development services in the fields of education, training, employment and social inclusion;
- To develop an international knowledge base on policies and systems for lifelong career development services;
- To make this knowledge available internationally; and
- To create learning links and partnerships between policy makers, researchers and expert sources.

Subsequent symposia have been held as follows: Australia 2006, UK 2007, New Zealand 2009, Hungary 2011, USA 2015, and South Korea, 2017. Hartung (current volume) also details significant international collaboration.

With authors from more than 14 countries, including several non North American and European countries, Professor Maree has certainly delivered a handbook which continues this global endeavour. In the pursuit of innovative approaches to all aspects of the career development field, chapters which demonstrate the importance of learning from shared and diverse challenges can only advance the reach and efficacy of the practice of career counselling.

Integration

While ongoing work toward the project of integration of career theories has been evident since the 1950s (see Patton & McMahon, 2014 for a summary), more focused attention began in the very early 1990s (Borgen, 1991; Hackett, Lent & Greenhaus, 1991; Osipow, 1990). Super (1990) commented on the understandable segmental nature of much theory development in the area of career psychology, "in view of the size of the problem" (p. 221). He acknowledged that theories which attempt to encompass too much may suffer from superficiality, and that future theories of career development "will be made up of refined, validated and well-assembled segments, cemented together by some synthesizing theory to constitute a whole which will be more powerful than the sum of its parts" (p. 221). A major development in the move toward theory integration was the convening of an international conference in 1994, acknowledged as the first attempt to facilitate "rapprochement among career theories" (Savickas & Lent, 1994, p. 5). Subsequently, multiple attempts to integrate theories have been developed (see Patton & McMahon, 2014 for a comprehensive summary).

A number of chapters within the current handbook further advance the integration discussion. Coetzee advances goal facilitation theory as relevant to career development, and Urbanaviciute, Buhlmann and Rossier propose an integrated theoretical approach focusing on micro- and macro-level actions which need to be implemented to promote sustainable careers and well-being. Duarte, Paixao and da Silva emphasize the importance of aligning converging epistemologies to advance a "shared scientific endeavour". Finally, in noting the importance of these actions for the growth and relevance of career development in these changing times, Young asserts "But it is precisely by drawing on these significant theoretical developments in adjacent sciences that we can hope to address the important issues in career, link career with counselling practice and the lives of our clients, and advance our discipline". What is emphasized throughout the book is the importance of past paradigms in career development, and the innovation of integrating the best from the past into the future.

In addition to focusing on integration of theory, authors within the handbook add to the project of integrating theory, research and practice which has aimed to advance each of those components of the discipline of career development (see Brown & Lent, 2005, 2013; Sampson Jr, Bullock-Yowell, Dozier, Osborn & Lenz, 2017). For example, McMahon, Watson and Abkhezr demonstrate theory and practice integration through systems mapping and narrative career counselling to facilitate successful integration with refugee resettlement. Osborn shows the integration of CIP theory with technology, emphasizing innovation in this approach. Riberio and Almeida discuss the concept of intersectionality, identifying it in their work as "a transdisciplinary theory aimed at capturing the complexity of identities and social inequalities through an integrated approach grounded in the interconnectedness of social class, gender and race/ethnicity". Their work demonstrates the integration of theoretical principles and technical principles.

Innovation

The book is a *Handbook of Innovative Career Counselling* and this innovation is reflected through all subsections of the book. In this section of this chapter I will draw from some of the book's authors to define and clarify innovation. Young proposes five questions pertinent to proposing an innovative theory of career, emphasising the importance of relevance to practice, complexity, meaning, and its role in capturing an individual's navigation of the future. Duarte and colleagues define innovating as "not so much a process aligned with the idea of finding the right answers for contemporary complex problems, but rather with adopting an interrogative stance that continually searches for the best questions that promote and expand the critical creative thinking needed to transform and move forward in the next decades the career counselling discipline". These authors go on to note that "In career counselling innovation can be seen as a theoretical reference that feeds off a dialogic relationship, through which we can define arguments, order them, and later transform into words which give meaning to the narrative of each" (current volume).

Chapters throughout the book demonstrate innovating technology, innovating research, and innovating diversity. Transitions throughout the lifespan and special populations all feature with examples of innovating thinking in practice. These chapters emphasize the increasing frequency and complexity of life career transitions and focus on children's career development building blocks, challenging transitions for young people, through to middle aged and older adults and bridging and retirement transitions. Bimrose and Frigerio feature theoretically informed innovation through a UK adaptation of the Career Adaptabilities Scale, and other chapters describe innovative sustainable career card sorts and an innovative moments model.

The increasing attention to innovating career counselling for diversity and context sees a focus on refugees, post-apartheid schools, young people in socio-economically challenged contexts, and challenges in employability for unskilled and unemployed young adults. Maree challenges our traditional practice in describing career counselling interventions in a deep rural context in South Africa.

Other innovative approaches incorporate creativity to counter traditional linear or quantitative rational approaches. In a number of cases authors offer personal stories to demonstrate a range of innovative career counselling approaches, including career writing within autoethnographic theoretical frameworks, story, career writing and poetic reflexivity, and art dialogue in theatre and play. Niles and Guttierez write about career counselling with soul, featuring meaning and hope in work, and describing strategies for self-clarity and self-reflection.

Connecting Integration, Internationalization and Innovation

A number of chapters focus on the life design paradigm (Nota & Rossier, 2015; Savickas et al, 2009) with authors noting it as "the next major evolution of the field" (Hartung, current volume)". What is noteworthy about this paradigm is that it is an outcome of the field's internationalization, innovation, and integration efforts. Hartung (2013) emphasized the derivation of this paradigm from matching and vocational guidance to life span development to meaning making, noting it also embraces constructivist and social constructionist approaches, including biographical hermeneutics and the narrative approach. Thus it embodies theory and practice integration.

The development of the life design paradigm was a result of an international project, with theorists, researchers and practitioners working together to develop an internationally constructed paradigm, thereby seeking to collaboratively innovate the field through international efforts examining practices and models from multiple contexts. Finally, the development of this paradigm is an example of innovation through providing a framework for development of innovative career counselling and practice methods. Its beginnings through work of an international group serves to continue to internationalize its development, and in turn career counselling for global challenges.

Concluding Comments

It has been an honour to read this book and offer this epilogue to its overall contribution. I am grateful to Professor Maree for inviting me to undertake this important task. Each of the chapters in this book demonstrate multiple and diverse approaches to innovation. In addition, they embrace what I call innovation in context—both micro and macro, acknowledging the diversity and multiplicity of the practice of career development. It is this contextual emphasis which makes the book so valuable. What is especially courageous of many authors within this handbook is their descriptions of modelling of approaches on themselves in detailing their own life career stories.

The themes of internationalization, integration and innovation have been strongly demonstrated throughout all chapters of this book. Each of the authors has shown that innovation in context can provide a new learning for their clients, their colleagues, and our discipline. In particular, all readers will find innovative ways to theorise, research and practice - the complexity of the current world of work demands new strategies and our field must continue to innovate to serve all clients experiencing challenging career life journeys.

References

Bezanson, L., & O'Reilly, E. (2002). (Eds.). *Making waves: Connecting career development with public policy* (Vol. 2). Ottawa: Canadian Career Development Foundation.

Borgen, F. H. (1991). Megatrends and milestones in vocational behaviour: A 20-year counselling psychology retrospective. *Journal of Vocational Behaviour, 39*, 263–290.

Brown, S. D., & Lent, R. W. (2005). *Career development and counselling: Putting theory and research to work*. Hoboken, NJ: Wiley.

Brown, S. D., & Lent, R. W. (2013). *Career development and counselling: Putting theory and research to work* (2nd ed.) Hoboken, NJ: Wiley.

Hackett, G., Lent, R. W., & Greenhaus, J. H. (1991). Advances in vocational theory and research: A 20-year retrospective. *Journal of Vocational Behaviour, 38*, 3–38.

Hartung, P. J. (2013). Career as story: Making the narrative turn. In W. B. Walsh, M. L. Savickas & P. J. Hartung (Eds.), *Handbook of vocational psychology* (4th ed., pp. 33–52). New York: Routledge.

Hiebert, B., & Bezanson, L. (2000). (Eds.) *Making waves: Career development and public policy, International symposium 1999, Papers, proceedings and strategies*. Ottawa, Canada: Canadian Career Development Foundation.

Nota, L., & Rossier, J. (2015). (Eds.). *Handbook of life design: From practice to theory and from theory to practice.* Boston, MA: Hogrefe Publishing.

Organisation for Economic Cooperation and Development. (2004). *Career guidance and public policy: Bridging the gap.* Paris: OECD.

Organisation for Economic Cooperation and Development and European Commission. (2004). *Career guidance: A handbook for policy makers.* Paris: OECD/European Commission.

Osipow, S. H. (1990). Convergence in theories of career choice and development. *Journal of Vocational Behaviour, 36*, 122–131.

Patton, W., & McMahon, M. (2014). *Career development and systems theory: Connecting theory and practice* (3rd ed.). Rotterdam, The Netherlands: Sense Publishers.

Sampson Jr, J. P., Bullock-Yowell, E., Dozier, V. C., Osborn, D. S., & Lenz, J. G. (2017). *Integrating theory, research, and practice in vocational psychology: Current status and future directions.* Tallahassee, FL: Florida State University Libraries.

Savickas, M. L., & Lent, R. W. (1994). (Eds.). *Convergence in career development theories: Implications for science and practice.* Palo Alto, CA: CPP Books.

Savickas, M. L., Nota, L., Rossier, J., Dauwalder, J-P., Duarte, M. E., Guichard, J., Soresi, S., Van Esbroeck, R., & van Vianen, A. E. M. (2009). Life designing: A paradigm for career construction in the 21st century. *Journal of Vocational Behaviour, 75*, 239–250.

Sultana, R. G. (2004). *Guidance policies in the knowledge society: Trends, challenges and responses across Europe*. Thessaloniki, Greece: European Centre for the Development of Vocational Training.

Super, D. E. (1990). A life-span, life-space approach to career development. In D. Brown & L. Brooks (Eds.), *Career choice and development: Applying contemporary theories to practice* (2nd ed., pp. 197–261). San Francisco, CA: Jossey-Bass.

Watts, A. G., & Fretwell, D. H. (2004). *Public policies for career development: Policy strategies for designing career information and guidance systems in middle-income and transition economies*. Washington, DC: World Bank.

Wendy Patton GAICD
Professor Emeritus
Queensland University of Technology
Kelvin Grove Campus QLD 4059
w.patton@qut.edu.au

Printed by Printforce, the Netherlands